HOW TO USE THIS BOOK

For ease of use, this book is organized alphabetically. Single word entries are straightforward, but it is not always obvious where a compound term should be listed. I have tried to list such entries more or less as they are used in normal speech or writing, that is, in the form in which they are most likely to be first encountered. For instance, *natural resources* and *strategic resources* appear, respectively, under "N" and "S" rather than "R." If readers fail to find an entry under the first part of the compound term they seek, they should simply try some other component of the phrase. Additionally, the book is heavily cross-referenced (all words in *italics*, thus). Also, some grammatical leeway has been taken, such as in cross-referencing *annex* as a guidepost to *annexation*. Readers are strongly advised to make use of the cross-referencing feature: checking cross-referenced terms will almost always provide additional information or insight, often from a different sub-field of international relations. Note, however, that rather than clutter the text unduly with italics, common references such as country names have been left in normal font. Yet, readers may rest assured that all countries are listed and that they will always be able to find additional information under country names, whether italicized or not. In rare cases, countries are deliberately highlighted with italics. This indicates that information highly relevant to the entry readers are perusing is available under the entry for the highlighted country. Also listed are virtually all other extant political entities, such as *associated states, city-states, colonies, condominiums, dependencies, microstates* and so forth. Lastly, quite a few *extinct* polities, whether *empires, federations, nations* or *unions* are listed (e.g., *Austria-Hungary; Ottoman Empire; Prussia; Senegambia; Soviet Union; UAR; Yugoslavia*). Also on the roster are the former and/or colonial names of newly independent nations.

To avoid confusion, foreign words and phrases have not been italicized so as not to send the reader on a fruitless cross-reference search. If they are italicized, then a cross-reference to the term or phrase exists because it has a special meaning for international relations. For example, a reference to "the domestic status quo" will not carry italics, whereas "after 1919 Britain was a leading *status quo power*" tells readers that they may find additional information under the italicized, compound term. The only time italics have been used grammatically is in the bold, alphabetically arranged entry titles themselves (whatever precedes the first colon in any given reference). But all italics within the text of an entry (whatever follows the first colon) serve a cross-referencing rather than a grammatical function. For example: *"status quo* power: Any *state* that seeks to preserve the political and *territorial integrity* of a *peace* settlement or established *balance of power*. The antonym is *revisionist power*." In this context, there is no additional reference to "status quo," but there are additional entries for the five italicized terms provided.

When searching for an acronym check under the full name of the organization, if known. Frequently used acronyms are cross-referenced for quick referral (e.g., *UNGA* will redirect readers to *United Nations General Assembly*). If the full title of an organization is unknown to you, it can be located by scanning all entries under its first letter. For instance, if looking for *ECOSOC* scan "E" until you come to *Economic and Social Council (ECOSOC)*. Exceptions to this rule are foreign language acronyms commonly used in English; these are listed under the acronym itself rather than a foreign spelling most likely unknown to the English language reader. Thus, the former Soviet security agency is listed as "KGB (*Komitet Gosudarstvennoy Bezopasnosti*)," not under "Komitet."

Crises and wars are inventoried by their conventionally accepted names. When readers are looking for a particular event but are unsure of the standard name, they should check a country entry of a known participant. This will also provide the precise main entry title for those crises or wars that have unusual names with which readers may, or may not, be already familiar. For instance, a non-specialist seeking information on China's wars with Japan might think such wars are usually called, and therefore are listed here as, the First and Second "Chinese/Japanese Wars" (of some given date). But in fact, these conflicts are most commonly referred to, in English, as the *Sino/Japanese War(s)*. Simply by looking up China (or Japan) readers can find these entry titles. Middle East wars are listed under *Arab/Israeli War(s)*, with cross-references from "Yom Kippur" or "Six Day" wars. In cases of special confusion a guiding cross-reference is also listed. For example, the *Iran/Iraq War* was called the *Gulf War* until that term was taken over by the multinational conflict with Iraq over its 1990 invasion and annexation of Kuwait. Readers will thus find an entry under *Gulf War (1980-88)* explaining the shift in nomenclature and redirecting them to the proper log-in; below that appears another entry, *Gulf War (1990-91)*, which synopsizes the UN/Iraq confrontation. Another contemporary example of confusing nomenclature is the war in Bosnia. Should it appear as "Bosnian Civil War," "Serbian/Bosnian War," or some other term? There is no agreed-upon title among the media, and the history books are as yet unwritten. Therefore, with an admitted measure of editorial license, it has been listed here under *Third Balkan War*. That reflects a deliberate intention to place the conflict in its wider historical context, and thereby draw readers' attention to its regional antecedents, impact and significance. Yet even those assertive, indeed impetuous, readers who have rushed right past this sparkling preface will have no trouble finding the listing, as it is cross-referenced under all the countries concerned (Bosnia, Albania, Croatia, Greece, Macedonia, Serbia, Slovenia and Turkey, among others), as well as related concepts (*peace enforcement*) and regional bodies like *NATO* or the *WEU*. Two final points: if a cross-reference that includes a country name is given in normal syntax,

readers should still look for it under the country (e.g., the *invasion of Grenada* is found under *Grenada, invasion of,* not under *invasion*). Lastly, please note that all *civil wars* are listed by country. Hence, *American Civil War* appears under "A" for American, not "C" for Civil War. In this case, and some others, I have accepted the wise advice of reviewers to cross-reference to vernacular usages. This will help direct more colloquial readers to the entries they seek. But *chauvinists* or *jingoists,* of whatever country or stripe, will still have to locate their nation's or ideology's proudest moments and conflicts cataloged by mere, even humbling, alphabetical order!

SPECIAL FEATURES

Biography: These are mainly political in nature, with personal detail kept to a minimum. Yet the peculiar, human element is not ignored where deemed revealing or relevant (e.g., the mysticism of *Nicholas I,* cruelty of *Idi Amin,* or *Stalin's* sadism). Most major power statesmen are included, among them American, Austrian, British, Chinese, French, German, Indian, Japanese, Ottoman, Russian and Soviet leaders. All UN *Secretaries General* are listed, as are most individual *Nobel Prize* (for Peace) winners, as well as institutional winners. Also included are prominent figures from smaller powers in Africa, Asia, Europe and Latin America, according to whether they had an impact on international affairs beyond their nation's borders.

Diplomacy: Entries include major concepts (e.g., *arbitration, conciliation, diplomatic immunity, good offices, mediation, sphere of influence*); major conferences (e.g., *Westphalia, 1648; Vienna, 1815; Paris, 1856; Berlin, 1878; Paris, 1919; Washington, 1922; Bretton Woods, 1944; San Francisco, 1945; Helsinki, 1973-75*); many practices and rituals of negotiation, and most diplomatic functions, offices, ranks and titles. Classical diplomatic terms (e.g., *cordon sanitaire, raison d'état, rapprochement, realpolitik, Weltpolitik* and so forth) are defined and examples are provided.

Intelligence: A sampling of major *intelligence agencies* is included (e.g.. *CIA, KGB, MI5/MI6, Mossad, NSA, STASI, Sûreté* and others), along with widely used intelligence terms and jargon.

International law: Included are numerous concepts, legal maxims, specialized terminology and illustrative examples, including multiple entries on *international criminal law, international customary law, international public law,* the *law of the sea,* the *law of war, recognition, sovereignty* and *treaties.* Numerous treaties,

from *arms control* to the several *UNCLOS* agreements, are listed. *Human rights* issues are also covered.

International organizations: Most major *multilateral* bodies and organizations have entries, going back even before and including those associated with the *League of Nations,* but concentrating on the *United Nations.* This includes all *specialized agencies* and important committees and commissions. There is comprehensive coverage of regional organizations (including several failed ones), whether organized around economic, political or security themes. A few prominent *nongovernmental organizations (NGOs)* are also listed.

International political economy: There are entries on economic institutions (*GATT, IBRD, IMF* etc.), associations (*ASEAN, CARICOM, ECOWAS, EEC, EU, NAFTA, OECD, OPEC* etc.) and on *MNCs/MNEs, foreign direct investment* and related concepts. There is solid coverage of basic economic concepts and specialized language (e.g., *adjustment, balance of payments, debt rescheduling, deficit financing, First Tranche, free trade agreements, oligopoly, structural adjustment*), and some economic history (*world depressions, Bretton Woods system, gold standard,* among other entries).

Maps: Nearly two dozen maps accompany the text. Half cover current world political divisions on a region-by-region basis. These are up-to-date to 1994. The rest illustrate major past events (e.g. the *occupation* of Germany after 1945; the rise and fall of the *Japanese Empire*) or longstanding controversies (e.g., the *Eastern Question*; the *Straits Question*), or outline salient contemporary conflicts.

Military: Included are major concepts (e.g., *envelopment, flanking, mobilization, strategy, tactics*), as well as *military ranks* and *units* and a limited number of entries on weapons systems, conventional and otherwise. Many wars are synopsized, including discussion of their course, causes and effects. *WWI* and *WWII* receive extended coverage. A number of pivotal battles are listed, and some generals or admirals of special note have earned separate biographical entries.

Political geography: There are entries on every nation, *colony,* possession or *protectorate.* Significant minority groups are listed (e.g., *Ibos, Karen, Kurds*). Some non-sovereign regions are cataloged, especially those with secessionist histories (e.g., *Ossetia, Nag-*

orno-Karabakh, Québec or *Shaba*). Country entries provide a synopsis history, description of major foreign policies pursued, alliances, major international associations, current population and level of military capability.

Political science: Major concepts, terminology and translations of jargon into plain English, including concepts and terms from *dependency, deterrence* and *game theory, decision making, just war theory, liberal-internationalism, marxism, perception/misperception theory, realism, strategic studies* and various *systems theories.* A few key political thinkers are also listed.

PRINCIPLES OF SELECTION

All states, including the *Great Powers*, operate within a wider *international system* with special features of its own. A full understanding of world affairs is incomplete without awareness of the historical evolution and contemporary nature of this system, in particular how it is made manifest in both cooperative and competitive relations in international economics, law and organization. Hence, there are multiple entries in all these areas, taking up a substantial share of the text. In addition, this book approaches contemporary world politics with a deliberate stress on international political and diplomatic history, and through it the essential continuity of events of our own day with great ideas and major occurrences of the past. It highlights the significance and impact of leading individuals, whether historical or contemporary, as well as key ideas, associations and organizations. It aims to present readers with a sense of the complex interweaving of causality in world affairs, past, present and across what political scientists have called the three *levels of analysis*: the individual, the state (or society) and the international system. But what is a great event or a leading individual? In making the inevitable choices required to reduce the many subjects treated in this book to manageable size, without sinking into merely subjective designations, I have been guided by the principles of selection laid out below.

Great Powers are the prime movers of world history and politics. Even small events in the affairs of the Great Powers may have a more vast--and often destructive--impact on the international system than signal events within or among smaller powers. Comprehensive coverage is therefore given not merely to the foreign policies and interactions of the most powerful states, but also to the dynamics that drive them, including economic, intellectual, political and social decay or innovation. This includes several former Great Powers, now *extinct* or declined from the first

rank, going back to the *Peace of Westphalia* and the emergence of the modern states system in 17th and 18th century Europe. Likewise, it is true that even lesser (whether in character or talent) individuals in charge of the affairs of Great Powers have a broad influence on world history and politics. Most often, this influence is weightier than that of even a moral or intellectual titan, confined to a Lilliputian land. Therefore, individuals who might be subjectively judged as of little personal consequence can be given great play in this book, owing to the indisputable public consequences of their choices, actions or omissions. More than one mediocre or downright appalling dictator, prime minister or president of a Great Power has slipped in through this back door, held ajar for them by the still pervasive importance of national power as a motive and moving force in the affairs of nations.

Yet the world is full of states and other economic, legal and political entities that do not number among the Great Powers. Whether *middle powers* or *regional powers*, small states may still be influential in the larger course of world history (if only, in some cases, as objects of *aggression* or other imperial misadventure). Also, they are often interesting or regionally important in their own right. Thus, all countries currently in existence are listed (as well as a number of extinct nations), receiving at least an entry that summarizes the main features of their national development, and often much more. Individual leaders from smaller countries have been treated this way: if they can be fairly said to have had an impact outside their own community, whether globally or on a particular region, they are given a separate biographical entry. If they have had a major impact on their own society but not on wider affairs, mention of this role is made in the country reference alone. And there are other "actors" on the stage that demanded and were given their due, whether they were *customs unions, multinational corporations, non-governmental organizations*, or the impressive host (angelic and otherwise) of *international organizations*.

Historical entries are of two basic types: (a) national histories; (b) more general international processes and events. Individual country histories abbreviate thousands of years in the case of major civilizations and religions, hundreds of years in the case of the Great Powers, and decades in the life of newer nations, though even for very young countries there may be considerably more historical depth on a case-by-case basis. Most historical entries listed separately from national histories concern the modern era (post-Westphalia). The focus is upon the rise of the Great Powers, their wars and other relations with one another, and the enlargement of the states system through *colonialism*, imperial wars and the expansion of market economics beyond Europe to Africa, Asia and the Americas. There is comprehensive coverage of Great Power relations after 1648, substantial reporting of colonial and other national experience after 1789, and universal review of the 20th century. As well, there has been a conscious effort made to cover regions that otherwise have been, at best, tributary streams of the riverine flow of world history. In addition to reporting how such areas were affected by ultimate inclusion in the state system and by international economic developments, the text attempts to communicate something of the flavor of their local histories. This is particularly true for such often neglected areas as pre-independence sub-Saharan Africa, the Islamic world, parts of Latin America, and especially the *associated states*, *microstates* and remaining *dependencies* of the South Pacific. Coverage of developments of world historical significance (the *Industrial Revolution, modernization, telecommunications, total war* and so forth) is extensive following the *French Revolution*. Two types of special circumstance were considered in making the decision as to whether historical summary should return to periods earlier than the founding of the states system after the *Thirty Years' War*, and its expansion globally in the 18th and early 19th centuries: (1) National histories may include very distant events if these are highly significant in the historical memory of modern peoples or provide intimations of the broad scope of a people's posture toward the outside world. For example, the *Tokugawa* period in Japanese history, and even much earlier periods, receives relatively extended coverage, just as the founding of the *Manchu* dynasty is detailed, prior to a summation of its response to external pressures and its decline and fall in China. (2) Certain intellectual revolutions of global historical significance are included, such as the *Renaissance*, *Reformation* and *Enlightenment*. While these tumultuous times were on the surface confined to Europe, it is noted how such upheavals in fact had profound effects on all international relations down to our own time, notably by their contribution to the development of *secularism* as a central principle of modern world political organization.

ACKNOWLEDGMENTS

The author and Longman gratefully acknowledge the efforts of the reviewers, who offered detailed and insightful comments:

Gary Baker--Virginia State University
Forest Grieves--University of Montana
Carl Hodge--Okanagan University College
C.L. Holoman--SUNY Buffalo
Kalevi Holsti--University of British Columbia
Brian Job--University of British Columbia
Joseph Lepgold--Georgetown University
Karen Mingst--University of Kentucky
John Outland--University of Richmond

Joseph Rudolph--Towson State University
Frank Sherman--Syracuse University
Alden Williams--Kansas State University

The author would also like to thank the editorial and production staff at Longman. Particular thanks to David Shapiro, without whose irrepressible enthusiasm and unfailing good cheer a task of this scope might have proven too daunting to the author, and the book may not have come to pass; and to Ann Kearns, who saw the ms. through the various stages of production with the utmost professionalism.

LIST OF MAPS

POLITICAL

Africa

Caribbean
Central America
North America
South America

Australasia and Oceania
Northeast Asia
Southeast Asia
Southwest Asia
Middle East

Europe
Russia and the Near Abroad

HISTORICAL

Eastern Question: 1683-1923
"America's Backyard" Chaos and Intervention: 1776-1994
The Straits Question: 1800-1994
Japanese Empire: 1895-1945
Occupied Germany: 1945
Cold War Crises: 1945-90
Korean Conflict: 1950-53
Indochina: 1954-79
Israel and the Occupied Territories: 1967-94
Gulf War: 1990-91
Bosnia: 1993

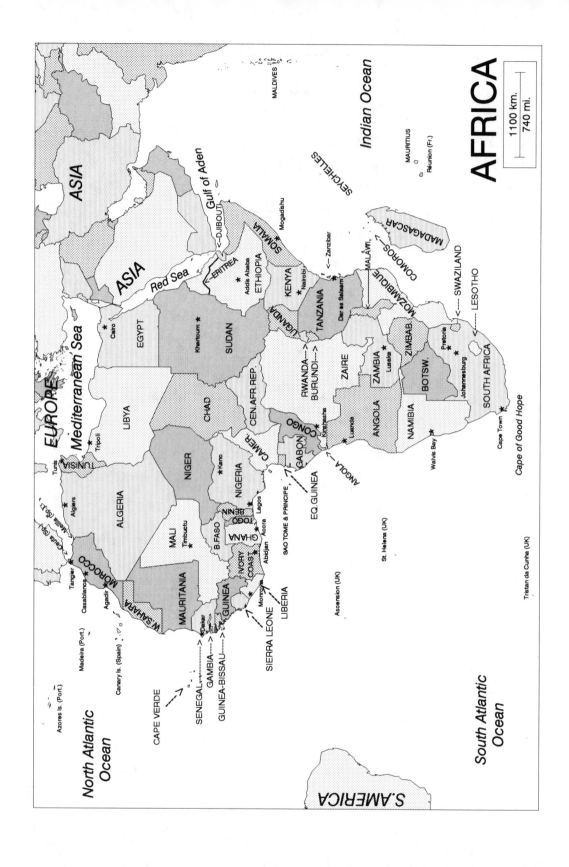

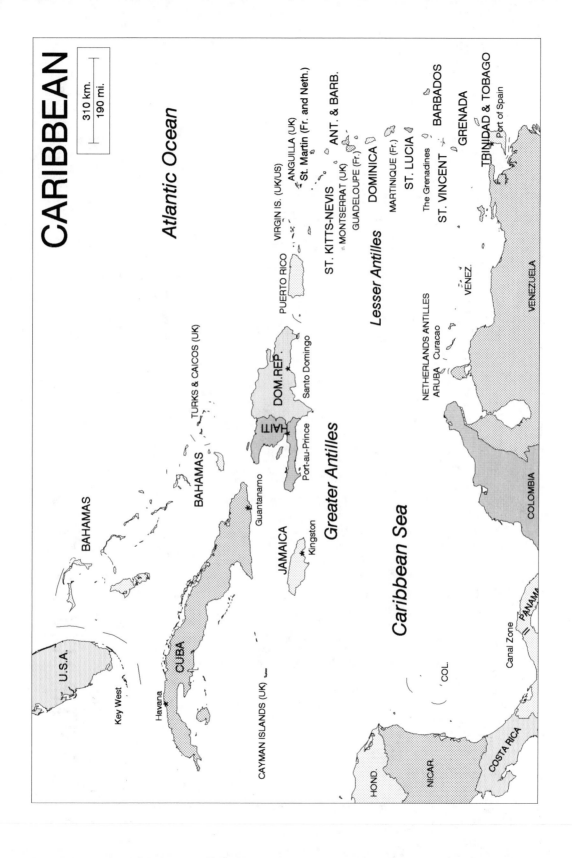

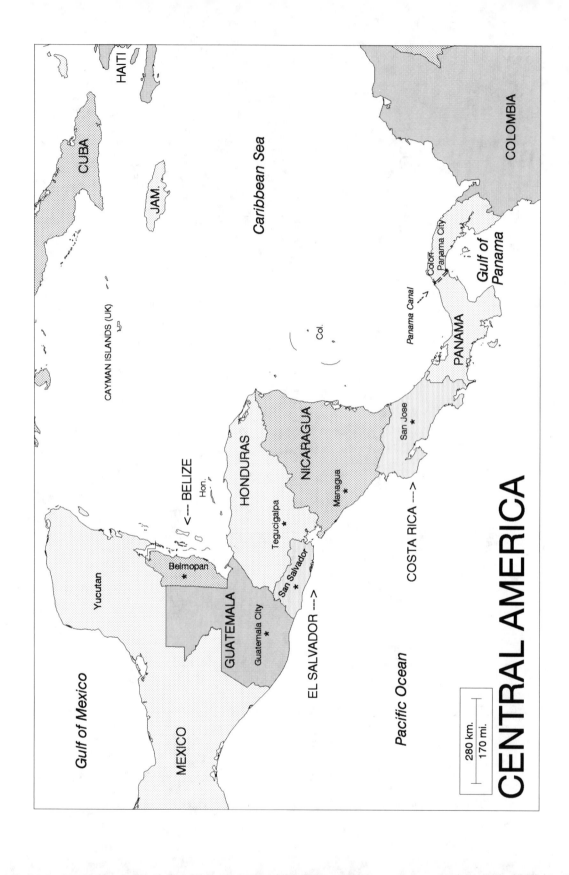

CENTRAL AMERICA

280 km.
170 mi.

Gulf of Mexico

MEXICO

Yucutan

CUBA

HAITI

JAM.

Caribbean Sea

CAYMAN ISLANDS (UK)

Col.

COLOMBIA

Panama City

Colon

Panama Canal

Gulf of
Panama

PANAMA

Belmopan
★

<-- BELIZE

Hon.

GUATEMALA

Guatemala City
★

EL SALVADOR -->

San Salvador
★

HONDURAS

Tegucigalpa
★

NICARAGUA

Managua
★

San Jose
★

COSTA RICA -->

Pacific Ocean

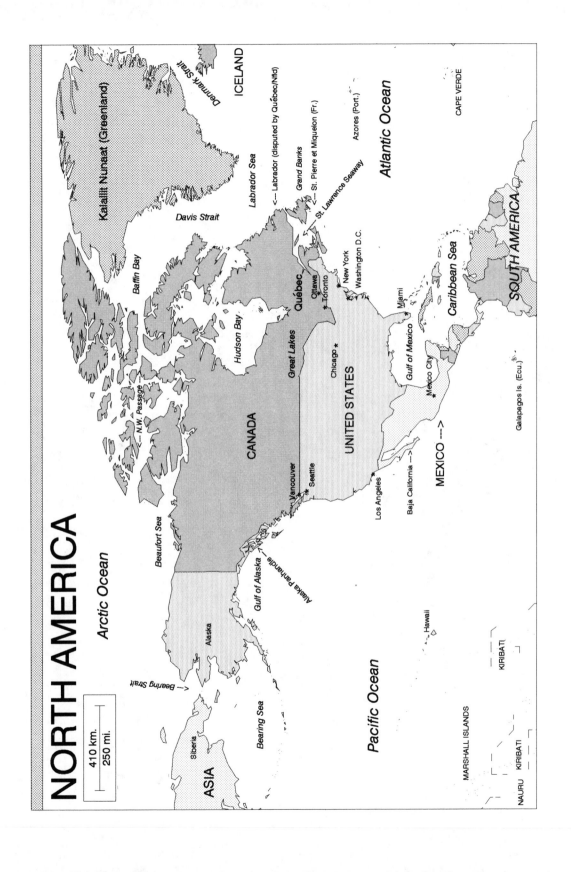

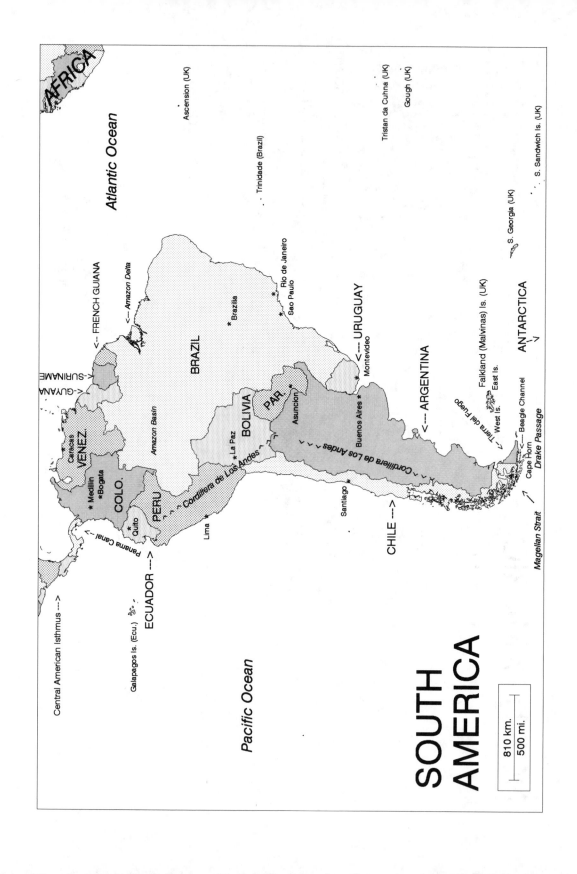

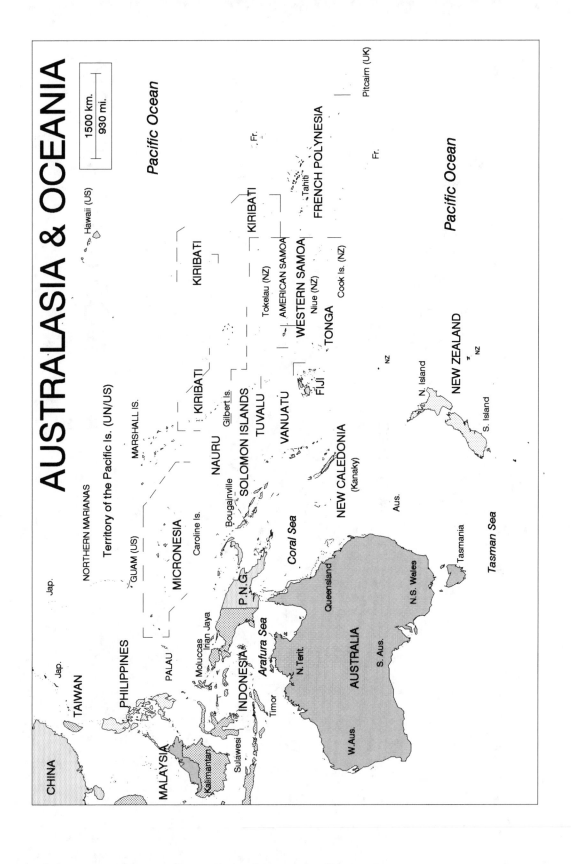

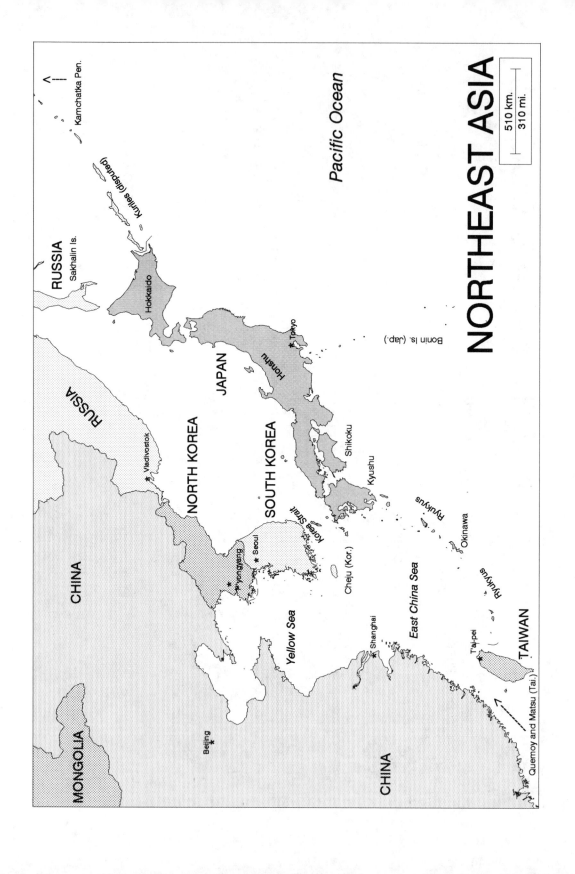

NORTHEAST ASIA

510 km.
310 mi.

Pacific Ocean

Kamchatka Pen.

Kuriles (disputed)

RUSSIA

Sakhalin Is.

Hokkaido

JAPAN

Honshu

Tokyo

Bonin Is. (Jap.)

RUSSIA

Vladivostok

NORTH KOREA

SOUTH KOREA

Shikoku

Kyushu

Pyongyang

Seoul

Korea Strait

Ryukyus

Okinawa

CHINA

Cheju (Kor.)

East China Sea

Ryukyus

MONGOLIA

Yellow Sea

Shanghai

Tai-pei

TAIWAN

Beijing

CHINA

Quemoy and Matsu (Tai.)

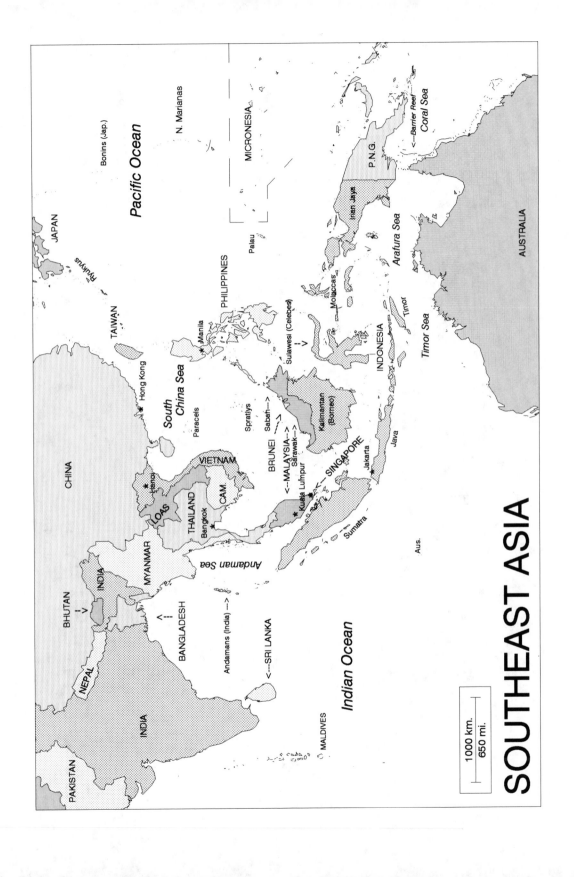

SOUTHEAST ASIA

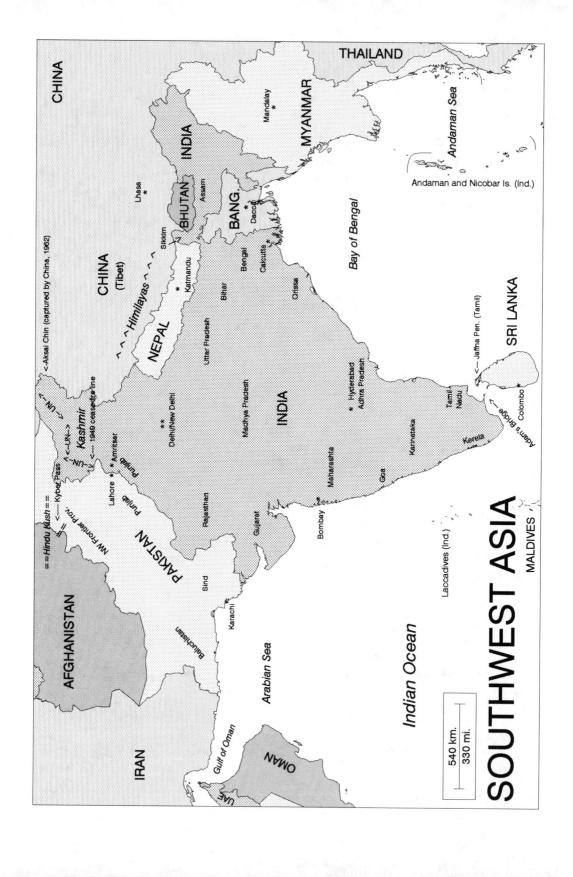

SOUTHWEST ASIA

CHINA

THAILAND

MYANMAR

Mandalay *

INDIA

Andaman Sea

*Lhasa

BHUTAN

Assam

BANG.

Andaman and Nicobar Is. (Ind.)

Sikkim

*Dacca

<--Aksai Chin (captured by China, 1962)

CHINA
(Tibet)

Katmandu *

Bengal

Calcutta *

Bay of Bengal

^^^ Himalayas ^^^

NEPAL

Bihar

Orissa

Kashmir

1949 ceasefire line

Uttar Pradesh

Jaffna Pen. (Tamil)

SRI LANKA

NN

<-- UN --

Delhi/New Delhi **

Madhya Pradesh

INDIA

*Hyderabad
Andra Pradesh

Tamil
Nadu

Adam's Bridge

Colombo *

<-- NN --

Lahore *

Amritsar *

Kerela

Karnataka

== Hindu Kush ==

<-- Khyber Pass

Punjab

Goa

Maharashta

Bombay

== Hindu Kush ==

NW Frontier Prov.

PAKISTAN

Rajesthan

Gujarat

AFGHANISTAN

Sind

Karachi

Laccadives (Ind.)

MALDIVES

Baluchistan

Arabian Sea

Indian Ocean

IRAN

Gulf of Oman

OMAN

UAE

540 km.

330 mi.

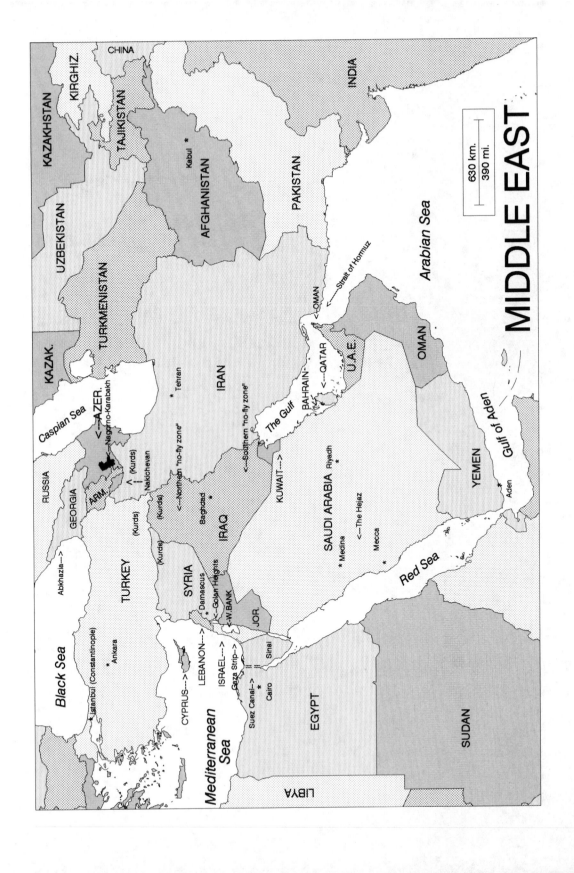

MIDDLE EAST

630 km.
390 mi.

CHINA
KAZAKHSTAN
KIRGHIZ.
TAJIKISTAN
UZBEKISTAN
TURKMENISTAN
KAZAK.
AFGHANISTAN
* Kabul
PAKISTAN
INDIA

RUSSIA
GEORGIA
Caspian Sea
AZER.
Nagorno-Karabakh
(Kurds)
Nakichevan
ARM.
(Kurds)
Tehran *
IRAN
<--Northern "no-fly zone"
<--Southern "no-fly zone"
Strait of Hormuz
OMAN
Arabian Sea

Black Sea
Abkhazia-->
TURKEY
Istanbul (Constantinople) *
* Ankara
(Kurds)
(Kurds)
(Kurds)
SYRIA
Damascus *
Golan Heights
<--W. BANK
Baghdad *
IRAQ
KUWAIT--->
BAHRAIN
QATAR
U.A.E.
The Gulf
Riyadh *
SAUDI ARABIA
OMAN
Gulf of Aden
YEMEN
Aden *

Mediterranean Sea
CYPRUS--->
LEBANON-->
ISRAEL-->
Gaza Strip->
Suez Canal->
* Cairo
Sinai
JOR.
EGYPT
SUDAN
LIBYA
<--The Hejaz
Mecca *
* Medina
Red Sea

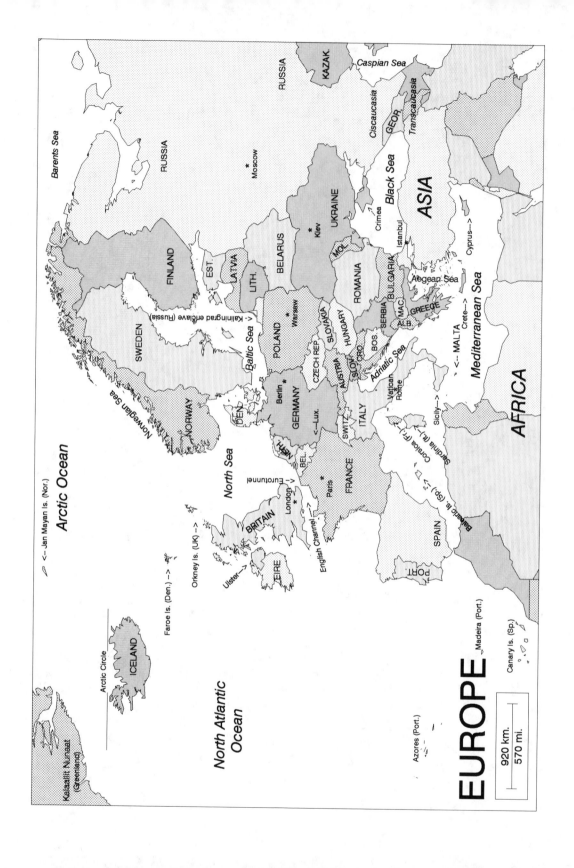

EUROPE

920 km.
570 mi.

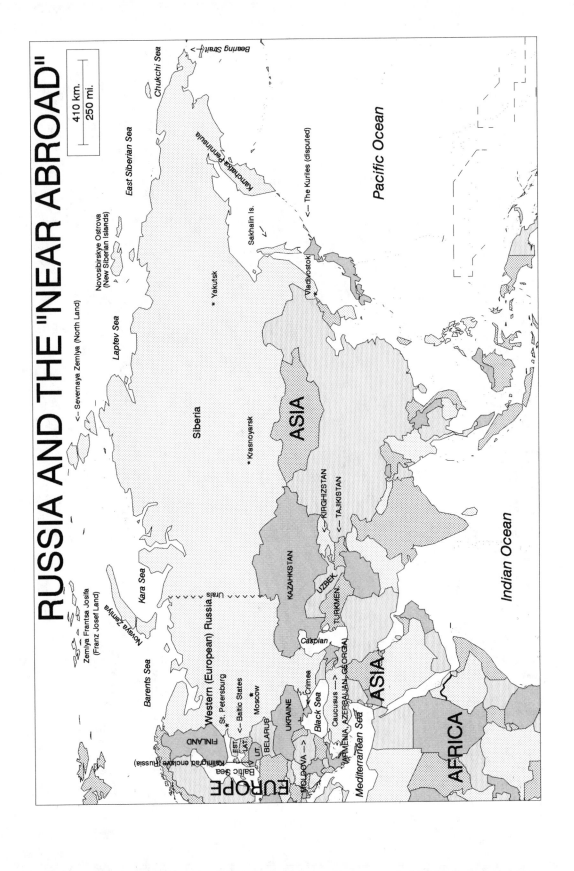

RUSSIA AND THE "NEAR ABROAD"

410 km.
250 mi.

Chukchi Sea

Bering Strait →

East Siberian Sea

Kamchatka Peninsula

Pacific Ocean

← Severnaya Zemlya (North Land)

Novosibirskye Ostrova
(New Siberian Islands)

← The Kuriles (disputed)

Sakhalin Is.

Laptev Sea

* Yakutsk

Vladivostok

Zemlya Frantsa Josifa
(Franz Josef Land)

Siberia

ASIA

Kara Sea

* Krasnoyarsk

Novaya Zemlya

KIRGHIZSTAN

← TAJIKISTAN

Barents Sea

Urals

KAZAKHSTAN

Indian Ocean

UZBEK

Western (European) Russia

Caspian

TURKMEN

St. Petersburg

Baltic States

* Moscow

Caucasus →
(ARMENIA, AZERBAIJAN, GEORGIA)

ASIA

FINLAND

EST.

LAT.

LIT.

BELARUS

UKRAINE

Crimea

Black Sea

Kaliningrad enclave (Russia)

Baltic Sea

MOLDOVA →

Mediterranean Sea

AFRICA

EUROPE

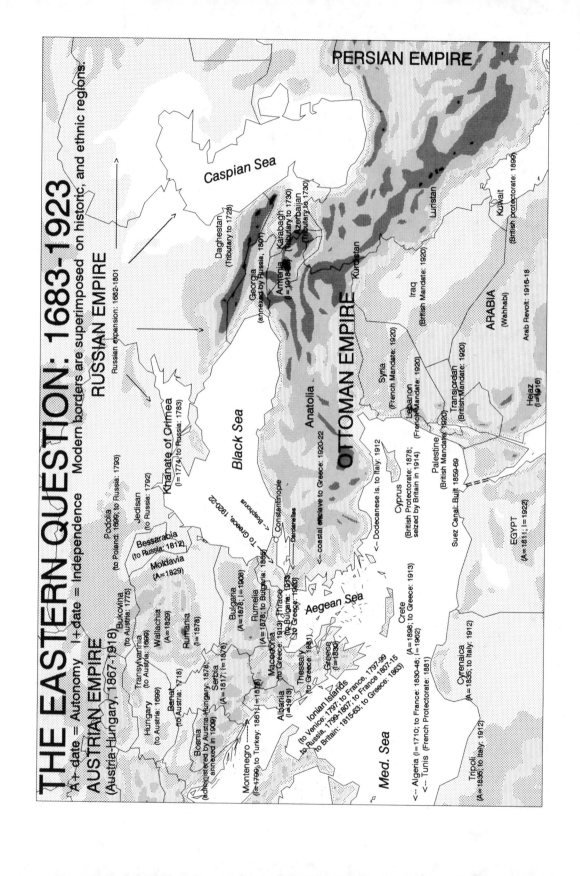

THE EASTERN QUESTION: 1683-1923

A + date = Autonomy   I + date = Independence   Modern borders are superimposed on historic, and ethnic regions.

PERSIAN EMPIRE

AUSTRIAN EMPIRE
(Austria-Hungary, 1867-1918)

RUSSIAN EMPIRE

Caspian Sea

Russian expansion: 1682-1801

Daghestan
(Tributary to 1723)

Karabagh
(Tributary to 1730)

Azerbaijan
(Tributary to 1730)

Georgia
(annexed by Russia, 1801)

Armenia
(I = 1918)

Luristan

Kurdistan

Kuwait
(British protectorate: 1899)

Khanate of Crimea
(I = 1774; to Russia: 1783)

Podolia
(to Poland: 1699; to Russia: 1793)

Jedisan
(to Russia: 1792)

Bessarabia
(to Russia: 1812)

Moldavia
(A=1829)

Bukovina
(to Austria: 1775)

Transylvania
(to Austria: 1699)

Hungary
(to Austria: 1699)

Banat
(to Austria: 1718)

Wallachia
(A=1829)

Rumania
(I=1878)

Black Sea

Anatolia

OTTOMAN EMPIRE

Syria
(French Mandate: 1920)

Iraq
(British Mandate: 1920)

Lebanon
(French Mandate: 1920)

ARABIA
(Wahhabi)

Arab Revolt: 1916-18

Transjordan
(British Mandate: 1920)

Hejaz
(I=1916)

Constantinople

Bosphorus

Dardanelles

To Greece, 1920-22

← coastal enclave to Greece: 1920-22

Bulgaria
(A=1878; I=1908)

Rumelia
(A=1878; to Bulgaria: 1885)

Thrace
(to Greece: 1913; to Bulgaria: 1915;
to Greece: 1920)

Macedonia
(to Greece: 1913)

Serbia
(A=1817; I=1878)

Bosnia
(administered by Austria-Hungary;
annexed in 1908)

Montenegro
(I=1799; to Turkey: 1861; I=1878)

Albania
(I=1913)

Thessaly
(to Greece: 1881)

Greece
(I=1830)

Aegean Sea

Crete
(A=1898; to Greece: 1913)

Dodecanese Is. to Italy: 1912

Cyprus
(British Protectorate: 1878;
seized by Britain in 1914)

Palestine
(British Mandate: 1920)

Suez Canal: Built 1859-69

EGYPT
(A=1811; I=1922)

Ionian Islands
(to Venice: 1797; to France, 1797-99;
to Russia, 1799-1807; to France 1807-15;
to Britain: 1815-63; to Greece: 1863)

Med. Sea

← Algeria (I=1710; to France: 1830-48;   (A=1830; I=1962)
← Tunis (French Protectorate: 1881)

Cyrenaica
(A=1835; to Italy: 1912)

Tripoli
(A=1835; to Italy: 1912)

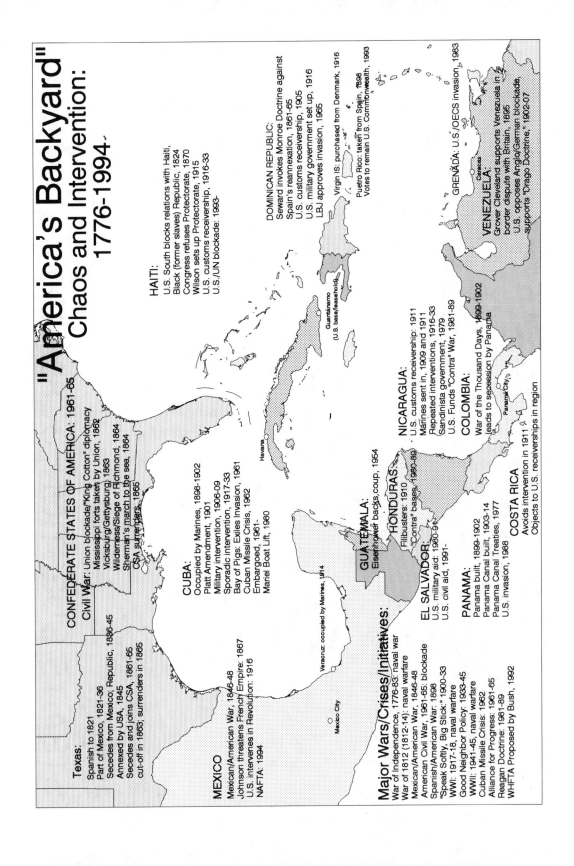

"America's Backyard"
Chaos and Intervention:
1776-1994

Texts:
Spanish to 1821
Part of Mexico, 1821-36
Secedes from Mexico; Republic, 1836-45
Annexed by USA, 1845
Secedes and joins CSA, 1861-65
cut-off in 1863; surrenders in 1865

MEXICO
Mexican/American War, 1846-48
Johnson threatens French Empire: 1867
U.S. intervenes in Revolution: 1916
NAFTA: 1994

Major Wars/Crises/Initiatives:
War of Independence, 1776-83: naval war
War of 1812 (1812-14): naval warfare
Mexican/American War, 1846-48
American Civil War, 1861-65: blockade
Spanish/American War: 1898
"Speak Softly, Big Stick," 1900-33
WWI: 1917-18, naval warfare
Good Neighbor Policy: 1933-45
WWII: 1941-45, naval warfare
Cuban Missile Crisis: 1962
Alliance for Progress: 1961-65
Reagan Doctrine: 1981-89
WHFTA Proposed by Bush, 1992

CONFEDERATE STATES OF AMERICA: 1861-65
Civil War: Union blockade/"King Cotton" diplomacy
Mississippi forts taken by Union, 1862
Vicksburg/Gettysburg, 1863
Wilderness/Siege of Richmond, 1864
Sherman's march to the sea, 1864
CSA surrenders, 1865

CUBA:
Occupied by Marines, 1898-1902
Platt Amendment, 1901
Military intervention, 1906-09
Sporadic intervention, 1917-33
Bay of Pigs: Exiles Invasion, 1961
Cuban Missile Crisis, 1962
Embargoed, 1961-
Mariel Boat Lift, 1980

GUATEMALA:
Eisenhower backs coup, 1954

HONDURAS:
Filibusters: 1910
"Contra" bases, 1980-89

EL SALVADOR:
U.S. military aid: 1980-91
U.S. civil aid, 1991-

PANAMA:
Panama built, 1899-1903
Panama Canal built, 1903-14
Panama Canal Treaties, 1977
U.S. invasion, 1988

COSTA RICA
Avoids intervention in 1911
Objects to U.S. receiverships in region

NICARAGUA:
U.S. customs receivership: 1911
Marines sent in, 1909 and 1911
Repeated interventions, 1916-33
Sandinista government, 1979
U.S. Funds "Contra" War, 1981-89

COLOMBIA:
War of the Thousand Days, 1899-1902
leads to secession by Panama

HAITI:
U.S. South blocks relations with Haiti,
Black (former slaves) Republic, 1824
Congress refuses Protectorate, 1870
Wilson sets up Protectorate, 1915
U.S. customs receivership, 1916-33
U.S./UN blockade: 1993-

DOMINICAN REPUBLIC:
Seward invokes Monroe Doctrine against
Spain's reannexation, 1861-65
U.S. customs receivership, 1905
U.S. military government set up, 1916
LBJ approves invasion, 1965

Virgin IS: purchased from Denmark, 1916

Puerto Rico: taken from Spain, 1898
Votes to remain U.S. Commonwealth, 1993

GRENADA: U.S./OECS invasion, 1983

VENEZUELA:
Grover Cleveland supports Venezuela in
border dispute with Britain, 1895
U.S. opposes Anglo/German blockade,
supports "Drago Doctrine," 1902-07

Guantánamo
(U.S. base/leasehold)

Havana

Veracruz: occupied by Marines, 1914

Mexico City

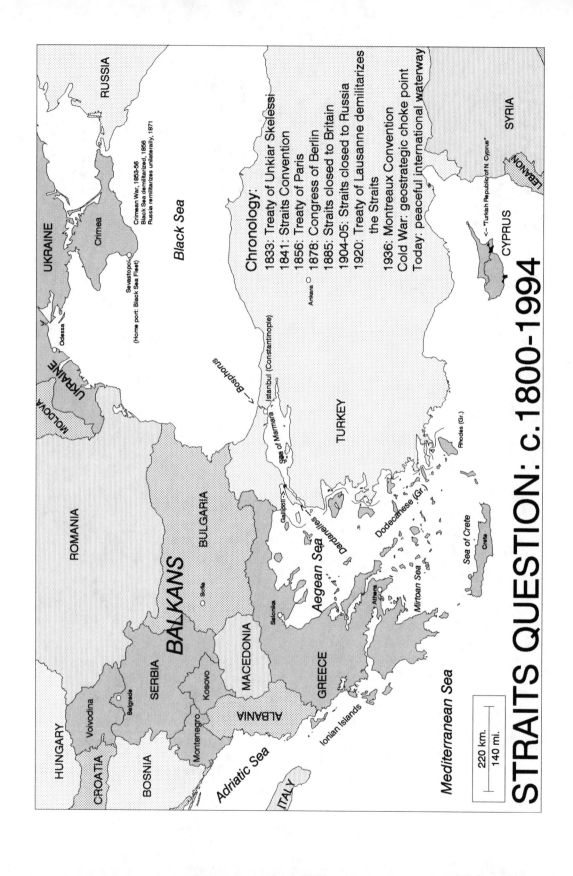

STRAITS QUESTION: c.1800–1994

RUSSIA

UKRAINE

Crimea

Sevastopol

(Home port: Black Sea Fleet)

Crimean War, 1853-56
Black Sea demilitarized, 1856
Russia remilitarizes unilaterally, 1871

Odessa

MOLDOVA

UKRAINE

Black Sea

Bosphorus

Istanbul (Constantinople)

Sea of Marmara

Ankara

TURKEY

Chronology:

1833: Treaty of Unkiar Skelessi
1841: Straits Convention
1856: Treaty of Paris
1878: Congress of Berlin
1885: Straits closed to Britain
1904-05: Straits closed to Russia
1920: Treaty of Lausanne demilitarizes
        the Straits
1936: Montreaux Convention
Cold War: geostrategic choke point
Today: peaceful international waterway

SYRIA

LEBANON

<-- Turkish Republic of N. Cyprus"

CYPRUS

HUNGARY

CROATIA

BOSNIA

Voivodina

Belgrade

SERBIA

Montenegro

Kosovo

ALBANIA

MACEDONIA

BALKANS

Sofia

BULGARIA

ROMANIA

Gallipoli

Dardanelles

Salonika

Aegean Sea

GREECE

Athens

Mirtoan Sea

Dodecanese (Gr.)

Rhodes (Gr.)

Sea of Crete

Crete

Ionian Islands

Adriatic Sea

ITALY

Mediterranean Sea

220 km.
140 mi.

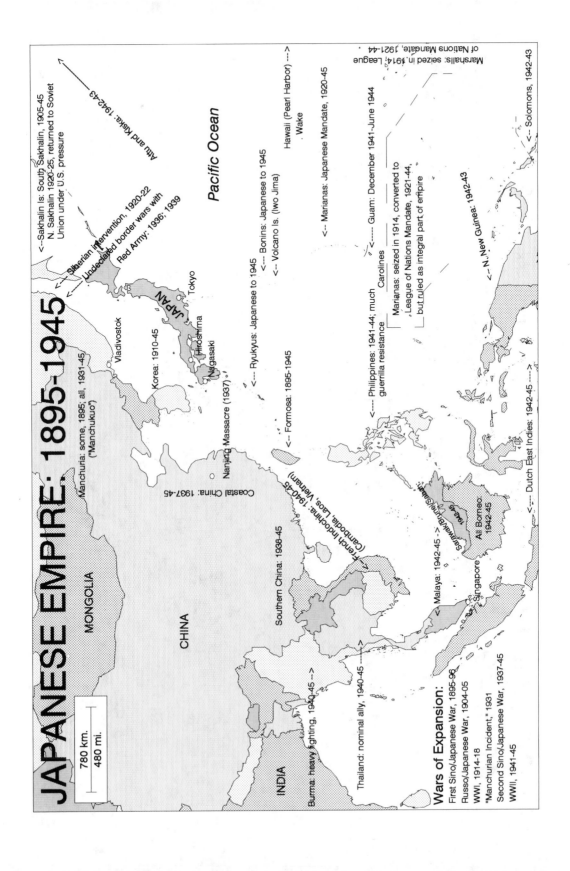

JAPANESE EMPIRE: 1895-1945

780 km.
480 mi.

MONGOLIA

CHINA

INDIA

Vladivostok

JAPAN
Tokyo
Hiroshima
Nagasaki

Korea: 1910-45

Manchuria: some, 1895; all, 1931-45,
("Manchukuo")

Siberian Intervention, 1920-22
Undeclared border wars with
Red Army: 1936; 1939

<-- Sakhalin Is: South Sakhalin, 1905-45
N. Sakhalin 1920-25, returned to Soviet
Union under U.S. pressure

Attu and Kiska: 1942-43 -->

Pacific Ocean

<-- Ryukyus: Japanese to 1945

<-- Bonins: Japanese to 1945

<-- Volcano Is. (Iwo Jima)

<-- Formosa: 1895-1945

Nanjing Massacre (1937)

Coastal China: 1937-45

Southern China: 1938-45

French Indochina: 1940-45
(Cambodia, Laos, Vietnam)

Thailand: nominal ally, 1940-45

Burma: heavy fighting, 1940-45 -->

<-- Philippines: 1941-44; much
guerrilla resistance

Carolines

<----- Guam: December 1941-June 1944

<-- Marianas: Japanese Mandate, 1920-45

Marianas: seized in 1914, converted to
League of Nations Mandate, 1921-44,
but ruled as integral part of empire

Hawaii (Pearl Harbor) -->
Wake

Marshalls: seized in 1914; League
of Nations Mandate, 1921-44 .

<-- Solomons, 1942-43

<-- N. New Guinea: 1942-43

<----- Dutch East Indies: 1942-45 ----->

All Borneo
1942-45

Sarawak/Brunei/Sabah
1942-45

Singapore

< Malaya: 1942-45 ->

Wars of Expansion:

First Sino/Japanese War, 1895-96
Russo/Japanese War, 1904-05
WWI, 1914-18
"Manchurian Incident," 1931
Second Sino/Japanese War, 1937-45
WWII, 1941-45

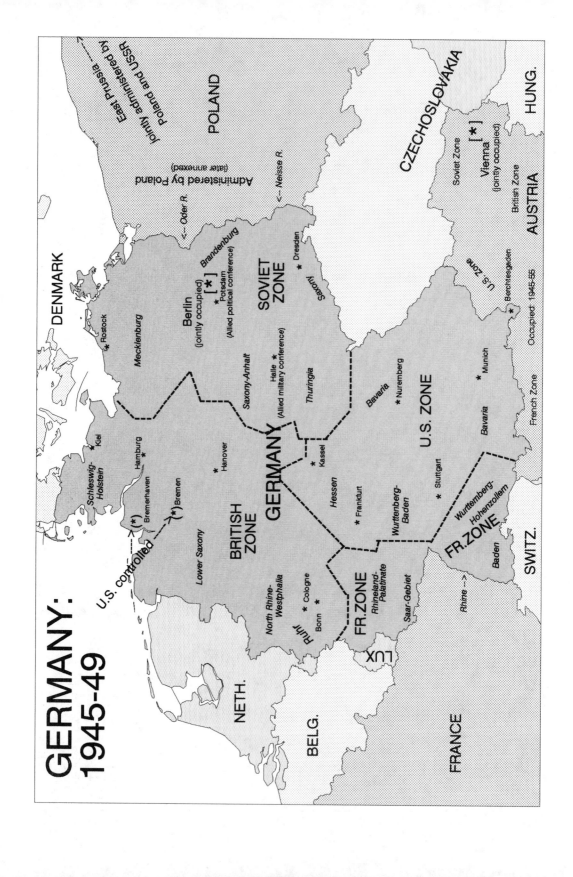

GERMANY: 1945-49

Soviet Union becomes extinct, on
December 25, 1991.

<-- Warsaw Pact (1955)

<-- NATO Alliance (1949) -->

1 Poland (1944-45, 1980-81)
2 Rumania (1944-45)
3 Iran (1946)
4 Greece and Turkey (1946-47)
5 Berlin (1948, 1953, 1958, 1962, 1989)
6 Czechoslovakia (1948, 1968)
7 Korean Conflict: 1950-53
8 Vietnam War: 1954-75
9 Hungarian Uprising (1956)
10 Quemoy and Matsu (1958)
11 Cuban Missile Crisis (1962)
12 Ussuri River clashes (1966, 1969)
13 Third Indo/Pakistani War (1971)
14 Fourth Arab/Israeli War (1973)
15 Soviet/Cuban aid to Angola (1975)
16 Ethiopia/Somalia War (1978-88)
17 Soviets invade Afghanistan (1979-89)
18 Euro-missiles Crisis (1979-82)
19 Fighting in Soviet periphery (1988)
20 Baltic States declare indep. (1990)
21 Pact of Paris ends Cold War (1990)

COLD WAR CRISES: 1945-90

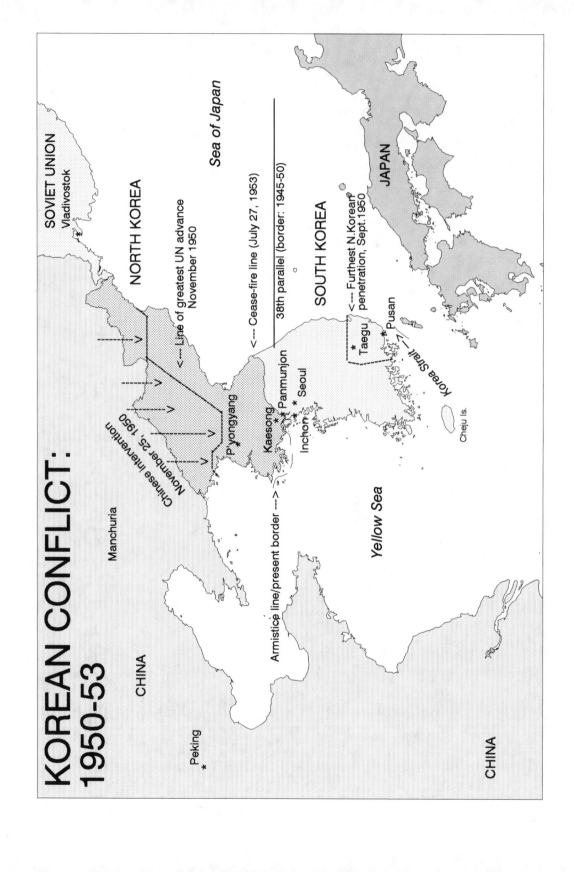

KOREAN CONFLICT: 1950-53

SOVIET UNION

Vladivostok

Manchuria

CHINA

Peking

NORTH KOREA

Sea of Japan

JAPAN

Chinese Intervention November 25, 1950

<-- Line of greatest UN advance November 1950

<-- Cease-fire line (July 27, 1953)

38th parallel (border: 1945-50)

P'yongyang

Kaesong

Panmunjon

Seoul

Inchon

SOUTH KOREA

<--- Furthest N.Korean penetration, Sept.1950

Taegu

Pusan

Korea Strait

Cheju Is.

Yellow Sea

Armistice line/present border --->

CHINA

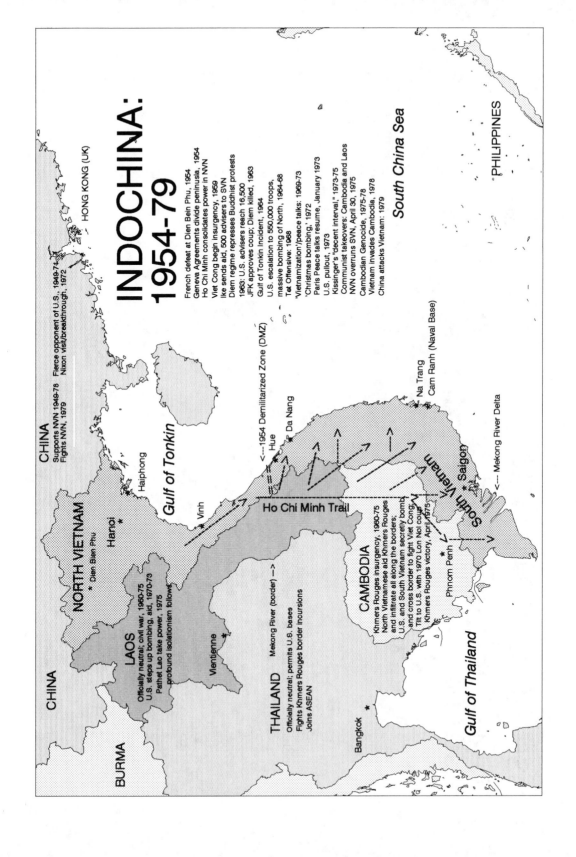

INDOCHINA: 1954-79

French defeat at Dien Bein Phu, 1954
Geneva Agreements divide peninusla, 1954
Ho Chi Minh consolidates power in NVN
Viet Cong begin insurgency, 1959
Ike sends aid, 500 advisers to SVN
Diem regime represses Buddhist protests
1963: U.S. advisers reach 16,500
JFK approves coup; Diem killed, 1963
Gulf of Tonkin Incident, 1964
U.S. escalation to 550,000 troops,
  massive bombing of North, 1964-68
Tet Offensive: 1968
"Vietnamization/peace talks: 1969-73
"Christmas bombing," 1972
Paris Peace talks resume, January 1973
U.S. pullout, 1973
Kissinger's "decent interval," 1973-75
Communist takeovers: Cambodia and Laos
NVN overruns SVN, April 30, 1975
Cambodian Genocide, 1975-78
Vietnam invades Cambodia, 1978
China attacks Vietnam: 1979

South China Sea

° PHILIPPINES

CHINA
Supports NVN 1949-78   Fierce opponent of U.S., 1949-74
Fights NVN, 1979   Nixon visit/breakthrough, 1972

HONG KONG (UK)

Gulf of Tonkin

CHINA

BURMA

NORTH VIETNAM
Hanoi *
* Dien Bien Phu

Haiphong

LAOS
Officially neutral; civil war, 1960-75
U.S. steps up bombing, aid, 1970-73
Pathet Lao take power, 1975
profound isolationism follows

Vientienne

Vinh

<--1954 Demilitarized Zone (DMZ)

Hue

Da Nang

Ho Chi Minh Trail

THAILAND   Mekong River (border) -->
Officially neutral; permits U.S. bases
Fights Khmers Rouges border incursions
Joins ASEAN

Bangkok
*

CAMBODIA
Khmers Rouges insurgency, 1960-75
North Vietnamese aid Khmers Rouges
and infiltrate all along the borders;
U.S. and South Vietnam secretly bomb
and cross border to fight Viet Cong;
Tilt to U.S. with 1970 Lon Nol coup;
Khmers Rouges victory, April 1975

Phnom Penh
*

South Vietnam

Saigon *

Na Trang
Cam Ranh (Naval Base)

<--- Mekong River Delta

Gulf of Thailand

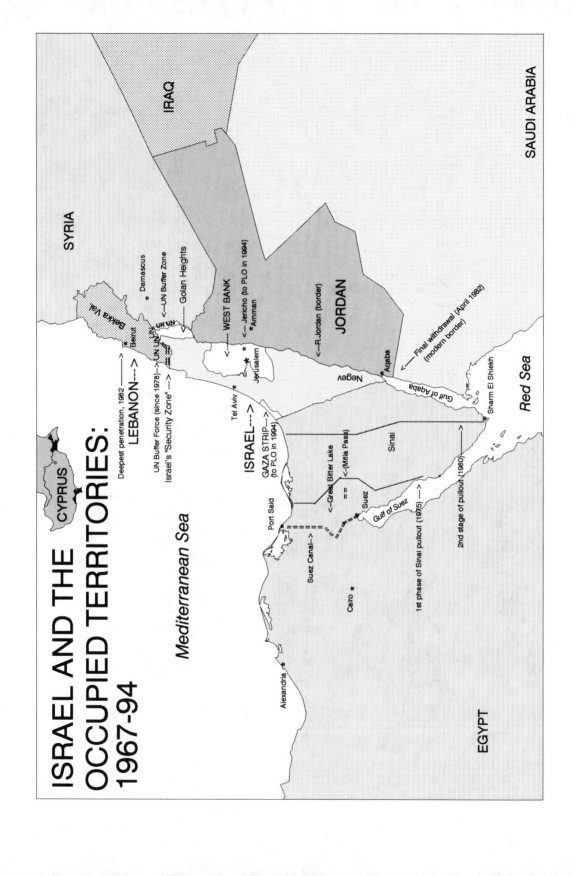

ISRAEL AND THE OCCUPIED TERRITORIES: 1967-94

CYPRUS

SYRIA

IRAQ

Mediterranean Sea

Damascus *

Deepest penetration, 1982 ------->

LEBANON--->

UN Buffer Zone

Golan Heights

UN Buffer Force (since 1978)--->

Israel's "Security Zone" --->

Bekka V'al

Beirut *

UN UN UN UN

WEST BANK

<--Jericho (to PLO in 1994)

*Amman

JORDAN

<--R.Jordan (border)

Jerusalem *

Tel Aviv *

ISRAEL--->

GAZA STRIP--->
(to PLO in 1994)

Negev

Aqaba *

Final withdrawal (April 1982)
(modern border)

Gulf of Aqaba

Sharm El Shiekh

Red Sea

<--Great Bitter Lake

<--(Mitla Pass)

Suez

Gulf of Suez

Sinai

Port Said

Suez Canal-->

Cairo *

1st phase of Sinai pullout (1975) --->

2nd stage of pullout (1980)
--->

Alexandria *

EGYPT

SAUDI ARABIA

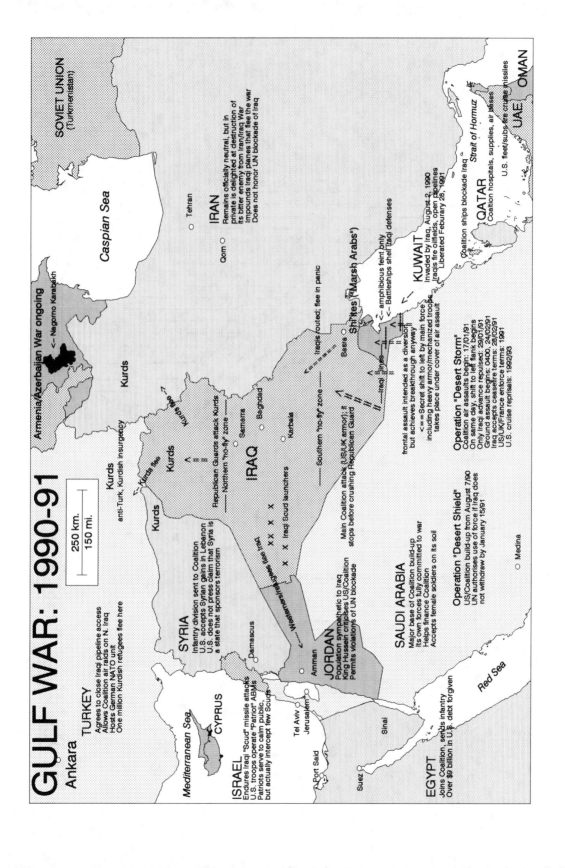

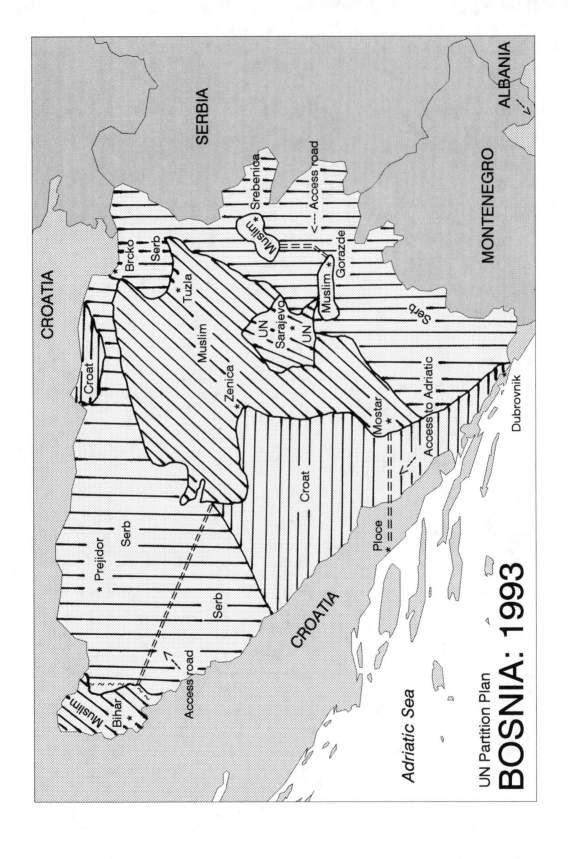

UN Partition Plan
BOSNIA: 1993

A

abatement: A controversial justification for *intervention*, holding that *anarchy* in a neighboring country compels *intervention* to abate the "intolerable nuisance" caused by a spillover of violent or anarchical activities. This is a common self-absolution given by *Great Powers* for their intervention in regional affairs. It may also serve as cover for *imperialism*.

Abdul Hamid II (1842-1915): Sultan of the *Ottoman Empire* from 1876-1909. He ruled during a period of agonizing decline in which most of Turkey's European *territory* was stripped away under Russian and Austrian pressure. He helped organize the *Armenian genocide* of 1895-96. Opposed to domestic reform, he was deposed by the *Young Turks*.

Abkhazia: With Georgia's *independence*, this NW region attempted *secession*, leading to armed hostilities in 1992. The local assembly asked Russia to either declare Abkhazia a *protectorate* or *annex* it. In June 1993, Russian troops entered as ostensible peacekeepers, but secretly aided the rebels. *Eduard Sheverdnadze* asked for Western help, but by October Abkhazia had broken away from Georgian control. An uneasy *peace* developed when Georgia acceded to a long-term Russian presence. Russia's interest remains access to Abkhazia's Black Sea coastline.

ABM: See *anti-ballistic missile, missile system.*

aboriginal: Issues of social, economic (often concerning land use), cultural or other concerns that pertain: (1) to the *indigenous peoples* of any country; (2) to the indigenous people of Australia.

absolute advantage: When one country or firm can supply *goods* or *services* below the costs to competitors. This is an aspect of the global division of labor. Cf. *comparative advantage; competetive advantage.*

absolute monarch: A *sovereign* unlimited by secular laws or a constitution, only conscience (if possessed) and the (putative) laws of God. See *absolutism.*

absolute responsibility: The legal doctrine that a state may be held accountable even without being directly guilty of a harmful action. Cf. *culpability.*

absolute right: An international legal right without impediment or restriction.

absolutism: Unrestrained authority in government, especially of a *sovereign*, but loosely applicable to any

tyrannical or *totalitarian* political system. In the heyday of European *state creation* it had as its legitimizing purpose the process of domestic political integration. Its economic analogue was *mercantilism.* Cf. *enlightened despotism; popular sovereignty.*

abstract: (1) Theoretical. (2) Existing solely as an idea. (3) A concise summary.

abstraction: (1) A general idea, not tied to specific time or place. (2) A visionary and unrealistic idea without practical significance.

abuse of rights: An international legal doctrine in which unreasonable exercise of an otherwise legal right may amount to an *illegal act.*

Abyssinia: The ancient name of Ethiopia.

Abyssinian War (1935-36): Border skirmishes with Italian troops in *Eritrea* occurred during the 1930s. Italy invaded without a *declaration of war* on October 3, 1935, using advantages in aircraft and *armor*, and even *poison gas*, against the lightly armed Ethiopians. The capital fell on May 5, 1936. The *League of Nations* denounced Italy as an *aggressor* but only authorized limited *sanctions* (excluding *oil*), as Britain and France feared pushing *Mussolini* closer to *Hitler.* This weak response further discredited the League as an instrument of *collective security.* As one result, Hitler concluded that the West was feeble, speeded his rearmament program, and moved more quickly to overturn the *Treaty of Versailles.*

accession: (1) When a state *adheres* to an already existing *treaty*, which requires prior *consent* of all other *treaty powers.* (2) Taking title to *territory* or political authority. (3) When a *sovereign* legally takes the reigns of *power*, upon the death or other passage out of power of the previous sovereign.

accidental war: The idea that *war* may occur without deliberate action by any *decision-maker*, by mistakes of *perception* as a crisis escalates out of control, or through technical failure. Given the speed of modern events and weapons the *Great Powers* have tried to prevent accidental war by improving communications and developing *Confidence and Security Building Measures (CSBMs).* These provide advance notice of *maneuvers*, permit observers and inspection, and otherwise aim to reduce *tension* and elevate trust.

accretion: When new *territory* is formed by natural

causes, such as alluvial deposits of a river delta or vulcanism, under *international law* it accrues to the state to whose territory it is connected and has been added. See also *avulsion; Thalweg*.

ace: By convention, a *fighter* pilot credited with five or more enemy aircraft "kills" (shootdowns).

Acheson, Dean (1893-1971): Assistant U.S. Secretary of State 1941; Under Secretary to *George Marshall* 1945; Secretary of State to *Harry Truman* 1949-53. He was a major player in such key policies of the early *Cold War* as the *Marshall Plan, containment*, the *Truman Doctrine, NATO* and support for Nationalist China. He has been criticized for misleading statements about the degree of U.S. support for South Korea, remarks said by some to have failed to discourage the North's *aggression*. He defended the State Department and (rightly or wrongly, courageously or foolishly) also his personal aide *Alger Hiss* from charges of disloyalty. See *McCarthyism; Wise Men*.

acid rain: High acidic content in rain, caused naturally by volcanoes and artificially by industrial pollutants, with devastating impact on flora and fauna. It is a growing subject of *negotiation* as pollutants cross boundaries, transferring costs of cleanup and recovery from polluter to neighboring states.

ACP Nations: African, Caribbean and Pacific states linked to the *EC/EU* by the *Lomé Conventions*. They numbered 49 in 1975 but reached 69 with the addition of Namibia in 1990.

acquiescence: When *tacit consent* is inferred from a *state's* silence on a given matter. See also *consent*.

Acquired Immune Deficiency Syndrome (AIDS): A disease that came to public attention in the mid-1980s, though it was incubating unnoticed for years before that. In the West it is largely confined to homosexual, hemophiliac, and intravenous drug-using populations. Elsewhere, it affects Haiti and sub-Saharan Africa in particular, due to poverty, the dislocation and ravages of multiple wars, and their attendant effects of reduced resistance and widespread rape and unprotected prostitution. Of 12 million cases known in 1993, eight million were in Africa. The epidemic is placing strain on the medical systems of even advanced countries, and is close to overwhelming several in Africa.

acquisitive prescription: When legal title to a given *territory* is conceded due to its long-term *occupation*.

Action Française: An extreme right-wing French

organization. It helped undermine *national morale* before *WWII*, and was a mainstay of the *Vichy* regime.

active defense: Interception and destruction of enemy forces and/or weapons before they reach their targets.

active measures: An *intelligence* term for direct action taken to influence events abroad, as opposed to merely gathering information. This may include *assassination*, bribery, *disinformation*, funding political parties or *guerrillas*, and *propaganda*. See also *agent of influence; penetration agent*.

act of state: Under *international law*, a doctrine denying to municipal courts *jurisdiction* on the legality of acts taken by foreign powers.

Act of Union: (1) 1707: It joined *Scotland* to *England*. (2) 1800: The legislation by which *Ireland* was joined to the *United Kingdom*. It followed the rising of the *United Irishmen*. Ireland was given 28 Peers and 100 seats in the House of Commons. *Pitt* pushed it through Parliament but was unable to obtain *Catholic emancipation* as promised. Most Irish never reconciled to what they regarded as an unnatural Act.

act of war: (1) An act of *aggression* constituting a *casus belli*. (2) Any act defined as warlike by the *laws of war*.

actor: Any player in *international politics*. These are most often the states but may be "*non-state actors*" as well, such as individuals, *ethnic groups, MNCs* or *nongovernmental organizations* involved with specific issues of policy or world affairs.

Adams, John (1735-1826): U.S. President 1796-1800. He served with distinction as the first U.S. Minister (Ambassador) to London. As President, he continued *George Washington's* policy of *neutrality*, but built up the navy to enforce claims to *neutral rights*. His election was viewed with hostility by the French *Directory*, and this along with the *XYZ Affair* almost brought the U.S. and France to war. By 1798 the navy was persevering against the French, but the main factor keeping peace was *Napoleon's* and *Talleyrand's* lack of desire for *war*. Adams' successor was *Thomas Jefferson*, the man he defeated in 1796. Jefferson would let the wooden navy Adams built rot in port, for which a price would be paid against the *Barbary States* and during the *War of 1812*.

Adams, John Quincy (1767-1848): U.S. statesman and *John Adams'* son. Secretary of State 1817-24; President 1824-28. He drafted the *Monroe Doctrine* and negotiated the transfer of the Floridas from Spain in the *Adams-Onis Treaty* (1819). As President, he sought but failed to obtain concessions from Britain concerning trade with the West Indies. Despite intense personal opposition to *slavery*, he upheld American claims to *neutral rights* against British demands to search U.S. ships that might be transporting slaves. He is usually listed among the most successful secretaries of state, though not presidents, for framing the American *realist* tradition in foreign affairs. His final years were spent fighting slavery from inside Congress.

Adams/Onis Treaty (1819): *John Quincy Adams* and the Spanish Ambassador Dom Louis de Onis agreed to set the boundary between the U.S. and *Spanish America* from the Floridas to the Pacific. Adams acquired the East Florida panhandle, West Florida (that is, southern Mississippi, Alabama and Georgia), and the *Oregon Territory*. He gave up only a vague claim to *Texas* that the U.S. would later revive anyway. A.k.a the Floridas or Transcontinental Treaty.

Adenauer, Konrad (1876-1967): West German Chancellor 1949-63. Mayor of Cologne during the *Weimar* period, he was removed from office by the *Nazis*. After *WWII* he became leader of the *Christian Democratic Union* and the first West German Chancellor. He worked with the U.S. to rebuild and rehabilitate *West Germany*, leading it back to full acceptance with entry into *NATO* in 1955. He embraced the *Schuman Plan*, Franco/German cooperation, and European federalism. During his tenure Germany became the locomotive of European recovery and prosperity. As Adenauer foresaw, it was soon a bulwark against Soviet political *influence* and exerted a magnetic attraction for moribund eastern economies. That reality was dramatized by *East Germany's* construction of the *Berlin Wall* a year before Adenauer's retirement.

Aden Protectorate: A onetime British *colony* and port, *annexed* in 1833 and made a Crown Colony in 1937. Set up as a *protectorate* in 1966, it combined several minor *sheikdoms* with the port of Aden. It was later absorbed into Yemen.

adherence: Acceptance of a *treaty* by additional states, with the *consent* of the original signatories.

ad hoc: For a particular purpose; temporary.

ad hoc chambers: See *chambers of the Court*.

adjudication: The settlement of (almost always) nonvital *disputes* through voluntary submission by all parties to a binding judicial decision.

adjustment: The way states use saving, production, and expenditures to correct deficits in their *current accounts*, and stabilize their *balance of payments*.

administration: A synonym for the U.S. *executive* branch or presidency alone, and even then usually just the top officers, not the government as a whole.

adoption: (1) A doctrine whereby *international laws* are incorporated into *municipal law* by custom or statute, but are not so incorporated automatically. (2) When states *consent* to a *treaty*.

Adowa, Battle of (1896): A decisive, humiliating defeat of Italian colonial forces by the Abyssinians (Ethiopians). This badly damaged Italian *prestige* and delayed *conquest* of Ethiopia until the 1930s.

adventurism: Rash or reckless pursuit of national ambitions, often *prestige* or *conquest*, that risks *war* though a *victory* is highly uncertain.

advisory opinion: The answer to inquiries put to an international court, that permits a court to issue a legal opinion without any case before it.

advisory services: Legal, technical and other specialized assistance offered to one state by another (or by a *multilateral* agency) to help the weak state meet its *treaty* obligations, or in the interest of *development*.

aerospace defense: An all-embracing term including measures to defend against aircraft, *missiles* or even space-based weapons systems.

affluent society: Advanced, post-*WWII* industrial societies that emphasize *consumer goods* and other material satisfactions.

Afghanistan: Location: Central Asia. Major associations: *NAM, UN*. Population: 16 million. Military: surplus Soviet and U.S. weapons systems left from the Soviet war, divided among warring factions; no offensive capability. An arid, mountainous, *Islamic* country lying along the historic Central Asian *invasion* route, and traditionally associated with Persia. It was a source of friction between Britain and Russia during the 19th century *Great Game*. It fell under British sway in 1857, but was never fully pacified. It achieved a fractious independence in the 1920s, and signed a *nonaggression pact* with the Soviet Union. Feudal *emirs* ruled in uneasy coexistence under a loose, central kingdom until 1973, when a *coup* led by Sadar Muhammad Daud Khan (1909-78) turned Afghanistan into a *republic*. It was a quiet member of the *Non-*

Aligned Movement until 1978, when a pro-Soviet coup led to Khan's death, drew Afghanistan into the *Cold War*, and generated large-scale internal unrest. A second coup led to a Soviet invasion in December 1979. Soviets and Afghan communists fought Afghan *mujahadeen*, who received significant U.S. assistance, for nine years. The *guerrillas* prevailed: the Soviets withdrew in 1989. Afghanistan then resumed its traditional *neutrality*. The mujahadeen took over the government in April 1992. Yet, the *civil war* continued along factional, religious and tribal lines. UN efforts to *mediate* proved fruitless into 1994.

Afghan-Soviet War (1979-89): A pro-Soviet *coup* in 1978 was partly reversed in a counter-coup in 1979. The second coup served as the pretext for a Soviet *invasion* over Christmas, that brought Babrak Karmal to power in Kabul. But what really sparked the invasion was a rebellion by the Afghan garrison in Herat, put down at a cost of 20,000 lives. For nine years the Soviets fought a brutal campaign against Afghan *guerrillas*, or *mujahadeen*, in which one million died. The Afghans received assistance from the U.S. Some Muslim nations also provided weapons and financing. The *CIA* supplied the ultimately decisive weapons: ground-to-air Stinger missiles that curtailed Soviet *air power*, and thousands of mules to haul supplies from Pakistan. In 1986 Muhammad Najibullah (the head of *KHAD*) replaced Karmal, but the fighting continued. A UN mediated *cease-fire* in 1988 led to full Soviet withdrawal by February 1989, and the return of several million *refugees*. The agreement was jointly guaranteed by the U.S. and USSR, but was rejected by the mujahadeen as long as Najibullah remained in power. The Afghan communists, who ultimately became just another faction in the civil war, were toppled in 1992. But that did not end the fighting, which moved into Kabul, hitherto relatively unscathed by thirteen years of *war*. As various factions contended for power, 30,000 were killed in Kabul alone and 100,000 injured in 1992-93. Fighting continued in 1994.

Afghan Wars: (1) 1832-42. (2) 1878-79. (3) 1879-80. (4) 1919. Fought between Britain and the Afghans, partly due to Britain's efforts to forestall Russian expansion toward the Persian Gulf and India, but also its own desire to control Afghanistan. The last was more repression of an Afghan *rebellion* than a full *war*.

Africa: The world's poorest and second most populous continent. It is bounded by the Atlantic and Indian Oceans and the Mediterranean Sea, and adjoins Europe and Asia via the Sinai. It is divided into North Africa, which is predominantly Muslim, Arab and Berber, and sub-Saharan Africa, which is predominantly black and divided into Muslims, Christians and Animists. There are also several white *enclaves*. Sub-Saharan Africa is also subdivided into East, West and Southern Africa. The continent is desperately poor: the total *GNP* south of the Sahara barely equals that of Holland or Belgium. See also *Sahel; sudan.*

African: Any native or citizen of a country in Africa, including the Arab and Berber states of North Africa, the large island of Madagascar, and several small island chains in the Atlantic and Indian Oceans.

African Development Bank: Headquartered in Abidjan, Ivory Coast, it was founded in 1965 by African states to assist in their *development* projects and attract outside *capital*. Besides meager start-up capital, it has received occasional infusions from non-African *donor countries*. It now includes some non-regional members, but remains the smallest and least well-funded of the several *regional banks*.

African National Congress (ANC): This multiracial, but mostly black, organization was created in 1912 to promote peaceful, democratic reform of South African society. It turned to armed action after the *Sharpeville massacre* in 1960. It made no secret of the joint membership of a number of its senior leaders (e.g., Joe Slovo) in the South African Communist Party, a fact that drew fire from some quarters in the West. It was banned in 1961 and its leadership, including *Nelson Mandela*, imprisoned. It drew support from the *front line states*, the *Soviet bloc*, and in its non-military aspects also from a number of Western countries and international *aid* agencies. Through the 1980s it carried out *guerrilla* attacks from bases in neighboring African states, while organizing in secret in the townships. In 1990 the ANC was legalized ahead of the release of Mandela and the opening of negotiations aiming at a multiracial constitution. It was drawn into a violent political struggle with unreconstructed whites, *Zulu* supporters of *Inkatha*, and the radicals of the *Pan-African Congress* who rejected any *power sharing*. It prevailed in the first free elections, in 1994.

Afrikaner (Boer): A white South African who speaks Afrikaans, usually of Dutch or French Huguenot lineage, and not including the ethnically English whites who live predominantly in the Cape Town area.

Afro-Asian bloc: A large *caucus group* formed in the UN and other *IGO*s. It presented a more solid front during the *Cold War* than presently.

afrocentrism: Viewing world affairs from the point of view of Africa and Africans.

Agadir: A *crisis* erupted over this Moroccan port in July 1911, when a German gunboat was dispatched to show the flag to the French, then expanding across North Africa. The British feared Germany's intent was to threaten their base at *Gibraltar*. The crisis was resolved, as only *prestige* was at stake, not *vital interests*. Yet it contributed significantly to prewar *tension*, and deepened distrust on all sides. It is sometimes referred to as the "Second Moroccan Crisis."

agency: When one state acts on behalf of another, because the second lacks representation or *diplomatic relations* with a third country.

agent: (1) An *intelligence* operative, especially if *covert*. (2) An element or component of *chemical, biological* or *nerve weapons*. (3) In international relations theory, a problem of *causality* arising where there is difficulty identifying the relative influence of the direct agent of an action and the deeper structure in which the action occurs. See also *agent of influence; agent provocateur; double agent; illegal agent; legal agent; penetration agent.*

agent of influence: An *agent* whose task is to spread *disinformation* or *propaganda*, or by insinuation into a position of influence to affect the decisions of key policy-makers. Cf. *mole; penetration agent.*

agent provocateur: An *agent* of some *secret police* or *intelligence service*, who incites selected persons to actions that make them liable to arrest, prosecution or political defeat.

aggrandizement: An increase in a state's *territory*, usually by *conquest*; if by one *Great Power* with the agreement of others, it may be accompanied by *compensation.*

aggression: In general, any unprovoked attack aiming at *expansion* or *conquest*. Aggressive *war* has been made illegal in the 20th century (hence, modern aggressors always maintain that they are acting defensively). The idea of aggression assumes that an *international society* exists, and that *states* within this society have certain rights and duties. The unprovoked use of *force* to strip away one such right, to *territorial integrity*, is deemed to be criminal (indeed, the only state-to-state crime), and justifies the use of force in *self-defense*. It has been encoded in *international law* that nothing but resisting aggression can justify war, and that aggressors may be punished unilaterally, collectively, or subsequently (in the form of *reparations*). For all that, a precise, binding legal definition still eludes consensus. The closest approximation is

from a UN Special Committee that adopted a nonbinding definition in 1974, declaring as aggression the use of force in any manner inconsistent with the *UN Charter*. It added a list of seven offenses that so qualified: (1) *incursion, invasion* or *occupation* of *territory;* (2) *bombardment;* (3) *blockade* of ports or a coastline, though not if undertaken with UN authority as a *police action;* (4) any unprovoked attack on the armed forces of another state; (5) using military bases in a second state to attack a third, without permission of the second; (6) allowing unprovoked military action against another state to be taken from one's territory, or otherwise aiding and abetting a second-party aggression; (7) sending armed irregulars or *mercenaries* to attack another state. See also *crimes against peace.* Cf. *indirect aggression.*

aggressor: A state that engages in an unprovoked attack on another, or otherwise engages in acts of *aggression.*

agitprop: Agitation and *propaganda* used against targeted countries to stir populations to civil unrest or *rebellion*. This tactic was developed by Russian, *marxist* revolutionaries in their domestic political struggles, and later added by them and others to the foreign policy arsenal of communist states.

agréation: The formal exchange of *diplomats* between and among *states.*

agrément: Formal acceptance of an accredited *diplomat* by a receiving (host) government.

agricultural revolution: (1) A shift in cropping practices and landholding systems, and technological innovations, that together greatly increased farm production in Europe in the 18th century, and later. It stimulated population growth while displacing people from the land to the new, rapidly growing cities. It led to rural unrest, underlay urbanization and urban poverty, and spilled Europe's overflow population into colonial enterprises on several continents. But it also contributed to new accumulations of capital and labor that stimulated industrialization and shifted the political balance among social classes. That sometimes resulted in revolutionary upheaval; other times in new social compacts where different classes shared the fruits of a foreign policy of *imperialism*. (2) The astonishing expansion in farm productivity and output since c.1940, especially in the U.S. and Western Europe, based upon industrialization of agriculture and new fertilizers and seed. It has had a global impact, paradoxically raising both population levels and living standards. Cf. *green revolution; Malthus.*

agriculture: See *agricultural revolution; CAP; collectivization; famine; FAO; food; GATT; green revolution; neo-mercantilism; Uruguay Round.*

aid: *Development*, economic, humanitarian or military assistance from one *state* to another, or *multilateral* assistance. The objectives vary with each relationship, but can include: *alliance* and political support; purchase of general *influence* over foreign policy; bribery on specific projects or issues; assurance of access to market share; development; *postwar reconstruction*; maintenance of economic stability; *debt* relief; or even altruism and humanitarianism. It became a prominent feature of world politics with the *Cold War*, which spurred the *ERP*, *Colombo Plan* and bilateral programs. Some types: (1) Development aid: *Soft loans* or grants to assist *LDCs* develop *infrastructure.* (2) Economic aid: Money or credit given to sustain the economy of a recipient, or meet *balance of payments* problems. Most economic aid is given by the *OECD* nations, lately joined by *OPEC*. There is a growing tendency to channel it through multilateral or *regional banks*, though the majority remains bilateral. (3) Humanitarian aid: Food, medicine, shelter or other *matériel* assistance given to support a civil population in times of national disaster, such as earthquake or *famine,* or to alleviate the suffering attendant on *war.* (4) Military aid: Money, matériel or technical advice given to support a recipient's military development, *deterrence,* or wartime operations. It can be given by virtually any state. Cf. *advisory services; aid burden; IBRD; IMF; ODA; NIEO; tied aid.*

aid burden: The extent to which *aid* draws upon a *donor country's* revenues as a proportion of *GNP*.

airborne troops: *Infantry* delivered to the battlefield by glider or parachute.

Airborne Warning and Control System (AWACS): Advanced radar and communications equipment based in aircraft. AWACS aircraft spot enemy targets and threats and direct strikes and counter-strikes. They are the key to complex air combat operations.

airburst: Detonation of a *nuclear weapon* above its target, to obtain maximize *blast* and *radiation effects.*

air cavalry: *Infantry* with independent air transport.

aircraft carrier: A large, *capital warship* with a flat deck and concealed hangers, capable of carrying a variety of aircraft and used to project *power* far from home waters. An "aircraft carrier battle group" is an arrangement developed by the U.S. Navy in which multiple ships of many types, protecting the aircraft carrier(s) at the center, move under a single coordinated command.

air drop: Dropping military or humanitarian relief supplies from the air.

Air Launched Ballistic Missile (ALBM): A *ballistic missile* carried by and fired from an aircraft, blimp or other airborne vehicle.

Air Launched Cruise Missile (ALCM): A *cruise missile* carried by and fired from an aircraft, blimp or other airborne vehicle.

air power: (1) A nation in the first rank in air force strength. (2) The ability to project *force* with aircraft, and now *missiles*. The effects of air power were small in *WWI*, but tactically if not strategically decisive by *WWII*, on land and at sea. There is some disagreement as to whether *aircraft carriers* and *cruise missile*-launching *submarines* should be classified as elements of air power or *sea power*. Cf. *land power.*

airspace: States claim and exercise *sovereignty* not just on, but also above and below their *territory*. The rules governing *civilian* use of national airspace, and the principle of free international airspace, were set in a 1944 *convention* that created a monitoring body, the International Civil Aviation Organization. Military transit of a country's airspace always requires advance permission. At sea, airspace corresponds to the *twelve-mile limit*. Also see *innocent passage.*

Air-to-Air Missile (AAM): A *guided missile* fired from an aircraft against enemy planes or *missiles*.

Air-to-Surface Ballistic Missile (ASBM): A *ballistic missile* fired from an aircraft at a ground or sea target.

Aix-la-Chapelle, Congress of (1818): Austria, Britain, Prussia and Russia met for the first time under the *Congress system*. France was brought back into the *Great Power* fold following its *defeat* in 1814-15. Aix also settled French *reparations*, fixed *Napoleon's* exile to St. Helena, and most unusual, gave a guarantee of civil rights to German Jews. Most important, it marked the beginning of Britain's shift away from the continental powers. London was moving back to its tradition of aloofness from continental entanglements in favor of overseas expansion, and it was concerned about restoration of the *balance of power*. Britain also opposed any extension of Russian *influence* into the west of the continent, under the guise of *intervention* to suppress outbreaks of *liberal* reform and *rebellion*.

Ajaria: A Georgian region that after 1991 sought to secede, but offered to settle for *autonomy*.

Akihito (b.1933): Emperor of Japan. He acceded to the throne in 1989 upon the death of his father, *Hirohito*. In 1993 he apologized to China and Korea for Japan's wartime *aggression* and atrocities.

Alabama claims: Generic term for a series of *disputes* arising from the *American Civil War*, taken from a commerce raider (CSS Alabama) built for the *Confederacy* by Britain, which had done great damage to *Union* shipping. All claims were settled by tribunal in 1871, marking an important advance for the principle of international *arbitration*. Along with the *Treaty of Washington*, the Alabama settlement signaled a shift from Anglo/American animosity toward the permanent *rapprochement* critical to the course of world affairs in the 20th century.

Aland Islands: Russia gained these Baltic islands, and Finland, in 1809. They were declared *neutral* as part of the settlement of the *Crimean War*. Their *occupation* by Sweden in 1918 provoked a brief German *intervention*. The *League of Nations* gave the islands to Finland in 1921, under conditions of *demilitarization* and *autonomy* for the predominantly Swedish population. Occupied by Germany from 1941 to 1944, they reverted to Finland in 1945. Finland wanted to exempt them from *EU* rules as it negotiated its own admission, because *Maastricht* threatened Aland *demilitarization* with its common defense policy.

Alaska: See *Russian-America*.

Albania: Location: *Balkans*. Major associations: *CSCE, UN*. Population: 3.3 million. Military: small, outdated. Ruled by the *Ottomans* for over 300 years and containing a large share of Europe's Muslims as a result, Albania became an independent principality in 1913, following the *Balkan Wars*. It quickly sank into *anarchy*. Nevertheless, its independence was confirmed in 1921 in an agreement between Italy, Greece and Yugoslavia, all of which coveted Albanian *territory* but could not agree on *partition*. Proclaimed a *republic* in 1925, it returned to *monarchy* under *King Zog I* (1928-39). Invaded and occupied by Italy in 1939, and Germany in 1940, it was freed by nationalist and communist *guerrillas* in 1944. Under the quixotic, *stalinist* dictator *Enver Hoxha*, it joined the *Soviet bloc* early in the *Cold War*. A schism over *de-stalinization* led to a break with Moscow in 1958. In 1961 Albania was expelled from *COMECON*, and in 1968 it withdrew from the *Warsaw Pact*. It then supported China and followed a policy of *autarky*. It

was the only European country not to sign the *CSCE* accords in 1975. Hoxha broke with China in 1978, after the death of *Mao Zedong*. That left Albania and North Korea the only remaining, staunchly stalinist states, and Europe's poorest and most repressive country. Hoxha died (utterly unmourned) in 1985. It was among the last communist states to break down during the upheavals of 1989-91, and there was significant bloodshed first. Albanian *boat people* crossed as economic *refugees* to Italy in 1991. That year, *James Baker* became the first U.S. Secretary of State ever to visit Albania. In 1993 the U.S. agreed to supply surplus light arms and equipment to replace Albania's obsolete (1950s) Chinese weapons, as Washington and Tirana drew together out of a shared interest in preventing the spread of *ethnic cleansing* by Serbs to the ethnic Albanians in *Kosovo* and *Macedonia*.

Aleutian Islands: An Alaskan archipelago extending toward eastern *Siberia*. During *WWII* the western Aleutians (Attu and Kiska) were occupied by Japan from mid-1942 to mid-1943, and only retaken with heavy loss of life. That *occupation* helped *postwar* acceptance of Alaskan statehood by the lower 48 states.

Alexander I, of Russia (1777-1825): *Tsar*. He is sometimes called "the enlightened despot" because of his early flirtation with social reform. He fought *Napoleon* in the *War of the Third Coalition*, made *peace* at *Tilsit* in 1807, fought again in 1812 and in the *War of the Fourth Coalition*. He rode into Paris at the head of a Russian army in 1814 and played a prominent role at the *Congress of Vienna*. (When *Stalin* was congratulated at *Potsdam* on his victorious presence in Berlin, he remarked: "Tsar Alexander got to Paris.") He extended Russian *influence* into Central Europe under the guise of a Polish *protectorate* and a conservative *coalition* with Austria and Prussia. Five years after *Waterloo* he still had a million men under arms. He championed *reaction* against the influence of the *French Revolution* when he founded the *Holy Alliance*. His reactionary rhetoric, *interventions* in Poland and Italy, and threat to intervene in Latin America pushed Britain out of the *Congress system* and provoked the *Monroe Doctrine*. He was followed by his even more reactionary brother, *Nicholas I*.

Alexander I, of Yugoslavia (1888-1934): Regent and later king of the *United Kingdom of the Serbs, Croats and Slovenes* from 1918 to 1929, when the name was changed to Yugoslavia. He was instrumental in establishment of the *Little Entente*, which he wanted to connect to France in a larger security arrangement. He was assassinated by a Macedonian *fanatic* while on a diplomatic mission to France in 1934.

Alexander II, of Russia (1818-81): He was made *Tsar* during the *Crimean War*. He responded to that disaster for Russia with a series of great reforms (including *emancipation* of the serfs, but without a corresponding grant of land), aimed at *modernization* of the economy, government and military. He was the *Union's* main support during the *American Civil War*, when France and Britain were flirting with *recognition* of the *Confederacy*. He wished the Union to serve as a commercial and geopolitical counterweight to Britain, to distract the British from his own designs on the *Ottoman Empire*. In 1867 he approved the sale of *Russian-America* (Alaska) to the U.S. Maintaining amicable relations with *Prussia*, he expanded into the *Balkans* under cover of *pan-Slavism*, and into *Central Asia* under cover of defending Christians against the Muslim Turks. That raised suspicion in London that his real objective was to capture India. This Anglo/Russian conflict deepened over Afghanistan during later decades. His assassination propelled Russia into *reaction*, including officially sanctioned *pogroms* that ultimately sent two million destitute Jews to the U.S.

Algeciras Conference (1906): An attempt to settle the *dispute* that led to the *Moroccan Crisis* of 1905. Contrary to Berlin's hopes and expectations, its main significance was that it brought France and Britain closer, and opened a channel between those powers and Russia as well. The conference also authorized France and Spain to "police" Morocco, which remained under nominal rule by its *sultan*. The Swiss acted as observers. The U.S. also signed, but said it would do nothing to enforce the *terms* (see *entangling alliances*).

Algeria: Location: North Africa. Major associations: *Arab League, NAM, OAU, OPEC, UN*. Population: 26 million. Military: regional capability. Ruled by the *Ottomans* from 1518 to 1830, it was for decades a base for Muslim *pirate* raids against a lucrative Mediterranean trade. It was seized by France in 1830, although resistance lasted until 1845. Algeria occupied a special place in French colonial history, as both a kind of French *Siberia*, full of political exiles, and a preferred locale of settlement by nearly one million French who migrated there. In 1871 it was formally "attached" to France. It was part of *Vichy* during *WWII* until Anglo/American troops forced a switch to the *Free French* side in 1942. French rule was fully restored in 1945, but local *nationalism* led to the *Algerian War of Independence* beginning in 1954, with cruel atrocities on both sides. The revolt brought down the *Fourth Republic*, already teetering from defeat in Indochina, and brought *Charles de Gaulle* to power in France. He accepted Algerian independence in 1962. That entailed departure of the French settlers ("pied

noir") and almost led to *civil war* in France itself. Ahmed Ben Bella (b.1919) was Premier, 1962-65; President, 1963-65. He was an *authoritarian* at home but *neutral* in the *Cold War*. He was ousted in a *coup* led by Houari Boumédienne (1927-78), dictator to 1978. Boumédienne toed a neutralist line, accepting *aid* from the West and the Soviets while opposing *peace* with Israel. He also sought a *pan-Arab* union in N. Africa. Algeria broke with the West in 1967, *declaring war* on Israel during the *Third Arab/Israeli War*. During the 1970s and 1980s it developed close ties with the *Soviet bloc*. Domestic unrest after 1988 led to a multiparty constitution and attempts to patch relations with the West in the early 1990s. Despite economic distress and collapse of its Soviet ally, it still criticized UN action against Iraq in the 1990 *Gulf War*, and subsequently. When Islamic *fundamentalists* won a first round of elections in 1992, the second was canceled and emergency rule instituted. This action was not greeted in the West with the same dismay that met cancelled elections elsewhere. Algeria accused Iran of funding the militants and broke *diplomatic relations*. It also *recalled its Ambassador* from radical, fundamentalist Sudan.

Algerian War of Independence (1954-62): Algerian nationalists in the FLN fought a *guerrilla* campaign against France that eventually pitched 100,000 irregulars against 500,000 French troops. In 1958 a *mutiny* within the French army threatened to spread the war to France itself. *Charles de Gaulle* was called back from the political wilderness, while the FLN set up a provisional government in Tunis. De Gaulle put down the mutiny and continued the war, but also offered *autonomy* to Algeria. That sparked a *terrorist* campaign within France and a revolt by French settlers, joined by units of the *Foreign Legion*. Settler bombs in Paris, rising casualties, and the viciousness of both sides changed French *public opinion*, and Algeria was given its *independence* in July 1962.

Algiers: Formerly one of the *Barbary States*; the city and its hinterland are today an integral part of Algeria. See *Tripolitan War*.

alien: Someone who is foreign born and not a *naturalized* citizen, and who therefore owes legal allegiance to another country. A resident/non-resident alien is one who has/has not taken up domicile. Among legal aliens are *diplomats, visa* workers and *tourists*. An illegal alien is a foreigner who enters without permission. An enemy alien is an alien present or residing in a country with which his or her own is at *war*.

alignment: The way *states* are arranged or arrayed according to their common enemies, *security treaties* and political interests. Cf. *alliance*

Allende Gossens, Salvador (1908-73): Chilean *marxist* elected President in 1970, after three earlier failures (1952, 1958, 1964). He encountered substantial domestic opposition to his program of *nationalizations*, and was opposed by several *multinational corporations* whose property was expropriated. Lastly, he was opposed by the *Nixon* administration. *CIA* support for strikes designed to undermine the Allende government has been confirmed. A CIA role in the 1973 *coup* that cost his life and presidency is widely alleged, but direct evidence for that charge is lacking. However, the evidence of earlier support for destabilization and the open hostility of the Nixon administration suggest that the coup had tacit U.S. support. In either case, it led to a repressive *junta* under Augusto Pinochet (b.1915), who ruled with an iron, indeed murderous, hand until 1989. In 1990 Allende's corpse was exhumed and given a *state funeral*, to honor his death while holding a democratic office.

alliance: A formal agreement between or among *states*, whether secret or open, in which military and security policy is coordinated with a common diplomacy. See also *ally; casus foederis; confederation; entangling alliance; league; pact; tacit alliance.* Cf. *alignment; nonalignment; neutrality.*

Alliance for Progress: An *aid* and *trade* initiative for Latin America that revisited the *Good Neighbor policy* of the 1930s. Announced by *John F. Kennedy* in March 1961, it was endorsed by the *OAS* states (except Cuba). It was premised on a "*takeoff*" theory of *development* that had a powerful administration advocate in Walt W. Rostow. It failed, largely because it was simultaneously underfunded and overly ambitious.

Allies, WWI: Common term for the allied powers who fought the *Central Powers*: the British Empire, France, Japan, Russia, Serbia, Italy, Belgium, Greece and Rumania. The U.S. called itself an "Associated Power" during the war and in the *peace treaties*, to uphold the fiction that it had not joined an *entangling alliance.*

Allies, WWII: Common term for the *WWII* alliance that was formally called the "*United Nations*," whose principal members were: the United States, the Soviet Union, Britain and China. Lesser powers included the *Free French*, and forty small nations and territories, of whom the more notable were: Australia, Belgium, Canada, Greece, Norway, Poland, South Africa and Yugoslavia (Serbia). A million Indian troops fought for the *British Empire*. Other than Ethiopians and South Africans, Africans who fought did so within various colonial forces. The formal name of the alliance was transferred to the postwar security organization founded in 1945 by these victors of WWII.

allocation of resources: How resources are apportioned within a national or international economy. For most traditional economists the primary interest is in questions of *efficiency;* more *radical* views focus on matters of social and *distributive justice.*

ally: (1) A *state* bound by *security treaty* to another. (2) Less commonly, a state that tacitly coordinates defense policy with another, without aid of any *treaty.*

Alsace-Lorraine: Alsace was *occupied* by France in 1648. Lorraine was *annexed* in 1766. After the *Franco/Prussian War*, Alsace and most of Lorraine were ceded to Germany in the *Treaty of Frankfurt* (1871). Recovery of the lost provinces became a central French *war aim* in *WWI*, a goal achieved in the *Treaty of Versailles* (1919). Reclamation of the territories then became a demand of German nationalists. In 1940 the territories were re-annexed by Germany. The provinces were *liberated* and returned to France in 1944. Today, their French status is assured by close Franco/German cooperation within the *EU* (not to mention the *force de frappe*).

Amal: A *shi'ite militia* active in the *Lebanese Civil War*, supported by Iran and fiercely opposed to Israel.

Amazon basin: The great drainage basin of the Amazon river system, with its several thousand tributaries. It lies mostly in Brazil but portions are found in nine different countries. It has become an increasing focus of environmental concern as *slash and burn* clearing continues, possibly adding to *global warming* and threatening *biological diversity*; and it is a place of severe mistreatment of *indigenous people.*

Amazon Pact: A 1978 treaty signed by most states with *territory* in the *Amazon basin*: Bolivia, Brazil, Colombia, Ecuador, Guyana, Peru, Suriname and Venezuela. It aims at joint development and management of the basin, and at regulation of water usage, navigation, transportation, research and *tourism.*

Ambassador: The highest rank of *diplomats*, historically considered the personal representative of a *sovereign,* or of a sovereign power. They are usually resident. If *ad hoc* or roving, they are called "Ambassador-at-Large" or "Special Ambassador." See *chargé d'affaires; consul; diplomacy; envoy extraordinary; high commissioner; nonresident ambassador.*

America: A commonly used alternative to "United States of America," even though the politically correct wince at this usage as supposedly exclusive of other *nations* of the *Americas.*

American Civil War (1861-65): It broke out after 11 slave-owning states seceded from the *Union* following the 1860 election of *Abraham Lincoln*, and formed the *Confederate States of America*, or Confederacy. *Secession* sprang from a deep conflict between the values and economics of the *slave states* and those of the industrialized, free labor Northern states (though it should be noted that several slave states stayed in the Union). That conflict had become irreconcilable with the application for admission of new states after the westward expansion occasioned by the *Mexican/American War*. The South enjoyed early successes owing to superior morale and inferior Union generalship. However, over time the natural advantages of the North in manpower and industrial capacity were brought to bear. The war was decided by two things: (1) a naval *blockade* which progressively strangled Confederate *trade* and led to an *inflation* crisis; and (2) *attrition* on the battlefield. The key battles were Vicksburg and *Gettysburg*, which took place within days of each other in 1863. Defeat in both turned back the high tide of the Confederacy and set the stage for *Ulysses S. Grant's* campaign of attrition. The main Union army under Grant pressed home the attack on *Robert E. Lee's* confederates during 1864-65, while William T. Sherman (1820-91, "war is hell") cut a swath of destruction deep through the Confederate heartland. Lee *surrendered* to Grant at Appomattox Court House on April 9, 1865. Lincoln was shot by an assassin within the week, dying on April 15. The Confederacy had failed to win foreign *allies* or *recognition* by France or Britain, always the key to its survival. The Union won by forcing the issue militarily, while modifying its diplomacy and principles just enough to placate European sensibilities and forestall outside *intervention*. Some 600,000 were killed, more than in all other American wars combined. Afterwards, Americans had little appetite for *annexation*: they opposed aquisition of Cuba or Santo Domingo, and called the purchase of Alaska "Seward's Folly."

americanize: To make similar to the customs of the U.S. in cultural, economic, political or social respects.

American Relief Administration (ARA): A *famine* relief agency set up after *WWI* to alleviate *postwar* starvation in Belgium and other parts of Europe, both for humanitarian reasons and to forestall the spread of *Bolshevism*. It was headed, very effectively, by *Herbert Hoover*. During the great famine in Russia from 1921-23 it fed, clothed, and provided medical treatment to tens of millions of Soviet citizens, quite possibly saving the *regime*.

American Revolution: See *American War of Independence.*

American Samoa: It was taken over by the U.S. 1900-04, by agreement with Britain (*compensated* in the Solomon Islands) and Germany (given *Western Samoa*). It was administered by the U.S. Navy until 1951, then by the Interior Department. Its first elections were held in 1978. It is an *unincorporated territory* of the United States. Samoans are "American nationals" but not *citizens*, which means they may come and go freely from the mainland and other U.S. *jurisdictions*, but may not vote. Of approximately 125,000 American Samoans nearly 70% have migrated to Hawaii or California.

American War of Independence (1775-83): The *war* between Britain and those thirteen of its seventeen North American *colonies* that joined in rebellion to secure independence (*Upper Canada, Newfoundland* and Nova Scotia remained loyal to Britain, while *Lower Canada* was effectively occupied). The immediate cause of the conflict arose from the outcome of the *Seven Years' War*, which by removing France from North America lessened the colonists' need for British protection, while simultaneously encouraging the British to impose greater *duties* on colonial *exports* and make the colonies pay for their own garrisons. After the Declaration of Independence, the main contribution made by *George Washington* and the Continental Army was simply to survive, and thereby sustain the *rebellion* until other powers *intervened*. Defeats of the British at Saratoga and at *Yorktown* were not decisive in themselves, but they gave Britain's European enemies the final push they needed to *recognize* the U.S. and enter the war. The decisive events actually took place in Europe, where France and the Netherlands *declared war* on Britain in 1778 and 1780 and brought to bear their combined navies to threaten British interests far more vital than retention of the American colonies. London therefore made *peace* on terms more favorable than American arms had won in the field, or at sea. About one-third of the U.S. population rejected *independence*. Some stayed anyway, but others returned to England, resettled in the Caribbean or went as *United Empire Loyalists* to Upper Canada and Nova Scotia, where some of their descendants still harbor anti-Yankee sentiments.

Americas: North, Central and South America, and their island extensions. See *New World.*

amerophile/phobe: One who admires/fears the United States, and/or things American.

Amiens, Peace of (March 25, 1802): A false settlement of Mediterranean issues that amounted to no more than a pause in the *War of the Second Coalition*. *Napoleon* violated the agreement within months by intervening politically in Germany, Switzerland and Italy. *War* between England and France resumed in May 1803.

Amin, Idi Dada (b.1926): Ugandan officer who took power in a *coup* in 1971. He became "dictator-for-life" and began an eight-year reign of savage butchery. However, his talent for titillating insults to the *West* often played well in Africa. He flirted with support for *terrorist* groups and drew financial support and even troops from Libya. In 1978 the U.S. imposed *sanctions* on coffee, which severely hurt Amin's regime. But he was ousted only after provoking neighboring Tanzania, which invaded in 1979. Amin fled to Libya, then Saudi Arabia, where he lives in comfortable exile. He left behind a *civil war* and *anarchy* from which Uganda took many years to recover. See *Entebbe raid*.

Amnesty International: A global *human rights* monitoring agency made up of private volunteers and a small corps of salaried officers. It works to free *prisoners of conscience* and for the right to a fair trial, and against *torture* and capital punishment. Its main tactic is publicity. In 1977 it was awarded the *Nobel Peace Prize*. It has official observer status at meetings of the *UNHRC*.

analyst: (1) In general: Any person who makes considered appraisals of the nature or course of world affairs, often on a professional basis. (2) In *intelligence*: A person with area, economic, language, scientific or technical expertise who interprets *raw intelligence*.

anarchical society: A depiction of world politics where *anarchy* is muted by decentralized "social" features among the states, such as *international law*, *international organization*, moral norms, and the *balance of power*. Cf. *world governance*.

anarchism: A 19th century political theory which looked to replace all *states* with idealized, voluntary social cooperation and saw government as the principal obstacle to *liberty*. Anarchist *terrorists* were very active at the end of the 19th century; they killed two tsars, an Austrian empress, an Italian king, a French president, U.S. President *William McKinley*, many lesser nobility and officials, and scores of innocent bystanders. Anarchism was important as a *dissident* movement in pre-revolutionary Russia, but as a mass political movement only in Spain before and during the *Spanish Civil War*.

anarchy: A social condition without government or law. By analogy, some see this as the underlying condition of international relations, in which the absence of a central authority means world politics approximates the *state of nature*, or "war of all against all," depicted by *Thomas Hobbes*. Others see that portrait as a crude view that does not account for extensive features of interstate cooperation, and propose instead that *states* exist in an *anarchical society*. Cf. *world community; world governance; world government*.

Anatolia: The broad plateau between the Mediterranean and Black Seas; a key region for the *Ottoman Empire*, it is now part of Turkey.

ancien régime: (1) The political and social system of France and Europe before 1789, marked by *absolutism* and *mercantilism*. (2) The world political and social order before *WWI*, dominated by conservative, *multinational empires* yet also filled with a sense of unfolding scientific and social progress. (3) Any era preceding a period of historic and revolutionary political and social upheaval.

Andean Common Market, a.k.a. Andean Pact: A sub-regional economic association agreed to in 1966 and set up in 1969, headquartered in Lima. It includes: Bolivia, Chile (withdrew in 1976; rejoined in 1990), Colombia, Ecuador, Peru and Venezuela (joined in 1973). Its "Foreign Investment Code" is among the more sophisticated, and pragmatic, Southern efforts to regulate *MNC* investment and activity. In 1989 it declared as goals: nuclear *non-proliferation*, regional development, and some level of political *integration*.

Andorra, Principality of: A political curiosity held over from the Middle Ages (1278), Andorra was for centuries a joint *sovereignty* co-ruled by France (until 1574, by the independent princedom, the Comte de Foix; after that passing to the French Crown, and then *state*) and the Spanish Archbishop of Urgel. A new constitution in 1993 gave it *autonomy*, and it joined the UN. Population: 51,000. Military: none.

Andropov, Yuri Vladimirovich (1914-84): Soviet statesman. He was Ambassador to Hungary during the Soviet *invasion* of that country in 1956. He headed the *KGB* from 1967 to 1982, when he was elected General Secretary of the *Communist Party* (CPSU). His drawn-out illness and death in February 1984, after just 14 months in office, set off a paralyzing succession crisis. Andropov wanted his friend and protégé *Mikhail Gorbachev* to take over, but the old guard elected *Konstantin Chernenko*. He proceeded to die after 11 enfeebled and ineffective months in power, and Gorbachev was at last elected.

angary, right of: In *international law*, the right of a *belligerent* to *requisition* or destroy the property of *neutrals* in accord with the doctrine of *necessity*. This must take place on one's own or on enemy *occupied* territory (no violation of the *territorial integrity* of the neutral is permitted), and must be accompanied at some point by full *compensation*. Previously, it included a claimed right to compel neutral ships and crews to carry the belligerent's troops or cargos, but in modern times it has been reserved to property, not persons. On land, there is a special *rule* concerning railways and rolling stock: under angary, a belligerent may seize neutral rolling stock that crosses onto its territory. However, as a neutral may retaliate by seizing the belligerent's trains on its territory, in practice this right tends to be applied sparingly.

Anglo/Egyptian Sudan: Sudan 1898-1955, during its period of *condominium* under Britain and Egypt.

Anglo/French *Entente*: See *Entente Cordiale*.

Anglo/German Naval Agreement (1935): Violating the *disarmament* clauses of the *Treaty of Versailles*, Britain agreed to German naval *rearmament* up to 35% of its own tonnage in *capital warships,* a figure German production could not even reach. More important, the agreement gave Germany equality with Britain in *submarines*, which would prove to be a critical weapon against British surface ships in *WWII*. In April 1939, Germany renounced the agreement, and began to build as many *warships* as its shipyards could turn out.

Anglo/German naval arms race (1895-1914): See *Dreadnought; Jutland; two-power naval standard*.

Anglo/Irish: Descendants of English/Scots settlers, mainly Protestants, living in Ireland. This minority has played a disproportionate role in Irish history, both on the side of *independence* and *republicanism* in the south, and in favor of retaining *Ulster's* ties to the English crown.

Anglo/Japanese Alliance (1902): A mutual assistance *pact* aimed at containing Russia in *Manchuria*, and confirming the integrity of China and Korea. From London's point of view, it precluded a Russo/Japanese *alliance* in Asia, and ended Britain's period of *splen-*

did isolation. For the Japanese, it opened the way to the surprise attack that started the *Russo/Japanese War.* It was redefined in 1905, in Japan's favor concerning Korea. Renewed for ten more years in 1911, it was replaced by the *Four Power Treaty*.

anglophile/phobe: A person who admires/fears Britain and things British.

anglophone: An English-speaking person or country.

Anglo/Russian Entente (1907-17): The easing of rivalry between Britain and Russia in the Mideast, Persia and Central Asia, brought about by the common threat from Germany. It established mutual *spheres of influence*, notably in Persia, and settled other outstanding questions. In September 1914, it was made into a formal, wartime alliance. See *Triple Entente*.

Angola: Location: Southern Africa. Major associations: *NAM, OAU, UN*. Population: 9 million. Military: engaged in *civil war*. Portuguese penetration began in the 16th century, although effective colonization did not take place until the 20th century. A multisided *guerrilla* war of *independence* started in 1961, but Portuguese rule only ended with a *revolution* in Lisbon in 1974. A civil war followed among the three main groups that had fought the Portuguese. The U.S. and South Africa backed UNITA, the Soviets supported the MPLA, and an independent FNLA guerrilla army struggled on without allies. Although a Cold War gloss of *ideology* was painted onto each faction, at root these groups represented regional and *tribal* interests. The MPLA crushed the FNLA by 1979 and took power in the capital with the help of Cuban troops, with UNITA retaining sections of countryside and its base in the south. In 1988 Cuba withdrew as part of a settlement with South Africa, the U.S. and the USSR, that included independence for *Namibia*. A *peace* agreement was signed in 1991 between the MPLA and UNITA. Following the MPLA's victory in internationally supervised elections in 1992, UNITA's Jonas Savimbi (b.1934) rejected the results. Russia, Portugal and the U.S. jointly warned Savimbi against restarting the war, but he defied them. Heavy fighting and casualties resumed in January 1993, literally over the heads of UN observers. UNITA no longer had foreign backers but still seized or destroyed important towns. In May the *Clinton* administration recognized the MPLA government, reversing 17 years of U.S. policy. UNITA made major territorial gains before the government resumed the offensive. By September 1993, the UN said 1,000 per day were dying, making Angola's the worst conflict in the world. The MPLA has *artillery* and *armor*, older model *MIGs*, weapons and a sizeable army. UNITA's supply lines have dried up, but its tribal support base is very strong.

Anguilla: This island in the *Lesser Antilles* has been a British colony since 1650. In 1958 it joined the *West Indies Federation*. In 1967 it declared *independence*, but Britain quietly put down the movement and it remains a *dependency*. Population: 7,000.

Annam: An Asian kingdom, and later a French *protectorate*, situated on the east coast of *Indochina*. It was split by the decision of the *Geneva Agreements* to divide Vietnam at the 17th parallel. With the *defeat* and *extinction* of *South Vietnam* in 1975, all Annam has been incorporated into a unified Vietnam.

annexation: When a state appends additional *territory* to itself that previously was claimed by another political authority, with or without legal sanction. From the Italian *Renaissance* to the settlement at the *Paris Peace Conference* in 1919, annexation was commonplace. The *Great Powers* seized or traded territory constrained by little other than threats and *retaliation* by their peers. Since 1919 the odd stab of public conscience has led to plebiscites on *self-determination*, but forcible annexations still abound. Some, such as *Nazi Germany's* seizures of 1939-41 and Iraq's 1990 annexation of Kuwait, have been generally rejected as illegitimate and were overturned when the opportunity ripened. Others fall into a gray area, where either the claims of the annexing state have some merit or the political reality is such that reversal seems impossible whatever the merits of the case. For instance, the 1938 German *Anschluss* with Austria and the Soviet annexations of 1939-40 (both since reversed); the Chinese takeover of *Tibet*; Israeli claims to Jerusalem and parts of the *occupied territories*.

Anschluss: The forced *union* of Austria and Germany by the *Nazis*, in March 1938. Union was forbidden by the treaties of *Versailles* and *St. Germain*, and in 1931 an attempt to establish a *customs union* was blocked by France. However, collaboration between Italy and Germany after 1936, and the internal ideological conflicts of the *Third Republic*, left Austria isolated. Chancellor Kurt von Schuschnigg (1897-1977) was forced out in favor of the Nazi Seyss-Inquart (1892-1946) on March 11, 1938. Seyss-Inquart then "invited" the German army to enter Austria, and the next day proclaimed the Anschluss. Britain, France and Italy did nothing. That enhanced Hitler's reputation within the army and *diplomatic corps*, and deepened his already profound contempt for the West. The Anschluss was reversed in 1945, with Austria *occupied* by the *Allies* until 1955 (separately from Germany).

Antarctic/Antarctica: The southern polar region/continent. Unlike the *Arctic,* it is not divided among the *states* but is governed by the *Antarctic Treaty system,* and it has no *indigenous peoples*. See also *whaling.*

Antarctic Circle: The circumpolar line at 23° 28' north of the South Pole.

Antarctic Treaty: Signed in late 1959 by 12 countries and in effect as of mid-1961, it bans nuclear tests, military activity, economic *exploitation*, and defers all *territorial* claims to the frozen continent (all enforced by on-site inspection). It allows scientific research stations as the only permanent installations. The original "Consultative Parties" retain full voting rights. They are subdivided into seven claimant states (Argentina, Australia, Britain, Chile, France, New Zealand and Norway), and five non-claimants. Other states joined the consultative group under the test of conducting "substantial research." All *states* may *adhere* as non-consultative parties. In 1991-92, it was renegotiated by 33 nations. The main amendment to the *regime* was the Madrid Protocol on Environmental Protection, banning mining and *oil* exploration for 50 years.

Antarctic Treaty system: The *Antarctic Treaty* and other *conventions* on marine conservation (flora and fauna in 1964; seals in 1972; marine living resources in 1982). A *moratorium* on mineral exploration and *exploitation* was set in 1977, and extended for 50 years in 1992. In 1988 the *UNGA* voted to include the *Secretary General* in the system, but this was not binding on the original *Treaty States*. Cf. *whaling.*

anti-ballistic missile, missile system (ABM): Defensive weapons designed to confuse, deflect or shoot down incoming *missiles*. The clumsy term arises as these missiles aim at *ballistic missiles*, not at "ballistics." *SDI* proponents said that the claimed success of the Patriot anti-aircraft system, converted to defend Israel and Saudi Arabia from Scud missile attacks during the *Gulf War*, showed that ABMs could be used against small, missile-armed powers. Others demurred. In any case, since 1991 new research on ABM systems has gotten underway in several major countries--including Japan, which is concerned about North Korea's missile and potential *nuclear weapons* capabilities. Cf. *ballistic missile defense.*

Anti-Ballistic Missile (ABM), Missile Treaty (1972): It was signed as part of the *SALT I* agreements, and came into force in October 1972. It limited the U.S. and USSR to two ABM sites (one capital and one silo) and 100 ABM *launchers* each. An ancillary *protocol* (1974) cut to one site each. The Soviets built theirs to defend Moscow. The U.S. began a site to protect part of its land-based *nuclear deterrent* but abandoned it as too expensive, and irrelevant to the reigning *strategic doctrine* of *Assured Destruction*. The *Strategic Defense Initiative* (SDI) program of the *Reagan* administration challenged the logic and renewal of the Treaty, as does the end of the *Cold War*.

Anti-COMINTERN Pact (November 25, 1936): A joint *declaration* by Nazi Germany and Imperial Japan affirming opposition to the *COMINTERN*. The soon-to-be Nazi Foreign Minister, *von Ribbentrop*, regarded this as a triumph worthy of exchanging German *recognition* of *Manchukuo*. Italy *adhered* the next year, also recognizing Manchukuo. The *pact* made Western powers nervous about German/Japanese collaboration, but did little more. In 1939 Hungary and Spain signed, followed in 1941 by Slovakia, Rumania and Bulgaria.

anti-dumping laws: National laws that ostensibly aim at foreign *dumping*, but are often so specific as to be actually *non-tariff barriers* to trade by legitimate foreign competition. They are part of the *new protectionism*. Regulations against the worst of such laws were included in the *Uruguay Round*, but were weakened in last-minute bargaining.

Antigua and Barbuda: Location: Caribbean. Major associations: *CARICOM, Commonwealth, OAS, UN*. Population: 82,000. Military: none. A British *colony* from 1632, it became independent in 1981. It maintains ties to Britain as an *associated state*, but has connections with the U.S. and Venezuela.

anti-personnel weapon: Any weapon designed to kill or maim people rather than disable equipment.

Antipodes: (1) Upper case: A small island group SE of, and belonging to, New Zealand. (2) Lower case: any two points diametrically opposite on the Earth's surface; from this and the *eurocentric* view of 16th and 17th century explorers of the *South Pacific*, any extremely remote and isolated *territory*.

anti-satellite system (ASAT): Any weapon designed to destroy enemy *satellites*, including anti-satellite mines, *missiles*, and hunter-killer satellites.

anti-Semitism: Hostility to Jews. In the late 19th century deteriorating conditions for Jews in the *Ottoman* and *Russian Empires*, and in Rumania, provoked international protests. After 1882 some two million destitute Jews fleeing *pogroms* in Russia arrived in the U.S., becoming an irritant in relations with Britain, Germany and Russia, and sparking a rise in anti-Sem-

itism in the U.S. itself. Protections for Jews were written into the *Minorities Treaties* with east European nations after *WWI*, but these proved of paper value only. During the 1930s anti-Semitism fed into the rise of *fascism* in Europe, leading to the *Holocaust*. Since then, anti-Semitism has been most important in the politics of the Middle East, although concern over Soviet policy also contributed to the decline of *détente* after 1972. Within the UN, an anti-*zionist* resolution was passed in 1975 but was repealed in 1991. In 1994 the *UNHRC* added anti-Semitism to its list of condemned, racist attitudes. Note: Arabs too are Semites, but this term has acquired a particular attachment to prejudice against Jews. Cf. *Aix-la-Chapelle; Birobizhan; Genocide Convention; Jackson-Vanik; Nuremberg Laws; Protocols of the Elders of Zion; zionism*.

anti-submarine warfare (ASW): All passive or active measures that defend against *submarines*. Among others: *convoy*, surveillance and hunter aircraft, underwater electronic *listening posts*, and hunter-killer subs.

antithesis: (1) In general: opposition or contrast; a direct opposite. (2) In Hegelian method: an opposing *thesis* to the original thesis. See *dialectic*.

ANZAC: The Australian and New Zealand Army Corps in *WWI* and *WWII*.

ANZUS: A 1951 *pact* coordinating Australian and New Zealand military policy with the U.S. It signaled displacement of Britain as the dominant naval power in the area. In 1985 New Zealand refused visitation to U.S. *warships* because of the U.S. "no confirm/no deny" policy regarding whether specific ships carried *nuclear weapons*. The U.S. renounced its obligations to New Zealand in 1986, effectively ending ANZUS (although formally, there is no mechanism to expel a member). In 1987 New Zealand declared itself a *Nuclear Weapons Free Zone*. The U.S. responded to that by downgrading its designation from "ally" to "friendly country." Washington maintains military ties with Australia, the main regional power. Cf. *Kiwi disease*.

apartheid: "Separateness." The system of racial segregation of blacks, coloreds (mixed race) and Indians, from whites instituted in 1948 in South Africa by the Afrikaner National Party. It included *Nazi*-like racial categories and assessments, a ban on miscegenation, and an effort to force the majority black population into *Bantustans*. Fundamentally, it was a means of preserving white privilege and a separate *Boer* identity while ensuring a large, floating pool of cheap black labor existed near, but not in the cities. It became the focus of *human rights* and *sanctions* campaigns orchestrated through the *UN, Commonwealth,* and bilaterally. A 1973 UN *convention* made it an international crime. That led to progressive sanctions and global shunning of South Africa. After 1976 the system became increasingly difficult to enforce, as the black middle class grew in number and the townships were rendered ungovernable. Legal apartheid was renounced by *de Klerk* in 1991, and dismantled by mid-1993. Multiparty elections were held in 1994. See *ANC.*

apparat: In the Soviet Union, the network of lower level *Communist Party* functionaries tied by relative privilege and reflected power to the *nomenklatura,* and responsible for carrying out in the regions and in local affairs all directives of the *Politburo.* It was the central nervous system of the Soviet body politic, identifying resistance and sending messages back to the muscles (the *KGB*) about *dissidents* and shortages.

apparatchnik/aparatchiki: A member of the *apparat.*

appeasement: Pacifying (buying off) an *aggressor* with concessions, often including on matters of principle. Morally, it challenges the presumption of a duty to resist evil (*aggression*) with the prescription that a higher duty is to seek *peace.* But that is a narrow, short term view, pointing as it does to an *international society* founded not on rights (*sovereign* or otherwise), but upon constant readjustments to threats and the naked exercise of *power.* Insofar as a policy of appeasement intends to avoid *war* at all costs it is more than likely to fail, and incur intolerable losses in the process. As an interim measure to gain time for *diplomacy, rearmament* or *alliance* building it may be a viable policy, but only if the time gained is used for those practical purposes. The most infamous example of appeasement as both a moral and practical failure was the *Munich Conference,* which gave the approach such a bad name that when practiced today it is always called something else.

application: A claim presented by a *state* before an international court. If a formal application is made, the full court sits in session. Cf. *chambers of the Court.*

appreciation: Increase in market value, over time.

appropriate technology: Smaller-scale and less sophisticated *technology* than the state-of-the-art variety, which therefore is said by its advocates to be more suitable to local economic and social conditions in a *developing nation.* It may be prefered for reasons of easy operation and repair, cheapness, use of a greater amount of *labor* in a labor-rich but *capital*-poor economy, or because it does not disrupt established social

patterns. In the 1980s the term stretched to cover "environmentally-sensitive" technologies.

Aquino, María Corazón (b.1933): President of the Philippines 1986-92. After the assassination of her husband and opposition leader, Benigno Aquino, on August 21, 1983, she took over leadership of the Philippine opposition to *Marcos.* She won the presidency in 1986 in a burst of popular support she called "People's power." She governed weakly, however, barely surviving six *coup* attempts and opposition from within her own *cabinet.* She promised to rule only one term, and did not stand for reelection.

Arab: Any member of the Semitic peoples of North Africa, the *Arabian peninsula,* Palestine, Lebanon, Syria, Iraq and northern Sudan.

Arabian peninsula: A West Asian peninsula constituting Bahrain, Kuwait, Oman, Qatar, Saudi Arabia, the United Arab Emirates (UAE) and Yemen.

Arab/Israeli War, First (May 15, 1948-June 1949): Fighting broke out between Arabs and Jews within *Palestine* in November 1947, and continued as preparations got underway for a *partition* brokered by the UN. On April 9th, elements of *Irgun* and the *Stern Gang* encountered heavy resistance at the village of Deir Yassin, after which they massacred 245 civilians. Panic spread among the Arabs, who believed there was a deliberate policy to terrorize them into leaving. Tens of thousands fled. The UN partition plan gave the Jews 55% of the land (but not *Jerusalem,* which was to be a *free city*). That disappointed Jews but outraged Arabs who noted that Jews formed less than one-third of the population. At midnight on May 14th the British *mandate* ended, and the State of Israel was proclaimed as the fulfillment, more or less, of *zionist* dreams. The next morning Arab armies from Egypt, Iraq, Lebanon, Syria and *Transjordan* all attacked. The fighting was often hand-to-hand. While massacres of *civilians* took place on both sides, it was the Arab population that fled, this time by the hundreds of thousands. Many still live a subsistence life in *refugee camps* because neither Israel nor the Arab states will accept them as permanent residents. *Cease-fires* were negotiated, starting with Egypt in February 1949. Israel had gained another 21% of Palestine, but also highly insecure borders. Cf. *Arab Legion; Count Folke Bernadotte; Jewish Agency; United Nations Relief and Works Agency.*

Arab/Israeli War, Second (October 29-November 5, 1956): Beginning in February 1955, *David Ben-Gurion* authorized a campaign of limited military action aimed at compelling the Arab states to make a formal *peace* with Israel. The Egyptians responded by setting up *fedayeen* units to escalate border warfare already underway. In September *Nasser* instituted a *blockade* of Israeli shipping through the Straits of Tiran and the Gulf of Aqaba, causing Israel to consider opening the *vital* passage by *force*. By 1955 France had surpassed even the U.S. as Israel's main sponsor, and with a U.S. arms *embargo* in place, as its main supplier of advanced weapons. The first French fighters (Mystères) arrived in April 1956, followed by British tanks and night-fighters. Meanwhile, in June-August 1956, the *Suez Crisis* rapidly developed between Egypt, Britain and France. In a series of secret meetings France agreed to supply Israel with more advanced weapons to counterbalance a major arms purchase from Czechoslovakia announced earlier by Nasser. On September 1st Israel was informed that France would welcome a joint attack on Egypt. From October 22-24, at Sèvres, British, French and Israeli representatives met, but could not agree on a joint attack. Instead, Israel attacked on its own, on October 29th, seizing *Gaza* and sending tank columns deep into the *Sinai*. Two days later Britain and France piggybacked their attack onto the Israeli thrust. With a huge domestic and international outcry against the triple *invasion*, and in particular fierce American opposition, all three countries were forced to cease operations within a week. The British and French pulled out, humiliated. Israel did better. It returned the Sinai in 1957 after a UN *peacekeeping* force was put in place, but it had secured its main *war aim* of opening the Strait of Tiran. Also in 1957, Egyptian government returned to *Gaza*, although the strip remained *demilitarized*. Despite this, another victor (politically speaking) was Nasser. He emerged as a hero of the Arab world, who had stood up to the hated foe in Israel and to the old, imperial powers.

Arab/Israeli War, Third (June 5-10, 1967): It is called by the Israelis, the "Six Day War." In the ten years since the last *war* Israel had developed into a formidable *regional power*. It also had begun to divert the Jordan River to "make the desert bloom." In 1963 that diversion led to border clashes with Syria. Again in January-March 1967, there were clashes between Israeli and Syrian border troops. In April the fighting escalated to tank and air battles. On May 16th, *Nasser* asked for partial withdrawal of the UN *peacekeeping* force in the *Sinai*, to enable Egyptian units to move into forward positions; he was told partial withdrawal was impossible. Two days later, under *Arab League* pressure, he asked for a total withdrawal of the UNEF. On the 22nd Egypt closed the Gulf of Aqaba to Israeli shipping. By the 24th Israel ordered *mobilization* of its *reserves*. In the next week a flurry of diplomacy made

it clear that the Western nations would not open the Gulf for Israel, but that they would not be heartbroken should it do the job itself. Meanwhile, Nasser and other Arab leaders indulged inflammatory and impolitic rhetoric about "pushing the Jews into the sea," destroying Israel, and so forth. Israel began to plan a *preemptive strike*. In the early hours of June 5th the Egyptian, Jordanian and Syrian air forces were caught on the ground and largely destroyed. In the subsequent ground fighting the professionalism of the Israeli army, and air superiority, quickly overwhelmed the Arab forces. On June 7th Jordan was pushed out of East *Jerusalem* and Israel captured the entire *West Bank*. The next day the Israelis secured *Gaza* and extended their hold on the Sinai to the *Suez Canal*. By June 10th, when a cease-fire took hold, Israel had also captured the *Golan Heights*. It was a humiliation for Arab arms so deeply felt that only a future victory, any victory, would salve the wound and open the way to *peace*. Also see *Resolution 242*.

Arab/Israeli War, Fourth (October 6-24, 1973): Called by Israelis the "Yom Kippur War" and by Arabs the "October War." On July 18, 1972, *Anwar Sadat* suddenly expelled 20,000 Soviet military and technical advisers from Egypt, but kept the military hardware they had supplied. On November 30, 1972, he made the decision for war. Sadat believed that *détente* between the *superpowers* meant Egypt's window of opportunity to change the situation in the Middle East might be closing. He assumed (correctly) that the superpowers would prevent either side from achieving a total *victory*. Yet he thought he needed a partial victory to restore Egyptian pride, and shake loose the *Suez Canal* from effective Israeli control: he intended to force Israel to the negotiating table by inflicting a shock to its sense of military invulnerability. This time, it was the turn of top Israelis to make impolitic remarks that aggravated tensions: *Dayan* spoke of how Palestine was "finished" and those in the *refugee camps* should just settle in other Arab countries and give up thoughts of returning. That helped firm up an Arab front in favor of war, with the Saudis agreeing to lead *OPEC* in an *embargo* of *oil* to the West when fighting broke out. Syrian and Egyptian officers began meeting in secret to complete war plans. In the final hours before the attack, on October 6th, Israeli officials finally realized it was coming and ordered *mobilization*. But it was too late to prevent breakthroughs, by the Egyptians across the Canal and the *Bar-Lev Line*, and the Syrians in the *Golan Heights*. After ferocious fighting the Israelis managed to stop, then drive back the Syrians (who had been joined by Iraqi and Jordanian units). In the *Sinai*, Israeli air and tank superiority was challenged by hand-fired SAM and anti-tank rockets. A huge tank-to-tank battle ensued, the largest since *Kursk* during *WWII*. Israel began to push the Egyptians back, at a huge cost in lives for such a small nation, and an even greater cost in matériel. Its losses were made up by a massive U.S. airlift ordered by *Richard Nixon*. A joint Soviet/American *cease-fire* proposal was accepted for the 22nd, but there were violations on all sides. Israeli forces continued their encirclement of the Egyptian Third Army, now trapped on the east bank of the Canal. The situation then began to spin out of control. The Soviets went on military alert, loaded troop transports, and insisted on immediate military *intervention* by both *superpowers*. Nixon countered with a global alert of U.S. forces on the 24th, as a *deterrent* threat. He and *Kissinger* simultaneously menaced Israel with threats not to re-supply its battlefield losses, even after the war, unless it stopped the attack in the Sinai. That day, a UN *cease-fire* resolution was put into effect. On November 5th Kissinger began his famous *shuttle diplomacy,* beginning the process that would end successfully, after his own time, in the *Camp David Accords*. A UN *peacekeeping* force was also put in place on the Golan Heights. Also see *Resolution 338*.

Arabist: A specialist in *Arab* affairs.

Arab League (League of Arab States): A regional organization formed in 1945 by Egypt, Iraq, Lebanon, Saudi Arabia, Syria, Transjordan and Yemen. It has since been joined by 12 more states: the *Gulf States*, Algeria, Djibouti, Libya, Morocco, Oman, Somalia, Sudan, Tunisia, as well as the *Palestine Liberation Organization*. Egypt was expelled for making peace with Israel in 1979, but was readmitted in 1987. The move of the League's headquarters from Cairo to Tunis was not reversed. The Yemens have merged and currently share one membership. The League split over the *Gulf War*, with a majority voting in favor of *multilateral* action to *liberate* Kuwait.

Arab Legion: The Jordanian army, commanded by a British officer, John B. Glubb, from 1921-56. It held the *West Bank* for *Transjordan* during the *First Arab/Israeli War* in 1948. Its English officers were dismissed in 1956.

Arab Revolt: The uprising by the Bedouin of Arabia, under *Ibn Ali Hussein* and others, against Turkey in 1916. It was abetted by the British. Its success gave birth to a new Arab *nationalism* (and the legend of *T.E. Lawrence, of Arabia*). But wartime promises to the Arabs were undercut by the terms of the secret *Sykes/Picot Agreement,* and the subsequent division of the Arab lands of the *Ottoman Empire* into *mandates*.

Arafat, Yassir (b.1929): Founder of *Fatah* in 1959, and since 1969 the oft challenged but still surviving head of the *PLO*. When the U.S. refused to *visé* him so he could speak to the *UNGA* in 1974, the meeting was moved to Geneva. He spoke wearing a holstered pistol. He kept the PLO intact and survived as leader despite its forcible, bloody expulsion from Jordan in 1971, and from Lebanon after the Israeli *invasion* in 1983. In 1974 he called for a *secular,* democratic *state* in Palestine (whether sincerely or not is open to question). In 1988 he implied that he would accept a two-state settlement. He supported Iraq during the *Gulf War*, a position that cost the PLO its Kuwaiti and Saudi financial support. Most Israeli leaders swore never to negotiate with him, or the PLO. Yet in private, he was a key influence on the Palestinians at the *peace talks* that began in 1992, and in 1993 shook hands with Peres and other Israeli leaders, sealing a peace accord. He escaped multiple assassination attempts, both Israeli and PLO. See *Gaza; West Bank*.

Aral Sea: An inland sea in Kazahkstan, drained by the Soviets in the 1960s and 1970s to irrigate crops in a near-desert zone. That led to environmental and economic disaster: excessive irrigation has caused it to dry up, and it may disappear entirely. An important fishing industry has been destroyed, with some ships dry-marooned over 100 miles from shore. Central Asia is therefore threatened with drought, future civil conflict and quarrels over a dwindling fresh *water* supply.

arbitrage: Purchasing *goods, services* or *currency* in one foreign market and selling them quickly in another, to take advantage of varying prices or rates.

arbitration: Peaceful settlement of *disputes* by submission of claims to binding judgment by a third party. See *compromis*. Cf. *mediation*.

arbitration clause: Inclusion in a *treaty* of the stipulation that in cases of interpretive disagreement the *states* concerned will submit to *arbitration*.

arbitration treaties: A host of pre-*WWI treaties* between both major and minor powers, promising to submit *justiciable disputes* to binding *arbitration*. It was hoped that this would avert military clashes. See *Permanent Court of Arbitration; Root Arbitration Treaties*. Cf. *cooling-off treaties*.

arbitrator: A neutral, third party usually specified in the *arbitration clause* of a *treaty*. It can be another state, *ad hoc* court, the *Secretary General*, or some mutually acceptable individual such as a former *head of state* or *government*. The pope has performed this function several times in Latin America; retired or third party justices may also act in this capacity.

archetype: An ideal model or pattern.

architecture: (1) A synonym for *grand strategy*. (2) A currently fashionable metaphor referring to the *regimes*, structures and institutions that support regional or global security and order.

archive: The stored diaries, memoranda, military plans, *diplomatic notes, treaties*, and related material of a state's foreign policy. This resource is used by *foreign services* and *statesmen* to ensure continuity, consistency of interpretation, and institutional and historical memory. Archives remain closed to scholars in the U.S. for 30 years in most cases, and for 50 years or more in Britain and elsewhere. They were shut until 1992 in the Soviet Union, but are now partly open. They remain forbidden in China, North Korea and other closed societies.

Arctic: The northern polar region. Unlike *Antarctica,* it is divided among the *Arctic nations* and has resident, *indigenous peoples.*

Arctic Circle: The circumpolar line at 23° 28' south of the North Pole.

Arctic nations: Those states with *territory* and/or *sovereignty* claims above the *Arctic Circle*: Canada, Finland, Iceland, Kalaallit Nunaat (Greenland), Norway, Russia, Sweden and the United States.

Ardennes: A wooded area of France, Belgium and Luxembourg, thought by French strategists to be impenetrable by *armor*. That belief was played upon by German generals, who in 1940 turned the flank of the *Maginot Line* and overwhelmed France. See *Battle of the Bulge.*

area defense: An *active defense* of a *strategic* area.

Argentina: Location: S. America. Major associations: *OAS, UN*. Population: 32.5 million. Military: regional capability. First entered by the Spanish in 1515 and colonized by them, it seized its independence by 1816. By the end of the 19th century most of its native population had been wiped out by disease or *genocide*, or was assimilated. From 1880-1916, it was ruled by a single party, controlled by the "2,000 families" of a ruling oligarchy. The 1920s saw mild reforms, but the landowners took power back in 1930. In 1943, *fascist* sympathizers in the military took over in a coup. In 1946 *Juan Perón* sidled into power, along with his

charismatic and ambitious wife, Eva (Evita). Perón was ousted in 1955, and there followed a succession of nondescript military and civilian governments. Perón returned from exile in 1973, but died in 1974. Another wife, Isabela, succeeded him but soon after was deposed. There followed the *dirty war* against leftist guerrillas, in which thousands of Argentines were "disappeared" (killed). The economy was badly mismanaged, and the junta sought to distract the public in 1983 by stirring nationalist sentiment with an invasion of the *Falkland (Malvinas) Islands*. After that *defeat*, a civilian government disavowed Argentina's secret *nuclear weapons* program and signed *non-proliferation* agreements with Brazil and the *IAEA*. Raul Alfonsin (b.1927) succeeded the generals who lost the war. He restored democracy and prosecuted some military for human rights violations, but declined to come to a final settlement with Britain over the Falklands. *Hyperinflation* threatened internal stability during the 1980s: in 1990 the inflation rate was 20,000%. Under President Carlos Menem, Argentina shifted toward the U.S. in foreign policy, restored relations with Britain (1990), and began an impressive economic recovery: by mid-1993 *inflation* was down to 13.4%. It was the only Latin American country to send troops to the *Gulf War*. It also sent peacekeepers to Croatia in 1991 and asked the OAS to intervene to restore democracy in Haiti. In January 1993, full *rapprochement* with Britain began with a visit by the U.K. Defense Minister. Even so, Argentina has not renounced its claim to the Malvinas.

armaments/arms: Weapons, of all types.

armed hostilities: Actual combat, whether legal and declared, or illegal. Cf. *war; warfare.*

armed intervention: See *intervention.*

Armed Neutrality: (1) League of: A group of north European naval powers (Denmark, Russia and Sweden) formed during 1780-81 to ensure *neutral rights* on the Baltic, as against Britain's effort to *blockade* their commerce with the U.S. during the *American Revolution*. It was revived by *Napoleon* in 1800 to try to break another English blockade of France. In the *Battles of Copenhagen*, the British destroyed the Danish fleet. (2) *Woodrow Wilson's* policy of: The arming of the U.S. *merchant marine* in 1917, announced within days of receipt of the *Zimmermann telegram*. (3) In general: A policy of *neutrality* in diplomacy, but backed up by a large military establishment that serves as a *deterrent* to potential *aggressors*. The two most successful practitioners of this policy historically have been Sweden since 1814 and Switzerland since 1815.

Armenia: Location: *Caucasus*. Major assocations: *CIS, CSCE, UN*. Population: 4 million, with 1.5 million ethnic Armenians in Azerbaijan (including *Nagorno-Karabakh*), Georgia, Russia, and Turkey. Military: inherited Soviet arms. Armenia has existed in some form since the 9th century B.C. In 300 A.D. most of its population converted to *Christianity*, a faith they preserved despite the subsequent conversion of most neighbors to *Islam*. It was brought under *Ottoman* rule as that *empire* rose after the 13th century. In 1828, northern Armenia was ceded to Russia, as the Ottomans declined. Russians ruled with a less heavy hand than did the Turks, who in 1895 and again during *WWI* carried out the *Armenian genocide*. Armenia was briefly independent 1918-20. It would have become formally independent by the *Treaty of Sèvres* (1920) had that agreement been ratified. Instead, it was partitioned between Turkey and Soviet Russia in 1921. In 1922 it was made part of the *Transcacasian SFSR*. In 1936 *Stalin* split Armenia from Azerbaijan, leaving Armenians in the *enclave* of Nagorno-Karabakh and Azeris in the exclave of *Nakhichevan*. In 1988 Armenia suffered a great earthquake. Then *war* flared with Azerbaijan, which cut off all land routes to Armenia and blocked *oil, food* and other deliveries. The Soviets were unable to sort out matters before both *states* became independent in 1991. With the collapse of the Soviet Union the *Armenia/Azerbaijan War* intensified. By 1994 Armenia had significantly expanded, *de facto*, at the expense of Azerbaijan.

Armenia/Azerbaijan War (1988-): In February 1988, an old *territorial* dispute between these two Soviet republics over possession of *Nagorno-Karabakh* flared into open *warfare*. Soviet *intervention* in 1988, 1989 and 1990 failed to prevent an increase in the fighting. With *independence* for both *nations* at the end of 1991 the war took on new significance and lethality, despite being overtaken in news coverage, and public and policy awareness, by the Balkan conflict that flared with the breakup of Yugoslavia. In May 1992, Armenia cut a six-mile-wide corridor to the *enclave*, forming a land bridge. Fighting then spilled into *Nakhichevan*. In April 1993, Armenian gains led Turkey to warn that unlike in Bosnia, it would not wait to intervene to stop dismemberment of Azerbaijan. In June Armenian forces consolidated their corridor to Nagorno-Karabakh, expelling most Azeris (900,000 have been made *refugees* by the war), and precipitating a brief *civil war* within Azerbaijan. *CIS* and *CSCE* mediation efforts failed to end the fighting.

Armenian genocide (1895-96; 1915): In 1895-96 massacres of Armenians by the *Ottomans* occurred, partly alienating the Western *Great Powers* that had support-ed Turkey against Russian *encroachment*. This was one of the first occasions when outside powers made *human rights* a direct concern in their foreign policy. The second episode may have killed as many as one million. Many were murdered but most died from neglect after being herded into *concentration camps* set up in the Syrian desert. Turkey still denies the extent of the carnage. That remains a source of contention with Armenians.

armistice: More than a *cease-fire*, an armistice is a suspension of hostilities with the expectation of proceeding to a compromise *peace* (though it may also precede a *diktat*). The most famous is that of *WWI*, declared for the 11th hour, of the 11th day, of the 11th month, 1918. That time is still marked by a minute of silence on "Armistice Day" in many nations that participated in the war. Cf. *peace treaty*.

armor: A generic term for steel plated and reinforced military vehicles, but usually referring to tanks. Tanks were first used in combat by the British, on the *Somme* and at *Cambrai* (1916), but were not decisive in *WWI*. In *WWII*, in contrast, the tank came into its own. The largest tank battle ever fought was *Kursk*. The *Third Arab/Israeli War* saw large tank battles, but also remarkably effective anti-tank warfare, both from *missile*-firing *infantry* and *air power*. In the *Gulf War*, Iraqi armor was so handily defeated by *Gulf Coalition* air power (especially helicopter gunships), that questions have been raised about whether the day of the tank is done, at least when it is put up against the air force of a first-rate military power.

arms buildup: Increasing the level of one's armaments and military preparedness, whether qualitatively or quantitatively. This does not necessarily occur in competition with any other *state* (for instance, it may reflect an overdue refit of old or technologically obsolete equipment). Nor must it imply threat and foreboding, as is the case in an *arms race*. See also *economies of scale*.

arms control: Mutually agreed-on restraints on the research, manufacture, or the levels and/or locales of deployment of troops and weapons systems. Note: This should not be confused with *disarmament*. See *ABM Treaty; Anglo/German Naval Agreement; Antarctic Treaty; arms race; Biological Warfare Treaty; Chemical Weapons Convention; Comprehensive Test Ban; continuity of safeguards; Conventional Forces in Europe Treaty; Disarmament in Europe Accord; Five Power Treaty; Four Power Treaty; Geneva Protocol; Hague Conventions; Intermediate-range Nuclear Forces Treaty; land mine; Moon Treaty; Mutual Force*

Reduction Treaty; National Technical Means of Verification; Nine Power Treaty; Nuclear Non-Proliferation Treaty; Open Skies; Outer Space Treaty; Partial Test Ban; Rush-Bagot Treaty; SALT; satellites; SDI; START; verification regime; Washington Conference; World Disarmament Conference.

arms exporting nations: Many countries are in the arms business. Here are some of the top exporters, in terms of 1994 gross volume of arms sales: U.S., Russia, Britain, France, China, Germany, Slovakia, Israel, Sweden, Brazil, North Korea, Canada. See *economies of scale.*

arms importing nations: Among the leaders in terms of gross volume of arms imports in 1994: Saudi Arabia, India, Greece, U.S., Japan, Indonesia, Iran, Vietnam, Cuba, China, Malaysia, South Korea.

arms limitation: A synonym for *arms control.*

arms race: Efforts by *states* to acquire a numerical and/or qualitative superiority in troops and weaponry over each other, accompanied by a sense of threat and fear of impending military conflict. In times of *crisis* or *tension*, this may contribute to a spiral of deployment and even use. See *security dilemma.* Cf. *arms buildup.*

Arnold, Benedict (1741-1801): American traitor. A much admired and decorated general in the colonial army during the *American War of Independence*, he tried to betray West Point to the British, then led a force against his erstwhile comrades.

Arrow War: See *Opium Wars.*

arsenal: (1) A storage place for arms, explosives and military supplies. (2) All weapons a state possesses.

artillery: Stationary or mobile weapons that fire explosive projectiles, and the troops and science of warfare that accompany these.

Aruba: This West Indies island split from the *Netherlands Antilles* in 1986. It is an *overseas territory* of Holland, with the same status as the Antilles.

Arusha Declaration: A set of loosely socialist and collectivist principles laid out by *Julius Nyerere* in 1967, and touted by him and others as a model for developing a unique brand of "African *socialism.*" It was widely popular at first for its egalitarian rhetoric, but was deeply resented in the implementation for its insistence on (often forced) resettlement of peasants in

"Ujamaa villages" (collectives). Its manifest failure as an economic strategy led to abandonment of the program after 1987. Cf. *collectivization.*

Aryan: (1) In demographic studies: ancient Indo-European, Sanskrit-speaking tribes that migrated to India c.1500 B.C., merged with the *indigenous* population, and contributed to the rise of classical Indian civilization. (2) In *Nazi* race theory and ideology: a non-Jewish caucasian; the "superior race" supposedly responsible for creating all higher civilization.

ASEAN: See *Association of South East Asian Nations.*

ASEAN Forum: The working name for a new Pacific *security* forum, founded in mid-1993. It consists of the *ASEAN* states as well as 11 other countries, including China, Japan, Russia and the U.S. It aims at cooperative, *preventive diplomacy* for the region.

Ashanti: (1) A former West African *empire.* (2) A British *colony*, now part of Ghana. (3) The main *tribe* (or *ethnic group*) in modern Ghana.

Asia: The world's largest, most populous continent. It stretches from Japan to the *Middle East.* By convention, it is subdivided into *Central Asia, East Asia, Northeast Asia, South Asia, Southeast Asia* and *West Asia.* Cf. *Asia/Pacific, Pacific Rim.*

Asia and Pacific Council (ASPCA): It was founded in 1966, to encourage regional economic and political cooperation among noncommunist Asian states.

Asia for Asians: The slogan under which Japan pursued *hegemony* in *East Asia.* At first it touched a responsive cord in a region dominated by white foreigners. After the conquests and brutal occupations of 1931-43, however, it was obvious to most that it really meant "Asia for the Japanese."

Asian Development Bank: Headquartered in Manila, it was founded in 1967 to finance regional *development* projects. It had $40 billion in *capital* funds in 1994. Extra-regional members include Britain, Germany, the U.S. and smaller *OECD* countries. The U.S. and Japan each had a 16% share in 1994.

Asian Tigers: Hong Kong, South Korea, Singapore and Taiwan; so-called owing to ferocious *GNP* growth rates that ate into world market shares in the 1970s and 1980s.

Asia/Pacific: The huge region comprising *East Asia* plus *Oceania.* Cf. *Pacific Rim.*

Asia/Pacific Economic Co-operation (APEC): A general forum for discussion of *Pacific Rim* economic issues, founded in 1989. It consists of all the major trading nations of the Pacific region: the six *ASEAN* members (Brunei, Indonesia, Malaysia, Philippines, Singapore and Thailand), together with Australia, Canada, China, Hong Kong, Japan, Mexico, New Zealand, Papua New Guinea, South Korea, Taiwan and the U.S. At *Bill Clinton's* suggestion, its 1993 summit in Seattle was for the first time one of *heads of state* rather than finance ministers (it was also the first time the three Chinas met formally). Its *Secretariat* is in Singapore, and it has agreed to hold every second meeting in a Southeast Asian nation. At the 1993 meeting APEC warned the *EU* not to block agreement on the *Uruguay Round* of *GATT*. At the theoretical level, there are murmurings of APEC forming a vast *free trade area* in the Pacific, but that seems a distant prospect at best. Still, the two sets of *NAFTA* countries are keenly interested in not being excluded from any alternative, all-Asian free trade regime. Other Pacific countries tried to join in 1993. Of these Mexico and Papua New Guinea were admitted; Chile was promised entry in 1994; and Peru and others were put on a three-year delay list. ASEAN, China, Japan and the U.S. are the key players on the APEC board.

Asquith, Herbert (1852-1928): British PM 1908-16. A successful domestic reformer, he was held responsible by many for the *stalemate* on the *western front* and was ousted in favor of *Lloyd George* (who promised a more vigorous war policy). In the 1920s his bitter dispute with Lloyd George split the Liberal Party, which ceased to be the main opposition to *Tory* rule.

Assad, Hafez al (b.1928): Dictator of Syria. He led a successful *coup* in 1963, becoming Defense Minister, and took full control in 1970 in another coup. He is from the minority Alawi sect. He had 50,000 killed to repress Muslim *fundamentalists* in the city of Hamma in 1982. Assad made Syria a Soviet *client state*, was a *hard-line* opponent of Israel, and reputedly sponsored *state terrorism*. He lost the *Golan Heights* during the *Third Arab/Israeli War*, and was unable to reclaim them during the *Fourth*. He *intervened* in the *Lebanese Civil War*, and achieved *influence* over events in Lebanon. Assad supported Iran in the *Iran/Iraq War*. With collapse of the Soviet Union he lost his main source of arms and technical *aid*. Growing more accommodating of Western interests, he joined the *Gulf Coalition* against Iraq in 1990-91. He subsequently joined Mideast *peace talks* in 1992, offering a compromise *peace* with Israel on the condition of return to Syria of all the Golan. He clung to power after 1980 despite increasingly frail health.

assassin: Anyone who murders a prominent person for political reasons. The term derives from a secret sect of *Ismaili* fanatics (hashshāshin, or "hashish eaters") who fought the Crusaders from the 10th to 13th centuries, often while high on God and hashish.

assassination: The murder for political reasons of a prominent public figure. Cf. *wet affair.*

associated state: A new type of *international personality* that has replaced the *protectorate*. Authority over foreign affairs is delegated to a *principal state*, but the associated state is treated as independent in the eyes of the law. Examples: *Cook Islands; Marianas; Marshall Islands; West Indies Associated States.*

Association of Southeast Asia (ASA): A subregional organization founded in 1961 by Malaya, Philippines and Thailand; since subsumed in *ASEAN.*

Association of Southeast Asian Nations (ASEAN): This regional body was established in 1967 by five noncommunist states (Indonesia, Malaysia, Philippines, Singapore and Thailand) to insulate themselves from the *Vietnam War* and the *Cold War* in Asia. They were later joined by Brunei, while Papua New Guinea attends as an observer. ASEAN has promoted limited economic cooperation and coordinated *diplomacy* toward regional issues. In 1980 it signed a trade cooperation agreement with the *EC*. In 1992 Vietnam signed a "Treaty of Amity and Cooperation" with ASEAN as a first step toward membership. Also, concerned by China's military assertiveness, ASEAN proposed *demilitarization* of the *Spratly Islands*. In 1993 it edged into security areas with the *ASEAN Forum*. It also functions as a *caucus group* within *APEC.*

Assured Destruction: A *strategic doctrine* that relies on assurance of massive destruction of enemy facilities, and indirectly of population, through launch of a *second strike* as the main guarantee of *deterrence*. It is usually converted by its critics to the pejorative (but not wholly inaccurate) MAD, or Mutual Assured Destruction. This doctrine emerged once American/Soviet parity in *nuclear weapons* was reached, and reflected a desire to stabilize that relationship. See *ABM Treaty; SALT.* Cf. *flexible response; massive retaliation.*

Aswan Dam: A 6,500 foot hydroelectric dam spanning the Nile. After the *West* refused to finance it, *Nasser* nationalized the Suez Canal Company, sparking the *Suez Crisis*. The dam was completed in 1971, with Soviet assistance, and heralded as an archetype of *Soviet bloc* aid to Third World countries. But both as a megaproject that Nasser hoped would propel Egypt into the first rank of nations, and a Soviet bribe of Egyptian fealty in the *Cold War*, it failed.

asylum: (1) Territorial: refusing to *extradite* an individual for civil, humanitarian or political reasons. Countries of "first asylum" are not necessarily countries of "final settlement." (2) Diplomatic: granting refuge to a national of a host state, within the domain of immunity of one's *embassy*; e.g., in the early 1980s Baptists were given sanctuary in the U.S. embassy in Moscow. For different reasons, President Manuel Noriega received temporary sanctuary in the Papal Legation during the 1988 U.S. *invasion* of Panama.

asymmetrical interdependence: When the effects of *interdependence* are felt extremely unequally, with one state experiencing much higher *vulnerability* than the other. It is *jargon*, and can be a misleading way to avoid saying that one state is dependent on another.

Atatürk, Mustapha Kemal (1881-1938): Turkish statesman whose adoptive name, Atatürk, meant "father of the Turks." He commanded at *Gallipoli*, and in the Greek/Turkish War of 1920-22. He founded the modern Turkish *state*, both *secularizing* and *modernizing* it, but ruling it as an uncompromising *autocracy*.

Atlantic, Battle of (1939-45): The great *WWII* contest for control of the Atlantic sea lanes supplying Britain and the Soviet Union from North America. Over its chill course the *Allies* lost 2,452 merchant ships and 175 *warships*, while the Kriegsmarine lost 696 out of 830 *U-Boats* (several German surface raiders were also sunk). The casualty rates on the U-boats were 63% dead, and another 12% captured (25,870 submariners killed out of 40,900 crewmen), the highest death rate of any arm of any service in the war. With U.S. entry into the battle in January 1942, the Allies turned the tide by mid-1943. The U.S. simply built more "Liberty Ships" than Germany could sink (averaging three months per ship and 1,500 per year at the height of production). U.S. naval shipyards also turned out 200 escort ships per year, and the Allies began to sink more U-boats than Germany could replace. Sonar and aircraft patrols from island bases, escort *aircraft carriers* (mass produced later in the war), and the *convoy* system finished the U-boat as a *strategic* force. They were reduced to a minor threat to lives and shipping by the end of 1943. This victory at sea permitted *Lend-Lease* to flow to Russia and Britain, and fed the buildup for *invasions* of North Africa (1942), Sicily and Italy (1943) and France (1944).

Atlantic Charter: A statement of principles drafted by *Franklin Roosevelt* and *Winston Churchill* in August 1941, at their meeting in Newfoundland. After U.S. entry into the war it was endorsed as a statement of *war aims* by the *United Nations alliance*. Its terms were *liberal*, even if all signatories were not: (1) no territorial *aggrandizement*; (2) border changes only following upon popular consent; (3) *self-determination*; (4) *free trade*; (5) economic cooperation; (6) freedom from want (poverty) and fear (of aggression); (7) *freedom of the seas*; and (8) *disarmament* of the *Axis* states. Like the *Fourteen Points*, it stirred public enthusiasm and fed illusions that the *peace* would be a liberal one. It found some resonance in the *Charter of the United Nations*.

Atlantic Community: The liberal-democratic nations of Europe and North America that share a political and cultural heritage and common economic and security interests. The notion has no institutional or organizational expression, yet is an influential idea in *NATO* relations, and more generally.

Atlanticism: (1) The tendency to see transatlantic connections as the most important in world affairs. (2) The tendency in foreign policy to view the U.S./Europe relationship as the main focus of *national security* and interests. Cf. *eurocentrism*.

Atlee, Clement (1883-1967): PM of Britain 1945-51. He replaced *Churchill* as PM in the middle of the *Potsdam Conference*. Mainly interested in Labour Party reforms at home, he started to shed the *empire* with *independence* for Burma, India and Pakistan in 1947. He approved withdrawal from (some say abandonment of) the *mandate* over Palestine. He was important in framing the U.K. response in the early *Cold War*, taking Britain into the *Brussels Treaty* and *NATO* and joining the UN forces in Korea.

atmospheric testing: Detonating *nuclear weapons* above ground. The practice was common in the 1950s but is forbidden to those states adhering to the *Partial Test Ban Treaty*.

atomic age: The present era, dating from detonation of the first *atomic bomb* on July 17, 1945.

atomic bomb: An explosive *fission* device, producing extraordinary destruction of lives and property, due to its *blast* and *radiation effects*. A *critical mass* of fissile material is forced together suddenly by a *conventional* explosion (acting as a trigger), producing an uncontrolled chain reaction. The first "Trinity" test was made by the U.S. at Alamogordo, New Mexico, on July 17, 1945. That was two months after the *surrender* of Nazi Germany, against which the race to build the bomb was run. These weapons have been used in *war* only twice, at *Hiroshima* and at *Nagasaki*. See also *fusion; hydrogen bomb; Los Alamos; Manhattan Project; Minatom; nuclear weapons; Peenemünde; plutonium*.

atomic demolition mine (ADM): A low-yield, *tactical*, defensive *nuclear weapon* for use against advancing troops and *armor* formations.

atomistic economy: One in which many small producers compete in every industry.

Atoms for Peace: A 1953 U.S. proposal for cooperation on the development of peaceful uses for nuclear technology. It led to creation of the *IAEA* in 1957.

attaché: Any specialist with a diplomatic mission representing and reporting on areas such as culture, trade or military affairs. For a military attaché appointed to an unfriendly state, and nowadays also for a trade attaché attached even to *allies*, this duty may amount to *espionage*. In *intelligence*, attaché positions are often preferred cover for a *legal agent*.

attrition: Wearing down an enemy by inflicting continuous damage and casualties, usually while suffering heavy losses to one's own forces. See *American Civil War; Iran/Iraq War; Verdun; Vietnam War; WWI*.

Aung San (1914-47): Burmese nationalist, PM in 1947. After fighting alongside the Japanese in *WWII*, he led a revolt against them in 1945. He gained the premiership during the struggle for power attendant on British withdrawal from Burma. He was, however, assassinated shortly after that.

Aung San Suu Kyi (b.1946): Daughter of *Aung San*, and today the leading opposition figure in Myanmar as well as a *Nobel Peace Prize* winner. She has been under house arrest since 1989.

Auschwitz: The largest and most notorious of the *death camps* set up by the *Nazis*, near a small Polish town from which it took its name. It was the site of obscene medical experimentation and the worst sadism; occasionally, there were scenes of saintly self-sacrifice. Just before its few surviving inmates were liberated by the *Red Army*, it was killing Jews at a rate of 20,000 per day, using Zyclon B gas pellets manufactured by the German petrochemical industry. That was too many dead for even its four massive crematoria to handle. See *anti-Semitism; Holocaust*.

Ausgleich: The "compromise" of 1867, converting the *Austrian Empire* into the *Dual Monarchy* of Austria-Hungary where each was *autonomous* domestically, but *foreign policy* was run from Vienna.

Austerlitz, Battle of (December 2, 1805): The key battle in the *War of the Third Coalition*. A French army under *Napoleon* defeated a larger but badly led Austrian and Russian force, knocking Austria out of the war and forcing a Russian *strategic* retreat.

Australasia: Australia, New Zealand, Tasmania and scattered islands. Cf. *South Pacific*.

Australia: Location: S. Pacific. Major associations: *ANZUS, Commonwealth, OECD, SPC, SPF, UN*. Population: 17 million. Military: small but first-rate and well-equipped; active in UN operations and as advisers regionally. It was explored by James Cook (1729-79) in 1770, and used as a penal *colony* by the British from 1788. By the 1830s white settlement took hold in the four Australian colonies (New South Wales, Tasmania, South Australia and Victoria) with the *aborigines* pushed onto reserves in the "outback." In 1850 the white colonies were given self-government in domestic affairs, but Britain retained control of foreign policy. In 1901 they were federated into a single Commonwealth of Australia, which fought as part of the *British Empire* contingent in the *Boer War* and again in *WWI*. The terrible casualties suffered at *Gallipoli* (1915) stimulated a new *nationalism* and sense of separate interest from Britain. After WWI Australia was treated as virtually independent. It attended the *Paris Peace Conference* and joined the *League of Nations*, though it had little influence over either. But it only took formal control of its foreign policy with passage of the *Statute of Westminster* in 1931. It fought against the *Axis* from 1939, and was an important base of Allied operations against Japan after the fall of the Philippines. John Curtin (1885-1945) was the wartime PM of Australia, 1941-45. While working well with the U.S. he sought to preserve the Commonwealth link to Britain as a counterweight to Australia's new security dependence on America. After *WWII* Australia persued a more homegrown foreign policy, but also shifted under the U.S. security umbrella as the *British Empire* rapidly receded from Asia. It joined ANZUS in 1951. It participated in the *Korean Conflict*, and sent troops to fight in the *Vietnam War*. Since the 1970s it has increasingly seen itself as a Pacific nation, rather than a European outpost in Asia. Under John Frazer (b.1930), PM 1975-83, Australia turned firmly toward the Asia-Pacific region in its foreign policy. A 1987 Defense White Paper identified its main security area as the SW Pacific, and a 1989 parliamentary committee called for regional leadership of the local island states. Yet, its security ties still reflect close coordination with the U.S. Australia was the *mandate* and then *Trustee Power* for Nauru and Papua New Guinea. It no longer has *dependencies*, but still oversees South Pacific island *territories*, including Norfolk, Coral Sea, Cocos, Kiritimati and the Ashmore and Cartier Islands. Most of its *aid* goes to the region. It has claims in *Antarctica*, where it is a *Treaty Power*. In 1993 it began a national debate over becoming a *republic*. It has taken a regular part in UN *peacekeeping* operations, including Cambodia and Somalia in 1993.

Australian New Guinea: The *mandate/trustee* name for Papua New Guinea.

Austria-Hungary: The *Austrian Empire,* after the *Ausgleich* of 1867 until its demise in 1918. See also *Dual-Monarchy.*

Austrian Empire: Austria was controlled by the *Hapsburgs* from 1300. Its domination of central Germany was confirmed by the *Thirty Years' War* and not broken until the 18th century. It was defeated by *Napoleon* during the *Wars of the First, Second* and *Third Coalitions* and forced to *terms*, but rejoined the anti-French side in 1813 to fight to *victory* in the *War of the Fourth Coalition*. It participated in the *Congress of Vienna* and the *Concert* system, and joined the *Holy Alliance*. Under the able Count *Metternich*, Austria exercised *influence* but also took on commitments well beyond its *capabilities*. It staggered through the *Revolutions of 1848*, mauled but intact. *Defeat* at the hands of *Prussia*, in 1866, ended the long competition for control of Germany and focused Vienna on the problem of keeping its hold on southeastern Europe. In 1867 Hungarians were given equal status with Germans in the *Ausgleich* that created the *Dual Monarchy*. That awkward arrangement signaled the internal decay and weakness of the Empire. Austria-Hungary thereafter became intensely conscious of its faltering position and jealous of any slight to its *prestige*. Thus, it was prepared to strike back hard at the Serbs, who foolhardily salted every imperial wound in July 1914, by sponsoring the assassination of the Austrian heir, Archduke *Francis Ferdinand*. Backed by Germany, Vienna *declared war* on Serbia, loosing the floodgates of *WWI*. Most Austrian fighting was against Serbia (which it defeated), Russia (which it held off only with German help), and Italy (which it humiliated at *Caporetto*, before succumbing). Only German aid and reinforcements prevented an early exit from the war. In the end, not even the German *alliance* was enough: the Austrian Empire shattered on the battlefields of WWI into several component nations. Austria itself was reduced to its present status of small *republic*. See *successor states*.

Austrian State Treaty (May 15, 1955): An agreement among the four occupying powers (Britain, France, the Soviet Union and the U.S.) to withdraw, on condition of creation of a *neutral, republican* Austria confined to its 1937 frontiers. It also banned another *Anschluss*.

Austria, Republic of: Location: Central Europe. Major associations: *CSCE, EFTA, EU* (1995), *OECD, UN*. Population: 7.6 million. Military: good quality, small numbers, and purely defensive. Proclaimed in Vienna in 1918, this rump *republic* was sanctioned as well as proscribed by the *Treaty of St. Germain* (1919). Politically unstable, it suffered a brief *civil war* in 1934 in which *Social Democrats* were ousted by Austrian *Nazis*. The Nazis murdered Chancellor *Englebert Dollfuss* later in 1934, and prepared the way for Hitler's takeover on March 13, 1938 in the *Anschluss*, or union with the *Third Reich*. Fully incorporated into Nazi Germany, Austria was invaded and occupied by the *Allies* in 1945. There was controversy over whether to treat it as a willing collaborator of Nazi Germany, or the first victim. Like Germany, it was divided into four *occupation zones*. Unlike Germany, the Allies agreed to early withdrawal in the *Austrian State Treaty* (1955). The *occupation* was ended on terms of permanent Austrian *neutrality* and *disarmament*, and *union* with Germany was forbidden. Austria was diplomatically shunned during the Presidency of *Kurt Waldheim*, who was under suspicion of *war crimes*. The end of the *Cold War* made neutrality problematic, as did acceptance into the EU (January 1, 1995), with its dedication to common foreign and defense policy.

autarchy: Absolute *sovereignty*. See *autocracy*.

autarky: The effort to achieve total, national *self-sufficiency* by imposing economic, political and cultural *isolation*. States attempting this included: Albania in its *communist* phase; post-*WWII* Burma; Cambodia under *Pol Pot*; China during the *Great Leap Forward* and *Cultural Revolution*; Japan under the *Tokugawa shoguns,* before its forced opening in the 19th century; Russia under *Nicholas I;* and the Soviet Union under *Stalin*, 1928-34. Note: This extreme policy should not be confused with more modest efforts at *self-reliance*, such as India's under the *Congress Party* before 1992.

authoritarianism: A style of government without regard for individual rights or representative principles, often military, and usually without much ideological content but capable of savage brutality and repression nonetheless. A controversial distinction was introduced by the *Reagan* administration between authoritarian and *totalitarian* regimes, in order to justify the *Reagan Doctrine* and waivers of *human rights* conditions on *aid* to authoritarian *allies*. It argued that such systems could be overthrown from within because they left large areas of social and economic life free of government control, but that totalitarianisms were so pervasive in their control of human activity the chance was close to nil opposition could build and reform take place. Therefore, outside pressure was necessary to topple them. The extent to which this idea was confirmed or denied by the events of 1989-91 remains subject to debate. Cf. *containment*.

authoritative interpretation: When a *treaty* is interpreted by the parties to a related, subsequent treaty.

autocracy: The *ideology* and system of government supporting rule by an *autocrat*. The idea stemmed from *absolutism*, but was modified into a fairly sophisticated theory of government by benevolent dictatorship, notably in *Austria-Hungary* and *tsarist Russia*.

autocrat: A ruler with nearly unrestrained political power, whose claim to *legitimacy* rests on *dynastic* or religious, not representative principles.

auto-interpretation: Interpretation of *treaty* or other legal duties by the obligated *state* itself.

autonomous development: A close synonym for *autarky*, but less extreme in the application.

Autonomous Soviet Socialist Republic (ASSR): An administrative unit of the *Soviet Union*, of lesser stature than a full *republic*. The Russian republic contained 16 of these; several proclaimed *independence* after 1991, but this has not been *recognized*.

autonomous variable: One that is not entirely dependent on the "objective factors" (say economic) being studied, but also on vagaries of human *volition* and psychological, religious or other motivation.

autonomy: When a *dependency* or other weak state is self-governing on internal matters, without a similar grant in foreign affairs.

Auzou strip: A patch of desert along the Libya/Chad border, part of Chad but coveted by *Muammar Quadaffi* for its rich deposits of *uranium*. Libya's *occupation* (1973-88) angered so many *OAU* states the 1982 summit in Tripoli was cancelled. See *Chad/Libya War*.

Avila, Camacho (1897-1955): Revolutionary leader

and President of Mexico 1940-46. He improved relations with the U.S., instituted major domestic reforms, and *declared war* on the *Axis* in 1942.

avulsion: When a *border* (boundary) river changes course suddenly but for natural reasons, the original boundary is left unaffected. See *accretion; Thalweg*.

axiom: (1) A self-evident truth. (2) A universally accepted rule or principle, whether true or not.

Axis: A term coined by *Mussolini* in 1936, purporting to describe how European and world history would from now on revolve around a Rome-Berlin axis. Formal *alliance* came later, in the *Pact of Steel* signed in May 1939. The term was extended to include Japan when it signed the *Anti-COMINTERN Pact*. Minor states that joined were: Bulgaria, Hungary, Rumania and the Nazi *puppet states* of Croatia and Slovakia. Finland is not normally numbered among the Axis powers. Yet for reasons pertaining to the *Russo/Finnish War*, it fought alongside Germany. Although not the formal name of the alliance opposed by the *United Nations*, "Axis" has gained wide currency as a term for the *coalition* of *fascist* states that lost *WWII*.

ayatollah: "The sign of God." A title of senior clerics within the *shi'ite* tradition of *Islam*. See *Iranian Revolution; Khomeini*. Cf. *caliph; imam; mahdi; sultan*.

Ayub Khan, Muhammad (1907-74): President of Pakistan 1960-69. He took effective control in 1954 as the Minister of Defense who imposed *martial law*, but only sought the presidency in 1960. His constant repressions alienated the Bengalis of *East Pakistan*. He provoked the *Second Indo/Pakistani War* in 1965, but his loss of men and *prestige* in the fighting weakened his hold on power. He was forced out in 1969.

Azaña, Manuel (1881-1940): President of Republican Spain 1936-39. He was unable to persuade the West to aid the republican cause, and fled to France with *Franco's* victory in the *Spanish Civil War*.

Azerbaijan: Location: *Caucasus*. Major associations: *CIS, CSCE, UN*. Population: 8 million. Military: Soviet arms; mauled by war with Armenia; ties to Iran, from where it draws some volunteers, and to Turkey. This Central Asian, mainly *Shi'ite* land was part of the Safavid Empire, which took it from Persia. It was overrun by Turkic invaders in the 11th century, and later became a province in the *Ottoman Empire*. It was divided between the Ottoman and Russian Empires in the 18th century, and fell fully under Russian control by 1815. It was Europe's main oil producing region before *WWI* (later surpassed by the Rumanian fields at Ploesti). It was briefly independent from 1917-20, but was reincorporated into the *Russian Empire* at the end of the *Russian Civil War,* after being invaded by the *Red Army.* Within the Soviet Union it formed part of the *Transcaucasian SFSR,* until separation and *partition* in 1936: *Stalin* fenced tens of thousands of Armenians in the *enclave* of *Nagorno-Karabakh* and left Azeris in the exclave of *Nakhichevan* between Armenia and Turkey. After 1988 violence flared with Armenia over control of Nagorno-Karabakh. In January 1990, riots in Baku led to a massacre of Armenians, intervention by Soviet troops, and further bloodshed.

With *independence* in December 1991, the *Armenia/Azerbaijan War* flared into full-scale fighting. In June 1993, a *civil war* broke out, bred of recrimination over looming *defeat* and the wider, personal ambitions of the Azeri leadership of Nakhichevan.

Azores: An island group in the Atlantic, under Portuguese control.

Aztecs: The Nahuatl people of Mexico, whose vast and complex *empire* was conquered with astonishing ease by *Cortés* and his band of holy, and unholy, cutthroats and brigands.

B

B-1 bomber: This *strategic,* intercontinental *bomber* was supposed to replace the aging U.S. fleet of *B-52s,* but initially reinforced it instead.

B-2 bomber: The most advanced U.S. *bomber* with *stategic* capability. As it used *stealth technology,* some critics worried it might be perceived by the Soviets as a *first strike* weapon. Budget cuts greatly reduced production of this $1 billion (each) weapons system.

B-52 bomber: The standard U.S. *bomber* with *strategic (nuclear* and *conventional)* capability, 1955-1990. it was used in the *Vietnam War* and in the *Gulf War.*

Baader-Meinhof gang, a.k.a. Red Army Faction: A West German nihilist group that undertook a brief but frenzied *terrorist* campaign in 1970-71, with small cells only active after that. Ulrike Meinhof (1934-76) committed suicide in prison; Andreas Baader (1943-77), too, was found dead in his cell.

Ba'ath (Arab Socialist Renaissance) Party: Founded as a *pan-Arabism* movement in the 1930s, it merged *marxist* analysis with Arab and Islamic *nationalism,* and promoted *union* of various Arab *states.* In time, however, it split along national lines. One branch took power in Syria in 1963, another in Iraq in 1968. Personal dictatorship (*Hafez al-Assad* in Syria and *Saddam Hussein* in Iraq) rather than Ba'ath *ideology* became the order of the day in both countries.

back-channel negotiations: Secret contacts between governments and/or other parties, which for political or public relations reasons are unable to negotiate openly. They involve using journalists, academics,

businessmen or third party governments as go-betweens, to relay messages and arrange other contacts. They may permit governments to bypass their own bureaucracies, publics, vested interest groups and/or policy *elites,* and thereby break negotiating or political logjams. But they risk making policy in a vacuum, in the absence of expert advice and public support.

Backfire bomber: This Soviet medium range *bomber* was controversial during the *SALT II* negotiations because Western *intelligence* thought it had secret, *strategic* (that is, intercontinental) capability.

backwash effect: In *dependency theory,* the idea that an inflow of expensive manufactured goods to *developing nations* stimulates export of *raw materials* at the expense of domestic *industrialization.*

bad actors: *Intelligence* slang for *terrorists.*

Badoglio, Pietro (1871-1956): Italian general. Governor of Libya 1929-33; conqueror of Ethiopia in 1936. He opposed the attack on France in 1940. He succeeded *Mussolini* in 1943, and negotiated with the *Allies* to take Italy out of *WWII.* The *armistice* led instead to German *occupation* of northern Italy, and to a *civil war* fought within WWII. Badoglio was then rejected by the Italian *resistance* and retired.

Baghdad Pact: A 1955 security *alliance* concluded by Iraq and Turkey at the instigation of the U.S., and then joined by Britain, Iran and Pakistan. The U.S. hesitated to join openly out of concern for adverse reaction among *radical* Arabs. Britain thus bore the brunt of *Third World* criticism, and of formal alliance commitments. In March 1959, Iraq withdrew, and the alliance was renamed the Central Treaty Organization (CENTO). It was meant to reinforce *containment*, but some analysts have criticized it for encouraging Soviet attention to, and penetration of, the *Middle East*. When Iran withdrew in 1979 CENTO was dissolved.

Bahamas: Location: Caribbean. Major associations: *CARICOM, Commonwealth, OAS, UN*. Population: 252,000. Military: minimal. A chain of hundreds of small islands, with but a handful inhabited. European settlement began in 1647, and the main islands became a British *colony* in 1783. *Autonomy* was granted in 1964, and *independence* in 1973.

Bahrain: Location: *Persian Gulf*. Major associations: *Arab League, OAPEC, OPEC, UN*. Population: just over 500,000. Military: small but well equipped. It was a British *protectorate* from 1861. *Oil* was discovered in 1932, giving this *microstate* sudden *strategic* importance. Independent by 1971, it participated in OPEC *embargoes* in 1973 and 1979. The *Iran/Iraq War* and *Gulf War* led it to *align* with Saudi Arabia and the West in search of protection against Iraq and/or Iran. With much of its oil reserve depleted, it now earns *foreign exchange* by processing and refining.

Baker, James (b.1930): U.S. statesman. He held various posts in the Ford, Reagan and Bush administrations, and authored the *Baker Plan* on *LDC* debt restructuring in 1985. As Secretary of State 1989-92, he oversaw major *arms control* agreements with the Soviet Union and its *successor states*. He kept a low profile during the *Gulf War*, but was active in the subsequent drive to arrange comprehensive *peace talks* for the *Middle East*. He resigned to take charge of the unsuccessful *Bush* reelection bid in 1992.

Baker Plan: Proposed by *James Baker* to the *IMF* and *IBRD* in September 1985. Its premise was that credit could only be restored to *LDC* borrowers through *growth*. It had three parts: (1) debtor nations must undertake market reforms to remove inefficiencies; (2) commercial banks should provide $20 billion in loans; (3) the IMF and IBRD should increase lending by $3 billion per year. It had mixed results--*structural adjustment* was unpopular (especially *subsidy* cuts), and *debt servicing* actually exceeded inflows from commercial banks.

baksheesh: In India and the Middle East, a tip or bribe often asked of foreign businesses before awarding a contract.

Bakunin, Mikhail (1814-76): Russian anarchist, active in abortive *revolutions* in Germany (1848) and France (1870). He had continent-wide influence, and was the personal and political bête noir of *Karl Marx* within the *First International*.

balance of payments: The annual tracking and measurement of all the economic transfers of a nation with the rest of the world economy, including *exports* and *imports* of *goods* and *services*, capital *investment*, and *reserve currency*. In addition to changes in price levels, international *capital* movements have long played a role in balance of payments *adjustment*. Indeed, in the confusion following collapse of the *Bretton Woods* system, *exchange rate* variation became a favored means of adjustment. When calculated globally, balance of payments surpluses and deficits equal zero. See also *current account; devaluation; IMF; macroeconomics; official financing.*

balance of power: (1) A policy of supporting the weaker side in a conflict, to maintain an *equilibrium*. (2) A condition in which the distribution of military and political forces among *nations* means no one *state* is sufficiently strong to dominate all the others. It may be global, regional or local in scope. Forming a balance may be a conscious policy, or occur reflexively as one state attempts to overthrow the existing balance. If a *revisionist power* is also a *Great Power*, an attempt to overthrow the balance will certainly propel other Great Powers together in spite of their differences (e.g., the U.S. and Soviet Union in *WWII*). The primary interest it protects is survival of the Great Powers, sometimes at the expense of smaller powers. (e.g., see *partitions of Poland*). It is conservative, in that it seeks to maintain the status quo (at least against violent change). The primary value it projects is Great Power order, not *peace* or justice. Concern for local justice or principles such as *self-determination* may be sacrificed to anxiety about international order. Similarly, peace may give way to the pressing interest of preserving or reestablishing a balance. Yet the moral content of the balance of power should not be overlooked: at its best it seeks not mere equilibrium, but just equilibrium. Nor is it necessarily opposed to *liberal-internationalist* or *Wilsonian* conceptions. It is both capable of underwriting and reinforcing a liberal-international order, and indeed, essential to that prospect: without a modicum of national justice, ethnic and other challenges arise that may overwhelm a given balance; but without attention to the balance of power policies that aim to enhance international justice may instead lead to chaos, upon which great injustices are usually in close attendance. Note: This term is subject to considerable abuse, and often takes on multiple meanings other than the primary ones given here; e.g., the declaration "we seek a favorable balance of power" nearly always masks a policy that seeks advantage, or even *preponderance*. Cf. *correlation of forces*.

balance of terror: When *equilibrium* and moderate behavior is produced because of shared, intense fear about the implications of a failure of *nuclear deterrence*. It is a far narrower notion than *balance of power*, focusing on just one type of weapon or source of *power*, and implying virtually no freedom of maneuver. The phrase is usually attributed to *Churchill*.

balance of trade: The difference between the values of *exports* and *imports*, described as "favorable" if the former exceed the latter. A surplus in the balance of trade was seen by *mercantilists* as a key to national economic health, and many countries still enact policies of *protectionism* in order to create a trade surplus. Yet there is nothing inherently undesirable about a trade deficit--it might, for instance, reflect a faster domestic *growth* rate; and of course, protectionism is sure to generate retaliatory barriers to one's exports.

balancer: A *state* that, like Britain at its peak, lends support to whatever is the weaker side to maintain a *balance of power*.

Baldwin, Stanley (1867-1947): British statesman. PM 1923, 1924-29, and 1936-37. He was mostly passive in foreign policy, responding without vigor to the key crises of the mid-1930s: the *Abyssinian War*, the *Rhineland* crisis; and the start of the *Spanish Civil War*. However, he began British *rearmament*.

Balfour, Arthur (1848-1930): British statesman. PM, 1902-05; First Lord of the Admiralty 1915; Foreign Secretary 1916-19. He was a key player during *WWI*, especially in coordinating relations with the U.S. He was active at the *Paris Peace Conference*, in the *League of Nations*, and at the *Washington Conference*. He is most famous for the declaration on Palestine that took his name.

Balfour Declaration: On November 2, 1917, *Arthur Balfour* wrote to a *zionist* leader that Britain favored a homeland for Jews located in *Palestine*. This declaration took on real meaning when the *Allies* endorsed it at the *Paris Peace Conference* in 1919, and later, when Britain inherited Palestine from Turkey and ran it as a *mandate territory*. It became the basis for zionist claims on Britain, as the mandate power.

balkanize: To divide a country or region into small, ineffective and quarrelsome *states*, such as those in the *Balkans*.

Balkan League: The *alliance* of Bulgaria, Greece and Serbia that fought against Turkey in the *First Balkan War*, but then broke apart and fell to fighting over division of the spoils.

Balkan pacts: Three major attempts have been made to settle *disputes* over *territory* and other *security* questions in the *Balkans*: (1) In 1933: *Alexander of Yugoslavia* tried to resolve disputes with Bulgaria, Greece, Rumania and Turkey. Bulgaria coveted too much of Macedonia to agree, but the others formed an *entente* that lasted to 1940. (2) In 1954: Greece, Turkey and Yugoslavia signed a *pact* that lasted only to the next *crisis* over Cyprus. (3) In 1988: Albania, Bulgaria, Greece, Rumania, Turkey and Yugoslavia met but failed to conclude an agreement; then things fell apart with the disintegration of Yugoslavia.

Balkans: The region below the Danube, surrounded by the Adriatic, Aegean, Ionian and Black Seas, and containing the *Balkan States*.

Balkan states: The *states* occupying the Balkan Peninsula of southern Europe: Albania, Bulgaria, Greece, Rumania, the European portion of Turkey, and Yugoslavia--since 1991 broken into *successor states* of Bosnia, Croatia, Macedonia, Serbia and Montenegro, Slovenia (and counting).

Balkan War, First (1912-13): Under Russian prodding, the *Slav* states Bulgaria and Serbia agreed to *partition* Macedonia, then an *Ottoman* province. They were joined by Greece and Montenegro in attacking Turkey. The *Great Powers* then *intervened* to force Turkey to cede most of its remaining holdings in Europe, the lion's share of which went to Bulgaria in exchange for agreeing to an independent Albania.

Balkan War, Second (1913): The creation of Albania frustrated Serb and Montenegran territorial ambitions. Bulgaria feared a secret deal between the other *regional powers* to exclude it from the *partition* of Macedonia. Within a few months of the settlement of the *First Balkan War*, it launched an attack on Greece and Serbia, its recent *allies*. It was immediately attacked in its turn by Rumania and Turkey. That created the unusual situation of the Turks, Serbs and Greeks being *de facto* allies against Bulgaria, in spite of being technically still in a *state of war* with each other. Bulgaria was *defeated*, and forced to surrender its earlier gains. In the *Treaty of Bucharest*, Serbia and Greece emerged with the most *territory*. Bulgaria was even forced to cede an eastern province to Rumania, held by Bulgaria before the Balkan Wars. It would try to retrieve these lands during *WWI*.

Balkan War, Third (1991-): Serbia supported attacks by ethnic Serb *militia* on Slovenia within days of that state's declaration of *independence* from *Yugoslavia*, on June 25, 1991. Fighting spread to Croatia, which also declared independence, then failed to honor a commitment to Slovenia. By December, 30% of Croatia was in Serb hands, and a so-called "Serb Republic of Croatia" declared (not *recognized*). In 1992-93 the war spread to Bosnia, where Serb militia declared a "Serb Republic of Bosnia," and besieged Sarajevo and other Muslim and Croatian *enclaves* in defiance of UN *resolutions*. President *Mitterand* of France personally flew to Sarajevo in June 1992, to arrange humanitarian relief; UN troops followed. In July the UN called off the airlift because of fighting near the airport. After a brief reopening, it closed again in September, after an Italian Air Force relief plane was shot down, with eleven dead. In August the *Security Council* called for a *cease-fire* and access to all detention centers, where it was suspected *genocide* was taking place. The UN next *embargoed* military supplies to all sides, giving an unintended advantage to the Serbs, who drew upon the huge Yugoslav army stockpiles in Serbia, particularly for *armor* and *artillery*. Croatia then entered the war, turning on its erstwhile Muslim allies in a tacit partition of Bosnia with the Serbs. By the end of 1992 nearly 70% of Bosnia was under Serb control. In March 1993, the *Vance/Owen peace plan* dividing Bosnia into ethnic *enclaves* but retaining a federal shell was set to fail, as the Serbs refused to sign. The UN passed tougher *sanctions*, while *NATO* discussed air strikes and lifting the arms embargo for Bosnia's Muslims. That forced Serbia to the table, and to sign (but not to respect) the Vance/Owen plan. In May, Serbia declared it was closing its border with Bosnia, whose "Serb parliament" still rejected the UN/EC plan. In August it was agreed to abandon the idea of a federal Bosnia and carve it into three ethnic states, with the Muslims reduced to a few enclaves. NATO again threatened air strikes, even while Britain and Canada openly discussed withdrawal of their *peacekeeping* forces and the Russian *Duma* warned off *intervention* against the Serbs. In the first half of 1994 Bosnian Muslims made some gains against Bosnian Croats, NATO finally forced an end to Serb *sieges* of Sarajevo and Goradze, and Muslims had joined in a loose *federation* with ethnically-related Croats.

ballistic missile: A *missile* that takes a ballistic trajectory (one influenced only by gravity and atmospheric friction), flying without power beyond the initial thrust of takeoff.

ballistic missile defense (BMD): Any complex of *ABM* systems, lasers, *charged particle beams*, projec-

tiles, target acquisition systems, tracking and fire-guidance radars for defense against *ballistic missiles*.

Baltic: The region in northern Europe bordering the Baltic Sea, not just the *Baltic States*.

Baltic States: Estonia, Latvia, Lithuania (and sometimes, but not usually, Finland).

Baluchistan: A mountainous region straddling SE Iran and NW Pakistan; the Baluchi people are similarly divided.

bamboo curtain: The policy of rigid secrecy and repression in China in the first decades of *communist* power. The term played on *Winston Churchill's* famous phrase about an *"iron curtain"* descending across east and central Europe, drawn down by *Stalin*.

banana republic: (1) A disparaging reference to the states of Central America, whose agricultural economies depend largely on the export of tropical fruits. (2) A disparaging reference to any state dependent both economically and politically on a larger power, especially if that power is the U.S.

Bancroft Conventions: Named for George Bancroft (1800-1891). These *treaties* reflected a rising respect for U.S. *power* after the *American Civil War*, and resolved longstanding disputes over *naturalization*. The first was signed with the *North German Confederation* in 1868, followed by other German and Scandinavian states. Another was agreed to by Britain in 1870, ending a dispute over naturalization that had helped cause the *War of 1812*. This was a historic, but not universal, victory for a right of *expatriation* over the doctrine of *indefeasible allegiance*. Disputes continued for decades between the U.S. and other states, particularly Russia, over the regular detention, imprisonment, and even *impressment* of naturalized Americans.

Bandung Conference (1955): The conference of African and Asian *states* that launched the main associations and themes of the *Non-Aligned Movement*: anti-*colonialism*, opposition to *racism* and *neutrality* toward the *Cold War*.

Bangladesh: Location: SW Asia. Major associations: *Commonwealth, NAM, SARC, UN*. Population: 120 million. Military: no offensive ability. Originally a Hindu area, it was conquered by Muslim invaders in the 12th century. The British ruled it as East Bengal, a province of the *Raj*, from the 18th century until their departure from the *subcontinent* in 1947. It became East Pakistan at the *partition* of India. It was ruled mainly by and for West Pakistanis from the *Punjab*, from which it was separated by 1,000 miles of Indian territory. In 1970 a cyclone took an estimated 500,000 lives, perhaps the greatest natural disaster in human history. The *separatist* Awami League gained control of the Assembly in 1971. The Pakistani army, largely West Pakistani in make-up, intervened. That provoked a declaration of *independence*, followed by a civil war that killed one million and created 10 million *refugees*, who mostly fled into India. On December 3, 1971, the *Third Indo/Pakistani War* began, ultimately ensuring that Bangladesh achieved independence. Desperately poor and doomed to suffer devastating annual monsoons, Bangladesh also suffered repeated *coups* and has been scene to extensive *human rights* violations. It was declared an "Islamic Republic" in 1988. A cyclone killed 125,000 in 1991, after which a new realism seemed to take hold: it accepted humanitarian assistance even when delivered by foreign (including U.S.) troops, and agreed to IMF *stabilization*.

Bank of International Settlements (BIS): Since the great crisis of the 1930s, European *central banks* have been meeting regularly (in Switzerland) to coordinate policy. The U.S. remained aloof until the Federal Reserve joined in 1960. The central banks of most major economic powers nowadays participate or tacitly coordinate with this important forum.

Bantustans: Ten so-called "homelands" of blacks in South Africa under *apartheid*. Four were ostensibly "independent" (Bophuthatswana, Ciskei, Transkei and Venda), but were never *recognized* internationally.

Bao Dai, né Nguyen Vinh Thuy (b.1913): Emperor of Vietnam from 1932-45. He adjusted his sails to whatever political wind was blowing: he *collaborated* with the French, the Japanese and then the communists. He abdicated in 1945, but in 1949 was made *head of state* by the French. When he was deposed in 1955, South Vietnam became a *republic*.

Barbados: Location: Caribbean. Major associations: *CARICOM, Commonwealth, OAS, UN.* Population: 260,000. Military: minimal. Settled by Britain after 1627, it developed a slave plantation economy until *emancipation* in 1834. *Independence* was granted in 1966. It sent a token force to the *invasion of Grenada*.

Barbarossa: Named for Frederick I (1123-90), Holy Roman Emperor, also called Barbarossa (the "Red Beard"). This was the code name for the German *invasion* of the *Soviet Union* by three million men, on June 22, 1941, the largest invasion in history. Stalin was caught unprepared, in spite of advance warnings

from *Churchill, Roosevelt,* and Soviet *intelligence* and border troops. *Stalin* ignored the warnings, thinking them a British provocation to bring Russia to blows with Germany. The Soviets were still supplying raw materials to Germany (as agreed in the *Nazi/Soviet Pact*) when the attack began. By Christmas German armies had taken Minsk and Kiev, begun their 900-day siege of Leningrad, and were shelling Moscow.

Barbary pirates: Actually, the navies of small Muslim rulers who in the 18th-19th centuries raided the commerce of Europeans, Russians, Americans and anyone else trading on the western Mediterranean. See *Tripolitan War.* Cf. *Trucial Oman.*

Barbary Coast/States: Small, *Islamic* states located along the western Mediterranean coast of Africa, and home in the 18th and 19th centuries to the *Barbary pirates: Algiers, Morocco, Tunis* and *Tripoli.*

Barents Sea: The N. Atlantic between Spitsbergen and the European continent. In 1920, some 39 states signed the Svalbard Treaty, regulating economic exploitation of the Svalbard archipelago and Barents Sea. Disputes subsided until a fisheries and boundary dispute between Norway and the Soviet Union, resolved *bilaterally* in a *treaty* in 1977. It was also the locale of shadow jousting by nuclear *submarines* during the *Cold War*, as it marked passage for Soviet naval vessels based in Murmansk.

Bar-Lev Line: Israeli fortifications along the *Suez Canal* 1968-73. The Egyptians crossed the canal and broke through the Bar-Lev Line in October 1973, stunning the defenders (who nonetheless later rallied).

barrage balloon: A large gas balloon held by wires and deployed near military installations or cities during *WWI* and *WWII*. They were used to deter enemy aircraft from accurate, low-flying bomb runs (for fear of hitting the cables).

barter agreements: Direct exchange of *goods* and *services* (e.g., plum jam for engine parts), without capital transfers. States short on *foreign exchange* or those in a forced *dependency* relationship use these to facilitate trade. For example, they became commonplace during the *Great Depression*, and were also extensively used within the *COMECON* bloc.

Baruch Plan: Named for Bernard Baruch (1870-1965), U.S. financier and statesman. It was a half-serious effort to snuff out the nuclear *arms race* before it got started. The U.S. asked for control of all atomic energy and research to be given to an international authority with unlimited powers of inspection. Once this agency had control, the U.S. would stop manufacturing *nuclear weapons* and destroy its stockpiles. The Soviet Union refused the plan, both because of the paranoia of *Stalin*, and more rationally, because the U.S. alone would retain knowledge of how to construct nuclear weapons, and in all likelihood would control the UN agency as well.

baseline: The inside limit for measuring the *territorial sea*, drawn from the low-tide mark. Under *UNCLOS III's* "archipelagic regime," in an archipelago the baseline would be measured from the outer edge of the outermost island. See also *contiguous zone; EEZ; internal waters; straight baseline*.

basic needs: In *development*, proposals to shift plans (and indices used to measure national development) from *macroeconomic* ends such as *growth*, to progress in meeting basic human needs for the general population, such as primary and secondary education, housing, nutrition and elementary health care. Also see *Human Development Index*.

basic rights: An approach to *human rights* stressing satisfaction of certain minimum physical needs (subsistence, housing, freedom from arbitrary arrest, detention or *torture*), before pressing for more ambitious rights, such as equitable pay, political representation, free speech and assembly. Not all *liberals* are comfortable with this approach. Some argue that prior guarantees of civil and political rights are the best way to ensure provision of subsistence rights, by setting up means for people to make effective, rights-based demands of their own societies.

Basque: An ethnic group numbering some 700,000 persons, not closely related to either the Spanish or French, living on both sides of the border in the western Pyrenees. Most supported the Spanish republic in 1936, in return for local *autonomy*. On the losing side of the *Spanish Civil War*, they were ignored or repressed by *Franco*. Some autonomy was granted in 1980. A radical independence organization, the *Euzkadi Ta Askatasuna (ETA)* keeps up low-level *terrorism*.

Basutoland: The former name of Lesotho.

Bataan death march: After the fall of the Philippines to Japan in 1942, American and Filipino soldiers were marched hundreds of miles to *POW* camps. Thousands died, brutalized along the way; stragglers were shot or bayoneted. This cruel story hardened anti-Japanese sentiment in the U.S. and the Philippines, both during and after *WWII*.

Batistá, Fulgencio (1901-73): Cuban military dictator 1934-40, and President 1940-44, 1952-59. His corrupt *regime* was overthrown by *Fidel Castro* during the *Cuban Revolution*. He went into comfortable *exile*.

battlecruiser: A *capital warship* that possesses the speed and firepower of a *battleship*, but with the lighter armor of a *cruiser*. Cf. *pocket battleship*.

battle fatigue: A *WWII* term for *shell shock*, or what is now called (post) *traumatic stress disorder*.

battlefield nuclear weapons: See *tactical nuclear weapons*.

battleship: A *capital warship* with good speed, maximum firepower and the heaviest feasible armor. Cf. *battlecruiser; Dreadnought; Five Power Naval Treaty; pocket battleship; two-power naval standard*.

Bavaria: A German Electorate in 1623 and an independent kingdom from 1805, it was incorporated into the German Empire in 1871. In 1918 a *soviet* republic was proclaimed, but was crushed. It was the site of early *Nazi* efforts to gain power. After *WWII* it was an influential state in West Germany. Largely Catholic, it continues to exert a broadly conservative pressure on German foreign and domestic policy.

Bay of Pigs: Two weeks before *Kennedy* took office *Eisenhower* cut relations with Cuba. Kennedy immediately approved ongoing *CIA* training of Cuban *exiles* for an *invasion* to overthrow *Fidel Castro*. On April 17, 1961, some 1,400 anti-Castro Cubans landed at the Bay of Pigs, armed and transported by the CIA. They hoped for a rising of the population that never materialized, and counted on U.S. air support that Kennedy, at the last minute, decided not to provide. Within three days most were dead or captured. The fiasco lowered U.S. *prestige* in Latin America, and generally. It may also have encouraged the Soviets to place *missiles* in Cuba, as *extended deterrence* against another attempted invasion of its *ally*, and/or because *Khrushchev* concluded that Kennedy had "blinked" during the Bay of Pigs operation, and could be bluffed and bullied into accepting the presence of Soviet missiles.

beachhead: A shoreline or transriverine area secured by an invading force, to await reinforcements.

Beaufort Sea: The Arctic Ocean NE of Alaska.

Bechuanaland: The former name of Botswana.

Bedouin: Nomadic tribesmen of the Arabian desert.

Bedouin joined the *Arab Revolt* against Turkey in *WWI*. Both Israel and Arab countries have forced them into settlements of late.

Beer Hall *putsch* (November 9-10, 1923): *Hitler's* first attempt to take power, in *Bavaria*. He thought the *Reichswehr* would join the revolt, but it sat aside. He, *Ludendorff* and other Nazi marchers were met by a hail of police bullets. Ludendorff went unscathed. The man beside Hitler was killed, pulling him to the ground, and safety, in a death spasm. Hitler was sentenced to five years in prison, but only served nine months, taking the time to write "Mein Kampf" (My Struggle). The *putsch* brought him and his *revanchist* message to national prominence. More important, it decided him against openly illegal methods. Afterwards, he sought the constitutional path to power, which he would attain in 1933.

beggar-thy-neighbor: Foreign economic policies that look to maximize domestic interests through aggressive *export* strategies, ranging from *import* controls, *tariffs*, export *subsidies*, *quotas* and other mechanisms that do not take due notice of the effect on the economies of trading partners. This often leads to mutual *retaliation* that hurts the very interests one is trying to promote. For example, see *Hawley/Smoot tariff.*

Begin, Menachem (b.1913): Israeli PM and statesman. He migrated to *Palestine* from *Nazi*-occupied Poland in 1942, where he headed the *Irgun*. He was involved in *terrorist* operations against British forces, most infamously destruction of the King David Hotel in Jerusalem, an action that killed 91 (including a number of Jews). He led *Likud* in government from 1977-83. His greatest moment came in 1978, when he signed a *peace* agreement with *Anwar Sadat* of Egypt, for which they shared the 1978 *Nobel Prize* for Peace. In 1982, he approved an *invasion* of Lebanon and shelling of Beirut that drove the *PLO* out of its bases all the way to Tunis, and set up an Israeli security zone in south Lebanon. But the war severely damaged Israel's image and support within the U.S. Begin quit suddenly in 1983, reportedly grief-stricken over the death of his wife, but also despondent over criticism of his conduct of the Lebanese war.

behavioralism: An approach to the study of international politics that regards only observed behavior as relevant and measurable. It stresses *quantification of variables* and the use of *causal modeling*. Its adherents tend to dismiss the role of *volition*, and reject as intuitive and unscientific--and therefore valueless--more historical and philosophical approaches. Cf. *post-behavioralism; traditionalism.*

Belarus: Location: E. Europe/*near abroad*. Major associations: *CIS, CSCE, UN*. Population: 11 million. Military: elements of the old *Red Army*, and for the moment both tactical and strategic *nuclear weapons*. Formerly Byelorussia. In the Middle Ages this area was disputed by Poland, Russia and Ukraine, but ultimately fell under the sway of the princes of Muscovy. It was for centuries a province of the *Russian Empire*, and became an "*autonomous republic*" within the Soviet Union in 1922. It straddles the natural *invasion* route into Russia from Europe (and vice versa). Its capital, Minsk, was burned during the *Napoleonic Wars*. Belarus was overrun by German troops in *WWI* and again in *WWII*, when its people suffered all the terrors of Nazi *occupation*. After the war its *territory* was much expanded at the expense of Poland. It also held (nominally) one of the three seats in the *UNGA* granted the Soviet Union in 1945. It is ethnically closer to Russia than is even Ukraine, and has never had a strong *nationalist* or *secessionist* movement. Yet, because the Soviet Union broke up along existing borders in 1991, somewhat to their surprise Belarussians became independent, and in charge of a nuclear state at that! It subsequently agreed to hand over all nuclear weapons to Moscow and to abide by both the *START* agreements. It retied its economy to Russia's with a 1993 trade agreement, and remains in the ruble zone.

Belgian Congo: Former name of the Republic of the Congo. See *Zaire.*

Belgium: Location: W. Europe. Major associations: *CSCE, EFTA, EU, NATO, OECD, UN, WEU*. Population: 10 million. Military: first-rate, NATO capable. Lying on a historic *invasion* plain, Belgium was the possession of various conquerors for 2,000 years: Romans, Franks, Burgundians, Spaniards, Austrians and French. It was joined to the Netherlands as part of the settlement of the *Congress of Vienna*. It revolted in 1830, becoming an independent, constitutional monarchy in 1831, and one of the most advanced industrial societies on the continent. Domestically, it must perpetually balance the interests of Flemish and Walloon. Its unusual international position in the 19th century was sustained by a British guarantee of *neutrality*, issued in the *Treaty of London* (1839), reaffirmed during the *Franco/Prussian War* (1870), and invoked in August 1914, when German troops invaded as part of the *Schlieffen Plan*. It cleaved to its *neutrality* in the *interwar years*, refusing cooperative defensive efforts, such as an extension of the *Maginot Line* along the Franco/Belgian border. It was invaded by Germany in 1940. Its *surrender* after just 18 days cut off Anglo-French armies and forced a mass evacuation from *Dunkirk*. Liberated in 1944 and 1945, it abandoned neutrality and joined NATO. Its colonial practices in the Belgian Congo (Zaire) ranked with the worst when King Leopold had personal control. Belgium abandoned the Congo in 1960, but has intervened militarily several times since in Africa. It was also the colonial power in *Rwanda* and *Burundi*.

Belize: Location: Central America. Major associations: *CARICOM, Commonwealth, OAS, UN.* Population: 180,000. Military: minimal; implicit *deterrent* of annual British *maneuvers,* and nearness of the U.S. Formerly British Honduras, it was the last British *colony* on the American mainland. It gained *independence* only in 1981, after which Britain maintained a garrison because Guatemala refused to *recognize* Belizean independence and laid claim to parts of its *territory.* In 1991, with an improved security climate in Central America, Guatemala at last extended *recognition.* Britain announced it could not afford its garrison, and pulled it out on January 1, 1994.

belligerency: (1) The actual or legal condition of being at *war.* (2) *Recognition* of a *state of war* within a society, which has the effect of giving international status to *insurgents.* This falls short of full recognition but still carries certain rights. For instance, the *Confederacy* was treated as a belligerent by Britain for purposes of trade, but was never recognized.

belligerents: Communities at *war.* See *recognition.*

belligerent rights: The legal rights accruing to a *state* that is formally at *war.* These include rights to *visit and search;* seizure of *contraband* trade with the enemy; to attack and destroy, under the *laws of war,* the productive capabilities and military forces and equipment of the enemy; and to have its soldiers treated in accord with the *Geneva Conventions.* See also *angary; blockade; booty; capture; levée en masse; occupation; prize; requisition;* Cf. *neutral rights.*

bellum justum: See *just war theory.*

Belorussia: See *Belarus.*

BENELUX: (1) Belgium, the Netherlands and Luxembourg. (2) A *customs union* established in 1948 and composed of those three *states.*

Beneš, Eduard (1884-1948): Czech statesman and twice President of Czechoslovakia. From 1918-35 he served as Foreign Minister, and was instrumental in coordinating Czechoslovak policy within the *Little Entente.* From 1935-38 he was President, resigning in disgust and bitter disappointment over the outcome of

the *Munich Conference.* After *WWII* broke out, he headed a Czechoslovak *government-in-exile* in Paris, which moved to London when Paris fell in 1940. He was President again from 1946-48, but was not trusted by, and could not sufficiently please *Stalin.* He resigned in June 1948, following a Soviet-sponsored *coup.*

Bengal: A large state in eastern India, divided in 1947 between India and *East Pakistan,* and now between India and Bangladesh.

Ben-Gurion, David (1886-1973): A *zionist* immigrant to *Palestine,* during *WWI* he raised a Jewish Legion to fight alongside the British against the *Ottomans.* In the 1930s he chaired the World Zionist Organization, headed the *Jewish Agency,* and was a key figure in Israel's struggle for statehood. He became its first premier and served from 1948-53, and 1955-63. He led it during the first two *Arab/Israeli Wars.*

Benin: A small West African kingdom, later incorporated into Nigeria and not to be confused with the modern *republic,* which it borders.

Benin, Republic of: Location: W. Africa. Major associations: *la francophonie, NAM, OAU, UN.* Population: 4.9 million. Military: no offensive capability. Formerly Dahomey, this *territory* came under French control in the late 19th century, and was incorporated into *French West Africa* in 1904. It achieved *independence* in 1960. A coup in 1972 led to a *marxist-leninist* regime in 1974, and a name change to Benin in 1975, under Ahmed Kerekou. In 1989, as his *Soviet bloc* allies collapsed, Kerekou formally renounced marxism-leninism and appealed for Western *aid.* In 1991 elections he was defeated by Nicephore Soglo.

Bentham, Jeremy (1748-1832): English utilitarian. His impact on international relations came through wide publicity for his views on *free trade,* his opposition to formal *international organizations,* and his active involvement with peace societies. His fully dressed mummy resides at University College, London, where it is still a dinner guest once per year.

Berber: The Hamitic peoples of North Africa living along the *Barbary Coast,* and penetrating as well into the Sahara desert.

Berchtesgaden: A Bavarian resort used as a southern headquarters by *Adolf Hitler.* The *Allies (WWII)* feared it would be used for a last-ditch, suicidal defense by the *SS* and other *Nazi* fanatics. It was not.

Beria, Lavrenti Pavlovich (1899-1953): Longtime

member of the *CHEKA* and *OGPU*. He headed the *NKVD* from 1938, overseeing its use of forced labor, executions, show trials and *purges*. He was notorious for using his police powers to satisfy gross sexual perversions, and was greatly feared by other Soviet leaders. After *Stalin's* death (1953) he briefly joined a ruling troika with *Malenkov* and *Molotov*. But he was soon arrested and shot, after the kind of "*treason* trial" and absurd charge (that he was a British spy) whose techniques he had pioneered and perfected.

Bering Sea: The north Pacific Ocean, next to the *Aleutians*.

Bering Strait: The passage between the Pacific and Arctic Oceans that separates *Alaska* from *Siberia*.

Berlin airlift: The Soviets *blockaded* the road and rail links to the city, from June 22, 1948, to May 1949, trying to force the Western powers to vacate their *occupation zones*. In the first great test of the *Cold War*, the city's inhabitants were kept alive, warm, fed and free, by a daunting display of *air power* and an impressive demonstration of U.S. and Western resolve. See also *Lucius D. Clay*.

Berlin-Baghdad Railway: Chartered by a German company in 1899, the British feared this was a German push into the *Middle East* aimed at confirming Turkey's *dependence*, and perhaps ultimately aimed at India. The more cynical saw it as entangling Russia (which also opposed it) with Germany, thus easing the strain on Britain and France.

Berlin Conference (1884-85): It was hosted by *Bismarck* and attended by the European colonial powers with the U.S. as an observer. It drew and confirmed the borders of Africa, including *internationalizing* the Congo River. Its great accomplishment, from Europe's perspective, was to resolve colonial *border* disputes short of *war*. However, no African was invited or present, and the Conference thus has been criticized for its arbitrary character and gross indifference to local conditions and ethnic divisions. Even so, most of the borders set at Berlin remain in place, accepted as legitimate boundaries in the Charter of the *Organization of African Unity* out of fear that to reopen the issue would *balkanize* the continent even further, and lead to untold bloodshed in multiple wars of *secession*. On the ground it is an entirely different matter, as many formal political divisions in Africa are rejected by the peoples that live astride them.

Berlin, Congress of (1878): This meeting of the *Great Powers* was called by *Bismarck* to revise the *Treaty of San Stefano* and address the regional *balance of power* in southern Europe, unsettled by the decline of the *Ottoman Empire* and *rebellion* in its European provinces. An *autonomous* Bulgarian principality was created and the *independence* of Serbia, Montenegro and Rumania was formally asserted. Russian control of the *Caucasus* was confirmed. Britain gained bases in Cyprus, and Austria received Bosnia-Herzegovina as *compensation* for Russian gains. While stability returned for several decades following this settlement, final resolution of the *Eastern Question* was postponed to 1915-18, and Ottoman *defeat* in *WWI*.

Berlin, division of: At the end of *WWII* it was decided to divide the German *capital* into three *occupation zones*: American, British and Soviet, in tandem with the larger division of Germany agreed at *Yalta*. A French zone was later carved out of the American and British. By 1949 the three western zones were united to form West Berlin, but the West German capital was moved to Bonn. The Soviet zone became East Berlin, and capital of *East Germany*. The failure to resolve the legal status of Berlin led to several crises: the *Berlin airlift* in 1948-49; Soviet denunciation of the occupation agreements in 1958; and building of the *Berlin Wall* in 1961. Tension over its four-power status was eased in the early 1970s by agreements reached under *détente* and through West German *Ostpolitik*. *Recognition* of both Germanies and agreement within the *CSCE* process to permit visitations and facilitate *family reunification* also eased tension. With the fall of the Berlin Wall the city was made whole. In 1991 the Bundestag voted to move the capital from Bonn to Berlin. However, budget problems and bureaucratic inertia suggest it may not move for years.

Berlin Wall: Beginning on August 13, 1961, *East Germany* constructed a fortified wall dividing the city of Berlin, and it reinforced fortifications along the intra-German border. The Wall was really a layers-deep barrier of concrete, barbed wire, watch towers, dogs, hidden mines, and guards ordered to "shoot-to-kill." The primary purpose of the Wall was to stop the hemorrhage of *East Germany's* population to the West (nearly 3.5 million had left since 1949, and over 200,000 in the first six months of 1961 alone). The Western powers chose not to confront this clear violation of four-power control, out of fear the crisis might escalate to a full *NATO* vs. *Warsaw Pact* confrontation. *Kennedy* later went to Berlin and declared that all free people everywhere were spiritual Berliners. The Wall succeeded in its purpose of stanching the outflow of population, but at the cost of open concession that the East German *regime* had no *legitimacy* among its people. Several thousand managed to escape in the years that followed, through a variety of ingenious methods; several hundred more were killed in the attempt. In time, the Wall achieved an impressive height and apparent permanence. It served for many in the West as a symbol of what was at stake in the *Cold War*: *Ronald Reagan* went to Berlin in June 1987, and challenged *Mikhail Gorbachev* to tear down the Wall and end the era of Cold War confrontation. Even so, it was a colossal shock when the Wall and the regime that built it collapsed in November 1989, after East Germany announced it was opening the border. On November 9th, newly made gates were opened. The next day the Wall was breached by hundreds of thousands, from both sides (most of whom ignored the gates). In the days that followed much of the Wall was torn down, literally by hand. Germany donated a large piece to the U.S. in symbolic gratitude for its long-term support for Berlin during the Cold War. It is on display at Fulton College, Missouri, site of *Churchill's* famous *iron curtain* speech.

Bermuda: A British colony in the Atlantic, off the coast of the Carolinas. During *WWII*, the U.K. leased a naval and air base in Bermuda to the U.S.

Bernadotte, Count Folke (1895-1948): Swedish statesman who attempted to act as mediator in both *WWI* and *WWII*. He was appointed by the UN to mediate the partition of *Palestine*. He was assassinated by Jewish zealots (the *Stern Gang*) in September 1948, in the midst of the *First Arab/Israeli War*.

Bernadotte, Jean-Baptiste (1763-1844): He was one of *Napoleon I's* marshals, but was elected heir-apparent to the Swedish throne (1810), and was made king in 1818, founding the dynasty of Ponte Corvo. He arranged Sweden's entry into the war against France in 1814, in exchange for acquisition of Norway from Denmark (a French *ally*). He then led a Swedish army against his erstwhile commander.

Bernstein, Eduard (1850-1932): German socialist who led the great democratic revision of *marxism*, which developed into a major stream of European *social democracy*.

besiege: Surrounding an enemy position with one's military forces, to better *bombard* or starve the enemy into submission.

Bessarabia: A disputed Rumanian province, parts of which changed hands with Russia several times between the *Crimean War* and 1920. It was taken along with *Bukovina* by *Stalin* in 1940, while *Hitler* was busy fighting in the west, returned to Rumania during

WWII, retaken by Russia in 1944, and later incorporated into the Soviet Moldavian Republic. When Moldavia became independent as Moldova in 1991, fighting broke out in Bessarabia. Russian army units (possibly rogue) supported ethnic Russians from *Trans-Dniestra* against ethnic Rumanians.

Bethmann-Hollweg, Theobald von (1856-1921): German statesman and Chancellor 1909-17. He was astonished that Britain *declared war* in 1914 over what he called "a scrap of paper" guaranteeing Belgian neutrality (the *Treaty of London, 1839*), which he had helped Germany violate. Despite pressure from *Tirpitz* he held back for two years from a policy of *unrestricted submarine warfare*, out of fear that it would bring the U.S. into the war and hence lose it for Germany. He was pushed aside by the military, which sensed victory in Russia and moved to break the *stalemate* on the *western front* with a full-scale *U-boat* campaign. Within a year his fears about the U.S. impact on the war were confirmed.

Bevin, Ernest (1881-1951): British Labour politician and Foreign Secretary 1945-51. After serving in *Winston Churchill's* wartime *cabinet*, he became Foreign Secretary in the *postwar* Labour government. He oversaw the *peace treaties* signed after *WWII* with the minor members of the *Axis* coalition (Bulgaria, Hungary and Rumania), and with Italy. He coordinated closely with the U.S. over *occupation* policy in Germany, and in the decision to rebuild and rearm West Germany and form *NATO*. He was responsible for coordinating mutual assistance under the *Marshall Plan*. He approved *independence* for India and Pakistan, setting the *British Empire* on the road to rapid *decolonization*. He also helped initiate the *Colombo Plan*. Yet he clung to the illusion that Britain had special *Commonwealth* ties, and so was more cautious than America, France or Germany on the prospect of European federalism and political *integration*. He also handed the issue of the British *mandate* in *Palestine* over to the *United Nations*, rather than devising a British solution or taking responsibility for *partition*.

BfV (Bundesamt für Verfassungsschutz): The (West) German security service charged with *counterintelligence*. During the *Cold War* it was often penetrated by the East German *HvA*. For instance, in 1954 the head of the BfV, Otto John, defected to East Germany. See also *BND*.

Bhopal, chemical accident (December 3, 1983): The worst industrial accident in history occurred when toxic gas leaked from a chemical refinery in this Indian city, killing 3,000 and seriously injuring 50,000

more. Compensation from Union Carbide took a number of years to arrange.

Bhutan: Location: SW Asia. Major associations: *NAM, SARC, UN*. Population: 1.6 million. Military: minimal. This kingdom was ruled from Tibet in the 16th century. It came under British control during the 19th century, and was made a formal *protectorate* in 1910. After British withdrawal from India, Bhutan was given its *independence* in 1949. But it quickly became dependent on India, around which it continues to orbit today. It is home to many *refugees* from Tibet.

Bhutto, Benazir (b.1953): PM of Pakistan 1988-90; daughter of *Zulfikar Ali Bhutto*. In 1986 she returned from *exile* to lead the opposition to dictator *Muhammad Zia ul-Haq*. In elections following Zia's death, she became that rarest of things in politics: a woman head of government in an *Islamic* country. Her brief tenure was marked by a flood of 3 million *refugees* from Afghanistan. She tried to patch relations with India and generally adopted a moderate foreign policy line. Dismissed for ostensible "abuse of power" and corruption in 1990, she was an influential leader of the opposition until her return to power as Prime Minister after elections in 1993.

Bhutto, Zulfikar Ali (1928-79): President of Pakistan 1971-73; PM 1973-77; Foreign Minister to *Ayub Khan* 1958-66. He improved relations with China, but resigned over the government's provocative policy on *Kashmir*. After the loss of *East Pakistan* (Bangladesh), he became President. He withdrew from the *Commonwealth* in 1972, when Britain *recognized* Bangladesh, yet he moderated *tensions* with India in the Simla Agreement. Economic failure and rampant corruption led to riots, a rigged election and a *coup* in 1977. He was later tried and hanged, ostensibly for complicity in a murder in 1974, despite worldwide efforts to have his sentence commuted. Cf. *Zia ul-Haq*.

Biafra: See *Nigerian Civil War*.

bicycle theory: Actually, a somewhat trite metaphor rather than a theory. It suggests *negotiations* are rather like riding a bicycle: if forward momentum slows, the talks will become unsteady and may collapse.

Bidault, Georges (1899-1982): *Resistance* leader; French statesman; founder of the MRP; PM of France in 1946, and again 1949-50; Foreign Minister 1944, 1947, and 1953-54. During his frequent visits to high office he was a supporter of European cooperation and *integration*, but he strongly opposed *independence* for Algeria even after settler *terrorist* attacks in France.

Charged with *treason*, he fled into *exile* from 1965-68, eventually returning without facing trial.

bigemony: Half *jargon*, half slang for the idea that the preeminence and *integration* of the American and Japanese economies necessitates joint management of the world economy. Others refer to this notion by the even more awkward "Amerippon." Cf. *hegemony*.

Big Five: Immediately after *WWII*: the United States, the Soviet Union, Britain, France and China.

Big Four: (1) At the *Paris Peace Conference*: *Vittorio Orlando, Lloyd George, Georges Clemenceau* and *Woodrow Wilson*. (2) During *WWII*: Britain, China, the Soviet Union and the United States.

Big Three: (1) The United States, the Soviet Union and Britain during *WWII*. (2) *Franklin Roosevelt, Joseph Stalin* and *Winston Churchill*.

Bikini Atoll: Part of the *Marshall Islands* chain. It was the site of U.S. *atmospheric testing* of *nuclear weapons* from 1946-58. The tests left a great deal of fallout, and almost left no Bikini at all.

Biko, Steven (1946-77): A South African student activist whose probable murder by security forces focused world attention on *apartheid* and spurred new calls for *sanctions*.

bilateral: Any arrangement, *dispute*, interaction or *treaty* between just two *states*. Cf. *multilateral*.

billets: Living quarters for troops in the field.

billiard ball model: A crude image of world politics that sees *states* as analogous to a game of surreal billiards; collisions that occur among balls (states) of varying weight and momentum (*power*) lead to outcomes decided by forces of action and reaction, rather than internal events or conscious *decision-making*. It is sometimes held up as an image of the state-centric approach to world affairs, in which states are *unitary, rational actors* and little or no account is taken of other factors that determine outcomes.

binary weapons: A type of *chemical agent/weapon* in which *agents* not in themselves lethal, but highly toxic when mixed, are stored in separate compartments in a *warhead* or shell, and mixed upon firing or detonation. They are considered less hazardous to store and transport than pre-mixed weapons.

biological agents/weapons: Bacteria, viruses or toxins used to kill or disable people, livestock or crops. By the end of *WWII* six countries are known to have researched such weapons: Britain, Canada, France, Japan, the Soviet Union and the U.S. Many more have since done so. Japan is known to have used such weapons against China, and to have performed experiments on *POWs* during *WWII*. Iraq is suspected of using them in the 1980s against Iran. Biological agents include anthrax, black rust, blight, foot-and-mouth disease, plague, rice blast and others. See below, and *chemical and biological warfare*.

biological diversity: Conserving many species. See *Earth Summit; Global Environmental Facility*.

Biological Warfare Treaty (1972): It prohibits research, production and stockpiling of *biological agents/weapons*, except for a giant loophole "for defensive purposes." It was boosted in the *ratification* process in 1969, when *Richard Nixon* announced that the U.S. would unilaterally renounce all biological weapons as well as *first use* of *chemical agents/weapons*. It was initially signed by 111 nations, with more *adhering* since. *Verification* of compliance is extremely difficult, especially given rapid advances in genetic engineering. It is now known that in 1973 the Soviets had *Minatom* set up an illegal biological weapons research center at Biopreparet. In 1979 dozens of civilians at nearby Sverdlovsk (Yekaterinberg) were killed by a release of anthrax. Work on this and even more virulent plagues continued while *Gorbachev* was in power. It was ordered ended by *Yeltsin*, but given ongoing administrative chaos in Russia, it may still be underway. In 1991 Russian *intelligence* reported that North Korea was field testing a range of biological weapons. Cf. *Geneva Protocol*.

bipolarity: (1) A theoretical *alignment* in which *states* cluster around two poles of *power*, said by some theorists to be the most stable of all possible *balance of power* systems. (2) Roughly, the *structure* of the international system during the *Cold War* 1947-89. Cf. *tripolarity; multipolarity; unipolarity*.

bipolycentrism: *Jargon*, purporting to describe the late *Cold War*, when the U.S. and Soviet Union were still in military balance but others were gaining in political and economic influence.

Birobizhan: The "Jewish Autonomous Region" in a desolate area along the Chinese/Soviet border, set aside by the *Bolsheviks* as a homeland for Russia's Jews. It was established in the 1920s by *Joseph Stalin* (then Commissar for Nationalities). Its purpose was to undercut the attraction of *zionism* for the *empire's* mil-

lions of Jews, and to treat them as just one among many minority nationalities of the empire. Only about 100,000 Jews migrated there.

Bishop, Maurice (1945-83): PM of Grenada 1979-83. His *socialist* government came to power in a *coup*, announced its *nonalignment*, and edged somewhat closer to Cuba. He was murdered during a coup by a more *radical* faction of his own "New Jewel" movement. That precipitated a U.S. and Caribbean *invasion*.

Bismarck, Otto von (1815-98): "The Iron Chancellor." German *statesman*. Minister (Ambassador) to Russia 1859, to France 1862. Recalled in 1862 to head the Prussian *cabinet*, he reorganized the army and bureaucracy and led *Prussia* into a brief *war* with Denmark over the *Schleswig-Holstein* question. After securing his eastern *border* with friendly ties to Russia, he moved to eliminate Austria as a rival within Germany. A dispute over division of the spoils from the Danish war provided the pretext for the astonishing *victory* over Austria in the *Seven Weeks' War* (1866). That confirmed Prussian mastery of Germany. In 1870 he deliberately provoked the *Franco/Prussian War* with the *Ems Telegram*. France was humiliated, *Louis-Napoleon* toppled and *Alsace-Lorraine* annexed. Prussia formed the German Empire in 1871, with Bismarck as Chancellor. He transformed his policy from *aggrandizement* to preservation of Germany's central place on the continent, through a series of secret *alliances* designed to isolate France: the *Dreikaiserbund*, with Austria and Russia; and the *Triple Alliance*, with Austria and Italy. His guiding light was to ensure Germany was "one of the three in an unstable system of five Great Powers." He presided over the *Berlin Congress* on the *Eastern Question*, and the *Berlin Conference* on Africa. Bismarck accepted some minor *colonies* for Germany, but thought the *scramble for Africa* foolish, yet useful to Germany if it kept France and Britain distracted from Europe. He strengthened the Prussian and then Imperial German state, attempting a *revolution from above*. After failing to win the *Kulturkampf* against German Catholics, he sought compromise with the middle classes. He also failed to reconcile the working classes. He saw *Wilhelm II* as impetuous and dangerously *adventurist*. He resigned in 1890, rather than be dismissed. Much of what he achieved for Germany was then gambled away by the Kaiser and the Prussian military class that upheld him, whose power Bismarck did so much to build and sustain. See *machtpolitik; realpolitik*.

Black 'n Tans: An auxiliary military force sent to Ireland during the *Irish War of Independence* 1918-21, and named for the motley nature of their uniforms.

They are still bitterly remembered by the Irish for their rough justice, and rougher injustice.

Black Hand: A secret Serbian society formed by young zealots in the *officer corps* in 1911. It promoted *irredentism* toward Serb lands in Austria and the *Ottoman Empire*, and was behind the assassination of *Francis Ferdinand*.

black market: One where *goods* and *services* are sold and purchased illegally, to avoid government *price controls*, *rationing* or taxes. Some analysts regard such markets as the "real" markets, where relations of *supply* and demand are what sets prices.

Black Sea: It lies between Europe and Asia, nestled by Bulgaria, the *Caucasus*, Ukraine, Rumania and Turkey. While landlocked, it is part of the *high seas*.

Black Sea Fleet: The main Russian (also Soviet) battle fleet, based at the *warm water port* of *Sebastopol*, except for a period of *demilitarization* following the *Crimean War*. With the breakup of the *Soviet Union* it became the subject of a bitter ownership dispute between Ukraine and Russia. In 1992 it was decided to divide the fleet (then comprising 21 *submarines*, 35 *battleships* and 250 *first-line* aircraft), but many crews refused to serve with Ukraine. In 1993 the Russian parliament claimed Sebastopol as Russian *territory*, thereby also claiming the fleet, but *Yeltsin* disavowed this move. It was agreed to place the fleet under joint command for three to five years, as part of a larger settlement. But in 1994 *secessionist* sentiment in the *Crimea* reopened the issue. See also *Straits Question*.

Black September: A Palestinian *terrorist* organization that carried out a massacre of Israeli athletes at the Munich *Olympic Games* in 1972. Participants were later identified by Israeli *intelligence*; it has been reported that all were killed by secret assassination squads, with the last dying in 1993.

blackshirt: (1) A member of the *fascist,* Italian *paramilitary* organization before *WWII*; (2) any fascist street thug. Cf. *brownshirt*.

Black Tuesday (October 29, 1929): The day the Wall Street *stock market* crashed (16 million shares were traded), setting off investor panic and precipitating a chain of events that built toward the *Great Depression*. It came on the heels of a multiyear speculative boom, before the market had modern protections on margins, credit and trading cutoffs during a panic.

blank check: The guarantee of German support to Austria, given by Kaiser *Wilhelm II* on July 5, 1914, in the event Austria should attack Serbia. See *mobilization crisis*.

blast effects: The immediate destruction caused by the concussive force of a *nuclear* bomb, as distinct from the lingering lethality of *radiation effects*.

Blenheim, Battle of: A key 1704 clash in SW Germany where a British army under Marlborough (John Churchill, 1650-1722) defeated a combined Bavarian/French force. It was one of several major setbacks Marlborough gave the ambitions of *Louis XIV*.

blitz: Slang for the bombing of London and other British cities, November 1940-May 1941. Derived from *blitzkrieg*.

blitzkrieg: "Lightning war." German term for the style of rapid attack inflicted on Poland, Norway, Denmark, the *Low Countries* and France in 1939-40. It involved constant movement to complete a rapid *flanking* maneuver, using air and *armor*. It grew out of new technologies of armored transport and the tank, both designed to avoid a descent into *trench warfare* as had happened in 1914, after the movement phase of *WWI*. By 1943 better defenses blunted fear of blitzkrieg, and then in 1944 the *Red Army* turned it against Germany.

bloc: An informal *coalition* or *alliance* (though it may also incorporate formal ties); some uses imly high rigidity in both *diplomacy* and military doctrine.

blockade: In *international law*, effective (not just declared) isolation of a port or coast and interception of all transiting ships and *goods*. (1) Pacific blockade: one applied in peacetime as a form of *reprisal*, and affecting mainly ships of the target country. Pacific blockades have been recently enforced under UN authority against Iraq (1990-), Serbia (1992-), and Haiti (1993-). (2) Paper blockade: a declared blockade that lacks effectiveness, and thus may be legally ignored by third parties. (3) Long-distance blockade: this reflects a rule that the distance of the blockading force from the coast is irrelevant for purposes of law, since the action is effective. (4) Land blockade: effective interception of commerce on land. There is no such thing as an aerial blockade, in law. In *warfare*, as in the application of *sanctions*, a blockade may be used to cripple the enemy's economy. The *Union* blockade of the *Confederacy* was a major factor deciding the *American Civil War*, though it was at first misapplied. Britain used this weapon against *Napoleon*, who counter-blockaded; and against Germany in both *WWI* and *WWII*, with Germany counter-blockading with *U-*

boats. See also *Third Balkan War; Battle of the Atlantic; Berlin airlift; Continental System; contraband; Cuban Missile Crisis; Gulf War; infection; Abraham Lincoln; ultimate destination; unrestricted submarine warfare*. Cf. *embargo; quarantine*.

Bloody Sunday (January 22, 1905): A massacre of over one hundred, and wounding of a thousand, peaceful petitioners outside the Tsar's Winter Palace in *St. Petersburg*. It was the spark that set off the *Russian Revolution of 1905*.

Blücher, Gebhart Leberecht von (1742-1819): Prussian Field Marshall. He fought in the *Seven Years' War*, but is most famous for his late yet decisive arrival that won the *Battle of Waterloo*, finally ending *Napoleon I's* career.

Blue Division: Spanish *fascist* volunteers, fighting alongside the *Nazis* on the *eastern front* in *WWII*.

Blue Shirts: Chinese *fascists*, organized in 1932 with *Nazi* help. They were responsible for many atrocities.

blue water navy: One that has ships capable of operating far from coastal waters, in the deep, "blue waters" of the oceans.

Blum, Léon (1872-1950): In 1936 he became the first socialist PM of France, heading a coalition government. He was unable to garner support for a policy of strong opposition to *Hitler*, because: (1) a mood of *defeatism* gripped national life; (2) the *Spanish Civil War* badly divided *public opinion*; and (3) the democratic right failed to see that the real danger to democracy was not French socialists, but German and Italian (and French) *fascists*. In 1938 Blum was again PM, but enjoyed almost no support for an active policy of resistance to Nazi Germany. Despising both his socialist politics and his Jewish faith, the far right in France even proclaimed the slogan: "Better Hitler than Blum." He was *interned* in Germany during *WWII* and tried by *Vichy*, but he masterfully turned the proceedings into a judgment on Vichy itself, leading to cancellation of the trial. He headed a caretaker government in 1946, but bowed to the constitutional chaos of the *Fourth Republic* that continued the moral and political paralysis of the *Third*.

BND (Bundesnachrichtendienst): The (West) German foreign *intelligence service*. During the *Cold War* it was deeply penetrated by the East German *HvA*. For instance, its head of section for Soviet *counterintelligence*, Heinz Felfe, was for years a *mole* who fed *disinformation* to Western services.

boat people: *Refugees* who take to the seas, often in unsafe boats, homemade rafts or just inner tubes, in the hope of sanctuary in a neighboring country. Participation is not always voluntary, and there have been uncounted deaths at sea. The most extensive migrations have been from Vietnam in the 1970s and 1980s, Cuba in the 1980s, and Albania and Haiti in the early 1990s. In 1979 Vietnam signed an agreement with the *UNHCR*, while *OECD* countries agreed to accept 250,000 refugees. Since 1989 the flow from Vietnam has abated. Cf. *humane deterrence; piracy*.

Boers: See *Afrikaner; Boer Wars*.

Boer War, First (1881): A short, sharp clash between the British and the *Boers*, who sought to renege on the surrender of their *independence* to Britain in 1877 that had been the price of British protection against the *Zulus*. In the Convention of Pretoria (1881), Britain granted the Boers *autonomy* in the *Transvaal*, with most limitations lifted by 1884.

Boer War, Second (1899-1902): Led by *Paulus Kruger*, *Boer* forces attacked the British to achieve full *independence*. After early victories, a successful British *counterattack* forced the Boers into *guerrilla* tactics. These were defeated by using *concentration camps* to collect Boer *civilians*, who suffered badly from a policy still not forgiven in the historical memory the Boers. The *war* ended with the Treaty of Vereeniging, which incorporated the *Transvaal* and *Orange Free State* into the empire. In addition to worsening relations with Berlin, the momentary possibility of a British war with Germany arising over the Boer War left London in a weak international position. It was so in need of U.S. *neutrality*, if not support, it bowed to American demands over a Venezuelan *boundary* dispute (where the U.S. was strongly backing Venezuela), the *Panama Canal* issue, and another dispute over the boundary between the Alaskan panhandle and British Columbia.

Bohemia: Formerly an Austrian province, and later forming western *Czechoslovakia*, today this region forms part of the *Czech Republic*.

Bohemia-Moravia: A *protectorate* set up by the *Nazis* during the German *occupation* in *WWII*, 1939-45. This *territory* reverted to *Czechoslovakia* after the war.

Bokassa, Jean Bedel (b.1921): Dictator of Central African Republic from 1965-79. He took power in a *coup*. He proclaimed himself *emperor* in 1976, in a coronation that took a quarter of the *GNP* in one of the world's poorest countries. He was a ruthless and corrupt tyrant whose *human rights* abuses were infamous, including a mass shooting of schoolchildren. Despite this, he had French support for years. In 1979 he was ousted in a coup that had French military help, and went into exile. Apparently mad, and a reputed cannibal, he returned in 1986 despite having been condemned to death *in absentia*. However, his sentence was commuted.

Bolívar, Simón (1783-1830): South American revolutionary, soldier and patriot, who led the region out from under Spanish rule and tried to create a great Latin *republic* modeled on the U.S. In 1821 he became President of Colombia (then comprising Colombia, *New Granada* and Venezuela). In 1822 Ecuador was added to this state. In 1824 he became dictator of Peru, the northern part of which was separated and renamed Bolivia in appreciation of his efforts. But things fell apart, owing largely to his dictatorial tendencies: Bolivia rejected Colombian troops, and in 1829 Venezuela severed its ties as well. The vision of a single Latin republic thus died with Bolivar.

Bolivia: Location: South America. Major associations: *LAIA, OAS, UN*. Population: 7.5 million. Military: defensive only. Spanish *conquest* of the Incas occurred in the 1530s, with the largely Indian population subsequently suffering a fall into political repression and economic *exploitation*. Under the leadership of *Simon Bolivar*, for whom the country is named, *independence* was proclaimed in 1825. In the *War of the Pacific* it lost *territory* to Chile. In the *Chaco War* it lost that rich area to Paraguay and other areas to Brazil. In total, it lost half its territory in a 50-year period. Usually under military rule (it had 189 *coups d'etat* in its first 168 years) and preoccupied with internal unrest and poverty, Bolivia has no international *influence*. In the 1980s it became associated with U.S. anti-drug efforts, as it was a main locale of the Latin cocaine industry. More important, in 1993 it embarked on an experiment in *democracy*, building on some years of sustained *growth*.

Bolshevik Revolution: The *coup d'etat* in Russia that took place in November 1917, and brought the *Bolsheviks* to power. See *Lenin; Russian Revolution, November (October) 1917*.

Bolshevik Russia: Not an official term, yet it was widely used in the *West* once Russia fell under rule by the *Bolsheviks*.

Bolshevik: "Majority." (1) The *radical* wing of the Russian Social Democratic Party, which split with the *Mensheviks* in 1903, forming a new party in 1912.

Under *Lenin* the Bolsheviks seized power in the *Russian Revolution, November (October) 1917*, and consolidated power during the *Russian Civil War*. During the 1930s most of the *Old Bolsheviks* were *liquidated* by *Stalin*. (2) Loosely, and usually derogatory, a person who sympathized with *Bolshevism*.

Bolshevism: The *ideology* and practices of the *Bolsheviks*, to wit: *expropriation* of private property, a *one-party state*, suspension of civil and political liberties, *liquidation* of state enemies, support for *subversion* of foreign powers and societies, *Red Terror*, tactical shiftiness, and veneration of *marxism-leninism* as a catchall economic, political and social doctrine.

bomb: *Ordnance* dropped from an aircraft. They are often crudely aimed and gravity directed, except for "smart bombs" which are guided to target by inboard TV cameras and/or lasers or electronic signals.

bombardment: Sustained shelling by *artillery* or the *navy*.

bomber: An aircraft whose primary function is to deliver *ordnance* to enemy targets, rather than destroy other aircraft as does a *fighter*. By convention, they are divided into heavy, medium and light classes, according to *payload* and range.

Bonaparte: See *Napoleon I (Bonaparte)*.

Bonapartism: Rule by a charismatic military leader, à la *Napoleon I* or *III*, who purports to rise above class and sectoral interests and embody the spirit and interests of the *nation* as a whole. It had a long history as a political possibility and sometime reality in France. Even in the *Fifth Republic*, some feared *de Gaulle*'s retailoring of the sentiment might be used to support a personal dictatorship (it was not). The term has also been applied to *Third World* societies plagued by military dictators, charismatic or not: e.g., *Saddam Hussein; Juan Perón; Quadaffi; Sukarno*.

Bonin Islands: A small island chain in the North Pacific. Japan retained "residual sovereignty" over this chain under terms of the *Japanese Peace Treaty*. The U.S. *occupied* them until full *sovereignty* was returned to Japan in 1968. The adjacent Volcano Islands, including battle-scarred Iwo Jima, were returned that year as well.

boom: Rapid economic *growth*.

boomer: Common navy slang for a nuclear *missile*-bearing *submarine*. Cf. *hunter-killer*.

booty: Moveable enemy property that is claimed as part of the spoils of *war*. See *laws of war*.

Borah, William Edgar (1865-1940): U.S. Senator (Idaho) 1907-40; Chairman of the Foreign Relations Committee 1924-40. He led the *isolationists* in the Senate who opposed the *Versailles Treaty* because it committed the U.S. to joining the *League of Nations*. He also opposed *Republican* Presidents in the 1920s who sought to have the U.S. join the *World Court*. In the 1930s he advocated *disarmament*, despite the *rearmament* programs of the *Axis*. See *Kellogg-Briand Pact*.

Borden, Robert (1854-1937): PM of Canada 1911-20. He led Canada during *WWI*, which saw a national crisis over *conscription*. He also was able to parlay its wartime contribution into a new status and voice within Empire affairs. He attended the *Paris Peace Conference*, where he won agreement to let the *Dominions* sign separately from Britain and join the *League of Nations* as individual *states*.

border: Any line marking the limit of *jurisdiction* between two distinct *territories* that may be *states, colonies, dependencies, protectorates*, or any of the above and *territorium nullius*. Borders are set by *conquest, diktat, negotiation*, military *stalemate, topography* or some combination of those considerations. Numerous borders are in *dispute*.

border states: The *slave states* lying between the *Union* and the *Confederacy* that sought compromise rather than *secession*: Delaware, Maryland, Kentucky and Missouri. Their populations split between North and South when *war* came.

Borneo: A large island in the Malay Archipelago, divided into *Sabah, Sarawak, Brunei* and *Kalimantan*; now divided among Brunei, Indonesia and Malaysia.

Bornu: Formerly an independent West African *emirate*; now part of Nigeria.

Borodino, Battle of (September 7, 1812): Russians under Kutuzov (1745-1813) and French, and others, under *Napoleon I*, fought this savage battle outside Moscow. While the Russian army later abandoned the city, it was not eliminated as an effective fighting force. During the *retreat from Moscow* it harassed and ultimately destroyed Napoleon's invading army.

Bose, Subhas Chandra (1897-1945): Indian nationalist. He opposed the non-violence of the *Congress Party*, preferring armed insurrection. During *WWII* he raised and led the "Indian National Army" to fight with Japan against the British in Burma and India. He died in Japan.

Bosnia-Herzegovina: Location: *Balkans*. Major associations: *CSCE, UN*. Population: 4.4 million (45% Muslim; 35% Serb; 20% Croat). Military: *civil war*. It was ruled by Croatians in the Middle Ages, then was briefly an independent duchy before falling under Turkish sway and becoming a province of the *Ottoman Empire*. In 1878 the *Congress of Berlin* gave Austria the right to administer the area. Austria formally *annexed* Bosnia in 1908, precipitating the *Bosnian Crisis*. It remained part of the *Austro-Hungarian Empire* until 1918, when it was incorporated into *Yugoslavia*. During *WWII* it was annexed by the Nazi *puppet regime* in Croatia, and was the scene of vicious *guerrilla warfare* and ethnic massacres. After the war it was again dominated by Serbia, within the remade Yugoslavia. In 1991 its parliament declared independence, following an earlier declaration by Croatia. In April 1992, its independence was *recognized* by the *EC* and the U.S. War followed, in which well-armed Bosnian Serbs pursued a policy of *ethnic cleansing* aimed at joining the lion's share of *territory* to Serbia. At the end of 1992 Croatia, too, carved out Bosnian land, leaving *enclaves* of Muslims cut off, starving and at the mercy of Serb and Croat *militia*. EC and UN mediators proposed *partition* into a patchwork of ethnically defined territories in a loose *federation*. UN troops were helpless to prevent fighting or deliver humanitarian aid, in the face of Serb militia refusal to permit access to the Muslim enclaves. In February 1993, the U.S. began to airdrop relief supplies. Six months later the UN still would not *intervene* with force, and all three ethnic groups engaged in intensified ethnic cleansing to secure as much land as possible before the expected partition. The *Vance/Owen peace plan* was then abandoned in favor of a three-way partition reflecting the reality of Croat and Serb gains. The Muslims objected, but the *Security Council* refused to lift the arms embargo. The *warlord* in one Muslim area, the enclave of Bihac, has also declared independence. In March 1994, *NATO* imposed a *cease-fire* on parts of Bosnia. See *Third Balkan War*.

Bosnian Crisis (1908): Austria annexed Bosnia in 1908, precipitating a crisis with Russia, which demanded *compensation*. Germany's threatening *intervention* and Britain's reluctance to see Russian *warships* in the Straits forced Russia to back down. The affair humiliated Russia and thereby raised *tensions* higher in the area where *WWI* would begin. See also *Eastern Question; Straits Question*.

Bosphorus: The narrow channel passing under the

walls of Istanbul (*Constantinople*), and linking the Black Sea with the Sea of Marmora, and through the *Dardanelles*, the Mediterranean as well. Its *strategic* importance to Russia and Britain made it the central issue in the *Straits Question*. See *Nelidov Project*.

Botha, Louis (1862-1919): South African general and statesman. He was commander-in-chief of *Boer* forces during the *Second Boer War*. In 1907 he became Premier of the *Transvaal*, which he represented at the Imperial Conferences in London in 1907 and 1911. In 1910 he was made the first premier of the Union of South Africa. During *WWI* he cooperated with the old enemy Britain, in conquering German South West Africa (Namibia), which later became a South African *mandate*. He attended the *Paris Peace Conference*.

Botha, Pieter Willem (b. 1916): PM of South Africa 1966-78, and President 1978-89. He was *hard-line* and repressive in support of *apartheid* at home, and supported aggressive *intervention* and *sabotage* of neighboring African nations, regardless of the consequences for negative world opinion about South Africa. His retirement opened the way to overdue reforms.

Botswana: Location: Southern Africa. Major associations: *Commonwealth, OAU, SADCC, UN*. Population: 1.3 million. Military: minimal defense force. Formerly Bechuanaland. A British *protectorate* from 1886, it was used as a defensive base against *Boer* and German *encroachments* on more important *territories* in East Africa such as Rhodesia and Kenya, and for offense against German *colonies* during *WWI*. It became independent as Botswana in 1966. It adopted a pragmatic approach toward *apartheid* in South Africa, reflecting an overall vulnerability to its large and powerful neighbor. Since the 1970s it has enjoyed high rates of *growth*, significant *foreign direct investment* and excellent returns on its diamonds.

Bougainville insurgency: In 1989-90 a *secessionist* movement sprang up among landowners on this Solomon island that belongs to Papua New Guinea. New Zealand and the Solomons hosted talks in 1990-91 that led to lifting of a *state of emergency* declared earlier. Talks broke off, but resumed in 1993.

boundary: See *border*.

Bourbon: The dynasty that ruled France from 1589-1792, with a brief restoration in 1814, and again from 1815-30; also, Naples from 1735-1806, and again from 1815-60; and Spain from 1700-1931. The Bourbons were noted for rigid conservatism in both political and social affairs.

bourgeoisie: (1) The middle class. (2) In *marxism*, the class that developed the capitalist *mode of production* and opposes the interests of the *proletariat*.

Boutros-Ghali, Boutros (b.1916): Egyptian and world statesman. Formerly Foreign Minister of Egypt, he became *Secretary General* of the *UN* at the beginning of 1992. He has been exceptionally active and unusually (some would say, refreshingly) blunt. He has publicly lectured states large and small, on their financial and other obligations to the UN. He has proposed an ambitious agenda of moving from *peacekeeping* to *peacemaking*, and has been strongly supportive of UN *intervention* and humanitarian efforts in Angola, Bosnia, Cambodia, Haiti, Somalia and elsewhere.

Boxer Rebellion (1900): With the tacit support of China's government, foreigners of all types were attacked by young "Boxers," or members of the secret "Society of Harmonious Fists," that opposed all foreign *influence* and presence in China. The German Ambassador was killed and foreign legations besieged. The *Great Powers* sent in troops to rescue their nationals and restore their economic and political privileges. Foreign *intervention* further weakened the hold of the *Manchus* and strengthened the *nationalist* movement led by Dr. *Sun Yat-sen*.

boyar: A Russian noble class, below the rank of prince, that perennially contested the power of the tsars. They were tamed by *Peter I (the Great)*, but still remained a drag on Russian *modernization* through the 19th century.

boycott: When nationals of one state refuse to buy *goods* or *services* from another. Some examples of boycotts: *Arab League* vs. Israel, 1948-93; U.S. vs. Cuba 1960- . An international boycott of South Africa ran from 1965-92. Although boycotts are supposed to imply voluntary action taken by private international actors for public policy reasons (and therefore lie outside the purview of *international law*), very often they are backed by governments and the term becomes interchangeable with *embargo*. Cf. *sanctions*.

Boyne, Battle of: In 1690 the Protestant king *William III (of Orange)* defeated the Catholic James II in this battle in *Ulster*. Protestants still celebrate the battle with annual parades, inevitably sparking bouts of intercommunal violence.

brain drain: An outflow of highly educated or skilled persons from one country to another, due to greater economic opportunity abroad or a wish to escape government repression at home. For example, before

WWII the U.S. became a major beneficiary of brilliant scientists (often Jewish) fleeing *fascist* persecution in Europe. After WWII the U.S. was able to attract foreign scientists, engineers, doctors and so on due to its high salaries and advanced facilities. Today, the loss of trained personnel to developed countries by the *Third World* is a major problem for those societies, as the costs of education are largely or wholly borne by the public but the gains made may be merely private.

Brandt, Willy (1913-92): German statesman. Active in the anti-Nazi *resistance* during *WWII*; Mayor of West Berlin 1957-66; Foreign Minister 1966-69; Chancellor 1969-74. He was a driving force behind *Ostpolitik* and *détente* in the early 1970s, for which he won the 1971 *Nobel Prize for Peace.* He was forced to resign after it was learned that a member of his personal staff was an East German *agent of influence.* Much admired in the *West* and the *South,* he later chaired the United Nations commission that bore his name.

Brandt Commission: A United Nations *ad hoc* commission headed by *Willy Brandt,* that reported in 1980 on *North/South issues.* It recommended a set of broadly *social democratic, multilateral* solutions to issues of *development, famine* and *North/South* trade. These proposals were much applauded within the *UNGA,* especially by the *Third World* states, but few were ever enacted.

Braun, Werner von (1912-77): German rocket scientist who headed the team that constructed the *V-1 and V-2 rockets* for *Adolf Hitler,* as well as the world's first jet fighters. Captured by the U.S. in 1945, he assisted in the rapid development of the American space program, in both military and civilian aspects.

Brazil: Location: South America. Major associations: *LAIA, NAM, OAS, UN.* Population: 160 million. Military: large, with a regional capability. It was first penetrated by the Portuguese after 1500. As it was settled over the next several centuries the native Indian population was either exterminated or pushed back into the *Amazon basin.* Brazil has the second largest black population in the world, mostly descendants of slaves. In 1808 the Portuguese King Dom Joao VI temporarily moved to Brazil, after Lisbon was captured by *Napoleon.* In 1822, following popular unrest, his son became Emperor Dom Pedro I, ruler of an independent Brazil until 1831 when he abdicated in favor of his five-year-old son. *Slavery* was abolished in 1888. Dom Pedro II was deposed by an army revolt in 1889 in favor of a *republic* called the United States of Brazil (changed to the Federative Republic in 1967). Brazil has been ruled for the most part by its

military since another major revolt in 1930, with brief periods of democratic experimentation from 1945-64 and 1985 to the present. Under the dictator Getulio Vargas (1930-45) Brazil had a quasi-*fascist* government, but nonetheless bent to U.S. pressure and *declared war* on the *Axis* in 1942, actually sending troops to Italy in 1944. Its economy has grown since the 1970s, and it has sought to exert leadership in Latin America, surpassing its rival, Argentina. It is emerging as a significant arms manufacturer and exporter, and is a rising industrial power. It faces criticism of its *development* policies, especially concerning the environment and *indigenous peoples.* It announced an Amazon environmental initiative in 1989, and hosted the *Earth Summit* in 1992. But it resists efforts to have the Amazon basin treated as a global, rather than a national resource. Brazil's ability to meet its foreign *debt service* payments was hampered in 1992 by an *IMF* decision to freeze a $2 billion loan, and delay renegotiation of another $44 billion of existing *debt* until the economy was stabilized. Other important decisions were held up by a simultaneous political crisis that only ended when President Fernando Collor was impeached, and replaced by Itmar Franco.

Brazzaville bloc: A regional association formed in 1960 by the new states in Africa, superseded by the *OAU* in 1963.

breeder reactor: A nuclear reactor built to produce *plutonium* for bomb construction or plutonium reactors by various enrichments of its uranium fuel.

Brenner Pass: The strategic Alpine pass between Austria and Italy, a major objective of both nations during *WWI.*

Brest-Litovsk, Treaty of (March 3, 1918): A separate and *Carthaginian peace,* signed by the *Bolsheviks* with Germany. It pulled Russia out of *WWI,* and gave Germany possession or control of nearly one third of Russia's *territory* (the *Baltic States,* the Caucasus, Finland, Poland and Ukraine), and one quarter of its *population.* The Bolsheviks needed to concentrate on consolidating power for the *Russian Civil War* then beginning; the Germans sought the full spoils of *victory,* but also wanted to end the fighting so they could transfer vast numbers of men to the *western front,* and attack before the arrival of U.S. troops denied them victory. The *treaty* caused great bitterness against Russia among the *Allies.* Britain and France tried to intervene against the Bolsheviks to keep Russia in the war, and secondarily to prevent establishment of a communist regime. The U.S. was at most a reluctant and minor participant in the *interventions,* and the first to pull out. German avarice at Brest-Litovsk (they took Russia's gold reserves and extorted massive *reparations*) set a precedent for the *diktat* on reparations at the *Paris Peace Conference*.

Bretton Woods system: A conference in Bretton Woods, New Hampshire in July 1944, laid the ground for creation of the *IBRD* and the *IMF*. The general purpose was to set up a cooperative system to monitor *exchange rates*, maintain *liquidity* and prevent *balance of payment* problems. In general, it worked by building the *postwar* monetary system on dollar convertibility to gold. The system evolved from a plan for limited international management to dependence on primary U.S. management. Yet it was greatly successful in aiding quick and sustained recovery among the *OECD* nations. It lasted until 1971, when *Nixon* took the U.S. off the *gold standard*. It has been replaced by a system of floating *exchange rates* and loose collective management. One Bretton Woods initiative, a proposed *International Trade Organization*, failed to get off the ground, and was partly replaced by the *GATT*.

Brezhnev, Leonid Ilyich (1906-82): First Secretary of the CPSU 1964-82, after he helped oust *Khrushchev* from power. His reputation within Russia is that of a stultifying bureaucrat, who delayed domestic reform for a whole generation. But that view underestimates the degree to which his foreign policy was one of *adventurism*: he threatened China with a *preemptive strike* in 1969, supplied *regimes* in the *Middle East* with advanced weaponry, intervened with military *aid* and Cuban proxies in the Horn of Africa and Arabia, and most disastrously, approved the *invasion* of Afghanistan in 1979. While opportunistic, his main purpose still seems to have been to consolidate rather than extend the gains made after *WWII*: he promoted the *Warsaw Pact* invasion of Czechoslovakia in 1968 to forestall reforms that might unravel Soviet control of Eastern Europe; cooperated with *Richard Nixon* and *Willy Brandt* in designing *détente* in the early 1970s, and pushed for the *CSCE* talks, hoping they would lead to formal *recognition* of Soviet postwar gains, as well as divide the U.S. from Western Europe. See *Brezhnev Doctrine*.

Brezhnev Doctrine: Advanced a month after the 1968 invasion of *Czechoslovakia*, it declared a right to intervene where Moscow deemed *socialism* was threatened by "*counter-revolutionary* forces." In short, Moscow viewed the *status quo post bellum* as irreversible concerning communist states, while supporting *wars of national liberation* and proclaiming *peaceful coexistence*. See also *East Germany; Jaruzelski; Prague Spring; Sinatra Doctrine; Soviet legal thought; Tito.*

Briand, Aristide (1862-1932): French statesman. Eleven times premier; Foreign Minister 1925-32. He shared the 1926 *Nobel Prize for Peace* with the great Weimar statesman *Gustav Stresemann*, for work on Franco/German *rapprochement* in the aftermath of *WWI*. He reluctantly coauthored the *Kellogg-Briand Pact*, which sought to outlaw *war* when what he really wanted was a security guarantee from the U.S. He gave what support French *public opinion* permitted to the *League of Nations*.

bridgehead: A tactical position gained on the enemy's side of a river, preparatory to bringing over more troops.

brinkmanship: Manipulating a crisis to the brink of *war*, to frighten an opponent into backing down. This dangerous style, including threatening to use *nuclear weapons*, was attributed to the conduct of U.S. foreign policy by *John Foster Dulles* in the 1950s, but it can be ascribed to many statesmen and crises.

Britain: See *Great Britain; United Kingdom.*

Britain, Battle of (July 11-September 17, 1940): This prolonged air battle between the *Luftwaffe* and the Royal Air Force (RAF) was just barely won by the RAF. The battle was the key to Hitler's planned *invasion* of Britain ("Operation Sea Lion"), and thus a major turning point in *WWII*: only if the RAF was eliminated would the German Navy be able to escort an invasion force across the *English Channel* with any chance of success against the *Royal Navy*. The key to the battle was a fateful decision to switch targeting from airfields to raids on British cities, which let the RAF survive. When air losses became intolerable, Hitler called off the invasion and turned to planning *Barbarossa*, his great attack on Russia set for June 1941. That left Britain to recover, and later to serve as a giant airfield for the deadly and punishing Anglo/American air raids of 1942-45, and as the supply base for the invasion of Europe and Germany, 1943-45.

Britannia: A female personification of the *British Empire*; from the Roman name for Britain.

British Antarctic Territory: A South Atlantic *colony* comprising several small and desolate island chains, near the much larger *Falkland Islands*.

British Broadcasting Corporation (BBC): A state radio and television service, broadcasting to all regions in many languages. Budget cuts have reduced its reach, but it remains one of the world's most respected and listened to electronic news services. For many people living under *regimes* of censorship, it is the main source of outside information. In 1993 it began to share resources with the American network ABC. Cf. *CNN; Radio Free Europe; Voice of America.*

British Cameroons: Part of this *colony* joined with the *French Cameroons* to form modern Cameroon in 1960, while the other part joined Nigeria in 1961.

British Commonwealth: See *Commonwealth.*

British East Africa: In disuse. It referred to *Kenya, Uganda, Tanganyika* and *Zanzibar.*

British Empire: The vast *territories* under the authority of the British Crown, once comprising a quarter of the world's *population* and stretching so far afield it was said (romantically by some, bitterly by others) that upon its shores "the sun never set." See *Dominions; imperialism; Raj; United Kingdom.*

British Guiana: Former name of Guyana.

British Honduras: Former name of Belize.

British India: The part of the *subcontinent* that before 1947 was subject to English law and governance, including most of modern Bangladesh, India and Pakistan, but excluding the *Princely States.*

British Indian Ocean Territory (BIOT): The Chagos Archipelago, south of the Maldives in the Indian Ocean. It is the last British possession in the region. One island, *Diego Garcia,* is leased to the U.S. which uses it as a naval and *satellite* base. The whole Chagos group is claimed by Mauritius.

British Isles: The islands of *Great Britain, Ireland,* the Orkneys, Isle of Man and small adjacent islands.

British Malaya: The British colonial possessions located on the Malay peninsula and archipelago that later became part of *Malaya,* and later still part of the Malaysian Federation. See *Sabah; Sarawak.*

British North America: (1) Before 1776: All seventeen British *colonies* in North America (excluding the Caribbean). (2) From 1783-1867: The *territories* now comprising Canada.

British North Borneo: Former name of *Sabah.*

British Raj: See *Raj.*

British Somaliland: A former *protectorate* in the Horn of Africa. In 1960 it joined with *Italian Somaliland* to the south to form Somalia.

British Togoland: A small possession, it joined the *Gold Coast* (Ghana) in 1957.

British West Africa: In disuse: *British Cameroons, Gambia, Gold Coast, Nigeria, Sierra Leone* and *Togo.*

British West Indies: A general reference to British colonial possessions in the Caribbean: Bahamas, Barbados, Jamaica, Trinidad, Tobago, and the Leeward and Windward Islands.

brownshirt: (1) A member of the Nazi *SA (Sturmabteilung)*; (2) any *fascist* street thug. Cf. *blackshirt.*

Brunei: Location: SE Asia. Major associations: *Commonwealth, NAM, UN.* Population: 375,000. Military: minimal; under nominal British protection. This small *state* was the site of a *sultanate* that controlled all *Borneo* from the 16th century. A British *protectorate* from 1888, it gained *independence* only in 1984. It followed an entirely pro-Western line in the 1980s, even donating funds to the Nicaraguan *Contras* at the request of the *Reagan* administration. Malaysia denies Brunei's *EEZ* and *continental shelf* claims and disputes one common land *border.*

Brüning, Heinrich (1885-1970): Chancellor of *Weimar Germany* 1930-32. Without a parliamentary majority, he chose to govern by decree, thus further weakening Weimar's shaky democratic credentials. Even so, he was unable to correct the collapse of Germany's economy and was forced out by *Hindenburg.* He fled to the U.S. in 1934.

Bruntland Commission: Named for Gro Harlem Bruntland, PM of Norway. It was a 1987 international commission that called for, and thereby gave prominence to, the idea of *sustainable development.*

Brussels, Treaty of (March 17, 1948): Precursor to *NATO,* it was a defense pact between Britain, France and the *BENELUX* nations. It arose from fear of Germany as much as it did from apprehension about the Soviet Union.

Bryan, William Jennings (1860-1925): Thrice defeated (1896, 1900 and 1908) Democratic candidate for President. He served as Secretary of State to *Woodrow Wilson* 1913-15. A passionate *pacifist,* he resigned over the second *Lusitania note* sent to Germany, which might have led to *war* had *Bethmann-Hollweg* not persuaded the German military to back down on the question of *unrestricted submarine warfare*. See also *cooling-off treaties; Open Door.*

Brzezinski, Zbigniew (b.1924): U.S. National Security Adviser, 1977-81. He was the foil to Secretary of State Cyrus Vance within the *Carter* administration. He consistently argued for a *hard-line* toward the Soviets, viewed *human rights* policy as primarily an instrument of ideological contest and engaged in a behind-the-scenes power struggle for control of foreign policy. He finally got his way in 1980, when Vance resigned. He began to institute a tough line in relations with Moscow, but shortly lost office to the even more uncompromising *Reagan* team.

Buchanan, James (1791-1868): U.S. President, 1857-61. As Minister (Ambassador) to Russia, he negotiated a *commercial treaty* that had eluded U.S. *diplomats* for over 30 years. He also became an apologist for Tsarism, including bloody repression of a *rebellion* in Poland in 1831. He defended *serfdom* in terms akin to his strong support for slavery. He served as Secretary of State to *James Polk*, settling the *Oregon Question*. During his term as President, he watched in inept and tragic befuddlement the great crisis that led to dissolution of the United States and to the awful carnage of the *American Civil War.*

Bucharest, Treaty of (1913): This *treaty* ended the *Balkan Wars* that preceded *WWI*. While its specific *territorial* adjustments would be overturned in that greater conflagration, it had two lasting effects: (1) it pushed Turkey out of its European holdings, except a small area around *Constantinople;* (2) it created a weak Albania, and set it tremorously in the midst of the territorial ambitions of the other *Balkan states.*

Buddhism: Founded in India by Buddha (Prince Siddhartha, 566?-480 B.C.), it grew out of *Hinduism*. It has since spread throughout Asia (Burma, China, Japan, Thailand, Tibet and Vietnam). In the 20th century it has even made minor inroads in North America and Europe. It offers self-perfection through prajna, or enlightenment, in which an end to suffering comes from the extinction of desire. It stresses personal discipline and self-correction. This leads through a cycle of reincarnations to nirvana (a condition of holiness, purity and release from the desires and travails of earthly life). One may halt the cycle of births and deaths only with full enlightenment and merger with the Buddha, the first being to achieve nirvana.

buffer state: A small, *neutral* state lying between two *Great Powers* and said to provide a cushion to absorb their potential hostility. In fact, such states can just as easily be a temptation to mutual *aggrandizement*, as the historical experience of Poland illustrates. Note: This term does not apply to weak, but *aligned* states trapped between large powers, as in Eastern Europe during the *Cold War.*

buffer stock: Reserves of commodities held by states or under *International Commodity Agreements*, purchased or released for sale from time to time as a means of evening out price fluctuations.

buffer zone: A *neutralized* and often *demilitarized* zone of *territory* lying between two hostile powers, created by agreement or just by one power in an attempt to insulate itself from attack. Examples include: *Heligoland,* the *Rhineland* 1919-36, and Israel's self-proclaimed "security zone" in southern Lebanon. Cf. *neutral zone.*

Bukovina: A Rumanian province, taken along with *Bessarabia* by *Stalin* in 1940 while *Hitler* was busy fighting in the west. Its southern portion is in Rumania still; the rest is in Ukraine.

Bulganin, Nikolai Alexandrovich (1895-1975): One-time mayor of Moscow, he was active in the Soviet Military Council during *WWII*. He was Soviet Defense Minister in 1946, Vice-Premier after *Stalin's* death in 1953, and a figurehead premier 1955-58.

Bulgaria: Location: *Balkans*. Major associations: *CSCE, UN*. Population: 9 million. Military: Balkan capability, with older, *Warsaw Pact* weapons. Conquered by the *Ottomans* in 1396, Bulgaria remained under Turkish rule for 500 years. In 1870 the Turks allowed the establishment of a separate branch of the *Orthodox Church* for their Bulgarian subjects (the Exarchate). This body led a nationalist revival, encouraged by Russia. The Turks sought to crush the movement in 1875-76, but that only led to *war* with Russia and Bulgarian *autonomy* in the *Treaty of San Stefano* in 1878, amended by the *Congress of Berlin* later that year. In 1885, in defiance of the *treaty* interests of the *Great Powers*, Bulgaria expanded into eastern *Rumelia*, inflicted a *defeat* on Serbia, and emerged as the largest of the new *Slav* states in the Balkans. It was dissatisfied with the territorial outcome of the *Balkan Wars* (1912 and 1913), and so it joined the *Central Powers* in 1915. It was badly beaten at Salonica in 1918. While its nationalists gained no satisfaction at the *Paris Peace Conference*, it did obtain less onerous terms in the *Treaty of Neuilly*. Boris III (1894-1943) was the last King of Bulgaria 1918-43. In *WWII* he allied with *Hitler*, whom some believe had him poisoned. This time, Bulgaria joined with Germany to invade Yugoslavia, in 1941. It sought to stay out of the German war with the Soviet Union, but in 1944 was invaded by the *Red Army* anyway. The Soviets set up a communist state, melding Bulgaria to the *Soviet bloc*. It joined the *Warsaw Pact* in 1955 and traded through *COMECON*. From Moscow's point of view, Bulgaria was the most stable and reliable of the satellite states in Eastern Europe, participating in the invasions of Hungary (1956) and Czechoslovakia (1968). Suspicion lingers that the Bulgarian KGB was behind an attempt to assassinate Pope *John Paul II*. Domestically, it was highly repressive of Muslim and Turkish minorities, and political *dissidents*. Several dissidents were assassinated overseas, one with a poisoned umbrella tip on a London street. In 1984-85 ethnic Turks (numbering one million) were forced to change their names to Bulgarian ones, and speaking Turkish was forbidden. In 1989 over 300,000 ethnic Turks were forced from their homes and herded to Turkey. In November, *Todor Zhivkov*, communist dictator for 35 years, was forced to resign by popular unrest. In January 1990, the National Assembly dismantled the communist state. In subsequent elections, however, old-style communists newly decked out in nationalist clothing did quite well.

Bulge, Battle of (a.k.a. Ardennes Offensive): The last German offensive in *WWII*, launched on December 16, 1944. *Hitler* threw in all his *reserves*, and German losses were so extensive that it later proved impossible to hold the Western *Allies* along the Rhine. The battle thus hastened the Nazi collapse by several months. That may have spared Germany the *atomic bombs* used against Japan: they became operational two months after Germany's surrender.

Bülow, Prince Bernhard von (1849-1929): German statesman. Foreign Secretary 1897; Chancellor 1900-09. He was frequently overruled or left uninformed by Kaiser *Wilhelm II* and the military High Command, and bore less than full responsibility for the aggressive and *adventurist* course of German foreign policy in the pre-*WWI* period.

Bunche, Ralph (1904-1971): U.S. and UN diplomat. After stints in the *State Department* and with the *Joint Chiefs of Staff*, he joined the UN, where he was responsible for *trusteeship* and *peacekeeping*. He was the first American black awarded the *Nobel Prize* for Peace (1950).

Bundesbank: The highly independent *central bank* of Germany, charged above all else with holding down Germany's rate of *inflation*. That policy is rooted in memory of the devastation of the economy, and Ger-

man politics and society, wrought by *hyperinflation* under *Weimar*.

Bundestag: (1) The Federal Diet in Prussia 1815-66. (2) Since 1949, the lower house in the bicameral German legislature.

Bundeswehr: The German armed forces. The term replaced *Wehrmacht*, which had too many *Nazi* connotations.

bureaucratic politics model: This *political science* theory posits that in complex, modern *states* policy is often not the result of *rational decision-making* by leaders, but of bargaining and competition among elements of the bureaucracy. This causes policy distortions, as bureaucratic struggles may have more to do with budgets and defense of internal turf than solving problems. Cf. *organizational process model*.

Burgenland: Part of Hungary under the *Dual Monarchy*, but ethnically German, it was transferred to Austria at the *Paris Peace Conference*. It was the only land so transferred between defeated states.

Burkina Faso: Location: W. Africa. Major associations: *la francophonie, NAM, OAU, UN*. Population: nine million. Military: minimal, no offensive capability. Formerly Upper Volta. It became a French *colony* in 1896. *Independence* was granted in 1960. A radical military clique took power in 1982, changing the country's name to Burkina Faso in 1984. Among the world's poorest states, and subject to severe drought, its inhabitants depend on foreign *aid* or repatriated earnings of family members working in the Ivory Coast, Ghana or Nigeria.

Burma: Former name of *Myanmar*, until 1988.

Burma road: The *supply line* to China used by the *Allies* in *WWII*. It was closed by the British, under Japanese pressure, for three months in 1940. It later became a vital link in the war against Japan.

Burmese Spring: A brief outburst of public demonstrations from March to September 1988, brutally crushed by Burma's military. See *Myanmar*.

Burundi: Location: Central Africa. Major associations: *NAM, OAU, UN*. Population: 5.7 million. Military: controlled by the Tutsi. A very small, poor and densely populated Central African state. It is peopled predominantly by Hutus, conquered in the 16th century by the unusually tall Tutsi (Watusi), who still dominate the country. It was taken over by Germany in

1899, but captured by Belgian forces during *WWI*. Belgium ran Burundi as a *mandate* under the *League of Nations* and as a UN *trusteeship territory*. Burundi was given *independence* in 1962. It has had almost no impact on affairs beyond its borders, nor have outside influences much penetrated the deeply unjust ethnic politics that characterize its society. It has suffered terrible *tribal* massacres, mainly of Hutu by the numerically fewer but dominant Tutsi, who conquered the region from the north several centuries prior: 150,000 were butchered after an abortive rising in 1965; another slaughter took place in 1972-73 (10,000 Tutsi and 100,000 Hutu died); and yet another massacre, of 5,000 Hutu, occurred in 1988. A peaceful election in 1993 brought the first civilian to power in 30 years: Melchior Ndadaye (a Hutu). But he was overthrown and killed in a *coup* less than three months later, as Tutsi military officers tried to prevent reforms aimed at bringing Hutu into the army. Some 800,000 (mostly Hutu) refugees fled Burundi, with about half fleeing to Hutu-run Rwanda. After sharp international protest, the coup faltered. Nonetheless, tribal killings in the villages continued for months, with estimates of the dead varying from 25,000 to 150,000. With Tutsi military abusing *hot pursuit* to drag Hutu back across the border to kill them, *war* threatened with Rwanda. In April 1994, the Rwanda and Burundi presidents (both Hutus) were killed while on the same aircraft, which might have been shot down by Tutsi rebels. That sparked a frenzy of intertribal killing in Rwanda and an international airlift was mounted to get all foreigners out. Belgium and France played the main role, and also sent troops into Rwanda and Zaire.

bus: Common slang for "Post-Boost Vehicle (PBV)." It is the part of a *missile* left after the booster rockets fall away. It carries the guidance packages and the re-entry vehicle(s) that convey the *warhead(s)* to target. The bus is critical to the operation of *MIRVs*: it contains the mechanisms that allow for independent targeting and sequential release of the warheads.

Bush, George (b.1924): U.S. President and statesman. He had more experience in foreign policy before becoming President than anyone before him. He was Ambassador to the *UN*, director of the *CIA*, Ambassador to China, and VP for eight years 1980-88. Elected as the hinge of history turned from the *Cold War*, he oversaw a transformation in U.S./Soviet relations, including breakthroughs on both nuclear and conventional *arms control*. Closer to home, he authorized the use of force against *Panama*, and helped wind down the long civil war in *El Salvador*. He contributed to a shift in the use of the UN on matters of *peace* and *security*, culminating in leadership of a great coalition of states during the *Gulf War*. He approved a UN request for U.S. troops in *famine* relief operations in *Somalia* in December 1992, but declined to enter the war in Bosnia. In 1991-92 he squeezed Israel by withholding loans to aid resettlement of Russian Jews, and put Mideast *peace talks* on track after a decade of neglect. He signed the *NAFTA* with Canada and Mexico, but did not fare as well in U.S./Japanese economic relations. His record was tarnished by constant doubts about his role in, and honesty about, *Iran/Contra*. He was defeated by *William Clinton* in 1992, in an election that rarely touched on foreign policy, where Bush was most comfortable. From 90% favorable in the polls during the Gulf War, his ratings fell precipitously. He was widely viewed by the electorate as a "foreign policy president." That, added to a lingering recession, a three-way electoral contest and a sense of national exhaustion with foreign policy problems, contributed to his popular free fall and defeat.

business cycle: Recurring fluctuations in a nation's overall economic activity, marking out periods of *growth* or *recession*.

Buthelezi, Gatsha Mangosuthu (b.1928): Leader of KwaZulu and *Inkatha*. He was expelled from the *ANC* in 1950. After 1986 his followers engaged in an increasingly violent political struggle with the ANC and other black groups in South Africa. He accepted secret funds for Inkatha from the government. In 1993 he agreed to ally with right-wing whites, who for reasons of their own shared his fear of one-person/one-vote politics. But he joined *Mandela's* government in 1994.

buyers' market: One where the prices of *goods* and *services* are low. The antonym is *sellers' market*.

Byelorussia: "White Russia." See *Belarus*.

Byrnes, James Francis (1879-1972): U.S. Secretary of State 1945-47. He supported *Truman's* policies on quick restoration of Germany as a bulwark against the Soviet Union, and the usefulness of the *UN*. He parted company with his president over the *Truman Doctrine*, and was replaced by *George C. Marshall*.

C

C³ (pronounced: "see-three"): Command, control and communication. See *C³I.*

C³I (pronounced: "see-three-eye"): Command, control, communication and *intelligence*: the several means by which a military commander plans, directs and controls field combat operations.

Cabinda: A Portuguese *colony* on the SW African coast; now an Angolan *enclave* north of that country.

cabinet: A council of ministers that advises the *sovereign*, the president or prime minister, according to the given form of government in a country.

cabinet noir: "Black chamber." A secret installation for intercepting and decrypting foreign *diplomatic* or *intelligence* correspondence. The term dates to the 19th century, where such *sigint* techniques were pioneered by the tsarist *Okhrana*.

Cable Network News (CNN): An all-news service that rose to global prominence in the 1980s because of its live coverage of unfolding international events. During the *Gulf War* it was widely watched not just by the public, but by leaders and officials of participating states and the UN. Cf. *BBC; Radio Free Europe; Voice of America.*

cabotage: In *international law* (maritime), a right of carriage of *goods* between ports of the same *state*.

Cadmean victory: One costing the winner nearly as much as the loser. Cf. *defeat; victory.*

cadres: Experienced military or *communist party* members, who also organize and train recruits.

Cairo Conferences (1943): (1) *Franklin Roosevelt* met with *Winston Churchill* and *Chiang Kai-shek* from November 22-26, 1943, en route to *Tehran* to meet *Stalin.* Their discussions dealt mainly with issues of the *war* against Japan. They issued the joint "Cairo Declaration" that stated four common positions on the postwar settlement in Asia: Japan would lose all islands in the Pacific it acquired since 1914, including the old German *mandates*; all lands taken from China were to be returned (including *Formosa, Manchuria* and the *Pescadores*); it was to be expelled from additional lands, including *Sakhalin* and the *Kuriles*; and *Korea* was to become independent "in due course." (2) Roosevelt and Churchill met again December 3-7, to discuss the *invasion* of Europe, set for spring 1944.

California: Russia laid claim to northern California early in the 19th century, but did not press its right after 1825. The south passed from Spain to Mexico, but remained largely unsettled. Its superb natural harbors attracted those Americans interested in the Asia trade. It was the secret objective of President *James Polk* in the *Mexican/American War*, and its acquisition gave the U.S. *vital interests* in the Pacific. It made a minor contribution to the *Union* in the *American Civil War*. After 1900 it pressed for *Oriental exclusion laws* (as did British Columbia in Canada), hurting relations with Japan. During the *Cold War* it was a center for *strategic* industries. If independent, it would place seventh among *OECD* economies with a *population* near 30 million (both figures well ahead of Belgium, Canada, Holland and other OECD states).

caliph: (1) A spiritual and temporal leader claiming succession from Muhammad in his political function, and thus the right to rule all Muslims. The main split in *Islam*, between *sunni* and *shi'ite* traditions, was occasioned by a dispute over the succession to the caliphate. The original, continuous line was overthrown by the Mongols in the 13th century. The title was picked up by the *Ottomans*, but they did not enjoy universal acceptance. There has been no recognized claimant at all since the title was renounced by Turkey in 1924. (2) The Ottoman rulers from 1571-1918. Cf. *ayatollah; imam; mahdi; mullah; sultan.*

caliphate: The jurisdiction of a *caliph.*

Callaghan, James (b.1912): British statesman. Chancellor of the Exchequer 1964-67; Foreign Secretary 1974-76, PM 1976-79. He was committed to *NATO*, and to an independent British nuclear force. He tried, but failed, to bring *peace* to *Ulster.*

call-up: Colloquial. Ordering *reserves* to military duty. See *mobilization.*

Calvo clause: Upheld by by most Latin American countries since c.1900, it states that a *host nation* has *jurisdiction* over any dispute arising from transactions with foreign corporations or persons, say over *compensation* for *nationalization*. That denies *parent countries* a right to *intervene* on behalf of their nationals, and hence the clause has been widely rejected outside Latin America.

Cambodia: Location: SE Asia. Major associations: *UN*. Population: 6.8 million. Military: in the process of forming a national army; some 10,000 *Khmers*

Rouges guerrillas still in the field. The Khmer Empire once stretched from Thailand across much of *Indochina*, lasting from the 9th to 13th centuries. Then it fell under Thai domination. The area of modern Cambodia became a French *protectorate* in 1863. It was occupied by Japan during *WWII*. *Independence* was granted in 1955 as part of the *Geneva Agreements*. Prince *Norodom Sihanouk* ruled conservatively under the French from 1941-55. He became *head of state* in 1960. Cambodia tried to escape the *war* in Indochina by proclaiming *neutrality*, *tilting* toward China, and turning a blind eye to *Viet Cong* enclaves along the *Ho Chi Minh Trail* that traversed its border. That did not prevent a communist *insurgency* by the Khmers Rouges In 1970, with U.S. backing, *Lon Nol* overthrew Sihanouk and abolished the monarchy. Sihanouk set up a *government-in-exile* in China. U.S. and South Vietnamese forces then secretly moved into Cambodia to cut the Ho Chi Minh Trail and cover U.S. withdrawal from the war. This *invasion* and secret bombing provoked a public backlash in the U.S. (though in terms of *international law*, the U.S. was fully within its legal rights in attacking an enemy on *territory* that had effectively ceased to sustain a claim to *neutral rights*). In April 1975, Khmers Rouges fighters entered the capital, Phnom Penh, and under *Pol Pot's* orders began the *Cambodian genocide*. Border skirmishes with Vietnam erupted into war in 1978, ending with a Vietnamese invasion that drove the Khmers Rouges from power and into bases along the Thai border. Despite the revelations about Pol Pot that followed, Vietnam faced strong international opposition to installation of a *puppet regime* under Heng Samrin, and continuing insurgency from the Khmers Rouges and other *guerrilla* groups. Sihanouk formed a coalition, including some Khmers Rouges, in 1982. After 14 years of war, with Vietnam's economy in shambles and its Soviet *ally* gone, Hanoi pulled out all forces in late 1992. The UN organized elections in May 1993. Participation was high, despite several murders of UN personnel and other efforts at intimidation. The country is again a constitutional monarchy. However, with renewed fighting in early 1994, it is unclear whether the specter of its long, national nightmare has yet been entirely exorcised.

Cambodian genocide (1975-78): *Khmers Rouges* (led by the megalomaniacal butcher *Pol Pot*) emptied Cambodia's cities after 1975 and *liquidated* all those perceived as "class enemies" of the party and peasantry. That included most persons who spoke foreign languages, had higher education, or even wore glasses (and thus were presumed to be educated). Over the next several years, in the "killing fields" of Cambodia (briefly renamed Kampuchea), anywhere from one to three million died. There was no international *intervention*, and the killings came to an end only with an *invasion* (for unrelated reasons) by Vietnam. In retreat, the Khmers Rouges herded many thousands of captive civilians with them into *refugee camps* along the Thai *border*, where they were kept from international humanitarian observation well into the 1990s.

Cambrai, Battle of (November 1915): This *WWI* battle witnessed the first extensive use of modern *armor* (tanks), by Britain.

Cameroon: Location: W. Africa. Major associations: *OAU, UN*. Population: 12 million. Military: local; no offensive capability. A locale of the *slave trade* before the 19th century, it was a German possession (*Kamerun*) from 1884-1916. Taken from Germany during *WWI*, it was divided north/south by Britain and France into approved *mandates* and then *trust territories*. The French portion became independent in January 1960. The British section split in 1961; one part joined Nigeria and the other French Cameroon. Ahmadou Ahidjo (1924-89) was President 1960-82. Cameroon has been relatively stable and prosperous, avoiding entanglement in wars in neighboring Chad and Nigeria. In 1994 it disputed an *oil field* with Nigeria (Bakassi), and accepted deployment of French paratoopers.

camouflage: The art of concealing troops and equipment from the enemy, historically by using foliage or painted patterns. A modern camouflager must contend with infrared scopes, supersensitive listening devices and radar. Cf. *stealth technology*.

campaign: A military operation with specific objectives, as in "the Manchurian campaign of the Japanese army," or over a season, as in "a spring campaign."

Campaign for Nuclear Disarmament (CND): An antinuclear organization that advocates unilateral *disarmament* for Britain. In the 1960s and again in the early 1980s, it generated significant public protests.

Camp David: A rural retreat near Washington, D.C. used by U.S. presidents to escape the pressures of their office, and sometimes as an informal setting for the conduct of diplomatic and other negotiations.

Camp David Accords: Signed at *Camp David* on September 17, 1978, by *Menachem Begin* and *Anwar Sadat*, they established *peace* between Israel and Egypt. They were overseen by *Jimmy Carter* and underwritten by U.S. *diplomacy* and massive financial and military *aid*. There were two Accords: (1) The first promised full *diplomatic relations*, Israeli withdrawal from the *Sinai*, and a *peace treaty*, which in fact followed on March 26, 1979. (2) A Framework Agreement designated *Resolution 242* as the basis for a comprehensive peace, and promised to resolve the Palestine problem, including negotiations on the status of *Gaza* and the *West Bank*. The thorny question of *Jerusalem* was tactfully deferred to another day.

Campo-Formio, Treaty of (1797): A temporary *peace* between Austria and France, arranged by *Napoleon* after his greatly successful Italian *campaign*. It transferred much of Belgium to France, established the fleeting "Cisalpine Republic" in Italy, and brought *Venice* into the Austrian *sphere of influence*. But as a general settlement, it did not survive renewal of the war between France and Austria a year later.

Canada: Location: N. America. Major associations: *Commonwealth, CSCE, G-7, la francophonie, NAADC, NAFTA, NATO, OAS, UN.* Population: 27 million. Military: NATO quality training; small numbers (80,000), with 4,000 dedicated to UN *peacekeeping* standby. Early Canada was divided into small, separately governed *colonies*: the British in Acadia, *Newfoundland* and *Upper Canada*; the French in *Lower Canada*. The British captured Québec City in 1759, and all *Québec* was ceded in 1763. These colonies did not join in the *American War of Independence*, which swelled their population by an influx of *United Empire Loyalists*. Canadians played a minor role in the *War of 1812*. In 1837 rebellions in both Upper and Lower Canada led Britain to unite the provinces. Modern Canada then took shape in 1867 under the British North America (BNA) Act, which set up a Confederation of four colonies: New Brunswick, Nova Scotia, Ontario and Québec. These were later joined by six more provinces and three northern territories.

Canada began the 20th century committed to the imperial tie. It fought as part of the empire contingent in the *Boer War*, while in 1911 a Liberal government fell over its proposal for *free trade* with the U.S. Canada found itself automatically at *war* with Germany and Austria in August 1914, upon Britain's *declaration of war. Conscription* was bitterly opposed in Québec, and badly divided the country. Heavy casualties, such as at *Ypres* and the *Somme*, stirred nationalist demands. But although Canada attended the *Paris Peace Conference* and sat separately in the *League of Nations*, foreign policy remained Britain's responsibility until the *Statute of Westminster* in 1931. In the *interwar years* it shared the *isolationist*, "fortress North America" outlook of its southern neighbor. Yet when Britain *declared war* on Germany in 1939, Canada followed suit, after a decorous delay to display symbolic and legal *independence*. Once again, conscription

split the nation and it fought until 1944 with an all-volunteer force that was undermanned, and hence took heavy casualties. Its main contributions came in the *Battle of the Atlantic*, in Normandy and in the *liberation* of Holland. After the war Canadians thought their efforts had earned them a greater voice in world affairs (especially at the UN, which they embraced). They were gravely disappointed to discover that other than Britain, the *Great Powers* had hardly noticed. Even so, the *postwar* years have gone down in Canadian nationalist lore as a "golden age" of global responsibility and creative diplomacy.

Canada shared the Western view of the *Cold War*, participating in the *Berlin air lift*, joining NATO, and fighting in the *Korean Conflict*. During the *Suez Crisis* PM *Lester Pearson* helped initiate UN peacekeeping operations, and Canada has been a mainstay of such efforts ever since. The *Vietnam War* opened a rift with the U.S., widened in the 1970s by a *protectionist* economic policy and a more narrow redefinition of foreign policy by *Pierre Trudeau*. Repeated efforts to diversify *trade* and political connections were unable to overcome the tug of economic *integration* with the U.S. A *separatist* ("sovereigntist") movement in Québec then focused attention on domestic unity. Election of a separatist government in that province in 1976 led to a defeated *referendum* on "sovereignty-association" in 1980. *Pierre Trudeau* then "repatriated" the BNA Act. However, Québec has not adhered to the new constitution and the idea it might yet leave still reverberates in national politics. In 1992 a referendum on an inclusive constitution was rejected by nearly every region. In 1988 Canada took a continental turn with a *free trade agreement* with the U.S., and subsequently signed NAFTA. It sent a small, support contingent to the *Gulf War*, but has pulled back its NATO forces from Germany. It has converted part of its military to a UN standby force, but also warned that it would no longer carry the same peacekeeping burden. For instance, in 1993 it announced that fiscal restraint and political frustration meant a pullout after 29 years of UN peacekeeping duty in Cyprus.

Canal Zone(s): (1) Panama: The ten-mile wide area straddling the *Panama Canal*, controlled by the U.S. A 1904 *treaty* was revised in 1979, promising to abolish the zone. Panama also received control of ports at either end, and the U.S. committed to a full handover in 2000. (2) Suez: The zone around the *Suez Canal*, occupied by the British under treaty from 1936-56, and contested by Israel 1967-79. It has been under full Egyptian control since the *peace treaty* with Israel.

Canaris, Wilhelm (1887-1945): German admiral who headed military *intelligence* in *WWII*, which had little success. He joined the *July Plot* to kill *Hitler*. He was slowly and cruelly executed, just before the *surrender*.

Canary Islands: Located in the Atlantic off West Africa, they are an overseas province of Spain.

Canning, George (1770-1827): British statesman, Foreign Secretary 1807-9 and 1822-27, and PM for just five months before his death. He moved Britain away from the *Congress system*, supported the Latin American *colonies* in their rebellion against Spain, and spurred the U.S. into taking its assertive position in the *Monroe Doctrine*. He became Foreign Secretary for the second time in 1822, after *Castlereagh*, with whom Canning dueled in 1809, committed suicide.

cannon: Any mounted weapon that fires heavy *ordnance*, such as a *howitzer* or mortar.

cannon fodder: (1) *Infantry*, fed to the enemy's cannons in the course of combat. (2) Any wasteful dissipation of military personnel.

cannon shot rule: Before the revisions made under *UNCLOS III*, a measurement of *territorial waters* by the range of a cannon shot from shore. Cf. *terrae dominium; three-mile limit; twelve-mile limit.*

CANZ Group: Canada, Australia and New Zealand. A compact, informal, small power *caucus group.*

capabilities: The material or tangible components of *power*: industrial capacity, military might, *natural resources, population,* advanced *technology, territory, topography* and wealth.

Cape Colony: Located on the Cape of Good Hope, it was captured from the Dutch by the British in 1795. It was permanently ceded to Britain in 1814, becoming the main British base in southern Africa. It took control of *Natal* in 1843, but was forced to concede *autonomy* to the *Boers* of the *Orange Free State* in 1854. *Cecil Rhodes* was premier from 1890-96, and sponsored raids into the *Transvaal*. In 1912, Cape Colony became part of the Union of South Africa.

Capetian: Of the dynasty that ruled France directly from 987-1328, and through the Valois and *Bourbons* branches until 1848 (interrupted during the *French Revolution* and *Napoleonic Wars*, 1792-1814, 1815).

Cape Verde: Location: off the W. African coast. Major associations: *OAU, UN*. Population: 340,000. Military: minimal. First settled by the Portuguese in 1460, slaves were brought from Africa and the populations

mingled. Little more of note occurred until *independence* was proclaimed in 1975. Although some thought was given to *union* with Guinea-Bissau, nothing came of this project. Elections were held in 1991.

capital: (1) Wealth, whether in money or *capital goods* used to produce other goods, and thus one of the *factor endowments* of an economy. It contrasts with income received during a given period (revenue). (2) An alternate in *marxism* for capitalists as a class, used pejoratively, as in "the selfish interests of monopoly capital." (3) A city made preeminent by hosting a country's seat of government. See below, and *foreign direct investment; infrastructure; investment; patient capital; profit; social overhead capital; venture capital.*

capital flight: When *capital* is moved in large volumes from a country whose economy is weakening, or whose political situation has become unstable. In a usage peculiar to some in the *Third World*, it may also refer to transfers of *foreign exchange* by national *elites* or corrupt governments into *hard currency* accounts abroad, as insurance against economic collapse or loss of political power.

capital formation: The increase in the *capital* stock of a national economy. Net capital formation subtracts *depreciation*, and the cost of repair and replacement, from the gross figure.

capital gain: Whatever is the increase in the value of assets, from when they are first purchased to when they are sold. It has particular relevance for investments in *stocks* and real estate.

capital goods: Machines, tools and other such primary goods used to produce secondary goods for sale; not for final use themselves. Cf. *consumer goods.*

capital intensive: Economic activity with high *capital* costs, relative to *labor*. See *comparative advantage.*

capital investment: The total of all funds invested in a firm or national economy.

capitalism: An economic system where wealth, investment, exchanges, distribution and ownership of property are mainly in private hands, there is basic reliance on market forces, and encouragement to free movement of *labor* and *capital*. This century there has been growing regulation of private economic activity in advanced capitalist societies. Also see *laissez-faire; liberalism; market economy; reform liberalism.* Cf. *marxism; mercantilism; socialism; communism.*

capitalist: A person with *capital* available for investment, who accepts risk of losses in exchange for the opportunity to earn *profits* (as distinct from wages or rents), through investment, management, and/or other participation in the expansion of productive economic activities in a *market economy.*

capitalization/capitalize: To supply with *capital.*

capital markets: Banks, insurance companies, trust societies and *stock exchanges* from whose holdings investment *capital* is transferred to commercial enterprises and manufacturers. Cf. *money market.*

capital warships: The largest *warships,* including: *aircraft carriers, battleships, battlecruisers,* and heavy *cruisers,* and now including nuclear *submarines.*

capitulations: (1) A rule by which Westerners (and later Japanese) were made exempt from local laws and *jurisdiction* in China. (2) Any similar rule, imposed by a strong *state* on a weaker state. Cf. *servitude.*

Caporetto, Battle of (October 24-November 12, 1917): The *Central Powers* broke through the Italian lines on the Isonzo River, routed the defenders who had stood for two years, and would have knocked Italy out of *WWI* had France and Britain not rushed in reinforcements. The defeat cost Italy at the *Paris Peace Conference,* and the national humiliation fueled later *fascist* propaganda. It was only partly redeemed by a victory at Venito Vittorio, in October 1918.

capture: The legal right whereby a state takes ownership of enemy property seized at sea in a *war.*

Caribbean: (1) The part of the Atlantic Ocean, contained by *Central America, South America* and the *West Indies.* (2) The political region comprising the *nations* and *dependencies* of the West Indies.

Caribbean Basin Initiative (1984): Announced in 1982 and in effect from 1984-96, it gives participating states *preferential tariff* treatment on certain goods in the U.S. market.

Caribbean Community and Common Market (CARICOM): It was established July 4, 1973 (by the Treaty of Chaguaramas) as the effective successor to *CARIFTA.* It aims at economic, social and technical cooperation, eventual creation of a full *customs union* and coordination of foreign economic policy. Members: Antigua, Bahamas, Barbados, Belize, Dominica, Grenada, Guyana, Jamaica, Montserrat, St. Kitts (St. Christopher and Nevis), St. Lucia, St. Vincent, Trinidad and Tobago. Observer status: Dominican Republic, Haiti, Suriname.

Caribbean Free Trade Association (CARIFTA): The predecessor of *CARICOM,* it was formed in 1968 to work toward a *free trade area* among former British colonies. It shares a *Secretariat* and much the same membership with CARICOM.

Carlists: Supporters of the line of Don Carlos (1788-1855), who claimed the Spanish throne in a succession struggle that led to *civil war* in 1834-37, and again in 1870-76. This quarrel kept Spain out of the larger political currents in Europe, heading to the plunge of the *Revolution of 1848,* but also held it back from faster *modernization* and *liberal* reform after that date.

Carlsson, Bernt (1938-88): Swedish diplomat. He headed the *Socialist International* 1970-76. As UN Commissioner for *Namibia* 1987-88, he helped negotiate the regional settlement that led to Cuban and South African withdrawal and Namibian *independence* in 1990. He was killed in a *terrorist* bombing of a Pan Am plane over Scotland.

Carnegie, Andrew (1835-1918): U.S. billionaire and philanthropist who made his billions in *oil,* iron and steel. He founded numerous endowments, included those dedicated to studying international conflict, ethics and *peace.*

Caroline Islands: Some 500 small islands off the Philippines. Settled by Spain, but sold to Germany in 1899. In *WWI* they were seized by Japan, and in 1921 made a *mandate territory.* During *WWII* the Japanese had a naval base on Truk. After 1947 they were made part of the *Trust Territory of the Pacific Islands.* See *Federated States of Micronesia.*

Carpatho-Ukraine: An alternate name for *Ruthenia,* ceded by *Czechoslovakia* to the *Soviet Union* in 1945, and now part of Ukraine.

Carranza, Venustiano (1859-1920): Mexican revolutionary and President from 1915-20, a period of U.S. *intervention.* He was opposed by *Pancho Villa* and especially *Emiliano Zapata,* after it became clear his dedication to agrarian reform was fairly shallow. He alienated *Woodrow Wilson* by his (entirely defensible) refusal to take Mexico into *WWI.* He was assassinated.

Cartagena Group: Also known as the "Group of Eight." It was formed in the 1980s to discuss matters of common regional and foreign policy interest. Its membership includes the larger countries and economies of Latin America: Argentina, Brazil, Colombia, Ecuador, Mexico, Peru, Uruguay and Venezuela.

cartel: A producers' organization that limits competition and sets high prices by creating artificial shortages through low production quotas. They may also seek to control the market through stockpiling (hoarding), and setting marketing quotas. However, cartels are inherently unstable: there is great temptation to defect from the quota system to take advantage of the high prices it has created; that results in falling prices for all members of the cartel, including those who stuck to the quotas, and hence causes discord among members. See *OPEC*.

Carter, James (b.1924): U.S. President 1976- 80. His foreign policy suffered from his inability to decide between the ultimately incompatible courses suggested by his key advisers, Cyrus Vance and *Zbigniew Brzezinski*. The main motif was *human rights*, but that was an insufficiently examined electoral promise that cut across too many policies and interests to be applied consistently. By 1978 it had largely subsided to rhetoric. His successes were negotiating the *Panama Canal* agreement, facilitating the *Camp David Accords*, and finishing the restoration of relations with China begun by *Richard Nixon*. His handling of U.S./ Soviet relations was less than stellar. He was unable to gain Senate consent to *SALT II*, was stunned by the *invasion* of Afghanistan and hobbled by the *sanctions* he introduced after that *invasion*. He was also weighed down by the *hostage crisis* in Iran that dogged his final year, and the prolonged *recession* and high interest rates that followed the *OPEC* oil price shock of 1979. Out of office, he has enjoyed more public respect for his many good works and his peace efforts than for his job performance when he was President.

Carter Doctrine: A proclamation issued in the wake of the Soviet *invasion* and *occupation* of Afghanistan. It stated that the U.S. would regard as a threat to its *vital interests* any Soviet *aggression* directed at the Persian Gulf. It led to development of the *rapid deployment force* (used in *Operation Desert Shield*). It reaffirmed the earlier *Truman* and *Eisenhower Doctrines*, and partly repudiated the *Nixon Doctrine*.

Carthaginian peace: A brutal *peace*, or *diktat*, imposed upon the vanquished by the victor: "Where they make a desert, they call it peace." Calgacus, to the Britons, about the Roman desolation of Carthage.

Casablanca bloc: See *Organization of African Unity*.

Casablanca Conference (January 14-24, 1943): *Franklin Roosevelt* and *Winston Churchill* met in N. Africa to discuss *Allied* policy; *Stalin* declined to attend. The main decisions taken were: (1) the demand for *unconditional surrender*; and (2) agreement on an *invasion* of Sicily and Italy, to precede the main invasion of Europe. The Sicilian invasion was the last time Britain prevailed in *Allied* counsels on a major *strategic* decision.

Casement, Roger (1864-1916): This former British consular officer spent much of *WWI* trying to recruit Irish *POWs* from the British Army to join an "Irish Brigade" in the German Army. Just before the *Easter Rising* he landed in Ireland from a German *U-boat*, hoping to deliver arms to the *IRA*. He was captured, convicted of *treason*, and hanged.

case study: (1) A history. (2) An in-depth examination of a given phenomenon (*crisis, war, negotiation, trade* system, etc.) or institution. (3) A method in *political science* that seeks to illustrate or discover causal connections by tracing them through a series of illustrative cases that are then compared.

Casey, William (1913-87): Director of Central Intelligence (DCI) 1981-87. He revived *covert action* by the *CIA*, in disuse after the 1970s. That move was heavily criticized by those who saw Casey as a key, though shadowy, figure in the *Reagan* administration, charged with circumventing the will of Congress and perhaps the law, too, by using the CIA and other channels to send secret aid to the *Contras*. More importantly, during his years as DCI the agency failed to correctly assess the rising crisis within the *Soviet Union*, or to predict the impending collapse of that *empire*.

Caspian Sea: The largest inland, salt sea in the world, located between SE Europe and SW Asia.

Castile: A onetime kingdom that led the campaign to expel the Moors from Iberia, and comprising the core of modern Spain.

Castlereagh, Robert Viscount (1769-1822): Secretary for Ireland 1798-1801; Secretary for War and the Colonies 1805-09; Foreign Secretary 1812-22. He worked for *union* of Britain and Ireland but resigned as Secretary when he met opposition to *Catholic emancipation*. In 1809 he dueled with *George Canning*, a remarkably foolish act which temporarily forced both men out of high office. As Foreign Secretary he ordered destruction of the Danish fleet at the *Battle of Copenhagen*, launched the *Peninsular War*, and was responsible for gathering the *coalition* that defeated *Napoleon*. He envisioned a just *balance of power* for Europe, and worked to this end at the *Congress of Vienna* and within the *Congress system*. As he grew disillusioned with the *reactionary* policies of the continental powers, he moved Britain out of the Congress system. He took his own life, with a penknife, in 1822.

Castro, Fidel (b.1927): Cuban revolutionary. PM of Cuba 1959-76; President since 1976. He organized and led the *rebellion* against *Batista* that turned into the *Cuban Revolution*. At first dynamic and charismatic, he soon revealed a deep and corrupting megalomania (his prolix nature is infamous, including six to eight hour harangues of sun-baked crowds). Castro tacked Cuba against a hostile U.S. gale for over 30 years, steering always to the *radical* (and dictatorial) left. To his chagrin, he played little role in the *Cuban Missile Crisis*. But in the 1970s he found an outlet for his ambitions (which far exceeded the island of Cuba) in *proxy wars* and *revolutions* in Angola, Mozambique and Ethiopia. In 1989 he publicly lamented the fall of the *Berlin Wall*, and bitterly criticized *Gorbachev* for *glasnost* and *perestroika*. As his Soviet *subsidies* disappeared, he grew more not less defiant of "*world public opinion*," taking extra repressive measures to quell dissent. Three things sustained him in power in the early 1990s: (1) his military; (2) the unpopularity among Cuba's poor of *exile* leaders in Florida, who threatened to return to reclaim their property rights; and (3) the U.S. *embargo*, that exacerbated the structural weaknesses of Cuba's *planned economy*, but also provided an external enemy upon which Castro could fasten blame for all internal failings.

casus belli: A justification or an event that occasions, or one that merely serves as a pretext for, *war*.

casus foederis: When obligations previously entered into under terms of an *alliance* must now be honored.

casus non praesatur: When unintentional failure to fulfill international legal obligations does not lead to liability for the *state* concerned.

Catherine II, of Russia (1729-96): "The Great." This German princess (with a prodigious sexual reputation) became Tsarina by marriage and Russian *Empress* in 1762, preceding by days the murder of her deposed husband, Tsar Peter III. She genuflected toward the *Orthodox Church*, but really fancied herself a child of the *Enlightenment* (she corresponded with *Voltaire* and other philosophes). During her reign Russia greatly expanded its territorial holdings. She oversaw the three 18th century *partitions of Poland,* and fought expansionist wars against the *Ottoman Empire* (1774 and 1792), and Sweden (1790). See also *Potemkin*.

Catholic Church: The largest Christian denomination, numbering 900 million people, holding to the apostolic succession of bishops and maintaining a vast scheme of moral and philosophical doctrine. Once a significant secular power in central Italy, today its temporal mandate is confined to the few hectares of the *Vatican*. Controversies of international significance involving the Catholic Church are legion. Among recent examples: the role of *John Paul II* in the *Solidarity* movement in Poland, and the possible involvement of the Bulgarian KGB in an attempt on his life; the development of a marxist strain of Catholicism in Latin America known as *liberation theology;* conflict between the Vatican and Israel; Papal opposition to birth control; and a growing schism between Rome and several national churches in Africa. See *concordat; Counter Reformation; Inquisition; John XXIII; Kulturkampf; Lateran Treaties; Old Catholics; Papal States; Pius IX; Pius XII; Reformation; Roman Question; Vatican Councils.* Cf. *Orthodox Church; Unitate Church.*

Catholic emancipation: An issue that dogged English/Irish relations from 1673, when a Test Act (requiring an oath on Anglican sacraments and doctrine) was passed that excluded Catholics, Jews and Nonconformist Protestants from sitting in Parliament. Bitterness increased when Britain failed to emancipate Catholics following the *Act of Union*. When civil war threatened, the Test Act was repealed in 1828. Catholic emancipation passed the next year. Cf. *Irish Question; William Pitt.*

Caucasus/Caucasia: The region between the Black and Caspian Seas, straddling the border between Europe and Asia. It is split by the Caucasus Mountains into *Ciscaucasia* in Europe and *Transcaucasia* in Asia. In all it comprises *Abkhazia, Armenia, Azerbaijan, Georgia, Kurdistan* and *Ossetia*.

caucus groups: Voting blocs in the UN, and other *multilateral* forums, that meet to plot common procedural strategy and map out arguments and positions. They may be regional (African, Asian, Latin American, Nordic, *WEOG*) or interest oriented (Arab, *Non-Aligned, Group of 77*).

causal modeling: The use of simulations or diagrams to illustrate the presumed relations among different *causes* (or *variables*).

causation: The direct or indirect relation of *cause* to *effect*: (1) necessary cause: one without which an effect will not occur, but not in itself enough to bring about an effect; (2) sufficient cause: one that in and of itself is said to produce an effect; (3) efficient cause:

that which triggers an effect; (4) permissive cause: that underlying an effect and permitting it to occur. For instance, "*Anarchy* is a permissive cause of *war*, but *national interests* and conflicts provide the necessary causes, while individual acts, decisions, personalities, ambitions and vanities are often the efficient causes. It cannot be fairly said that any one thing is a sufficient cause of all war, though it may be said of a given war." Another way of differentiating: (5) primary: the key agency producing an effect; (6) secondary: that reinforcing a primary cause, but less influential in and of itself; (7) tertiary: one that helps produce an effect, but clearly not of the first or second order of influence. Cf. *post hoc ergo propter hoc; sine qua non; variables.*

cause: Any agency (instrumentality) that produces an *effect*. See *causation; variable.*

cavalry: Historically: (1) horse-borne soldiers. Today: (2) mechanized or airborne *infantry.*

Cavour, Count Camillo (1810-61): Italian statesman. A liberal PM of *Piedmont* from 1852-61, he sought unification of all *Italy*. He entered the *Crimean War* in order to gain a place at the conference table. He allied with *Napoleon III* in a short war against Austria in 1859. In 1860 he sent troops into the *Papal States* but stopped short of the *Vatican* to avoid antagonizing Catholic opinion in Europe. He then joined forces with *Garibaldi*, mainly to forestall him from proclaiming a separate, southern *republic*. Instead, they proclaimed the unified Kingdom of Italy on March 17, 1861. He died shortly thereafter.

Cayman Islands: Three West Indies islands; they are *dependencies* of Jamaica, and an off-shore banking center.

cease-fire: A *truce*, or temporary halt in fighting. It may be a prelude to a *peace treaty*, or merely a pause during which wounded are removed and resupply takes place. See *war termination*. Cf. *armistice.*

Ceausescu, Nicolae (1918-89): Rumanian dictator 1967-89. He was courted by the *West* because he took a somewhat independent line from Moscow in foreign policy, such as keeping ties to China and Israel and denouncing the 1968 *invasion* of Czechoslovakia by the *Warsaw Pact*, to which he refused to send troops. At home, he was brutal, corrupt, inept and increasingly megalomaniacal. His regime left bitter divisions between ethnic Rumanians and Hungarians, and tens of thousands of orphans born of an idiosyncratic ban on contraception. After a *summary* trial, he and his

similarly corrupt and vicious wife were shot, much to their surprise, on Christmas Day, 1989.

censure: To express disapproval, as in a vote criticizing a *state* for *human rights* abuses, *aggression*, or disregard of UN *resolutions*. It is a large step from censure to *sanctions.*

center: See *core.*

Center, Moscow: The command headquarters of the Soviet *secret service*. See *KGB.*

Central African Federation: An alternate name of the former *Federation of Rhodesia and Nyasaland*, 1953-63. It broke into the component parts of Malawi, Zambia and Rhodesia (Zimbabwe).

Central African Republic: Location: Central Africa. Major associations: *la francophonie, OAU, UN*. Population: 3 million. Military: minor. Formerly Ubangi-Shari, it was a French *colony* from the end of the 19th century until *independence* in 1960. Under President David Dako Chinese *influence* grew until a break in relations in 1965, when Dako's cousin, *Jean Bedel Bokassa*, seized power. In 1976 Bokassa proclaimed himself *emperor* and renamed the country Central African Empire. He was ousted (with French help) in 1979, and Dako resumed the presidency. The economy was badly damaged by Bokassa's depredations. In 1981 another *coup* ousted Dako. CAR remains among the world's poorest countries.

Central America: The portion of North America comprising Belize, Costa Rica, El Salvador, Guatemala, Honduras, Nicaragua and Panama.

Central American Common Market (CACM): It was founded in 1960 by Costa Rica, El Salvador, Guatemala, Honduras and Nicaragua to create a *customs union*, with a parallel scheme to rationalize industrial development in the region. After early success into the 1970s, efforts at economic *integration* were blocked in the 1980s by several crises: *revolution* in Nicaragua, *civil war* in El Salvador, and *guerrilla* conflicts in Honduras and Guatemala.

Central Asia: The region lying between the Arabian Sea and the southern border of Russia, defined at its broadest to include the *Caucasus*, to wit: Afghanistan, Armenia, Azerbaijan, Georgia, Iran, Kazahkstan, Kirghizstan, Pakistan, Tajikistan, Turkmenistan and Uzbekistan. Cf. *Turkestan.*

central bank: A government chartered and run national bank. It does not lend money to individuals as do other banks. It issues *currency*, lends to governments and to private banks, and in general oversees and manages the national financial system, with special regard for the money supply, *interest rates*, and the relative value of the national currency. See *BIS*.

Central Intelligence Agency (CIA): The only *civilian*, and not the largest, of the American *intelligence* agencies. It was created in 1947 to adapt to peacetime the work of the wartime *Office of Strategic Services* (OSS), and to undertake *covert* political support for U.S. *containment* policy. Its budget is secret ("black"), but it shared in some $30 billion for 1993. It is best known to the public for covert operations that failed, such as the *Bay of Pigs* or *pacification* in Vietnam. It is also known for its previous *interventions* in the *internal affairs* of several nations, including: early Italian elections to keep communists from power; Iran, where it lent support to the Shah against *Mossadegh*; Guatemala, where it helped overthrow Jacobo Arbenz; and Chile, where it was involved in destabilizing the government of *Salvador Allende Gossens*. More recently, it has provided security training to Georgia, and other former Soviet or *Warsaw Pact* republics. Its covert successes, by definition, remain mostly unknown and unheralded. Perhaps the best known was *overt/covert* aid to the *mujahadeen* during the *Afghan/Soviet War*. Yet to concentrate on covert actions is largely to miss the point about the CIA: its main task is not *secret diplomacy*, but analysis of traditional and nontraditional sources of economic, social and political information. Thus, it has been most strongly criticized in official circles for failing in its main role during the *Cold War*: to gather and accurately analyze information about the *capabilities* and intentions of the Soviet Union, and other designated hostile states. CIA estimates of the Soviet economy were consistently--even grossly--wrong, and (like everyone else) it failed to predict the collapse of the *Soviet bloc*. Facing budget cuts and revelations that it was badly penetrated by *moles* working for the *KGB*, since the end of the Cold War the agency has sought a new role in countering *terrorism*, *economic espionage*, tracking *proliferation* and monitoring the rise of *fundamentalism*. Cf. *National Security Agency*.

Central Powers: (1) An alternate term for the *Triple Alliance* of Austria, Germany and Italy, from 1882-1914. (2) Austria, Germany, Turkey and Bulgaria in *WWI*. Italy declined to fight in 1914, enticed by secret promises into joining the *Entente* in 1915. See *Constantinople Agreement*; *Treaty of London (1915)*.

central strategic systems: In U.S. *strategy* during the

Cold War, those systems considered essential to maintaining the nuclear *balance of power*.

Central Treaty Organization (CENTO): See *Baghdad Pact*.

cession: Transfer of *territory* by mutual agreement. For instance, see *Crimea*; *Louisiana Purchase*.

Cetewayo (b.? d.1884): *Zulu* chief recognized by Britain as King of the Zulus in 1872. He fought the British in 1878-79, was captured and held prisoner in *Cape Colony* (1879-82), and taken to England (1882). An attempt by Britain to reinstate him failed.

cetirus paribus: "All other things being equal." A common qualifier in international legal judgments.

Ceuta: A Spanish *enclave* in Morocco, which has tied its future to Spain's efforts to reclaim *Gibraltar* from Britain. Cf. *Melilla*.

Ceylon: The former name of *Sri Lanka*.

Chaco War (1932-35): A bitter *war* fought between Bolivia and Paraguay for control of the border Chaco area. Paraguay won and was able to keep most of the *territory*, an outcome *mediated* and ratified by a commission of the U.S. and five Latin American states in 1938. The war denied Bolivia an outlet to the Pacific. Some 100,000 died, on all sides.

Chad: Location: W. Africa. Major associations: *la francophonie, OAU, UN*. Population: 5.1 million. Military: small but relatively well equipped; access to French *air power* and troops. Lying along the historic trans-Sahara salt and Arab *slave trade* routes, Chad was made a French *colony* around 1900. It was given *independence* in 1960, but remained a desperately poor, *Sahel* nation. By 1966 there was steady fighting between northern Muslims supported by Libya and southern Christians and animists, supported by the French. The *civil war* lasted until 1982, when Hissène Habré took control of the capital. The 1980s saw severe drought, the effects of which were aggravated by continuing low-level fighting and the overlap of the *Chad/Libya War*, waged on and off until 1987. An OAU military force tried to police the *peace* after 1988, but Chad remained too ethnically and religiously divided, north vs. south. Heavy fighting resumed in 1991, when Habré's Western backers were preoccupied with the *Gulf War*, and he was deposed.

Chad/Libya War (1973-88): In 1973 Libya took advantage of the *civil war* in Chad to invade and occupy the

Auzou strip. In 1980, seeking to protect this claim, Libya arranged an "invitation" to send troops into Chad from one faction in the still ongoing civil war. When it was announced that the two countries would form a *union*, international opposition increased. The key was the effort of Libya's strongman, *Quadaffi*, to obtain *uranium* for his *nuclear weapons* program from the Auzou strip, and create a *client state* in Chad. Protests over the proposed union from surrounding African states and the dispatch of French troops forced the Libyans to pull back in 1981. In June 1982, southern rebels under Hissène Habré took the capital, ending the civil war but launching a new phase of the conflict with Libya. With French support, including air cover and several thousand troops, Habre took the offensive in 1983. France and Libya agreed to withdraw in September 1984, but Libyan troops stayed in the Auzou strip, which Quadaffi said was *annexed* to Libya. In 1987 Chadian forces inflicted a decisive *defeat* on the Libyans, who fled, leaving behind thousands of dead and over $1 billion in military equipment.

Chamberlain, Austen (1863-1937): British statesman, son of Joseph Chamberlain. Secretary for India 1915-17; member of the War Cabinet in *WWI*; Foreign Secretary 1924-29. He helped devise the *Locarno* agreements in 1925. That year he shared the *Nobel Prize* for Peace, for the *Dawes Plan*.

Chamberlain, Houston Stewart (1855-1927): An English philosopher who was rabidly anti-English, his ramblings were picked up by the *Nazis*, then in search of intellectual cover for their specious race theories.

Chamberlain, Joseph (1836-1914): British statesman. He was a fierce opponent of *Home Rule* for Ireland. In 1895 he became Secretary for the Colonies. He oversaw colonial policy during the *Second Boer War*, and worked for an imperial federation in Africa. He once declared: "The day of small nations has long passed away. The day of Empires has come." Thus blinded by imperial ambition, he saw France as the main enemy of Britain's *vital interests*, and actually tried to influence policy toward an *alliance* with Germany. His scheme for an *imperial tariff* was carried out by his sons, *Austen* and *Neville*.

Chamberlain, Neville (1869-1940): British statesman. Son of *Joseph Chamberlain* and half-brother of *Austen Chamberlain*. As *Chancellor of the Exchequer* in 1932 he helped implement his father's scheme for a preferential, *imperial tariff*. As PM from 1937-40, he took total and inflexible control of foreign policy, such that several top advisers resigned. Although inexperienced in *diplomacy* he was convinced he could avoid *war* by

face-to-face *negotiations* with *Hitler*. He will be forever remembered as the main dupe of the *Munich Conference* (1938), where he betrayed *Czechoslovakia* by handing the *Sudetenland* to Germany. Back in London he announced: "peace with honor; it is peace for our time. . . . Go home and get a nice quiet sleep." His animosity for the *Soviet Union* prevented an *alliance* with that state, then the one continental power with the *capabilities* to oppose Germany, and which prior to Munich had sought such a compact with the West. His *appeasement* policy was so discredited by subsequent events statesmen have ceased to use the term, for fear of association with him and Munich. He abandoned appeasement when Hitler occupied the rump of Czechoslovakia in 1939, and belatedly offered security guarantees to Greece, Poland and Rumania. With deep reluctance, he led Britain into *WWII* when Germany attacked Poland in September 1939, but he was weak and indecisive during the *Phony War*. He resigned in May 1940, as Germany attacked in the west. He was replaced by his old political nemesis, *Winston Churchill*. He died shortly thereafter.

chambers of the Court: When justices numbering less than the full complement of the *International Court of Justice* gather to hear a *dispute*. This permits the *states* concerned a say in the composition of the adjudicating panel. It was first used in 1981, by Canada and the U.S. to resolve a fisheries/boundary matter. Cf. *application*.

Chanak crisis (1922): Britain and Turkey almost went to war over *Atatürk's* opposition to Britain's presence in Chanak, the eastern shore of the *Dardanelles*. It was resolved by giving Turkey *territory* in exchange for *internationalization* of the Dardanelles and the *Bosphorus*, a deal confirmed in the *Treaty of Lausanne* in 1923.

Chancellor of the Exchequer: The U.K. Finance Minister.

Channel Islands: British possessions in the *English Channel*, near France: Alderney, Guernsey, Jersey and several smaller islands. They were the only part of the UK *occupied* by Germany during *WWII*.

Channel Tunnel Treaty (February 12, 1986): It was signed by France and Britain to support a private venture to build a tunnel under the *English Channel*. The project was first proposed in the late 1870s, but was long opposed by Britain for *strategic* and *security*, as well as cultural reasons. Construction of the main rail line of the "Chunnel" was completed in late 1993. Construction on other lines continued into 1994.

chargé d'affaires: The 4th rank of *diplomats*, accredited by and to *foreign ministers*, not *heads of state*.

chargé d'affaires ad interim: (1) A *diplomat* placed in charge of a post in the absence of the *ambassador*. (2) A diplomatic *envoy* sent to a posting where there is no ambassador.

charged particle beam: An experimental weapons system, researched under *SDI*, that uses channeled, concentrated beams of subatomic particles, produced by nuclear explosions, to destroy targets. See *Teller.*

Charles, of Austria (1887-1922): Emperor for two years 1916-18, he tried to secretly negotiate a *separate peace* for Austria with the British and French in *WWI*. The effort led to tighter German control of Austrian policy and even field operations. He died in *exile*, embittered at the end of the *empire* and his throne.

Charles IV, of Spain (1784-1819): His reign was dominated by the politics of the *French Revolution*: his fleet was destroyed along with the French fleet at *Trafalgar*, and in 1808 he was forced to abdicate by *Napoleon I.* That weakening of Spanish power during his rule opened the door for the *independence* movement in Latin America.

Charles XII, of Sweden (1682-1718): At age 15, he led an army against a combined Danish, Polish and Russian attack. He defeated the Danes, humbled the Russians at *Narva*, and deposed the Polish king. In 1708 he invaded Russia, nearly capturing *Peter I* (the Great). He marched all the way to Ukraine, was beaten at *Poltava* and fled into Turkey, where he was imprisoned. Escaping, he returned to Sweden, raised a new army and attacked Norway in 1716. His ambitions went so far as a scheme to displace the Stuarts from the Scottish throne. He was killed in battle, in Norway. His wars crippled Sweden and dropped it permanently from the ranks of the *Great Powers.*

Charles XIV: See *Bernadotte, Jean-Baptiste.*

charter: {1} A *declaration* of principles (e.g., *Atlantic Charter.* {2} A *treaty* setting out the constitution of an *international organization* (e.g. *Charter of the UN*).

charter colony: Those founded by grant of a Royal charter, or license; e.g., Virginia.

Charter of the United Nations: The *treaty* outlining the constitution of the UN, hammered out at *Dumbarton Oaks* in 1944 and revised at *San Francisco* in April-June 1945. It outlines the *rules* and procedures governing the UN and its *specialized agencies*, and declares as its purposes: (1) maintaining *peace* and *security* through collective measures; (2) promotion of *self-determination*; (3) promotion of economic, social and cultural cooperation; (4) promotion of respect for fundamental *human rights* and freedoms. See *aggression; Four Freedoms; law-making; neutral rights; Outer Space Treaty; self-defense; trust territory.*

Charter '77: In 1977, some 700 Czechoslovak human rights campaigners founded this *Helsinki watch group.* All were eventually imprisoned. See *Václav Havel.*

chauvinism: Assertive, even belligerent *nationalism*; from Nicolas Chauvin, a loud and zealous fan of *Napoleon I.* Cf. *jingoism; nationalism; patriotism.*

CHEKA (*Chrezychainaya Kommissiya*): Full title: "All Russian Extraordinary Commission for the Suppression of *Counter-Revolution* and *Sabotage.*" This was the *Bolshevik* secret and political police from 1917-22, later renamed the *OGPU, NKVD*, and finally the *KGB.* It conducted the *Red Terror* and the confiscations of *food*, seed and fuel that contributed to privation and then starvation in the countryside, 1919-23. In *Lenin's* time, and under *Felix Dzerzhinsky*, it executed at least 200,000 (as compared with 14,000 executed in *tsarist Russia* in the preceding 50 years).

chemical agents/weapons: Those instruments of *war* that use chemical compounds to asphyxiate, poison, corrode or burn the lungs or flesh. The ancient Greeks and others sometimes poisoned the water supply of cities they besieged, but chemical compounds and gases as *weapons of mass destruction* came into their own only with the mass production of the *Industrial Revolution*, in particular the invention of dyes that produced large amounts of poisonous chlorine gas as a by-product. The 1899 *Hague Convention* pledged 25 states to abstain from using such weapons. Germany broke the taboo during *WWI* and the *Allies* followed suit: chlorine, phosgene and *mustard* gases became the most hated weapons of that war. When opposing troops took simple *countermeasures*, adamsite (which induces vomiting) was added to force soldiers to remove their gas masks and inhale the main, deadly agents. Chemical weapons were not used in *WWII* as most militaries deemed them ineffective. Non-lethal types were used by the U.S. in Vietnam (psychedelic "BZ," tear gas, and "Agent Orange" defoliant). Lethal gases were probably employed by Vietnam in Laos and Cambodia, likely used by the Soviet Union in Afghanistan ("yellow rain"), and certainly were fired by Iraq against Iran and its own *Kurd* population. See *binary; gas; incendiary* and *nerve weapons.*

chemical and biological (CB) warfare: Waging *war* with *chemical weapons* or *biological weapons*. They include: blister agents that corrode and blister the skin or lungs (e.g., "oderless dust" and *mustard gas*); blood agents that asphyxiate by inhibiting the blood's ability to convey oxygen (e.g., hydrogen cyanide); choking gases (e.g., phosegene); diseases (e.g., anthrax); incapacitators (e.g., psychedelic agents); *nerve agents*; and toxins (e.g., fungi extracts).

Chemical Weapons Convention (1992): In August 1992, after 24 years of negotiations, this *treaty* banning *chemical agents/weapons* was agreed upon at the UN Disarmament Conference in Geneva. It supersedes the 1925 *Geneva Protocol*. States will have to declare stockpiles and destroy them within 10 years (with a possible 5-year extension). There are strong enforcement provisions: an organization will be created to oversee implementation, states will be able to call for "challenge inspections" of suspected cheaters, and non-signatories may be subjected to *embargo* on chemical exports. The treaty identifies 29 chemicals and 14 chemical families subject to international supervision. It will enter into effect in 1995.

Chen Yi (1901-72): Chinese communist general. He was a leading figure in the *war* against Japan and in the *Chinese Civil War*. He was Defense Minister from 1958-66, but was stripped of power and humiliated during the *Great Proletarian Cultural Revolution*.

Chernenko, Konstantin Ustinovich (1911-85): General Secretary of the CPSU, February 1984-March 1985. His brief and ineffective tenure merely delayed an improvement in U.S./Soviet relations, and the succession from *Andropov* to *Gorbachev*.

Chernobyl nuclear accident (April 28, 1986): A partial core meltdown and explosion at this Soviet facility near Kiev had multiple effects: (1) It produced a radioactive cloud that traveled over several countries. (2) It further delegitimized the Soviet system at home, when it emerged that official secrecy had exposed tens, perhaps hundreds, of thousands to deadly radiation for several days longer than necessary. (3) It brought severe international criticism over the delay in reporting (Sweden, not the Soviet Union, announced detection of the cloud). (4) It led to agreement on environmental notification procedures within the *UNEP*. On April 6, 1993, a smaller reactor explosion occurred in Russia, at Tomsk. It was promptly reported, even though it occured at a hitherto secret *Minatom* installation.

Chetniks: Serbian nationalists who fought the *Otto-*

mans before 1918, and led by General Mihailović, fought the Germans in *WWII*. Many thousands were *liquidated* by *Tito* after the war.

Chiang Kai-shek, a.k.a. Jiang Jieshi (1887-1975): Chinese Nationalist leader. Effective ruler of China 1928-46; President of the Republic of China (Taiwan) 1950-75. He set out to unify China by military means in 1926, bloodily purged the *Guomindang* of communists after 1927, and defeated the last northern *warlords* by 1928 (although there were still warlord *rebellions* intermittently until 1937). He led the Guomindang forces in the *Chinese Civil War*. Nationalist and Manchurian troops were unhappy that Chiang insisted on pursuing a vigorous war against the Chinese communists. A Manchurian unit detained him at the end of 1936, and held him for nearly two weeks. He finally agreed to meet *Zhou Enlai* and to join forces with the communists to fight the Japanese. This tenuous agreement was more or less kept, until Japan's *defeat* in 1945. After coming to terms with the communists he led the Guomindang in the *Second Sino/Japanese War* and *WWII*. Chiang attended the *Cairo Conference*, and in *Roosevelt's* eyes at least was seen as one of the *Big Four.* But his regime was so corrupt the war effort was badly weakened, and U.S. support waned after 1945. Defeated in the renewed civil war by 1949, he led the Nationalists to Taiwan, from where they vainly sought to continue the fight. He and his American-educated wife remained favorites of the U.S. right-wing until his death.

chicken: In *game theory*, a *mixed motive game* with two players and the following set up: If A alone swerves, B scores 4 and A scores 2 (and vice versa); if both swerve, each scores 3; if neither swerves, each scores -1. The worst outcome occurs when neither cooperates in avoiding a collision. It is said, by some, to apply by analogy to the structure of certain crises.

Children's Vaccine Initiative (CVI): A major program aimed at developing new, more robust vaccines, and possibly a combined antigen that would reduce transportation risks and administrative costs while targeting multiple diseases. It was begun in 1990 with funding from divers private and public sources, ranging from the Rockefeller Foundation to the *World Bank*. The *WHO* agreed in 1993 to merge the resources of its Expanded Program on Immunization with the CVI.

Chile: Location: South America. Major associations: *LAIA, OAS, UN*. Population: 13 million. Military: regional capability. The Spanish *conquest* of the Incas took from 1536-40 in the north of modern Chile. Indian *resistance* continued until late in the 19th century in the south. A war of *independence* was fought against Spain from 1810-18. Chile fought and won *expansionist* wars against Bolivia and Peru in 1836-39, and again in the *War of the Pacific,* 1879-84. It evolved one of the few stable democracies in Latin America. However, by the 1950s class and ideological differences were dividing Chilean society. Montalva Eduardo Frei (1911-82) was President 1964-70. He was a severe critic of the *Alliance for Progress.* In 1970 *Salvador Allende* won the presidency with a plurality of the votes. He was killed in a *coup* in 1973 that installed a repressive *junta* led by Agusto Pinochet (b.1915). Over the next several months and years this cruel dictatorship arrested more than 100,000 persons, tortured many, and killed several thousand *desaparecidos*. Yet its economic policies made Chile one of the region's fastest growing economies. In a 1988 *plebiscite,* Chileans rejected Pinochet's bid to be installed as president-for-life: despite successful economic policies he was a widely despised and feared man. To get his agreement to free and fair elections it was found necessary to pardon the military criminals, if not the crimes, of his *regime* and retain him as head of the army. In 1989 elections he was beaten for the presidency by Patricio Aylwin. The return to democracy enhanced Chile's growing reputation as a regional *development* model. To the mid-1990s its *inflation* rate was low and its *growth* rate high.

China: Location: East Asia. Major associations: *UN (permanent member of the Security Council).* Population: 1.15 billion. Military: See *PLA.* (1) Imperial: China has the longest recorded history of continuous civilization and government of any human society. Imperial rule dates back some 4,500 years to the Shang dynasty, and progressed through several Chinese and Mongol dynasties, ending with the *Manchus.* The first significant contacts with the modern *West* came under the Manchus. Despite the brilliance of its classical civilization, for several centuries China had been stagnating compared to the West, especially in government, navigation and *technology*. It suffered extraordinary internal convulsions and peasant uprisings, such as the *White Lotus Rebellion* and the *Taiping Rebellion.* These upheavals left millions dead and the country weakened and vulnerable to external powers. Over the course of the 19th century China felt the effects of its backwardness and the advanced technology of the West. Britain, France, Germany, Russia and the U.S. forced open its *trade*, and even ruled its coastal cities. After the *Opium Wars,* China's subjugation was symbolized by the humiliating *terms* forced upon it in the *Treaty of Nanking,* and other *unequal treaties*. Japan joined the scramble for *spheres of influence* and exclusive trade in the *First Sino/Japanese War* (1895),

in which China lost control of *Korea, Taiwan* and *Manchuria*, and began its final descent into *revolution*.

(2) Republican: After the failed *Boxer Rebellion*, a revolution led by Dr. *Sun Yat-sen* and the *Guomindang* (Nationalists) overturned the Manchu dynasty in 1911. A Republic was established in 1912. But the decentralization that had begun with the Taiping Rebellion now culminated in a China divided among competing *warlords*. The Guomindang could not sustain national unity. During *WWI* Japan expanded its holdings by expelling Germany from *Shantung*. With that Japan emerged as the central threat to Chinese *peace, security* and *independence*. Tokyo's ultimate ambition to dominate all China was exposed in the *Twenty-One Demands* (1915). At the same time, the U.S. moved into the vacuum left by European preoccupation with WWI to defend its interest in an *Open Door* in China, and to support the Asian *balance of power* by supporting China against Japan. In foreign policy the 1920s were quiet, but at home the civil war continued, with the Guomindang pursuing and finally defeating the last of the northern warlords in 1928. But a new *Chinese Civil War* broke out almost immediately, between the Nationalists and the Chinese communists. The Japanese, who attacked Manchuria in 1931, took advantage by moving against China proper in 1937, starting the *Second Sino/Japanese War* that later merged with *WWII*. The Communists and Nationalists put aside most of their differences to fight the Japanese, whose brutal *occupation* and disregard for Chinese lives was symbolized by the *sack of Nanking*. During WWII China held down the bulk of the Japanese Army, with logistical and air support from the U.S. and Britain. With the *defeat* of Japan in 1945 the civil war in China resumed. It was won by the Communists under *Mao Zedong* in 1949, and the "People's Republic" was proclaimed. There followed an orgy of executions until 1955, taking at least several million lives (some estimates go over 10 million). With the Nationalists brooding in Taiwan it looked for many of those years as though the civil war was unfinished business, but in fact it was over.

(3) The People's Republic: China entered the *Korean Conflict* when U.S. and UN forces failed to heed its warnings and came close to its *border* with North Korea, in November 1950. It then fought U.S. and UN forces to a standstill, though it took very heavy casualties. Despite sharing communist *ideology*, relations with the Soviet Union worsened steadily. By the late 1950s a *Sino/Soviet split* was apparent. It flared openly in 1966 and again in 1969, when Chinese and Soviet forces clashed bloodily along their lengthy, disputed border. China made some effort to challenge the Soviets for leadership among more radical *Third World* countries, but it did not have the same resources to

commit, or appear quite as serious about projecting *power* beyond its immediate neighborhood. However, it did achieve an independent nuclear capability, which made the conflict with Russia dangerous in the extreme. The so-called *Great Leap Forward* (1958-60) failed to advance China's *industrialization*. Meanwhile, a *fanatic* and brutal effort to coerce the peasantry into joining "Peoples' Communes" met fierce resistance. It may have taken as many as 27 million lives, through persecution and massive *famine* in the countryside. During the 1960s China aided North Vietnam against the U.S., and armed the *Khmers Rouges* in their *insurgency* in Cambodia. It also entered another period of internal chaos, the *Great Proletarian Cultural Revolution* (1965-78), in which hundreds of thousands were *purged* and killed, and millions sent to political *reeducation camps*. In 1971 the UN ousted Taiwan from the China seat in the *UN General Assembly* and *Security Council*, and the People's Republic emerged as a major diplomatic player. In a stunning *rapprochement* in 1972, *Nixon* visited China. Formal U.S. *recognition* came in 1978. Relations with Vietnam deteriorated with the end of the *Vietnam War*, and were openly hostile after Vietnam invaded Cambodia. China attacked across the border in 1979, to "punish" Vietnam for toppling *Pol Pot*, but the Vietnamese were not intimidated and it was the *People's Liberation Army* that was bloodied. Concerning its other neighbors, China invaded Tibet in 1951, and ever since ruthlessly crushed Tibetan *nationalism* and *Buddhist* practices. It also won the short, sharp *Indo/Chinese War* (1962) and allied with Pakistan to counterbalance India's *alliance* with the Soviet Union. From the end of the Korean Conflict to the early 1990s it supported North Korea, but dropped trade privileges since then. It continued in a state of suspended hostility with Taiwan, and had uneasy but coolly cordial relations with Japan. After Mao passed from power, the disastrous policies of the Great Leap Forward and the Cultural Revolution were disavowed. After purging the party of the *gang of four*, China's new leaders moved to reform the state, economy, scientific research and armed forces (the *four modernizations*). By 1988 the economy was booming, but political tensions were also building. A student movement for democracy, centered on *Tiananmen Square* in Beijing, was crushed by PLA tanks and troops in two June days of internationally televised repression. The collapse of the Soviet Union in 1989 led to warmer relations with Russia and Japan, and even India. Relations with the U.S. were good, despite protests over Tiananmen, but deteriorated in 1994 over *human rights* questions. By that year, parts of Chinese society had been effectively decommunized by market reforms: *guanxi* was more important than *ideology*, for foreign investors and Chinese them-

selves. Between 1990 and 1993, China's *defense spending* doubled. Combined with events elsewhere, that gave it the world's numerically largest military, part of which it used against Vietnam in the *Spratlys* in 1992. The PLA also spoke ominously in 1993 of claims to all the islands in the South China Sea, and even to the Malacca Straits, and began to acquire a *blue water navy*. On the other hand, in November 1993, China signed an agreement with Vietnam renouncing the use of force over border disputes.

China/Japan Peace and Friendship Treaty (1978): This agreement represented the beginning of a slow *rapprochement* in Sino/Japanese political relations, and a new trading relationship, following the death of *Mao Zedong*.

China, Republic of: See *Taiwan*.

Chinese Civil War (1927-49): In 1926 China was reunified after defeat of northern *warlords* by the *Guomindang* (Nationalists), under *Chiang Kai-shek*. He then split with and turned on the Communists in the *Shanghai massacre*. Surviving Communists founded the *Jiangxi Soviet* in 1931. By 1934 Nationalist attacks forced them into the *Long March* to the northwest. During that harsh trial, *Mao Zedong* emerged as an able field commander and a leading political boss on the Communist side. Chiang pressed the fight, insisting on eliminating domestic enemies before fully engaging Japan. But at the end of 1936 he agreed to join forces with the Communists. When the Japanese attacked China in 1937, following the *Marco Polo Bridge incident*, Communists and Nationalists combined to resist the invader, or more accurately, ceased fighting each other and fought the Japanese in parallel *campaigns*. WWII had two critically important consequences for China's internal divisions: (1) the Japanese drove the Nationalists far inland from their coastal bases, and (2) the Communists were able to move out from enforced isolation into central China, pick up support among the peasantry, and increase the size of their army tenfold in eight years. With the defeat of Japan the civil war resumed in 1946, but on more nearly even terms. The U.S. supported Chiang and the Nationalists, while the Soviets backed Mao. The civil war was won by the Communists in 1949, following the Huai-Hai campaign (November 1948-January 1949), the decisive action during the end game to the war. In successive engagements during that campaign the Guomindang lost nearly half a million troops, killed or captured, and its will and physical ability to resist further was fatally diminished. The defeat forced remaining Nationalist forces to retreat to *Taiwan* (Formosa). There they regrouped and rearmed, in hope of carrying on the fight, and one day returning to the mainland. However, thereafter they received only enough U.S. support to survive on Formosa, never to seriously contemplate restarting the war.

Chinese Revolution, 1911: The *Manchu* dynasty was in the end fairly easily overthrown, by rival factions of revolutionaries led by General Yüan Shih-k'ai and *Sun Yat-sen* In 1912 the child Emperor *Pu Yi* abdicated and a *republic* was declared. The Nanking Constitution of that year was supposed to establish China as a democracy. However, real power was in the hands of various *warlords*, some of whom defied the national government in Nanking until 1928, when *Chiang Kai-shek* finally brought them to heal. Classical, Confucian, traditional China was no more. Ahead lay decades of bloody unrest, *civil war*, Japanese *aggression* and then communist dictatorship.

Chou En-lai: See *Zhou Enlai*.

Christian Democracy: Moderate Catholic political parties, formed in many countries in Europe and Latin America in the 20th century.

Christian Democratic Union (CDU): The main center-right party of the Federal Republic of Germany since 1949. Founded by *Konrad Adenauer*, during the *Cold War* it cleaved to a pro-American position on *NATO* and relations with the *Soviet bloc*, and strongly supported European *integration*. It guided the extraordinary German recovery from *WWII*, and was the governing party for most of the period since 1949. Under *Helmut Kohl*, it oversaw the reunification of the two Germanies in 1989-90. It took the lead on more activist foreign policy in the post-Cold War period, especially toward the breakup of *Yugoslavia* and the *Maastricht Treaty*. It has recently moved to undercut *neo-nazi* positions and complaints by other *EU* members by tightening immigration policy to keep out economic *refugees* from *Eastern Europe*.

Christianity: Originating among the Jewish subjects of the Roman Empire, today it comprises 1 billion Catholics and hundreds of millions of Protestants, Orthodox and others. It is related to and has been deeply influenced by *Judaism*, and later and to a much lesser extent by *Islam*. Its central beliefs: messianism, and specifically, the divinity and sanctifying life of Jesus Christ; monotheism; the historical and divine role of prophesy; and various conceptions of social justice. It is subdivided into three major camps: Catholics, Orthodox and Protestant, with the latter subdivided into numerous denominations and sects. Catholics and Orthodox are far more internally cohesive groups than

Protestants, but both also face constant schismatic tendencies. Until the 17th century the Orthodox were the most numerous of Christians. But the expansion of Catholics into the Americas, and parts of Africa and Asia, that accompanied Western European *imperialism* made Catholicism the largest faction. See also *Catholic Church; Coptic Church; Counter Reformation; Inquisition; Orthodox Church; Reformation; Uniate Church*.

Christopher, Warren (b.1925): U.S. Secretary of State 1993- . A long-serving *diplomat* in subordinate roles, he was heavily criticized--fairly or not--during his first year in office for: a lack of *strategic* vision; an elevation of Asian and *trade* concerns over Europe and *security* issues (despite the *war* in Bosnia); failure to keep focused on a few key, specific goals; painful and excessive caution; needlessly damaging relations with China; and an inability to obtain or keep sufficient attention by his president (*Clinton*) on foreign affairs.

Chue Teh: See *Zhu De*.

Churchill, Winston Spencer (1874-1965): British statesman. First Lord of the Admiralty 1911-15, 1939-40; Minister of Munitions 1917; Secretary for War 1918-21; *Chancellor of the Exchequer* 1924-29; Minister of Defense and PM 1940-45; PM 1951-55. Abrasive, often drunk, switching political parties twice, he was nonetheless one of the outstanding *statesmen* of the 20th century. During *WWI* he headed the *Royal Navy*, but was forced to resign in 1915 over the fiasco of *Gallipoli*, a *campaign* he had urged. He returned to the War Cabinet in 1917, but in a diminished role. In the *interwar years* he voiced two unpopular opinions that helped keep him out of high office: (1) he refused to support concessions to India on self-rule, and (2) he repeatedly warned against taking *Hitler* lightly, and called for stepped-up preparations for yet another *Great War*. He found his personal destiny as a national leader in wartime. Britain's "finest hour" in 1940 was also his: there can be no doubt about the value of his leadership when Britain stood alone against Hitler's legions that summer, or his contribution to civilization itself in keeping alive armed resistance to *nazism* until the Soviet Union and the U.S. entered the war, and *victory* became possible. He was deeply frustrated after 1943 by the decline of Britain's relative *power* among the *Allies*, and thus the fading of his own *influence*: he thought he understood better than *Franklin Roosevelt* the nature of *Stalin's* regime and ambitions. He participated in the conferences at *Cairo, Casablanca, Tehran* and *Yalta*. Dismissed by the British electorate in the moment of triumph in 1945, while at *Potsdam*, he was thereafter most popular in America.

His powerful, anti-Soviet voice was influential in persuading the American public to endorse *Cold War* policy. But he also failed to recognize that the *British Empire* had entered terminal decline, and to adjust his policy to that reality. His motto: "In War: Resolution. In Defeat: Defiance. In Victory: Magnanimity. In Peace: Goodwill." See also *Atlantic Charter; balance of terror; bamboo curtain; Declaration on Liberated Europe; English Channel; Halifax; iron curtain; second front; unconditional surrender; Warsaw Rising.*

CIA: See *Central Intelligence Agency.*

Ciano, Galeazzo (1903-44): Son-in-law to *Benito Mussolini* from 1930; Italian Minister of *Propaganda* 1935; Foreign Minister 1936-43. He supported the *Axis* with Germany, an *expansionist* foreign policy, *annexation* of Albania, and the attack on Greece. His diary records growing disillusionment with Mussolini, whom he voted to overthrow in 1943. As things fell apart he fled, only to be captured by *partisans* and summarily tried and shot.

cipher: An encoded message. Some diplomatic, most military, and virtually all *intelligence* messages are sent in cipher. A common technique is the "one-time pad," which is a cipher book (pad) specific to a given mission, that does not depend on a preset, general (and therefore crackable) master code.

cipher clerk: An *embassy* or *intelligence* officer whose function is to encrypt and decode *ciphers.*

CIS: See *Commonwealth of Independent States.*

Ciscaucasia: The European portion of the *Caucasus,* lying north of the Caucasus Mountain range.

citizen: A native born or *naturalized* person who has rights against but also duties to a *state,* such as military service in time of *war.* The antonym is *alien.* See *jus sanguinis; jus soli.* Cf. *statelessness.*

citizenship: The legal status of being a *citizen.* It delimits rights and obligations of individuals vis-à-vis specific *states.*

city-state: A small *state* that does not extend much beyond the confines of a single city and its supporting, agricultural hinterland. This was a common political entity until the 18th century, when most were incorporated into national states. The closest approximations in modern times are *Singapore* and the *Vatican.* See also *city-state system; Hanseatic League.* Cf. *free city; microstate.*

city-state system: A political subsystem, protected by geography or luck from outside powers, where the main players are *city-states.* In classical Greece, Athens and Sparta contended for dominance of other city-states, mostly isolated from the larger conflict of the Persian Empire and Indian *subcontinent.* Similarly, for 100 years *Renaissance* Italy was shielded from the great contest between the *Hapsburg* house of Spain and its great rival in France. Hence, it saw the struggles of Italian city-states, whose *machiavellian* intrigues later found resonance in *Great Power* statecraft. *Venice* was the greatest of the Italian cities, but no matter: after defeating Spain, French armies poured into the peninsula and ended the era of the city-states.

civil defense: All measures to protect the *civilian* population, such as evacuation of cities or cover in shelters. While still feasible in *WWII* or modern *conventional* conflicts, it is near to hopeless in a nuclear scenario.

civilian: (1) All non-military aspects of a nation's life and economy. (2) In *just war theory* and the *laws of war,* any person who is not a soldier, and who therefore may not be deliberately killed or targeted.

civilian primacy: The Anglo/American, and broadly democratic, tradition whereby the military is expected to take its ultimate orders from the *civilian,* constitutional authority.

civilized states: A classical term for those states that seek, or say they seek, to maintain minimal moral and legal rules and standards, based on *consent, reciprocity* and voluntary compliance with law, rather than primary reliance on force. See *Treaty of Paris (1856); world community.* Cf. *outlaw state; pariah state.*

civil war: Armed conflict within a state, usually over control of the apparatus of government of that state, or on behalf of one region's desire to secede. Civil wars frequently attract *intervention* by outside powers, which can be decisive to the outcome. See specific conflicts, listed by country. Cf. *rebellion.*

clash of civilizations: See *secularism.*

class: (1) A social group sharing certain attributes or interests, as in "landowning class" or "entrepreneurial class." (2) In *marxism,* a group identified by its relationship to prevailing *modes of production,* such as the *bourgeoisie* or *proletariat.*

classical: (1) That which has stood the tests of time and circumstance. (2) Previously widely accepted.

classical school (of liberalism): Adherents believe that the best economic and governmental systems are those with the least intrusive governments, in which harmony is a natural by-product of self-interest. Historically, they have supported *free trade, laissez-faire* and the *gold standard.* Cf. *reform liberalism.*

class struggle: In *marxism,* the (putatively) mortal struggle carried on between antagonistic social classes for control of the *means of production,* which must culminate in the triumphal establishment of *communism* by the *proletariat.*

classified information: Knowledge deemed key to *national security,* and kept hidden by a government under its prevailing system of secret classification. Even in the top ranks of officialdom, access to information is restricted by degrees of classification. Cf. *archive.*

Clausewitz, Karl von (1780-1831): A Prussian strategist whose great work "Vom Kriege" (On War) influenced all subsequent thinking on the topic. His main accomplishment was to convincingly demonstrate that *war* is fundamentally a continuation of political struggle by alternate (violent) means, rather than an utter break with peacetime politics among nations. He never held an active, combat command, serving instead on the Prussian *General Staff,* and teaching at the Army school. He died rather ingloriously, from cholera.

clausula rebus sic stantibus: A legal doctrine that a *treaty* remains binding only so long as no vital changes occur to conditions that all parties had assumed. The claim such changes have occurred may be genuine, or invoked to cover a desire to discard a treaty commitment for other reasons. See *pacta sunt servanda; validity.*

Clay, Lucius D. (1898-1978): American soldier. He was an engineer by training and an administrator rather than combat soldier by inclination and talent. During *WWII* he was in charge of the massive procurement program that kept the war effort going, not just for U.S. troops, but through *Lend-Lease* for Britain, the *Soviet Union* and other *allies.* His most public role came as U.S. Military Governor in Germany 1945-49. He worked hard but unsuccessfully for German unity. Getting along well himself with Soviet military counterparts in occupied Germany, he found it difficult to understand why his superiors could not achieve the same easy relations with *Stalin.* Yet once the irrevocable break came, he adjusted masterfully. He was in charge in western Germany during the most tense days of *occupation,* and the *Berlin air lift* (which he inspired and oversaw). As Military Governor he had

virtually unlimited powers (he once reportedly joked to his secretary, "take a law"). Under his stern but not unkind guidance, *West Germany* laid the basis for a renaissance into a prosperous, *capitalist* democracy. On that project he worked closely with *Konrad Adenauer.* Retired from the army after 1949, he remained close to *Eisenhower,* playing *éminence grise* from 1952-61. A nonpartisan personality, from 1961-62 he was *Kennedy's* personal representative in Berlin.

clean bomb: A *nuclear weapon* with minimal *radiation effects.* Cf. *dirty weapon; neutron bomb.*

Clemenceau, Georges (1841-1929): French statesman. Premier 1906-09, 1917-20. His caustic tongue earned him the sobriquet "The Tiger." The nation turned to him to reverse a turn toward *defeatism* in 1917, when *mutiny* swept the trenches and *victory* seemed unattainable. Something of a *Jacobin* in temperament, he used heavy-handed methods. He executed traitors, spies (such as Mata Hari), and mutineers. When asked his policy, he said: "Home policy? I make war! Foreign policy? I make war! All the time, I make war!" His major influence came at the *Paris Peace Conference,* where he was often *Woodrow Wilson's* foil and always his personal bête noir. He worked for a punitive *peace,* pressing for separation of the *Rhineland* from Germany and high *reparations.* He wanted Allied *intervention* in the *Russian Civil War,* but could not convince Wilson. Despite his stern performance at Paris the French public judged him too soft on Germany; he was ousted in 1920. *John Maynard Keynes* said of Clemenceau: "He had one illusion, France; and one disillusion, Mankind, including Frenchmen." Cf. *cordon sanitaire; Fourteen Points.*

Cleveland, Grover (1837-1908): U.S. President 1884-88, 1892-96. In a quiet foreign policy era, he opposed a rising tide of *imperialist* sentiment in the U.S. Yet he also invoked the *Monroe Doctrine* against Britain when it disputed a *boundary* between *British Guiana* and *Venezuela.* London was astonished at this pugnacious twist in what had been improving relations since the end of the *American Civil War.* Britain conceded, restoring good relations.

client state: A smaller power beholding to a larger power for *aid,* military supplies, or diplomatic support. It gives diplomatic support in return; e.g., Cuba's relations with the Soviet Union after 1958, or more loosely, Philippine relations with the U.S. Cf. *satellite state.*

Clifford, Clark (b.1906): U.S. diplomat. He was one of the *Wise Men* who advised successive presidents, from both parties. He was *Lyndon Johnson's* Secretary of

State in 1968, and helped change course in the *Vietnam War* by convincing Johnson to stop the bombing campaign. In 1992 his reputation suffered from suggestions he was implicated in an international bank scandal, but he was cleared the next year.

climate: An underlying factor affecting national *power* (for instance by limiting the *food* supply), but about which nothing can be done on a national basis. Some theorists have suggested climate as the main reason why most historic *Great Powers* have been temperate zone countries. *Global warming* due to atmospheric pollution, and likely adverse effects on agricultural production and rising sea levels, is now a topic of *multilateral* negotiation. A *convention* on climate was agreed to at the *Earth Summit*.

Clinton, William (b.1946): U.S. President, 1993- . In his first year he concentrated on domestic affairs, but was repeatedly forced to address foreign policy. He approved cuts in *NATO* forces in Europe, to a force level of 100,000 by 1995. His administration set out to cut *defense spending* to a level where the U.S. could fight two *Gulf War*-size conflicts simultaneously. It also slashed *SDI* while seeking to modernize, streamline and provide high-tech equipment to the armed forces. He reversed some positions taken by the *Bush* administration at the *Earth Summit*, and on Angola. He appeared sincerely to embrace *multilateralism* as a general guide, but also as a cover for inaction toward Bosnia. He became more cautious as U.S. lives were lost in Somalia, but still committed naval forces to UN *blockades* of Serbia and Haiti. He approved air strikes and other forceful actions, but also allowed Bosnia and Haiti to slip from presidential and public attention. After some hesitation, he came out strongly in favor of *NAFTA*, *free trade* in general and completing the *Uruguay Round* of *GATT*. In 1994 he ended the *embargo* against Vietnam, criticized China on *human rights* and pressed North Korea on nuclear *proliferation*. If his foreign policy had any overall coherence, and many doubted this, it followed these principles: viewing the *national interest* in a revitalized economy as a prerequisite to engaged foreign policy, pragmatic rather than doctrinal assessment of when to intervene, and a limited effort to move beyond *containment* to "enlargement" of the community of democratic, market economy nations. See also *Armenia/Azerbaijan War; Rushdie; Thatcher*.

Cloroflurocarbons (CFCs): Used in refrigerants and aerosols, CFCs are thought to be a major contributor to depletion of the *ozone* layer.

closed economic system: See *collectivization; COM-*

ECON; five-year plans; planned economy. Cf. *market economy*.

clothing: See *textiles*.

Club of Rome: An influential group of economists making analyses and predictions about future world trends and problems. It has been accused by critics of spreading *neo-malthusian* fears about growth.

coalition: An *alliance* of more than two states, made to perform some joint action or fight a specific enemy. Coalitions may be *ad hoc* and include highly disparate states. They are often fragile and temporary, unlike a *treaty* alliance. For instance, see *Gulf Coalition; Napoleonic Wars; United Nations alliance*. Cf. *Central Powers; NATO; Triple Entente; Warsaw Pact*.

coastal states: Those with ocean coastlines, and hence claims to *territorial sea/waters* and *EEZs*.

cobelligerency: Relations between *combatants* on the same side, but not joined in a formal *alliance*; e.g., the United States was an "Associated Power" in *WWI*.

Cochin China: It was once an independent kingdom that for many centuries fought against absorption by the neighboring kingdom of *Tonkin*. It was made part of *French Indochina*, and is now within Vietnam.

codification: Systematic enumeration, in written form, of international rules and/or principles.

Cod War (1972-76): The fishing rights *dispute* between Britain and Iceland, in which naval vessels sometimes escorted fishing boats. It was settled by a compromise that favored Iceland. The only blood shed involved the cod.

coercion: The use or threat of *force* to obtain another state's compliance with a desired objective.

coercive diplomacy: Intimidation, or threat of punishment, to force an adversary to undo an action already taken. This contrasts with *deterrence*, where the threat is to retaliate for action that might be taken. Advocates portray coercive diplomacy as defensive, distinct from bullying or blackmail. Cf. *compellence*.

cognition: The act of knowing, and the processes of perception. See *cognitive dissonance; misperception*.

cognitive dissonance: A psychological theory that says individuals will tend not to believe, accept, or even perceive information that is contrary to their preformed notions. Instead, they screen out such information, or reinterpret it so that it does not contradict preferred beliefs. Applied to *decision-making*, it suggests that conflicts may be exaggerated out of *misperception* of an opponent's actions or intentions.

coimperium: Joint control of a *territory* by two powers, with neither claiming it as their exclusive, *sovereign* possession. Cf. *condominium*.

cold launch: A launch-safety system that uses an external power supply to eject a missile from its silo prior to igniting inboard thrusters. Cf. *hot launch*.

cold war: Intense rivalry and conflict among *nations* that falls short of active, *armed hostilities*.

Cold War: The period in world affairs from c.1947-90, marked by ideological, economic and political hostility and competition between the U.S. and the Soviet Union, and drawing in other powers at various levels of involvement. Among other entries, see *Afghan/Soviet War; Angola; Berlin airlift; Berlin, division of; Berlin Wall; Brezhnev; Brezhnev Doctrine; Bush; Cambodia; Carter; Carter Doctrine; Castro; China; CIA; communism; containment; Cuban Missile Crisis; Cuban Revolution; Czechoslovakia; détente; double containment; Eisenhower; Eisenhower Doctrine; ERP; Ethiopia; flexible response; Ford; France; Germany; Grenada; Gorbachev; Hungarian Uprising; Lyndon Johnson; Kennan; Kennedy; KGB; Khrushchev; Korean Conflict; Laos; liberal-internationalism; linkage; Marshall; massive retaliation; NATO; Nitze; Nixon; Nixon Doctrine; national liberation; Non-Aligned Movement; NSC-68; peaceful coexistence; Potsdam; Quemoy and Matsu; revisionism; Reagan; Reagan Doctrine; Russia; SALT; Sinatra Doctrine; Sino/Soviet split; Soviet Union; space race; SPUTNIK; Stalin; START; Taiwan; Truman; Truman Doctrine; two-plus-four talks; UK; US; Vietnam; Vietnam War; Warsaw Pact; Wisconsin School; X article; Yalta; Yeltsin.*

collaboration: Voluntary cooperation with the officials of an *occupation* power, usually taken as implying sheer opportunism on the part of collaborators. Real, or just accused, collaborators are often subjected to rough justice following *liberation*. Cf. *fraternize*.

collateral damage: The unintentional destruction of people or property caused by weapons not directly aimed at them, but at nearby targets. In *just war theory*, this may be permissible under certain circumstances. In actual *warfare*, it happens all the time.

collective goods theory: Analysis of payment for and allocation of *public goods*, or goods that are jointly provided and from which it is difficult or impossible to screen out noncontributors; e.g., the *balance of power; liquidity*. Cf. *free rider problem*.

collective security: A theory that aims at preservation of *peace* through shared *deterrence* of *aggression*. It offers an advance guarantee that overwhelming diplomatic opposition, *sanctions* and, ultimately, *force* will be brought to bear against the *aggressor*. It was the central *security doctrine* of the *League of Nations*. However, that organization never met the precondition of participation by all the *Great Powers*, suffered from a lack of will among the Western powers and had to face several powerful *aggressors* all at once: Japan (1931), Italy (1935), Germany (1939) and the Soviet Union (1940). The *UN Charter* contains some modified collective security provisions.

collective self-defense: Assistance given by other states to a state acting in self-defense, under Article 51 of the UN Charter. Note: Not to be confused with *collective security*.

collectivization: Under *communism* and some variants of *socialism*, moving from private to collective (which often means state) ownership of property and the *means of production*, and compelling the adoption of new social, work and even living arrangements on all those "collectivized." At the extreme, it means forcible elimination of all private ownership; at the least, it means heavy government regulation of economic activity, usually including setting of prices and wages. Its most destructive applications have come in peasant *agriculture*, including in the 1930s in the Soviet Union, where it was wedded to a brutal campaign against the *kulaks* and Ukrainian *nationalism*; in the 1950s in *Mao's* China; in the 1970s in Cambodia under the *Khmers Rouges;* and in the 1980s in Ethiopia. Many tens of millions died savage, thoughtless, futile deaths in those campaigns. Lesser efforts have taken place under non-communist, but still socialist governments, as in Tanzania in the 1960s and 1970s. Some force was used there, too, but nowhere near the levels used in the campaigns in China, Russia or even Ethiopia. Cf. *expropriation; nationalization; privatize*.

Colombia: Location: S. America. Major associations: *G-8, OAS, UN*. Population: 32.7 million. Military: Small, *counterinsurgency* focus, with ties to the U.S. Originally, the vast area comprising modern Colombia, Ecuador, Panama and Venezuela, conquered in the 1530s and ruled by Spain for 300 years. It gained its *independence* in 1819 as part of the wave of successful Latin American *rebellions* against Spain. Ecuador and Venezuela broke off in 1829-30, forming separate states. With U.S. connivance, Panama broke away in 1903. One of Latin America's more successful democracies, Colombia still suffered a period of violent upheaval from 1948-58, simply called "La Violencia," in which as many as 200,000 died. It remains a deeply divided society, with enormous gaps between living standards of different classes. Since the 1970s it has had to contend with *drug cartels* whose huge profits enable them to corrupt the legal and political system, distort the normal economy, and hire what amount to private armies. In 1989 one drug baron, Pablo Escobar of the Medellín Cartel, ordered the assassination of a presidential candidate and began a terror bombing campaign to intimidate the country into abandoning anti-cocaine policies. Caesar Trujillo, who opposed the drug cartels, was elected anyway. Colombia cooperates with the U.S. military to combat the cocaine trade. In 1993 the government finally caught up with and killed Escobar. See *narco-terrorism*.

Colombo Plan: A model for early foreign *aid*, focusing on the Pacific region, first developed by the *Commonwealth* in 1950. Japan, the U.S. and other states joined later. Japan is currently the major donor.

colonialism: Extending one's *sovereign* authority over new territory, by *conquest* if populated, by settlement if not. *Third World* opposition to colonialism came to dominate the *UNGA* in the 1960s and 1970s. The issue has faded to rhetoric, as most colonies are now independent. Cf. *neo-colonialism*.

colony: (1) A group of settlers in a new *territory* who are subjects of a parent state. (2) Any territory not connected to, but ruled by, a distant power.

combatant: (1) A *nation* or other identifiable group at *war*, not a *neutral* party. (2) In *international law* and in *just war theory*, persons enlisted for or actively engaged in *warfare*, as distinct from *civilians*.

combat area: In *international law*, part of the *high seas* designated by a *belligerent* as forbidden to *neutrals* under rules of *blockade*.

COMECON: Council for Mutual Economic Assistance. It was set up in 1949, ostensibly to increase trade within the *Soviet bloc* as a substitute for the *Marshall Plan* aid that Moscow forced its east European *satellites* to forgo. A handful of other states became associated with COMECON later, all of which were Soviet *clients*: Cuba, Finland (a special case), Iraq, Laos, Nicaragua and Vietnam. Albania was expelled in 1961. It collapsed in 1990, and dissolved in 1991.

COMINFORM: *Commun*ist *Inform*ation Bureau. Established by nine European *communist parties* ostensibly to coordinate information and policy, but really to permit *Stalin* to extend his political influence into Western Europe. It lasted from 1947-56.

COMINTERN: See *Third (Communist) International*.

comity of nations (*courteoisie*): Practices of reciprocal courtesy among nations; e.g., not publishing each other's correspondence. These practices have no binding character: violations may be seen as unfriendly, but not as a *casus belli*, and will not support claims for *damages*.

command economy: One wherein the key economic decisions about production and distribution of *goods* and *services* are made by centralized, government authorities. Their records, as in the *Soviet bloc* or China under *Mao*, were unenviable. A synonym is *planned economy*. See *five-year plans*. Cf. *market economy*.

commando: A military unit trained to conduct lightning raids, such as against coastal installations or *terrorist* camps. See *Dieppe; Entebbe*.

commerce: Trade, or the interchange of *goods* and *services*. This is distinct from manufacturing industry.

commercial treaty: A *treaty* governing *trade*, usually intended to lower mutual *tariff* and other barriers to freer exchange of *goods* and *services*.

commissioned officer: One holding command by virtue of a commission (a certificate of presidential or other formal authority).

Committee of Permanent Representatives (COREPER): A committee of the *European Council*. Once it emerged from the *Luxembourg Compromise*, most major decisions, proposals and initiatives on *integration* in the *EC/EU* have come from this committee.

Committee on Disarmament (CD): An *arms control* body that comprises all acknowledged *nuclear states* and some 35 interested states. It meets in Geneva to discuss issues of *proliferation* and *nonproliferation*.

commodity: Any *good* available for trade or sale. Cf. *factor endowments*.

commodity agreement: See *International Commodity Agreement (ICA)*.

common heritage principle: By analogy to the feudal

idea of common grazing lands, the idea that certain resources fall outside the *domain* of *sovereignty*, and belong instead to humanity as a whole. The idea has application to *multilateral* approaches to global problems, such as marine pollution or *global warming*. It is put forward assertively by *LDCs* as a vehicle for claims for *distributive justice* and greater economic *aid*. Cf. *Antarctic Treaty; Moon Treaty; Outer Space Treaty; res communis; Seabed Treaty; UNCLOS III.*

Common Agricultural Policy (CAP): Agreed upon by the *EEC* in 1968 as a *protectionist* system for farmers, it was only partly modified by the *Uruguay Round.*

common market: This goes beyond a *customs union* in that besides internal *free trade* and common external *tariffs*, it seeks to harmonize financial policy.

Commonwealth: A loose association of most of the former territories of the *British Empire. Queen Elizabeth* is its titular head. *Heads of state* or *government* meet once per year. Its finance ministers also meet, and it maintains a *secretariat* in London. It divided badly over *apartheid* (South Africa withdrew, 1961-94). In the 1960s it nearly split over the question of *UDI* by Rhodesia. It had 51 *sovereign* members in 1994 plus small *dependencies* and *protectorates.*

Commonwealth of Independent States (CIS): It replaced the *Soviet Union* upon its *extinction* (11 of the 15 former Soviet republics joined the CIS. Those that did not were the *Baltic States* and Georgia. It tries to coordinate policy, in particular on *currency* and trade issues, through *heads of government* meetings. It is headquartered in Minsk, Belarus. By early 1994 six members had signed defense *pacts* with Russia (the central Asian states plus Armenia). Moldova threatened to leave over Russian *aid* to *secessionists*, and Georgia made a desperate offer to join in an unsuccessful bid to stave off Russian aid to rebels in *Abkhazia*. Cf. *near abroad; Newly Independent States.*

commonwealth status: The constitutional association of a *microstate* with a former colonial or *trusteeship* power. There is internal *autonomy* but little to no control of foreign policy, and direct inclusion in the larger economy. See *Marianas Islands*. Cf. *free association.*

Communauté Financière Africaine (CFA): "African Financial Community." Founded in 1948, it connects France to its former African *colonies* by linking a common *currency* (the CFA franc) to the French franc. The rate was unchanging at 50:1 from 1948-94, when the CFA was devalued by 50 percent. *Devaluation* was a response to *IMF* and *IBRD* pressure, and

economies floundering under over-priced exports. In exchange for the devaluation, France wrote off all bilateral *debt* from countries in the CFA zone, and the IMF extended new credit lines.

Commune, Paris: *Defeat* in the *Franco/Prussian War* stimulated a *radical* rising in Paris in 1871, lasting several months. It was crushed after bitter street fighting. It left 20,000 dead and a legacy of class hatred. It also fed a legend of *proletarian* fervor important to revolutionary *socialists* in Europe.

communism: (1) A theory of social organization based on collective ownership of the *means of production*, and rational and equitable redistribution of *goods, services* and wealth. (2) An actual system of social and political organization in which ownership of property resides with a centralized and *totalitarian state*, run in the name of the *proletariat* by a highly privileged, ideological and managerial *elite*. (3) Whatever a ruling communist party says it is. See the cross-references listed under *marxism.*

Communist Manifesto: A long pamphlet issued by *Karl Marx* and *Friedrich Engels* in 1848, sparked by the upheavals of that year and exhorting Europe's *proletariat* ("workers of the world") to unite and overthrow the *ancien régime*. It was no more than a statement of general principles. Marx's major analytical work came years later, in "Das Kapital."

communist parties: Those advocating theories of *communism*, and especially of *marxism-leninism*, but including variants that reflect specific leaders such as *maoism*. The term was not widely used until after the *Bolsheviks* split from the Russian Social Democratic Party. (1) Communist Party of China (CCP): Founded in 1920 with the help of Soviet advisers, at first it supported the *Guomindang*. It split in 1927 after the *Shanghai massacre* of its supporters. It took power in China in 1949, and has yet to relinquish it. It carried out major land reforms, but also the disastrous *Great Leap Forward* and the *Cultural Revolution*. After 1978 it moved briskly toward market economics, but continued to repress nearly all political dissent. (2) Communist Party of the Soviet Union (CPSU): The ruling party from 1920-91 (though the name was changed to CPSU only in 1952). It conducted forced *collectivization, purges* and *five-year plans*, led the country through *WWII* and waged the *Cold War*. It also created a legacy of anger, entrepreneurial lethargy and backwardness, and deepened national and ethnic divisions. It was left without an *empire* to rule with the *extinction* of the Soviet Union. Some of its most prominent members have been since charged with crimes, economic and political. It was banned for a time in Russia in 1993, and remains banned in several other former Soviet republics, but its cohorts still wield considerable power within the bureaucracy and in outlying regions. (3) Other: Communist parties (though not all used the name) were entrenched in power by the Soviet Union in Bulgaria, Czechoslovakia, East Germany, Hungary, Mongolia, Poland and Rumania. They came to power more or less independently in Albania, Angola, Cambodia, China, Cuba, Ethiopia, Laos, Mozambique, Vietnam, Yemen and Yugoslavia. They were influential in France, Weimar Germany, Italy, India, Indonesia and Spain. See *eurocommunism; Partai Kommunis Indonesia (PKI); Pathet Lao; Viet Minh.*

Comoros: Location: Indian Ocean. Major associations: *OAU, UN.* Population: 460,000. Military: minimal. This island *nation* was ruled by independent Muslim *sultans* prior to being made a French *protectorate* in the late 19th century. One island, Mayotte, is predominantly Catholic. A *referendum* in 1976 confirmed its preference to stay attached to France rather than the Muslim Comoros, which declared *independence* in 1975. A leftist clique ruled from 1975-78, when it was deposed in a *coup* that had support from France. A *mercenary* regime took control briefly in 1989, but was overthrown by direct French military *intervention.*

compact: A binding contract between or among nations. A synonym for *treaty.*

comparative advantage: The idea that an economy benefits from *trade* in situations where it has a relative advantage in the *efficiency* with which it produces a *service* or *good.* This is the underlying assumption of advocates of *free trade.* It is said that each country in a pure free trade system will tend to use its comparative advantages to provide the goods and services where it is the most efficient producer. Thus, countries with plentiful, cheap *labor* will focus on labor-intensive goods, while high technology economies will maximize that advantage. Of course, even free trade states actively seek to protect those sectors where the comparative advantage of others threatens domestic production, job creation and perhaps a government's political base. Cf. *competitive advantage.*

compellence: The use of threat, intimidation and ultimately *force* to make (compel) an adversary do or undo something. It incorporates notions of *coercive diplomacy*, but also of bullying and blackmail.

compensation: (1) In *diplomacy: territorial*, financial or other inducements given by one *state* to another, to gain acquiescence to an act of *aggrandizement* or other territorial adjustment. (2) In *international law:* funds paid by *belligerents* to *neutrals* under the right of *angary*, for property that has been *requisitioned* for wartime use. (3) In *economics*: monies paid to a firm (foreign or domestic) whose assets have been *nationalized.* Cf. *expropriation; indemnity.*

compensatory financing: Stop-gap loans or grants to *LDCs* made on highly advantageous terms to compensate for shortfalls in export earnings that result from "Acts of God" (or nature) like floods or drought, or from a global recession. The *IMF* began a scheme in 1963. *COMPEX* and *STABEX* are run by the *EU.*

competitive advantage: The idea that global market forces and new technologies mean that the classical measures of *comparative advantage* (e.g., *labor* costs or skills) are no longer adequate. Instead, it is recommended that nations develop grand strategies (national industrial plans) to develop competitive superiority in selected industries. Some critics of the idea argue that pragmatism and overall adjustment to market forces are more important than pre-set and possibly distorting "national strategies."

competitiveness: A measure of the *efficiency* of an enterprise or national economy when compared to its competitors. This measure looks at overall, national economic performance, especially at levels of productivity, *standards of living*, and *export/import* ratios.

COMPEX: A *compensatory financing* scheme set up under the *EC* and maintained by the *EU* for those *LDCs* not party to the *Lomé Conventions.* It operates like *STABEX*, but is smaller.

complex interdependence: A situation in which two (or more) countries have multiple networks of contacts and transactions, ranging from government to private economic exchanges, and all types of social and cultural activity. Each is therefore highly *sensitive* to events and policies in the other country. Under these conditions, existing between Canada and the United States or members of the *EU*, it is said that *power* must be measured differently than in "normal" international relations: *low politics*, not *high politics*, will tend to dominate, and small is not the same as weak.

composite state: An entity composed of more than one *state*, such as a regional *federation* or a *union.*

comprador class: In *dependency theory*, an *elite* within the *periphery* that owes its privileges (and even its social manners) to cooperation with the elites of the *core*, which it helps to more thoroughly exploit local resources and *labor*. They are depicted in dependency theory and other variants of *marxist* analysis as a social product of the *world capitalist system*.

comprehensive security: (1) A *CSCE* doctrine holding that threats to *security* may arise from a multitude of sources. (2) A doctrine developed in the 1980s suggesting that Japan's security required a regional presence via cultural, diplomatic and economic initiatives, but with military activity still restricted to defense of the *home islands*. Cf. *Kuranari Doctrine*.

Comprehensive Test Ban (CTB): A proposal to extend provisions of the *Partial Test Ban Treaty* to underground testing. It aims to snuff out *vertical proliferation* in *nuclear weapons*. It was opposed by the *Bush* administration, but a majority of signatories of the PTBT have warned they may make it a precondition of renewal of that treaty in 1995.

compromis: Agreement to submit a *dispute* to *arbitration*, that sets terms and conditions of the resolution process and appoints the arbitration court (often on an *ad hoc* basis). Not to be confused with "compromise."

compulsory jurisdiction: A misleading but widely used term referring to the *Optional Clause of the Statute of the ICJ* (Article 36), granting advance jurisdiction, without requiring specific agreement. It only applies in cases where both states have accepted the clause. In short, giving the court compulsory jurisdiction is actually voluntary. Some states have retracted their prior *consent*. Cf. *limited jurisdiction*.

compulsory rules: Those applying irrespective of formal *consent*. Cf. *jus cogens*.

concentration camp: (1) A detention center set up to concentrate the *civilian* population under military control, usually intended to deny support to *guerrillas*. In their modern form, they were invented by the British for use against the *Afrikaner* population during the *Second Boer War*. They have been used since by many armies fighting guerrillas or *partisans*. Indeed, the barbed wire and guard towers typical of such camps have become something of a visual metaphor for the 20th century. (2) The *death camps* set up by the *Nazis* during *WWII* to exploit *slave labor* and exterminate the Jews of Europe. See *Auschwitz; Dachau; ethnic cleansing; Holocaust*.

concept: A general idea; an *abstract* construction.

conceptualize: To think of as an *abstraction* (*concept*), or generalization.

concert: (1) A common plan or accord among several *states*. (2) Harmony among states. Cf. *cold war*.

Concert of Europe (c.1815-53): The informal system of consultation set up by the *Great Powers* (Austria, Britain, France, Prussia and Russia) to manage the *balance of power* at the end of the *Congress system*. It confirmed their *condominium* over the smaller powers on matters of international significance, but helped keep the *peace* for decades. Most historians date it from the *Congress of Vienna* in 1815, though some prefer 1822 (when Britain pulled out of the Congress system). It ended with the breakdown of Great Power consensus in the *Crimean War* (1854-56). *Realists* have admired its high degree of Great Power cooperation and its relative unconcern with ideological disputes. Liberals have often found its abjuring of principle morally repugnant and practically dangerous. Insofar as it worked (and many other factors besides the Concert prevented war during this time), it did so because all the Great Powers accepted the principle of the balance of power. They also agreed that any gain by one of their number must be by consensus, and be accompanied by *compensation* to the rest. Sometimes this compensation was had at the expense of hapless smaller powers, caught between the driving hammer of one Great Power's ambition and the anvil of another's resistance. More often, it was had outside Europe, in the form of colonial swaps and/or *de jure* acceptance of each others' *de facto*, territorial *conquests*. Cf. *Holy Alliance; Quadruple Alliance*.

conciliation: When a commission makes non-binding recommendations on settling a *dispute*.

concordat: A *treaty* between the *Vatican* and another *state* concerning church affairs, but often social and educational policy as well. Major concordats were signed with France (1801), Spain (1851), Fascist Italy (1929), Nazi Germany (1933) and Poland (1993).

conditionality: When qualifications (conditions) with respect to fiscal policy, consumer *subsidies*, and other national government economic policies are required by a lending agency, especially a *multilateral* agency such as the *IMF* or *World Bank*. See *First Tranche; stabilization program*.

condominium: (1) The idea that the *Great Powers* should act together to impose orderly solutions to questions of international *peace* and *security*. (2) In *international law*, the exercise of joint or shared *sovereignty* over a *territory* by two or more *states*; e.g., the Anglo-Egyptian Sudan 1899-1955. Note: this is quite different, legally at least, from *occupation*.

Condor Legion: The German air force "volunteers" fighting on the *fascist* side in the *Spanish Civil War*.

confederacy: (1) An alternate term for *alliance*. (2) The *Confederate States of America*, 1861-65.

Confederate States of America (CSA): The eleven southern states that seceded from the U.S. between November 1860 and February 1861, rather than accept the presidency of *Abraham Lincoln*: Alabama, Arkansas, Florida, Georgia, Louisiana, Mississippi, North Carolina, South Carolina, Tennessee, Texas, and most important, Virginia. It sought but failed to obtain international *recognition* of its *independence*. After four years of *war* with the more populous and industrialized *Union*, in which early victories turned into grinding, bloody and bitter *defeat*, it was dissolved in April 1865. See *American Civil War.*

confederation: See *union of sovereign states*.

Confederation of the Rhine: Created by *Napoleon I* in 1806, it was a failed effort to make permanent French *hegemony* over western Germany. It fell apart in 1813, during the *retreat from Moscow*.

conference diplomacy: *Multilateral* negotiation in public or open sessions. The public twist given to conferences in the 20th century came from the *Hague Conferences*, and the influence of *Woodrow Wilson* and those liberal-internationalists who demanded "open covenants, openly arrived at." It sprang from broad democratic pressures within several *Great Powers*, and the widespread belief that secret *treaties* had helped precipitate *WWI*. It then achieved permanence with the Assembly of *League of Nations*, the *UNGA*, the *CSCE* and most recently, *APEC*.

Conference on Security and Cooperation in Europe (CSCE): From 1973-75 all European states (except Albania), plus the U.S. and Canada met to discuss regional *security*. The Soviets wanted *recognition* of their *postwar* gains; the West Europeans wanted to expand *détente*, as did most *neutrals*. All participants agreed on the *Helsinki Accords*. Follow-up conferences were held (13 between 1975-89). After 1990 much changed. The *Charter of Paris* was adopted and a Conflict Prevention Center (CPC) set up (in Vienna). The CSCE moved to implement *CSBMs* and coordinate some *peacekeeping* and many election *observer* missions. Helsinki 1992 set up new structures--a *Secretariat* and Permanent Committee (in Vienna), and an Office for Democratic Institutions and *Human Rights* (ODIHR) in Warsaw. The CSCE accepted the *successor states* of the *Soviet Union* and *Yugoslavia*, rising

to 52 members. It also *suspended* Serbia. Japan and Macedonia (whose entry was vetoed by Greece under the *unanimity rule*) have observer status--they attend but do not speak or vote. The U.S. is very active, as is Russia; the *EU* acts as a *bloc*, and often a drag.

Confidence and Security Building Measures (CSBMs): Practical steps taken to reduce levels of *tension* in a hostile relationship where there is no apparent or immediate solution to the basic *conflict*. They include exchanging military observers, giving advance warning of military *maneuvers*, and avoiding maneuvers in border areas to lessen the risk of *accidental war*. But they may be virtually any other political or even social measure seen as a building block of trust necessary to eventual resolution of the underlying issues. They are most developed within the *CSCE*, but other countries have adopted them because of their practical utility. For example, India and Pakistan have agreed to some advance notification of maneuvers, local *hot-line* communications between commanders and so forth, concerning their *dispute* over *Kashmir.*

conflict: A given instance of the endemic antagonism in political life between various interests or principles.

conflict management: The idea that management of persistent *conflicts* that defy resolution, rather than construction of *grand strategy*, is the most practical contribution to the maintenance of *peace*. Students of conflict management mainly examine structures of *decision-making, negotiation* and *crises*, looking for techniques that are conducive to peaceful outcomes.

conflict of laws: When different municipal laws, specific to the *nations* concerned in a claim, apply to the same case. Cf. *private international law.*

Congo: Location: Central Africa. Major associations: *OAU, UN*. Population: 2.3 million. Military: minor. France took over this *territory* in 1885, granting *independence* in 1960. A *coup* in 1963 set up a *marxist-leninist* regime that invited assistance from both the Soviet Union and China. But France remained the dominant *influence* on Congo's economic and social life, as it continued to provide *ODA* and to be the major trade partner. In 1990 Congo's leftist regime underwent an economic epiphany, renouncing marxism-leninism and moving toward a multiparty system. Note: Not to be confused with the Belgian Congo, which later became Zaire.

Congo crisis (1960-65): Belgium abruptly left its Congo *colony* in 1960, without advance preparation for *independence*. Within weeks the resource-rich

Katanga province seceded under *Tshombe*. The UN sent in *peacekeeping* troops, but they could not prevent the Congo from splintering into several more parts: a rival government to the federal government at Leopoldville was set up at Stanleyville, under the radical, Federal PM *Patrice Lumumba*. Tshombe's troops captured and murdered Lumumba in 1961, and then UN forces came under attack. *Dag Hammarskjöld* was killed in a plane crash on his way to meet Tshombe. The UN prevailed in heavy fighting against Katanga's largely white, *mercenary* army by mid-1963, and it was rejoined to the Congo. Intermittent fighting continued until 1965, when *Mobutu Sese Seko* took power in a *coup*. In 1971 the Congo was renamed *Zaire*.

Congress: (1) A formal meeting of international *envoys*, usually very senior *diplomats* or *foreign ministers*. (2) The legislative branch of the U.S. government, comprising the Senate and the House of Representatives.

Congress of Vienna: See *Vienna, Congress of*.

Congress Party (of India): The main nationalist party of India before *independence*, founded in 1885. It has been the usual governing party, with some interruptions, since independence. From the 1920s it was dominated by the personality and policies of *Mohandas Gandhi*, then by *Nehru*, his daughter Indira Gandhi and grandson *Rajiv Gandhi*. All stressed *self-reliance*. In 1969 and again in 1978, important factions split from the party. Its secular agenda, long attractive to minority Muslims, has recently being challenged by Hindu *fundamentalism*.

Congress system: The practice of *diplomacy* by *congress*, 1815-22, by the four *Great Powers* that defeated *Napoleon*: Austria, Britain, Prussia and Russia. There were five congresses: *Vienna* 1814-15; *Aix-la-Chapelle* 1818; *Troppau* 1820; *Laibach* 1821; and *Verona* 1822. France used them to return to the good graces of the three conservative powers. Britain attended only as an observer from Troppau on, and left the system at Verona. Austria, Prussia and Russia met again in St. Petersburg in 1825, but the system was then abandoned in favor of the *Concert of Europe*, which included Britain.

conquest: Military *occupation* of *territory* of another *state*. It may precede *annexation* or *subjugation*.

conquistador: One of the Spanish conquerors of the Americas. See *Cortés*.

conscientious objector: Someone who declines to

fulfil national military obligations for moral, philosophical or religious reasons.

conscript: A drafted soldier; not a volunteer.

conscription: Compulsory military service, rare before the *French Revolution* and the *levée en masse*, but used extensively ever since. A popular American synonym is "the draft." Among the *Great Powers* universal conscription was introduced first in those nations that suffered great *defeats*: in Prussia (1814), and Austria-Hungary (1867). France introduced conscription in 1889, lengthening service to three years as its *population* declined relative to Germany's. During the *American Civil War*, after a brief spell of using volunteers (with three-month enlistment periods!) the *Union* introduced conscription. Yet the wealthy could purchase replacements for themselves or their sons. The *Confederacy* originally relied on volunteers, but by the end of the war was conscripting less enthusiastic whites and even some slaves (used mainly in garrison duty that freed white troops for combat). Russia was a special case: the gentry served as officers under a system of near-feudal obligation. In 1715 conscription was introduced on the basis of one draftee for every 75 serf households (the ratio applied as well to state peasants), with conscripts serving for 25 years in exchange for freedom, should they survive.

consent: A cardinal principle of *international law*, by which changes in *rules* require consent by the parties concerned to be legally binding. Some theorists suggest that consensus among the states, rather than consent by every state, is becoming the standard by which a rule is considered generally binding and an obligation incurred. See also *liberum veto; unanimity rule*.

Conservative Party, of Britain (Tories): It was founded in 1832 as a successor to the *Tory* Party. It considers itself the "natural governing party of Britain" and with good reason: it ruled sternly for parts of the 19th century, under Peel and *Disraeli*, and from the moderate center during most of the 20th. A strong supporter of anti-Soviet policies in the *Cold War*, under *Margaret Thatcher* in the 1980s it grew leery of European *integration* and turned harder right at home. In the 1990s it moved toward the center, and became more accepting of Britain's place in Europe. But it still tends to look to a "special relationship" with the U.S. that has had decreasing reality since the *Suez Crisis*.

Constantinople: The city founded by Constantine the Great that served for a millennium as the great capital and center of learning of the Byzantine Empire, and for centuries more as the capital of the *Ottoman Em-*

pire. It lost its status as the Turkish capital in 1923, when the seat of government was moved to Ankara to signal a break from the religious and imperial pretensions of the Ottomans. Its name was changed to Istanbul in 1930.

Constantinople Agreement (1915): A secret *treaty* wherein France and Britain promised Russia the city of *Constantinople* and its *hinterland*, if Russia stayed in *WWI*. It was a mark of the frustration of the *stalemate* on the *western front*, and of the importance of Russia to the Allied cause, that France and Britain thus quit their traditional policy on the *Eastern Question*. It was among the secret pacts published by the *Bolsheviks* in 1918, to the embarrassment of the *Allies*.

consul: A non-diplomatic, official representative who still may enjoy *diplomatic immunity*. Posted to *consulates*, they see to *trade, immigration*, assistance to *citizens* traveling or residing abroad and other mundane matters. See *representation; Vienna Convention*.

consulate: (1) The diplomatic premises occupied by a *consul*, usually in cities other than the *capital* and concerned with nonpolitical matters like *trade*, assisting nationals and processing *immigration*. (2) The system of government in France under *Napoleon I*, from September 1799 until he was crowned Emperor in May 1804. Cf. *embassy; legation*.

consul general: The senior consular officer.

consumer goods: Final *goods* ready for use, or consumption, and not for use in any further production. Cf. *capital goods*.

consumer price index (CPI): A composite statistic measuring prices over a range of consumer *goods* and *services*. It is used by firms and unions in planning investment or negotiating wages, and by governments to help set *macroeconomic* policy. Some criticize it for overestimating the true rate of *inflation*, for instance by not adjusting fully for improvements in the quality of goods and services.

Contadora Group: An *ad hoc* association formed in 1983 by Colombia, Mexico, Panama and Venezuela to *mediate* the *conflicts* in Central America. In 1987 it backed a *peace* plan framed by President Oscar Arias of Costa Rica. But as the *Reagan* administration did not welcome the initiative, it made little headway.

containment: (1) A foreign policy that aims at preventing expansion of an imperialist adversary by supporting its weaker neighbors and otherwise blocking opportunities for *aggrandizement*; e.g., British policy toward Russian ambitions to acquire the *Ottoman* lands and parts of the *Balkans* in the 19th century; U.S. policy toward Iran after 1979. (2) The policy pursued by the U.S. toward the Soviet Union, c.1947 to c.1989. Its premise was that denying Moscow opportunities to expand its political influence would force it to abandon *imperialism* and address internal contradictions. Its main instrument was the *Marshall Plan* to aid recovery of Germany and Europe, and bilateral *aid* to Japan. Rapid recovery of these former enemy states and their incorporation into a U.S.-led trading and financial system addressed U.S. interests in trade. But it also denied Moscow *influence* over a poor, hungry and potentially radicalized postwar populaces. *NATO* merely reinforced political and economic containment as a form of prudential military insurance against the unlikely possibility that Moscow planned an assault on Western Europe. In short, NATO was to counterbalance Soviet military advantages in Europe, enabling the U.S. to play its trump card--a vastly more efficient economy--through the reconstruction of Germany, Western Europe and Japan. However, the *Korean Conflict* encouraged a *militarization* and globalization of containment that was not part of its original conception. It thus helped stimulate an expensive *arms race* after 1950, and became extended to areas beyond the West's *vital interests*. It was most tragically misapplied to local or merely perceived, communist threats in Latin and Central America, Africa, and especially throughout Indochina. See *George Kennan; NSC-68; Paul Nitze; X article*. Cf. *double containment*.

contiguity: Basing claims to neighboring *territory* or *territorial seas* based upon physical connection to one's own. Cf. *propinquity*.

contiguous zone: Formerly 12 nautical miles from the *baseline*, it was extended by *UNCLOS III* to 24 nautical miles. Within this zone, of what are otherwise the *high seas*, *states* claim limited *jurisdiction* for specific purposes, such as interception of illegal *immigration* or smuggling. See *hot pursuit; territorial sea*.

continental shelf: The part of any continent or *island* contiguous with a coast and submerged in shallow water (up to 200m). A prime source of fish and sometimes *oil*, rights to this region were a major concern of the *UNCLOS III* talks. When it extends beyond the *EEZ*, the effective rights of an EEZ state are "prolonged" to the edge of the shelf. Cf. *islet*.

Continental System: The *blockade* of Britain instituted by *Napoleon* in November 1806, that aimed at closing Europe's northern ports to British commerce to force London to negotiate. Russia was added briefly after the agreement at *Tilsit* in 1807, and *Iberian* ports were closed in 1808. It was resisted by traders all across Europe and the U.S. and Napoleon was required to abandon it as ineffectual by 1809.

continuity of safeguards: A concept related to *nonproliferation,* and in particular the *Nuclear Non-Proliferation Treaty,* and more generally to *arms control* agreements. It refers to acceptance of the principle of continuous, and even surprise, inspections as a means of *verification,* rather than permitting occasional or *pro forma* inspections to serve as a cover for violations. It was expanded after the *Gulf War.* See *IAEA.*

continuity of states: Maintaining the legal identity of *international personalities* following a *revolution, territorial* change or military *occupation.*

continuous voyage: See *ultimate destination.*

contraband: (1) Smuggled or illegal *goods.* (2) Goods supporting an enemy's war effort that another country declares contraband under the law of *blockade.* The definition has stretched with the expansion of accepted legitimate targets, until it can mean virtually anything, including *food.* See *infection; noncontraband.*

contra proferentum: In cases of ambiguity a *treaty* is interpreted against the party that drafted it, and which might have been more precise. Cf. *obscuritas pacti.*

Contras: The anti-*Sandinista* force that fought a harassing *guerrilla war* in Nicaragua in the 1980s, backed by the *Reagan* administration. See *Nicaragua.*

Control Commission, Allied: The command structure, or Kommandatura, set up by the four occupying powers in Germany after *WWII.*

control experiment: In *quantitative analysis,* when one *variable* is held constant (unvarying) to observe and measure the effects it has on other variables.

controlled response: The attempt to limit one's military reply to an attack, in the hope of preventing *escalation* to all-out *war* by giving an adversary time to reconsider and withdraw. Cf. *escalation control.*

control test: A wartime test used to establish the legal status of a firm or property, by assessing which state exercises preponderant influence over it.

convention: A *multilateral* agreement (*treaty*) that is concerned with a specific problem or issue. Topics are as diverse as civil aviation, epidemic diseases, postal service or *genocide.*

Conventional Forces in Europe, Treaty (1990): It set out reduction targets in *conventional weapons* and troop levels, and called for phased and equal reductions over four years. It was signed by the *NATO* countries and six remaining *Warsaw Pact* states. Its obligations have been passed, proportionately, on to the *successor states* to the Soviet Union.

conventional war: (1) Waging *war* with *conventional weapons.* (2) War against *regular,* conventional forces; that is, not against *terrorists* or *guerrillas.*

conventional weapons: All weapons except *biological, chemical, gas, nerve* or *nuclear weapons.*

convergence: A once fashionable academic theory, positing that *capitalist* and *communist* societies were growing more alike in response to the shared circumstances of modernity. It did not survive past 1989.

conversations: A diplomatic term referring to exchanges of views and information between governments. Less formal than *negotiations,* they also do not necessarily aim at any agreement. Cf. *Military Conversations.*

convertibility: When a *currency* is freely exchanged for another, according to market *exchange rates.*

convictio juris sive necessitatis: The conviction that a legal duty exists to obey a (specific) *rule.* Note: Only if this applies can a rule be said to derive from *international customary law.*

convoy: When merchant ships in wartime travel in groups, under escort if possible. The convoy system was controversial in *WWI,* but by *WWII* was accepted as the best defense against *submarine* warfare, and used by all seafaring *belligerents.* It worked by lowering the probability that a submarine would spot a merchant ship: 100 ships sailing individually along a known *trade route* present 100 possible instances of making contact with a target; but 100 ships sailing together present only one opportunity. The Germans countered this in WWII by developing the *wolf pack.* The *Allies* then took such *countermeasures* as more *destroyers* and escort *carriers* to seek out submarines.

Cook Islands: Location: S. Pacific. Major associations: *SPC, SPF.* Population: 18,000. Military: none. This island group was made a British *protectorate* in 1888, and after 1901 a *dependency* of New Zealand.

Since 1965 it has been self-governing in *free association* with New Zealand. Note: Not a *UN* or *Commonwealth* member; nor is it *recognized* by Japan as an independent *state*. Yet it has *diplomatic relations* with a dozen other countries, and belongs to several *IGOs*.

Coolidge, Calvin (1872-1933): U.S. President 1923-28. He was a passive administrator in both domestic and foreign affairs. The most significant diplomatic developments came from subordinates: (1) *Frank B. Kellogg*, who signed the *Kellogg-Briand Pact*; and (2) Charles Dawes (1865-1951), who developed the *Dawes Plan*. The Coolidge administration decreased U.S. *intervention* in the Western Hemisphere, and managed to keep out of *civil wars* in three areas where some Americans wanted armed action: China, Mexico and Nicaragua. Opposed to the *League of Nations*, Coolidge yet approved U.S. application to the *World Court*. However, conditions on U.S. *adherence* imposed by Congress proved unacceptable to other states. He called for *disarmament* and sponsored a naval conference in Geneva in 1927, but there was no agreement with Britain on *cruiser* limits. Relations with Japan deteriorated when Congress overrode him and continued *Oriental exclusion laws*.

cooling-off treaties: This was the popular name for some 30 bilateral "Treaties for the Advancement of Peace" negotiated by the U.S. with other nations, Germany being the major exception, during the first term of the *Wilson* administration. Wilson embraced the idea, but even he could not outdo for enthusiasm his ebullient Secretary of State, *William Jennings Bryan*. The first was signed with El Salvador in August 1913. They committed signatories to almost nothing. They asked that on *disputes* involving "national honor" or otherwise not solvable, the case be referred to an *ad hoc* international commission whose recommendation would be non-binding. During a one-year period of investigation neither party was to use *force* to resolve the dispute. Cf. *Root Arbitration Treaties*.

Coordinating Committee (COCOM): Set up in 1949 under U.S. pressure, it coordinated Western *embargoes* of *goods* with *strategic* value to the *Soviet bloc*. This was intended to stall the Soviet Union's military advances, cripple it economically and further isolate it politically. It dissolved in 1994, without immediate agreement on replacing it with a new organization, to include Russia as a member. Cf. *containment*.

Copenhagen, Battles of: (1) April 2, 1801: The *Royal Navy* destroyed the Danish fleet in Copenhagen harbor, ending the threat that *Napoleon I* might revive the *League of Armed Neutrality* to break the *blockade* of

his *Continental System*. (2) September 5-7, 1807: The British bombarded the rebuilt Danish fleet over three days, denying it to Napoleon but thereby confirming Denmark as an enemy power.

Coptic Church: The indigenous Christian church in Egypt. It has a distinctive rite and hierarchy. Copts constitute about 1/7th of the Egyptian population.

Coral Sea: Part of the Pacific between Australia, New Guinea and the Solomons, and site of a U.S. naval victory over Japan in 1942, one of the first for the Americans in *WWII*.

cordon sanitaire: A buffer of small *states* between two large, hostile states or camps. *Clemenceau* proposed that Eastern Europe serve this purpose concerning the Soviet Union, in a metaphor likening *Bolshevism* to a communicable disease, requiring quarantine. In 1993 Russia's policy toward *Central Asia* and the *Caucasus* suggested it sought a cordon sanitaire along its southern border, to contain Islamic *fundamentalism*.

core: In *dependency theory*, the center of the *world capitalist system* whose ruling *elites* are said to benefit from exploitative organization of the global economy. It is sometimes used as a synonym for those elites.

Corfu incident (August 27, 1923): After several Italian officers were shot while on an *observer mission*, Italy occupied the island of Corfu. Greece took the issue to the *League of Nations*, which successfully pressed for Italian withdrawal.

Corfu, Pact of (July 20, 1917): An agreement among *exile* leaders of the south *Slavs* that Croatia, Montenegro, Serbia and Slovenia should unite against Austrian rule, under the Serbian king. It led to *Yugoslavia*.

corporatism: (1) The vague *ideology* of Italian *fascism* that viewed society as an organic whole with mutually reinforcing, functional parts called syndicates or corporates. (2) In political science and Latin American studies in the 1950s-1970s, this was the idea that all significant interest groups were created and controlled by the state.

correlation analysis: The quantified search for associations between a dependent *variable* and an *independent variable*, over time, that may suggest a causal relationship. When more than one independent variable is used the technique is called, prosaically enough, "multiple correlation analysis."

correlation of forces: A Soviet concept akin to, but

wider than, the *balance of power*. It included the role of political, social, economic and morale factors in calculations of relative *power*, and did not just rely on estimates of military balance.

Corsica: A large island in the Mediterranean comprising an offshore province of France. A movement for *secession* has on occasion led to violence. It was the birthplace of *Napoleon*.

Cortés, Hernando (1485-1547): He began Spain's *conquest* of the *Aztec* Empire in Mexico in 1519. One honest *conquistador* of the 550 who accompanied him to *plunder* the halls of Montezuma said: "We came here to serve God and the King, and also to get rich."

cosmopolitan values: Global or universal principles; those belonging to the *world community* ("cosmopolis"), not a specific culture or *state*. See *cultural relativism; human rights; Kant; secularism*.

Cossack(s): (1) Turkic and Slavic horsemen from south Russia who formed the core of tsarist cavalry. (2) A derogatory term meaning an uncouth barbarian.

Costa Rica: Location: Central America. Major associations: *CACM, OAS, UN*. Population: 3 million. Military: none. Conquered by the Spanish in 1502, it gained *independence* in 1821. It joined the Central American Federation, but left that association in 1838. It suffered a brief civil war in 1948-49, but since then has managed to escape the violence that has troubled nearly all its neighbors and to sustain a peaceful democracy. It maintains no permanent military, and poses no threat to its neighbors. It relies on U.S. and perhaps OAS *intervention* for defense. In 1987 President Oscar Arias won the *Nobel Prize* for Peace, for a peace plan he promoted for Central America, which was supported by the *Contadora Group*.

cost/benefit analysis: Any systematic, not necessarily *quantitative*, evaluation of the losses and gains to be had from a given economic or foreign policy.

Côte d'Ivoire: Location: W. Africa. Major associations: *la francophonie, OAU, UN*. Population: 12 million. Military: small, French supported. Formerly the Ivory Coast (the name change was made in 1985). The area was penetrated by Portuguese traders in the 16th century, but became a French *protectorate* in 1842 and a *colony* in 1893. It was briefly joined to *Upper Volta* and part of *French West Africa*, but gained *independence* in 1960. It retained close ties with France under the paternalistic leadership of Félix Houphouët-Boigny (1905-94). It was among the most prosperous and peaceful of post-colonial African states, and one of the most pro-Western. That led it to be seen by some as a model of how Europe might better have *decolonized* Africa. By 1994 its economy was failing, the *CFA* was devalued, but the links to France remained strong.

Council for Asia-Pacific Economic Cooperation (CAPEC): This consultative body was formed in 1989 by the *ASEAN* states, plus Australia, Canada, Japan, South Korea and New Zealand.

Council of Europe: See *European Council*.

Council of Ministers: The organ of the national governments of the *EC*, established in 1958 by the *Treaty of Rome* and connected to the *European Commission* by a consultative Committee. In 1965 France boycotted its meetings for seven months over the *CAP* and the degree of *supranational* control and *integration* within the Community. The main instrument of the Council is *COREPER*. With the *Luxembourg Compromise* the Council began to act more like a real executive, overtaking the Commission. In 1993 it restyled itself an organ of the *EU*.

counterattack: One made in reply to a prior attack.

counterbalance: Supporting the weaker side in a disturbed *balance of power*, in order to reestablish *equilibrium*. Cf. *balancer*.

counterespionage: See *counterintelligence*.

counterforce targeting: Aiming solely at C^3, weapons or troops (which takes highly accurate weapons). Cf. *countervalue targeting*.

counterinsurgency: Political and combat tactics specifically designed for fighting against *guerrillas*.

counterintelligence: Detection, blocking, turning into *double-agents, disinformation* and deliberate deception of an adversary's spies or saboteurs. Many of the same techniques can be used against *terrorists* (or less happily, *dissidents*).

countermeasure: Any *tactic* or *technology* employed in response to enemy tactics or technology. For instance, if an opponent's *BMD* proposed to shoot down missiles with lasers, a simple countermeasure might be to spin the missiles or give them reflective surfaces.

counterpart funds: Local funds given by an *aid* recipient to a *donor nation*, in exchange for *hard currency* aid. Control of such funds may over time give donors a considerable say in a recipient's national economy, through control of large holdings of its *currency*.

Counter Reformation: The Catholic effort to reverse the political and doctrinal changes of the Protestant *Reformation*. Backed by the *Hapsburgs*, it led to destructive, sectarian wars. It climaxed, and ended, with the *Thirty Years' War*. See *ecumenism; Inquisition*.

counter-revolution: Originally a *Bolshevik* concept, it is in effect anything identified by a reigning *communist party* as actively opposing, or just passively countering, the principles or policies it has laid out.

counter trade: A generic term for a variety of exchanges that take place directly, without a transfer of money in return for *goods* or *services*. See *barter*.

countervail: To oppose with equal *force* or *influence*.

countervailing duty: A tax imposed on imported *goods* said (truly or not) to be unfairly advantaged or subsidized by a foreign power as compared to domestic goods (for which *subsidies* are, of course, seen as entirely reasonable and fair).

countervalue targeting: Aiming at population and economic centers that constitute the "social value" of an adversary. This does not require highly accurate weapons, but does ask for blunted moral sensibility. Cf. *counterforce targeting*.

coup d'etat: A sudden strike for power, usually by the military, in which mass violence is avoided by a small group acting to decapitate the old political leadership from the body politic. Coup is the standard short form.

coup de théatre: An unexpected diplomatic or political foray that captures widespread attention and acclaim; e.g., *Nixon's* stunning trip to China (1972); *Sadat's* courageous visit to Israel (1977); *Peres* and *Arafat* shaking hands on *peace* in *Palestine* (1993).

coupling: (1) A synonym for *linkage*. (2) The *NATO* doctrine of linking a Soviet conventional *invasion* of Europe to a *strategic nuclear response*.

Court of St. James: Diplomatic term for the British crown and government, as in the expression "she was appointed Ambassador to the Court of St. James."

covenant: A formal, written agreement among states specifying mutual legal and political obligations. A synonym for *treaty*, but used most often about multilateral arrangements.

Covenant of the League of Nations: That portion of the *Treaty of Versailles* laying out the rules and authority of the *League of Nations*. Its inclusion in the text of the treaty had two deeply unfortunate effects: (1) it alienated Germany from the League by making it appear as an instrument for enforcing the hated peace settlement (which it was, in the eyes of the French at least); and (2) it meant the U.S. never joined the League, after "twelve wilful men" in the Senate blocked *consent* to the Versailles Treaty.

covert action: Concealed, low-level uses of *agents of influence, disinformation* or more rarely, of limited force. See also *overt/covert; secret diplomacy*.

cover-up: To conceal information, scandal or illegal foreign policy actions from public scrutiny.

credibility gap: The distance between *Assured Destruction* and the likelihood an adversary will be deterred from certain actions by what amounts to a threat to commit mutual suicide.

credible threat: One taken seriously by an adversary, because it is believable it will be carried out. This is a critical notion in *deterrence*: if a threat is not credible, it is--by definition--not a deterrent.

Crete: Taken from the Venetians by the *Ottomans* in 1669, and ruled by Egypt from 1824-40, it was made part of Greece in 1913. It was captured by Germany in the first ever paratroop assault, in 1941. In 1945 it reverted to Greece.

Crimea: The peninsula that juts south into the Black Sea. It was part of Russia for centuries, since it was taken from the Crimean *Tartars* by *Catherine II (the Great)* in 1783. The Crimea has served as home base for the *Black Sea Fleet*, except for a period of *demilitarization* following the *Crimean War*. The Tartars were forcibly deported to Siberia by *Stalin* during and after *WWII*. In the 1950s Russia "gave" the Crimea to Ukraine, never considering that Ukraine might one day split from Russia (which it did at the end of 1991). The Tartars began to return from their enforced Siberian exile in the late 1980s to a mixed welcome from Russians and Ukrainians alike. In January 1994, a *secessionist* candidate (Mykola Bagrov) won local elections, and called for reunification with Russia. Crimea has 2.5 million people, of whom 600,000 are ethnic Ukrainians, 300,000 are Tartars and the remaining maority are ethnic Russians.

Crimean War (1853-55): In September 1853, Russia provoked war with the *Ottoman Empire*, proclaiming as its *casus belli* the need to protect Turkey's Christian minority from Muslim persecution. Britain opposed Russia's real design, which was to *partition* parts of Turkey, and *declared war* in March 1854. France followed suit, mainly so *Napoleon III* could ingratiate himself with Britain, and *Piedmont-Sardinia* declared war to ingratiate itself with France. An Anglo/French *invasion* fleet arrived after the Turks had repelled the Russians. In search of a battlefield, it sailed to the *Crimea*. Other than some naval skirmishes in the Baltic, fighting was limited to the Crimean peninsula. *Trench warfare* and *stalemate* proved a precursor to *WWI*, with both sides suffering under awful conditions and worse commanders (the flavor of this contest can be had from Leo Tolstoy's "Sebastopol Stories"). When the Tsar died and Austria, too, threatened to declare war, Russia agreed to terms in February 1856. They included limitation of armaments and the *demilitarization* of the Black Sea (which lasted only 15 years). The war shattered the consensus underlying the *Concert of Europe* and left Russia an embittered and *revisionist* power. *Defeat* also set Russia on a course of internal reform, under *Alexander II*. The impact on Britain and France of their hollow *victory* was rather less: both continued in military complacency, blithely unaware of what was quietly happening in Prussia (military reform and *modernization*) while they frittered away resources on a futile and distant war. The only real winner was Piedmont, and that hardly mattered. Also see *jingoism; Treaty of Paris (1856)*.

crimes against humanity: In a "London Agreement" signed by the major *Allies* in 1945, and in several conventions since *WWII*, certain acts have been defined as crimes against humanity itself. This category is intended to elevate the notion of *human rights* to a new plateau, but by a focus on murderous or other heinous acts against whole *civilian* populations, rather than individuals. It includes: enslavement, extermination, forcible *deportation* and *genocide*. The charge was first made at the *Nuremberg* and *Tokyo war crimes trials*. In 1994 France convicted a WWII *collaborator* on this charge. Cf. *crimes against peace; war crimes*.

crimes against peace: In a "London Agreement" signed by the major *Allies* in 1945, certain acts have been defined as crimes against *peace*. The definition, which was vague and remains controversial, included: "planning, preparation, initiation or waging a *war of aggression*." Since aggression remains ill-defined in law, and because preparations for *self-defense* may look rather similar to preparations for offense, many legal thinkers reject this category. See also the *Nuremberg* and *Tokyo war crimes trials*. Cf. *crimes against humanity; nullem crimen; war crimes*.

crisis: The decisive point in a serious *conflict* between *states*, potentially leading to *war* if pertaining to *security* policy, or to some major change in relations if concerning economic or other non-military conflict. It also represents an opportunity for resolution of the conflict, by focusing attention on it. Cf. *tension*.

crisis management: As the term implies, efforts to control the degree of hostility engendered during a *crisis*, and in particular to abort the tendency toward *escalation*. Theoretical studies of crisis management tend to stress either altering the structure of the confrontation or somehow adjusting the psychology and perceptions of the participants. Critics object that such volatile situations cannot be "managed" by preset schemes, or in accord with a flow chart; they must instead be addressed through creative intuition and *diplomacy*, and great political flexibility.

crisis stability: The assumption that the *balance of terror* is such that neither side has any incentive to use *nuclear weapons*, even in a severe crisis.

Crispi, Francesco (1819-1901): Italian statesman. PM 1887-91, 1893-96. He started Italy on the path of overseas *empire* with the acquisition of *Eritrea*. He then overreached the country's abilities, suffering a humiliating *defeat* at *Adowa* (1896).

critical mass: The amount of enriched uranium or *plutonium* needed to sustain a nuclear chain reaction, and so produce an *atomic bomb*.

Croatia: Location: *Balkans*. Major associations: *CSCE, UN*. Population: 4.8 million (20% Serb; 80% Croat). Military: fighting Serbs in east Croatia, supporting Croats in Bosnia. For 800 years (1102-1918) this largely Roman Catholic area was joined to Hungary, enjoying limited *autonomy* after 1868. In 1917 its exiled leaders signed the *Pact of Corfu* setting in motion the creation of *Yugoslavia*. In 1939 Croat *fascists* led by Ante Pavelic launched a *terrorist* campaign aiming at *secession*. In 1941 they formed a *puppet regime* under *Nazi* authority and commenced atrocities against Serbs, Jews, Muslims and communist *partisans*. Croatia was forced back into Yugoslavia in 1945. On June 25, 1991, it again declared *independence*, but soon faced *war* with its ethnic Serb minority in *Krajiina*, who had the support of Serbia proper. By the end of 1991, 30% of Croatia was in Serb hands, and a so-called "Serb Republic of Croatia" declared in Krajiina. In January 1992, it was *recognized* by the *EC*, at Germany's urging. It then entered the war in next-door Bosnia to protect Croats from Serb *ethnic cleansing*, but also to carve up Bosnia in tacit concert with Serbia. In January 1994, as Bosnian Muslims retook lands seized earlier by Croats, Croatia threatened to intervene with its army; *NATO* warned it not to do so. See *Third Balkan War*.

cruise missile: A guided or remote, air-breathing, pilotless missile that is capable of delivering *conventional* or nuclear *ordnance*. It may be fired from a ship, aircraft or *submarine*. It is not a *ballistic missile*. Instead, it hugs terrain using TV, satellite guidance and inboard computers. Cruise missiles were deployed by *NATO* in the 1980s. They were used against ships in the *Falklands War*, and had a devastating impact on land targets in the *Gulf War* and in punitive attacks against Iraq in 1992-93. See *terrain contour matching*.

cruiser: A medium tonnage and medium-armored *warship*, capable of high speeds and extended tours of duty. A heavy cruiser generally sports eight-inch guns; a light cruiser is mounted with six-inch guns.

cryptology: The science and study of cryptanalysis (all procedures and methods used in code-breaking and analysis of secret writing), and cryptography (all procedures and methods of code-making, *ciphers* and other secret writing).

CSBMs: See *Confidence and Security Building Measures; CSCE*.

CSCE: See *Conference on Security and Cooperation in Europe*.

CSIS: Canadian Security and Intelligence Service. It was set up in the 1980s to take over from the *intelligence* division of the RCMP, which had been discredited by a scandal over illegal operations against *separtists* in *Québec* in the 1970s. It is confined to *counterintelligence,* and even then may not act abroad. Its main focus is counterterrorism.

Cuba: Location: Caribbean. Major associations: *UN*. Population: 10.6 million. Military: very large relative to *population*, but now with outdated *Warsaw Pact* arms and no sure resupply lines; battle-experienced in Africa, and a pillar of the Castro regime. It was charted and claimed for Spain by Christopher Columbus in 1492. Slaves were imported from West Africa to sustain a plantation economy. It remained a *colony* until the *Spanish/American War* in 1898 (with the exception that the British occupied Havana from 1762-63). In 1868 a 10-year uprising against Spanish rule began without exciting U.S. opinion. *Slavery* was abolished in 1886. Another *rebellion* began in 1895, under Jose Marti. By 1898 U.S. opinion favored *intervention*, which was sparked by the sinking of the *Maine* in Havana harbor. The war forced Spain to renounce all claims to Cuba. Cuban *independence* was granted with the proviso that the U.S. retained a right of intervention (the Platt Amendment). U.S. marines accordingly intervened in Cuba in 1906, 1913, 1917 and 1933. In 1934 the U.S. gave up its right to intervene as part of the *Good Neighbor policy*. In 1952 *Fulgencio Batista* seized power. He favored foreign investor (and Mafia) interests, and ran a corrupt administration. In 1956 a rebel, communist uprising began, led by *Fidel Castro* and *Che Guevara*. Batista fled in January 1959. Castro became premier in February, and moved to repress all opposition. In short order, executions began and the count of *political prisoners* rose. He also *nationalized* the economy, mostly without *compensation*. In the next years hundreds of thousands of Cubans fled, settling in nearby Florida, where they formed an important lobby group stiffening U.S. policy toward Cuba. In 1961 *CIA*-trained Cubans landed at the *Bay of Pigs* in an attempt to overthrow Castro, who was steadily moving Cuba into the *Soviet bloc*. In 1962 *Kennedy* imposed a trade *embargo*, severely damaging Cuba's economy (the U.S. was its natural export market), and pushing Castro even closer to the Soviet Union. In October 1962, the *Cuban Missile Crisis* brought the world to the brink of all-out *nuclear war*. In the early 1970s, U.S./Cuban relations remained tense over Castro's support for left-wing guerrillas in South and Central America. In 1975 Cuba sent troops to fight in civil wars in Angola and Mozambique, and in 1977 it helped Ethiopia's *marxist* regime defeat Somalia. In 1977 Cuba and the U.S. established diplomatic contact but did not restore full relations. In the *Mariel boat lift* of 1980, hundreds of thousands of Cubans left for the U.S. In 1983 Cuban military engineers and U.S. troops clashed during the *invasion of Grenada*. Cuba withdrew from Africa when a regional settlement was reached on Namibia, and the *revolution* in Ethiopia collapsed. After 1990, with Soviet aid gone, Castro introduced severe rationing but refused to renounce the *Cuban Revolution* or introduce democratic reforms. An election was held in March 1993, but only Castro's list of candidates was permitted. Note: The U.S. maintains a naval and marine base at *Guantánamo* Bay.

Cuban Missile Crisis (October 1962): U.S. spy planes discovered Soviet nuclear *missile* bases under construction in Cuba. *John F. Kennedy* announced this discovery, imposed a *quarantine* and demanded removal of the missiles. The *crisis* lasted two weeks, and raised global *tensions* over the possibility of *nuclear war* as Soviet ships closed on the U.S. *blockade* line, and U.S. forces prepared to invade Cuba to take out the bases. On several occasions Soviet and U.S.

units were engaged and casualties were incurred, though this was not announced at the time. The crisis was resolved by Soviet agreement to withdraw the missiles in exchange for a public pledge by the U.S. not to invade Cuba, and a secret agreement to remove comparable U.S. missiles from Turkey within six months. In 1990-91 it was suggested that the crisis was even more serious than had been known: a Soviet official said that Russian troops had operational, *tactical nuclear weapons*, and that orders had been issued releasing these to the discretion of the local commander. This implied that had a U.S. *invasion* taken place, it would likely have been met with *nuclear weapons*: use of such weapons within 90 miles of Florida, and against American troops, would likely have required a comparable response, perhaps from Turkey or Europe. However, this claim is under dispute, as it lacks documentary support and appears contrary to the known Soviet practice of tight central control of nuclear firing decisions, especially during a *crisis*.

Cuban Revolution: It began with a 1956 rebel, *communist* rising, led by *Fidel Castro* and *Che Guevara* against the government of *Batista*. When Castro became premier in 1960 the *revolution* moved into a highly repressive stage, and development of a *cult of personality* from which it never really emerged. There was large-scale *nationalization* of the economy and an across-the-board shift to the *Soviet bloc*, in part driven by a U.S. *embargo* and diplomatic hostility. The revolution provided literacy and primary health care to many, surpassing most other states in the region in these areas at least. It firmed up this base of domestic support with tenant reform and land redistribution. But its repressive side never eased, and by the 1990s an aging Castro and stagnating revolution saw increasing opposition, as disintegration of the Soviet bloc ended the huge *subsidies* that for 30 years had artificially sustained the Cuban economy and social welfare system, and thereby, the Castro regime.

culpability: In *international law*, a doctrine whereby responsibility (guilt) is established by reference to intentionality or negligence.

cult of personality: Concentration of political authority in a single individual within a *totalitarian* state, and near-deification of that individual in state *propaganda*. Leaders are portrayed as superhuman in their heroism, knowledge, wisdom or any other virtue called upon by the political needs of the moment or *regime*. This serves to sustain them in power, deter criticism and legitimate whatever policies shifts and twists they feel compelled to make. Among the more infamous and pervasive cults this century: *Hitler, Ho Chi Minh,*

Kim Il Sung, Mao, Mussolini, Pol Pot, Saddam Hussein and *Stalin*.

cultural exchanges: Encouragement or sponsorship of private exchanges of artistic, literary, musical or scientific activities. They may be used to soften respective *public opinion* and enhance a *rapprochement*, or as *propaganda*. See *ping pong diplomacy*.

cultural imperialism: When the values of one *nation* or social system are deliberately imposed on another, e.g., *russification*. Imprecisely, but often, the term is used about a strong and dynamic culture that undermines and threatens to displace a weak or static culture, e.g., *americanization*. It implies a conscious, morally reprehensible policy. Yet, it more often happens without conscious design. In any case, it can provoke *protectionist* policies, such as censorship or *tariffs* against importing cultural goods such as films or mass media. See also *human rights; Uruguay Round*.

cultural relativism: See *relativism*.

cultural revolution: (1) A policy adopted by the *Bolsheviks* from the end of the *New Economic Policy* c.1928 to c.1932, when the deleterious effects of *Stalin's* edicts against the *kulaks* and in favor of forced *collectivization* were evident in the deaths of millions by deportation, execution and *famine*. It signaled a return to the spirit of class warfare that had characterized *war communism*. Failures to meet production quotas were blamed not on the planner who set them too high (Stalin), but on "wreckers," "kulaks," and other supposed enlistees in the army of *counter-revolution*. (2) For the similarly disastrous experience in China, see *Great Proletarian Cultural Revolution*.

curfew: A military or emergency order confining a population to certain zones or hours of public intercourse. A common feature of *occupation*, it may also be used domestically to quell civil unrest or dissent.

Curragh incident: A mass resignation (in effect, a *mutiny*) of British officers in March 1914, in Ireland, when faced with having to use *force* to make *Ulster* accept *Home Rule*. London backed down, and the outbreak of *WWI* rendered the immediate issue moot.

currency: The physical component of a nation's money supply, composed of banknotes and coins, as well as government bonds.

current account: All financial flows resulting from trade in *goods* and *services*, including interest, *profits* and *remittances*. A current account deficit is when exports and financial inflows, from both private and public sources, are exceeded by the value of imports and financial outflows from private and public sources. Cf. *balance of payments.*

Curzon, George (1859-23): Viceroy of India, Foreign Secretary 1919-24. He fought with his PM, *Lloyd George*, and opposed French ambitions to create a separate Rhenish (*Rhineland*) state. He subsequently lent his name to the *Curzon Line.*

Curzon Line: A proposal for settlement of the frontier question between Poland and Russia. It was designed to adhere roughly to principles of *self-determination* by excluding from Poland eastern areas populated by non-Poles. But Poland rejected the proposal, keeping and expanding those *territories* in the *Polish/Soviet War* of 1920. In 1939 the Curzon Line served as the *boundary* between *Nazi Germany* and the *Soviet Union*, after Eastern Europe was divided in the *Nazi/Soviet Pact*. In 1945 it became the border between the new Poland and a greatly expanded Soviet Union.

customary law: See *international customary law.*

customs: Duties, or *excise*, imposed by national governments or by *customs unions* on *imports*; very rarely, duties may be imposed on *exports.*

customs union: An arrangement among *states* that lowers, regulates and "unifies" their *tariffs* vis-à-vis states not in the union. It aims at removal of all barriers to trade between two or more states, in which a common external tariff is kept up against other states. Cf. *free trade area.*

cybernetic theory: A communication and control theory concerned with the comparative study of automatic systems. It was first developed to study neurology and mechanics. By analogy, cybernetic theory is applied to so-called automatic, or routine, though still complex foreign policy decision-making. See *feedback; decision-making theory.*

Cyprus: Location: Mediterranean. Major associations: *Commonwealth, UN.* Population: 710,000 (including 20% who are Turks). Military: the important ties are to Greece and Turkey. In 1571 Cyprus was captured from the Venetians by the Turks, who held it within their *empire* until 1914. It was protected by the British under terms of the *Cyprus Convention* of 1878. When *war* broke out in 1914, Britain took over the island. It was made a Crown Colony in 1925. Greek Cypriots agitated for *enosis*, or union with Greece, an idea opposed by Turkish Cypriots. This was resisted by the

British until after *WWII*, when violence erupted. A compromise was reached among Britain, Greece and Turkey setting up an independent *republic* in 1960, with Archbishop Makarios (leader of the enosis movement) as President, 1960-74. Communal conflict led to a UN *peacekeeping* force in 1964. In July 1974, Greek officers attempted a *coup*, which forced Makarios to flee and sparked an *invasion* by Turkey. Turkish troops occupied its northern half, and in 1975 Turkish Cypriots founded a separate government there. Greeks were expelled from the Turkish side of the *green line* between the communities. Makarios returned to the presidency of the Greek side in 1975, dying in 1977. The *Turkish Republic of Northern Cyprus* declared *independence* in 1983, but it remains a *vassal* of Istanbul and does not enjoy world *recognition.*

Cyprus Convention (1878): By this agreement Britain was permitted to station troops on the *strategic* Mediterranean island of *Cyprus*, then controlled by the *Ottoman Empire*. In exchange, London guaranteed Turkey from Russian attack.

czar: "Caesar." An archaic spelling of *tsar.*

Czech Legion: A military force of volunteer *POWs* organized by *Tómaš Masaryk* in 1917. It was trapped in Russia by the *Bolshevik Revolution*, then became embroiled in the *Russian Civil War* as it tried to fight its way out via *Siberia*. One of the declared purposes of the *Siberian intervention* was to rescue this corp of some 70,000 former allies from *WWI.*

Czechoslovakia: Location: Central Europe. Bohemia, Moravia and Slovakia were parts of the *Austrian Empire* for centuries, but in modern form this country only appeared in 1918 with the collapse of Austria in *WWI*. Led by *Tómaš Masaryk* and *Eduard Beneš*, this civilized, democratic *republic* joined the *Little Entente*. It also sought security guarantees from the Western democracies as Nazi agitators stirred *secessionist* sentiment in the ethnically German *Sudetenland*. At the *Munich Conference* in September 1938, to which Czechoslovakia was not invited, the Sudetenland was awarded to Germany by France, Britain and Italy. *Hitler* rolled over the rump of the country in March 1939. It was split into *fascist, puppet states*, 1940-45. The *Red Army* arrived in 1944, and Beneš returned as President. In 1946 he appointed a communist PM, *Klement Gottwald*. In February 1948, a communist *coup* forced Beneš to resign, to be replaced by Gottwald, a harsh *Stalinist* who brought the country fully into the *Soviet bloc*. In 1968 the *Prague Spring* swept through the country, now headed by *Dubček*. But the Soviet Union and four *Warsaw Pact* armies (from

Bulgaria, East Germany, Hungary and Poland) crushed the reforms. In 1977 *human rights* campaigners founded *Charter '77*; also crushed. The 1989 *velvet revolution* forced the communists out and led to restoration of democracy in 1990. Human rights activist *Václav Havel* became President. After the fall of the communists regional differences appeared between Czechs and Slovaks over the speed of adjusting to a *market* economy, as most of the old, Soviet-style heavy industries were concentrated in Slovakia. By agreement, the federation suffered *extinction* (a "velvet divorce") with the turn of the year to 1993, breaking into the *Czech Republic* and *Slovakia*.

Czech Republic: Location: E. Europe. Major associations: *CSCE, UN*. Population: 10.5 million. Military: small. Formerly a province of the *Austro-Hungarian*

Empire, after *WWI* it was the lead part of *Czechoslovakia*. After the fall of the communists in Czechoslovakia regional differences appeared between Czechs and Slovaks over the speed of adjusting to a *market economy*. The Czechs wanted to move faster with basic reforms, while in Slovakia a revived ethnic spirit was stoked by newly-elected, conservative leaders. The modern Czech republic came into being simultaneously with *Slovakia* at the stroke of midnight on December 31, 1992, with the *extinction* of Czechoslovakia. *Václav Havel* took office as republic President with promises of rapid conversion to market economics and closer ties to the West. The Czech republic immediately applied for the *partnerships for peace* program of *NATO,* and to the *EU.* The gap between its rapidly reforming economy and Slovakia's more sluggish efforts widened in 1994.

D

Dachau: A *death camp* just outside Munich. Inhabitants of that city claimed they knew nothing about what had gone on in Dachau. After its *liberation* in 1945 the *Allies* ordered Germans walked through, so they could never deny what had been done within range of the spring breezes that carried the stench of the dead to their homes. Cf. *Auschwitz; Holocaust.*

Dahomey: Former name of Benin.

daimyo: The feudal lords of Japan. As a class, they were effectively eliminated during the *Meiji* period.

Daladier, Édouard (1884-1970): Premier of France 1933, 1934, 1938-40. He played second fiddle to *Chamberlain's* lead at the *Munich Conference,* supporting *appeasement,* though without the same public enthusiasm. In 1942 he, *Léon Blum* and General Gamelin were put on trial by *Vichy* for alleged treasonable responsibility for the *defeat* of France. The trial was cancelled when Blum turned it into a showcase against Vichy's own extensive *collaboration.*

Dalai Lama: The title of the religious leaders of Tibet, from the 17th century until a failed revolt against Chinese rule in 1959, when the current Dalai Lama was forced into *exile*. The reigning Dalai Lama is the fourteenth (b.1935). He works to keep Tibet's case before world opinion. He won the *Nobel Prize* for Peace in 1989. At the *World Human Rights Conference* (1993), China prevented him from addressing official sessions, though in a compromise he spoke to *NGO* delegates.

Dalhousie, James (1812-60): Viceroy of India 1847-56. He was an active imperialist, conquering the *Punjab* and annexing several *Princely States.* He also built irrigation canals and the telegraph system, and moved against female infanticide, suttee, the thuggee and the *slave trade.* The year after his departure, the *Indian Mutiny* took place, partly in reaction against his reforms. In 1858 *direct rule* was instituted.

damage: Injury suffered through the *illegal act* of another state, for which *damages* may be exacted.

damage limitation: (1) In *warfare*: efforts to reduce the operational impact of enemy fire by using *preemptive strikes* and *active defense* measures. (2) In *statecraft*: efforts to reduce the harm to policy or the impact on *public opinion* of an opponent's actions, or one's own mistakes (say, by blaming a subordinate).

damages: Compensation for *damage.* See *ne judex.*

Daman: See *Portuguese India.*

Danton, George Jaques (1759-94): *Jacobin* leader. A major figure in the *French Revolution,* he voted to execute *Louis XVI,* and as head of the Jacobin Club repressed the *Girondins* during the *Terror.* When he moved toward reconciliation, he fell out of favor with *Robespierre,* who had him guillotined.

D'Annunzio, Gabriele (1863-1938): Italian nationalist. He urged *war* against Austria in 1915, and was wounded when war came. In 1919 he led a handful of *fanatics* in the seizure of *Fiume*. He held the city for a year, in spite of the opposition of the *Allies*. Fiume was long coveted by Italian nationalists but was not ceded to Italy as hoped for at the *Paris Peace Conference*, causing the Italians to storm out of the conference in April 1919. *Mussolini* learned much from D'Annunzio's tactics, and shared his contempt for the Western democracies. See also *mutilated victory*.

Danubian principalities: Moldavia and Wallachia, which stand astride the *strategic* mouth of the Danube River. Russia tried to make them a *protectorate* in 1856, but they were instead given a joint guarantee of *autonomy* by the *Great Powers* in the *Treaty of Paris (1856)*. In 1858 they formed *Rumania*, though still within the *Ottoman Empire*. Outright *independence* was granted in 1877, and confirmed at the *Congress of Berlin*. See *Eastern Question*.

Danzig (Gdansk), Free City of: This German town, once a center of the *Hanseatic League*, was obtained by Prussia at the *Congress of Vienna*. It was declared a *free city* at the *Paris Peace Conference* in 1919, under administration of a commissioner appointed by the *League of Nations*. Poland was placed in charge of *foreign policy, customs* and *exports*, and gained access to the sea through the *Polish Corridor*. German/Polish relations suffered over Danzig, especially when local *Nazis* agitated for reunion with Germany. On September 1, 1939, Germany attacked Poland, ostensibly to free the "persecuted" population of Danzig. In 1945 Danzig reverted to Poland, which was itself moved northwest by the Soviets, and the German population was expelled. Renamed Gdansk, in the 1980s it was the center of dissent and the *Solidarity* movement.

Dar al-Harb: "Area of War." In *Islam*, all *territory* not occupied or ruled by Muslims. The implication is that in the fullness of time, it will be. The idea dates to the era of militant Islamic expansion a millennium ago, and should not be mistaken for a present-day threat to non-Muslims, except in rare instances.

Dar al-Islam: "Area of the Faithful (Submission)." In *Islam*, all *territory* occupied or ruled by Muslims.

Dardanelles: The narrow channel that links the Aegean with the Sea of Marmara, and via the *Bosphorus*, connects to the Black Sea. Its status within the tottering *Ottoman Empire* was a major *geopolitical* question of the 19th century. Britain kept Russia from passage to the Mediterranean through the Dardanelles, but used them itself during the *Crimean War*. Other times, Turkey denied passage to Britain. During *WWI*,

Allied failure to get past Turkish defenses led to the disaster at *Gallipoli*. Russia gained the right to send *warships* through in the *Montreux Convention* of 1936. During the *Cold War*, the regular passage of the Soviet *Black Sea Fleet* was monitored by *NATO*. Since 1989, they have declined in geopolitical, but not in economic, importance. Cf. *Straits Question*.

Darlan, Jean Louis (1881-1942): French admiral and *Vichy* leader in Algeria. A willing *collaborator* with *Nazi Germany*, he was in Algiers when Anglo/American forces landed in 1942. He ordered French troops to fire on the invaders, but they had not the stomach for more than brief resistance, and many went over to the *Allied* side. Darlan traded a *cease-fire* for recognition of his authority over Algeria. Shortly after that he was assassinated (which rendered his ambitions moot).

dark continent: Africa to the 19th century; so-called by Europeans as they knew so little about it (which raises the question of who was more in the dark).

Davis, Jefferson (1808-89): He was the only President of the *Confederacy*, 1861-65. Vain and meddlesome in military affairs, his *diplomacy* was based on disastrous, romantic delusions such as the idea of *King Cotton*. He lived in quiet retirement for a quarter century after the end of the *American Civil War*.

Dawes Plan (1924): Drafted by Charles Dawes (1865-1951), it stabilized Germany's runaway economy by developing a reasonable schedule for it to meet *reparations* obligations after *WWI*, and authorizing large private loans from 1924-29. It set in motion a recycling of reparations dollars from Germany to Britain and France, to America in the form of *war debts* payments, then back to Germany as loans.

Dayan, Moshe (1915-81): Israeli soldier. Chief-of-Staff 1953-58; Agriculture Minister 1959-64; Defense Minister 1967-74; Foreign Minister 1977-79. He gained much of the credit for the success of Israeli arms in 1967, when he was the main advocate of a *preemptive strike*. However, in the lead-up to the *Fourth Arab/Israeli War* he made dangerously impolitic remarks about how Israel would remain on the *West Bank* forever, and that helped solidify an Arab front favoring *war*.

D-day: (1) Any specific date set for launch of a military operation. (2) June 6, 1944, when the Western *Allies* secured a beachhead in Normandy and began their *invasion* of Europe; that ended with *defeat* of Nazi Germany 11 months later, and a linkup with the *Red Army* in the center of Germany and Europe.

dead letter drop: In *intelligence*, a site for exchanging messages where those doing so do not meet and cannot be easily compromised.

death camps: The network of extermination and *slavery* camps set up by the Nazis during *WWII*, whose purpose was to kill all the Jews of Europe and Russia. The most infamous was *Auschwitz*. See *anti-Semitism; concentration camp; Dachau; Holocaust.*

death squad: *Paramilitary* units, often associated with or directly tied to security forces, whose task is elimination of the *regime's* political opponents. The term became current during the *dirty war* in Argentina, was used in El Salvador and elsewhere in Central America in the 1980s, and is now generally applied to this phenomenon, wherever it appears.

Debayle, Anastasio Somoza (1928-80): Nicaraguan dictator. Son of *Anastasio Somoza*. President 1967-72, 1974-79. He inherited his father's National Guard while his older brother, Luis, became President. When Luis Somoza died in 1967 Debayle won a rigged election (his family was well practiced at that). His regime was so corrupt that even international, earthquake relief funds were pirated to personal use. By 1979 his army and National Guard were defeated by the *Sandinistas*, and he fled. He was assassinated in Paraguay in September 1980.

debellatio: Elimination of an *international personality* by the utter destruction of its machinery of state.

debrief: In *intelligence*, close scrutiny of the account of actions and recollections of an *agent*, or *defector*.

debt: The total money owed by a given state to foreign lenders, whether private banks, international banks or other governments. Cf. *debt service.*

debt crisis: Unprecedented levels of *Third World* (and other) foreign *debt* reached by the 1980s. It followed *OPEC* price increases (1973, 1979) and commodity price falls, which led to massive borrowing to finance *development* plans or to continue consumer *subsidies* and social welfare spending. That was attended by a rising inability of *G-77* and other nations to meet *det service* obligations. See also *IMF; scissors crisis.*

debt-equity swaps: Exchanging bank *debt* for equity investment in the local *currency*, with government guarantees. This permits a bank to reduce exposure to possible bad debt, and even convert it into a valuable local asset. The *debtor nation* lowers its overall debt load, and obtains needed investment.

debt fatigue: The process whereby continuing austerity programs designed to reduce *debt* create political, social and popular resistance. It may result in unilateral suspension of *debt service* payments, as happened in 1987 when Brazil and a number of smaller countries announced a *moratorium* on payments. The U.S. and other Western governments put heavy pressure on Brazil to resume payment, and the banks refused to yield. The moratorium ended with a *debt rescheduling* agreement.

debtor cartel: Much debated but never tried, this is the notion that *debtor nations* should simultaneously announce a *moratorium* on *debt service* payments, to extract better financing terms or partial loan forgiveness from creditors.

debtor nation: A country that is in *debt* to foreign governments and/or private or international banks.

debt rescheduling/restructuring: When a *debtor nation* and foreign lenders agree to renegotiate existing loans, to draw out the repayment schedule, reduce interest charges or both.

debt service: The total principal and interest owed on borrowed funds, to be paid over a year; not total *debt*. The "debt service ratio" is the amount of *export* earnings that must go simply to service the debt.

Decembrist revolt: An attempted *coup* in Russia by young, liberal army officers, upon the *accession* of Tsar *Nicholas I* in 1825. It was crushed. Some executions followed.

decision-maker: (1) Any person with the final say in formulating or implementing foreign policy: the *head of government* and his or her staff, and relevant *cabinet* officers and senior bureaucratic officials. (2) Any person with the final say in formulating or implementing policy decisions for any major *actor* in international relations, including *international organizations* and/or private concerns such as *MNCs*.

decision-making theory: An alternative form of analysis that focuses on individual *decision-makers*. It is mainly interested in the subjective concerns of decision-makers, as primary causes of the decisions taken. It argues that the objective reality within which decisions are made may not be correctly, or even at all, perceived by the statesman, and thus has lesser explanatory value than a tight focus on the internal dynamics of decision-making. Cf. *bureaucratic politics; cognitive dissonance; cybernetic theory; game theory; groupthink; ideology; image; instrumental rationality;*

misperception; pluralism; SOPs; organizational process model; rational actor model.

decision theory: A branch of mathematics concerned with optimal choices where, unlike in *game theory* situations, outcomes of decisions do not depend on the choices of other players, but on *exogenous* factors determined by probabilities.

declaration: A non-binding statement of policy or intent by one or more states. Even when *multilateral* these have, at most, quasi-legislative authority under *international law.* For instance, the *Universal Declaration of Human Rights* is seen by some legal scholars as having gained standing in *international customary law* since its adoption in 1948, but others insist it remains non-binding. Cf. *resolution; treaty.*

declaration of war: A formal act (under the *Hague Convention III* of 1907) by which one *state* opens *armed hostilities* with another, and claims the rights and privileges of a *belligerent* power. As surprise and *blitzkrieg* can decide *victory* quickly, and *aggression* has been made illegal this century, declarations of war are now seldom issued; or they are held back until after the first surprise attack has been made. For example, Japan struck thrice without a declaration of war: against Russia in 1904, China in 1937 and the U.S. in 1941; and Germany attacked Poland in 1939 and the Soviet Union in 1941 without warning. Since 1945, no war has begun with a formal declaration.

Declaration on Liberated Europe: A promise of free elections to be held in *Eastern Europe* after *WWII,* signed at the *Yalta Conference.* It was highly controversial during the *Cold War,* with charges made that the Soviets had wilfully violated it, and on the hard right, that *Roosevelt* and *Churchill* had somehow "sold out" Eastern Europe (were guilty of *appeasement*).

decline of the West: (1) An argument of Oswald Spengler (1880-1936) in a 1922 book of that title, arguing that democracy was decadent and for the overthrow of the *Weimar Republic.* (2) A recurring motif among intellectuals and social critics who mistake contemporary manifestations of the usual quota of human greed, venality and ignorance as signs of the terminal cultural illness of Western civilization.

decolonization: (1) Shedding one's colonial possessions. (2) When a *colony* becomes *independent* after a period of rule by a foreign power. The important North American colonies were let go by Britain in 1783; Latin America broke free of Spain and Portugal 1810-25. Africa and Asia were mostly decolonized

after *WWII.* Britain, Belgium and the Netherlands departed with varying degrees of ease, if not grace. France had difficulty adjusting to loss of *empire,* and tried to return by *force* in *Indochina* until 1954, and to hang on in Algeria until 1962. Portugal clung to empire the longest. Only after its *revolution* in 1974 were its colonies freed; several collapsed into immediate *civil war.* The end of the Soviet/Russian empire has largely completed the decolonization process. However, new, smaller and more informal imperial formations may well be in the offing (such as *Greater Serbia, Greater Syria* or the *near abroad*). See *mandated territories; neo-colonialism; self-determination.*

decommission: To retire, say a *warship* or an *officer.*

deepening vs. enlargement (widening): The perennial question facing the *EC,* and now the *EU*: should it concentrate on advancing *integration* of existing members in all its aspects (deepening, as in *Maastricht*), or add new members even beyond *les petite riches* (widening)? Reunification of Germany is seen by some as requiring widening to balance the Community. The current "solution" is a Europe of concentric rings: the EU states, other (non-EU) *EEA* states, and dependent east European economies.

de-escalation: Reducing *tensions* or military readiness; winding a *crisis* or *conflict* down, level by level.

de facto: "In fact." (1) Existing regardless of legal status, and even especially if unlawful. (2) *Recognition* granted to a regime that exists in fact, by virtue of its control of a given *territory. De jure* recognition may, or may not, follow. See *sovereignty.*

default: Failing or refusing to meet one's foreign *debt* repayment schedule. Most defaults are temporary, pending negotiations on *debt rescheduling.* See *Drago Doctrine.* Cf. *debtor cartel.*

defeat, in war: When one is compelled to concede an opponent's physical (military) superiority by *asking for terms,* with the consequence that one's interests in the *dispute(s)* occasioning the *war* are harmed while one's opponent makes gains. Most defeats are partial and relative (e.g., Germany in *WWI*), though some are absolute (e.g., Germany in *WWII*). In general, a decisive defeat is the more likely to discourage efforts to revise the status quo, by clarifying for all participants the realities of their relative *power.* A partial defeat may accomplish that, but can also stimulate *revanchism.* Thus, criticism of the putative harshness of the *Treaty of Versailles* (compared with the rehabilitation of Germany and Japan after WWII) likely mistakes *cause* and *effect*. That *treaty* was, in fact, relatively temperate (especially as compared to the *diktat* Germany imposed on Russia at *Brest-Litovsk*). Instead, it was the absence of an awareness of defeat within Germany that provoked subsequent demands for revision. Similarly, in addition to the rehabilitation of the *Axis* states after 1945 it was their absolute defeat and deliberate *occupation* that smothered all yearning for a military revision of the status quo, and turned those nations away from their imperial paths. Liberal-capitalist institutions and prosperity then held out a positive alternative, while the Soviets posed an altogether different, and less attractive, choice. Cf. *victory*.

defeatism: A pervasive attitude of pessimism and anticipation of inevitable *defeat*. It can seriously undermine *national morale*. See *Maginot spirit*.

defection: (1) From *game theory*: the notion that it may be the most rational choice for a *state* to "defect" from cooperation and go it alone, rather than take the chance that another player will be the first to defect. It has some implications for the idea of a *security dilemma*. (2) In *intelligence*: asking for *asylum* in exchange for being *debriefed* on all one knows about an adversary's operations.

defector: A person who abandons the cause of one country to embrace another (or just for money or from spleen), and who asks for *asylum*. Defectors are a constant, if minor, feature of world affairs.

defense: (1) Resistance, or all measures taken in preparedness to resist or preempt, a real or anticipated attack. (2) Weapons procurement and deployment, *logistics*, research, training, military *intelligence*, and all other aspects of *war planning*.

defense area: That part of the *high seas* that a *belligerent* declares out-of-bounds to *neutral* shipping.

defense-in-depth: Establishing several defensive lines rather than one, to blunt, absorb and weaken an enemy's advance.

Defense Planning Committee (DPC): Founded with *NATO* in 1949, it meets weekly to discuss Alliance business. Unlike the *North Atlantic Council*, which includes all members, France did not participate in the DPC after formal withdrawal from the military side of NATO in 1966. However, in 1993 it began attending to discuss NATO's role in regional *peacekeeping*.

defense spending: The portion of a national budget allocated to military expenditures.

deficit spending: When a government's total annual expenditures exceed total revenues. Cf. *current account deficit*.

defilade: Shielding a position from enemy view, either by using natural cover or *camouflage*.

deflation: A decline in prices, related to a contraction of the money supply and reduced credit. Cf. *inflation*.

deforestation: Denuding an area of its trees and other vegetative covering. It is a contributing cause of the advance of deserts, soil erosion, destruction of coastal fisheries and extinction of many species. See *Sahel*.

De Gaulle, Charles André (1890-1970): French general, war theorist, *resistance* leader, *statesman* and President 1958-69. He developed a theory of tank tactics in the *interwar years* that was ignored by his superiors but studied closely by German *Panzer* commanders such as *Guderian*. His was one of the few units to advance against the Germans during the battle for France in May/June 1940. Refusing to accept defeat or *Vichy*, he fell back to Britain and called French patriots to rally to his *Free French* movement. A prickly personality at best, he got on badly with *Churchill* and worse with *Roosevelt*, who froze him out of the North African landing in Algeria in 1942. After patching relations, he received *Allied* support and entered Paris a day after it was retaken by Free French forces in 1944. He then led a *provisional government*. But he was thought by many to have a strong *authoritarian* streak, and was forced to withdraw from the political sidelines. The parliamentary chaos of the *Fourth Republic*, and the war in *Algeria*, led to his return to politics in 1958. He wrote the constitution of the *Fifth Republic*, and ruled for the next decade. His decision to accept Algerian *independence* in 1962 led to several assassination attempts by the *Organization de l'armée secrèt (OAS)*. He sought a "third way" for France and Europe between Moscow and Washington, looking to a Paris/Bonn political axis and an independent French nuclear force to help provide it. He distanced France from *NATO's* military wing, but cooperated at other levels. He twice vetoed Britain's membership in the *EC*: fearing a rival, he argued that Britain was not really committed to Europe, and that it might act as a "Trojan Horse" for the U.S. He put his presidency on the line in a *referendum* in 1968, after student riots and labor unrest. When he lost, he resigned. In his principled actions during *WWII* he rescued a measure of honor for France from the sting of *defeat* and the shame of *collaboration*. Afterward, he guided it through a painful *decolonization*, and may well have saved it from dictatorship and perhaps even *civil war*.

de jure: "By right." (1) According to law. (2) In *recognition*, when a *state* is given status as a *subject of international law* with which *diplomatic relations* are instituted. Cf. *de facto; sovereignty.*

de Klerk, Fredrik Willem (b.1936): South African statesman. President 1989- . He dismantled *apartheid*, thereby ending *sanctions* against South Africa. He released *Nelson Mandela* in 1990, unbanned the *ANC*, opened multiparty and multiracial talks, and agreed to free elections, held in 1994. He was awarded the *Nobel Prize* for Peace, jointly with Mandela. In 1994 he became a deputy PM in Mandela's unity government.

Delcassé, Théophile (1852-1923): French statesman, Foreign Minister 1898-1905, 1914-15; Naval Minister 1913-15. He promoted *rapprochement* with Britain over disputes in Africa, leading to the *Entente Cordiale* and a fresh focus on the problem of Germany. He was forced out of office during the *First Moroccan Crisis* (1905). He helped bribe Italy away from the *Central Powers* into the *Triple Entente.*

Delhi: Capital of the Mogul Empire in India; administrative seat of the British *Raj*, 1912-29.

delict: A breach or offense against *international law.*

démarche: In *diplomacy*, some major change in policy or course of action requiring a significant effort to alter international views and (or) domestic opinion.

demilitarize: (1) To place a country under *civilian* control. (2) To remove all weapons, troops and military infrastructure from an agreed area. See *DMZ.*

demilitarized zone (DMZ): An area where no *state* is permitted to keep military equipment or perform military operations. Cf. *buffer zone.*

demobilization: Disbanding an army (usually of *conscripts*) after a *war* has been won, or lost.

democracy: Government through elected representatives, based upon the theory of *popular sovereignty* and reinforced with *liberal* notions of the *human rights* of individuals and citizens. Along with *fascism* and *communism*, democracy has been one the central ideas at contest in the great ideological wars of the 20th century. Cf. *end of history; liberalism; liberal-internationalism; majority rule.*

Democracy Wall: In 1957, 1978 and again in 1988, Beijing students posted criticisms of the Chinese *Communist Party* on a "democracy wall." In all instances,

after a brief and confused tolerance the government moved to repress this free expression. The most bloody scene was at *Tiananmen Square.*

democratic centralism: In *marxism-leninism*, concentration of power in the hands of the top party leadership. It worked by permitting discussion of options until a decision was taken, after which no dissent was tolerated. It was a term used by *Lenin* and his successors to conceal from the more naïve in the party the reality of collective dictatorship.

democratic deficit: The perceived gap between elected representation in the *European Parliament* and actual decision-making by non-elected officials within the *European Community*. It has narrowed somewhat with the creation of the *European Union.*

Democratic Party: Founded by *Thomas Jefferson*, until 1830 it was known as the Republican Democrats, when it was given a populist twist by *Andrew Jackson*. It split in 1854 over the issue of *slavery*, opening the middle for the 1860 victory by the new *Republican Party* led by *Abraham Lincoln*. Identified with slavery and the south, the Democrats were kept out of office until 1884. *Woodrow Wilson* put his stamp on the party before and during *WWI*. Yet it was *Franklin Roosevelt* who made over the modern party, sweeping into power in response to the *Great Depression* and holding the presidency for an unprecedented four terms. Since the *Truman* years, the party has usually enjoyed majorities in both houses of Congress but has had trouble with the presidency. After taking the U.S. into the *Vietnam War* under *Kennedy* and *Johnson*, it split profoundly over that war. It retook the White House in 1976 with *Carter*, when the Republicans were hobbled by a messy endgame in Vietnam and by the *Watergate scandal*. Out of power for the 1980s, *William Clinton* won the presidency in 1992. That was only the second Democratic win in seven elections.

democratize: To cause to take on the values and characteristics of democracy, such as was accomplished through *Allied* occupation and administration of Austria, Italy, Japan and *West Germany* after *WWII.*

demography: The study of *population* patterns, with special regard for national cycles of births and deaths. Cf. *Malthus.*

demonetize: (1) To divest a monetary standard of its value. (2) To reduce the available supply of money.

denationalize: To return to private hands a property or enterprise previously controlled by the state.

denaturalize: To revoke *citizenship* previously given to a *naturalized* (as opposed to native-born) subject.

Deng Xiaoping (b.1904): Chinese communist leader and statesman. A veteran of the *Long March*, he was *purged* in the *Cultural Revolution* (also, his son was thrown from a window by *Red Guards* and paralyzed for life). Deng was later *rehabilitated*. Purged again in 1976, he was again rehabilitated and by 1978 he was first-among-equals within the leadership. He moved to take China off the careening course it endured under the tiller hand of the "Great Helmsman," *Mao Zedong*. Deng launched a drive for *four modernizations* of Chinese national life, encountering conservative resistance at every turn. He apparently agreed to crush the student movement in 1988 at *Tiananmen Square*. Still, by 1993 Deng had more truly revolutionized Chinese life and society than perhaps anyone in its long history. The changes he promoted were a new openness to market forces and foreign trade, and acceptance of considerable decentralization in economic affairs (with political decentralization implicit in the process).

Denmark: Location: W. Europe. Major associations: *CSCE, EU, NATO, Nordic Council, OECD, UN*. Population: 5.2 million. Military: small, but NATO proficient. Originally a Viking state, as late as the 17th century it controlled parts of Norway, Sweden and north Germany. It was pounded by the British at the *Battles of Copenhagen*. A French *ally* in the *Napoleonic Wars*, in 1815 it lost Norway and its German possessions. It tried to reclaim *Schleswig-Holstein* in a *war* with neighboring German states in 1848-49. Bismarck forced Denmark to forfeit its claim in a sharp war in 1864. Neutral in *WWI*, it was awarded the northern part of Schleswig in 1920, after a *plebiscite*. Germany invaded and occupied Denmark from 1940-45. King Christian X (1870-1947), to his lasting credit, defied *Nazi* orders to round up Danish Jews and refused *collaboration* with the *occupation*. Many Danes followed his lead and hid the majority of the small Jewish community from the *Gestapo*. In 1944 Iceland declared *independence*, under Anglo/U.S. pressure (it was being used as a major *Allied* naval base). Denmark was a charter member of NATO. After joining the *EFTA* in 1960, it became a full member of the *EC* in 1973. It incorporated Greenland (now *Kalaallit Nunaat*) directly under its constitution in 1953, but granted it *Home Rule* in 1979. It shook Europe in 1992, when a *referendum* turned down *Maastricht*. In another referendum in May 1993, it voted to approve the treaty, sparking anti-EU riots in Copenhagen.

dense pack: Placing *nuclear*-tipped *missiles* in clusters (which is cheap, but makes them vulnerable),

rather than using a wide dispersal pattern (which is costly, but safer). Cf. *fratricide*.

denuclearization: See *Nuclear Weapons Free Zones*.

Department of Defense (DOD): The U.S. department headed by the Secretary of Defense. It commands the Air Force, Army, Marines and Navy, and is headquartered in the *Pentagon*. It is responsible for all matters relating to defense, including procurement and *war-planning*; until *WWII* called the "War Department."

Department of State: The U.S. federal bureaucracy headed by the Secretary of State, responsible for formulating and implementing *foreign policy*. In fact, its policy suggestions must compete with a wide range of other bureaucratic and political centers of power, such as the president's top advisers, *Congress*, the *Treasury, Defense*, the *National Security Council*, foreign lobbyists, and the personal contacts and political cronies of all the above.

Department of the Treasury: The arm of the U.S. Federal government headed by the Secretary of the Treasury that controls collection, management and distribution of federal revenues. See *secret service*.

dependence: In general, high *vulnerability* to decisions, policies, interests, markets, and so forth in other countries. Cf. *dependency; dependency theory*.

dependency: (1) Territorial: a weak area subject to rule by a foreign power. (2) Economic: a condition in which key decisions affecting weak national economies are made in foreign capitals and/or financial markets. (3) In *dependency theory*: the condition described in #2 is said to be a product of *imperialism*, and unredeemable and unreformable as long as weak societies remain tied to the *world capitalist system*.

dependency theory: In this view of the *international system, states* are not primary. The nature and operations of the *world capitalist system* are the focus of analysis. Moreover, the world is divided not into *blocs, alliances* or regions, but into *core, semiperiphery*, and *periphery*. The central concern is identification of the interests and operations of a global capitalist class, and efforts by the periphery to break free of the *exploitation* of its resources and *labor* by dominant *elites* controlling the core and local elites cooperating with the system. The capitalist system is said to be so corrupt, exploitative and inherently unfair that it is beyond reform, and the advice of dependency theorists has been alternately withdrawal from the system or its overthrow. These premises gained currency during the 1960s (when the notion of economic dependence was effectively juxtaposed with the more recent achievement of political *independence* throughout the *Third World* via *decolonization*). By the 1990s most southern states that once operated by the firefly glow of dependency theory abandoned it in favor of seeking access to global markets, *capital* and *technology*. See *autarky; comprador class; dependent development; development; MNC/MNE; neo-colonialism; neo-imperialism; reformism; self-sufficiency; semiperiphery; underdevelopment; uneven development.* Cf. *barter; COMECON; imperialism; post-imperialism.*

dependent development: The idea that *industrialization* and *modernization* of sectoral areas within economies in the *South* have the net effect of increasing economic and political dependence on the *North*.

dependent state: One submitting to the legal control of another state. See *dependency; protectorate.*

dependent variable: A phenomenon to be explained, the value of which is discovered by analysis of the role of *independent* and *intervening variables*. More simply, it is the *effect* for which one looks to find primary and secondary *causes*. See *causation.*

deportation: (1) Expulsion of undesirable *alien*, criminal or other persons, with or without due process of law. (2) Forcible transfers of whole populations. Cf. *collectivization; ethnic cleansing; repatriation; Stalin.*

deportee: A person already, or due to be, deported.

depreciation: A fall in the worth of fixed assets.

depredation: Laying waste, *plundering*, ravaging and killing; the general atmosphere in which *war crimes* or other atrocities take place.

depression: A severe, extended decline in economic activity, rates of production and investment, and a severe contraction of credit. This leads to corresponding rises in unemployment and bankruptcies.

depressions, world: (1) 1873-96: A severe downturn in finance, trade, prices and *labor* markets, felt most keenly in Britain, but also affecting France, Germany, Russia, the U.S. and the smaller trading nations. (2) 1929-39, the "Great Depression." Its effects were felt in all economic subfields and all countries, but most disastrously in Germany. Unemployment levels soared (reaching 17 million in the U.S. alone), prices severely contracted, banks collapsed, farm income plummeted and world trade fell off sharply. It soured relations among trading nations, including the industrial democracies. There were mutually debilitating quarrels over *reparations, war debts, tariff* policy and closing of markets. It radicalized politics everywhere to some degree, and in key countries such as Germany it was closely related to the rise of *fascism*.

depth charge: An explosive dropped overboard by a surface ship to concuss and otherwise damage, surface or sink a *submarine*. Today, some are nuclear.

deregulation: Cutting back on bureaucratic and legislative oversight of economic activity. This trend began in the 1980s, markedly so in the U.S. and Britain, then spread and continued into the 1990s as numerous governments sought to free market forces from central controls. Cf. *free trade; GATT; protectionism.*

dereliction: Abandoning legal title to a *territory.*

derogation: Declaring a *reservation* on a clause of a *treaty* (if permitted), so that signature and *ratification* of the whole treaty may proceed without a state being bound or blocked by that one clause.

desaparacidos: "Disappeared ones." First used about unaccounted-for victims of the *dirty war* in Argentina, the term has currency beyond Latin America as a marker of suspected victims of *death squads.*

desertification: The expansion of desert at the expense of grasslands or other *ecosystems* better able to sustain *agriculture* and human and animal settlement. It is both a naturally occuring phenomenon, and one abetted by human activity (modern mechanized farming, traditional *slash and burn* land clearance, *overpopulation*, using sparse trees as firewood and so forth). This is a major problem in Africa, especially.

desk officer: Within most *foreign services*, an official in charge of coordinating policy and information toward a specific country or region, or overseeing an "issue desk" such as *human rights* or *arms control.*

despot: A tyrant or *autocrat.* Cf. *absolutism; despotism; enlightened despotism.*

despotism: The political system and values associated with a *despot*, to wit: absolute authority; arbitrary whim; personal favoritism; vainglory; and often, incompetence or madness. Cf. *enlightened despotism.*

de-stalinization: (1) The partial opening of Soviet society after 1953, and the end of the reign of terror that characterized even personal life under the great tyrant whose name it celebrates. It was a main element of the *thaw* following the secret speech by *Nikita Khrushchev* at a closed session of the 20th Congress of the CPSU in 1956. (2) Similar liberalization in any Soviet-style system. Cf. *de-stalinization; Hungarian Uprising; Prague Spring; stalinization.*

destroyer: A small, fast *warship* used primarily for escort duty and in *anti-submarine warfare (ASW).*

destroyers-for-bases: In 1940 *Franklin Roosevelt* sent 50 *WWI*-vintage *destroyers* to Britain for use in *convoy* duty, in exchange for leases on several naval bases. It was a clever way around the *Neutrality Acts,* but also spoke to FDR's interest in permanent expansion of American *sea power.*

desuetude: No longer in being or practice. A legal doctrine holding that if a *treaty* has been disregarded for some time it falls into permanent disuse. It is used to give *tacit consent* to termination of a treaty.

détente: (1) Relaxation of international *tension*; an abatement of hostility, but not resolution of *conflict,* between or among antagonistic powers. (2) The reduced tension in East/West relations from 1969 to 1973 (some say 1979). See *Brandt; Brezhnev; Nixon.*

detention center: A camp or other place where *refugee* claimants may be held pending a hearing of their case, or relocation or *deportation.*

deter: Discouraging an undesirable or hostile foreign policy action by another *state* by encouraging fear of damaging *retaliation.* See *deterrence.*

determinism: (1) Theory or doctrine that holds social and historical phenomena are caused by preceding events or the putative laws of god or history, and are largely unaffected by acts of will (which are themselves determined by unseen structures). Theorists usually deny that their ideas are deterministic. Yet their statements about *causation* may nonetheless reflect an unconscious proclivity toward determinism in thought or language. (2) A disposition to see multiple effects as flowing from a single cause, that is used to explain all change. See *economic* and *structural determinism; historicism.* Cf. *volition.*

deterrence: The policy of maintaining a large military to discourage *aggression.* It works by raising the costs of success to an *aggressor,* even when the outcome might still be *defeat* for the defender. For example, Sweden historically might have been overrun by either of its more powerful neighbors (Germany and Russia),

but a large military threatened to make the effort expensive in lives and national treasure. Some species of the genus: *extended; intrawar; minimum* and *nuclear.* See also *Assured Destruction; humane deterrence; opportunism; qui desiderat; retaliation; second strike.*

deterrent: (1) Any military force capable of forestalling an attack by the credible promise it makes of retaliatory destruction. (2) Any retaliatory threat.

devaluation: Reducing *currency* value relative to other currencies, or to the *gold standard.* This is done by decree where the currency is *soft* and the government *pegs* its value; or in advanced, *hard currency* economies, by a lessening of market support by the *central bank,* which lets markets set *exchange rates* at lower levels. This lowers the price of *exports* and thus increases volumes of exports, and it raises the cost of *imports,* reduces consumption, and thereby helps erase the country's *balance of payments* deficit. However, competitive devaluation may result, as nations try to outdo each other's devaluations to gain an advantage for their own balance of payments problem.

developing nation: One that has begun the process of exploiting its resources and *labor* to allow a sustained increase in production and wealth, but has not yet achieved *modernization* in major areas of its national life. It will generally have a low per capita income compared with developed, or *OECD* states, and shortages of *capital* and skilled labor. Most are located in Africa, Asia and Latin America, but some are in the *Balkans,* the *CIS* region and Eastern Europe. An alternative term, now falling into disuse as a supposed pejorative, is *underdeveloped nation.* Even older terms, long in official disuse as politically insensitive, included "poor nations" and "former colonies." See also *LDC; Third World.* Cf. *Fourth World.*

development: There is no consensus about the general meaning of this term, or even which *indicators* should be used to assess it. Yet it is often used in *North* and *South* alike to mean the building of institutions and economic *infrastructure* to steer the *modernization* of traditional societies. It is closely associated with *industrialization* and urbanization. For variants, see *autonomous, dependent, reflexive, sustainable* and *uneven development.* See also *basic needs; HDI; IBRD; IMF; LDC; regional banks; self-reliance; underdevelopment.*

DEW (Distant Early Warning) Line: A radar warning system stretching across Alaska and Northern Canada, to provide early notice of hostile aircraft or *missiles* traversing the *Arctic.* For 36 years it was under U.S. control and command. From 1988-93, it was phased out in favor of the more modern *North Warning System*, which also introduced separate national control of bases on national territory. The DEW Line was shut down in July 1993. See *NORAD; North American Air Defense Command.*

Dewey, George (1837-1917): U.S. admiral who destroyed Spain's fleet and captured Manila in the *Spanish/American War*, without a single U.S. casualty. The *victory* made the U.S. both a colonial and Pacific power, to the surprise of most Americans.

dhow: A generic term for Arab sailing vessels that dominated trade between Africa, Arabia and the *subcontinent* before the 20th century.

diachronic study: *Jargon* for analysis of a broad phenomenon over a lengthy period, such as a general study of *industrialization* or *war* (as opposed to studies of discrete industries or wars).

dialectic: (1) In formal reasoning: proceeding via a dialogue, or conversation. (2) In Hegelian method: reasoning where a *thesis* is opposed by an *antithesis*, forming a higher *synthesis* which serves as a higher thesis, and so on.

dialectical materialism: In *marxist* usage, the application of the logical model of the *dialectic* to history, and the study of the "iron laws" of *class struggle* and change that supposedly derive from the material basis of reality. Once in power, the mask of materialism has often slipped to reveal the more driving motive force among dedicated revolutionaries: a deep romanticism about human nature, and savage determination to employ whatever means are necessary and at hand to force unwilling human beings into the *procrustean* theoretical beds prepared for them.

diaspora: (1) The scattering, through migration forced or voluntary, of a people from their original home to far-flung lands, such as happened to Africans, Chinese, Irish, Jews and, more recently and for different reasons, Russians. (2) The whole body of such people living in new countries.

Díaz, José de la Cruz Porfiro (1830-1915): President and dictator of Mexico 1877-80, 1884-1911. He fought the French under *Maximilian*, alongside *Juárez*. He kept up good relations with the U.S. and other *Great Powers*, thereby insulating Mexico from *intervention* and overseeing a significant rise in *foreign direct investment* and the *standard of living* of some social classes. He was overthrown in the Mexican Revolution of 1911, and fled into *exile*. See *Mexico.*

dictatorship: A political system where power is exercised arbitrarily by an individual, clique or party.

dictatorship of the proletariat: (1) In the theory of *marxism-leninism*: a transitional phase between the overthrow of the capitalist *mode of production*, the establishment of *socialism*, and the achievement of *communism*. (2) In practice: in the Soviet Union in the 1920s-1930s, a justification of ruthless one-party rule where opponents of the regime were labelled "class enemies" and *liquidated*, and the *Bolsheviks* instituted a *revolution from above* in agriculture and then industry that cost millions of lives. See *collectivization; five-year plans; kulaks; war communism.*

Diego Garcia: An island detached from the jurisdiction of Mauritius in 1965 by the British, and leased to the U.S. for use as its major naval and *satellite*-tracking base in the Indian Ocean. In 1982 the British agreed to pay *compensation* to former plantation workers *deported* to make way for the U.S. base.

Diem, Ngo Dinh (1901-1963): PM of *South Vietnam* 1954 (under *Bao Dai*); President and dictator 1955-63. Seen as both corrupt and inept, he was deposed and killed in a *coup* tacitly authorized by *John F. Kennedy* (just three weeks before his own assassination). That furthered the sense that the *Vietnam War* was becoming an American conflict, rather than a war for the South Vietnamese to fight with U.S. *aid.*

Dien Bien Phu, Battle of (March-May 1954): This defeat of French forces by Vietnamese communists was the final straw convincing France to pull out of *Indochina*. The French were cut off in a forward firebase and took extremely heavy casualties before surrendering to General *Giap*. See Indochina map.

Dieppe: A large *commando* raid on *occupied* France in April 1942. It was a disaster: 6,000 men, mostly Canadians, caught on the beaches; over half were slaughtered or captured. However, much was learned that proved useful on *D-Day*. See *Mountbatten.*

Diet: The legislative body in Japan.

dignitary: A person with high government or ceremonial rank.

diktat: A harsh, dictated settlement imposed upon a defeated nation; not a negotiated *peace*. For instance, *Brest-Litovsk*. Cf. *Carthaginian peace.*

Dimitrov, Georgi Mihailov (1882-1949): Bulgarian communist. Charged by the *Nazis* in 1933 as one of those responsible for setting fire to the *Reichstag*, he was acquitted and later became a Soviet citizen. From 1934-43, he was titular director of the *COMINTERN*. He was installed as Bulgarian Premier by *Stalin*, an office he held from 1946-49, and which he used to ruthlessly *sovietize* the country.

Diomede Islands: Two barren islands in the *Bering Strait*, four miles apart, and separated by the International Date Line. The big one is Russian and the little one American, which was more a curiosity than problem during the *Cold War*.

diplomacy: (1) A synonym for a state's *foreign policy*. (2) The art of *negotiation*. Harold Nicolson argued that modern diplomatic practice evolved out of five distinct periods, or styles: (1) Greek: There were no permanent missions, so diplomacy was by conference. Yet there were developed principles governing *declarations of war, peace treaties, ratification, arbitration, neutrality* and even certain rudimentary *laws of war*. (2) Roman: the *jus gentium* governed relations between Romans and foreign citizens, and there was respect for elementary *good faith, reciprocity* and sanctity of contracts. (3) *Renaissance*: This period witnessed the introduction of "written instructions" to *ambassadors*, highly developed ceremonial and ritual, and the first permanent missions; *archives* were kept, to confirm histories of negotiation; *raison d'etat* was elevated to a cardinal principle; duplicity, short-term agreement (faithlessness), *espionage* and bribery became ubiquitous tools of the diplomat. (4) French: *Richelieu* recognized that negotiation was a permanent activity; that it should aim at durable arrangements; that the interests of the state were paramount over religion or ideology; that *treaties* are sacred; that ambassadors ought not exceed their instructions; and that foreign policy should be conducted by a single, national ministry and by a corps of professional diplomats. (5) Modern: Colonial expansion, democratic idealism and a revolution in communications dramatically altered diplomacy. Europe united the globe through its imperialist thrust, and thereby brought non-European peoples into a diplomatic system that was hitherto regional. After *WWI* democratic sensibilities demanded that negotiations be more public, which led to a return to *conference diplomacy*, and ultimately the permanent conferencing of the *League of Nations* and *UN*. Insistence on the fiction of interstate *equality*, such as at the *Hague Conferences*, had eroded the notion that the *Great Powers* should have special rights because they have unique responsibilities. The U.S. failure to *ratify* the *Versailles Treaty*, negotiated personally by a President, shook confidence in the sanctity of contract, as did later Nazi and Soviet prac-

tice. Communications technology has lessened the independence and importance of ambassadors by: (a) increasing the role of *public opinion*, including direct *propaganda* appeal to each other's publics; (b) quickening the *decision-making* process for all concerned; and (c) permitting instantaneous, direct talks between *heads of government* or other *decision-makers*. Cf. *Aix-la-Chapelle; attaché; chargé; coercive diplomacy; Congress of Vienna; consul; consulate; embassage; embassy; envoy extraordinary; gunboat diplomacy; mediation; minister plenipotentiary; nonresident ambassador; plenipotentiary; preventive diplomacy; protocol; representation; Vienna Conventions.*

diplomat: An accredited representative of a nation and its foreign policy visiting or resident in a foreign land, or resident in the home country but who helps maintain political, economic and social relations with foreign governments. To Sir Henry Wotten (1568-1639) is attributed the most cuttingly humorous and risqué definition: "An ambassador is an honest man, sent to lie abroad for the commonwealth." See *representation*.

diplomatic bag: Any receptacle (not necessarily a bag) subject to *diplomatic immunity* from inspection or seizure.

diplomatic corps: (1) The body of resident *diplomats*, from all countries. By tradition, the "dean of the diplomatic corp" is the *ambassador* who has been longest at his or her post, no matter the significance or insignificance of the country represented. (2) All the diplomatic officials and employees of a given *state*.

diplomatic courier: An *envoy* charged with delivery of state papers, and enjoying limited *diplomatic immunity* in that task.

diplomatic credentials: See *letters of credence*.

diplomatic immunity: The exemptions from local civil and criminal *jurisdiction* enjoyed by a properly accredited *diplomat*, including freedom from all search or inspection, seizure of property, arrest or prosecution, and taxation. Note: *consular* officers do not enjoy these immunities in law, but frequently do as a matter of courtesy and mutual consular convenience. Immunity rights were explicitly laid out in two 1961 *Vienna Conventions*. Cf. *state immunity*.

diplomatic intervention: The effort to persuade rather than compel a foreign power to alter some policy, or undo some action it has taken toward a third party.

diplomatic note: A formal statement of policy delivered, usually in private and not for publication, directly to a foreign government. It may concern arrangements of mutual interest, in which case it is less than a *treaty* or *executive agreement* but still a statement of official policy. If a protest note, it serves as an instrument of frank understanding.

diplomatic protection: When a state intercedes on behalf of its own nationals. This is permissible only after the individual(s) concerned have reached *exhaustion of local remedies.*

diplomatic protest: A formal objection to some policy or action, say an abuse of *human rights* or an *incursion* onto one's *territory*, made to a senior representative of a foreign power. It may, or may not, be *pro forma.*

diplomatic relations: (1) Formal *recognition*, courtesies, ambassadorial rights and privileges, means of communication and especially the acknowledgement of *sovereignty* that *states* extend to one another. These relations can be broken in whole or part to signal deep displeasure with some conduct or policy, but can also remain in place even when states are in conflict (as during the *Gulf War*, when the coalition allies did not sever relations with Iraq). If no formal relations exist, another state may deliver messages, threats and so forth. (2) Formal, government-to-government contact. Cf. *foreign relations; relations officieuses.*

directed trade: Any form of government *intervention* that prevents full and open *free trade*. It may be done to consolidate *alliance* commitments, carry out a *boycott* or support domestic constituents. A synonym is *managed trade*. Cf. *protectionism.*

Directory: The five-man executive body that governed France from 1795-99. Under the Directory, France at first enjoyed major *victories* against other powers. But it also suffered through savage repression of a Catholic revolt in the *Vendée*, and then setbacks in the *War of the Second Coalition*. It was overthrown by *Napoleon I* in a *coup d'etat* ("a whiff of *grapeshot*").

direct rule: (1) In colonial administration: when there was no local intermediary between the colonial government and the governed population. (2) In *Ulster*: the closing of the Stormount Parliament to rule directly from London, as a response to rising *IRA* and other violence in the mid-1970s. Cf. *indirect rule.*

dirigisme/dirigiste: "Direction." From the French economic theory and practice of state-guided industrial and national *development*, which denies moral phe-

nomena and goals can be radically separated from economics, and aims at minimizing "collective losses." More broadly, an ethos of *elite*, bureaucratic prerogative concerning major decisions about national economic and social policy.

dirty float: When a *state* that says it is letting its currency *float* secretly *intervenes* in the marketplace to influence the direction of *exchange rates.*

dirty war: The campaign, replete with *death squads*, carried out by the military against political opposition in Argentina from 1976-82. After the military was humiliated in the *Falklands War*, several top officers were tried and imprisoned for their part in the dirty war. See *desaparacidos.*

dirty weapon: A *nuclear weapon* yielding very high *radiation effects*. Cf. *clean bomb.*

disarmament: Inaccurately, but commonly, used as a synonym for *arms control*. It means the elimination of all offensive arms, either unilaterally (in the hope that one's example will be followed, as some *peace* activists have suggested), or reciprocally. The UN has, formally at least, set as its goal "General and Complete Disarmament," which supposedly means that all *states* are one day to be reduced to levels of weaponry sufficient only to maintain internal order.

Disarmament Conference, Geneva (1932-34): The *Geneva Protocol (1925)* called for a full *disarmament* conference, but this was delayed to 1932 when it met in Geneva, with 59 states attending (the largest international gathering to that point in history). It was sponsored by the *League of Nations* but non-members like the U.S. and Soviet Union also participated. It floundered on French insistence on a prior, general scheme of *international security*, and beached on the ascent to power of *Hitler*, who pulled Germany out in October 1933.

Disarmament in Europe (CDE) Accord: It arose out of the Stockholm conference of the *CSCE*, 1984-86. It sought to reduce the chance of military misunderstanding or miscalculation by introduction of such *CSBMs* as advance notice of *maneuvers* by the *Warsaw Pact* and *NATO*, and on-site weapons and *arms control* inspections. Cf. *transparency; verification.*

discovery: Historically, a means by which *states* acquired new *territory* by claiming it as *terra incognita* (usually ignoring the cries and claims of its *indigenous people*). Now that the globe is fully mapped it is also fully claimed (except for the *global commons*). Moreover, the principle of discovery appears earthbound: the U.S. declined to claim the moon when its astronauts landed there in 1969, a self-denial later codified more generally in the *Moon Treaty*.

disengagement: The physical separation of two previously hostile, engaged militaries. This is an essential prelude to ending armed conflict. Note: This may precede, but is different from and more limited than, *demilitarization*.

disinflation: A downward movement of wages and prices, raising the purchasing power of a *currency*. Cf. *deflation*.

disinformation: The deliberate provision of misleading or false information, say as part of a *covert operation* to confuse an opponent's political strategy, military *intelligence* or *counterintelligence*. It is different from *propaganda* in that it is done in secret and not (usually) intended for a mass audience.

disinvestment: When a firm divests itself of ownership and involvement in an enterprise or project in which it previously had an *investment* stake. In the 1980s the term took on the additional meaning of private *boycott*, with particular application to South Africa: public and in some cases stockholder pressure was placed on *MNCs* to divest their holdings and plants in South Africa, as a way of reinforcing internationally agreed, public *sanctions*. See *capital flight*.

dispatch: A diplomatic or military communication.

displaced person (DP): An archaic, sometimes derogatory term for *refugee*.

dispute: Any point of significant legal or political disagreement between or among *states*. See *frontier dispute; justiciable dispute* and *nonjusticiable dispute*.

Disraeli, Benjamin (1804-81): British statesman and *Chancellor of the Exchequer* 1852, 1858-59, 1867; PM 1868, 1874-80. A leading foe of *free trade*, as PM he also followed an assertive imperial policy. He was able to avoid *war* with Russia over a *crisis* in Bulgaria and the *Dardanelles* by personally attending the *Congress of Berlin* (1878). He won Russian confirmation of British interests in the *Straits Question* and achieved the *Cyprus Convention*. Rebuffs in Afghanistan and South Africa, and world *depression* after 1873, cost him high office.

dissenting opinion: When an international justice disagrees with a court's judgment, and submits an opinion providing alternate reasoning and/or a different conclusion.

dissident: A person who disagrees with national policy, often suffering persecution as a result. Outside concern for dissenters has grown in recent decades, but still generally leads to nothing more dramatic than *diplomatic intervention*.

distributive justice: The moral questions about global allocation of wealth, especially as affecting North/South relations.

Diu: See *Portuguese India*.

diversionary war: One started to deflect public attention from domestic troubles; e.g., *Falklands War*.

divide et impera: "Divide and rule." The political maxim of *Niccolo Machiavelli*, and the political practice of many an *empire* or *despot*.

divine right of kings: A pre-*French Revolution* political doctrine that held a *sovereign's* right to rule derived directly from God. Cf. *popular sovereignty*.

Djibouti: Location: *Horn of Africa*. Major associations: *Arab League, OAU, UN*. Population: 540,000. Military: minimal/French. It became a *colony* (French Somaliland) in piecemeal fashion, 1862-1900. Its population is divided into two main groups: Issas (akin to Somalis) and Afars (akin to Ethiopian tribes). Ethiopia and Somalia claimed portions of its *territory*, and there was some interethnic violence prior to *independence* in 1977. However, these claims were renounced under international pressure. France keeps a *deterrent* force in Djibouti nonetheless.

Dobrynin, Anatoli Federovich (b.1919): Soviet diplomat; longtime Ambassador to the U.S., including during the *Cuban Missile Crisis*, when he negotiated secretly with Robert Kennedy the quid pro quo that enabled both sides to *save face*. His was one of the most familiar names and faces of the *Cold War*.

Dodecanese: An island group in the Mediterranean, formerly part of the *Ottoman Empire* but taken by Italy after it defeated Turkey in 1911-12. They were ceded to Greece in one of the *Treaties of Paris (1947)*. They are partly *demilitarized*.

Doenitz, Karl (1891-1980): German admiral who built up the *U-boat* fleet and directed the *wolf packs* during the *Battle of the Atlantic*. In 1945 he was briefly commander of what remained of all Nazi forces and the last *head of state* (after *Hitler's* death) of *Nazi Germany*. Tried at *Nuremberg*, he was imprisoned for 10 years for *war crimes*.

dog fight: Aerial combat; named for its vicious, tangled maneuvering. In the modern era, *air-to-air missiles* have rendered such combat nearly obsolete.

Dogger Bank incident (October 21, 1904): The Russian Baltic fleet, en route to the Pacific to take part in the *Russo/Japanese War*, fired on British fishing boats in the *North Sea*, thinking they were Japanese attack boats. Public opinion in Britain reached a war pitch and was only cooled by Russian acceptance of responsibility, and later agreement to make *reparations*.

dollar convertibility: Under the *Bretton Woods* regime, a commitment of the U.S. to convert foreign held dollars into a fixed price of gold, providing *liquidity* and *adjustment* for the whole system.

dollar diplomacy: (1) The use of financial power to promote other *national interests* in one's foreign policy, through *investment* or the use of *aid* to gain voting support within the UN, or on regional issues. (2) The use of foreign policy resources to support the private business interests of a state's citizens.

dollar gap: In disuse. The difference between a state's *exports* and *investments* in the U.S. and what it owed to the U.S. It was important in the immediate post-*WWII* decades when the dollar was the unchallenged, international monetary standard.

Dollfuss, Englebert (1892-1934): Chancellor of Austria, May 1932-July 1934. Suspicious of democracy, he used the army freely against demonstrators. He set up a *fascist* constitution in 1934, then was killed in a failed *Nazi* attempt to seize power.

domain: (1) The area under the *sovereign* or effective control of one government, as in "China has Tibet under its domain." (2) The reach or range of *international law*, to the point where it is limited by *sovereignty, jurisdiction, consent* and so on.

domestic jurisdiction: The range of internal activities of states entirely free from the *domain* of international law. In some areas, such as *human rights*, boundaries are no longer clear.

dominant power: This may be a local, regional or (rarely) global status enjoyed by a powerful state, where it has no clear rivals and its foreign policy preferences usually hold sway.

Dominica: Location: *Lesser Antilles*. Major associations: *CARICOM, Commonwealth, OAS, OECS, UN*. Population: 85,000. Military: minimal. It became a British *colony* in 1805. As a member of the *West Indies Associated States* it was given local *autonomy* in 1967, gaining full *independence* in 1978. A hurricane devastated its plantation economy the next year. *Coup* attempts failed in 1980 and 1981. Dominica took the lead in obtaining support from the OECS for the U.S. *invasion of Grenada* in 1983.

Dominican Republic: Location: *Greater Antilles*. Major associations: *CARICOM* (observer status), *OAS, UN*. Population: 7.3 million. Military: for internal use. It is part of the island of *Hispaniola*, stumbled upon by Columbus in 1492. A Spanish *colony* from that date, it boasts in Santo Domingo the oldest permanent European settlement in the Western hemisphere. The western portion was ceded to France in 1697, and became *Haiti*. France took the remainder of the island in 1795, but lost it to Haiti following a successful slave *rebellion* there in 1801. Spain regained control briefly, from 1803-21. Haiti again took over the eastern half, from 1822-44. Spain returned a third time, from 1861-63. The U.S. then displaced Spain from the hemisphere in 1898. It sent in marines to occupy and administer the Dominican Republic from 1916-24. In 1930, Rafael Trujillo (1891-1961) became President and dictator. He ruled with an iron fist until assassinated in 1961. There was a prolonged succession crisis. Juan Bosch (b.1909) was elected President and served for seven months in 1963, until he was overthrown in a U.S.-supported *coup*. Agitation for his return to power led to a U.S. *invasion* in 1965, despite a 1940 *treaty* in which the U.S. relinquished a right to *intervene*. The country has since stayed quietly within the U.S. orbit, under Joaquin Balaguer (b.1907).

Dominican Republic, intervention in (1965): In April 1965, a revolt took place led by young army officers seeking to restore deposed President Juan Bosch (b.1909), a liberal who had been elected in December 1962, but had been deposed seven months later. The group was reported to involve some communists, and that sparked U.S. *intervention*. President *Lyndon Johnson* sent in 23,000 marines, accompanied by token units from five *OAS* countries and with the somewhat reluctant voting support of the OAS. The intervention marked a shift in U.S. policy away from the *Alliance for Progress*.

Dominion: A class of states within the *Commonwealth* that accepted the British monarch as their *head of state*, as represented by a Governor-General. Before *WWII* they were: *Australia, Canada, Eire, Newfound-*

land, *New Zealand* and *South Africa*. Some post-WWII Dominions, such as India, later became *republics*, accepting the Queen solely as titular head of the Commonwealth. Others, such as Eire, became republics and left the association.

domino theory: A *strategic* metaphor in which it is argued that the loss of influence or control over one state to an adversary will lead to the loss of adjacent states, which will fall "like dominoes." At the extreme, it can blind one to the relative insignificance of certain states. For instance, during the *Vietnam War* this idea inflated U.S. perceptions of the importance of *Indochina* to the *balance of power*, and thereby led to an overcommitment of resources and *political capital*. Yet the Soviets accurately saw their own outer *empire* as a set of dominoes: reform in one state might (and did) lead to a toppling of the whole, rickety, imperial edifice. In turn, that might (and did) threaten the *Soviet Union* itself. Thus, until 1989, Moscow acted out the *Brezhnev Doctrine*.

donor country/nation/state: One that gives *aid*.

Doolittle Raid (April 18, 1945): This first bombing of Japan in *WWII* was conducted soon after *Pearl Harbor*, to bring home to Americans and Japanese alike that the *home islands* of Japan would be pounded by U.S. *air power*. Using land-based, *heavy* bombers (B-25s) launched from an *aircraft carrier*, the raid achieved total surprise. Most planes made it to safety in China, but some captured crews were executed by the Japanese, in spite of their status as *POWs* and in violation of the *Geneva Conventions*. The raid helped provoke *Yamamoto* and the Japanese navy into the disastrous attack on *Midway*.

double agent: A spy working for two countries simultaneously. He or she may have real loyalty to one nation, or just be a clever *mercenary*.

double containment: The idea that including West Germany in *NATO* served two vital purposes: bolstering West European defense against the Soviets, and locking Germany itself into a watchful and controlled security setting. It recognized that German military revival was inevitable, but ensured that when it came Germany's military would be under NATO command and closely integrated with other NATO militaries.

double cross: A betrayal; from the highly successful British *disinformation* campaign against German *intelligence* in *WWII*, code-named "XX."

double standard: When a foreign policy is applied unevenly, across the range of a state's *diplomatic relations*. Thus, economic *sanctions* over *human rights* violations may be applied against one state and not a second, because the second is too powerful to be influenced in that way, too unconnected for the sanctions to have any real bite or too important to other foreign policy goals to risk giving too much offense.

doublethink: In *propaganda*, simultaneous acceptance of mutually contradictory ideas, where one has been preconditioned to ignore what to others appear as obvious contradictions; drawn from the brainwashing process used on William Smith ("Everyman") in George Orwell's classic novel "1984." Cf. *groupthink*.

Dowager Empress: See *T'su Hsi*.

draft: See *conscription*.

draft dodger: A *conscript* who does not report for service, for whatever reason (U.S. usage). Such a person may or may not also be a *conscientious objector*.

Drago Doctrine: Announced by Argentina in 1902, and backed by the U.S., it said that mere *default* on national *debt* was insufficient reason for foreign *intervention*. It was provoked by a *blockade* of Venezuela by several European powers, after Venezuela had defaulted. The U.S. took direct control of the *customs* of several smaller countries to ensure payments and forestall additional interventions.

Dreadnought: A class of *battleship* named for H.M.S. Dreadnought, first launched by Britain in February 1906. The heavy armament and guns of these ships made all other battleships obsolete overnight. Yet their construction actually weakened Britain's advantage: it placed the *Anglo/German naval arms race* on even terms, at least in battleships, and undercut Britain's policy of keeping a *two-power naval standard*. In fact, these mighty weapons platforms were hardly used. There was only one major naval engagement in *WWI*, at *Jutland* in 1916. That war also witnessed the emergence of the dominant ships of the 20th century: *submarines* and *aircraft carriers*. See *Scapa Flow*.

***Dreikaiserbund* (1873-87):** "League of the Three Emperors." A system of consultation and later formal cooperation between Austria, Germany and Russia concerning Turkey. It was a successful effort by *Bismarck* to forestall a French attempt to reverse the defeat of the *Franco/Prussian War*, by denying France its needed ally to the east of Germany. It lapsed when Austro/Russian tensions over changes in the Balkans began to outweigh mutual interests toward Turkey.

drug cartels: Private drug production and smuggling operations run out of several Latin American and Asian countries. Extensive profits allow them to hire private armies, buy local police, judges and politicians, distort the national economy and block effective *development* programs in the countryside. They are increasingly a target of both national and cooperative international military operations. See *drug trade; narco-terrorism.*

drug trade: The export of illegal narcotics, or other banned substances such as steroids, from one country to another, via roundabout routes and devious means. In the 19th century the main importer was China and the trade was openly controlled by Western states (see *Opium Wars*). In the late 20th century, the main importers are Western countries, although the calamitous social effects of drug abuse are beginning to be felt globally, while the major suppliers are in the *Third World*. Because the trade is illegal its scope is difficult to estimate. However, some specialists place it as the second largest (after *oil*) export from the Third World to the *OECD* nations.

Druse: A small, secretive sect, in schism from mainstream *Islam* since the 11th century, now living in Israel, Lebanon and Syria. Left in their mountain isolation by the *Ottomans*, they opposed French colonization of Syria after *WWI*. Druse have fought for Israel, and against Israel or anyone else seen as threatening their independence. They remain blood enemies of the Maronite Christians, whom they fought in the *Lebanese Civil War*. See *Druse rebellion.*

Druse rebellion (1925-27): A revolt against the French *mandate* in southern Syria. The *Druse* captured Damascus, but in fierce fighting France later reclaimed the city and crushed the rebellion.

Dual Alliance: (1) The secret, Austro/German *alliance* of 1879, which later became the *Triple Alliance* with the addition of Italy. (2) The Franco/Russian alliance of 1890, strengthened with a military *convention* in 1893-94, that lasted until 1917.

dualism: (1) In *development* literature: where urban *modernization* is juxtaposed with rural backwardness and neglect. (2) In *international law*: the doctrine that international law and *municipal law* are unrelated. Cf. *monism.*

dual key: The *NATO* practice, developed during the 1960s, of placing U.S. nuclear *warheads* on a second country's *launchers*, with the U.S. retaining one "key" (set of launch codes) and the host country another. As the keys only worked in tandem, actual launch authority would have to satisfy the command and control concerns of both nations. The Soviets, in contrast, kept control of all launch keys to themselves.

Dual Monarchy, of Austria-Hungary: It was created in 1867 by the *Ausgleich* that followed Austria's *defeat* at the hands of *Prussia*. This rickety state survived as one of the *Great Powers* into *WWI*, but not beyond. Its breakup was already underway by 1918, and thus was sanctioned (but not decided, as is often wrongly charged) at the *Paris Peace Conference*. See *Austria.*

dual nationality: When an individual has legal *citizenship* in two states.

dual use technology: Any technology with both military and civilian applications. For example, a boost vehicle/missile *launcher* or civilian/breeder reactor, or advanced computers or bioengineering.

Dubček, Alexander (b.1921): Czechoslovak *communist party* leader who supported the liberalization movement known as the *Prague Spring*. He promised "socialism with a human face." But that effort was dispatched, and he was detained in the Soviet Union, following the *Warsaw Pact* invasion in July 1968. He was treated as a national hero during the *velvet revolution* of 1989, and later elected to chair the first genuinely democratic national parliament.

Dulles, John Foster (1888-1959): U.S. statesman. He served on the U.S. delegation to the *San Francisco Conference* on the founding of the *UN*, and then as U.S. representative to the UN from 1946-50. During the 1952 presidential campaign he led a savage *Republican* attack on *containment*, as an immoral policy that abandoned millions of east Europeans to *tyranny*. He was a conservative internationalist, like *Vandenberg* and *Eisenhower*. That meant he actually had more in common with liberal Democrats who originally framed containment policy, *NATO* and the *Marshall Plan*, than with the still *isolationist* right-wing of his own party. As Secretary of State 1953-59, he held to containment, although adjusting it to a *strategic doctrine* of *massive retaliation* and indulging inflated rhetoric. He has been accused of playing the dangerous game of *brinkmanship*. Yet during the 1953 *Berlin crisis* and 1956 *Hungarian Uprising* he acted with deliberation and restraint. It was once thought that he was highly independent, but it is now known that little was done in foreign policy without Eisenhower's prior knowledge and approval.

Duma: The Russian parliament, created in the wake of

the *Russian Revolution (1905)*. It was at best a weak restraint on the *tsar*. However, when *Nicholas II* tried to dissolve it in 1917, it formed the core of the *Provisional Government* that replaced him. In 1993 a State Duma replaced the old Soviet parliament, following *Yeltsin's* assault on the *White House*.

Dumbarton Oaks Conference (August-October, 1944): A meeting of the *Big Four* to draft the constitution of the UN. Most of the major decisions about division of powers, representation and guiding principles were taken here, by the *Great Powers* alone. That left minor adjustments and amendments for the *San Francisco Conference* of 1945, with two key exceptions: (1) the scope of the *veto* power of *Permanent Members of the Security Council*; and (2) the question of separate representation for each of the fifteen Soviet republics, over which *Stalin* threatened to scuttle the UN (later settled by a compromise of three Soviet seats). The U.S. alone lobbied for *human rights* in the *UN Charter* at Dumbarton Oaks, succeeding (with small power assistance) at San Francisco.

dumping: Selling an *export* below the cost of production to increase market share, or create a *monopoly* prior to raising prices. It may also be done to clear surplus stock produced by government *subsidies*. See *anti-dumping laws*.

Dunkirk: The evacuation of 300,000 British, *Commonwealth* and French troops, mostly without their equipment, to England, at the end of May and early June 1940. It was made necessary by the *surrender* of Belgium, and accomplished with the aid of hundreds of civilian craft, of all types. The British turned this military defeat into a psychological victory ("the Dunkirk spirit") important in sustaining *national morale* after France, too, surrendered.

Dunkirk, Treaty of (1947): A defense and security *pact* between Britain and France, aimed at Germany rather than the Soviet Union. It was superseded by the American policy of rapid rehabilitation of Germany, and then by the *Brussels Treaty* and *NATO*.

durable goods: By convention, those expected to last longer than three years, such as cars or houses.

Durham Report: Named for Earl Durham (1792-1840), sent to Canada in 1838 in the wake of rebellion there. It called for responsible local governments in the major *colonies*, rather than continued rule by a powerful governor. It was a radical proposal that set the *British Empire* on the road to *Commonwealth*, by giving real *autonomy* to the *Dominions*.

Dutch Borneo: A Dutch *colony* on *Borneo*, now in Indonesia.

Dutch East Indies: A Dutch *colony*, now the major part of Indonesia.

Dutch Guiana: Former name of Suriname.

Dutch New Guinea: Former name of West Irian, now in Indonesia.

Dutch West Indies: Former name of the Antilles.

dyad/dyadic: *Jargon* unplain and unsimple: it means "a pair." See *obscurantism*.

dyarchy: The compromise government in India between 1919-35, which granted limited *autonomy* to the states on specific issues. See *India Acts*.

dynastic war: One prosecuted to expand or extend the narrow interests of a given *dynasty*, not that of the *state* or *nation*.

dynasty: A series of rulers from the same family.

Dzerzhinsky, Felix (1877-1926): Founder of the *CHEKA* and leading member of the *Bolshevik* inner circle under *Lenin*. He oversaw the *Red Terror* following a failed attempt on Lenin's life, and carried out the food seizures and executions that marked *war communism* as much as it had the *Russian Civil War*. He was an early supporter of *Stalin* as successor to Lenin. He was a near-cult figure within the *OGPU* (and later, the *NKVD* and *KGB*). His austere statue brooded over KGB headquarters in Moscow until 1992, when an angry crowd of former victims, and relatives of victims, manhandled it to the ground, decapitated and otherwise despoiled it.

E

Earth Summit: See *UN Conference on the Environment and Development.*

East: (1) Historically: Looking from Europe, Asia in general, but especially China ("Cathay"). (2) During the *Cold War:* a term loosely applied to the *Soviet bloc,* including China before the *Sino/Soviet split.* Cf. *Far East; Middle East; Near East.*

East Aden Protectorate: A British possession on the Saudi peninsula, now part of Yemen.

East African Community: From 1967-77, Kenya, Tanzania and Uganda formed a *common market.* However, it ultimately floundered over their quite different paths to *development,* and owing to the ascent to power of *Idi Amin* in Uganda.

East Asia: *Northeast Asia* plus *Southeast Asia.*

East Berlin: The Soviet *occupation zone* in Berlin (as distinct from *East Germany*) after 1945, and the capital of East Germany. See *Berlin air lift; Berlin Wall.*

East China Sea: That part of the N. Pacific lying between China, Japan, Korea and Taiwan.

Eastern Church/Eastern Orthodox: Alternates for the *Orthodox Church,* or churches that follow the Byzantine rite and Nicene creed.

Eastern Europe: Bulgaria, Czech Republic, Estonia, Hungary, Latvia, Lithuania, Poland, Rumania and Slovakia; some usages include Belarus and Ukraine. During the *Cold War* the term included *Czechoslovakia* and *East Germany* (both now *extinct*), but excluded the *Baltic States* (then part of the Soviet Union).

eastern front: In *WWI* and *WWII,* the *front line* between Russian forces and those of Germany and its minor allies.

Eastern Question: "Who will inherit the non-Turkish provinces of the *Ottoman Empire,* as the center weakens?" With the failure of the Ottoman assault on Vienna in 1683, *Hapsburg* Austria began its assault on Turkish power and possessions in Europe. Under *Peter I (the Great)* Russia, too, began to whittle away at Turkey's Balkan provinces and Central Asian allies (various, small Khanates). Under *Catherine II (the Great)* Russia made major gains, playing upon quasi-religious concern for Christians under Muslim authority, and playing to the *pan-Slavism* movement. By the

19th century the question changed to one of decay from within, rather than *conquest* from without. The empire was hurt after 1804-17 by Serb revolts, and the *Greek War of Independence,* 1821-29. In the 1830s *Mehemet Ali* of Egypt, ostensibly an Ottoman vassal, broke away from the sultan's control. The Eastern Question was further complicated by the competing interests of the Great Powers over the *Straits Question.* A major episode was the *Crimean War,* in which Britain and France shored up Turkey against Russia. Internal and Russian pressures on Turkey increased after 1870, contributing to the breakaway of new but unstable states, namely Rumania (1878) and Bulgaria (1886). Several powers sought to freeze the Eastern Question with the *Mediterranean Agreement.* It was at the heart of the *Balkan Wars* of 1912 and 1913, and was an underlying cause of *WWI.* It was resolved not with the end of the Ottoman Empire in 1918, but the creation of modern Turkey by *Atatürk* in 1923 and renunciation of the imperial pretensions of the sultans. Disputes over the breakup of *Yugoslavia* are modern echoes of the Eastern Question. See map and *balkanization; Congress of Berlin; Münchengrätz Agreements; Treaty of Paris; Treaty of San Stefano.*

Easter Rising (April 24-29, 1916): An *insurrection* in Dublin by the Irish Volunteers (Irish Republican Brotherhood), forerunner to the *IRA.* It aimed at securing Irish *independence* during Britain's moment of difficulty in *WWI,* with anticipation of *aid* from Germany that never materialized. The execution of 14 of its leaders gave Irish nationalists yet another round of martyrs to keen ("a terrible beauty is born," in the famous words of W. B. Yeats), and stimulated armed resistance during the *Irish War of Independence.*

East Germany: See *German Democratic Republic.*

East India Company: This giant trading corporation was chartered by Britain in 1600. It grew to dominate the Indian *subcontinent,* until introduction of *direct rule* after the *Indian Mutiny.* It was dissolved in 1874. Note: Other countries chartered East India companies, notably France and the Netherlands, but the term usually refers to the British company.

East Indies: This term, never uniformly applied, has fallen into disuse: (1) Pre-*decolonization* term for lower, *Southeast Asia.* (2) The islands and territories of the Malay archipelago. (3) Some islands of modern Indonesia.

East Pakistan: Now *Bangladesh,* from 1947-71 it was

divided from West Pakistan by 1,000 miles of Indian territory.

East Prussia: The key province in Imperial Germany, it exercised through its contribution to the officer and *diplomatic corps* a disproportionate influence on military and foreign policy. After *WWI* it was separated from Germany by the *Polish Corridor.* After *WWII* it was divided and *annexed* by Poland and the Soviet Union, and most of its German population forcibly deported westward. See *junkers.*

East Timor: A Portuguese holding on the island of *Timor,* annexed by Indonesia in 1975. Since then, Indonesian troops have faced a *guerrilla* campaign. Until the end of the *Cold War* the brutal repression of Timorese *human rights* went largely uncriticized by the West, for whom Indonesia was an important regional ally; or by the *South,* for whom it was a leader. In 1993 the UN and western states suggested that Indonesia was engaged in near-*genocide* on the island.

East-West conflict: An alternative term for the *Cold War* between the *West* and the *Soviet bloc.*

Eban, Abba (b.1915): Israeli statesman. Ambassador to the UN 1949-59; Ambassador to the U.S. 1950-59; Foreign Minister, 1966-74. He played a key role in gaining UN support for Israel in the 1950s, and in formulating foreign policy during the *Third* and *Fourth Arab/Israeli Wars.* He once said *international law* was "the law which the wicked do not obey and which the righteous do not enforce."

Ebert, Friedrich (1871-1925): President of the *Weimar Republic* 1920-25. He laid the basis of what might well have evolved into parliamentary democracy in Germany, but was never able to escape from the shadow of *Versailles,* and fell victim to *hyperinflation.*

EC: See *European Community.*

econometrics: The use of statistical and other mathematical methods in exploring and testing economic propositions.

Economic and Social Council (ECOSOC): A major UN organ coordinating the *specialized agencies.* Its main function is to foster economic and social *development.* Since the 1960s it has evolved an emphasis on development issues in the *Third World.* It has 54 members serving rotating terms. It oversees a vast array of programs and commissions, including on *human rights* and *refugees.* The *UNDP* and *UNEP* are also run under its auspices. It reports to the *UNGA.*

Economic Community of West African States (ECO-WAS): Founded in 1975, under Nigerian leadership, to promote regional *trade* and *development.* It aims at a *customs union,* but has enjoyed only limited success.

Economic Cooperation Organization (ECO): Founded in the 1960s by Iran, Pakistan and Turkey. It was moribund until after the *Cold War,* when it expanded to comprise ten non-Arab, Muslim countries: the original three, plus Afghanistan, Azerbaijan, Kazahkstan, Kirghizstan, Tajikistan, Turkmenistan and Uzbekistan. In part, it represents a competitive effort by the original three to provide regional leadership, but it also is quiet acknowledgement of the fact that none of these nations (except perhaps Turkey) stands to gain admittance to the *EU.*

economic determinism: An analytical tendency that views social, political and even intellectual forms as ultimately decided by underlying economic factors. Cf. *Kondratieff cycles; marxism.*

economic espionage: The use of the various tools and resources of *intelligence* to spy out discoveries, trends and developments of economic rather than political or military importance. It implies its antonym: economic *counterespionage.*

economic indicators: See *indicators.*

economic integration: See *integration.*

economics: The field of study concerned with production, distribution, and consumption of *goods* and *services.* Reflecting on its often baleful conclusions and the uneven social consequences of economic realities, Thomas Carlyle once famously (though rather unfairly) called it "the Dismal Science." Inter alia, see *absolute advantage; adjustment; agriculture; aid; allocation; anti-dumping laws; APEC; arbitrage; autarky; backwash effect; Baker Plan; balance of payments; balance of trade; Bank of International Settlements; barter agreements; basic needs; beggar-thy-neighbor; black market; Black Tuesday; boom; boycott; Bretton Woods system; buffer stock; business cycle; buyers' market; CACM; capital; capital flight; capital formation; capital gain; capital goods; capital intensive; capital investment; capitalism; capitalist; capital markets; CARICOM; cartel; central bank; CFA; classical school; class struggle; collective goods theory; COMECON; command economy; commodity; common market; communism; comparative advantage; compensation; compensatory financing; competitive advantage; competitiveness; conditionality; consumer price index; convertibility; cost-benefit analysis; coun-*

terpart funds; counter trade; countervailing duty; currency; current account; customs union; debt; debt crisis; debt-equity swaps; debt fatigue; debtor cartel; debt rescheduling; debt service; deficit spending; deflation; demonetize; dependency; dependency theory; depreciation; depression; depressions (world); devaluation; developing nation; development; dirigisme; dirty float; disinflation; disinvestment; dollar convertibility; dollar diplomacy; drug trade; dumping; durable goods; EC; econometrics; ECOSOC; economic determinism; economic espionage; economies of scale; economy; ECSC; ECU; EEA; EEC; EEZ; efficiency; EFTA; elasticity of demand; EMI; EMS; EPZ; ERM; ERP; EU; eurobond markets; eurocurrencies; exchange controls; exchange rate; excise; exploitation; export-led growth; expropriation; factor analysis; factor endowments; factors of production; fair trade; final goods; finance; First Tranche; fiscal policy; five-year plans; fixed currency; floating currency; foreign direct investment; foreign exchange; foreign exchange reserve; forward market; free enterprise; free market; free rider problem; free trade; FTA (1); FTA (2); fungible; G-5; G-7; G-8; G-10; G-77; GATT; GDP; GNP; gold standard; goods; graduation clause; green loans; growth; guanxi; Hawley/Smoot tariff; hard currency; hard loan; hot money; human development index; hyperinflation; IBRD; ICA; IDA; IFAD; IFC; IMF; imperialism; import quotas; import substitution; indicators; Industrial Revolution; inflation; informal sector; infrastructure; input; integration; interdependence; interest rates; intermediate inputs; internalization theory; investment; invisible trade; IPC; ITO; Kennedy Round; Keynes; keynesian economics; Kondratieff cycles; labor; labor theory of value; LAFTA; LAIA; laissez-faire; land; LDC; leading indicators; leaseholds; liberalism; licensing; linkage; liquidity; macroeconomics; managed trade; Manchester school; market economy; marxism; marxism-leninism; mass production; means of production; mercantilism; microeconomics; MITI; mixed economy; MNC/MNE; mode of production; modernization; monetarism; monetary policy; money market; monopoly; monopsony; most-favored-nation; NAFTA; nationalization; natural resources; NDP; new protectionism; NICs; NIEO; Nixon shocks; NNP; non-tariff barriers (NTBs); OAPEC; OECD; OEEC; official financing; oil; oil shocks; oligopoly; OMAs; OPEC; Open Door; outputs; patient capital; pegging; petrodollars; physiocrats; planned economy; Plaza Agreement; political economy; portfolio investment; poverty; preferential tariff; price controls; price elasticity; price supports; primary producer; primary products; private sector; privatize; product cycle theory; productivity; profit; protectionism; protective tariffs; public goods; public sector; pump priming; quotas; raw materials; reces-sion; reciprocity; reflation; reformism; reform liberalism; refugees; regional banks; remittances; reserve currency; revaluation; rising expectations; sanctions; scissors crisis; SDRs; sellers' market; sensitivity; services; short-term capital account; slump; SNA; social overhead capital; soft currency; soft good; soft loan; spot market; STABEX; stability; stabilization program; stages of growth; stagflation; stagnation; standard of living; stock; stock exchange; strategic materials; strategic stockpiles; structural adjustment loan; subsidiary; subsidy; Super 301 Procedures; supply; supply side economics; surplus value; sustainable development; sustainable growth; takeoff; tariff; tax haven; technology transfer; terms of trade; textiles; tied aid; tied loan; Tokyo Round; tourism; trade; trade balance; trade barrier; trade routes; turn-key factory; underground economy; uneven development; Uruguay Round; venture capital; visible trade; VERs; vulnerability; water; WHFTA; world capitalist system; world system theory; zaibatsu.

economies of scale: The greater the amount of production (scale) of a given item the lower the cost-per-unit will tend to be, as start-up, design and research and development (R&D) costs are averaged over all units produced. This encourages production at large volumes, and requires a sizeable home market and/or an assertive export strategy to dispose of any *goods* in excess of what the national market can absorb. This phenomenon has an impact on arms exports as well as regular goods. For example, if a country wishes to maintain independence of foreign suppliers in its defense industries it must sell a certain number of fighters (or tanks, or *missiles*, or whatever) abroad to keep the costs-per-unit affordable for its own defense needs, and production lines rolling. In short, it may be driven to become an arms exporter as well as producer. This has been the case both for small arms producers such as Israel, and larger ones like France.

economy: (1) The structure of economic life and activity in a country, region or historical period. (2) The sum total of a nation's economic resources and activity, measured in terms of *GNP*.

ecosystem: A biological system of interactions and interdependent processes of a community of organisms, and their surrounding environment. Concern for the viability and integrity of ecosystems is a rising issue in global environmental politics.

Ecuador: Location: S. America. Major associations: *OAS, OPEC, UN*. Population: 10.5 million. Military: minor. The Incas of this country on the west coast of South America were conquered by Spain c.1633. It was ruled by Madrid until 1822, when it broke free as part of the original state of *Colombia*. It seceded from Colombia in 1830, and afterward kept up a boundary *dispute* with Peru. It alternated between civilian and military dictatorships for many decades, but has made progress toward democratic rule since 1979. It has had a rising *debt* burden since the 1960s. In 1987 it briefly, though unilaterally, suspended repayment of its debt, due to declining *oil* revenues and *infrastructure* repair costs brought on by a large earthquake.

ecumenism: A drive to reunite the world's Christian churches, despite doctrinal differences. An older term for the ideal of a single, universal church was "catholic". See *Catholic Church; Orthodox Church; Reformation; Vatican Councils; World Council of Churches.*

Eden, Anthony (1897-1977): British statesman. Foreign Secretary 1935-38, 1941-45, 1951-54; PM 1955-56. He resigned in 1938 over disagreements with PM *Neville Chamberlain*, including treatment of Italy but also *appeasement* of Germany. During *WWII* he was a close aide to *Churchill*. He led Britain's delegation to the *San Francisco Conference*. He helped arrange the *peace* in Korea in 1953, and French withdrawal from Vietnam in 1954. His reputation was permanently hurt by the 1956 decision to invade Egypt, which set off the *Suez Crisis* that brought down his government. He has been faulted for wrongly viewing *Nasser* as another *Hitler*.

EEZ: See *Exclusive Economic Zone*.

effect: Any consequence or result that proceeds from an agency, or *cause*. See *causation*.

efficiency: (1) In economic theory: a measure of the costs of production: *capital, labor,* research and any other costs; and an assumption that prices reflect real, basic information. (2) In statistics and *econometrics*: an evaluation of the relative merits of *parameters*.

Egypt: Location: N. Africa/Middle East. Major associations: *Arab League, OAU, UN*. Population: 55 million. Military: among the best in the Middle East. One of the world's oldest civilizations started here, more than 4,000 years ago. It has historically been divided into Lower Egypt (the Nile Delta), and Upper Egypt (Cairo to the Sudan). Egypt was repeatedly conquered, by Persians; Greeks; Romans; Arab Muslims who converted most of its population to *Islam*; and the *Ottoman Empire*, which ruled it from 1517-1882. *Napoleon* invaded Egypt in 1798, but it reverted to Ottoman control in 1802. Under *Mehemet Ali* it broke free of the Ottomans, *de facto*. French *influence* was exten-

sive during most of the 19th century, leading to the *Suez Canal* being built by a French charter company. After anti-European demonstrations occurred in 1882, Britain intervened to make Egypt a *protectorate*. Yet it remained formally connected to the Ottoman Empire until 1914, when it was seized by Britain after war broke out. It became independent in 1922, but hosted British military bases until after *WWII*. A 1936 *treaty* left British troops in Egypt to guard the canal and set up a British/Egyptian *condominium* over Sudan, then still attached to Egypt. (Sudan became a separate state in 1956.) Egypt was one of the Arab states that attacked Israel in 1948, but was defeated. A nationalist revolt in 1952 overthrew King *Faruk I* and established a *republic*. In 1953 *Nasser* became premier; in 1956 he was made President. He tilted toward the Soviet Union, which gave him arms and some economic *aid*. He ordered British troops out of the *Canal Zone* and *nationalized* the Suez Canal Company in 1956, which led to the *Suez Crisis* and the discretely caused but related *Second Arab/Israeli War*. The U.S. forced Britain and France to withdraw, and a UN *peacekeeping* force was put in place along the Israeli border. Nasser ordered it out in 1967, precipitating the *Third Arab/Israeli War*, in which Egypt was badly defeated and lost the *Sinai*. Next came the *War of Attrition*. Nasser died in 1970. In 1973 *Anwar Sadat* launched a surprise attack, beginning the *Fourth Arab/Israeli War*. Afterward, he moved Egypt into the U.S. camp. In 1977 he flew to Israel, opening *peace talks* that led to the *Camp David Accords* and a formal *peace treaty* in 1979 that returned the Sinai. For making *peace* Egypt was expelled from the Arab League, and Sadat assassinated by Muslim *fundamentalists*. Egypt slowly regained acceptance among Arab states (readmitted to the Arab League in 1989). In 1990-91 it sent 20,000 troops to fight in the *Gulf War* against Iraq. In 1992 it joined in U.S.-sponsored peace talks for the whole region, and sent troops to aid in the UN relief effort in Somalia. It is currently at odds with Iran, Libya and Sudan, but is again a leader in the Arab world. Internally, it is facing Muslim fundamentalists whose random killing of tourists severely undermines revenues, but who really threaten the regime because they have gained support among Egypt's millions of poor.

Eichmann, Adolf (1906-62): Nazi commandant in the *death camp* system. He escaped to Argentina after *WWII*. He was kidnapped by *Mossad* agents in 1960, taken to Israel, tried and executed in 1962. The social philosopher Hannah Arendt observed Eichmann at the trial and concluded that the most remarkable thing about him was the "banality of evil."

Einstein, Albert (1879-1955): Physicist, *peace* activist.

He wrote to *Franklin Roosevelt* in 1939 to inform about the theoretical possibility of an *atomic bomb*, that Germany was probably working on such a device, and urging that a U.S. program get started. That led to the *Manhattan Project*. The following remark is often (mis)quoted: "The unleashed power of the atom has changed everything save our mode of thinking, and we thus drift toward unparalleled catastrophes."

Eire: The Gaelic name of the Republic of Ireland.

Eisenhower, Dwight (1890-1969): U.S. general and statesman. Supreme Commander of Allied Forces in Europe, 1944-45; first commander of *NATO* 1950-52; President 1953-61. After ending the *Korean Conflict*, he rode out the *McCarthyism* bluster at home, working to preserve presidential discretion in foreign policy from the right-wing of his own party. He strove constantly for *arms control*, but achieved very limited success. Yet he made proposals such as *Open Skies*, which would be accepted when conditions changed in the 1980s. One of the last fiscal conservatives in the White House, he kept *defense spending* fairly low. [Note: In percentage terms, his defense budgets were higher than in later years; but that is deceptive as it fails to take into account an absolute increase but relative decline in defense spending due to huge increases in social and other government spending after 1961.] While he oversaw a significant *arms buildup*, it did not approach the levels to come under his successors. That left an opening for *John F. Kennedy* to (falsely) claim a "missile gap" in the 1960 elections. Eisenhower used *John Foster Dulles* to make tough policy declarations and public threats while he played the role of senior statesman, in a type of good cop/bad cop routine that was often highly effective. His administration relied on *massive retaliation* as its *strategic doctrine*. He warned against getting involved in a land war in Asia. While providing *logistical* support to the French in Indochina and then to South Vietnam, when he left office there were fewer than 600 U.S. advisers in that country, and no combat troops. But he was not loathe to use *force*: he supported a *coup* in Guatemala in 1954, sent marines into Lebanon in 1957 and twice threatened China, possibly with *nuclear weapons*, over *Quemoy and Matsu*. In his Farewell Address he revisited his small-government, Republican roots by warning against the rise of a *military-industrial complex*. His historical reputation has risen steadily, in no small part related to the precipitous decline of *Kennedy's*.

Eisenhower Doctrine: Issued January 5, 1957, in the wake of the Anglo-French fiasco during the *Suez Crisis*. It promised U.S. military *aid* to victims of *aggression* in the Middle East. It aimed at forestalling Soviet penetration of the region. It was invoked toward Jordan (1957) and Lebanon (1958).

ejus est interpretari legum cujus est condere: "Who has the power to make a law, has the power to interpret it." Legal maxim.

El Alamein, Battle of (October 23-November 4, 1942): Fought less than 100 km from Alexandria, Egypt, it turned back the *Axis* threat to Egypt and the *Suez Canal*, cost *Hitler* valuable manpower and equipment (200,000 men), ended *Mussolini's* pretensions to imperial greatness, helped clear the Axis from North Africa, bolstered British and *Allied* morale and set the stage for the *invasion* of Italy. It was the first substantial victory over the *Wehrmacht* (soon followed by the even greater German defeat at *Stalingrad*), but also the only major British victory of *WWII* won over the Germans without large-scale U.S. help.

elasticity of demand: The rate at which demand for a *good* changes in response to changes in price or *supply*. "High elasticity" means that a small change in price or supply leads to a large change in demand; "low elasticity" is of course the reverse relation. High elasticity can wreak havoc on national budgets and forward economic planning, as operating assumptions may be invalidated almost overnight.

Elba: A small Italian island next to Corsica, in the Mediterranean. *Napoleon I* was *exiled* there in 1814, with his title intact and an honor guard of 1,000 men. He escaped in 1815 to begin the *Hundred Days*.

elder statesman: (1) In general: A retired or onetime *statesman*, called upon to give foreign policy advise to a current policymaker. (2) In Japan: A group of senior politicians who derived great influence over policy from their control of the *emperor's* Privy Council, especially between 1898-1914. Cf. *Genro*.

electronic countermeasures (ECM): Jamming and other devices used to confuse enemy radar, signals and communications, or to confuse, trick and deflect incoming *missiles*.

elint: "Electronic intelligence." Any and all information gathered in secret by electronic means. Its advocates regard it as highly reliable as compared to *humint* or even *sigint*. Its main drawbacks are that it is extremely expensive to gather information this way, and that one can be lulled into a possibly misleading sense of information security.

elite: (1) Of merit: The most knowledgeable, skilled

and capable in a given society. (2) Of birth: Those who inherit inordinate influence, power or wealth, but not necessarily any talent. (3) Of power: The small, inner circle of persons from government, business and (rarely) academia, who actually make decisions that affect national policy, whether they are formally and legally charged with this task or not. Such persons are usually familiar to each other, are often non-partisan in a party political sense, and move in and out of senior government and private sector positions with relative ease (if not always with grace).

elitism: (1) In general: The practice of, or belief in, rule by an *elite*, whether of merit, birth or power, and whether open or secret ("power elite"). (2) In *diplomacy*: The belief that foreign policy should be made and carried out by an elite corps of professional diplomats (a *foreign service*); or previously, by an aristocracy charged with feelings of "noblesse oblige" and prepared for the task with a privileged, advanced education. (3) In the *Security Council*: Formal recognition, through *permanent member* status and the *veto*, that *Great Powers* have special obligations in world affairs, and that it only follows they should have special rights as well (to better enable them to fulfill their duty to uphold *international security*). Cf. *pluralism*.

Elizabeth II, of Great Britain (b.1926): Queen of the *United Kingdom* (1952-), Australia, Canada, New Zealand and many minor territories; titular head of the *Commonwealth*. Her role is strictly ceremonial. The Royal House was called Saxe-Coburg-Gotha, but the name was changed to Windsor (after the summer castle) in 1917, successfully concealing the German roots of the British Royal Family.

El Salvador: Location: Central America. Major associations: *CACM, OAS, UN*. Population: 5.2 million. Military: downsizing from *civil war*, with incorporation of some former *guerrillas* into civil police force. It broke away from Spain to join the Central American Federation in 1822. In 1839 it left the federation to become fully independent. In 1969 it fought the so-called *Soccer War* with Honduras. From 1979 it was in a state of civil war, in which U.S. and Soviet funding played a significant role, and some 80,000 died. Its worst feature was the rampaging of *death squads*, mainly associated with the military but operating at arms length from official orders. (In 1993 a UN *human rights* special committee laid the blame for 90% of death squad killings at the feet of the military, with 10% attributed to the guerrillas; *State Department* and published *CIA* documents roughly concurred.) The U.S. provided large amounts of financial and military assistance to the government, especially after the 1984

election of the relative centrist, José Napoleon Duarte (1926-90) and the Christian Democratic Party. Duarte led what few moderates there were in El Salvador's 11-year civil war. The guerrillas (an eclectic mix of communists, peasant rebels in search of land reform, and native Indians) received *aid* from Nicaragua, Cuba, the Soviet Union and some Western governments and *nongovernmental organizations*. The war ended in a *stalemate* in the field, and political exhaustion on all sides. The UN mediated the *peace* settlement from 1991-93. That was made possible as the collapse of the Soviet Union meant neither Russia nor the U.S. any longer saw El Salvador as crucial to their *national interests*, and worked with the UN to end the war. In January 1991, a *cease-fire* was agreed; a formal peace settlement followed in January 1992. The guerrillas were disarmed in five stages, and the armed forces cut in half. First, each side retreated to pre-selected sites; next they agreed to stop patrolling; then weapons were turned in to UN officials, and supervised elections were scheduled. Some death squad activity resumed, however, toward the end of 1993.

emancipation: Freeing a repressed and exploited class of people, such as Russian serfs (1861) or American slaves (1863).

embargo: A refusal to sell *goods* or *services* to another country. (1) Absolute: A declaration by a *state* prohibiting all goods, shipping or aircraft from specified countries from entering or leaving its ports or airports. This is an extreme policy, rarely tried, and in this first form only also involves a *boycott*, or refusal to purchase the target state's goods (e.g., the over 30-year U.S. embargo of all trade with Cuba). (2) Limited: A prohibition, finite in scope and purpose, of specified exports. During the *Cold War*, the *West* banned computer and high technology exports to the *Soviet bloc* through *COCOM*. *Nuclear states* block the export of nuclear fuel and technology (and the *IAEA* monitors this), and advanced military states routinely embargo their latest weapons systems, with exceptions for close allies. See also *Thomas Jefferson; King Cotton; Abraham Lincoln*. Cf. *blockade; quarantine*.

embassage: Archaic: the instructions given an *ambassador*.

embassy: (1) The *diplomats* of one state accredited to a foreign government, as well as their buildings and staff. (2) A mission undertaken by an *ambassador*. Cf. *consulate; legation; special interest section*.

emergency session: When the UN calls an unscheduled sitting during a crisis. See *Uniting for Peace*.

emigrant: A person who departs his or her native land intending never again to domicile there.

emigré community: A group of *emigrants* living in the same quarter, or in close contact, and still with political interests in the old country. For instance, Russian revolutionaries found in tearooms and salons all over Europe before 1917; *White Russian* communities in Western Europe after 1920; Cubans in Miami after 1959; *overseas Chinese* and so forth.

éminence grise: "Gray eminence." (1) Informal salutation of the monk Père Joseph (Francois du Trembley) who served as confidant and adviser to the French statesman *Richelieu*; taken from the color of his monk's robes. (2) From #1, a person with quiet, and especially secret, influence over foreign policy.

éminence rouge: "Red eminence." (1) Cardinal *Richelieu*, manipulator of *nations* and destroyer of the power of *Hapsburg* Spain; taken from the color of his cardinal's robes. (2) From #1, an exceptionally independent and powerful adviser on foreign affairs.

emir: A *Muslim* chieftain or prince. Cf. *sultan*.

emissary: An *envoy* sent from one *state* to another, especially if on a secret diplomatic mission.

emperor/empress: The title of the male/female ruler of an *empire*; above a king/queen in ceremonial rank.

empire: (1) A great political community containing more than one *nation* or *tribe*, yet under the rule of a single *sovereign*. (2) A vast, far-flung *state* comprised of conquered *territories* and/or distant *colonies*.

empirical: Relying on observation or experience; not theoretical. Cf. *abstract; normative*.

empiricism: (1) A doctrine that regards all knowledge as derived from sensory experience. (2) A practice of, and analytical tendency toward, empirical research methods. (3) A preference for observation over deduction as the main basis for reasoning.

emplacement: A platform or reinforced position supporting an *artillery* piece.

Ems telegram: A message from the King of Prussia (later *Kaiser*) Wilhelm I to *Bismarck* concerning a meeting with France's ambassador at the spa at Ems, on July 13, 1870. Bismarck altered the text to make it appear that the king had treated the ambassador with disrespect, and released it to the press. French opinion rose to the bait, within a week forcing the *declaration of war* Bismarck wanted. That launched the *Franco/Prussian War*, which led to the fall of the *Second Empire* and European dominance by Imperial Germany.

enceinte: (1) A fortified enclosure. (2) A rampart.

enclave: A state or portion thereof, surrounded by another country. For example, *Lesotho*, *Goa* or *Walvis Bay* or some *protectorates*. Ethnic enclaves are common features, as in *Bosnia-Herzegovina* or *Nagorno-Karabakh*. The synonym "exclave" may also be used.

encroachment: When one *state* trespasses, especially with military units, across the *border* of another state. This may happen without intent, as say by a confused pilot; or deliberately, as part of the threat and counter-threat that usually accompanies a *crisis*.

end of history: The argument that with the triumph of the democratic states over *fascism* and *communism* in the 20th century, history (in *Hegel's* sense of an unfolding of contending, ideal forms) has come to its close. Henceforth, public events (*wars* and such) will still occur, but there will be no ideal *antithesis* thrown up to contest the triumph of liberal democracy, revealed now as the final *synthesis* of historical processes. At a political level, this fancy (if not fanciful) notion epitomized Western triumphalism at the end of the *Soviet bloc* and *empire*, and celebration of the currently unchallenged ascendancy of liberal-market societies and ideas after nearly a century of fierce ideological contest, as well as actual *warfare*. At a philosophical level, where it was first pitched, it was a rather hoary effort by neo-hegelians to stand poor Hegel back on his feet, his having once been famously (and quite rudely) stood on his speculative head by *Karl Marx*.

endogenous factors: Originating from within; elements of an explanation of events said to be internal to the system.

enemy prisoner of war (EPW): This term came into general and media currency when used by the U.S. during the *Gulf War*. However, it has not entirely displaced the venerable *prisoner of war (POW)*.

enfilade: A military position in which fire can be directed from along a whole trench, or line of troops.

enforcement procedures: Whatever mechanisms, punishments, *reprisals* or other means of *reciprocity* an agreement says states party to it can use against a transgressor. These may range from nothing, to automatic penalties and fines; e.g., see *GATT*.

Engels, Friedrich (1820-95): German socialist, friend of *Karl Marx* and collaborator on the 1848 "*Communist Manifesto*." He was a synthesizer of marxist thought, rather than an original thinker.

England: The dominant political territory within the *United Kingdom*, or Britain. Historically a separate *nation*, it was only partly conquered by the Romans, who built Hadrian's Wall across the country to protect their settlements from the barbarian *tribes* to the north. After the Norman Conquest (1066 A.D.) English kings held vast swaths of *territory* in France. They were pushed from these by the end of the *Hundred Years' War.* After that, England developed primarily as a maritime, trading nation. As its power grew it conquered and absorbed Wales, *Scotland* and lastly, *Ireland.* It challenged Spain commercially and in the New World, while facing down the Spanish Armada in home waters. It subsequently headed great *coalitions* against French ambitions to dominate Europe and expand overseas, into the Americas and India, under *Louis XIV* and then *Napoleon.* In the process, it built the most far-flung *empire* the world has yet seen. After 1707 this island power is more often and properly referred to as *Great Britain*, with "England" reserved to mainly domestic and cultural divisions from the Gaelic peoples of the *British Isles.* See also *Industrial Revolution; Napoleonic Wars.*

English Channel: The *strait* that divides France from England, and has along with the *Royal Navy* kept the island of *Great Britain* free from foreign invaders since the Norman conquest of 1066. It blocked the Spanish Armada, *Napoleon I* and *Hitler.* Its *strategic* importance was made clear as France fell under the Nazi jackboot and German *armor* raced for Paris in June 1940. *Churchill* flew over the Channel to offer Anglo-French *union* and convince the French government to fight on from Britain and the outposts of the French Empire. *Pétain*, deep in the throes of his *defeatism*, shot back that it was alright for Britain to fight on, as the Channel made a "fine anti-tank ditch," but France could do no more and would *surrender.*

Enhanced Radiation Weapon: See *neutron bomb.*

Eniwetok: An atoll in the *Marshall Islands* chain. It was the site of U.S. *atomic bomb* tests from 1947, and the first test of a *hydrogen bomb* (1952). It is presently uninhabitable.

enlightened despotism: An 18th century style of government in which absolute rulers refused to surrender their formal, legal powers, in return for governing less arbitrarily and with the welfare of their sub-

jects (or at least, the aristocracy and middle classes) foremost in mind. It was an unstable transition stage between *absolutism* and *popular sovereignty.*

Enlightenment: A philosophical, then cultural and social movement in 18th-century Europe, that argued for the elevation of reason and science as higher standards of knowledge, and against superstition, intolerance and established religion. In its call for the progressive encroachment by reason upon the unknown, and the exposure of cherished untruths, it was more than international; it was truly *cosmopolitan.* Among its leading lights were Diderot, *Kant*, Montesquieu, *Rousseau* and *Voltaire.* See also *secularism.*

enmity: Ill will between or among nations.

enosis: The demand of Greek Cypriots for *union* with Greece.

entangling alliance: Originally, a warning by *George Washington* to avoid "permanent alliances," thereby keeping America out of the *Napoleonic Wars* (the phrase "entangling alliance" was actually *Jefferson's*). Later, a near-ritual incantation by *isolationists* about the putative wisdom of not concerning oneself with foreign, and in particular, European affairs. Thus, during *WWI*, and in the *Treaty of Versailles*, the phrase "Associated" rather than "Allied" power was used to refer to the U.S. (as a sop to public opinion). The first entangling, that is, peacetime *alliance* the U.S. joined was the *Rio Pact* in 1947, followed by *NATO* in 1949.

Entebbe raid (July 4, 1976): An Israeli *commando* rescue of Jewish passengers of a *hijacked* Air France flight, flown to Entebbe in Uganda with the connivance of *Idi Amin.* The hijackers were all killed, with just three Israeli deaths (one an elderly woman left behind and later murdered, possibly by Amin). Efforts were made by some in the *UNGA* to condemn the raid as a violation of *sovereignty* and *territorial integrity*, but it was defended by others as extended *self-defense.*

entente: An accord between or among states reflecting a shared understanding that they have complementary *foreign policy* and *security* goals and interests.

Entente Cordiale: An agreement between France and Britain signed on April 8, 1904. It settled a series of minor *disputes* over fishing and colonial *boundaries*, but most importantly assigned Egypt to Britain's *sphere of influence* and Morocco to that of France. The Entente was not an *alliance*, did not involve the close collaboration of the later *Military Conversations* and was not aimed at Germany. But it set the stage for full Anglo/French *rapprochement* when Germany's subsequent actions threatened both. It has sometimes been confused with the formal Anglo/French military alliance that was actually signed only after the outbreak of fighting in 1914. (Hence, the common depiction of *WWI* as a product and clash of rigid alliances is, at least on a technical level, false.) A separate, Anglo/Russian *entente* was signed on August 31, 1907. It defined spheres of influence in Afghanistan, Persia and Tibet. It too was not anti-German, although as a matter of standing policy both Russia and Britain wanted to block Germany from influence in the Middle East. These two ententes are at times melded together and called the *Triple Entente.*

enterprise: A firm, organized to pursue commercial activities.

enthrone: To invest with *sovereign* authority.

entrench: To dig into a defensive position.

entrepreneur: A risk taker who organizes a firm.

envelopment: To threaten or attack both *flanks* of an enemy's position.

Enver Pasha, a.k.a. Enver Bey (1881-1922): Turkish statesman. A leader of the *Young Turks* rebellion in 1908, he became Minister for War in 1914. He fled to Russia in 1918 to avoid imprisonment after Turkey's *surrender.* He was killed during a failed *insurrection* in central *Turkestan* in 1922.

environmental security: The idea that changes to a nation's environment may seriously threaten its national well-being. For instance, a rise in sea levels would cause great harm to island or *coastal states,* especially those like Bangladesh or Egypt that have large populations living on low-lying river deltas. Of a different order are questions surrounding defense of nuclear, chemical or other sensitive facilities from environmental *terrorism.* It remains moot whether environmental security should be seen as a wholly new concept requiring a basic redefinition of *security,* or an addition to the list of traditional security notions and issues. See *deforestation; ecosystem; Euphrates; water.*

envoy (envoyé) : See *representation.*

envoy extraordinary (envoyé extraordinaire): A *diplomat* next in rank to an *ambassador,* accredited by, but not usually taken to be the personal representative of, a *sovereign* or *head of state.* Diplomats of this rank may also be called *minister plenipotentiary.*

epiphenomenon: Any secondary or less significant phenomenon, as in the view by some *marxists* of the *states* as epiphenomena produced by the more important, underlying structure of global *capitalism.*

equality: The legal right of a *sovereign* entity to be treated as a formal equal with all others. For example, each *state* is entitled to one vote in the *UNGA,* no powerful state may legally claim *jurisdiction* over a weak state, and no state is bound by any law without its *consent.* There are important exceptions: see *servitude; veto; weighted voting.*

Equatorial Guinea: Location: W. Africa. Major associations: *OAU, UN.* Population: 360,000. Military: minimal. A coastal *enclave,* it includes the offshore island of Fernando Po. It was colonized by Portugal during the late 15th century but was ceded to Spain in 1778. It was ruled from Madrid until 1968, when it received *independence.* Tensions exist between the more developed island and the poor and backward mainland enclave, called Rio Muni. In 1972 a mainlander, Maise Nguema Biyongo, declared himself president-for-life. He embarked on a brutal repression of all dissent and a debasement and corruption of nearly all national life. In 1976 his brutality led European settlers to flee. He then expelled tens of thousands of Nigerian migrant workers. In 1979 he was overthrown and executed. His nephew, Teodors Nguema Mbasogo, replaced him, retaining the one-party system but ruling with less naked brutality. Ostensibly free, multiparty elections were held in 1993, but opposition parties boycotted the process and fewer than 30% of the population voted.

equilibrium: A *balance of power* across a region or the whole *international system.*

equity: The requirement that an international court use fair play, balance and impartiality in its *judgments.*

equivalence: See *essential equivalence.*

Erfurt conference: A meeting between Tsar *Alexander I, of Russia* and *Napoleon I,* in October 1808. Napoleon wanted a comprehensive settlement with Russia in Eastern Europe and toward Turkey. But Alexander, who was secretly told of French plans by *Talleyrand,* was able to evade any commitment. Having thus failed to placate Russia and secure his eastern *flank,* Napoleon would strike out at Alexander in 1812. See *Tilsit.*

Eritrea: Location: *Horn of Africa.* Major associations: *OAU, UN.* Population: 3 million, and 500,000 refugees in Sudan. Military: 100,000 troops; *demobilizing,* with a clear ability to defend against Ethiopian *revanchism*. An Italian colonial possession from 1890, it was used as a base from which to attack Ethiopia in 1935. It was taken from Italy by the *Allies* during *WWII*, and its fate handed to the UN in 1945. It was federated with Ethiopia by UN order in 1952, to give that country access to the sea. A *guerrilla* movement developed from 1962, when Ethiopia abrogated the *autonomy* promised Eritrea by the UN. Fighting continued through a terrible *famine* and forced *deportations* of Eritrea's *civilians* during the 1980s. It obtained *de facto* independence after the collapse of the Ethiopian Revolution. In April 1993, a *referendum* produced a 99% vote in favor of *independence*. It gained *de jure* acceptance the next month and joined the UN. It is one of the world's poorest states: 75% of its population in 1994 was dependent on foreign *aid* to survive.

error: An error of fact or deliberate fraud may, if discovered, invalidate a *treaty*. See *validity*.

escalation: Increasing the level and/or the scope of conflict. See *horizontal escalation; vertical escalation*.

escalation control: An idea connected to theories of *limited nuclear war*, in which escalation to *strategic nuclear weapons* is carried out in a careful and planned way. Some critics dismiss this notion as both politically and psychologically absurd.

escalation dominance: The effort to keep military superiority over an opponent at all levels of conflict and confrontation, as one moves up the ladder of *escalation* during a conflict.

escape clause: A clause inserted into trade agreements to permit cancellation of agreed *tariffs*, following formal *notification*. It is an instrument of qualified *protectionism*.

escrow: When a *state* keeps the assets of another state in a kind of trust account, pending resolution of a *dispute*; e.g., after *WWI* the *Allies* kept in escrow Russian gold that Germany had taken from the *Bolsheviks* under the *terms* of *Brest-Litovsk*. During the 1979-80 *hostage crisis*, the U.S. placed in escrow Iranian assets amounting to several billion dollars. This money was returned when Iran agreed to pay *compensation* to American businessmen whose property had been *nationalized* or destroyed.

espionage: The use of *elint, humint, sigint* or other means to discover economic, military, political and scientific secrets of other countries. See the cross-references under *intelligence; intelligence services*.

esprit de corps: High morale, or a sense of common purpose, in a nation's military or *foreign service*.

essential equivalence: In *strategy* and *arms control*, treating different weapons systems as effectively equal, so that they cancel each other out. For example, *warheads* with larger *yield* on one side might be seen as balanced by more accurate *missiles* on the other.

Estonia: Location: *Baltic*. Major associations: *CSCE, UN*. Population: 1.6 million. Military: minimal; Russian troops still in-country. One of the *Baltic States*, and a Russian province after 1721, it was occupied by Germany during *WWI*. When German troops withdrew it declared *independence*, and with Russia deep in *civil war* until 1920, succeeded in asserting that claim by force of arms. In 1940 it was seized by the Soviet Union under *terms* of a secret *protocol* to the *Nazi/Soviet Pact*. The U.S. and some other Western powers refused to recognize that *annexation* as legal, and continued to maintain ritualistic, formal *diplomatic relations* with an Estonian *government-in-exile*. But most non-Western states simply accepted Estonia as part of the Soviet Union. In March 1990, its legislature reasserted independence, describing the country as an "occupied nation." During the August 1991 *coup* attempt in Russia, Estonia declared itself fully independent and demanded that Russian troops leave. This was accepted by *Gobachev* and Estonia was *recognized* by the Western states in September, months in advance of the *extinction* of the Soviet Union.

estoppel: This legal doctrine underlies *good faith*: *states* cannot disavow earlier statements made by their representatives, or facts they have led other states or *international personalities* to believe.

ethics: Moral principles; that is, principles concerned with right and wrong conduct (the common usage "morals and ethics" raises a distinction without a difference). This *normative* dimension of international affairs cannot be fruitfully studied without reference to historical and empirical dimensions, and their hard realities; nor can it be ignored (as it too often is) if one wishes a complete understanding. Moral reasoning about politics is a vital corrective and a refreshing complement to approaches that concentrate on appraisals of *power* and material interests. It is as well a rich and persistent tradition in its own right. Among other entries see *aid; anarchical society; cosmopolitan values; crimes against humanity; crimes against peace; distributive justice; genocide; Grotius; Hobbes; human rights; humanitarian intervention; international law; just war theory; Kant; norm; laws of war; liberal-internationalism; liberal peace program; Machiavelli;*

machiavellian; outlaw state; pacifism; raison d'état Rousseau; realism; slave trade; slavery; state obligations; terrorism; torture; war crimes; war crimes trials; weapons of mass destruction; world community.

Ethiopia (Abyssinia): Location: *Horn of Africa*. Major associations: *OAU, UN*. Population: 52 million. Military: contracting and demoralized. It was the only African nation that stayed independent during imperial penetration of that continent. It resisted the Portuguese, and held off Italian *conquest* from 1882-1936. Italy's move into neighboring *Eritrea*, which the Abyssinians also coveted, led to a decisive *defeat* of the Italians at *Adowa* in 1896. Border skirmishes continued to the 1930s, when the dispute was referred to the *League of Nations*. Italy invaded in 1935, starting the *Abyssinian War*. Emperor *Haile Selassie* was deposed, and fled. The League denounced this *aggression*, but imposed only weak *sanctions*. Selassie returned in 1941, with *liberation* by a combined British/Ethiopian force. Eritrea was taken from Italy and joined to Ethiopia by the UN in 1952. The U.S. maintained a base at Kagnew 1962-74, when Selassie was overthrown by a leftist *coup* that moved Ethiopia firmly into the Soviet camp and forced the U.S. to a former Soviet base at Berbera, Somalia. Helped by Sudan and Somalia, *guerrilla* campaigns in Eritrea and the Ogaden continued to destabilize the country. In 1977 large numbers of Cuban troops arrived. They were unable to defeat the rebels, but did make headway in the *Ethiopia/Somalia War*. In 1984 relief efforts were mounted in response to a terrible *famine*, caused in part by forced *deportations* and made worse by government refusal to allow food into rebel areas. In 1988 a formal *peace* was agreed with Somalia. In 1991 a *coalition* of six guerrilla armies overturned the revolutionary *regime*. Eritrea's *de facto* independence was accepted by the new government in 1992. The next year its *de jure* independence was accepted, again cutting Ethiopia off from the sea. By 1993 famine had returned to threaten millions.

Ethiopia/Somalia War (1977-88): Somalia laid claim to the Ogaden region of eastern Ethiopia, where mostly ethnic Somalis lived, and where local *guerrillas* were already in *rebellion* against Addis Ababa. On July 23, 1977, Somalia invaded. After initial successes, it was pushed back by Ethiopian troops who enjoyed the help of some 11,000 Cubans and a fair number of *Soviet bloc* advisers. Somalia expelled its Soviet advisers in November 1977, and switched to the Western camp in the *Cold War*. In March 1978, its forces were broken. It asked for a *cease-fire* and withdrew, but supported guerrillas who continued fighting for the next 10 years. Meanwhile, some 1.5 million *refugees* poured into Somalia. *Terms* of a *peace* settlement were finally agreed in 1988.

ethnic cleansing: A term in currency since the start of the *Third Balkan War*, but a practice that has gone on for centuries. It refers to the forcible *deportation* and intimidation of the *civilian* population "pour encourager les autres" (to encourage the others); that is, to expel or frighten people from one *ethnic group* into abandoning *territory* coveted by another. It can include use of terror tactics, mass rape and *summary execution*. At its most extreme it reaches *genocidal* proportions. Some examples: forcible transport of *indigenous peoples* in North America, and elsewhere, onto reservations; the *Armenian genocide* (1915); all Nazi racial policy; mass deportations of ethnic Germans from East and Central Europe after *WWII*; the human calamity of the *partition* of India (1947); elements of *apartheid*; and of course, more recent fights over *Nagorno-Karabakh* and in *Bosnia*. See also *Holocaust; lebensraum; war crimes; war crimes trials.*

ethnic group: A self-conscious community that shares race, or religious or cultural values. Cf. *nation; tribe.*

ethnocentrism: Viewing and judging the world from the perspective of one culture, often taken to be superior, without due empathy for alternate views. This goes beyond pride in one's nation or culture to imply exclusivity and a blinkered, parochial worldview. Note: Having "due empathy" does not require sinking into *cultural relativism*. Also, any culture may produce persons with ethnocentric views. Cf. *Afrocentrism; Atlanticism; chauvinism; cosmopolitan values; Eurocentrism; fundamentalism; jingoism; nationalism; négritude; pan-Africanism; pan-Americanism; pan-Arabism; pan-Slavism; racism; xenophobia.*

Eupen and Malmedy: A *border* area between Belgium and Germany, given to Belgium at the *Paris Peace Conference*, retaken by Germany in 1940 and returned to Belgium in 1945.

Euphrates River: It runs through Turkey, Syria, Iraq and Iran. In the 1980s and 1990s Turkish irrigation and hydro dams significantly reduced the flow volume, raising questions of *environmental security* for downstream states.

Eurasia: *Europe* and *Asia* considered as one.

eurobond markets: Transactions for bonds held outside the European country of issue.

eurocentrism: Viewing events from the point of view

of *Europe*, or seeing European interests as always at the center of world affairs.

eurocommunism: The post-1962 effort by West European *communist parties* to establish separate, "national paths to *communism*," rather than slavishly follow the *party line* laid out by Moscow, as most had done previously. The trend was first and most strongly evident in Italy, and most resisted in France. The Soviet *invasion* of *Czechoslovakia* in 1968 was a turning point, drawing rebukes even from the French. The main tenets were ostensible acceptance of pluralism and a parliamentary path to *communism*. This switch in tactics did not avert electoral decline in the 1980s, or extinction of this ideological dinosaur by conversion to a softer leftism in the 1990s.

EUROCORPS: It started in 1990 with a Franco/German brigade (unilingual soldiers, bilingual officers). It was pushed hard by the French as the core of an independent (of the U.S.) European military. In 1993 Belgium joined. By 1995 it aims to have 50,000 troops. Curiously enough, when all else fails its *lingua franca* is English. Events on the ground in Europe blunted the initial enthusiasm of France for a wholly separate force. In 1993 it was agreed that under specified conditions the EUROCORPS may come under *NATO* command, which may represent a step back toward military *integration* by Paris.

eurocurrencies: *Currencies* held in accounts outside the country of issue as a medium of international *liquidity*, credit and exchange, usually free of strong national controls. The important ones are eurodollars, euromarks, and eurofrancs (Swiss). By 1990 the eurocurrency markets reached $5 trillion.

Euro-MP: A member of the *European Parliament*.

Europe: The western continent located on the Eurasian land mass, bordered to the south by the Mediterranean, Caucasus Mountains, the Black and Caspian Seas, and to the east by the Urals. For cultural and even religious reasons, most historical and political usages exclude Russia (the western third of which is geographically part of Europe), and almost all emphatically excluded the *Soviet Union*. Similarly, Turkey is often excluded even though it was a major European power as the *Ottoman Empire*, and still has *territory* in Europe near Istanbul (*Constantinople*). There is also the occasional, quixotic exclusion of Britain (usually by the British themselves), as in the quaintly nationalistic usage "Europe and Britain."

European Atomic Energy Commission (EURATOM):

Established in 1958, under the *Treaty of Rome*. It coordinates *civilian* nuclear research, development and economic applications. In 1965 it was merged into a single executive with the *ECSC* and the *EEC*, all under the *European Commission*.

European Coal and Steel Community (ECSC): It was established in 1952 by a *treaty* among Belgium, France, Germany, Italy, Luxembourg and the Netherlands. It was the first major move toward European *integration*, pooling coal and steel resources under a High Authority that aimed at eliminating *tariffs* on these key industries, but also at political *union*. In 1967 it merged with the *EEC* and *EURATOM*. See *European Commission; European Communities; European Community.*

European Commission: A quasi-*executive* set up by the *Treaty of Rome* in 1958. At first, it had nine members, one for each of the original six, plus additional commissioners for the larger states of France, Italy and West Germany. Its main duty was to administer the *treaty*. In 1967 it took over *EURATOM* and the *ECSC*, although the latter was still answerable to its High Authority. It is a vehicle of cooperation among national governments, rather than a *supranational* body. That reality was confirmed in the *Luxembourg Compromise* of 1966, which derailed the fast track toward political *union*. The commission grew weaker with expansion, as complex monetary and other issues fell outside its brief.

European Communities (EC): Some, especially in Britain, still prefer this term to make the point that there is not one community, but a galaxy of organizations and functional communities such as *EURATOM*, *ECSC* and the *EEC*. The *European Court of Justice* also maintains this distinction. For the rest of us, these three formed the core of the *European Community* in 1965, when they came under a shared *executive* authority (implemented, July 1967). In 1993 the political/terminological debate shifted further, with creation of the *European Union*.

European Community (EC): (1) The collective name of the *European Communities*, beginning with the 1967 merger into a single *executive* organ of *EURATOM, ECSC* and the *EEC*, and the creation of a single Community by 1970. It included the whole complex of *IGOs* related to European *integration*. (2) A looser term referring to the member *states* working together toward a target of European economic and political *integration*, and federal *union* as the long-term goal. It had six original members: Belgium, France, Italy, Luxembourg, the Netherlands and West Germany.

Britain applied in 1961, but was rejected by a French veto in 1963, and again in 1966-67. Three other states had attached their applications to British entry, Denmark, Ireland and Norway, and these were blocked too by *De Gaulle's* opposition to Britain. With De Gaulle's resignation in 1969 the six moved quickly to reopen Britain's application. It joined in 1973; with it came the other three applicants of 1963 and 1966, but Norway balked at the last, and decided not to join. In 1981 Greece was admitted, and in 1986 Portugal and Spain joined. States that sought association with the end of the *Cold War* included: Austria, Finland, Norway, Sweden (all slated to join in 1995), the *Baltic States*, Czech Republic and Turkey. In 1992, Swiss voters rejected the idea of joining the EC. With the *Maastricht Treaty* the EC added a higher decision-making layer in the form of the *European Union (EU)*. Other states are attached to the EC/EU at an associate level through the *Lomé Conventions* and the *EFTA*. See *deepening vs. enlargement; petites riches*.

European Convention for the Protection of Human Rights and Fundamental Freedoms: Launched in November 1950 and in force as of 1953, this is the most advanced of all regional *regimes* on *human rights*. In 1954 it set up protective machinery, including a commission, that permitted individual *petition* to the *European Court of Human Rights*.

European Council: The name given meetings of the *heads of government* of the *European Community/ Union (EC/EU)*. These had no official status in the *Treaty of Rome*. But after 1974 they became an institutionalized feature of the EC, and continued into the EU. Meetings are usually twice per year. It was given legal recognition (without definition of powers) by the *Single European Act*. Its presidency rotates every six months among all members on an equal basis. This can raise very small nations, even Luxembourg, into the world limelight during a time of *crisis* if they happen to be hosting the presidency. After 1974 the Council was the only body that could set targets or guidelines for the Community. Furthermore, it was not tightly bound by *inter se* treaties, and therefore heads of government were free of the authority of both the *European Commission* and the *European Parliament*. In the 1980s the Council evolved from a brake on *integration* to a force pushing for it, as in the *Single European Act* and *Maastricht Treaty*, which modified its relation to the Commission and Parliament.

European Court of Human Rights: Set up in 1950 under the *European Convention on Human Rights*, and based in Strasbourg, it is empowered to make binding decisions in the event complaints cannot be resolved at the national level. The *Council of Ministers* supervises compliance with these decisions, which may also be addressed by the *European Court of Justice*.

European Court of Justice: Its formal name is still "Court of Justice of the European Communities," reflecting its relations with the *ECSC* and *EURATOM* as well as the *EEC* and *EU*. It was established by the *Treaty of Rome* in 1958. Its seven judges serve six-year terms. It hears *disputes* between members of the several communities, particularly those relating to *treaties*. Its *judgments* are binding, but ultimately have to be interpreted by national governments and courts. Still, from 1958-94 the Court found against every EC member in some case or other. Already by the 1970s, it was established as an important *intergovernmental* (not *supranational*) instrument. In 1994 the EU took Greece before the court over its policy on *Macedonia*.

European Currency Unit (ECU): See *European Monetary System*.

European Defense Community (EDC): It derived from a French proposal for a European army. It met resistance from Britain and Scandinavia, and so was joined only by the six members of the *ECSC* in 1952. Its purpose was to forestall an independent German military by compelling Germany to base all its military within the EDC while the other members would place only a portion each of their armies under EDC authority. *Adenauer* supported it as a way of quickly rehabilitating Germany. The Soviets tried to block it with an insincere offer of early German unification. The EDC never got beyond the planning stage because it conflicted with *NATO*, but even more because the French parliament ultimately balked at any German rearmament and refused *ratification* of the *treaty*.

European Economic Area (EEA): It began as a 1988 proposal to extend free market rules, but not full *EC integration*, to the *EFTA* nations. It became entangled with the question of *deepening vs. enlargement,* but still came quietly into effect on January 1, 1994. It is the largest *free trade area* in the world, with 17 member states, 375 million people and close to $7 trillion collective *GDP*. In 1992 Switzerland voted, in a *referendum,* against membership. Due to their shared *customs union,* that also denied membership to Liechtenstein. Legal disputes over *EU* rules against *monopolies* and state *subsidies* led to a compromise: the *European Court of Justice* will rule in the EU zone, and a "surveillance authority" will rule in the EFTA zone (incongruously, it is located in Switzerland). Four EFTA states (Austria, Finland, Norway and Sweden) applied to join the EU and were accepted for January 1, 1995.

European Economic Community (EEC): Established in March 1958 by the *Treaty of Rome*, it created a *customs union* of six nations by 1968 that grew to include 12 members by 1986, with four more slated to join in 1995. It is associated with the members of the *EFTA*, and by the *Lomé Conventions* with states in Africa and the Caribbean. It came under the authority of the *European Commission* in 1967.

European Free Trade Association (EFTA): It was established in 1960 as a counter to the *EEC*, which Britain had not joined. It included: Austria, Denmark, Norway, Portugal, Sweden and Switzerland. It aimed at industrial *free trade* by 1970, but not at political *integration*. It opened a rift within Europe between those eager for *supranational* integration down the road, and a minimalist goal of a set of *sovereign* states sharing free trade and *functional agencies*, but not in any way surrendering national *sovereignty*. Finland joined, first as an associate member, in 1961; Iceland joined in 1970. In 1973 EFTA lost three members to the EEC (Britain, Denmark and Ireland). The EFTA and EEC established a "special arrangement" in 1972, leading to a wider *free trade area* in 1984. In 1989 work began on a *treaty* of limited *union* with the EEC. However, the wider events of that year upset the negotiation, raising anew the question of *deepening vs. enlargement*. In 1994 most EFTA states agreed to form the *EEA* with the *EU;* but four also applied to the EU.

European Monetary Institute: It first met in January 1994. It is designed to one day become a *central bank* for the *EU*. At present, it is a forum where the governors of members' central banks sit on a council with ill-defined powers. As new member states join the EU, their central bankers join the EMI. Its vague mandate is to increase cooperation among the central banks.

European Monetary System (EMS): The idea was first broached in 1978 as a means of providing some predictability to *exchange rates* through an *Exchange Rate Mechanism (ERM)*, whereby *currencies* would be permitted to fluctuate only within a specified range. In addition, a European Currency Unit (ECU) was created to stand beside the various national currencies, guaranteed by a general fund to which members contributed a share of their gold and financial *reserves*. Under the ERM each currency was assigned a central rate relative to the ECU. If the floor or ceiling of a permissible range was reached, the *central banks* would *intervene* to keep currencies within the proscribed ranges. This was intended to provide stability, head toward a common *monetary policy* and prepare the way for full monetary union. In practice, only the second objective was really striven for, until the

Maastricht Treaty tried to push forward the third despite German reunification and differential growth undermining the first. The entire EMS idea was brought into question by a monetary crisis in September 1992, and was preserved only by widening the permissible range of currency fluctuation beyond any regulatory meaning (from 2.25% to 15% from center). This again raised the prospect of a *two-speed Europe*.

European Parliament: Established by the *Treaty of Rome* in 1958, it was to have consultative rights and powers of recommendation within the *EC*. It later received some minor budgetary powers and theoretically could dismiss the *European Commission*. It ached to become a true parliament for Europe, and pushed for an enlarged role based on its claims of democratic legitimacy. This effort was greatly aided by a 1974 decision to hold direct elections to the Parliament. The first took place in 1979. Yet this popularly elected Parliament was not given more powers. Also, the elections divided Europe, with Social Democrats doing well on the continent just as Britain moved into a more conservative phase under *Margaret Thatcher*, and toward a sustained defense of the higher legitimacy of national parliaments. In 1982 *Euro-MPs* held up the EC budget to show displeasure that the *Council of Ministers* had ignored their earlier recommendations. But in the end the Parliament was revealed to have representation, but no power of taxation or decision. Voter participation fell in EC elections, which were often viewed (and fought) merely as midterm comment on national governments. *Maastricht* gave the Parliament more powers within the *EU*, but whether these can be exercised against a prevailing mood of national assertion is moot. See *democratic deficit*.

European Political Community (EPC): An early proposal for comprehensive federation, above the *EDC* and the *ECSC*. It went down along with the EDC when France failed to ratify the latter in 1954.

European Recovery Program (ERP): Official name of the "Marshall Plan." It was a program of financial and other economic *aid* proposed by U.S. Secretary of State *George C. Marshall* in 1947, to formalize and expand assistance and *investment* already underway. It came into effect in 1948. To administer it, the *OEEC* was set up. Marshall aid was offered to all European *states* that had suffered from *WWII*, including those moving into the *Soviet bloc*. Czechoslovakia and Poland showed interest, but were compelled to withdraw by Moscow. The ERP provided *liquidity* and was a vital catalyst to rapid *postwar* recovery. It brought Germany and Western Europe into an American-led, international monetary and trading system. And it led to an elevated appreciation, perhaps even an overestimation, of the efficacy of foreign *aid* as a tool of *diplomacy*.

European Union (EU): The successor to the *European Community (EC)*, which it partly superseded without supplanting. Formed by the *Maastricht Treaty* on November 1, 1993, to the original 12 EC members it added four in 1995. It has the same structures as the EC, but not the same legal persona (e.g., only the EC can make binding agreements). Yet it went beyond the EC by adding to the project of economic and social *integration* a higher promise to have the EU, as Maastricht put it, "assert its identity on the world scene, in particular through the implementation of common foreign and security policy including the eventual framing of a common defense policy." It also seeks unified standards of justice and enhanced police cooperation. Its aim of more complete European federation stood in sharp contrast to critical reactions against Maastricht in several key countries. Four more states were admitted as of January 1, 1995, all affluent *EFTA* states: Austria, Finland, Norway and Sweden. Others from Eastern Europe and the Baltic may follow suit.

Euzkadi Ta Askatasuna (ETA): A *Basque* nationalist and *terrorist* organization, less active in the 1990s than in the 1970s or 1980s due to Spain's new prosperity, democracy and membership in the *EU*.

events data: Gathering and analyzing information on a range of newsworthy (that is, non-routine), singular events. Events are chosen according to their salience for transactions among *states* or societies, whether economic, social, communication, political, diplomatic or military. The idea is to build a picture (one pixel at a time?) of the *international system*, as reflected in its notable, or at least public, transactions. This research also seeks to isolate changes that surround *crises*, in the hope of developing a predictive *model*.

Évian agreements (1962): Secret accords between *De Gaulle* and the Algerian leadership that ultimately led to *independence* for Algeria, and almost led to *civil war* in France.

ex aequo et bono: Fair *judgment*, based on fairness rather than law. This idea seeks to go past mere textual judgment to a concept of justice, but can be invoked by the court only with mutual *consent* of the *states* party to the case.

exceptio rei judicatae: When a *judgment* in the same case is had elsewhere, such as a national court or *arbitration* body, this plea ends legal proceedings.

excess of authority: (1) When domestic legal authority is exceeded by a government in pursuit of some international aim, some maintain that this is irrelevant for purposes of *international law* (others disagree). (2) When an international court exceeds its *jurisdiction* the act invalidates its *judgment*.

exchange controls: Government interference in the market that sets the *exchange rate*, up to totally fixing rates and refusing to permit conversion or export of a national *currency*.

exchange rate: The price a *currency* will fetch in gold or in *hard currencies*. (1) Fixed: When a currency is supported by a government commitment to peg and keep it at a specific value. (2) Floating: When the market decides the actual value of a currency compared with other currencies.

Exchange Rate Mechanism (ERM): Created in 1979, its members reduced *inflation* and the wild fluctuations of European *exchange rates*. But the costs of German unification placed enormous strains on the system, changing the economy that had supported it into a source of instability. In September 1992, a major crisis led to the ejection of the British and Italian *currencies, devaluation* of several others, and a radical shift in exchange rate policy. See *European Monetary System*.

excise: Tax or duty applied to *commodities*.

Exclusive Economic Zone (EEZ): A 200 nautical mile (from the *baseline*) zone of exclusive economic rights granted to *coastal states* by *UNCLOS III*. In these zones states control mineral and fishing rights on the *continental shelf* and have obligations concerning marine conservation and pollution. But they must permit free passage to international shipping and in all other respects the waters remain part of the *high seas*. EEZ claims overlap, as lines project out from irregular coastlines. Conflicts may be resolved by drawing medians through the zones, or by *arbitration*. About 1/3rd of the world's oceans fall under EEZs, including entire seas such as the *Caribbean, Caspian, Mediterranean, Black, Red* and *Yellow Seas*, among others. Some South Pacific *microstates* control vast EEZs. Competition to claim EEZs around hitherto valueless atolls is intensifying, as with the *Spratlys*. See also *island; islet*.

exclusive jurisdiction: See *domestic jurisdiction*.

excuse: Escaping blame for breach of a legal *rule* or obligation by pleading *force majeure*.

executive: The administrative authority of a *state* (or *union* etc.). In the U.S. this is the branch of government under the direct authority of the president.

executive agreement: Agreements between *heads of government* that serve in effect as *treaties* but do not require *ratification* (though they may need enabling legislation), and are more easily revoked. They are usually concerned with mundane matters, such as consular arrangements, but can also be highly significant. U.S. presidents frustrated by the *treaty power* process have at times used these to bypass congressional oversight or avoid rejection of a political or diplomatic settlement (e.g., *Yalta*). From 1952-54 conservatives and *isolationists* failed to amend the constitution to put these on the same footing with treaties.

exequatur: Formal acceptance of a *consular* officer.

exhaustion of local remedies: See *remedy*.

exile: Someone living abroad because expelled from, or denied re-entry to, his or her native land.

existence: Under *international law*, the recognized (and obvious) necessity and right of an *international personality* to continue to exist in order to enjoy all other rights bestowed by that status.

exogenous factors: Those springing from external causes; elements of an explanation of events that are external to the *system* under study.

expansion/expansionism: A practice/policy of *conquest* or *aggrandizement*. Cf. *encroachment*.

expatriation: The voluntary renunciation or involuntary revocation of one's *nationality*. Cf. *Bancroft Conventions; deportation; exile; naturalization*.

exploitation: (1) Using something, such as a *labor* or a *natural resource*, to make a *profit*. (2) Using other people's labor or resources to make an unfair profit.

export: Any *commodity* or *service*, including information and *technology*, sent abroad for sale or exchange.

export control: See *embargo*.

Export-Import Bank (EXIMBANK): A U.S. government bank set up in 1934 and reincorporated in 1945. It provides credit to domestic exporters and loans to foreign governments or firms, under the condition that the funds must be used to purchase *goods* or *services* in the United States.

export-led growth: When a national economy, particularly in the *South*, is outward oriented, seeking to capture a share of world markets by *exploiting* its own *comparative advantages* to export *goods* or *services* and earn *foreign exchange*. Cf. *import substitution; NICs*.

Export Processing Zones (EPZs): Areas set aside by *LDCs* to encourage foreign manufacturing *investment*, local employment, *technology transfers* and other benefits, by making *imports* and *exports* free of *tariffs*. Additional incentives to *foreign direct investment* in these zones might include ready *infrastructure*, cheap *labor* and a streamlined bureaucracy.

expressio unius est exclusio alterius: "Listing of one thing implies the exclusion of another (not listed)." Thus, an international *human rights* covenant implicitly excludes some rights by listing others.

expropriation: When one *state* seizes the property of nationals of another state, or of an enterprise, without due *compensation*. Cf. *nationalization*.

expulsion: The legal technique of extreme censure of a miscreant *state* by declaring it outside the company of *civilized states*. For example, in the UN a state may be expelled by a majority vote of the *UNGA*, following recommendation of the *Security Council*. The procedure has been used by the UN only regarding *Taiwan* (October 21, 1971), and that was a very special case. South Africa was effectively suspended for a time by the UNGA Credentials Committee refusing to accredit its delegates, but not expelled for *apartheid*. The *Soviet Union* was the only state expelled by the *League of Nations*, for its unprovoked *invasion* of Finland. Cuba was expelled from the *OAS* at American insistence. Egypt was expelled from the *Arab League* for making *peace* with Israel (later readmitted). Serbia was suspended, not expelled, by the *CSCE* for its Balkan *aggression*. Cf. *suspension; withdrawal*.

extended deterrence: (1) Using threats of nuclear *retaliation* to protect a third party from a nuclear *first strike*, as in the U.S. *strategic* commitment to Western Europe during the *Cold War*, or to Japan and South Korea regarding a possible North Korean attack. (2) Any guarantee (not necessarily nuclear) to defend a small power in case of attack, such as was belatedly offered by Britain and France to Poland in 1939.

external affairs: A synonym for *foreign affairs*.

external indebtedness: See *debt; debt crisis; debt fatigue; debtor cartel; debt rescheduling; debt service*.

extinction: When one or more *states* absorb the *international personality* of another by *conquest*, dissolution, *federation* or *union*. For example, the *partitions of Poland;* Soviet *annexation* of the *Baltic States;* China's conquest of *Tibet;* West Germany's union with *East Germany;* dissolution of the *Austro-Hungarian, Ottoman* and *Soviet* empires, or of *Czechoslovakia* and *Yugoslavia.* Cf. *debellatio; state succession.*

extinctive prescription: When by *consent* or acquiescence the loss of a claim is incurred through failure to assert it over a long period.

extradition: The handing over of a fugitive or other person by one *state* to another, usually under *terms* of bilateral *treaties* set up to handle such cases, and usually non-political. *War crimes* are not considered political offenses, and hence suspected war criminals may be extradited (in practice, however, this right is often waived, for a variety of reasons). Also, extradition

treaties among *belligerents* are normally only suspended in wartime, not terminated. Cf. *asylum.*

extraterritoriality: (1) An exemption from local *jurisdiction;* e.g., *capitulations.* (2) The attempt to make one's own domestic laws apply in the *territory* of other *states;* e.g., U.S. insistence that its *MNCs* should not permit foreign-based *subsidiaries* to trade with a country under a U.S. *embargo.* That was tried toward several communist countries during the *Cold War,* including Cuba and Vietnam. But it raised protests from friendly states such as Canada that hosted subsidiaries of American MNCs and accepted *COCOM* restrictions, but never accepted the U.S. embargoes against Cuba or Vietnam. Cf. *servitudes.*

extremism: Immoderation in one's foreign policy, intellectual, political or social opinions and judgments. See *chauvinism; fanatic; fundamentalism; ideology; jingoism; radical; reactionary; secularism.*

F

fact-finding mission: An investigative mission undertaken by a disinterested party on the assumption that *conflicts* may be the product of *misperception* or lack of information, and that once the facts are uncovered rational solutions become possible. The *League of Nations* made use of such missions, sometimes with success. However, one that led to a mild rebuke of Tokyo's 1931 invasion of *Manchuria* occasioned Japan's withdrawal from the League. The *UN* and *CSCE* also use such missions to defuse local conflicts or investigate *human rights* complaints.

factor analysis: A *quantitative* approach to explaining causal connections, or "factors," said to underlie an observed economic, political or social problem.

factor endowments: The share of a nation's *inputs* required to produce a *commodity: capital, labor, land* (*natural resources*). The amounts and interrelations of these factors determine price and the commodities produced by a given *economy.* The term is a near synonym for *factors of production.*

factors of production: All *factor endowments*, plus *entrepreneurial* abilities and management skills.

fail-safe: Any mechanism or system to prevent accidental or unauthorized use of a *nuclear weapon.*

fair trade: (1) Trade that takes place under an agreement that sets specific prices, below which trading cannot occur. (2) Very often, a euphemism for *protectionism.*

Faisal I (1885-1933): King of Iraq and the *Hejaz* 1921-33. He fought with *T. E. Lawrence* against the Turks in *WWI.* Briefly King of Syria (a title claimed in wake of the collapse of the *Ottoman Empire*), he was deposed when it became a *mandate.* He spoke for the *Arab Revolt* at the *Paris Peace Conference.*

Faisal II (1935-58): King of Iraq 1953-58 (child king from 1939); grandson of *Faisal I.* He objected to *union* of Egypt and Syria in the *United Arab Republic*, and associated Iraq with Jordan. Faisal and his family were killed in a *coup d'etat* that ended the *monarchy* and established Iraq as a *republic.*

fait accompli: "An accomplished fact." Used about a unilateral action taken to resolve a *crisis* in one's own favor. One near-antonym is *negotiation.*

Falange: The *fascist* political party founded in 1933 by José Primo de Rivera (1903-36). It opposed the Spanish Republic and threw its support behind *Franco's* rebellion during the *Spanish Civil War.* Having used it to attain and consolidate power, in the latter

1940s Franco moved away from the Falange, sending it into terminal decline.

Falasha: The "Black Jews" of Ethiopia who practiced *Judaism* in isolation for two millennia. Persecuted in their native land, many were flown to Israel under the *law of return* beginning in the mid-1980s. In 1991 Ethiopia reneged on its agreement to allow their *emigration*, but with U.S. assistance the few remaining thousands were transferred to Israel. Since then other Ethiopians, and some Somalis, have rather more dubiously claimed a Jewish lineage.

Falkenhayn, Erich von (1861-1922): German general. He commanded on the *western front* early in *WWI*. He committed the German army to *Verdun*, trying to knock France out of the war by a ruthless *strategy* of *attrition*. Failure to break the *stalemate* in the West cost him his command.

Falkland Islands (Malvinas): Two main and over 100 small islands in the S. Atlantic. Originally uninhabited, between 1765-67 French, British and Spanish settlers all tried to gain a toehold. Britain left in 1774; Spain kept a garrison there until 1810, and then also abandoned the islands. Britain reestablished its claim and a permanent settlement after 1833. Argentina asserted that it inherited Spain's claim, challenged British possession and coveted the islands. Nonetheless, they became a British *dependency*. They were the scene of a naval battle in 1914 in which the British sank four German *cruisers*; and they saw the *Falkland Islands War*. Population: 2,000 people; 100,000 sheep.

Falkland Islands War (1982): British control of the *Falkland Islands* was disputed since 1833 by Argentina, which calls them the Malvinas. After decades of legal wrangling formal talks began in 1965. The talks were generally proceeding toward Argentine *sovereignty* over the islands, when the situation for the *junta* leaders in Argentina deteriorated badly. Looking for a foreign distraction, they played the nationalist card by invading the Falklands on April 2, 1982. Apparently, they miscalculated that Britain would not fight for what it had been about to surrender through *negotiation* anyway. But fight Britain did. It sent a naval taskforce to the islands, cheered out of port by the populace in a style not seen since *WWI*. But it also took a month to arrive. In the interim, the U.S. tried to *mediate*. In the end, however, the U.S. backed Britain, its close *NATO* ally, with *intelligence* and *logistical* support. Argentina tried to invoke the *Rio Treaty*, but got little response. The *Soviet Union* stayed out of a conflict that was beyond its reach and outside its declining imperial interests. A highly professional British

land force routed the Argentines (who were mostly unenthusiastic *conscripts*) within 25 days. All Argentine land forces surrendered on June 14th. At sea, French-built, Argentine "Exocet" *missiles* sank one aluminum, British *destroyer* and set afire several other ships (leading to reconsideration of ship materials and design by all modern navies). Britain sank an aging Argentine *warship*, incurring high loss of life. The war toppled General *Galtieri* but helped reelect British PM *Margaret Thatcher*. The Falklands remain disputed, but Britain now garrisons them.

fallout: Dust and other material irradiated by a nuclear explosion, that falls back to the surface where it poisons animals, people and plants for years and even decades afterwards.

falsification: The effort to prove a *hypothesis* or *theory* incorrect to exclude it as an explanation. The term was introduced by philosopher of science Karl Popper (b.1902), who argued that this was the only way scientific knowledge accumulates: proving theories true is not possible; one can only prove them false, that is, partial or incomplete. Cf. *paradigm*.

family reunification: (1) In *immigration*: A basic principle for permitting follow-up immigration once a primary family member has become established. (2) In *human rights*: An issue over which *diplomatic intervention* frequently takes place, where governments plead with other *states* on humanitarian grounds not to divide families by refusing exit *visas* to some members. It was very important to Germany during the *Cold War*, and therefore became a central weave in the human rights "basket" of the *Helsinki Accords*. It remains a concern in numerous *civil wars* and interethnic conflicts.

famine: Food scarcity, to the point of starvation for large numbers of people. Famine was a chronic problem in China, especially in the 18th and 19th centuries, and again in the 20th following the dislocations of *war* and *revolution*; Europe into the 19th century, where it underlay the *Revolutions of 1848* and mass *migration* from Ireland and elsewhere; Russia and the Soviet Union, which had major famines in 1890-91, 1919-22 and 1931-33 (the second partly man-made, the third entirely so); and India. Yet there has been tremendous progress, and famine no longer threatens these regions. The *Sahel* was famine-stricken in the 1980s due to a prolonged drought, overpopulation, overcropping, overgrazing and several wars. Recent famines there that provoked international responses include Ethiopia in the mid-1980s and Somalia in 1992-94. Famine can be natural or artificial. The latter sort may be an unintentional consequence of human action, or deliberate. Famine has been used frequently as a conscious instrument of war and repression, and in the 20th century also resulted from social experiments such as *collectivization*. More often, political factors convert what otherwise would remain chronic hunger and food deficiency into famine. It should be noted that famine is but the most visible (that is, newsworthy) aspect of the much greater problem of hunger. In fact, more deaths occur from chronic malnutrition, undernutrition and seasonal hunger than from famine. See also *food*.

Fanon, Franz (1925-61): Algerian revolutionary. A medical doctor, he joined the Algerian *rebellion* against French rule. He was famous for his anti-colonial writings, promoted during the war (which he did not survive) by leading French intellectuals. Contrary to classical *marxism*, with its emphasis on the role of the *proletariat* as the revolutionary class that is destined to build *socialism*, and dismissal of the peasantry as either a *reactionary* or politically unconscious mass, Fanon said that peasant *revolution* was the only option for *Third World* colonial nations. He went further than *Lenin* or even *Mao* in this regard, openly distrusting the urban working classes as having interests opposed to the peasantry. He was also original in his frank discussion of the role of race in politics. He had an almost *fascist* admiration for violence as a social "purgative," and a vision of himself and other revolutionaries as doctors to the colonial body politic.

Far East: The core of the Orient: *China, Japan, Korea, Siberia* and what is today called *Southeast Asia*.

Faroe Islands: N. Atlantic islands under Danish control, of which a mere 18 are (sparsely) populated. They enjoy considerable *autonomy*. They declined to join the *EC*, mainly due to a fisheries *dispute*.

Faruk I (1920-65): King of Egypt, 1936-52. He hated the British and was sympathetic to the *Axis* during *WWII*. The loss to Israel in 1948 exposed the ineptitude and corruption of his reign. He abdicated in 1952, replaced by a military *republic* under *Nasser*.

fascism: The term came from the "fasces," a sheaf of rods carried as a symbol of office by Roman consuls, and adopted by the movement that brought *Mussolini* to power in Italy in 1922. Yet it is most often applied to *nazism*, and may refer to comparable movements in Croatia, Rumania, Spain, and on a smaller scale all across Nazi-occupied Europe. Burma, China, India and Japan all had fascist movements and parties as well. Milder variants spread to Latin America, and else-

where. Fascism is a *totalitarian,* romantic *ideology* that looks to a strong dictator and veneration of the *state* and/or *nation,* and emphasizes *militarism, chauvinism* and usually *racism,* too. Its revolutionary character and ambitions ought not to be underestimated: it is not simply "more conservative" conservatism or far-right *reaction* (an abusive misuse common in contemporary, pejorative speech and writing). Rather, it is an utter rejection of democratic norms in favor of mass worship of, and personal surrender to, the ethnic collective. It vehemently repudiates both *capitalism* and *marxism* (though in practice, it has proven more comfortable with the former), and views *democracy* and the search for tolerant social consensus as weak and decadent. Its great appeal to millions in the 1920s and 1930s also should not be underestimated: it was found greatly attractive by all those, mainly in the middle classes but also among the rural population, who wished to dissolve class conflict, personal misfortune, and national economic woes into an "organic" community based upon the nation (defined ethnically or even racially). That longing to surrender individuality to some putatively higher, collective purpose was made acute by the travails of the *Great Depression,* during which fascism presented itself as a distinct alternative to the promotion of class conflict by the extreme left, while still offering revolutionary answers to problems that were defying solution by traditional, democratic means. Others were (are) attracted to fascism for its celebration of the irrational, its declaration of the superiority of emotion, intuition and will over intellect, its shrill insistence on direct action as against reason, or just because they enjoy anti-social violence and belonging to a herd. See *neo-nazism; social imperialism*.

Fashoda incident (1898): In the Sudan, source of the White Nile, a clash of imperial interests almost led to *war* between Britain and France. London feared a dam on the upper Nile would hurt its interests in Egypt, and was the more forceful of the two in the confrontation. Paris ultimately backed down and renounced claims to the Nile Valley.

Fatah (al-Fatah): A *Palestinian* organization set up in 1957. It began *guerrilla* operations against Israel in 1964. Under *Arafat* it became the core of the *Palestine Liberation Organization* put together in 1969. Expelled from Lebanon along with the PLO in 1982, it relocated to Syria, then Tunisia. In 1993 it endorsed the PLO *peace* agreement with Israel.

February Revolution: See *Russian Revolution, March (February) 1917*.

fedayeen: A generic term for an Arab *guerrilla* fighting Israel, especially one willing to sacrifice his or her life on a suicide mission.

Federalists: One of the first two U.S. political parties, organized around the intellect and political ambitions of *Alexander Hamilton*. It was dedicated in foreign policy to the idea that America's interests were *rapprochement* with Britain and an end to the *alliance* with France. The Federalists were bitterly opposed by *Jefferson*, and the *Democratic (Republican) Party*.

Federal Republic of Germany (FRG): See *Germany*.

Federated Malay States: Former name of *Malaya*.

federation: (1) A composite association of *states*, which maintain common institutions under a divided *sovereign* or constitutional authority. (2) A *union* of previously separate states, fused into a single *international personality*.

feedback: In *systems* and *cybernetic theory*, return to the policy maker of evaluative information about the effects of a decision.

feint: A false attack, aimed at one point of an enemy's position to distract from the main attack to take place elsewhere.

Feisal, Ibn Abdul al-Aziz Al Saud (1905-75): King of Saudi Arabia 1964-75; son of *Ibn Saud*. Feisal turned to the *West* for *arms* and diplomatic support without conducting a pro-Western *diplomacy*. He opposed *Nasser* for his *secularism* and *pan-Arabism*. He backed Syria and Iraq in the *Third Arab/Israeli War*, and helped *mediate* the Jordanian/PLO war of 1970. He was instrumental in organizing the *OPEC* oil *embargo* in 1973. In 1975 he was assassinated, by a deranged nephew.

fellow traveler: A person who, although not a member of a political party, mouths or supports its positions and ideals; usually used in the pejorative.

female circumcision: Surgical alteration of the female genitalia, a practice that afflicts millions of women and children in over 40 *African*, *Arab* or *Islamic* countries. Always a major health problem, it emerged in the 1980s as a highly contentious *human rights* issue. There are three types: (1) sunna: cutting the prepuce or hood of the clitoris; (2) excision: cutting the clitoris and labia minora; (3) infibulation (pharonic): removing the clitoris, labia minora and labia majora. Criticism has met fierce opposition on grounds of *cultural relativism*. See also *World Health Organization*.

Fenians: Irish nationalists who in 1866-68 raided Canada from upper New York state. Their military excursions were trivial, but aroused *Gladstone* to reconsider the *Irish Question*.

Ferdinand II, of Spain (1452-1516): King of Aragon; Naples; Sicily; and with Isabella I, joint ruler of *Castile*; conqueror of the last Moorish states in Iberia; and sponsor of expeditions by Christopher Columbus, among others, to the *New World*.

Fernando Po: An island off the Nigerian coast. Formerly an overseas province of Spain, it is now part of Equatorial Guinea.

Ferry, Jules (1832-93): French statesman. PM 1880-81, 1883-85. As a deputy, he voted against *war* with *Prussia* in 1870. As PM, he was an active *imperialist*. He acquired *Tunis*, fought a war to add *Tonkin* to *French Indochina* and obtained parts of the Congo and Madagascar. But these adventures were undertaken at a cost of neglect of interests in Europe, which undermined his support from the nationalist right. He was murdered in 1893, but not for political reasons.

Fertile Crescent: The prime agricultural area between the Nile, the Tigris and the Persian Gulf.

field artillery: Mobile guns light enough to accompany *infantry* on the march.

fifth column: Traitors and/or saboteurs behind the lines prepared to help an enemy force. The term derives from the *Spanish Civil War:* General Queipo de Llano, commanding four *fascist* columns advancing on Madrid, was asked which one would take the city. He is said to have replied, with arrogant swagger: "The fifth, which is already there."

Fifth Republic: France, since the installation of its most recent constitution in 1958.

fighter: Any small, fast aircraft designed to hunt and destroy other aircraft.

fighter-bomber: An aircraft that combines the main functions of a *fighter* and a light *bomber*.

Fiji: Location: S. Pacific. Major associations: *NAM, SPC, SPF, UN*. Population: 700,000. Military: little offensive capability. Populated for 2,000 years by *Polynesians* and *Melanesians*. Before becoming a British *colony* (1874), these 300 islands fought *wars* with *Tonga*. Fijian troops helped suppress a communist *insurgency* in Malaya in the 1950s and 1960s, leaving a legacy of Malaysian interest in Fiji, including several technical, cultural and trade agreements. Upon its *independence* in 1970 it joined the UN and *Commonwealth*, quickly becoming the most diplomatically active of the region's island states. In 1971 it joined the *South Pacific Commission*. In 1972 it helped establish the *South Pacific Forum*. It has sent UN contingents to Lebanon, Sinai and Kuwait, partly to earn *foreign exchange*, and is active within *ECOSOC* and *UNCLOS*. Its racial divisions are a major foreign policy problem. Native Fijians attached to the land resented a more entrepreneurial Indian population, descended from contract laborers brought in by Britain in the 19th century. In 1987 two pro-native *coups* brought threats of international *intervention*. The second led to declaration of a *republic*, a lapse in Commonwealth membership and a racially biased constitution. Most Western countries cut military and economic *aid* to Fiji, distressed that it was the first state in the region to retreat from democracy. Some have since restored economic aid. India was drawn in by concern for the rights of the Indian minority. It blocked Fiji's re-entry into the Commonwealth in 1990, which led to a breach in relations. Relations with Australia and New Zealand remain cool, but the *ASEAN* states have moved into the trade vacuum.

final act: A summary statement of any international conference; a *declaration* rather than a *treaty*. See also *Helsinki Accords*.

final goods and services: Those intended for end use or consumption, requiring no further processing.

final solution to the Jewish problem: "Endlösung." The *Nazi* euphemism for the *genocide* they conducted against the Jews of Europe. The decision was taken at the secret Wannsee Conference in January 1942. There never was before in history such a chilling meeting: functionaries of one of the world's great nations sat at a conference table and coldly, clinically and methodically planned the mass murder of millions of fellow human beings. They talked as though the issues at stake were nothing more than logistics--of transport, rail schedules, construction contracts for the *death camps* and the instruments of murder, personnel problems, pay rates, and the liklihood of their own personal advancement should they complete their appointed task at the speed requested and to the full satisfaction and pleasure of their masters in Berlin. When these gangsters were done three years later, over six million Jews had been sacrificed at the altars of hatred and ambition. See also *anti-Semitism; Auschwitz; concentration camps; Dachau; Himmler; genocide; Gestapo; Göring; Hitler; Holocaust; National Socialism;*

SS. Cf. *Armenian genocide; Burundi; Cambodian genocide; collectivization; ethnic cleansing; Rwanda.*

finance: The management of matters concerning money, especially those touching on public affairs such as regulatory policy toward banking and *investment*.

financial veto: When a large, contributing *state* withholds funds from an *international organization* to register disapproval of some vote, or extract concessions on procedural or substantive issues. If the monies withheld are so large as to render impossible any implementation of the decision concerned, an effective veto has occurred. Cf. *weighted voting*.

fin de siècle: (1) The close of the 19th century, with its decline of faith in science, progress and human perfectibility. (2) A pose of fashionable melancholy.

FINEFTA Treaty (1961): This agreement gave Finland associate membership in the *EFTA*, while allowing it to maintain its *preferential trade* scheme with the Soviet Union.

Finland: Location: *Baltic/Scandinavia*. Major associations: *CSCE, EFTA, EU* (1995), *Nordic Council, OECD, UN*. Population: five million. Military: small, top-quality defense force. It was part of Sweden from 1154-1809, when it was transferred to Russia, with a grant of *autonomy*, as the Grand Duchy of Finland. During the late 19th century policies of *russification* wore down Finnish autonomy and stimulated a nationalist revival. On December 6, 1917, Finland seized the chance offered by the chaos of *revolution* in Russia and declared *independence*. Led by Baron *Carl Mannerheim*, Finnish *Whites* fended off the *Red Army*, at first in *alliance* with Germany. *Peace* was agreed in 1920. In the *interwar* period it maintained an uneasy *neutrality*. In 1939-40 it fought and lost the *Finnish/ Soviet War*. In 1941 it attacked the Soviet Union in alliance with Nazi Germany, trying to recover its lost *territory*. It signed an *armistice* with Russia in 1944, and then *declared war* on Germany. U.S. support for Finnish independence helped prevent its complete incorporation into the Soviet bloc after *WWII*. It lost more territory to Russia, but was compelled only to toe the Soviet foreign policy line, in exchange for something like its old domestic autonomy. In 1961 it signed the *FINEFTA Treaty*. It also developed trade ties with the *EC* and joined the EFTA. With the collapse of the Soviet Union it was freed in foreign policy, and was accepted into the EU. But down the road it is likely to keep a fairly close eye on Russia, its inescapably large and dominant neighbor regardless of regime. See also *Aland Islands; finlandization.*

finlandization: When small countries adopt a foreign policy of *neutrality* or subservience under *Great Power* pressure, but keep their internal *autonomy*. Derived from Finnish/Soviet relations 1944-91.

Finnish/Soviet War (1939-40): Also called the "Winter War." In November 1939, *Stalin* demanded that Finland cede that part of *Karelia* where the border came within 30 miles of Leningrad. Concerned about a German attack from so close a point, he reportedly said: "We cannot move the city, so we must move the border." Finland refused to cede any portion of Karelia or to permit Soviet bases on its soil, as Stalin also demanded. Russia therefore attacked on November 30, 1939, in a bitter winter *campaign* that badly damaged its relations with Britain and the U.S. For nearly four months the Finns held out, actually enjoying early successes then falling back to defend the *Mannerheim Line*. The apparent weakness of Soviet arms impressed *Hitler*, and may have hastened his decision to attack eastward before he had eliminated Britain and the chance of a *second front*. But in the end Soviet manpower told the tale, and Finland was forced to *ask for terms* and cede part of Karelia. In 1941 Finland joined the attack on the Soviet Union. But when Germany began to lose the war and Soviet forces punched a gap through the Mannerheim Line in 1944, Finland was forced into a *separate peace*. It surrendered more of Karelia to the Soviet Union, and agreed to provide Moscow with military base facilities. This was confirmed in a *peace treaty* in 1947.

firebreak: Slang for the perceptual and psychological line between waging *conventional* and *nuclear war*.

First Empire: The French Empire of *Napoleon Bonaparte* 1804-14. It included *territories* in Italy, as far north as the Baltic and as far east as Dalmatia.

first line: Top quality troops or equipment.

First Reich: The retroactive name given by German nationalists to the *Holy Roman Empire*.

First Republic: France, from the deposing of *Louis XVI* in 1792, to the coup by *Napoleon* of 18 Brumaire (July 1799). See *France*.

first strike: A surprise, nuclear attack on an enemy's *missiles* that aims to win by eliminating the enemy's *second-strike capability*. Cf. *first use*.

first-strike capability: The ability to preempt enemy *retaliation* by eliminating all or most of its *nuclear weapons*, including its *second strike* weapons. Seeking

such a capability within a relationship characterized by *Assured Destruction*, such as existed between the Soviets and Americans during the latter decades of the *Cold War*, was widely considered destabilizing. That may not be the case where a large nuclear power is facing a state with but a few nuclear-tipped missiles, or other *weapons of mass destruction*.

First Tranche: The right to draw credits from the *IMF* up to the limit set by one's quota (determined mainly by contributions and extant *debt*). Beyond this, conditions on government *subsidies, fiscal policy, exchange rates* and so forth are attached by the IMF to further borrowing; thus, the higher the tranche the greater the conditionality of the loan.

first use: The initial move from *conventional* to *nuclear weapons* (or other *weapon of mass destruction*) in battle. The *Warsaw Pact* gained in public relations by renouncing first use. *NATO* refused to follow suit, arguing that this option provided a *deterrent* against a lightning thrust by much more massive, Warsaw Pact conventional forces. In 1993 the hypocrisy of "no first use" was dropped by Russia, which laid out a defensive doctrine that included possible first use, as other *nuclear states* have done. Conversely, India renounced first use in 1994. Cf. *first strike*.

First World: (1) In origin, a *Cold War* term referring to the industrial democracies. (2) A synonym for the *West* or *North*, with both terms including Japan, Australia and New Zealand.

fiscal policy: A *macroeconomic* device to control expenditure by means of taxes or *deficit spending*.

fission: Splitting the nucleus of an atom. When it leads to an uncontrolled chain reaction within a *critical mass* of fissile matter (e.g., *plutonium*), it causes a catastrophic release of energy in the form of *blast* and *radiation effects*. It is the basic process within an *atomic bomb*, and sometimes the trigger mechanism for a *fusion* explosion. Cf. *hydrogen bomb*.

Fiume, seizure of (1919-20): *Gabriele D'Annunzio*, the Italian poet and *irredentist*, and a handful of *fanatics* seized the city of Fiume in 1919 and held it for a year, in spite of the opposition of the *Allies*. Fiume had not been ceded to Italy at the *Paris Peace Conference* as Italians hoped, causing Italy to storm out of the conference. The Fiume incident, which ended with D'Annunzio's expulsion in 1920, inspired *Benito Mussolini* and other interwar *fascists*. It presaged the success of lawless political techniques later used in Italy and Germany, and revealed the *defeatist* mood and vulnerability to *stormtrooper* tactics of the Western democracies. In 1924 *Yugoslavia* agreed to cede the major part of Fiume to Italy. Returned to Yugoslavia in 1946 and renamed Rijeka, it is now in Croatia.

Five Power Naval Treaty (1922): Negotiated at the *Washington Conference*, it set up a ten-year *moratorium* on building *capital warships*, and established a *battleship* and *aircraft carrier* ratio of 5:5:3:1.75:1.75 (corresponding to ships permitted to the navies of the United States, Britain, Japan, France and Italy). This was hailed as a great breakthrough for *disarmament* as it forestalled an Anglo/American naval race, appeared to prevent a Pacific race of Britain and the U.S. against Japan, and capped the extant race in the Mediterranean between France and Italy. However, it actually permitted Japan more *warships* than it could build in the time allotted, and left out entire classes of auxiliary warships, notably *destroyers* and *submarines*. In addition, Tokyo only accepted the ratio in exchange for agreement that certain territories be excluded from *fortification*, to wit: for the U.S., the Aleutians, Guam, Midway, Pago-Pago, the Philippines and Wake; for Britain, Hong Kong and most possessions east of 110 degrees longitude (those near Australasia and Canada were excluded); for Japan, the *Bonins, Formosa,* the *Kuriles, Pescadores* and *Ryukyus. Hawaii* and *Singapore* were excluded, with fortification improvements permitted on both. At Geneva in 1927 an attempt was made to extend the 5:5:3 ratio to other ships in the Pacific, but this failed. A compromise was reached at the *London Naval Disarmament Conference*, but it did not last long into the crisis-riven 1930s. When the Five Power Treaty expired on December 31, 1936, a broad naval *arms race* was already underway on all the main oceans. See also *Shantung.* Cf. *Dreadnought; two-power naval standard.*

five-year plans: The periodic setting by the Soviet leadership of goals and production targets for national economic and industrial *development*. The first was announced in 1929 (backdated to run 1928-32). Production targets were set absurdly high, and then frequently reset to even higher levels by *Stalin* personally. When the inevitable failure to reach these quotas arrived, managers, workers, and even *apparatchiki* were subjected to charges of *counter-revolution*, or of being "wreckers" (saboteurs), "right-deviationists," "trotskyites" or other imaginary villains. Stalin's five-year plans thus fed the fires of the *purge trials* and thereby overfilled at least one quota: the prisoner and death count totals in the *GULAG archipelago.* Tens of millions more, left in place to work, suffered great privation and lived in a state of constant fear. In short, the spirit of the first plans was that of a revival

of *war communism,* and marked the definitive abandonment of the *New Economic Policy* that followed Stalin's utter triumph over first the left and then the right wing of the Party. For all that, the first plans led to a remarkably rapid conversion of the Soviet Union from an agrarian to an industrial society. None of the targets were actually reached (though in *propaganda,* all were exceeded). Nonetheless, almost all sectors of heavy industry (power production, machine tools, automotives, steel, petrochemicals) saw huge percentage increases in output. While this enabled Russia to become a major industrial and thereby military power by the end of the 1930s, the plans also led to permanent social dislocation, perpetually falsified production figures and other endemic administrative malpractices. Later plans led to less spectacular gains, but always similarly exaggerated claims. They were standard in the *planned economies* of other communist states after *WWII,* which all tended to emphasize heavy industry megaprojects at the expense of consumer goods.

fixed currency: One supported by a government commitment to *peg* and keep it at a specific value. Cf. *exchange rates; floating currency.*

fixed satellite: One that remains over a fixed point on earth, in geosynchronous orbit. They are used for mundane purposes such as meteorology; as spy platforms over *strategic* installations; or to support a *verification regime* set up by an *arms control* treaty.

flag officer: In the navy, any *officer* ranking above a captain.

flag of convenience: Ships must register with a home country, whose flag they normally fly, if they are to avoid *visit and search,* charges of *piracy* and administrative inconvenience. Yet certain *states* (notably Belize, Cyprus, Honduras, Liberia, Panama, Sierra Leone and Vanuatu) permit foreign vessels easy registry even though after the first visit these ships may never make another port of call in their "home waters." Such ships hence fly under a foreign flag, at the convenience of the owner. The states concerned gain revenues, while shipowners gain low registration fees and taxes, cheap *labor* and perhaps lax environmental laws. A rare exception to the host country rule is permission given to ships operated by the *UN, IAEA* and some other *international organizations* to use the flags of those bodies.

flag of truce: A (generally) white flag, displayed to call for a parley or to arrange a *surrender.*

flagship: A *warship* flying colors of the commander of the fleet.

flak: Anti-aircraft fire in the form of high-altitude *shrapnel.*

Flanders: A region in Belgium, parts of France and the Netherlands. During *WWI,* and less so in *WWII,* the Belgian portion was the scene of very heavy and bloody fighting.

flank: (1) The side or wing of a military position. (2) A maneuver in which one seeks to face the side of an enemy position, to bring maximum firepower to bear where it cannot.

flank speed: The top speed of a *warship.*

flattop: Naval slang for *aircraft carrier.*

flexible response: The U.S. and *NATO* doctrine that advocated meeting possible Soviet *aggression* at the precise level of that aggression: *conventional* vs. conventional or *nuclear* vs. nuclear, escalating only in case of failure to match forces adequately at lower levels. It was developed by *Robert McNamara* for the *Kennedy* administration, to escape what had become a non-credible threat of *massive retaliation.*

floating currency: One left to find a level in international *exchange* markets according to *supply* and demand, without artificial *intervention* or controls. Cf. *exchange rate; fixed currency.*

flotsam and jetsam: The wreckage of a ship, particularly its cargo, found floating (flotsam), sunken or ashore (jetsam). It may be freely claimed by anyone discovering it.

Flying Circus: In *WWI,* any squadron of aircraft, but especially that of Baron Manfred von Richthofen (1892-1918), a.k.a. the "Red Baron." His command not only eschewed *camouflage,* its planes were provocatively multicolored. The last commander of this most famous air unit of the war was *Herman Göring.*

Foch, Ferdinand (1851-1929): French marshal in *WWI.* He commanded field units at the *Marne* in 1914, and at *Ypres* and the *Somme,* after which he was retired. He was brought back as an aide to *Pétain* in 1917, then given command of *Allied* forces in 1918 with the rank of supreme Allied *generalissimo.* He pressed home the offensive that broke German resistance and led to the *armistice.* Foch served on the French delegation at the *Paris Peace Conference.* He accurately, albeit gloomily, predicted that the *Treaty of Versailles* did not mean real *peace,* but was merely "an *armistice* for twenty years."

Foggy Bottom: Widely used, affectionate slang for the U.S. *State Department;* from the nearby neighborhood.

food: Food supply is an underlying component of national *power,* and thus securing or *interdicting* an enemy's food supply, even to the point of causing *famine,* has been a common objective in *war.* In *WWII* Hitler's drive into Ukraine was partly an effort to secure an independent food supply for his *empire* that the British and Americans could not interdict, as they had during *WWI.* Conversely, German *U-boats* tried to starve Britain into submission. Similarly, Japanese imperialists wanted access to the rice paddies of China and Korea, and tropical supplies of SE Asia. Food is also a political weapon within countries: denying food for political reasons killed seven million in Ukraine from 1930-33, spread famine in Ethiopia in the mid-1980s, and again in Somalia and Sudan in the 1990s.

Food and Agriculture Organization (FAO): It was set up in 1943 and later became a UN *specialized agency.* Its purpose is to develop and promote improvements in the production of foodstuffs. It has played a significant role in *famine* relief, and agricultural research, education and *advisory services.* It is the largest of the specialized agencies, with over 160 member states. It has taken important initiatives in conservation of plant genes, early-warning systems on global food stocks and eradication of locust and other farm pests.

food security: The idea that all people have a right to levels of daily nutrition that permit their full physical and mental development.

foot soldiers: *Infantry;* the term derives from their means of locomotion.

Forbidden City: The section of Beijing (Peking) that contained the Imperial Palace and court buildings, forbidden to commoners or foreigners.

force: The use of military power (that is, violence) to coerce or punish, conquer or resist *conquest.*

force de frappe: The French *capability* and doctrine of maintaining a *nuclear weapons* force to serve as an independent *deterrent* against nuclear attack and a prop for national *prestige.*

forced labor: See *five-year plans; GULAG; Holocaust; kulaks; Peenemünde; prisoner of war; Vichy; war communism; war crimes.* Cf. *slavery.*

force majeure: "Superior force." (1) In general: any peerless force to which one must bend, regardless of right or principle. (2) In *international law:* any "act of God" (that is, nature) that overwhelms and therefore *excuses* one party from otherwise valid international legal obligations to another.

Force Nucléaire Strategique (FNS): The nuclear forces of France (currently being expanded).

Ford, Gerald (b.1913): U.S. President 1973-76. A respected figure in the Congress, he replaced Spiro Agnew as VP, after Agnew pleaded "no contest" to an income tax charge and resigned. He then replaced *Nixon* as President, when Nixon resigned under threat of impeachment. Ford was thus the only non-elected president in U.S. history, a fact that gravely handicapped his presidency. He accepted the *Jackson-Vanik Amendment* to the 1974 trade bill, leading to Soviet rejection of the trade agreement, and a cessation of Jewish *emigration*. In 1974 he became the first president to visit Japan. He placed curbs on the *CIA* and other security agencies, though not as many as some in Congress called for, and accepted a more constrained presidential role on foreign policy in the face of an "imperial Congress" still feeling its oats after toppling Nixon. Ford retained *Henry Kissinger* as Secretary of State, and continued Nixon's major initiatives toward China and the Middle East. After the collapse of Cambodia and the fall of South Vietnam in March 1975, he tried to show U.S. resolve in the "Mayaguez affair." But he was unable to convince Congress to *intervene* more forcefully in Angola. He endorsed the *Helsinki Accords*, for which he was heavily criticized within his own party. He was defeated by *James ("Jimmy") Carter* in 1976, in part due to a gaffe in the second presidential debate when it was clear (he was asked twice) that he did not know Poland was a Soviet *client* even though he had visited it as president.

foreign affairs: (1) The total activities, interests, and dealings of a *state* with other states, and other *international personalities.* (2) A rough synonym for *world affairs* or *international relations.*

foreign aid: See *aid; ODA.*

foreign correspondent: A journalist who reports on the political and other affairs of foreign states.

foreign direct investment: When a *multinational corporation* invests in the physical resources of a local corporation or starts a new plant, in a country where it is not headquartered. Cf. *portfolio investment.*

foreigner: From the viewpoint of any country toward all others: a non-native, and non-*naturalized* person.

foreign exchange: (1) Balancing international commercial accounts, especially when such transactions involve different *currencies.* (2) Foreign currency, or short-term credit payable in foreign currency.

foreign exchange reserves: The amount of foreign *hard currency* or credits held by a national bank. It is used to stabilize one's own *currency*, if *floating*, by buying or selling at low and high points within a preferred range.

Foreign Legion: A volunteer force within the French Army, made up mostly of foreigners with dubious or lonely pasts, or a taste for *martial* adventure. It has fought in all French wars since it was formed in 1831 (nearly 30 in all), suffering 36,000 dead. It was based in Algeria until it joined the colonists in *rebellion.* After Algerian *independence* it was transferred to France. In 1993 it served with UN *peacekeeping* forces in Cambodia.

Foreign Minister: In most countries, the cabinet officer in charge of foreign policy. In the U.S. the title used is Secretary of State.

Foreign Ministry: In most countries, the *executive* department concerned with *diplomacy.* In the U.K. it is called the Foreign Office; in the U.S. it is the Department of State.

foreign policy: (1) The complex of decisions and actions taken concerning one's position in world affairs, especially those pertaining to other *states* and *international personalities.* (2) Any stable goal, and the strategy to achieve it, followed by a state in the conduct of its *diplomacy.*

foreign relations: A looser term than *diplomatic relations*, this refers as well to relations that states welcome or encourage but do not necessarily initiate or conduct; e.g., international cultural, scientific or other *NGO* affairs and contacts.

foreign service: The corps of *diplomatic* and *consular* personnel in the field, as well as counterparts and support staff within a given state's *foreign ministry.*

foreign service examinations: Highly competitive, comprehensive written and oral exams that one must pass to qualify for admission to the professional *foreign service* of most *states.* Of course, another option is to ensure that a highly placed member of the government is a close relative or family friend.

foreign service officer (FSO): The basic title of employees of a *foreign service* in English-speaking, Western countries.

Formosa: A large island off the coast of China. See *Taiwan.*

Formosa Strait: It connects the East and South China Seas. For the "Crises of Formosa Strait" see *Quemoy and Matsu.*

fortification: (1) The military art and science of constructing defensive works, strengthening a set position and so forth. (2) A bolstered, defensive position.

forward-based delivery systems: *Artillery* or *missile* units, or any other delivery system for firing *tactical nuclear weapons,* based near the *front line*; that is, in forward positions.

forward defense: The *NATO* doctrine of meeting Soviet forces as far to the east as possible. It was designed to placate German fears of abandonment, and to avoid being overrun in a Soviet *blitzkrieg.*

forward market: Agreement to buy or sell at a future date and at a fixed price. Cf. *spot market.*

Four Freedoms: A vague set of postwar aims announced by *Franklin Roosevelt* on January 6, 1941: freedom of speech and religion, freedom from want (poverty) and fear (of *aggression*). They set the tone for declarations of *war aims* and the *Atlantic Charter,* and found some resonance in the *Charter of the UN.*

four modernizations: Fundamental, modernizing reforms begun in China in 1978 by *Deng Xiaoping,* in agriculture, industry, space and the military. Of these, military expenditure and doctrine was left till last, but caught up quickly after 1990. See *guanxi.* Cf. *Mao.*

Four Power Treaty (1922): Negotiated at the *Washington Conference,* it abrogated the *Anglo/Japanese Alliance,* which in 1922 could only aim at U.S. interests. Britain, France, Japan and the U.S. agreed instead to mutual guarantees of the Pacific status quo, including promises of China's continuing *independence* and the *Open Door.* It was an effort to freeze the colonial race in Asia the same way its sister agreement, the *Five Power Naval Treaty,* tried to freeze the naval *arms race.* Although Canada was not invited to the conference, it was greatly relieved: the pact removed even the slim chance it might find itself part of an Anglo/Japanese alliance in a *war* with the U.S.

Fourteen Points: The definitive statement of U.S. *war*

aims in *WWI.* It was later begrudgingly adopted by the *Allies* as a basis for negotiations with Germany. It was announced by *Woodrow Wilson* on January 8, 1918, in response to the *Bolshevik Revolution.* The immediate aim of the address was to keep Russia in the war, but the real significance lay in its comprehensive plan for *peace,* and in its setting the agenda for the *Paris Peace Conference.* The Fourteen Points were: (1) an end to secret *diplomacy,* or "*open covenants, openly arrived at*"; (2) *freedom of the seas*; (3) *free trade*; (4) *arms control*; (5) impartial adjustment of all colonial questions; (6) *liberation* of Russia; (7) restoration of Belgium; (8) liberation of France and the return of *Alsace-Lorraine*; (9) readjustment of Italy's *borders* in accordance with the principle of *self-determination*; (10) self-determination of the various peoples of the *Austrian Empire*; (11) evacuation by Austria of Rumania, Serbia and Montenegro; (12) *independence* for the non-Turkish peoples of the *Ottoman Empire,* and *internationalization* of the *Dardanelles*; (13) an independent Poland with access to the sea though *Danzig*; and (14) formation of a *League of Nations* to guarantee the independence of all *states.* Wilson scholar Arthur S. Link suggests that there was an implied fifteenth point: as far as it was still possible given Germany's *defeat,* the U.S. did not intend to impose a *diktat* on the *Central Powers.* The Fourteen Points became a moral standard around which Allied *public opinion* rallied. Governments were another matter, as reflected in the attitude of that brilliantly acerbic wit, *George Clemenceau.* He said in private of Wilson and his Fourteen Points: "God himself had only ten."

Fourth International: A small group of *radical* socialists organized by *Leon Trotsky* in 1936, and anti-Soviet in character and purpose. It had little influence other than to feed Trotsky's delusions about his own importance, and *Stalin's* delusions about a hidden *trotskyite* faction working to sabotage his *five-year plans.* Its main impact was that it probably helped Stalin decide to have Trotsky killed. It expired in 1953.

Fourth Republic: France, from 1946-58. Emerging from the *defeat* and *collaboration* of *WWII,* it was dominated by a fractious parliament and by losing and divisive colonial wars in *Indochina* and *Algeria.*

Fourth World: An alternate term for *Least Developed Countries (LDCs),* or the poorest of the poor, where *aid* may be all that prevents mass starvation or economic collapse; e.g., Somalia or Bangladesh.

Four Tigers: See *Asian Tigers.*

France: Location: W. Europe. Major associations:

CFA; CSCE, EU, la francophonie, G-5, G-7, NATO, OECD, UN (permanent member of the Security Council). Population: 57 million. Military: first-rate; #5 *nuclear state* in the world. (1) 1648-1815: France has numbered among the *Great Powers* since the *Thirty Years' War,* from which it emerged the main victor. Under a succession of brilliant *statesmen* its kings challenged and overtook Spain as the Great Power *primus inter pares* in Europe. From the *Peace of Westphalia* on, policy aimed at dynastic *aggrandizement* and the continuing division of Germany as the best hope of French *hegemony.* But *Louis XIV* overreached both himself and France: his quarter century of *dynastic war* and ambition raised in opposition a sequence of *coalitions,* under stern English leadership. His ever-longer wars drained the treasury, and he left France at his death in 1715 no better off territorially than when he began. The remainder of the 18th century saw French power slip vis-à-vis Russia and even *Prussia,* but most of all *England,* then a rising maritime nation. This shift was obscured by the *French Revolution,* which temporarily inflated French power by enlisting the full resources of the nation in the interests of an explosive *imperialism* within Europe itself, carried to its farthest reaches by *Napoleon I.* The other Great Powers still relied on *mercenary* armies and outdated tactics, but they eventually learned the lessons of *Napoleonic warfare* and the *levée en masse.* Thus, France was again overmatched by an English-led coalition in 1814, and for good and all in 1815. It never again challenged for dominance, though it remained a Great Power.

(2) 1815-1945: After Napoleon, France was preoccupied with political reform. It changed systems several times, from the *Restoration,* to *Second Republic,* to *Second Empire* and *Third Republic.* In foreign affairs it was taken with *empire* building in Africa and Asia, and overtaken in Europe by *Bismarck's* Prussia. It was badly beaten in the *Franco/Prussian War,* ceding *Alsace-Lorraine.* Yet it still flirted with *war* with Britain over colonial issues as late as 1905. At last drawn into mortal conflict with Germany in 1914, France was bled white at *Verdun* and all along the *western front* of *WWI.* It would have lost the war without U.S. *intervention* in 1917-18. This near-defeat and horrific loss of manpower made it the most intransigent victor at the *Paris Peace Conference.* It tried to enforce the *Treaty of Versailles* unilaterally in the 1920s, by occupying the *Saar* and the *Rhineland,* but it could not sustain the effort without British and American help. With U.S. failure to join the *League of Nations,* and Russia too isolated under the *Bolsheviks,* France was bereft of its two great *allies*--and without their huge reserves of industry and *population*--when Germany rose again in the 1930s. Its effort to build up the *Little*

Entente in Eastern Europe was a poor substitute for the vast numbers of the Russian army and industrial might of America. The *Maginot spirit* set in, leading to adoption of a wholly defensive posture in military planning and to *appeasement* in *diplomacy.* When war came anyway in 1939, French armies sat in their bunkers during the *Phony War,* while *Hitler* carved up their only eastern ally, Poland. When real war crossed the border in 1940, French resistance collapsed in just six weeks. During the *occupation,* a majority reluctantly accepted *Vichy* and accommodation to a German-run Europe, while minorities either willingly embraced *fascism* or joined the *Allies* and the *Free French.* With *liberation* in 1944 came retribution, and very nearly open *civil war.* Reconciliation was achieved around the legend of the wartime *Resistance,* a collective forgetfulness about the real extent of *collaboration,* and the charismatic personality of *Charles de Gaulle.*

(3) Since 1945: After 1945 France attempted to return to Great Power status. The effort to reclaim its empire led to two bloody but unsuccessful colonial wars, in *Indochina* until 1954, and in *Algeria* 1954-62. In Europe, it was greatly ambivalent about the U.S. desire to rebuild Germany as a bulwark against the Soviets. But then it embraced the idea of European *integration* and took the lead in construction of the *EC,* into the mid-1960s. While it withdrew its troops from NATO's integrated command in 1966, it continued to attend NATO political functions and to coordinate military policy less formally. However, it was highly jealous of its *force de frappe* and *Force Nucléaire Strategique.* During the *Cold War* French policy was broadly independent and could seem, though it was not, anti-American. The basic assumption of French diplomacy was that European integration offered a "Third Way" to *superpower* status, between Washington and Moscow. But belief that a unified Europe must necessarily revolve around a Paris/Bonn axis was shaken by German unification, and by 1994 France began to elevate its relations with the U.S.

France remains a colonial power in the South Pacific, where it integrated several possessions directly under its own constitution. It tests its *nuclear weapons* in the region, at Mururoa and Fangataufa atolls, with support facilities at Tahiti. Since 1989 Paris has tried to start a European army (see *EUROCORPS*), but also recommitted to NATO. It joined the *Gulf Coalition* with a degree of enthusiasm that surprised many observers; and while it sent its forces into *Yugoslavia* under a UN flag, it was more assertive than other European states about using *force.* It continues to intervene in its old colonies in Africa, most recently in in Zaire (1993) and Cameroon (1994). It was a strong supporter of the *Maastricht Treaty,* and moved to shore up the *EMS* and Franco/German cooperation after a monetary crisis in 1992. In 1993, the left was crushed in national elections and the French re-entered a period of "cohabitation," as only they could call a mixed or coalition government. Also see, *Bidault; Blum; Briand; Clemenceau; Dien Bien Phu; Foch; French Empire; Laval; Mitterand; overseas departments; overseas territories; Pétain.*

Francis Ferdinand (1863-1914): Archduke and heir to the Austrian throne. He and his wife were assassinated in *Sarajevo* on June 28, 1914, by a Serb *fanatic* society (the *Black Hand*). The plot was devised by the head of Serb *intelligence*. That provoked an *ultimatum* from Austria to Serbia that set in motion the chain of events leading to the *mobilization crisis,* and to *WWI.*

Francis Joseph (1830-1916): Emperor of Austria 1848-1916; last of the major *Hapsburg* rulers. His style was that of a benevolent *autocrat*, his ambition to preserve the *empire*. Yet by 1914 his age and fragility symbolized the decrepitude of Austrian rule, and its and his dependence on the more youthful and *adventuristic* German Kaiser. In his personal affairs he suffered nearly unbearable tragedies: his brother *Maximillian* was executed in Mexico; his son committed suicide; his wife was murdered by an *anarchist*; and his nephew *Francis Ferdinand*, with whom he quarrelled bitterly over the empire, was assassinated. The *Austrian Empire* disintegrated at the end of *WWI*, within two years of his death.

Franco, Francisco (1892-1975): Spanish dictator. In 1936 he flew from the Canaries to Morocco, where he rallied troops to land in Spain to overthrow the Republic, beginning the *Spanish Civil War*. With help from *Mussolini* and *Hitler*, he led the *fascist* armies to *victory* in 1939. While clearly pro-German, he skillfully kept Spain out of *WWII* (save for the "volunteers" of the *Blue Division*). He reingratiated Spain with the *West* during the *Cold War* by providing U.S. bases. He never relaxed his *authoritarian* rule at home, however. Spain experienced a democratic and economic renaissance in the 1970s and 1980s, after his death.

francophile/phobe: A person who loves/fears France and things French.

francophone: A French-speaking person or country.

la francophonie: Founded in 1958, it includes all the *overseas departments, overseas territories* and *dependencies* of France, also former French *colonies* that chose to remain associated. At first directly tying these areas to France in a neocolonial arrangement, it has since evolved into a French version of the *Common-*

wealth with mainly fully *sovereign* members rather than *associated states*. Cf. *Communauté Financière Africaine.*

Franco/Prussian War (1870-71): France *declared war* in the wake of the *Ems telegram*, but its basic cause was *Bismarck's* intent to have *Prussia* dominate *Germany*, and Germany displace France as the dominant power in Europe. The *campaign* was one of the first in which the new German railways were used, and to great effect. Within six weeks France was beaten, with Emperor *Louis Napoleon* captured and the main French army surrendering at *Sedan*. A second French army, at Metz, surrendered shortly after that. Only Paris held out under *siege* until the end of January 1871 (it was eventually stormed by French troops, who crushed the *Commune*). Terms were agreed on March 1, 1871, and written into the *Treaty of Frankfurt*. The war met all Prussian goals: the German Empire was proclaimed (at *Versailles*), and Bismarck stood at the tiller of the *balance of power*. The war's brevity misled strategists into belief that the offense was advantaged, and that wars among *Great Powers* could be waged and won quickly. That mistake led to calamity and carnage all around, in 1914.

Frankfurt, Treaty of (May 10, 1871): It set the terms on which the *Franco/Prussian War* ended: France lost *Alsace-Lorraine*, was required to pay an *indemnity* of five billion francs, and had to accept the humiliation of a German *occupation* army until the *reparations* were paid in full.

Frank, Hans (1900-46): Nazi Justice Minister (yes, that was indeed his formal title, sick joke though it was). He was a savage, utterly unmerciful governor of Poland during *WWII*, inflicting many *reprisals*. Convicted of *war crimes* at *Nuremberg*, he was hanged.

Franklin, Benjamin (1706-90): U.S. statesman. His first diplomatic mission was in 1757, when he was sent to England by the colonies to press the case for taxation to support the *French and Indian War*. In 1764 he was sent back to argue for representation on matters of taxation. After aiding in the Declaration of Independence, he went to France to seek help in the *American War of Independence*. In 1778 he secured America's first *alliance*, with France. After the war he was Minister (Ambassador) in Paris, serving to 1785. He was three-time elected President of Pennsylvania.

fraternize: To associate with the enemy, especially sexually. Cf. *collaboration.*

fratricide: The assumption that an enemy nuclear

explosion may so disturb "brother" incoming *missiles* as to make them inoperative or destroy them. This provided rationalization for the *Reagan* administration's effort to place the MX missile in a *dense pack* formation, to save the money necessary for more extended deployment. It was rejected by the Congress.

Frederick I, of Prussia (1657-1713): He backed *William III's* attempt to claim the English throne. He expanded *Prussia's* domain, and was the first head of that resource-poor state proclaimed "King."

Frederick II, of Prussia (1712-86): "The Great." King of *Prussia* 1740-86. Trained in the stern, Prussian military style, in 1740 he made *war* on Austria and seized part of *Silesia*, setting off the *War of the Austrian Succession*. In a second war over Silesia, from 1744-45, he further augmented Prussia's holdings. For the next decade he concentrated on consolidation of gains and reforming the army. In 1756 a third war over Silesia, part of the *Seven Years' War*, saw new gains and a reputation for military genius. In 1772 he participated in the first *partition of Poland*. By then, Prussia had emerged as a serious rival to Austria for leadership within Germany. Upon his death he left the kingdom doubled in size, a full treasury, and the most modern and advanced army in Europe. Yet some blame him for permanently discrediting the *balance of power*, by changing it (regarding Poland) into an offensive doctrine.

Frederick III, of Germany (1831-88): Kaiser of Germany and King of *Prussia*, 1888. He commanded an army in the *Franco/Prussian War*, gaining the rank of Field Marshal, but he abhorred *war*. He also favored constitutionalism, sought to reform and liberalize Germany in spite of the reactionaries among the Prussian ruling classes, and was pro-British in foreign affairs. But he ruled for just 99 days, and was succeeded by his son *Wilhelm II*, who shared neither his father's horror of war nor his love of constitutional liberties.

Frederick VI, of Denmark (1768-1839): He abolished *serfdom* at home and banned the *slave trade* in the Danish *colonies*. He joined the *League of Armed Neutrality* with Prussia, Russia, and Sweden in 1800, which led to the first *Battle of Copenhagen*. He refused to join with Britain in opposing *Napoleon*, leading to a three-day *bombardment* of Copenhagen by a British fleet in 1807. That confirmed him within the French camp. At the *Congress of Vienna* he was accordingly punished by the loss of Norway. He ruled quietly and fairly liberally after that.

Frederick-William, of Brandenburg (1620-88): "The Great Elector." He led recovery from the *Thirty Years' War*, making peace with Sweden. In the *Treaty of Westphalia* he recovered Pomerania and secured *independence* for the (then poor and insignificant) Duchy of Prussia. He helped organize a league of powers to fight *Louis XIV*, and fought off a Swedish *invasion* of Brandenburg that was backed by France. Lacking full support of the other German princes, he was compelled to accept *terms*, after which he devoted his energies to *internal affairs*. His efforts laid the foundation for his son, *Frederick I*, to become King of Prussia.

Frederick-William III, of Prussia (1770-1840): He *declared war* on *Napoleon I* in 1806, only to suffer crushing defeats at Jena and Auerstädt (1806), after which Napoleon occupied Berlin. At *Tilsit* in 1807, *Alexander I, of Russia* and Napoleon stripped *Prussia* of its western *territories*, and of its share of Poland. For five years Frederick-William reorganized the Prussian army and state, drawing upon the example of France. As Napoleon fell back after his disastrous *invasion* of Russia in 1812, Frederick-William struck out at the French with his new army. He scored a major victory as part of the *coalition* at *Leipzig* in 1813, and marched into Paris the next year beside Russians and British. His troops arrived just in time to turn the tide at *Waterloo* in 1815. At the *Congress of Vienna* he regained all his lost territories, and some additional central European lands, but gave up his Polish possessions to Russia. Frederick-William then joined with Alexander in casting a *reactionary* blanket over the continent. He was forced to adapt to some internal reform after 1830, but always ruled from a deeply conservative instinct.

free association: When a small *nation* freely chooses formal association with a larger power. There is domestic *autonomy*, but foreign policy is conducted within the parameters set by the larger power's interests. This may occur when a *trustee power* fulfills its obligations under the *Charter (UN)* and *UNGA* resolutions Nos.742, 1514, and 1541, which provide that the form of *self-determination* in continuing association must be genuinely voluntary and democratic, culturally respectful, and deemed acceptable by the UNGA. See *associated state; commonwealth status*.

free city: One that by international agreement forms a limited political entity, usually is kept open to world commerce, and lies outside the *territorial jurisdiction* of any one state; e.g., *Danzig, Tangier* or *Trieste*. This was proposed by the UN for *Jerusalem* in 1948, but was not carried through. Note: This is not the same as a *city-state*.

freedom of the seas: A fundamental principle of *international law*, holding that all shipping may by right sail the *high seas* without any interference in peacetime, and permitting only limited interference with neutral shipping in wartime.

free enterprise: A system in which economic activity is primarily in the hands of individuals responding to forces of *supply* and demand, without heavy regulation by the state. See *laissez-faire; liberalism; market economy; reform liberalism.*

Free French: The French forces that refused to accept the surrender of June 1940. They were led by *Charles de Gaulle*, and continued the fight from Britain and bases in the *French Empire*. Relations with the U.S. were shaky, but in 1943 de Gaulle secured *Allied* recognition as head of the *provisional government*. A Free French division spearheaded the *liberation* of Paris on August 25, 1944.

free market: One where buying and selling takes place unencumbered by governmental regulation and forces of *supply* and demand set prices for *goods* and *services*. See *black market; market economy.*

free rider problem: When *collective goods* are used even by states that do not fully contribute to them, such as when a small country by virtue of its *location* near a *Great Power* is defended automatically, and which hence spends relatively small amounts on its own defense--for example, Canada or Ireland.

free soil: *Territory* where *slavery* was illegal, especially in the U.S. before the *American Civil War.*

Freetown colony: See *Sierra Leone.*

free trade: A trading system in which imported *goods* are exempt from *excise* in exchange for reciprocal treatment of one's own *exports*, and where *free markets* prevail over government regulation. Proponents argue that this is mutually beneficial as it increases the volume of trade; and that it is conducive to *peace* as it creates shared interests and expands contacts among *nations.* Critics point to local job losses and the inequality and uneven productivity of national economies. The major free trade nations in history have been maritime, industrial powers: Britain in the 19th century, the U.S. in the 20th. Free trade was abandoned by the major trading nations during the *Great Depressions* of 1873-96, and 1929-39. Since *WWII* major trading nations have worked toward global free trade in specific commodities through the *GATT.* The *EEC* and the *EFTA* aim at regional *free trade areas*, as

does *NAFTA.* See also *APEC; ASEAN; CARICOM; fair trade; FTA; LAIA; mercantilism; non-tariff barriers; Open Door; protectionism; tariffs; WHFTA.*

Free Trade Agreement (FTA), Canada/US: It was implemented in January 1989, establishing a *free trade area* between the U.S. and Canada, with full *tariff* elimination slated for January 1, 1999. It was reinforced by, but remains distinct from, *NAFTA.*

free trade area (FTA): More than a *preferential tariff* but less than a *customs union*, a free trade area is one in which states agree to eliminate most *tariffs* and *non-tariff barriers.* See *EFTA; NAFTA.*

free will: Voluntary choice, not decisions predetermined by supposed divine intervention, or underlying and immutable economic or structural factors.

***Freikorps* (Free Corps):** Right-wing *militia* in *Weimar Germany*, and other countries, drawn mainly from unemployed veterans of *WWI.* They put down attempts at left-wing *revolution* in the period of *postwar* chaos. In Italy they helped propel *Mussolini* into power in 1922. In Germany, where the term is most properly applied, they participated in the street combats of the 1920s and early 1930s, but after 1933 were banned and/or absorbed into the Nazi *SA* and *SS*, and then the army. The German freikorps were a specific example of a general phenomenon: angry men used to combat and the comraderie of the barracks, but no longer in military service and posing a real threat of deadly political violence, and even revolution, following a great *war.* Europe was flooded with such rootless, rancorous souls after both the *Thirty Years' War* and the *Napoleonic Wars*; after the *American Civil War* unreconstructed *Confederates* formed the Ku Klux Klan to terrorize poor blacks as "night riders," abusing skills learned on raids into *Union* territory; and in Russia, post-WWI politics was about loose and independent *paramilitary* units as well as about class warfare. In modern Africa, Asia and Central America, too, disbanded *guerrilla* or other armed forces have proven exceedingly tough for civil society to digest.

FRELIMO: The *guerrilla* organization that fought the Portuguese in Mozambique from 1964, and formed the ruling party after *independence* in 1975.

French and Indian War (1754-60): A conflict between the American colonists and French troops and their Indian allies. It was precipitated by American advances into the Ohio valley that threatened French claims to the whole interior of North America, and historic Indian lands. The fighting widened with the dispatch of British troops to aid the colonists. It fed into the more general and important conflict, the *Seven Years' War* between France and Britain. It thus was one of very few colonial conflicts to actually trigger a *Great Power* war.

French Army mutinies (April-May 1917): A revolt behind the lines, and in some cases in the lines, following yet another failed and bloody French offensive during *WWI*. The mutineers were encouraged by the example of Russian troops *voting with their feet* for home and *peace*. Thousands were arrested and dozens were executed.

French Cameroons: It was formed out of the German *protectorate* of *Kamerun* in 1919, and remained a French *mandate* and *trusteeship territory* 1919-61. It is now part of *Cameroon*.

French Community: See *la francophonie*.

French Congo: French *colony* and former name of the Republic of the Congo.

French Empire: After the loss of *New France* to Britain and the sale of *Louisiana* to the U.S., France constructed a second great *empire*, whose major possessions were: *Algeria, French Indochina, French Equatorial Africa, French West Africa* and other, lesser territories in the Caribbean, South America and the South Pacific.

French Equatorial Africa: A *federation* of French *colonies* in central Africa 1908-58: *Chad, Gabon,* the *French Congo* and *Ubangi-Shari.*

French Guiana: An *overseas department* of France, in S. America. It has fewer than 100,000 residents, but direct representation in the French parliament, (one Senator and one Deputy). It was the site of the infamous penal colony, Devil's Island, until 1951.

French Guinea: French *colony* and former name of The Republic of Guinea.

French India: Five French *enclaves* in India: Chandernagor, Karikal, Pondicherry, Yanaon and Mahé. From 1952-54, they were peacefully returned to Indian *jurisdiction*.

French Indochina: A conglomerate French *colony*; its construction was complete toward the end of the 19th century. It comprised *Annam, Cambodia, Cochin China, Tonkin, Laos* and the *leasehold* on Kwangchowan. During *WWII* it was *occupied* by Japan, with the con-

nivance of *Vichy* officials. The French tried to return in 1945, but ran into heavy nationalist/communist resistance. In the 1955 *Geneva Accords* it was divided into North and South Vietnam (now just Vietnam), Laos and Cambodia. Cf. *Indochina*.

French/Indochina War (1946-54): The French effort to return to *empire* after the humiliation of *WWII* led to disaster in *French Indochina*, where it conflicted with rising local *nationalisms*. With Chinese material assistance, Vietnamese communists inflicted the decisive *defeat* at *Dien Bien Phu* in 1954. The *Geneva Accords* followed.

French Oceana: Former name of *French Polynesia*.

French Polynesia: It was a *protectorate* from 1847, and a *colony* from 1880. Made an *overseas territory* in 1977, it comprises 130 islands in a sprawl of five archipelagos in the *South Pacific*: the Austral Islands, Gambier Islands, Marquesas Islands, Society Islands, Tuamotu Archipelago, and Windward and Leeward Islands. It has a governor and a local assembly that meets on Tahiti, the main island. France keeps 5,000 (very happy) troops there.

French Revolution (1789-99): State finance problems (related to the wars of *Louis XIV* and later), unjust taxation, and a crisis of *rising expectations* on social, economic and political matters helped cause the French Revolution. It began with the meeting of the Estates General at *Versailles*, May 5 to October 15, 1789, where demands were made for conversion of France into a constitutional *monarchy*. The Third Estate, representing the middle classes, demanded that it be convened as a National Assembly. The King, *Louis XVI*, agreed to that demand in June. On July 14th, however, the *citizens* of Paris took a hand by raiding the Bastille prison, ever since a focus of *nationalism* and revolutionary élan. It would not be the last time Paris decided the course of the *revolution* and the future of France. The King and Assembly were obliged to relocate there, and the process of radicalization of the revolution began in earnest that winter. For the next 18 months the Assembly proceeded to transform national laws and life, and it looked as though France might emerge reconstructed along the English model of constitutional monarchy. But during 1791-92 a growing movement favoring a *republic* took hold within the Revolutionary Convention (the renamed Assembly). It was fed in part by the King's obvious desire to return to the old, *absolutist* ways. When Louis tried to flee France with his aloof Austrian wife, Marie Antoinette, he cinched his own fate. *War* was declared on Austria on April 20, 1792; Prussia joined with Austria to invade France and restore Louis. Under threat of *invasion*, the King and his conspiratorial family were jailed, the monarchy was abolished, from September 2-6 royalist prisoners were massacred, and France became a republic on September 21, 1792. The next year, Louis and his wife were executed for *treason*, by the *Girondins*. That regicide, and the promise of some *radicals* to export the revolution to all the peoples of Europe, raised a great *coalition* against France. By 1793 it was at war with Austria, Britain, the Netherlands, Prussia and Spain. The sense of siege this created helped further radicalize events.

In October 1793, the Girondins were overthrown and most executed by a more radical group, the *Jacobins*. The *Terror* had arrived. During 1793-94, two Jacobins struggled to ride the tiger of radical change and seize the reigns of power: the hot-blooded *Danton* and the brooding, cold-blooded *Robespierre*. When the latter won, he sent Danton and his supporters to the guillotine. In Georg Büchner's famous phrase, the revolution had begun to "eat its own children." While the revolution triumphed in foreign wars, greatly aided by the *levée en masse*, it bloodily repressed the *Vendée* and held the blade of terror over Paris and other cities. When the last laws protecting the innocent went down before Robespierre's puritanical fury, members of the Revolutionary Convention feared for their own lives, and overthrew the Jacobins on July 28th. The radical phase ended when Robespierre's head, too, looked up from a wicker basket. After 1794 France turned right, to government by a conservative *Directory*. The period of the Directory witnessed great military and diplomatic victories for France, and for an up-and-coming young commander who proved his mettle in *campaigns* in Egypt and in Italy: *Napoleon Bonaparte*. But the Directory did not enjoy popular support, was plagued by peasant and royalist revolts and began to suffer military setbacks. It was ended by Napoleon's *coup* ("a whiff of *grapeshot*") in 1799.

The Revolution changed France forever. It had cycled from an absolutist state, to a constitutional monarchy, to a constitutional republic, to a radical republic, to a conservative Directory, to a military dictatorship and then an empire. But it came far more than full circle. It permanently empowered and enriched the bourgeoisie and professional classes, and stripped real power from the landed aristocracy. It also set the stage for the rise of Napoleon, with all that name portended. Through its celebration of the ideals of the *Enlightenment* and the idea of *popular sovereignty*, and its challenge to the *Westphalian* principle of *nonintervention*, truly it remade international and even all politics, in Europe in the 19th century and globally after that. It added much fuel to the *liberal* assault on *absolutism*

that swept Europe in the 19th century. It also witnessed the world's first encounter with modern *nationalism*, in the *chauvinistic* and bloody garb that has become so familiar, but which then still had power to shock and repulse the imagination. It caused enormous military changes, too, moving *warfare* from the small, professional and *mercenary* armies of the 18th century toward mass *mobilization* in the 19th and 20th. It thus ended the era of *dynastic wars* and launched one of wars of nation vs. nation, culminating in *total war* between entire civilizations 100 years later. See also *Napoleonic Wars; Napoleonic warfare*.

French Somaliland: A former French *colony* that became independent as Djibouti.

French Soudan: Former name of Mali.

French Southern and Antarctic Lands: A composite *overseas territory* of France, comprising claims in *Antarctica* and four island groups in the Indian Ocean: Kerguelan Archipelago, made up of one large and 300 small islands; Crozet Archipeligo; St. Paul; and Amsterdam.

French Togoland: The eastern part of *Togo* colony taken by France from Germany as a *mandate territory*. It became Togo in 1960. Cf. *British Togoland*.

French Union: The constitutional association of France and its overseas *colonies* and possessions set up under the *Fourth Republic* from 1946-58. It was superseded by the *French Community*, under the *Fifth Republic* from 1958.

French West Africa: A colonial *federation* from 1895, embracing Dahomey (Benin), French Guinea, French Soudan (Mali), Ivory Coast, Mauritania, Niger, Senegal Dakar and Upper Volta (Bourkina Fasso).

French West Indies: Martinique, Guadeloupe and even smaller dependencies.

friendly fire: Shelling or any other *ordnance* coming from one's own side in a battle. This can lead to accidental infliction of casualties on one's own troops, or those of one's *allies*, in the confusion of combat.

Friendly Islands: Tonga.

friendship treaty: An agreement declaring non-hostility between or among *states*. Such *treaties* usually are vague, and intended more to send political signals to other states than to resolve outstanding issues (e.g., the Indo/Soviet friendship treaty signed in 1971, or the

China/Japan treaty of 1979). More specific agreements may tackle longstanding problems, placing them on a new footing (e.g., German/Polish acceptance of the *Oder/Neisse line* in 1990). Some *realists* scoff at the term and idea, arguing that states have no permanent friends or enemies, just permanent interests. Cf. *non-aggression pact*.

frigate: From the 17th to 19th century, a fast *warship* with rows of heavy guns at two levels, but somewhat smaller than a *man-of-war*.

FROLINAT: A Muslim *guerrilla* organization founded in northern Chad in 1966. For years it fought against southern-based, Christian and animist-dominated forces. These latter usually controlled the government, and had French support. FROLINAT broke down into competing factions in 1976 under the strain of the long *civil war*, Libyan *intervention* in its *territory* in the North and continuing French *aid* to the Chadian government. Yet it continues to provide an umbrella organization for Muslim and northern opposition to the government. See *Auzou strip; Chad/Libya War.*

Front de Libération du Québec (FLQ): A small, amateurish, *Québec* terrorist group. Its bombs, kidnappings and occasional murders provoked a brief period of *martial law* in Canada (in October 1970), after which the FLQ's few members were imprisoned or *exiled* to Cuba, by agreement with Canadian authorities.

frontier dispute: This occurs when two or more *states* disagree about where the *boundaries* between them lie. There are scores of disputed borders, both from previous conflicts and successive waves of *state creation* from the 1950s to 1990s.

front line: (1) The line across which troops from different armies face or fight each other. (2) A synonym for *first line*. Cf. *no-man's-land, trench warfare.*

front line states: Those African countries bordering or near South Africa, which in the 1970s and 1980s were subject to attacks and *sabotage* financed or directed by Pretoria: Angola, Botswana, Mozambique, Tanzania, Zambia and Zimbabwe (after 1980). They successfully pressured for Zimbabwean *independence*, and during the end game to *apartheid* they were helpful in negotiating a regional settlement regarding *Namibia*. However, several suffered from internal conflicts, which limited their *influence*. See also *Swaziland.*

Fuchs, Klaus (b.1911): Soviet atomic spy, attached to the British team at *Los Alamos*. His information was critical to early Soviet construction of an *atomic bomb*. He fled upon discovery. He was subsequently decorated by, and worked in the weapons programs of, the *Soviet Union* and *East Germany*.

Führerprinzip: "Leader principle." The idea in *Nazi ideology* that the entire *nation* should be organized along military lines, and ultimately answer with absolute obedience to one national leader. The leader was thus conceived as rather a combination of tribal chieftain, high priest and *warlord*. See *Hitler.*

Fulani: A Muslim people who used *cavalry* in the 18th and 19th centuries to found a far-flung West African *empire*. Thereafter, they mingled with the *Hausa* and other local *tribes*. Their imperial expansion was interrupted in its advance southward by two things: (1) the tse tse fly, which bore sleeping sickness that killed Fulani horses, eroding their military advantage; and (2) the British and French, both building their own empires northward from the coast, and both militarily and technologically superior.

full powers: When an individual other than the *head of state* has authority to negotiate final *terms* of a *treaty* or other agreement on behalf of a *state*.

functional agencies: Those established by the *states* to perform non-political tasks, or functions, where *national interests* cannot be satisfied separately. See *public international unions; specialized agencies.*

functionalism: A *grand theory* that intimates *world governance* is best achieved by an incremental approach based on interrelated and interacting institutions. It suggests focusing *international organizations* in the short-run on specific purposes and problems, but with a long-term view to ever greater international *integration*. The essential idea is that if states organize to perform non-political tasks, or functions, in the fullness of time they will move toward structural changes that permit elevated economic, political and security cooperation as well, even to the point of *union*. Functionalism theory has been criticized for failing to note just how difficult it is in practice to separate social and economic from political tasks, underestimating the resilience of *sovereignty*, and underplaying the key role of dynamic leadership and/or external threat in bringing about basic political change. See *spillover.*

Functionally Related Observable Differences (FRODs): Weapons design features that are essential to specific combat functions, and therefore give away the purpose of, say, an aircraft, to foreign observers. FRODs are used (for instance in *SALT*) to help verify compliance with *arms control* agreements.

functional protection: The legal right of an *IGO* to intercede on behalf of staff as though they enjoyed *diplomatic immunity*.

fundamentalism: The tendency among religious believers to stress strict adherence to a set of principles derived from a scripture such as the Bible, Koran or Torah that is interpreted literally, and often exclusively of other social groups and more pluralistic points of view. Christian fundamentalists gained some influence over aspects of U.S. policy in the 1980s, such as concerning the UN's population control program. In the early 1990s Islamic fundamentalists of one stripe controlled the governments in Iran and Sudan, and threatened several others with violent *rebellion* (notably Algeria and Egypt). Muslim fundamentalists of an entirely different sort have dominated Saudi Arabia and the *Gulf States* since their founding. Jewish fundamentalists exercised a near veto over Israeli settlement and *peace* policies until 1992, owing to influence well beyond their numbers in the population, exercised under a system of proportional representation in the *Knesset*. Hindu fundamentalism has flared from time to time in India; a political party and movement favoring a Hindu rather than a secular nation rose in popularity in India in the early 1990s. Cf. *secularism*.

funerals: The death in office of a governing or former statesman presents unique opportunities for *diplomacy*, and may be more useful than a *summit*. That is why, besides reasons of *protocol* and unease over their own mortality, *heads of state* or *heads of government* (or top surrogates) attend *state funerals* on short notice. Funerals permit a "quick read" on the new leader and perhaps a sense of policy shifts to come. Also, in an age when *negotiation* often takes place in front of TV cameras, ministers may conduct substantive discussion with their foreign counterparts without the hampering glare of publicity. They may thus avoid the pitfalls caused at summits by a media tendency to conclude that unless something concrete is agreed, a face-to-face meeting must have been a failure.

fungible/fungibility: The ability to convert something (say, money or *power*) into something else (say, production or a desired political outcome).

fusion: A thermonuclear reaction that fuses rather than splits or divides atoms as in *fission*. If uncontrolled within a *critical mass*, say of *plutonium*, fusion releases huge amounts of energy in the form of *blast* and *radiation* effects. This is the central process within a *hydrogen bomb*. Controlled, hot fusion research may promise a partial solution to national energy shortages, as well as problems of pollution, but most scientists agree that it remains a long way off.

G

G-5: See *Group of Five*.

G-7: See *Group of Seven*.

G-8: See *Cartagena Group*.

G-10: See *Group of Ten*.

G-77: See *Group of Seventy-Seven*.

Gabon: Location: central Africa. Major associations: *la francophonie, OAU, OPEC, UN*. Population: 1.1 million. Military: minor. A French *colony* from the late 19th century, in 1910 it was joined to *French Equatorial Africa*. It has been independent since 1960. Its dominant *ethnic group*, or *tribe*, is the Fang. Yet for most of its independence it has been dominated by the minority Beteke. It has prospered due to *natural resources*, including *oil*, that attract *foreign direct investment* (mainly French). In 1968 it became a corrupt, elitist, *one-party state* led by Omar Bongo (b.1935). In 1990 a multiparty system was reinstated (local wags soon dubbed this "Bongostroika"). But in 1993 hope for change was dashed when Bongo claimed he won the election with 51% of the vote. Riots ensued, and those Gabonese who wished to march to the beat of a different drummer accused Paris of preferring Bongo's stable dictatorship to promoting real democracy.

Galapagos Islands: An archipelago 600 miles west of, and belonging to, Ecuador.

galleon: From the 15th to 19th centuries, a large sailing ship used as a *warship* or in the *merchant marine*.

Gallipoli, Battle of (April 25, 1915-January 9, 1916): British and *ANZAC* forces attempted to seize this approach to the *Dardanelles* to open a southern, warmwater *supply line* to Russia. The Turks successfully resisted. The battle made one political career, that of

Atatürk, and nearly destroyed another, that of *Winston Churchill*. ANZAC forces took terrible casualties, weakening commitment to imperial ties that bound.

Galtieri, Leopold (b.1926): Argentine general. President 1981-82. He was in charge of the army during the *dirty war*. He is most notable for heading the *junta* that attempted to distract from its own economic ineptitude (and moral turpitude) by invading the *Falkland Islands* (Malvinas) in 1982, provoking *war* with Britain. After a humiliating *defeat*, he was toppled. He was later sentenced to 12 years in prison.

Gambia: Location: West Africa. Major associations: *Commonwealth, OAU, UN.* Population: 900,000. Military: minor. It was Britain's first African *colony* (1843), a riparian *territory* penetrated by traders and explorers as early as 1588. Although Gambia shares ethnic affiliations with Senegal, which surrounds it, a British colonial history means the Gambian national elite is mainly *anglophone*, whereas Senegalese are predominantly *francophone*. It gained *independence* in 1965, and became a *republic* within the Commonwealth in 1970. It has been a splinter of *democracy* in a forest of *one-party states* and personal dictatorships, despite experiencing a *famine* in 1977-78. In 1982 it joined Senegal in a *confederation* called *Senegambia*, but that experiment failed and was dissolved in 1989.

game theory: A branch of mathematics concerned with games of probability, wins and losses, and accompanying strategies used by players. It is employed by some political scientists to assess and weigh optimal choices in decision situations, where each player's choice influences outcomes for all other players. Applied to *economics* or *foreign policy*, it is said by these analysts to highlight how the structure of conflicts influences *decision-making* and *negotiation*. See *chicken; decision theory; maximizing; minimax; minimum winning coalition; mixed motive; n-person; positive sum; prisoner's dilemma; satisficing; side payments; variable-sum; zero-sum.*

Gandhi, Indira (1917-84): PM of India 1966-77, 1980-84; stateswoman. Daughter of *Jawaharial Nehru*. She cleaved to her father's effort to develop *self-sufficiency*. She negotiated a *friendship treaty* with the Soviet Union in 1971. Also that year, she approved an attack on Pakistan in December, in a decisive *intervention* that permitted *Bangladesh* to break free of *West Pakistan*. She shook Indian democracy in 1975 when she introduced emergency rule, provoking nationwide protest. A forced sterilization program, part of a major population control initiative, was subjected to intense domestic and international criticism. Thrown out in

elections in 1977, she split the *Congress Party* and was reelected in 1980. She opposed *Sikh* separatists and crushed a rising in *Punjab* in June 1984, approving a military raid on the holiest Sikh shrine, the Golden Temple, where militants were headquartered. In October, she was assassinated by one of her Sikh bodyguards; thousands died in the riots that followed.

Gandhi, Mohandas Karamchand (1869-1948): "Mahatma" (Great Soul). Indian nationalist leader and social reformer. *Hindu* by upbringing and a lawyer by training, he first organized a civil disobedience (satyagraha and ahimsa) campaign among South African Indians, which won some concessions. Back in India by 1915, he emerged as a leader of the *Congress Party*. He used *boycotts* to great effect, went on hunger strikes several times, and organized the *salt march*. He was arrested and jailed repeatedly by the British. In 1931 he attended the *Round Table Conference*. He was jailed again during *WWII*, during which he asserted his fundamental *pacifism*, but also kept a prudent silence about the war. He assisted in the 1947 British withdrawal from India, although he opposed *partition*. He did more than anyone to bring the Indian masses into politics and alleviate the awful conditions of the Harijans ("*untouchables*"). He was grief stricken over partition and the extreme violence that accompanied *independence*. Gandhi was assassinated by a Hindu *fanatic*, who saw his concern to accommodate Muslims and Sikhs as traitorous. Cf. *Ali Jinnah.*

Gandhi, Rajiv (1944-91): PM of India 1984-89. He reluctantly succeeded his mother but carried forward her policies, until he lost the 1989 election. He was assassinated during a subsequent campaign, by a woman suicide bomber.

gang of four: Four radical supporters of *Mao Zedong* and the *Great Proletarian Cultural Revolution*: Jiang Qing (Mao's widow), Wang Hongwen, Yao Wenyuan, and Zhang Chungqiao. They were *purged* when Mao died, and sentenced to death (later commuted) for *treason,* after a *show trial* in 1980.

Garibaldi, Giuseppe (1807-82): In 1849 he organized the defense of the short-lived Roman *republic* against French *intervention*. In 1860 he and a force of "One Thousand Redshirts" invaded Naples and Sicily, trying to unite all Italy. He delivered up his *conquests* to the King of Piedmont, whose armies then completed Italian unification.

gas weapons: Those that kill by asphyxia, corrosion or poisonous gaseous emissions. See *Abyssinian War; chemical weapons; Chemical Weapons Convention;*

Geneva Protocol; mustard gas; nerve weapons; Iran/ Iraq War.

GATT: See *General Agreement on Tariffs and Trade.*

Gauleiter: A regional party chief in *Nazi Germany,* head of an administrative unit called a "Gau."

Gaullism: Principles of nationalism, conservative, technocratic government and a Europe-centered foreign policy, all after the manner of *Charles de Gaulle.*

Gaza Strip: Part of the 1919 *mandate* over *Palestine* awarded to Britain. Assigned to the *Arabs* upon *partition* in 1948, it was occupied and administered by Egypt. In 1956, during the *Second Arab/Israeli War,* it was captured by Israel, who handed it to the UN in 1957. It reverted to Egyptian administration until 1967, when it became the smaller of the *occupied territories* taken by Israel in the *Third Arab/Israeli War.* Its 800,000 Arabs are often barred from entering Israel, which is for many the sole locale of employment. Many Gaza youths joined the *Intifada.* In August 1993, Israel and the PLO settled on limited *autonomy* for Gaza and the city of Jericho, the first step in a five-year *peace* plan. Isreali troops left in May, 1994.

GDP: See *Gross Domestic Product.*

General Agreement on Tariffs and Trade (GATT): The most important mechanism regulating world trade. It was founded by *treaty* in 1947 as a temporary measure, but replaced the failed *International Trade Organization* by default. It has since become a full-fledged instrument, with its own *Secretariat* and complaint procedures. GATT reflected a prevailing postwar consensus on *free trade,* and U.S. leadership of a *liberal-international* trade *regime.* Its purpose is to reduce *tariffs* and *non-tariff barriers,* and develop a trade system based on two rules: (1) the nondiscrimination principle, or *most-favored-nation (MFN)* status for members; (2) *reciprocity.* Members must agree to tax and regulate affected *imports* according to GATT schedules, with the ultimate aim of treating imports as if they were domestic products. Permitted exceptions to the MFN and reciprocity rules are *customs unions* (e.g., *BENELUX*), and *free trade* associations (e.g., *EFTA* or *NAFTA*), or other such regional arrangements that lower internal tariffs without setting up external trade discrimination. Also permitted, as of 1971, is the *Generalized System of Preferences (GSP).* Eight rounds of talks have been held, each more complex and difficult but also advancing past the previous on tariff reductions. Only 23 states participated in the first GATT round in Geneva in 1947; some 116 countries were part of the latest, *Uruguay Round,* concluded in December 1993. Major exclusions before Uruguay were: (1) agricultural products; (2) *services*; (3) intellectual property, weakly regulated by *WIPO,* partially included in Uruguay; (4) China and the *Soviet bloc.* China was a signatory in 1948, but its membership was withdrawn by *Chiang Kai-shek* after his defeat in the *Chinese Civil War.* In 1987 the People's Republic asked to rejoin, but talks have made only slow progress. Since 1989 former *Soviet bloc* republics have moved into the system at varying speed. The main benefits of GATT for large economies are defused trade tensions; reduction (but not elimination) of the influence of *protectionist* lobbies, which are less able to manipulate bilateral trade; and assured access to the markets of major trade partners. Smaller economies gain greater entry to large markets than they could hope to achieve bilaterally (but see *graduation clause*). On January 1, 1995, GATT becomes the World Trade Organization. See also *Kennedy Round; Tokyo Round.*

general debate: A misnomer: it is not a debate so much as a series of formal speeches. This procedure is used during opening weeks of the *UNGA's* annual sessions, in which each member may expound upon the state of world affairs, as well as UN agenda items. Most speeches merely restate known policy, but they may also be used to launch new policies (or enhance political careers) before a global audience.

generalissimo: (1) In certain armies, a supreme commander. (2) The supreme commander of several armies, acting in concert; e.g., *SACEUR.*

generalization: An general idea, example or principle.

Generalized System of Preferences (GSP): In 1968 agreement in principle was reached on a scheme of preferences for *Third World* exporters. In 1971 *GATT* waived its *most-favored-nation* requirement to allow this. However, it is not really a general scheme, but a waiver that permits *OECD* states to set different preferences. Each scheme is temporary, subject to *quotas,* may exclude certain products (often where southern *comparative advantage* is greatest), and be unevenly applied to different regions. Many southern countries are thus effectively excluded and trade without meaningful preferences. Yet, GSP trade reached $90 billion by the 1990s. It is also linked to *ILO* standards.

general principles (of international law): Principles abstracted from the national legal systems of the *states.* That is, principles drawn from legal rules that are widely regarded in *municipal law* or drawn from Roman law and *natural law.*

general retaliatory response: The launch of a full-scale *reprisal* for a nuclear attack, rather than trying *escalation control*. See *second strike*.

General Staff: Officers who help the highest ranking commanders prepare *logistics, mobilization, tactical* and *strategic* war plans. Invented by the Prussians, the General Staff was adopted by all modern armies.

general strike: The idea that simultaneous strikes by all a nation's workers might force major economic or political reforms. Though attempted a few times, notably in France and Spain, it never met the high expectations of various *labor* movements. See *Solidarity*.

Geneva Agreements (July 20, 1954): They ended the French phase of the 30-year-long war in *Indochina* by *Great Power* agreement on *independence* for Cambodia (*neutralized*), Laos (neutralized) and the division of North from South Vietnam. That division was to be healed by an open election, but it never took place. The conference also discussed the situation on the Korean peninsula, with no success.

Geneva Conventions: A series of agreements setting out the humane and permissible treatment of individuals in wartime, drawing often from the tenets of *just war theory*. The first was in 1864. Others followed in 1906 and 1929. Superseding these were the four summary conventions of 1949 (the "Red Cross Conventions"), stipulating correct treatment of the wounded and sick in the field, and at sea; treatment of *prisoners of war*, and protection of *civilians*. Two more *protocols* were drafted in 1977. The first dealt with limits to methods of war that harm the environment, and thereby harm the civilian population. The second extended traditional protections to *civil wars* and wars of *national liberation* See *Red Cross*.

Geneva Protocol (1925): In response to *WWI*, it banned use of "asphyxiating, poisonous, or other gases, and all analogous liquids, materials or devices," as well as all "bacteriological methods of warfare." However, it said nothing about making or storing such weapons. See *Chemical Weapons Convention*.

genocide: Deliberate, systematic extermination of an ethnic, national or religious group. In law, though not in practical effect, *liquidation* of a social class does not appear to qualify as genocide. See *Armenian genocide; Burundi; Cambodian genocide; ethnic cleansing; Genocide Convention; Holocaust; indigenous peoples; international criminal law; Newfoundland; Rwanda.* Cf. *collectivization; Great Leap Forward; Great Proletarian Cultural Revolution; kulaks*.

Genocide Convention: Adopted by the *UNGA* in 1948 in response to the horrors of the *Holocaust*, it entered into effect in 1951. It criminalizes acts of *genocide* by stripping away the traditional defense against *extradition* of claiming genocidal acts are political in nature. And it includes provision for holding individuals directly accountable by national courts, but without corresponding international enforcement. While it advanced *codification* of moral norms and standards of state conduct, it has had little practical impact. It defines acts of genocide broadly, to include: (1) killing; (2) causing serious mental or physical harm; (3) deprivation of the "conditions of life" sufficient to cause physical destruction of the group; (4) efforts designed to prevent births within the group; (5) forced transfers of children outside the group. By 1993 over 120 states had either acceded or succeeded to the Convention. Also see, *crimes against humanity; ethnic cleansing; war crimes*.

Genro: The *elder statesmen* in Japan, 1889-1940. They had constitutional status and significant, though after 1920 declining, influence on policy.

geographical pivot (of history): The thesis that great turning (or pivotal) points in world history occur with changes in whichever *state* or civilization controls the *Heartland*, or central core of *Eurasia*. Cf. *geopolitics; geopolitik; Mackinder*.

geographic escalation: See *horizontal escalation*.

geopolitics: (1) The legitimate study of *climate, location, natural resources, topography*, etc. to assess how these influence the *power, foreign policy* and military *strategy* of *states*. (2) A late 19th and early 20th century pseudoscience that treated geography as the paramount, even sole, source of the power of nations; at the least, it offered geography as the prime mover (*cause*) of large-scale historical and political events.

geopolitik: A skewed variant of *Halford Mackinder's* thesis about the *Heartland*. This adaptation, devised by Karl Haushofer (1869-1946) and other German academics, encouraged *Hitler* to develop notions like *lebensraum* for the German people and inflamed his pathological insistence on economic *autarky*. Such theories reinforced the *social darwinism* already evident in Nazi *ideology*, such as the idea that an "organic state" must grow (expand) or die. Unlike Haushofer, who feared attacking the great expanse of Russia, Hitler's *fanatic* belief in this romantic nonsense encouraged him to launch *Barbarossa* against the Soviets.

Georgia: Location: *Caucasus*. Major associations: *CIS*,

CSCE, UN. Population: 5.6 million. Military: in a three-way *civil war*, incapable of sustained resistance to Russian *intervention*. It was an ancient Christian kingdom that was conquered by *Muslim* Arabs, but not converted, in the 8th century. It was also overrun by Mongol and then Turkic invaders. For centuries a province of the *Ottoman Empire*, it worked its way to semi-*autonomy*, only to be annexed by Russia in 1801. Georgia remained an integral part of the *Russian Empire*, undergoing some *russification*. It remained in the *Soviet Union* after the *Bolshevik Revolution*. From 1922-36 it was part of the *Transcaucasian SFSR*. There were disturbances in Georgia in 1988-89, and the *Red Army* was used to repress demonstrators. Its parliament declared *independence* in April 1991, but this was not *recognized* by the international community until the *extinction* of the Soviet Union in December. Georgia declined membership in the *CIS*. Civil war broke out almost immediately. President Gamzakhurdia was forced to flee in January 1992, and *Eduard Sheverdnadze* became President. He was faced with a continuing civil war when Gamzakhurdia returned at the head of a rebel army to western Georgia in mid-1993 (he committed suicide in January 1994, when the invasion failed). As well, attempts at *secession* developed in *Ajaria, Ossetia* and *Abkhazia*. By October 1993, Abkhazia had effectively broken away, with the aid of Russian "volunteers." In November Georgia was forced to invite in Russian troops to end the civil war, and was coerced into the CIS. The UN placed 100 military observers in Georgia in 1993.

geostrategic: Any consideration of diplomatic, political or military *strategy* drawn across a global canvas or having worldwide implications.

German Confederation: Created at the *Congress of Vienna*, it was composed of some 39 separate German *states* without any central authority. Until the creation of the German Empire in 1871, it was the locale of conspiracy, rivalry and then *war* between Austria and Prussia, who competed to lead/absorb it.

German Democratic Republic (GDR): It was created out of the Soviet *occupation zone* in Germany on October 7, 1949. At first the Soviets stripped their zone of all industrial plant and even rail lines, in lieu of *reparations* promised at *Potsdam*. But by 1948 it was already clear to Moscow that deindustrializing what would become the GDR would be more costly in the long run than letting it rebuild and integrate into the Soviet camp. However, the communist regime that ran *East Germany* was hobbled by chronic illegitimacy in the eyes of its own people. When *West Germany* joined the *European Defense Community* in 1952, the

GDR decreed a three-mile deep "prohibited zone" along the border. In 1953 there were serious riots in East Berlin. In 1955, after West Germany joined *NATO*, the GDR joined in formation of the *Warsaw Pact* (Soviet troops were already stationed there). Another *crisis* over Berlin took place in 1958. By 1961 the steady drain of young, skilled refugees *voting with their feet* for life in the West led to construction of the *Berlin Wall*, a concrete admission of political illegitimacy and failure. The GDR was not recognized by NATO countries, and like West Germany was not permitted to sit in the UN until agreement was reached under the *Ostpolitik* initiative of *Willy Brandt* in 1972. Under *détente* in the 1970s, it opened somewhat to the West, and was drawn partly into the West German economic orbit, also introducing a "new economic system" at home. Yet, overall it remained one of the most *hard-line* states within the Soviet bloc. It kept up shoot-to-kill orders at the Wall under the authority of *Erich Honecker*, in power from 1976 to 1989. After *Gorbachev* took power in Moscow, Honecker objected to *glasnost* and *perestroika* and maintained a tough line. But in 1989 he was unable to stop a tide of *refugees* leaving through rents in the *iron curtain* opened by reforms in Hungary and Czechoslovakia. After Gorbachev visited to say that the GDR was on its own, that the *Sinatra* not the *Brezhnev Doctrine* would apply, it was only a matter of time until the *regime* collapsed. Honecker was forced to resign on October 18th. The border with Czechoslovakia was opened on November 4th, to ease pressure on the failing regime. Instead, the end came with unexpected suddenness on November 9th, with the announcement that the Wall was to be opened to intra-German traffic. The *two-plus-four talks* followed. On August 23, 1990, the GDR's parliament agreed to reunification. Pushed hard by *Helmut Kohl*, merger of the Germanies took place on October 3rd. See also *CSCE; Hallstein Doctrine; Helsinki Accords; regulated coexistence*.

German East Africa: A former German colony consisting of *Burundi, Rwanda* and *Tanganyika*, under the control of the German East Africa Co. from 1884-90, when it was taken over by Berlin as a state colony. It was the scene of fairly heavy fighting in *WWI*, during which a German colonial army held off an Allied force 10 times its size until just days before the *Armistice* in Europe. Taken from Germany after the war, it was broken into several *mandates* following the *Treaty of Versailles*.

German SW Africa: Former name of Namibia.

Germany: Location: Central Europe. Major associations: *CSCE, EU, G-5, G-7, NATO, OECD, UN, WEU.*

Population: 80 million. Military: first rate, NATO capable; non-nuclear. (1) The Rise of *Prussia*: At the *geopolitical* heart of Europe, Germany has been historically more often divided than united. The *Thirty Years' War* was fought largely in and over Germany, which emerged from it still *partitioned* into hundreds of *states*, *free cities* and statelets. France's aim of sustaining this division was aided by the regional and dynastic conflicts within Germany. *Frederick-William of Brandenburg* managed to raise the resource-poor, northern state of Prussia slowly from obscurity. Under *Frederick II* ("The Great"), it emerged as a new power in the northeast, based largely on its highly professional army. It numbered among the *Great Powers* by the time of the *French Revolution*. Yet modern Prussia emerged only after being severely defeated by *Napoleon* (who occupied Berlin). That moved *Frederick-William III* to adopt wholesale economic, social and military reforms that enabled him to strike back at France from 1813-15, and propelled Prussia to predominance in the 19th century. From 1815 to 1866, Austria and Prussia competed for influence over the central and south German states. *Bismarck* settled the issue of who would rule Germany, and of Prussia's place in Europe, in three sharp victories: over Denmark in 1864; over Austria in the *Seven Weeks' War*, in 1866 (leading to the *North German Confederation*); and by crushing France in the *Franco/Prussian War* 1870-71, thereby creating the German Empire.

(2) Imperial Germany: After the *defeat* of France, Bismarck transformed his policy from *aggrandizement* to seeking preservation of Germany's central place on the continent. He did so through *alliances* designed to isolate France: the *Dreikaiserbund* with Austria and Russia, and the *Triple Alliance* with Austria and Italy. However, by 1890 a brash new Kaiser, *Wilhelm II*, was pushing for a policy of *Weltpolitik*. Bismarck resigned. The 1890s saw Germany involved in a major arms race on land, and with the coming of the *Dreadnoughts* it entered full force into the *Anglo/German naval arms race*, too. By 1900 Germany had become the greatest industrial and military power in Europe. In *WWI* it was the heart of the *Central Powers* alliance, propping up *Austria-Hungary*, the *Ottoman Empire* and several lesser allies. It defeated Russia in 1917, and almost won in the west in 1918. Nearing domestic revolt and with the *Allies* poised to cross Germany's borders, the military advised the civilians to *ask for terms*. The Kaiser abdicated and fled into *exile* in Holland, the army *surrendered* and the Weimar Republic stumbled into existence in November 1918.

(3) The Weimar Republic: Germany's initial experiment with *democracy* was an ill-fated one. Weimar politicians could never shake the accusation from the far right that in signing the *Armistice* they had lost the war for Germany through a *"stab-in-the-back"* of the army. And they were saddled with blame for the *Versailles Treaty* (arguably also incurred by the army), especially the deeply unpopular *war guilt clause* requiring Germany to pay *reparations*. In 1922 there was *rapprochement* with Russia in the *Treaty of Rapallo*. Germany defaulted on its reparations, leading to French and Belgian *occupation* of the *Ruhr* in January 1923. Greater bitterness was to follow, as Weimar experienced *hyperinflation*: the mark had been 4:1 to the American dollar in 1914, but reached 160,000:1 in July 1923, and 130,000,000,000:1 (in short, it was worthless) by November 1923. The economy was rescued only by the *Dawes Plan*, and hefty American loans. Matters were improving in the late 1920s. Under *Gustav Stresemann* there was economic recovery, the success of *Locarno*, entry into the *League of Nations* and better relations with France. But the *Great Depression* did irreparable harm to Weimar's tenuous hold on democracy. A financial crisis of the first order was coupled with a dramatic rise in unemployment and hopelessness. The *republic* was further weakened by an inability of any of the democratic parties to secure a majority, and faced unremitting, open hostility from center-right and conservative parties, and the *Freikorps*. By 1930 there was a sharp rise in street violence and political murders. *Paramilitary* groups supporting the various political parties clashed bloodily, especially the Nazi *SA* and the Communist Red Front, the organized thugs from the two parties who most gained at the polls from the atmosphere of despair (the Nazis rose from 12 to 109 seats in 1930, and to 230 in 1932--making them the largest party in the *Reichstag*). Weimar was deeply handicapped by having as its president in these turbulent times the vain, authoritarian and increasingly senile monarchist, *Paul von Hindenburg*. On January 30, 1933, power was handed to *Hitler* by the conservatives, who thought they would use and control "the Bohemian corporal." Seldom have men been so awfully wrong in their political judgment. Within six months, Hitler destroyed Weimar and with it any hope of German democracy or peaceful adjustment to Versailles. Within six years, he would lead Germany into a *war* that killed eight million of its citizens, destroyed its cities, and left it divided and occupied by foreign armies.

(4) The Third Reich: Inside a month of taking power the Nazis used the Reichstag fire as an excuse to ban the *communist party* and suspend civil liberties. In March they pushed through an "enabling law," giving Hitler dictatorial powers for four years. On April 1st anti-Jewish regulations passed, mapping out the start of the road to the *Holocaust*. All other parties were banned by July. The next year the *Night of the Long Knives* bought peace with the army. In August

1934, Hindenburg finally died, and Hitler added the title President to that of Chancellor. In January 1935, a *plebiscite* in the *Saar* rejoined that *territory* to Germany. Come March, Hitler repudiated all *disarmament* clauses of the Versailles Treaty, introduced *conscription* and announced plans for a peacetime army of one million men. In June, Britain aided Hitler tear up Versailles with the *Anglo/German Naval Agreement*. In September, the *Nuremberg Laws* were passed, stripping Jews of their few remaining legal protections. Hitler gave diplomatic support to *Mussolini* in the *Abyssinian War*. Then in March 1936, he took his biggest gamble: he remilitarized the *Rhineland*. That November the *Axis* was proclaimed, and Hitler and Mussolini sent aid to *Franco* in Spain. Hitler next took personal control of the armed forces, exacting a loyalty oath from the *officer corps*. In March 1938, the *Anschluss* with Austria took place, and soon the Nazis in the *Sudetenland* were told to agitate for their own Anschluss. Germany *mobilized* in April, but stood down in September when the *Munich Conference* delivered the Sudetenland without any military effort. The Nazis were jubilant, celebrating the year's triumphs with that obscene premonition of horrors yet to come, *Kristallnacht*. In March 1939, Germany occupied the rump of Czechoslovakia, displaying utter contempt for the Munich agreements. At last the West began serious preparation for war and extended guarantees to Poland. But it was too late to try *deterrence*: in August, Germany signed the *Nazi/Soviet Pact*, and on September 1st it invaded Poland. Britain and France delivered *ultimata* that expired two days later. *World War II* had begun.

Over the next two years Germany overran Poland, Norway, Denmark, Holland, France, Belgium, Greece, Yugoslavia, chased the British from the continent and attacked and conquered one-third of European Russia. The Nazis also began the systematic *liquidation* of the Jews of Europe, as well as of Gypsies, communists, "mental defectives" and homosexuals. Nazi Germany also reintroduced *slavery* to areas that had not seen it for 1,000 years; by war's end the slave labor system would use up and discard millions of human beings from nearly all the occupied nations, but especially from Russia. But Hitler's mistakes were mounting: by 1943 Germany was also at war with the U.S., had been halted by the British at *El Alamein* and by the Soviets at *Stalingrad*, and was being pounded by Anglo-American *thousand bomber raids*. By mid-1944 it was in a *two-front war*, the Kaiser's great error that Hitler had sworn to avoid (actually, there were four fronts, if one counts Italy and the Balkans). By the winter of 1944-45 its armies were retreating across German soil for the first time in the war. In April 1945, the Russians entered Berlin, while the Americans swept through Bavaria into western Czechoslovakia and the British pushed across the Rhine. On April 30, 1945, Hitler and others of the Nazi leadership killed themselves; many more fled or were captured in later days and weeks. On May 2nd, Berlin fell to the *Red Army*. Six days later Germany accepted *unconditional surrender*. The Nazi dream of a "Thousand Year Reich" had lasted but 12, nightmarish years.

(5) The Federal Republic: Germany had been defeated by the armies of over 40 nations: there could be nothing to follow that but a *diktat*. Austria was separated and *neutralized*; the Sudetenland was returned to Czechoslovakia, which promptly *deported* its German population; and *East Prussia* and *Silesia* disappeared into Poland and the Soviet Union, their German populations also expelled. What was left of Germany was then administratively divided and occupied by Britain, France, the Soviet Union and the U.S. (see map). But the *Allies* fell out, and two German states eventually emerged: the *German Democratic Republic* (see separate entry) on October 7, 1949, preceded by announcement of West Germany, or the Federal Republic (FRG), on May 23rd. The FRG became fully independent of Allied controls in 1955, and joined NATO, but the Saar was returned by France only in 1957. Already an economic powerhouse, in 1957 it signed the *Treaty of Rome*. *Konrad Adenauer* served as Chancellor from 1949-63, a period of sustained economic recovery and growing global legitimacy, but also crises over the uncertain status of *West Berlin*, in particular with construction of the *Berlin Wall*. The 1960s and 1970s were years of improved Franco/German relations and joint leadership of the *EC*. In 1970 *Willy Brandt* initiated his *Ostpolitik* toward the Soviet Union. The two Germanies signed *friendship treaties* in 1972, somewhat normalizing their relations and permitting each to join the UN. In 1973-75, the FRG successfully pushed for the *Helsinki Accords*. In 1983 it was convulsed by opposition to new American and NATO *missile* systems, deployed in response to a previous Soviet deployment. Other strains were felt during the 1980s over what was seen in West Germany as a lack of U.S. leadership and understanding of the importance of *détente*. In 1989 the GDR unexpectedly collapsed. In February 1990, *two-plus-four talks* began preparatory to unification. The Soviet Union agreed that united Germany could remain in NATO. Monetary union came on July 1st, and political merger on October 3, 1990.

(6) Germany since 1990: Since reunification Germany has been increasingly absorbed with integrating the East German economy and population, and with a consequent rise of *inflation*, unemployment and *neo-nazi* racism. It has thus shown at best an intermittent inclination to take up a new international role. It

stayed out of the *Gulf War* in part due to constitutional barriers, only sending a token air squadron to NATO bases in Turkey. While it avoided combat, it provided considerable financial support to the *Gulf Coalition*. It was diplomatically assertive over *recognition* of Croatia and Slovenia, pushing the U.S. and the other EC states to move faster than they wished. But it then refused military *intervention* when war broke out in Bosnia. In April 1993, it reluctantly acceded to NATO's first-ever combat operation, enforcing *no-fly zones* in Bosnia. It is interested in becoming a *permanent member of the Security Council* but has pushed the issue less hard than Japan. The *Maastricht Treaty*, its major effort at leadership within Europe, ran into deep trouble. See also *double containment; Hallstein Doctrine; Kapp putsch; Köhl; Marshall Plan; Minorities Treaties; Morgenthau plan; Napoleonic Wars; National Socialism; Nuremberg Rallies; Potsdam; realpolitik; regulated coexistence; Schmidt; Social Democracy; Tilsit; Yalta.*

Gestapo: "*Geheime Staatspolizei.*" The Nazi *secret police*, properly infamous for barbarism and sadism. Under *Himmler,* it terrorized Europe and helped run the *death camps*. See *Holocaust*. Cf. *SA; SS.*

Gettysburg, Battle of: One of the decisive battles of the *American Civil War*, fought in and around this small Pennsylvania town on July 1-3, 1863. The *Union* army under George Meade barely held off *Robert E. Lee's* Confederates. The third day witnessed the sick pathos of "Picket's Charge," in which a Confederate division was cut to pieces inside 30 minutes. Gettysburg finished Southern hopes that a great victory might bring European *intervention*. Lee never again invaded the North, and the South thereafter went over to the defensive.

Ghana: Location: West Africa. Major associations: *Commonwealth, OAU, UN*. Population: 15.3 million. Military: enmeshed in politics. Formerly the Gold Coast. It was established as a British *colony* in 1874, but not pacified (the main resistance came from the dominant *tribe*, the Ashante) until 1900. It merged with *British Togoland* in 1956, and was renamed Ghana upon *independence* in 1957, after the historic *empire* of that name on the Niger River (c.400-1240 A.D.). It became a *republic* within the Commonwealth in 1960. Its first president was *Kwame Nkrumah*, who was courted by the *Soviet bloc* and accepted *East German* and Chinese advisers and *aid*. He was overthrown in a *coup* in 1966. Since then, Ghana has been racked by chronic instability, with coups in 1972, 1978, 1979 and 1981, the last two led by a charismatic army officer, Jerry Rawlings (b.1947), who had several previ-

ous Presidents unceremoniously executed despite protests from the OAU. In 1991 it joined the five-nation mission (ECOMOG) that interceded in Liberia's civil war. In 1994 ethnic violence broke out in the north.

Ghent, Treaty of (1814): It ended the *War of 1812*, in December 1814, with the aid of Russian *mediation*. Reflecting *stalemate* on the battlefield, it froze the *peace* by avoiding the main points at issue in the *war*. Anglo/American relations thus remained troubled for decades afterward.

Giap, Nguyen Vo (b.1912): Vietnamese general. A brilliant tactician, but also unsparing of the lives of his troops. He fought the Japanese during *WWII*, led the *victory* over France at *Dien Bien Phu*, and oversaw the extended *campaign* against U.S. and South Vietnamese forces 1961-75. He then fought campaigns in Cambodia and directed the defense against China's attack along the northern border in 1979.

Gibraltar: Since 1704, a British *colony* and fortress guarding the *strait* of the same name connecting the Mediterranean and Atlantic. Of enormous *strategic* importance in successive British wars, its ownership is still disputed by Spain, which imposed a "*siege*" in 1967 after Gibraltar chose to stay British in a *referendum*. Spain's entry into the *EC* has eased *tensions* over Gibraltar (an agreement was signed in 1984), and Britain has reduced its military presence.

Gierek, Edward (b.1913): Polish dictator 1970-80. He succeeded *Gomulka* as First Secretary following an outbreak of serious rioting. His fall from party grace was precipitous: the birth of *Solidarity* led to his ouster, following which he was expelled from the ranks, arrested and interned.

Giolotti, Giovanni (1842-1928): Italian PM 1892-93, 1903-05, 1906-09, 1911-14, and 1920-21. He led a successful *war* against Turkey in 1911-12, seizing Libya for Italy. He supported the *Triple Alliance* with Germany. Out of power during *WWI*, his return to office was unsuccessful: he failed to arrest the decay of public life and civic violence symbolized by the seizure of *Fiume,* and gave way to *Mussolini.*

Girondins: A political faction of moderate republicans within the French Assembly that took control of public affairs 1792-93. They took France into *war* with Britain, the Netherlands and Spain. When there were defeats, the mob turned on the Girondins, encouraged by the more radical *Jacobins*. By October 1793, most Girondin leaders had been guillotined. See *French Revolution; The Terror.*

Gladstone, William (1809-98): British liberal states-man. As *Chancellor of the Exchequer* 1852-55 and 1858-66, he vigorously pushed *free trade*. He first served as PM in 1868, responding to the *Fenian* raids on Canada by disestablishing the Irish Church and introducing limited land and tenant reform in Ireland. He was defeated in 1874, with the votes of dissatisfied Catholic members telling the tale. Returned in 1880, he was drawn into the *First Boer War*, and felt com-pelled to introduce tough measures in Ireland. With the death of *Gordon* at Khartoum, his government fell. Returned in 1886, he tried to give Ireland *Home Rule*. His bill carried the Commons but not the Lords, and split the party, with a faction led by *Joseph Cham-berlain* vehemently opposed. He returned for a fourth term 1892-94, but again floundered on Home Rule. He had championed *liberal* causes, such as Italian unity, Home Rule, and Bulgarian *independence* from Turkey. He thus was among the first Western statesmen to ex-pound *human rights* as a general principle with which foreign policy should be concerned, and may even have been genuinely concerned to further those causes illuminated by a refined conscience.

glasnost: "Openness." A term introduced by *Mikhail Gorbachev* about his post-1985 opening of Soviet society to *dissidents*, public criticism and limited ad-mission of past Soviet mistakes. Cf. *perestroika*.

global commons: See *Antarctica; common heritage principle; Moon Treaty; Outer Space Treaty; res com-munis; Seabed Treaty; UNCLOS III*.

Global Environmental Facility: Founded in 1990 and jointly managed by the *IBRD*, the *UNEP* and the *UNDP*, it is concerned with financing *green loans* and more generally linking development and environmental issues. Its main task is to pay the "incremental costs" of environmental protection that accompany *develop-ment*, which *LDCs* cannot afford. Its probationary period runs until June 1994, after which it takes over financing of the *Earth Summit* treaties on Biodiversity and Climate Change.

global village: The idea that modern communications give such immediacy to events they bring previously isolated societies, cultures and individuals into effec-tive proximity. The term is often used to imply direct *interdependence*, and shared interests and purposes. However, it might be suggested that "global New York" or "global Calcutta" is more apt: a world me-tropolis where extremes of wealth and poverty coexist, violence is rampant, *anarchy* is not far distant, and in-habitants may choose to help or step over and past the less fortunate. In short, not all facets of interdepen-dence are benign: we may have a new interdependence of global problems without a corresponding sense of community or shared solutions.

global warming: The theorized general raising of the Earth's average temperatures by a *greenhouse effect*. If true, it may potentially melt part of the polar ice caps, raise ocean levels and lead to massive flooding in coastal and river delta states. It could also alter crop cycles and viability, and affect climate patterns. All that could cause massive demographic shifts, with unpredictable economic and political consequences.

Gneisenau, August Wilhelm von (1760-1831): The general who organized the new Prussian army for *Frederick-William III*, and helped command it in the *campaigns* of 1813-15.

GNP: See *Gross National Product*.

Goa: See *Portuguese India*.

Goebbels, Joseph (1897-1945): Nazi Minister of En-lightenment and Propaganda 1933-45, and member of *Hitler's* innermost circle. His street name was "the poison dwarf." He took a doctorate in philosophy at Heidelberg, but drifted until he met Hitler, who con-firmed his rabid *anti-Semitism* and gave him Nazi Party responsibilities. During *WWII* he ran much of the domestic side of *Nazi Germany*, and all its *pro-paganda*. His main technique was the "Big Lie," a tale so monstrous as to be unbelievable that yet is believed through constant repetition. He also pioneered the use of radio to reach a mass audience (one can only shud-der at the thought of what he and Hitler could have done with television). In the final days in Berlin he and his wife poisoned their six children, whom they could not imagine living "in a world without Hitler," and then killed themselves.

Golan Heights: A high plateau in *Palestine* that com-mands the Galilee and the Jordan Valley. It was cap-tured by Israel from Syria in the *Third Arab/Israeli War* (1967). It was formally *annexed* in December 1981. In 1993 Israel for the first time showed a will-ingness to return some or all the Golan, in exchange for a secure *peace* with Syria, which also showed flexibility (under considerable American and other Western coaxing and pressure) for the first time in nearly three decades.

Gold Coast: (1) The former name of Ghana. (2) Part of the West African coast of modern Ghana, named for the *primary product* taken from it; nearby sections were known as the *Ivory* and *Slave Coasts*.

gold standard: A monetary standard in which the value of *currency* is *fixed* in terms of the price of gold, first introduced by Britain in 1821. In theory, currency so *pegged* is convertible to gold. It was abandoned with the outbreak of *WWI*. Britain tried to lead a return to the gold standard in 1925, but that effort failed by 1931. *Roosevelt* took the U.S. off gold in 1933. Re-established after 1945, the U.S. went off gold again in August 1971. See *Nixon shocks.*

Gomulka, Wladyslaw (1905-82): Polish communist dictator. Distrusted and arrested by *Stalin*, he yet emerged as leader during the Polish/Soviet *crisis* of 1956. He was able to keep up a limited *autonomy* domestically by keeping loyal to Moscow in foreign policy. He resigned in face of wide unrest in 1970.

good faith: A fundamental principle of *international law*, it calls for the exercise of legal rights in accord with minimum and internationally accepted reciprocal standards. In short, it assumes that agreements are made with the honest intention of being kept.

Good Neighbor policy: Initiated by *Harding* and practiced by *Hoover* after 1930, it was taken up and expanded by *Franklin Roosevelt* after 1934. It promised, and delivered, an end to the previous era of U.S. military *intervention* and running of customs receiverships in Central America, and led as well to better relations with all of Latin America.

good offices: The attempt by a third party, such as the *Secretary General* or a UN or regional body, to bring enemies together to resolve a *dispute*. It offers the chance to *save face* for one or both parties.

goods: Physical merchandise or tangible products. See also *durable goods; soft good.* Cf. *services.*

Gorbachev, Mikhail Sergeyevich (b.1931): Soviet statesman. His ascent to power in 1985 marked a major departure in Soviet and *Cold War* history. He engaged in an array of *arms control* agreements with the West, including the *INF Treaty,* and generally warmed relations. His frank renunciation of the *Brezhnev Doctrine* was critical to the *revolutions* of 1989 in *Eastern Europe*. Most important, he agreed to allow German unification, within *NATO*. Yet his vague plans to reform, modernize and partly decentralize the Soviet system only loosed nationalist and regional forces that tore that empire apart. More admired abroad than at home, he was awarded the 1990 *Nobel Prize* for Peace. Increasingly challenged by the Soviet republics, he began to shift back to the *hardliners*, authorizing the use of some force against demonstrators in Lithuania and rioters in Azerbaijan. He was shocked by the sudden resignation of his friend and Foreign Minister, *Eduard Sheverdnadze*, who warned that Gorbachev was courting favor with the right, and that dictatorship threatened. Gorbachev survived an attempted *coup* by the communist old guard in 1991, but was after that made irrelevant by rapid decentralization, and was left without a country when the Soviet Union became *extinct* later that year. While he introduced more *glasnost* (openness), there was little fundamental restructuring of the economy (*perestroika*) until after the accession to power of *Boris Yeltsin*, long his personal as well as political bête noir.

Gorchakov, Alexander (1798-1883): Russian statesman. Ambassador to Austria during the *Crimean War*; Foreign Minister 1856-82; and Chancellor 1863-82. Other than *Bismarck*, he had no rival for influence among the *Great Powers*. He kept Austria from entering the *Franco/Prussian War*, and by working with Bismarck, freed Russia from the constraints imposed by the *Treaty of Paris (1856)*. He took Russia into the *Dreikaiserbund*, but toward the end of his career he grew bitterly jealous of the power of Germany and prestige of Bismarck. He was ineffectual at, and after, the *Congress of Berlin*.

Gordon, Charles (1833-85): British general. Sent to Sudan in 1884 to repress the *Mahdi* revolt, he underestimated the Mahdi's forces. He was caught in a 10-month *siege* at Khartoum, at the end of which he and his garrison were killed. His death brought down *Gladstone's* government.

Göring, Herman (1893-1946): Nazi Air Minister 1933-45. An *ace* in *WWI*, he joined the party in 1922. Elected in 1928, he became President of the *Reichstag* in 1932, and later Minister President in Prussia. He helped found the *Gestapo* and the *concentration camp* system, and was overall a (rather large) pillar of the *Hitler* regime. His star began to slip with the failure of the *Luftwaffe* to win the *Battle of Britain*. He failed again at *Stalingrad*, and never recovered his earlier stature. He once said, citing a common Jewish name: "If a single bomber reaches the *Ruhr*, you can call me Meier!" From 1943 on, Germany's cities were pounded by *thousand bomber raids*. Germans huddled in their shelters, muttering: "Where is Meier?" Vain, corpulent, corrupt and endlessly ostentatious, he was convicted of *war crimes* at *Nuremberg*. He managed to cheat justice with smuggled poison, only a few hours before he was due to hang.

Gossens, Salvador Allende: See *Allende, Salvador;* and see also, *Chile.*

Gottwald, Klement (1896-1953): President of Czechoslovakia 1948-53. Returning from wartime *exile* in Moscow, he formed a coalition government with *Eduard Beneš*, whom he replaced after the communists took power in a 1948 *coup*. He utterly subjugated *Czechoslovakia* to *Stalin* and the *Soviet Union*.

government-in-exile: One forced temporarily abroad by an *invasion* and *occupation* of its home *state*.

graduation clause: Inserted in the *GATT* over *G-77* objections, it permits developed countries to almost unilaterally decide when Southern economies have "graduated" to the point they should no longer enjoy the special advantages of the *GSP*, and must become full GATT members bound by *reciprocity* and the *MFN* principle. For example, in 1989 the U.S. dropped the *Asian Tigers* and other *NICs* from its GSP list.

grammatical interpretation: Resolving ambiguities in interpretation of a *treaty* by looking at its syntax.

Grand Alliance: See *Quadruple Alliance*.

Grand Mufti: Formerly, the spiritual leader of Muslims in Jerusalem. The Grand Mufti in office during *WWII* secretly conspired with *Nazi Germany*, in search of aid for his opposition to Jews in *Palestine*.

grand strategy: The long-term-vision, if any, and relation of goals to means underlying a state's foreign policy. A synonym for *architecture*.

grand theory: Theory at the highest, or at least broadest, level of generalization. It seeks to explain the largest phenomena of human and world affairs, and to spin off subordinate theories. For example, *dependency theory; marxism; realism*. Cf. *paradigm*.

Grant, Ulysses S. (1822-85): U.S. general; President 1868-76. Dismissed early in the *American Civil War*, he later won a great victory in the west at Vicksburg. Over *cabinet* opposition, *Lincoln* appointed him to the command of the Army of the Potomac. He was the first to grapple with *Robert E. Lee* and refuse to disengage, thus bringing to bear the weight of superior *Union* manpower during 1864-65. He accepted Lee's surrender at Appomattox Court House. His first term as President was more successful than his second, which is mostly remembered for its scandals. As memory of Lincoln faded, the country--and perhaps Grant too--drifted into the bitterness of *Reconstruction*. Then a world *depression* began to bite into its ideals. Yet, Grant and Secretary of State Hamilton Fish were quietly successful in settling the *Alabama claims* with Britain in the *Treaty of Washington* and avoiding war with Spain over Cuba. His attempt to *annex* Santo Domingo as a naval base was rebuffed when the Senate refused take-over of a self-governing, black nation.

grapeshot: Iron balls, nails, chain links or other scrap metal fired from a cannon. It was devastatingly effective against *infantry* at close range.

Great Britain: (1) A large island off Western Europe. (2) The name used since 1707 for the island power that brought *Ireland, Scotland* and Wales (and minor, offshore islands) under *England*. From 1800-1922 it included all Ireland; after 1922 it retained just six of the nine counties of *Ulster*. See *United Kingdom*.

Great Depression (1929-39): See *depressions, world*.

Greater Antilles: The islands of Cuba, Jamaica, Hispaniola, Puerto Rico and some smaller *dependencies*.

Greater East Asian Co-Prosperity Sphere: The Japanese euphemism and slogan used to mask the reality of brutal imperial expansion into China and the Pacific 1937-45. Cf. *Asia for Asians*.

Greater Israel: The ambition of radical *zionists*, and the ultra-Orthodox, to expand Israel until it is coextensive with the biblical nation, entailing incorporating all of the *West Bank* and *Gaza* and driving out the *Arab* population. From 1967-92 the notion was a powerful impetus behind Israel's settlement policy as implemented by *Likud*. In 1993 the Labour government took a different path: it chose to exchange *land for peace*.

Greater Serbia: The longstanding ambition of Serb nationalists that all ethnic Serbs, and the *territory* they occupy in whole or in part, should be brought under Belgrade's control. See *Balkan Wars; ethnic cleansing*.

Greater Syria: A nationalist vision, at the extreme incorporating all *Lebanon* and *Palestine* within Syria.

Great Fear: A peasant revolt against the chateaux in France from 1788-89. Once peasant anger was spent, the *French Revolution* shifted to Paris. See *jacquerie*.

Great Game: A long struggle in the 19th century between Britain and Russia for influence in *Central Asia*, the borderland area between respective *empires*.

Great Leap Forward (1958-61): *Mao Zedong's* slogan for the attempt to expand production in China by replacing market incentives with compulsory revolutionary ardor, rural *collectivization* and rural *indus-*

trialization. Mao thought he could mobilize the peasantry for modern economic production in the same manner he had mobilized them for *war* (he is known to have referred to "General Steel, General Coal, and General Grain" as his commanders in this crackpot enterprise). The scheme fell down on several levels, not least the attempt to increase production in traditional, heavy industries by using large numbers of small-scale "backyard" foundries that produced brittle and unusable steel where quality was to be had from a few large and efficient plants. Convinced that China's poor harvests were the result of sparrows eating the grain, rather than his policies of forced collectivization, Mao organized tens of millions of peasants to kill off these winged *counter-revolutionaries*; that only freed truly damaging insect pests to consume what was left of the crops. In combination with fierce peasant resistance and several bad harvests, this produced a devastating *famine* in the countryside that took many millions, and perhaps tens of millions, of lives. Mao's "Great Leap Forward" was, in short, an utter disaster, constituting in fact a great leap backward and a national and human tragedy of mind-boggling proportions, rather than any kind of advance. Nevertheless, Mao and his most loyal *cadres* would try again a few years later to severely radicalize Chinese society, in that second disaster of unchecked, secular romanticism known as the *Great Proletarian Cultural Revolution.*

Great Man (approach to history): The study of the history of *nations* and societies by primary concentration on individuals of influence, and their preferences, policies and choices.

Great Patriotic War: Russian name for the Nazi/Soviet war fought within the larger contest of *WWII.*

Great Powers: This term was used in a *treaty* for the first time only in 1815, but for centuries before that it was understood to mean those states whose economy, size and military capability made their interests and policies an inescapable concern to all other powers in the system. Until modern *technology*, and even more so *war*, created a single world political system in the late 19th century, the term "Great Powers" was applied solely to the dominant powers of Europe. Since then it has become universal. (1) 17th century: Austria, France, the Holy Roman Empire, the Netherlands, the Ottoman Empire, Spain and Sweden. (2) 18th century: Austria, England, France, the Ottoman Empire, Prussia and Russia. (3) 1815-1918: Austria; Britain, France, the Ottoman Empire, Prussia (German Empire 1871-1918), Russia and less clearly, Italy (1861), the U.S. (1865) and Japan (1895). (4) 1919-1945: Britain, France, Germany, Italy, Japan, the So-

viet Union and the U.S. (5) 1945-1991: Britain, China, France, Germany (c.1955), Japan (c.1964), the Soviet Union and the U.S. (6) Post-1991: Britain, China, France, Germany, Japan, Russia and the U.S. Possible future additions, depending on the measure of *power* one uses, might include Brazil, India and Indonesia. Some listed as still Great Powers, such as Britain (largely because of its large nuclear force and *Security Council* seat), are already in relative and likely in terminal decline from that status. Cf. *superpower.*

Great Proletarian Cultural Revolution: It began in 1966, yet its full fury was not spent until *Mao Zedong* died in 1976. Gangs of young thugs were organized into the *Red Guards*, and sent out to *purge* the party and society of pragmatists and others who opposed Mao's radical egalitarianism. They "criticized," humiliated, and often killed anyone who dared go against the "Great Helmsman." Nearly five million were purged from the party and bureaucracy. Rank or past service to the revolution or party provided no sure defense against arbitrary mistreatment. They destroyed universities, shrines, temples and the daily practices of China's ancient culture. By 1968 *civil war* threatened, and the *PLA* was brought into the center of Chinese politics to restore order. The Cultural Revolution, before it ran its course, severely damaged the economy, led to gross injustice and persecution of millions, and paralyzed the educational system. It cost China a full generation of stable development. See also *cult of personality.* Cf. *cultural revolution.*

Great Purge: See *Yezhovshchina.*

Great Trek (1836-38): The migration of *Boer* families from *Cape Colony* to the Orange River and *Natal,* under Andrius Pretorius (1799-1853). The story of Voortrekker hardships and battles against the *Zulu* forms a central legend of Boer *nationalism.* Their descendants still congregate in annual convention at the Voortrekker monument.

Great War: A term used about *WWI*, until the world was again astonished and broken by the even greater horror, destruction and shaking of *nations* of *WWII.*

Greece: Location: *Balkans.* Major associations: *CSCE, EU, NATO, OECD, UN.* Population: 10 million. Military: below NATO par; regional range. Greece was conquered by the *Ottomans* in the 15th century. With Russian help, it fought the *Greek War of Independence* with Ottoman Turkey, 1821-29. It was ruled by a German King, Otto of Bavaria 1832-62. He was succeeded by a Dane, King George, 1863-1913 (assassinated). In 1863 it was given the Ionian Islands, previously under British protection. The Turkish possession Thesaly was added in 1881. Greece added Crete in 1913, and from the *Balkan Wars* it gained part of Macedonia and Thrace. It joined the *Allies* in *WWI*, but only in 1917 when it sensed gains might be made. It remained a kingdom until 1924, when it became a *republic*. The *monarchy* was restored in 1935, and made peace with the semi-*fascist* regime of General Metaxas (1871-1941). In 1940 Greece was attacked by Italy. Its successful resistance brought in German and Bulgarian troops, who occupied it until 1944 when it was *liberated* by the British. Monarchist and British forces then fought local communists. From 1947-49 a *civil war* raged between Greek communists with Soviet support, and monarchists and others aided by the U.S. under the *Truman Doctrine*. Greece (and Turkey) joined NATO in 1952. But once *Yugoslavia* broke with Moscow the strategic importance of Greece declined, a process accelerated by disputes with Turkey in the Aegean (and over *Cyprus*). The U.S. saw Turkey as strategically more important and a more stable and reliable security partner. In April 1967, a *coup* began harsh dictatorial rule by "the colonels." In 1973 the monarchy was again abolished. Greek officers on Cyprus attempted a coup and *enosis* in July 1974, but their actions only provoked a Turkish invasion of Cyprus and collapse of the *junta* in Athens. A shaky but working democracy was restored. In 1981 Greece joined the *EC*. That year, socialist Andreas Papandreou won the presidency and Greece became a vocal critic of U.S. policy. Cooperation with NATO declined, but despite talk, Greece did not withdraw from the alliance. During the 1980s it was widely criticized for its lax anti-*terrorist* record, and for taking more than it gave to the EC. Greece took a singular attitude toward the breakup of Yugoslavia, tacitly supporting Serbia because both opposed independence for *Macedonia*. When that came anyway, it blocked Macedonia's admission to the UN until April 1993, insisting that it change its flag and name; in 1994 it unilaterally sanctioned Macedonia, over EU objections. Greece maintains interests in Cyprus and the *Dodecanese*, and retains muted hostility for Turkey and Macedonia.

Greek/Turkish War (1921-22): An ambitious, romantic Greek attempt to "reclaim" historic, Hellenic possessions near *Constantinople* was thoroughly rebuffed by the Turkish Army, under *Atatürk*.

Greek War of Independence (1821-29): A Greek revolt against *Ottoman* rule broke out first in 1821. It gained sympathy and support from European liberals (Lord Byron died fighting for Greece). Heavy fighting raged from 1822, with the *Great Powers* proclaiming their *neutrality*. *Alexander I, of Russia*, well into his

reactionary phase, preferred to see the principle of *monarchy* protected even over gains at the expense of Turkey. But *Canning* favored *independence*. In 1827 he agreed with the Russians (Alexander was dead) to set up an *autonomous* Greek *state* under an Ottoman *suzerain*. The Sultan balked, and called on his Egyptian vassal, *Mehmet Ali*, for aid. Britain and Russia then together sank the Ottoman and Egyptian fleets at *Navarino* in 1827. *Wellington* succeeded Canning and broke off talks with Russia. Russia *declared war* and in 1829 Greece became independent. Turkey accepted this *de jure* in the Treaty of Constantinople in 1832.

greenhouse effect: The theory that Earth's atmosphere may be so changed by pollutants that excess heat (solar radiation) will be trapped and lead to *global warming*. From the 1980s it became the subject of negotiation over reduction of harmful, gaseous emissions, particularly *CFCs*.

Greenland: (1) Former name of *Kalaallit Nunaat*. (2) The largest island in the world (840,000 sq. miles), most of it covered by a permanent ice pack.

green line: (1) The disputed, but UN-policed boundary between the Greek and Turkish communities on Cyprus. (2) The divide between Israel and the Arab states, set by the UN in 1949. (3) The line in Beirut dividing Christian and Muslim sections.

green loans: *Development* loans made by *donor countries* or banks with an eye to the environmental impact of financed projects, or made specifically for corrective, environmental purposes.

Greenpeace: Founded in Canada in 1971, it is a leading pressure/activist group on environmental issues. Its early focus was on the whale and seal hunts, and opposition to nuclear tests. It dismissed extremist members who advocated or used violence ("eco-terrorism"). It relies mainly on education, *propaganda* and non-violent publicity stunts. See *Rainbow Warrior.*

green revolution: The major increase in crop yields and food production in parts of the *Third World* that began in the 1950s and 1960s. It resulted from the introduction of genetically engineered varieties of grains, the use of advanced fertilizers in some countries, and reorganizing landholding patterns for greater *efficiency*. It was most successful in India, where *famine* (if not *hunger*) was eliminated. *Radical* critics, in contrast, suggest that it represented an effort to provide a quick technical "fix" for what is essentially a long-term social and political problem, that of equitable (not just efficient) land reform.

Greens: Political activists/fringe parties prominent in the 1980s, especially in Europe. They emphasized, often to the point of exclusivity, environmental issues and concerns. With the end of the *Cold War* the soft, anti-*capitalist*, anti-*growth* message of the Greens lost much of its electoral appeal, particularly in Germany.

Grenada: Location: *Lesser Antilles*. Major associations: *CARICOM, Commonwealth, OECS, OAS, UN*. Population: 86,000. Military: minimal. Columbus charted the coast of this Caribbean island in 1498, but Europeans did not settle there until after 1650. It repeatedly changed hands between Britain and France until 1784, when the British secured it permanently. Grenada was given *independence* and joined the *Commonwealth* in 1974 as the least populous nation in the Americas, with fewer than 90,000 people. It drifted toward *alignment* with Cuba under the faintly *marxist* government of *Maurice Bishop*. He was overthrown on October 14, 1983, and murdered five days later by a more *radical* faction of his own "New Jewel Movement." On October 25th the U.S. and token forces from six Caribbean states invaded. They later oversaw free elections, and left in 1985. Since then Grenada has sunk back into international obscurity. Its controversial airport, started by Cubans and finished by U.S. military engineers, is used for charter tourist flights.

Grenada, invasion of: On October 21, 1983, the *OECS* requested U.S. *intervention* in Grenada. The OECS states claimed that the overthrow of *Maurice Bishop* in a *coup* threatened *security* and *stability* in the area. Four OECS states sent token forces, joined by troops from Barbados and Jamaica, to support the main U.S. *invasion* on October 25th. The *Reagan* administration justified intervention on the grounds that an airfield under construction by Cuban engineers was designed for military purposes, and that the safety of several hundred American medical students was at stake--it was said the students might be taken *hostage* by *radicals*, in a repeat of the *hostage crisis* in Iran. After several days of small-scale fighting, including against the Cubans, resistance ended. The students returned home, and U.S. *aid* flowed to the island. Polls showed an overwhelming majority of Grenada's population approved of the invasion. American troops remained until elections were held, departing in June 1985. While Grenadians and the OECS states approved, the *OAS* denounced the invasion, invoking the principle of *nonintervention*.

Grey, Edward (1862-1933): British statesman. Foreign Secretary 1905-16 (the longest continuous service by any British foreign secretary). Originally an enthusiastic imperialist, the *Second Boer War* dulled that

sentiment and made him concentrate on building up the *Royal Navy*. He welcomed closer relations with the U.S. and the *Anglo/Japanese Alliance* of 1902. Once in office, he completed the *Entente Cordiale* in 1907 and approved the *Military Conversations* with France, Belgium and Russia. He refused to conclude formal *alliances* with these powers, because he wished to deter Germany, not encourage France and Russia into *adventurist* policies. He was also a supporter of *arbitration treaties* before *WWI*. He strove vigorously to avoid *war* during the *mobilization crisis*, but argued urgently for a *declaration of war* once Germany violated Belgian *neutrality*. Until fired by *Lloyd George*, he worked to fend off *Wilson's* mediation offers without cutting Britain's lines of supply to U.S. credit and goods. After the war, he was a vocal supporter of the *League of Nations*.

Gromyko, Andrei Andreovich (1909-89): Soviet diplomat. At the Washington embassy from 1939, and Ambassador from 1943; UN Ambassador 1945-52; Ambassador to Britain 1952-54; Foreign Minister 1957-85; figurehead President of the Soviet Union 1985-88. He was a permanent fixture during the *Cold War*. While always near the center of events, he was but a gray, accomodating man who rarely had decisive influence (that being the likely secret of his longevity).

Gross Domestic Product (GDP): The total value of a nation's output of *goods* and *services* over one year, but confined to domestically located *factor endowments*. Thus, GDP is *GNP* minus "net factor incomes" (*profits* and wages) *repatriated* from abroad. See *GNP; remittances*. Cf. *NNP; SNA*.

Gross National Product (GNP): The total value of a nation's output of *goods* and *services* over one year, measured not territorially as with *GDP*, but including all value produced by the *factor endowments* of that country, wherever they may be located. It is often used as an indicator of *growth* and *development*. It is calculated in two ways: (1) at *factor* cost: or earnings on production factors such as wages, interest, *profits* and *remittances*; and (2) at *market* cost: where expenditures are added, such as consumption, *investment* and public spending. When divided by the total population, the figure arrived at is cited as the per capita GNP. Comparative GNP figures are first converted to a single *hard currency* value, usually in U.S. dollars, and adjusted for *inflation*. Note: This concept has been criticized for excluding valuable but non-monetary services, such as unpaid work in the home, while including without qualification production that may have hidden costs, such as environmental degradation. Also, there can be considerable distortion when one uses a figure that measures economic activity as an indicator of economic welfare. Cf. *Net National Product; SNA*.

Grotian: Drawn from the theories of *Hugo Grotius*.

Grotius, Hugo, né Huig van Groot (1583-1645): Dutch jurist, humanist and diplomat (in the Swedish service). His great work, "De jura belli et pacis" (On the Law of War And Peace), is widely regarded as a landmark in the development of *international law*. His writings drew deeply from the well of *natural law* theory, as well as utilizing the new idea of *social contract* (still germinating in his day, and flowering fully only with the *Enlightenment*). He devised from these sources general, rational principles, which he then put forward as the basis for a system of law between and among nations. Of these, four key ideas have been bequeathed to modern legal and political discourse: (1) States ought not to seek to impose their *ideologies* (in his day and corner of the world, Catholicism and Protestantism) upon each other, but should instead abstain from interference in each others' *internal affairs*. (2) A "law of nature" exists separate from and higher than human affairs, but it is knowable by human intellect and reason. (3) General elaboration and acceptance of this *natural law* is the only path to escape from *anarchy*. (4) An "assembly of the nations" ought to be created to enforce these laws drawn from nature by reason. He profoundly influenced thinkers as diverse as *Hobbes* and Locke, and to some degree, almost all subsequent writers on the law of nations.

ground zero: The exact point at which (or below which, if an *airburst*) a nuclear explosion occurs.

Group of Eight: See *Cartagena Group*.

Group of Five (G-5): (1) The five largest industrial democracies, which attempt to coordinate *monetary policy* and collectively manage the global financial system: Britain, France, Germany, Japan and the United States. Increasingly, management falls to the three largest economies: the U.S, Japan and Germany. (2) The name of the *G-7* before the admission of Canada and Italy. See also *Plaza Agreement*.

Group of Seven (G-7): The club of the world's leading industrial democracies (not, as often said, its largest economies): Britain, Canada, France, Germany, Italy, Japan and the United States. Since the mid-1980s the G-7 has held annual *summits* of *heads of government*. It also sponsors regular meetings of foreign and finance ministers. To sustain collective *growth*, the G-7 monitor basic economic policies and performance and recommend voluntary remedial actions, if one member's domestic policy is deemed harmful to others. Current disagreements include the continuing problem of the U.S. *deficit*, and German *interest rate* policy. *Boris Yeltsin* showed up uninvited at the Tokyo summit in 1993 (he did not attend the meetings), where he confidently predicted that in due course Russia will join a renamed "Group of Eight."

Group of Seventy-Seven (G-77): A *caucus group* of *Third World* states formed in 1964 to present a bargaining front against the industrial *North* at the *UNCTAD* conferences and other *multilateral* negotiations. It promoted the *NIEO* demands of the 1970s. Named for the number of its original members, its membership rose by 1994 to 128 nations.

Group of Ten (G-10): A management group formed in 1961 by Belgium, Britain, Canada, France, Germany, Italy, Japan, the Netherlands, Sweden, and the United States. It addresses *exchange rates* and *monetary policy*. It also established a common fund for exchange rate management (the "General Arrangements to Borrow"), expanded in 1983 to include *IMF* members whose problems might threaten the system.

groupthink: A criticism of *rational decision-making* explanations. It argues that in small groups under intense pressure, as in a *cabinet* during a major *crisis*, there develops a stronger tendency to form a consensus and then resist criticism of the core position and to disregard "disconfirming" information, than to realistically evaluate options. Cf. *cognitive dissonance*.

growth: An increase in the volume of the *economy*, usually measured in terms of expansion in the size of the *Gross National Product*. It is considered a key *indicator* of a healthy national economy. Note: Growth is measured against the previous performance of each national economy, not a single standard. Hence, a 10% growth rate in a small economy, while an outstanding figure in itself, will still indicate a smaller amount of absolute economic activity than a 2% or 3% growth rate in a much larger economy. See also *export-led growth; import substitution; NICs*.

GRU (Glavnoye Rasvedyvatelnoye Upravlenie): The Soviet military *intelligence service*, charged with gathering information about the military *capabilties* and intentions of adversaries of the *Soviet Union*, particularly the U.S. and *NATO* but also China.

Guadalupe Hildago, Treaty of (1848): The *peace treaty* to the *Mexican/American War*, on *terms* wholly favorable to the U.S., which gained Arizona, California and New Mexico, and confirmed its hold on Texas. The border was set at the Rio Grande. Cf. *Zimmermann Telegram*.

Guadeloupe: An *overseas department* of France, located in the *West Indies*. It has been a French possession since 1635.

Guam: Part of the *Marianas* group first colonized by Spain after 1668. It was an *unincorporated territory* of the U.S. after the *Spanish/American War*. Seized by Japan in December 1941, it was retaken by U.S. forces in July 1944. U.S. *citizenship* was not granted until 1950, along with limited local government. In a 1977 *plebiscite* Guam rejected *independence*. In a set of *referendums* in 1982, 73% chose *commonwealth status*; this is still being negotiated. It claims *Wake Island*, which is also claimed by the Marshall Islands. Population: 132,000. Military: U.S. base.

Guandong (Kwantung) Army: The main Japanese force on the Asian mainland, placed in *Manchuria* after 1905 and soon virtually independent of civilian, or even central military control. It was a major influence pushing Japan toward imperial expansion. It staged the *Mukden incident* and invaded Manchuria in 1931, and it attacked China in 1937. It fought on the mainland until the Japanese *defeat* in 1945.

Guantánamo: The U.S. received a lease from Cuba in 1903 (renewed 1934) for this marine base. It remained in U.S. hands during the *Cold War* and *Castro* years.

guanxi: "Connections." A term used by foreign businesses for knowledge of persons and routines necessary to doing business in China post-1980. It implies considerable corruption, but also an ideological pragmatism about working within the realities of China's "socialist market economy" where party officials continue to pose formidable barriers to the *private sector*.

Guatemala: Location: Central America. Major associations: *OAS, UN*. Population: 9.3 million. Military: *counterinsurgency* focus; enmeshed in politics. A Spanish *colony* from 1524-1821, when it joined a doomed federal experiment called the United States of Central America. It became a separate *republic* in 1839. It briefly experimented with *democracy* in 1945, but has seen efforts at social and land reform thwarted by repeated military *rebellion* and *coup d'etat*. Jacobo Arbenz (1913-71) was a genuine reformer as President, 1950-54. But he was ousted by military and landowner opponents supported by the *Eisenhower* administration, which viewed Arbenz as a communist dupe. In 1975 a peasant insurgency began ("The Army of the Poor"). The government response grew espe-

cially brutal when the revolt spread to Guatemala's sizeable Indian population: *death squads* roamed freely with government support, and *torture* was unstated policy. Several more coups occurred in the 1980s, and several hundred thousand Guatemalans fled to Mexico. Civilian government was reintroduced in 1986, but the military continues to play a dominant role in Guatemalan domestic affairs.

Guderian, Heinz (1888-1954): German general. He studied *de Gaulle's* ideas on tank combat, and adapted them for use by the *panzers* he commanded that overran Poland and then France in 1939-40. Less successful in Russia, he was dismissed at the end of 1941, but returned in 1943. He was intensely loyal to *Hitler.* See *blitzkrieg*.

Guernica: A Basque city, the first to ever taste the ferocity of mass aerial attack, when it was bombed by *Nazi* "volunteers" during the *Spanish Civil War*.

guerrilla: Irregular fighters organized in small units to harass the enemy. See *guerrilla warfare*. Cf. *partisan*.

guerrilla warfare: From the Spanish for "little war," the term developed from the practices of Spanish and British units during the *Peninsular War* in Iberia, against *Napoleon*. Since then it evolved to mean quick, surprise engagements and *sabotage* attacks by small bands of irregular fighters, with the aim to either force *negotiations* or so weaken the opposing military force that a switch can be made to the next level of warfare: a *conventional* civil war where *territory* is taken and held, opposing forces are met on equal terms and an alternative government is set up. In the 20th century *Mao* emerged as both a "theorist" and practitioner of guerrilla warfare, predicating success on intense, advance political work among the peasantry (the guerrilla, he said, is a fish swimming in the great ocean of the peasantry). *Che Guevara* thought political work could follow direct action, but learned otherwise --at the cost of his life--in Bolivia. Guerilla armies must achieve outside *recognition* and *aid* to have any hope of ultimate success. See *counterinsurgency*.

Guevara, Ernesto "Che" (1928-67): Argentine-born revolutionary and *guerrilla warfare* commander. He fought alongside *Castro* in Cuba. He occupied an important post in Castro's *regime*, but while he enjoyed making *revolution* he was quickly bored and frustrated by what his revolution had made. He quit the Cuban government and returned to the gun, fighting in the Congo and Latin America. He was killed in an ambush while trying to foment an uprising among broadly indifferent peasants in Bolivia. He became something of a cult figure for the campus left in the West in the late 1960s, but inspired few emulators on the Latin left.

Guiana: The tropical region of NE South America.

guided missile: Any *missile* steered in flight by television signal, radio signal, wires or other mechanical controls.

Guinea: Location: W. Africa. Major associations: *OAU, UN*. Population: 7.3 million. Military: enmeshed in government. This extremely poor state became a French *colony* in stages from 1849-98. It was given *independence* in 1958, but was the only one of France's African possessions to reject membership in the *French Community*. France then withdrew all *aid* and *investment*, and Guinea's economy collapsed. Ahmed Sekou Touré (1922-84), a dedicated *marxist* and President from 1958-84, obtained aid from the *Soviet bloc*. His *one-party state* during the 1960s and 1970s was one of the most avowedly anti-Western in Africa. After a failed, Portuguese-inspired effort to invade Guinea from neighboring Guinea-Bissau, Touré's regime became more repressive. He died in 1984 and the military took control. Economic recovery has been slow.

Guinea-Bissau: Location: West Africa. Major associations: *OAU, UN*. Population: 1 million. Military: local capability. A center of the Portuguese *slave trade* from the 15th century, it was colonized only in the 19th century. In the early 1960s a *guerrilla* movement began to fight for *independence*, just as similar *rebellions* against Portuguese rule were occurring in Angola and Mozambique. Many independent African *states* *recognized* the rebel movement as the *legitimate* government, long before it took control in 1974, following *revolution* in Portugal itself. In 1980 a *coup* set up a *one-party state*.

GULAG archipelago (*Russ Glavnoe Upravlenie Ispravitel'notrudovykh LAGeri*): "Main Administration of Corrective Labor Camps." An archipelago of the mind's eye (as seen by *Alexandr Solzhenitsyn*), but made up of the very real prison camp and *slave labor* system of the *Soviet Union*. Located mainly in *Siberia*, in its heyday it contained 12 million or more *political prisoners* and "de-kulakized" peasants used as slave laborers, though usually the numbers stayed at three to four million (the numbers varied from year to year). It is estimated that some 40 million cycled through the GULAG, with perhaps 80% dying there. Inmates were used on construction of *Minatom* projects as well as heavy industry and other *infrastructure*. This labor was a critical component of several *five-year plans*, making up over 1/10th the labor force and costing the Soviet state less than 1/3rd as much to maintain each worker. The camps were emptied of most political prisoners after *Stalin's* death, but criminals used as forced laborers and some political prisoners could still be found in isolated camps even in *Gorbachev's* time. After the failed communist *insurrection* of 1993, *Boris Yeltsin* announced that Russia would abolish all forced labor, ending 1,000 years of the heinous practice.

Gulf Coalition: The military and political coalition assembled under UN authority, but not acting as the direct agent of the UN, that under U.S. leadership defeated Iraq during the *Gulf War*. It comprised more than 600,000 troops, about 2/3rds American with the rest drawn from 28 countries, including major contingents from Britain and France. Other states involved included the *Gulf States*, Egypt, Saudi Arabia and Syria. Small units came from another dozen countries, and non-combat units from still more nations provided medical and *logistical* support. Germany and Japan each provided billions of dollars to underwrite the coalition. Its commander was *Norman Schwartzkopf*.

Gulf Cooperation Council (GCC): It was set up in 1981 in response to the *Iran/Iraq War* by Bahrain, Kuwait, Oman, Qatar, Saudi Arabia and the United Arab Emirates. Its purpose is to promote regional cooperation in economic *development*, defense and foreign affairs. In 1984 it agreed to coordinate peninsular defense with the U.S. by hosting bases for the *rapid deployment force*. It supported the *Gulf Coalition* during the *Gulf War.*

Gulf States: Bahrain, Kuwait, Oman, Qatar and the United Arab Emirates. A distinction is sometimes made between the smaller Gulf states and Oman.

Gulf War (1980-88): See *Iran/Iraq War.*

Gulf War (1990-91): Iraq attacked and overran Kuwait on August 2, 1990. In an *emergency session* of the *Security Council* on August 6, the UN imposed an immediate *embargo* of all trade with Iraq. The U.S. began to airlift troops into Saudi Arabia (*Operation Desert Shield*), to bases prepared in advance to receive the *Rapid Deployment Force*. On August 28th, Iraq announced it had annexed Kuwait, which henceforth it called "Province 19." Westerners, including children, were taken *hostage* for use as "human shields" in case of U.S. or other attacks on Iraqi military installations. After intense negotiations, all were released. Kuwaiti officials were highly visible at the UN and the *Arab League*, and ran a very successful publicity campaign about Iraqi atrocities and looting. The *Security Council* set a January 15th deadline for Iraqi withdrawal, after which it authorized member states to use *force*. On January 16th, the U.S. led *Gulf Coalition* began air and *cruise missile* attacks on Iraqi positions (*Operation Desert Storm*). The Iraqi air force was mostly destroyed, or fled to Iran. Iraq responded with indiscriminate Scud *missile* attacks on Saudi Arabia and Israel (the latter was not a member of the coalition, and never joined the war). The ground offensive began on February 27th. Within hours the Iraqi army crumbled, and within three days it *surrendered*. As it ran it conducted a *scorched earth* policy, setting the Kuwaiti oil fields afire, and spilling crude into the Gulf. The *cease-fire* terms set by the UN, and agreed to by Iraq, included long-term inspection to ensure elimination of all Iraqi *weapons of mass destruction*. In the following months, the U.S., France and Britain jointly declared *no-fly zones* over northern Iraq, to protect the *Kurds*, and southern Iraq, to protect the *shi'ite* Marsh Arabs. Despite this, Iraq pursued the Kurds on the ground, chasing one million *refugees* to Turkey and Iran. Iraq intermittently refused to cooperate with UN weapons and cease-fire inspection teams. In December 1993, Iraq formally agreed to abide by the cease-fire resolutions and accepted long-term weapons inspections. But it was so little trusted that the embargo remained in place, despite objections from some quarters that it was unduly punishing the Iraqi civilian population. Both before and after *William ("Bill") Clinton's* inauguration on January 20, 1993, U.S. cruise missile attacks occurred, to coerce Iraq into compliance with the cease-fire resolutions, and also to punish it for an apparent plot to kill *George Bush*. See map and *oil; Republican Guard; Resolutions 660, 678*.

gunboat diplomacy: Sending elements of the navy to a hostile coast or port to display resolve, and *capabilities*, in order to compel or deter some action. Cf. *coercive diplomacy*.

gunnery: The art and science of designing, making and/or firing large guns.

Guomindang (National People's Party), a.k.a. Nationalists: A Chinese nationalist party formed in 1891 by Dr. *Sun Yat-sen*. After leading the *Chinese Revolution* of 1911, it failed to win control over the many *warlords* that sprang up throughout China. With military training from Soviet advisers in the early 1920s, under *Chiang Kai-shek*, Guomindang forces fanned

out from Canton and suppressed even the northern warlords by 1928. The party, which was partly built around a *leninist* model, set up a national government in Nanking. Then Chiang turned on the communists, precipitating the *Chinese Civil War* that continued (interrupted by the *Second Sino/Japanese War*) until the communist *victory* in 1949. The Guomindang retreated to *Taiwan*, where it was the dominant party into the 1990s.

Gurkhas: Nepalese *mercenaries* assimilated into and traditionally associated with the British army. They last fought for Britain in the *Falklands War*.

Gustavus Adolphus (1594-1632): King of Sweden. He recovered Sweden's Baltic provinces from Denmark, and in a *war* with Russia he took parts of Finland (1617). He made *peace* with Poland only to regroup and conquer more *territory* in 1629. In 1630 he intervened in the *Thirty Years' War*, becoming champion of the Protestant cause in Germany. He pushed the *Hapsburg*, Catholic armies back to Leipzig, where he fell in battle.

Guyana: Location: S. America. Major associations: *Commonwealth, OAS, UN*. Population: 800,000. Military: minimal. This Amazonian *territory* on the north coast of South America was a Dutch *colony* from the 17th century. Its economy was plantation, using extensive African *slave labor*. Britain took control in 1815 and abolished slavery, instead importing Indian indentured laborers. Modern Guyana, an extremely poor state with little arable land, became independent in 1966. Linden Forbes Burnham (1923-85) was PM from 1964-80. Diplomatically, he moved it toward Cuba and the *Soviet bloc*. Domestically, his "cooperative socialism" led to economic stagnation. Venezuela claimed a share of Guyana's western territory, but agreed to suspend this claim in 1970. However, in 1982 Venezuela revived its claim. Suriname disputes the eastern border.

Guyane: See *French Guiana*.

Gypsies (Roma): One of Europe's last nomadic peoples, they have suffered persecution and ill-will for centuries. *Hitler* sent hundreds of thousands to the *death camps*. Some six million survive, mainly in Eastern Europe but also Spain and as far west as Ireland, where they are known as "Tinkers." In 1994 they were again openly persecuted, this time in *Slovakia*.

H

Haganah: A *paramilitary* established in the 1920s to protect Jewish settlers in *Palestine*. It was more moderate than other paramilitaries, like the *Stern Gang* or *Irgun*, in the fight against the British. It became the nucleus of the Israeli Defense Force.

Hague Conferences: *Nicholas II* proposed these conferences on limiting the international *arms race* then underway, largely because Russia was having difficulty financing its military expenditures. (1) First (1899): This conference did little to slow the arms race, but was notable for the first-time participation of smaller powers, and of the United States and Japan. With 26 nations attending, it was an augury of the era of *conference diplomacy* to come, and a signal of the beginning of the end of the formal dominance of world politics by the European *Great Powers* alone. It set up the *Permanent Court of Arbitration*. (2) Second (1907): Small power and extra-European participation further expanded (some 44 states took part), but this handicapped discussions on matters of *vital interest* to the Great Powers. Still, a series of *Hague Conventions* were signed dealing with aspects of the *law of war*. These conferences were precursors to the assemblies of the *League of Nations* and *United Nations*. Cf. *Root Arbitration Treaties*.

Hague Conventions: Three sets of conventions dealing with the *law of war* fall under this rubric: those of 1899, 1907 and 1954, of which the first two are the most important. The conventions deplore the necessity of *war*, but recognize that when an appeal to arms occurs it is still in the interest of humanity and civilization to limit the extent and conduct of war. They follow three basic principles: (1) They do not claim to be exhaustive; the proper limits of war and the interests of humanity extend to additional rules not made explicit in *treaty* form. (2) The right of a *belligerent* to inflict harm is upheld but limited. (3) It is forbidden to use arms to cause "unnecessary suffering" to enemy soldiers or *civilians*. Parties to these conventions--and membership is not universal--must make a prior and reasoned *declaration of war*, or issue an *ultimatum* with a conditional declaration of war and communicate this to *neutral* powers. Who does and does not have *belligerent rights* is defined, and *POW* rights are spelled out. Among the acts forbidden by the Conventions are the following: the use of *poison gas*, killing or wounding enemies who have surrendered, not giving *quarter*, use of a white flag to deceive, use of the enemy's flag or uniforms, use of the *Red Cross* emblem to deceive, *bombarding* undefended towns, *pillage*, applying penalties to enemy civilians in reprisal

for enemy military acts, and refusing to care for enemy wounded. The 1954 convention dealt with protection of cultural property in wartime. See *Geneva Conventions; just war; war crimes.*

Hague Tribunal: See *Permanent Court of Arbitration.*

Haig, Alexander (b.1924): U.S. general. Adviser to *Richard Nixon* 1969-73; *SACEUR* 1974-79; Secretary of State 1981-82. He played a key role in holding the Nixon administration together during the final days of *Watergate.* As Secretary of State, he was more moderate than some in the first *Reagan* term, especially over the Polish crisis of 1980-81. He strongly supported Israel during its *invasion* of Lebanon. He was unable to prevent the Argentine invasion of the *Falklands* from turning into *war*, despite strenuous effort. His disagreements with others in the administration grew to be too many by 1982, and he resigned.

Haig, Douglas (1861-1928): British Field Marshal. He was made Commander-in-Chief of the British Expeditionary Force (BEF) in 1915. His inability to adjust to the realities of *trench warfare* led to repeated, bloody frontal assaults on the German lines that seldom gained or held ground before the summer counteroffensive of 1918. Despite leading the BEF into such disasters as the *Somme*, and despite many quarrels with *Lloyd George,* he kept command until the end of the war.

Haile Selassie, né Ras Tafari Makonnen (1892-1975): "The Lion of Judah." Emperor of Ethiopia 1930-74. Early on, he was a modernizer and reformer, though he fell away from that habit in later life. He became a symbol of Ethiopian resistance after his country was invaded by Italy in 1935. Forced into *exile* in 1936, he poignantly warned the Assembly of the *League of Nations,* "everyone is someone's Ethiopia." He returned in the wake of a joint Ethiopian/British force in 1941. He was a prominent leader in the early decades of the *Organization of African Unity.* He was overthrown by *marxist* revolutionaries in September 1974. He became a figure of veneration for a Caribbean religious movement (Rastafarianism), but had nothing to do with its founding.

Haiti: Location: *Greater Antilles.* Major associations: *OAS, UN.* Population: 6 million. Military: 8,500 troops, used solely for domestic repression; no offensive capability. The island of *Hispaniola* was discovered by Columbus in 1492. Haiti, comprising its western third, it was ceded to France in 1677. African slaves were imported in large numbers, to work a plantation economy. In 1791, under *Toussaint L'Ouverture*, the slaves rose against the French. They ultimately won freedom by 1804. In 1798 the former slaves joined with the French to repel British and Spanish forces. L'Ouverture defeated all white and colonist resistance by 1800, and applied to France for *recognition*. But *Napoleon* was now emperor in Paris, and he tried to reintroduce *slavery* and regain control of Haiti as a Caribbean base against England. In 1802 L'Ouverture was defeated, betrayed, shipped to and imprisoned in France. Tropical disease and superior motivation helped the Haitians turn back a Napoleonic army of some 20,000 troops. In 1804 Jean Dessalines (1758?-1806) proclaimed himself emperor, only to be assassinated two years later. Haiti remained proudly independent, the only *state* established by a slave revolt in a hemisphere replete with slavery for most of the 19th century. Tales of Haitian horrors were spun in the bedrooms of Dixie, reinforcing deep fears of a slave rebellion in the U.S. South and encouraging southerners to support the status quo in the Caribbean. But northern, abolitionist support for Haiti helped preserve it from *intervention*. The U.S. first intervened in 1915, in response to large-scale unrest and out of concern that Imperial Germany might attempt to establish a naval base there. U.S. troops were withdrawn in 1934 as part of the *Good Neighbor policy*, although the U.S. continued to oversee Haiti's fiscal affairs until 1947. François Duvalier ("Papa Doc") was elected president in 1957. He quickly established a brutal tyranny, ruling through the combined ruthlessness and voodoo mysticism of his "Tonton Macoutes," a vicious *paramilitary* and secret society that manned the *death squads* and kept the military in check. His son, Jean-Claude ("Baby Doc"), took over in 1971. Following two years of unrest he was deposed and fled into comfortable *exile* in France in 1986. Elections in 1988 were overturned by successive *coups*. In 1990 a Catholic priest, Jean-Bertrand Aristide, was elected president. When he too was overthrown in a coup, there was international outrage. The U.S. and OAS kept up pressure for his reinvestiture. In 1993 the *Security Council* imposed mandatory *sanctions* pending restoration of Aristide. The Haitian military agreed to his return and sanctions were lifted, but the military soon went back on its agreement. "Attaches," successors to the Tonton Macoutes, killed those loyal to Aristide and threatened UN workers (including American and Canadian police advisers). The UN reimposed sanctions and U.S., French, Canadian and Venezuelan *warships* enforced a *pacific blockade*, an action fully endorsed by the Security Council. In June 1994 the U.S. and Canada cut off all air and commercial contacts.

haj: A pilgrimage to visit the *Muslim* holy sites at *Mecca*. Prescribed rituals and prayers at the Kaaba (which houses the famous black stone), around which pilgrims circumambulate, complete the haj and earn a devout pilgrim the honorary title "al-Hajji." Since the *Iranian Revolution* the absolute proscription on political activities during the haj has several times been violated by Iranian demonstrators, over 400 of whom were killed by Saudi security in 1987.

Halifax, Edward Wood (1881-1959): Viceroy of India 1926-31; Foreign Secretary 1938-41; Ambassador to Washington 1941-46. He encouraged *Neville Chamberlain* to take a tougher line toward *Hitler*, and what backbone there was in British foreign policy after *Munich* can be attributed to him. *Churchill* kept him on as Foreign Secretary, then dispatched him to the critically important post in Washington during some of the darkest days of the war, when U.S. *aid* was vital to Britain's survival.

Hallstein Doctrine: Enunciated in 1957 by Germany's Foreign Minister Walter Hallstein, it declared that (other than the Soviet Union), West Germany would refuse to have *diplomatic relations* with any state that extended *recognition* to *East Germany*. See also *regulated coexistence; Ostpolitik*.

Hamas (*Harakat al-Muqawama al-Islamiyya*): "Islamic Resistance." A *fundamentalist* movement formed during the *Intifada*, which it saw not as a tactic to force concessions but as a *jihad* that must end in the destruction of Israel. In 1993 a diplomatic crisis developed over Israel's decision to expel 400 Hamas supporters, depositing them in southern Lebanon (they were allowed back at the end of the year). Most important, its rising support in the *occupied territories* encouraged both Israel and the *PLO* to make *peace*.

Hamilton, Alexander (1755-1804): Personal aide to *George Washington* 1777-81; contributor to the "Federalist Papers"; Secretary of the Treasury 1789-97. He advocated a strong federal government for the new Union, *protective tariffs* for the manufacturing sector, *rapprochement* with Britain, construction of a strong navy and *war* with France, if necessary. He greatly distrusted the rhetoric and ambitions of the *French Revolution*, and *Napoleon*. He was bitterly opposed by *Jefferson*. He was killed in a duel by another rival, Aaron Burr (1756-1836). His policies melded into the *Whig* tradition in American foreign policy.

Hammarskjöld, Dag (1905-61): Secretary General of the UN 1953-61. He earned worldwide respect for his handling of the *Suez Crisis*, where along with Canada's *Lester Pearson* he helped introduce the idea of

UN peacekeeping. However, he was bitterly criticized by the Soviets during the *Congo crisis*. He was killed in a plane crash while on his way to negotiate a resolution of that crisis. He was posthumous recipient of the *Nobel Prize* for Peace (1961).

Hanseatic League: A loose, medieval, north European association of *city-states* that shared trade and limited, mutual defense. Among its main centers were Bremen, Brunswick, Breslau, Cologne, Cracow, *Danzig*, Hamburg, Lübeck and Magdeburg. Some analysts view this type of weak international association as a possible *model* for a world order "beyond the *nation-state*."

Hapsburgs: The great dynastic House surviving from 1282-1918; rulers of the *Holy Roman Empire* 1438-1740, 1745-1806. They divided into Austrian and Spanish branches, representing the two great centers of temporal Catholic power in Europe. *Francis Joseph* was the last, enfeebled *emperor* in the Austrian line.

Hara Kei Takashi (1856-1921): PM of Japan 1918-22. He was unable to restrain the militarists in Japan from intervening in *Siberia*, during the *Russian Civil War*. His rule was pivotal, as he was the first commoner to be PM (with the brief exception of the Okuma-Itagki in 1898); that signified the end of the era of the *Genro*. He was readying to circumscribe the independence of the *Guandong Army* when he was assassinated.

hard currencies: Freely convertible national *currencies*. Reserves are held in *foreign exchange* accounts and used to finance trade, or *intervene* in the money markets to support a *floating* currency.

hardening: Reinforcing *missile* silos or other facilities to withstand nuclear attack. It produces "hard targets."

hard goods: See *durable goods*.

Harding, Warren (1865-1923): U.S. President 1920-23. Before, during and after *WWI* he opposed *Woodrow Wilson's* efforts to drag America into active involvement in world affairs. He took the country back onto the path of *isolationism* after 1920, vehemently opposing membership in the *League of Nations*. Even so, he tried (but failed) to obtain Congressional approval for U.S. membership in the *World Court*, and he continued to seek *arms control* agreements, as in the *Washington Conference* of 1921-22. He also attended to some necessary foreign policy housekeeping, after the fits and starts of too many initiatives by Wilson. He thus ordered separate and immediate *peace treaties* with the defeated *Central Powers*, with whom the U.S. remained technically at war into 1921, having failed to

ratify the treaties negotiated at the *Paris Peace Conference;* and he set about orderly arrangements for repayment of European *war debts*. Harding and his competent Secretary of State, *Charles Evans Hughes*, repaired relations with Mexico, which had been left in shreds by Wilson. They also began a partial military disengagement from Central and Latin America, notably from the Dominican Republic and Haiti. And they agreed to patch relations with Colombia by paying *compensation* for U.S. involvement in the *secession* of Panama. They even promised to reconsider the *Monroe Doctrine*, and apply it sparingly. Those were initiatives that would find resonance ten years later in the *Good Neighbor policy*. Much of that record has been obscured by Harding's early death, and a spate of domestic scandals (including Teapot Dome) that tattered his reputation posthumously.

hard-line: Rigid, tough, unforgiving, persistently unyielding, even *fanatic*. Most often used as a pejorative to characterize the style of harsh ideologues or national leaders, as in the *Cold War* usages "hard-line communist" and "hard-line anti-communist."

hard loan: Money lent to a state on market terms, and repayable in *hard currency*. Cf. *soft loan*.

Harmel Report (1967): Issued by *NATO* after France withdrew from military cooperation, it argued that NATO had two basic purposes: (1) maintain *deterrence* against a possible Soviet attack; and (2) create a stable environment in Europe in which political and other issues could be addressed and resolved.

Harriman, W. Averell (1891-1986): U.S. diplomat. He was sent to London in 1940-41 by *Franklin Roosevelt* to oversee the crucial *Lend-Lease* program. He was Ambassador to the Soviet Union 1943-46, the most critical years in the origins of the *Cold War*. He attended *Teheran, Yalta* and *Potsdam,* growing increasingly suspicious of *Stalin's* postwar intentions, and warning Roosevelt and then *Truman* that the only way to deal with the Soviets was from a position of firm resolve and resistance to bullying. He entered domestic politics, serving as Governor of New York 1954-58. But he remained one of the *Wise Men*, advising presidents of both parties on foreign policy. He served in the *Kennedy* administration as Assistant Secretary of State. He had a hand in the 1963 *Nuclear Test Ban Treaty* and in unsuccessful negotiations on ending the *Vietnam War*.

Hashemites: A line of Arabian *emirs* claiming descent from Muhammad, some serving for generations in *Mecca* under the *Ottomans*. This branch was pruned by the defeat of *Ibn Ali Hussein* by *Ibn Saud*. However, the line survived in Iraq until 1958, and in *Transjordan* (Jordan) to the present day.

Hassan II (b.1929): King of Morocco 1961- . He presented himself, with dubious success, as a bridge between the Arabs and Berber of North Africa and the black populations of sub-Saharan Africa. He maintained close ties with the old colonial power, France. His insistence on annexing the *Western Sahara* led to a protracted *war*, soured relations with Algeria and split and paralyzed the *OAU*, from which he withdrew Morocco in 1984.

Hausa: A widespread, mainly Muslim people, concentrated along the southern tier of the Sahara desert. The Hausa were the main backers of the Federal side in the *Nigerian Civil War*. Their language remains widely used for commerce across the *Sahel*, the Sahara and some points south. They were conquered by and merged with the *Fulani* in the 19th century.

Havel, Václav (b.1936): *Human rights* activist, dramatist, President of Czechoslovakia 1989-92, and President of the Czech Republic, 1993- . He was twice jailed by the former *communist* regime. Havel, contemporary circumstance and Czech history all tilted the Czech Republic firmly toward the *West*.

Hawaii: Formerly the Sandwich Islands. American settlement began in the 1820s, with annexationist fever high by the 1890s. After U.S. settlers overthrew the native Polynesian *monarchy*, Hawaii was *annexed* to the U.S. in 1898. *Pearl Harbor* became a forward base for the U.S. Pacific fleet before *WWII*, and was attacked by Japan on December 7, 1941. Hawaii became a state within the American union in 1959.

Hawley/Smoot tariff (1930): A high *tariff* wall against nearly all imported *goods*, enacted by the U.S. Congress in response to the *Great Depression*. It greatly exacerbated the depression by reducing world trade, and provoking a round of retaliatory *tariffs* from all other, major trading states. It most severely hurt U.S. trade with Canada and the Latin American countries.

head of government: The person wielding supreme, recognized and legal political power in a given country. Such a person may or may not also be the *head of state;* e.g., the British PM, rather than the monarch.

head of state: The person embodying or just symbolically representing the *sovereignty* of a state; not necessarily the *head of government*; e.g., the British monarch, rather than the PM.

Heartland: In the *geopolitics* of *Halford Mackinder*, the central part of the Eurasian landmass historically unreachable by *sea power* (no longer true in the age of *missiles*), from the Volga to the Yangtze, and northern India to the Arctic Ocean.

Heath, Edward (b.1916): British PM 1970-74. A centrist *Tory* and strong supporter of the *EC*, he secured membership for Britain in 1973. He improved relations with China over *Hong Kong,* but was weakened by domestic strife, including switching to *direct rule* in *Ulster*. After losing an election in 1974, he was replaced by *Margaret Thatcher*.

heavy (bomber, cruiser, missile, etc.): Those above an arbitrary size or weight. This designation may appear in an *arms control* agreement, for purposes of classification and elimination of agreed-upon systems.

Hegel, George (1770-1831): German philosopher. His theories of idealism (*history* as the manifestation of abstract principles greater than mere material existence) and of the *dialectic* powerfully influenced *Karl Marx*, among others. His philosophical speculations and system have often been seen as supporting *authoritarian* traditions, and as opposed to 19th century *liberalism*. In particular, he has been accused of expressing and reinforcing Prussian veneration for the *state*. He was himself a stern, Prussian nationalist. See also *end of history*.

hegemon: (1) Traditional usage: a dominant *regional power*. (2) Currently fashionable usage: a dominant *world power* that sets the *rules* and largely decides the distribution of *collective goods* for the whole *international system*. See below. Cf. *preponderant power*.

hegemonic stability: The theory that when there is a global *hegemon* the *international system* is more stable than when several *Great Powers* compete for *influence*. Why? Because from its own interests a powerful country will set *rules* and maintain *collective goods* that benefit the system as a whole, as well as coerce obedience. Cf. *imperial overreach; world power*.

hegemony: The *preponderance* of one nation, and its interests, over others. Cf. *bigemony; hegemon; hegemonic stability; sphere of influence*.

Hejaz: The historic region within Saudi Arabia, briefly independent in the 1920s, containing the holy cities (for Muslims) of *Mecca* and Medina.

Heligoland (also Helgoland): This North Sea island was taken from Denmark by Britain in 1807. It was ceded to Germany in 1890 as part of the *Schleswig-Holstein* settlement, in exchange for *Zanzibar*. It became an important German naval base after 1900; was *demilitarized* by the *Treaty of Versailles*, but remilitarized in 1936; became a target for British bombers in *WWII*; was demilitarized again in 1947, and was returned to West Germany in 1952.

Helsinki Accords: Alternate term for the *Final Act* signed at the 1975, summary meeting of the *Conference on Security and Cooperation in Europe*, that divided issues into three "Baskets." (1) Peace and security: This confirmed *postwar* borders, set up *Confidence and Security Building Measures (CSBMs)* in the CSCE, and attempted to regulate military affairs in the Mediterranean. (2) Social and economic affairs: It proposed a range of cultural exchanges, trade missions and *technology* transfers. (3) Human rights: The focus was on *family reunification* and the free flow of ideas and information. The central principle of the Accords was that state borders ought not to present barriers to free movement of *goods*, ideas or people.

Helsinki watch groups: Private *human rights* bodies set up in dozens of countries to monitor compliance with the *Helsinki Accords* of 1975. Most of those within the *Soviet bloc*, such as that led by *Andrei Sakharov* or *Charter '77* in Czechoslovakia, were banned and members arrested by 1979.

Helvetic Republic (1798-1802): A *puppet state* set up by *Napoleon I* in Switzerland.

Herrenvolk: "Higher peoples" or "master race." In *nazism*, any of the *Aryan* peoples considered racially and culturally superior to Jews, *Slavs* and other so-called *Untermenschen*.

Herzel, Theodor (1860-1904): Leading *zionist*. He called for creation of a Jewish state, founded the Zionist Congress in 1897, and was first president of the World Zionist Organization.

Herzen, Alexander (1812-70): Russian thinker and journalist. His liberalism grew increasingly *radical*. He went abroad in 1847, and never returned, but his writings influenced several generations of reformers and revolutionaries.

Hertzog, James (1866-1942): PM of South Africa 1924-29, 1933-39. A fierce nationalist, he fought the British during the *Second Boer War* and opposed support for Britain during *WWI*. When he again opposed supporting Britain at the start of *WWII*, he was forced to resign.

Hess, Rudolf (1894-1987): Nazi Party member #16. He rose to deputy party leader and was *Hitler's* designated successor. He signed the *Nuremberg Laws*. On May 10, 1941, he flew a *fighter* to Scotland and then parachuted down on a "mission of humanity" to *Churchill*, who refused to meet him. It is unclear on what authority, if any, he offered an *alliance* against the Soviets. The British concluded he was demented and/or simple-minded, and imprisoned him. The Soviets were more suspicious. Tried at *Nuremberg*, he was convicted of fomenting *aggression* but acquitted of *crimes against humanity*. He spent the rest of his life in Spandau prison in Berlin, where after 1967 he was the sole prisoner (the Soviets refused clemency). It was announced in 1987 that he committed suicide.

heuristic device: (1) Any technique or argument used in teaching that stimulates the student to pursue knowledge independently of the teacher. (2) An illustration or schematic presentation of a set of *variables*; less than a *model*.

Hezbollah: "Party of God." Lebanese radical *shi'ites*, joined by *fundamentalists* from Iran in 1982, who formed a *militia* that fought in the *Lebanese Civil War*. It was backed by Syria. In July 1993, Hezbollah launched rockets into northern Israel, leading to a six-day Israeli *retaliation* that was the most extensive in 11 years, and drove hundreds of thousands of civilians north to Beirut.

high command: (1) The top leadership in any military. (2) The main headquarters of a military force.

high commissioner: (1) In *multilateral diplomacy*: the head of an agency or program, such as the *UN High Commissioner for Refugees*. (2) In imperial relations: the usual title, if not governor, given to the head of a *colony, protectorate* or *mandate*. (3) In the *Commonwealth*: an ambassadorial-level *diplomat*. The title *ambassador* is not used among Commonwealth nations that share Queen *Elizabeth II* as their *head of state*, although that is exactly what high commissioners are.

highly enriched uranium (HEU): See *plutonium*.

high politics: All matters relating to *security, strategy, defense* and other *geostrategic* aspects of war and peace. Cf. *low politics.*

high seas: Under *international law*, all open water beyond *territorial waters*. Historically, that meant beyond the *three-mile limit* (see *cannon shot rule*); now it is generally beyond the *twelve-mile limit*. The fundamental principle is *freedom of the seas*. The most recent *codification* of law on the high seas is *UN-CLOS III*, which states "the high seas are open to all *States*, whether coastal or land-locked," and assigns legal freedom to: (1) navigation, (2) overflight, (3) lay submarine cable and pipeline, (4) construct "artificial islands" and other installations, (5) fishing, (6) scientific research. It also reserves the high seas to peaceful purposes, and denies any state the right to claim any portion for its *sovereignty*. In addition, landlocked states have been given a right of access, and most controversially, to "an appropriate" share in *exploitation* of the living resources of *EEZs* of *coastal states* in the same region. See *hot pursuit; law of the sea.*

hijacking: The violent (forcible) seizure of vehicles, ships, but especially aircraft. Air hijacking (a.k.a. air piracy) has increased in conjunction with *civilian* air travel. Motives are mixed: flight from a repressive regime, *terrorism* or perhaps just mental instability. At first, requests for *asylum* were heard according to the merit of each case. But as the perception grew that hijacking poses a general threat to life, property and good international order, states have agreed that no cause, however just, warrants this act. In a 1970 *convention* and another in 1971, hijacking was declared a crime under *international criminal law*, regardless of motive. A clarifying *protocol* was added in 1988. See also *Entebbe raid.* Cf. *piracy.*

Himmler, Heinrich (1900-45): Head of the *SS* 1929-45; head of the *Gestapo* 1934-45; Minister of the Interior 1943-45. He ran all the police in Germany after 1936, and was largely responsible for their reign of *torture* and terror. He was, in short, one of *Hitler's* head butchers, taking personal interest and direction of the *death camps* and *"final solution to the Jewish problem,"* and overseeing revenge for the *July Plot.* In 1945 he tried to negotiate with the *Allies* without Hitler's knowledge. Captured by the British, he committed suicide before he could be tried and executed.

Hindenburg, Paul von (1847-1934): German general, President of the *Weimar Republic* 1925-34. With *Ludendorff*, he won the great victory over Russia at *Tannenberg* in 1914, and in 1918 they imposed the *diktat* of *Brest-Litovsk* on Russia. But their spring offensive in the West in 1918 failed, and he told the civilians to *ask for terms.* He served *Weimar* reluctantly, and badly. He defeated *Hitler* in presidential elections in 1932, but agreed to appoint him Chancellor in 1933. He may have been senile toward the end of his life.

Hindenburg Line: German *fortified* positions along the French/Belgian border in *WWI.* The Germans fell back to these positions in February 1917, to shorten their *supply lines* and await an offensive. The *Allies* did not break through until September 11, 1918, but that advance convinced the German *high command* to tell the civilians it was time to sue for *peace.*

Hinduism: An umbrella term for the varied beliefs of 80-85% of India's population. It is polytheistic, within a view of all subdeities as different aspects of the trinity of Brahma, Vishnu and Shiva. It suggests reincarnation as a pathway to eventual perfection of the spirit and unity with the deity (godhead). The main books of scripture are the "Veda," the "Upanishad" and the "Bhagavad-Gita." These works and intellectual tradition established Indian law, taught tolerance and respect for life, but for millennia also supported and underwrote the caste system.

hinterland: An inland region, behind a coastal settlement. In the days of colonial expansion the doctrine of a hinterland was important for agreeing on *spheres of interest*, so as to limit imperial conflict.

Hirohito (1901-89): Emperor of Japan 1926-89. A figure of continuing controversy, his exact role in Japan's imperial surge between the wars is unknown (many records were destroyed). Similarly murky is the extent of his culpability in Japanese *war crimes* during *WWII.* He later portrayed himself as a simple gardener (he was an amateur botanist) who kept aloof from all politics and military decision-making. Yet his reign was marked by savage *aggression* against *Manchuria* and China, *alliance* with the *Axis*, expansion into Southeast Asia and the attack on the U.S. at *Pearl Harbor.* He intervened with the military in 1945 to prevent the suicidal heroics and mass slaughter that would have accompanied Allied *invasion* of the *home islands.* He was not tried at the *Tokyo war crimes trials*, mainly out of U.S. concern over permanently alienating Japan, and over the objections of most American allies in the Pacific (especially Nationalist China) who wanted him tried. The condition of his continuing to reign was renunciation of his status as a divinity and acceptance of a democratic constitution. Once a smart military dresser, after 1945 the ever-adaptable Hirohito wore only civilian clothes.

Hiroshima: On August 6, 1945, this hitherto undamaged Japanese city experienced the first use of an *atomic bomb* in wartime. A single U.S. bomber, with *fighter* escort, dropped "Little Boy," as the bomb was code-named. Some 75,000-80,000 were killed outright; another 50,000-60,000 died within 12 months, from radiation burns or poisoning. Many thousands have died since from cancers, and genetic mutations are expected to last for several generations. Cf. *Nagasaki.*

Hispaniola: One of the larger Caribbean islands, it was the part of the *Americas* Columbus stumbled upon in 1492. The part that forms the Dominican Republic today is the oldest permanent European settlement in the Western hemisphere. The western third of the island was ceded to France by Spain in 1697, and later became Haiti.

Hiss, Alger (1904-91): *State Department* officer. He was accused by an admitted Soviet agent, Whittaker Chambers, of being a spy for the Soviets, a charge Hiss always denied. He was convicted of perjury and served time 1950-54. He was defended by *Dean Acheson* in face of fierce attacks from the right. The case helped elevate *Richard Nixon* to national prominence. In 1990 Oleg Gordievsky, a high-ranking KGB defector, stated that Hiss was indeed a *penetration agent.* Even so, the charge remains moot--as espionage cases often do.

historical interpretation: Interpretation of a *treaty* with explicit reference to its *negotiation* and drafting.

historical method: The intellectual endeavor of constructing general principles to explain human political and social behavior, via a systematic study of historical facts.

historicism: (1) In its primary sense, this is one of the great intellectual sins a historian, political scientist or any other student of *history* or *politics* may commit. It means to argue without regard for *volition*, in such a way that history is presented as driven by forces beyond human agency. (2) A theory that says past eras should be treated as unique, even discrete phenomena, without attempting to graft onto them judgments that derive from contemporary experiences and culturally flavored values. Cf. *determinism; relativism.*

historiography: Principles, theories and techniques related to the formal study and writing of history.

history: That branch of knowledge concerned with past events. Since the innovations introduced by Leopold von Ranke (1795-1886), history as an academic discipline has become intensely concerned with accuracy of sources and systematic, detailed explanations of the past, and less with *grand theory*. More recently, there has been a trend among academic historians away from the *Great Man approach* toward social history, which deals more with the affairs of common folk and of social groups. However, the shock waves reverberating from the end of the *Cold War* may turn the tide of international history writing back some way toward large-scale explanations of the lives of nations.

Hitler, Adolf (1889-1945): *"der Führer"* (leader). Austrian-born (his father's original surname was Schicklgruber), German dictator 1933-45. He avoided *conscription* in the *multinational* Austro-Hungarian army, not wanting to serve with *Slavs* or Jews, but volunteered for the German army in 1914. He served bravely during *WWI*, seeing much action; he was twice wounded and twice decorated (once on the recommendation of a Jewish *reserve* officer). That wartime experience was formative: he always spoke of WWI as the happiest time of his life, and never once is known to have regretted its destruction of lives, property and decent social relations. He seems to have found in *martial* life the comraderie (but not friendship, which he shunned) and sense of purpose that had eluded him in his impecunious and secretive youth as a failed artist in Vienna. He worked as a propagandist for the Army in Bavaria after the war, but as an embittered *nationalist* and pathological *anti-Semite* he was drawn to become *Nazi Party* member #7 in 1919. Hitler quickly made the ragtag party his own, and began to draw attention for his spell-binding rhetoric (he poured hours of study into perfecting his monstrous gift for oratory). His *Beer Hall putsch* failed in 1923, leading to nine months in jail writing his autobiographical diatribe "Mein Kampf" (My Struggle). Propelled to national prominence by the *Great Depression*, he was defeated for President in 1932 by *Paul von Hindenburg*, who dismissed him prematurely as "that Bohemian corporal." After the Nazis emerged as the largest party on the right in the *Reichstag* in 1932 elections, Hindenburg appointed him Chancellor on January 30, 1933. Within months he abolished all political opposition and established a party and then absolute, personal dictatorship. When the old general died on August 2, 1934, Hitler proclaimed himself President. To placate the Army's concern about the *SA* he ordered the *Night of the Long Knives*, showing thereby both great political flexibility and a fathomless capacity for ruthlessness. He sought to destroy the *Versailles* settlement but did so cautiously at first, moving only when Western resistance was low. He greatly stepped up the secret *rearmament* of Germany already underway--before he was finished the *Wehrmacht* would emerge as perhaps the greatest beneficiary of the Nazi revolution. In 1936 he occupied the *Rhineland*, sent aid to *Franco* and negotiated the *Axis* with Italy. In 1938 he completed the *Anschluss* with Austria. He took the *Sudetenland* through threat and intimidation at *Munich*, and the rump of Czechoslovakia in March 1939, by force. That year he threw all caution to the winds, giving in to a megalomania that had haunted him even in his Viennese obscurity. In August he concluded the *Nazi/Soviet Pact*, which freed him to attack Poland. For the first years of *WWII* he let the army lead Germany to triumph upon triumph, content to give general *strategic* direction. Then he took personal command (in November 1941), making even *tactical* decisions. Out of great hubris feeding on a sense of personal destiny, but also from a profound fascination with destruction, his decisions brought Germany to crushing defeats and then utter disaster. Through it all, he and his murderous henchmen pursued their fanatic hatred of the Jews and other so-called *Untermenschen*. He enthusiastically followed reports on the progress of the *Holocaust*, to which he insanely dedicated transportation and other resources badly needed by the military. He barely survived the *July Plot* in 1944, exacting a terrible vengeance and further imposing his will on the Wehrmacht. The mad evil of the man brought him to his end in a bunker in Berlin, with that great city, the nation and continent in ruins about him. With the *Red Army* a mere 100 meters away, Hitler (by then an impotent drug addict) married his mistress, Eva Braun. Knowing what Italian *partisans* had done to the corpse of his friend, *Mussolini*, he ordered his body burned. On April 30, 1945, Eva Braun took poison and he shot himself, through the mouth. His *SS* guard, loyal past the end, poured petrol on and set fire to the twisted couple, adding their flames to the city's. Here is historian Alan Bullock's memorable epitaph for Hitler in 1945, borrowed from history's judgment of Sir Christopher Wren (creator of the stone wonder of St. Paul's Cathedral), and posted instead over the physical and moral rubble of Nazi Germany: "Si monumentum requiris, circumspice" (if you seek his monument, look around). See also *anti-Semitism; fascism; geopolitik; Germany; lebensraum; National Socialism; Nazi/Soviet Pact; Nuremberg Laws; Nuremberg Rallies; Third Reich.* Cf. *Mao; Stalin.*

Hoare/Laval Pact (1935): An agreement between the British Foreign Secretary, Samuel Hoare (1890-1959), and the French Foreign Minister, *Pierre Laval*. It proposed to *partition* Ethiopia as a means of appeasing *Mussolini* during the early stages of the *Abyssinian War*. Public outrage forced renunciation of the pact, and Hoare's resignation.

Hobbes, Thomas (1588-1679): English political philosopher. His most famous work, "The Leviathan," depicted life in the hypothetical *state of nature* as "solitary, poor, nasty, brutish and short," a condition escaped only by construction of the "Leviathan," or *unitary state*. World politics is often depicted, especially by *realists*, as without an equivalent Leviathan, and thus akin to a Hobbesian state of "war of all against all." Foreign policy, some realists argue, must therefore emphasize the unblinking pursuit of self-interest and the *balance of power*, not *Grotian* solutions of

international law or *Kantian* notions of *cosmopolitan* moral norms. Yet while it is true that Hobbes was a "minimalist" about permanent solutions to the problems of *anarchy* and *war*, he conceded that states had some mutual interests, and fought wars and conducted their affairs with a certain *prudence*.

Hobbesian: Characteristic of, or deeply influenced by, the political thought of *Thomas Hobbes*.

Ho Chi Minh, né Nguyen Tat Thanh (1890?-1969): President of North Vietnam 1945-69. His adopted name meant "he who brings/seeks enlightenment." A communist party organizer from his student days in Paris and Moscow, in 1943 he returned to Vietnam to organize *resistance* to the Japanese *occupation*. In August 1945, he proclaimed Vietnamese *independence* from France, which led to a bitter *war* from 1946-54, culminating in *Dien Bien Phu*. After the *Geneva Agreements* he continued to work for unification of all Vietnam under his regime. He maintained close relations with China and the Soviet Union despite the *Sino/Soviet split*, while defying the U.S. during the 1950s and 1960s. At home, he encouraged a *cult of personality* and engaged in the usual *stalinist* practices of forced *collectivization*, and *purges* and *liquidation* of class and political enemies. There was much debate then and since whether he was a communist or a nationalist. He was, of course, both. See *Vietnam; Vietnam War.*

Ho Chi Minh Trail: A complex of roads, trails, depots and bunkers from North to South Vietnam, traversing also eastern Laos and Cambodia. During the *Vietnam War* it was the main *supply line* for the *Viet Cong*, and the target of intense bombing and *search-and-destroy* raids by the U.S and South Vietnam. See *Indochina* map.

Hohenzollern: A European royal family that formed the Prussian House 1701-1870, and then ruled Imperial Germany from 1871-1918. A Rumanian branch lasted from 1866-1947.

Holland: See *Netherlands*.

Holocaust (1933-45): In its primary sense, the persecution, then *genocide* against the Jews of Europe conducted by the *Nazis*. Some reserve the term exclusively for the virulent hatred and deliberate planning with which the Nazis hunted down and murdered Jews. But in a wider sense it includes non-Jews who were systematically, rather than individually, murdered by the Nazis, such as *Gypsies*, homosexuals and the severely mentally or physically handicapped. Still,

Jews were always the central focus of the hatred. From street violence by the *SA* and *SS* before the Nazi ascent to power, persecution progressed through the passage of the *Nuremberg Laws,* confiscation of property, ostracism, economic boycott, ghettoization and frequent murder. Once the war started to go badly after 1941, the ghettos were emptied into the *concentration camps,* and the full nightmare was reached. The explicit decision to exterminate the Jews of Europe, the so-called *"final solution to the Jewish problem,"* was laid out at the Wannsee Conference in January 1942. What happened next had no precedent in history: the utter dehumanization of Jews in Nazi *propaganda* and the systematic horrors of the *death camps.* That meant transport by cattle car, deliberate severing of families, sadistic medical experimentation, *slave labor,* starvation, mass hangings and shootings, and the gross obscenity and indignity of the gas chambers and crematoria. In all, some six million Jews died. Another three million to four million non-Jews must be added to the list of victims, mainly Russians and Poles starved or worked to death, but some also shot or gassed. In the scale of lives lost, the Holocaust has been surpassed only by *Stalin's* war against the *kulaks* and *Mao's* depredations against the Chinese peasantry. But in ferocity, hate, sadism and horror, the Nazi genocide of the Jews of Europe has no peer. Contemporary efforts by *neo-Nazis* and their *fellow-travelers* to deny the historical reality of the Holocaust are utterly spurious. Worse, they are indicative of the very mentality that brought it about. See also *anti-Semitism; Auschwitz; concentration camps; Dachau; Gestapo; Göring; Himmler; Hitler; kristallnacht; righteous Gentiles; social darwinism.*

Holy Alliance: A compact between Russia, Austria and Prussia, signed in 1815 at the behest of *Alexander I, of Russia.* It was not an *alliance* so much as a vague promise to govern according to Christian principles, hence the exalted claim of its title. Britain refused to join, as did the U.S. and the pope, all for different reasons. The *Ottoman* sultan was snubbed. Several small powers joined, some for cynical, others for defensive reasons. The Holy Alliance should not be confused with the *Quadruple Alliance* or *Quintuple Alliance* that underwrote the *Concert of Europe,* and to which Britain did belong. Cf. *Monroe Doctrine; Münchengrätz Agreements.*

Holy Roman Empire: A mainly Germanic *empire* established in 962 A.D. by Otto I. For centuries it competed with the papacy for ultimate authority over Christendom, while simultaneously cooperating with the popes to prevent the rise of local powers. From 1273 it was ruled by the *Hapsburgs,* and dominated much of central Europe and the Balkans. Sectarian control of the HRE was the original issue in the *Thirty Years' War,* which greatly accelerated its long decline. It lasted until *Napoleon* contemptuously dismissed it from its shrunken existence in 1806. *Voltaire's* famous epigram sums up its decadent, truncated final days: "It is neither holy, nor Roman, nor an empire." See also *Renaissance.*

home front: The *civilian* aspects of conducting a *war,* especially regarding *national morale.*

home islands, of Japan: By convention, Hokkaido, Honshu, Kyushu and Shikoku.

Home Rule: (1) In general: The phrase used by those demanding *autonomy* from colonial rule, and genuinely representative government in the *colonies.* It represented a lesser demand than outright *independence,* though some nationalists saw it merely as a stepping-stone to full *sovereignty.* (2) In Ireland: This issue dogged Anglo/Irish relations for most of the 19th century, following the *Act of Union.* Its central demand was a separate Irish parliament in Dublin. *Gladstone* took up the cause, but met with bitter opposition (the Protestant cry was "Home Rule is Rome Rule!"). Three failed Home Rule bills (1886, 1893, 1912) left Ireland on the verge of *civil war* in 1914, when the movement was interrupted by *WWI.* The *Easter Rising* and the animosity of *Ulster's* Protestants to government from Dublin led to *partition* after the war, the *Irish War of Independence* and the *Irish Civil War.*

Honduras: Location: Central America. Major associations: *OAS, UN.* Population: 5.3 million. Military: reduced capability from 1980s; *counterinsurgency* focus. This part of Central America was a province of the pre-Columbian Mayan Empire. It then fell under Spanish rule for several centuries after Columbus arrived on its coast in 1502. It became *independent* in 1821, as part of the Federation of Central America. Honduras left that *federation* in 1838, but the new *republic* quickly fell under the hold of a succession of military dictators. For much of this century its economy was dominated by the United Fruit Company, a giant U.S. *multinational corporation.* Honduras fought the so-called *Soccer War* with El Salvador in 1969. During the 1980s the U.S. provided assistance to the Honduran military in exchange for tolerance of the presence of Nicaraguan *Contras.* In 1988, after a border crossing by Nicaraguan troops, the U.S. sent 3,200 troops to bases in Honduras. As late as 1990 some 10,000 U.S.-supported Contras were using Honduras as a base for attacks on Nicaragua. But U.S. policy shifted with the end of the *Cold War.* From 1990 to 1993, American military aid fell from $40 to $2 million. Honduras held free elections in December 1993.

Honecker, Erich (1912-94): East German leader 1971-89. A life-long *communist*, he was imprisoned by the *Nazis,* 1937-45. He was in carge of erecting the *Berlin Wall.* He ruled as a *hard-liner* after coming to power, grudgingly accepting *détente* and *Ostpolitik.* He objected to *glasnost* and *perestroika,* clinging to *stalinist* habits. He was bewildered by *refugees* fleeing *East Germany* via breeches in the *iron curtain* opened by reforms in Hungary and Czechoslovakia in 1989. Soon after *Gorbachev* visited and said that East Germany was on its own, that the *Brezhnev Doctrine* no longer applied, Honecker was also cut loose by his own *regime* and party. After communism and the Berlin Wall both fell, he fled to the Soviet Union. But change kept reaching after him, and caught him when it arrived in Moscow: Russia agreed to *extradite* him to face trial in Germany. He tried to flee again, to China, but he was returned to stand trial in 1992. As he was dying of cancer, the proceedings were suspended without result and he was permitted to leave with his wife for Chile. By that act Germany showed more compassion for him (and unease about itself) than he ever showed thousands, perhaps millions, of his countryfolk.

honey trap: Beguiling a foreign *agent,* government or military official, or some other target of *espionage* or counterespionage into compromising positions with a man, woman, boy, girl or other sexual enticement measured to personal taste or tastelessness. The target is then blackmailed into cooperation and betrayal.

Hong Kong: This portion of the Chinese coast was seized by the British in 1841 during the first *Opium War,* with Kowloon added in 1860, during the second. Britain compelled China to issue a 99 year lease on Hong Kong, Kowloon and the attached "New Territories" starting in 1898. In 1925 Chinese workers began a year-long strike to protest wages, conditions and the *Shanghai massacre.* It was awhile before Britain reestablished its authority. The colony was attacked by Japan the day after *Pearl Harbor;* it was captured within two weeks. Britain reclaimed it in 1945. From then on it prospered, becoming an *Asian Tiger.* In 1984 Britain agreed to return Hong Kong and the New Territories to China on July 1, 1997. In return, China agreed to maintain Hong Kong's "social and economic systems." In 1992-94, under Governor Chris Patten, a major controversy developed as democratic reforms were introduced to the colony prior to its return to China. It was not clear that China would agree to view these changes as covered by the 1984 agreement. Hong Kong is a member of *APEC.*

honor and vital interests: Before 1914 this reservation was often added to *treaties* to exclude from *arbitration* select or important matters, on the ground they touched upon the "honor" or *vital interests* of a *state.*

Hoover, Herbert (1874-1964): U.S. statesman. Head of Belgian Relief 1914-17, and of the *American Relief Administration* (ARA) 1917-21; President 1929-33. He first came to international prominence for his relief efforts in wartime Belgium, and then in Western Europe after *WWI,* where he refused to let the Germans starve (as some French leaders suggested). He did withhold food from *Béla Kun's* regime in Hungary, contributing to its fall, but did so only after large-scale executions had begun. He was instrumental in getting food to 30 million starving Soviets from 1921-23, as head of the ARA. Although he championed the *League of Nations* during *Wilson's* administration, he did not advocate joining after he became President. His foreign policy was overwhelmed by the onset of the *Great Depression.* As financial markets collapsed and *defaults* began on *war debts* and *reparations,* he announced the *Hoover moratorium.* His Quaker roots led him to embrace the work of the *London Naval Disarmament Conference,* but also led to his weak response to the rise of Japanese *aggression* in China: the ineffective *Hoover/Stimson Doctrine.* In later life he moved to the right, advocating *isolationism* both before and after *WWII.* But his independence of mind was ever apparent, as in his criticism of the *atomic bomb* attacks on Japan. See *Good Neighbor policy.*

Hoover moratorium (on debt repayments): A one-year postponement on *debt* repayments, mostly owed to the U.S., announced by *Herbert Hoover* in June 1933. It aimed at temporarily easing both the *war debts* and *reparations* burdens in Europe, but soon became permanent. It helped ease, but did not end, the financial crisis.

Hoover/Stimson Doctrine (January 7, 1932): An announcement by President *Herbert Hoover* and Secretary of State *Henry Stimson,* in response to the *Mukden incident* and Japan's invasion of *Manchuria:* they declared that the U.S. would refuse to *recognize* any arrangements in China that ran contrary to the *Open Door.* That was an ineffective compromise between Hoover's caution and Stimson's desire to carry out *sanctions* (even though the U.S. did not belong to the *League of Nations*). It widened the breach with Japan without affecting Tokyo's plans for expansion at China's expense.

Hopkins, Harry (1890-1946): U.S. statesman. He was a close friend and adviser of *Franklin Roosevelt,* serving as his *envoy* to *Stalin* and *Churchill* and as a top adviser at *Yalta*. He was opposed to the *hard line* toward the Soviet Union suggested by *W. Averell Harriman*, and others. He was active at the *San Francisco Conference*, and attended *Potsdam* with *Truman*. He became a hated figure to the American far right, taking much of the blame for the supposed "sell-out" of *Eastern Europe* at Yalta.

horizontal escalation: Widening a combat area geographically, instead of stepping up destructive levels of military response. Cf. *vertical escalation*.

horizontal proliferation: Acquisition of weapons systems by *states* or private groups or persons (such as *terrorists*), that did not have them before. Cf. *vertical proliferation*.

Hormuz, Strait of: A narrow *strait* connecting the *Persian Gulf* and the Gulf of Oman. Gulf tanker traffic must pass through it on the way to the Americas, Africa, Europe or Japan. It thus is a *strategic* and economic choke point of global interest.

Horn of Africa: The subregion of East Africa formed by Djibouti, Kenya, Ethiopia, Eritrea and Somalia.

hors de combat: Something, or someone, removed from the fight; a disabled vehicle or wounded soldier.

Horthy de Nagybána, Miklós (1886-1957): Hungarian regent and dictator 1920-44. In 1920 he crushed the Hungarian *soviet* set up by *Béla Kun*. He formed an *alliance* with Germany in 1941, sending troops to fight in *Yugoslavia* and against the *Soviet Union*. He tried to withdraw and negotiate a *separate peace* in 1944, as Germany began to fall back along the *eastern front*. He was captured by the Nazis, then the Americans when Germany fell. He died in *exile* in Portugal.

hostage crisis (November 4, 1979-January 20, 1980): Iranian students and Revolutionary Guards seized the U.S. embassy in Tehran, taking 66 Americans hostage (another six went into hiding, and later escaped using false Canadian passports). All diplomatic efforts and one rescue attempt failed. The crisis damaged the re-election chances of *James ("Jimmy") Carter*, making him appear inept and weak. An agreement was finally reached, but the Iranians waited to release the hostages until just minutes after Carter ceased to be President. That was likely done out of personal spite for Carter on the part of *Ayatollah Khomeini*. Speculation that a secret deal was cut with *Ronald Reagan* to keep the hostages until after Carter was defeated (as Republicans supposedly feared an "October surprise" release

might help Carter win) is not supported by any compelling evidence.

hostage taking: Taking hostages in peacetime has been a crime under *international criminal law* since 1979, when a *convention* was passed to that effect. The 1980s saw multiple cases. The most famous was the *hostage crisis* between the U.S. and Iran, but *war* in Lebanon also led to even more drawn-out affairs (seven years in one case), usually involving Westerners as captives. Iraq's 1990 declaration that some 21,000 foreigners from hostile nations (the *Gulf Coalition*) would be detained as "human shields" was the largest hostage taking in modern history. UN troops were taken hostage in Somalia and Bosnia in 1994.

hostilities: (1) *Acts of war.* (2) A euphemism for *war.*

host nation: One housing a foreign *MNC* plant, or a *subsidiary*. Cf. *Calvo clause; parent country.*

hot launch: When a *missile* ignites thrusters while still in its *silo* or *launcher*. Cf. *cold launch.*

hot line: A direct communications link between the *White House* and the *Kremlin*, set up by agreement on June 20, 1963, in the wake of the *Cuban Missile Crisis*. In January 1994, the U.S. and Russia agreed to another hot line connecting the *Pentagon* to the Russian Ministry of Defense. The U.S. has lines to other major capitals, and they exist between other states.

hot money: Speculative *capital* that plays the *foreign exchange* markets.

hot pursuit: The right to pursue on the *high seas* a foreign vessel that has violated *municipal laws*. Pursuit must begin in *contiguous* and *territorial waters*, and be continuous (that is, it cannot be resumed once it has been broken off).

hot war: Open conflict; *hostilities; war.* Cf. *cold war.*

Houphouët-Boigny, Félix (1905-90): President of *Ivory Coast* 1960-90. He offered a great contrast in *decolonization* styles to that of *Kwame Nkrumah*. Rather than *radical* confrontation, he chose to keep intimate links with France, and was a centrist on most African issues.

household guard: Those troops, usually hand-picked for loyalty, protecting the person of the *sovereign* or ruler. Most democracies and other modern *states* have dispensed with this institution, in favor of a *civilian* security service.

howitzer: A short-barreled cannon that fires high-elevation shells, used to *bombard* concealed positions.

Hoxha, Enver (1908-85): Quixotic, *stalinist* dictator of Albania 1945-85. He led the *resistance* to Italian *invasion* during *WWII*. He joined Albania to the *Soviet bloc* early in the *Cold War*. A doctrinal schism over *de-stalinization* led to his break with Moscow in 1958, formalized in 1961 with Albania expelled from *COMECON* and later the *Warsaw Pact*. He formed a new *alliance* with China, and moved closer to *autarky*. He broke with China in 1978, following the death of *Mao Zedong*. Albania was Europe's poorest and most repressive country under Hoxha.

Huggins, Godfrey (1883-1971): PM of Southern Rhodesia 1933-53; PM of the Central African Federation 1953-56. He was a strong supporter of the tie to Britain, but also of cooperation with neighboring black-ruled states, in spite of his personal racial prejudice. His successors in *Rhodesia* did not display the same flexibility or imagination, or ability to overcome their baser instincts.

Hughes, Charles Evans (1862-1948): U.S. statesman. Secretary of State 1921-25; Chief Justice 1930-41. He was an advocate of membership in the *League of Nations,* but the *nation* and the two presidents he served, *Harding* and *Coolidge,* were unconvincable. He patched relations with Mexico, negotiated the *treaty* with Germany formally ending *WWI* for the U.S., and otherwise tied up loose ends left by *Woodrow Wilson* (except for Russia, from which he continued to withhold *recognition*). He organized and hosted the *Washington Conference*, 1921-22.

Hughes, William Morris (1864-1952): Australian PM 1915-23; Minister for External Affairs 1937-39; Minister for the Navy 1940-41. He was a fierce proponent of Australia taking its dutiful place within the *British Empire*. He introduced *conscription* in 1916, responding to criticism with characteristic petulance and political reprisal. He supported a "White Australia" policy, opposed *Wilsonian* idealism at the *Paris Peace Conference* and gave great offense to Japan. His exclusive, racist vision for Australia now seems a distant illusion.

Huk (*Hukbalahap*) rebellion: A left-wing *guerrilla* movement in the Philippines that began as part of the anti-Japanese *resistance* 1943-45. From 1946-50 the Huks took over most of the island of Luzon. After the outbreak of *war* in Korea the U.S. encouraged the Philippine government to move forcefully against the Huks. Unlike local communists in *Indochina*, the Huks were isolated from *supply lines* to China and the Soviet Union, and were crushed by 1954. A successor movement, the *New People's Army*, resumed fighting in the 1970s and was still making occasional forays in the mid-1990s.

Hull, Cordell (1871-1955): U.S. Secretary of State 1933-44. He fleshed out the *Good Neighbor policy* begun by *Harding* and *Hoover*, encouraged *Roosevelt* to open full diplomatic and economic relations with the Soviet Union, sought to counteract the harmful effects of the *Hawley/Smoot tariff*, and continued with the *Hoover/Stimson Doctrine* toward Japanese *aggression* in China. One of his greatest contributions was to begin early work on planning for a *postwar* security organization to replace the failed *League of Nations*. During *WWII*, however, Roosevelt largely froze him out of major *decision-making*, preferring to use personal *envoys* and conduct face-to-face negotiations with *Churchill* and *Stalin*. Even so, Hull was awarded the 1945 *Nobel Prize* for Peace.

Human Development Index (HDI): A statistical measure of average life expectancy, degree of schooling, literacy and income in a given *nation*. It is an attempt to provide a more nuanced gauge of *development* than the crude figures of comparative *GNP*.

humane deterrence: A policy attributed to the *ASEAN* nations, but not admitted by them, whereby *boat people* from Vietnam were discouraged from arrival by making *refugee camps* as austere and prison-like as possible. Its claim to be humane sprang from the effort to discourage *refugees* from even undertaking a voyage often plagued by storms or pirates, that had already proven fatal to thousands.

humanitarian intervention: (1) *Diplomatic protests, sanctions* or of late, even military *intervention* that aims at stopping gross and persistent abuse of *human rights*. Such activities normally constitute interference in *internal affairs*. However, there is controversial but clearly increasing acceptance by *states* (witness UN actions in Somalia) that humanitarian considerations sometimes outweigh the privileges of *sovereignty*. (2) All aid given benevolently to alleviate some great disaster such as earthquake or *famine*.

human rights: The idea that all human beings, irrespective of race, sex or creed, share certain fundamental rights that emanate not from any *social contract* or grant from a *sovereign*, but from the essence of their humanity. It is a concept steeped in *natural law* conceptions. Because of its *universalism*, it is a notion inherently controversial in a world of parochial, sovereign *states*. For the same reason, human rights are often subversive of established cultural practices and political systems, be they feudal, *authoritarian* or *totalitarian*. The oldest stream of international conceptions of human rights flows from the ideals of the *French Revolution*, 19th century *liberalism* and *Wilsonian* idealism; that is, the stress is on civil and political liberties of the individual, and rights are seen as held against the *state*, not by it on behalf of the *nation*. Human rights issues were discussed at the margins during the *Congress of Vienna* and at the *Paris Peace Conference*. In the 19th century the great human rights campaigns were against the *slave trade* and then for the abolition of *slavery*, and against child labor. Other issues of which one or more of the *Great Powers* took note in their *diplomacy* included persecution of Jews under the *Ottoman Empire*, and in Rumania and Russia; the *Irish Question*; persecution of Christians in Japan; racially discriminatory immigration laws in Australia, Canada, New Zealand and the United States; persecution of Christians and Armenians by Turkey; and mistreatment of natives in the Congo (Zaire). Since *WWI* the list has been expanded to include social and economic rights, but drawing far more upon the *social democratic* than the *communist* tradition. Issues of racial equality were broached by Japan and China after c.1905. The real breakthrough on human rights came at the *Dumbarton Oaks* and *San Francisco conferences*, where the *Charter of the UN* was imbued with the rhetoric of rights at U.S. and to a lesser extent, small power insistence. The *Universal Declaration* came in 1948 and the *International Bill of Rights* in the mid-1950s. Often overlooked as a source of internationalization, human rights articles were included in the *postwar* constitutions of, and *treaties* with, the defeated *Axis* powers. Departing imperial powers also set human rights articles in the constitutions of former *colonies* (raising a standard they had seldom themselves observed--which is often the case on this issue, where a "ratchet of hypocrisy" operates). Subsequently, even states that did not intend to respect the rights of their citizens began to incorporate proclamations or charters in their domestic legislation and constitutions; some of them have even been required to live up to these provisions on occasion. *Decolonization* and *development* as rights were on the agenda of *non-aligned* states after 1955. Special legal protections for women and children are also recent additions. Today, there is nearly universal rhetorical acceptance of human rights. However, enormous differences over definition, application and priority to be given different categories of rights quickly surface in any multilateral discussion. It should be stressed, too, that the state system has since 1945 incorporated a new legal emphasis on respect for human rights without incurring a fundamental challenge to its core principle of *sovereignty*. Also see *Amnesty International; Atlantic Charter; basic needs/rights; crimes against humanity; Declaration of the Rights of Man and Citizens; European Court of Human Rights; expressio unius; Four Freedoms; Fourteen Points; Geneva Conventions; genocide; Genocide Convention; Hague Conventions; Helsinki Accords; Helsinki Watch Groups; Minorities Treaties; nonintervention; self-determination; torture; UN Human Rights Committee; UN Human Rights Commission; just war theory; Red Cross; sanctions; World Human Rights Conference*.

humint: "Human intelligence." Any and all information secretly gathered from people, whether *agents* or informers. It is generally easier to provide *disinformation* through humint than *elint* or *sigint*. Hence, there is commonly a division within the *intelligence* community over humint. At the extremes, it is seen as either unreliable to the point of being useless, or the most vital and incisive form of intelligence, when accurate.

Hundred Days (February 26-June 22, 1815): A frantic period marking *Napoleon's* return from *exile*, his reclaiming of the title "Emperor," rallying of the army for a last effort to force his own peace *terms, defeat* at *Waterloo* on June 18, 1815, and his abdication for a second time four days later.

Hundred Flowers campaign (1956-57): A brief renaissance of dissent within China, launched by *Mao Zedong* as a way of stirring erstwhile revolutionaries who were fast becoming staid bureaucrats, but also as a trap to expose those who would criticize him. While criticism focused on the lower *cadres* in the *Communist Party* Mao was content; but when it turned on his own leadership, he uprooted the "hundred flowers and a hundred schools of thought" that had appeared on wall posters, and in more courageous newspapers, and tossed away their authors like so many weeds. Half a million died in the *purges* that followed. Rather than feeling shame over this betrayal, Mao later boasted of his revolutionary ruthlessness.

Hundred Years' War: The running conflict between England and France, 1337-1453. Its main issue was a contest for control of Normandy. It ended with England's expulsion from the Continent, a feat that marked the beginning of the ascent by France to predominance over Europe.

Hungarian Uprising (October 23-November 4, 1956): When Hungary's *communist* regime began *de-stalinization* in the wake of *Khrushchev's* secret denunciation of *Stalin* in February 1956, Hungarians embraced the process and made it their own. *Imre Nagy* and *János Kádár* formed a coalition government on October 24th, following a massive street demonstration in which the Hungarian Army joined, suggesting it might support a *counter-revolution* against the communists. When the new government announced it was withdrawing from the *Warsaw Pact* and following Austria into *neutrality*, Kádár fled, soon to return with Soviet tanks and troops to crush the uprising. Hungarians appealed for U.S. assistance, but that was never seriously contemplated by *Eisenhower* or *Dulles*. Nagy and others were secretly executed, violating Soviet promises of safe conduct. Meanwhile, the uprising was overtaken in world attention by the *Suez Crisis*.

Hungary: Location: E. Europe. Major associations: *CSCE, UN*. Population: 10.6 million. Military: former *Warsaw Pact*, presently downsizing. Settled in the 9th century A.D. by Magyar nomads from out of Central Asia, Hungary became a sizeable Christian kingdom during the Middle Ages. It was repeatedly invaded by Turkish armies from the 15th-16th centuries, being finally conquered in 1526. The Turks were defeated by the Austrians 1686-97, who took control of Hungary. During the *Revolutions of 1848*, Hungary rose against *Hapsburg* rule, under the leadership of *Lajos Kossuth*. In 1867 the *Dual Monarchy* was created in the *Ausgleich* with Austria. In the wake of *defeat* in *WWI*, *Béla Kun* briefly set up a *soviet* republic. This was quickly overthrown in favor of a kingdom, set up as a front for the personal dictatorship of the Regent *Horthy*, from 1920-44. Hungary was subject to the strictures of the *Treaty of Trianon*, set at the *Paris Peace Conference*. As in Germany, there was much bitterness over the *terms*. In the 1930s Hungary drifted into the Nazi orbit, cooperating with the dismemberment of Czechoslovakia in 1938 and again in 1939. It also joined Germany in its assaults on Yugoslavia and the Soviet Union, both in 1941. When matters along the *eastern front* began to go badly, Hungary sought unsuccessfully to negotiate a *separate peace* with the Soviets. The Soviets occupied Hungary at the end of 1944, and installed a coalition *provisional government*. During 1946-47 the coalition partners of the Hungarian *communists* were forced out. Hungary was firmly within the *Soviet bloc* by the end of 1948, and undergoing thorough *stalinization*. The ruling party fractured after the death of *Stalin*, with *Imre Nagy* leading a reform bloc that was repressed by the end of 1955. In October-November 1956, the *Hungarian Uprising* occurred, ending with a Warsaw Pact *invasion*. Subsequently, the Hungarian regime mellowed (comparatively), and sought to incorporate some non-communist elements, notably in the economy. During the 1970s and 1980s this trend continued, although the

experience of 1956 meant that Hungarian reformers moved with little speed and much caution. Domestic reform was aided by a strict pro-Soviet line in foreign policy. Also in the 1980s, there developed a rising conflict with Rumania over persecution of ethnic Hungarians in *Transylvania*. During 1988-89 there was a rapid dismantling of the Soviet-style political system. In turn, the opening of Hungarian borders led to mass flight of East Germans into Austria, that helped topple the German domino as well. Free elections were held in early 1990, and under Jozef Antall (1932-93) Hungary embarked on a painful but relatively successful transition to a market democracy. In 1993 it announced that given the breakup of *Yugoslavia* it no longer feels bound by the borders set in the *Treaty of Paris* (1947), and its nationalists mumbled about Trianon. In 1994 former communists did well in open elections.

hunger: See *famine; food*.

hunter-killer: A sleek, fast *submarine* that is used to locate, tail and when necessary "kill" other submarines (especially *boomers*).

Husak, Gustav (1913-91): President of *Czechoslovakia* 1975-89. He took over with Soviet support following the ouster of *Dubček* in 1969. He was thrown out by the *velvet revolution* in 1989.

Hussein, Ibn Abdul (1882-1951): King of *Transjordan*, which he led in the *First Arab/Israeli War*. He aspired to *pan-Arab* leadership, but was resisted by other Arab *states*. He was assassinated in 1951.

Hussein, Ibn Ali (1856-1931): Sherif of Mecca and "King of the Hejaz." He joined the *Arab Revolt*, but his ambition to lead the *Arabs* was dogged by the similar ambition of *Ibn Saud*. He was bitter over the *Sykes-Picot Agreement*. In 1924 he claimed the title *caliph*, but was overthrown when Ibn Saud invaded the *Hejaz*. He retired to Cyprus. His sons ruled awhile longer, in Iraq and *Transjordan*.

Hussein, Ibn Talal al-Hashemi (b.1935): King of Jordan since 1953. He retained power despite Egyptian intrigues against him (after the ouster of his father), by using the strength of the *Arab Legion* and drawing support from the U.S. and Britain. He invited British troops to Jordan during the 1958 crisis in Lebanon. He was a reluctant participant in the *Third Arab/Israeli War*, pushed into combat by his *Palestinian* subjects. During 1970-71 he fought a sharp and bloody *war* against the *PLO*, then based in Jordan. He reconciled with the PLO in 1985. In 1988 he renounced Jordan's claims to the *West Bank*, opening the way for possible creation of a Palestinian state there. He has maintained a careful balancing act between the radicalism of many among his population, and his interest in keeping close ties to Washington and the West. This tenuous policy was most evident during the *Gulf War*, in which he first sought to *mediate* a resolution then supported *Saddam Hussein* rhetorically and with some *sanctions* busting. Subsequently, he repaired relations with the West but lost his funding from Saudi Arabia and the *Gulf States*. In September 1993, following the Israeli/PLO peace agreement, he too moved to normalize relations with Israel.

Hussein, Saddam Sadisavan (b.1937): President and dictator of Iraq. He fled Iraq after participating in a failed *Ba'ath* coup in 1959, returning in 1963 after the ouster and murder of *Abdul Kassem*. Emerging from prison he helped lead the 1968 Ba'ath *revolution*, assuming power behind the scenes. In 1979 he became President, henceforth wielding power openly. He set up a *Nazi*-style regime that eliminated all manifestations of dissent. He sought to crush, even exterminate, the *shi'ite* "marsh Arabs" of southern Iraq, and the *Kurds* of northern Iraq. Captured documents and film reveal that in the 1980s there was a campaign of *genocide* against the Kurds, with at least 200,000 killed, including through use of *chemical weapons*. There have been many attempts to kill Saddam, but he has elaborate security and is protected by the praetorian *Republican Guard*. In 1980 he tried to take advantage of Iran's revolutionary turmoil to seize *territory* and *oil* fields in the south, beginning the *Iran/Iraq War* that took over one million lives. In 1990 he invaded and annexed Kuwait, leading to the destruction of his armed forces and much Iraqi infrastructure in the *Gulf War*. He was then faced with *rebellions* of the shi'ites and Kurds. He tried to repress both, but was unable to reestablish control over northern Iraq. He has since repeatedly tested U.S. and *Security Council* resolve regarding implementation of *cease-fire* agreements. So far, he has met a solid front and several punishment raids. In June 1993, he was accused by the U.S. of masterminding an attempt to assassinate former President *George Bush*. In *retaliation*, the U.S. hit some of his *intelligence* installations with *cruise missiles*.

Hu Yaobang (1915-89): Chinese reformer. A veteran of the *Long March*, his career is closely associated with that of *Deng Xiaoping*, with both suffering great vicissitudes of personal and political fortune under the erratic leadership of *Mao Zedong*. Having survived the *Great Proletarian Cultural Revolution*, he was made the scapegoat for student unrest in 1987, and dismissed. Two years later his death sparked the demonstrations that culminated in the massacre at *Tiananmen Square*.

HvA (*Hauptverwaltung Aufklärung***):** The foreign *intelligence service* of the *German Democratic Republic*. It was highly successful in penetrationg West Germany's intelligence services (*BfV* and *BND*), government and industry.

Hyderabad: One of the largest *Princely States* in India. In 1948 it joined India (under considerable pressure from Britain and the *Congress Party*). In 1956 it was broken up under administrative reforms that carved it into several states.

hydrogen bomb: Also called "thermonuclear weapons." The second generation of *nuclear weapons*, using a *fusion* rather than a *fission* reaction. First, fission energy comes from rapidly compressing a core of *plutonium* or uranium, encased in lithium and deuterium (heavy hydrogen). Neutrons released from the plutonium split lithium atoms into helium and tritium (another form of heavy hydrogen). It is the tritium and deuterium that fuse, again producing helium and other by-products plus the extraordinary energy of a hydrogen bomb explosion. These devices have been detonated by the U.S. (1952), the Soviet Union (1953), Britain (1957), China (1967) and France (1968). Hydrogen bombs are far more massive than *atomic bombs*. The Soviets built 150 *megaton* bombs (about 10,000 times more powerful than the atomic bomb dropped on *Hiroshima)*, and are thought to have planned, but not built, bombs 10 or more times that size. See also *charged particle beam; radiological weapons*.

hyperinflation: Runaway *inflation* that can reach figures of thousands or millions of percent per year, or even per month. Few *regimes* can long survive the destruction of personal wealth and economic planning such inflation causes, particularly for the middle classes. Hyperinflation has plagued many *Third World* states, but among the most spectacular examples was the inflation that devastated *Weimar Germany*. Runaway inflation also threatened reforms in several former communist countries, including Ukraine. For different reasons, Serbia's inflation hit four quadrillion percent per year in 1993/94. At such a point of absurdity, hyperinflation doubles back and reinforces itself, as people lose all remaining faith in the *currency* (and often in the government as well). When that happens a new currency must be introduced, with believable guarantees that it will not simply suffer the same fate.

hypothesis: (1) In *quantitative analysis*: a tentative assumption about causal relations put forward as an equation, to explore and test its logical and *empirical* consequences. (2) In formal reasoning: any proposition set forth as a provisional conjecture to guide further reasoning. (3) In unexamined argument: an unstated assumption implicit in one's premise. (4) In daily discourse: a naked best guess, often overdressed as a trenchant insight. Cf. *null hypothesis.*

I

IAEA: See *International Atomic Energy Agency.*

IB (Intelligence Bureau): The *intelligence service* of India, concerned mainly with: targeting Pakistan's *nuclear,* and other, weapons programs; China; and domestic dissent and *terrorism.*

Iberia: The peninsula comprising Portugal and Spain.

Ibo (Igbo): A West African people that during the *Nigerian Civil War* formed the core of the *Biafra.*

IBRD: See *International Bank for Reconstruction and Development.*

ICBM: See *Intercontinental Ballistic Missile.*

Iceland: Location: N. Atlantic. Major associations: *NATO, Nordic Council, OECD, UN.* Population: 260,000. Military: NATO and U.S. bases. It was an independent *republic* from 930-1262 A.D., when it fell to Norwegian Vikings. It had representative government for centuries: the Althing is the oldest, continuous parliament in the world. It was linked to Denmark from 1380-1918, enjoying *autonomy* under the Danish crown in the *interwar years.* It severed ties with the Danish crown in 1944, under *Allied* pressure during *WWII* (when Denmark was occupied by Germany). Iceland was a major naval base during the *Battle of the Atlantic,* occupied first by British, and then American forces. This tiny outpost was a charter member of NATO. During the *Cold War* it deferred in foreign policy to the U.S., which kept major naval and *submarine* monitoring bases there. From 1972-76 it engaged in the so-called *Cod War* with Britain. In 1986 it hosted a summit between *Reagan* and *Gorbachev.*

ICJ: See *International Court of Justice.*

idealism: An approach to world politics that emphasizes the key role of *volition* and ideas as capable of bringing about progressive change (more peaceful and prosperous relations) in world affairs. A variant of *liberal-internationalism,* it stresses the positive role of *diplomacy, international law* and *international organization* over *force.* Moderate idealists keep their goals of enhanced cooperation and reduced international violence to the fore, without neglecting pragmatic considerations of the *struggle for power.* Utopian idealists often overlook the persistence of relations of *power,* placing at peril their ideal systems (and much else besides). In both cases, idealists tend to be more accepting of abstract motivations and theory than the more empirically minded adherents of *realism.* Note: for an entirely different usage see *end of history; Hegel.*

idealpolitik: A policy driven by abstract goals or principles; usually pejorative. Cf. *realpolitik.*

ideologue: A *fanatic* adherent of any given *ideology.*

ideology: A set of systematic ideas about political, economic and social conditions, often visionary and highly theoretical. Among other entries, see *absolutism; communism; dependency theory; fascism; fundamentalism; maoism; marxism; national socialism; secularism; stalinism.* Cf. *human rights; image; liberal-internationalism; paradigm; realism.*

IGO: See *International Governmental Organization.*

Île des Faisans: "Isle of Pheasants." A political/legal curiosity, and since 1856 a tiny *condominium* on the French/Spanish border.

illegal (agent): A spy, with neither official cover nor *diplomatic immunity.* The term "illegal" refers more to a lack of formal status than to *espionage* activities. Cf. *legal (agent).*

illegal act: A deliberate action, or an act of omission, that breaches a *state's* legal obligations under a *treaty* or under *international customary law.*

image: (1) A softer term than *ideology,* referring to the perspectives on world affairs of *decision-makers,* said to act as a filter organizing incoming information. (2) Sometimes used as a synonym for *paradigm,* or the general approaches used by those who study world affairs. (3) A set cognitive structure in the mind of a decision-maker, said to restructure incoming information in ways that hardly resemble the information itself, so that evidence that confirms preset views is strongly perceived and accepted, while disconfirming evidence is neglected, explained away or repressed. See *misperception*.

imam: (1) In the *sunni* tradition: the head of a mosque and a prayer leader. (2) In the *shi'ite* tradition: a Muslim leader said to have direct succession from Muhammad, and therefore in theory the divinely appointed and rightful ruler of the faithful, above all secular authority. A quasi-messianic variant of this tradition, called "Twelfth-imam shi'ism," or even just "Twelvers," recognizes 11 specially annointed imams while awaiting the return of the 12th, or "Hidden Imam," who is the true *caliph*. In contrast, *Ismailis* (Fatamid) are sometimes called "Seveners" because they believe the rightful succession stopped in 765 A.D. with the death of the sixth caliph, the last visible to earthly eyes after Muhammad. Some Ismailis (Nizari) divided even further, following only until the fourth caliph.

IMF: See *International Monetary Fund.*

immigration: The arrival in a country of non-natives or non-*naturalized* persons, for the purpose of taking up permanent residence.

Imperial Conferences: These were held to discuss affairs of the *British Empire* in 1911, 1921, 1923, 1926, 1930, 1932 and 1937. They signified the growing foreign policy independence of the *Dominions* within the empire, but also their desire to continue to coordinate *tariff* and other economic policy.

imperialism: The policy and practice of extending the *power* and domination of one *nation* over another, especially by territorial *conquest*. It is as old as recorded history, whether of the Aztecs or of Babylon, Byzantium, China, ancient Egypt, the Indus valley, classical Greece, Rome, the Mongol Khans, Muscovy or the Zulus. Its adherents have come from all races, all colors and most faiths. There have been *empires* built by great individuals like Alexander of Macedon, or imperial aristocracies, oligarchies, and theocracies. There have even been imperial democracies. Imperialism has myriad causes: cultural or religious missionary zeal; defensive expansion; exporting surplus *population*; racial arrogance; competition for scarce resources; *prestige*; *strategic* interests, real or imagined; *trade*; and the personal or collective vanity of dictators, national *elites* or *peoples*. Such facts should be born in mind, as too often imperialism as a general phenomenon is underestimated by banal reference to historically parochial developments, such as the rise of *capitalism*. (1) Modern: The first wave of modern empire building began in the 16th century, when the British, French, Portuguese, Spanish and Dutch penetrated the *Americas*, parts of *India* and *Southeast Asia*, while Turkey clung to its hold over the *Middle East* and Russia expanded into *Central Asia* and *Siberia*. The second wave saw British conquests in India and the consolidation of French and British *colonies* in North America, mostly lost in the *Seven Years' War* and *American Revolution*. The British--arguably the greatest imperialists of any age--fought multiple *wars* and otherwise schemed, plotted and manipulated nations and events to secure a route to India protected by bases at *Gibraltar, Malta, Suez* and *Aden*; they secured the Cape route by taking South Africa. The third wave came in the 19th century, as Europeans carved up the interior of Africa at the *Conference of Berlin*. They were joined in late century by Japanese and Americans in Asia, with the Pacific islands and China the main targets. Often overlooked is that Europe itself was the target of the greatest and most destructive imperial ambitions and wars: those of *Louis XIV, Napoleon,* two 20th century German drives and post-*WWII* Soviet expansion as far west as central Germany. (2) In *marxism-leninism*: Imperialism is the final stage of *hegemonic* expansion of the capitalist system, which but temporarily prolongs the final crisis of capitalism by exporting surplus production to the *Third World*. This is said to lead to wars among capitalist powers (notably *WWI*) that improve the chances for revolutionary success by destroying social cohesion at home. See *dependency theory; Eastern Question; Fulani; Greater East Asia Co-prosperity Sphere; imperial overreach; jingoism; lebensraum; Lenin; manifest destiny; Mfecane; mission civilatrice; pan-Slavism; Shaka Zulu; social darwinism; social imperialism; white man's burden.* Cf. *dollar diplomacy; hegemony; neo-imperialism; post-imperialism; Wisconsin school.*

imperial overreach: When commitments to *security* and economic support for an empire's maintenance greatly exceed the economic and other benefits of that empire. Some see this as a recurring pattern of all empires: costs one day will exceed benefits, and contraction or collapse must follow. This was said by some to be happening to the U.S. in the mid-1980s. It much more clearly happened to the *Soviet Union* at the end of that decade. Cf. *hegemonic stability*.

imperial tariff: Also called "imperial preference." Treating all the *British Empire* as a single economic unit. This large-scale *protectionism* was proposed *Joseph Chamberlain* and his sons, and later by Canada, and adopted by British imperialists as a substitute for *free trade*. It was implemented by the *Commonwealth* after an *Imperial Conference* held in Ottawa in

1932. Modified under U.S. pressure with the creation of the *Bretton Woods* system, it was not entirely abandoned until Britain joined the *EC* in 1972.

Imperial Way (Kodo-ha): An extreme faction in the Japanese Army in the 1920s and 1930s that aimed at aggressive expansion at China's expense. On February 26, 1936, they attempted a *coup*, killing several top Japanese leaders but failing to take control of the country. Most of the faction's leaders were executed, and the imperial cause within the army passed over to the slightly less extreme Control Faction (Tosei-ha). In the end, this may have been a distinction without much of a difference.

imperium: The jurisdictional and other legal rights of a state. See *territorial jurisdiction*.

import: Any *good* or *service* purchased or accepted from a foreign supplier.

import duty: A tax imposed on *imports*.

import quotas: A *non-tariff barrier* limiting *imports* by arbitrarily capping their permitted quantity.

import substitution: An attempt to conserve *foreign exchange* and develop an indigenous industrial base by subsidizing local production of *goods* and *services* that are otherwise imported. A.k.a. "import substitution industrialization." Cf. *autarky; export-led growth; self-reliance*.

impressment: Involuntary military service, sometimes under a foreign flag. Impressment of U.S. citizens by Britain was one *casus belli* of the *War of 1812*.

imputability: An idea basic to the notion of state responsibility under *international law*, it holds that acts by officials or state organs that injure resident *aliens* may be legally attributed to states, which then become responsible for *redress*. See also *act of state; exhaustion of local remedies*.

in absentia: "In the absence of (someone)." Legal proceedings undertaken without the accused present. This procedure was used in *war crimes trials* prior to 1993, when a UN commission recommended not pursuing charges in the absence of the defendant.

incendiary: Weapons that involve destruction with fire. Perhaps the first incendiary was the "Greek Fire" used by Athens against the Persian navy over 2,000 years ago. In the Middle Ages, burning oils were pumped through pipes or poured over walls on attack-

ing soldiers, while African and American native troops used flaming arrows against fortifications or villages. Any urban *guerrilla* or *partisan* can make a *Molotov cocktail*, while better equipped troops and tanks have sported flamethrowers. In modern times, thermite has been employed in bombs and shells, while napalm has proven an all-purpose incendiary.

incorporation, doctrine of: Within the Anglo/American tradition, this is the notion that *international customary law* is incorporated into domestic law (is part of common law), and therefore is to be enforced by domestic authorities. Cf. *consent*.

incursion: A hostile raid or other limited military action by the forces of one *state* across the *border* of another. It may be designed as a *provocation*, or as *saber rattling* to intimidate an opponent into a political outcome they oppose. It is less than, but may be precursor to, an *invasion*. Cf. *intrusion*.

indefeasible allegiance: A doctrine that holds *nationality* cannot be voided or annulled by the will of individuals. Also called "indelible allegiance."

indemnity: *Compensation*, or *damages*, paid voluntarily or as *reparations*.

independence: (1) The ability to manage domestic affairs free of outside interference, which is a main prerequisite of *sovereignty* and *recognition*. (2) The legal right of a *state* with recognized *international personality* to conduct its *foreign policy* free from supervision. It requires of other states the duty to refrain from such interference. See also *associated state; servitudes*.

independent variable: The factor explaining change in the *dependent variable*. In short, it is the primary *cause* thought to explain the *effect* one is studying.

indeterminate solution: When outcomes cannot be predicted owing to random changes in the *variables* (it really means you are left just guessing).

India: Location: SW Asia. Major associations: *NAM, SARC, UN*. Population: approx. 900 million. Military: over one million troops but outdated Soviet equipment; dominates the Indian Ocean area; *nuclear* and *missile* capable. (1) Classical period: The Indian subcontinent is home to one of the world's oldest and greatest civilizations, also several of its major religions. *Hindu* civilization dates back at least 5,000 years, and probably more. The classical period is usually dated from c.1500 B.C., with the infusion of *Aryan* tribes that led to a florescence of high culture.

From the 3rd century B.C. much of India was ruled by Asoka; this period also witnessed the development of *Buddhism*. During the Gupta era, 4th-6th centuries A.D., Hindu culture revived and flourished. In the 8th century, *Islam* arrived in the form of *Muslim* invaders who penetrated the north, and by the 12th century had divided it into Muslim kingdoms. The great Mogul Empire ruled from 1526-1857, but was in precipitate decline from the 17th century, opening a door to European penetration and dominance.

(2) The *Raj*: The Portuguese came first (Vasco da Gama), setting up coastal trading posts from 1498. They were followed by the Dutch and the British, and much later, the French. Great trading houses were established, of which by far the most successful was the British *East India Company*. Behind this expanding enterprise the British ultimately came to control most of India, ruling through local princes, or by direct administration. *Direct rule* was established following the *Indian Mutiny*. Through the *Indian Army*, a mere 100,000 British ruled some 400 million Indians, divided into *British India* and the *Princely States*. By the end of the 19th century the empire in India was under threat from rising *nationalism*. That was partly of British making, through the creation of a middle class of educated administrators that gathered in reformist political parties, of which the greatest was *Congress*. A separate Muslim movement started in 1905: the *Muslim League*, under *Ali Jinnah*. Both focused on representation for Indians within the empire, and on inequitable, imperial economic arrangements. India's contribution to Britain's war effort in *WWI* was considerable (it would be even greater during *WWII*), and it felt the effect of new ideas about *self-determination* of nations drifting in from the *Paris Peace Conference*. This increased pressures for reform. The first *India Acts* did not devolve power quickly enough to satisfy the nationalists. *Mohandas Gandhi* rose to leadership in the Congress Party just as confrontation between Indians and their British overlords was rising. The situation was made irretrievable by the Amritsar massacre (April 13, 1919): British troops fired on a peaceful crowd of demonstrators, killing nearly 400 and wounding 1,200 more. The massacre greatly accelerated moves toward *independence*, both shocking British liberal opinion and galvanizing Indian outrage. Gandhi brought the Indian masses into the nationalist movement through a series of brilliant stratagems, such as the *salt march*. Before that Congress was a rather elitist, even effete, party of polite pamphleteers, lawyers and negotiators. An effort to deflate the growing conflict took place with the *Round Table Conferences*, but the British remained unconvinced their day was done. WWII delayed progress toward independence, and then accelerated it: full application of the 1935 India Act was postponed, but India's contribution to the war, and Britain's exhaustion by it, made withdrawal from the empire inescapable. The end came (with *partition* from *Pakistan*) on August 15, 1947.

(3) Republic of India: For three years India was a *Dominion* within the *Commonwealth*, with the last Viceroy, *Louis Mountbatten*, serving as the first Governor-General and the British monarch as Indian king. It became a *republic* on January 26, 1950. But a more pressing problem than republicanism delayed was the fierce sectarian hatreds that sprang up between Hindus and Muslims (and *Sikhs*) accompanying partition: 12 million were forcibly relocated in a massive example of *ethnic cleansing*, and several hundred thousand died in sectarian massacres. After partition the cankerous dispute over *Kashmir* remained, leading or contributing to *war* with Pakistan in 1947, 1965 and 1971, and nearly leading to war in 1992. Under Congress, led next by *Nehru* and then *Indira Gandhi*, India embarked on a decades-long attempt at *self-sufficiency*, carried out the *green revolution* and assumed a leadership role in the *Non-Aligned Movement*. China's *annexation* of *Tibet* and then the *Indo/Chinese War* in 1962 over a disputed border pushed India toward the Soviet Union, and to become a *nuclear state* (1974). That led to a deterioration in relations with the U.S.

The 1970s were consumed by a prolonged domestic crisis over Indira Gandhi's proclamation of emergency rule. There was also a growing sense that the governing classes operated outside the law, and were exempt from such onerous policies as forcible sterilization. The 1980s witnessed continuing *ethnic* tensions throughout the *subcontinent*. The most prominent examples were in Assam (where Bengali refugees poured in after 1971), Kashmir and the *Punjab* (where Sikh *radicals* agitated for a separate state). Neighboring Sri Lanka attracted Indian diplomacy and then troops. It *intervened* at Sri Lankan invitation against the *Tamil Tigers* in 1987, but withdrew in 1990. The end of the *Cold War* and China's rapid economic advances convinced India to abandon self-sufficiency in favor of full entry into the global marketplace. In 1991 a severe economic crisis compelled it to accept a *stabilization program* from the *IMF*, and introduce market reforms. By 1993 India had partly opened its trade and made the rupee convertible. It began naval maneuvers with the U.S., but relations remained strained over American opposition to Indian purchase of Soviet missile technology.

India is legally a *secular*, not a Hindu state. However, it is currently experiencing a revival and politicization of Hindu *fundamentalism* that threatens to replace its secular, and perhaps also its democratic, traditions. In March 1993, Hindu *fanatics* destroyed a mosque they claimed was built on the site of an an cient Hindu temple, leading to religious rioting and aggravating tensions with Pakistan. Despite massive problems, India has achieved success in agriculture (*famine* has been eliminated), creation of an urban middle class, and some land reform. It preserves the world's largest democracy, albeit one shaken by assassination, undermined by corruption and capable of ignoring huge social problems that hide behind fundamentalist religious protection. See also *Aden; Bangladesh; Burma; Dalhousie; Rajiv Gandhi; Goa; French India; Hyderabad; Indian Mutiny (Sepoy Rebellion); indirect rule; Indo/Pakistani Wars; McMahon Line; Sikkim; untouchables.*

India Acts: These were four Acts of the British Parliament over 40 years that devolved self-rule on the *subcontinent.* (1) 1909: Indians were given a limited say in local governing councils. (2) 1919: It set up a compromise system of government in India (*dyarchy*) between 1919-35 that granted limited *autonomy* to the states on specific issues, and established a national parliament. (3) 1935: It proposed transforming the empire into a *federation*, with representation for *Princely States* as well as provinces of *British India.* The scheme was postponed due to *WWII*, but much *autonomy* was granted. Also, *Aden* and *Burma* were severed from Indian jurisdiction. (4) 1947: It proclaimed the independent *states* of *India* and *Pakistan*, dividing assets between them. It permitted the Princely States to choose India, Pakistan or *independence*, contributing to the bloody dispute over *Kashmir.*

Indian Army: The large force with which Britain kept control of the Indian *subcontinent*, and manned other posts of its vast *empire* (particularly in Afghanistan, Egypt, Palestine and Persia). Until *WWI* the ranks were Indian but the officers exclusively British. Indian officers were moved into the force after that. During *WWII* the Indian Army was instrumental in holding off the Japanese advance, and then in retaking Burma. In 1947 it too was divided between India and Pakistan. See also *Indian Mutiny.*

Indian Mutiny, a.k.a. Sepoy Rebellion (1857-58): An *Indian Army* revolt that soon became a full-scale *rebellion.* It began with anger over the reforms of cultural practices introduced by *Dalhousie*, combined with rumors about forcible conversions to Christianity, and more rumors that British cartridges were greased with cow and pig fat (offending Hindus and Muslims respectively, as cartridge wrappings were bitten off before loading). It took the British over a year to repress the rebels and retake *Delhi* and other cities. Afterward, the *East India Company* lost its charter and *direct rule* was instituted.

indicators: Mechanisms that measure levels of economic activity, or national *development.* (1) Economic gauges are *commodity* price indices, consumer price indices, *gross domestic product, gross national product, growth,* industrial production, *inflation, leading indicators, net domestic product, net national product,* demand and jobs, aggregate prices and wages, producer price indices, retail sales, *system of national accounts,* and unemployment. (2) Gauges of development include health services, daily caloric consumption, the *Human Development Index,* energy consumption, *infant mortality rate,* life expectancy, literacy (general and adult); scientists, doctors, engineers and other (useful) professionals per 1,000 of general population, percentage of boys/girls in primary and secondary education, percentage of the labor force still in agriculture, sanitation, and personal and national *standards of living.* Cf. *industrialization; modernization.*

indigenismo: A cultural, nationalist movement in Latin America prominent especially in the early decades of the 20th century. It upheld pre-Columbian models of Indian societies as more "authentic" than the dominant Latin cultures of most Latin American countries. Cf. *négritude.*

indigenous peoples: The native peoples of colonized lands, primarily in *Australasia,* the *Americas,* the *Arctic* and the *South Pacific,* but also China and Japan, *Indochina, Siberia* and elsewhere. They tend to exist on the margins of modern economic and political life, though in some countries (among others, Canada, New Zealand, the U.S. and most recently, Australia) they have won significant land claims settlements. They have often been subject to *genocide* or near-genocidal policies. For instance, the natives of *Newfoundland* were hunted down and exterminated entirely; the *conquests* of the American west and Russian east were accompanied by *ethnic cleansing* and/or extermination of some natives; parts of South America were denuded of their indigenous populations by disease, but also mass murder. And this still happens: in Brazil in 1993, gold miners were charged with genocide for the deliberate killing of whole villages of Amazonian Indians, to undermine their land claims. Treatment of indigenous peoples has come under increased *UNHRC* and *NGO* scrutiny.

indirect aggression: Not readily defined in law, this term is used about a set of actions that may include *covert action, subversion,* military *aid* to a third *state* that commits direct *aggression*, or support for a *guerrilla* or *secession* movement in another state.

indirect rule: When an imperial power governs a

colony through local intermediaries, in return for leaving unchanged the local social arrangements. The British did this with the *emirs* of northern Nigeria and the maharajahs (princes) of India. Cf. *direct rule*.

indiscriminate bombing/fire: Bombing or shelling populated areas without due regard for *just war* distinctions between *civilians* and *combatants*.

individualism: Political and social theory, and practice, encompassing express individual freedoms, privileges and rights, as against the claims of groups (including majorities), and especially against onerous burdens or tyranny erected over individuals by the *state*. These ideas and practices were first developed and are still most advanced in the *West*, but arguably have exhibited near-universal appeal since they began to spread with the *Enlightenment* and *French Revolution*. See also *capitalism; Declaration of the Rights of Man; democracy; human rights; laissez-faire; liberalism; popular sovereignty; Renaissance; secularism*. Cf. *collectivization; communism; fascism; fundamentalism; nationalism; self-determination*.

Indochina: The SE Asian peninsula comprising Burma, Cambodia, Laos, Malaysia, Thailand and Vietnam. Cf. *French Indochina*.

Indo/Chinese War (October 20-November 22, 1962): China's seizure of *Tibet* aggravated relations with India, and created a long, disputed *border* in the Himalayas. China had long claimed that the *McMahon Line* demarcating Tibet's border with India had been unfairly set by the British. When India refused to accept China's interpretation, it attacked, catching the Indians off guard and throwing them back on two fronts. Once its limited objectives were achieved, China proclaimed a unilateral *cease-fire*. That left India unable to do more than protest. The lasting impact of this brief clash was threefold: (1) a worsening of relations between the two giants of Asia; (2) a regional realignment of India with the Soviet Union, which China countered by supporting Pakistan; (3) India's decision to acquire *nuclear weapons*. The border remains disputed, with China occupying its claimed territories (Arunachal Pradesh) and a salient that juts into *Kashmir* (Aksai Chin). In 1993 it was agreed to respect the status quo, pending final settlement.

Indonesia: Location: SE Asia. Major associations: *ASEAN, OPEC, UN*. Population: 193 million (more than all the rest of ASEAN combined). Military: currently expanding and rearming. Formerly the Dutch or Netherlands East Indies, this sprawling archipelago was divided in pre-independence times between Britain, Germany, Holland and Portugal, but was mainly controlled by the Dutch. *Hinduism* and *Buddhism* arrived from India over 2,000 years ago; they were followed by the spread of *Islam* in the 14th-15th centuries, which followed in the wake of Muslim traders. In the 16th century the Portuguese established a trading presence, but in the 17th century they were supplanted by the Dutch, who took control of Java in 1750. It was only in the 20th century that modern Indonesia was first united under a single political authority. A communist-led revolt against the Dutch failed in 1926, after which Dutch rule was maintained through fairly ruthless methods. Indonesia was captured from the Dutch by Japan in 1942, and held until their *surrender* in 1945. *Sukarno* proclaimed *independence* before the Dutch returned, but when they did, fighting broke out. An interim agreement placed Indonesia in a "special relationship" with Holland, but this agreement quickly broke down and fighting resumed. The measures used by the Dutch were so severe the UN and U.S. became involved, with the U.S. brokering a *cease-fire* in December 1947. Meanwhile, Indonesian nationalists (republicans) began fighting the *Partai Kommunis Indonesia (PKI)*, which tempted the Dutch to break the cease-fire and resume their *campaign* against the republicans. Under sustained international criticism for the brutality of their methods and the untenable position they were seeking to defend, the Dutch finally agreed to depart, doing so on December 27, 1949. Modern Indonesia formed out of the main islands of Celebes, *Java*, Sumatra, Kalimantan (on *Borneo*) and some 3,000 smaller islands. Instead of a *federation*, a *unitary state* under the dictatorship of Sukarno was established, with Java the political heart of the country. In 1965 an attempted *coup* provided the pretext for annihilation of the PKI by *Suharto*; several hundred thousand were slaughtered. Sukarno pulled Indonesia out of the UN in 1965, but Suharto (who deposed Sukarno in 1967) rejoined. Indonesia later became a contributor to UN *peacekeeping* forces. It has pursued opportunistic *expansionism* since its formation. It forced the *cession* of *Irian Jaya* from Holland in 1963, was blocked by British and Malay troops from acquiring *Sabah* and *Sarawak* during the *Konfrontasi*, invaded and annexed *East Timor* in 1975 and is pursuing claims to the *Spratlys*. It improved relations with Malaysia after 1967 and led in the formation of ASEAN. It has come under criticism for its poor *human rights* record, especially in East Timor, where some *NGOs* have said *genocide* is occurring. It faces *insurgencies* in East Timor, Irian Jaya, Aceh on Sumatra, and in Ambon and the Muluccas. It normalized relations with China in 1990. In 1993 it purchased one-third of the old *East German* navy (some 39 surface ships).

Indo/Pakistani War, First (1947-49): In 1947 *Kashmir's* Hindu maharajah tried to avoid a choice of association with either predominantly Hindu India or Muslim Pakistan. Fighting broke out between Muslim tribesmen from the north, and the Hindus of Jammu. The maharajah asked for military aid from India, which agreed on condition Kashmir accept sovereign association. This was intolerable to Pakistan, and large-scale fighting erupted. Neither side prevailed. India brought the matter before the *Security Council* in January 1948. Pakistan countered witn an accusation of *genocide*. A UN commission investigated and brokered a *cease-fire* in January 1949. That left one-third of Kashmir with Pakistan and the rest with India, but with neither side really accepting the outcome.

Indo/Pakistani War, Second (1965): The *war* was preceded by an incident in the isolated and sparsely populated "Rann of Kutch," where Indian and Pakistani patrols clashed repeatedly. In a brief encounter Pakistani forces enjoyed quick, though merely local victory. Pakistan emerged from this engagement over-confident of its *martial* prowess and India was left seeking revenge. In August, *Ayub Khan* sent *guerrilla* fighters into *Kashmir*. India countered by occupying several mountain passes. On September 1st Khan raised the stakes by sending troops and tanks across the 1949 *cease-fire* line. On September 5th India widened the war by attacking directly into *West Pakistan*. A *stalemate* soon took shape. The war ended with *mediation* by Soviet Premier *Aleksei Kosygin*, at a conference in Tashkent. *Peace* (of a kind) was restored. But the problem of Kashmir had been merely set aside, not resolved.

Indo/Pakistani War, Third (1971): The Bengali-controlled Awami League gained control of the *East Pakistan* Assembly in 1971. The Army, 95% *West Pakistani* in makeup, intervened and began indiscriminate killings of the Bengali population. That provoked a declaration of *independence* by East Pakistan (Bangladesh), followed by a *civil war* that killed one million and created 10 million *refugees*, who mostly fled into India. Pakistani troops also engaged in *hot pursuit* of Bengali *guerrillas* across the Indian border, sometimes clashing with Indian border patrols. On August 9th, India signed a 25-year *friendship treaty* with the Soviet Union: New Delhi was clearly preparing to *deter* Chinese *intervention*, should it decide to attack Beijing's *ally*, Pakistan. The Indians now more openly aided the Bengali *secessionists*. Pakistani leaders did not read the messages from New Delhi correctly, continuing both the repression in East Pakistan and the provocative practice of hot pursuit. A cyclone struck in November, killing thousands of Indians as well as Bangladeshis. The economic burden of caring for refugees from two major cyclones and an ongoing war proved too much for India to bear. At the same time, the temptation to weaken permanently its old enemy by aiding the secession of East Pakistan became irresistible. At the end of November, *Indira Gandhi* ordered limited strikes against the Pakistanis, but in East Pakistan only. On November 30th, Indian troops penetrated five miles into Pakistan. The U.S. countered with an announced *tilt* toward Pakistan (Washington perceived the conflict in *Cold War* rather than regional terms). The next day Gandhi issued an *ultimatum* demanding withdrawal of all Pakistani forces from East Pakistan--in effect, she demanded Bangladeshi independence. On December 3rd, Pakistan launched what it hoped would be a *preemptive strike* against India's air force. An Indian *counterattack* overwhelmed the Pakistanis, and in the end it was India that dictated *cease-fire* terms: it took 2,500 square miles of *territory* from West Pakistan as *damages* (*reparations*), retained 93,000 Pakistani *POWs* until 1973, and oversaw the independence of Bangladesh.

industrialization: See *Industrial Revolution; UNIDO.*

Industrial Revolution: The conversion of a national economy from an agrarian to a manufacturing base, usually attended by increased ecological damage and population increase, but desirable to most people for its stimulative effect on *modernization,* urbanization and rising *standards of living.* The usual schoolbook models in *anglophone* countries are the United Kingdom after 1760, and the United States in the 19th century, both of which emphasized *laissez-faire* principles. Yet most large industrial economies developed with the *state* at or near the center of planning and *investment.* That was true in China, France, Germany, Japan and Russia. Cf. See also *mass production; dirigiste; power; slave trade; total war; UNIDO.*

industrial triangle: A 1991 proposal by Indonesia, Malaysia and Singapore to link their disparate resources for joint industrial *development.* The core idea was to connect Singapore's strength in *capital* to the large *labor* pool in the other two nations.

inelasticity: See *elasticity of demand.*

infant mortality rate: The ratio of infant (less than one year old) deaths to live births, usually expressed in terms of numbers per thousand, or hundred thousand. It is a pretty sharp indicator of the basic welfare of a population, remaining high in poor societies or those touched by *famine,* disease or *war,* and falling with *industrialization,* social welfare spending and general rises in the *standard of living* across a national population.

infantry: Soldiers who maneuver and fight on foot.

infection: An international legal doctrine under which *contraband* is said to "infect" *noncontraband* goods on the same ship, so that the latter may also be rightfully seized by a *belligerent.*

inflation: A continuing rise in the price of *goods* and *services* that undercuts the value and purchasing power of a national *currency.* It has shattered more than one society or political system (thus, the *Bundesbank* still governs *fiscal policy* influenced by memory of *hyperinflation* in the 1920s). Cf. *deflation.*

influence: The capacity to cause wanted changes in the behavior of others through indirect, and usually intangible, means. Cf. *coercion; power; soft power.*

informal sector: Those precincts of the economy that are unreported, unregulated and untaxed (e.g., private *barter* transactions, migrant *labor* exchange, the *drug trade* or activity on the *black market*).

information technology: Any means, but especially mechanical or electronic, for the storage and communication of information. It has been especially effective in developing scientific underpinnings for specific international initiatives, such as on global environmental questions. It has also made it more difficult for societies to remain closed to outside cultural and other foreign influences. For example, the economic and political ramifications of new communications technology helped force open the *Soviet bloc,* and continues to put pressure on the domestic practices of China and other still closed societies.

infrastructure: Facilities like communications, transportation systems (airports, seaports, rails, roads), electricity, and other public services necessary to economic activity and *modernization.* "Social infrastructure," a.k.a. *social overhead capital,* includes education and health care, which are necessary to a productive and efficient workforce. A synonym is *public goods.*

infringe: To transgress another *state's* legal rights, as in such-and-such an action "infringed upon its *sovereignty.*"

Inkatha: A *Zulu* organization in South Africa with a *tribal* rather than *democratic* vision of post-*apartheid* South Africa. Its leader is Chief *Gatsha Mangosuthu Buthelezi* (b.1928). After 1986 Inkatha engaged in an increasingly violent political struggle with the *ANC* and other black groups. It is known to have accepted secret funds from the South African government. In 1993-94 it allied with extreme right-wing whites, who shared Butehelezi's fear of democracy. At the last minute it agreed to join the elections, but fared poorly.

Inner Mongolia: See *Mongolia.*

innocent passage: The right of foreign ships to transit *territorial waters,* if without ulterior motive (such as *espionage* or fishing). *UNCLOS III* would greatly lengthen the list of prohibited activities. Note: There is no right of innocent passage for aircraft through national *airspace.* States may and do require *civilian* aircraft to enter and depart by designated corridors, and usually insist on prior notification. Military aircraft may pass over only with explicit permission.

Inönü, Ismet (1884-1974): Turkish statesman. PM 1923-37, 1961-65; President 1938-50. He fought the Greeks in *Anatolia* in 1921-22, built up the Turkish army and led the diplomatic mission that negotiated the *Treaty of Lausanne.* He succeeded *Atäturk,* and maintained his policies of *secularization* and *modernization.* During *WWII* he expressed sympathy for the *Allies,* but declined to enter the war until March 1945, just before the German collapse. To his great credit, after WWII he accepted domestic political reform and even ouster in elections in 1950. He returned to office in 1961. When *Lyndon Johnson* prevailed upon him to cancel a planned *invasion* of Cyprus, he paid a heavy political price at home.

input: (1) In economics: any *good* or *service* used to create a secondary product (*output*). (2) In political science: *jargon* for virtually anything that is considered by a *decision-maker* in the course of arriving at a decision. Cf. *intermediate inputs.*

Inquisition (1480-1834): The Catholic Inquisition, especially in Spain and its possessions, used *torture* and mass executions to ferret out and repress all religious dissent and indirectly, all political opposition to the *Hapsburgs.* It was most ruthlessly applied during and after the final years of *conquest* of Muslim Spain. With the fall of the last Muslim state, Granada, in 1492, forcible conversions of Muslims and Jews became mass expulsion orders, followed by executions of those who refused. For Muslims, it was the end of centuries of civilized life and independence in *Iberia*; for the Jews, it proved a second *diaspora* that sent many hundreds of thousands into Central and Eastern Europe, and into Russia and Ukraine. And for Spain, it proved an end to the vibrant intellectual life that

Muslim and Jewish scholars and communities had provided, and the beginning of its long, dark night of orthodoxy. In the long-term it contributed to Spain's relative decline, as northern neighbors embraced the secular and classical knowledge that Moorish and Jewish scholars had kept alive in translation. The Inquisition was subsequently carried to Africa, the Americas and Asia by missionaries, the Jesuits in particular.

instrumental rationality: The assumption that a *decision-maker* always chooses, when presented with options, the path that maximizes interests. See *cognitive dissonance; groupthink; minimax principle; misperception.*

instruments of ratification: Documents that formally confirm that a *state* accepts a *treaty*, delivered to other states if concerning a bilateral treaty, or to the *Secretary General* of the UN in the case of some *multilateral* treaties.

insurgency: (1) A condition of armed *rebellion* short of full *civil war;* a synonym for *guerrilla war.* (2) The legal status of *guerrillas* or violent revolutionaries that falls short of *belligerency* but whose actions are beyond merely municipal, criminal law.

insurrection: An armed uprising against an established, *recognized* government.

Integrated Program for Commodities (IPC): It was proposed by *UNCTAD* as part of the *NIEO*, and has been ill-received by the *OECD* states. It calls for the creation of *ICAs,* and a Common Fund to help pay for *buffer stocks.* Agreement was finally reached on a modest program, when the recession of the early 1980s hit, drastically reducing *commodity* prices and shifting attention to the *debt* problem. The Common Fund was established in 1989, and only a handful of ICAs were in place by the early 1990s.

integration: Increasing the quantity and quality of interconnections among *states*, at a minimum by cooperation in *functional agencies,* and at the maximum through economic and political *federation* or even *union.* Some writers look to "transaction flows" (financial, mail, telephone, tourism, trade) as key *indicators* of the level of integration. Others question whether such flows precede and *cause*, or merely stem from, processes of integration with deeper causes. For example, much integration theory has been criticized for neglecting the role of external conflict and common enemies as a key stimulus to cooperation. Yet the basic impetus toward real integration is likely a com-

bination of security and economic concerns. At the economic level, integration increases the home market through combination; augments bargaining position relative to actors outside the system; and should in theory reduce inefficiency and streamline industries by eliminating duplication within the larger, single market (this latter effect can be seriously counteracted by government policy that protects politically sensitive sectors; e.g., the *CAP*). See *Andean Common Market; ASEAN; BENELUX; CARICOM; Central African Federation; common market; complex interdependence; customs union; deepening vs. enlargement; ECOWAS; European Community; European Union; functionalism; LAFTA; LAIA; Mali; NAFTA; Ruhr; spillover; two-speed Europe; world federalism.*

intelligence: Information public and secret about enemies real or potential, all activities necessary to gathering such information, and conclusions drawn from its systematic study. At its best, intelligence is accurate knowledge, and some foreknowledge, of the state of the outside world, and should be part of the prelude to any major foreign policy decision. However, in practice it is often partial, unreliable, suspect or just plain ignored by *decision-makers* overconfident of their own talents and insights. See also *active measures; agent of influence; agent provocateurs; agitprop; assassination; cabinet noir; counter-intelligence; covert action; cipher; cryptology; dead letter drop; debrief; disinformation; double agent; double cross; economic espionage; elint; honey trap; humint; illegal agent; intelligence services; legal agent; listening post; mole; overt/covert; penetration agent; persona non grata; psychological warfare; raw intelligence; safe house; sabotage; satellites; secret diplomacy; sigint; spies; station; surveillance; tradecraft; wet affair.*

intelligence services: The government agency(ies) charged with gathering and analyzing *intelligence*, usually subdivided into military and *civilian* (economic and political) intelligence. Most states maintain at least *counterintelligence* services, while many are also active intelligence gatherers, and a few undertake *covert action.* Selected examples only have been included here. See *BfV; BND; CHEKA; CIA; CSIS; GRU; HvA; IB; KCIA; KGB; KHAD; MI5/MI6; Mossad; NKVD; NSA; OGPU; Okhrana; OSS; SDECE; SIS; STASI; Sûreté.*

Inter-American Development Bank: Incorporated in 1960, headquartered in Washington. It is a *regional bank* for the *Americas.* Its *capital* fund is over $100 billion, reflecting U.S., *EU* and Japanese participation.

inter bellum et pacem nihil est medium: "Between

war and *peace* there is no intermediate state." Legal maxim. Cf. *status mixtus*.

Intercontinental Ballistic Missile (ICBM): A *strategic weapon* capable of hitting targets on a different continent from where it is fired (the most accurate can strike within 100 meters of the target). They may carry single *warheads* or be *MIRVed*. *SALT* defined them as land-based, *ballistic* systems with a range of more than 3,000 miles. They are the main instruments of strategic *nuclear deterrence*. Tipping ICBMs with *hydrogen bombs* and placing them on undetectable nuclear *submarines* (as SLBMs, or submarine launched ballistic missiles) altered the whole character of *Great Power* war, certainly making it unwinnable if not quite yet unthinkable. See also *Einstein*.

intercourse: The unfettered right of an *international personality* to incur obligations and make transactions with others of its kind, and with private concerns.

interdependence: Mutual dependence. That is, relations between countries, markets or societies with high levels of *sensitivity* and *vulnerability* to each others' policies and internal events. Cf. *asymmetrical* and *complex interdependence; global village; MNC*.

interdiction: (1) Cutting or destruction of a military *supply line*. (2) Air strikes aimed at C^3 and supply behind the enemy's *front line*. (3) Interception, inspection and, if necessary, seizure of *contraband* under the rules of *blockade* or *embargo*. (4) Peacetime stopping of commercial traffic while enforcing *sanctions*.

interest group: Any group of persons who share (or think they share) common interests and that seeks to influence *foreign policy* to favor those interests, by lobbying, other participation in the political process or by direct corruption of officials. Interest groups may form around any conceivable interest, whether export/ import, ethnic, ideological, industrial or agrarian. Or they may focus on issues, from particular countries to general concern for the environment or *human rights*.

interest rates: The cost of borrowing money, derived from market processes, and expressed on bond and *money markets* as a percentage over time.

intergovernmental: Transactions between, or organizations set up by and answering to, governments. Cf. *nongovernmental; supranational; transnational*.

intermediate inputs: Partly manufactured goods used to make finished goods, such as copper ingots (not copper ore) used to make wiring.

Intermediate-Range Nuclear Forces (INF): *Ballistic* or *cruise missiles* with less than *intercontinental* ranges (not exceeding 1,500 miles). In *arms control* discussions before 1977 these weapons were called MRBMs (Medium-Range Ballistic Missiles), or IRBMs (Intermediate-Range Ballistic Missiles).

Intermediate-Range Nuclear Forces (INF) Treaty (December 8, 1987): Signed by Presidents *Reagan* and *Gorbachev*, and *ratified* within six months, it eliminated all U.S. and Soviet intermediate *ballistic* and *cruise missiles* in Europe. With the missiles went nearly 500 U.S. and 1,600 Soviet nuclear *warheads*. It was the first agreement to eliminate an entire class of *nuclear weapons*.

internal affairs: Those matters claimed by *states* to lie beyond the strictures laid down by *international law*. Once a blanket claim covering all domestic activities, the scope of this area has shrunk, particularly concerning issues such as environmental disasters and *human rights*. See *intervention*.

internalization theory: The idea that firms move to multinational activity in order to "internalize" markets. That means setting up *subsidiaries* in order to maintain a *monopoly* on *technology* and all aspects of production of a product, to limit competition and ensure market share. Cf. *MNC; product cycle theory*.

internal waters: Those on the interior side of the *baseline*, as well as inland waterways and lakes. Cf. *territorial sea/waters*.

International Atomic Energy Agency (IAEA): It was established in 1957 to promote the use of nuclear energy for peaceful purposes. Its more important function is monitoring the *Nuclear Non-Proliferation Treaty*, including on-site inspections of designated facilities. See also *continuity of safeguards; plutonium*.

International Bank for Reconstruction and Development (IBRD): Also called the World Bank. An *international public corporation*, and UN *specialized agency*, founded at the *Bretton Woods* conference as a global lending agency associated with, but not under the effective authority of, the *UN*. It was designed to aid recovery of the industrial nations from the *Great Depression* and *WWII* by providing international *liquidity*. The IBRD is dedicated to promotion of *market economics, free trade* and high rates of *growth*. It uses *weighted voting*. In 1956 the *International Finance Corporation* was created as an affiliate; in 1960 the *International Development Association*, another affiliate, was established. In the 1990s it began to focus on "poverty reduction" as a measure of its new mandate on *development*. That meant projects were to be assessed for their impact on the poor. It has boosted lending on primary health and education and begun to address what it calls "the social dimensions of adjustment" in poor countries. Cf. *IMF; regional banks.*

International Bill of Rights: The somewhat misleading name given to the *Universal Declaration of Human Rights*, the Covenant on Civil and Political Rights and the Covenant on Economic, Social and Cultural Rights, taken together. In fact, the first is a *declaration* not a binding *treaty*, and the second and third are related but discrete treaties states *sign* and *ratify*, or not, separately. The confusion arises from the initial intent to have both *covenants* in a single bill. However, that idea did not survive *Cold War* and other disagreements over content and definitions, leading to a split of the bill into disconnected covenants in 1952.

International Brigades: Foreign volunteers for the Republican cause in the *Spanish Civil War*. Many were *liberals* or *democratic socialists*, while some were *communists*; but all were jeered as communist dupes upon their return home. However, their choice and (lost) cause was then vindicated by the character of *WWII*, that even greater contest against *fascism*.

international city: See *free city*.

International Civil Aviation Organization (ICAO): A *specialized agency* of the *United Nations*, established in 1947 to oversee the regulation and safety of civil air transportation. It operates under terms of a 1944 (Chicago) convention and several supplementary conventions. It is headquartered in Montreal.

international comity: See *comity of nations*.

international commodity agreement (ICA): Unlike a *cartel*, such agreements include consumers as well as producers, all with a shared interest in stabilizing prices. ICAs use *buffer stocks* and export *quotas* to try to even out fluctuations within an agreed range for the price of a given *commodity*. See *Integrated Program for Commodities (IPC).*

International Court of Justice (ICJ): Also known as the World Court. The principal judicial organ of the *United Nations* system. It meets at The Hague. It is the direct successor to the *Permanent Court of International Justice*. As its founding statute is contained in the *Charter of the UN*, all members of the UN belong to the ICJ (non-UN members may also join). Its 15 judges are elected by the *Security Council* and

General Assembly, voting independently of each other. They are supposed to represent not merely a high level of legal competence, but also the world's major civilizations and legal systems. While the ICJ has procedures permitting *compulsory jurisdiction*, most cases are brought before it voluntarily when both parties to a *justiciable dispute* agree to seek a ruling. It may also issue *advisory opinions* upon the request of the General Assembly, individual states or any of the *specialized agencies*. Its *judgments* must reflect the tenets of *international law*. See *chambers of the Court; error; ex aequo; excess of authority; Optional Clause.*

international criminal law: A rare area where individuals are explicitly subject to *international law*. It falls into two categories: (1) Crimes of war: *aggression, war crimes* and *crimes against humanity*. (2) Crimes in peacetime: *apartheid, genocide, hijacking, hostage taking, piracy, slave trade, terrorism* and *torture*.

international customary law: Established, historical conduct that has come to be accepted by the great majority of *states* as legally binding, even without *codification* in a *treaty*. To establish a customary practice as a binding *rule*, besides following regular patterns of conduct states must accept a legal obligation to do so. See *consent; convictio juris; declaration; illegal act; incorporation; judicial legislation; jus cogens; law creating processes; necessity; remedy; transformation; UNCLOS III; Vienna Conventions.*

International Development Association (IDA): It was established in 1960 as an affiliate of the *IBRD*, to offer *soft loans* to *Third World* countries for *development* purposes. Membership is nearly universal among *states*. Its lending conditions tend to be on much easier terms than regular IBRD loans.

International Finance Corporation (IFC): It was created in 1956 as an affiliate of the *IBRD*. It is concerned with cofinancing private investment in member countries, especially in *LDCs* where private *capital* is not so easily procured. *State* membership is nearly universal. In 1994 it began securitizing its loans. In addition to its own lending, it has cofinanced loans with commercial banks, thereby providing long-term *debt* financing to LDCs. It also promotes equity *investment*.

International, First: An organization of *socialists, anarchists* and other revolutionaries, founded by *Karl Marx* in 1864. It failed to reconcile personal and doctrinal differences between Marx and anarchist *Mikhail Bakunin*, and collapsed amidst discord in 1876.

International, Fourth: See *Fourth International*.

International Fund for Agricultural Development (IFAD): A *specialized agency* of the UN, operating under *ECOSOC*. This agency was an initiative growing out of the World Food Conference in Rome (1974), and the terrible *famine* in the *Sahel*. Besides traditional Western *donor countries, OPEC* members have made substantial contributions to the Fund.

International Governmental Organization (IGO): Any international body or agency set up by the *states*, controlled by its member states, and dealing primarily with their common interests. See *international organization*. Cf. *nongovernmental organization*.

internationalism: Belief systems or ideas that look to common interests beyond the *nation* or *state*. (1) Liberal: Principles of *international law* and *international organization*, renunciation of *force* as an instrument of national policy, *human rights* and faith in the existence of fundamental, shared interests across all humanity. (2) Communist: Belief in the universal interests of the *proletariat*, as against the *world capitalist system*. Cf. *fascism; isolationism; nationalism*.

internationalize: To place under international, rather than *sovereign*, authority. For example, *Antarctica*; some cities; and several key waterways, such as the *Dardanelles, Bosphorus*, the Scheldt and the Rhine.

International Labor Organization (ILO): A *specialized agency* that preexisted but was brought under the *League of Nations* at the *Paris Peace Conference* and later brought into the *UN system*. It has a unique tripartite representation, with workers' and employers' groups sitting alongside state representatives. It is charged with monitoring *labor* conditions, standard setting, and research and technical cooperation. It has developed an elaborate Labor Code that is widely *ratified*, if not yet actually respected by *states*. It won the *Nobel Prize* for Peace in 1969.

international (public) law: The customs, *norms*, principles, *rules* and other legal relations among states and any other *international personality* that establish binding obligations. International persons are the main, some say the only, *subjects of international law*. Usually, individuals and non-state entities (ships, corporations, etc.) are its *objects*. However, of late it has become more concerned with individuals as subjects, as in the area of *human rights*. It exists in a separate realm from *municipal law*, though with some overlap. Customarily, the following are listed as its fundamental principles: *consent, freedom of the seas, good faith, recognition, responsibility, self-defense* and *sovereignty*. It lacks centralized enforcement, yet is respected by

most states on most issues, most of the time. Its sources are: *treaties, international customary law*, the writings of accepted jurists, binding *resolutions* of the *Security Council* and the *judgments* of international courts and *arbitration* bodies. Two major subdivisions are: (1) *Law of the sea:* see *baseline; blockade; belligerent rights; cabotage; canal zones; cannon shot rule; capture; combat area; continental shelf; contraband; EEZ; embargo; equity; flag of convenience; flotsam and jetsam; high seas; hot pursuit; innocent passage; internationalize; international waterway; neutral rights; piracy; privateer; prize; Seabed Treaty; slave trade; territorial sea; three-mile limit; twelve-mile limit; UNCLOS I, II, and III*. (2) *Laws of war:* see *aggression; angary; armistice; belligerent rights; blockade; booty; capture; Chemical Weapons Convention; civilian; combatant; crimes against peace; declaration of war; Geneva Protocol; Geneva Conventions; genocide; Genocide Convention; Hague Conventions; incursion; intrusion; invasion; jus ad bellum; jus in bello; just war theory; Kellogg-Briand Pact; letters of marque; levée en masse; neutral rights; nuclear weapons free zones; Nuremberg trials; occupation; Declaration of Paris (1856); peace; piracy; POWs; privateer; prize; recognition; requisition; retaliation; rules of engagement; rule of 1756; state of war; status mixtus; visit and search; war crimes; war crimes trials; war zone*. See also *International Court of Justice; international criminal law; international legislation; Optional Clause; representation; Soviet legal thought; Treaty of Paris (1856); validity; world community*.

International Law Commission: An advisory body set up in 1947 to provide legal advice, comment on draft *conventions* and make occasional recommendations to the *UNGA*, whose creature it is.

international legislation: An alternative term for *treaty* law. This is somewhat misleading, as such law binds only those *states* party to a given *treaty*.

International Maritime Organization (IMO): A *specialized agency* of the UN, approved in 1948 and coming into existence in 1958. It is concerned with safe navigation, and now also with maritime pollution, *oil spills* and environmental issues.

International Military Tribunals: See *war crimes*.

International Monetary Fund (IMF): An *international public corporation* founded at the *Bretton Woods* conference. It is a global lending agency associated with, but not under the authority of, the *UN* (it is one of the *specialized agencies*). Its immediate purpose was to aid recovery of the industrial nations from the

Great Depression and *WWII*, by assisting with *balance of payments* problems. It is dedicated to promoting *market economics, free trade* and high rates of *growth*. From the 1960s on, *Third World* states pressured the IMF to become more concerned with their *development*. In 1963 the IMF introduced a *compensatory financing* facility that was expanded and liberalized in 1976. Its involvement with weaker economies broadened with the onset of the *debt crisis* and the realization of *OECD vulnerability* that crisis brought home. Yet, it remains primarily an instrument of economic management by and for the *OECD* nations. The IMF uses *weighted voting*, and lends based on acceptance of its management and free market principles. See *First Tranche; SDRs; stabilization program.*

international minimum standard: The minimum conduct required toward nationals of a foreign power, established in a *bilateral* treaty or by *international customary law.*

international morality: *Norms* of conduct that states accept as ethically, but not necessarily legally, binding. There has been a progressive *codification* of these norms during the 20th century. See *aggression; ethics; genocide; human rights; international society; just war theory; self-determination.*

International Nongovernmental Organization (INGO): A *nongovernmental organization* with ties to several nations, such as *Amnesty International; COMINTERN; Red Cross; World Council of Churches.*

international order: (1) A specific distribution and *balance of power*, as in the phrase "the *postwar* international order." (2) A theoretical construct concerned with the large-scale institutions supporting the *structure* of the *international system*. (3) In *international law*, the doctrine that certain principles are so fundamental no one state can abrogate them. See *jus cogens; international public policy.*

international organization (IO): (1) The way *economics* and *politics* are organized at the international level, especially the evolution of means and agencies of *world governance*, whether formal or informal. (2) Associations that are set up by states, varying from sub-regional and regional bodies to nearly universal agencies enjoying the status of *international personality*. Among others, see *APEC; ASEAN; CIS; EU; IBRD; ICJ; IMF; League of Nations; NATO; OAU; OAS; OECD; regional banks; specialized agencies; SPC; SPF; UN.* Cf. *functionalism; integration.*

international personality: All entities that enjoy rights and have duties under *international law*, especially the *states* but including in a partial sense certain *specialized agencies* and *international organizations*. Traditionally, these rights are said to be: *equality, existence, independence, intercourse, self-defense* and *sovereignty*. In 1974 the UNGA passed a non-binding *resolution* enumerating putative economic rights and duties of states. However, beyond the *Third World* this is seldom cited and does not enjoy legal acceptance. Some collective associations such as the *EEC* have limited personality, in that they may make binding arrangements with states, and dispatch and receive diplomatic representatives.

international political economy (IPE): See *political economy.*

international politics: An academic focus on specifically political facets of *world affairs*. It is a field greatly eclectic in its approaches, interests and conclusions. See *international relations; world politics.*

international public corporations: Organizations like the *World Bank* or *IMF*. They do not enjoy a status of *international personality*, and while they are immune from suit or judicial processes, their officials do not enjoy the full privileges of *diplomatic immunity.*

international public policy: In *international law*, the doctrine that certain *rules* are so basic to orderly relations among *nations* they override *treaties* with which they cannot be reconciled. Cf. *international order.*

international relations: The whole complex of cultural, economic, legal, military, political and social relations of all *states*, as well as their component populations and entities. Some undergraduate major, huh?

International, Second: See *Second International.*

international security: Issues of *multilateral* security concern, rather than security matters and issues that pertain to a single nation. For instance, *aggression; alliances; balance of power; collective security; intervention; nonproliferation; peace enforcement; peacekeeping; spheres of influence.* Cf. *national security.*

international society: (1) The *states*, and all the institutions, laws, mechanisms and *norms* they have developed to regulate their interactions. (2) The inescapable political environment within which law, moral principles and a rudimentary social order are developed by, influence and temper the conflict and conduct of states. Cf. *anarchical society; world community; world governance; world public opinion.*

international system: World affairs viewed as a system; that is, as a complex of regular patterns, relations and interactions among *states* and all other significant international political, economic or social actors. Any *abstraction* about *world politics* that attempts to develop an overall or general theory must end by describing the international system. Such descriptions usually center on the states (as in *realism*), but they may focus on class (as in *dependency theory*), markets (as in *interdependence* theory), or another central construct. Cf. *endogenous; exogenous; systems analysis.*

International Telecommunications Union (ITU): A *specialized agency* of the UN, set up in 1932 as successor to the *International Telegraph Union*. As one of the most useful *functional agencies*, it enjoys near universal state membership. See *radio*.

International Telegraph Union (ITU): A *public international union* set up in 1865 in response to new communications technologies of the 19th century; succeeded by the *International Telecommunications Union*.

International, Third: See *COMINTERN*.

International Trade Organization (ITO): The *states* represented at *Bretton Woods* succeeded in setting up a new *postwar* monetary order. It was expected they would go on to establish a new *international organization* to regulate *trade*, but this they did not do. The U.S. and U.K. dominated negotiations, but not even the U.S. in its heyday could make *free trade* prevail over the disparate interests and *protectionism* of most states (and its own Congress). The British clung to the *imperial tariff*, while other states worried about their *balance of payments* or uncompetitive industries. Still, a charter for the proposed ITO was achieved by 1947. Then the U.S. Congress refused consent to the treaty: the ITO was stillborn. The focus of trade negotiations thereafter shifted to the *GATT*. In the *Uruguay Round* negotiations began to reform GATT into a World Trade Organization (WTO), in the spirit of the ITO.

international waterway: A river or *strait* that has been placed under *multilateral* authority (*internationalized*) by *treaty*: the *Panama Canal* (and formerly, the *Suez Canal*); the *Bosphorus* and *Dardanelles*; and natural passages through the *high seas*, such as the *Northwest Passage* or various straits. Many are governed by legal *regimes* separate from *UNCLOS I, II* or *III*.

internment: When the *citizens* of *belligerent* states are trapped by events or otherwise travel to *neutral* countries, they may be legally confined for the duration of the *war*. The purpose of internment is to maintain strict *neutrality* by avoiding suspicion that trade in *contraband* or information, or any other *unfriendly act* is occurring. Also called "administrative detention."

INTERPOL (International Criminal Police Organization): Set up in 1923, it coordinates police information concerning criminal, not political activity. Most *states* are members, though the degree of cooperation varies.

interposition forces: Third-party forces interposed between hostile parties. Archaic; see *peacekeeping*.

inter se: Relations or *treaties* among members of a given community, such as the *EU* or *ASEAN*, as opposed to relations with non-members.

intervening variable: One that modifies the effects of the *independent variable* on the *dependent variable;* or in plain English, a secondary *cause*. See *causation*.

intervention: (1) Technical: participation in a *dispute* before an international court by a third party that it is affected by the dispute. (2) Lawful: entering a conflict in accordance with rights granted by prior *treaty*, including military intervention by invitation or to protect specific interests or enforce terms of said treaty; or by way of *remedy*, compelling another state to respect *customary international law*; or to protect one's nationals in another state, after *exhaustion of local remedies*. (3) Unlawful: dictatorial interference in the *internal affairs* of another state (not simple interference). (4) Armed: it may be lawful (by invitation) or unlawful (unilateral). (5) Collective (a.k.a. "universal sanction"): when a group of states assert a higher international interest as justification for direct intervention in a local or regional affair; this may be lawful or unlawful. (6) In *economics*: any buy or sell action taken by a *central bank* to influence *exchange rates*. See also *abatement; Bosnia; Brezhnev Doctrine; collective security; Concert of Europe; Congo crisis; diplomatic intervention; Drago Doctrine; Good Neighbor policy; human rights; Hungarian Uprising; Korean Conflict; Monroe Doctrine; near abroad; neo-colonialism; Nixon Doctrine; security zone; Somalia, UN intervention; Spanish Civil War; sphere of influence; Third Indo/Pakistani War; Truman Doctrine;* and related crises and wars. Cf. *noninterference; nonintervention*.

interwar years: In Asia, 1919-37 for China and Japan, 1919-41 for the rest; in Europe, 1919-39; for the U.S., 1919-41.

***Intifada* (1988-):** The term, meaning "shivering" or "shaking," was first used by Arabs fighting Jewish settlement in *Palestine* in the 1920s and 1930s. Today it refers to the uprising against Israeli control of the *occupied territories* that began spontaneously among the young in *Gaza* and the *West Bank* in 1988. This rising, comprised at first mainly of jeers and stone throwing, was quickly organized in secret by a range of radical Palestinians, including *Hamas,* who viewed the *Palestine Liberation Organization* as too cautious and conservative. As stones were exchanged for knives and a few guns, Israel responded with deliberate, retaliatory violence: many hundreds of Palestinians have been killed by the Israeli Army, including scores of children; thousands more have been seriously injured. In turn, the Intifada spread into Israel proper, with killings of and by Jewish citizens. Intifada leaders also targeted Palestinians, killing those identified, correctly or not, as "*collaborators*" with Israel. The Intifada made the occupied territories ungovernable by Israel. It thus succeeded in its less radical ambitions, by finally convincing most Israelis to trade *land for peace.* However, its more radical leaders still promoted violence after the 1993 peace agreement in order to undermine the *peace* process. Note: Under *levée en masse,* Intifada fighters did not enjoy rights bestowed by the status of *belligerent.* Although Israel was bound by laws on *human rights* and by its own domestic code, it was not obliged to apply the special protections of the *Hague* or *Geneva Conventions.*

intra virus: "Within the *jurisdiction*" (of a court).

intrawar deterrence: Trying to prevent *escalation* when *hostilities* are already underway by making threats of even higher escalation; that is, by threatening to use even more destructive weapons against more valuable targets.

intrusion: Unauthorized penetration of national *airspace* by foreign aircraft. The affected country has the legal right to impound the plane if it lands, intercept and force it to fly out again, or even shoot it down, though that can have enormous political costs, especially if it is a *civilian* craft. See *U-2 incident.*

invasion: Crossing into another state's *territory* with one's armed forces, for the purpose of *conquest* or *counterattack.* Cf. *incursion.*

investment: The inflow of *capital* to fund productive activity in return for a share in any *profits.* This is distinct from financial transactions relating to the *balance of payments.* See also *foreign direct investment; patient capital; venture capital.*

inviolability of territory: Under *international law,* states claim this from each other in times of *peace.* It

means permission is required for any use or transit of another state's *territory.* Cf. *servitude.*

invisible trade: Trade in intangible *services;* not material *goods.*

Iran: Location: Middle East/Central Asia. Major associations: *Islamic Conference, ECO, OPEC, UN.* Population: 56 million. Military: exhausted by the Iran/Iraq War, but rearming. (1) Ancient Persia: The Persians settled in this area about 2000 B.C., arriving from India (they were *Aryan,* not *Arab*). They soon conquered the earlier Babylonian Empire, establishing their own. They were defeated by the Greeks under Alexander of Macedon (the Great) in 333 B.C., but regained their *independence* with the collapse of the Greek Empire. Two great Persian *dynasties* followed: the Parthians for nearly 500 years, and then the Sassanians in 226 A.D. In the 8th century, Zoroastrian Persia was forcibly converted to *Islam* by Arab conquerors. This was a key period in the life of the Persian nation and of Islam, for within a generation of the Prophet Muhammad's death Islam divided into *sunni* and *shi'ite* traditions, with the Persians cleaving to the minority shi'ite branch. This split has deepened over the centuries, adding to the ethnic differences that divide modern Iran from the predominantly sunni and Arab nations to the west. In the 9th century the underlying Persian culture was reasserted, though now in Muslim form. From the 12th century the Mongols ruled Persia, though without much influencing its culture or people (this was the era of the "Golden Horde"). They melded with Turkish overlords until 1502, when a Persian dynasty was reasserted. Persia managed to avoid being absorbed into the *Ottoman Empire,* even at its height (another distinction from the Arab lands). During the 19th century, with the Ottomans in fast decline across the region, the British and Russians vied for influence in Persia and Central Asia, with the British separating the *vassal state* of Afghanistan from Persia in 1857.

(2) Modern Iran: Around the turn of the 20th century *oil* exploration began in Persia, adding to the country's *strategic* value. The *Anglo/Russian Entente* (1907) divided it north/south into Russian and British *spheres of influence.* But after the *Bolshevik Revolution,* the British moved into all of Persia, even intervening in the *Russian Civil War* from Iranian bases. In 1925 Britain helped *Reza Pahlavi* make himself Shah. He began to *secularize* and *modernize* the country, changing its name from Persia to Iran in 1935. But in *WWII* the new Shah backed the *Axis* powers, thinking they would win, and the British and Soviets jointly deposed him in favor of his son, *Muhammad Reza Pahlavi.* After the war, the Soviets applied pressure on

northern Iran, but the British and Americans propped up the young Shah and resisted Russian *encroachment*. British and Soviet troops both withdrew in 1946. The Shah faced rising domestic opposition, especially to his links with Britain, the U.S. and Western oil companies, which dominated Iran's economy. In 1951 he reluctantly appointed *Mossadegh* as PM, but sacked him in 1953, with the backing of British and American *intelligence services*. The Shah then propelled Iran down a path toward full modernization, using dictatorial powers to force major economic and social changes (including the legal *emancipation* of women, in 1963) on a deeply conservative and increasingly anti-Western nation. He was pleased to have Iran serve as the West's "policeman" in the Middle East, acquiring a vast arsenal of modern weaponry. His *regime* grew ever more unpopular; he ruled increasingly through the threat of military force and the reality of police and *secret police* (SAVAC) persecution. In 1975 Iran was declared a secular state. Yet a combination of middle class frustration at the lack of political representation, and surging peasant unrest stoked by *fundamentalist* clerics, led to open dissent and public demonstrations in 1977-78. In 1979 elements of the army joined the opposition, and the Shah fled.

(3) Islamic Republic of Iran (Jomhori-e-Islami-e-gin-Irân): *Ayatollah Khomeini* returned from an enforced *exile* to lead the clerical faction in the *Iranian Revolution*, eventually assuming dictatorial powers (despite the fiction of ruling through an Islamic parliament, the *Majlis*). Iran took a radical, anti-Western, and specifically anti-American turn (the U.S. was, and still is, known as "the Great Satan") symbolized by the *hostage crisis*. But Iran's new fundamentalism and its old geopolitical situation meant that it could not move too close to the *Soviet bloc* either. Lastly, Iran repelled much of the sunni *Islamic world* through its radical shi'ism, particularly in the Gulf region; and it could not penetrate the Arab world owing to the Persian ethnicity of its people. The inevitable outcome was increasing isolation from much of the *world community*. Moreover, it was plunged into a bitter war with Iraq, when attacked by *Saddam Hussein*. The *Iran/Iraq War* raged for eight years, killed nearly 750,000 Iranians, and maimed many more in body or mind. Iran was further distanced from the *Gulf States* by their support for Iraq, and by the misbehavior of its pilgrims during the *haj* to *Mecca*. It introduced draconian domestic legislation, including the rule of *sharia* law, and gained an even worse *human rights* reputation than the Shah's. It supported fundamentalist groups throughout the Arab and Islamic worlds, and it lent support to a variety of *terrorist* groups and actions. Yet its reach extended little beyond Lebanon and Yemen. In 1986 the *Reagan* administration sold it *arms*, in the vain

hope this would end the hostage crisis (see *Iran/Contra*). With the death of Khomeini in 1989 Iran slowly edged toward reacceptance by the West, under the leadership of *Rafsanjani*. However, into the mid-1990s it remained a designated "terrorist state," refused to lift its call for the murder of *Salman Rushdie*, and in a display of diplomatic schizophrenia, habitually used derogatory rhetoric about states and leaders it was courting on other issues. During the *Gulf War* it profited by condemning the UN action against Iraq while quietly gloating over the destruction of the armed forces of its hated enemy, Saddam. It also kept the many Iraqi aircraft that flew into Iran to escape the war. It was less pleased with the arrival of refugee *Kurds*, fleeing Saddam's *depredations* in the wake of his *defeat*. With the collapse of another old enemy, the Soviet Union, Iran positioned itself to compete with Turkey for leadership of the emergent Central Asian republics and Afghanistan. In short, in the 1990s it moved to reestablish its historic sphere of influence above its northern border. Iran remains hostile to Saudia Arabia and the Gulf States. In 1993 it purchased three Kirov-class *submarines* from Russia, as well as longrange bombers, which would permit it to project force over the Gulf. The U.S. announced it would base a countering submarine force in the region. There are persistent rumors that Iran is seeking to build/purchase *nuclear weapons*.

Iran/Contra: In November 1986, senior members of the *Reagan* administration secretly traveled to Iran, bearing an assortment of odd gifts and in search of "moderates" within the Iranian government. They offered to sell Iran a limited amount of specialized weaponry, needed in its *war* with Iraq (toward which the administration was then *tilted*). In exchange, assistance was requested in obtaining the release of U.S. *hostages* in Lebanon, over whose captors it was thought Tehran had *influence*. This part of the scheme was definitely stupid--because it ran contrary to administration policy on the *Iran/Iraq War*--but it was not illegal. However, the proceeds of the arms sales were then secretly funneled to the *Contras* in Nicaragua, which almost certainly was illegal. When the story broke it became the major scandal of the Reagan presidency, implicating several high foreign policy officials (including VP *George Bush* but excepting Secretary of State George Schultz), and causing one to attempt suicide. Years of hearings and special investigations led to many resignations and a few, minor convictions.

Iranian Revolution: Shah *Muhammad Reza Pahlavi* grew unpopular for his use of *secret police* (SAVAK), *torture*, and political repression, and for his insistence that Iran develop as a *secular*, even *westernized*, nation. The lack of political representation helped tip the middle class and the students against the Shah. But the real fuel that fed the opposition was in the countryside: the *revolution* represented in large part a rural reaction against the secular and developmental excess of the cities, and general peasant frustration that was played on by those who pointed to Western *oil* companies and interests as the putative source of rural poverty. This grassroots unrest, fed upon by *fundamentalist* clerics, led to massive public demonstrations in 1977-78. Elements of the army joined the opposition, and the Shah fled on January 16, 1979. A rapid consolidation of clerical power, under the iron rule of *Ayatollah Khomeini*, drove *Kurds* and Iran's *communists* (the Tudeh Party) into *rebellion* in the north of the country. The new regime responded with mass executions. Introduction of religious police and of the *sharia*, which led to public flogging and even execution for relatively minor offenses, alienated the secular middle classes. Meanwhile, student radicals and Revolutionary Guards, in a hysteria of anti-Western and anti-American rage, seized the U.S. Embassy and began the *hostage crisis*. The revolution reached a fevered pitch after Iraq attacked in September 1980, beginning the long and bloody *Iran/Iraq War*. After that, any dissent could be labeled both un-Islamic and unpatriotic. In June 1981, Khomeini ordered the relative moderate president, Abol Hassan Bani Sadr, arrested; but he escaped to France. His successor was killed, with most of the *cabinet*, in a gigantic bomb explosion on August 30th. Each of these episodes fed a bloody spiral of persecution, recrimination, reprisal and murder. The revolution at first enthused Iran's young to fight a *jihad* against Iraq, and against the "Great Satan" (America), and the minor satan, Israel. Yet, crusading for *Islam* in time lost its appeal for all but the most *fanatic*. As the enormous body count from the war mounted and the maimed and wounded returned in their tens of thousands to pious towns and villages, the war became a burden to avoid, not a collective triumph to celebrate. The national energy and treasure that might have gone into land reform and other schemes was consumed by the war effort, and by 1988 Iranians had enough. Khomeini was forced to accept a *stalemate* that left the hated enemy, *Saddam Hussein*, still in power in Iraq. With the death of Khomeini in 1989 there was a last, great outpouring of nationalist and religious hysteria--replete with mass, self-flagellations. Since then Iran has acted increasingly like a "normal" nation, looking to its national interests as defined by economics, geography and security, and (almost) leaving Allah to his own devices.

Iran/Iraq War (1980-88): Also widely known as the Gulf War, prior to the 1991-92 *Gulf War.* When the *Iranian Revolution* brought chaos to Iran, and confrontation with its old patron the United States, *Saddam Hussein* pounced. He attacked in a bid to quickly secure control of three islands in the *Strait of Hormuz*, and the *Shatt-al-Arab* waterway. Iraq was initially successful, capturing *territory* and a few cities, notably Abadan. Saddam then offered a *cease-fire*, but this was rejected by *Ayatollah Khomeini*, who called for *jihad* and the destruction of Saddam's *regime*. In May 1982, an Iranian *counterattack* pushed Iraq back from some of its earlier gains, but at the cost of many lives. Iran used massed and poorly trained *infantry* to assault well-*entrenched* Iraqi positions (the *tactical* success of his defenses would later delude Saddam into thinking he could repeat the effort against modern Western armies during the Gulf War, inflicting massive casualties at which the West might balk). The major powers imposed an arms *embargo* on both sides, but France and China continued to make significant sales, and the U.S. secretly arranged the minor arms transfer of *Iran/Contra*. A rough *stalemate* and consequent war of *attrition* developed. That led to indiscriminate attacks on the cities, including use of missiles by both sides, and *chemical weapons* and poison gas by Iraq. Before 1987, however, there was a tacit agreement not to attack oil shipments on the *Persian Gulf.* But as Iran grew more desperate it started to attack not just Iraqi but also Kuwaiti and other shipping, with *mines* and small assault craft. The world's major naval powers, the U.S., the Soviet Union, France, Britain and others, joined to enforce the *neutrality* of *international waterways* in the Gulf, leading to exchanges with Iranian boats and two tragic incidents: the USS Stark was hit by an Iraqi missile (a French-made Exocet) in May 1987, losing 47 crew; that contributed to a worse disaster, where an American ship shot down a Iranian passenger airliner, killing the passangers, after mistaking it for an attacking bomber (a Pan Am airliner was subsequently blown up over Lockerbie Scotland, in apparent retaliation). In 1988, with Iranian *national morale* collapsing and Iraq unable to make any further gains, both sides agreed to *mediation* by *Pérez de Cuéllar*. The cease-fire took hold on August 20th. In all some one million died, with about 3/4 of all casualties Iranian.

Iraq: Location: *Middle East*. Major associations: *Arab League, OPEC, UN*. Population: 19 million. Military: still sizeable, still seeking *weapons of mass destruction*, and capable of internal repression but no longer a major threat to Iraq's neighbors. Iraq was once the seat of the great pre-Islamic, Mesopotamian civilization of Sumeria, one of the oldest on record (c.3000 B.C.). The area was successively overrun by ancient Persians and Greeks, then Arabs who brought with them a new religion, *Islam*. During the first centuries of the Islamic era Baghdad was home to the *caliphs*, to great universities (madrasa), and a florescence of ancient science and learning. After a prolonged decline under the Mongols it became a province of the *Ottoman Empire*, known as Mesopotamia from 1638-1918. It was part of the secret *Sykes-Picot Agreement*, leading in 1920 to Iraq becoming a British *mandate*. In 1930 it gained *independence* as an Arab kingdom under the *Hashemite*, Faisal I. Modern Iraq is a polyglot country, with a large *Kurd* minority in the north (in rebellion from 1922-32, 1961-79, 1991-), and a sizeable "marsh Arab," *shi'ite* minority in the south. *Oil* was discovered in 1927. In 1941 a pro-Nazi *coup* was foiled by British *intervention*. Iraq then entered the war against the *Axis* in 1943. The British army stayed in place until 1947. *Faisal II* tried to associate Iraq with Jordan, but was killed in a coup, led by *Kassem*, that established Iraq as a *republic* in 1958. In 1963 another coup killed Kassem and instituted *Ba'ath Party* rule. A third coup, in July 1968, established a brutal military dictatorship. *Saddam Hussein* emerged from the background to assume the presidency in 1979. In 1980 he attacked Iran, beginning the *Iran/Iraq War*. At home he established a crude *cult of personality*, repressed all dissent, conducted *genocide* against the Kurds, hanged a shi'ite *ayatollah* and members of his family, and generally indulged in *torture* and *summary execution* to a degree that revealed a sadistic passion for both. On June 7, 1981, Israel bombed a nuclear reactor outside Baghdad, setting back by a decade the Iraqi *nuclear weapons* program. *Peace* with Iran came in 1988, but not *demilitarization*: by 1990 Iraq could put in the field an army numbering close to one million troops, though its quality was uncertain. On August 2, 1990, it invaded Kuwait, later annexing it as "Province 19." That naked *aggression* provoked the *Gulf War*, in which Iraq's military was reduced from a threat to its neighbors to a threat to its citizens. The UN *embargoed* Iraq, pending full compliance with the *cease-fire* resolutions passed by the *Security Council*, especially those pledging to eliminate all *weapons of mass destruction*. The *sanctions* hurt severely, and made it difficult to complete civilian *reconstruction* even while they had the desired effect of hamstringing the military. Iraq still placed obstacles in the way of UN inspection teams, leading several times to U.S. and other countries conducting punishment raids. In June 1993, the U.S. unilaterally fired 23 *cruise missiles* at Iraq's *intelligence* headquarters in *retaliation* for what it said was an Iraqi plot to assassinate former President *George Bush*. In December 1993, Iraq finally agreed to long-term UN monitoring of its weapons programs, bringing it into technical compliance with the *cease-fire* resolutions.

Ireland: A large island off the west coast of Europe, comprising the *Republic of Ireland (Eire)* and *Ulster*.

Ireland, Republic of (Eire): Location: W. Europe. Major associations: *CSCE, EU, OECD, UN*. Population: 3.6 million. Military: minor. After centuries of conflict, colonial plantation, forced resettlement, *rebellion* and *war*, Ireland was joined with Britain by the *Act of Union* of 1800 (effective 1801). It suffered through a terrible *famine* in the 1840s (the "Great Hunger"), losing half its total population of eight million to starvation or *emigration*. That was a decimation from which it has never recovered, and which deepened demands for *Home Rule* in later decades. Anti-British sentiment was also carried overseas by the Irish *diaspora*, notably to America. It was automatically embroiled in *WWI*, as part of Britain. After the unsuccessful *Easter Rising* of 1916, and then the successful *Irish War of Independence*, the lower 26 counties of the island were given *Dominion* status in 1921, while six counties stayed with Britain as *Ulster*. That gave rise to the *Irish Civil War*. In 1937 a new constitution prepared by *Eamon de Valera* proclaimed Irish *sovereignty* over the whole island (including Ulster) and renamed the country Eire. Ireland remained *neutral* in *WWII*, fending off British plans to take control of its southern ports for use in the *Battle of the Atlantic*. Its neutrality was supported by Irish *emigré* opinion, which greatly influenced U.S. policy. In December 1948, Eire declared itself a *republic* and left the *Commonwealth* (both actions were accepted by Britain in 1949). Its economy, however, remained tied to Britain's. Recognizing this, it signed a *free trade* agreement with Britain in 1965. It then followed Britain into the *EC* in 1973, after two earlier applications were withdrawn when *de Gaulle* vetoed British entry. It has mostly stayed clear of the sectarian fighting that broke out in Ulster after 1969, though its *territory* is used as a sanctuary by the *Irish Republican Army*. In 1986 it signed the "Hillsborough Agreement" with Britain, giving it a voice in Ulster's affairs. In 1993 it signed a "Framework Agreement" concerning Ulster's future. It must now reconsider its *neutrality* as the EU inches toward a common defense and foreign policy. Irish troops have several times served as UN *peacekeepers*. See also *Catholic emancipation; Fenians; Gladstone; Irish Question; United Irishmen*.

Irgun (*Zvai Leumi*): Founded by militant *zionists* in 1937, this *paramilitary* organization used terror tactics against the British and the Arabs in *Palestine*. It was led by *Menachem Begin* after 1941. One of its most effective actions was to flog captured British officers, causing London to drop the practice of flogging Arabs and Jews. Just before the *First Arab/Israeli War* began, it participated in a massacre of Arabs at the village of Deir Yassin. It later merged with the Israeli Defense Forces.

Irian Jaya: Formerly West Irian, and a Dutch *colony*. Indonesia placed severe economic pressure on Dutch property after 1958, when Holland refused to resume negotiations over transfer of the *territory* to Indonesia. After U.S. *mediation*, it was ceded to Indonesia by the Netherlands in 1963.

Irish Civil War (1921-22): Following the proclamation of the *Irish Free State* a diehard faction of the *Irish Republican Army (IRA),* led by *Eamon de Valera*, refused to accept the treaty with Britain. That agreement entailed *partition* of six of *Ulster's* nine counties to create a gerrymandered Protestant majority, but also gave *Home Rule* to the southern 26, mostly Catholic counties. The youthful Michael Collins (1890-1922), PM of the Free State, had represented Ireland at the *peace talks* that led to *independence*. He was assassinated by his old comrades-in-arms, but the "Free Staters" prevailed, as public revulsion for the violence increased and the IRA lost its stomach for the fight.

Irish Free State (1921-36): Established by the *treaty* that ended the *Irish War of Independence,* this state comprised the *autonomous* southern 26 counties. However, part of the *IRA* rebelled against the settlement, provoking the *Irish Civil War.* That faction lost the war but later turned to parliamentary tactics, winning a majority in 1932. In 1936 they changed the name of the Irish Free State to Eire. The modern *republic* was declared in April 1949.

Irish Question: (1) Before 1829: *Catholic Emancipation,* or whether Irish Catholics should be granted civil and political rights roughly equal to those enjoyed by Anglicans in Britain, including representation in Parliament; (2) 1829-1916: demands for *Home Rule* for *Ireland*; (3) 1916-21: demands for *independence*; (4) since 1922: the status of *Ulster* within the *United Kingdom*, and its relationship to Ireland (Republic of).

Irish Republican Army (IRA): It grew out of the Irish Republican Brotherhood (IRB), a nationalist *paramilitary* organized before *WWI* as tensions over *Home Rule* built. The IRB fought in the *Easter Rising.* In 1919 it was reorganized into the IRA by Michael Collins, and fought Britain in the *Irish War of Independence.* Even then, political assassination and killings of informers and policemen were used to supplement *guerrilla* attacks on the British military. The IRA split over the settlement that created the *Irish Free State.* Over the next decades the unreconstructed, extreme *nationalist* and increasingly *marxist* element in the IRA threatened civil order in Britain and Ireland with bomb attacks. In 1968 a Catholic civil rights movement in *Ulster* was seized upon by the IRA, especially after *"Bloody Sunday,"* and it resumed *terrorist* attacks. In May 1972, the IRA split again. One faction (Officials) accepted an end to the bombing campaign, while another ("Provisionals" or "Provos") vowed to intensify it. The Provos have since pursued a crude, marxist/nationalist program and placed virtually no humane limits on their tactics. They accepted financing from Libya and developed ties with other terrorist groups. Another source of the IRA's funding has been Irish *emigré communities*, particularly those in the U.S. and Canada. In 1993 *Sinn Féin*, the IRA's political arm, joined secret *peace talks* with Britain.

Irish War of Independence (1918-21): A *guerrilla* campaign sparked in part by a British decision to execute the leaders of the *Easter Rising,* thus making them nationalist martyrs. Its main source was anger over the unfinished business of *Home Rule*, postponed since before *WWI.* The campaign escalated with ambushes and assassinations by the *Irish Republican Army*, and reprisals and murders by less-than-disciplined British forces such as the *Black 'n Tans.* It ended with a 1920 agreement to *partition* Ireland between *Ulster* and the *Irish Free State.* That gave rise to the *Irish Civil War.*

ironclads: The first 19th century *warships* to use armor plating (literally, were wooden ships clad in iron) to protect against incoming *ordnance.* The first was the CSS Merrimack, built by the *Confederacy* during the *American Civil War.* It savaged the wooden ships of the *Union* until it met its match in an inconclusive battle with the USS Monitor off the Virginia coast, in July 1862. The Union rapidly outbuilt the South, compiling an impressive ironclad fleet by war's end. Britain and other European naval powers looked on in astonishment at the overnight obsolescence of their fleets, then rapidly converted to iron ships.

iron curtain: The rigid secrecy and repression of the *Soviet bloc*, especially its comprehensive barriers to the free flow of people, *goods* and ideas. The term was made famous by *Winston Churchill* in a speech at Fulton, Missouri, in 1946, that had prior approval from *Truman.* Cf. *bamboo curtain; Berlin Wall.*

Iron Guard (*Garda de Fier*): A Rumanian *fascist,* peasant, and nationalist organization founded in 1927. It was a viciously *anti-Semitic.* It rose against the government in 1941. Quite to its surprise, its *insurrection* was crushed with the aid of German troops. That happened despite earlier Guardist massacres of thousands of Rumanian Jews, carried out for hate's sake, and in the expectation of ingratiation with the Nazis.

iron rice bowl: A guarantee of lifetime employment and economic *basic needs*--though not basic civil or political rights--for China's workers, made by *Mao* and the *Communist Party*. The term was also used about the Vietnamese communist system. The idea of an "iron rice bowl" of security, regardless of worker or industry productivity, began to break down in the 1980s with the *market economy* reforms introduced by *Deng Xiaoping*.

irredentism: From *Italia irredenta*. At first expressive of the demands of Italian nationalists, it now refers to the demand of any *ethnic group* for acquisition of *territory* claimed as part of its historic homeland, or populated by ethnic cousins.

Islam: "Surrender (to the will of God)." The faith of one billion Muslims, of whom 85% are *sunni* and 10% *shi'ite*. The most important holy sites for Muslims are *Mecca*, Medina and *Jerusalem*. Islam is closely related to *Judaism* and *Christianity* in its history and central beliefs: monotheism; the succession and revelatory role of prophets, with Muhammad (570-632 A.D.) the last and greatest; social justice; and for some, messianism. Its scripture is al Qur'an (the Koran). Islam derives its legal code (*sharia*) from the Koran and the Sunna, or accepted interpretations by its leading religious scholars of the life and practices of Muhammad. Islamic countries have not, with the exceptions of Turkey and briefly Iran, accepted the separation of religion and state that occurred in the *West* with the Protestant *Reformation*. New interpretation has not been permitted since the first two centuries following Muhammad's death. That produced a rigidity in social custom and public (including financial) institutions that handicaps Islamic countries in adjusting to secular forces of modernity, and competing with non-Islamic nations on a range of issues. Islam offers equality to all men under Allah (God), which made it a greatly attractive faith over the centuries to the socially disadvantaged in rigid, hierarchical cultures. It thus continues to make converts in Africa, India and elsewhere. But in more *fundamentalist* guises it offers a distinctly lesser place to women, in both family law and public life. That may put it into conflict with both international conceptions of *human rights* and the needs of economic efficiency. See *assassin; ayatollah; caliph; Druse; haj; imam; Ismaili; mahdi; mullah; Wahhabi*.

Islamic Conference: An association of over 40 nations with sizeable Muslim populations, mainly in North Africa, the Middle East and Central Asia. In 1993 it offered 17,000 peacekeeping troops for Bosnia, but this offer was deflected by the UN.

Islamic world: Nearly 50 countries where *Islam* is predominant, and others where it is a significant cultural and political force. It stretches from Africa to Central Asia, and as far afield as Indonesia and parts of the Philippines.

islamicize: To imbue with the values and traditions of *Islam*, particularly its emphasis on *sharia* law and pervasive intrusion of religious authority into private as well as public affairs.

island: In *international law*, a *territory* surrounded by water that due to size and availability of potable water is able to sustain human life. Offshore islands complicate the demarcation of *EEZs* by extending the *baseline* claims of *coastal states*. This is not true of *islets*.

islet: In *international law*, land surrounded by water that due to small size, non-arable soil or lack of potable water is unable to sustain human life. Offshore islets (known as rocks to those innocent of the law) do not affect the *baseline* or demarcation of an *EEZ*.

Ismaili: A sect of *shi'ite* Muslims who once controlled the *caliphate* and continue to emphasize the sufi (mystic) tradition. Subsects or offshoots historically included the *Druse* and *Assassins*. They are today concentrated in the Indian *subcontinent* and *Central Asia*, with smaller communities scattered across the Middle East and North and East Africa. See *imam*.

isolationism: A policy (or just advocacy) of minimal participation in military *alliances, noninterference* and *nonintervention* in the *internal affairs* or external *wars* of other *nations*, and avoidance of entangling *treaties* or security commitments such as those required by *collective security*. It is most famously identified with the United States from c.1793-1917, and 1919-41. Yet other nations, too, have adopted this stance. China, Japan and Russia have experienced periods of even more extreme isolationism than the American variety, though each grew out of a different cultural heritage and geopolitical situation. Small states such as Burma, Canada or Ireland, as well as much of Latin America, have had isolationist periods. Are there general traits? Yes. Isolationists tend to a parochial concentration on the culture of a single national community, they are often highly suspicious of *international law* and *international organizations*, often fail to recognize the wider interests of their nation, and may at the extreme suffer from *xenophobia*. See also *autarky; entangling* *alliance.* Cf. *internationalism; intervention; nationalism; splendid isolation.*

Israel: Location: *Middle East.* Major associations: *UN.* Population: 4.4 million. Military: the best in the *Middle East,* technologically and in war-fighting capability (an edge the U.S. is pledged to maintain), with approximately 120 (unacknowledged) *nuclear weapons.* After 1900 *zionist* immigration to *Palestine* grew. The *Balfour Declaration* spurred hope for a Jewish state, but also increased Arab resistance. *Guerrilla warfare* was waged by Jewish settlers against both British and Arabs in the 1930s and 1940s. The British abandoned their *mandate* and the *territory* was *partitioned* in accordance with UN *resolutions.* Israel was established on May 14, 1948. The Arab countries refused to extend *recognition,* and within hours fighting was underway in the *First Arab/Israeli War.* A *cease-fire* held after June 1949, but no peace settlement followed. Instead, more wars ensued: the *Second* (1956), *Third* (1967), and *Fourth Arab/Israeli Wars* (1973), as well as the *War of Attrition.* In the 1967 war Israel captured the *occupied territories* (see map). That led to a new type of confrontation, with the *PLO* and later still the fighters of the *Intifada.* Israel has enjoyed high levels of Western and especially American support, but simultaneously was fiercely, even ritualistically condemned by the *Soviet bloc* and *Third World* majorities in the *UNGA.* In 1982 it sent its army to *intervene* in the *Lebanese Civil War,* to chase the PLO from its bases in Lebanon. The image of Israeli *artillery* shelling Beirut, and a massacre of *civilians* at the Shabra and Shatilla *refugee camps* by Lebanese Christian *militia* allied to Israel, soured relations with traditional supporters in the West. By 1985 it had suffered its own, mini-*Vietnam War* at the hands of *shi'ite* militia, and pulled its troops back to a "security zone" along its northern border. The logjam remained unbroken in the 1980s, partly due to the *hard-line* character of Israel's government, and partly because the *Reagan* administration showed only occasional interest in resolution of the region's most persistent conflict.

Much changed with collapse of the Soviet Union, and then the *Gulf War* (which Israel stayed out of, despite being hit by unprovoked Scud *missile* attacks from Iraq). A new *balance of power* was established in the region; and the Soviet Union, traditional supplier of Israel's Arab opponents, was no longer playing the game of disruptive diplomacy. U.S. policy also changed: the *Bush* administration called in decades of chips, signaling through a withholding of $10 billion in resettlement money for Russian Jews that it wanted a settlement based on a trade of occupied *land for peace.* The result was a set of *multilateral* talks sponsored by Washington that for the first time included

all the major players in the Middle East (with the PLO formally excluded but acting behind the scenes of the Palestinian delegation, with Israel's knowledge). That set the stage for *back-channel* talks brokered by Norway that led to a breakthrough in September 1993: mutual recognition by Israel and the PLO. Domestically, Israel preserves the only democracy in the Middle East, albeit one that often overrode the rights of Arab subjects and the population of the occupied territories (as in discriminatory water rights rationing, or formally, its an aggressive settlements policy).

issue area: Any set of related issues that are usually viewed or dealt with collectively.

Italia irredenta: "Unredeemed Italy." Ethnically Italian areas mainly in Austria and *Yugoslavia* that nationalists wished to join to Italy. To wit: *Fiume,* Gradisca, Gorizia, Istria, South Tyrol, Trentino and *Trieste.* Cf. *irredentism; revanchism.*

Italian East Africa: A short-lived *union* of Italy's east African possessions, *Eritrea, Italian Somaliland* and the newly but only briefly conquered *Ethiopia,* from 1936-42 (subtracting *liberated* Ethiopia in 1941).

Italian Somaliland: An Italian *protectorate* between the world wars, it was the only *trusteeship territory* that was not a former *mandate.* Also unusual was that Italy, the former imperial power, became the *trustee power* (from 1950). In 1960 it joined *British Somaliland* to form Somalia.

Italo/Ethiopian War: See *Abyssinian War.*

Italo/Turkish War (1911-12): Under PM Giovanni Giolitti (1842-1928) Italy waged a successful *war* against the *Ottoman Empire,* gaining control of the *Dodecanese* and *Tripoli* (Libya). Italy would later face local *guerrilla* resistance in Tripoli, and conduct a brutal war of repression.

Italy: Location: Mediterranean. Major associations: *CSCE, EU, G-7, NATO, OECD, UN, WEU.* Population: 58 million. Military: NATO quality. After years of incremental union of smaller Italian states to Piedmont, *Cavour* climaxed the *risorgimento* by sending troops into the *Papal States* in 1860. He then linked with Garibaldi's forces approaching from the south, and proclaimed the Kingdom of Italy on March 17, 1861. Unification was completed with the addition of *Venice* in 1866 and Rome in 1870, the latter at cost of a 60-year quarrel with the popes. Italy is thus one of Europe's youngest countries, and its weak sense of national, as opposed to provincial, identity reflects that fact. It was allied with Austria and Germany in the *Triple Alliance,* but in 1914 declined to join them in offensive war. In 1915 it was bribed into the war on the Allied side with offers of gaining all *Italia irredenta.* Italy did badly on the battlefield, particularly at *Caporetto,* and was bitterly disappointed at its meager gains from the *Paris Peace Conference.* In 1922, following the *march on Rome,* the figurehead King *Victor Emmanuel III* made *Mussolini* prime minister. He instituted a *fascist* state that lasted until 1943. In 1929 the *Lateran Treaties* were signed with the *Vatican.* Outside the peninsula, Mussolini engaged in aggressive diplomacy. He lost to Greece over the *Corfu incident* but consolidated colonial holdings with a savage war in Libya, and expanded them in the *Abyssinian War.* That was a critical turning point, moving Italy out of the *Stresa Front* and into *alliance* with, and dependence on, Nazi Germany. At the *Munich Conference* Mussolini joined in the betrayal of Czechoslovakia to *Hitler.* Yet when war broke out in 1939 Italy remained *neutral,* for despite Mussolini's swagger, the Italian army was woefully underequipped for modern combat. As Hitler rolled up victories and brought France to its knees in 1940, Italy *declared war* on France and Britain to pick up easy spoils (in fact, the French badly bloodied its troops on the southern front). Italy subsequently attacked Greece and Yugoslavia, where yet again its armies were beaten back and had to be rescued by the Germans. Within two years Italian armies were defeated in East Africa (Eritrea, Ethiopia and Somalia), North Africa (Libya), Greece and Yugoslavia. In 1943 Anglo/American forces landed in Sicily. Mussolini was dismissed in a palace *coup* that had the support of his own son-in-law, *Ciano. Badoglio* made peace with the Allies and declared war on Germany on October 13th. But the Germans moved into northern Italy and set up Mussolini, a shadow of his former self, to head a *puppet regime.* Italy was then torn apart by what amounted to a *civil war* fought within the confines of *WWII.* With war's end, reconstitution of the fascist party was forbidden. The *communist party* emerged as the country's largest. This alarmed Britain and the U.S., which covertly *intervened* to ensure that the communists were excluded from government. Indeed, most of Italy's *postwar* political history was a game of successive coalitions each of which kept the communists from real power--but it was as much the politics of corruption as ideology. That was even more true after 1974, with the development of *eurocommunism* and Italian communists' acceptance of NATO. In 1949 Italy had joined NATO and helped found the several *European Communities.* It grew prosperous in spite of its farcical political system (50 governments in 45 years) and the heavy burden of the Mafia (in 1990 alone organized

crime murdered over 2,000 Italians). In the 1970s and 1980s Italy faced down the terrorist threat of the *Red Brigades.* In 1991 it joined the *coalition* that fought the *Gulf War.* That same year, 20,000 refugees arrived from Albania; while most were shipped back, Albanians continue to seek a better life in Italy. In 1993/94 the political system finally collapsed under the weight of a corruption scandal that exposed hundreds of politicians at the highest levels (including Guilo Andreotti, b.1919, a seven-time PM). This development threatened to exacerbate *secessionist* tensions in the north. Also, in 1993 Italy broke with the UN in Somalia (its former *colony*), objecting to the use of heavy force against uncooperative Somali *warlords.*

Ito, Hirobumi (1841-1909): Japanese statesman. A prime mover in the effort to *modernize* and *westernize* Japan. He was the founder of the modern Japanese navy that proved its mettle during the *Russo/Japanese War* (which he opposed). He was assassinated by a Korean nationalist while serving as governor of Japan's Korean *colony.*

Ivan III (1440-1505): "The Great." He succeeded in throwing off the "yoke of the *Tartars"* from Muscovy and began the policy of expansion that would ultimately result in creation of the vast *Russian Empire.*

Ivan IV (1530-84): "The Terrible." He was the first to assert the title *Tsar.* He conquered the *Tartar* Khanates of Astrakhan and Kazan, beat back Polish and Lithuanian assaults (by the Livonian Order), and began a creeping *annexation* of *Siberia.* Increasingly paranoid, he launched a reign of brutal terror against the *boyars* and those cities he suspected of harboring rebellious intent. In a fit of mad rage he killed his own son, an act that haunted his final days. In Ivan's time contacts were first made with Elizabethan England, whose sailors arrived in Archangel seeking trade.

Ivory Coast: (1) Part of the West African coast in colonial times, named for its primary product; nearby were the *Gold* and *Slave Coasts.* (2) Former name of *Côte d'Ivoire.*

Izvestia: "The News." The official mouthpiece of the Soviet government for seven decades. Cf. *Pravda.*

Izvolski, Alexander (1856-1919): Russian statesman. Foreign Minister 1905-10; Ambassador to France 1910-16. Following the *Russo/Japanese War* he sought to repair relations with Japan, and to shore up Russia's building *entente* with Britain. As Ambassador in Paris before and during *WWI* he played a key role, including negotiating the *Constantinople Agreement.*

J

Jackson, Andrew (1767-1845): "Old Hickory." U.S. general; President 1828-36. He commanded at the futile *Battle of New Orleans,* and led the *conquest* and *pacification* of the Floridas, 1818-23. Jackson reshaped domestic politics, giving it a western and populist turn. That significantly altered the character of the presidency by providing popular legitimacy, expanding the veto power, and making it more interventionist in legislation; and he advanced the development of the two-party system. In foreign affairs he vacillated between prickly defense of minor principle and cautious pragmatism on larger issues. But he opened up foreign trade, securing a *commercial treaty* with Russia that had evaded U.S. negotiators for 35 years. With the British he arranged for trade in the highly profitable West Indies markets (cf. *Jay's Treaty*). With Turkey he gained entry to the Black Sea, and with Siam he signed the first ever U.S. *treaty* with an Asian nation. At home he resisted *annexation* of Texas, fearing war with Mexico and division of the *Democratic Party* over the admission of another *slave state* (this although he himself owned slaves). Less happily, he imposed new removal laws on the frontier Indians, forcibly displacing most eastern and midwestern *tribes* to areas west of the Mississippi. That prompted several bloody wars, including the Blackhawk War (1832) and the Seminole War (1835).

Jackson/Vanik Amendment: An amendment sponsored by Senator Henry ("Scoop") Jackson and Representative Charles Vanik, attached to *Nixon's* omnibus 1974 trade bill. It linked Soviet compliance on free emigration for Jews to access to U.S. *trade, technology* and credits. The bill was intended as the carrot in Nixon's strategy of *linkage* of trade with Soviet foreign policy restraint, but Congress linked trade instead to internal policies. The Soviets rejected the bill and stopped Jewish emigration entirely for several years. It thus marked a turning from *détente,* as well as new salience for conflict over *human rights* in U.S/Soviet relations. Because it linked human rights to trade with all communist countries, in the 1990s it continues to raise an annual problem regarding *MFN* for China.

Jacobins: A *republican* political club that quickly grew into the most *radical* faction in the *French Revolution*. Dominated by *Danton* and *Robespierre*, from 1792 the Jacobins conducted the *Terror,* provoking the reaction of *Thermidor* in 1794.

jacquerie: A bloody, peasant rising in France in 1358, aimed at the chateaux and taxation; from this, any similar outburst of mass peasant violence.

Jamaica: Location: Caribbean. Major associations: *Commonwealth, OAS, UN.* Population: 2.6 million. Military: minimal self-defense. The island was sighted by Columbus in 1494. Subsequent Spanish rule was harsh, and the local Indian population was soon completely wiped out. Jamaica was captured by Britain in 1655, and became a *colony* valued both for its fine tropical products and its *strategic* location. It received a good measure of *autonomy* after *WWII,* but only became independent in 1962. From 1958-62 it belonged to the ill-fated *West Indies Federation*. Since independence, it has maintained a shaky democracy, where elections are often rocked by deadly violence and challenged by stories of vote fraud. Jamaica has tended to swing widely between conservative, pro-American governments under Edward Seaga (b.1930), and more *radical* governments under Michael Manley (b.1923). Under the former, it severed ties with Cuba and sent a contingent to *Grenada* in 1983; under the latter, it embraced *nonalignment* and resisted calls by the *IMF* for an austerity program.

Jamieson Raid (December 29, 1895-January 2, 1896): L. Storr Jamieson (1853-1917), who worked for the British South Africa Company, took a ragtag force of close to 500 men on a misconceived adventure that aimed at the overthrow of the government of the *Transvaal*. Its failure encouraged the *Boers* to think they could resist *regular* British forces, and toppled *Cecil Rhodes* from his perch as premier of *Cape Colony*. Cf. *Boer War, Second; Kruger Telegram*.

Janissaries: These soldiers recruited from the Christian population of the *Ottoman Empire* formed its paramount military corps. Over the centuries their power grew until they could, and did, topple *sultans* and dictate policy. In 1826 they revolted, and were utterly wiped out by *regular* Ottoman troops, assisted in the massacre by an angry mob of citizens from *Constantinople*.

Japan: Location: N.E. Asia. Major associations: *APEC, OECD, UN.* Population: 125 million. Military: 240,000 strong, first-rate and expanding. (1) Traditional/feudal: *Sinification* dominated the Asuka (or Suiko) period, 552-645 A.D. but *Buddhism* was also introduced around the 6th century (by convention, in 552). Chinese influences continued to be the strongest formative force in the Hakuho period (645-710). Over these centuries, Japan took from China its writing, an early constitution and the Taiho code. During the Nara period, 710-94, the Yoro code was adopted, and a flowering of the arts and letters took place. Heian

Japan (794-1185) was characterized by local *warlords* and *samurai* dominating political life, and the burden of taxation falling more heavily on the peasantry. Buddhism continued to advance among the populace, absorbing local cults and conditioning arts, law, literature and politics. But *Shinto* also penetrated and altered Buddhist ideas and practices. Civilian families lost even more ground to the military castes, commercial activity boomed, and despite the rise of the bushi, or warrior lords, the pacifistic faith of Buddhism flourished. Kamakura Japan (1185-1333) saw steady development of *infrastructure*, and effective if unspectacular government. It may even have been a time of consolidation and advance, rather than an interregnum between supposedly better times. Politically, indirect rule by the emperors and *shoguns* was the order of the day, but this proved decreasingly effective. The Ashikaga period, 1333-1603, saw chaos and strife, with *civil war* nearly destroying the imperial capital, Kyoto, during the Onin War (1467-77). This period also saw the arrival of the first Westerners. Portuguese traders landed in 1542, followed by Jesuit missionaries. The Spanish arrived in 1581. In 1587 all Christian missionaries were ordered to leave by Toyotomi Hideyoshi (1536-98). He also invaded Korea, and planned a great *empire* to include Indochina, the Philippines, and *Siam*. In 1597 he ordered mass executions of Christians, whom he feared would serve as a *fifth column* for foreign conquerors. In 1600 the first Dutch traders arrived. But just as Western trade and influence appeared about to make real headway, Tokugawa Ieyasu (1542-1616) became Shogun, moved the center of power to Edo (Tokyo), and forced Japan onto the path of *autarky* it followed for the next 250 years.

(2) Tokugawa period (1603-1868): Faced with endless civil wars and the arrival of strange and perhaps threatening foreigners, the Tokugawa Shoguns chose to resist all change. They offered political stability, although harshly enforced, and seclusion from foreign influence. The price was suppression of most creative social forces and a self-imposed, growing technological and military inferiority to the West. Westerners met increasing harassment and were generally discouraged from a permanent presence (the English arrived in 1612, but left in 1623; the French established no real trade links, and Americans would not arrive until 1791). After 1613 Confucianism was proclaimed an official religion, and Christians were again persecuted. In 1618 most missionaries were killed or forced to leave. In 1637-38 Christian peasants rebelled in Shimabara, aided by some Europeans. Many thousands were *liquidated* after the *rebellion* failed. With the dissolution of organized Christianity most foreign trade fell away: Spanish traders were expelled in 1624, and the Portuguese in 1638. Only the Dutch were left,

at a single post (Deshima). Chinese merchants were more welcome, but they too were controlled in their movements and trade. In 1637 the Tokugawas went further: Japanese nationals were forbidden to leave the islands and shipbuilders were ordered not to construct vessels capable of ocean trade; another major industry was thus blindly retarded. Yet the policy worked: for over 200 years Japan avoided *civil war, revolution*, or even significant social unrest. Stable, but secluded and conformist, the nation was largely unaware of the global historical currents about to burst upon its shores, with more force than a great tsunami.

Even under the Tokugawa, foreign ideas seeped into Japan through the Dutch outpost at Deshima. What is more important, changes in the West itself meant that Japan could no longer resist a much more powerful set of nations demanding access to its markets. In 1720 the Shoguns lifted the ban on importing foreign books (except Christian texts, which remained under interdict). Some samurai began to worry about falling too far behind foreign powers militarily; others grew concerned over Japan's ability to sustain its population without trade and overseas expansion. By the mid-19th century Japan faced a crisis born of domestic discontent with failure to *modernize*, and the growing threat of Western power and pressure. Just then, on July 8, 1853, Commodore *Matthew C. Perry* steamed into Edo Bay and demanded a *commercial treaty*. His squadron of well-armed ships that could sail against the wind made a real impression: when he returned the next year he got his vague, but still breakthrough treaty. The first cracks in the isolationist seawall appeared: the limits on shipbuilding were lifted. In 1858 a full-scale commercial treaty with the U.S. was agreed, and treaties with other Western states quickly followed. But the Japanese *elite* remained divided over the wisdom of making such contact, and in 1863 one *daimyo* shelled Western ships. The U.S. responded with a *warship*, in a basic display of *gunboat diplomacy* that was endorsed by the French (who sent two). In 1864, 17 warships (American, British, Dutch and French) imposed a settlement on the daimyo.

(3) Meiji period (1868-1912): This display of Japanese vulnerability sparked a fundamental political upheaval. Power was restored to the emperor in 1868 after a long-building revolution. The shogunate was abolished. With it, over time, went the samurai. In their place Japan embraced *modernization* and the ways of the West, seeking out knowledge of both and applying it to one of the most remarkable national transformations in all history. In just 45 years it fundamentally changed its economic, political and social institutions, and achieved the status of a modern *Great Power*. It then put that newfound power to *expansionist* purposes in the *First Sino/Japanese War*, the begin-

ning of a 50-year assault on its giant neighbor. In 1902 it formed the *Anglo/Japanese Alliance* with Britain. It next attacked Russia, starting the *Russo/Japanese War.* Japan *annexed* Korea in 1910. By 1911 it had eliminated all *unequal treaties* forced upon it earlier by foreign powers, and readied to impose its own on China. No longer isolated, it had become a naked expansionist power, with major holdings on the Asian mainland and a great hunger for more. Relations with Russia were repaired in 1907, with a secret *spheres of influence* agreement dividing *Manchuria.* In 1910 it was agreed to consult on Asian issues; in 1912 another agreement divided Inner Mongolia; and in 1916 Japan pledged war supplies to Russia. In contrast, relations with the U.S. after 1905 grew worse. Besides the irritant of *Oriental exclusion laws,* the U.S. had new strategic interests in the Pacific since the acquisition of the Philippines in 1898. Moreover, it was suspicious of Japan's intentions to close the *Open Door* in *Manchuria* and China. Yet the U.S. also accepted some Japanese expansion--such as annexation of Korea--in the *Root/Takahira Agreement,* contributing to confusion in Tokyo about American intentions in Asia.

(4) Imperial Japan 1912-45: The Emperor Meiji died in 1912, beginning a period of relative *liberalism* (Taisho Japan 1912-22), and the epochal premiership of *Hara Kei Takashi.* Foreign policy was basically concerned with China. Thus, Japan entered *WWI,* although Britain preferred not, invoking the *Anglo/Japanese Alliance* in order to seize German interests in Shantung. In 1915, with Europe distracted, Japan tried to force the *Twenty-One Demands* on China. That further raised U.S. ire and opposition. At the *Paris Peace Conference* Japan had three goals: gain control of the former German islands in the Pacific; win *recognition* of its 1914 gains in China; and obtain international acceptance of the principle of racial equality. It was partially successful on the first two, but was rebuffed on the third, at which it took great national umbrage. In 1918 Japan sent a large force into *Siberia* and did not pull out until 1922, long after the other powers had withdrawn. It was a major player at the *Washington Conference,* which forced it to retrench but not to give up its consistent ambition of achieving *hegemony* on the Asian mainland. During this time Japanese liberals differed from militarists not in their goals, but in their preference for diplomacy over direct action: as long as international cooperation worked, the sword could remain sheathed. Japan also sought *rapprochement* with Soviet Russia, recognizing the *Bolshevik* regime in 1925. But civilian ascendancy came to an end in the 1930s, with the rapid growth of *militarism* and *fascism* in Japan. In 1931 elements of the *Guandong Army* staged the *Mukden incident,* and

subsequently set up the *puppet state* of *Manchukuo.* Young officers killed PM Inukai Tsuyoshi in 1932, effectively ending the party system and replacing it with military rule. Japan left the *League of Nations* in March 1933, and launched a propaganda/policy called *Asia for Asians.* Between 1932-37 it consolidated its gains. An attempted *coup* in February 1936, by the *Imperial Way* faction of the Japanese military, was repulsed. However, the imperial ambitions of the military and other elites continued to drive policy. In 1936 Japan joined the *Anti-COMINTERN Pact.* In 1937, following the *Marco Polo Bridge incident,* it attacked China proper, beginning the *Second Sino/Japanese War.* From 1937-39 Japanese forces clashed with the Soviets in a bloody, undeclared border war along the Amur River. However, the surprise of the *Nazi/Soviet Pact* made the Japanese cautious: fearing Russia might now be free to attack, Tokyo became less provocative, and turned its attention southward (in April 1941, it signed a five-year neutrality pact with Moscow). It signed the *Tripartite Pact* in 1940. Also in 1940, France was forced to allow Japanese troops into northern *Indochina*; in 1941, they marched south and took Saigon. They also threatened the *Dutch East Indies* (Indonesia), but were unable to gain access to those resources until they attacked in 1942. The U.S began to selectively *embargo* war matériel in 1940. Japan attacked *Pearl Harbor* on December 7, 1941. [At this point, refer to *WWII,* and see the map of the *Japanese Empire.*] After the sudden shock of *Hiroshima* and *Nagasaki,* on August 6 and 9, 1945, Japan surrendered on August 15th, and was then occupied by the U.S. Japan was to lose a great deal by virtue of decisions taken at *Casablanca, Yalta* and *Potsdam.* It was, in fact, about to be shrunk back to its pre-Perry borders.

(5) Modern Japan 1945- : From August 1945-April 28, 1952, Japan was occupied by the U.S., technically in consultation with an Allied Council for Japan (Britain, China, France and the Soviet Union). In fact, the *occupation* was nearly exclusively an American effort (with some *Commonwealth* participation), under *Douglas MacArthur.* The nation was *demilitarized,* and a democratic constitution introduced that made the emperor a figurehead monarch and limited the military to self-defense (interpreted until 1992 as blocking any deployment of Japanese troops overseas). At first, an effort was made to break up the *zaibatsu,* but already by 1947 this stopped as the U.S. emphasis shifted from reform to recovery, to make Japan a bulwark in Asia against the Soviet Union. Perhaps the major achievement of the occupation, besides democratization, was land reform. In 1951 the *Japanese Peace Treaty* was finally signed. On the same day, a *security treaty* with the U.S. established American bases and military cooperation, and required some

rearmament by Japan. Not entirely popular, the treaty was renegotiated in 1960 to make it more of a genuine partnership, and to exclude *nuclear weapons* from Japan's soil, unless with its permission. The U.S. also provided *reconstruction* funds, a protective blanket of *preferential tariffs,* and market access that permitted the Japanese economy to boom. Japan spent the 1950s and most of the 1960s as a quiet, U.S. *client state.* In 1956 the Soviets finally dropped their veto of its entry into the *United Nations.* Japan's full reemergence into the *world community* was symbolized by the 1964 *Olympics,* which it hosted. By 1970 it was an important partner with the West on economic matters, but remained a diplomatic dwarf. Where its relations with the Soviet Union were frosty, particularly concerning the *Kuriles,* they were normalized regarding China in September 1972. Postwar relations with most Southeast Asian nations reflected tensions born of Japan's remembered *aggression* and its rising economic stature. North Korea is a special case: its threat to go nuclear could well force Japan down the same road, and/or into developing a limited, land-based *SDI* system to protect against missile attack. Until the *Cold War* ended, Japan was content to let the U.S. conduct extra-regional diplomacy. Yet already by the 1980s Japan was more diplomatically active, even becoming the world's largest *aid* donor. With the *Gulf War* further adjustments began. Japan refused to send troops (citing Article Nine of its constitution), but did ante up a great deal of money. In June 1992, its Self-Defense Force was authorized to join UN *peacekeeping* troops in Cambodia, the first overseas deployment since WWII. In fact, Japan led the effort to restore peace to Cambodia. It also announced a desire for status as a *permanent member of the Security Council,* to give it diplomatic influence commensurate with its economic power. See also *Akihito; Asia for Asians; Bataan death march; Sato; fact-finding mission; Genro; Greater East Asia Co-Prosperity Sphere; Hirohito; Ito; Treaty of Kangawa; kamikaze; Kishi; Lansing/Ishii Agreement; MITI; Supreme Command of Allied Power; Tojo; unconditional surrender; VERs; Yamagata; Yamamoto; Yamashita; Yoshida.*

Japanese Peace Treaty (September 8, 1951): It was signed with Japan by 49 states (the Soviet Union and several others refused, while both Chinas were excluded). Among other features, it contained a promise to uphold *human rights.* Japan renounced all *territorial* claims beyond the *home islands* (and minor attachments), as decided at *Cairo* and *Potsdam*; to wit: all Antarctic claims, and all claims to China, *Formosa,* Korea, the *Kuriles,* the Pacific *mandates,* the *Paracels,* the *Pescadores,* the *Spratlys* and South *Sakhalin.* Japan retained merely "residual *sovereignty*" over the

Bonins and *Ryukyus.* It retained a right of *self-defense* of the home islands, but was required to renounce all other use of force in its foreign policy. In return, the *occupation* armies withdrew. Japan was also pledged to join the *free trade* bloc of nations, and *reparations* were prescribed, but payment indefinitely postponed. It received all necessary *ratifications* by April 28, 1952. Countries not signing, but later negotiating *ad hoc* settlements with Japan included: India (1952), Burma (1954), the Philippines and the Soviet Union (1956), Indonesia (1958).

jargon: (1) Rhetoric or writing typified by convoluted syntax and/or highly pretentious language. (2) Using nonce words or phrases (those coined for a single occasion; e.g., "complex neo-hegemonic regime"). Such practices cause loss of meaning and may result in the speaking and writing of gibberish. International relations, like most advanced study, requires some specialized terminology (e.g., *détente, Great Power, sphere of influence*). But once complexity in language is introduced merely for its own sake one has entered the murky realms of jargon, where words become barriers instead of bridges to understanding. When a writer is so tempted to impress by cultivating obscurity, it might do to recall the ancient cartographer's warning to sailors who wandered too far out from the known world: "Cave! Hic dragonis" (Beware! There be dragons). Cf. *obscurantism.*

Jaruzelski, Wojciech (b.1923): Polish general. PM 1981-89; President 1989-90. This dour soldier conducted the first ever displacement of a *communist party* within the *Warsaw Pact* that did not end with a Soviet *invasion.* By that action, he unintentionally demonstrated the hollowness for the 1980s of the *Brezhnev Doctrine.* He declared *martial law* (to July 1983) in a failed effort to stem the rise of the *Solidarity* movement, but then he cooperated in easing the transition to government by Solidarity. Many Poles and other observers remain ambivalent about his role, as his takeover may have forestalled invasion; at least, that is his best defense.

Jaurès, Jean (1859-1914): French socialist. He led the *social democratic* wing of the French left before *WWI,* which he opposed. He worked within the *Second International* to gain approval of what would later be called *Popular Fronts,* but never held office. He tried to convince German and French workers to strike rather than accept *mobilization* during July 1914, but on the 31st he was assassinated by a nationalist zealot.

Java: The main, heavily populated island of Indonesia, which dominates that nation's national life.

Jay's Treaty (1794): An agreement between Britain and the U.S. reestablishing trade relations, broken during the *American War of Independence*. It began a partial *rapprochement,* set trade on a *most-favored-nation* basis, but limited U.S. trade in the Caribbean to the British East Indies, excluding it still from the more lucrative West Indies. These terms lasted until the time of *Andrew Jackson*.

Jefferson, Thomas (1743-1826): U.S. statesman. Minister to Paris 1785-89; Secretary of State 1789-93; President 1801-09. His education, intellectual predilections, and his time in France made him a lifelong *francophile* and an admirer of the *French Revolution*. He resigned as Secretary of State, objecting to the influence over policy of *Alexander Hamilton*, whom he suspected of backing an *alliance* with Britain. He supported *George Washington's* policy of *neutrality* toward the *Napoleonic Wars* despite his deep ideological affinity for France and his *anglophobia*. As President he successfully negotiated the *Louisiana Purchase*, and continued *neutrality*. However, he allowed serious deterioration in relations with Britain. He so little appreciated the need for America as a maritime nation to have a strong navy that he let its ships literally decay and rot in port; and he did so in spite of a prolonged contest with the *Barbary pirates*, his aggressive posture in the deepening crisis over U.S. claims to *neutral rights*, and the *impressment* controversy with Britain. In desperation, he placed an *embargo* on all U.S. trade with Britain or France, and their empires. That served to reinforce the French and British *blockades* he was trying to break, bankrupted many trading houses (with which, as an agrarian idealist, he was not overly concerned), and nearly led to the *secession* of New England. He left office widely unpopular, with the nation vastly expanded but also more seriously divided than before his watch. He also left relations with Britain in tatters and heading toward the crisis of 1812. His foreign policy failures are overlooked in American popular memory, due to celebration of his role in drafting the Declaration of Independence and other domestic accomplishments.

Jerusalem: "City of Peace." This ancient Jewish city remains of central importance to *Judaism*, for it contains the Wailing Wall (reputed to be the only surviving wall of the Temple built by Solomon). It is also prominent in *Christianity* as the site of Christ's public life and death. Lastly, within *Islam* it is revered as the locale of the Dome of the Rock, from whence it is believed Muhammad ascended directly to heaven. At the *partition* of *Palestine* Jerusalem was to have become a *free city*. Instead, the fighting of the *First Arab/Israeli War* left the west in Jewish hands. The eastern half (containing the Old City and the Wailing Wall) was then quickly annexed by *Transjordan*. In the *Third Arab/Israeli War*, East Jerusalem was captured by Israel and the whole city was annexed to that state. Israel has sought but has not generally received *recognition* of Jerusalem as its capital. The status of this city remains the single greatest obstacle to a comprehensive *peace*.

jetsam: See *flotsam and jetsam*.

Jewish Agency: A quasi-government set up to buy land and assist Jewish *immigration* to *Palestine*, with the approval of the British *mandate* authorities and the *League of Nations*. Many of its officials moved directly into government service upon creation of Israel. It now coordinates relations with the *diaspora*.

Jewish Autonomous Region: See *Birobizhan*.

Jiang Jieshi: See *Chiang Kai-shek*.

Jiangxi Soviet: From 1931-33, Chinese communists fleeing pursuing *Guomindang* armies settled in this region and declared they had established a *soviet*. Some land reform was introduced, and as one result the communists began to attract significant peasant support. After fending off several attacks they were forced to evacuate, which led to the *Long March*.

jihad: "Holy war." A term used by militant Muslims when a *war* is undertaken, or is portrayed as undertaken, for religious principles. It is a common, even trite, practice for leaders of Muslim countries to try to rally public support by asserting that the *dynastic* or *national interest* being advanced by a war is also, or even mainly or solely, a holy cause. Yet it should be noted that other faiths, too, support the notion of religious war, though they use different terms: e.g., Constantine the Great (c.274-337 A.D.) had as his motto: "In hoc signo vinces" (in this sign shall you conquer), referring to the Christian cross. That was also the motto of the Christian Crusaders against *Islam* in the Middle Ages. Cf. *WWI*.

jingoism: Extreme *patriotism*; unthinking *chauvinism*, usually characterized by bellicose posing, and a tendency to deflect internal social tensions outwards into a pugnacious foreign policy. It derives from a music hall ditty popular in England just before the *Crimean War:* "We don't want to fight, but by jingo if we do, we've got the men, we've got the ships, we've got the money too!" Cf. *social imperialism*.

Jinnah, Muhammad Ali (1876-48): "Quaid-i-Asam."

Pakistani statesman. He split with the *Congress Party* to form the *Muslim League* in 1934, demanding creation of an independent *state* for Indian Muslims, called *Pakistan* ("Land of the Pure"), in whose formation he was the key figure. He thought *Mohandas Gandhi's* policy of non-violent resistance to the British was insufficient. During *WWII* he curried favor by supporting the British war effort (whereas Gandhi refused, and was jailed). Jinnah was at least partly responsible for inciting the interfaith rioting and killing that preceded the extraordinary *partition* of India in 1947. He was briefly Governor-General of Pakistan, but died after slightly more than a year of contentious and, for him, truncated independence.

Jodl, Alfred (1892-1946): German general. A key figure in the German *High Command* during *WWII*. He was the top operations planner and key military adviser to *Hitler* (who personally assumed overall command in 1941). Jodl recommended the terror bombing of British and other cities, and signed orders for the execution of *POWs*, among other atrocities. At the end of the war he signed the instrument of *surrender* on behalf of the German military. Convicted of *war crimes* at *Nuremberg,* he was hanged. In 1953 a Munich court posthumously declared that he was not, after all, a "major offender" as the court at Nuremberg had found. That reversal, too, is moot.

Joffre, Joseph Jaques (1852-1931): French marshal. He was instrumental in saving Paris from capture during the *Marne* in 1914, but he was unable to adjust to *trench warfare*. He was promoted out of the lines in 1916, after the disasters of the *Somme* and *Verdun*.

John XXIII, né Angelo Roncalli (1881-1963): Pope 1958-63. He partly opened the *Catholic Church* to a spirit of *ecumenism*. He also called the *Second Vatican Council*, and instructed, and to a degree inspired, its liberalizing efforts. But he did not live to see its conclusion, and was succeeded as pontiff by a much more dour and deeply conservative man, Paul VI.

John Paul II, né Karol Wojtyla (b.1920): Pope since 1978. A Pole, he is the first non-Italian to be pope since 1522. His election inspired a nationalist outpouring in Poland that aided the rise of *Solidarity* and inhibited Soviet action. His energetic travels led to huge rallies in many countries, notably Ireland, where 1/4 of the population gathered to hear him speak. In 1981 he was shot, by a Turk who claimed to be working for the Bulgarian KGB. His policies have been rigidly conservative on the role of women, abortion and contraception. He has also pressed traditional Catholic social criticism of both *communism* and *capi-*

talism as inadequate systems, on moral and economic grounds. He pushed the church hierarchy to openly denounce the deep legacy of Catholic *anti-Semitism*.

Johnson, Andrew (1808-75): U.S. President 1865-69. While he sought to carry forward reconciliation as part of *Reconstruction*, the assassination of *Lincoln* radicalized Northern opinion and made a gentle peace impossible. Over his veto, Congress insisted on continuing for awhile military government in the defeated South. He faced an impeachment trial, but was acquitted. He threatened to use *Union* veterans against *Maximillian* and the French in Mexico, sending 50,000 to the border; France withdrew and the Mexican *revolution* proceeded. He was reelected to the Senate in 1875, but died soon thereafter.

Johnson, Lyndon Baines (1908-73): U.S. statesman. President 1963-68. As Senate majority leader he assisted in developing and managing the bipartisan approach to foreign policy during the *Eisenhower* years. He was *John Kennedy's* VP, but was kept poorly informed of policy. He became President on November 22, 1963, when Kennedy was *assassinated*. He kept on most of Kennedy's key advisers and promised to fulfill the dead President's mandate, which included support for South Vietnam as well as *détente* with the Soviets (after 1962). Johnson sought more than he achieved from *arms control*, but set in motion the negotiating process that led to breakthroughs in the 1970s. He became extremely activist in domestic affairs following his landslide mandate in 1964. That year he also escalated American involvement in the *Vietnam War,* without ever telling the truth about this commitment to the public. In 1965 he authorized *intervention* in the Dominican Republic, in effect abandoning the *Alliance for Progress*. His legislative record is unparalleled since FDR: he passed historic bills on civil rights, social welfare and other programs he collectively called "the Great Society." But Vietnam continuously drained his energies and the nation's resources (he once said the Great Society was his real love, but he had to spend all his time "with that bitch, Vietnam"). As opposition to the war built, he asked for and received advice from the *Wise Men*. They told him he was right and to continue the fight (George Ball was a courageous exception), which he did. In 1968, when he asked them again, they told him to end the war, but not how. Confused, deeply depressed, and beset by challengers within his own party, he decided not to run again. As he contemplated his record he revealed in private that his greatest political fear was to end up seen as "the mistake between the Kennedys" (John and Robert). He left office a deeply depressed man, and a widely unpopular President. Some seek to lay blame for Vietnam squarely, even solely, at his door. To do so is to ignore a broad consensus within the foreign policy *elite* (some Cassandras aside), and sustained support for the war by a majority of the public at least until the *Tet offensive*. Vietnam was not "Johnson's War" (nor "*Nixon's* War," for that matter). For good reasons and for bad, it was America's war. See *McNamara; Pearson; Tonkin Gulf Resolution*.

Joint Chiefs of Staff (JCS): The U.S. *General Staff*. It combines the chiefs and staff of the Army, Air Force, Marine Corps and Navy.

Jordan: Location: *Middle East*. Major associations: *Arab League, UN*. Population: 3.1 million. Military: small, defensive posture. "Hashemite Kingdom of Jordan." This historically *Arab* area was conquered by the *Ottoman Empire* in the 16th century, and remained an Ottoman province until 1918. It was part of the secret *Sykes-Picot Agreement*, and became a British *mandate* after *WWI*, under the name *Transjordan* until 1949. In 1946, with the British pulling out of *Palestine*, it became a *Hashemite* Kingdom. Under King *Ibn Talal Hussein*, Jordan was ever at odds with Egypt under *Nasser*, turning for support to the *Arab Legion* and to the U.S. and Britain. In 1958 Jordan and Iraq briefly attempted *union*, but this failed with a radical *coup* in Baghdad. Jordan was badly defeated in the *Third Arab/Israeli War*, losing control of the *West Bank*. During 1970-71 it experienced a sharp war against the *Palestine Liberation Organization*, then largely based in Jordan and existing almost as a state-within-a-state. Hussein reconciled with the PLO in 1985. In the *Third Arab/Israeli War* Jordan limited itself to a few troops on the Syrian front, choosing not to engage along the whole of its border with Israel. In 1974 the PLO was accepted by most Arab countries as the sole representative of the population on the West Bank; Jordan acquiesced in this decision. In 1988 Hussein renounced remaining claims to the West Bank, opening the way for creation of a Palestinian *state* there. During the *Gulf War* Jordan remained *neutral*, but most of its public supported *Saddam Hussein*. Subsequently, it repaired relations with the West, but support for Iraq cost Jordan greatly needed aid from Saudi Arabia and the *Gulf States*, especially as some 750,000 *refugees* from Kuwait (expelled Palestinians) and Iraq flooded into Jordan. In September 1993, following the Israeli/PLO *peace* accord, Jordan began direct *peace talks* with Israel. That year it also held the first multiparty elections since 1956.

Joseph II (1741-90): Holy Roman Emperor 1765-90. He ruled the *Hapsburg* lands as an *enlightened despot*; e.g., he abolished *serfdom*. His unsuccessful wars with Turkey further weakened Austria, just before the coming of *Napoleon*.

Juan Carlos I (b.1938): King of Spain 1975- . He was crowned upon the death of *Franco*. He gained great stature, domestically and internationally, when he helped thwart an anti-democracy *coup* in 1981.

Juárez, Benito (1806-72): Mexican revolutionary. He led a successful revolt against the clergy and landowners in 1854, but his reforms provoked a *civil war* from 1857-60. When he suspended payments of Mexico's foreign *debt*, *Napoleon III* took advantage of the preoccupation of the U.S. with its own civil war to intervene and set *Maximillian* up as "Emperor." Juárez fought the French from 1861-67, when U.S. threats of *intervention* forced Napoleon to withdraw. Juárez was again President of Mexico 1867-72.

Judaism: Originating among the slaves of ancient Egypt, its adherents have shown a remarkable tenacity in the face of perhaps the world's most virulent and persistent form of hate: *anti-Semitism*. Judaism is divided into two main groups, the Ashkenazi (predominantly European in origin) and Sephardi (predominantly Middle Eastern in origin), and into the three streams of Orthodox, Conservative and Reform. It follows the teachings of scripture (Torah), as well as venerated oral traditions (Mishnah and Talmud). The entire body of tradition, oral and written, is called the Halakah. Judaism is closely related to, has deeply influenced, and to a lesser extent has been influenced by, *Christianity* and *Islam*. With those faiths it shares much history and several core beliefs: monotheism, the divine authority of prophets, messianism and a tradition of social justice springing from belief in the essential equality of all humanity in the eyes of God. More problematically, it proffers that Jews are God's "chosen people" given the light of special revelation, but also a people sorely tested in their faith by collective ordeals comparable to the sufferings of Job, as they await the arrival of the messiah. See also *Falasha; fundamentalism; Israel; Jerusalem; Judea*.

Judea and Samaria: The SW of ancient *Palestine* (Judea) and the center (Samaria), forming today part of the *occupied territories*. Orthodox Jews insisted that the whole of the biblical area must become part of modern Israel, and promoted exclusively Jewish settlements there, on land long since occupied by Arabs.

judgment: A binding decision by an international court.

judicial legislation (decision): Development of new

rules by decisions of international courts that are then accepted into *international customary law*. Note: Such decisions do not have status as precedent, as do the decisions of domestic courts under the doctrine of *stare decisis*. At best, therefore, this is an indirect and ancillary source of lawmaking.

judicial settlement: A binding decision by a permanent, as opposed to an *ad hoc*, international court.

July Monarchy/Revolution: France from 1830-48, a period that witnessed the displacement of the *Bourbons* and creation of a constitutional *monarchy* under the "bourgeois king" Louis-Phillipe (1773-1850).

July Plot (July 20, 1944): The nearly successful plot by the anti-Nazi German *resistance* that wounded and shook, but did not kill *Hitler*, with a bomb. It was to have led to a new government and a negotiated end to *WWII*. The *Nazis* took terrible vengeance on the survivors, butchering several thousand.

Junkers: The east-Prussian landed aristocracy who manned the upper civil service and *officer corps* of Prussia and then Germany. Conservative and agrarian, they were increasingly at odds with the state they served as Germany *industrialized*. Their influence only ended with the *Allied* occupation after 1945, and the *annexation* of much of what had been *East Prussia* into Lithuania, Poland and the Soviet Union.

junta: A small military clique that governs a state although lacking any proper, constitutional authority.

jura novit curia: "The court knows the law." Maxim.

jurisdiction: (1) The scope of competence of an international court. (2) The right of a *sovereign* state to exercise exclusive control over its own *territory* and *population*. See *accretion; airspace; baseline; border; cession; contiguous zone; continental shelf; conquest; discovery; domestic jurisdiction; EEZ; human rights; municipal law; occupation; prescription; servitudes.*

jurisprudence constante: The accepted or settled practice of international courts, established through sequentially consistent opinions on related cases.

jus ad bellum: "The right to make *war*." It incorporates notions of just cause, right intention, right authority, *proportionality* and the requirement that the decision for war be taken as a last resort. Fundamentally, jus ad bellum says that one may only go to war for just reasons, such as *self-defense* or last resort resistance to great evil; it is never permissible to make war for bad reasons, such as *conquest* or collective theft. Cf. *aggression; jus in bello; just war theory.*

jus civile: The civil or domestic law that each state creates for itself. The term is drawn from the law that applied solely to the citizens of Rome (excluding slaves and women), as distinct from the *jus gentium*.

jus cogens: Principles of law binding despite objection by any one *state* or *treaty* to the contrary. To satisfy jus cogens a norm must be peremptory, derive from *international law*, be accepted by the *world community*, not be subject to *derogation* and cannot be modified save by the incontrovertible rise of new peremptory norms. For example, *freedom of the seas.*

jus gentium: "Law of the peoples." The principles of law prevailing among *nations*, as drawn from Roman law and practice. It was based on ideas of justice derived first through reason, but also the pragmatic practice of Roman relations with the divers peoples of their vast, *multinational* empire. Cf. *jus civile.*

jus gestionis: When a *state* acts in a non-*sovereign* capacity.

jus imperii: When a *state* acts in its capacity as a *sovereign*.

jus in bello: "The law of (making) *war*," or the law of actual *warfare*. Its cardinal principles are: (1) discrimination between *civilians* and *combatants* (with the latter constituting the only morally permissible targets). But note that *collateral damage* may be permitted if targets are selected with "right intent." (2) *Proportionality*, or the requirement that violence used be proportionate to the injury suffered. Jus in bello thereby seeks restraints on the extent of harm done even in a *just war*, and to limit the means by which even that permissible harm is performed. Cf. *jus ad bellum.*

jus in re: A legal right held against everyone.

jus naturale: "Natural law." The Roman modification of the original body of ideas developed by the ancient Greeks, who believed a native sense of justice had been implanted in humans by the gods. This influential idea reflects a conviction that there exist eternal or ideal principles of justice and right action, which are discernible by right reason, or one's natural moral faculties. See *Hugo Grotius; human rights; natural law.*

jus sanguinis: "Law of the blood." The principle that a child's *nationality* is the same as its parents (with exceptions). Cf. *jus soli.*

jus soli: "Law of the soil." The principle that *nationality* is set by the territory where a child's birth occurs (with exceptions). Cf. *jus sanguinas*.

justiciable dispute: Any *dispute*, generally non-political in nature, that states agree can be settled by referring to decision by an international court under principles of *international law*; a near-synonym for *legal dispute*. Cf. *nonjusticiable dispute; political dispute*.

justification: Those exceptional instances when a *state* may claim exemption from obedience to a legal *rule*, as may be occasioned by recourse to *self-defense*.

just war theory: This body of thought is centuries old. While rooted in religious (mainly Christian, but also Islamic) thought, it also has an impressive international legal pedigree. Even in its religious guise it is, at base, a practical understanding of *war*, born of historical experience rather than dogma. It recognizes that political communities will on occasion resort to war to advance their interests. Rather than railing ineffectually against that reality, it seeks to limit the number of such occasions by establishing agreement on *jus ad bellum*, or the right to make war, when it may be made, and in what moral context. It also seeks, not to put too fine a point on it, to justify the inevitable killing and destruction that must accompany even a just war. This aspect is the *jus in bello*, or the search for justice in the prosecution (conduct) of war. Just war theory is sophisticated: for a war to be just, both jus ad bellum and jus in bello requirements must be met; it is hence possible to wage war unjustly, in terms of means, in a just cause (e.g., did even the evil of the *Nazi* regime justify *thousand bomber raids* on German cities?). Just war theory requires moral distinctions be made between *aggressor* and victim, and may require one (morally speaking) to do violence in aid of a victim of an unjust war. It proposes that no war can be just on both sides, while allowing that a war may be unjust from all points of view. In making such distinctions it differs strikingly from another venerable tradition of moral discourse about war: *pacifism*. See also *Geneva Conventions; genocide; Hague Conventions; indiscriminate bombing; laws of war; necessities of war; Nuremberg trials; prohibited weapons; Red Cross; standards of civilized behavior; superior orders; Tokyo trials; war crimes*.

Jutland, Battle of (May 31-June 1, 1916): The main naval action of *WWI*, other than the *submarine* campaigns. Although the Germans under Vice Admiral Scheer (1861-1928) achieved a *tactical* draw with the larger British fleet, under Admiral Jellicoe (1859-1935), they withdrew to port, from whence they never ventured again prior to a fleet *mutiny* in November 1918. This long-awaited clash of the *Dreadnoughts* was thus something of an anti-climax. The more important and sustained naval *campaign* was against the German *U-boats*.

K

Kádár, János (1912-89): Hungarian communist leader 1956-65; PM 1956-58, 1961-65. During the *Hungarian Uprising* he participated in early reforms, then fled Budapest as the movement evolved into an anti-communist *rebellion*. Reappearing in eastern Hungary, he proclaimed a new government in collusion with the Soviet *invasion*. He again submerged his inclination to reform during his first premiership. His second saw some liberalization at home, but Hungary remained loyal to the *Soviet bloc* in foreign affairs.

Kaiser: "Caesar." (1) Title of three German emperors, 1871-1918. (2) All Austrian emperors, to 1918.

Kalaallit Nunaat (Greenland): This huge, sparsely populated *colony* was incorporated into Denmark in 1953, but then given *home rule* in 1979. Four-fifths of the island is under the permanent icecap. It cooperates with other arctic communities on environmental, cultural, fishing and *indigenous peoples* issues. In 1985 it dropped association with the *EC*.

Kalimantan: A large portion of the island of *Borneo*; formerly a Dutch possession, now part of Indonesia. It is also the Indonesian name for all Borneo.

Kaliningrad enclave: Captured and *annexed* from Germany in 1944, it was cut off from Russia by Lithuanian *independence* in 1991. See *East Prussia*.

Kalinin, Mikhail Ivanovich (1875-1946): Soviet statesman. Head of state 1922-46. He survived the *purges* by sheer toadyism, supporting *Stalin* at every opportunity, and on occasion inventing some of his own.

Kamerun: A German *protectorate* in West Africa

1884-1919. It was divided into British and French *mandates* in 1919.

kamikaze: "Divine wind." *WWII* Japanese suicide pilots who flew planes loaded with *ordnance* into *Allied* ships. Two thousand kamikaze met a U.S. *invasion* fleet off *Okinawa*, sunk or damaged 200 ships but failed to stop the invasion. They were named in remembrance of a typhoon that destroyed the invasion fleet of the Mongol *warlord* Kublai Khan (1214-94).

Kampuchea: See *Cambodia*.

Kanaky: The name of *New Caledonia* proposed by its Kanak population, should it achieve *independence* from French colonial rule.

Kangawa, Treaty of (March 31, 1854): The *commercial treaty* forced on a reluctant Japan by Commodore *Perry*, granting *trade* access to the U.S. It opened up Japan to the West, as it was quickly followed by similar agreements with other trading nations.

Kant, Immanuel (1724-1804): 18th century philosopher and the greatest thinker of the Ideal School in German philosophy. His most important work on *international relations* was "Zum ewigen Frieden." He advocated a world *federation* of constitutional *republics*, bound by respect for the rule of law and a shared interest in free commerce. His writings have had a profound impact on those concerned with *international organization* and *international law*. Recently, his ideas have influenced those concerned with *cosmopolitan* underpinnings for notions of *human rights*.

Kapp putsch (March 1922): A failed *coup* attempt against the *Weimar Republic* by some of the *Freikorps*. The supporters included *Ludendorff,* but the main leader was the journalist Wolfgang Kapp (1868-1922). The rebels briefly held Berlin but fled when popular support failed to develop. Although it failed, the *putsch* revealed how thin was support for Weimar.

Karelia: The Finnish peninsula and isthmus that comes within range of *St. Petersburg* (then, Leningrad), part of which *Stalin* forced Finland to cede in 1940, and again in 1945.

Karen: A minority ethnic group in both *Myanmar* and *Thailand*. In both countries, the Karen have waged *guerrilla* campaigns dating back to the 1940s. In Myanmar, however, the Karen opened *peace talks* in January 1994.

Kashmir: A largely *Muslim, Princely State*. In 1947 its *Hindu* maharajah, Hari Singh, tried to avoid a choice of either Hindu India or Muslim Pakistan. Fighting broke out immediately between Muslim tribesmen from the north, and the Hindus of Jammu. The maharajah asked for military *aid* from Delhi, which agreed on condition he accept association with India. This was intolerable to Pakistan. A *cease-fire* agreement brokered by the UN in 1949 placed most of Kashmir under Indian administration, and UN *peacekeepers* on the ground. In 1957 India *annexed* its part, over Pakistani and UN protests. In 1962 China seized a part, Aksai Chin, in the *Indo/Chinese War.* The *Second Indo/Pakistani War* (1965) broke out over Kashmir. There was more fighting in the *Third Indo/Pakistani War.* In 1989 a *secessionist* movement in Kashmir led to clashes between the Indian Army and *civilians*. Since then, *Amnesty International* and Western countries have charged India with *human rights* abuses. On January 1, 1994, direct discussions with Pakistan began, but were broken off after just two days.

Kassem, Abd al-Karim (1914-63): Dictator of Iraq 1958-63. He headed the *coup* that overthrew the *monarchy* in 1958. Refusing to follow *Nasser's* lead, he suppressed nasserites within Iraq. He also fought the *Kurds*. In June 1961, he proclaimed that *Kuwait* was really part of Iraq (to which it had been connected under the *Ottoman Empire*). However, British and then Arab troops arrived in Kuwait to prevent him from seizing it. He was deposed and shot in 1963.

Katanga (Shaba): A province in SE Zaire, rich in ores. It has a *secessionist* history. See *Congo crisis*.

Katyn massacre/controversy: In April 1943, the *Nazis* announced they had uncovered a mass grave of Polish *officers* they said had been murdered by the Soviets. Moscow denied the charge, accusing the Germans in turn. The Polish *government-in-exile* in London was suspicious, as Russia had never made an accounting of the 15,000 Polish officers it captured during its attack on east Poland in 1939. *Stalin* used a request for a *Red Cross* investigation as an excuse to break relations with the London Poles, preferring the in-house, communist Poles he would later plant as a *puppet regime* in the eastern Polish city of Lublin. This move, rather than the massacre per se, caused the first real rift among the *Big Three.* The massacre was a focal point of historical controversy for decades. However, in 1989 the Polish government released long-suppressed evidence that pointed to Moscow. In April 1990, as part of *glasnost,* the Soviets at last admitted guilt. See also *Sikorski*.

Kazahkstan: Location: Central Asia. Major associations: *CIS, CSCE, UN*. Population: 16.5 million (45% Kazahk; 40% Russian; 10% Volga German). Military: inherited units of the old Red Army; tactical and strategic *nuclear weapons* to be returned to Russia or dismantled. Kazahkstan was long part of the Mongol domains. Then it enjoyed *independence* as a *Muslim* khanate, allied to the *Ottoman Empire*. Russian expansionist pressure was felt after 1730, but the Kazahks did not succumb until the mid-19th century. It remained attached to Russia all through the Soviet period. Attempts at *russification* continued in these years, and large-scale Russin *immigration* threatened to make the Kazahks a minority in their own land. It gained independence with the *extinction* of the Soviet Union on December 25, 1991. Unexpectedly, it was a major *nuclear power*, as thousands of Soviet *warheads* remained on its soil. However, it agreed to abide by *SALT* and *START,* and in late 1993 it joined the *NPT*. It is large, rich in *natural resources*, and competes as regional cultural and political leader with Uzbekistan. In January 1994, it signed a limited *free trade* agreement with Uzbekistan.

Kellogg, Frank B. (1856-1937): U.S. statesman. Ambassador to London, 1923-25; Secretary of State to *Calvin Coolidge,* 1925-29. He won the 1929 *Nobel Prize* for Peace for his efforts on the *Kellogg-Briand Pact.* He kept up his predecessors' policy of *nonrecognition* of the Soviet Union. From 1930-35 he served on the *Permanent Court of Justice* at the Hague.

Kellogg-Briand Pact (1928): Formal title: "General Treaty for the Renunciation of War," a.k.a. the "Pact of Paris." In March 1927, French Foreign Minister *Aristide Briand* proposed a defense *pact* with the U.S. through the American media, calling for joint renunciation of *war* as an instrument of national policy. Secretary of State *Frank Kellogg* and President *Calvin Coolidge* were at first annoyed by the idea. They objected to Briand appealing over their heads to American *public opinion*, and thought his proposal might represent an *entangling alliance*. It was *William Borah,* the powerful Senate *isolationist*, who suggested deflecting the initiative into a multilateral *declaration* outlawing war. The French were greatly displeased. However, as holder of the 1926 *Nobel Prize* for Peace Briand could hardly spurn a pact renouncing war--no matter how little he actually believed in its efficacy. After delaying for months, France agreed to a *multilateral* pact, though with reservations that suggested to close observers that it reserved the right to use *force* (for "legitimate *self-defense*"). Kellogg, who at first supported the pact by ulterior design, came to genuinely believe it would be a benediction for humanity, and embraced the cause with enthusiasm. It was duly

agreed by some 65 states, including later *aggressors* such as Italy and Japan. It had no provision for enforcement. It has been touted by more naïve *liberal-internationalists* as a great advance for moral consciousness among states, and criticized by harsher *realists* as a prime example of legalistic folly in *diplomacy*. Neither view seems entirely merited: it was instead a clever security gambit by Briand, who only did not foresee that *isolationists* in the U.S. might deflect it into an innocuous public relations bonanza. Despite this checkered history, the pact achieved much public acclaim, and was subsequently cited in the *Nuremberg war crimes trials*. See also *crimes against peace*.

Kemal, Mustapha: See *Atatürk*.

Kennan, George Frost (b.1904): U.S. statesman. During the 1920s he was trained as a Soviet specialist. He joined the *embassy* staff in Moscow in 1933, with the opening of *diplomatic relations*. He was deeply affected by the *Yezhovshchina*, and grew more disaffected with *Franklin Roosevelt's* approach to Soviet policy. His strongly anti-Soviet views had little influence until after *WWII*, when he authored the *X article* and the more important and weighty *Long Telegram*. He was sent back to Moscow as Ambassador in 1952, but retired from the service the next year. He then became an enormously influential academic (at Princeton), and critic of U.S. *Cold War* policy. His later views often seemed to contradict his earlier work, which either reflects an open and flexible mind or raises doubts that he ever believed anything very deeply.

Kennedy, John Fitzgerald (1917-63): U.S. President. Elected by an extremely narrow margin over *Richard Nixon*, he immediately inherited *Eisenhower's* plan for a proxy *invasion* of Cuba at the *Bay of Pigs*, which most observers agree he handled ineptly. Perception of his failure during that *crisis* encouraged *Khrushchev* to attempt to bully him over *Berlin*. His greatest test came during the *Cuban Missile Crisis*. He has been alternately greatly praised for cool *prudence*, or severely criticized for *escalating* that confrontation to extremely dangerous heights. After that, he moved toward a limited *détente* with the Soviets, including setting up the *hot line*, and signing the *Partial Test Ban Treaty*. He also presided over the greatest *arms buildup*, to that point, in U.S. peacetime history. His policy toward the *Third World* placed greater overt emphasis on promoting *democracy* than had that of his predecessors. He introduced the *Peace Corps* and tried with limited success to reorder relations with Latin America in the *Alliance for Progress*. Yet he was not loathe to try to have *Castro* killed. He shared the consensus view on the nature of the *Cold War*, and hence on the need to defend perceived U.S. interests from local *communists*, even in far-flung corners of Africa and Asia. He inherited a fairly limited commitment to South Vietnam, which he greatly increased by approving the *coup* that cost *Diem* his life, further Americanizing the *Vietnam War*. By the time of his *assassination* (November 22, 1963), he had increased the number of U.S. advisers in Vietnam over 30-fold (from 500 to 16,500). Hollywood films notwithstanding, available documentary evidence suggests that he was, at best, uncertain over what to do about Vietnam, and seemed just as intent to "stay the course" as his successor. His historical reputation remains inflated among the public and media by emotion surrounding the events of his death (and as well, by early hagiographies written by academics once part of his administration, or of a generation that felt itself bereft of heroes). Among more recent histories his reputation has gone into precipitate decline, aided by release of hitherto classified documents. See also *flexible response; Lyndon Johnson; Nassau Agreement.*

Kennedy Round: A major round of *GATT* negotiations, held from 1964-67. It was the apex of U.S. global trade management among *OECD* countries. Although *agriculture* was excluded, *tariffs* on non-agricultural products were reduced by 1/3rd. The U.S. continued to accept asymmetrical benefits in order to sustain European and Japanese *postwar* recovery, within the context of also providing economic buffering of those areas from Soviet political *influence* during the *Cold War*. In exchange, it was assured that as Europe moved toward *integration* it remained open to free, *multilateral* trade and *liberal* political values. This round also introduced rules against *dumping*.

Kenya: Location: E. Africa. Major associations: *Commonwealth, OAU, UN.* Population: 26 million. Military: moderate defense force. Britain and Germany competed for *trade* and *influence* in this region until 1886, when they agreed to divide their interests into a British *sphere* in Kenya and a German sphere in *Tanganyika*. Kenya was controlled by the British East Africa Company until 1893, when it became a part of the East Africa *protectorate*. Some local government was permitted the white settlers, and Kenya became a Crown Colony in 1920. From 1952-54 Kenya suffered through the *Mau-Mau rebellion*, in which *nationalists* (mainly Kikuyu) organized in secret societies and began attacks on Europeans and their property. The British response was severe, including the use of forced confession, which led to many deaths in detention. Some 14,000 died in all, about 80% killed by the British and the rest by the Mau Mau. Kenya achieved *independence* in 1964, under *Jomo Kenyatta*. It was

widely cited in those years as a model of relative tribal tolerance and free market development. In 1978 Daniel Arap Moi (b.1924) became President. Under his stewardship Kenya became more repressive, its economy declined, and it entered into confrontation with *donor nations* and the *IMF*. Under international pressure, Moi agreed to hold multiparty elections in 1993. But when the outcome did not suit his tastes, he canceled the results within 24 hours. Later in the year the aid *boycott* ended anyway, and nearly $1 billion was pledged to Kenya for 1994.

Kenyatta, Jomo (1895?-1978): Kenyan statesman. President 1964-78. Active in the *independence* movement from the 1940s, he denounced the violence of the Mau Mau (see *Kenya*), but still spent a decade in a British jail. As President, he steered Kenya on a moderate, pro-Western course.

Kerensky, Alexander (1881-1970): From July 1917, PM of the *Provisional Government* that took charge when the *Tsar* abdicated in February (March) 1917. His fatal mistake was to launch a summer offensive against Germany that so weakened his government it was threatened on all sides politically, and ultimately fell to the *Bolsheviks* in the *October (November) Revolution*. He lived out his days in academic *exile*.

Keynes, John Maynard (1883-1946): British economist. His theories about the *business cycle* and underlying causes of unemployment have been greatly influential since *WWII*. On the other hand, his criticism of the *reparations* set out in the *Treaty of Versailles*, while widely accepted in the 1920s, has since been shown wrong (Germany could have borne the burden). Keynes's main influence stemmed from the argument that public works spending could stoke an economy into recovery and stimulate full employment. Added to that was his considered rejection of the assumption of *classical liberalism* that the best market was a self-regulating one. He led the British delegation to the *Bretton Woods* conference, where in the wake of the *Great Depression* and the need to stimulate recovery from *WWII*, his theories were well received. See also *Georges Clemenceau; Keynesian economics.*

keynesian economics: The enormously influential theories developed by *John Maynard Keynes* and his devotees. To wit: increased savings (Keynes thought excessive saving severely damaged an economy) must be offset by enhanced *investment* to maintain levels of employment; savings will in general tend to exceed new investment. That must lead to stagnant *growth* and high unemployment unless governments *intervene* to stimulate investment, if necessary through *deficit* *spending* that also stimulates consumer spending. This was the first time anyone had proposed that markets tended to find equilibrium between savings and investment at levels below full employment. It was also new to propose that if mass unemployment in a *recession* times was to be corrected, then governments would have to be active players in a *market economy*. This approach was broadly applied to the problem of *postwar*, economic *reconstruction* in 1945. Cf. *laissez-faire; monetarism; supply side economics.*

KGB (*Komitet Gosudarstvennoy Bezopasnosti***):** "Committee on State Security." Formerly the *CHEKA*, *OGPU,* then *NKVD.* The name was changed to KGB in 1953. It was the Soviet *secret police*, and "shield and sword" of the *communist party*. Its main function was internal security: that is, repressing dissent, holding down ethnic unrest, monitoring the military and party *cadres*, running the *GULAG*, conducting the *purges*, and later, protecting *nuclear weapons* sites. But it also had a *counterespionage* and *espionage* function. It was widely respected by its opponents as among the toughest, most capable and ruthless *intelligence services* in the world. In 1992, to live down its unsavory past, its name was changed to the Federal Security Agency (SBRR). It is the world's largest security service (120,000 officers, excluding *paramilitary* and border guards). See also *Felix Dzerzhinsky; Alger Hiss; McCarthyism; Nazi/Soviet Pact.*

KHAD (*Khedamat-e Etela'at-e Dawlati***):** The Afghan *intelligence service* from 1980-92. It was trained by the *KGB*, and engaged in systematic *torture* of *mujahadeen* fighters, real or suspected, and their family members. It was headed by Muhammad Najibullah until he became president in 1987.

Khmers Rouges: "Red Khmer." The Cambodian *communist* movement led by *Pol Pot*. It engaged in *guerrilla* attacks from 1963-75. In the wake of the U.S. withdrawal from *Indochina* and the collapse of the South Vietnamese resistance, it took power and set in motion the *Cambodian genocide*. Thrown out by the Vietnamese *invasion* of Cambodia in 1978, the Khmers Rouges returned to *guerrilla warfare*, from bases in Thailand where it again imprisoned hundreds of thousands of Cambodian civilians. In 1992 its commanders accepted a UN plan for elections, but then threatened a massacre and began killing ethnic Vietnamese. Yet, in some areas, Khmers Rouges lined up to vote. After the election some 3,000 Khmers Rouges fighters deserted, with some permitted to enlist in the new Cambodian army being formed with UN help. In January 1994, sporadic fighting broke out between the Cambodian army and the remaining Khmers Rouges.

Khomeini, Ruhollah (1900-89): "Ayatollah Khomeini." A puritanical *Islamic* cleric and leader of the *Iranian Revolution*, 1979-89. He was *exiled* to Turkey by the Shah 1964-65, but moved to Iraq 1965-78, and to Paris 1978-79. Upon his return to Iran he established a harsh *theocracy*, introducing the *sharia* and reversing the Shah's *emancipation* of women. He declared the *Iran/Iraq War* a *jihad* that could end only with the destruction of *Saddam Hussein*. When circumstance compelled him to accept a UN-brokered *armistice*, he lamented that *peace* was for him "a cup of bitter poison." Just before he died he called on Muslims to murder *Salman Rushdie*, whom he accused of blasphemy. Khomeini's death occasioned an outpouring of mass hysteria, self-flagellation and expressions of deep *xenophobia* in Iran. The news was received with considerably more equanimity elsewhere.

Khrushchev, Nikita Sergeyevich (1894-1971): Soviet statesman. PM of Ukraine 1944-47; First Secretary of the Soviet Union 1953-64; Premier 1958-64. He helped get rid of *Beria* during the succession struggle following *Stalin's* death in 1953. His pursuit of *de-stalinization* after his 1956 secret speech denouncing Stalin was brave, but did not spring from a *liberal* conscience: it enabled him to take control of the *communist party* by moving his own supporters into *purged*, though no longer "*liquidated*," positions. He was first among equals in the *Politburo* by 1957. His recklessness was legendary. At home he began the Virgin Lands project, which proved an expensive disaster and has since led to evaporation of the *Aral Sea*. Abroad, he indulged in *saber rattling* over Berlin (1958) and during the *Cuban Missile Crisis*, before moving to a limited *détente* with the U.S. He handled problems with China more quietly, but they grew to dominate his concerns. Deposed in 1964, he became a virtual "*non-person*" in his enforced retirement. His memoirs were smuggled out and published in the West. See also *Bay of Pigs; Berlin; Molotov; national liberation, wars of; Open Skies; peaceful coexistence; Solzhenitsyn; U-2 incident; Zhukov.*

Khyber pass: The key passage (33 miles) through the mountains between Afghanistan and Pakistan.

Kiachow incident (November 1897): The German navy seized this Chinese coastal area, ostensibly in *retaliation* for the killing of German missionaries. It became the basis for their larger *sphere of influence* in *Shantung*. The actual seizure of Chinese *territory* caused a rush of emulation by the other *Great Powers* during 1898. Caught unawares and preoccupied with the *Spanish/American War*, the U.S. vainly protested about maintaining the *Open Door* in China. The base was later captured by Japan (1914), returned to China (1922), retaken by Japan (1938), and finally returned to China in 1945.

kiloton: A measure of nuclear explosive power: the equivalent explosive force of 1,000 tons of TNT. See *megaton*.

Kim Il-Sung (b.1912): "The Great Leader." North Korean dictator. Premier 1948-72; President 1972- . He came to power in the North with the aid of Soviet diplomacy and the *Red Army*, in which he had served (he is reputed to have also served as an informer for the *NKVD*). In 1993 Soviet documents finally resolved an old question of whether Kim started the *Korean Conflict* with *Stalin's* approval or not. They show he was primarily responsible for starting the war, gaining Stalin's reluctant support only after intense lobbying (48 telegrams to Moscow). But the Soviet Union then provided the necessary military buildup, including technicians and later, pilots and gun crews. Stalin also pressured *Mao Zedong* to support Kim, as a means of himself keeping a safe distance from direct military conflict with the U.S. After the war, Kim imposed a rigid, *stalinist* regime on North Korea. And he subjected it to a grotesque *cult of personality* (including hundreds of thousands of oversize statues of himself, and ritual praise songs made mandatory for every "street committee"). His policy must be described as extreme *autarky*, his personality as quixotic bordering on mad, and his rule as perverse and destructive. While driving his nation into extreme poverty, he sought all types of *weapons of mass destruction*. It has long been thought that he planned for his younger son, Kim Jong Il, to succeed him. However, at the end of 1993 an elder son, Kim Yong Yu, was made Vice President after 18 years of utter absence from public view.

King Cotton: The astoundingly nearsighted policy of the *Confederacy*, which *embargoed* and burned cotton in the vain hope that a shortage of the "king of commodities" would force Britain and France into diplomatic *recognition*. Of course, it should have traded its cotton for guns and ships before the *Union* could make an effective *blockade*. The move brought Dixie economically to its knees by depriving the army of supplies, eroding morale and destroying the economy. Besides overestimating the importance of cotton, it was not considered that the Europeans had accumulated *strategic stockpiles* as well as tapped into new sources in India and elsewhere.

King George's War (1744-48): The North American phase of the *War of the Austrian Succession*, waged by Britain and its colonists against France. In 1745 American *militia* and British *regulars* captured the great fortress of Louisbourg in Nova Scotia (formerly, Acadia). But the larger war in Europe ended in *stalemate*, and by the Treaty of Aix-la-Chapelle (1748) Britain handed Louisbourg back to France in exchange for *territory* to its ally in Holland. That shook the confidence of American colonists that in fighting for Britain their own interests would be tended to as well. It thus accelerated the process whereby they would one day seek to separate from the British Crown.

King, William Lyon Mackenzie (1874-1950): Canadian PM 1921-26, 1926-30, 1935-48. An *isolationist* during the 1930s, he supported the British policy of *appeasement* and opposed an *alliance* with the Soviets against *Nazi Germany*. Nevertheless, he brought Canada into *WWII* shortly after the British *declaration of war*. Erring always on the side of caution, he avoided *conscription* until 1944. His anti-communism meant Canada only opened *diplomatic relations* with the Soviet Union (a wartime ally from 1941) in 1943. He was forever offended at his exclusion from the councils of the *Great Powers*, where he believed Canada could play an intermediary role. Belatedly discovering untapped virtue in Moscow, he refused to believe and then failed to press in 1945 on a major atomic *spy* ring discovered in Canada. His diaries revealed a man subject to delusions of personal grandeur and steeped in obscure mysticism (he conducted regular seances). His foreign policies were reactive, and seldom creative. It has been justly said that he never did anything by half measures that he could do by quarters.

King William's War (1689-97): The North American phase of the *War of the Grand Alliance*, waged by England, its colonists and Indian *allies* against the French. The French, and their Indian allies, invaded Maine, New Hampshire and New York. American *militia* countered with an *invasion* that captured Port Royal in Acadia (Nova Scotia), but otherwise failed to meet its objective.

Kirghizstan: Location: Central Asia. Major associations: *CIS, CSCE, UN*. Population: 4.4 million (54% Kirghiz; 22% Russian; 16% Uzbek). Military: converted *Red Army* units. Along with other parts of *Central Asia*, this area was overrun in the Middle Ages by successive waves of Mongol and Turkic peoples. It was governed by various Muslim khanates until annexed by Russia in 1864. It was held in the empire by the *Red Army* during the *Russian Civil War,* and incorporated into the *Soviet Union* after 1920. It declared *independence* after the August 1991 *coup* attempt in Russia, but this was not widely *recognized* until *extinction* of the Soviet Union in December.

Since then it has been the most economically liberal of the Central Asian *republics*, and the most open to foreign *investment* and *trade*. It has even been praised by the *IMF* for its far-reaching reforms. While still underdeveloped and poor, it has rich deposits of *natural resources*. Politically, it has remained quiet. Thus, so far it has not drawn in Russian attention or troops.

Kiribati: Location: S. Pacific. Major associations: *ACP nations, Commonwealth, SPC, SPF, UN*. Population: 65,000. Military: none. This *microstate* is isolated from major population centers, cut off from main sea lanes and lacking in mineral resources. However, it claims a large *EEZ* with potential *seabed* resources and rich fishing grounds. It was a British *protectorate* from 1892 as part of the Gilbert and Ellice Islands, and a *colony* after 1916. Occupied by Japan early in *WWII*, it was *liberated* and occupied by the U.S. from 1943-45. A UN supervised *referendum* in 1974 led to a split with the Ellice Islands (*Tuvalu*), and the Gilberts became independent as Kiribati in 1979. As it maintains no foreign posts, Britain represents its overseas interests. In 1979 it signed a *friendship treaty* with the U.S. Washington dropped its claims to 14 islands in the Line and Phoenix group, in exchange for a guarantee that no foreign power would use those islands for military bases.

Kirov, Sergey Mironovich (1886-1934): *Old Bolshevik,* and potential rival to *Stalin's* leadership within the *Communist Party*. He was murdered on Stalin's orders. The killing was blamed on a monstrous (but imaginary) plot, and used as an excuse to launch the *Yezhovshchina*.

Kishi Nobusuke (1896-1987): Japanese statesman. PM 1957-60. He eased tensions with Japan's Asian neighbors left over from *WWII*. From necessity as well as inclination, he continued close relations with the U.S. and revised the U.S./Japan *security treaty*.

Kissinger, Henry (b.1923): U.S. statesman. National Security Adviser 1969-73; Secretary of State 1973-76. His conservative, *balance of power* diplomacy derived in part from his admiration for *Metternich*, whose system he wrote about in "A World Restored" (1957). He helped *Nixon* wind down the *Vietnam War* by first easing *tensions* with North Vietnam's principal sponsors, China and the Soviet Union, through policies of *détente* and *linkage*. He sought to limit U.S. security commitments, which he believed had been grossly exaggerated by *Kennedy* and *Johnson*. He did so, by overt attention to principles of *realpolitik*, disengaging from Vietnam to return *containment* to its original reliance on economic and political pressure. He hoped

thereby to free resources to buffer *NATO*, and allow the U.S. to focus on the core areas of *strategic* concern in industrialized Europe and Asia. He also pushed for acceptance of *SALT I*. He did not view foreign policy as a contest of *ideologies*, but of *nations*. Therefore, he arranged *Nixon's* breakthrough trip to China, then hostile to the Soviet Union. That, he said, "reduced *Indochina* to its proper scale--a small peninsula on a large continent." He won the *Nobel Prize* for Peace (shared with the North Vietnamese negotiator, *Le Duc Tho*) for the agreement ending the American phase of the *Vietnam War*. He returned it after North Vietnam conquered the South. He took a tough stance against Israel during the *Fourth Arab/Israeli War*, warning it to cease operations or risk fracturing the U.S. alliance. He was often accused of amoralism in his conduct of *diplomacy*, a charge he always and vigorously denied.

Kitchener, Horatio Herbert (1850-1916): British Field Marshal. He commanded British forces in the *Second Boer War*, where he was heavily criticized for using *concentration camps* to enclose *Boer* civilians, with many dying of disease and neglect. He also commanded in Egypt and India before *WWI*. Appointed to the War Cabinet in 1914, he proved unable to grasp the political side of the war, and was sent off to Russia on a diplomatic mission in 1916. He never arrived, drowning en route when his ship hit a *sea mine*.

Kiwi disease: Slang for U.S. fear that a "contagion" of states declaring *nuclear weapons free zones* might occur, on the New Zealand model. See *ANZUS*.

Knesset: The Israeli parliament. It has a history of paralysis due to Israel's system of proportional representation that gives undue influence to minor parties, in particular those of the Ultra Orthodox.

Kohl, Helmut (b.1930): German Chancellor 1982- >. He chose to rush reunification of the Germanies in 1989-90, and was rewarded with a massive electoral victory in the former *East Germany*. That popularity later waned. He held back during the *Gulf War*, choosing not to press the constitutional issue by sending troops to support the *Gulf Coalition*. Yet he argued, not without merit, that Germany was doing its share for world stability by absorbing East Germany and aiding *Eastern Europe* and the *Soviet Union* while other Western states were preoccupied with the Gulf crisis. He displayed what some saw as reckless haste to *recognize* Bosnia, Croatia and Slovenia, in a rush to judgment resisted vainly by the *EC, UN* and U.S. After that, his critics say, he showed little to no ability for leadership regarding the *Third Balkan War,* or to have Germany play a role on the world stage commensurate with its economic stature.

Kolchak, Alexander Vasilievich (1874-1920): Russian admiral. Commander of the *Black Sea Fleet* during *WWI*. He became leader of the Siberian *Whites* in the *Russian Civil War*, gaining notable victories. He had pretensions to become dictator of all the Russias, but was betrayed to the *Bolsheviks*, who had him shot.

Kondratieff cycles: Theorized "long waves" of economic fluctuations lasting from 50-60 years, in which levels of production, prices and trade are supposedly determined by forces intrinsic to the underlying structure of *capitalism*. The "waves" are characterized (or labeled) by a given period's major inventions (e.g., steam power, mass production or the automobile). In this example of *economic determinism* (there is little room here for *volition*) national policies, technological advances and even wars are seen as by-products of the "long waves." Expanding economic forces in the ascending wave are said to lead to invention, but also *revolution*, interstate *conflict* and *war*.

Konfrontasi (1963-66): "The Confrontation." The tense standoff and brooding threat of *war* between Indonesia and Malaysia following the latter's *federation* in 1963. It stemmed from Indonesian designs on *Sabah* and *Sarawak*. British and *Commonwealth* troops came to Malaysia's assistance, and proved a sufficient *deterrent* that war was avoided.

Koniev, Ivan Stepanovich (1897-1973): Soviet general. He was a successful commander in *WWII*, after which he served as head of the *Red Army* 1946-55, and first commander of the *Warsaw Pact*.

Korea: Location: East Asia. "The Hermit Kingdom." Made a tributary of China in 1637, as China weakened Korea became a pawn of *Great Power* intrigue. China and Japan signed a *convention* on Korea in 1885, and it was made nominally independent by the *Sino/Japanese War* of 1894-95. It was steadily penetrated by Japan from the south and Russia from the north, leading to the *Russo/Japanese War* of 1904-05. After 1905, Japan took over Korea's diplomacy, and ended the fiction of *independence* by formally *annexing* it in 1910. Korea remained under Japanese *occupation* until 1945. During this time it developed in many respects, but always to the advantage of the Japanese rather than the native population: Japanese language was made compulsory; agricultural production increased, but was skimmed off to feed Japan; and harsh military control was maintained. At the *Cairo Conference* in 1943, it was decided that Korea should become independent "in due course." At *Potsdam* it was decided to divide the *surrender* of Japanese forces in Korea with the Americans taking control south of the 38th parallel, while the Soviets accepted the surrender in the north. The Soviets and Americans duly occupied the peninsula after the war. But unification fell victim to the burgeoning *Cold War:* on August 15, 1948, the *Republic of Korea* (South Korea) was proclaimed; on September 9th that was matched by declaration of the *Democratic People's Republic* (North Korea). On June 25, 1950, the *Korean Conflict* broke out. The issue was decided by 1951, but the fighting did not stop until July 1953. The *Geneva Agreements* in 1954 failed to bring about reunification. The *DMZ* between the Koreas remains volatile in the 1990s, bristling with troops and weapons. See *Root/Takahira Agreement*.

Korea, Democratic People's Republic (North Korea): Location: East Asia. Major associations: none. Population: 23 million. Military: it had in 1994 the world's fifth largest military at 1,130,000 troops (larger are China, India, the U.S. and Russia). Its best *missile*, the Rodong-1, has a 1,000-km range. Proclaimed in the Soviet administrative zone on September 9, 1948, in 1950 it invaded *South Korea*, starting the *Korean Conflict*. It has remained for decades a harsh, *stalinist* state, under the control of *Kim Il-Sung*. It officially followed a policy of "juche" (*self-reliance*). Throughout the *Cold War* it was allied closely with China and the Soviet Union, directing over 95% of its trade to those countries but managing not to take sides in the *Sino/Soviet split*. On the other hand, it was not recognized by the U.S. As South Korea began to pass it by in economic development, the North grew more not less *xenophobic, autarkic* and *militaristic*, and sponsored *terrorist* attacks against the South. With the collapse of the Soviet Union the North lost its major market; China too, ended trade at "friendship prices." The North therefore reached an economic crisis of catastrophic proportions. Its response was a marginal domestic *thaw*, a few joint ventures, and a diplomatic offensive proclaiming a new openness. Meanwhile, it increased *arms exports* (including missile technology to Iran), and speeded completion of its *nuclear weapons* program. In 1992 Russia suspended all military shipments, depriving North Korea of replacements for its advanced, *MIG-29* fighters. In January 1993, Russia announced a unilateral revision of its *friendship treaty*, removing a clause committing it to aid North Korea in the event of *war*. Then Russian *intelligence* reported that North Korea was testing *chemical and biological weapons* on offshore islands, including anthrax, cholera, bubonic plague and smallpox. On April 1, 1993, the *IAEA* reported North Korea's refusal to submit to inspection to the *Security Council*, whereupon the North announced it would withdraw from the *Nuclear Non-Proliferation Treaty*. It warned the UN not to impose *sanctions*. In 1993 the *CIA* suggested that the North had already built one or two atomic *warheads*. In January 1994, North Korea agreed to limited IAEA inspections of its *plutonium* production, and the principle of *continuity of safeguards*. Even so, it continued to deny effective monitoring in practice.

Korean Central Intelligence Agency (KCIA): The main *intelligence agency* of South Korea, originally modeled on, and maintaining close links with, its American namesake. Its main role has been *counterintelligence* against its North Korean counterpart. In a bizarre incident in 1979, the head of the KCIA assassinated President *Park Chung Hee*.

Korean Conflict (1950-53): In January 1950, *Dean Acheson* made an impolitic statement in which he appeared to leave *South Korea* out of the defense perimeter to which the U.S. had declared it would commit troops. On June 25th, the *North Korea's* army attacked, overrunning Seoul within 72 hours and routing the South Korean defenders. The U.S. began to send *aid* and supplies from Japan, while seeking UN authorization for a larger engagement. With the Soviets boycotting the *Security Council* over the issue of China's representation, the U.S. obtained the desired *resolution* and some 15 nations committed themselves to repel *aggression* against South Korea (the Soviets never missed another meeting). Still, the bulk of the fighting was done by U.S. and Korean troops. General *Douglas MacArthur* was placed in overall command. On September 15th he landed a force behind the overextended North Korean lines, at Inchon. Now the Northern army was routed in its turn. The UN goal was satisfied and several member states wanted to stop at the 38th parallel. But *Truman* pressed ahead, aiming at unifying Korea under a single, pro-Western government. MacArthur was under orders to stay clear of tangling with the Chinese, but as his forces approached the border he suppressed *intelligence* about a Chinese troop buildup. At the end of November, 300,000 Chinese "volunteers" stunned his troops and pushed them back into the south, in the longest retreat in U.S. military history. After several more months of back-and-forth fighting, the war settled into a protracted *stalemate* near the original border at the 38th parallel. For two years desultory fighting continued for this hill or that valley, but the front hardly moved. With the death of *Stalin* and the election of *Eisenhower*, the diplomatic logjam was broken and a *cease-fire* agreement reached. Efforts at a *peace treaty* failed, however, leaving the peninsula in a state of apprehended conflict ever since. At least 3 million died, mainly

Korean *civilians*. Casualties included unknown numbers of Chinese, and 30,000 American dead (108,000 wounded) in the "forgotten war," as well as 15,000 more dead and many more wounded from other UN contingents. The U.S. experience with Chinese *intervention* was a major factor in the refusal at any point in the *Vietnam War* to cross with ground forces into North Vietnam. Note: On the matter of responsibility for the war see *Kim Il-Sung*. See also map.

Korea, Republic of (South Korea): Location: E. Asia. Major associations: *APEC*. Population: 44 million. Military: currently upgrading; qualitatively superior to the North, but smaller. Proclaimed on August 15, 1948. Its first President was *Syngman Rhee*. After the *Korean Conflict*, the South slowly rebuilt under a U.S. security and, to a lesser extent, economic umbrella. Simultaneously, it was not *recognized* by the *Soviet bloc*. It was handicapped by millions of *refugees* and by the rampant corruption that attended Rhee's government. The army seized power in 1961, and while it ruled with an iron hand it also oversaw revival based on an export-oriented economy. In the early 1970s South Korea emerged as an *Asian Tiger*. By 1980 domestic prosperity had produced a vibrant middle class that began to insist on representative institutions, a demand echoed by the *Carter* administration in the U.S. The army gave way only slowly, and not without bloodshed: in the city of Kwangju hundreds of demonstrators died at the army's hand. The crisis was exacerbated by a bitter personal rivalry between the main opposition figures (the "two Kims"), Kim Dae Jung and Kim Young Sam. Nonetheless, in 1987 free and fair elections were held. Korea then used the 1988 Seoul *Olympics* as a symbol of its acquisition of *First World* status. The collapse of the Soviet Union led to *diplomatic relations* with Russia and the other *successor states*. Korean relations with Japan are close due to trade interests, but not untroubled by charges of Japanese *racism* against ethnic Koreans (brought to Japan as *slave laborers* after 1910). There are lingering worries about a revival of Japanese *militarism*. All U.S. *nuclear weapons* were removed, by agreement, by December 1991. South Korea continued military exercises with the U.S. but offered to cease these if it received assurance that the North would not obtain nuclear weapons. As of 1995, the combined Korean/American force is to be commanded by a Korean.

Kosciuszko, Tadeusz (1746-1817): Polish revolutionary who fought in the *American War of Independence*. He led a rising against Russia in 1794 that garnered sympathy, but no help from the powerless and *isolationist* U.S. He went into *exile* in France, refusing to help either the Russians or the French control Poland.

Kosygin, Alexei Nikolayevich (1904-81): Soviet PM 1964-80. He helped *Brezhnev* oust *Khrushchev* in 1964, and was rewarded with the premiership. He was most interested in domestic affairs, particularly in improving the rate of production of *consumer goods*, but neither he nor the system enjoyed much success.

Kosovo: Violence erupted in this onetime Yugoslav province in 1968, and again on a larger scale in 1981, when its population demanded to be upgraded to the status of a *republic* within *Yugoslavia*. Instead, in 1989 its *autonomy* was stripped away and it became a mere province of Serbia. It is 95% Albanian, but after the breakup of Yugoslavia this majority found itself a despised minority still tied to Serbia. In 1992 *George Bush* warned Serbia that any attempt at *ethnic cleansing* in Kosovo would lead to direct U.S. *intervention*. Why such concern while *war* was allowed to rage in Bosnia? Ankara had indicated that a Serbian attempt to expel the Kosovo Albanians (who are mostly Muslim and desire *union* with Albania) would bring Turkish intervention. If that happened Greece, too, would have been drawn in, and a general war might have engulfed the region. In mid-1993 Serbia ordered *CSCE* observers to leave Kosovo.

Kossuth, Lajos (1802-94): Hungarian *patriot* who led the *Revolution of 1848* that was crushed by the troops of Tsar *Nicholas II*. A U.S. *warship* was dispatched to fetch him from a Turkish prison, and he toured the U.S. seeking financial and military aid. Other than polite applause and a county in Iowa named after him, he got little real assistance and returned to Europe.

kowtow: Touching the head to the floor when in the presence of a *Manchu* emperor. It was a practice demanded of foreign *emissaries* to signify that the Chinese court regarded other *sovereigns* as supplicants, not equals. When foreigners began to refuse the kowtow in the 19th century, it was a sure sign that China's relative power was in steep decline.

Krajiina: A strip of *territory* in Croatia along the north and west borders of Bosnia. In March 1994, a UN-brokered *peace* left it 70% controlled by ethnic Serb *militia*, who were backed by Belgrade in their declaration of a so-called "Serb Republic of Krajiina."

Kremlin: "The Citadel." (1) The exceptionally ornate citadel, with accompanying churches and living quarters, built by the Muscovite princes. It was used by them, the Tsars and the Soviets as the administrative center of the *Russian Empire*. It is now used by the President of Russia. (2) A synonym for the Russian state, its dreams, plots and policies. Cf. *White House*.

Kremlinology: The study, during the *Cold War*, of the politics and government of the *Soviet Union*.

Kremlin watching: Intense concentration by Western *analysts* during the *Cold War* on shifts and tendencies in Soviet policy revealed by the nuances of leadership behavior. Who is up, down, in or out? Is anyone not present? Is anyone dead? These were the topics of conversation every *May Day*, as Kremlinologists scrutinized the closeness to the top leaders of lesser lights during appearances of the Soviet leadership on the wall of the Kremlin during the parade.

***kristallnacht* (November 9-10, 1938):** "The night of broken glass." The *Nazis* arranged this orgy of rape and murder of Jews, and pillaging of Jewish shops and property, that marked the beginning of Germany's final descent into barbarism. The terror of those nights was named for the shards of thousands of broken windows from Jewish shops, littering the streets of German and Austrian towns. The *pogrom* was a signal, if one was still needed, that the position of Jews under the *Third Reich* was about to deteriorate dramatically: thereafter, they could not make a living or feel secure on the streets, in their persons or their homes. Those who could cashed in whatever they had and bought their way out of the country. The Nazis, with characteristic cynicism, encouraged this by maintaining a "Ministry for Jewish Emigration," which they used to extort the last pfennig from departing Jews. *WWII* and plans for the *"final solution to the Jewish problem"* yet to come would close down even this trickle of escapees.

Kruger, Paulus (1825-1904): *Afrikaner* leader, President of the *Transvaal* 1883-1900. As a boy, he made the *Great Trek;* as a man, he led the *Boers* in both *Boer Wars* against Britain. He is a towering figure within Afrikaner nationalist circles.

Kruger telegram (January 3, 1896): A message of congratulations on the defeat of the *Jamieson Raid* sent by Kaiser *Wilhelm II* to *Paulus Kruger*. Typical of the Kaiser's gestures, it gave offense to Britain without gaining anything for Germany. It also falsely encouraged the *Boers* into thinking they would have real support from Germany in any *war* with Britain.

Krupp, Alfred (1812-87): German *arms* manufacturer. He developed the vast Krupp steel and *armaments* works that fed the German war machine during its expansion under *Bismarck*, and in both world wars. His descendants made the firm the largest armaments conglomerate in the world. Several were accused of *war crimes*, including the use of *slave labor* from the *concentration camps* in Krupp factories and mines.

Alfred Felix Krupp (1907-67) served four years, but was pardoned and released in 1951 and played a lead role in West Germany's industrial revival. The Krupp firm became a public corporation in the 1960s.

kulaks: "Tight-fisted ones." A *Bolshevik* pejorative for the richer peasants (such as those with property beyond subsistence, or employing farm laborers) who had benefited most from the agrarian reforms of 1906, and also 1917. They bitterly resisted the *collectivization* drive of 1931-33, when *Stalin* ordered kulaks *"liquidated* as a class" and the "dekulakization" of Soviet agriculture. Actually, the term "kulak" was never precisely defined, which suited Stalin's simultaneous and more general campaign against *nationalism* in Ukraine, and his paranoid delusions that failure to meet unrealistic requisition quotas was due to kulak *sabotage* and *counter-revolution*. As a result, middle peasants were also swept into the net and destroyed. By 1933 the scale of peasant resistance and state repression approached that of *civil war.* Some 14.5 million--including large numbers of children--died (roughly equivalent to the total killed on all sides in *WWI*). Hundreds of thousands were shot; millions more were worked to death in the *forced labor* camps of the *GU-LAG*. At least five million were left to starve in their homes after their cattle and grain were confiscated. At the height of the *famine* the *Red Army* hemmed in the entire Ukraine to prevent food smuggling or flight, while *OGPU* units and Young Communist volunteers seized the grain and dealt out "revolutionary justice" (otherwise known as murder). Two million more from accused kulak families were *deported* by cattle car to arid, infertile lands in *Central Asia* and *Siberia*, where at least half died from starvation or exposure. As the *depredations* worsened, kulak sabotage became a self-fulfilling prophesy: the peasants slaughtered their pigs and cattle and burned the grain, rather than hand it all to the collectives. Still, Stalin had his way: within five years the peasants who survived had been cowed and driven into the collectives. Soviet agriculture never recovered from the destruction of property and dispiriting of the countryside this savage campaign caused. It took 25 years simply to return to precollectivization numbers of livestock, while peasant trust and incentive was gone, perhaps forever. Undeterred by these facts, *Mao* would later model his rural "reforms" on this *stalinist* example, with comparable disastrous results.

Kulturkampf (1872-87): "Cultural struggle." The conflict between *Bismarck* and German Catholics, following the declaration by the *First Vatican Council* of the popes' putative infallibility. Bismarck failed to impose his will, but the contest was superseded by his concern at the rise of an organized, working-class movement.

Kun, Béla (1886-1937): Hungarian communist who set up a *soviet* in Hungary that lasted from March-August 1919. It was invaded by the Czechs and the Rumanians, and *civil war* also broke out. He fled to the Soviet Union, where he was later *purged*, dying unheralded somewhere in the *GULAG*--another nameless number, afterward misplaced, in the *slave labor* system run by the gray men he had so admired and so long served.

Kuranari Doctrine: Enunciated by the Japanese Foreign Minister in 1987, it declared that in the *South Pacific* Japan respected island *autonomy* and *independence*, and offered greater economic assistance to assure regional political stability.

Kurdistan: The would-be state of the *Kurds*, and a region spanning parts of Armenia, Azerbaijan, Iraq, Iran, Syria and Turkey.

Kurds: Kurdish-speaking peoples (numbering perhaps 20 million) in *Kurdistan*. Many are pastoral; others have moved into the cities. The *Treaty of Sèvres* created an independent homeland for the Kurds, but it was never ratified. (1) In Iraq: Forming nearly 1/5th of the population, from 1922-32 the Kurds fought an unsuccessful *war* for an independent *state*. Again in 1961 they rose, led by Mustapha Barzani (1901-79), Kurdish nationalist and able *guerrilla* leader who led Iraqi Kurds in a sustained but unsuccessful *rebellion*, 1961-79. In 1970 Baghdad conceded *autonomy*, but when this promise was not kept, fighting resumed. With support from Iran, Kurds won further concessions in 1975. But when the Shah dropped his support they were crushed by then General *Saddam Hussein*. Under Saddam's iron regime a *genocide* was conducted against Iraq's Kurds, with some 200,000 dying, many in *chemical weapons* attacks on their villages. With Saddam's defeat in the *Gulf War* the Kurds rose yet again, but the *Republican Guards* forced nearly a million to flee to Iran, Turkey, and into the hills. The U.S., Britain and France declared a *no-fly zone* over the Kurdish region of northern Iraq, effectively guaranteeing (for the moment) Kurdish autonomy. (2) In Turkey: A full-scale revolt in 1925 was crushed. A policy of state persecution then aimed at wiping out the Kurdish culture and language and forcing assimilation. The Kurds revolted again in 1944-45, and 1978-79. At the present time, many Kurds have assimilated, but since 1984 others have supported a radical group that is waging a guerrilla campaign in the southeast part of Turkey. Turkey has claimed *hot pursuit* in crossing into northern Iraq to bomb and shell guerrilla encampments. (3) In Iran: The Soviets promoted a Kurdish state in northern Iran at the close of *WWII*, but it collapsed when they pulled out under Anglo/

American pressure in 1946. The Kurds have faced persistent persecution in Iran that only deepened since the *Iranian Revolution*. In 1993 representatives from Iran, Syria and Turkey met in Damascus to coordinate policies to prevent a Kurdish state emerging from the autonomous zone in Iraq.

Kuriles (Chishima): An island chain just north of the Japanese *home islands*, taken from Japan by decision of the *Cairo* and *Yalta Conferences* and given to Russia. They were not included in the *Japanese Peace Treaty*, as the Soviets did not sign it. The Russians pledged to return Habomai and Shikotan once a separate treaty could be negotiated (partially achieved in 1956). In 1960 they added the condition of prior abrogation of the 1951 Japan/U.S. *security treaty*, a proviso quietly abandoned by 1973. Regarding Etorufo and Kunashiri, the Soviets were adamant that return was out of the question. With the breakup of the Soviet Union the Kuriles (the "Northern Territories" to Japan) remained a bone of contention. Japan refused to consider *aid* to Russia until the islands were returned; but Russia both was interested in extending its fishing rights into the Sea of Okhotsk, and feared opening border questions with other neighbors, notably China. Only great pressure from the *G-7* led to moderation of Japan's position in mid-1993. The issue remains a serious barrier to warmer Japanese/Russian relations.

Kursk, Battle of (July 1943): A major turning point on the *eastern front*. After *Stalingrad, Hitler* ordered a mass of *armor* and the *Luftwaffe* to cut to pieces a Russian salient, some 100 miles deep, at Kursk. The Germans were met by even larger, but hidden, Soviet tank and air formations under *Zhukov*. The largest tank battle in history resulted, involving over 5,000 tanks as well as many thousands of lesser armored vehicles. The Germans lost so many tanks and planes (Soviet equipment had by then surpassed German in design) that they were never again able to go on the offensive in the east. After Kursk the Soviets faced a long, bitter and bloody, but also unstoppable, march to the *Führer* bunker in Berlin.

Kuwait: Location: *Middle East*. Major associations: *Arab League, Gulf Cooperation Council, OAPEC, OPEC, UN*. Population: two million Kuwaitis, and an equal number of foreign workers. Military: rapidly rearming with top equipment, but based on a tiny population grown indolent with great wealth. A small, desert nation ruled by the al-Sabah dynasty (and extended family *elite*). It was founded in 1759 as a province within the *Ottoman Empire*. It was made a British *protectorate* from 1899-1961, when it was given *independence*. *Oil* production began in 1936, making Kuwait attractive to Iraq, which claimed it in 1961 on the ground they had once been linked under the Ottomans. The British sent troops back to Kuwait as a *deterrent*; they were replaced by an Arab force following *mediation* of the conflict. During the 1960s and 1970s Kuwait prospered, sending only token forces to fight against Israel in 1973. By the 1980s it was one of the wealthiest (per capita) nations in the world, and imported *Palestinians* and others to do manual labor, while dispensing wealth to and repressing dissent by Kuwaitis. It supported Iraq during the *Iran/Iraq War*, for which the al-Sabah family earned the permanent enmity of Iran. However, Iraq too turned on the Kuwaitis: on August 2, 1990, *Saddam Hussein* sent his army into Kuwait, despoiled it, and announced it was now Iraq's "Province 19." The *Gulf War* followed. Liberation came on February 27, 1991. Retribution came the next day: Palestinians were expelled for supporting the Iraqis, and Kuwaiti *collaborators* were executed. However, the al-Sabah family did not return for over a month, waiting until their palaces were cleaned and restocked with creature comforts. Reform and democratization was reluctantly promised, and has been slow arriving. Since the war, Kuwaiti foreign policy has become enthusiastically pro-Western, and has dropped its *neutrality* in favor of close military cooperation with Saudi Arabia and the *Gulf States*.

Kwantung Army: See *Guandong Army*.

Ky, Nguyen Cao (b.1930): South Vietnamese general. He participated in the *coup* that overthrew *Ngo Dinh Diem*, heading the *junta* that then took power. He has been heavily criticized in the U.S. for his conduct of the war. His retort is that Americans were guilty of heartless abandonment of the South during the collapse of 1975 when they (and he) fled, along with the human *flotsam and jetsam* of the South Vietnamese regime. He went into commercial business in America.

L

laager: A *Boer* term for an encampment of circled wagons, a *tactic* used against the *Zulu* before the 20th century; used subsequently as a metaphor for a *siege* mentality, such as contributed to *apartheid*.

labor: (1) One of the *factor endowments* of an economy. It is any productive work or activity done by wage workers. (2) The overall labor capacity of an economy, whether employed or latent. Cf. *slave labor*.

labor theory of value: The theory, not originally but most famously propounded by *Karl Marx*, that the entire value of a *commodity* is derived from the *labor* that goes into its production. Despite the gaping oversight of not accounting for *capital*, management skills, marketing and other factors that add real value, it was the main premise of *Soviet bloc* economic theory.

lacunae: Gaps, or issues not covered by *international law* or in a theory.

Lafayette, Marquis de (1757-1834): He fought in the *American War of Independence*, then commanded the French National Guard from 1789-92, providing a living link between the American and French revolutions. An unflagging *liberal*, in 1830 he tried to rally U.S. support for a Polish revolt against tsarist rule.

Laibach, Congress of (1821): Austria, Prussia and Russia met, with Britain and France as observers, for the third time in the *Congress system*. It dealt with *liberal* revolution in the Italian and *Iberian* peninsulas. Britain confirmed the agreement of *Troppau* that Austria should intervene in Italy, but again rejected the premise of a general right to *intervention* by the *Great Powers* in the *internal affairs* of small states.

laissez-faire: The theory/doctrine that the most efficient, equitable and productive economy is one where the government interferes (acts, owns and regulates) the least, so that market forces are permitted to operate nearly unhindered. There are also public policy variants that prefer private charity and philanthropy to government social programs, and react strongly against efforts to regulate private behavior or morality. See *liberalism; market economy; physiocrats; reform liberalism*. Cf. *dirigisme; industrial revolution*.

land: One of the *factor endowments* of an economy. It comprises unused and agricultural land, all properties that produce rent and all *natural resources*.

land for peace: The idea that in cases of territorial dispute it is in the long-term interest of the power controlling the disputed land to give up some or all of it in exchange for a verifiable, secure *peace*. See also *occupied territories; Resolutions 242 and 338*.

landing craft: Flat-bottomed ships used to bring troops, vehicles and equipment onshore, from where they drive inland to press home an amphibious assault.

land mine: An explosive set to trigger on contact, or upon the weight of a soldier or vehicle. Their use against *civilians* was prohibited by a *protocol* attached to the 1983 Convention on Inhumane Weapons, but to little practical effect--the land mine is inherently indiscriminate. Indeed, its use has spread from defense to a means of *ethnic cleansing*, terror and *reprisal*. Their advantage is cheapness (some cost but a few dollars). A major disadvantage is the high cost of later removal (on average, up to $1,000 each). Wide removal techniques have not advanced much beyond the crude and dangerous feel-and-mark methods of *WWII*. As a result, many people are killed by mines for years after a war ends. *Human rights* groups want mines banned. Others view a ban as unenforceable but suggest, as a pragmatic first step, making them detectible by insertion of a metal strip (because many are now plastic, they cannot be located with metal detectors). Experiments with microwave detection are also underway. In 1993 the U.S. announced a three-year extension of its unilateral, 1992 *moratorium* on export of anti-personnel mines, and called for a total export ban.

land power: One in the first rank in army strength.

Lansing, Robert (1864-1928): U.S. statesman. He replaced *William Jennings Bryan* as *Wilson's* Secretary of State 1915-20. An *anglophile*, he pressed for early U.S. entry into the war, secretly assuring the British that this would be the ultimate outcome of U.S. policy. He disagreed vehemently with Wilson's conduct of the *Paris Peace Conference*, and subsequently was sharply and openly critical of his old boss.

Lansing/Ishii Agreement (October 31, 1917): In December 1916, the Western *Allies* asked the U.S. to block Japan's advances in China through *dollar diplomacy* to forestall Japanese economic dominance of the region. European *capital* was tied up in the war effort; American capital was thus the only freely available and abundant supply. Japan asked for a statement of U.S. policy. A meeting was arranged between Ambassador Kikujiro Ishii and Secretary of State *Robert Lansing*. They agreed to a *protocol*, kept secret for 18 years, promising neither party would seek special privileges that might abridge the rights of other states (under existing *servitudes*) in China. Next, they publicly reaffirmed respect for the *Open Door* and the *territorial integrity* of China. But in a controversial phrase, the U.S. accepted that "territorial *propinquity* creates special relations between states," and hence that Japan had special interests in China. This ambiguity between the public and secret accords allowed each side to interpret the understanding differently, and thus rendered it more of a misunderstanding: the U.S. thought it had obtained a Japanese pledge to respect the Open Door and China's integrity; Japan thought it had obtained U.S. recognition of its own *hegemony* over China. In 1922 the U.S. thought it abrogated the secret protocol (by then seen as a mistake) in the *Nine Power Treaty*. When Japan contested this interpretation, the U.S. threatened to publish the protocol. Japan reluctantly and resentfully consented to formal cancellation, in an exchange of *diplomatic notes* in April, 1923. The end result of the Lansing/Ishii agreement, meant to clarify positions and avoid conflict, thus was a worsening of relations.

Laos: Location: SE Asia. Major associations: *UN*. Population: 4.4 million. Military: outdated weapons, small numbers. For centuries Laos was divided among small, independent kingdoms that struggled to remain independent of Siamese (Thai) influence. It was unified by the French, who made it a *protectorate* in 1893. In 1947 it was made *autonomous* within the *French Union*. It became an independent, *neutral* kingdom by the *terms* of the *Geneva Agreements*. The conflicts of its neighbors, Cambodia and Vietnam, spilled into Laos, which also faced a home grown *insurgency* by the *Pathet Lao*. A low-level *guerrilla* campaign sputtered on for over two decades. It was worsened by the abuse of Laotian *neutrality* by the North Vietnamese, who ran the *Ho Chi Minh Trail* through Laos and Cambodia. In turn, the trail was bombed and raided in secret by the U.S. The Pathet Lao took power in Vientianne in 1975, simultaneously with the collapse of South Vietnam. King Savang Vatthana (1907-?) was sent to a *reeducation* camp, where it is thought he died or was murdered. As with other communist states, the collapse of the Soviet Union and changes in China compelled a reevaluation of the international position of Laos, and of its domestic policy. Since 1987 there has been a moderation of repression and a slow move toward market openness, with heavy reliance on the *Asian Development Bank*. Yet Laos remains among the world's poorest nations.

Lapland: The northern portions of Finland, Norway, Russia and Sweden, traditionally the land over which the nomadic Lapps have followed the reindeer. It is a cultural, rather than a political, term.

Lateran Treaties (1929): These agreements between the Italian state and the papacy finally resolved the conflict that had dragged on since the days of *Pius IX*. They established the *Vatican* as an independent *city-state* within the larger city of Rome, and granted generous financial compensation to the popes for their lost territories. See *Roman Question*.

Latin America: The part of the Americas south of the U.S. where Latin, or romance, languages (Spanish, Portuguese and French) are dominant. Therefore, Latin America is not just the continent of South America, but also Mexico, Central America (excluding Belize) and some Caribbean islands (including Cuba and all Hispaniola). Aslo, see *Alliance for Progress; Amazon Pact; Calvo clause; Cartagena Group; Contadora Group; Good Neighbor policy; LAFTA; LAIA; Monroe Doctrine; OAS; Rio Pact.*

Latin American Free Trade Association (LAFTA): It was set up in 1960 (Treaty of Montevideo), and aimed at a *free trade area* for Latin America within just 12 years. Its lack of success was due largely to an overly ambitious timetable, a failure to distinguish among the levels of economic development of its member states, and rising *debt* and *protectionism*. Failure led to creation of the successor *Latin American Integration Association*.

Latin American Integration Association (LAIA): This organization was set up in 1980 as the successor to the *Latin American Free Trade Association*. It introduced more flexibility by dropping LAFTA's precise deadline for success, and by formally differentiating among member states, ranking them according to their levels of *development*. During the 1980s members remained preoccupied with the *debt crisis*. The move toward hemispheric *free trade* then somewhat preempted LAIA, with signature of *NAFTA* and proposals for a *Western Hemisphere Free Trade Association*.

Latvia: Location: *Baltic*. Major associations: *CSCE, UN*. Population: 2.7 million. Military: *militia* only; Russian troops still in-country. This *Baltic State* was long a battleground for German, Swedish and Russian princes. It was made a Russian province in the 18th century. After fending off both the *Red Army* and lingering German forces, it enjoyed *independence* from 1921-40. However, by 1934 hard times led to institution of an *authoritarian* regime. It was secretly assigned to the Soviet *sphere of influence* by the *Nazi/Soviet Pact* in 1939. Latvia was occupied by the Soviets in June 1940, and annexed in August. The Germans occupied it from 1941-44, when Soviet control was reestablished. The U.S. and some other Western countries never accepted the legality of the Soviet *annexation*. Instead, they maintained formal ties with a paper *government-in-exile* that had an *embassy* in Washington throughout the *Cold War*. During the August 1991, *coup* attempt in Russia, Latvia declared its independence. It reemerged as an undisputed *sovereign* nation with the *extinction* of the Soviet Union on December 25, 1991. See *near abroad*.

launcher: The lift vehicle that launches a *missile* on its flight path (as distinct from the *warhead*, which is the missile's ultimate raison d'être). Launchers can be land-based (ICBM), submarine-based (SLBM) or loosed from an aircraft (ALBM and ASBM).

launch on warning: Firing a *retaliation* (retaliatory) strike once incoming *missiles* have been confirmed but before their *warheads* detonate, so that one's own missiles are not destroyed in the enemy's *first strike*. It is a *strategic* posture that strains toward the possibility of *accidental war*. Cf. *second strike*.

Laurier, Wilfred (1841-1919): PM of Canada 1896-1911. He was the first French-Canadian to serve as PM. He agreed to an *imperial tariff*, and to send troops to fight in the *Second Boer War*. However, when he sought a *free trade* arrangement with the U.S. his government fell. Out of office, like most others from *Québec*, he opposed *conscription* during *WWI*.

Lausanne, Treaty of (July 24, 1923): The second, and final, *peace treaty* formally ending *WWI* between the *Allies* and Turkey. It replaced the *Treaty of Sèvres*. Turkey gave up all claim to the old *Ottoman* lands in Europe, except a small area around *Constantinople*; Greece received most of the Aegean islands, but returned Smyrna (Izmir); Britain's control of *Cyprus* and Italy's of the *Dodecanese* was confirmed; the *Bosphorus* and *Dardanelles* were *demilitarized*; and in a milder version of *ethnic cleansing*, a transfer of Greek and Turkish populations was effected, totaling nearly 1.5 million persons. The big losers were the *Kurds*, who lost the homeland promised them by Sèvres.

Laval, Pierre (1883-1945): French traitor; *Vichy* politician. Originally a *socialist*, he drifted to the right in the 1920s and then raced there in the 1930s. He was PM 1931-32, 1935-36; Foreign Minister 1934-36. He negotiated the *Hoare-Laval Pact* on Ethiopia. He was PM of Vichy 1942-44. Laval enthusiastically *collaborated* with the *Nazis*, shipping Jews and French *forced labor* to Germany. Always the schemer, he adopted a

more neutral stance after *D-Day*, for which he was briefly arrested by the Germans. He fled to Spain, but upon his return to France in 1945 he was executed for *treason*. Cf. *Vidkun Quisling; Wang Jingwei*.

law-creating processes: Making new *international law* via *law-making treaties, international customary law* or extrapolation from *general principles*.

law-making treaties: *Treaties* are the major instrument for creating *international law*. Even *bilateral* treaties may have universal effects, if the principles they apply are repeated in other such agreements. In addition, there are deliberate "law-making treaties." These are *multilateral* agreements in which states set out to codify new *rules* in the hope and expectation that most other states will *adhere* customarily or formally. Examples include: the *Geneva, Red Cross* and *Hague Conventions;* the *Covenant of the League of Nations* and the *Charter of the United Nations*.

law of return: Passed in 1950, it gives all Jews a right to *immigrate* to *Israel*. It has been amended several times, each time to narrow it toward the Orthodox definition of who is a Jew. See *Falasha; judaism*.

law of the sea: The oceans and waterways of the world are of concern here, as are the ships that ply and the industries that mine them. This is both the oldest and most well-developed branch of *international law*. That is probably because *nations* have for centuries encountered each other in non-hostile pursuits, particularly commerce and fishing, on the great ocean trade routes. Of course, they have also made *war* at sea, and that branch of law, too, is highly developed. See *baseline; blockade; belligerent rights; cabotage; Canal Zones; cannon shot rule; capture; combat area; continental shelf; contraband; EEZ; embargo; flag of convenience; flotsam and jetsam; high seas; hot pursuit; innocent passage; internationalize; international waterway; neutral rights; piracy; privateer; prize; Seabed Treaty; slave trade; straight baseline; Straits Question; territorial sea; three mile limit; twelve-mile limit; war crimes; war zone; UNCLOS I, II, and III*.

Lawrence, T. E. (1888-1935): "Of Arabia." An *Arabist* seconded by the British to *Ibn Ali Hussein*, whom he convinced to join the *Arab Revolt* (and later helped become King of the *Hejaz*). He coordinated Arab irregular attacks with the British advance on Damascus. He was revolted by revelation of the *Sykes-Picot Agreement*. After the war he withdrew from public life, assuming several false identities. He reenlisted under an assumed name at a lower rank, but published a successful memoir ("Seven Pillars of Wisdom").

laws of war: These are positive *rules* of practical *statecraft*, not the *normative* tradition of *just war theory*. Yet, they draw deeply from that well, especially the *jus in bello*. The great legal writer of a previous generation, H. Lauterpacht, identified three principles underlying the laws of *war*: (1) *States* may use all necessary force to pursue their ends in war. (2) That right is conditioned by humanitarian concerns, and by requirements of *proportionality* in the use of force and meeting out punishments. (3) Even in the conduct of war there is room for the virtues of chivalry (honesty, mercy, gallantry). For specific rules see *aggression; angary; armistice; belligerent rights; blockade; booty; capture; cease-fire; chemical weapons; civilian; combatant; crimes against humanity; crimes against peace; declaration of war; gas; Geneva Conventions; genocide; Hague Conferences; Hague Conventions; incursion; intrusion; invasion; jus ad bellum; Kellogg-Briand Pact; letters of marque; levée en masse; neutrality; neutral rights; nuclear weapons free zones; Nuremberg trials; occupation; Paris, Declaration of (1856); peace; peace treaty; piracy; POWs; privateer; prize; prohibited weapons; recognition; requisition; retaliation; rule of 1756; rules of engagement; state of war; status mixtus; Tokyo trials; visit and search; war; war crimes; war crimes trials; war zone.*

LDC: (1) Less Developed Countries: Those not at *OECD* or comparable levels of *development*. (2) Least Developed Countries: This UN designation refers to societies where the level of development is so low and economic *growth* and progress so minimal it is considered inappropriate to include them among even *developing countries*. Some of the *indicators* of this status include per capita *GDP* in the few hundreds of dollars, little manufacturing activity, low levels of literacy and high *infant mortality rates*. Cf. *Fourth World*.

leading indicators: Statistical measures of the performance of dominant sectors of an economy, say housing starts, business failures or unemployment, that suggest the direction and rate of *growth*. See also *indicators*.

league: (1) A synonym for *alliance,* where the connections are very close because a definite object is in view, like mutual defense or *aggrandizement*. (2) A loose, *multilateral* association under a shared *covenant*, where the profession of common interests may be more *pro forma* than real. For instance, see *Arab League; League of Nations*.

League of Nations: The first permanent (sitting in peacetime), *international security* organization. It was the innovation *Woodrow Wilson* most wanted from the *Paris Peace Conference* and *Treaty of Versailles*. Its *Covenant* was an integral part of that *treaty*, and other treaties with the defeated *Central Powers*. It first met in 1920, at Geneva. At no time were all the *Great Powers* members: the U.S. never joined; the Soviet Union only joined in 1934, and was expelled in 1940 over its unprovoked attack on Finland; Germany (1933), Japan (1933) and Italy (1937) all withdrew, as did some minor powers. The League hence never met even the least conditions of *collective security*, its cardinal security doctrine. Other measures it took sometimes seemed designed to prevent not the next, but the previous *war*: (1) *Fact-finding* and *good offices* were to lead to a "cooling-off" period in a crisis, so that states would see reason and submit to *arbitration*. This approach reflected the widespread belief that *WWI* had been a great accident, planned by no one. It achieved minor successes in the Balkans and Latin America, but not among the Great Powers. (2) *Disarmament* conferences were held to end all *arms races*, which many thought had led to WWI. One result of this preoccupation was that *public opinion* was utterly unprepared to face the crisis of the 1930s. In that decade several powerful states set out to rearm as part of deliberate plans for *aggression*, which meant *deterrence* rather than disarmament was the policy called for by the facts, which hardly needed finding out. Instead, the League was not used in any significant way to affect the outcomes of the Japanese *conquest* of *Manchuria*, the *Abyssinian War,* or the *Spanish Civil War.* It never enjoyed the confidence of the *fascist* states, and quickly lost that of the Soviets and the Western powers (a by-product of the latter's failure to use the League). During *WWII* it existed as a shadow of its former self, concentrating on *functional agencies* in a dysfunctional time. It was replaced by the UN, as the Soviets would not consent to rejoining an association that had so shamed them with *expulsion*, the U.S. did not wish to relive the failed *ratification* debate of 1919, and *"world public opinion"* was uninspired by its record. The League was formally dissolved in 1946. Still, the UN carried forward many of the League's basic structures and ideas. See also *Corfu; Danzig; ILO; liberal peace program; public international unions; sanctions.*

League of the Three Emperors: See *Dreikaiserbund*.

leaseholds: Areas clearly the *territory* of one *state*, but governed or *exploited* by another power which holds an agreement to "lease" the area, and where it enjoys an economic *monopoly*. Previously, leaseholds provided legal cover for what otherwise amounted to *occupation zones* by imperial powers. But China in the 1990s introduced a new type of leasehold as an enticement to *foreign direct investment*. In these zones the companies and trade of a single country predominates. See *Hong Kong; Shantung; unequal treaties.*

Lebanese Civil War (1975-90): Fighting broke out in 1975 between the *PLO* and the Christian (Maronite) *Phalange*. In June 1976, Syrian troops *intervened* in support of the PLO. In 1977 Israeli moved into south Lebanon and established a "security zone" along the border, following PLO raids that killed 37 and left 76 wounded. The UN sent in a *buffer* force that soon proved more buffeted about, by all sides, than forceful. Israeli and Syrian *intervention* in the *civil war*, via arms and financial support for various groups, kept the fires burning. In June 1982, Israel launched a full-scale *invasion* that reached Beirut, which was heavily shelled and bombed for over two months, and Syria and Israel came close to *war*. The PLO was forced to relocate to Tunis and the Israelis withdrew to their security zone, and to face an internal crisis over the war. As they left, Phalangist *militia* allied to Israel massacred 1,000-2,000 Palestinian *civilians* in the Sabra and Shatila *refugee camps*. Also in 1982, Syria permitted Iranian radicals to enter Lebanon. These *fanatics* merged with Lebanese *shi'ites* to form the fiercely anti-Israeli *Hezbollah*. They then joined some 15 separate militia engaged in a potpourri of fighting, including several PLO factions that turned against *Arafat*. American, British, French and Italian troops entered Beirut as a multinational *peacekeeping* force. On April 18, 1983, the U.S. embassy was bombed, killing 46. On October 23rd, suicide bombers exploded themselves and their trucks inside the American and French headquarters, killing 265 U.S. marines and 58 French soldiers. The U.S. *retaliated* with naval *bombardment* of Lebanese militia positions. In February 1984, the multinational force withdrew. In 1987 Amal and the PLO reached an uneasy *truce*, but Amal and Hezbollah began fighting the next year. By July 1990, Syria or its proxies gained control of most of Beirut, essentially ending the war. In May 1991, following Syria's support for the U.S. in the *Gulf War*, a "Treaty of Brotherhood" was signed between Syria and the Lebanese government. It essentially made Lebanon a Syrian *protectorate* (above the Israeli security zone).

Lebanon: Location: *Middle East*. Major associations: *Arab League, UN*. Population: 3.5 million. Military: some *militia* disarmed, others with secret arms caches; Syrian troops in-country in the north and west; Israeli troops occupy the south. This small nation sits on a natural *invasion* route (through its interconnected valleys and along its coast) at the intersection of Africa, Asia and Europe. Over the centuries it has been passed through and marauded over by countless ar-

mies, among them: Greeks, Arabs, Crusaders, Turks and British. More recently, Americans, Syrians, Israelis, *Palestinians, Druse*, Maronite Christians and Iranians have fought in and over Lebanon. For several centuries it was an Ottoman province (1516-1918). In 1860 the area became a French *protectorate*, though still within the *Ottoman Empire*. France claimed full possession by the *Sykes/Picot Agreement*, but instead Lebanon became a French *mandate*. In 1926 it became a *republic*, but without full *autonomy*. In 1940, with the fall of France to the *Wehrmacht*, it came under the control of *Vichy*. But in 1941 *Free French* forces took over, with British support. In 1946 Allied troops withdrew and it became independent. It joined in a minor way in the *First Arab/Israeli War*. After that it developed into a prosperous, regional banking and trade center. But always Lebanon's own precarious ethnic and religious balance threatened instability, a factor complicated by the arrival of hundreds of thousands of impoverished Palestinian *refugees*. In 1958 *civil war* was averted only by the *intervention* of U.S. troops. In 1970 the *PLO* moved into south Lebanon after being expelled from Jordan. Over the next 12 years the PLO and Israel fought each other across the Lebanese border. The multisided *Lebanese Civil War* erupted in 1975, lasting until 1991. Israel invaded in 1982, driving the PLO from Lebanon and enlarging the "security zone" it had proclaimed five years earlier. Decisive Syrian intervention occurred following the *Gulf War*, a fact some interpret as evidence of a deal between the U.S. and Syria concerning Lebanon. While Beirut and northern Lebanon began to rebuild, the south remained mired in conflict. In 1993, Israel launched its biggest operation since 1982, which aimed at crushing *Hezbollah*. In 1994, Lebanon broke relations with Iraq.

lebensraum: "Living space." The Nazi euphemism for land to be taken by force from the *Slavic* peoples of *Eastern Europe* and Russia, and resettled by Germans. See *ethnic cleansing; geopolitik; social darwinism.*

Le Duc Tho (1911-90): Vietnamese statesman. He headed the North Vietnamese negotiating team that met with the Americans at Paris from 1968-73, arranging the *cease-fire* agreement that permitted the U.S. to withdraw prior to the North's resumption of the war. He was awarded the *Nobel Prize* for Peace, jointly with *Henry Kissinger*, but he refused it (Kissinger later returned his).

Lee Kuan Yew (b.1923): PM of Singapore 1959-90. He was active in the independence movement, and helped negotiate entry into the Malaysian Federation in 1963, and then out again in 1965. He developed an autocratic style of government that was often overlooked (or looked away from) in the West, because it was so successful in economic terms. Under his stewardship Singapore developed a prosperous *mixed economy*, and emerged as an *Asian Tiger.*

Lee, Robert E. (1807-70): *Confederate* general. He fought as a young officer in the *Mexican/American War*, and led the force that captured John Brown at Harpers Ferry, and later hanged him. He was offered a senior command by *Abraham Lincoln*, but chose to serve his native Virginia, and hence the *Confederacy*, which Virginia joined once it seceded from the American union. He was a brilliant tactician, frequently defeating larger *Union* armies commanded by inept or overly cautious generals. Lee twice invaded the North in attempts to win a decisive *victory* that might provoke European *intervention*. But he was turned back decisively at *Gettysburg* in 1863, and after that went over to the defensive. He met his equal in *Ulysses S. Grant*, who in 1864-65 did what no other Union general dared do: grapple with Lee and refuse to disengage, thereby bringing to bear the crushing superiority of Northern manpower and war matériel. Lee surrendered to Grant at Appomattox Court House, on April 9, 1865. He died in quiet, academic retirement.

Leeward Islands: A onetime composite British colony, comprising Anguilla, Antigua, Barbuda, British Virgin Islands, Montserrat, Nevis and St. Kitts.

legal (agent): An officially accredited foreign representative, who happens also to be a *spy*. The term "legal" refers to formal status, not *espionage* activities. If uncovered, they may be declared *persona non grata* and expelled. Cf. *illegal (agent)*.

legal disputes: Disputes pertaining to the rights and obligations of states, as laid out under both general and *treaty* law; a synonym for *justiciable dispute*. Cf. *political disputes*.

legalism: The tendency in *statecraft* or foreign policy analysis to concentrate on strict adherence to the letter of *international law*, at the expense of broader interpretations that allow a wide range of policy choices, up to and including the use of *force*. Usage is often pejorative.

legate: A diplomatic *envoy*.

legation: The office of an *ambassador* and his or her staff. Cf. *consulate; embassy*.

legitimacy/legitimate government: One *recognized* by most or all members of the community of states. Prior

to the 20th century, usage in no way implied moral approval; it merely signified legal acceptance of a *de facto* situation. That is still its primary meaning, but ideological warfare among *communists* and *fascists* and especially the emergence of several democratic *Great Powers* meant that the form of government is now sometimes considered as well. The first example of this new phenomenon came in 1913, when the U.S. refused to recognize the Mexican revolutionary government as legitimate because *Woodrow Wilson* disapproved of it. The main cases since then have occurred owing to ideological hostility between democracies and other states, notably the Soviet Union in the first years following the *Bolshevik Revolution* (to 1924, in most cases; 1934 for the U.S.), and China (from 1949-72/78, for the U.S. and some other states). Neither Germany was recognized until the breakthrough of *Ostpolitik*; and the two Koreas remained in recognition limbo for the whole *Cold War*. Among recent examples are Haiti, where a military *coup* met with *Security Council* sanctions in 1993 and demands for restoration of the civilian government. Perhaps the single most quixotic case of withholding recognition concerned Greece and *Macedonia*, dating from 1993, where the main objections were by the former to the latter's name and flag. See also *nonintervention*.

Leipzig, Battle of (October 16-19, 1813): A.k.a. "Battle of the Nations." The major battle of the *War of the Fourth Coalition*. British, Prussian and Russian troops broke the French Army, cleared Germany of the French and opened the way for the final advance on Paris in 1814. In the middle of the battle some of *Napoleon's* minor German allies changed sides, creating a position untenable even by his skills.

Lend-Lease: President *Franklin Roosevelt* was desperate to extend aid to Britain against *Nazi Germany*, but he faced enormous opposition within Congress. In a close vote in March 1941, he obtained authority to extend matériel assistance to all countries he deemed "vital to the defense" of the U.S. *Aid* went to Britain and China immediately, and to the Soviet Union after it was attacked in July (but not before Roosevelt engaged in some creative deceit to undercut Catholic opposition to aiding *Stalin*). This had four critically important effects on the outcome of *WWII*: (1) It provided Britain with badly needed war supplies, particularly ships and aircraft, far beyond its ability to pay or produce. (2) It placed the U.S. economy on a near-war footing, and started the vital conversion of factories to full war production many months before the U.S. entered the war. (3) It helped save the Soviet Union during the desperate days of 1941-42, when its own factories were being relocated behind the Urals. (4) It matched Soviet manpower with American industrial might in a decisive combination that proved lethal to German ambitions. Among the items Lend-Lease delivered to Russia alone (not including pre-Lend-Lease aid or the aid Britain trans-shipped): 15,000 aircraft, 8,000 tanks, 2,000 train engines, 11,000 rail cars, 50,000 jeeps, 380,000 trucks, 16 million pairs of boots, several million uniforms, and millions of tons of rails, steel, explosives, food and various minerals. Lend-Lease ended abruptly in 1945, causing rancor in Moscow for which some have criticized the *Truman* administration. That criticism ignores the fact it was always intended to be a strictly wartime program, and that it was also cut off to Britain and 36 other nations.

Lenin, Vladimir Ilyich, né Ulyanov (1870-1954): Russian revolutionary. His brother was executed in 1887 for plotting to kill the *tsar*, an event that seared Lenin's youth. He spent many years abroad, in London and Geneva, writing pamphlets and publishing a newspaper. He led the *Bolsheviks* in their break with the *Mensheviks* and in the *Russian Revolution (1905)*. In 1917 he was smuggled into Russia, by the German *High Command*, in a sealed train. He fled to Finland after an abortive *coup* attempt in July, but returned to lead the *Bolshevik Revolution* in November. He agreed to a *Carthaginian peace* at *Brest-Litovsk*, so he could consolidate Bolshevik power and prosecute the *Russian Civil War*. He instituted *war communism*, approved the *Red Terror* and *expropriation* of food from the peasants, personally ordered the execution of the Royal Family (confirmed from Russian sources only in 1992), and set up a brutal dictatorship. In 1921, facing total economic collapse and a massive *famine*, he reversed course. He accepted market-style reforms in the *New Economic Policy* and turned to the West for food *aid*. What land reform he did achieve was later reversed under the policy of *collectivization*. Before dying, he warned against the ambitions of *Stalin*, whom he had earlier cultivated and promoted. His activism and leadership of a *marxist* party to power was a historical first. Indeed, he seems to have seen (perhaps only subliminally) the self-conscious "*vanguard*" party, rather than deep social forces or the existing *mode of production*, as the main engine of history. While his influence on the practice of marxist *states* is undoubted, his reputation as an original thinker is probably inflated. His most widely influential, theoretical writings were on *imperialism* as the "final stage of monopoly *capitalism*," yet even that idea was largely cobbled from the English economist, John Hobson (1858-1940). Lenin's greatest impact came from his acts, not his writing. He showed that a marxist movement might seize power under conditions of social chaos, even where *Marx* had said a socialist

revolution should not yet be possible--in a backward, peasant society on the fringe of capitalist Europe. See also *leninism; marxism-leninism; Petrograd Soviet*.

Leningrad: The name of *St. Petersburg* 1924-91.

leninism: The philosophy of government and society taught and enacted by *Lenin*, in particular his emphasis on establishing the *dictatorship of the proletariat* through the actions of a *vanguard* party. See *marxism-leninism*.

Lesotho: Location: Southern Africa. Major associations: *OAU, UN*. Population: 1.9 million. Military: small, and for internal use only. Formerly called Basutoland. It was made a British *protectorate* in 1868, during the early struggle between Britain and the *Boers*. It became an outright British possession in 1884. The British kept it administratively separate from the Union of South Africa, formed in 1910, which completely surrounds the *enclave* of Lesotho. In 1966 it became an independent *monarchy*. The constitution was suspended in 1970. In 1986 South Africa imposed a *blockade* on Lesotho, accusing it of harboring anti-*apartheid* guerrillas. After just three weeks a *coup* was carried out, and Lesotho agreed to expel all identified by South Africa as *terrorists*. The old king (Moshoeshoe) was expelled in 1990 and his son placed on the throne, but behind the scenes the military remained in real command.

Lesser Antilles: Numerous, small, East Caribbean islands under varied *jurisdiction* (British, French, U.S. and independent). Cf. *Greater Antilles*.

letter of credence (*lettre de créance*): Identification and authority papers (credentials) issued to *diplomats* for presentation to foreign governments, or to representatives of other *international personalities*.

letters of marque (and reprisal): A license given by a state to a *privateer* permitting the capture or destruction of enemy shipping. Captures would then be adjudicated by a *prize court*.

Levant, the: The region bordering the eastern Mediterranean and Aegean Seas, to wit: Israel, Lebanon, Syria and Turkey. Some usages limit it to Lebanon and Syria.

levée en masse: "The mass arising." (1) In history: The compulsory enlistment for military service of August 1793, declared by the Committee on Public Safety during the *French Revolution*. It vastly increased French *power* by enlisting large numbers of *citizens* to do battle with the smaller, professional armies of European monarchs. It was eventually copied by other powers, especially those (such as Prussia) France had defeated. (2) In *international law*: armed resistance by a civil population against a *occupation* army, lawful under the *Hague Conventions* only if offered from unoccupied *territory*; those resisting within occupied territory thus do not enjoy the rights bestowed by the status of *belligerent*. See *Intifada*.

levels of analysis: In *political science*, three widely accepted levels of generalization: the individual, *state* (society) and *international system*. A given argument will tend to emphasize one more than others: in *misperception* and *decision-making theory* generally, the individual is central; for *bureaucratic politics* the state is key; while for the *balance of power, development theory* or *Kondratieff cycles*, systemic causes are primary. A well-rounded study of complex world events will utilize elements of explanation at all three levels, integrated into a compelling argued whole (but alas, this is all too rarely done). Some suggest as additional levels *cognitive* processes, dynamics of small group interaction or patterns of *transnational* relations.

leverage: When one *state* has sufficient *influence*, whatever the source, to alter the actions or policy of another state. See *capabilities; coercion; compellence; linkage; power; sanctions; soft power.*

Leviathan: The *state*, especially if *unitary* and tyrannical. See *Thomas Hobbes.*

lex domicilii: The law of the place of domicile.

lex ferenda: The law it is hoped to establish.

lex fori: The law of the *jurisdiction* of whatever court is hearing the case.

lex lata: The law actually in force.

lex loci contractus: The law of the place where the contract in question was made.

lex loci delicti: The law of the place where the breach (*delict*) in question was committed.

lex loci res sitae: The law of the place a thing is (situated).

lex loci solutionis: The law of the place where the contract at issue will be carried out.

lex posterior derogat priori: A general principle in

international law that says a later law drafted on the same subject overrules a prior law.

lex societatis: The law governing an organization.

lex specialis derogat generali: A special (or specific) statute overrules a general statute.

liaison: In the military, keeping contact among different units, in order to coordinate attack, defense or movement.

Liberal Democratic Party (Japan): It formed in 1955, and held power from then until July 1993. Its policies included: close cooperation of government with industry to develop global leadership in selected industries; protection of domestic markets, especially in agricultural and fisheries products; close *security* cooperation with the U.S., but an increasingly independent approach to *trade* and *Asia/Pacific* affairs. It governed at first largely through persuasion and genuine representation, and lack of a serious electoral alternative. But in the 1970s it grew ever more reliant on patronage, and then outright corruption. It lost its majority in 1993 after a series of scandals revealed that this corruption went to the very top, including one serving and several former prime ministers.

liberal-internationalism: An approach to world affairs that seeks to construct a society of *interdependent*, democratic political communities that resolve disputes in acccordance with *international law*, supported by a mutual interest in free commerce. See *free trade; human rights; idealism; internationalism; Kant; liberalism; liberal peace program; Woodrow Wilson.*

liberalism: A political philosophy championing: freedom of the individual; constitutional enshrinement of civil and political liberties, and other *human rights;* and *laissez-faire* economic arrangements, including *free trade*. Attitudes toward laissez-faire have been modified for most modern liberals by acceptance of varying degress of economic regulation and social guarantees of minimum living standards, all supported by representative government erected on a base of *popular sovereignty.* Cf. *individualism; liberal-internationalism; liberal peace program; reform liberalism.*

liberal peace program (1914-18): The main elements of this program, backed by international peace societies and much *public opinion* in the *Allied* countries, were: (1) an end to secret *alliances*, thought to have led to the outbreak of *WWI* during the *mobilization crisis* in August 1914; these to be replaced by one, universal alliance (a.k.a. *collective security*); (2) general *disarmament*; (3) creation of a *League of Nations* to resolve problems rationally and peacefully, and to deter *aggression*; (4) an end to the *balance of power* and *spheres of influence*, and enshrinement of liberal and democratic principles as the new governing *norms* of international relations, especially the rights of *self-determination, free trade*, and *freedom of the seas*; (4) *peace* without *indemnities* (no *reparations*); (5) territorial transfers only with the consent of affected populations; (6) an immediate *cease-fire*; (7) a peace conference dedicated to a "peace without victors" and abjuring border changes; (8) *casus belli* such as *Alsace-Lorraine* or *Italia irredenta* to be redressed by *plebiscites*. See also *Fourteen Points; open covenants; Paris Peace Conference; Woodrow Wilson.*

liberation: (1) Military: expulsion or *defeat* of a foreign army of *occupation*. (2) Political: This usage can mean a multitude of things. For some, it is formal *sovereignty*, whether or not accompanied by real *independence*; others use it to mean complete freedom from foreign *influence*; and the most *radical* mean by it not just political independence, but social (and often, *socialist* as well) *revolution*. Cf. *self-determination.*

liberation theology: A social/theological movement within the *Catholic Church* in Latin America, blending the social teachings of Catholicism with *marxist* analysis of *capitalism* and the origins of poverty. It was not accepted by the hierarchy in Rome or Latin America (with rare exceptions). The Catholic Church as a whole remains politically and philosophically anti-communist and anti-marxist.

Liberia: Location: W. Africa. Major associations: *OAU, UN*. Population: 2.7 million. Military: no central force; three factions in *civil war*, and fighting ECO-MOG (an OAU *peacekeeping* force). It was founded in 1822 by freed American slaves, sponsored by northern philanthropists (in the 1820s not even abolitionists yet thought that the races could or should intermingle in America). The project was approved by President *James Monroe*, after whom the capital Monrovia is named. The colonists settled mainly in the coastal areas, setting up a republic in 1847 modeled on the U.S. It was not long before the settlers established their own dominion over the native population, a position they maintained by controlling the police and the law in a manner all too familiar to blacks left behind in America: natives were not permitted to vote or hold high office. In the 1920s the Firestone company set up a plantation economy, which further reinforced the differences between coastal settlers and interior natives. In 1980 the conflict flared into violence, with a *coup* led by Sgt. Samuel Doe and other junior and

noncommissioned *officers*. In 1989 civil war broke out. Doe was captured and killed in 1990. In 1991 a regional peacekeeping effort (ECOMOG) was mounted by five West African states, with OAU and UN approval. Nigeria dominated this group, which became involved in heavy fighting during 1992-93. Several truces were arranged but broken. By 1994 the civil war had taken nearly 200,000 lives, and Liberia's descent into *anarchy* was nearly complete.

liberté, égalité, fraternité: "Liberty, equality, fraternity." The famous slogan of the *French Revolution*. It resonated among 19th century *liberals* despite the corruption of those ideals in the *Terror*, and by *Napoleon I*. The phrase inspired both imitative cant and genuine emulation in later decades.

liberty: (1) Personal: freedom from bondage and tyrannical government, and freedom of thought and direction of one's own life. (2) National: freedom from foreign rule; *independence; sovereignty*. See *human rights; self-determination*. Cf. *slavery*.

liberum veto: A by-product of situations where the *unanimity rule* is in effect, under which any one state's refusing *consent* to an agreement blocks or invalidates that agreement. See *veto*.

Libya: Location: N. Africa. Major associations: *Arab League, Maghreb Union, OAU, OAPEC, OPEC, UN*. Population: 4.3 million. Military: old Soviet weapons, but lots of them; seeking *chemical, nerve* and *nuclear weapons*. As Tripoli, it was once part of the Carthaginian Empire, then the Roman and several Arab Muslim successors, until it fell under *Ottoman* rule in 1551. In the 18th and 19th centuries it was home to the *Barbary pirates*, local Muslim fiefdoms that paid lip service to Ottoman authority. It was taken by Italy after the *Italo/Turkish War* of 1911-12. From 1922-30 Italy was faced with a *guerrilla* uprising in Tripoli. During *WWII* the Italians were pushed out by the British. German troops (the Afrikakorps) then fought the British and Americans, but were defeated by 1943. Libya was under Allied military government until 1951, when it became a constitutional *monarchy* under King Idris. *Oil* was discovered in 1959. During the 1960s Libya held to a moderately pro-Western policy while modernizing at home (e.g., women were *emancipated*). In 1969 the monarchy was overthrown by a clique of young officers led by *Muammar Quadaffi*. He proclaimed a *revolution* based on his personal epiphany about how to blend *Islam, democracy, capitalism* and *socialism* (laid out in his "Green Book"). By 1971 Libya was purchasing arms from the *Soviet bloc*, and had begun to arm and train *guerrillas/terror-*

ists from Chad, Egypt, Tunisia and Sudan. It also trained and helped arm the *IRA, PLO* and other groups. In 1973 Quadaffi *nationalized* the oil industry. In 1977 Libyan and Egyptian troops clashed along the border. Continuing Libyan *incursions* into Chad and its support for *subversion* elsewhere in Africa led to increasing isolation within the African and Arab worlds, as well as from the West. In 1979 Quadaffi sent troops to help *Idi Amin*, but they were slaughtered by Tanzanian troops even as they arrived at Entebbe airport in Uganda. His ambitions next sparked the *Chad/Libya War* 1980-87, which cost Libya dearly in blood and treasure. Relations with major western countries deteriorated sharply in the 1980s. In 1981 Libyan jets were shot down by the U.S., which challenged the *line of death* drawn by Quadaffi in the *Gulf of Sidra* (Sirte). In April 1984, Britain broke relations after a London policewoman was shot to death by a Libyan diplomat. In 1986 *Reagan* imposed *sanctions* and ordered all Americans to leave; on the night of April 14/15th the U.S. bombed Libya in *retaliation* for its support of terrorist actions against Americans in Europe. Libya was highly critical of the *Gulf Coalition* in 1990-91, but moderated this stance with criticism of Iraq as well. In 1992 the *Security Council* initiated arms and aviation *sanctions* for Libya's refusal to hand over suspects implicated in a 1986 terrorist bombing of a Pan Am airliner over Scotland.

licensing: A *non-tariff barrier* by which *import* companies may trade only under state license and according to government *quotas*. When applied to *exports*, licensing becomes a device for carrying out a limited *embargo*, say on military hardware or *dual technology* transfers to designated unfriendly states.

Liechtenstein: Location: Europe. Major associations: *EFTA*. Population: 30,000. Military: none. This *microstate* became an *autonomous* principality in 1868, with Austria-Hungary in administrative control until the end of *WWI*. It forms a postal and *customs union* with Switzerland, and is thus blocked from joining the *EU*.

Lie, Tygve (1896-1968): World statesman. Norwegian Foreign Minister (*government-in-exile*) 1940-45; UN *Secretary General* 1946-53. He unsuccessfully supported admission of *mainland China* to the UN. With the outbreak of the *Korean Conflict* he strongly supported UN assistance to South Korea, but opposed *MacArthur's* unilateral extension of the war into the North. His support for *intervention* cost him the support of the *Soviet bloc*, and he subsequently resigned rather than seek a third term.

like-minded states: (1) A loose association, such as

a *caucus group*, with common interests or views. (2) Small Western countries, such as Ireland, the Netherlands and the *Nordic Council* states, that cooperate on issues on which they share perspective. They have sometimes sought to play an intermediary role between larger Western states and the *Third World*.

Likud: A parliamentary coalition formed in Israel in 1973. It formed several governments under *Begin* and *Shamir* from 1977-84, and again under Shamir as part of the National Unity government from 1986-92. It supported an aggressive settlements policy on the *West Bank,* and encouragement of Jewish *immigration* from Russia. It presided over the 1982 *invasion* of Lebanon that shattered Israel's foreign policy consensus. After the *Gulf War* its rigidity on settlements led to a sharp deterioration of relations with the *Bush* administration. It opposed the 1993 peace accord with the *PLO*.

limitations (of state jurisdiction): Boundaries placed around *state* action by *international law*, such as in definition of *territorial* extensions, and rights and duties on matters of interest to other states.

limited jurisdiction: The range of competence of an international court or other body to deal with *legal disputes*.

limited nuclear war: One that is confined to a certain *theater* of operations, or not escalated to the maximum exchange of available *nuclear weapons*. Many critics hold that this notion is both politically and psychologically impossible to carry out for great nuclear powers. Even if that is true, it is conceivable that small nuclear powers might engage in geographically, numerically or otherwise limited nuclear war. Cf. *limited war.*

limited war: One fought with less than total means, on a less than total scale, and for less than total *strategic* purposes. From the *Peace of Westphalia* to the *French Revolution* wars were limited by a relative absence of ideological conflict, by a common warrior class with an interest in self-preservation, and because crude and limited means were available with which to wage them. The rise of *nationalism, industrialization* and 20th century ideological competition greatly expanded *war*. When those phenomena were coupled with revolutionary developments in ballistic science, explosives and metallurgy, even minor conflicts moved toward *total war* in both their inspiration and application. The development of, and *stalemate* caused by, *nuclear weapons* revived interest in devising limited war-fighting *capabilities*. See also *limited nuclear war.*

Lin Biao, a.k.a. Lin Piao (1907-71): Chinese marshal.

He commanded a corps during the *Long March,* and held combat commissions again in the *Sino/Japanese War.* When the *Chinese Civil War* resumed, his army made major gains in *Manchuria,* securing the north for the communists. He also commanded in the *Korean Conflict.* He backed *Mao* and the *Great Proletarian Cultural Revolution,* rising to be Mao's designated successor. But his base in the *PLA* was seen as threatening Mao with a new *"warlordism."* Moves were afoot to have him *purged* when he died or was killed while fleeing to the Soviet Union (the story has never been publicly confirmed). He became a figure of utter vilification in subsequent Maoist *propaganda.*

Lincoln, Abraham (1809-65): U.S. statesman. He was President during the greatest crisis the country ever faced: the *American Civil War* (1861-65). He was not a "fire-eating" abolitionist: he did not number among those who wished to end *slavery* immediately, rents in the national fabric be damned. But he hated and opposed slavery nonetheless. His solution was to refuse slavery in any new state admitted to the *Union,* without proposing immediate abolition in those states where it already existed. He knew that without further expansion slavery would wither on the cotton bush within a few decades--an obnoxious anachronism barricaded into the agrarian, southeast corner of a great industrial and commercial nation. Yet precisely because proslavery forces knew that too, his election hastened the *secession* of 11 states, which then joined to form the *Confederacy.* He was determined that the Union not fire the first shot, to preserve Northern public support and gain the moral high ground. Confederate hotheads obliged when they attacked Fort Sumter, which he had ordered provisioned. He immediately made a terrible mistake: he declared a *blockade* of southern ports. That unintentionally elevated the Confederacy to the status of *belligerent,* and opened the way for a serious confrontation with Britain. (The alternative was to make a blockade without actually declaring it, through the fiction of announcing that all southern ports were from now on under a total *embargo.*) He was rescued more than once from confrontation with Britain, for instance during the *Trent Affair,* by his shrewd Secretary of State *William Seward.* On the other hand, Lincoln's well-timed *emancipation* proclamation (after Antietam) undercut those in Britain and France who wished to *intervene* by appealing directly to anti-slavery opinion. Lincoln was afflicted with excessively cautious generals. He was thus taken with the verve shown by *Ulysses S. Grant* at Vicksburg and elsewhere, and appointed him to command the Army of the Potomac, facing *Robert E. Lee's* Army of Northern Virginia (the Union named its armies for rivers, the Confederacy called its after states).

When the straightlaced, Christian gentlemen in the Union *cabinet* vehemently objected to Grant's infamous drunkenness, Lincoln curtly shot back: "Find out what he drinks, and send a case to each of my generals." He planned a tolerant, forgiving *Reconstruction.* But less than a week after war's end, on April 14, 1865, he was shot, the needless victim of a conspiracy of misfit Confederates. He died the next day.

line of death: A *baseline* drawn by *Muammar Quadaffi* across the *Gulf of Sidra* (Sirte), which he claims as Libyan *territorial waters* but other powers insist is part of the *high seas.* Libyan attack boats have tried to enforce the line. The U.S. has deliberately crossed it with naval or air forces several times. When challenged, it has shot down or sunk Libyan interceptors.

lingua franca: Literally, "the French language," but in effect whatever is the main language used to conduct *diplomacy* and other facets of international affairs. The lingua franca of any given age is inevitably that of its dominant *Great Power(s).* Hence, French was the tongue of diplomacy in the time of *Richelieu.* It had displaced Latin, the high language of the *Catholic Church* and *Holy Roman Empire,* in tandem with the ascendancy of France over those declining powers. This situation continued for 200 years, reflecting the dominance of France in *Great Power* affairs and then the world, to the Age of *Napoleon.* So pervasive was this trend Russian nobility at *Catherine II's* Court conversed solely in French, unable to speak their native tongue, or that of the serfs they owned (the burning of Moscow by the French in 1812 cured that fetish!). English began to compete with French in the 18th century, with the rise of Britain as a great imperial and commercial rival. It surpassed French in the 20th century, when the U.S. joined Britain as the two dominant powers in *commerce, war* and *diplomacy.* German, Russian, Chinese, Spanish and Japanese have all competed with English to some degree, but have not mounted an effective challenge to its practical utility for business and politics. The UN has seven official languages. However, a move is afoot--driven by financial pressures of simultaneous translation, publication and archiving--to reduce this to two or three.

line officer: One serving in command of a combat unit ("in the line of fire"). Cf. *staff officer.*

linkage: (1) In foreign policy: tying another state's behavior on one issue to reward or punishment on a second, as when *foreign aid* is linked to respect for *human rights,* or trade access is tied to a move away from regional *adventurism.* Linkage was a prime component of *Nixon's* policy of *détente.* However, Congress shifted the emphasis on economic rewards for the Soviets from foreign policy to domestic policy, through the *Jackson/Vanik Amendment*. More recently, the UN linked *sanctions* on Iraq and Serbia to compliance with *cease-fire* resolutions and cessation of territorial *aggression*, respectively. (2) In economics: when success or failure of one industry has a major impact on another, particularly when it stimulates growth of new industries.

liquidate: (1) A euphemism often used when whole classifications of human beings are murdered by the *state*. (2) Pay off a debt. (3) Convert assets to cash.

liquidity: Convertibility of assets into cash or cash equivalents to transact business, repay loans and so forth. It is the lubricant of international economics. From 1947-58 the U.S. provided liquidity for the world economy (excluding the *Soviet bloc*), through a huge outflow of dollars in the *Marshall Plan* and other *aid* programs. Liquidity also came from expenditure on procurements for *NATO* and the *Korean Conflict*. Today liquidity is provided by the sum of *hard currencies, regional banks*, the *IMF* and *IBRD*, and through *SDRs* and the *eurocurrency markets*.

listening post: (1) In the military: a forward position connected to even more forward, hidden microphones or vibration detectors, where the enemy's movements are listened to and charted. (2) In *intelligence*: any secret sites in or near a target country, where events are monitored and *raw intelligence* is collected to be shipped home for full analysis.

literal interpretation: Reading a *treaty* in light of the strict or normal meaning of the words it uses.

Lithuania: Location: *Baltic*. Major associations: *CSCE, UN*. Population: 3.7 million. Military: minimal. It was a *regional power* in Central and Eastern Europe during the middle ages, dominated the Baltic and Poland. After 1569 it was linked to Poland. As a result, it too was extinguished with the *partitions of Poland* and absorbed by the *Russian Empire*. Parts of it were occupied by Germany during *WWI*, but when German troops withdrew in 1918 it declared *independence*. With Russia deep in *civil war* until 1920, it succeeded in asserting that claim by force of arms. During that conflict its ancient capital at *Vilna* was taken by Poland. In 1923 Lithuania seized *Memel*, which was a point of friction with Germany throughout the *interwar* period. Lithuania was assigned to Germany under terms of a secret *protocol* to the *Nazi/Soviet Pact*, but within a few weeks was traded to Moscow for eastern Poland. In August 1940, it was

annexed by the Soviet Union. It was occupied by Germany 1941-44, then retaken by the Soviets. Most non-Western states simply accepted Lithuania was a province of the Soviet Union. The U.S. and some other Western powers refused to recognize the *annexation* as legal, and continued to maintain formal *diplomatic relations* with a *government-in-exile* until the 1990s. The nationalist movement, Sajudis, became prominent (under Vyautas Landsbergis), and in 1989 demanded independence. In March 1990, the legislature reasserted independence. *Gorbachev* responded with an economic *blockade* and a threat to use force, briefly cowing the Lithuanians. Under U.S. pressure, and with Lithuania more compliant, the blockade was lifted in June. During the August 20, 1991, *coup* attempt in Moscow it again declared independence and demanded that Russian troops leave. It reemerged as an undisputed *sovereign* nation with the *extinction* of the Soviet Union. The last Russian troops left in August 1993, moving west to the *Kaliningrad enclave*.

Little Entente: The system of interwar *alliances* between *Czechoslovakia* and *Yugoslavia* in 1920 and both those powers and Rumania, in 1921. The separate agreements were incorporated into a single *treaty* in 1929. The main purpose was to prevent Austria or Hungary from attempting to reclaim the old *Hapsburg* lands taken away in the *Treaties of St. Germain* and *Trianon*. After the rise of *Hitler,* efforts were also made to negotiate mutual defense arrangements with France. The turn to the right in Yugoslavia after the assassination of *Alexander I*, especially its growing willingness to collaborate with plans for *aggrandizement* by Nazi Germany, shook the Little Entente. The *Munich Conference* then gutted it of any use it might have had against Germany, by removing Czechoslovakia from the board. It was dissolved in February 1939. Cf. *Balkan Pacts*.

Little Russia: A colloquial term for Ukraine, though not one favored in that country.

Litvinov, Maxim Maximovich (1876-1951): Soviet diplomat. Deputy Foreign Commissar 1921-30, 1939-46; Foreign Commissar 1930-39; Ambassador to the U.S. 1941-43. He consistently argued for closer ties to the West and for *collective security* through the *League of Nations*. But after *Munich* he was replaced by *Molotov* to signal *Stalin's* interest in a deal with Germany, negotiated a few months later in the *Nazi/Soviet Pact*. His survival of Stalin's *purges*, given his Western leanings and his heritage as a Jew, was itself a singular accomplishment.

Liverpool, Robert Banks (1779-1828): British statesman. Foreign Secretary 1801-04; Secretary of War 1809-12; PM 1812-27. He was closely involved with the whole course of the British conflict with *Napoleon I*, and the reconstruction of European order after 1815. However, British policy in this period is typically ascribed almost exclusively to the influence of *Castlereagh* and *Canning*, whom Liverpool proved shrewd enough to employ in high office.

living off the land: When an army on the march resupplies its food, fuel and shelter needs by *requisition* of matériel from the civil population.

Lloyd George, David (1863-1945): British statesman. Chancellor of the Exchequer 1908-15; Minister of Munitions 1915-16; Secretary for War 1916; PM 1916-22. He opposed the *Second Boer War*. He took charge during *WWI* (replacing *Herbert Asquith*), with a promise to wage vigorous *war*, which he did. He also finally closed a contentious debate over whether to adopt a *convoy* system. A major figure at the *Paris Peace Conference*, he tried to work for a more moderate *peace* against his own electoral promise to "squeeze Germany, until the pips squeak." He fought against Irish *independence*, then bowed to the inevitable in 1921, agreeing to *partition* of *Ulster* from *Ireland*. In the 1920s his running dispute with Asquith split the Liberal Party, which ceased to be the main opposition to *Tory* rule in domestic or foreign affairs. The Liberals never ruled Britain again.

local remedies: See *exhaustion of local remedies*.

Locarno, Treaties of (1925): (1) In the West: The Belgians, French and Germans agreed on the permanence of their mutual frontiers, and the *demilitarization* of the *Rhineland*. The *treaty* was guaranteed by Britain and Italy. No one would enforce this treaty when *Hitler* sent troops into the Rhineland in 1936. (2) In the East: Germany signed treaties of *arbitration* with Czechoslovakia and Poland. Those states were in turn assured by French treaties of guarantee; these promises were never kept, in the Czech case.

location: A state's geographical place, that may significantly affect its *power* and *foreign policy*. For example, Belgium and Poland are located in low-lying areas that have served as *invasion* routes for larger powers; Russia's flat expanses offered no natural barriers to invasion, or to *expansion*; much of Africa was for centuries isolated by the Sahara from the main flow of *history* and *technology*; Britain, Japan and the U.S. enjoyed periods of isolation from continental conflicts due to ocean barriers; and some areas, such as Egypt or South Africa, were colonized primarily because of

their position along key *trade routes*. See also *English Channel*. Cf. *topography*.

locus regit actum: "The place rules the act." A legal maxim that holds *jurisdiction* concerning some legally significant act resides under the laws of the *state* (or other place) where the act was done.

Lodge, Henry Cabot (1850-1924): U.S. senator. He chaired the Senate Foreign Relations Committee during the great debate over the *Treaty of Versailles*, which he vigorously opposed (in its unamended form). His was also a powerful voice favoring *protectionism* and a postwar return to the *gold standard*.

logical interpretation: Reading a *treaty* according to logic, or formal reasoning.

logistics: That branch of military art, science and operations concerned with transporting military personnel, and maintaining, procuring and supplying their equipment.

loiter time: The period for which an aircraft can circle or hover before having to attack or disengage. For some *missiles* with this capability, it is the time when primary and secondary targets are selected.

Lomé Conventions: Aid and *preferential trade* treaties that also established *STABEX*, signed in 1975 between the *EC* and 49 *ACP Nations*. Designed to encourage *export* earnings by *Third World* nations, they were championed within the EC mainly by France, for which they also supplemented *neo-colonial* ties to *la francophonie*. The original convention was revised and redrafted in 1979, 1984 and 1989 (with 69 ACP countries). They permit preferential access to *EC/EU* markets for ACP goods, including manufactured and agricultural produce; offer marketing assistance; grant some *technology transfer* and waive requirements of *reciprocity*. A limited amount of EU *aid* (and *soft loans*) is also available.

London Declaration (July 6, 1990): A formal statement by *NATO* that might well be taken as the definitive end of the *Cold War*. It said: (1) NATO and *Warsaw Pact* nations were no longer enemies; (2) NATO was to shift to lower levels of *conventional* forces; (3) *nuclear weapons* would only be used by the Atlantic alliance as an ultimate, "last resort."

London Naval Disarmament Conference (1930): A follow-up to the successful *Washington Conference* and a failed Geneva conference. Several *treaties* were agreed by the Britain, Japan and the U.S. extending variations of the Washington ratio for *battleships* (5:5:3, in numbers) to heavy *cruisers* (18:15:12, in numbers), light cruisers (1:1.5:0.75, in tonnage), *destroyers* (1:1:0.66, in tonnage), and *submarines* (parity). This victory for *arms control* and general moderation in Tokyo was short-lived: the agreement was abrogated by Japan in 1936.

London, Treaty of (1839): It settled a decade-long *dispute* between Belgium and the Netherlands, granting Belgium recognized *independence* and providing *Great Power* guarantees of its *neutrality*. It also confirmed the status of Luxembourg as a Grand Duchy, connected to Holland. It was the "scrap of paper" infamously referred to by *Bethmann-Hollweg* the night of the British *declaration of war* in 1914.

London, Treaty of (1915): A secret *treaty* in which Britain, France and Russia bribed Italy into *WWI* with offers of Austrian *territory*. The lands promised included the full extent of *Italia irredenta*, as well as parts of Dalmatia, Albania and all of *Tripoli* (Libya). In the event, Italian entry into the war proved more a burden than a help, as the *Allies* had to send reinforcements to the southern front in 1917, after *Caporetto*. The treaty's implicit assault on the principle of *self-determination* angered *Woodrow Wilson*, and liberal opinion, after its text was released by the *Bolsheviks* early in 1918. The terms were not kept at the *Paris Peace Conference* due to Wilson's stern opposition and to Allied discounting of Italy's contribution to the *victory*. In consequence, Italy stormed out of the conference, returning only to sign the several *peace treaties*. See *Constantinople Agreement; mutilated peace*.

long-cycle theory: The notion that *Great Powers*, and in particular *preponderant powers* or *"hegemons,"* rise and fall in regular (by one account, precisely 107 years!) cycles, that form one of the largest patterns of all world affairs. The existence (or not) of these cycles is a subject of merely academic controversy.

Long March (1934-35): The long, fighting retreat of 100,000 Chinese communists following withdrawal from the *Jiangxi Soviet*. During the Long March, which covered some 6,000 winding miles to Ya'nan (Yenan), *Mao Zedong* emerged as a principal leader and tactician of the Chinese communist movement. The ordeal (at least 60,000 died along the route), became a central legend of the communist *revolution* and *regime*, serving as a heroic example of the triumph of will over harsh reality. Mao, ever the romantic, would utilize that image in his subsequent, unforgiving demands for a superhuman effort from the peasantry and party to *modernize* China. Despite the aura attached to

Long March veterans, many discovered that their participation and service to the party were not enough to save them from being *purged* during the *Great Proletarian Cultural Revolution*.

long peace (1945-): The present era, which is the longest period of *Great Power* peace in history.

Long Telegram (February 1946): A multipage, encrypted cable sent by *George Kennan* from the Moscow Embassy to the State Department. It portrayed a dark picture of Russian history and the nature of the Soviet system. It then described *Stalin's* foreign policy intentions as *fanatic* and ruthlessly *expansionist*, but also as internally logical and influenced toward caution when it met firm external resistance. With prescience, Kennan noted the grave internal weaknesses of the Soviet system, reflected on its problem with post-war *imperial overreach* (although that was not the term he used), and called for a firm policy of *containment*. The missive was highly influential in helping to crystallize similar views already being formed at top levels in Washington. Cf. *X article; NSC-68*.

Lon Nol (1913-85): Cambodian general and statesman. PM 1966-67; President 1972-75. He was a staunch anti-communist with experience fighting the *Khmers Rouges* in the 1950s and 1960s. He opposed *Sihanouk's* neutralism toward the wars in Laos and Vietnam, and helped overthrow him in 1970, realigning the country with the U.S. and South Vietnam. The timing of that adjustment was clearly off, as within five years he was forced to flee in face of the U.S. withdrawal, the fall of South Vietnam and the temporary, nightmarish ascendancy of the Khmers Rouges.

Los Alamos: The main U.S. atomic research center (located in New Mexico). During *WWII* its scientists and engineers developed the first *atomic bomb*. It also played a key role in development of the *hydrogen bomb*, and in weapons research during the *Cold War*. Cf. *Manhattan Project; Minatom; Peenemünde; Strategic Defense Initiative*.

Louis XIV (1638-1715): "The Sun King." King of France. His life was spent at *war*, and for half a century he so dominated the affairs of Europe *Voltaire* named the Age itself for him. He was deeply affected in his youth by the "Fronde," a *civil war* (1648-59) occasioned by a *rebellion* of the French nobility. He reacted to that with characteristic verve born of an *absolutist* temperament: "L'Etat, c'est moi" (I am the state). He never said it, but he may as well have. The country was at first prosperous under his bracing *despotism*. He put the state's commercial and financial affairs in order, built *Versailles* and reigned in cultural splendor, though with little regard for the welfare of his subjects. He wanted *hegemony* over Europe. To get it, he embarked on a series of costly, *expansionist* wars. The span of his ambition and the power of France combined to bring great *coalitions* against him, in a classic example of the workings of the *balance of power*. In the War of Devolution (1667-68) he took border posts in Flanders from Spain. But in the Dutch War (1672-78), his policy brought together *England* in alliance with *William I (of Orange)* of Holland, with consequences that still echo in the life of NW Europe (including faraway *Ulster*). There was no decisive *victory* and the apex of Louis' reign had in fact passed, but no one noticed. Instead, bigger, longer, more destructive but still futile wars ensued: the *War of the Grand Alliance* (a.k.a. *League of Augsburg*), 1688-97; and the *War of the Spanish Succession*, 1701-13, ending with the *Treaty of Utrecht*. For all the wasted blood and treasure France had gained almost nothing. It was still *primus inter pares* among the *Great Powers*, but the treasury was drained, its people exhausted and its enemies legion and more powerful than before (that was especially true of England and *Prussia*). For the remainder of the 18th century France would have to fight off the English lion tearing at the vitals of its empire, while holding the Prussian eagle from its throat. Thanks in good measure to the wasted time and resources of Louis' reign, it would stumble domestically, all the way into the *French Revolution* and then the disaster of the *Napoleonic Wars*.

Louis XVI (1754-93): King of France 1774-92. He compromised in the first days of the *French Revolution*, then sought to flee the country with his Austrian Queen, Marie Antoinette, to organize a *counter-revolution* with foreign help. They were captured and returned to Paris. They watched the radicalization of the revolution from a prison cell, from where they were taken to the guillotine in 1793.

Louis XVIII (1755-1824): King of France 1814-15, 1815-24. Restored to his dead brother's throne by the *coalition* that defeated *Napoleon I*, he did not enjoy loyalty from the army or middle class, those two great beneficiaries of the *French Revolution*. He fled France in early 1815, during the *Hundred Days* that culminated in Napoleon's final *defeat* at *Waterloo*. Again restored in 1815 by foreign armies, in foreign policy he deferred to *Talleyrand* and others who successfully moved France back into the *Great Power* club.

Louisiana: A French *colony* in N. America, stretching from the Mississippi to the Rockies, and from the Gulf of Mexico to western Canada. Unlike *Québec*, it was mostly untouched by French settlement. See *Louisiana Purchase*.

Louisiana Purchase: *Thomas Jefferson* bought *Louisiana* for the U.S. from *Napoleon* for $15 million in 1803. Napoleon feared he would lose it to Britain anyway, and sold it (with deliberately ambiguous *borders*) both for the cash, and in the hope it might bring the U.S. into conflict with Britain over the Canadian border (it did, but eventually caused more trouble with Mexico). The sale completed the French withdrawal from *empire* in North America that began with their defeat in the *Seven Years' War*, and it marked a major milepost in the continental empire building of the United States.

Louis-Napoleon: See *Napoleon III*.

Low Countries: The lowland region adjacent to the North Sea, forming the basin of the Rhine, Meuse and Schledt rivers, and corresponding to modern Belgium, Luxembourg and Holland.

Lower Canada: The populous portion of *Québec*, from 1791-1841. At the time it was a British *colony*, captured from France as part of the settlement of the *Peace of Paris* (1763). Cf. *Upper Canada*.

low-intensity conflict: (1) Wars that do not involve direct, antagonistic engagement of the forces of large, military powers; instead, a large *state* might engage a smaller state, not with its maximum military *capabilities* but roughly at a level just superior to the forces of the smaller state. (2) Using military forces in small units and in short, sharp, limited engagements, either in defense against *guerrillas* or in emulation of them. Development of war-fighting theories that suggested major military powers could fight and win on the same level as guerrillas signaled a new respect by *conventional* forces for the effectiveness of guerrilla *tactics*, and the failure of older means of countering them, such as *pacification*.

low politics: Socioeconomic or *distributive justice* issues. The traditional distinction from *high politics* is blurring, as individuals become *subjects of international law*, and as patterns of *complex interdependence* emerge among societies.

Ludendorff, Erich Friedrich Wilhelm von (1865-1937): German general. With *Hindenburg*, he won the great victory at *Tannenberg* in 1914. Also with Hindenburg, after 1916 he took greater control of the whole war effort, pushing civilians like *Bethmann-Hollweg* into supporting roles. He was behind the plan to transport *Lenin* to Russia in a sealed train, and later forced upon Lenin the harsh terms of *Brest-Litovsk*. He planned the spring offensive of 1918 that broke the German army, instead of the *Allied* front. After the war he championed *reaction* and the *Freikorps,* joined the *Kapp putsch* and the *Beer Hall putsch* against *Weimar,* and overall was active on the far right.

Luftwaffe: "Air weapon." The German air force in *WWII.* It dominated the skies over Europe, North Africa and Russia until 1942, when it was thrown increasingly on the defensive. It was the first air force to utilize jets, but had these in insufficient numbers and too late in the war to turn the tide. See *blitz; blitzkrieg; Battle of Britain; Göring; Kursk; Malta; Stalingrad; thousand bomber raids.*

lumpenproletariat: In *marxism,* the loose, rootless class of manual workers who do not have the full status of members of the *proletariat,* and do not necessarily share working-class values and aspirations.

Lumumba, Patrice (1925-61): Premier of the Congo for a brief period, 1960-61. During the *Congo crisis* he called for UN *intervention* upon the *secession* of *Katanga.* A radical nationalist, he sought to rally the Congolese against white *mercenaries* and Belgian interference, but the fighting soon developed along tribal lines. He was dismissed as PM and later captured and murdered by *Tshombe.* Patrice Lumumba University, outside Moscow, was for several decades a training center for Africans the Soviets hoped to continue to influence after graduation.

Lusitania notes: The British passenger liner Lusitania was sunk off the Irish coast by a German *U-boat* on May 7, 1915, with a loss of 1,198 lives, including 128 Americans. The liner was carrying some 4,200 cases of ammunition and was in a declared *war zone* when torpedoed, which made it (technically) a legitimate target. Even so, *public opinion* viewed the action as mass murder. *Woodrow Wilson* sent a protest *note*, but found the German reply unsatisfactory. He drafted a second, much harsher note demanding an apology and *reparations,* and insisting Germany abandon its policy of *unrestricted submarine warfare.* Secretary of State *William Jennings Bryan* resigned, saying the note

might lead to war. It was sent anyway, on June 9th. Germany saw the note as a hostile act (designed to take away a vital weapon) and a sign the U.S. was not truly *neutral.* It refused to back down publicly, but in private issued orders to its U-boat captains to avoid passenger ships. Even so, more ships were sunk with more American lives lost, to eager U-boat captains. War was avoided--but only for the moment--when Germany apologized on February 4, 1916, though without ever admitting that the sinkings were illegal.

lusophone: A Portuguese-speaking person or country.

Luxembourg: Location: W. Europe. Major associations: *CSCE, EU, NATO, OECD, UN.* Population: 400,000. Military: small, but NATO caliber. Part of the *Holy Roman Empire* until that anachronism was extinguished by *Napoleon,* this tiny Grand Duchy was placed under Dutch control in 1815. In 1890 it became independent because there was no male heir to the Dutch throne, and it was decided that a Dutch Queen could not also serve as Grand Duke of Luxembourg. It was overrun by the Germans (who hardly noticed they had done so) in 1914. It regained its *independence* in 1918. Marched through by German troops again in 1940, it was annexed to *Nazi Germany* 1942-45. After the war, it joined the *BENELUX*. It signed the *Treaty of Brussels* in 1948 and joined NATO in 1949. It is a significant banking center. Also, as one of the founding members of the *EC*, and given its central location, it hosts several important EU organs.

Luxembourg Compromise (1966): A formula by which any member of the *EC* could *veto* a proposal that it believed touched upon its vital *national interests.* It increased the power of the national governments compared with the *European Commission* and *Parliament.*

Luxemburg, Rosa (1870-1919): "Red Rosa." German *marxist* and co-leader of the *Spartikists.* She opposed *WWI,* proposed a *general strike* in Germany, and was critical of *Lenin* and the *Bolsheviks.* With Karl Liebknecht (1871-1919), she led an abortive, communist uprising in Berlin in 1918. After surrendering they were both murdered on the way to prison by thugs from the *Freikorps.*

M

Maastricht Treaty (December 1991): The formal title is the "Treaty on European Union." It was the culmination of the proposals of the *Single European Act*, aiming at creation of a fully integrated *common market* free of *tariffs* and restrictions on movement of *capital* and *labor*. It enhanced the *supranational* aspects of the *European Community*, converting it (at least in name) to the *European Union*. It promotes the *WEU* for collective defense. It calls for a unified *currency* by 1997-99 and shared *foreign policy*. It provoked a sharp popular reaction in several countries, catching Europe's *elites* by surprise. The most notable response was in Denmark, where a referendum narrowly rejected Maastricht; after concessions to the Danes it passed a second referendum in 1993. In Britain, PM *John Major* faced an internal party revolt. In France, the majority in favor of Maastricht was much smaller than expected; and in Germany it had to pass a constitutional challenge. The debate revealed deep tensions within the Community over the wisdom of real political and monetary *union*, and suggested the possibility of a *two-speed Europe*. Nonetheless, Maastricht came into effect on November 1, 1993.

Macao: A Portuguese *colony* on the China coast, near *Hong Kong*. In 1974 it was given local *autonomy*. It will be returned to China in 1999.

MacArthur, Douglas (1880-1964): U.S. general. A prickly prima donna but brilliant tactician, in 1935 he succeeded his father as commander of the Philippine Army. Pushed out of the Philippines by the Japanese *invasion* in 1942, he pledged with characteristic egoism: "I [not we] shall return." He commanded Allied land forces in the Pacific *theater* from 1942-45. However, he bridled under the knowledge that it was Admiral Chester Nimitz's naval forces that controlled the *campaign*, and that the entire Pacific played second-fiddle to the war in Europe in *Allied* strategy, and in public perception. In 1944 he returned to the Philippines, wading ashore twice to ensure the newsreels caught the historic moment. He accepted the Japanese surrender in Tokyo Bay, on September 2, 1945. Appointed to head the *occupation*, he enjoyed the powers and status of a Roman proconsul. He moderated demands for punishment (e.g., refusing to let *Hirohito* be tried as a war criminal), and imposed a democratic and anti-militarist constitution on Japan. Recalled to active duty in the *Korean Conflict*, he took command of UN forces and saved South Korea by the extraordinary feat of an amphibious landing at Inchon, 200 miles behind North Korean lines. He then advocated forceful unification of Korea, while lying to *Truman*

about reports of Chinese troop concentrations as the UN approached the Yalu River. His forces were nearly overwhelmed when 300,000 Chinese "volunteers" suddenly poured south. When MacArthur went public with demands that the war be brought home to China, with *nuclear weapons* if need be, Truman fired him. The decision was unpopular: MacArthur returned to a New York ticker tape parade and widespread adulation. After an embarrassingly inept run at the presidency he "just faded away," into quiet retirement.

Macedonia: Location: *Balkans*. Major associations: *CSCE, UN*. Population: 2 million, 1/3rd Albanian. Military: minimal. For five centuries an *Ottoman* province (1380), it became the target of Bulgarian annexationist designs in the 1870s, and again during the *First* and *Second Balkan Wars*. It was incorporated into the new state of *Yugoslavia* after *WWI*, with a portion left in Greece and another in Bulgaria. In 1946 it was made a republic within the Yugoslav *federation*. It broke with what was left of Yugoslavia (Serbia and Montenegro) in 1992. Greece blocked it from *EC* and UN recognition, on the ground it has a province of the same name and fears Macedonia's historic claim to that province. In March 1993, Athens agreed to UN membership for Macedonia on condition its flag not fly outside the UN building, as it is the emblem of Alexander of Macedon (the Great) who ruled Greece in the 4th century B.C. The UN solution to this surreal dispute was to use a formula pioneered by the *IMF*, to wit: admit Macedonia under the cumbersome, but temporary name, "Former Yugoslav Republic of Macedonia," with the problem of terminology to be worked out with Greece later. In April 1993, it became the 181st member of the UN. In July, 300 U.S. troops arrived as UN peacekeepers, to deter Serbian *aggression*. Like other tenuous, new European countries, it asked to join *NATO* but has not been accepted.

Machel, Samora (1930-86): President of Mozambique 1975-86. He was commander of FRELIMO, a nationalist *guerrilla* movement, during its fight with Portugal from 1964-74. He governed from a doctrinaire, *marxist* perspective. His *expropriations* of foreign companies alienated many in the West. However, he was seen as a hero within southern Africa for supporting the *ANC*. Faced with South African economic *sabotage* and military *incursions*, he accommodated to geopolitical reality and signed the "Nkomati Accord" (1984) with the *apartheid* regime. He was killed in a plane crash, just inside South African *territory*.

Machiavelli, Niccolò di Bernardo (1469-1527): Florentine political thinker. Like Jonathan Swift, he has been more often misinterpreted and vilified for his honesty than understood or appreciated for his insight. Some regard him as the founder of *political science* (in its classical concerns with governance, *power, ethics* and diplomacy, not later preoccupations with arcane methodological disputes). He lived in greatly turbulent and violent times, when Italy was overrun by clashing armies of the *city-states* as well as foreign invaders, and diplomacy was a prime instrument of *statecraft* in a "red in tooth and claw" (Tennyson) battle for survival. He was imprisoned and tortured by the Medici, the ruling family of Florence. His thinking reflected those realities. His most famous, and still widely read, works are "De Principatibus" (The Prince) and "The Discourses." In them he laid out a broad understanding of politics, expressing a terror of *anarchy*; expedience in choice of means as a regrettable, but unavoidable, requirement of successful political action; and the equivocal nature of public as opposed to personal moral judgments. Less widely recognized, he wished for the successful and even ruthless exercise of power by princes not for its own sake or in a vacuum of values. Rather, he yearned to see princely power advance specific causes he regarded as having inherent moral content, including *republicanism* and the *liberation* of Florence--and perhaps Italy-- from foreign control. He is justly famous for his depiction of the workings of power in the real world. His awareness of the *balance of power*, and his sense of how the lust for power lies naked beneath the covers of even the most silken idealism, was instinctive, instructive and brilliant. Cf. *machiavellian; realism; realpolitik; Renaissance.*

machiavellian: (1) Philosophical: akin to the principles of *Niccolò Machiavelli*, in particular his emphasis on expediency over absolute conceptions of morality, his pessimism about the quality of human nature, and about the possibilities for success of schemes of social organization that do not rely ultimately on fear and force. (2) Pejorative: unscrupulous and dishonest; excessively cunning and full of intrigue; merely self-interested, without higher purpose.

machtpolitik: "Power politics." A celebration of conflict among *nations* as the forceful assertion of national will, as embodied in the *state*. Distantly related to *realpolitik*, this Prussian notion grew in part out of simple, sober recognition that the German Empire had been constructed by force of Prussian arms. Yet it also reflected a romantic view of *martial* virtues, and the belief that international struggle was morally redemptive. For example, *Helmut von Moltke* (the elder), principal architect of Prussia's *victories* over Denmark

(1864), Austria (1866) and France (1870-71), once said: "war is a link in the divine order of the world." Cf. *social darwinism.*

machtstaat: "Power state." In *nazism* and more generally in German history, an exaltation of the *state* as a *reified*, organic whole, with a moral force and worth unto itself that far exceeded that of any individual. This view of the German state underlay much of the Nazi appeal to extreme *nationalism*, and lent support to their assertive and then aggressive foreign policy.

Mackenzie, William Lyon (1795-1861): Canadian rebel, and Scottish-born MP. He joined forces with French Canadian rebel Louis-Joseph Papineau (1789-1871), who objected to the *union* of the Canadas and to British government in *Québec*. Their joint *rebellions* in *Upper* and *Lower Canada* failed. Mackenzie formed a rebel government in Buffalo, New York, and with aid from Irish-Americans launched cross-border raids from a base in the Niagara region. In *retaliation,* a British military party sank a rebel ship, the Caroline, while it was berthed in American waters, killing one U.S. *citizen*. Hotheads on both sides called for *war*, before cooler minds prevailed and the issue petered out into stiff *diplomatic protests*. The episode deepened Canadian suspicions that the U.S. secretly wanted to *annex* Canada. It also left unsettled U.S. claims for *reparations*, adding another load to the desultory cargo of Anglo/American relations.

Mackinder, Halford (1861-1947): British geographer who posited the *geographical pivot of history* and ideas of the *Heartland* and *World Island*, from which he derived the rule: "Who rules east Europe commands the Heartland; who rules the Heartland commands the World Island; who rules the World Island rules the world." His theory was most influential in Germany, where it affected Imperial *war plans* and later fed into *Nazi* ideas about *lebensraum* (though he personally had no sympathies in that direction). He also influenced American naval *strategy* between the wars, and during the early *Cold War*. However, he failed to account for the fact that the following powers controlled much of the "Heartland" without dominating the world: tsarist Russia 1815-1917; Germany 1941-44; the Soviet Union 1920-41, 1945-91. Most glaringly, his theory could not explain why the U.S. was completely separate from the World Island, yet was the *preponderant power* for most of the 20th century. He also badly neglected *air power*. Cf. *geopolitics; geopolitik; Rimland.*

MacMahon, Patrice (1808-93): French general. Governor of Algeria 1864-70; President of France 1873-

79. He held France together after its *defeat* in the *Franco/Prussian War*, crushing the *Paris Commune* and trying vainly to restore the *monarchy*.

MacMillan, Harold (1894-1986): British statesman. Minister of Defense 1954-55; Foreign Secretary 1955; PM 1957-63. He coordinated British diplomacy in North Africa during *WWII*, and helped negotiate the *Austrian State Treaty* after it. As PM he sought to play a role as mediator between Moscow and Washington. He was ineffective because he took office just as Britain's *influence* began to plummet because of the *Suez Crisis*, and because he was so personally and politically close to U.S. leaders. In 1960 he spoke in South Africa of the "winds of change" sweeping that continent and Asia (that is, *decolonization*). While that remark has been cited as perspicacious and daring, it can also be seen as just a pithy observation of unfolding events. He endorsed the *Partial Test Ban Treaty*.

macroeconomics: A subfield of economics that analyzes large-scale *indicators* and processes, such as a nation's total foreign *debt, GDP, GNP, money supply, balance of trade* and *balance of payments*.

macropolitical perspective: Analyses that attempt to view world political and economic affairs from the vantage point of the *international system* as a whole.

Madagascar: Location: Indian Ocean, off the E. African coast. Major associations: *OAU, UN*. Population: 12 million (an admixture of South Asian, Polynesian, Arab and African ethnic groups). Military: small, self-defense forces only. This large island was originally settled by Malays and Polynesians. It was made a French *protectorate* at the end of the 19th century, and a formal *colony* in 1896. In 1945 it was made an *overseas territory*, but it gained *autonomy* in 1958 within the *French Community,* and *independence* in 1960 as Malagasy (the name was changed back in 1975). Unrest at continuing French dominance led to a *coup* in 1972, and a radical regime that *nationalized* French property and sought close ties with China. In 1979 all foreigners were expelled. In 1990 the regime cracked and a multiparty system was introduced. Peaceful elections were held in 1993.

Madison, James (1751-1836): U.S. statesman. Secretary of State, 1801-09; President, 1909-17. He was among those who saw success in the *American War of Independence* as requiring a strong central government, but preferred this to be Congress rather than the *executive* power favored by *Alexander Hamilton*. He was involved in the *Louisiana Purchase* and in the *embargo* imposed by *Jefferson*, 1807-09. As Secretary

and as President, Madison looked to republican (Jeffersonian) substitutes for *force* in foreign policy. Facing the chaos and danger of the *Napoleonic Wars*, in which American citizens were *impressed*, ships seized, and trade interfered with, he failed to prepare the nation for *war* or to provide an effective *deterrent* to Britain and France. For 12 years he searched for a form of peaceful coercion, a republican solution to war, and thought he found it in a denial of *trade*. What he failed to realize was that Britain and France were locked in mortal combat in which trade was a weapon of *war*, not a tool of peacemaking. Moreover, he regarded Britain as the greater threat, mainly because its ships were the most evident and its *blockade* the most effective; he did not seem to grasp the long-term threat to the U.S. should France have achieved *hegemony* over Europe. Most important, his policy of bluff and bluster failed because the U.S. remained a small and weak nation, without a navy or other means to enforce its threats. But instead of accommodating to that reality and compromising on *neutral rights*, Madison chose to shout loudly at London although all he carried was a gentleman's walking stick, and when his adversary had the rather more impressive club of the *Royal Navy*. With the country ill-prepared and virtually unarmed, he asked Congress for a *declaration of war*, commencing the *War of 1812*. Hoping for a quick seizure of *Upper Canada* so he could trade it back to Britain for maritime concessions, he authorized an invasion. It fizzled. The next year, battle-hardened British troops, veterans of the *Napoleonic Wars*, landed and burned Washington; Madison fled the city, to wander the Virginia countryside for three days. Worse might have come had not the *Treaty of Ghent* been agreed: before the *Hundred Days* in Europe, the British were beginning transfers of troops from France, amidst public calls for vengeance against the former, upstart *colony* that had attacked while they fought (or so it was thought in London) to defend international liberties from the great tyrant just exiled to *Elba*. From the U.S. point of view, victory in the *Battle of New Orleans* (actually irrelevant to the outcome of the war and the peace), meant that "Mr. Madison's War" could be proclaimed a triumph, even a "second war of independence." It was no such thing. It was more a close escape from the consequences of a disastrously naïve and ideological diplomacy, that having blundered into war was fortunate not to have had a draconian peace imposed upon the land.

Mafeking, siege of (1899-1900): One of several *sieges* of British garrison towns by the *Boers*, during the *Second Boer War*. The siege was finally lifted and the Boer army crushed, forcing the Boers into dropping *conventional warfare* in favor of *guerrilla* tactics.

Maghreb: Traditionally, the western part of North Africa, populated mainly by *Arabs* and *Berber*, and including modern Algeria, Libya, Morocco and Tunisia.

Maghreb Union: A loose association of Algeria, Libya, Mauritania, Morocco and Tunisia. It was founded in 1989 to coordinate on matters of regional interest.

Maginot Line: French *fortifications* running from Belgium to Switzerland, built 1929-34, and named for André Maginot (1877-1932), Minister for War. The Belgians refused to continue the line, insisting on returning to *neutrality* (which would fail them, again, in 1940). German *armor* went around the line, through the supposedly "impenetrable" *Ardennes*. Many French guns never fired, and hundreds of thousands of defenders surrendered after offering no more than token resistance, and some not even that.

Maginot spirit: A mood of *defeatism* pervading France between the world wars, symbolized by the defensive posture of the *Maginot Line*. The idea that France could never take the offensive against Germany paralyzed its diplomacy and army, contributed to the *appeasement* of the 1930s, the *Phony War* and the French collapse and *surrender* in 1940.

magyars: (1) Native Hungarians. (2) The Hungarian landed aristocracy.

Mahan, Alfred Thayer (1840-1914): American naval strategist. He wrote several enormously influential books on the notion of *sea power*. His great work, "The Influence Of Sea Power On History, 1660-1783," helped shape naval thinking and policy for several *Great Powers*. He argued that contrary to most theories emphasizing *land power*, history showed that the dominant powers in every age were great sea powers with strings of overseas possessions and bases. He maintained that despite advances in weaponry, the basic principles of naval *strategy* and *warfare* remained constant, and that dominant power was linked to commercial and martial command of the seas. Some have attributed to his theories the interest of both Germany and Britain in naval dominance. Others point to American interest in a large navy and overseas bases, and view Mahan as contributing to U.S. imperial expansion during and after the *Spanish/American War*. But perhaps his greatest influence was posthumous: U.S. *containment* policy during the *Cold War* involved setting up a circle of *alliances* around the Soviet Union, each supported by naval forces.

mahdi: "The Guided One." The title taken by several historical figures who have claimed to be the fulfill- ment of the messianic tradition in *Islam* (especially the *shi'ite* branch). That tradition looks to a temporal ruler who will bring a reign of righteousness to the world. The most important was the Sudanese "Mahdi of Dongola" (Muhammad Ahmed)," active from 1840-85. His "whirling dervishes" clashed bloodily with the British, killed *Gordon* (among others), and toppled *Gladstone*. His great-grandson, Sadiq al-Mahdi, set up a *theocracy* in Sudan in 1986. In 1980 a Chadian refugee was acclaimed mahdi by his followers in Nigeria, and as many as 10,000 died. Another claim led to bloodshed in *Mecca* in 1979, and so on.

Mahmud II (1785-1839): Sultan of Turkey 1808-39. He temporarily stemmed the decline of the *Ottoman Empire*, through reforms and destruction of the *Janissaries*. But he fought a losing *war* with Russia 1809-12, and lost control of Serbia and Greece 1821-29. He was increasingly challenged by *Mehemet Ali* of Egypt.

Maine (sinking of): This U.S. *warship* was blown up, cause unknown, in Havana harbor on February 15, 1898, killing 260 sailors. The slogan, "Remember the Maine!" became a rallying cry of the *yellow press* calling for *intervention* in Cuba against Spain, and a *casus belli* for the *Spanish/American War*. Theories about the cause of the explosion vary from a faulty boiler (in which case the U.S. casus belli was spurious), to a mine or torpedo (planted either by Cubans, to draw the U.S. into their rebellion, or the Spanish, for unclear motives).

mainland China: Sometimes used about the People's Republic of China, to distinguish it from Taiwan.

Majlis: An *Islamic* parliament, especially the one in Iran, but also in several other Muslim countries.

majority rule: (1) A basic principle of representative government, resting legitimate authority in the expressed will of an adult majority, with respect for rights of minorities. (2) Rule by the black majorities that followed a transition from white, minority or colonial regimes in Africa. (3) When *multilateral* decisions are taken by majorities, rather than under the *unanimity rule*. Cf. *elitism; popular sovereignty; power sharing*.

Major, John (b.1943): British PM, November 1990- . He succeeded *Margaret Thatcher*, and to the surprise of most observers and pollsters, he won the next general election. He led Britain during the *Gulf War*, and was a firm supporter of UN resolutions on Iraq. After wavering on the *Maastricht Treaty*, he put his career and government on the line in July 1993, by threatening his own party with a snap election it would surely lose if backbenchers failed to vote to ratify Maastricht. That maneuver somewhat undercut earlier criticism about political weakness. He authorized secret talks with the *IRA* in 1993, and signed a breakthrough with Ireland, regarding *Ulster.*

Malacca Straits: A strategic and heavily traveled waterway located between Malaysia and Sumatra.

Malagasy: The name of Madagascar, from 1960-75.

Malan, Daniel F. (1874-1959): South African PM 1948-54. A racist ideologue convinced he knew the will of the deity, and that God insisted on the separation of the races. He accordingly introduced *apartheid* to South Africa, after leading the *National Party* to electoral victory. The country was thus set face against the prevailing winds of *self-determination* and *decolonization*. Several decades of deepening isolation from the *world community* followed.

Malawi: Location: Central Africa. Major associations: *Commonwealth, NAM, OAU, SADCC, UN.* Population: nine million. Military: minimal. Formerly Nyasaland. Arab slavers raided the Bantu of Malawi in the 19th century, but the *slave trade* was eradicated and a British *protectorate* proclaimed by the 1890s. It joined the *Central African Federation* 1954-63, but gained its independence in 1964 and became a *republic* in 1966 under Hastings Banda Kamuzu (b.1900?), PM and then president-for-life from 1963. He bought *peace* for his regime at the price of much accommodation of South African interests, and considerable repression at home. Although a *front line* state, Malawi mainly kept a low foreign policy profile and stayed out of the many *regional wars.* A 1993 *referendum* called 63% for a pluralist democracy. In May 1994, Banda was thrown out in Malawi's first multiparty election.

Malaya: British *colonies* were set up on parts of the *Malay archipelago* from the late 18th century, with full control by 1867. After *WWII* it was thought advisable to federate these, and a British *protectorate* was set up (Federation of Malaya) from 1948-57. During these years British and *Commonwealth* troops defeated a *communist* insurgency. Malaya was an independent *republic* 1958-63. It then joined with *Sabah, Sarawak* and *Singapore* to form *Malaysia.*

Malay archipelago: The SE Asian island group comprising the principal islands of Borneo, Celebes, the Moluccas, the Philippines, Sumatra and Timor, and many smaller islands.

Malaysia: Location: SE Asia. Major associations: *ASEAN, NAM, UN.* Population: 17 million. Military: currently upgrading. A Federation comprising *Malaya, Sabah* and *Sarawak* (*Singapore* was an original member, but left in 1965). Tunku Abdul Rahman (1903-90) was PM of Malaya 1957-63; PM of Malaysia 1963-70. His was a voice for moderation, whether of internal ethnic conflicts between Chinese and Malays, or interstate conflict. He oversaw the founding of the Malay and then Malaysian Republic. The latter *union* was met by Indonesian hostility in the *Konfrontasi.* There was also *tension* with the Philippines. Malaysia was a founding member of ASEAN, through which it sought to insulate itself from the *war* in *Indochina*, and in which it prospered. Even with the departure of Singapore, Malaysia remains ethnically divided between Malays and Chinese. It lays claim to some of the *Spratlys.* In the 1980s it led an unsuccessful drive to open the *Antarctic* to mineral exploitation on the basis of the *common heritage principle*, and raised objections to Western notions of *human rights* at the *World Human Rights Conference.* In 1993 it said it would increase defense spending from 2% to 6% of GNP over the next 10 years, to keep pace with the new Asian *arms race.* In 1994 relations with Britain worsened.

Maldives: Location: western Indian Ocean. Major associations: *Commonwealth, NAM, SARC, UN.* Population: 225,000. Military: minimal. Formed out of some 2,000 islands, this Muslim archipelago was a British *protectorate* from 1887-1965, enjoying some *autonomy* after 1948. In 1965 it resumed a status as an independent *sultanate*, but in 1968 it became a *republic.* In 1988 India's intercession prevented an *invasion* by a ragtag band of *mercenaries* from succeeding.

Malenkov, Georgi Maximilianovich (1902-88): Premier of the Soviet Union 1953-55. He helped *Stalin* destroy the *kulaks*, and was always close to the great dictator after 1930. He succeeded Stalin as Party Secretary in 1953, but within weeks was relegated to a figurehead position, then suffered repeated demotions. In 1957 he was expelled from the Central Committee and became a *non-person.*

Mali: Location: W. Africa. Major associations: *la francophonie, OAU, NAM, UN.* Population: 9.5 million. Military: poor; embroiled in domestic politics. A Muslim *empire* was ruled from Mali until the 15th century, with its capital at Timbuktu, site of a great university of Arab and Muslim learning. The area was ruled from Morocco until the 19th century, when French *influence* penetrated from the coast and it became the "French Soudan." In 1898 it was incorporated into *French West Africa.* In 1946 it was declared an *overseas territory*, but in 1958 it became *autonomous* within the *French Community* as the Soudan Republic. In 1959 it attempted a *union* with Senegal (the "Mali Federation") but this soon broke up and it changed its name to Mali in 1960. This desperately poor, desert country has, along with the rest of the *Sahel*, suffered through three decades of drought. That destroyed its economy, made *refugees* of many of its *citizens* and has kept its politics unstable.

Malta: Location: Mediterranean. Major associations: *Commonwealth, NAM, UN*. Population: 360,000. Military: minimal. It was ruled by the Maltese Knights (of St. John) from 1530-1798, when *Napoleon* captured the island. The British successfully *blockaded* and captured Malta in 1800, and *annexed* it in 1814. It became a major British naval base in the Mediterranean, second only to *Gibraltar*. In the 1920s and 1930s Britain warded off demands by *Mussolini* that Malta be ceded to Italy. From 1940-43 it stood against constant Italian and then German air attacks, and played a vital role in disruption of the *Axis* sea *supply lines* in N. Africa. It was next used in launching the *invasions* of Sicily and Italy (the entire island was later given a decoration for valor). It gained *independence* in 1964, and became a *republic* in 1974. Britain closed its naval base in 1979, ending a 180-year presence, and Malta became *non-aligned*. From 1980-85 it was involved in a *dispute* with Libya over *oil* exploration within conflicting claims to *EEZs*, in which Libya used its navy to prevent Maltese drilling. The dispute was resolved by a compromise in 1985. In 1989 Malta declared itself a *nuclear weapons free zone*.

Malvinas: See *Falkland Islands*.

Malthus, Thomas Robert (1766-1834): English economist. He argued that optimism about the perfectibility of the human condition, such as characterized the *Enlightenment*, was misplaced. Instead, there was a tendency in nature for *population* to increase faster than the means of subsistence. Population grows, he said, geometrically, while *food* supplies grow only arithmetically. The inevitable result must be the ride of the Four Horsemen of the Apocalypse: *war*, disease, *famine* and death. Malthus did not take joy from this gloomy forecast, though like Jonathan Swift's his reputation has ever since suffered from misplaced accusations of misanthropy. Latter-day "Malthusians" converted his observation into a justification for social inaction concerning poverty, public health and starvation. Charles Darwin was influenced in another direction, toward the theory of natural selection as a response to population increase and competition for scarce food supplies. Concerning human populations, Malthus' predictions have not been lived out: agricul-

tural and technological advances, from draining swamps to new crop varieties, along with widespread birth control in industrial societies, has changed the equation. Cf. *agricultural revolution; green revolution; population*.

malthusian/neo-malthusian: A shorthand term used to describe the dire possibility that population increase in the *Third World* may one day exceed *food* supply, leading to *famine*. Critics point out, with considerable justice, that a focus on reproduction deflects attention from underlying economic and social problems that may be more important to long-term population control. See *Malthus*.

managed trade: Where *states* agree to mutual *quotas* and other mechanisms for controlling the flow of trade. A synonym is *directed trade*. It is often just a euphemism for *protectionism*. Cf. *free trade*.

Manchester school: A 19th century school of economic theory that argued for British leadership in establishing international *free trade*, and adopted a *laissez-faire* attitude on questions of social reform.

Manchukuo: A Japanese *puppet state* set up in occupied *Manchuria* 1932-45. *Pu Yi*, the last *Manchu*, was installed as "emperor." Only the *Axis* states ever recognized it. It was overrun by the Soviets and Chinese at the end of *WWII*.

Manchuria: The area to the northeast of historic China. The Russians penetrated it economically and built roads and rails across it toward the end of the 19th century; they *occupied* it after the *Boxer Rebellion*. Japan seized a portion after the *First Sino/Japanese War*, but was forced to give this up by the *Triple Intervention*. Japanese forces then attacked the Russians in Manchuria in 1904. The province was returned to China in the *Treaty of Portsmouth*, with both Japan and Russia retaining transit rights and stationing troops there. In 1906 Japan constructed the Manchurian Railway, which enabled it to fully penetrate the region and support its *Guandong Army,* and ensured an ongoing conflict with China. In 1907 Japan and Russia secretly divided Manchuria into N/S *spheres of influence*. With the *Russian Revolutions of 1917*, Japan increased its presence. In 1931 the Japanese staged the *Mukden incident*, invaded Manchuria and set up the *puppet state* of *Manchukuo*. In 1945 Manchuria was returned to Chinese control, though the border with Russia remained in dispute. See also *Treaty of Peking*.

Manchus, a.k.a. Ch'ing dynasty: A mongolian people

from *Manchuria*, they conquered China and established a dynasty that ruled from 1644-1911. The greatest of the Manchus was the K'ang-hsi emperor (1661-1722), who subjugated southern China, conquered Mongolia, gave support to law and the arts, and began a reign of relative *peace*. His grandson, the Ch'ienlung emperor (1736-96), made Tibet a *protectorate*, and advanced *conquest* as far as *Turkestan*. The Manchus repressed the *White Lotus Rebellion* after 1796. They were not so able to fend off foreign *influence*, however, especially after their humiliation in the *First Opium War* (1839-42), and failure in the *Second Opium War* (1856-60) to overturn the *unequal treaties*. For ten years they lost effective control of much of southern China during the *Taiping Rebellion*. That rising was put down only by a significant surrender of central Manchu power to regional gentry and *warlords*. The *Dowager Empress* made one last attempt to expel the hated foreigners in the *Boxer Rebellion*, but when that too failed it was clear that fundamental reform was both necessary and inescapable. After a few years of half-hearted trying, the Manchus, in the person of the child-emperor *Pu Yi*, were overthrown by the *Chinese Revolution*.

mandates/mandated territories: *Colonies* and other territories taken from the *Central Powers*, and administered under Article 22 of the *Covenant of the League of Nations*, by appointed *states* as diverse as Australia, Britain, France, Japan and South Africa. There were three kinds: Class A (limited mandates), expected to soon advance to *independence*; Class B (indefinite mandates), to be governed like colonies; Class C (indefinite mandates), to be governed as if they were indistinct from the *metropolitan power*, with little thought of *independence*. They later became UN *trust territories*. States that were not members of the *League of Nations* negotiated separate *recognitions* of League mandates. As with *Yap Island*, this process did not always go smoothly. The mandate system can be viewed as a reasonable, because achievable, compromise between the continuing realities of *imperialism* and the new ideal of *self-determination*.

Mandela, Nelson (b.1918): South African nationalist. He was a principal organizer of the *ANC* in the 1950s, facing arrest and trial several times. He was imprisoned from 1962-90, becoming the most famous political prisoner in the world. As his sentence lengthened his stature and reputation for integrity grew. Released in 1990, he instantly became the spokesman for black civil rights and a negotiated end to *apartheid*. By mid-1993 all of apartheid's pernicious legal forms had been abolished, and agreement was reached to hold free and fair, multiracial elections in 1994. Mandela became

South Africa's first truly democratically elected President in May 1994. He was awarded the *Nobel Prize* for Peace, jointly with *F. W. de Klerk*.

maneuvers: *Tactical* exercises essayed to test equipment and troops, and gain simulated experience of large-scale operations in wartime. They can be air, land or naval exercises.

Manhattan Project: The code name for the Anglo/American *atomic bomb* project during *WWII*. In 1939 *Albert Einstein* wrote *Franklin Roosevelt* warning that a *fission* bomb was possible, leading to this top-secret research project in 1942 at Chicago; Oak Ridge, Tennessee; and *Los Alamos*, New Mexico. It was a race against German scientists working at *Peenemünde*. An American team, with some Canadian and British help, was the first to test an atomic bomb on July 17, 1945. The Soviets were not included or informed until *Potsdam*, though it was later learned they had highly successful *spies* in position the whole time. Two bombs built by the project, "Little Boy" and "Fatman," were dropped on Japan on August 6 and 9, 1945. The project was disbanded in 1946. Cf. *Minatom*.

manifest destiny: An 1840s notion that it was the historic destiny of white, democratic, American civilization to expand over the breadth of the North American continent. That such was the will of Providence, it was said, was manifest in the endless bounty and evident success of the United States, and its character as a self-governing society of free men--slaves, and women, were simply overlooked in this flattering self-appraisal. Besides, the rich lands spread out to the west were empty, more or less--Indians also did not count in these assessments. When Indians made themselves noticed, say by resisting *conquest*, the argument was made that they should forfeit the land anyway, because they did not work and exploit it to create prosperity, as Providence clearly intended. Similarly, Mexican claims to *Texas, California* and the Pacific coast could be swept aside, as that people did not enjoy divine favor--after all, they were Catholic, non-white and ill-governed, were they not? The idea of a manifest national destiny became immensely popular, rising to its peak following the *Mexican/American War* (as a post facto justification for expansion at a neighbor's expense). It was not applied to Canada, however, by any but the most extreme: that *colony* was seen as white and reasonably democratic, if curiously ill-governed and stubbornly anti-republican. Not of minor account, it was also defended by Britain, although that was an uncomfortable fact that could hardly be admitted in polite, expansionist company when one was discussing the marvelous unfolding of a divine plan for an "empire of democracy" in the *New World*. The idea of manifest destiny did not survive the *American Civil War*, though the basic impulse that gave rise to it found continuing expression in the looser notion of Americans' "moral exceptionalism." Cf. *mission; mission civilatrice; white man's burden*.

manned penetrator: Military *jargon* for a piloted aircraft, as opposed to drones, assigned to penetrate enemy defenses and press home an attack on selected targets. When political correctness reaches the *Pentagon*, no doubt this already awkward term will become the even more ungraceful "personed penetrator."

Mannerheim, Carl Gustaf (1867-1951): Finnish statesman. He served in the Russian army 1889-1917, then led Finnish *Whites* in the *war* that freed Finland. He was President of Finland 1919-20. He headed Finnish defenses, and led the army in another war with Russia 1939-40. He agreed to an anti-Soviet *pact* with Germany, and fought Russia again, 1941-44. He signed an *armistice* as the *Red Army* advanced, then took Finland into the war against Germany in March 1945.

Mannerheim Line: Finnish defensive positions on the *Karelia* peninsula that held the Soviets up for three months during the *Winter War*.

man-of-war: The largest *warship* during the age of sail. First built by the Portuguese, it was a mobile *artillery* platform capable of bringing to bear multiple decks of cannon in a devastating broadside or *bombardment*. Cf. *sloop-of-war*.

Mao Zedong, a.k.a. Tse Tung (1893-1976): "Great Helmsman." Chinese dictator and statesman. Active in revolutionary politics from 1911, he was a leader in the *Jiangxi Soviet*. He solidified his position in the *Long March*, during which he displayed a talent for innovative *guerrilla* tactics and an appreciation of peasant grievance as a springboard to power in China. Once in *Yenan* he concentrated on party work while *Zhu De* commanded the *PLA* and *Zhou Enlai* handled diplomacy. He became Chairman of the People's Republic upon its founding in 1949. One of his first acts was to consolidate the *revolution* by *radical* land reform, modeled on *Stalin's* treatment of the *kulaks*, in which the peasants were forced onto Peoples' Collectives. That draconian and often brutal coercion of the peasantry took over a decade to complete, led to enormous social and economic dislocation and a major *famine*, and cost by some estimates over 25 million lives. It has been confirmed (from Soviet *archives*) that Mao came under strong pressure from Stalin to back North Korea, and later approve Chinese *interven-*

tion in the *Korean Conflict*. By the mid-1950s his disdain for the post-*stalinist* Soviet Union was evident (Mao considered Soviet *revisionism* about Stalin not merely wrong, but a threatening example to his own *cadres*). By 1958 the *Sino/Soviet split* was well advanced, as was Mao's own *cult of personality*. His effort to woo Chinese intellectuals with the *Hundred Flowers campaign* ended in further revelation of his extremely narrow tolerance for dissent, and his cunning about exposing opponents. His policies were: emphasis on the role of the peasant in an adapted, *marxist-leninist* model of *development* that stressed collective will and revolutionary commitment; radical egalitarianism; *collectivization* of agriculture; state control of *capital* accumulation and allocation, and of the *labor* supply; rejection of *peaceful coexistence;* dictatorship by the *Communist Party,* and over the party by himself as a latter-day *Manchu* in all but name; *peoples' war; cultural revolution;* and the disastrous, backyard industrialization schemes of the *Great Leap Forward*. Temperamentally, he was a radical puritan and romantic, who judged social and political behavior by moral and ideological intent rather than practical outcome. He little understood economics, viewing deep problems of China's lack of agricultural and industrial *modernization* as amenable to military-style commands and methods of *mobilization*. He cared nothing for the welfare of individuals: he once shocked his personal doctor by remarking that he hoped the U.S. would use *nuclear weapons* to kill 20-25 million Chinese, so that the truth of the turpitude of the capitalist nations might be revealed to all and sundry. He was responsible for tens of millions of deaths; the exact number remains unknown, but probably exceeded the totals run up even by *Hitler* and Stalin. He was a visionary but also a dogmatist; a charismatic leader for many, but a bloody tyrant to more; and finally, a moral monster. See also *gang of four; Lin Biao; Red Guards*.

maoism: The ideas and practices of *Mao Zedong*, and of various groups that later took up the banner of maoism. See *collectivization; Great Leap Forward; Great Proletarian Cultural Revolution; Hundred Flowers Campaign; people's war; Red Guards; reeducation; Sendero Luminoso*. Cf. *Franz Fanon*.

Maori: The *indigenous people* of New Zealand.

Maori Wars: (1) First, 1843: A *Maori* rebellion occasioned by disregard for land settlements the Maori had accepted in the *Treaty of Waitangi*; British troops suppressed the rising. (2) Second, 1860-70: A *guerrilla* campaign undertaken by the Maori, mainly on North Island. Again, the central issue was a dispute over native land claims. See *tribe*.

march on Rome (1922): A central myth of Italian *fascism*, inflated in the retelling far beyond its import or heroic content (which was minimal). In fact, it was rather more of a hesitant shuffle by Italian *blackshirts*, while *Mussolini* negotiated for control of the government. He actually arrived in the capital by train, better rested and in advance of more pedestrian fascists.

Marco Polo Bridge incident (July 7, 1937): Near Beijing, shots were exchanged between a Chinese garrison and Japanese troops on *maneuvers*. China apologized, but Japan attacked in force anyway (it had been longing for a pretext). Thus began the *Second Sino/Japanese War.*

Marcos, Ferdinand (1917-89): Dictator of the Philippines 1965-86. He fought in the *resistance* against Japan, though his claim to leadership is doubtful. His first term as President saw increasing repression, until in 1972 he declared *martial law* (lifted only in 1981). While domestic opposition grew, his strong ties to the U.S. and the *strategic* importance of the Philippines meant there was little more than rhetorical pressure from Washington to reestablish democracy. Things began to fall apart after he had the opposition leader, Benigno Aquino, murdered as he stepped off a plane in Manila. The *Reagan* administration threw its support to the opposition at a critical moment in 1986, and by "peoples' power," Marcos was forced from office and out of the country. The corruption of his regime was symbolized by discovery of his wife's (Imelda) shoe closet, containing over 3,000 pairs in a nation where too many children grow up barefoot. He spent his final days in Hawaii. In September 1993, the Philippines finally permitted return of his remains.

mare clausum: "Closed sea." A navigable body of water enclosed by, and therefore under the sole *jurisdiction* of, a single *state*.

mare liberum: "Free sea." A navigable body of water open to all nations, under the *jurisdiction* of none.

mare nostrum: "Our sea." Used by the Romans about the Mediterranean. For them, it was not an idle boast. It was a *strategic* condition sought and most nearly achieved by the British in the 19th century; it was also aspired to by *Mussolini* prior to *WWII*.

Marianas Islands: Location: Pacific. Colonized by Spain after 1688, *Guam* was ceded to the U.S. and the other islands sold to Germany in 1899. They were seized by Japan in 1914. In 1921 they became a Japanese *mandate territory*, but were administered as though they were an integral part of the Japanese

Empire. During *WWII*, they were captured by the U.S. and later administered as part of the *Trust Territory of the Pacific Islands*. In 1975 a UN *referendum* led to *commonwealth status* for the Northern Marianas, in association with the U.S. In 1990 the Security Council ended the trusteeship, and the population (43,000) became U.S. *citizens*.

Maria Theresa (1717-80): Archduchess of Austria and Queen of Hungary, 1740-80. She led the Austrian *Hapsburgs* in the *War of the Spanish Succession*, but lost badly for Austria in the *Seven Years' War*. She joined in the 1772 *partition of Poland*. After 1756 she ruled jointly with her son, *Joseph II*.

Mariel boat lift (1980): Hundreds of thousands of *boat people* left Cuba for the U.S., many voluntarily, others under compulsion. Cynically included by the *Castro* government were several thousand criminals and mentally ill. These were *interned* in the U.S. and returned to Cuba in an *immigration* agreement signed in 1987.

marine sovereignty zone: See *territorial sea.*

maritime frontier: The limit to a *state's* claims of *jurisdiction*, extending from the coast out to sea. See *baseline; straight baseline; territorial sea.* Cf. *EEZ.*

market economy: One in which the forces of *supply* and demand are given relatively free reign as to production, distribution and consumption of *goods* and *services*. Of course, in the real world even *OECD* market economies reflect a significant degree of non-market activity and influence, such as government intervention through *protectionism*, regulation and/or *subsidy* to specific sectors or industries. Cf. *reform liberalism; planned economy.*

Marne, Battles of: (1) September 5-19, 1914: This battle took place with the Germans in sight of Paris. The arrival of French reinforcements by any and all means of transport lent it the popular name "battle of the taxis." It stopped the *Schlieffen Plan* short of its goal, and thereby led everyone into the unanticipated horror of *trench warfare.* (2) July 15-August 7, 1918: The final offensive of the German Army in *WWI*, which took it across the Marne before being halted and thrown back in unredeemable *defeat.*

Marshall, George Catlett (1880-1959): American statesman. Chief of Staff 1939-45; Secretary of State 1947-49; Secretary of Defense 1950-51. He was intimately engaged in all wartime military *strategy*, and attended all the important conferences, including *Tehran, Yalta* and *Potsdam*. He backed the *Truman Doc-*

trine and fathered the *Marshall Plan,* perhaps his single greatest achievement. He was closely involved in the *Berlin air lift;* creation of *NATO;* and the early planning in the *Korean Conflict.* He won the *Nobel Prize* for Peace in 1953, the only professional warrior ever to do so.

Marshall Islands: Location: Pacific. Major associations: *SPC, SPF, UN.* Population: 43,000. Military: U.S. missile range. Made a German *protectorate* in 1886, in 1921 they became a Japanese *mandate territory.* During WWII they were *occupied* by the U.S. and after 1947, administered as part of the *Trust Territory of the Pacific Islands.* They rejected a 1969 offer of *commonwealth status,* opting instead for *free association,* signing a compact in 1982 (ratified by *referendum* in 1983). The UN *Trusteeship Council* endorsed the change, and in 1990, the Security Council formally ended the *trusteeship.* While efforts have been made to diversify foreign relations, the U.S. performs most *consular* and diplomatic functions. In 1991 they joined the UN. See also *Bikini Atoll; Eniwetok.*

Marshall Plan: See *European Recovery Program.*

martial: Warlike; pertaining or disposed to war.

martial law: The imposition of strict military rule over a *civilian* population by a national government, during an emergency, during or following a *coup,* or by a foreign army setting up an *occupation.*

Martinique: An *overseas department* of France, located in the West Indies. It has been a French possession since 1635.

Marx, Karl (1818-83): German philosopher. He enthused over the *Revolutions of 1848,* for which with *Engels* he coauthored the most famous pamphlet in history: "*The Communist Manifesto.*" Much of his life he spent in *exile* in London, writing his magnum opus "Das Kapital." He founded the *First International,* but his bitter personal rivalry with *Bakunin* destroyed it. Reflecting on what he saw as the obtuseness of many of those who became devotees of his ideas, he once stated: "I am not a marxist." See *marxism.*

marxism: The philosophical system, *grand theory,* and *ideology* originating in the analysis of *history* and industrial *capitalism* undertaken by *Karl Marx.* It has since evolved into a greatly diverse set of theories and speculations about the main topics of *politics,* philosophy and all the social sciences. Its basic premise is the use of Hegelian logic (the *dialectic*) to study history: in every historical epoch the dominant class (*the-*

sis) is inevitably confronted by another class, generated by the prevailing system of economic relations and representing an opposing idea of social organization (*antithesis*); the clash that results produces a breakthrough to a higher level of human social life (*synthesis*); this forms a new thesis (a class-based idea, moving not just in, but also shaping history itself) that is opposed by a new antithesis, and so on. Subordinate ideas include the argument that the "superstructure" of social and political forms, customs, ideas and relations is determined by the "economic base" of human life. The superstructure then reinforces and reproduces the relations of production that brought it into being. This relationship advances through knowable stages, from primitive or "natural communism" to *slavery,* feudalism, capitalism and *socialism,* until it reaches its culmination in the liberation of the human body and spirit under mature *communism* (though Marx himself had little to say about the form this idealized, communist society would take). Then the tyranny of the *state,* necessary during the penultimate period of the *dictatorship of the proletariat,* will "wither away" and each person will take only what they need (will not hoard the "surplus" produced by the labor of others). Marx claimed that unlike "*utopian socialism,*" his vision was scientific, and rooted in the "iron laws of history." His many followers took his theories in a variety of new directions: the *Bolsheviks* first looked to *permanent revolution* to counteract the effects of "*uneven development*" they said was the product of capitalism; then they looked to *socialism in one country.* The Chinese communists turned directly to the peasantry, rather than the urban working class, as the basis for their revolution, as did other communist movements in *Vietnam* and elsewhere. Surely among the greatest ironies produced by this body of theory that looked to the end of the 19th century state, along with capitalism, was the actual construction in the 20th century of *totalitarian* societies that elevated the state to a hitherto unknown plane of domination in human social relations. See also *Albania; Allende; Berlin Wall; Benin; bourgeoisie; Bulgaria; Cambodia; Castro; China; class struggle; Cold War; collectivization; COMECON; COMINTERN; Communist Manifesto; Communist Parties; Cuba; Czechoslovakia; dependency theory; dialectical materialism; East Germany; economic determinism; Engels; Ethiopia; eurocommunism; First (Second; Third) International; five-year plans; Franz Fanon; grand theory; Grenada; Honecker; Hungary; ideology; imperialism; industrial revolution; Khmers Rouges; labor theory of value; Laos; Lenin; leninism; liberation theology; lumpen proletariat; Mao; maoism; marxism-leninism; means of production; Mensheviks; mode of production; Mugabe; New Economic Policy; Nicaragua; party line;*

peaceful coexistence; PKI; Poland; Pol Pot; Popular Front; Prague Spring; proletarian revolution; reeducation; rehabilitation; revisionism; Rumania; Russia; Russian Revolutions (1905; 1917); secularism; social democracy; social fascism; Solidarity; Soviet bloc; soviets; Stalin; stalinism; surplus value; Tito; Trotsky; trotskyites; vanguard; voting with their feet; war communism; wars of national liberation; Yemen; Yezhovshchina; Yugoslavia.

marxism-leninism: Adaptations of basic *marxism* made by *V. I. Lenin*, which emphasized the role of a ruthless *vanguard* party in establishing the *dictatorship of the proletariat*. Lenin turned *Marx* on his head by proclaiming that the vanguard did not have to await the production of the *proletariat* by *capitalism* to succeed at *socialist* revolution: it could take advantage of the calamity of *WWI* to seize power in even so backward a *state* as Russia. That war, said Lenin, was born of *imperialism*. It and future imperial conflicts would hasten the day the capitalist edifice came crashing down (this in contrast to Marx's stress on internal *revolution*). This was perhaps his most important (though not his original) idea: by focusing on imperialism as a projection of *class struggle* to the world stage, Lenin gave marxism an international dimension that Marx had almost completely ignored. He also provided the impetus for the Soviet Union to move down the path of support for *wars of national liberation*. That turned out to be a dead end, but one littered with corpses and broken nations, for both of which Lenin may be given some credit. This body of doctrine drew as well upon the dizzyingly adaptable, or better said, callously expedient policies and practices enacted by Lenin and the *Bolsheviks* within Russia itself, ranging from *war communism* and the *Red Terror*, to the *New Economic Policy*.

Masaryk, Jan (1886-1948): Czech statesman, and son of *Tómaš Masaryk*. Ambassador to Berlin 1925-38; Foreign Minister 1939-48 (*government-in-exile* 1939-45). He resigned the ambassadorship to protest the rape of Czechoslovakia at *Munich*. After *WWII*, he wanted to accept *Marshall Plan* aid, but *Stalin* prevented that. Still in office after the communist *coup* in 1948, he either fell or was hurled to his death from a window in the Foreign Ministry.

Masaryk, Tómaš (1850-1937): Czech statesman. In 1917 he went to Russia, where he organized the *Czech Legion*. He then traveled to the U.S., where he may have deeply influenced the views of *Woodrow Wilson*, who at the least accepted Masaryk's claim to head an independent Czechoslovak *republic*. He was President from 1918-35.

Mason-Dixon Line: The boundary surveyed 1763-67 by Charles Mason and Jeremiah Dixon, mainly between Pennsylvania and Maryland. It was widened in the popular imagination to become the marker between North and South, free and slave, in the period before the *American Civil War*.

massive retaliation: A *strategic doctrine* most closely associated with *John Foster Dulles* and the *Eisenhower* administration, which held that any Soviet *aggression* would be met with the full nuclear retaliatory capability of the U.S. arsenal. This doctrine severely limited options, as it appeared to lack credibility. It gave way to the idea of *flexible response*.

mass production: The production of standardized *consumer* or other *goods* by machine and assembly line; one of the cardinal features of the *Industrial Revolution*. The development of new technologies and organizational principles, from the 19th century to the present, has permitted manyfold increases in *productivity*. This has transformed the material basis of the daily lives of a growing percentage of the human population. It has also helped make possible modern *totalitarianism* and *total war*. Cf. *economies of scale*.

master race: See *Herrenvolk*.

Mau-Mau rebellion: See *Kenya*.

Mauritania: Location: W. Africa. Major associations: *Arab League, Maghreb Union, OAU, UN*. Population: 2.1 million. Military: poor quality, ill-equipped. This drought-stricken *nation* became a French *protectorate* in 1903. In 1920 it merged with *French West Africa*. It gained *autonomy* within the *French Community* in 1958, and *independence* in 1960. In 1976 it divided the *Western Sahara* with Morocco, but gave up its claims to *POLISARIO* in 1980. Mauritania is racially and religiously divided between Muslim Arabs (moors) and Christian and animist blacks. The latter historically were slaves of the former. The moors still hold political power and have declared an "Islamic republic." In the 1970s and 1980s, it participated in a *World Bank* irrigation scheme involving nine countries. This raised land prices near the rivers, and in 1989 violence exploded between displaced black fishermen and farmers and moorish speculators. The dispute led to a border *war* with Senegal after Mauritania stripped 60,000 blacks of *citizenship* and *deported* them to Senegal (they were ethnically Senegalese).

Mauritius: Location: Indian Ocean. Major associations: *Commonwealth, OAU, UN*. Population: 1.1 million. Military: minimal. This island was uninhabited when settled by the Dutch, after 1638. France seized it in 1721, and imported African slaves to work a sugar plantation economy. In 1810 Britain took over and having banned the *slave trade*, imported poorly paid Indian laborers instead. It was given *independence* in 1968. In the 1980s it developed as an offshore banking center. It claims the *British Indian Ocean Territory* (Chagos archipelago), including *Diego Garcia*, where the U.S. has a naval base.

maxim: A pithy statement of diplomatic, legal, political or other principle.

Maximilian, Ferdinand Joseph (1832-67): Emperor of Mexico 1864-67; brother of *Francis Joseph*. Placed on the Mexican "throne" by *Napoleon III*, he was left to his own (rather poor) devices when the U.S. threatened to *intervene* and the French withdrew military support. Refusing to flee, he was captured by *Juárez*, and later shot.

maximizing: In *game theory*, a strategy that seeks the greatest gains possible while minimizing losses, and all under conditions of uncertain knowledge. This is different from *optimizing*.

May Day: May 1st, widely celebrated as a day of workers' solidarity by organized *labor* (outside Canada and the U.S., which have Labour/Labor Day in the fall). *Soviet bloc* countries made use of the holiday to display their industrial and military might in the form of production and *martial* parades, as a means of enhancing their international *prestige*. These occasions were attended by foreign *military attachés*, and observed by *Sovietologists* and *Kremlinologists*.

Mayotte: It has been an *overseas department* of France since 1976, when its *Catholic* population voted in a *referendum* to merge with France rather than remain with the largely *Muslim*, and newly independent, Comoros Islamic Republic.

Mazzini, Giuseppe (1805-72): Italian, *liberal* revolutionary. He founded the "*Young Italy*" movement, hoping to create a unified *republic*. He was part of a revolutionary government that briefly seized Rome in 1848. His influence extended well beyond Italy.

McCarthyism: Making charges of disloyalty and *treason* against high officials, particularly of secret attachment to *communism*, based on circumstantial or no evidence. The term derives from the scurrilous practices of Senator Joseph McCarthy (1909-57), R-Wisconsin. During 1952-53 he rode a campaign of slander and smear out of political obscurity into national pro-

minence, when he charged that the *State Department* was riddled with communists. *Truman* delayed facing him down, as did *Eisenhower*. However, *Dean Acheson* strenuously defended his department and, more problematically, *Alger Hiss*. The increasingly wild, alcoholic McCarthy was eventually censured by the Senate, without ever identifying a single communist *agent* in the U.S. government. But his fall from media and political grace did not take place before a wave of red-baiting hysteria had destroyed many reputations and careers. The real causes of this phenomenon were of course bigger than the excesses of one rogue senator with a fifth of bourbon rather than evidence in his valise. They had to do with the "loss" of China to the communist camp in 1949, with how badly the war was going in Korea and with Soviet detonation of an *atomic bomb*, well ahead of expectations. For many Americans such catastrophic events understandably required villains (that is, scapegoats). McCarthy easily tapped into this rich vein of fear and confusion, and set off his explosive charge that treason and conspiracy were behind all the ills of American foreign policy. Note: Although McCarthy's charges were entirely groundless, it is of course true that Soviet *spies* were in place within the U.S. and other Western governments (just as the reverse was true). What was pernicious about McCarthyism was not the charges of *espionage* or disloyalty per se, but his insistence on deciding guilt by association (or just innuendo), and the shocking failure of *elite* opinion to stand against such unprincipled, star-chamber procedures. The experience made it less acceptable among American intellectuals to be avowedly anti-communist, and in that respect McCarthy was among the best friends the *KGB* ever had (as one KGB defector later noted).

McCloy, John Jay (b.1895): U.S. statesman. Despite his "outsider" origins (a trait he shared with *George Kennan*), he built on his identity as a *Republican* internationalist and rose on his own merits to become one of the *Wise Men* of American foreign policy during the *Cold War*. serving His most important role came as U.S. High Commissioner to Germany during its transition to liberal-democracy. He worked closely with *Adenauer*, ensuring Germany's readmittance to the club of *civilized states*, its *integration* into Europe, and its membership in *NATO*. He has been criticized for not rigorously pursuing denazification. He later advised successive presidents on policy toward Germany and the Soviet Union, as well as on the *Vietnam War*.

McKinley, William (1843-1901): U.S. President 1896-1901. As America emerged from the *depression* of the early 1890s, his administration kept up a high *tariff* wall. It was also the most *expansionist* since the *Am-*

erican Civil War, annexing *Hawaii* and maneuvering to obtain a *sphere of influence* in China. McKinley's greatest failure was his inability to resist the pressures of an aroused *public opinion* and Congress, both of which wanted war with Spain in 1898. He feared the public would punish his party electorally if war was not forthcoming, and so he gave it the *Spanish/American War*. Americans thereby acquired the *Philippines, Puerto Rico* and *Guam* as a result of a pugnacious crusade to free Cuba, accompanied by something approaching national innocence about the consequences of self-indulgent exercise of great power. Many were left baffled (but impressed) at how their "splendid little war," as *Elihu Root* called it, in "America's backyard" had made the nation a Pacific and imperial power. Less spectacularly, McKinley protested to the Tsar about mistreatment of Jews, who were flooding into the U.S. in ever larger numbers, and in an increasingly destitute condition. He was also concerned about Russian expansion in Asia, and leaned toward Japan's cause in *Korea* and *Manchuria*. He was assassinated on September 6, 1901, by an anarchist. *Teddy Roosevelt* succeeded him.

McMahon Line: The *boundary* between Tibet and India, marked out by the British, Chinese and Tibetans in 1914. China negotiated an agreement on the line with Nepal and Burma in 1960 and 1961, and with Pakistan in 1963. But India refused to accept China's interpretation or claims. The line was overrun by Chinese troops during the *Indo/Chinese War.*

McNamara, Robert Strange (b.1916): U.S. statesman. Secretary of Defense 1961-68; President of the *World Bank* 1968-81. He promoted *flexible response* as a replacement doctrine for *massive retaliation*. He supported *intervention* in Vietnam, and was a principal advocate of using massive bombing to coerce the North into a settlement. He tried to apply his Harvard Business School background and *econometrics* training to the war, developing the idea of a "body count" of NVA and *Viet Cong* dead as a measure of whether it was being won or not. He grew disillusioned and resigned in 1968. At the World Bank, he was instrumental in adding poverty alleviation to the list of funding criteria. Despite his deep unpopularity among Vietnam veterans and others, he continues to write and speak, rather adamantly, about U.S. foreign policy.

means of production: (1) In *marxism*, the factors essential to the production of goods, especially *labor* and *capital*. (2) A synonym for *technology* in the broadest sense. Cf. *mode of production.*

measures short of war: Unilateral, diplomatic or forceful actions essayed by a state in defense of its legal rights, to wit: imposing a pacific *blockade*, making a *diplomatic protest*, severing *diplomatic relations*, proclaiming an *embargo*, carrying out an *occupation* or making a *retorsion* or *reprisal*. Cf. *self-help.*

Mecca: This Saudi Arabian city is capital of the *Hejaz* and a main spiritual center for the *Islamic world*. In November 1979, *fundamentalist* followers of a self-proclaimed *mahdi* seized the Grand Mosque. Hundreds were killed in the fighting that followed. In 1988 some 400 Iranian demonstrators were killed by Saudi police. Mecca is forbidden to non-Muslims, but millions of Muslims visit it annually during the *haj.*

mechanical majority: (1) The position enjoyed by the U.S. in the *UNGA* during the 1950s, when it could count on nearly automatic voting support from Latin American countries. (2) The position enjoyed by *Third World* states in the UNGA after c.1965.

mediation: When a third party tries to reconcile *states* engaged in a *political dispute*. Unlike *arbitration*, there is no promise of a binding solution in mediation; but unlike *good offices*, the mediator does offer real, substantive proposals aiming at a solution.

Mediterranean Sea: It is enclosed by Africa, Europe and western Asia, and is therefore of enormous *strategic* and commercial importance. For much of the 18th and 19th centuries it was effectively controlled by Britain, which held *Gibraltar* and worked to close the *Bosphorus* and *Dardanelles* to Russia. After construction of the *Suez Canal* the Mediterranean became even more important. It was the scene of major naval commitments in both world wars, and in the *Cold War*. Today the major threat is pollution, demanding *multilateral* action from the many states that share its waters. See also *mare nostrum; Mediterranean Agreement; Straits Question.*

Mediterranean Agreement (1887): Austria-Hungary, Britain, Italy and Spain secretly agreed to consult on ways to defend the *status quo* in the Mediterranean. The understanding aimed at preventing either France or Russia benefiting from any change in the status of *Ottoman* holdings. *Bismarck* apparently knew about and approved of the agreement.

megaton: One million tons of TNT equivalent; a measure of the energy of a nuclear explosion. Cf. *kiloton.*

Mehemet Ali (1769-1849): Viceroy of Egypt 1805-48. An Albanian who became Egyptian governor for the *Ottomans*. He grew increasingly independent of the

Ottoman *sultans*. In 1820-22 he conquered Sudan, *plundering* it for slaves but also founding Khartoum. He sent his fleet and army to aid Turkey fight Greek *independence* 1823-28, but it was sunk at *Navarino*. He then turned against Turkey in a *war* that won him Syria 1832-33. He took more land 1939-41, but was forced by the *Great Powers* to cede his earlier *conquests* back to the Ottomans (whom Britain was trying to prop up against Russia). In exchange, his family became hereditary rulers of Egypt. Meanwhile, he went slowly mad.

Meiji Restoration: The period of dramatic reform and change in Japan from 1868-1912, or the reign of Emperor Mutshuhito (1852-1912). See *Japan*.

Meir (Myerson), Golda, née Mabovitch (1898-1978): PM of Israel 1969-74; Ambassador to the Soviet Union 1948-49; Foreign Minister 1956-66; stateswoman. She worked for the *Jewish Agency* before *independence*, and later helped found the Labour Party. As Foreign and Prime Minister, she cultivated ties with the emerging nations of Africa. Her greatest success came in securing Israel's ties to the U.S. (she enjoyed a close working relationship with *Richard Nixon*). She has been criticized for being caught unawares by the start of the *Fourth Arab/Israeli War*.

Melanesia: One of the subdivisions of *Oceania*, consisting of the *South Pacific* island groups NE of Australia, including New Guinea, whose *indigenous peoples* are ethnically distinct from *Polynesians*.

Melian Dialogue: See *Peloponnesian Wars*.

Melilla: A Spanish *enclave* in Morocco, whose future status is tied to Spain's efforts to reclaim *Gibraltar* from Britain. It and *Ceuta* are the last European possessions in Africa.

Memel: A *condominium* run by the *Allies* from 1919-23, it was seized by Lithuania. Recovered to Germany in 1939, it was *annexed* by the Soviet Union in 1945. It is today within Lithuania, renamed Klaipeda.

Mensheviks: "Minority." The "moderate" faction of the Russian Social Democratic Party, from which *Lenin* led the *Bolshevik* split in 1903, and formally in 1912. The main points at issue were Lenin's insistence on a dictatorship within as well as by the party, and his call for an *insurrection* in 1917. The more doctrinaire Mensheviks argued that a *bourgeois*, democratic *revolution* must of historical necessity precede any *proletarian* revolution or creation of a *socialist* state. After the *Russian Revolution of 1917* these old com-

rades of the Bolsheviks were briefly tolerated, then savagely repressed; many died in the *GULAG*.

Menzies, Robert (1894-1978): Australian statesman. PM 1939-41, 1949-66. He led Australia into *WWII*, but was ousted in 1941. After the war, he shifted Australia under an American *security* umbrella, joining *ANZUS* and *SEATO*.

mercantilism: A 16th to 18th century economic doctrine that saw *politics* as dominant over *economics*, and competition among *states* over the distribution of wealth as the main force in world *political economy*. It argued for a national policy of accumulating wealth by maintaining a favorable *balance of trade* through high *tariffs*, and by hoarding precious metals, especially gold. It was assumed that such hoarded wealth translated into enhanced national *power* (and in an age of *mercenary* armies, that point was not without merit). Mercantilist theories initially stimulated rapid *growth*, and drove the creation of colonial *empires* as sources of rare metals, markets for *exports* and supports for political *self-sufficiency*. However, as gold was in limited supply, mercantilist practices exacerbated interstate conflict while encouraging low domestic consumption and leading to high *inflation*. Mercantilism did not survive the *rebellion* of the American *colonies* against its strictures, the rise of national armies around the time of the *French Revolution*, or most important, the *Industrial Revolution* and *liberal* trade *regime* promoted in the 19th century by Britain. Its antonym is *free trade*. Its political analogue was *absolutism*. See also *neo-mercantilism*.

mercenary: A soldier who fights for money or plunder, not for a national or political cause or because he is a *conscript*. Mercenaries dominated warfare in Europe until the *French Revolution*, and in other parts of the world long after that. Their role in the 20th century has been limited, yet mercenaries have fought in several African wars, notably the *Congo crisis* and *Nigerian Civil War*. Drawn to war, they also appeared in Lebanon in 1982, and most recently, in Abkhazia, Moldova and the *Third Balkan War*. See also *Comoros; Maldives; Seychelles*.

merchant marine: The fleet of *civilian* ships that carries a nation's trade. Cf. *navy*.

metastrategy: In *game theory*, one conditional upon expectations about the choices made by other players.

metropolitan power: (1) The dominant or imperial power in a colonial relationship. (2) The home or original country of a *multinational corporation*.

Metternich, Prince Klemens (1773-1859): Austrian statesman (though not of Austrian nationality). Foreign Minister 1809-48; Chancellor 1821-48. He first worked for the small German state of Westphalia, but entered Austrian service in 1801. He directed Austrian policy during the *War of the Fourth Coalition*, and at the *Congress of Vienna*. Subsequently, he presided over the so-called "Metternich system" wherein conservative monarchs and classes cooperated to maintain *balance of power* diplomacy, but also repression of *liberal* reform in home affairs. Even so, his personal reputation for *reaction* is sometimes overdone, as he was never permitted (because he was a foreigner) to guide Austria's domestic affairs. After 1815 his diplomacy focused on Italy and the *Balkans*, leaving intra-German politics more to *Prussia* than had his predecessors. His office and his system were overthrown by the *Revolutions of 1848*. He went into *exile* in England, but returned in 1849 to take up the role of *elder statesman* to the whole of Europe.

Metz: A French fortress that witnessed battles between French and German forces in 1870 (*Franco/Prussian War*), 1918 (*WWI*), 1940 and 1944 (*WWII*). In the last battle, the French were joined by other *Allies*.

Mexican/American War (1846-48): After the U.S. annexed Texas in 1845 relations with Mexico deteriorated rapidly. President *James Polk*, who had already decided on *war* as the only means of acquiring *California*, sent troops into a disputed area in a clear *provocation*. When the Mexicans dutifully attacked, he asked Congress to *declare war*. He was opposed by the *Whigs*, but rode a cresting wave of public support. One young Whig congressman, *Abraham Lincoln*, challenged Polk's *expansionism* and belligerence without success. The resulting military clash was among the most one-sided *victories* in American history. U.S. forces captured Vera Cruz and Mexico City, forcing on Mexico the onerous terms of the *Treaty of Guadaloupe Hidalgo*. The humiliation left Mexico embittered toward the U.S. and weakened *Santa Anna's* hold on power. But America's victory soon turned to ashes in the mouth: within a decade the newly acquired lands were asking for statehood and admission to the Union, raising the great question of *"slave state* vs. *free soil"* that hastened the awful carnage of the *American Civil War*. See also *manifest destiny*.

Mexico: Location: North America. Major associations: *APEC, NAFTA, OAS, OECD; UN*. Population: 90 million. Military: midsized, without an offensive tradition. The *Aztec* Empire of Mexico fell 1519-21, with almost ridiculous ease to the marauders who landed with *Cortés*. It gained *independence* from Spain in 1821 as a constitutional *monarchy*, but became a *republic* in 1824. Mexico was dominated by *Santa Anna* for the next several decades. It lost Texas to *secession*, and then saw *California* and other *territory* north of the Rio Grande stripped in the *Mexican/American War*. In 1855 Mexican liberals under *Juárez* drove Santa Anna from power, but then faced a French *invasion* and the "empire" of *Maximillian*. War against the French continued until 1867. From 1876-1911 there was relative peace and prosperity under *Porfirio Diaz*, but that was followed by the turmoil of the Mexican Revolution (1911-20) and U.S. *intervention* in 1916. Mexico stayed out of *WWI*. The *revolution*, a series of agrarian uprisings under leaders as varied as *Venustiano Carranza, Pancho Villa* and *Emilio Zapata*, ended in a *civil war* among the victorious revolutionaries, and then the dictatorship of Plutarco Calles (1877-1945) from 1924-28. Since 1929 Mexico has been ruled by a single party, the Institutional Revolutionary Party, which has kept up a leftist rhetoric while running conservative policies. The country concentrated on incremental *modernization* in the 1950s and 1960s, encouraged by steady *oil* revenues, but it ran up an enormous *debt* through excessive borrowing in the 1970s. Under President Luis Echeverria 1970-76, it engaged in a more activist and leftist diplomacy. In the 1980s it sought to *mediate* conflicts in Central America. In 1993 it joined NAFTA. On January 1, 1994, a brief *uprising* of *indigenous people* took place in southern Mexico; its declared and perhaps its proximate cause was the NAFTA accord taking effect, but its root causes lay in rural poverty and discriminatory landholding laws. Also in 1994, Mexico joined the OECD.

Mfecane: "Time of Troubles." The astonishingly brutal *imperialism* of the *Zulu*, launched against the other *tribes* of southern Africa from 1816-28, under the leadership of *Shaka Zulu*. See also *Swaziland*.

MI5/MI6: The twinned British *intelligence* and security services. The first handles *counterintelligence* and counterterrorism within Britain; the second is the overseas, information and *covert action* branch. Since *WWII*, when British intelligence enjoyed its own finest hour, MI6 has been racked by scandal and controversy. The worst was over defections to the *Soviet Union* of the high-profile "Cambridge Comintern" of Burgess, Maclean and Philby, the confession of their friend Anthony Blunt, and persistent rumors about a "fifth man" (identified in 1990 as John Cairncross).

MIA: "Missing in Action." A designation used of soldiers who cannot be located among the dead, wounded, deserted or captured. After a suitable period has passed they are (usually correctly) presumed dead.

Suspicion about unreturned MIAs from the *Vietnam War* long prevented a *rapprochement* between the U.S. and Vietnam. That reflected deep distrust on the part of many Americans toward the Vietnamese regime, and toward their own government. The belief was fed by occasional reports (whether true or not) of "sightings" and of concealed information, including one by *Boris Yeltsin* in 1993. At another level, it represented a naïve, albeit understandable, unwillingness to accept that a tropical jungle does not easily give up its dead.

microeconomics: A subfield of *economics* that looks at the market behavior of individuals and enterprises, especially as to how this affects *supply*, demand and production costs.

Micronesia ("the little islands"): A subdivision of *Oceania*, consisting of island groups N of the equator and E of the Philippines: the *Carolines, Marianas, Marshalls* and the remaining *trust territories.*

Micronesia, Federated States of (FSM): Location: Pacific. Major associations: *SPC, SPF, UN.* Population: 113,000. Military: U.S. base. Once a Japanese *mandate*, during *WWII* these four islands (Kosrae, Pohnpei, Truk and *Yap*) were *occupied* by the U.S. Later administered as part of the *Trust Territory of the Pacific Islands*, they rejected a 1969 offer of *commonwealth status*, opting instead for *free association* with the U.S. They signed a compact in 1982 (ratified by *referendum* in 1983) that granted *autonomy* but left the U.S. in charge of *defense*. The UN *Trusteeship Council* endorsed the change, and in 1990 the *Security Council* ended the trusteeship. In 1991 Micronesia joined the UN, as one of its smallest members.

microstate: A tiny nation with an extremely small area and/or population; a.k.a. dwarf states: *Andorra; Dominica; Kiribati; Liechtenstein; Monaco; Maldives; Nauru; San Marino; Tuvalu.* See *associated states.*

Middle East: Looking from Western Europe the "Middle East" historically was the great Muslim domain stretching from India to Persia, the Arabian desert, Syria, Palestine and Egypt. It refers now mainly to the states clustered near the eastern Mediterranean: Egypt, Iran, Iraq, Israel, Jordan, Lebanon, Saudi Arabia, the Gulf States, Syria and Turkey. Some usages include Cyprus, Libya and the *Maghreb.*

middle power: One not ranked among the *Great Powers*, but whose *capabilities*, interests and *influence* clearly rank it ahead of small powers. But "middle-powermanship" is also something of a national (or *elite*) state of mind. It implies a *multilateral* slant to foreign policy and a readiness to perform tasks according to one's *functional* abilities, including *mediation, good offices, advisory services* and so forth. For instance, Canada and Sweden rank among the middle powers in part because that is how they view themselves, which makes the ranking something of a self-fulfilling prophesy through efforts to live up to it. Of course, this effort also involves a considerable craving for *prestige*. In 1945 Canada led an effort to obtain official recognition of this term and status within the UN, but was rebuffed by all the Great Powers.

Midway, Battle of (June 4, 1942): The decisive naval engagement in the Pacific in *WWII*. The American and Japanese fleets never sighted each other, making this the first sea battle in history decided solely by naval *air power*. While the U.S. base on *Midway Island* was heavily pounded, the Americans sank four Japanese *aircraft carriers*, losing just one themselves. That turned the tide in the Pacific, forcing Japan over to the defensive within just six months of *Pearl Harbor.*

Midway Island: This N.Pacific island was acquired by the U.S. in 1867. With no *indigenous* population, it is administered by the U.S. Navy, which has a base there. See *Battle of Midway.*

MIG: Soviet-built *fighters* named for the aircraft designers (Mi)koyan and (G)urevich. Currently, the most advanced model is the MIG-31.

migration: The voluntary relocation of people within or across national borders (involuntary migrants are called *refugees*). Migration occurs mainly for climatological (drought, flood) and for social or economic reasons (discrimination at home, or better opportunities elsewhere), but ethnic conflict and *human rights* violations also greatly contribute. Migration poses major questions of *immigration* policy, *indigenous peoples'* rights, regional *development*, and international as well as internal race relations. Some current examples: 25 million Russians who migrated within the old empire now find themselves stranded in the *near abroad;* Chinese internal migration is running poor/north to advantaged/south, peasant/interior to urban/coast, causing severe regional tensions; millions of East Europeans and North Africans are seeking entry to Western Europe; and millions more Central Americans, Cubans, Haitians, Mexicans and others wish to follow those who migrated to the U.S. (and to a lesser extent, also Canada) in recent decades.

militarism: This term is often used loosely, and nearly always in the pejorative. (1) Maintaining a large military, even when to do so absorbs much of the material wealth of a nation. (2) A spirit or habit of mind that regards the rigors and virtues of military life as both an individual and national ideal. See *fascism; Imperial Way; National Socialism; Potsdam Declaration; social darwinism; WWII.* Cf. *pacifism.*

militarist: A person who espouses a policy or exhibits a spirit of *militarism.*

militarize: (1) To suffuse a population with a spirit of *militarism.* (2) To enlist or equip a region with military supplies. Cf. *demilitarize.*

military attaché: See *attaché.*

Military Conversations (1906-14): Talks between the British and French *General Staffs* (also including the Belgians) that aimed at increasing army cooperation in the event of *war* with Germany. Naval talks did not begin until 1912, and with Russia not until June 1914. This was as close as these powers came to *alliance* before September 1914, when in the aftermath of *hostilities* a formal *pact* was signed. See *Entente Cordiale; Triple Entente.*

military government: (1) A domestic *regime* where the military has seized power and rules by issuing decrees enforced by draconian punishments. (2) A temporary situation during an *invasion* or *occupation*, where the local population is placed under foreign military authority. Cf. *Berlin; Lucius Clay; Douglas MacArthur; martial law.*

military-industrial complex: A phrase first used by *Dwight Eisenhower* in his 1961 "Farewell Address." He warned the American people not to permit their most important national decisions to be skewed by the narrow, special interests of a large military and the defense industries that support it. The warning reflected Ike's small-town, *Republican Party*, and fiscally conservative values, now threatened by *Cold War* requirements of a larger peacetime military than had been the historic American experience. The phrase has since been expanded to refer to the symbiotic relationship between certain industries and the military in most major powers. It is often used as a pejorative, sometimes without due discrimination. See *Minatom.*

military law: (1) A synonym for *martial law.* (2) The discrete code of professional and legal conduct applied to serving officers and troops, but not *civilians.*

military necessity: The plea made when claiming a waiver of normal moral guidelines to carry out destruction of a *military objective.* Cf. *just war.*

military objective: Any target whose loss or damage would reduce the military performance or *capabilities* of the enemy. Cf. *collateral damage.*

military ranks: {A} In most armies: (1) private: a soldier of any of the three lowest grades; (2) corporal: a *noncommissioned officer* of the lowest rank; (3) sergeant: a noncommissioned officer above corporal (sergeant-major is the highest grade within the sergeant classification, as well as the highest grade of NCO); (4) lieutenant: the lowest class of ranks of *commissioned officers*; (5) captain: above lieutenant, in command of a company; (6) major: above captain, in command of a battalion; (7) colonel: a rank forming several grades between major and general, usually in command of a brigade; (8) general: several grades of officer of the second highest rank (first in the U.S.), usually in command of a division or larger unit; (9) marshal: the highest possible rank, ranging in Britain, Germany and some other armies to a grade of field marshal (the U.S. does not use this rank). {B} In most air forces: (1) flight commander: an officer in charge of a flight; (2) wing commander: an officer in charge of a wing of aircraft. {C} In most navies: (1) sailor: equivalent to private; (2) warrant officers: all noncommissioned officers; (3) ensign: the lowest ranked commissioned officer; (4) lieutenant: ranked above ensign; (5) commander: the third tier of officer grades; (6) captain: an officer in command of a *warship*, ranking below admiral; (7) admiral: several grades of the highest rank, peaking at fleet, rear or grand admiral in some navies; usually commanding a fleet. See also *flag officer; officer; officer corps; petty officer.*

military science: The professional study, undertaken mainly by various *officer corps*, of the causes, tactics and nature of *war.*

military spending: All spending on *arms, logistics* and support (housing, uniforms, food and pay) of military personnel. Global military spending is a major sector of the world economy, valued at many hundreds of billions of dollars per year.

military units: {A} In most armies: (1) squad: a group of approximately 10 soldiers; (2) platoon: three or four squads and a local headquarters; (3) company: usually four platoons and a headquarters (in the *artillery*, a battery); (4) battalion: four to five companies and a headquarters; (5) brigade/regiment: three battalions and a regimental headquarters; (6) division: three brigades or regiments and a divisional headquarters, usually with combat support personnel, artillery batteries, and transport units attached; (7) corps: two or three divisions, and a corps headquarters, field hospitals, and so on; (8) army: two or more corps, and a major headquarters with support staff, artillery divisions, and often control of air units as well. {B} In most air forces: (1) flight: the smallest air unit, often used for specific missions or routine patrolling; (2) squadron: the foundation unit of an air force; (3) group: two or more squadrons, and a substantial headquarters; (4) wing: a large unit, though varying in size and number of aircraft from air force to air force, and war to war; (5) division: the largest manageable air formation. {C} In most navies: (1) squadron: a small unit of ships, often assigned to a specific patrol or mission; (2) flotilla: a small fleet, containing two or more squadrons of ships; (3) fleet: the largest naval unit under the command of a single officer, usually an admiral. An alternate meaning of fleet is the total naval forces of a nation, as in "the Japanese fleet."

militia: (1) A military *reserve*, called up only during emergencies. (2) A private military force. (3) A nonprofessional army, *mustered* from citizen volunteers. See *levée en masse.* Cf. *partisans; Resistance.*

Milošević, Slobodan (b.1941): Serb statesman. He came to power in large part because *Tito* cleared the path for a character like him by *purging* reform-minded Serb communists in the 1970s. He consolidated his power 1987-88, around an expedient conversion to *nationalism* as *Yugoslavia* began to break up. He appears to have counted on *war* to keep him in power after the federation dissolved. He aided Serb *militia* in their fight for *territory* and their *ethnic cleansing* in *Croatia* and *Bosnia,* and kept a grip on *Kosovo.* He has been accused of *war crimes,* but the success of Serbian arms allowed him to slip into peacemaker's clothes even as the fighting continued in 1993/94. His policies brought disapprobation and *sanctions* down upon Serbs. He gave them *hyperinflation,* shortages, poverty and many dead. But he may also have given them what they wanted most--*Greater Serbia.*

Minatom: Code named the "Ministry for Medium Machine Building" during the *Cold War,* since renamed Ministry of Nuclear (Atomic) Energy, or Minatom. A top secret arm of the Soviet *state,* and now a somewhat more open ministry of the Russian government. It was set up by *Lavrenti Beria* in 1942 to begin a crash research program into building a Soviet *atomic bomb;* it later expanded into *missile* and other weapons research, design and manufacture. In its early work at least, it drew heavily upon information obtained through *espionage* against the *Manhattan Project.* Relying on *slave labor* from the *GULAG,* Beria built a vast complex of secret cities, some reaching populations (of scientists, engineers and their families)

over 100,000 without appearing on Soviet maps. This *elite* lived pampered lifestyles and enjoyed great prestige within the *nomenklatura,* supported by state funds and GULAG labor in return for top secret weapons work. At least 10 large cities were constructed, and perhaps more, with Minatom's population reaching maybe 800,000. In all, nearly 90 secret Minatom installations and weapons factories have been publicly identified since the end of the *Cold War. Sakharov* worked on the *hydrogen bomb* at one, Arzamas-16. With development of the *ICBM,* the system was spread out over Russia's vastness owing to fear of a U.S. *first strike.* Minatom kept its disasters secret too: it presided over numerous nuclear accidents, several larger than *Chernobyl.* In 1957 nearly half a million people were irradiated by an accidental release of radioactive material; they were never informed of their danger. On April 6, 1993, at Tomsk, a major accident occured; this one was reported by Russia to its neighbors, unlike the delays that attended Chernobyl.

mine: See *ADM; ASAT; land mine; sea mine.*

minimax principle: From *game theory:* shorthand for "minimum of the maxima," or the payoff to which the *minimizing* player can limit the *maximizing* player in a *zero sum game.* It applies only to such games, and is useful only if the opponent is fully rational and the strategy is applied over a series.

minimizing: From *game theory:* choosing the option with the least risk, rather than ones promising greater gain at higher levels of risk.

minimum deterrence: Forestalling an attack with limited rather than massive retaliatory force.

minimum winning coalition: From *game theory:* the smallest number of players necessary to implement a winning strategy in a multi-player game.

minister: (1) A member of the *executive,* with full *cabinet* rank. (2) The usual title of *ambassadors* until well into the 19th century.

minister plenipotentiary: See *envoy extraordinary.*

ministers resident: A class of *diplomats* below *ambassador* and *envoy extraordinary.*

Ministry of Trade and Industry (MITI): Japan's superministry charged with coordinating foreign economic policy, domestic industrial policy, and business *growth.* It aids in coordinating private research and development (R&D) with public and private financing.

It also acts as management consultant. Its influence has been great, but is also often exaggerated; it has even been feared by some. Its role was much greater in the first decades of *postwar* recovery than today, in Japan's increasingly sophisticated and complex economy. In 1993-94 MITI shifted partway from large conglomerates toward encouraging *venture capital*.

Minorities Treaties: On the insistence of *Woodrow Wilson* and other *liberals*, the post-*WWI* settlement included clauses in special *treaties* with the new states of East and Central Europe granting full rights to ethnic and religious minorities, to be guaranteed by the *League of Nations*. There was considerable popular concern in the U.S. for the treatment of Jews in Poland and Rumania. But for France and Britain, it was hoped that guarantees of minority rights to the Germans cut off by *Versailles* from Germany proper might help Weimar accept the larger settlement. Germany itself, therefore, was not required to grant such rights to its own minorities. Cf. *Volksdeutsche*.

Minuteman: (1) A member of the *militia* in the *American War of Independence*. (2) An *ICBM* first deployed in the 1960s; it formed the core of the land-based U.S. *nuclear deterrent*.

Miranda, Francisco de (1756-1816): South American revolutionary. A controversial adventurer, he fought for the U.S. after 1776, and France from 1793-94. He returned to Venezuela, his birthplace, upon its declaration of *independence* in 1811, and took command of its army. In 1812 he surrendered, an act that earned him contempt from *Bolivar* and others. He died in a Spanish prison.

mirror images: In *misperception* theory, the propensity of *decision makers* to see an opponent just as one is seen by that opponent (as hostile, aggressive, uncompromising and so forth). In one of the more trite uses of this idea, which is otherwise not without merit as a description of one possible psychological state during a *crisis*, it was suggested by some that the *Cold War* could be reduced to the self-reinforcing perceptual image U.S. = S.U. Cf. *moral equivalence*.

MIRV: See *Multiple Independently Targetable Re-entry Vehicle*.

misperception: The inability to accurately perceive or interpret incoming information, particularly concerning an opponent's intentions. Some argue that misperception is a key cause of failures of *deterrence*, and therefore a proximate cause of *war*. See *causation; cognitive dissonance; decision-making theory; fact-finding*

mission; image; levels of analysis; mirror images; rational decision-making.

missile: Any guided, projectile weapon. See *ABM; ballistic missile; BMD; bus; cruise missile; hardening; ICBM; launcher; MIRV; SDI; terrain contour matching; V-1 and V-2 rockets; warhead*.

mission civilatrice: "Civilizing Mission." Closer to the idea of *white man's burden* than *manifest destiny*, this concept grew from a conviction that French culture was the highest expression of Western civilization. That implied an obligation to carry enlightenment to what were seen as less civilized, non-European peoples (having lost the *Napoleonic Wars*, the French had given up trying to civilize the English, Germans and other nearby barbarians). Where necessary--and oddly enough, it was usually found to be necessary--this grand mission would have to be accomplished via *colonialism*, accompanied by missionary work, the benefaction of French manufactures, and one day, assimilation of native *elites* into the main flow of French culture itself. In short, the idea of a civilizing mission to Africa and Asia merely clothed as a noble venture a French imperial policy that otherwise would have discomfited the sensitive, by exposing itself as a naked commercial and geopolitical undertaking.

mission, sense of: Almost all great (that is, important) and some smaller *nations* have developed a sense of historic mission their people, or at least their *elites*, feel called upon to perform. Such notions are usually developed as a justification for self-interested policies (such as imperial expansion or regional dominance) that are generally if loosely supported by the populace, but would be found distasteful if presented in such plain, and hence unpalatable, form among polite company. The common denominator of senses of national mission is an ideological cloak that covers the naked pursuit of *dynastic* or *national interest*, but yet is light and attractive enough to beguile many into genuine belief in its more noble aspects. Cf. *Asia for Asians; manifest destiny; mission civilatrice; pan-Africanism; pan-Arabism; pan-Slavism; white man's burden*.

Mitteleuropa: (1) The nationalist dream of a Germanic superstate in central Europe and the Balkans. *Bismarck* rejected the notion as romantic, far-fetched and dangerous, but it was taken up by *Wilhelm II* and embraced by the *Nazis*. (2) German, for Central Europe.

Mitterand, François Maurice (b.1916): President of the *Fifth Republic* 1981- . An active *Resistance* fighter during *WWII*, he was a stubbornly independent politician in the 1950s, while simultaneously working for a grand coalition on the left. He rode an electoral alliance with the *communist party* into the presidency, but split with the communists in 1984 when economic reality forced him to reverse his program of *nationalization* and high *deficit spending*. After 1986 he was a much diminished figure, as the socialists lost their majority in the National Assembly. Yet he was reelected in 1988. He kept up a pose of independence during the *Cold War*, and was a strong proponent of the *force de frappe*. He adjusted quickly to German reunification, supporting *Maastricht*, proposing a Franco-German *EUROCORPS*, and increasing cooperation with the U.S. in the *Security Council*. He led France in a major contribution to the *Gulf Coalition*. In 1994 he encouraged a French *rapprochement* with *NATO*, and NATO enforcement of *no-fly zones* in Bosnia.

Mixed Arbitral Tribunals: An international tribunal composed of representatives of the parties to a *legal dispute*, and a third party.

mixed economy: One with features drawn from theories of both *socialism* and *capitalism;* this is actually the case in most advanced, industrial societies. Cf. *liberalism; reform liberalism.*

mixed motive game: In *game theory*, a *variable sum game* in which players have both competitive and complementary interests.

MNC/MNE: See *Multinational Corporation/Enterprise.*

mobile launchers: Any surface means by which *missiles* may be transported (to protect them or move into firing range), and launched.

mobilization: To assemble the armed forces so that they are ready for active service. It involves calling up *reserve* units, checking and preparing equipment, arranging transportation, moving troops closer to the likely locales of combat, putting units on alert status, issuing marching orders and the like.

mobilization crisis (June 28-August 4, 1914): On June 28th, in the Bosnian capital *Sarajevo*, the heir to the Austrian throne, *Francis Ferdinand,* was assassinated. The assassin was a 24-year old Serb *fanatic* (Gavrilo Princip, 1894-1918) who had help from the Serbian *secret police*. On July 5th Austria consulted with Germany, and was promised Berlin's full support for whatever actions Vienna might choose to take (this was the infamous *blank check*). Austria then delivered an *ultimatum* to Serbia, consisting of multiple conditions and designed to court rejection. Serbia conceded nearly every point, despite having its own guarantee of support from Russia. But Austria was intent on humiliating Serbia and *declared war* on July 28th, though *mobilization* would require another two weeks to complete. Russia ordered mobilization against Austria; but the Tsar was then told he had to mobilize against Germany too, as the plans and timetables were too complex to alter and delay might brook defeat should Germany enter the war. The Tsar reluctantly agreed to mobilize against his German cousin, *Wilhelm II*. Germany sent an ultimatum to Russia on July 31st demanding that mobilization stop. Meanwhile, Berlin sought assurances from France that it would not support Russia in case of war, and from Britain that it would remain *neutral*. It got neither. France and Germany both ordered mobilization on August 1st, and Germany declared war on Russia later that day. On August 2nd, Britain at last announced its decision to support France (its delay had greatly contributed to tensions, particularly in Berlin, born of uncertainty about what London would do). German troops crossed into Luxembourg and demanded a right of military transit across *neutral* Belgium. When Brussels refused, Germany invaded, declaring war on Belgium and France on August 3rd, and putting into operation the *Schlieffen Plan*. The British Empire declared war on Germany on August 4th, in accordance with the *Treaty of London (1839)*. Most of the main players of *WWI* were now assembled, and the carnage commenced. Italy, Turkey, the U.S. and various smaller powers entered the war later, each for reasons of its own.

Mobutu Sese Seko, né Joseph Desiré (b.1930): Dictator of Zaire. After heading the armed forces during the *civil war* (see *Congo crisis*) he launched a *coup* in 1965. He has run the country as a personal fiefdom ever since, relying on patronage of the military to stay in power. The level of corruption under his regime is staggering: his personal wealth, stored in foreign accounts, is said to run into the billions. While Belgium abandoned him in 1993, France appeared to lend support when *Mitterand* met with him at the *summit* of *la francophonie.*

model: An *abstract* representation of a set of causally related *variables.*

mode of production: In *marxism*, the general organization of a society (and especially of *labor*) for the production of *goods*, marked out by progressive historical stages reflecting dominant classes: *slavery*, feudalism, *capitalism, socialism* and finally *communism*, which is to be classless.

modernization: An inherently controversial idea, but one generally taken to mean the process of changing traditional societies into modern (meaning industrial and urban) economies and societies. It is more than just the process of development of *infrastructure*. It includes the fundamental transformation of traditional attitudes, habits of mind and patterns and institutions of authority. It is not universally seen as desirable. See also *development; indicators; Industrial Revolution; rising expectations; secularism; stages of growth; technology.* Cf. *Westernize.*

Moldavia and Wallachia: See *Danubian principalities; Rumania.*

Moldova: Location: Eastern Europe/Near Abroad. Major associations: *CIS. CSCE, UN.* Population: 4.5 million (65% Rumanian; 15% Ukrainian; 15% Russian). Military: unable to repress *rebellion* in the east or stand up to the Russian army. The Russian part of this region on the borders of the *empire* (located along the Dniester River) was merged with ethnically Rumanian *Bessarabia*, after that area was annexed by *Stalin* in 1940. The next year the whole region was *occupied* by Rumania, then in *alliance* with *Nazi Germany.* The Russians retook Moldova and Bessarabia in 1944, and merged them into a single "autonomous republic" within the USSR. Following a failed *coup* in Moscow in August 1991, Moldova declared *independence.* However, this was not *recognized* until, along with other *successor states*, it was set loose by the *extinction* of the Soviet Union on December 25, 1991. Within a few months fighting erupted in eastern Moldova, or *Trans-Dniestra.* Ethnic Ukrainians and Russians feared Moldova's Rumanian speakers wanted to merge with Rumania, and sought to secede (as the "Trans-Dniester Republic") and rejoin Russia or Ukraine; they had help from the Russian 14th Army. Russian troops remained in the area, as did CSCE monitors, in 1994.

mole: Slang for *penetration agent.*

Molotov, Vyacheslav Mikhailovich, né Scriabin (1890-1986): "Mr. Nyet." Soviet statesman. Premier 1930-41; Deputy Premier 1941-57; Foreign Minister 1939-49, 1957; Ambassador to Mongolia 1957-60. His adopted name meant "The Hammer." From 1921 onward he was one of *Stalin's* closest supporters. He helped direct the *collectivization* of agriculture, *liquidation* of the *kulaks* and artificial *famine* that killed millions (especially in Ukraine) in the 1930s. And he again did bloody work during the *Yezhovshchina.* In his memoirs and end-of-life interviews he never expressed regret for these actions. Rather, he defended them vehemently, even while recalling that had Stalin lived another year, he might not have. The measure of Molotov's abject sycophancy came during the *purges,*

when Stalin ordered him to divorce his wife and have her sent to a labor camp; he complied without question (but he took her back after the old tyrant died). He negotiated the *Nazi/Soviet Pact* (also called the "Molotov/*Ribbentrop* Pact") in 1939, was present at all the major conferences of *WWII* (*Tehran, Yalta, Potsdam*) and signed various *postwar* treaties with *Soviet bloc* allies/vassals. With Stalin's death Molotov's power waned, despite his briefly forming part of a ruling troika. His last major act was to negotiate for the Soviet Union concerning the *Austrian State Treaty* in 1955. Seen as a rival by *Khrushchev*, he was shunted aside--all the way to political exile as Ambassador to *Outer Mongolia.* The indignities continued when he was stripped of party membership in 1962 (reinstated in 1984). Cf. *Beria; GULAG; Litvinov, Vyshinsky.*

Molotov cocktail: A homemade *incendiary* weapon constructed from gasoline, detergent and rags; named during *WWII* for *Vyacheslav Molotov.*

Moltke, Helmuth von (1800-1891): German strategist. As chief of the Prussian *General Staff*, he reorganized the army and devised the war plans for *Bismarck's victories* over Denmark (1864), Austria (1866) and France (1870-71). But like Bismarck, after 1871 he became cautious, even fearful of Germany's exposed position and the possibility of a *two-front war.* He proposed a defensive posture should *war* come: Germany should hold against France, while attacking Russia only in its Polish provinces, and just to trade *territory* in return for acceptance of the *status quo ante bellum.* Cf. *machtpolitik; von Schlieffen.*

Moltke, Helmuth von (1848-1916): Chief of the German General Staff 1906-14; son of the elder von Moltke. He was dismissed from command after the failure of the *Schlieffen Plan* in 1914 led to a prolonged, *two-front war.*

Monaco: Location: Western Europe. Major associations: none. Population: 32,000. Military: none. Bordering on the SE Mediterranean coast of France, this *microstate* (principality) is barely 1/2 square mile in *size*, and yet has remained more or less independent for three centuries. It was a *protectorate* of *Piedmont-Sardinia* until 1861, when it was transferred to France as a reward for *Louis Napoleon's* support for Italian unification under the crown of Piedmont. Its main industry is *tourism.*

monarchy/monarchism: A political system in which political and legal authority is vested in the person of a *sovereign.* While *republicanism* has outstripped monarchism as the preferred government for most societies in the last two centuries, there are still monarchies among the states. Most of these are constitutional, where the monarch has strictly ceremonial, or even touristic functions (e.g., Britain). Yet kings still rule directly in several countries, notably in the Arab world and Africa. See also *nonintervention*.

monetarism: A theoretical challenge to *keynesian economics* that stresses a return to *laissez-faire* models, but with the government continuing to intervene to moderate extreme fluctuations in the *business cycle*, and control *inflation* via control of the money supply and a reduction in discretionary government spending. See also *supply-side economics*.

monetary policy: A *macroeconomic* device that aims at controlling the *balance of payments*, or levels of *inflation* or unemployment by means of interest rates and limiting the money supply.

money market: International *hard currency* markets where lending tends to be short-term and contract volume is high. See *capital market*.

Mongolia: Location: E. Asia. Major associations: *UN*. Population: 2.3 million. Military: minimal. A region in Asia comprising the *state* of Mongolia but also the province of Inner Mongolia in China and the former Tuva Autonomous Soviet Republic, now in Russia. One of the greatest *empires* in history was carved out by the Mongol khans in the 12th-14th centuries, though one merely of *conquest* not of building or lasting achievement. The modern state was a Chinese province known as Outer Mongolia until 1911, when it broke away with tsarist assistance. It immediately fell prey to *warlords*, leading to the chaos that local communists rode into power with Soviet aid in the early 1920s. It was then renamed the Mongolian People's Republic. Its independence was disputed until 1950, when China and the Soviet Union signed a joint guarantee of Mongolian *independence*. It spent the rest of the *Cold War* as a quiet backwater. In 1990, with the breakdown of the *Soviet bloc*, it held its first open elections; the old, communist authorities switched to nationalist clothing, and won handily. After 1990 Mongolia experienced a revival of traditional culture, including a *revisionist* celebration of the great khans.

monism: The doctrine that *international law* and *municipal law* are inseparable, or part of the same legal order. Note: Advocates of this doctrine may hold one or the other superior. Cf. *dualism*.

Monnet, Jean (1888-1979): French diplomat and economist. He served in the *League of Nations* 1919-23,

and was head of the National Planning Council 1945-47. His chief contribution was to press for the idea of *integration* of the French and German economies through the *Schuman Plan*, on the way to a wider *EC*. He was a major figure in the founding of the *ECSC*, serving as its President 1952-55.

monopoly: When one firm controls the license, production or transport, and thus effective pricing, of a *commodity* or *service*. Cf. *monopsony; oligopoly*.

monopsony: When only one buyer exists, and therefore effectively sets the price. Cf. *monopoly*.

Monroe, James (1758-1831): U.S. statesman. Secretary of State, 1811-17; Secretary of War, 1814-15; President, 1817-25. He began the negotiations that led to the *Rush-Bagot Treaty* that *demilitarized* the Great Lakes. That was part of his larger effort to improve U.S. defenses in the wake of *invasion* during the *War of 1812*. He provided for a larger army, and for coastal fortifications. He was a Virginia slave owner, who yet opposed retaining *slavery* in America (as threatening to the Union), and agreed with *Jefferson* that the solution was to ship all the slaves back to Africa. He therefore facilitated a settlement of freed slaves in West Africa. That was the beginning of *Liberia* (the name means "Freedom"), with its capital Monrovia. He was also an avid expansionist. He obtained the Floridas and settled a long simmering border dispute with Spain over *Louisiana*. His native *republicanism*, and instincts, encouraged him toward early *recognition* of the new republics in Latin America, but he held back upon the advice of Secretary of State *John Quincy Adams* until their viability was established. He then drafted and issued the *Monroe Doctrine*, again with the more than able assistance of Adams.

Monroe Doctrine: A statement opposing extra-hemispheric *intervention* in the Americas, drafted by *John Quincy Adams* and announced by President *James Monroe* on December 2, 1823. It said: "The American continents . . . are henceforth not to be considered as subjects for future colonization by any European power . . . . We should consider any attempt on their part to extend their system to any portion of this hemisphere as dangerous to our peace and security." It was stimulated by a threat from the *Holy Alliance* to reinstate the Spanish *monarchy* in the newly independent Latin American *republics*. A secondary interest was Russia's hint that it would expand its holdings in northern *California*. Monroe declared the *Americas* off-limits to *colonialism* by any European power, because of supposedly incompatible political systems between the *Old* and *New Worlds;* and he warned that the U.S.

would regard any attempt to interfere in the Americas as a direct threat to itself. Actually, it was the *Royal Navy* that defended Latin America from intervention, and the threat may not have been great in any case. The Latin republics were soon recognized generally, and in 1825 an accord with Russia marked out the *Northwest Frontier*. The Monroe Doctrine was mostly ignored until it gained teeth after the *American Civil War*. In the 20th century, the Roosevelt and Lodge Corollaries amended it, respectively, to authorize unilateral use of *force* and extend its prohibition to non-European powers (that is, Japan). It was given special status in the *Treaty of Versailles*, and was reasserted before *WWII* and during the *Cuban Missile Crisis*. But that *crisis* also breached the Monroe Doctrine by leaving a Soviet base in Cuba. Increasingly seen as anachronistic by Latin American states, it now belongs more to history than to policy, though it is still ritualistically invoked in public debate. See also *isolationism*. Cf. *near abroad; Rio Pact; sphere of influence.*

Monrovia bloc: See *Organization of African Unity.*

Montenegro: A distinct principality from the 14th century, Montenegro utilized its mountainous terrain to ward off the *Ottomans*, gaining independence in 1799. Reconquered in 1852, it regained independence in 1878. It entered the *First* and *Second Balkan Wars*, and joined *WWI* in support of Serbia. It was *occupied* by Austria in 1915. Its connection to Serbia was accepted at the *Paris Peace Conference*, and it became part of *Yugoslavia*. There was fierce *guerrilla* fighting there during *WWII*. Upon the breakup of Yugoslavia it remained tenuously attached to Serbia.

Montezuma II (c.1470-1520): He was the last *Aztec* emperor of Mexico 1502-20. He was overthrown and murdered, and his *empire* destroyed by a few hundred Spanish invaders, led by *Cortés*.

Montgomery, Bernard Law (1887-1976): British Field Marshall. He won at *El Alamein* and in Sicily, but has been heavily criticized by some Americans and other *Allies* for excessive caution in the Normandy campaign, followed by excessive ambition in the bloody and failed attempt to cross the Rhine in 1944 ("a bridge too far"). He is considered to have commanded well during the *Battle of the Bulge*. His personal and professional rivalry with *George Patton* was legendary. He was deputy commander of *NATO*, 1951-58.

Montreux Convention (1936): Turkey called an international conference to adjust the *Straits Question*, fearing Italian ambitions in the region. It was agreed that Turkey could remilitarize the straits, in exchange for allowing all light foreign *warships* to pass through during peacetime. At *Potsdam* it was agreed to revise the convention in favor of the Soviet Union, but the Soviets soon demanded full control of the straits from Turkey, and exclusion of the British. The U.S. sent a flotilla to Turkey to signal its objections, and the Soviets backed down.

Montserrat: A British island *colony* in the West Indies, population 14,000.

Moon Treaty: Originally proposed by the Soviet Union in 1971, it was then delayed over Soviet reluctance to accept the *common heritage principle*. It was finally agreed that neither the surface nor the subsurface of the moon are to be subject to exclusive or territorial claims by any state. It was passed by the *UNGA* in 1979, and came into force in 1984. Few states have signed it, with France the only space-capable nation to have done so to date.

Moors: The mixed, Berber and Arab peoples of N. Africa, who once ruled much of Spain and the *Maghreb*. The last Moorish kingdom on the Iberian peninsula, Granada, was *defeated* by the Spanish in 1492. Thereafter, a terrible persecution of Jews and Muslims followed, under the Catholic *Inquisition*.

moral equivalence: The argument that both sides in the *Cold War* were equally culpable, and indeed evil, in their propagation of the conflict. Ironically, some analysts who adopted this view were led to purely structural explanations of the conflict in which the role of *volition* and the *normative* realm in general were curtly, even cavalierly, dismissed. Cf. *mirror images.*

moratorium: A delay or suspension of some action, such as *nuclear weapons* testing or *debt* repayment, either undertaken unilaterally or in tandem with other *states*. It is a device used to test the efficacy of certain arrangements in the absence of a *treaty*, and to test political will. If successful, it may lead to the greater permanence of a formal treaty. Or it may be abused, as a *propaganda* ploy by an insincere government.

Moravia: An Austrian province taken by Czechoslovakia in 1918, an action confirmed by the *Treaty of St. Germain* (1919).

Morgenthau plan: Named for Henry Morgenthau (1891-1967), U.S. Secretary of the Treasury 1934-45. It proposed the "pastoralization" of Germany, in part to ensure it would not rise again as a military threat, and partly to punish the German population for what many among the *Allies* believed was its willing collaboration with the Nazi regime. *Roosevelt* signed on briefly in 1944, and the Soviets and some French were enthusiastic. But it was soon rejected by cooler and wiser minds as requiring a permanent Allied effort to feed, clothe and house the destitute population it stood to create. Also, by 1945 even Roosevelt was becoming concerned about *Stalin's* intentions, and realized that so draconian a treatment of Germany stood to render its *postwar* population susceptible to the lure of *communism*, by leaving them impoverished and hopeless.

Moroccan Crisis, First (1905): Secret agreements between Britain, France and Spain to *partition* Morocco led to German plans to split the *Entente Cordiale,* by demonstrating to France that the British *alliance* was unreliable. Thus, when Kaiser *Wilhelm II* put ashore in *Tangier,* he declared support for Moroccan *independence*, a deliberately provocative act that resulted in a *crisis.* Britain moved to support France. The crisis was resolved at *Algeciras,* but not on the terms the Germans anticipated.

Moroccan Crisis, Second (1911): See *Agadir.*

Morocco: Location: N. Africa. Major associations: *Arab League, UN.* Associate member of the *EU.* Population: 26.5 million. Military: mainly *counterinsurgency.* In the 11th and 12th centuries all N. Africa and part of Spain was ruled by a *Berber* empire centered on Morocco. After that, it went into a long decline, paralleling the rise of Spanish power. It was reduced to a Muslim princedom, one of the *Barbary States,* by the early 19th century. By 1905 it had become the target of French colonial ambitions, and stimulus to two major international crises before *WWI.* In 1912 it was *partitioned* between France and Spain, and *Tangier* was made a *free city.* Morocco saw the *Rif Rebellion* from 1922-26, led by Abd-el Krim (1881-1963). He was overthrown and captured by a Franco/Spanish force in 1926, and foreign rule returned. Moroccan troops fought in the *Spanish Civil War,* mainly on the side of *Franco.* In 1956 both France and Spain withdrew, and it became independent (incorporating Tangier as well). The Spanish *enclave* of Ifni was added in 1969. In 1976 Morocco annexed a mineral-rich part of the *Spanish (Western) Sahara,* partitioning that former *colony* with Mauritania. It then became embroiled in a protracted *war* with *POLISARIO.* In 1979 Mauritania quit the war, and Morocco occupied the whole of Western Sahara. A *cease-fire* was signed in 1990 under UN auspices, but real *peace* remains elusive. The war isolated Morocco from its neighbors and within the *OAU,* from which it withdrew in 1984. But its pro-Western policies during the *Cold War* assured it of U.S. support.

Moscow, retreat from (1812): When the French captured Moscow in September they found it virtually empty. Within days, a fire swept through its wooden buildings, leaving the French troops few billets and less sustenance. On October 18th, *Napoleon* ordered a retreat. Some 100,000 men, weighed down with *booty,* had to recross lands that had been subject to Russian *scorched earth* tactics. Winter weather and Russian *partisans* took an immense toll. Napoleon was almost captured fleeing ahead of his army, of which barely 1,000 men were still in fighting fit when they left Russia. The pathos and human meaning of this catastrophic clash is well captured in Leo Tolstoy's deservedly famous novel "War And Peace."

Mossad: The Israeli civilian *intelligence* agency.

Mossadegh, Muhammad (1880-1967): PM of Iran 1951-53. In 1925 he opposed the *accession* of the first Shah, and all his public life he objected to foreign control of Iran's *oil* industry and assets. In 1951, shortly after becoming PM, he *nationalized* the Anglo/Iranian Oil Company. He was overthrown in a *coup* that had support from *MI5* and the *CIA.* He is looked upon by some Iranians as a symbol of what might have been: a nationalist leader who could have avoided the extremes of both the *Pahlavis* and the *Ayatollah Khomeini.* Others see him as an emotionally and politically unstable character.

most-favored-nation (MFN): This status, granted to most trading partners, says that trade will take place on the same terms as are given to the most favored trading partner. It aims at *tariff* reduction and the avoidance of trade blocs. Yet MFN is really a misnomer, as under the *GATT* (and even outside it) most trading partners enjoy MFN. It does not, therefore, imply special preferences so much as mean that no uncommon discrimination is permitted. For example, if Australia permits imported toy cars from Korea or other countries to enter at a 10% tariff, then it must not impose a higher tariff on Chinese toy cars, if China enjoys MFN status. Should Australia revoke China's MFN, it can then apply whatever tariff it likes, subject to China's ability to retaliate.

Mountbatten, Louis (1900-79): British statesman; grandson of Queen *Victoria*; uncle of Queen *Elizabeth II.* During *WWII* he commanded in SE Asia, making a solid reputation in the Burma *campaign.* In 1947 he became the last Viceroy of India, overseeing the *partition* of the *subcontinent,* which he instructed should take place according to a strict timetable. In 1948 he became India's first Governor General. While on holiday off the Irish coast in 1979 he was blown up with his boat, by the *IRA*. Recent *revisionist* history has blamed him for the disaster at *Dieppe*.

Mozambique: Location: Southern Africa. Major associations: *OAU, SADCC, UN*. Population: 15 million. Military: factionalized. Portuguese traders began to penetrate this area in 1505, and Portugal subsequently colonized it. A *guerrilla war* began in 1964, led by the *marxist/nationalist* FRELIMO, that with other colonial wars helped bring about the collapse of the Portuguese dictatorship in 1974. Mozambique became independent in 1975 under President *Samora Machel*. Until 1980 it faced repeated border *incursions* from Rhodesia, and until a 1984 accord was signed it was raided by South African troops and had to fend off guerrilla attacks sponsored by Pretoria. The war cost many lives and the economy virtually collapsed; this was followed by a protracted *civil war*. Former guerrilla leader Joaqum Alberto Chissan (b.1939) became President in 1986. During the civil war he opened negotiations with South Africa in an effort to undercut its support for his opponents. Besides *famine, civil war* and internal *refugees*, Mozambique was hard hit by the spread of *AIDS*. A *peace* agreement was reached at the end of 1992, supported by a team of 7,000 observers and troops from the UN. In 1993 talks began on eventually holding UN-supervised elections.

Mubarak, Muhammad Hosni (b.1928): President of Egypt 1981- . Head of the air force 1969-75; VP 1975-81. He succeeded *Anwar Sadat*, upon his assassination. A supporter of the *Camp David Accords,* he oversaw the return of the final third of the *Sinai* in 1982. He was a strong supporter of the UN coalition in the *Gulf War*, committing significant forces, but also arranging a quid pro quo whereby $10 billion in debt was forgiven by the U.S. In 1993 he began all-out repression of Egypt's *Muslim Brotherhood*.

Mugabe, Robert (b.1924): PM of Zimbabwe. He helped set up political and *guerrilla* opposition to white rule in Rhodesia, and was imprisoned there 1964-74. He won Zimbabwe's first election, in 1980. An avowed *marxist*, his economic approach is increasingly at odds with a recent trends in Africa. However, he has shown a strong pragmatic side in the past, and may yet make necessary adjustments to retain power.

mujahadeen: "Holy warriors." *Islamic* fighters who are, or who say they are, engaged in a *jihad*.

Mukden incident (September 18, 1931): Japanese troops of the *Guandong Army* staged an explosion on the railway they controlled at Mukden, *Manchuria's* capital. They then blamed the Chinese, and invaded.

By early 1932 they controlled the whole of Manchuria. When a *fact-finding* mission sent by the *League of Nations* mildly criticized Japan, it withdrew from the League. Japan then set up the *puppet regime* of *Manchukuo*. Also see, *Hoover/Stimson Doctrine*.

mullah: In *Islamic* nations, this is a title of respect for persons learned in the *sharia* law.

Mulroney, Martin Brian (b.1939): Canadian PM 1984-93. After the *Trudeau* years of intermittent confrontation with the U.S. over energy, *investment* and *security* policy, and a decade long search for a "Third Option," Mulroney gave Canadian foreign policy a continentalist turn. He institutionalized this with an agreement creating a *free trade area* between the U.S. and Canada, and later signed *NAFTA*. He enjoyed close personal relations with two presidents (*Reagan* and *Bush*). He led a reluctant Canada into the *Gulf War*, although its contribution to the *coalition* was minor (mainly in *logistical* support and *blockade* functions). As the *Cold War* ended he announced a pullback from *NATO* deployments in Europe and an upper limit to Canada's traditional *peacekeeping* service. In 1990 he also overturned decades of hesitation and took Canada into the *OAS*. Domestically, he raised taxes, cut programs, and tried but failed to complete the Canadian constitution. He left office deeply unpopular.

multiethnic: A *nation* composed of two or more *ethnic groups*; e.g., Canada, India, Indonesia, most African *states*. With rising *immigration* even once homogenous states are becoming multiethnic; e.g., Germany or France. Some resist such pressures with tight *immigration* laws and discriminatory social practices; e.g., Australia and the U.S. previously, Japan today.

multilateral: Among more than two *states*.

multilateral aid: *Development* aid channeled through and administered by *international organizations*, such as the *IBRD, IMF* or various *regional banks*.

multilateral diplomacy: Diplomacy conducted by large numbers of *states*, often in public, as opposed to *bilateral* and secretive *negotiations*. See *conference diplomacy; public opinion*.

Multilateral Trade Negotiations (MTN): The rounds of *GATT*. See *Kennedy, Tokyo* and *Uruguay Rounds*.

multinational corporation/enterprise (MNC/MNE): A firm with production, marketing and distribution facilities located in several countries, and highly flexible in moving around *capital, goods* and *technology* to match market conditions. It also "thinks globally," or has no specific loyalty in making these decisions, which are based instead on questions of *economies of scale*, taxation policy and *repatriated* profits. This feature has led to criticism from *host countries* about insensitivity to local needs and interests, and on occasion about MNC interference in domestic political affairs. Some effort has been made to develop an international code of conduct for MNCs, but the most effective measures so far have been unilateral. The expanding wealth and role of MNCs stems from the very processes that produce modern economic benefits, as well as global *interdependence*. But this causes tension with national governments that are losing *autonomy* and local economic control to larger market forces. More enthusiastic advocates of MNCs see this decline in effective *sovereignty* as both inevitable and a good thing. They argue that it increases the quotient of human welfare by promoting interconnected growth and political homogenization. Fiercer critics, frequently drawing upon *dependency theory*, see MNCs as extending the tentacles of capitalist domination, producing hierarchical rather than interdependent relations, and promoting private power and gain at the expense of public welfare. Most governments have learned to take a pragmatic, middle road: they encourage MNC *investment* within whatever national guidelines they are able to impose, adjust to global economic and technological shifts by merging their bargaining power through regional economic *integration*, and slowly open to wider benefits through moves toward regional and global *free trade*. See also *Andean Common Market; foreign direct investment; internalization theory; portfolio investment; product cycle theory*.

multinational empire/state: A political entity composed of several *nations*, though most often organized to greatly advantage one, dominant *ethnic group* (e.g., the Germans in *Austria-Hungary*, the Serbs in *Yugoslavia* or the Russians in the *Soviet Union*). Multilateral empires dominated world history over the past 500 years. With the passing of *colonialism* and of the Soviet Union, that era appears to be ending.

Multiple Independently Targetable Re-entry Vehicle (MIRV): When a single *launcher* carries a *bus* that delivers two or more *warheads* to different targets. Its introduction in the 1970s eroded *SALT I* and seriously complicated *arms control* talks.

multipolarity: A metaphor drawn from magnetism depicting the distribution of *power* among *states* when there are several *Great Powers* of roughly equal strength or weight. Each has *preponderant* influence over lesser powers within its *sphere of influence*, and

is seen as repelling other Great Powers from that zone (as might a magnetic pole attract/repel objects within the range of its influence). Some theorists maintain that an *international system* with five "poles" is inherently the most stable; others argue for one, or for two. Yet it can be suggested that all such preferences are merely parochial. The widely held view of five as the optimum number might be dismissed as an untenable generalization because it is based upon a single example, that of the *Concert of Europe*. Similarly, a theoretical preference for just one *preponderant power* overseeing international order has no factual referent, even though it is often presented with overeasy reference to the Roman Empire, or even more ahistorically to the U.S. c.1945 or again in 1990. Yet Rome actually ruled but a corner of the world (and faced many powerful enemies on its periphery); and U.S. influence was for decades closed out of vast areas of the world's economy, politics and land surface. Lastly, to abstract from the example of the *Cold War* a firm generalization about the supposed inherent stability of a *system* of two dominant powers borders on crude *determinism*. Among other things, it ignores the vivid possibility that another such conflict could have a quite different outcome (as could have the Cold War itself!), depending on the choices made by *decision makers*, the virulence of ideological or other competition, altered *technology* or other circumstance, or just dumb chance. Cf. *bipolarity; tripolarity; unipolarity*.

Münchengrätz Agreements (1833): *Metternich* and *Nicholas II* met and agreed to act in concert should the *Ottoman Empire* appear about to collapse and be *partitioned*, and guarantee each other's Polish possessions against *rebellion*. A follow-up agreement included Prussia in a *declaration* that all three would aid any *sovereign* opposed by a *liberal* or *radical* revolt.

Munich Conference (September 29-30, 1938): This infamous conference, called to address the building crisis between Germany and Czechoslovakia, was attended by *Neville Chamberlain*, PM of Britain; *Édouard Daladier*, PM of France; *Benito Mussolini*, PM of Italy; and *Adolf Hitler*, Chancellor of Germany. It is permanently associated with the failure of the West's policy of *appeasement*. The *Sudetenland* was cravenly handed to Hitler; other parts of Czechoslovakia went to Hungary and Rumania. What was left of that benighted country was guaranteed protection by the four signatories. Chamberlain flew home to proclaim "peace with honor," and was received with great acclaim. The accolades lasted only until March 1939, when Hitler moved into the rump of Czechoslovakia, finally shocking the West into all-out preparations for *war*. Munich stunned the Soviets, who were excluded along with the Czechs, Poles and other vitally interested parties. *Stalin* ceased sending security feelers westward, sacked *Litvinov* and moved to make a separate deal with Hitler. One result of Munich was thus the *Nazi/Soviet Pact*, and the outbreak of *WWII* with the great anti-German *coalition* of *WWI* shattered by mutual suspicion. See also *Little Entente*.

Munich putsch: See *Beer Hall putsch*.

municipal law: Domestic law, *sovereign* and distinct from *international law*.

munitions: Matériel used in war: equipment and supplies, but especially *arms* and ammunition.

Munster, Treaty of (1648): A *peace treaty* between *Hapsburg* Spain and the *Netherlands*, through which an end was made of the "Eighty Years' War" (1568-1648), Dutch *independence* was accepted, and limited freedom of religion was granted to Spaniards conducting business in the Netherlands, and vice versa. It was part of the general settlement surrounding the end game to the *Thirty Years' War* and the *Peace of Westphalia*.

Murat, Joachim (1767-1815): Marshal of France; King of Naples. One of the greatest of *Napoleon's* marshals, and his brother-in-law, he was rewarded for both positions with an Italian throne. He commanded the French *cavalry* during the *invasion* of Russia in 1812, and less gloriously, during the *retreat from Moscow*. For rallying to his old commander during the *Hundred Days*, he was arrested by the *Restoration* authorities, tried for *treason*, and executed.

Muscat and Oman: See *Oman*.

Muslim: A believer in *Islam*. Among other entries, see *ayatollah; caliph; fundamentalism; haj; imam; Iranian Revolution; Ismaili; Mecca; mullah; Muslim Brotherhood; shi'ia Islam; sultan; sunni Islam; Wahhabi*.

Muslim Brotherhood: A *fundamentalist* movement within *Islam*, founded in Egypt in 1928 by Hassa al-Banna (1906-49). It has engaged in assassination of *secular* Arabs (and other *Muslims*) as part of a campaign to substitute the *sharia* for secular law and political authority in Muslim countries. For this it has been banned in several countries (in Egypt, as early as 1954). Al-Banna was himself assassinated by the Egyptian government in retaliation for the killing of a prime minister. While its radicalism and anti-secularism have earned it disapprobation internationally, its promotion of grassroots public works and Islamic

revival have earned it a substantial following among the poor, notably in Algeria, Egypt, Sudan and Syria.

Muslim League: The political party that founded *Pakistan*. It split from the *Congress Party* of India, under the ambitious leadership of *Muhammad Ali Jinnah*. By the late 1960s it was displaced by the Awami League in *East Pakistan*, and by the Pakistan People's Party in *West Pakistan*.

Mussolini, Benito (1883-1945): "Il Duce" (the Leader). Dictator of Italy, 1922-43. His political career was spent in pursuit of *martial* and imperial greatness for the Italian *nation*, an irony no doubt driven in part by his having fled Italy at age 19 (in 1902) in order to avoid military service. He abandoned his early, radical *socialism* for the crudest *militarism* and *nationalism* with the outbreak of *WWI,* in which he enlisted and was wounded. By the end of the war he had moved to embrace a new radical fetish: *fascism*. He borrowed heavily from *Gabriele D'Annunzio*, and was deeply influenced in both political tactics and style by that zealot's seizure of *Fiume*. Mussolini became PM in 1922, following the so-called *march on Rome*; he was outright dictator from 1925. He finally settled the Italian state's dispute with the *Vatican* in the *Lateran Treaty* and *concordat* of 1929. Though one is tempted to dismiss his foreign policy as mere bombast from a balcony (his favored locale for public strutting), it was in fact opportunistically *expansionist*, cost many lives, and in the end left Italy a shattered and occupied nation. He tried to take *Corfu* in 1924, but backed down. He invaded Ethiopia in 1935 (see *Abyssinian War*), and he pursued a long and brutal campaign of repression in *Tripoli* (Libya). He signed the *Axis* pact with *Hitler* and *intervened* in the *Spanish Civil War*, both in 1936, and took Italy out of the *League of Nations* in 1937. After that, he fell increasingly under Hitler's personal influence in what one historian has aptly called "the brutal friendship." He joined the *Pact of Steel* in 1939, the same year he invaded Albania. He treacherously attacked France as German tanks were rolling through Paris in 1940 ("I need 1,000 Italian dead to sit at the peace table"); invaded Greece, lost badly and was bailed out by Hitler, also in 1940. His armies suffered from poor equipment and low morale, and were easily thrown out of East and North Africa in 1941-42, mainly by the British. His *declaration of war* on the United States was deeply unpopular with the millions of Italians with family in America. He lost Sicily and southern Italy in 1943 to invading Anglo/American forces. With the *Allies* moving on Rome he was dismissed by his own fascist inner circle. Arrested in a palace *coup* led by *Pietro Badoglio*, whom he had once appointed governor of Libya, he was imprisoned. However, he was soon freed by German paratroopers in a daring *commando* raid. Still suffering from a fatal attraction to Hitler, he was briefly installed as a tattered Nazi puppet in north Italy. Captured by *partisans* in 1945 while trying to flee Italy (appropriately, disguised in a German uniform), he underwent *summary execution* on April 28th--just two days later his friend in Berlin blew his own brains out. Mussolini's body, and that of his murdered mistress, were hung by the feet, left for public display and vile, personal abuse in Milan's Piazza Loreto.

mustard gas: A liquid *agent* that when exposed to air turns into a noxious yellow gas (hence the name). It blinds and scorches the lungs and flesh of any who encounter even minute particles. It was used during the later part of *WWI*, a hated and much-feared weapon among the troops in the trenches. Yet, it proved so entirely indecisive that, despite stockpiling, it was not used again by any side in *WWII*.

muster: To assemble troops for battle. To muster in/out means to enlist/discharge from the military.

mutatis mutandis: "With the required changes made." An operational assumption commonly made in economic and statistical analysis.

mutilated victory (*vittoria mutilata*): A famous complaint about Italy's putative mistreatment by the other *Allies* at the *Paris Peace Conference*. First made by D'Annunzio, it echoed through Italian politics in the immediate postwar period, undermining stability by its implicit damnation of all who had taken Italy into and through *WWI*, to such little final purpose or accomplishment. The main complaint of nationalists was that at Paris, Italy had been refused its demand for *Italia irredenta*. This *territory* had been explicitly promised in the once secret *Treaty of London (1915)*, published by the *Bolsheviks* in 1918, to the great dismay of Britain and France, and provoking even greater anger and opposition to Italy's claims on the part of *Woodrow Wilson*. Also, Italy gained neither *colonies* nor *mandates*. Its representatives had stormed out of the peace conference on a point of principle and "national honor," and returned only after the spoils had been divided among the other victorious powers. See also *Fiume*. Cf. *stab-in-the-back; victory, in war*.

mutiny: A revolt of troops (or marines, *militia*, sailors and so forth), against the legally constituted military authorities that command them. Mutiny plays an unheralded role in world affairs, given that it often reflects the state of *national morale* as well as the mood of the principal internal threat--the military--to any

government suffering from a crisis of legitimacy. When it affects *front line* troops the effects can spell national disaster. For example, in *WWI* the spreading mutiny within the Russian army took the country out of the war and when it contaminated the navy, too, propelled Russia into the *Bolshevik Revolution*. Elements of the British and French armies also mutinied in 1917, bringing down the government in France and momentarily threatening the whole *Allied* war effort. The German military mutinied on the *home front* in 1918, which helped to topple the *Kaiser* and hastened signature of the *Armistice*. In 1956 a mutiny in the Hungarian army sparked the *Hungarian Uprising* and eventually, Soviet *intervention*. In the *Vietnam War*, the low morale of some American *conscripts* led to incidents of "fragging," a euphemism for wounding or even murdering one's own *officers* if they showed themselves too aggressive in going after the enemy. See also *Algerian War of Independence; Clemenceau; French Foreign Legion; Indian Mutiny; Jutland; Russian Revolutions (1917); voting with their feet*.

Mutual Assured Destruction (MAD): See *Assured Destruction*. Cf. *deterrence; Strategic Defense Initiative (SDI)*.

Mutual Force Reduction (MFR) Talks: Negotiations that began in 1973 between *NATO* and the *Warsaw Pact* concerning *conventional weapons* and reducing troop levels. The talks went virtually nowhere until the end of the *Cold War*, when agreement was reached across the board on massive conventional cutbacks.

Myanmar: Location: SE Asia. Major associations: *UN*. Population: 42 million. Military: new connections to China; anti-*guerrilla* experience. Called Burma until 1989. Once an independent kingdom, it was later ruled for centuries as a Chinese province. It fell under British control in three successive wars: 1824-26, 1852 and 1885. Britain governed it as part of its larger *empire* in India. From 1931-33 Burmese peasants resisted British rule and land policy. In 1937 it was separated from India. During *WWII* it was overrun by the Japanese, then retaken by British and Indian troops in vicious jungle fighting. Some Burmese, led by *Aung San*, fought alongside the Japanese then in 1945 revolted against them. *Independence* was achieved by negotiation with Britain in 1948. Aung San would have become PM, but he was assassinated six months before formal independence. Early agreements to respect the rights of Burma's multiple ethnic minorities were largely tossed aside in the 1950s, as Burma turned increasingly inward and overtly encouraged Burman *nationalism*. That led to decades of *guerrilla warfare*, with several ethnic groups (among them, the

Arakanese, Kachins, *Karen*, Mon, Shans and Wa) in long-term revolt against the central government. In addition, a low-level communist *insurgency* smoldered in the north (hampered by its own internal divisions). In turn, the government used the several insurgencies to justify repression of civil and political rights even to the Burman majority. In 1962 *Ne Win* led a coup that established an *autarkic* regime that ruled until 1988. It openly discriminated against ethnic Chinese and Indians, thereby undermining both the economy and the civil service. In foreign policy, Burma remained strictly *neutral*--for instance, it never joined *ASEAN* or *SEATO*--until the early 1990s, when it moved closer to China and opened discussions about leasing military bases and other forms of military cooperation. It has also moved to a *rapprochement* with Thailand. Burma was a strong supporter of the UN, even providing a *Secretary General, U Thant*. More recently, it has bristled under international criticism of its *human rights* practices. At home, it descended under its misfit rulers and "four-year plans" from one of the wealthiest new nations at independence, to one of the poorest Asian nations today (the UN has designated it a *LDC*). Since 1988 it has been under *martial law*, but has also partly opened to *foreign direct investment* and market reforms. It was renamed Myanmar in 1989. Elections held in 1990 were simply voided by the military. The *IMF* and *IBRD* spurned Myanmar's requests for loans, both for economic and political reasons. Civil rights activist, opposition leader, and *Nobel Prize* for Peace winner *Aung San Suu Kyi* (daughter of Aung San), who led the opposition coalition forces in the 1990 elections, was still under house arrest in 1994 despite international protest. The *junta* opened *peace talks* with Karen rebels in January 1994. At the same time, it showed no leniency toward *dissidents* and pressed ahead with plans to entrench a permanent political role for itself in a new constitution.

My Lai massacre (March 16, 1968): American GIs under Capt. Ernest Medina entered the village of My Lai in search of *Viet Cong*. They *tortured* the men for information, and then murdered over 100 unarmed men, women and children. After the story broke My Lai reinforced a growing perception that the *Vietnam War* had gone terribly wrong, and was tragically corrupting America's young men along with its national life and politics. Twenty-five men were originally charged, but just six actually came before a court-martial. Five were acquitted. Only Lt. William Calley was convicted. He was sentenced to life, had this reduced to 20 years hard labor, overturned on appeal, reinstated, and was then paroled in 1975. The trial was most notable for the court's rejection of the defense of *superior orders*, a decision implicitly upholding the precedent of the *Nuremberg war crimes trials*.

N

NAFTA: See either (1) *New Zealand/Australia Free Trade Agreement*, or (2) *North American Free Trade Agreement*.

Nagasaki: This Japanese city experienced the second, and to date, last use of an *atomic bomb* (code named "Fatman"). Dropped by the United States on August 9, 1945, it killed 40,000-60,000 outright, with perhaps 100,000 more dying lingering deaths in the years that followed. The attack came one day after the Soviet Union entered the war in the Pacific, and just three days after the first atomic bomb was dropped on *Hiroshima*. In combination, those events broke Japanese will to resist, already wavering other than among the most *fanatic*. Japan agreed to *terms* on August 15th.

Nagorno-Karabakh: An ethnically Armenian *enclave* of some 200,000 souls entirely within modern Azerbaijan. For centuries it was governed by Armenian princes, until taken over by Russia. During the chaos of the *Ottoman* collapse in 1917, it tried to join Armenia but was prevented from doing so by Azerbaijan (with Turkish aid). In 1918, with the collapse of all Ottoman power, it tried again to join with Armenia, then briefly independent; this time it was prevented from *union* by Britain. In 1920 the Soviets re-established Russian control. In 1921 the *territory* was ceded to Soviet Armenia, but within days protests from Soviet Azerbaijan overturned the decision. *Stalin* enforced a false peace on the region, setting the modern borders in 1936. In 1963 anti-Azeri riots broke out. In 1988 *Gorbachev* agreed to consider a transfer to Armenia, and the Assembly in Nagorno-Karabakh voted 110-17 to accept such a transfer. But the Soviet committee studying the question bent to Azeri pressure, and said no. Sectarian riots then broke out across the region, generating fears of *genocide*. Anti-Armenian *pogroms* began in Baku. Soviet troops tried unsuccessfully to intervene in 1988 and 1989, after sporadic fighting began. In 1990 they occupied Baku, site of massacres of Armenians. In January 1989, Gorbachev placed the enclave under direct administration from Moscow. That was opposed, and he quickly reversed the decision. By early 1991 the Russians could no longer enforce peace, and when the Soviet Union collapsed at the end of the year, they ceased trying. Rifles were soon supplemented by tanks and *artillery*, and the *Armenia/Azerbaijan War* spread and deepened. Russia has stayed out of the conflict. Turkey and Iran, on the other hand, have threatened *intervention* if Armenia attempts *annexation*. The enclave was 80% Armenian before fighting began. By 1994 *ethnic cleansing* raised that figure to 95%. Cf. *Nakhichevan*.

Nagy, Imre (1896-1958): PM of Hungary 1953-55, 1956. He was purged from the Communist Party in 1955 on charges of *titoism*. He returned to power in the spring of 1956 and with *János Kádar* stepped up the changes that led to the *Hungarian Uprising*. When the *rebellion* was crushed by the Soviet Union he was arrested, and later shot.

Nakhichevan: A non-contiguous part of Azerbaijan, forming an Azeri *enclave* between Armenia and Turkey. Fighting during the *Armenia/Azerbaijan War* spilled into this area in 1992. In 1993 rebel Azeri from this enclave fought a brief, successful *campaign* against the Azeri government, ostensibly to protest its poor management of the war with Armenia.

NAM: See *Non-Aligned Movement*.

Namibia: Location: Southern Africa. Major associations: *OAU, UN*. Population: 1.4 million. Military: minor. Formerly German South West Africa, a German colony from 1884-1915, when it was captured by British and South African troops during *WWI*. It was *mandated* to South Africa by the *League of Nations* in 1920. In 1946, with the *extinction* of the League, South Africa declined to transfer Namibia to the authority of the UN *Trusteeship Council*. In 1960 an *independence* movement, SWAPO, was founded. In 1966 it moved to *guerrilla* attacks aimed at pressuring Pretoria into conceding independence, with support from the *front line states*. In 1971 the *ICJ* ruled that South Africa's continued refusal to grant UN authority over Namibia was illegal. A UN "Contact Group" comprising Canada, Britain, France, Germany and the U.S. was formed to negotiate a settlement. In 1980-81 South Africa invaded southern *Angola* in a bid to eliminate SWAPO bases. Subsequently, it linked elections in Namibia to withdrawal of Cuban troops from Angola. Final settlement came in 1988 when the Cubans pulled out and South Africa, about to undergo massive change, permitted independence in March 1990. In 1993 *Walvis Bay* was ceded to Namibia.

Nanking (Nanjing), sack of: On December 13, 1937, the Japanese took Nanking, then capital of *Nationalist China*, during the opening phase of the *Second Sino/Japanese War*. Over the next two weeks they systematically slaughtered more than 200,000 men, women, children and infants, and *pillaged* and burnt the city. This barbarism shocked international opinion, severely damaged the image of Japan, and further hardened American attitudes toward Tokyo's thrust into China. Even Nazi Germany made a humbug protest.

Nanking (Nanjing), Treaty of (1842): This agreement ended the *Opium War* by ceding *Hong Kong* to Britain, forcing open five coastal cities to foreign trade, and imposing a low *tariff* on British goods. It marked the beginning of China's long obeisance to foreign powers, especially as it was copied by other foreign powers on the *most-favored-nation* principle. It was the first of the *unequal treaties* with China.

Napoleon I, Bonaparte (1769-1821): Emperor of France 1804-15. Born in Corsica, he made his early reputation in Italy and Egypt. He took power in a *coup* on "18 Brumaire" (July 1799). During his *Consulate*, he made major domestic reforms. After the *War of the Second Coalition* he crowned himself *Emperor*. His greatest victories came in the *War of the Third Coalition*, 1804-07, in which he defeated Austria and forced a *spheres of influence* arrangement on Russia at *Tilsit*. He invaded Russia in 1812, capturing Moscow. But in the *retreat from Moscow* he left most of his army to the untender mercies of Russia's winter and its *partisans*, barely escaping personal capture. His power was further drained by *attrition* in the *Peninsular War*. He was defeated in the *War of the Fourth Coalition*, abdicated, and was *exiled* to *Elba*. But he returned for the spectacular failure of the *Hundred Days* that ended at *Waterloo*. Exiled again, he died on *St. Helena*. His corpse was later returned to Paris, where it lies in state. He left a legacy of authoritarian *Bonapartism* to compete with *monarchism* and rule by the parliament (*parlement*) in France. He revolutionized *warfare*, and thereby accelerated the centralization and *modernization* of the *state* in Europe. See also *Napoleonic warfare; Napoleonic Wars.*

Napoleon II, Bonaparte (1811-32): "King of Rome" 1811-14; son of *Napoleon I* and Marie Louise of Austria. When she divorced the father, the son was taken to Vienna and raised as an Austrian prince. While Bonapartists accepted him as heir, he was sickly and died in his youth. He is included here not for reasons of historical importance (he had none), but because nearly everyone who reads of the 1st and 3rd Napoleons asks, "who was the 2nd?"

Napoleon III, a.k.a. Louis-Napoleon (1808-73): Emperor of France 1852-70; nephew of *Napoleon I*. He twice tried to seize power (1836 and 1840), but his *treason* was treated mildly by those who feared his uncle's legend. Elected President of the *Second Republic* in 1848, three years later he launched a *coup*, and one year after that proclaimed the *Second Empire* (on December 2nd, the anniversary of his uncle's coronation). He said: "The Empire is peace." But erratic and vainglorious, within two years he joined in the *Cri-*

mean War against Russia, more to appease Britain than defend French interests. He schemed constantly over Italy, set *Maximillian* on the "throne" of Mexico in a costly and foolhardy adventure, was out-flanked by *Bismarck* during the *Seven Weeks' War*, and destroyed by him in the *Franco/Prussian War*. He was captured at *Sedan* and spent his final days in brooding *exile* in Britain. His only son was killed fighting for Britain against the *Zulus*, ending the Napoleonic line.

Napoleonic warfare: More than anything *Napoleon's* martial success came from his emphasis on mobility on, and on the way to, the battlefield. He insisted on *living off the land*; an army, he once mused, "marches on its stomach." He used *cavalry* not just to scout or even *flank* the enemy, but as a shock force during critical points of a battle. His use of concentrated cannon fire and light, mobile *artillery* were other innovations, permitting the French to appear with unexpected suddenness and force. He was further aided in the early years by the revolutionary élan of his troops, and by his qualified merit system for choosing commanders: every foot soldier, he told them, "carries a marshal's baton in his knapsack." He was thus blessed with able commanders, where opposing armies might be led by tactical dolts who happened to be some aristocrat's son or nephew. However, others learned from his success and emulated his techniques, particularly the Prussians, so that by 1813 Napoleon no longer enjoyed all these advantages. Even so, the legend of his facility with movement would fixate much military thinking in later decades. The *rifled bore* musket and cannon, widespread by 1850, rendered Napoleon's tactics outdated by extending the range of effective defensive fire. He certainly would have adjusted, but hardly anyone else even noticed. That mistake contributed to the many futile, bloody charges and offensives of the *Crimean War, American Civil War* and *WWI*.

Napoleonic wars: See *Napoleon Bonaparte; Napoleonic warfare; Peninsular War; Quasi War; Wars of the First, Second, Third* and *Fourth Coalitions.* Cf. *French Revolution; War of 1812.*

narco-terrorism: Use of *terrorism* techniques by *drug cartels*, with the aim of intimidating the civil authorities into abandoning anti-drug policies.

narodniki: "Go to the people." A Russian populist movement active in the 1870s, made up of idealistic students who went into villages to persuade rather bemused peasants to emancipate themselves.

narrative: The story of a historical event. A good narrative history goes beyond a mere accounting or recital to discuss *causality*, possible larger meanings and connections to other events.

Nassau Agreement (December 18, 1962): *Harold Macmillan* met *John Kennedy* in the Bahamas (such *summit* locales were among the pleasant perks of *empire*), where they agreed to arm British *submarines* with nuclear-tipped *missiles*. *De Gaulle* cited the agreement as an example of Britain still being unready for Europe, when he vetoed UK entry into the *EC*; whether he was sincere or not is unclear.

Nasser, Gamel Abdel (1918-70): Egyptian statesman. PM 1954-56; President 1956-70. He was one among several leaders of the *coup* that overthrew *Faruk* and the Egyptian *monarchy*. His policy sprang from a vision of Egypt as the heart of three mutually reinforcing cultures: *African, Arab* and *Islamic*. Of these, his *pan-Arabism* predominated. He broke with the *West* in 1955, seeking and securing arms and diplomatic support from the *Soviet bloc*, including assistance in building the *Aswan Dam*. He led Egypt during the *Suez Crisis,* and the *Second* and *Third Arab/Israeli Wars,* gaining enormous *prestige* from the first two conflicts, but losing much of what he had gained by the third. He played a key role in founding the *Non-Aligned Movement*. In the name of pan-Arabism he attempted *union* with Syria from 1958-61, but it failed. His assertion of Egyptian leadership of the whole Arab world won him more enemies than allies. His last days were spent conducting the *War of Attrition*.

Natal: A British *colony*, and later a province in the eastern part of *South Africa*.

nation: (1) An imagined, self-conscious community composed of people who share ethnicity, language or culture but may or may not possess a *state*; e.g., Kurds or Palestinians. (2) A community that need not share common race, language or culture, but holds a defined and *recognized* piece of *territory* and shares a common government and a degree of common purpose; e.g., Belgium, Canada or India. (3) Often loosely used as a synonym for *state*. Cf. *nation-state; tribe*.

national debt: The debt of a national government, not the total of all debt held by all levels of government of a nation; it is smaller than the *public debt*.

National Front governments: Those with all (or nearly all) party participation, formed to deal with a *war* or other national crisis. Such governments were assembled in Britain and elsewhere during the *Great Depression* and again in *WWII*. They reflect a public demand and a real need to submerge normal partisan politics beneath genuine concern for *national security* in wartime, or another vital endeavor. It is a term seldom used in or about the U.S., where "bipartisanship" is the preferred nomenclature (without necessarily implying an emergency situation). Note: This is not the same as a *Popular Front*.

national interest: A conception drawn from classical *realism* where it means, in its rawest form, national survival. Once this is secured, lesser interests can also be addressed by foreign policy. Yet, even the classical meaning is far more expansive than sometimes depicted by its critics. It includes security for a nation's institutions, population and cultural values. How? By whatever measures improve its (absolute and relative) *power* position vis-à-vis other *states*, whether in the military, political, economic or other realm. The cardinal moral virtue upheld by statesmen pursuing the national interest is said to be *prudence*, and the yardstick of final judgment is success, not personal righteousness or purity of motive. Sophisticated usages add pursuit of enlightened self-interest in *international security, peace* and *distributive justice* as components of the national interest, insofar as these goals might help create a wider environment in which the nation is more secure. However, it is important to note that this narrow, classical, even classroom sense is not the way the term is generally used in daily discourse on world affairs, or a given nation's foreign policy. Instead, there is an inescapable political tendency to frame virtually any momentarily favored interest or policy option put forward by a government, or by interest groups competing for attention in foreign policy, as an element of the national interest. That is done whether it is truly a common and permanent (that is, national) interest or merely a special or even private interest overdressed in grandiose pretensions. For example, does a given *casus belli* truly represent a national grievance, or merely a powerful sectoral one? Or is a *free trade* agreement or heavily *protectionist* legislation in the nation's interest, or mainly in the interest of specific groups (say, exporters in the first case, and inefficient industries in the second)? Despite--or perhaps because of--this ambiguity, debate over what specific interests are also national interests, and whether they are so in the short or long-term, is at the center of nearly all discussion of foreign policy.

nationalism: Loyalty and devotion to a *nation*, and/or to the *state* that houses it. Nationalism frequently shades into *chauvinism*, in which one's nation is exalted above others. It has been a force of political construction since the 16th century, building new communities in previously decentralized or even ungoverned locales. But it has also been a force of great destruction, tearing apart *multinational empires*, dividing existing states, and blocking advance to greater regional or global *integration*. Cf. *jingoism; patriotism*.

Nationalist China: All China, 1928-49; Taiwan alone, 1949- . Republican China dates from the fall of the *Manchus* in 1911 to the ascendancy of the communists in 1949. See *China; Chinese Civil War; Chinese Revolution; Guomindang; Second Sino/Japanese War; Taiwan*.

Nationalists, in China: See *China; Chinese Civil War; Chinese Revolution; Guomindang; Second Sino/ Japanese War; Taiwan*.

nationality: The legal tie between *states* and firms or persons, deciding to which states duties and rights are owed or held by such persons or firms. Cf. *citizenship; dual nationality; expatriation; statelessness*.

nationalization/nationalize: To take under state control and ownership a property or enterprise that was previously privately owned. It is usually confined to industries or resource sectors thought key to *national security* or economic independence. To avoid being mere *expropriation*, it should be accompanied by fair *compensation*.

national judge: A Justice of the *International Court of Justice* who sits on a case involving the state of his/her nationality. See *chambers of the Court*.

national liberation, wars of: A Soviet *strategic doctrine* drawing upon *Lenin's* portrait of *imperialism*, and supporting anti-colonial *insurgencies* as threatening the weakest link in the chains bolstering world *capitalism*. Although *Khrushchev* gave it open voice, it was an idea already rooted in notions of *class struggle* and the putative common interests of all workers. It was also a resort to which the Soviets were driven by the logic of *peaceful coexistence*. Cf. *just war; marxism-leninism; Reagan Doctrine*.

national morale: The degree to which a population supports *foreign policy*. It is a broader idea than *public opinion*, as even the most absolute dictatorships must take it into account. When it collapses it does so with terrific speed and major consequences, such as when Russian morale collapsed during *WWI*, or Iranian morale fell at the end of the *Iran/Iraq War*. When it is high, as in France during the years of the *French Revolution* and under *Napoleon*, it enhances *diplomacy* by aiding the *state* marshal the full resources of the *nation*. When it is low, as in France during the years of the *Maginot spirit*, it can fatally undermine a more

forceful diplomacy just when strength is most required. Cf. *mutiny*.

National Party (South Africa): The all-white, predominantly *Afrikaner* party that won power in 1948 and introduced *apartheid*. It held power from 1948-93. It was opened to black membership in 1992, but for obvious reasons struggled with recruitment, even while losing white voters to more extremist parties.

national security: Foreign policy issues pertaining directly or indirectly to matters of defense of a given country. *Alliances, conscription*, overseas commitments, military expenditures, procurement policies and *strategic doctrine* are all obvious components of national security. Less plain, but no less vital, are considerations about the economic underpinnings of national *power* such as *competitiveness, deficit spending*, and *productivity*. Cf. *international security*.

National Security Agency (NSA): The largest and best funded U.S. *intelligence service*. It is headquartered at Fort Meade and is mainly concerned with *sigint* and *elint*. Less well known than the smaller *CIA*, an anonymous (could it be any other way?) wag once said its acronym really stood for "No Such Agency."

National Security Council (NSC): A subdivision of the *executive* branch in the U.S., set up in 1947 as an advisory body to the president on all matters relating to *national security*. It brings together the top U.S. foreign policy officials, including the president, the secretaries of state and defense, the *Joint Chiefs*, and the director of the *CIA*. The NSC grew increasingly important during the *Cold War* as a policy-making and coordinating body, often outstripping in influence, and even public profile, the *Department of State*. Its most important single directive was *NSC-68*.

National Security Council Directive #68 (NSC-68): Issued in April 1950, it was the most influential policy statement in U.S. *Cold War* diplomacy. Its principle drafter was *Paul Nitze*, who gave it a dramatic, even sinister language not usually encountered in internal memoranda. It portrayed the *Soviet Union* as fundamentally bent on *aggression* and relentless expansion, necessary to sustain the system at home. *Containment*, already the watchword of Washington's political and economic policy in Europe and Japan, was thereby given a dangerously militarized and global twist. NSC-68 went on to sanction the use of almost any available means to defend the interests of the democracies. It was different from the *X article* and *Long Telegram* in its tone, the scope of the threat it depicted, and its contention that a Soviet offensive against the West had become global. Just months later North Korea attacked South Korea, in apparent confirmation of NSC-68's warning. The Cold War moved center stage to Asia; before long its impact would be felt on every continent save *Antarctica*.

national security state: The idea that national life is grossly distorted in *states* that are involved in sustained international *tension*, such as characterized the *Cold War*, because of the requirement to divert social spending and national energies to matters of *national security* and military exigency. See also *military-industrial complex; Minatom*.

National Socialism: See *nazism*.

National Technical Means of Verification (NTM): All nonhuman, non-*multilateral* means of *verification* of *arms control* agreements that remain in the hands of a single country: *satellites*, radar, *listening posts* and so forth. See *elint; sigint*.

national treatment: In *international law*, the requirement to treat foreign nationals by the same legal rules and standards one affords one's own *citizens*.

nation-state: This malapropism is often used as a synonym for *state*, when it is really a term drawn from the state-building phase of modern European history. Destruction of the feudal order leading to centralized political authority and the rise of the modern state first took place in Europe. But this term implies that states are coterminous with single *nations*, when even most European states are polyglot ethnic and political communities. The confusion arises from the fact that on the whole, one ethnic group tends to dominate in any given state (other than explicitly *multinational* states), to impose and uphold its values as national ones and to project its own image internationally. Thus, in Britain the English historically have dominated the Irish, Scots and Welsh; France has marginalized and to a degree assimilated its Basque, Norman and other minorities; and the *Balkans*, Eastern Europe and Russia remain ethnic patchwork quilts. Similar situations abound in Asia, where non-Han Chinese and Tibetans are repressed in China, Punjabis dominate the other peoples of Pakistan, no one group controls India and the Persians of Iran silence large Azeri and Kurdish minorities. In Latin America the culture of *indigenous peoples* has, in many countries, been crushed under imported *Iberian* traditions. In Africa, it is common for myriad ethnic groups to share a single state, but rare for *public goods* to be allocated equitably.

NATO: See *North Atlantic Treaty Organization*.

naturalization: Conferring rights of *nationality*, usually meaning the full rights of *citizenship* (in those countries where citizens have rights, and not just duties). This may or may not involve renunciation of previous citizenship, and may or may not extend to children, depending on bilateral agreement between the countries involved in a given case. Most states historically held to a doctrine of *indefeasible allegiance*. After 1867, however, the U.S. gained some acceptance for a right of *expatriation*, a campaign in which it was supported by other *immigrant* nations. See *Bancroft Conventions*.

natural law: In *international law* and moral reasoning, an approach holding that universal principles can be devined from human nature or "the mind of God" through the application of reason, and are binding on human communities both in the absence of, and in addition to, *positive law*. This approach informs concern for *human rights*. See *jus naturale*.

natural resources: Wealth inherent to the *land* and *water* of a country: mineral ores, productive soil, fresh water, fish, forests and so on. See also *oil; power*.

Nauru: Location: Pacific. Major associations: *Commonwealth, SPC, SPF*. It declined membership in the *UN*. Population: 8,000. Military: none. This Micronesian *microstate* is the smallest independent *state* in the world, with a combined native and foreign population of just 8,000. It was a German *colony* from 1888-1914, when it was captured by Australia. In 1921 it became a *mandate territory*, jointly administered by Australia, Britain and New Zealand. Japan occupied it from 1942-45, when it became a UN *trusteeship territory*, under the same three powers. It became a *republic* and a *special member* of the Commonwealth in 1968. Rich in phosphates, it is the only island state to give others *aid*. In 1993 Australia agreed to pay *compensation* for earlier mining practices that left 4/5ths of the atoll uninhabitable.

naval power: See *sea power*.

Navarino, Battle of (October 20, 1827): When Turkey refused to accept Greek *independence*, a combined fleet of British, French and Russian *warships* met in battle with the Turkish fleet and that of *Mehemet Ali* of Egypt. The Turkish and Egyptian fleets were annihilated, with heavy loss of life. This action was much criticized on *realpolitik* grounds in Britain, where concern over the *Eastern Question* was on the rise.

navicert system: It was first developed by Britain as a means of assuring itself that *goods* shipped by its own merchants or by *neutrals* did not end up with its enemies. It involved inspection of cargos and issuance of letters of assurance that the *ultimate destination* was friendly or neutral *territory*. The U.S. began to use a similar system, calling the credentials navicerts, in early 1916.

navy: All *warships* and auxiliary (support and supply) ships operated by a state, as well as officers, crews, *High Command* and the *strategic doctrine* it follows, and supporting bureaucracy. Cf. *merchant marine.*

navy yard: A government operated shipbuilding and repair dock, for servicing ships of the *navy.*

Nazi Germany: The period from January 1933, when *Adolf Hitler* became Chancellor, to early May 1945, when the Nazi leadership surrendered, escaped or committed suicide, and Germany accepted *unconditional surrender.* See *Germany.*

nazism (National Socialism): Political, social, economic and racial doctrines of the NSDAP (Nationalsozialistische Deutsche Arbeiterpartei, or National Socialist German Workers' Party), the governing party of the *Third Reich* 1933-45. Its tenets and characteristics included: assertion of the racial superiority and right of *"Aryans"* to European and world dominance; subjugation of the individual to the group, of class conflict to a single national purpose, and of the nation to the *Führerprinzip; totalitarian* supremacy of the state; ruthless political will, utterly unimpeded by conventional morality or respect for the rule of law, coupled with a perverse insistence on making even the most foul atrocity legal; denial of all civil rights, and even of humanity for some, up to and including *slave labor* and physical extermination for "lesser races," such as *Slavs* and *Gypsies,* but especially the Jews; glorification of *militarism,* of physical activity over things intellectual and of Germany's pre-Christian history, heroes and myths; destruction of non-Aryan, and hence "decadent," art and literature; assertion of cultural and racial superiority for the *Volksdeutsche;* unification of all the Volk in a single, enlarged Germany; *lebensraum* for the German people at the expense of East European states and of Russia; and surrender to the personal and supreme will of *Adolf Hitler.* See *anti-Semitism; Beer Hall putsch; death camps; Eichmann; fascism; Freikorps; geopolitik; Gestapo; Goebbels; Göring; Herrenvolk; Hess; Himmler; Holocaust; kristallnacht; Krupp; nationalism; neo-nazism; Night of the Long Knives; Nuremberg Rallies; Nuremberg Laws; Nuremberg Trials; SA; SS; Untermenschen.*

Nazi/Soviet Pact (August 23, 1939): Formally called the "Russian/German Treaty of Nonaggression," it was negotiated and signed by *Ribbentrop* and *Molotov.* Only part of it was published, that portion stipulating a 10-year *nonaggression* agreement and pledging *neutrality* should either party go to *war* with a third state. That alone shocked the world, including many a loyal nazi and communist who had been told they were each other's mortal enemy. More important, it opened the way for *Hitler* to launch his *blitzkrieg* on Poland two weeks later. But the *pact* also contained a secret *protocol* agreeing to a fourth *partition of Poland,* and to divide Eastern Europe into German and Russian *spheres of influence.* Germany took western *Poland* and *Lithuania,* while the Soviets were granted control of *Bessarabia, Estonia, Finland, Latvia* and eastern Poland, and agreed to supply Germany with *food* and other resources on advantageous terms. An addendum at the end of September traded eastern Poland to Germany in return for Lithuania. The immediate victim was Poland, attacked first by German and then Russian armies moving to a prearranged *partition* line. The fallout did not end there. A Soviet attack followed on Finland (see *Winter War*), and while Germany was occupied in France and the *Low Countries* in May-June 1940, the Soviet Union completed its acquisition of the *Baltic States* and Bessarabia, all of which it annexed. Hitler's purpose in agreeing to the pact was to clear the way to destruction of Poland, and to avoid a *two-front war.* Yet he always intended to attack Russia in the end. *Stalin's* purposes are less clear. Until the very hour of the German attack on Russia on June 22, 1941, he continued to send trainloads of supplies to Germany, and to refuse to countenance any reports that it was preparing to attack. It seems likely that his main motives were to simultaneously avoid a war with Germany for which the Soviet Union was not ready, and to turn Hitler westward in the hope that the draining slaughter of *WWI* might be repeated, so that all his enemies to the west might destroy each other. The unexpectedly rapid collapse of France changed everything, however. It left the Soviet Union to face the onslaught of *Barbarossa* less than two years after it signed the pact, without a continental *ally.* Less directly, the pact made the Japanese cautious about provoking Russia and thus helped turn them southward toward *Indochina,* the Philippines, and *Pearl Harbor.* Postscript: The secret protocol was uncovered when U.S. troops captured the Nazi archives in 1945. For decades, the Soviet Union denied it ever signed such an agreement with the enemy it fought so bitterly in the *"Great Patriotic War."* In 1991, the *Kremlin* finally accepted the authenticity of the German documents; the *KGB,* however, said it was still looking for the Russian-language copy (which, it was implausibly asserted, might have been misfiled).

near abroad: A Russian term for the other *successor states* to the old *Soviet Union*. Relations with these states are viewed by Moscow as special, and distinct from relations with other foreign states. This is because of historic links through the old Russian and Soviet *empires*, the contemporary fact that some 25 million Russians live in the "near abroad" and the persistent reality that Russia regards these areas as within its historic *sphere of influence*. The idea may yet amount to a modern, Russian version of the *Monroe Doctrine*. Cf. *cordon sanitaire*. See map.

Near East: Archaic. Looking from Western Europe, the "Near East" historically referred to North Africa and the contemporary *Middle East*, sometimes including the *Balkans*.

near-nuclear states: Those suspected of being close to achieving a *nuclear weapons* capability, or having secretly done so: Argentina, until it signed *nonproliferation* agreements and opened itself to *IAEA* inspections in the late 1980s; Brazil, whose *civilian* government renounced a secret nuclear program by the military; India, which tested a bomb in 1974 but denies it keeps any in stock (it is thought to have the parts ready to assemble); Iran, which is clearly seeking such weapons; Israel, thought to have about 120 warheads; North Korea, which in 1993 refused *IAEA* inspectors and renounced the *NPT*; Pakistan, which the *CIA* in 1990 said was nuclear capable, leading to a suspension of *aid*; and South Africa, which early in 1993 announced it had built six bombs in the 1980s, but dismantled them before joining the NPT in 1991.

necessary representation: In *international law*, acceptance of the fact that corporate entities such as *states* or *MNCs* must act through individuals.

necessities of war: *Derogation* from accepted international moral standards under the claim that the requirements of making *war* force a waiver of those standards. Cf. *standards of civilized behavior.*

necessity: When exceptional circumstances lead to waiver of the otherwise illegal character of an act. This assertion is made by *belligerents*, as a *justification* for breaches of customary legal obligations they take in the prosecution of a *war*. See also *angary.*

negotiation: The discussion of a *dispute* through diplomatic representatives, with the aim of resolving it peacefully, say in a *treaty*. See *diplomacy.*

négritude: A celebration of the heritage of the black peoples of the world, not just of sub-Saharan Africa.

Following the wave of *independence* for African *nations* in the 1960s it fed into *pan-Africanism*. It was promoted by *Léopold Senghor*, among others, in his twin capacities as respected poet and President of Senegal. Its advocates were anti-colonial, but tended also to be conservative in their views of how independent black societies should be organized and governed, and to favor the *West* in the *Cold War*.

Nehru, Jawaharal (1889-1964): "Pandit" (teacher/guide). Indian statesman. PM 1947-64. A close confidant of *Mohandas Gandhi*, he became a leader of the *Congress Party* after the Amritsar massacre (1919). He was the main figure on the Indian side in the *partition* negotiations in 1947, although he was neither Hindu nor Muslim, but a confirmed agnostic. He served both as PM and his own Minister of Foreign Affairs. He conducted India through the *First Indo/Pakistani War*, the *Indo/Chinese War* and the *occupation* of *Goa* and other French and Portuguese *enclaves*. He was a founding member and leading figure in the *Non-Aligned Movement*. His daughter, *Indira Gandhi*, and several of his grandchildren followed him into high office, but never achieved his high stature.

ne judex ultra petita partium: "A judge must not award more than the aggrieved party has claimed." Legal maxim guiding *damages.*

Nelidov Project: Seriously considered but never tried, this was a secret Russian plan to seize the *Bosphorus*, devised and proposed by Ambassador Alexander Nelidov in 1896.

Nelson, Horatio (1758-1805): British admiral. He lost an eye in one battle against the French, and an arm in another. He destroyed a French fleet heading for Egypt in 1798. For nine months in 1805 he pursued a French *invasion* fleet, to South America and back to Europe. He then destroyed it at *Trafalgar*, losing his life in the battle.

nemo judex in re sua: "No one [state] can judge [its] own cause." Legal maxim.

neo-colonialism: The idea that the former colonial powers exercise indirect control of their former possessions, either through economic domination or co-opting local *elites* (in *dependency theory*, the *comprador class*), and by occasional military *intervention*. A looser usage refers to skewed economic relations that either continue or reinforce the structural *dependency* of parts of the *Third World*. The term is used to portray unequal economic relations as a result of deliberate policy by the *North*, including those areas where traditional economic analysis views economic weakness in the *South* as deriving from local causes.

neo-imperialism: The domination of one *nation* by another by indirect control of its economic and political operations. For most analysts, this must be deliberate to be imperialistic; otherwise it is seen as a structural feature. Yet the more doctrinaire tend to see all unequal economic relationships as imperialistic, whatever their socioeconomic or historical origin.

neo-malthusian: Advocacy of control of *population* growth, usually by contraception or sterilization, based on dire projections of populations outstripping local and/or global resources. See *Indira Gandhi; Malthus*.

neo-mercantilism: (1) Modern belief in that aspect of *mercantilism* that sees shifts in *power* among *nations* as driven by a recurring cycle of ascendancy and decline of economic *hegemons*. (2) When *states* aggressively pursue a trade surplus, leading to trade deficits among their partners. Japan is frequently accused of this, but all major exporters practice it (or would like to) in key portions of their economy, especially automotives, steel, computer chips and *agriculture*. For example, see *CAP; MITI; voluntary export restraints*.

neo-nazism: Characteristic or celebratory of some or all the tenets of *nazism*, but subsequent to the destruction of *Nazi Germany*. It became a major social problem in Germany following reunification in 1989, where it fed off unemployment and anti-immigrant anger in the former *East Germany*, especially. This led to a deterioration of Germany's foreign image, and to strained relations with Turkey, after Turkish women and children were killed in fire-bomb attacks.

neo-realism: An approach that emphasizes the *structure* of the system as the determinant of *state* action, and views states as *maximizing, rational actors*. Perhaps its main accomplishment has been to focus on *international political economy* questions in a way that classical *realism* seldom did. However, it has been criticized for neglecting the social dimension and insights into human nature of classical realism, the moral and cooperative concerns of *liberal-internationalism*, and more radical views of the global economic system upheld by *dependency theory*. In general, it de-emphasizes the realm of free choice available to *statesmen* through a stress on the large-scale structures of international relations. At its worst, this approach tends to *determinism*. Also called "structural realism."

Nepal: Location: Major associations: *SARC, UN*. Population: 19.5 million. Military: minimal. A mountain-

ous kingdom dominated by the *Gurkhas* since the 18th century. Isolated in its mountain fastness, it forged an *alliance* with Britain in the 19th century, sending many Gurkha sons to fight and die in Britain's *wars*. From 1950-90 its traditional, absolute *monarchy* underwent some relaxation and reform. King Bir Bikram Shah Deva Birenda (b.1945), had steered a careful course of *nonalignment* in the *Cold War*. He does so now regarding Nepal's giant neighbors, India and China. In 1990 a move to multiparty democracy began. Parties were unbanned and elections held in 1991.

nerve agent/weapon: A *chemical agent*, often in gaseous form, that kills or immobilizes by attacking the nervous system of people or animals, resulting in paralysis, heart failure or seizures. Chemically related to pesticides, they are absorbed through the skin.

Nesselrode, Karl Robert (1780-1862): Russian statesman. Foreign Minister 1822-56; Chancellor 1845-62. He advised *Alexander I* at Paris in 1814, and played a lead role at the *Congress of Vienna*. He was not an adventurer. He sought to restrain *pan-Slavism* and ambitions to control the *Balkans*, conciliated Turkey, opposed the *Crimean War* and opposed further expansion into Asia (*Siberia* and *Manchuria*). But as a deep conservative he endorsed *Metternich's* system, approving repression of Poland (1831) and Hungary (1849).

Net Domestic Product (NDP): The *GDP* minus *depreciation* of *capital goods* used in production. See *NNP*.

Netherlands: A historic region of Western Europe, roughly corresponding to modern *Belgium, Luxembourg* and the modern *Kingdom of the Netherlands* (Holland). It was a *Hapsburg* possession until the Dutch revolted in 1579. See *Low Countries*.

Netherlands Antilles: An *overseas territory* of the Netherlands, consisting of two island groups in the West Indies. Population: 190,000.

Netherlands East Indies: A Dutch *colony*, now forming the core of Indonesia.

Netherlands Guiana: Former name of Suriname.

Netherlands, Kingdom of: Location: W. Europe. Major associations: *BENELUX, CSCE, EU, NATO, OECD, UN*. Population: 15 million. Military: small, but NATO capable. Two-thirds of Holland is land reclaimed from the sea over the centuries, leading to the saying: "God made the world, but the Dutch made Holland." These *Low Countries* were under the rule of the *Hapsburgs* in Spain for centuries. But during the

Reformation the Dutch provinces became a leading Protestant and maritime commercial center. In 1579 William the Silent, Prince of Orange (1533-84) led the Netherlands in revolt and to the formation of the Union of Utrecht, which repudiated the tie to Spain in 1581. The United Dutch Republic lasted until 1795, when *Napoleon* overran it and made his brother king. Holland was *annexed* by France in 1810, with the brother abdicating in the French emperor's favor. The *Congress of Vienna* sanctioned creation of the Kingdom of the Netherlands, which contained modern *Belgium* and *Luxembourg* as well. In 1830 the Belgians seceded; this was accepted in the *Treaty of London (1839)*. During the 18th and 19th centuries the Dutch constructed a significant overseas *empire*, mainly in *Southeast Asia*. Luxembourg became an independent Grand Duchy in 1890, when the male line in Holland failed and it was decided a woman could not succeed to the dukedom. Neutral in *WWI*, it escaped that holocaust. But *neutrality* in *WWII* did not prevent a German *invasion* and *occupation*. Some Dutch embraced *fascism*, joining as invited ethnic cousins and fellow "*Aryans*" in *Hitler's* "higher cause." Most bitterly resented the German occupation, and the Dutch *resistance* and public welcomed the *Allied* armies in 1944. A sentimental relationship with Canada dates from this period, both because the Dutch royal family took refuge there and due to the fact it was the Canadian First Army that did much of the fighting that *liberated* Holland in 1944/45. The Dutch fought against independence for *Indonesia* until 1949, and have faced occasional *terrorism* from South Moluccans. Otherwise, since *WWII* the Netherlands has enjoyed peace and great prosperity as a member of the BENELUX, NATO, and the *EC* (now the EU).

Netherlands New Guinea: Old name of *West Irian*.

Net National Product (NNP): The *GNP* minus *depreciation* costs of *capital goods* used in production. The reasoning behind this figure and the *NDP* is an effort to arrive at working assessments of what is available for consumption and production, after subtracting from the gross figures what is necessary just to maintain the productive capacity of the economy. Cf. *System of National Accounts (SNA)*.

Neuilly, Treaty of (November 27, 1919): Drafted at the *Paris Peace Conference*. Bulgaria was not treated as severely as the other *Central Powers* by this *treaty*, out of fear of creating a new unstable situation, and possibly *war*, in the *Balkans* such as preceded *WWI*. It lost minor *territories* to Greece, Rumania and Serbia, had to pay some *reparations*, and was limited to a *self-defense* force.

neutral: (1) Any state not a *belligerent* when a *war* is ongoing, or a member of an *alliance*. (2) States such as Cambodia, Ireland, Finland or Sweden that historically proclaimed they would not side with any military or political alliance. Cf. *Non-Aligned Movement*.

neutrality: (1) A permanent status and attitude proclaimed by a state, such as Switzerland, rejecting adherence to any *alliance*. (2) The status of any state not at *war*, implying an obligation to be impartial toward all *belligerents* and to restrain its own nationals from taking directly hostile acts.

Neutrality Acts (1935-40): A series of acts by which the U.S. Congress prohibited all loans or credits or sales of war matériel to all *belligerents,* no matter what the cause or *war*. Thus was rejected the moral premise of *collective security*, and indeed of prudential foreign policy, that said it was wise and proper to make distinctions between *aggressor* nations and their victims. As a result, the U.S. gave no *aid* to China in the opening years of the *Sino/Japanese War,* to Ethiopia in the *Abyssinian War* or to Republican Spain (which American Catholics opposed anyway) in the *Spanish Civil War*. In 1939 Congress partly lifted the ban to help Britain. But this had the unintended sideeffect of also helping Japan in its *aggression* against China. That was so because to avoid the *WWI* dilemma of American ships being sunk while carrying *goods* through *war zones*, Congress said foreign powers must collect the goods themselves. This the British and Japanese could do, but the Germans and Chinese could not. When Congress sought to correct its mistake by selective legislation aimed at denying war matériel to Japan (aircraft, steel and *oil*), Tokyo viewed these selective *embargoes* as hostile acts.

neutralization: (1) An agreement between *belligerent powers* to exclude a given *territory* from *war*, such as the Gulf waters in the *Iran/Iraq War*. (2) The involuntary assumption of *neutrality* by a state, imposed by outside powers. For example, Belgium (1831), Congo (1885), Laos (1962) and Switzerland (1815).

neutral rights and duties: The concept of rights and obligations of neutral *states* in time of *war* evolved as a set of practical and legal *norms*, laid out in several *conventions* in the 19th and early 20th centuries. However, in *WWI* these finely defined legal rights were severely eroded, while before and during *WWII* they were nearly totally ignored (mainly by the *Axis* states). They were respected only toward the larger neutrals (such as the U.S.), and then only as a prudential matter when such a powerful neutral insisted on its legal rights and backed its claims with *force*. The 1945 creation of *UN Charter* obligations to assist resistance to *aggression* has qualified the conception of neutral rights in theory, but less so in practice. What are these rights and duties? (1) In all respects: by the rules of the *Treaty of Washington* (1871), the *Hague Conventions* (1907) and other such agreements, neutrals must exercise "due diligence" and exercise all "means at their disposal" to ensure their *territory* is not used by *agents* of *belligerents* or their own *citizens* to wage war or otherwise directly aid *combatants* (say by gathering *intelligence*). Neutral governments may not sell or export *arms* to belligerents. Note, however, that the sale of arms or other supplies by private persons is not prohibited. Legal *blockades* must be respected, whether enforced on land or at sea (there is no such thing as an aerial blockade, at least in law). But neutrals retain the right to use force to defend their just neutral claims, without this being taken as an act of war or declaration of belligerency. (2) On land: Neutral territory is held to be inviolable. Recruitment of neutral nationals is forbidden to belligerents, though individuals may travel abroad and then enlist. If soldiers or citizens (other than diplomats, the sick or wounded) of belligerents arrive on neutral soil, the neutral is obliged to *intern* them. (3) At sea: *Territorial waters* are also inviolable. Neutrals may prohibit belligerent *warships*, should they so choose, from their waters and/or their ports. Yet *innocent passage* may be permitted. However, warships may not abuse neutral waters to seek refuge from combat or *capture*. The U.S. added the proviso before WWII that all belligerent *submarines* were barred, except in cases of *force majeure,* when they were required to travel surfaced. Nor may enemy vessels transfer to a neutral registry or flag. Otherwise, at sea the laws of blockade are the main guideposts to neutral rights. (4) In the air: A convention drafted in 1923 has never received sufficient *ratifications* to enter into effect. Nonetheless, certain customary rules apply that parallel land and sea warfare: neutral airspace is inviolable, crews and aircraft must be interned and so on. See also *Armed Neutrality; Belgium; Bosnia; Burma; Cambodia; Continental System; contraband; embargo; Laos; Lusitania notes; navicert system; Panama Declaration; ultimate destination; Sweden; Switzerland; undeclared submarine warfare; Quasi War; War of 1812.*

neutral zone: A *buffer* area between two states that has been *demilitarized* by *treaty.* For example: (1) Iraq/Saudi Arabia: It was created by the Treaty of Mohammura in 1922, confirmed in 1938, but was divided by agreement in 1975. (2) Kuwait/Saudi Arabia: Set up in 1922 and confirmed in 1963, the zone was *partitioned* in 1966, but not annulled. The Kuwaiti half was occupied by Iraq during the *Gulf War.*

neutron bomb: An "enhanced radiation weapon" that destroys life by releasing a massive shower of neutrons and other radiation, but with reduced *blast effects.* It was designed by *NATO* for battlefield use. After the destruction of large military formations (say a *Warsaw Pact* tank division advancing into Germany), one's own troops could use the bombed area without suffering radiation poisoning, and *collateral damage* to *civilian* areas would be reduced. If used on cities it would kill the people but leave property intact. This feature led some critics to portray it as inherently evil, more so than other types of *nuclear weapons.* That reaction baffled those who pointed out that a "normal" nuclear weapon would both kill people and destroy their homes, as well as render the surrounding land poisoned and uninhabitable for years. Faced with aroused public opposition, particularly in Western Europe, the *Carter* administration backed away from production or deployment in 1978. That damaged the U.S. reputation for leadership within NATO and hurt *Helmut Schmidt* politically (he had expended a great deal of *political capital* supporting the project). Meanwhile the Soviets very effectively (in *propaganda* terms) dubbed it the "perfect capitalist weapon."

New Caledonia ("Kanaky"): Location: *South Pacific.* Acquired by France in 1853, it comprises the large island of that name and its *dependencies*: Loyalty Islands, Isle of Pines, Huon Islands and the Chesterfield Islands. It was used as a penal *colony* from 1864-96. The Kanaks revolted in 1878 and again in 1917. It was occupied by the U.S. 1943-45, then returned to France. After it rejected *independence* in a 1958 *referendum,* where non-Kanaks swayed the vote, it became an *overseas territory* of France. It is an important repository of minerals, in particular nickel. Relations between French workers and settlers and the Kanak population were hostile in the 1980s. In 1988 some devolution of power was agreed to, and a referendum on *self-determination* set for 1998. It is a member of the *SPC.* Some *SPF* members support Kanak observer status; Kanak parties are shadow members of the *Spearhead Group.* In 1986 the *UNGA* reinscribed New Caledonia on its list of *trusteeship territories.*

New Economic Policy (NEP): Limited, market-style reforms introduced by *Lenin* in March 1921, to alleviate the distress and dislocations caused by the *Russian Civil War,* famine and *war communism.* It lasted until the first *five-year plan* in 1929. By opening internal trade and reducing the role of bureaucratic middlemen it eased the food shortage, but it did not reverse the centralized control of the economy inaugurated by the *Bolsheviks.* In the 1980s *Mikhail Gorbachev* claimed to be returning to Lenin's NEP example with his *perestroika* reforms. Perhaps that was the very reason they failed.

Newfoundland: England's first *colony* in the Americas, established to exploit the rich fish grounds of the Grand Banks. It was secured by Britain in the *Treaty of Utrecht* (1713). Its native population was hunted down and exterminated, after which mainly Scots and Irish settlers eked out an isolated existence from coastal fisheries, far from the mainstream of North American development. In the 19th century it evolved local *autonomy*. It lost that status in 1934, after a total economic collapse. It fought in *WWI* and *WWII* within the British Empire forces, taking heavy losses. After a close *referendum*, it joined Canada in 1949.

New France: The French *colonies*, possessions and claims in North America. Acadia (Nova Scotia) and Hudson's Bay were lost to England in the *Treaty of Utrecht* (1713); *Québec* was captured during the *Seven Years' War*, its loss to the British confirmed in the *Peace of Paris* (1763). The *Louisiana Territory* was surrendered to the Spanish (also in 1763).

New Granada: A Spanish composite *colony*, comprising present-day Colombia, Ecuador, Panama and Venezuela.

New Guinea: The large South Pacific island divided between *Irian Jaya* and *Papua New Guinea*.

New Hebrides: A Pacific group that from 1906-80 was an Anglo/French *condominium*. See *Vanuatu*.

Ne Win (b.1911): Burmese dictator 1962-88. He was Chief of Staff in the army of *Aung San*, and thus he too fought against the British from 1943-45, and with them against the Japanese in 1945. After a *coup* in 1962 he expelled all foreigners (destroying the economy in the process) and imposed a rigid *autarky* on Burma. He was forced out in 1988 following massive street demonstrations. His colleagues restored military control, but did not return him to power.

New International Economic Order (NIEO): A *G-77* campaign to effectively replace the extant world economy with centrally managed policies on a global scale, taking much greater account of questions of *distributive justice* than of market forces. Supporting reforms included demands for guaranteed prices and markets for *commodities*, heavy regulation of *MNCs*, *technology transfers*, alterations to *IMF* and *IBRD* voting rules and expanded *LDC* access to private *capital* funds. The program never really extended beyond *resolutions* in the *UNGA* and *UNCTAD*, although marginal chang-

es were made to the lending policies of the IBRD and IMF. There followed a decade of rhetorical confrontation amidst a crisis of deepening *debt*. By the mid-1980s the *debt crisis* led to a new pragmatism about mutual interests between the G-77 and the *OECD*.

newly independent states (NIS): A term that by self-definition is destined to a short shelf-life: it refers to all the *republics* formed out of the former *Soviet Union*, not just those that joined the *CIS*.

newly industrialized countries (NICs): Those with economies previously at *LDC* levels of output, but now achieving or approaching *OECD* levels of production and wealth, through *export-led growth*. See Brazil, Mexico, Portugal and the *Asian Tigers*.

newly industrialized economies (NIEs): A synonym for *newly industrialized countries*.

New Order: *Hitler's* nightmare vision of a racially "purified" social and political order in Europe, and perhaps the world, centering on an ascendant *Third Reich* and its *Aryan* allies. This idea fed directly into plans for *conquest*, especially of Russia, and into the *Holocaust*. See *nazism*.

New Orleans, Battle of (January 8, 1815): Due to a delay in news crossing the Atlantic of the *peace treaty* signed at *Ghent*, this needless battle (in which American troops defended against and routed a large British force), was fought after the formal end of the *War of 1812*. Its main effects were to inspire a nationalist legend and aim *Andrew Jackson*, commander of the Americans, at the presidency.

New People's Army (NPA): Filipino communist *guerrillas* who took up the old fight of the *Huks* in the 1970s, gaining support from the peasantry due to the slow pace of land reform, especially on the island of Mindanao, and the repression of the *Marcos* regime. By the late 1980s their resistance was faltering, undercut in part by the reformist government of *Corazon Aquino*. By 1993 it had largely ended, leaving only a desultory Muslim *insurgency* against the government.

new protectionism: The rise of *non-tariff barriers* against more efficient foreign competition, including *anti-dumping laws, voluntary restraint agreements (VERs), quotas, procurement policy*, and odd customs and environmental standards. These challenge *GATT*, as they are not easily regulated and their impact is harder to assess. Still, some rules against them were added to the *Uruguay Round*. The multiplication of such practices is a backhanded compliment to the success of GATT, and of regional *free trade areas*, in reducing *tariff* barriers to *free trade*.

New Spain: The Spanish possessions in the Western hemisphere, at their imperial height stretching from Mexico (including Arizona, *California*, the Floridas, New Mexico and Texas), through Central America to *New Granada*. It included most of South America except Brazil (which was Portuguese). It existed in some form or other from 1492-1898, though it was severely truncated by Latin *independence* after c.1821.

New World: The *Americas* as a whole, not just the U.S. The term connoted to Europeans images of easy riches, vast space and vaster opportunity, and fresh starts in culture, industry and politics. For Americans, the unlimited bounty of their continent fed a quasi-religious sense of serving as a "New Eden," where Providence had supposedly set them to perfect a redemptive, national *mission*. For the political consequences of this essentially cultural/religious phenomenon, see *manifest destiny*. Cf. *Old World*.

New World Information and Communication Order (NWICO): A *Third World* proposal made within *UNESCO* in the mid-1970s. It aimed at international regulation of news gathering and reporting to correct a putative bias toward Western interests and perspectives. Its declared intent to license journalists meant that for most Western countries the NWICO arrived stillborn. It shows no more sign of life in the post-*Cold War* world, when Western notions of freedom of information are ascendant, and are seen to have economic utility, than it did in the ideologically contentious 1970s-1980s.

new world order: (1) A cliché phrase, usually used after some tidal shift in *world politics*, to indicate that fundamental modifications in the *balance of power* and other *international security* and economic matters are underway. (2) A term used by *George Bush* to describe the changes in world politics after the collapse of the *Soviet bloc*. It hinted at reinforcement of *liberal* economic, political and security norms already extant in the *international system*. As yet, it has no consensual or tangible meaning.

New Zealand: Location: *Australasia*. Major associations: *Commonwealth, OECD, SPC, SPF, UN*. Population: 3.4 million. Military: small defense force; well-equipped and trained. Originally settled by the *Maori* from Polynesia, the first European to chart these islands was Capt. James Cook (1729-79), who explored from 1769-70. British settlers arrived from the 1820s-1840s, and were granted *autonomy* in 1853-56. In

1843 and again from 1860-70, the *Maori Wars* were fought, ending with British domination. *Federation* with Australia was considered, and rejected in 1901. In 1907 it became a *Dominion* within the Commonwealth. It was automatically a belligerent in *WWI*, with the British *declaration of war*. Although the *Statute of Westminster* applied also to New Zealand, full *independence* did not come until 1947. In *WWII* it again fought on the British side, but the threat from Japan woke it from its colonial doldrums and brought home the reality that it is an Asian power rather than a European outpost. Since WWII it has become more committed to the Pacific: it switched from the British to the American security umbrella by joining *ANZUS* and *SEATO*, and sent troops to fight in both the *Korean Conflict* and the *Vietnam War*. Since the 1970s it has tended to see its Pacific interests as less than compatible with *Great Power* involvement in the region. It has objected to American, British and French nuclear tests (with a serious breech occurring over French *covert action* in the *Rainbow Warrior incident*). This change reflects its *location*, large Polynesian minority, and more open *immigration* policy. It maintains commitments to the *Cook Islands*, *Niue* and *Tokelau*, which it has administered since 1925. Lastly, it administers the Ross Dependency in the *Antarctic*. From 1975 it pushed for the South Pacific *nuclear weapons free zone (NWFZ)*. The next year, it began a major reorientation of its defense and foreign policy toward the South Pacific, confirming this in a 1987 defense "White Paper." It lent *good offices* (and a *warship*) to Papua New Guinea to assist in negotiating a *cease-fire* in the *Bougainville insurgency*. In 1980 it backed a "Regional Trade and Economic Cooperation Agreement." Under David Lange (b.1942), PM 1984-89, its assertive non-nuclear policy pleased domestic and regional opinion, but saw conflict with France, the end of *ANZUS* and a downgrading of New Zealand's relations with the U.S. In 1990 it set up a regional export assistance program. More than 2/3rds of its *foreign aid* goes to the region. The U.S. resumed high-level political talks with New Zealand on regional affairs in 1994. New Zealand also has differences with Japan on fishing and *whaling* policy.

New Zealand/Australia Free Trade Agreement (NAFTA): Agreed to in 1965, it began a slow process of *tariff* reduction between these South Pacific neighbors. In 1982 a deeper and more comprehensive "Closer Economic Relations (CER)" agreement was reached, which has progressively moved the pair closer to genuine *free trade*.

Ney, Michel (1769-1815): Marshal of France. Perhaps *Napoleon's* greatest marshal, he retained his titles by serving the *Restoration*, 1814-15. During the *Hundred Days* he promised *Louis XVIII* to bring Napoleon to Paris "in an iron cage," but his troops embraced their old emperor, and Ney--"loyal and neutral in a moment" (Macbeth, II, iii)--joined them. After *Waterloo* his renewed avowals of hidden royalism were dismissed, and he was quickly executed.

Nicaragua: Location: Central America. Major associations: *OAS, UN*. Population: 3.7 million. Military: downsized from 100,000 to 15,000 by mid-1993. Conquered by Spain in 1522, it did not gain *independence* until 1821. Briefly attached to Mexico, and then part of an ill-fated attempt at Central American *federation*, it was fully separate by 1838. Nicaragua conquered the coastal Mosquito Indians in the 1890s. U.S. *intervention* began in 1909, with overthrow of the dictator José Zelaya. For 10 years he waged petty wars against neighboring Honduras and El Salvador, after which he made the mistake of threatening U.S. interests. An attempt was made to regulate Nicaraguan customs, but the U.S. Senate rejected the idea. In 1912 U.S. marines quelled a new uprising, and 100 were stationed there to discourage *rebellions*. The marines were pulled out in 1925, but returned almost immediately as another *revolution* broke out. They left again in 1933 with the *Good Neighbor Policy*. Nicaragua was ruled by the family of dictators headed by *Anastasio Somoza* from 1936-56, and by his two sons from 1957-79. After 1961 peasant and left-wing *guerrilla* movements organized into the Frenté Sandinista de Liberacíon Nacional (FSLN). The rebels overthrew the Somoza family in 1979. They then split into a faction that favored a constitutional democracy, and a *marxist* faction led by *Daniel Ortega* which soon took control. At first the revolution was greatly popular, and its land reform program won the *Sandinistas* permanent allies among the peasantry. But the middle classes grew increasingly alienated, with many fleeing to Mexico or Miami where they lobbied the U.S. for *intervention*. The *Reagan* administration supplied and sustained an *insurgency* by *Contra* guerrillas, mined Nicaragua's ports in 1984 and placed an *embargo* on trade, loans and credits. With the end of Soviet *aid* what was left of the economy collapsed in 1988, and Ortega agreed to hold free and fair, internationally supervised elections in 1990. They took place in the shadow of the U.S. *invasion* of Panama. The Sandinistas lost, but retained a respectable share of the vote. That helped them negotiate a *power sharing* coalition with President Violetto Chamoro in which they retained control of the police and army. The Contras and excess Sandinista troops were *demobilized*, and U.S. *aid* resumed. However, in 1993 guerrilla attacks began from small groups of former Contras and Sandinistas, sometimes

in opposition to each other and sometimes in concert, to protest the failure of a promise to provide land in exchange for laying down arms. Also, elements within the U.S. Congress spoke of cutting off all aid as long as even one Sandinista remained in the government. See also *Iran/Contra; Reagan Doctrine*.

Nicholas I (1796-1855): Tsar of Russia 1825-55. He was a harsh *reactionary* and *anti-Semite* who repressed the *Decembrists*, closed Russia to foreign influence, opposed mass education, crushed revolts in Poland (1831) and Hungary (1849), and enforced brutal domestic *ukase*, especially against the Jews. He pressured Turkey into *war* in 1853, leading to the disaster for Russia of the *Crimean War* with Britain and France, during which he died in his bed.

Nicholas II (1868-1918): Tsar of Russia 1894-1917. A weak and indecisive leader, subject to the influence of mystics such as his wife and *Rasputin*. He called the first *Hague Conference* in 1899 to try to end an *arms race* Russia could not afford. His regime was shaken by the loss of the *Russo/Japanese War*, after which he waved at reform in public while privately supporting arch-*reactionary* and *anti-Semitic* groups. He moved Russia into *tacit alliance* with France and Britain after 1907, and secretly patched relations with Japan over *Manchuria*. He took personal command of the Russian armies in 1915, and so was blamed for the *defeats* of 1916. He abdicated after the *February (March Revolution)* in 1917. His entire family, including several small children, was executed by the *Bolsheviks* in July 1918. In 1992 it was revealed from *KGB* files that the order for that atrocity came directly from *Lenin*, a fact denied for 74 years. The bodies were exhumed from an unmarked grave and forensically identified in 1993.

NIEO: See *New International Economic Order.*

Nietzche, Friedrich (1844-1900): German philosopher. Among other ideas, he developed the idea of a revolutionary *elite* led by the "superman" (Übermensch), a perfectly free creature unencumbered by conventional political morality. Some have traced certain notions in *nazism* and *fascism* to his writings. He went completely insane in later life.

Niger: Location: W. Africa. Major associations: *ECOWAS, OAU, UN*. Population: 8 million. Military: minor. This impoverished desert region became a French *colony* at the turn of the 20th century. While the *Hausa* and *Fulani* population was subjugated, intermittent fighting continued against fierce Tuareg nomads into the 1920s. It was made part of *French West Africa* in 1922, it was given *autonomy* within the

French Community in 1958, and outright *independence* in 1960. It has maintained a quiet existence, staying out of wars in neighboring Nigeria and Chad. There was a peaceful election in 1993.

Nigeria: Location: West Africa. Major associations: *ECOWAS, OAU, OPEC, UN*. Population: 100 million. Military: large, well-equipped, but subject to internecine quarrels and prone to *coups*. Ancient enmities dot Nigeria's history. For centuries *Yoruba* kingdoms in the southwest warred among themselves, feeding the transatlantic *slave trade* out of the *Slave Coast* with their captives. To the north lay the great *Fulani* empire. The Fulani conquered the *Hausa* and other northern tribes by the 19th century when their southward expansion was stopped by the tse-tse fly that bore sleeping sickness to their *cavalry*, and the British, whose own imperial bite was even more lethal to Fulani ambitions. After 1900 the British proclaimed two Nigerian *protectorates*, one in the south under *direct rule* and one in the north where they used the local *sultan* and *emirs* to run a system of *indirect rule*. These were fused in 1914 to form Nigeria. Nigerians served in the British army in both world wars. After *WWII* the demand for *independence* grew apace with the global *decolonization* movement. In 1960 Nigeria became independent, and in 1963 a *republic* divided into three regions. Part of *Cameroon* joined in 1961. Tension between the major *tribes* (Hausa/Fulani, Yoruba and *Ibo*) was only exacerbated by rising oil revenues, with the oil concentrated in the Ibo southeast. In 1967 the Southeast region seceded, sparking the *Nigerian Civil War*. Under Yakubu Gowon (b.1934), President 1966-74, the nation managed to reconcile and avoid a feared bloodbath after the *Biafran* capitulation. With peace in 1970, Nigeria entered a boom decade, cashing in on the OPEC oil price rises. But it spent its billions unwisely, and saw corruption rise to staggering levels. A series of military coups ended in 1979 with an attempt to return to *civilian* rule. However, the civilian government of Shehu Shagari (b.1925) proved even more corrupt, and another coup displaced it in 1983. In 1985 yet another coup brought General Ibrahim Babangida (b.1941) to power. He provided some *stability* and redressed some of the country's economic problems by adhering to the spirit (though he refused the letter) of a *stabilization program* designed by the *IMF*. After several cancellations, elections were held in June 1993. Then Babangida indulged a flair for opéra bouffe: he canceled the results and called new elections while banning the old candidates, and all in spite of the fact international observers said the original elections were free and fair. A non-elected, civilian government eventually took charge, followed by yet another coup. Nigeria thus continues to stagger

from political instability, which reduces its ability to play the conservative, foreign policy role of "Africa's natural leader" that it sees for itself. Still, it *mediated* a long-standing conflict in Chad, took the lead in regional *intervention* in the war in Liberia 1990- , and joined the UN effort in Somalia in 1993.

Nigerian Civil War (1967-70): In 1966 and 1967 there occurred a series of massacres of *Ibos* working in the north of Nigeria, by Muslims from the *Hausa* and *Fulani* tribes. Ibos fled back to the SE region, which was dominated by their *tribe* and contained most of Nigeria's known *oil* reserves. When the SE region seceded (May 30, 1967) under the name Biafra, *civil war* broke out. After a brief Biafran offensive, the superior manpower and resources of the Federal forces led to a grinding war of *attrition*, in which Biafra was *blockaded* and slowly compressed. When the world was confronted with pictures of starving Biafran children in a shrinking *enclave*, the response was mixed. Most African states supported the Federal side, with only four members of the *OAU* recognizing Biafra, and that mainly in a last-minute attempt to save lives. France gave minimal support to Biafra out of flirtation with the idea of dividing Nigeria, which was larger than all the French nations in West Africa combined. The U.S. and the Soviet Union did not get involved, insulating the war from the *Cold War* and leaving the decisive role to the old colonial power, Britain. The UK fully supported the Federal side diplomatically, and with financial and military *aid* and sales. Private aid agencies and some *mercenary* forces came to Biafra's assistance. A highly successful *propaganda* campaign suggested that a war of *genocide* was being waged against the Ibo, generating public protests in many Western countries. The war dragged on until 1970, pushing even Vietnam off the TV screens on a few nights, but mostly it was waged outside the mainstream of world affairs. In the end, the Ibo were hemmed into a pocket around their capital, Enugu. When it too gave way, hostilities ended abruptly. One million had died, mostly by starvation. To Nigeria's lasting credit there was a generous *peace*, and the Ibos were more or less reintegrated into Nigerian society. Even the Biafran leader, Colonel *Ojukwu*, was pardoned and allowed to return in 1982.

Night of the Long Knives (June 30-July 2, 1934): A weekend of killing without even the pretense of legality, when *Hitler* purged Ernst Roehm and the *SA*, using *Himmler's* new and more sinister *SS* to do the deeds of murder. Its purpose was to placate the army, which was worried that the SA sought to displace it, and thereby to clear the way to Hitler's assumption of the presidency. Within months he became commander-in-chief besides being Chancellor. Several hundred were killed (the exact figure is unknown). Hitler personally gave the bloody night its name. While it shocked many in the West it was well-received in Germany, where the SA was despised. Also, *Stalin* reportedly admired its verve and decisiveness.

Nine Power Treaty (1922): Negotiated at the *Washington Conference,* it internationalized the principle of the *Open Door,* at least concerning China. It was signed by all powers with significant Asian interests, to wit: Britain, Belgium, China, France, Italy, Japan, the Netherlands, Portugal and the U.S. It also guaranteed China's administrative and *territorial integrity,* formally slapping down Japan's *Twenty-One Demands.* The *treaty* tried to make long-standing American principles binding on all major Asian powers (except the Soviet Union). But in 1937, when a conference was called to discuss Japan's attack on China, the Japanese contemptuously stayed away and the conclave solved nothing.

Nitze, Paul (b.1907): He was not influential in the early stages of the *Cold War,* but then he succeeded *George Kennan* as head of the *State Department's* Policy Planning Staff. His major impact was felt through *NSC-68.* Subsequently, he remained a powerful, anti-Soviet voice within the inner circles of U.S. policy. He was one of the so-called *Wise Men.*

Niue: Location: S. Pacific. Major associations: *SPC, SPF.* Note: Niue is not a *UN* or *Commonwealth* member; nor is it recognized by Japan as fully independent. Population: 52,000. Military: none. Formerly called "Savage Island." A British *protectorate* from 1900, this *microstate* was annexed to the *Cook Islands* by New Zealand in 1901. Since 1974 it has been *autonomous* in *free association* with New Zealand; its people are also New Zealand *citizens* (three times as many Niueans live in New Zealand as in Niue).

Nixon, Richard Milhous (1913-94): U.S. statesman. VP 1953-61; President 1969-74. Along with *Henry Kissinger,* his immediate aim upon taking office was to wind down the *Vietnam War.* By that he hoped to reorient *containment* policy back to its original focus on blocking Soviet advances into the industrial centers of Asia and Europe, with primary reliance on political pressure and economic inducements rather than military force. Despite his long career as an anti-communist he did not view foreign policy through an ideological prism. He took a *realpolitik* approach, assessing and weighing relative power and actual intentions. Yet he believed he could end the war in Indochina without losing it, through a policy of *Vietnamization* to take place simultaneously with a phased U.S. with-

drawal. He understood that he needed cooperation on this from China and the Soviet Union, the only states capable of bringing sufficient pressure to bear on the North Vietnamese to get them to cooperate in allowing an American pullout. Therefore, he developed *détente* with the Soviets after 1970 and made his extraordinary breakthrough trip to China in 1972. He kept up the pressure on Vietnam by invading Laos and Cambodia in an effort to cut the *Ho Chi Minh trail,* actions for which he has been severely criticized. He also authorized several rounds of bombing of northern cities, including a so-called "Christmas bombing" in 1972 which he claimed forced Vietnam back to the peace table in Paris. Yet détente was not merely designed to end the war. It aimed as well at a lasting reduction in *tensions* with Moscow, *arms control* and a limit to Soviet *adventurism* when it came to regional conflicts. It also sought to appease West European (and especially West German) demands for a partial *rapprochement* with the East bloc. He was a strong supporter of Israel, yet played hardball with Tel Aviv (and Moscow) in the *Fourth Arab/Israeli War* when the Soviets threatened to *intervene* directly to support their Egyptian *ally.* He also supported *Reza Pahlavi,* viewing the Shah's Iran as an island of *stability* for the Middle East. On economic policy, he shifted from *keynesian* social spending toward fighting *inflation,* and then *stagflation,* and took the U.S. off the *gold standard.* His second term was hamstrung and then destroyed by the *Watergate scandal.* He was the only president to resign (on August 9, 1974). See *Jackson/Vanik; Nixon Doctrine; Nixon shocks; SALT I; Sino/Soviet split.*

Nixon Doctrine: A retrenchment from global security commitments, brought about by the *Vietnam War* and *Richard Nixon's* sense that the globalization and militarization of *containment* policy had taken U.S. diplomacy off course. The doctrine established that the U.S. henceforth would support those fighting local *communist* movements, but would not itself become directly involved in the fighting, and by implication, was prepared to let some minor countries fall to the other side in the *Cold War.* It thus rejected the *domino theory* and sought to refocus on the *strategic* regions of Europe and Asia, and to return containment to reliance on America's great advantages in economic and political *linkage,* rather than brute military force.

Nixon shocks (August 15, 1971): In the spring of 1971 there was a run on the dollar and the U.S. first showed a trade deficit. Gold stocks were in decline, and *stagflation* was developing. *Nixon* suddenly announced, without consulting major allies, a new economic policy that radically transformed the international monetary system. He took the U.S. off the *gold* *standard*, and imposed a 10% surcharge on imported goods. Thus ended the *Bretton Woods* era.

Nkrumah, Kwame (1909-72): *Gold Coast* PM, 1957-60; President of *Ghana,* 1960-66. He was the best known African statesman of his time, championing *pan-Africanism* and *decolonization.* However, in his actual policies he distrusted the surrounding *francophone* African nations and resented other African *statesmen* as rivals to his own, pan-African leadership. Domestically, his regime disintegrated under a weight of corruption and inefficiency that seemed to grow in direct proportion to Nkrumah's megalomania (a phenomenon masterfully portrayed in Ayi Kwei Armah's novel "The Beautiful Ones Are Not Yet Born"). Nkrumah was overthrown in 1966, while visiting Hanoi. He died in a Rumanian sanatorium. See also *OAU.*

NKVD (*Narodnii Kommissariat Vnutrennikh Del***):** "People's Commissariat of Internal Affairs." The Soviet *secret police* from 1935-53, including during the *Yezhovshchina.* Previously, it was the *CHEKA* and the *OGPU.* Subsequently, it was renamed the *KGB.* It was responsible for millions of deaths among the *kulaks* during forced *collectivization.* See *Beria; Stalin.*

Nobel Prizes: Prestigious awards given annually from the funds generated by the estate of Alfred Nobel (1833-96), a Swedish *munitions* manufacturer who became fascinated by controlled explosions while working in his father's nitro-glycerine factory. He made his money from inventing and selling dynamite, blasting jellies and smokeless gunpowder. He left a large share of his estate to fund annual prizes in chemistry, literature, medicine, *peace* and physics. In 1969 a memorial prize was added for *economics.* In recent decades the "Nobel Prize for Peace" has been given on a broadened definition of peace, to include humanitarian and *human rights* work as well as attempts to resolve internecine or interstate conflicts.

no-fly zone: A ban on military, or even all, flights in a given area, enforced by *multilateral* action. Southern and northern Iraq were so designated in 1991 to prevent *Saddam Hussein* from attacking *shi'ites* and *Kurds*, respectively. Bosnia was declared a no-fly zone by the *Security Council* in October 1992, to prevent the resupply of Serb *militia. NATO* was selected to enforce the zone, its first-ever combat duty.

no-man's-land: From *WWI,* a term denoting the space between the trenches on the *western front* that neither side controlled, but both sides patrolled. Pock-marked with thousands of shell holes and marked out by barbed-wire borders, it was regarded by troops of all

armies with fear and loathing. It was the place of greatest exposure to enemy fire once troops went "over the top" of the trenches, and the site of awful suffering and death.

nomenklatura: Originally, the 5,500 top *Communist Party* officials in the Soviet Union whose appointment was controlled by the party's central organs. That increasingly meant they were beholden to *Stalin,* who used his administrative power to take control of the party from 1924-29. The most powerful were regional party secretaries who controlled lower levels of the *apparat,* upon which the center depended to implement its policies. Later the term came to include all highly placed and privileged members of the bureaucracy, party and military in *Soviet bloc* countries.

nonaggression pact: A *treaty* between or among states declaring that no signatory will attack another. In any given case its utility and reliability are dependent on *good faith.* Some pacts outline *spheres of influence* agreements; others are close synonyms to *friendship treaties.* See *Nazi/Soviet Pact*

Non-Aligned Movement (NAM): A mainly, though not exclusively, *Third World* movement started at *Bandung* in 1955. Its major themes were anti-*colonialism,* opposition to *racism* and formal *neutrality* toward the *Cold War.* It brought together *states* that wanted to raise economic and social issues onto the agenda of *international organizations,* where larger powers were otherwise preoccupied with security concerns. Thus, it promoted the *NIEO* in the 1970s. It suffered a chronic lack of unity born of the following factors: (1) Some of its members were clearly supporters of either the U.S. or Soviet camp (e.g., the Philippines and Cuba), and acted as Trojan horses for the varying agendas of the *superpowers.* (2) Differences in levels of *development, ideology* and regional animosities among members were too great for NAM to present a genuinely united negotiating front. (3) The rise of *OPEC* and the southern *NICs* exacerbated these differences and divided the movement over the issue of *oil* prices and commodity *cartels.* In the early 1990s, with the original purpose of NAM fading into irrelevance and regional animosities resurfacing, the movement appeared adrift.

nonalignment: A diplomatic stance of not taking sides in a protracted *conflict* between two formal *alliances;* from the practice of the *Non-Aligned Movement.* Cf. *alignment; neutrality.*

nonbelligerency: Legal *neutrality* toward a given *war,* whether this sentiment is real or feigned in practice. It is almost more a political than a legal term.

noncombatants: In *international law* and in *just war theory:* (1) *neutral* states; (2) *civilians.*

noncommissioned officer (NCO): An enlisted person ranked above *private*, but not holding a commission (a certificate of presidential or other formal authority); to wit: all *military ranks* of corporal and sergeant.

noncompliance: Failure to observe *treaty* obligations, *Security Council* resolutions and other legal duties.

nonconcessional loans: See *hard loans.*

noncontraband: *Goods* without military utility (such as vaccine) destined for an enemy port, that may not be seized under the law of *blockade.* Cf. *contraband.*

nondiscrimination: See *most-favored-nation.*

nongovernmental organization (NGO): Any private organization involved in activities that have *transnational* implications. Cf. *INGO; non-state actor.*

noninterference: (1) Respect for *sovereign* rights and *independence* of another *state*, in deed as well as word, particularly when a *Great Power* so respects the cultural, economic, legal, political and *territorial* rights of a smaller power. (2) A term oftimes used as a euphemism for refusing to become involved in a foreign *dispute*, such as over respect for *human rights*, a *civil war* or an interstate *war* that remains localized. A near synonym is *nonintervention.* See *Brezhnev Doctrine; Congress system; Good Neighbor policy; Kuranari Doctrine; Monroe Doctrine.* Cf. *nonintervention.*

nonintervention: The legal obligation to abjure involvement in the domestic *jurisdiction* of other states. It was developed in the *Peace of Westphalia*, where it served to preserve religious independence from either meddling neighbors or the universal claims of popes and holy roman emperors. The *French Revolution* set up a challenge by endorsing competing views of political *legitimacy* (*republicanism* vs. *monarchism* and *absolutism*) that contended in the 19th century. In the 20th, the principle was eroded by the rise of democracies to global prominence. Concerning *human rights*, claims that such-and-such a practice falls under the protection of *internal affairs* are now routinely rejected on such *basic rights* as freedom from *torture*, though respected on issues that remain (arguably) a matter of culture or faith. Cf. *noninterference.*

nonjusticiable disputes: Those disputes unamenable to settlement by reference to *international law*; a synonym for *political disputes.* Cf. *justiciable.*

non liquet: When the absence of clear *rules* makes it impossible to reach judgment based on the law.

non-person: A state of political and social limbo in the post-*stalinist* Soviet Union, in which purged party members were not killed but disappeared from mention in the Soviet media (and sometimes were erased from photographs). Among others, this happened to *Khrushchev* and *Malenkov.* Even *Stalin* disappeared from official view for two decades, but only postumously, which is not the same thing.

nonproliferation: Curbs on the spread of weapons systems. See *arms control; IAEA; Nuclear Non-Proliferation Treaty.* Cf. *proliferation.*

nonrecognition: See *recognition.*

nonresident ambassador: A *diplomat* accredited to more than one foreign *nation*, but who can be resident only in one and therefore travels back and forth to the others. States are increasingly turning to this mechanism as a cost-cutting measure in regions where their interests or resources are not deemed sufficient to warrant individual representatives in each country. Some states also have begun to trade information and expertise. For example, Australia and Canada have agreements to swap information on Asia and Europe, respectively, where each regards the other as better informed and with more dedicated resources.

non-state actor: Any player in international politics that is not a government, or an organization created by and serving governments, including *nongovernmental organizations* and *multinational corporations.*

non-tariff barriers: Any mechanism used to protect domestic markets and producers by limiting imports through means other than *excise.* They include: *licensing; quotas; voluntary restraint agreements*; procurement policy that insists on domestic-only goods; and purposeful obscurity in customs, regulatory or environmental standards.

non-zero-sum game: See *variable sum game.*

Nordic Council: An association formed in 1952, aiming at a *free trade area* in *Scandinavia.* With the creation of the *European Free Trade Association*, and application by Denmark and Norway to join the *EC*, it evolved into a mainly cultural association. Its members: Denmark, Finland, Iceland, Norway and Sweden.

norm: (1) An accepted and expected rule of interstate conduct, which may underwrite the workings of certain international *regimes.* (2) A moral principle. (3) In *international law*: see *jus cogens.* See also *ethics.*

normalize relations: To restore formal, if not amicable, *diplomatic relations* after a period of elevated *tensions* over a *dispute,* a *crisis* or following a *war.*

normative: Relating to, or derivative from, moral standards; the ethical content of foreign policy and world affairs. See *ethics.* Cf. *empirical.*

North: (1) The *OECD* nations. (2) The *West* plus Japan. (3) The *Union* during the *American Civil War.*

North Africa: The northern tier of African *states* comprising the *Arab* and *Berber* peoples of Algeria, Egypt (west of the *Suez Canal*), Libya, Morocco, Tunisia and Western Sahara.

North America: *Central America,* plus Canada, Mexico, the United States and various island attachments.

North American Aerospace Defense Command (NAADC): Founded as *NORAD* in 1957 to oversee the *DEW Line,* it is headquartered in the U.S. but includes Canadian personnel as well. In 1981 the name was changed to North American Aerospace Defense Command (NAADC). See also *North Warning System.*

North American Air Defense Command (NORAD): See *NAADC.*

North American Free Trade Agreement (NAFTA): A comprehensive agreement setting up a *free trade area* among Canada, Mexico and the United States, distinct from the already existing Canada/U.S. *Free Trade Agreement.* NAFTA aims at 99% *tariff* reduction to be phased in over 15 years beginning January 1, 1994. It was signed in 1992, but faced great *protectionist* opposition in both Canada and the U.S. (Mexico embraced it) before acceptance in 1993. It created a trade area second in combined *GDP* and population only to the *EEA.* Among its key provisions: all tariffs on cars and parts to be eliminated (10 years); 100% of tariffs on *agriculture* phased out after 15 years, 94% after 10, and 57% immediately; tariffs on *textiles* shed within 10 years; opening up of *foreign direct investment* rules in Mexico, including banking, securities and insurance. "Side agreements" set up two commissions with formal powers to impose fines, and at the extreme curtail trade privileges in cases of abuse of the environment, worker health and safety, child labor or minimum wage laws. During the debate over U.S. *adherence,* the *Rio Group* called for NAFTA as a step toward a hemisphere-wide trade agreement.

North Atlantic Cooperation Council (NACC): It was founded by *NATO* on March 10, 1992, to promote *CSBMs,* contacts on civil/military relations, air-traffic coordination, defense conversion and *peacekeeping.* It involves all former *Warsaw Pact* states, and Albania.

North Atlantic Council: Founded in 1949 along with *NATO,* it sits in permanent session, meeting weekly to discuss alliance business. Unlike the *Defense Planning Committee,* in which France did not participate 1966-93, it has always included all NATO members.

North Atlantic Treaty Organization (NATO): One cliché wrapped around a grain of truth is that NATO was formed to "keep the Soviets out, the Germans down, and the Americans in [Europe]." In 1948 five West European signatories of the *Treaty of Brussels* (Britain, France and the *BENELUX*) asked for U.S. security assistance, and an *alliance* then concerned as much with Germany as the Soviet Union. The Brussels states joined Canada, Denmark, Iceland, Italy, Norway, Portugal and, most critically, the U.S. in signing the North Atlantic Treaty in 1949. It was a major departure by the U.S. from its historic abstention from *entangling alliances* in peacetime. Greece and Turkey joined in 1952. West Germany adhered in 1955, prompting the Soviets to form the *Warsaw Pact.* Spain joined in 1982. France withdrew from NATO's unified command structure in 1966, but remained in the political alliance, tacitly coordinating military policy as well. That crisis prompted the *Harmel Report.* Disputes in the Aegean and over Cyprus between Greece and Turkey, forced Greece outside the unified command from 1974-80. In 1990 NATO foreign ministers arranged the inclusion of united Germany. Moscow approved the plan. It was then announced by NATO that the Soviet Union was no longer considered a hostile state. In 1990 it approved the *London Declaration.* With the subsequent dissolution of the Warsaw Pact, NATO began to redefine its role. At the Rome summit (November 1991) it elevated liaison with former members of the Warsaw Pact, agreed to develop a "European pillar" to handle regional problems and provide more equitable burden sharing with the U.S., and endorsed establishment of a *rapid reaction force.* In the entire *Cold War,* NATO never fired a shot in anger. In 1993 the *Clinton* administration announced it would cut U.S. forces in Europe to 100,000 by 1995 (1/3rd of 1989 levels). NATO also undertook its first combat mission, agreeing to enforce UN *no-fly zones* in Bosnia. It has ruled out admitting East European countries to the "distant future," but in 1993 offered them and Russia *partnerships for peace.* Also, France resumed attendance at meetings of the military committee when *peacekeeping* was the topic. NATO has set up joint task forces and placed some of its assets as the disposal of the *WEU*. See also *containment; double containment; dual key; EUROCORPS; flexible response; massive retaliation*.

Northeast Asia: China, Japan, the Korean peninsula, Mongolia, Eastern Siberia, Taiwan and various islands (Sakhalin, the *Ryukyus* and several small groups). Along with *Southeast Asia*, it forms *East Asia*.

Northern Ireland: See *Ulster*.

Northern Marianas Islands: See *Marianas Islands*.

North German Confederation: It was assembled by *Bismarck* after the defeat of Austria in the *Seven Weeks' War*. Frankfurt, Hanover, Hess-Cassel, Hesse-Nassau and *Schleswig-Holstein* were *annexed* to Prussia, though they retained some formal *autonomy*. The south German states of Baden, Bavaria and Württemburg were connected by secret *treaty* (deliberately undercutting creation of a South German Confederation). In 1871 this assemblage was converted into the *Second Reich*, incorporating the south German states.

North Korea: See *Korea, Democratic Republic*.

North Sea: The Atlantic between Britain and Europe, once called the "German Ocean." Large deposits of *oil* were discovered on the *continental shelf* in the early 1960s. Norway and Britain got the lion's share, with Denmark and the Netherlands also gaining. An *ICJ* ruling in 1969 expanded West Germany's zone. It has been the locale of fierce fishing disputes.

North/South issues: Economic, cultural, political and, to some extent, security issues salient in relations between the *OECD* nations and the *Third World*. See *aid; apartheid; debt crisis; decolonization; distributive justice; ECOSOC; G-77; GATT; IBRD; IMF; intervention; Lomé Conventions; NIEO; nonproliferation; stabilization program; UNCTAD; UNDP; UNGA*.

North Vietnam: See *Vietnam*.

North Warning System: An early-warning radar system, mostly automated, of some 54 sites stretching from *Alaska* to *Newfoundland*, and jointly operated by the U.S. and Canada. It was phased in from 1988-93, replacing the old *DEW Line*.

Northwest Frontier/Question: The Pacific *territories* of North America under dispute by Britain, Russia and the U.S. during the 19th century. U.S./Russian claims were settled in a 1825 *convention*. But the Northwest

Question exacerbated relations with Britain until the *Oregon Territory* settlement. It was put to rest only with the *Treaty of Washington* (1870).

Northwest Passage: It runs through the Arctic Ocean, above Canada. The U.S. insists it is an *international waterway*, and has sent ships through it; Canada claims it as *internal waters*.

Norway: Location: *Scandinavia*. Major associations: *EFTA, EU* (1995), *NATO, Nordic Council, OECD, UN*. Population: 4.2 million. Military: small, but NATO quality. A province of Denmark until it was severed during the *Napoleonic Wars*, gaining *autonomy* in 1807. With the defeat of Denmark (*Napoleon's* ally), it was attached to Sweden in 1814. In 1905 it split peacefully from Sweden and a Danish prince . became king. It was neutral during *WWI*. In *WWII*, it was attacked by Germany in April 1940, in a complete surprise aided by Norwegian *Nazis* who served as *fifth columnists*. A British force landed at Narvik was badly beaten by the Germans, and pulled out when *Hitler* invaded France later that summer. Norwegian *partisans* kept up resistance to the puppet regime of the traitor *Quisling*. The monarchy returned with *liberation* in 1945, and in 1947 Norway joined the *European Recovery Program*. It joined NATO in 1949 and the EFTA in 1960. It was accepted into the *EC* in 1972, but declined membership following a *referendum*; it reapplied to the EU for 1995. During the 1980s it engaged in marine pollution and fishing disputes with Britain and the Soviet Union. In 1993 Norway received widespread criticism for a decision to resume *whaling*, then praise for *good offices* in brokering a peace agreement between Israel and the *PLO*.

notification: When a state informs another state of some legally relevant fact, such as its intent not to renew a *treaty*, or an alteration in its interpretation of an extant agreement. Cf. *nullification*.

notoriety: Publicity attendant upon *occupation* of a *territory*, preparatory to acquisition of title.

Novotný, Anton (1904-75): President of Czechoslovakia 1957-68. A *hard-line* communist whose repression and ineptitude in running the economy did much to generate the opposition that flowered into the *Prague Spring*. He provoked that crisis by calling in the army to repress peaceful demonstrations in February 1968. When it refused his orders, he resigned.

n-person game: From *game theory*, one with more than two players, the complex structure of which makes probabilities extremely difficult to calculate. By analogy: conflicts with many states where estimating outcomes is difficult, and *rational decision-making* becomes correspondingly harder.

NPT: See *Nuclear Non-Proliferation Treaty*.

NSC: See *National Security Council*.

NSC-68: See *National Security Council Directive #68*.

nuclear deterrence: Preventing a nuclear attack by threatening *retaliation* that will produce levels of unprecedented and unacceptable destruction on the *territory* of the attacking power. An emerging problem in both theoretical literature and policy consideration is that most thinking about *deterrence* done during the *Cold War* assumed an effectively *bipolar* nuclear world. Adjustments must now be made to the reality of multiple nuclear powers. On the other hand, levels of hostility among the *Great Powers* that are also *nuclear states* are, at the moment, nothing like the animosities of the Cold War. Cf. *deterrence*.

Nuclear Non-Proliferation Treaty (NPT): Signed on July 1, 1968; in force from March 1970. It aimed at limiting *nuclear weapons* to the five states that acknowledge having them: the U.S., Soviet Union, Britain, France and China. The latter two refused to sign, but the others undertook not to help additional states acquire such weapons. The non-nuclear NPT states agreed, in turn, not openly or secretly to seek to acquire nuclear weapons or weapons technology, and to permit *IAEA* inspections of their facilities. India, long a critic of the perpetual nuclear monopoly the NPT implies, was the first to defy the *regime*. It exploded what its press release called a "peaceful nuclear device" in 1974 (in the land of *Mohandas Gandhi* one does not build *atomic bombs*, even when one does). South Africa secretly built six weapons in the 1980s, but destroyed them and joined the NPT and IAEA in 1991. China and France at last joined in 1992. Ukraine, Belarus and Kazahkstan, the newest certain *nuclear states*, have applied. Ukraine has also indicated an interest in retaining some of its weapons. Iraq was found in violation in 1991, following IAEA inspections after the *Gulf War*. North Korea shocked many by threatening to withdraw, giving the required six-months notice on March 12, 1993, just before an IAEA inspection deadline. It recanted "provisionally," then again refused cooperation. In January 1994, it agreed to the principle of *continuity of safeguards*, then refused inspections. Until Iraq showed that the old inspection regime was inadequate, the IAEA could only visit declared sites. In 1991 it was given new powers, and may now make special inspections of

NPT states, including of research and production sites that are undeclared. However, attempting to use those powers is precisely what provoked North Korea's animosity toward the NPT.

nuclear parity: See *essential equivalence; strategic nuclear parity*.

nuclear reprocessing: Separating spent fuel from fissile material. See *plutonium*.

nuclear states: States admitting to building and/or stockpiling *nuclear weapons*: U.S. (1945); the Soviet Union (1949), succeeded by Belarus, Kazahkstan, Russia and Ukraine in 1991 (with only the first two committed to surrendering those weapons and becoming non-nuclear, under *START*); Britain (1952); France (1960); China (1964); and India (1974), which tested one, but claims not to keep any in stock. In 1993 South Africa admitted that it had built six bombs after 1979, but dismantled these before signing the *NPT* in 1991. See also *near-nuclear states*.

Nuclear Test Ban: See *Partial Test Ban Treaty*.

nuclear war: War fought with *nuclear weapons*, besides or in lieu of *conventional weapons*. There has been only one nuclear war, thus far: *WWII* was principally a conventional conflict, but ended with *Hiroshima* and *Nagasaki*. There have been many *crises* where the use of such weapons was a real possibility. Several occurred between the U.S. and the Soviet Union, but others occurred between the U.S. and China, and between the Soviet Union and China. It is also thought that India and Pakistan came close to a nuclear exchange, over *Kashmir* in 1992. A nuclear confrontation is also possible on the Korean peninsula, should North Korea achieve a weapon.

nuclear weapons: They can be *bombs, land mines, depth charges, warheads* or even non-explosive *radiological weapons*. *Atomic* and *hydrogen bombs* are 1st and 2nd generation, ranging from battlefield devises with low *yield*, to hydrogen bombs with many times the destructive power of *Hiroshima*. To them add 3rd generation *neutron bombs* (not deployed). The 4th generation is already on the drawing board: *charged particle beam* weapons that channel and focus the elemental by-products of nuclear explosions. See *IAEA; ICBM; limited nuclear war; Manhattan Project; Minatom; near-nuclear states; Nuclear Non-proliferation Treaty; nuclear states; Nuclear Weapons Free Zone; Peenemünde; plutonium; SALT; SDI; START*.

Nuclear Weapons Free Zone (NWFZ): Any region

where *nuclear weapons* have been banned by international agreement: *Antarctica*, the *South Pacific, Latin America*, the ocean floor and space. Not all states respect or acknowledge the legality of such bans. Also, some agreements ban transit by nuclear weapons ships, but others do not. Some municipal governments, including in *NATO* countries, have declared local nuclear free zones in defiance of national policy. Unlike state-to-state agreements, such local declarations have no standing in *international law* or in *diplomacy*, and almost certainly no real meaning beyond local emotional gratification. See also these treaties: *Antarctic; Outer Space; Seabed; Rarotonga; Tlatelolco.*

nuclear winter: The idea of some scientists, given wide publicity during the 1980s, that an all-out nuclear exchange between the *superpowers* would raise such an amount of dust into the upper atmosphere that enough sunlight would be blocked to cause rapid global cooling, with a consequent dearth of plant life and breaking of the food chain (an effect comparable to a large asteroid impact). Other scientists counter that the result would more closely approximate a "nuclear autumn." In either case, much *public opinion* in the 1980s embraced the notion as a further inducement to *disarmament.*

nulla poena sine lege: "No punishment without a prior law." Legal *maxim.* Cf. *nullum crimen sine lege.*

null hypothesis: A proposition in which no relation among *variables* is specified, in contrast with one's working *hypothesis*, in which such a relation has been specified. Cf. *falsification.*

nullification: Cancellation of a *treaty*, or of a less formal interstate understanding. Cf. *notification.*

nullity of judgment: Some circumstances render void a *judgment* by an international court. For example, see *error; excess of authority.*

nullum crimen sine lege: "Where there is no law, there is no crime." A legal *maxim* held by some to have been violated by the procedures and charges brought at the *Nuremberg* and *Tokyo war crimes trials.* Cf. *nulla poena.*

nullum crimen sine poena: "No crime without punishment." A controversial, even mischievous, *maxim* promoted by the *Soviet bloc.* It was not widely accepted by states, and even less so among legal thinkers.

nuncio: A permanent representative of the pope; the title used by papal, or Vatican, *ambassadors.*

Nuremberg (*Nürnberg*) Laws: A series of decrees against the Jews announced at the 1935 *Nuremberg Rally.* They were later enacted by unanimous vote of the rubber-stamp, Nazi-controlled *Reichstag.* They stripped German Jews of all civil rights; forbade Jews from entering or practicing the professions (a decree welcomed by more jealous doctors, judges, lawyers and academics eager for promotion than those professions yet feel comfortable admitting); and declared illegal all sexual intercourse or marriage between Jews and "*Aryans.*" This enforcement of a two-class citizenship system in Germany was just the beginning of the process of dehumanization that led ultimately to the *death camps* of the *Holocaust.*

Nuremberg (*Nürnberg*) Rallies: Mass, *Nazi* propaganda festivals held in and around the football stadium in Nuremberg from 1933-38. They were famous for their torchlight parades and trumpet fanfares, and for careful concentration on bending the young to the Nazi message. Many Germans later remembered them as thrilling events that evoked a sense of oneness with the *nation.* They culminated weeks of cultural and sports activities, including Wagnerian music festivals, athletic competitions, air shows, hiking and other seemingly innocuous, but always Nazi-inspired events.

Nuremberg (*Nürnberg*) war crimes trials (1945-47): American, British, French and Soviet judges (that is, the victors in Europe in *WWII*) sat in judgment of Austrians and Germans accused of *crimes against humanity, crimes against peace* and *war crimes.* Out of 177 tried, 142 were convicted and 35 acquitted. Of the convicted, 97 received varied sentences, 20 were given life sentences and 25 "major criminals" were condemned to death (two, including *Göring*, would cheat the hangman by committing suicide). The trials and executions have been criticized as an example of *victor's justice.* Others counter that even if that is true, still it was justice. See also *Doenitz; Frank; Hess; Göring; Jodl; nullum crimen sine lege; Ribbentrop; superior orders.* Cf. *Tokyo war crimes trials.*

Nyasaland: Former name of *Malawi*, 1907-64.

Nyerere, Julius (b.1922): Tanzanian statesman. He was active in the *independence* movement in *Tanganyika*, becoming its PM in 1961. In 1964 he oversaw the *union* with *Zanzibar*, and became President of the new nation of Tanzania. He championed *pan-Africanism* and a variant of "African socialism" based on historic, communal property patterns, all laid out in the *Arusha Declaration* of 1967. He had many admirers in the West, including among *aid* agencies, who pointed to his emphasis on *self-reliance* and grass roots, rural development. He became an articulate spokesman for a *basic needs* approach to Africa's problems. But he also had critics who pointed to his less-than-stellar *human rights* record, and during the 1970s the worsening performance of the Tanzanian economy. Still, surrounded by regional conflicts he kept Tanzania relatively peaceful, even while becoming a leader of the *front line* states in their opposition to *apartheid* and to *UDI* in Rhodesia. He was a harsh critic within the *Commonwealth* of British refusal to impose comprehensive *sanctions* on South Africa. But he was himself forced, by geographical and economic reality, to deal with the apartheid regime from time to time. He was one of only a handful of African leaders to grant *recognition* to *Biafra*. He launched the *invasion* that overthrew *Idi Amin*, for which he was criticized within the *OAU* but much praised in the *West*. After he retired in 1985 many of his domestic programs were overturned, as Tanzania moved to a *market economy*. In 1993 the old man was called back to mediate a serious constitutional dispute between *Tanganyika* and *Zanzibar*.

O

OAS: See *Organization of American States*.

OAU: See *Organization of African Unity*.

obiter dictum: A judicial opinion not essential to a decision. Cf. *stare decisis*.

objectivity: In the social sciences and in *history*, objectivity is striving for emotional, intellectual and personal detachment from the facts, in order to permit them to "speak for themselves." But of course, that is precisely what facts never do. Historical, political and even economic statements and assumptions are usually laden with the values of supposedly objective observers and analysts (even those who honestly strive for detachment rather than merely make a humbug bow in its general direction). This problem is a by-product of the inherent uncertainty of knowledge in these fields. "If you would know history, know the historian." That is also sound advice concerning *economics* and *political science*. In the final analysis, the best guard against subjective distortion masquerading as objective truth is a critical intelligence and skeptical (but not cynical) attitude toward intellectual authority; which, by the way, should include any pale authority ever imputed to entries in this book! See also *paradigm*.

object of international law: Any person or thing, such as a ship, plane or firm, that does not enjoy the status of an *international personality*, yet is regulated under *international law*.

obscurantism: Deliberate obscurity in speech or writing. This pernicious disease breeds in academe. It is often carried by professors and has been known to be communicable to bureaucrats, journalists, politicians and students. It is advisable to keep exposure to a bare minimum. Note: infection may be warded off through exercise--of a sense of humor. Cf. *jargon*.

obscuritas pacti nocet ei qui apertius loqui potuit: "When there is ambiguity in a *treaty*, it works against the party that could have been more clear." Note: the same is true of exams, term papers or business reports.

observer mission: An international team with reporting powers alone, sent in to observe compliance with a given agreement (such as a *cease-fire*). First instituted by the *League of Nations*, they have become a fairly common feature of *multilateral diplomacy*. See *good offices; human rights; mediation; peacekeeping*.

Occam's razor: Named for the English scholastic William of Occam (d.1349?), this parsimonious principle (of argument) says the assumptions underlying an explanation ought not to be multiplied beyond necessity.

occupation: (1) Physical control of part, or the whole, of an enemy's *territory* by military means. (2) Acquisition of legal title to a territory, by virtue of effective and sustained possession. See *Spratly Islands*.

occupation zone: An area of one *state* controlled by the military forces of another. This is usually a temporary situation occurring after *defeat* in a war (e.g., Germany and Japan after *WWII*), or pending a *peace treaty* and restoration of an acceptable (to the conqueror) local authority. If permanent, it will shade into *annexation*, either declared or *de facto*.

occupied territories: (1) In *international law*: *territories* of one *state* controlled by a foreign military, but not *annexed*. (2) In the *Middle East*: the Arab lands captured by Israel but not annexed: the *Sinai* (since returned to Egypt), *Gaza* and the *West Bank*. The *Golan Heights* were annexed by Israel, but in April 1993 Tel Aviv suggested it might return this area to Syria in exchange for a secure peace.

Oceania: An alternate term for the South Pacific, used mainly in France, Japan and by certain *multilateral* agencies. It refers to the south and central Pacific, including *Australasia, Melanesia, Micronesia* and *Polynesia*.

October Revolution: See *Russian Revolution, November (October) 1917.*

October surprise: See *hostage crisis.*

October War: Also called "Yom Kippur War." See *Fourth Arab/Israeli War.*

Octobrists: (1) Members of the right wing of the constitutional movement in Russia, who split from the Kadets in 1905. (2) A huge Soviet youth organization.

Oder-Neisse Line: The frontier between Germany and Poland, agreed at *Yalta* and *Potsdam* as a provisional settlement. It followed the Oder and Neisse Rivers. After *liberation* millions of Germans were *ethnically cleansed* from what had been *East Prussia* (given to Poland), while the same happened to Poles in the eastern part of Poland (annexed by the *Soviet Union*). The *de facto* border gained some legal *recognition* from *West Germany* in 1970 as part of the *Ostpolitik* opening; *East Germany* had always accepted it. It was confirmed in 1990 in a formal agreement made to ease nervous tensions among Poles raised by sudden German reunification.

OECD: See *Organization for Economic Cooperation and Development.*

Office of Strategic Services (OSS): The wartime, civilian *intelligence service* of the United States, set up in June 1942. It supported Yugoslav and Italian *partisans* as well as lesser partisan groups in Bulgaria, Hungary and Rumania. Its more important activities lay in code breaking, although here U.S. army and naval *intelligence* was vastly more effective. The OSS made at best a marginal contribution to the war effort (despite this, it has an inflated reputation). It was disbanded in October 1945. The *CIA* replaced it in 1947.

officer: Any person holding a commission in a regularly constituted military force, or a commander in a *guerrilla* army acknowledged by the troops as a legitimate *combat* or *logistics* authority with the right to issue orders. See *commissioned officer; flag officer; noncommissioned officer; military ranks; petty officer.*

officer corps: The whole body (corpus) of *officers* in a regularly constituted military force.

Official Development Assistance (ODA): Financial or technical *aid* given by a developed *state*, or an *OPEC* member, to a *developing nation* (or *LDC*). It may be in the form of credits, grants, loans, or material assistance or expert personnel. Note: The *OECD* defines it narrowly, as concessional grants or loans where interest is set below prevailing market rates.

official financing: Financial transactions by a government, usually through its *central bank* but possibly including *IMF* facilities, aiming at prevention of gross fluctuations in the value of the national *currency* occasioned by surpluses or deficits in the *balance of payments.* If deficits persist, *foreign exchange reserves* may become exhausted and/or *debt* increase.

OGPU (*Obyedinyonnoy Gosudarstvennoe Politicheskoe Upravlenie*): "United State Political Administration. The *CHEKA*, or Soviet *secret police*, from 1923-34; later the renamed *NKVD*, and later still the *KGB*.

Okhrana: The tsarist *secret police*, founded in 1881. It pioneered many modern techniques of *counterespionage* in its efforts to monitor and repress the Russian democratic, *anarchist* and *socialist* opposition. It also developed a number of foreign *intelligence* methods, including early *sigint* such as the *cabinets noirs.* The *Bolsheviks* inherited both traditions--repression and espionage--and carried them forward in the *CHEKA.*

oil: The single most *strategic* item in the world in the last 150 years. The importance of oil is directly related to the *Industrial Revolution* and its appetite for fossil fuels, and to the invention of industrial, mechanized warfare. Oil thus underlies both the global economy and the capacity to wage modern *war* on a vast scale. The desire and need to control the supply of oil has lain behind *coups* (e.g., Iran 1953), *cartel* formation and the *debt crisis* (e.g., the *oil shocks* of the 1970s), and *war* (e.g., in *WWII* Hitler's eastern *strategy* had much to do with securing the only European oil fields within his reach, at Ploesti in Rumania; the *Gulf War* was as much or more about keeping control of oil supplies out of *Saddam Hussein's* hands as it was the liberation of Kuwait). Cf. *natural resources; water.*

oil shocks: The dramatic increases in the global price of *oil*, and consequent massive transfers of *capital* from the *OECD* countries to *OPEC* members, in 1973 and again in 1979. They resulted in an extraordinary flow of wealth into the oil-producing states, high *inflation* in the industrialized world and the rise of a huge *debt* burden in many *Third World* economies.

oil spills: Efforts to regulate oil spills and assign liability include a 1954 convention, amended in 1962. *UNCLOS III* lists 42 articles concerned with marine controls, monitoring, pollution and enforcement, but as these powers are assigned to a "Seabed Authority" that is not generally accepted by the major maritime nations, the proposals have to date had little effect. *Bilateral* agreements on coastal spills and pollution have arisen as stopgap measures.

Ojukwu, Chukwuemeka (b.1933): President of the *secessionist* nation of *Biafra*, May 1967 to January 1970. He became Military Governor of the Eastern Region of Nigeria following the "Ibo *coup*" of 1966. After thousands of *Ibos* were massacred in the north he led his region into secession as Biafra, and commanded throughout the *Nigerian Civil War*. A greatly charismatic figure, he helped sustain Biafran morale long after any hope of *victory* had disappeared. As the rag-tag Biafran army finally succumbed, he fled to the Ivory Coast where he was granted *asylum*. Pardoned in 1982, he returned to Nigeria.

Okinawa: This Japanese island (the largest of the *Ryukyus*) was captured by U.S. forces in 1945 after heavy fighting and loss of life, including many *civilians* who committed suicide. Waves of *kamikaze* met the *invasion* fleet, and damaged or sunk nearly 200 ships. The U.S. occupied Okinawa until full *sovereignty* was returned to Japan in 1972, and still has important military bases there.

Old Believers (*Raskolniki*): Russian *Orthodox* who refused to accept the reforms or rulings of the Council convened by Patriarch Nikon (1605-81), clinging instead to the old rituals. They were severely persecuted in *tsarist Russia*. From 1707-09, Old Belief helped feed a *cossack* rebellion that swept into arms perhaps 100,000 peasants as well. It was crushed by the better trained and more disciplined soldiers and ruthless generals of *Peter I (the Great)*.

Old Bolsheviks: The original *Bolshevik* leaders and party members. Most were *liquidated* by *Stalin* in the *Yezhovshchina* of the 1930s.

Old Catholics: Catholics in schism from Rome over the results of the first *Vatican Council* of 1869-70, especially its proclamation of papal infallibility; prominent in Austria and Germany, in particular.

Old World: Asia, Europe and North Africa (that is, the "known world" for Europeans before the discovery and charting of the *Americas*). In politics the term has traditionally connoted to Americans images of *machiavellian* intrigue, lack of principle, and conflict and war in Europe. To Europeans, who often incorrectly regard it as applying only to themselves, it suggests cultural conservatism and traditional social values.

oligopoly: When several firms together control the production and pricing of a *commodity*. Cf. *monopoly*.

Olympic Games: A modern revival (since 1896) of ancient Greek, ritual athletic competitions. They have long since expanded beyond recognition by the athletes of Athens and other Greek *city-states* (e.g., the inherent absurdity of "solo synchronized swimming" was an official event in 1992). They have been held every four years, suspended only during *WWI* and *WWII*. They were intended to promote peaceful competition among *nations*. Several games have been highly political. The most infamous was the 1936 Berlin Olympics, where the *Nazis* attempted to illustrate their racial theories and bolster domestic opinion by achieving international prominence in sport. However, the triumph of the would-be *Herrenvolk* had to be postponed due to one of the greatest Olympic track performances of all time. Jesse Owens (1913-80), a self-effacing black American who was the grandson of a Georgia slave, won four gold medals, besting a great German competitor in the long jump (afterwards, they became lifelong friends). That accomplishment caused *Hitler* to stomp out of the stadium in an *Aryan* huff. Less dramatic but just as political, the 1964 Tokyo Olympics were used by Japan as something of a national coming-out celebration, for its full reacceptance after WWII into the *world community*. The 1972 Munich Olympics were the most tragically marred, when Palestinian *terrorists* took *hostage* and then murdered Israeli athletes (*Mossad* took the next 21 years to hunt down and kill all those involved.) The 1976 Montreal Olympics were boycotted by African states protesting sport contacts with South Africa; the 1980 Moscow Olympics were boycotted by many Western and Islamic countries, protesting the Soviet *invasion* of Afghanistan; and the 1984 Los Angeles Olympics were boycotted by the *Soviet bloc* in retaliation for 1980. South Korea used the 1988 Olympics to improve relations with North Korea, enhance its global profile, and gain *prestige* as a rising economic powerhouse. Throughout the *Cold War* Americans and Soviets competed fiercely, while certain smaller countries sought to make up in sports achievement what they lacked in political *legitimacy* or national self-confidence. Of these, the most spectacularly successful was

East Germany. But Cuba, Rumania and other *Soviet bloc* nations also placed a premium on the political prestige thought to come with Olympic success. The Winter Olympics, which began in 1924, have never been as popular or well-attended as the Summer Games; the Jamaican bobsled team notwithstanding, it is understandably hard to get warm weather populations to compete in (or watch) events like the luge and speed skating. Nor have the Winter Games been as political as the Summer Games. The notable exception has been ice hockey, where politics was to the fore between the Soviets and Czechoslovakia at Grenoble in 1968, and between Soviets and Americans at the Lake Placid Olympics in 1980. That national sentiment is still to the fore after the Cold War was evident in China's intense 1992-93 bid to host the 2000 Olympics in Beijing. It lost to Sydney, reputedly owing in part to China's poor *human rights* record.

Oman: Location: *Arabian peninsula.* Major associations: *Arab League, UN.* Population: 1.4 million. Military: minor. Formerly Muscat and Oman. This was the most powerful *state* in *Arabia* after it overthrew Persian rule in the mid-18th century and became an independent *sultanate.* It dominated the nearby seas with its navy, and ruled far off *Zanzibar,* which it ran as a slave gathering *colony.* In 1861 it lost control of Zanzibar to the British, who ended the *slave trade.* Tensions between interior *tribes* of Arab nomads and the mixed, Arab and Indian population of the capital Muscat, led to violence in the mid-1950s. This was repressed with British assistance. *Oil* was also discovered, changing the basis of the Omani economy and reinforcing the dominance of Muscat. In 1970 the old *sultan* was deposed by his son, who engaged in a more explicitly pro-Western policy. During the *Iran/Iraq War* Oman did as most *Gulf States* and supported Iraq. In the *Gulf War* it permitted the use of its airfields to the *Gulf Coalition,* and has since moved closer in security affairs to the West and to Saudi Arabia.

omission: When a state fails to meet its *treaty* or other legal obligations through lack of positive action.

one-party state: Any state, regardless of ideological orientation, where only one political party is permitted by law or in fact. The one-party states of the *Soviet bloc* collapsed from 1989-91; and some *Third World* states experimented (sincerely or not) with *democracy,* as *OECD* states made this a partial condition of *aid.*

OPEC: See *Organization of Petroleum Exporting Countries.*

open covenants, openly arrived at: Part of the *lib-eral peace program* before and after *WWI.* It was an idea championed in a qualified sense by *Woodrow Wilson,* who coined the phrase, at the *Paris Peace Conference.* This demand arose out of fear that secret *alliances* might lead to another world war (it was widely believed they led to the first). Also contributing was shock and disgust at publication by the *Bolsheviks* of secret *treaties* and cynical *territorial* swaps made by Britain and France with Italy (to get it into the war), and with Russia (to keep it in the war). The idea of "open diplomacy" posits that *public opinion* is inherently *pacifist,* and thus a powerful check on the intrigues of diplomats. That contributed to a new emphasis on *conference* over *quiet diplomacy,* including the permanent conferencing of the *League of Nations* and *UN General Assembly.* See *Constantinople Agreement (1915); registration; Treaty of London (1915).*

open diplomacy: See *open covenants.*

Open Door: A principle of *free trade* championed by the U.S. toward China from c.1850-1949, which called for treating all foreign nationals and firms on a *most-favored-nation* basis, or one of equality rather than special rights. It was made explicit in the *Open Door notes.* Following the *Twenty-One Demands,* Secretary of State *William Jennings Bryan* announced that the U.S. would not accept any alteration in Asia that adversely affected American rights, impinged upon the *territorial integrity* of China, or sought to close the Open Door of competitive trade. The Open Door was of cardinal concern in the *Lansing/Ishii Agreement.* The principle was internationalized in the *Nine Power Treaty* in 1922 (and in a distant sense, also in *GATT).* Some in the *Wisconsin school* have seen this theme as a cover for American *imperialism* in Asia; others, notably *realists,* view it as an example of naiveté in U.S. diplomacy in the face of actual European and Japanese imperialism toward China. Liberal/nationalist historians tend to view it as an example of the (supposed) moral exceptionalism of American politics and civilization, and the pursuit of enlightened self-interest at the core of U.S. foreign policy. See also *capitulations; free trade; unequal treaties.*

Open Door notes: These *diplomatic notes* were sent by Secretary of State John Hay (1838-1905) to the European powers and Japan, in September and November 1899. They called on all powers with *spheres of influence* in China to respect the principle of the *Open Door,* not to stand in the way of China's collection of *customs* duties, and to cooperate with the U.S. in ensuring all other powers adhered to the Open Door. Only Italy, which had no sphere in China, embraced the notes; most others were polite but non-committal.

Nonetheless, Hay declared that he had secured international respect for the *territorial integrity* of China. In fact, the hard realities remained that spheres of influence would be defended by force (as the *Russo/Japanese War* would demonstrate), and that *free trade* was not widely accepted. The 1899 notes revealed that American interests had expanded greatly in Asia, even if U.S. policy was as yet little more than a missal of ineffectual pieties. In 1900 Hay issued more notes, unilaterally declaring for the Open Door and China's territorial integrity. The other *Great Powers* were again more polite than they needed to be: the U.S. had in the past itself impinged on Chinese *sovereignty*, and was at that moment closing the Open Door in the Philippines. The notes are perhaps most important for signaling a new engagement by the U.S. in world affairs. Unexpected by most, this had come about not through entanglement with the Great Powers of Europe, but via commercial interests in Asia. The notes also gave sign that despite its newfound power and importance, the U.S. still intended to uphold the fiction of its moral exceptionalism in dealings with the wider world. The national style of American diplomacy was thus to the fore: *national interests* were overdressed in a cloak of principle, and escorted about in a hansom cab of abstractions. Cf. *idealpolitik*.

Open Skies: A proposal for a *verification regime* to reduce *tension* over a possible *first strike* by either side, made by *Dwight Eisenhower* to *Nikita Khrushchev* at their 1955 Geneva summit. It was elegantly simple: each side would allow surveillance overflights by the other. The Soviets rejected the proposal, fearing the U.S. would discover just how far behind their missile program really was, and because of historic paranoia about foreign observance of Russian internal conditions. In a sense, the idea was implemented unilaterally by the U.S. in the form of *U-2* overflights. The rapid development of satellites by both sides in the 1960s rendered aerial reconnaissance less important. However, in the altered climate of the late 1980s, *George Bush* revived the open skies proposal and finally secured Soviet agreement. American and Soviet (then Russian) overflights are by now almost routine. Russian observers have actually been flown over American bases and missile silos in American planes, as their own equipment proved below standard.

operational code: *Jargon* for the worldview of a foreign policy *decision-maker* or *elite*.

operationalize: Some researchers like to say they "operationalize" a *variable* by finding ways to measure it.

Operation Desert Shield (August 7, 1990-January 16, **1991):** The buildup of *Gulf Coalition* forces from 28 nations, but mostly Americans, that reached over 600,000 troops. It began within days of Iraq's *invasion* of Kuwait, once the U.S. secured Saudi approval to base troops in-country. It had two purposes: (1) *deterrence* of Iraqi *aggression* against Saudi Arabia and the Gulf States; (2) preparation for expulsion of Iraq from Kuwait should it fail to comply with *Resolutions 660* and *678* voted by the *Security Council*.

Operation Desert Storm (January 17-February 27, 1991): The offensive against Iraq by the *Gulf Coalition*. It had two distinct phases: (1) an aerial and artillery *bombardment* to soften Iraqi positions and eliminate most *armor* and air cover; (2) a ground attack starting on February 24th, that swept around Iraqi ground forces in a great *flanking* maneuver and compelled Iraqi *surrender* within 100 hours.

Opium Wars: (1) 1839-42: The main issue was *trade*, of which opium was but a symbol. Chinese leaders were concerned at the growing numbers of addicts ("opium eaters") in the country, and the penetration of their country by foreign traders and influences. When they declared the death sentence for trafficking and confiscated a shipment of opium that British merchants were planning to market, Britain asserted the *extraterritoriality* of its laws, denied *jurisdiction* to China and demanded return of the opium and the merchants. China opened *hostilities* in November 1839, firing on British ships and *embargoing* trade with Britain. The British then shelled Canton and seized the coast around the village of *Hong Kong*. The war continued until China was compelled to accept the hard terms of the *Treaty of Nanking (1842)*, and pay full *compensation* to the British merchants for their lost opium. The opium trade thus continued, and even expanded under the license offered to foreign merchants enjoying *capitulations*. (2) 1856-60: The British won this contest too, which arose from the same commercial causes as the first. They were joined by the French in launching two punitive expeditions, the first after the original British attack was repulsed; the second after the Chinese court refused to accept the onerous terms of the *Treaty of Tientsin* (1858), which had followed the first Anglo/French raid into the interior. Peking was occupied in the second campaign, in 1860, and the court folded its resistance. The second Opium War is sometimes called the "Arrow War," after the British *casus belli:* China's boarding and seizure of the opium ship Arrow, in a Chinese port, and arrest of its crew for *piracy*.

Oppenheimer, J. Robert (1904-67): Nuclear physicist. In 1942 he joined the *Manhattan Project* and the next year he headed its *Los Alamos* base, driving its scientists to completion of the world's first *atomic bomb* while playing liaison with the military. When the first bomb was tested his internal reaction as he gazed on the fireball was to quote from the Bhagavad-Gita (*Hindu* scripture): "Now I am become death, the destroyer of worlds." He came to deeply regret the bombings of *Hiroshima* and *Nagasaki*, and called for joint control of nuclear technology with the Soviet Union. In 1953, under a cloud of *McCarthyism*, his past associations with some American communists led to his suspension from all atomic research. A man of some considerable conscience, he died emotionally broken. Cf. *Edward Teller.*

opportunism (in foreign policy): When a *state* with a general *expansionist* thrust to its diplomacy bides its time, advancing only when meeting weak or no resistance, as opposed to embarking on frank *aggression*. If this conclusion is reached about an opponent's intentions the logical counterpolicy is firm support for *deterrence*. Many *intelligence* and other *analysts* in the West during the *Cold War* saw this as the prime characteristic of Soviet policy. They rejected cruder, even hysterical, views that portrayed the Soviets as relentlessly aggressive and ever-ready to use force, as *Nazi Germany* had been. But they also dismissed as naïve, or worse, portrayals that ignored or denied the expansionist motif in Soviet policy.

opposable: In *international law*, a statement or act that one *state* may not regard as the exclusive concern of others.

optimize: In *game theory,* to choose the option that represents the greatest advantage, or the one with the highest payoff. Cf. *maximizing.*

Optional Clause (of the Statute of the *International Court of Justice*): Article 36. It stipulates that *states* may agree in advance to submit to *compulsory jurisdiction*. Those accepting do so on the basis of *reciprocity*. The U.S. made a *reservation* (the Connally Amendment, 1946), asserting a right to exclude disputes regarded as under *domestic jurisdiction*. This has been much criticized in legal circles by those who believe compulsory jurisdiction is highly desirable. Yet the Connally Amendment is in line with similar reservations taken by 90% of states accepting the clause so far. A further, more contentious modification was made by the *Reagan* administration in 1984, to deny the court *jurisdiction* in a case charging *indirect aggression*, brought against the U.S. by Nicaragua.

Optional Protocol: An addendum to a *treaty* that signatories are not bound to accept. *Adherence* to such a protocol is a separate act from *ratification* of the *covenant* to which it is attached.

optional rules: See *consent.*

oral history: (1) Historical lore passed from generation to generation by the spoken word. (2) Interviews, tape recorded or videotaped by historians, of persons thought to have led significant lives, or who have been witnesses to important events.

Orange Free State: An independent *Boer* republic 1854-1900. It was renamed the Orange River Colony by the British 1900-1910, and then incorporated into the Union (later Republic) of South Africa.

Orangemen: Named for Prince *William III (of Orange)*. (1) Members of a secret society organized in *Ulster* in 1795 to defend the union with Britain, promote Protestantism and hold power over the native, Catholic Irish. (2) Loosely, Ulster Protestants in general. (3) More precisely, a synonym for *Unionists*.

orderly market arrangements (OMAs): Alternative *jargon* for *voluntary export restrictions (VERs)*.

ordnance: Bombs, bullets, explosives, grenades, projectiles, shells, torpedoes or any other lethal device dropped on or fired at the enemy in *warfare*.

Oregon Question/Territory: "Where to draw the western border between Canada and the U.S.?" The absence of settlers meant it was left unresolved until the 1840s. Pressures then built in Britain to claim the whole Columbia River basin, and in the U.S. to assert extreme territorial claims, for some under the slogan "54/40 or fight!" (in reference to their preferred latitude of settlement). The dispute over Canada was aggravated by tensions over American expansionist pressure on Mexico, then a British *client state*. In 1846 agreement was reached by which the U.S. gained what later became Idaho, Oregon and Washington, and Britain (Canada) received British Columbia and Vancouver Island. That left as the only outstanding border issue the question of the Alaskan panhandle, settled in favor of the U.S. after a bit of *saber rattling* in 1902.

organizational process model: Institutional routines and *standard operating procedures* of bureaucracies are said to skewer foreign policy decisions during implementation, in ways that may surprise and frustrate the *decision-maker* and be misinterpreted by foreign leaders. This *model* may have relevance for assumptions about *rational decision-making*.

***Organization de l'armée secrèt* (OAS):** An illegal military cabal formed by French colonial officers, and supported by settlers from Algeria (the so-called "pied noir"). The OAS refused to accept *independence* and tried several times to assassinate *Charles de Gaulle.*

Organization for Economic Cooperation and Development (OECD): It succeeded the *OEEC* in 1961, to expand beyond European recovery into a harmonization of economic policy in industrialized countries. Its main purposes are: (1) to facilitate *sustainable growth*; (2) to assist economic *development*, even for non-members; (3) to encourage expanded *trade* among the world's major trading nations. Membership as of 1994: Australia, Austria, Belgium, Britain, Canada, Denmark, Finland, France, Germany, Greece, Iceland, Ireland, Italy, Japan, Luxembourg, Mexico (joined in 1994, the first new member in 21 years), the Netherlands, New Zealand, Norway, Portugal, Spain, Sweden, Switzerland, Turkey and the United States.

Organization for European Economic Cooperation (OEEC): It was set up in 1947 to facilitate delivery and oversee administration of massive *Marshall Plan* aid flowing into Western Europe from the U.S. In 1961 it was superseded by the *OECD.*

Organization of African Unity (OAU): It was founded in 1963 by 32 member states (it now has over 50 members). It aimed at speeding the *decolonization* of the continent, discouraging *secession,* encouraging *pan-Africanism* and enhancing Africa's diplomatic voice in *multilateral* negotiations. It found unity around the issues of decolonization of what remained of European rule, especially that of Portugal and Spain, and opposing *apartheid.* However, it quickly divided into two *blocs*: the smaller Casablanca bloc, led by *Kwame Nkrumah,* that promoted *pan-African* solutions and upheld a confrontational style in relations with the *West*; and the majority Monrovia bloc, led jointly by *Haile Selassi* of Ethiopia and various leaders from Nigeria, that took a more conservative and nationalist line on most issues. The OAU later divided over such regional conflicts as the *Nigerian Civil War,* the *Chad/Libya War* and the Tanzanian invasion of Uganda in 1979. In the 1980s it was severely split over Libya's *aggression* against its neighbors, Moroccan refusal to let go the *Western Sahara,* the *Ethiopia/Somalia War, secession* in *Eritrea* and civil wars in Angola and Mozambique. In fact, so bitter was the feeling over the admission of *POLISARIO* in 1982, annual summits were temporarily suspended. In 1992 the OAU proved unable to mediate an end to Somalia's civil war, agreeing to UN and U.S. *intervention* as an "interim measure."

Organization of American States (OAS): The regional organization for the Western hemisphere, founded in 1948 by 21 original members. It is headquartered in Washington, D.C. It has the full paraphernalia of a council of ministers and assembly. For its first two decades it was preoccupied with the perception of a communist threat to the region, and was (formally) fairly accepting of U.S. *intervention.* The apex of OAS cooperation on security issues came during the *Cuban Missile Crisis,* when it voted unanimously to support the U.S. response. In 1965 an OAS military mission also went into the *Dominican Republic* after U.S. assertions of a communist threat. However, during the 1970s and 1980s the OAS divided over U.S. intervention in Central America, and unanimously opposed the *invasion of Grenada,* on which it was not consulted. The OAS played a constructive role in winding down the several civil wars in Central America in the early 1990s. Canada joined only in 1990. *Castro's* Cuba was expelled, at the behest of the U.S.

Organization of Arab Oil Exporting Countries (OAPEC): It was founded in 1968 by Kuwait, Libya and Saudi Arabia. Most of the *Gulf States* have since joined. As the title suggests, it is confined to Arab states that also export oil, thus excluding Arab countries such as Jordan (no oil) or oil nations like Nigeria (non-Arab). See *OPEC.*

Organization of Central American States (ODECA): A subregional organization founded in 1951 by Costa Rica, El Salvador, Guatemala, Honduras and Nicaragua. The ODECA states were far too divided by internal and cross-border conflicts in the 1980s to advance their declared goals of enhanced economic cooperation and coordinated diplomacy. See also *Central American Common Market.*

Organization of East Caribbean States (OECS): Founded in 1981 by Antigua, Dominica, Grenada, Montserrat, Saint Lucia, Saint Vincent, St. Kitts/Nevis and the Grenadines. In 1983 it requested U.S. *intervention* in Grenada, on the ground that events had begun to threaten regional *security* and *stability.* Four OECS states joined Barbados, Jamaica and the U.S. in the *invasion of Grenada.*

Organization of Petroleum Exporting Countries (OPEC): It was founded in 1960 by Iran, Iraq, Kuwait, Saudi Arabia and Venezuela, at the behest of Venezuela, to try to raise oil prices. Subsequently joining were: Qatar (1961); Libya (1962); Indonesia (1962); Abu Dhabi (1967); Algeria (1969); Nigeria (1971); Ecuador (1973); and Gabon (1975). The *influence* of OPEC was not really felt until 1973, when its Arab members convinced the others to impose an oil *embargo* against Western states that supported Israel during the *Fourth Arab/Israeli War*. When prices leaped upward, several Western states shifted their diplomatic positions, leading some analysts to proclaim the arrival of an era of paramount "resource power." In 1978/79 OPEC cut exports again, leading to another price rise. This time Western states were less affected, as the earlier experience had stimulated new exploration and production by non-OPEC members (e.g., Britain, Mexico and Norway), and some conservation. The real losers were Third World importers: the OPEC price rise was one of the major factors behind the *debt crisis* of the 1980s. OPEC's ability to act jointly was severely damaged by the *Iran/Iraq War*, which divided its membership as the *Gulf States* supported Iraq and thereby earned the enmity of Iran. The *Gulf War* exacerbated divisions by alienating smaller Arab exporters from Iraq as well. More damaging is that world oil prices have been flat since 1989, as a result of which OPEC has begun to suffer from the inherent instability of all *cartels*.

Orient: The eastern hemisphere; Asia. See *East*.

Oriental exclusion laws: Racially discriminatory legislation introduced in Canada and the U.S. from c.1900-1947. They aimed at limiting Japanese and Chinese settlement on the west coast of North America. In 1924 the *immigration* code in the U.S. was changed to totally exclude Asians, by votes of 308-62 (House) and 68-9 (Senate). This deeply embittered relations with Asian nations, especially Japan. Canada still legally discriminated against orientals, including native-born Asians, into the 1950s.

Orlando, Vittorio (1860-1952): Italian statesman. PM 1917-19. He led the Italian delegation to the *Paris Peace Conference*, led it out in protest when *Woodrow Wilson* refused Italy's exaggerated territorial claims, and then back in just before its closing.

Ortega, Daniel (b.1945): Nicaraguan *guerrilla* commander, then President 1985-90. He headed the *Sandinista* government in its 11-year confrontation with the U.S. and *war* against the *Contras*. He was seen as a charismatic reformer by some, but as a rigid and doctrinaire, *marxist* ideologue by others. He reoriented the country toward the *Soviet bloc* out of political conviction, and from economic necessity once a U.S. *embargo* was declared. Defeated in 1990 elections, he still remains a figure of considerable political influence within Nicaragua. See *Sandinistas*.

Orthodox Church: The several national churches of

Eastern Europe but especially Russia, which follow the Byzantine rite and Nicene creed (a statement of fundamental principles set at the Nicene Council, in 325 A.D.). The Russian church was made subservient to the state by *Peter I*. The *Bolsheviks* persecuted it on all fronts. However, during *WWII* it was found politic by *Stalin* to reopen the churches as a spur to nationalism and inspiration to resistance against the Tutonic invader. Since the collapse of the Soviet Union the Church has experienced a revival of attendance, with *Boris Yeltsin* and other politicians paying clumsy, ill-practiced homage to its renewed influence over the Russian people.

Ossetia: A region in the *Caucasus*, formerly within the *Soviet Union*. It was divided upon that *empire's* breakup into North and South Ossetia (in Russia and Georgia, respectively). In 1992 a movement for *secession* began in South Ossetia. As fighting increased some Russian army units supported the Ossetians. The *rebellion* abated in late 1993, but could flare again.

Ostpolitik: "Eastern policy." The opening to *East Germany* and to Moscow initiated by *Willy Brandt*, which led to *peace treaties* with Poland and the *Soviet Union*, acceptance of the *Oder/Neisse line* as the German border, and admission to the UN of the two Germanies in 1972. It was further developed within the *CSCE*. It went beyond *regulated coexistence*, and completely overturned the *Hallstein Doctrine*.

Ottawa Agreements: See *imperial tariff*.

Ottoman Empire: Actually, the Turkish Empire 1300-1919, ruled by the Ottoman (Osmanli) dynasty, named for its founder Osman, a.k.a. Othman (1259-1356). By the 14th century it had grown to dominate Asia Minor and the *Balkans*, and indeed most of the *Islamic world* west of Persia, and all the *Arab* lands. In 1453 the Ottomans captured *Constantinople*, and moved their capital there. The cultural peak of Ottoman civilization came in the time of Suleiman the Magnificent (1520-66). Its military high tide came in 1683, when its troops washed up against the walls of Vienna, only to begin a centuries-long recession from Europe. In the 17th and 18th century it fought defensive campaigns, not always losing, against Austria, Hungary, Poland, *Venice* and especially Russia. By the 19th century the problem was more internal decay and disintegration than foreign *aggression*. Britain and France began to prop up the Ottomans against Austria and Russia, as in the *Crimean War*. But by *WWI* Germany dominated Turkey both economically and militarily. The Ottomans joined the *Central Powers* in a last, great gamble to cease the erosion of their empire. They lost. See also *Abdul Hamid II; Arab Revolt; Anatolia; Armenian genocide; Balkan Wars; Crimea; Dodecanese; Eastern Question; Italo/Turkish War; Janissaries; Mahmud II; Mehemet Ali; Navarino; Sublime Porte; Straits Question; Young Turks* and various lands and countries once part of the Ottoman lands, such as *Albania; Algeria; Arabia; Armenia; Azerbaijan; Bessarabia; Bosnia; Bulgaria; Cyprus; Egypt; Georgia; Greece; Hejaz; Hungary; Iraq; Kuwait; Libya; Macedonia; Nagorno-Karabakh; Palestine; Rumania; Serbia; Syria; Transylvania* and *Tunisia*.

Outer Mongolia: See *Mongolia*.

Outer Space Treaty: In 1961 the UNGA declared that the principles of the *UN Charter* extended to space. Another, non-binding *declaration* followed in 1963. Reflecting an interest in snuffing out any extension of the *arms race* to space, a binding *treaty* stipulated: (1) prohibition of space-based *nuclear weapons*; (2) a ban on military uses of the moon or planets; (3) exploration of space to take place in accordance with the *common heritage principle*; (4) a ban on *territorial* or other *sovereign* claims; (5) cooperation on peaceful *exploitation* of space; (6) liability for harm caused by objects launched into space; (7) people in space, of whatever nation, were to be considered representatives of all humanity, and as such all states are bound to aid them when in duress; (8) launching states to retain ownership and *jurisdiction* no matter where a space vehicle comes down. Adopted unanimously by the UNGA in 1966, it entered into force in 1967. Related agreements exist on Rescue of Astronauts (1968); Liability for Space Objects (1972); Peaceful Uses of Outer Space (1976); and a *Moon Treaty* (1979). See also *satellites; SDI*.

outflank: (1) In the military: to maneuver around the *flank* of an enemy's position, thereby threatening lines of retreat and supply and a multisided assault. (2) Colloquial: to outmaneuver an opponent.

outlaw state: (1) In *international law*: an extremely remote possibility that a *state* might forfeit its status as an *international personality* due to persistent disrespect for the law. (2) In rhetoric: states that act outside accepted *norms*, say by sponsoring *terrorism* or flouting *Security Council* resolutions. Cf. *pariah state*.

outliers: Single observations that are anomalous compared to the other data used in a *regression* analysis.

out-of-area: Military *theaters* where a security organization has no legal *jurisdiction* or *geostrategic* interest in operations. For example, before 1993 *NATO*

never operated outside its Atlantic/member countries zone. Since then it has agreed to a UN request to enforce a *no-fly zone* over Bosnia.

output: (1) In *economics*: any *service* or *commodity* produced and put on the market for sale. (2) In *political science*: *jargon* for the policy decisions that are yielded from a mix of considerations (*inputs*) fed into the *decision-making* process.

overpopulation: When the number of persons in a given *territory* or *state* is too great for that area to support at subsistence levels. Beyond subsistence, this becomes a relative concept: how many is too many depends on one's subjective sense of what level of *exploitation* of *natural resources* is possible and/or necessary for a desirable *standard of living*.

overproduction: Producing *goods* or *services* in excess of demand.

overseas Chinese: The Chinese *diaspora*, especially in SE Asia, where ethnic Chinese form a distinct, concentrated, influential, but also persecuted minority in several countries. Cf. *boat people*.

overseas departments (of France): Off-shore administrative units for lands incorporated under the French constitution that participate directly in French government through elected representatives. See *French Guiana, Guadeloupe, Martinique, Mayotte, Réunion* and *St. Pierre et Miquelon*.

overseas territories: (1) Colonial possessions not contiguous with a *metropolitan power*. (2) A type of direct *dependency*, in which certain islands are constitutionally part of the home country: e.g., *French Polynesia, French Southern and Antarctic Lands, Netherlands Antilles, New Caledonia (Kanaky)*, and the *Wallis and Fortuna Islands*.

overt-covert operations: A clumsy phrase to describe *covert* operations that are openly admitted because they are successful or publicly approved, and therefore good for the *intelligence agency's* image; e.g., *CIA* aid to Afghan *guerrillas* (or *mujahadeen*), 1979-89.

ozone depletion: The thinning of the protective ozone layer in the upper strata of the atmosphere, especially the opening of "ozone holes" over both poles due to release of volcanic gases, *CFCs* and other chemical pollutants. In 1984-87, the Vienna and Montreal Conventions on ozone depletion were negotiated and signed. A convention on climate change was also signed at the *Earth Summit*.

P

pacification: (1) In general: A euphemism used by governments to conceal their violent repression of armed resistance or political dissent. (2) In the *Vietnam War*: A U.S. policy of winning back the countryside from the *Viet Cong* (VC) by a combination of aid, *propaganda* and provision of village-level security by physical elimination of the VC, both through conventional military means and via a selective *assassination* program run by the *CIA* (code-named "Phoenix").

pacific blockade: See *blockade*. Cf. *quarantine*.

Pacific Rim: Geographically, all *territory* with a Pacific coastline. However, the term is used politically to depict the Pacific as a transportation freeway connecting *states* in *interdependent* relations, instead of holding them at vast distances as it once did. It is sometimes used to imply a regional community, parallel to the *Atlantic Community*, whether that exists in fact or not. Some prefer the term "Asia/Pacific" as a way of focusing on Asia (and excluding South America). In Canada and Japan, but less so elsewhere, "North Pacific" is used to focus even more tightly on the seven northern hemisphere states of Canada, China, the two Koreas, Japan, Russia and the U.S.

pacific settlement of disputes: See *peaceful settlement of disputes*.

pacifism: The position that all *war*, and all involvement in war, should be resisted as a moral evil. Sentimental pacifism is common in peacetime, but usually dissolves rapidly as the ethnic, national or religious passions of those holding such views are engaged and inflamed by war. Philosophical pacifism is more serious, and therefore more rare. Many individuals of refined conscience, including *Mohandas Gandhi*, have been pacifists; but many persons of conscience have not been pacifists. In terms of groups, pacifism has been promoted most consistently by Quakers. *Just war theory*, arguably the most sophisticated moral examination of the problem of war, rejects pacifism as failing to make key moral distinctions. It argues that there are crucial differences between *aggressor* and victim that may at times oblige direct action by either the victim alone or even by third parties. In contrast, pacifism appears nearly always to counsel passivity. Pacifists reply that any notion of just war is an oxymoron, as all war is seen by them as inherently unjust. They therefore also tend to support calls for general *disarmament* and *arms control*, to oppose military preparedness and to propose such non-violent means of conflict resolution as *arbitration* and *mediation*.

pact: An alternate term for *treaty*; usually reserved for military agreements, *alliances* aimed at specific adversaries or *multilateral* arrangements.

pacta sunt servanda: "Treaties are binding." Legal *maxim* affirming that *treaties* firmly bind *states*, and require them to observe all *terms* on which *reservations* have not been accepted. Furthermore, treaties bind states, not mere, transitory governments: a successor government, even a revolutionary one, may not (legally) renounce binding international agreements. Treaties also bind *successor states*, though with modifications according to the nature and degree of succession. Thus, the former Soviet republics each accepted shares of the rights and obligations of the *extinct* Soviet Union, but Russia assumed the main burden of obligation and the main advantages (such as the *veto* in the *Security Council*). For limitations, see *validity*.

pacta tertiis nec nocere nec podesse possunt: "Treaties impose no burden and confer no benefits beyond contracting parties." A legal *maxim* affirming the crucial rule that *treaties* create rights and binding duties only for *states* party to them. See *consent*.

Pact of Paris: See *Kellogg-Briand Pact*.

Pact of Steel (May 22, 1939): A 10-year *nonaggression pact* signed by Germany and Italy in the run-up to *WWII*. It formalized the Rome-Berlin *Axis*. See also *Tripartite Pact*.

pactum de contrahendo: The agreement that announces the intention of states to draft a *treaty*.

Pahlavi, Muhammad Reza Shah (1919-80): Shah-in-Shah of Iran 1941-79. He succeeded his father, who was deposed by the *Allies* during *WWII*. He allowed the Allies to tranship *Lend-Lease* from Iran. In 1946 he asked for, and received, Western help to resist Soviet *encroachment*. He nearly lost power in 1953, in a crisis over *nationalization* of Iran's oil facilities by *Mossadegh*. He hung on with the help of U.S. and British *intelligence*. In 1955 he took Iran into the *Baghdad Pact*, and built it into a major regional power. He continued *modernizing* and *secularizing* reforms of his father, but as domestic opposition grew, he turned increasingly to his *secret police* (SAVAK) to repress dissent. Sick with cancer, on January 16, 1979, he fled into *exile*, first to New York, then Mexico, Panama and finally to *Sadat's* Egypt, where he died.

Pahlavi, Reza Shah (1878-1944): A Persian army officer who launched a successful *coup* in 1921, and in 1924 with the support of Britain was crowned Shah of Persia. He began major *secularizing* and *modernizing* reforms (the "White Revolution"). He ruled Iran--the name was changed in 1935--until 1941, when his pro-*Axis* sympathies led to joint British/Soviet military intervention, and forced abdication in favor of his son, *Muhammad Reza Pahlavi.*

Pakistan: Location: SW Asia. Major associations: *ECO, NAM, SARC, UN.* Population: 115 million. Military: Well-equipped since the 1980s but still over-matched by India's; probably nuclear capable. Pakistan was founded as a *Muslim* state (the name means "Land of the Pure") at the insistence of the *Muslim League* and *Muhammad Ali Jinnah.* That required the *partition* of India in 1947 into three main parts, with *East Pakistan* and *West Pakistan* divided by 1,000 miles of Indian *territory.* That odd beginning was de-signed to separate the *subcontinent's* Muslim from Hindu areas, but nonetheless left more Muslims in India than the total population of Pakistan (then still including *Bangladesh*). The first *Indo/Pakistani War* immediately broke out over *Kashmir* (1947-49), fol-lowed by the *Second* (1965) and *Third* (1970). Domes-tically, Pakistan stumbled though these years from one state of emergency and one military dictator to the next. It became a republic in 1956 (it had been a *Do-minion*). *Ayub Khan* introduced *martial law* and an aggressive swagger to foreign policy. Civilian rule re-turned in the wake of the loss of East Pakistan in 1971, when *Zulfikar Ali Bhutto* became President. Bhutto was overthrown in 1977, and subsequently executed by *Muhammad Zia ul-Haq*, who reintroduced martial law 1981-86. The Soviet invasion of Afghani-stan and India's *tilt* toward the *Soviet Union* made Pakistan more important in the eyes of U.S. strategists. Aid flowed in by the billions in exchange for facilitat-ing arms supplies to the Afghan *mujahadeen*, whom Pakistan supported anyway out of fear of the Soviet thrust into Central Asia. Zia was assassinated in 1988, to be succeeded in time by the daughter of the man he had killed: *Benazir Bhutto.* She was sacked in 1990 on what may have been trumped-up charges and an un-constitutional process, but in 1993 she returned to power. Pakistan withdrew from the Commonwealth in 1972, after that organization admitted Bangladesh; and it continues to harbor ambitions of getting back some more or even all of Kashmir. In 1990 the U.S. sus-pended aid both because the Soviets had pulled out of Afghanistan and because Washington suspected Kara-chi of having constructed a *nuclear weapon.*

Palau: Location: Pacific. Major associations: *SPC.* Population: 26,000. Military: U.S. 50-year base lease.

After *WWII* it was made part of the *Trust Territory of the Pacific Islands*, administered by the U.S. In 1978 it rejected *commonwealth status.* In a 1979 *referendum* it approved by 92% a non-nuclear constitution. The U.S. removed the anti-nuclear clauses and resubmitted, but this time only 30% approved. With anti-nuclear clauses restored, it passed by 78% in 1980. Palau then asked for self-government in *free association* with the U.S., which insisted on a naval base agreement. Palau also agreed not to undertake *defense* arrangements in-compatible with U.S. interests. In a 1983 referendum a majority approved the compact, which included a nuclear ship visitation clause, but the vote fell short of the 75% required by the Palau constitution. While the *Federated States of Micronesia* and the *Marshall Is-lands* achieved free associated status by Senate con-sent in 1986, Palau did not. It had *autonomy*, but re-mained suspended in a legal limbo between the status of *trust territory* and independent *microstate.* In Nov-ember 1993, it voted in another referendum (this one requiring only a simple majority and supervised by the UN) to accept free association with the U.S.

Palestine: An ancient Asian country known in biblical times as Canaan. This *territory*, which included mod-ern *Israel, Jordan* and the *occupied territories*, be-came an *Ottoman* province in 1517. It remained under Turkish rule until 1918, when it was overrun by the *Arab Revolt* and the British advance on Damascus. *Zionists* began to migrate there in small numbers at the turn of the 20th century. In 1917 its future course was dramatically altered by the *Balfour Declaration* promising a Jewish homeland in Palestine. It was made a British *mandate territory* in 1920, but the Balfour Declaration, and rising Jewish immigration, dogged all its politics. Arabs and Jews both sparked sectarian riots in the 1920s and 1930s. More intense violence erupted in 1937-38. Independence was de-layed by *WWII*, but in 1947 the UN voted to *partition* Palestine into Jewish and Arab states. Britain walked away from the mandate in 1948, leading to three-way partition (Israel, the *West Bank* to Jordan, and *Gaza* to Egypt), the *First Arab/Israeli War* and the exodus of hundreds of thousands of Palestinian Arabs to *refugee camps* in other Arab countries. Since 1988 Palestine has experienced the violence of the *Intifada.* Modern conceptions of Palestine range from the extreme Israe-li view that Jordan is already a Palestinian state, to the extreme Palestinian view that a new Palestine must be erected on the whole territory of the old mandate, which requires the utter elimination of Israel. More moderate voices prevailed in September 1993, with an agreement between Israel and the *PLO* for a trial peri-od of *autonomy* in Gaza and Jericho, with security guarantees to and from Israel.

Palestine Liberation Organization (PLO): Founded in 1964, it is governed by the Palestine National Council, a quasi parliament. *Fatah* joined in 1968, followed by other *guerrilla/terrorist* groups that formed its armed wing and conducted raids into Israeli, or against Jewish targets in third countries. It was expelled from Jordan after a bloody confrontation in 1970, settling in Lebanon, where it became embroiled in the *Lebanese Civil War*. In 1974 the Arab states collectively announced that they regarded the PLO as the official body responsible for all Palestinian issues; since then some 100 states *recognized* it as representing the Palestinian people. In 1982 it was attacked in Lebanon by Israel and compelled to evacuate to Tunisia, where it is still headquartered (and where Israel bombed it in 1985). It was caught unawares by the *Intifada*, and while trying to catch up and lead the *uprising* from behind, found itself challenged within the *occupied territories* by *Hamas*. The PLO lost key support within the Arab world by backing Iraq in the *Gulf War*, but it never lost its status for Arabs as the recognized voice of Palestine. Israel consistently refused to negotiate with the PLO, stating it would only talk to Palestinians who resided in the occupied lands; Israel was even able to get the U.S. to adopt the same policy, a fact that enormously complicated and delayed the peace process. However, behind the scenes of *multilateral* talks underway since the end of the Gulf War the PLO was formulating the Palestinian position. In September 1993, after months of *back-channel negotiations* (in Norway), it agreed to an accord with Israel, which was finding the PLO moderate as compared to the irreconcilables in Hamas. See also *Yassir Arafat*.

Palestinians: (1) Pre-1948: All inhabitants of prepartition *Palestine*, whether Jew or Arab. (2) Post-1948: The Arab population of prepartition Palestine, now scattered in a *diaspora* of their own. There are approximately 5 million Palestinians, of whom some 2.3 million live in Israel or the *occupied territories,* many in *refugee camps*. Another 1.3 million live in Jordan, a number swollen by those expelled from Kuwait in 1991 for welcoming Iraqi invaders in 1990.

Palme, Olaf (1927-86): Swedish statesman. PM 1969-76, 1982-86. A major figure in international *Social Democracy*, he was an active advocate of opposition to *apartheid* and of *arms control* (despite Sweden's record as a quiet but major *arms exporting nation*). He was critical of the U.S. during the *Vietnam War.* He headed the Palme Commission in 1980 on global *disarmament*. He also served on the *Brandt Commission*, and on a UN *fact-finding* and *mediation* mission that sought an end to the *Iran/Iraq War*. He was shot on the way home from an outing with his wife. A de-

ranged man was convicted of the killing in 1989 (later overturned). It is not thought to have been a political assassination.

Palmerston, Henry John (1784-1865): British statesman. First Lord of the Admiralty 1807-09; Secretary for War 1809-28; Foreign Secretary 1830-34, 1835-41, 1846-51; PM 1855-58, 1859-65. On occasion, he promoted *liberal* causes through his foreign policy, moving further from the *reactionary*, continental powers; e.g., he supported Greek independence in the 1820s, secured Belgian independence in 1831 and *recognized* Italy in 1861. But more often he acted out of a strict sense of British *national interest*. While joining the *Quadruple Alliance*, he yet supported the *Ottomans* against both *Mehemet Ali* of Egypt and *Nicholas I* of Russia. He fought the *Opium Wars* against China, and suppressed the *Indian Mutiny* of 1857. With difficulty, he kept Britain out of the *American Civil War*. He left a more lasting mark than anyone else on the diplomacy of the greatest power of the 19th century.

Pamyat: A Russian, *fascist* political movement founded as the *Soviet Union* was collapsing, dedicated to *slavophile* values and hostile to democracy. It has called for new *pogroms* against Russia's Jews.

Pan-African Congress (PAC): A radical splinter group that broke with *Mandela* and the *African National Congress* in 1959. There was a brief coming together in 1990. But by 1993 the ANC and PAC again divided over the pace of change to a multiracial society, and the degree of *power sharing* with whites that should be accepted: PAC wanted no delay and no power sharing.

pan-Africanism: Social, cultural or political movements that seek to span the political divisions of the African continent (sometimes applied only below the Sahara), through appeal to a continental supernationalism. A pan-Africanist conference was held in 1945, and the movement was influential in several *independence* movements. It received rhetorical support within the *OAU* in the 1960s, contributing to formation of a minority *bloc* within that organization. But once power was won by various African *elites* on a national basis, the movement ceased to have real political meaning and subsided into a cultural ideal. Cf. *négritude*.

Panama: Location: Central America. Major associations: *NAM, OAS, UN*. Population: 2.5 million. Military: small, and under far more political restrictions than previously. With U.S. encouragement and naval support, it became independent from Colombia in 1903 following the *War of the Thousand Days*. It immediately signed a *treaty* with the U.S. permitting construction of the *Panama Canal*, and granting control of the *canal zone* to Washington. Until the announcement of the *Good Neighbor policy*, U.S. marines routinely *intervened* in Panama's volatile domestic politics. During *WWI* the U.S. had a heavy military presence in Panama, protecting the vitally important canal. Relations with the U.S. were broken from 1963-64 over Panama's demand for return of the canal Zone (and its revenues). An agreement was reached with *Jimmy Carter* from 1977-79, though not without a great deal of opposition to returning the canal from the Republican right ("it's ours; we built it" said *Ronald Reagan* during the debate). During the 1980s the Panamanian military, under Manuel Noriega, ran guns to the *Contras* in Nicaragua and drugs to the addicts of Miami, Orlando and points north. It did both with the knowledge of the *CIA*. In 1988 Noriega launched a *coup* and assumed the presidency after the President tried to fire him. The U.S. imposed *sanctions*, and Noriega was indicted by a Miami court on drug charges. Elections were set for May 7, 1989. When Noriega announced he had won, international observers cried fraud. It did not help matters that the real winner (Guillermo Endara) was beaten bloody by Noriega's thugs before a worldwide TV audience. An attempted coup on October 3rd failed, and there was considerable criticism of *George Bush* for failing to lend at least *logistical* support to the coup planners. In November and December, a U.S. marine from the canal Zone was killed and others harassed by Panamanian soldiers. The war of words and mutual *saber rattling* intensified, with Noriega at one point ramming a resolution through his Assembly that seemed to *declare war* on the United States. On December 20th the U.S. obliged, with an airborne *invasion* of some 25,000 troops that included the first-ever combat use of *stealth technology* aircraft. Noreiga sought *asylum* with the papal *nuncio*, but after 10 days he surrendered (January 3, 1990) and was taken to Miami to stand trial. Endara was installed as President, and U.S. aid and advisers arrived to help with *reconstruction*.

Panama Canal: This 40-mile-long passage across the Panamanian isthmus was built from 1903-14 by U.S. Army engineers, after *Teddy Roosevelt* maneuvered a Panamanian revolt and *secession* from Colombia (*War of the Thousand Days*). The U.S. quickly obtained rights to garrison the *canal zone*, but also accepted a self-imposed *servitude* that it would keep the canal open to all ships in peacetime. It was once of great *strategic* importance, permitting the U.S. Navy to easily reinforce its Pacific from its Atlantic fleet, and vice versa. But the greater size and draft of modern *warships*, tankers and merchant ships, has reduced its

significance. The 1904 agreement was revised in two *treaties* in 1979. One promised to eventually abolish the canal zone and remove U.S. troops by midnight, December 31, 1999; gave Panama *jurisdiction* over most of the canal zone, including the ports at either end; but it also reserved the right of defense of the canal to the U.S. The second treaty will come into effect on January 1, 2000. It declares the canal *neutral*, and assigns a right of defense to both Panama and the U.S., to be exercised jointly or severally.

Panama, Declaration of (1939): An effort by the American republics, but led by the United States, to keep *WWII* in Europe distant from the shores of the Americas. It declared a *neutral zone* 300 nautical miles around the Americas (excepting Canada, which was already a *belligerent*). This *declaration* was rejected by all the major naval powers in the Atlantic region (Britain, France, Italy and Germany).

pan-Americanism: Social, cultural or political movements that seek to span the political divisions of the Americas. The term sometimes excludes Canada, the United States, and the non-Latin Caribbean.

pan-Arabism: Social, cultural or political movements that seek to span the political divisions of the Arab *peoples*. When *fundamentalists* include an emphasis on the majority's common *Islamic* religious and political traditions, *Copts* from Egypt, Maronite Christians from Lebanon, and others, may be excluded.

pan-Slavism: (1) Social, cultural or political movements that seek to span the political divisions of the *Slavs*. (2) A *tsarist* foreign policy of support for Slav nationalism (always excepting Poland) in lands occupied by the *Ottomans* or *Austria*. Its purpose was to inspire *secession* by the Slav areas, and thereby weaken regional enemies and perhaps prepare *territory* for *annexation*. Cf. *slavophile*.

Panzer: In *WWII*, German *armor* divisions made up primarily of tanks, but including mechanized support troops, and capable of powerful assaults and rapid advances. See *blitzkrieg*.

Papal States (755-1860): *Territories* in central Italy under the temporal authority of the popes. During the *Renaissance* they intrigued to expand, as did the other *city-states*. They *declared war* on France in 1793, opposing the *French Revolution*'s radical *secularism* and confiscation of church property. *Napoleon I* occupied the Papal States (twice). There were several rebellions against the popes in the 19th century. As late as mid-century the Papal States spanned 16,000 square miles and contained over 3 million souls (as the popes might put it). Their takeover by the Italian state in 1870 caused a 60-year rift between Italy and the papacy. Today, only the vestigal hectares of the *Vatican* remain under the temporal control of the popes. See also *Catholic Church; Pius IX; Roman Question.*

Papandreou, Andreas (b.1919): PM of Greece 1981-89; 1993- ; son of *Georges Papandreou.* His premiership was marked by rhetorical confrontation with traditional, Western *allies.* In turn, he was criticized for a slack policy toward *terrorism.* His government fell in a swirl of financial and sex scandal. Without demur, Greeks reelected him to a majority in 1993.

Papandreou, Georges (1888-1968): Greek PM 1944, 1963-65. He was active in the anti-Nazi *resistance* during *WWII.* He was a popular politician, but one dogged by the problem of *Cyprus* and consistently opposed by the army. The latter launched the "colonel's coup" in 1967 to prevent his return to office.

Papua New Guinea: Location: Pacific/SE Asia. Major associations: *ACP, Commonwealth, NAM, SPC, SPF, UN.* Population: 3.6 million. Military: 5,000 personnel, coastal guard, few aircraft; Australian, New Zealand, British, *Gurkha* and U.S. training programs. The Dutch claimed the western half of the island in the 19th century. The eastern half was divided by the British and Germans in 1884. The British transferred the SE portion (Papua) to Australia in 1905, and Canberra seized the rest of eastern New Guinea from Germany in 1914. It was made a "Class C" *mandate* under Australian administration from 1920. From 1942-44 it was *occupied* by the Japanese. Australia returned as the *trustee power* from 1946-75, when PNG achieved independence. It maintains close relations with the Commonwealth, yet its diplomacy focuses on Australia, Indonesia, and Micronesia. It keeps up a joint defense arrangement with Australia. In 1979 it signed a border agreement with Indonesia. In 1984 some 11,000 *West Irian* rebels fled into its *territory.* At the invitation of Indonesia, it became an observer at *ASEAN.* In 1988 Indonesia made *incursions* in *hot pursuit* of rebels from West Irian, damaging relations. By 1991 relations with Indonesia warmed again, but the possibility of border conflict remains. In 1980 PNG sent 400 troops to *Vanuatu* to help suppress a *secessionist* movement. It took the lead in *Melanesia* further when it helped launch the *Spearhead Group* in 1986. It fought its own campaign against secessionists in the *Bougainville insurgency*, a problem that still simmers despite negotiations with the aid and *good offices* of New Zealand and the Solomon Islands. PNG is poor, underdeveloped and premodern in its interior

areas. But it is large, rich in *natural resources* and likely to emerge in time as one of the natural leaders in the South Pacific.

Paracels (a.k.a. Xisha or Hoang Sa): These small islands and reefs lie in the South China Sea. Vietnam and China fought a sharp battle over the *Spratlys* and Paracels in 1974. China pushed Vietnam out of the latter in another clash in 1982, but final ownership remains hotly disputed.

paradigm: An underlying, *grand theory* that guides research and the accumulation of scientific knowledge. The idea was developed in the 1960s by historian of science Thomas Kuhn to explain "scientific revolutions" such as the Copernican. He argued that scientific knowledge does not develop in a linear fashion. Instead, it builds up contradictions of an existing grand theory and then suddenly overturns it, by serving as a better predictor of experimental outcomes and accounting for more known phenomena with greater elegance and simplicity. Both the orthodox view being challenged and the discomfiting theories threatening it, he called paradigms: ultimately incommensurate views of the same reality, that highlight different features of a subject of inquiry, point to dissimilar problems as the key ones, and potentially distort perception of puzzles and disconfirming evidence, even so far as to blind researchers to alternative explanations. The idea thus suggests that the sociological, non-objective component of even "hard science" knowledge is far more important than most researchers dedicated to the scientific method would like to admit. How much more true was all this of the social sciences! Yet, undeterred by this context, many social scientists declared that their subjects and efforts were "preparadigmatic" scientific inquiries, implying that full status as predictive sciences (and of course, full stature as scientists) only awaited further accumulation of a "critical mass of data," after which a true grand theory (full paradigm) would be sure to emerge. But Kuhn never meant the term for the social sciences (or *history*), because they represent a different form of knowledge and follow a different epistemology (or should). He regarded this usage as corrupted, inappropriate and misleading, and said so. Nonetheless, a debate raged within the social sciences for nearly 10 years. It has since cooled, its origins largely forgotten. Today "paradigm" has deteriorated into little more than *jargon* for an academic's general theoretical perspective (e.g., *behavioralist, neo-realist, marxist*), which may be used to select interesting (or not) problems for research.

Paraguay: Location: South America. Major associations: *LAIA, NAM, OAS, UN.* Population: 4.6 million.

Military: no offensive capability; mainly of domestic significance. Its *indigenous*, Indian population was subjected to an overlay of Spanish settlement after 1535. It broke away from Spain in 1811. It was badly defeated in the *War of the Triple Alliance, 1865-70*, in which it lost so much *territory* and *population* it never recovered its previous *power* position and was left economically destitute and politically unstable. During the 1920s there was a series of border conflicts and crises with Bolivia that erupted into the bloody *Chaco War* in 1932, from which Paraguay gained some territory back but deepened its domestic problems. In 1954 General *Alfredo Stroessner* seized power. His stern rule was wielded through the compliant and longstanding "Colorado Party," but relied ultimately on the military and support from major landowners in Paraguay's near-feudal rural areas. He was not deposed until 1989, by a *coup* led by General Andés Rodriguez (subsequently elected president).

parameter: (1) A constant whose assigned values are set out at the beginning of a formal analysis, and proscribe its limits. (2) Outside limits (of an issue).

paramilitary: Any private (non-state) armed force, organized along military lines. Cf. *Freikorps; militia.*

parent country: One where an *MNC* originated and is headquartered. Cf. *Calvo Clause; Drago Doctrine; host nation.*

pariah state: A state that has stepped outside *international law*, for instance by supporting *terrorism* or by flaunting accepted legal and diplomatic *norms, regimes* or conventions. Cf. *outlaw state.*

par in parem non habet imperium: "Equals hold no *jurisdiction* over one another." A legal maxim formulating a key aspect of *sovereignty*.

Paris, Charter of (1990): A *declaration* by the *CSCE* that formally ended the *Cold War* and promised future relations would be based on principles of the *Helsinki Accords.* It sprang partly from the *two-plus-four talks.*

Paris, Declaration of (1856): This was the first major effort by the *Great Powers* to set out the *rules* of naval warfare. It proclaimed four basic principles: (1) *privateering* was made illegal; (2) *neutral* flags protected enemy *goods*, except for *contraband*; (3) neutral goods other than contraband were exempt from *capture*; (4) *blockades* had to be effective, or they were not binding. Naval warfare was briefly addressed by the *Geneva Convention* (1864), and more fully by the *Hague Conference* (1907). A major conference was held at London (1908-09). It laid out elaborate rules, but did not touch upon *submarines* and went unsigned by the major *sea power* of the day, Britain.

Paris Peace Accords (1973): A set of agreements completing complex negotiations from 1968-73, ending the American phase of the *Vietnam War*, signed by Britain, China, France, the Soviet Union, the U.S., North Vietnam and the National Liberation Front (*Viet Cong*). The accords came on the heels of the "Christmas bombing" of Hanoi ordered by *Richard Nixon*, who later claimed that action had forced the North to the table. They were torn up within two years, as the North completed the unification of the peninsula by a full-scale *invasion* of the South. See also *Henry Kissinger; Le Duc Tho.*

Paris Peace Conference (January 18, 1919 to January 20, 1920): The victorious powers of *WWI* met in Paris to arrange the *postwar* settlement, and set *terms* for the defeated *Central Powers*. It decided the *Treaties of Neuilly, St. Germain, Trianon* and *Versailles,* and set up the *League of Nations*. Though it began with great expectations of a *liberal* and cooperative peace, it ended in considerable acrimony between the erstwhile *Allies*. Elections in Britain, France and the U.S. showed that the populations of all three countries wanted a harsher peace than *Woodrow Wilson* was prepared to oversee. Italy stormed out after failing to get all its *territorial* demands, promised in the secret *Treaty of London (1915)*. It rejoined the conference just before *signature* of the treaties, but in its absence the other major powers divided the *mandates* among themselves, excluding Italy in punishment for its walkout. Japan was also miffed, especially over its failure to obtain international acceptance of the principle of the equality of races. Also troubling the conference, *Weimar Germany* agreed to *terms* only under duress and over rising internal opposition. The conference struggled with the issue of *self-determination*, granting *recognition* to (not creating, as has been falsely charged) the weak *successor states* of the *Austrian Empire*. Lastly, Russia was in the throes of civil war from which it would emerge under the *Bolsheviks* opposed to the entire settlement framed at Paris. It sent no representative, despite two efforts by Wilson to bring the warring Russian factions together. See *Clemenceau; Fiume; Fourteen Points; Lloyd George; Keynes; mutilated victory; Orlando; reparations.*

Paris, Treaty of (1763): Britain and France made a *peace* in which France got back the Caribbean sugar islands it had lost in the previous fighting, and Britain acquired legal title to *Québec*. French power was finally expelled from North America. That opened the way to a rising dispute--in the absence of a common enemy--between Britain and its American colonies.

Paris, Treaty of (1783): Britain accepted the *sovereignty* of the United States, agreed to frontier borders at N. Florida, the Mississippi and the Great Lakes, and granted the U.S. fishing rights off *Newfoundland*.

Paris, Treaty of (1856): This agreement ended the *Crimean War* on terms of the territorial *status quo ante bellum*, except the loss of south *Bessarabia* and control of the mouth of the Danube by Russia. It also dissolved the Russian *protectorate* over, but confirmed the *autonomy* of, the *Danubian principalities*; and it *neutralized* the *Black Sea*, with neither the Russians nor the Turks permitted to maintain forts or navies there. It also declared the Black Sea part of the *high seas*, except of course for coastal, *territorial waters*. Russia broke the *demilitarization* clause of the *treaty* when it pressed ahead with naval construction on the Black Sea after 1870, while Europe was being alternately appalled and dazzled by *Bismarck's* remarkable victory over France. The treaty also abolished the right of *reprisal* by individuals, reserving it to the *states* alone, and thereby ending hundreds of years of quasi-legal, private warfare. And it set out the law of *blockade* in near-modern terms and abolished *privateering*, in the *Declaration of Paris*. Most important, it began the formal expansion of the *world community*, or that circle of *civilized states* bound by *international law*, by admitting the *Ottoman Empire* as a full member.

Paris, Treaties of (1947): After six months of negotiations *terms* were agreed in February 1947, for the five minor *allies* of *Nazi Germany* in *WWII*: (1) Bulgaria: returned to its frontiers in January 1941, before its participation in the *invasion* of *Yugoslavia*. (2) Finland: ceded part of the *Karelia* Peninsula to the Soviet Union, otherwise returned to the frontiers of 1940 set after its defeat in the *Finnish/Soviet War*. (3) Hungary: limited to the frontiers set in the *Treaty of Trianon*, except for *territory* surrendered to Czechoslovakia. (4) Italy: ceded some Adriatic islands and small peninsular territories to Yugoslavia, transferred a small border area to France, and relinquished the *Dodecanese* to Greece; *Trieste* was declared a *free city*. (5) Rumania: the cession of *Bessarabia* and *Bukovina* to the Soviet Union was confirmed; otherwise, Rumania returned to its interwar boundaries. The *Japanese Peace Treaty* was negotiated separately in 1951. No *peace treaty* was signed with Germany, as with its *de facto* division by the *Cold War* there was no one German government capable of signing, nor the possibility of Allied agreement on terms. However, an interim legal settlement was achieved much later in the *Helsinki Accords*.

parity: Rough equivalence or correspondence in military force levels, equipment and weapons. See *essential equivalence; strategic nuclear parity*.

Park, Chung Hee (1917-79): South Korean statesman. President 1963-79. He ruled harshly, with diminished respect for *human rights*, but oversaw a dramatic expansion of the economy and the country's emergence as an *Asian Tiger*. In 1979 he was assassinated by the head of his own *KCIA*.

parley: Talks with an enemy while under a *truce*, to arrange exchanges of the wounded and/or *prisoners of war*, or to discuss terms of *surrender*.

Parnell, Charles Stuart (1846-91): Irish nationalist. His campaign for *Home Rule* through parliamentary politics was building steam when it was ruined by scandal. In a predominantly Catholic country, he could not survive politically once it was made known he was having an affair with a married woman, Mrs. Kitty O'Shea, who was also the wife of a friend.

parsimonious theory: One that explains much with little, like this.

parsimony, law of: See *Occam's razor*.

Partai Kommunis Indonesia (PKI): It was founded in 1920 as a communist/nationalist movement to agitate for *decolonization* from the Dutch. During *WWII* it joined other Indonesians in *guerrilla* resistance to the Japanese. In 1948 fighting broke out between the PKI and the Indonesian nationalists (republicans). The PKI enjoyed considerable electoral success after *independence*, but never threatened to form a majority and never renounced its call for violent *revolution*. When the PKI attempted to seize power in 1965 ("the year of living dangerously") it was put down with ruthless brutality: hundreds of thousands were rounded up and slaughtered by the Indonesian army--including many innocents--destroying the PKI, at the time the third largest *Communist Party* in the world.

Partial Test Ban Treaty (1963): Signed by Britain, the U.S. and the Soviet Union in the *thaw* that followed the *Cuban Missile Crisis*, it limits signatories to underground tests of nuclear weapons, banning tests in the atmosphere, the oceans and space. France ceased atmospheric tests in 1974; China continued until 1980. Negotiations on a comprehensive test ban treaty (to include cavern tests) have so far been stymied by the felt need of some signatories to maintain a margin of *deterrence* credibility, and weapons safety, by occasional testing. A *moratorium* that lasted two years expired in October 1993, after China, which may test for the additional reason of *prestige*--displaying its status as a major nuclear power--exploded a bomb.

patient capital: Long-term *capital* invested abroad in the expectation that *profit* taking will not occur for some years. See *foreign direct investment*.

Parti Québecois (PQ): A *secessionist* party in *Québec* founded in 1968 by René Lévesque (1922-87). It formed a government in 1976 and held a *referendum* in 1980 on what it called "sovereignty-association" with Canada, a form of halfway *independence* that would retain such links as a common *currency, passport* and army. Despite this proposal to have one's gateau and eat it too, the referendum was defeated 40% Oui to 60% Non. After that rebuff the PQ split, into a minority of irreconcilable nationalists and a majority reconstituted into a moderate, *social democratic* party. That looked to be the future of the party. However, with the failure of constitutional reform in Canada in a national referendum in 1992, the PQ enjoyed a revival. It is dedicated to a clear *sovereignty* referendum should it regain office in Québec. It also gained an important ally in the form of a large bloc of *separtist* MPs in the federal parliament, elected in 1993.

partisan (partizan): A *guerrilla* fighting behind the enemy's *front line*. The term originated concerning the Russian irregulars who harassed and destroyed French formations during the *retreat from Moscow*.

partition: Dividing *sovereign* control of a given *territory*. Most partitions have been by agreement of the *Great Powers* over the heads of the population of the concerned territory. Others have been by unilateral *force*. In the 20th century a new method was introduced: partition according to the principle of *self-determination*, usually following a *plebiscite*, as in *Cameroon* or *Schleswig-Holstein*. Where a plebiscite is impossible, as with India, partition follows a best guess at sectarian divisions on the ground. But this innovation should not be overestimated: the old, forceful ways still are favored by many as a means of settling territorial disputes. See *Abkhazia; Bosnia; Eritrea; Eastern Question; ethnic cleansing; Kashmir; Nagorno-Karabakh; Nazi/Soviet Pact; Ossetia; partitions of Poland; secession; Third Balkan War; Ulster.*

partnerships for peace: *Bilateral* agreements offered as of 1993 by *NATO* to the former members of the *Warsaw Pact*, and as well to some *successor states* to *Yugoslavia* and the *Soviet Union*. They permit participation in some NATO functions, such as *war games* and conferences, but do not offer a firm security commitment by the alliance. These may one day serve as an entry vehicle into the alliance, or not.

party line: Cleaving to the doctrine of a party or leader on a given issue of the day, and shifting positions in tandem with that leader or party, no matter in how tortuous a position one ends. It is used especially about the rigid loyalty (c.1920-70) of a number of foreign communist parties to the doctrines laid down by Moscow. Cf. *eurocommunism*.

Pašić, Nikola (1845-1926): Serb statesman. Ambassador to Russia 1883-89, 1893-94; Serb Prime Minister 1891-2, 1904-08, 1910-18; Chief Minister of Yugoslavia 1921-26. He led Serbia during the *Balkan Wars*, the confrontation with Austria in 1914, in *WWI*, in negotiating the *Corfu Pact* and at the *Paris Peace Conference*. His policy after 1921 always favored the Serbs, striving for *Greater Serbia* at the expense of other Balkan and Yugoslav peoples.

Passchendale, Battle of (July 31-November 10, 1917): *Douglas Haig,* the British Field Marshal in overall command, was not convinced even by the *Somme* that frontal assaults against an *entrenched* enemy were fatal mainly to the attacking side. He thus sent tens of thousands more to fruitless death in this prolonged offensive centered on the village of Passchendale. Casualties were particularly heavy among Canadian units. In addition to sheer bloodiness, the battle was notable for the first use of *mustard gas* on the *western front*, by the Germans.

passive defense: Any measure taken to protect military or other *strategic* targets by dispersal, *hardening* or *camouflage*.

passport: An official document issued to private citizens (but usually remaining the property of the government), authenticating identity, offering *diplomatic protection* and requesting other states to extend to the bearer due courtesy and respect. In the 19th century only Russia required passports, and insisted on their use even for internal travel by its own subjects. The move by other states to a passport system came with *WWI*, when tens of thousands of *aliens* were caught by the start of the war on what overnight had become enemy *territory*. This was a problem for the U.S. in particular, whose *dual citizens* visiting their native lands were often dragooned into military service. Some countries have since eliminated the need for passports for citizens of specified second countries; e.g., Canada and the U.S.; all members of the *EU*.

Pathans: A Muslim people straddling the mountainous borderlands of Afghanistan and Pakistan. While there has been some agitation for a separate state, this seems at best a far distant prospect.

Pathet Lao: A Laotian *communist/nationalist* movement that sponsored *guerrilla* resistance to a post-*WWII* return of French rule in Laos, and launched attacks against the government set up in Vientianne by the *Geneva Agreements*. During the *Vietnam War* the Pathet Lao allied with the *Viet Cong* and North Vietnam, and helped with the operation of the *Ho Chi Minh Trail*. In 1975 it seized power in the wake of the collapse of South Vietnam.

patriotism: Devotion to the cause of one's own country that may, or may not, be uncritical and unthinking. Cf. *chauvinism; jingoism; nationalism.*

Patton, George (1885-1945): "Old Blood and Guts." American general. The single best field commander in the U.S. Army, and perhaps on the *Allied* side, in *WWII*. While he has been--probably justly--criticized for disregarding casualties in the interest of spectacular maneuvers, he delivered results: in North Africa, Sicily and then in southern France, Germany and into Czechoslovakia, forces under his command smashed German defenses, took territory and killed or captured over a million enemy troops. He has also been criticized for a lack of concern for Allied units on his *flanks*. His retort was that he took "calculated risks. That is quite different from being rash." He was frequently in trouble with superiors for his off-the-field behavior. He was relieved of command as a military governor in Germany in October 1945, after making impolitic remarks about attacking the Soviets, and for not removing *nazis* from office with due speed. He died ingloriously, in a car accident.

pax americana: "The American peace." The international security guaranteed to parts of Europe and Asia by the power of the United States during the *Cold War*, ending perhaps with the Bosnian war. Cf. *hegemony; long peace; preponderant power.*

pax britannica: "The British peace." The relative lack of *Great Power* conflict from c.1815-53, if solely, then falsely, attributed to British *preponderance*, for it was underwritten by the *Concert of Europe* as a whole. Cf. *hegemony; preponderant power.*

pax romana: "The Roman peace." The hard but long lasting peace imposed upon the subject peoples of the Mediterranean by the military power of the Roman Empire, under which there flourished the rule of law and the encouragement of civilization. For variations

on this theme, the model for all comparisons, see *pax americana, britannica* and *sovietica.*

pax sovietica: "The Soviet peace." The relative order and peace imposed by Soviet military power on bordering regions, in particular the *Caucasus* and parts of *Central Asia* and *Eastern Europe*, c.1922-88. It ended with the *Armenia/Azerbaijan War* and a blaze of brush wars in the *near abroad*. Cf. *Sonnenfeldt Doctrine.*

payload: Any kind or amount of *ordnance* carried by an aircraft or *missile*.

peace: (1) In lay terms, an agreement to end hostilities, often just with an *armistice* or a *cease-fire*. (2) The legal condition reestablished among former *belligerents* only upon their *signature* and *ratification* of a *peace treaty*. (3) A prolonged lull between armed conflicts, whether under terms of a peace treaty or not. (4) The complete absence of *war* and the expectation of war. (5) A period of balance, security or order, where *international law* is broadly respected and *disputes* are settled by *adjudication, arbitration, conciliation, diplomacy* and *negotiation*, and the only force used or legally permitted in interstate relations concerns cases of limited *reprisal*.

Peace Corps: Established by *John F. Kennedy* in 1960, this program sends young Americans to developing, and now former *communist*, countries to teach or help in social or economic *development* projects. Other nations have similar programs.

peace enforcement: A post-*Cold War* notion that the *Great Powers*, and other states of the *world community* already enjoying *peace*, should act through the UN to end *civil wars* and other conflicts, even when not requested to do so by the contending factions. That is, the UN should not simply seek to keep warring parties apart (*peacekeeping*), or prevent them from expanding through the use of UN forces as police and relief workers, and offers of *good offices* (*peacemaking*), but should actively seek to suffocate civil or smaller interstate conflicts by military *intervention* and imposition of a political solution. In Bosnia (1992-), the UN has used its largest-scale forces since the *Congo crisis* (where they were badly bloodied), not merely as *interposition forces*, but to provide humanitarian relief and a modicum of civil order. In Somalia (1992-), helicopter gunships, *missiles* and *infantry* fighting under the UN flag were involved in heavy fighting as they sought to disarm Somali factions (clans) and provide *famine* relief. Meanwhile, UN diplomats conducted talks on rebuilding Bosnian and Somali government and society. In 1993 *Boutros-*

Ghali called for the creation of "Peace Enforcement Units" (national forces on standby for UN duty). The response to date has been lukewarm, at best.

peaceful coexistence: A security doctrine openly enunciated by *Khrushchev* in 1956, but part of Soviet practice before that date. It adjusted the orthodox *marxist* prediction of ineluctable conflict between *capitalism* and *socialism* to the reality of the Soviet Union's nuclear confrontation with the West. It gave birth to a policy of support for *wars of national liberation,* by which the capitalist world could be prodded at its (putative) weakest point, colonial *dependencies,* while the socialist motherland and the *dialectic* of history were alike spared from ending in a puffery of mushroom clouds. Cf. *regulated coexistence; Sino/ Soviet split.*

peaceful settlement of disputes: Non-violent conflict resolution. See *adjudication; arbitration; compromis; compulsory jurisdiction; conciliation; diplomacy; good offices; fact-finding mission; justiciable dispute; legal dispute; mediation; negotiation; nonjusticiable dispute; observer mission; political dispute; treaty.*

peacekeeping: The use of what were once called *interposition forces* by UN member states, inserted by mutual consent as a buffer between contending parties. During the *Cold War* it was standard to exclude troops from the *superpowers,* and to "balance the ticket" by troops from *NATO,* the *Warsaw Pact* and the *Non-Aligned Movement.* UN peacekeeping forces were used under restrictive *rules of engagement,* and could be withdrawn simply upon the request of one of the warring parties (as in *Suez,* in 1967). They were used mainly in those conflicts not central to the Cold War, such as *Cyprus.* UN peacekeepers were awarded the *Nobel Prize* for Peace in 1988. After 1988, requests for peacekeepers (and the peacekeeping budget) increased exponentially, and strictures on using American or Russian units were discarded. Also discarded were narrow rules of engagement, the light equipment and small size of previous forces and the idea that prior consent of both contending factions was required to legitimate *intervention* by a UN force. But even as peacekeeping began to shade into *peacemaking,* some countries (notably the U.S.) warned against the UN assuming too many burdens, at too bloody and dear a cost. Note: Peacekeeping is not confined to the UN. Several regional bodies have undertaken missions, though they use variations of UN methods and rules. Also, *ad hoc* missions have been assembled, for instance in Liberia and the Middle East.

peacemaking: This concept remains ill-defined, but seeks to go beyond merely keeping opposing sides in a conflict apart with *peacekeeping* forces. Instead, it searches for a UN-brokered, political solution to the underlying conflict. This means abandoning the tradition (some would say fiction) of outside *nonintervention* in favor of *conciliation, mediation* and *good offices* by the *Secretary General* and various UN agencies. It may also mean a significant military deployment to establish law and order in an anarchical situation, provide assurances of security to all sides, insist on a cessation of fighting even when the *United Nations presence* is not welcomed on the ground, and see to the material and medical needs of the *civilian* population. See *peace enforcement.*

peace talks: *Negotiations* ostensibly or actually aimed at ending *armed hostilities;* they may result in an *armistice, cease-fire, truce* or even a *peace treaty.* See *war termination.*

peace treaty: The only mechanism, other than *subjugation,* by which a *war* may be legally terminated. It reestablishes *diplomatic relations* on a full peacetime basis, in terms of legal rights and obligations between and among formerly hostile states. Unless the *terms* of a peace treaty state otherwise, all prior agreements (usually suspended during hostilities) resume their full legal status and effects. A peace treaty thus goes well beyond any provisions contained in an *armistice, cease-fire* or *truce* that may have preceded it. Quite a few wars, such as the *Korean Conflict, WWII* or the various *Arab/Israeli Wars,* ended in cease-fires or truces that left the *combatants* in a legal state of war for decades. See also *POWs; war termination.*

peak tariffs: Very high *protective tariffs,* by convention those pegged at 15% or higher. They are a particular target of the *GATT.*

Pearl Harbor (December 7, 1941): The U.S. Pacific fleet was moved to this shallow harbor from San Diego as a *deterrent* to a Japanese assault on *Southeast Asia.* Instead, the U.S. fleet was caught unawares by a naval air attack on a sleepy Sunday morning. The Japanese fleet that launched the several waves of attack aircraft sortied from the *Kuriles* on November 26th, flying the famous "Z" flag that had fluttered above naval victories over Russia in 1904-05. But as early as July 2nd, an Imperial Conference in Tokyo had decided on a drive into Southeast Asia. On November 1st Admiral *Yamamoto Isoroku,* who opposed the war, ordered the attack on Pearl. He intended to immobilize the Americans during a period of consolidation of the gains to come in Indochina, Indonesia, the Philippines and so forth, but warned he could only promise victories for six months to one year. Washington had broken the Japanese diplomatic (but not military) code, and sent warnings to Pearl and Manila of an anticipated assault; but the attack was expected by all to fall on the Philippines, with no one considering that the Japanese might be so daring as to hit Pearl itself. Within hours of the first explosion 19 U.S. *warships* were sunk or badly damaged, more than 120 aircraft were destroyed and 2,400 Americans were dead. The Japanese lost a mere 29 planes, attacking without a *declaration of war*. But the U.S. *aircraft carriers*, the primary targets sought by Yamamoto, were at sea and were spared. Four days later, for quixotic reasons, Germany and Italy declared war on the U.S. (even though Japan stayed out of the war with the Soviet Union). Pearl Harbor was followed by uninterrupted Japanese victories in the Pacific. Yet within six months, after the evasive American carriers won decisively at *Midway*, Japan would find *victory* most elusive. In the U.S., recriminations followed the attack. There were even suggestions by the conspiratorially minded that *Franklin Roosevelt* had connived to allow it as a means of bringing America into *WWII* via the Asian backdoor. Besides the fact that he was deeply worried the Japanese attack might deflect American attention away from the real threat (which was clearly from Germany) toward the secondary threat in the Pacific, there is simply no solid evidence to substantiate the charge, and much that refutes it.

Pearson, Lester B. (1897-1972): Canadian statesman. Ambassador to Washington 1945; Minister for External Affairs 1948-57; PM 1963-68. He was always a strong proponent of *multilateral diplomacy*, and especially of the *UN*. He was critical of the U.S. decision to push north during the *Korean Conflict*. He became the only Canadian ever to win the *Nobel Prize* for Peace, for his *peacekeeping* initiative during the *Suez Crisis*. In the 1963 elections he ran on a pro-*nuclear weapons* platform, but later declined to so arm Canadian *missiles*. He broke sharply with the *Johnson* administration in 1965, when he delivered a speech at Temple University critical of U.S. policy in *Vietnam*. It has been reported that the next day, on a balcony outside the Oval Office, Johnson repeatedly shouted and cursed at Pearson, even lifting him off his feet (Pearson was much the smaller of the two) to do so.

Peenemünde: Baltic site of German development and testing of the *V-I and V-2 rockets* during *WWII*; work was also done on the world's first jet fighters, and on an *atomic bomb* for *Hitler*. *Slave labor* was used extensively there. Some heroic Jews and other prisoners were able to *sabotage* rockets and other equipment, slowing weapons production; the *Allies* also heavily bombed Peenemünde. Most of the German scientists were captured either by the Americans or Russians after the war, and became instrumental in the U.S. and Soviet space and weapons programs. Cf. *Los Alamos; Manhattan Project; Minatom*

pegging: (1) Attaching a weak *currency* to changes in the *exchange rate* of a stronger one, rather than letting it *float* independently. For example, the Irish pound's sometime pegging to sterling; or African *CFAs* pegged to the French franc. (2) When a government artificially fixes the price of bonds and other securities, say during a *war*, to guarantee itself a steady and abundant supply of cheap money.

Peking (Beijing), Treaty of (1905): Between China and Japan: it confirmed Chinese acceptance of the gains Japan had made in *Manchuria* and North China as a consequence of the *Russo/Japanese War*.

Peloponnesian War: It was fought between Athens and Sparta, 431-404 B.C. and resulted in Sparta's triumph. The great history of this conflict was written by Thucydides (c.460-c.400 B.C.). His rendition is widely read, in particular the "Melian Dialogue" wherein representatives of the city of Melos appeal unsuccessfully to the better nature of the Athenians (their city was sacked anyway, after futile resistance). This episode is held up by *realists* as an example of the persistent reality that in politics "the strong do what they will and the weak suffer what they must." Others note that the Melian prediction came true: other *city-states* grew to fear and distrust Athens for what it did to Melos, and the great, imperial democracy of the classical age was thereby left to face Sparta alone, and was itself conquered.

penetration agent: A *spy* sent or recruited abroad but left inactive for many years, who seeks by career choice and promotions to one day be insinuated into a position of trust, influence, power or even just access to *classified information*.

penetration aids: Any device, such as chaff, dummy warheads or *stealth technology*, that helps an aircraft or *missile* penetrate enemy defenses.

Peninsular War (1809-14): The name given the bloody *campaign* fought by Spanish and Portuguese irregulars, with British support under *Wellington*, against the *occupation* forces sent to *Iberia* by *Napoleon*. The term "*guerrilla war*" dates from this conflict. The contest drained French *reserves* at a time when Napoleon was overextended by his Russian campaign. While British historians tend to regard it as a major reason for the defeat of Napoleon, others have not been as deeply impressed.

Pentagon: The building housing the *Department of Defense*. The term is often used as a synonym for the U.S. military *high command* and its policies.

Pentagon Papers: A *classified* study of U.S. involvement in the *Vietnam War* leaked to the "New York Times" by Daniel Ellsberg. He was a Pentagon employee who asserted a crisis of conscience as his motivation. The office of Ellsberg's psychiatrist was later burgled by the White House "plumbers" of *Watergate* fame, trying to find information with which to smear him. Publication revealed a pattern of government deceit about the costs of the war, and private doubts among high officials about the possibility of *victory*. In turn, that raised public doubts about the wisdom of U.S. involvement, and stimulated even stronger opposition to continued American involvment in Indochina.

people(s): The entire body of persons who form, or feel they belong to, a given ethnic community, such as a *nation* or *tribe*, whether living in the same political community or *territory* or not; e.g., Arabs, Chinese, Jews, Palestinians, Russians.

People's Bureaus: Under *Muammar Quadaffi,* this has been the quixotic term used by Libya for its foreign *embassies*.

People's Liberation Army (PLA): The army of the *Communist Party* that fought in the *Chinese Civil War* and the *Sino/Japanese War*, and then became the armed forces of the People's Republic of China. Since it was called in to suppress the *Red Guards* during the *Great Proletarian Cultural Revolution*, it has been a mainstay of communist power. In 1988 part of the PLA balked at crushing the pro-democracy movement in *Tiananmen Square*, but other units were brought in to do the job. Numbering more than four million strong, the PLA is the largest armed force in the world today. Note: the PLA includes all the armed forces of China, not just the army. While its equipment and doctrine are outdated (a fact made clear by the easy destruction of a similarly armed and commanded force during the *Gulf War*), it is rapidly rearming. The PLA already controls medium range *missiles* and *nuclear weapons*, with approximately 200 warheads and rising. It has begun to acquire a *blue water navy*.

people's war: From *maoism,* the doctrine that a communist movement could ride to power on the back of an aroused peasantry educated in revolutionary tactics and led by party *cadres*. Once the *Communist Party*

took power, the doctrine was adapted to make a military virtue out of China's huge manpower reserves: its lack of technical expertise and advanced weaponry was downplayed by the typically maoist, romantic claim that *peoples*, not armies, are decisive in warfare.

peremptory norms: See *jus cogens*.

Peres, Shimon (b.1923): Israeli statesman. Deputy Minister of Defense 1959-65; Minister of Defense 1974-77, 1992- ; PM 1984-86. He is widely seen as a more moderate PM than was *Begin* or *Shamir*. He helped keep close ties to France and the U.S. He was a strong supporter of Israeli military superiority in the region, and of its secret *nuclear weapons* program. He appeared ready from 1992 to trade *land for peace*, joining in the U.S.-sponsored, *multilateral* peace talks that followed the *Gulf War*. He also oversaw an improvement of relations with Russia. In July 1993, he authorized shelling of southern Lebanon in response to *Hezbollah* rocket attacks, creating several hundred thousand more Arab refugees. But in August he met secretly with *PLO* officials to arrange a historic breakthrough on Palestinian *autonomy*.

perestroika: "Restructuring." A term used by *Mikhail Gorbachev* to describe his (rather vague) plans to reform, modernize and partly decentralize the Soviet economy. While he introduced more *glasnost,* or openness, there was little fundamental restructuring of the economy until the accession of *Boris Yeltsin*.

Pérez de Cuéllar, Javier (b.1920): Peruvian and world statesman. *Secretary General* of the UN 1982-92. Despite or perhaps because of his Latin American background, he made little headway with an offer of *good offices* to resolve the Argentine/British dispute that led to the *Falklands War.* He was much more successful brokering an end to the *Iran/Iraq War*, the phased Soviet withdrawal from Afghanistan, resolution of Namibian independence and *mediation* of the civil war in El Salvador. Overall, his efforts brought new prestige to the office he occupied, and made diplomatic activism by the Secretary General not merely an accepted but an expected innovation.

periphery: In *dependency theory*, the outlying areas of the *world capitalist system* comprising the poor countries of Africa, Asia and Latin America. It is depicted as controlled, and its resources and labor as cruelly exploited, by the *elites* that control the *core*.

Permanent Court of Arbitration: Set up by the first *Hague Conference* in 1899, it led to a spate of bilateral *arbitration treaties* before *WWI*. While that cataclysm dampened enthusiasm for such agreements as a realistic means of avoiding *war*, the court survives because of its utility in resolving *disputes* that do not touch *vital interests*. See *Root Arbitration Treaties*.

Permanent Court of International Justice: Also known as the World Court. The world's first standing international court. It operated under the auspices of the *League of Nations* from 1922-46. Up to 1940 it delivered decisions in 29 cases and gave 27 *advisory opinions* to the League. It was replaced by the *International Court of Justice*.

permanent members of the Security Council: There are five permanent seats on the *Security Council*, but in a sense there have been seven occupants: Britain; the *Republic of China* (Taiwan) before October 25, 1971, the People's Republic of China (mainland) after; France; the Soviet Union until the end of 1991, and Russia since; and the U.S. These states are the only ones with the ability to exercise a *veto* through casting a "no" vote on issues of substance (not procedure).

permanent revolution: The policy backed by *Trotsky* and the "Left Position" in the *Bolshevik* Party during the power struggle that followed *Lenin's* death. It argued for "permanence" in two senses: First, the *revolution* should proceed directly from its democratic (*bourgeois*) phase to its socialist (*proletarian*) phase. Second, it posited that *socialism* in Russia would fail without a transition from a national to an international stage (if it did not lead to socialist revolutions in other countries than Russia). The implication was that Soviet foreign policy should aggressively export revolution, almost as a means of *self-defense*. Trotsky lost the debate (and later his life) to *Stalin* and the doctrine of *socialism in one country*.

Perón, Juan (1895-1974): President of Argentina 1946-55, 1973-74. In 1943 he was part of the *junta* that seized power in Argentina and established a semi-*fascist* regime (Perón was an admirer of *Mussolini*, and to an extent of *Franco* and *Hitler*). He was elected President in 1946. With his famous wife Eva (Evita, 1919-52) he ran a populist regime that employed left and right policies in an eclectic mix whose catalytic ingredient was opportunism. His foreign policy was mainly rhetorical, emphasizing opposition to the involvement of Britain (with which Argentina disputed the *Malvinas*) and the U.S. in Latin American affairs. Deposed in 1955, he spent two decades in Spanish exile before returning to a hero's welcome in 1973. His third wife, Isabel, ruled briefly after his death.

Perry, Matthew C. (1794-1858): American naval offi-

cer. He served off Africa in the 1840s, helping to suppress the *slave trade*, and fought in the *Mexican/American War*. On July 14, 1853, his four-ship squadron steamed into Edo (Tokyo) Bay, and Perry demanded a *commercial treaty*. He went to China to give the Japanese time to consider. When he returned he obtained the *Treaty of Kangawa*, signed March 31st, and ratified July 11, 1854. Afterward, he became an avid overseas expansionist who lobbied (unsuccessfully) for the U.S. to acquire the *Bonins, Ryukyus* and *Formosa*.

Persia/Persian Empire: See *Iran*.

Persian Gulf: An arm of the Arabian Sea, some 600 miles in length, lying between Iran and Arabia. It is highly *strategic*, as it is the passage for much of the world's supply of *oil*.

persona grata: A *diplomat* acceptable to one *state* as a representative of another, or any other person who may enter freely.

persona non grata: A *foreigner* deemed unacceptable by a *state*, for criminal or political reasons. The term is also used as a euphemism for *diplomats* apprehended as spies, and signals that they have been or are about to be expelled. See *legal agents*.

persuasive precedent: In *international law*, when in support of a decision a judgment relies on the internal logic and force of argument, not the formal existence, of a previous judgment.

Peru: Location: S. America. Major associations: *LAIA, NAM, OAS, UN*. Population: 22 million. Military: *counterinsurgency* and *narco-terrorism* focus. In pre-Columbian times Peru was the seat of Inca power (at Cuzco) over a vast South American *empire*. Starting in 1532 with the arrival of Francisco Pizarro (1478-1541), the Spanish began costly raids into Peru in search of gold and precious stones. That exacerbated the Inca *civil war*, and eventually led to outright Spanish *conquest*. In 1821 *San Martin* proclaimed Peru an independent *republic*, but it was not made fully secure until 1824. The economy went into steep decline following its loss of territory to Chile in the *War of the Pacific*, 1879-84. Peru was ruled conservatively for decades, until a left-wing *coup* in 1968 placed in power a *junta* that tried to *nationalize* foreign industries and assets. Civilian rule did not return until 1979, just as Peru experienced a severe *debt crisis* born of the *oil shocks* of the 1970s. The 1980s were marked by a consolidation of democracy and swings between the austerity of adjusting to a *stabilization program*, and radical initiatives such as bank *nationalizations*. There was also the persistent violence of the quirky, *maoist* movement *Sendero Luminoso*. President Albert Fujimori, an elected *autocrat*, reintroduced *IMF* inspired austerity and stabilization programs in 1990, including a *debt rescheduling* agreement. Investor confidence was further increased with the 1992 capture of Sendero Luminoso's founder, Abimael Guzmán. That curtailed killings by the radical left for awhile, but it did not end *human rights* abuses by the state, which grew worse as Fujimori revealed himself to be no lover of civil liberties.

Pescadores: An island chain off the SE Chinese coast, ceded to Japan after the *First Sino/Japanese War*. They were returned to China after the *defeat* of Japan in 1945.

Pétain, Henri (1856-1951): Marshal of France, President of *Vichy* 1940-44. He was the hero of *Verdun*, France's great defensive victory in *WWI*, and the successor to *Foch*. He headed French defenses in the 1920s, and put down the *Rif Rebellion* in Morocco. His *defeatism* grew apace, however, and ultimately led him to accept quick *surrender* and *collaboration* with the Germans in 1940. Even after Vichy was overrun, he continued to collaborate. In 1944 he was required to retreat to Germany as the *Allies* and *Free French* advanced. Convicted and sentenced to death for *treason* in 1945, his age and past services to the nation led to commutation of sentence to life imprisonment. See also *English Channel*.

Peter I, of Russia (1672-1725): "The Great." He took full power after ousting his sister, who was regent, with the help of foreigners in the Russian service. He devoted himself to *modernization* of Russian national life, concentrating foremost on the army and navy. In 1696 he made *war* on Turkey, seizing Azov. He then secretly traveled abroad, even working for a time as a shipwright in Amsterdam, and visiting England. These voyages confirmed him as a *westernizer*. He brought back hundreds of foreign artisans and engineers, and began several great construction and educational projects. He founded schools and universities, and he built a new capital (at the cost of many lives), *St. Petersburg*. He also crushed the rebellious gentry (streltzi), symbolically shaving their beards to show them there was no going back to their old, *slavophile* ways. Through all this he did not neglect foreign affairs. In 1700 he attacked Sweden, but was defeated at Narva. In fact, he lost battle after battle to the Swedes, except the final one at *Poltava*, dropping Sweden from the ranks of the *Great Powers* by 1709. He then turned on the *Ottoman Empire*, but was less successful in the south, losing Azov again. At home he ruled

with a mailed fist: he had his own son, who conspired against him, put to death. In 1721 the reversal of relative power vis-à-vis Sweden was confirmed by *cession* of the *Baltic States* and parts of Finland. He spent his final years in more enlightened pursuits, but that was largely due to the greater security he had given Russia through ruthless destruction of its (and his) enemies.

les petites riches: "The little, rich ones." Cultivated slang for the wealthy, developed economies of the *EFTA*: Austria, Finland, Iceland, Norway, Sweden and Switzerland. Most of them were front of the line to join the *EU* in 1995. See *deepening vs. enlargement*.

petition: A formal request from an individual, group, or state for a hearing of a grievance by an international *human rights* body. Few *covenants* permit petition from other than states, and those that do use an *Optional Protocol*. As a result, very few states afford this option to their *citizens*. On the other hand, several countries have responded with legislation to international criticism of some specific practice, after the issue arose in an individual petition (among them, Canada, Finland and Sweden).

petitum: The *object* of an international legal claim.

petrodollars: U.S. *currency* held by *oil*-producing *states* (but often redeposited in Western banks and other financial institutions). The term was in wide use in the 1970s and early 1980s, when *OPEC* price increases led to a massive transfer of *hard currency* to OPEC states from the *OECD* countries and oil-poor *Third World* states.

petty officer: The naval equivalent of a *non-commissioned officer* in the army.

Phalange: A right-wing Lebanese *militia* founded in the 1930s to defend against Syrian *annexation*. In 1975 it fought the *PLO* in Lebanon. In 1982 it allied with Israel in the *Lebanese Civil War*. It was the main loser in that war, forced in the end to accept a lesser share of power and a Syrian presence.

Philippines: Location: Pacific. Major associations: *APEC, ASEAN, NAM, UN*. Population: 68 million. Military: *counterinsurgency* focus. Long a *colony* of Spain (1565-1898), these islands were ceded to the U.S. after the *Spanish/American War*. The Filipinos, who had been doing quite nicely against the Spanish on their own and did not regard the arrival of U.S. marines as *liberation*, rejected the change of colonial masters. Under Emilio Aguinaldo (1870-1964) they switched their *guerrilla* campaign to American targets.

Fighting lasted until 1902, with the U.S. adopting some of the same tactics (e.g., *concentration camps*) against which it had ostensibly fought Spain in Cuba. The U.S. was moving toward granting *independence* to the islands (Jones Act, 1916; Tydings/McDuffe Act, 1934) when *WWII* interrupted the process. The Philippines were invaded and occupied by Japan 1941-44. Guerrilla fighting continued throughout the *occupation*, and Japanese rule and reprisals were brutal. In 1943 the U.S. committed to full independence upon *liberation*, which came with *Allied* landings and a bloody *campaign* from June 1944-July 1945. The U.S. carried through on its promise of independence on July 4, 1946. Until 1950 the Philippines faced the *Huk Rebellion*, but Filipino conservatives retained control of most of the country. In 1965 *Ferdinand Marcos* was elected and began to entrench himself as dictator. He declared *martial law* from 1972-81. Also in the 1970s, a left-wing *insurgency* resumed in the form of the *New People's Army (NPA)*. In 1986 Marcos was overthrown by a peaceful, grassroots rebellion ("people's power") led by *Corazon Aquino*. With the end of the *Cold War* and slow but steady land reform, the NPA insurgency faded into *peace*, leaving only a Muslim insurgency still smoldering on the large island of Mindinao; a pact was signed with the Muslims in 1993. Philippine *nationalism* also grew more assertive vis-à-vis the U.S. In 1992, after considerable controversy and in spite of the loss of foreign *currency* earnings, it was decided not to renew the leases on the U.S. bases at Clark Air Field (which was then destroyed by a volcano anyway) and Subic Bay. The Philippines lays claim to part of the *Spratlys*.

Phony War (September 3, 1939-May 10, 1940): The period of inactivity along the *western front* following the expiration of British and French *ultimata* to Germany over its *invasion* of Poland. The British at least began the fight at sea and assembled a force to help Norway. But the bulk of the French Army sat or drilled in the deep bunkers and fortifications of the *Maginot Line*, a picture of magnificent ineffectiveness in their sky-blue tunics. This futile activity frittered away morale, cost the French Army its fighting edge, and infected the British Expeditionary Force keeping it company on the Belgian *flank*. It ended with the Nazi *blitzkrieg* in May and June, 1940, that captured Paris and knocked France out of the war, and Britain off the continent. Cf. *sitzkrieg*.

physiocrats: An 18th century French school arguing that *land* was the sole basis of productive wealth, and thus against doctrines that stressed the role of *trade*. They also averred a *laissez-faire* attitude that influenced *Adam Smith* and other *classical liberal* writers.

Piedmont-Sardinia, Kingdom of: These Italian *territories* were united in 1748, conquered briefly by *Napoleon*, but restored in 1814. After 1850 they led the drive for Italian unification, largely achieved in 1861, and completed with the incorporation of Rome into the Kingdom of Italy in 1870. See *Sardinia*.

pillage: To rob with violence; to *plunder*, as did the Iraqi army in Kuwait in 1990. It is forbidden by the *Hague Conventions*. Cf. *requisition*.

Pilsudski, Josef (1867-1935): Polish statesman. He asked the Japanese to help a Polish *rebellion* in 1904. During *WWI* he led a Polish unit in the Austrian Army, against Russia. When Germany showed before and at *Brest-Litovsk* that it was more interested in its own eastward expansion than Polish emancipation, he protested and was arrested. Elected President of Poland after the German *defeat* in 1918, he commanded in the expansionist *Polish/Soviet War*, 1919-20. From 1926-34 he was increasingly dictatorial, and his voice alone spoke for Poland in foreign affairs. It was raised early and often about the danger that *Hitler* posed, but such warnings fell on deaf Western ears.

ping-pong diplomacy: (1) The preliminary softening-up of both American and Chinese *public opinion* preparatory to a coming *rapprochement*, by a series of ping-pong matches (China handily won almost every game) from 1970-71. This was the first direct, public contact between the two countries since the *Korean Conflict*. (2) Derived from the above, use of interstate sports contacts to break down hostile *images* of opponents and soften public opinion, prior to some diplomatic *démarche* or *coup de théâtre* that might shock "plain folks" were they not so prepared.

piracy: (1) In *international law:* [A] The use of private force to kidnap persons or detain a vessel, on the *high seas*, in the air or anywhere else outside the *territorial jurisdiction* of states, where the intention is to *plunder*. There are two types: {i} statutory: defined variously in discrete, national legal codes; {ii} piracy jure gentium ("under the law of peoples/nations"): defined in a 1934 decision as "any armed violence at sea that is not a lawful act of war," and amended under *UNCLOS III* to mean any such acts committed "for private ends." Sea pirates continue to operate, with their usual casual brutality, off the West African coast, near Thailand and off Celebes. Thousands of Vietnamese *boat people* were killed or abducted into *slavery* by pirates in the 1980s, and incidents still occur in the 1990s. [B] Setting up illegal, private, commercial *radio* or TV stations off a nation's *territorial waters* in order to broadcast to that country free of licensing, taxation or regulation. A number of states have taken forceful action against pirate radio stations (which are often immensely popular with listeners); nature itself has acted against others, by sinking ships or overturning oil rigs from which the stations operated. (2) In *economics*: The practice (but as often, merely a rhetorical charge) of illegal or unfair trade practices that aim at capturing a *monopoly* over a given market. Cf. *Barbary pirates; dumping; hijacking; international criminal law; Tripolitan War; Trucial Oman.*

Pitcairn Island: The last British *dependency* in the *South Pacific*, this tiny, isolated island has a population of fewer than 100.

Pitt, William (1759-1806): "The Younger." British statesman. PM 1783-1801, 1804-06. The youngest ever British PM, at just 24. He failed to obtain *Catholic Emancipation*, owing to a royal veto, but pushed through *union* with Ireland in 1800. He supported the anti-*slavery* campaign, and passed reforms for Canada and India. He led Britain in the first years of its great contest with Revolutionary France. He is not to be confused with his father, "Pitt the Elder" (1708-78), also the King's First Minister.

Pius IX, *né* Giovanni Ferretti (1792-1878): Pope 1846-78. He was in constant struggle with the Italian state over control of the *Papal States* and after 1870, the temporal status of the *Vatican*. He was forced to flee Rome during the *Revolutions of 1848*, but returned with French military backing. *Napoleon III* supported him from 1850-70, when Rome was united with the rest of Italy in the wake of France's *defeat* by Prussia. Pius called the *First Vatican Council*, which declared him (and his successors) "infallible" on matters of faith and doctrine. That caused severe political problems in Austria and Germany. In general, he was something of a throwback to the days of the "church militant," and much at odds with the new *nationalism* in Italy. His successors have not, on the whole, emulated his irascible style, even when they have taken his positions. See also *kulturkampf; Old Catholics.*

Pius XII, *né* Eugenio Pacelli (1876-1958): Pope 1939-58. His failure to speak publicly against the *Holocaust* is criticized by Christians, Jews and others. His reticence may have been motivated by political calculations relating to the position of the *Catholic Church* in *nazi*-occupied Europe and his deep detestation of *communism* and the *Soviet Union*, rather than any personal antipathy for Jews. But even if that is true, his silence still deafens. During the early *Cold War* he did much to persuade lay Catholic opinion that opposition to communism amounted to an absolute religious duty.

Plains of Abraham, Battle of (1759): A field near Québec City, abutted by a steep cliff, which an English army scaled to achieve its *victory* over French forces. Both commanding generals, Wolfe for the British and Montcalm for the French, were killed. The battle secured *Lower Canada* for England, a transfer confirmed in the *Peace of Paris (1763).*

planned economy: Where major decisions as to *capital* and *labor* supply are not left to the market, but are set and controlled according to certain social objectives or with bureaucratic interests foremost in mind. Typical examples of this were the *Soviet bloc* economies, and China before 1978. See *five-year plans; rationing*. Cf. *command economy; market economy.*

Plaza Agreement (September 1985): A key meeting was held in the Plaza Hotel in New York, attended by American, British, French, German and Japanese officials. They agreed to cooperate on management of international *monetary policy*. This was highly significant for two reasons: (1) it ended a post-*Bretton Woods* era of U.S. neglect of global economic mangement; and (2) it represented the definitive entry of Japan as a full partner in that management. See *G-5.*

plebiscite: A synonym for *referendum.*

plenipotentiary: A *diplomat* of *ambassadorial* or *cabinet* rank, with full powers to negotiate substantive agreements on behalf of the *state* he or she represents.

PLO: See *Palestine Liberation Organization.*

plunder: When an army steals massively from the people of an area it passes through or *occupies*. It does not carry the connotations of murder, rape and other violence that *pillaging* does. Cf. *requisition.*

pluralism: (1) A view of foreign policy *decision-making* in democratic states that argues against the control of policy by *elites*, in favor of the competition of *public opinion* and *interest groups* in developing a grand compromise that informs policy. (2) A view of the *international system* as populated by many more *actors* than just the *states*, and that does not necessarily see *security* as the main issue in *world politics*. Cf. *elitism; MNCs; nongovernmental organizations (NGOs); transnational actors; turbulence.*

plural nationality: See *dual nationality.*

plutocracy: Rule by a wealthy *elite.*

plutonium: Named for the planet Pluto, itself named

for the ancient Greeks' god of the underworld. Plutonium is a radioactive element that can sustain a chain reaction sufficient to bring about a massive, *fission* explosion, and has a fissionable isotope of prime importance in the *nuclear age*: PU^{239}. It is similar to uranium in its atomic chemistry, and is formed by bombarding the element neptunium with deuteron (or within pitchblende, where slow decay of neptunium produces U^{235}). "Ivory" plutonium is near pure PU^{239}, and is the deadliest, most poisonous substance known to humanity. It is found mainly in Russia, which built new *warheads* with fresh stocks and stored the old bombs, plutonium and all. Plutonium and highly enriched uranium (HEU) are both used to make *atomic bombs*, and the triggering component of *hydrogen bombs*. Uranium has two main isotopes: U^{235} and U^{238}. The first is the bomb-grade material. For the second to be used in weapons it must be enriched with U^{235}, producing HEU. It takes about 35 kg (77 lbs.) of civilian plutonium to make a *Hiroshima*-sized bomb, but only about 5 kg (11 lbs.) of military grade metal. There is presently in the world about 1,000 metric tonnes (2,200,000 lbs.) of plutonium and 2,000 metric tonnes (4,400,000 lbs.) of HEU. Of the HEU, 95% is held by the U.S. and Russian militaries combined. Thus, only 1% falls under *IAEA* inspections and safeguards. Yet it only takes about 220 kg of HEU (and less than 45 kg of metal if one uses plutonium), or 0.01% of the total stock to make a new *nuclear state*. The majority of plutonium is actually in various civilian hands, with only about 30% under IAEA or other safeguards. Military plutonium production is abating, as the U.S. and Russia move toward agreement on no longer making it. But civilian production is increasing as "fast" or breeder reactors enrich old plutonium and HEU to make it viable for power generation (and coincidentally, for weapons manufacture). The U.S. has agreed to buy surplus Russian stocks of HEU for civilian use. Some have proposed developing "mixed-oxide fuel" (MOX), in which surplus plutonium is blended with HEU for civilian reactors. This may be important, as there is a paradox of nuclear *arms control* unfolding: some 700-800 metric tonnes of HEU presently in bombs is due for release (through dismantling) under *START*. But there is no safe place to put it, either in terms of the environment or security from theft, and as yet no commercial use for it.

pocket battleship: A *battleship* in all respects except tonnage, due to limitations placed on displacement (ship size) by several *treaties*.

pogrom: "Devastation." This Yiddish term entered most Western languages after physical attacks on Jews and their property in *tsarist Russia* in 1881-82, when Jews were blamed for the assassination of *Alexander II* (a false charge). The carnage engaged European and U.S. attention due to a massive outflow of destitute *refugees* (from 1881-1920, over two million Jews fled to the U.S. alone). The pogroms increased in ferocity after the *Russian Revolution (1905)*. Pogroms also took place in Poland, Rumania, Hungary and the Soviet Union in the 1920s and 1930s. Some were spontaneous, springing from peasant bigotry and superstition, but many were government inspired. During 1990 there were rumblings from *Pamyat* about a new pogrom, but none materialized. See also *anti-Semitism; kristallnacht.*

Poincaré, Raymond (1860-1934): French statesman. PM 1912, 1922-24, 1926-29; President 1913-20; Foreign Minister 1922-24. He improved the *alliance* with Russia and *entente* with Britain before *WWI*. As President, he stood above the turmoil of wartime policy. He approved *occupation* of the *Ruhr* in 1923, but without either American or British approval could not buttress that stratagem, and resigned.

poison: Under terms of the *Hague Conventions*, poison as a weapon of *war* (for use against, say, a city's water supply system) is illegal. Yet, the limited utility of poisons, rather than their illegality, is probably the main cause of their restricted use in warfare. See also *chemical weapons; gas weapons; nerve weapons.*

poison gas: See *gas weapons.*

Poland: Location: E. Europe. Major associations: *CSCE, UN.* Population: 40 million. Military: *Warsaw Pact* equipment; downsizing as part of the CFE agreement. A *Great Power* in the Middle Ages, in an effort to arrest mutual decline it joined for a time with Lithuania. But the decline continued, and Poland found itself as barley, caught between the great millstones of *Prussia* and *Russia*. It disappeared from the maps with the three *partitions of Poland* 1772-95. Two great rebellions in the 19th century, in 1831 and 1863, were both crushed by Russia. An independent Poland did not reappear on the map until 1918, and then was enriched with *territory* taken from Germany at the *Paris Peace Conference* to create the *Polish Corridor*. It made its presence felt in the east with the expansionist *Polish/Soviet War*, and membership in the *Little Entente*. Until 1934 *Pilsudski* dominated Polish politics and foreign policy. In all discussions of collective defense in the 1930s, Poland refused to consider transit for the *Red Army* heading for the Czech/German frontier to repel a German *invasion*. That was one reason no eastern defense pact was agreed. Instead, Poland became the main target of the *Nazi/Soviet Pact*, which cleared the way for Germany to attack on September 1, 1939. Two weeks later the *Red Army* crossed the border not as defenders against, but as collaborators with, the Germans (and the *NKVD* followed, and following them, the massacre at *Katyn*). The Nazi *occupation* of Poland was horrific: millions of its *citizens*, including most of its Jewish citizens, were murdered. But not all Poles mourned the loss of the Jews, and some even *collaborated* in their extermination: the country had a history of deep *anti-Semitism*. The Red Army returned in 1944, this time as liberator and occupier rolled into one. It paused to permit the Germans to crush the *Warsaw Rising*, then installed a communist government at Lublin that would displace the *government-in-exile* in London after the war. Poland was a major topic of discussion at *Teheran, Yalta* and *Potsdam*. In 1945 it was reconstituted on the *Oder-Neisse Line* in the west and the *Curzon Line* in the east. Millions of Poles moved westward, expelling the Germans of *East Prussia* and *Silesia*, the innocent along with the guilty, in punishment for what their Nazi masters had done to 10,000 Polish towns and villages, and six million or more compatriots. By the end of 1946 Poland was firmly within the *Soviet bloc*, with successive governments towing the *party line* as set in Moscow: It joined the *Warsaw Pact* in 1955 and participated in the invasion of Czechoslovakia in 1968. Serious rioting occurred across Poland in 1956, and again in 1970, both times leading to cosmetic changes. A tidal shift came after 1976, when *John Paul II* (a Polish cardinal) was elected pope. A surge of *nationalism* combined with pent-up economic frustration to give birth to the extraordinary national movement *Solidarity*, led by *Lech Walesa*. In 1980 more strikes and violence erupted, culminating in the displacement of the *communist party* by the Polish military under General *Jaruzelski*, the declaration of *martial law* from 1981-82 and U.S. trade *sanctions*. The communist facade cracked, revealing a crumbling foundation as well. In 1989 Solidarity was legalized, multiparty elections held and effective Polish independence reestablished. In 1990 Walesa was elected President. After three years of economic *shock treatment* on the way to a *market economy*, by 1993 *inflation* began to recede and Polish *GNP* and industrial output began to grow again. In the process, Solidarity moved back into opposition and both it and Polish national unity shattered into the inescapable quarreling factions of normal politics. That was only made more clear by 1993 elections, out of which came a coalition government formed of two parties with roots in the old communist system, a clear reaction against the harsh--though unavoidable--deprivations of the transition period.

Poland, partitions of: (1) 1772: Portions of Poland were *annexed* by Austria, Prussia and Russia. (2) 1793: Austria was excluded from a round of annexation by Prussia and Russia, with the latter acquiring the lion's share of *territory*. (3) 1795: Poland was extinguished, again divided between the three eastern powers. Together, these three partitions of one of Europe's largest *states* destroyed the myth that the *balance of power* system was a natural, and naturally benevolent, mechanism working to preserve the *independence* of *sovereign* states. Instead, it appeared to be essentially a device for preserving *equilibrium* among the *Great Powers*. (4) 1815: From 1807-14 a French vassal state, the Duchy of Poland, made a brief appearance, but it was eliminated at the *Congress of Vienna*. In 1815 Prussia and Russia rearranged their Polish holdings, with more territory going to Russia. (5) 1939: Germany and Russia divided Poland (which had reappeared in 1918) in the *Nazi/Soviet pact*, an agreement nullified by *Barbarossa* in July 1941. (6) 1944-45: Poland was moved 200 miles west and north, at the behest of *Stalin*. It was *compensated* for its eastern losses with western provinces taken from Germany. The respective German and Polish populations were expelled, or *ethnically cleansed* as one might euphemistically say in the 1990s.

polar regions: See *Antarctic; Arctic.*

police action: A euphemism for the use of force to bring about compliance with *Security Council* resolutions. Most famously, the *war* in Korea was called a police action, thereby avoiding the need to *declare war* (which involves time-consuming debates). The term also implies a UN role as "globocop."

police activities (on the high seas): See *hot pursuit; piracy; slave trade; visit and search.*

police state: One in which *secret police* or the military enforce draconian restrictions on civil, political and personal liberties.

POLISARIO: The *independence* and *guerrilla* movement in *Western Sahara* that forced Mauritania to abandon its claim 1976-79, and has fought Morocco since then. Its prime backer is Algeria. It has been *recognized* by many countries as the *government-in-exile* of Western Sahara.

Polish Corridor: A narrow strip of *territory* cutting through *East Prussia* near the Vistula, given to Poland at the *Paris Peace Conference*. It permitted Polish goods access to the seaport of *Danzig*. It was a serious irritant in German/Polish relations during the *interwar years*. *Nazi* demands for "*liberation*" served as the excuse for the German attack of September 1, 1939, which was the proximate cause of *WWII*.

Polish/Soviet War (1919-20): With Russia in the throes of the *Russian Civil War*, the Poles struck east in a bid for *territory*. Led by *Pilsudski* and in *alliance* with Ukrainian *Whites*, they overran much of Ukraine. They briefly captured Kiev itself in May 1920, before being repulsed and driven deep into Poland by the *Red Army*, fresh from its victories over Crimean *Cossacks* and Ukrainian Whites. A second Polish offensive, in August, pushed the Russians back and retook much eastern territory lost in the spring. In the Treaty of Riga (March 1921) Poland accepted portions of western Byelorussia and Ukraine. These areas were not recovered by the *Soviet Union* until it attacked Poland in September 1939, fulfilling the *Nazi/Soviet Pact*.

Politburo (*Politichekoye*): "Political Bureau." The governing council of the Soviet *Communist Party* and system. In 1952, just before *Stalin's* death, it merged into the Presidium. But that represented a cosmetic change only; after *Khrushchev's* fall from grace and power even the name was changed back.

political capital: A metaphor wherein political influence is likened to *capital* reserves, in that its present sum and future purchasing power decline with expenditure (use or application). However, it should be noted that political capital is rather more like money kept in a mattress than a portfolio: if not invested or spent, it will only depreciate (and very rapidly, as *George Bush* learned from 1991-92).

political dispute: One that by its contentious nature is considered inappropriate for legal settlement; a synonym is *nonjusticiable dispute*. Cf. *legal dispute*.

political economy: (1) In modern usage: {A} study of the interrelatedness of *politics* and *economics*, whether at the domestic or international levels; {B} the use of economic models of rational choice to explain political decisions and actions; {C} the actual structures of interrelated, global (or regional or national) political and economic activity and phenomena, including but not limited to world markets, production and consumption patterns, global financial and trade institutions, *MNCs*, and the *states*, their governments and myriad economic regulations. (2) In the 19th century: a social science that developed into the modern discipline of *economics*. (3) In the era of *mercantilism*: A body of thought about how best to manage national society to maintain wealth, relative to other states.

political prisoner: A person incarcerated for political beliefs or acts. Legality is broadly unimportant in this concept, as repressive societies often ban in law actions that in a free society are taken as normal, or at least as protected, exercise of civil rights (e.g., printing and circulating pamphlets, organizing political rallies or joining a strike). A political prisoner may or may not, therefore, have advocated the use of violence against a repressive system. This term is generally used without reference to democratic states, where mechanisms of free speech, assembly and political representation exist, and where violent opposition to the existing state of political affairs is therefore widely (and correctly) viewed as both criminal and illegitimate. Cf. *prisoner of conscience*.

political science: A social science concerned with the systematic study of public affairs. At its best, it draws questions from the conversation across time of the great political thinkers, as well as from current policy debates. Its methodology is necessarily eclectic, drawing on such fields as economics, geography, history, law, philosophy, psychology, sociology and statistics. It is usually subdivided into comparative politics, international relations, political economy, political philosophy and political theory. Concerning political science and world affairs see *anarchical society; anarchy; behavioralism; bureaucratic politics; case study; cognitive dissonance; cybernetic theory; decision-making theory; dependency theory; deterrence; end of history; events data; falsification; game theory; geopolitics; grand theory; Hegel; hegemony; hegemonic stability theory; Hobbes; idealism; input; instrumental rationality; international organization; international system; jargon; Kant; levels of analysis; liberal-internationalism; long-cycle theory; Machiavelli; Marx; marxism; marxism-leninism; misperception; mirror image; neo-realism; objectivity; obscurantism; organizational process model; paradigm; pluralism; post-behavioralism; power; qualitative analysis; quantitative analysis; rational decision-making; realism; realist; regime; regression analysis; Rousseau; scientism; standard operating procedure; structuralism; systems theory; taxonomy; theory; traditionalism; units; variables*. Cf. *economics; history*.

politics: (1) The art and science of governance, by consent, force, intrigue, manipulation and stratagem, and embracing the whole complex of public affairs within and among societies. (2) "Who gets what, when and how" [Harold Lasswell]. (3) "The authoritative allocation of values" [David Easton]. (4) "That realm where conscience and power meet, where the ethical and coercive factors of human life interpenetrate and work out their tentative and uneasy compromises" [Reinhold Niebuhr].

polity: (1) A synonym for both *state* and a given *regime*. (2) Any organized political community.

Polk, James Knox (1794-1849): U.S. statesman. President, 1845-49. He was elected as an *expansionist*, specifically on the issue of admitting *Texas* to the Union as a *slave state*. Polk is most remembered for deliberately provoking the *Mexican/American War* by advancing troops to the border, and other incitements. He played upon submerged, romantic and expansionist sentiments (that later surfaced as *manifest destiny*) among the public. His private objectives were more prosaic: he wanted to acquire the deep harbors of *California* for the U.S. as a stepping stone to becoming a great commerical nation on the Pacific, as it already was on the Atlantic. He succeeded, in a shatteringly one-sided war that permanently scarred U.S./Mexican relations and brought vast new *territories* under the American flag. Yet it also greatly deepened the national crisis over *slavery* by raising the question of the admission of several new states carved from the Mexican lands as *slave state* or *free soil* applicants.

Pol Pot, né Saloth Sar (b.1926): Cambodian communist. See *Cambodian genocide; Khmers Rouges.*

Poltava, Battle of (1709): Russians under *Peter I (the Great)* defeated Swedes under *Charles XII* near this Ukrainian city. It knocked Sweden from the ranks of the *Great Powers* and confirmed Russia's rise.

polycentrism: (1) Archaic: allowing for national differences in the implementation of communist theory. (2) A synonym for *multipolarity*. It is not quite as excessive a bit of *jargon* as *bipolycentrism.*

Polynesia: The sea and islands east of *Melanesia* and *Micronesia*, extending N/S from Hawaii to Australasia. Its *indigenous peoples* are ethnically distinct.

Pompidou, Georges (1911-74): French statesman. PM 1962-68; President 1969-74. A loyal follower of *de Gaulle*, he negotiated the Algerian *cease-fire* in 1961, and served as de Gaulle's compliant PM. However, as president he took the important step of reversing the *veto* of Britain's entry into the *European Community.*

pontoon bridge: A floating, makeshift military bridge, where track is laid over boats or other floats.

pooled sovereignty: The partial surrender of decision-making over traditionally domestic matters, to consensus procedures with other states, as in the *EU.*

Popular Front governments: Coalitions of *liberals,* socialists and *communists* formed in France and other European countries in the 1930s to address the *Great Depression,* and to a lesser extent to fend off the rise of *fascism*. See *social fascism.* Cf. *National Front.*

popular sovereignty: (1) An *Enlightenment* political doctrine that was really launched with the American and more importantly the *French Revolution*. It holds that a *sovereign's* right to rule derives from the people, and rejects the older, absolutist notion of a *divine right of kings*. It revolutionized international relations by challenging the *ancien régime* with ideas of democracy and *self-determination*. (2) In the pre-*Civil War* U.S. this term was used by *states' rights* advocates to deny federal jurisdiction over *slavery* issues.

population: The number of people in a given *territory*. By convention, this is one of the tangible components of national *power*, with the equation assumed to be: larger population = increased power. That notion derives from military competition within Europe in the 19th century, particularly the experience of France, which fell behind Germany in its birth rate and hence saw its relative military power decline (fewer potential *conscripts* in each intake year). However, the impact of population cannot be evaluated discretely from the ability of the country to sustain it. That is one reason China and India introduced draconian population control programs. Nor may it be divorced from intangibles such as *national morale*, the quality of one's *diplomacy,* access to *natural resources, standards of living* and so forth. See *famine; food; industrialization; infant mortality rate; Malthus; malthusian; ZPG.*

population explosion: The idea that uncontrolled population growth will lead to calamitous economic, social and political effects. See *Malthus; malthusian.*

Port Arthur (a.k.a. Darien; Ryojun): A major *warm water port* on the Liaotung peninsula, in northern China. Russia based its far eastern fleet there after 1897, and that was where the Japanese found and sunk it in a surprise attack in 1904. Japan took possession under the *Treaty of Portsmouth*, and later forced the Chinese to issue a 99-year lease. The Soviets retook the port in 1945. They returned it to China in 1955.

portfolio investment: When foreign investors buy shares in national firms, but do not take control or provide *infrastructure*. Also, government bonds and loans. Cf. *foreign direct investment.*

Portsmouth, Treaty of (1905): Russia was racked by *revolution* in 1905, but Japan was nearly bankrupt, and could not make headway on land in the *Russo/Japan-*

ese War. Tokyo therefore asked *Teddy Roosevelt* to *mediate* an end to the conflict. The parties met at Portsmouth, New Hampshire. *Manchuria* was returned to nominal Chinese control (that is, neither side won its major aim, which was to secure Manchuria). Russia agreed to acknowledge a Japanese *sphere of influence* in Korea, transfer *Port Arthur* and the Liaotung peninsula to Japan, as well as southern *Sakhalin Island.* But no *indemnity* was paid. That led to anti-American riots in Japan when Japanese leaders transferred the blame for a less-than-triumphant *peace* to Roosevelt, via a concerted *propaganda* effort.

Portugal: Location: W. Europe. Major associations: *CSCE, EU, NATO, OECS, UN, WEU.* Population: 11 million. Military: among the smaller and less well-equipped NATO forces. Portugal has been an independent *state* for over 850 years. In the 15th and 16th centuries it numbered among the great maritime powers, sending explorers along the coasts of Africa, India and Latin America. These expeditions were soon followed by traders, missionaries, soldiers and settlers, as Portugal built an overseas *empire* on three continents, often connecting the different bits through the *slave trade.* As it declined if fell increasingly under the influence of Britain, a rising maritime power. Portugal was invaded and occupied by *Napoleon,* and subsequently was drawn into the *Peninsular War.* It lost Brazil in 1822, but clung to its possessions in Africa and India. The *monarchy* was overthrown in 1910. Portugal stayed out of *WWI,* but in 1926 its democracy was overthrown and a military dictatorship installed. In 1932 Portugal was converted to a quasi-*fascist* dictatorship under *Salazar.* It again was neutral in *WWII.* It was a charter member of NATO. In 1961 it lost *Portuguese India.* From 1964-74 it faced *guerrilla wars* in its African colonies (Angola, Guinea-Bissau and Mozambique), allying itself with Rhodesia and South Africa. From 1974-76 Portugal underwent great domestic turmoil, from which it emerged a stable democracy and during which it shed its African colonies. It retained *Macao.* It joined the *EC* in 1986, and has enjoyed increased prosperity since 1975.

Portuguese East Africa: Now *Mozambique.*

Portuguese Guinea: Now *Guinea-Bissau.*

Portuguese India: A composite *colony* consisting of the tiny *enclaves* of Daman, Diu and Goa, under Portuguese control from c.1510. All three were forcibly retaken by India in 1961.

Portuguese West Africa: A *colony* of Portugal, now independent as *Angola.*

positive control: Military jargon for *fail-safe* systems. These require a definite "go" command that must be authenticated before weapons are launched.

positive law: Law that is written down, or otherwise clearly established or recognized by governments, usually in *treaty* form. Cf. *natural law.*

positive sum game: A *variable sum game* where the outcomes for all players sum greater than zero.

positivism: (1) In general: a theory about knowledge that rejects all intuition as mere metaphysics, is unconcerned with ends or origins, and holds that the only real knowledge possible must be based on the *empirical* study of positively ("objectively") existing phenomenon. (2) In *international law:* an approach that insists legal *rules* exist only if states have given their *consent,* and that new rules cannot be made by reasoning alone or be said to lodge in the supposed eternal verities of *natural law.*

post-behavioralism: (1) A general trend in the social sciences away from strict *behavioralism* as an approach to the study of world affairs, toward a mix of methodologies and theoretical "*paradigms.*" Post-behavioralism has shifted contemporary research from an often fruitless and contentious debate over methodology back to a concern with substantive matters. But in the process it has carried along a number of *quantitative* techniques, and uses these alongside more traditional, or *qualitative,* approaches (though this eclecticism should not be mistaken for synthesis). (2) An effort within the academy to hive off *international relations* as a distinct field of study, drawing upon *economics, history, political science* and other disciplines, but separate from them in its central questions and interests. (3) A rather pretentious term for otherwise welcome calls for philosophical, historical and policy relevance, and the use of less arcane methods and language in political science and other academic research about world affairs.

post-boost vehicle (PBV): See *bus.*

post hoc ergo propter hoc: "After this, therefore because of it." A famous logical fallacy in which the mere fact that one event precedes another leads to the assumption that the first caused the second. For example, it is true enough that *arms* manufacturers tend to profit from increased *military spending* during a *war* (or *arms race*). But while it may be true, it does not necessarily follow that they had any hand in bringing the war (or arms race) about. Or, because a nation acquired *territory* in the settlement of a war it has won, it may, but it does not necessarily, follow that the acquisition of territory was its reason for going to war in the first place. In short, it may or may not be true that prior event A caused subsequent event B, but it is certainly false to assume it is true.

post-imperialism: An academic theory developed after c.1975 in response to: (1) major changes in the world economy attendant on the *OPEC oil shocks* and the rise of the *NICs;* (2) the growing unattractiveness of *dependency theory* for *Third World* elites (and for different reasons, not a few academic *radicals*); and (3) the abject failure of dependency prescriptions (such as *autarky* from world markets) in practice. Its basic premise is that *imperialism* was a historic phase that is now effectively finished. Hence, it suggests, theories that depict the Third World as locked into perpetually exploitative relations by *neo-colonial* structures generated by modern *capitalism* are at odds with reality. The continuing expansion of capitalism is not to be seen as necessarily imperialistic. Instead, *MNCs, foreign direct investment* and other features of *North/South* economic relations are viewed in a much more positive light than that cast by dependency theorists. Capitalism is portrayed as potentially unifying Third World national economies, and reorganizing them to participate in the world economy according to the mutually beneficial dictates of *comparative advantage*. It is also already acting as the main source of *technology transfer* and *capital,* and the capitalist nations are the main markets for Southern exports. Many *developing countries*, and especially the NICs, are described as run by elites that appreciate the mutuality and positive *interdependence* of North/South connections. This stands in stark contrast to the dependency/*marxist* view of such elites as *comprador classes*. Note: some "post-imperialist" writers represent the above, fairly traditional and *liberal* view of capitalism as relatively benign. But others are quite radical, using this thesis not to point out that dependency theory has overplayed its negative portrayal of the effects of capitalism so much as to note development of a global capitalist class, against which they urge others to direct political and analytical fire.

postlaunch survivability: The ability of an aircraft or *missile* to survive enemy defenses and complete its mission of attack. Cf. *prelaunch survivability.*

postliminium: Returning an *occupied territory* to its previous legal status.

postwar: (1) The period immediately following any *war,* usually characterized by political uncertainty, even instability, in at least the losing country and often on both sides. This is caused by a lack of clarity about what the outcome of the war actually is. As far more wars end in relative shifts in the *balance of power* than in total *victory* for one side (e.g., *WWI*), it takes time to figure out just what the degree of shift is. And those few wars that do end in absolute victory (e.g., *WWII*) also cause uncertainty, by rendering unclear the relative gains and losses of each member of the winning coalition and their new relationship toward one another. Furthermore, for some years there may be no one in the losing state(s) sufficiently acceptable to the winners with whom to make the inevitable and necessary *rapprochement.* (2) A cultural marker for an extended period following a great war, where politics and/or social life are notably different from the antebellum period. See also *diktat.*

Potemkin, Grigori Alexandrovich (1739-91): Russian statesman. He directed Russia's affairs under *Catherine II* (the Great). His particular charge was the southern lands newly conquered from the Turks. He participated in several southern wars, in nominal command over *Suvorov.* For Russia and himself, he conquered the *Crimea* and much of the Black Sea region, even founding the great port city of *Sebastopol.* The famous story of his erecting false towns ("Potemkin villages") to deceive Catherine as to the condition of the peasants is probably apocryphal, but usefully illustrates both her distance from the Russian people and his political sagacity and talent for self-promotion.

Potsdam, Conference of (July 17-August 2, 1945): The final wartime conference of the *Big Three* in *WWII,* held just outside the ruins of Berlin. While *Joseph Stalin* was an old hand at wartime *diplomacy,* it was *Harry Truman's* first conference. Upon losing a general election, *Winston Churchill* found himself replaced halfway through by *Clement Atlee.* One day before the meetings began the first *atomic bomb* was detonated in the New Mexico desert. When Truman informed Stalin of this he was perplexed that the great dictator was not surprised. (It was learned later that Stalin knew of the secret *Manhattan Project,* if not of the actual test, through Soviet *agents* who had penetrated it.) Truman and Churchill agreed that the news meant the vast reserves of Russian manpower would no longer be needed to defeat Japan; but Russia would enter the eastern war anyway, as agreed at *Yalta.* It was decided to *disarm* and *demilitarize* Germany, as well as *purge* it of Nazis and set up *war crimes* tribunals, but to treat it as a single economic and political unit. There was a continuing quarrel over the degree of *reparations* to be exacted from Germany, and deeper quarrels over interpretation and carrying out the Yalta agreements on Eastern Europe. A particular problem was the *Oder-Neisse Line*, which the Western allies refused to recognize as other than temporary. The discussion of these issues always assumed that a set of *peace treaties* would follow in due course (they did for the smaller *Axis* powers, but never for Germany and separately for Japan). Also rejected by the Western powers were Stalin's demands for control of the *Dardanelles* and of the Italian *colony* of *Tripoli* (Libya). On Asia, the U.S. was to receive the Japanese *surrender* in Korea south of the 38th parallel, in the Pacific Islands, the Philippines and Japan itself. The Soviets were to take control of the *Kuriles* and *Sakhalin*, Korea north of the 38th parallel and *Manchuria*. The Chinese were to accept surrender of all Japanese forces in China, and in Indochina to the 16th parallel. The British were to receive all surrenders in Southeast Asia. Finally, it was agreed to issue the *Potsdam Declaration* on the war against Japan. Potsdam was conducted in an air of deepening acrimony, and revealed many of the *Cold War* divisions to come. See *Japanese Peace Treaty; Paris Treaties (1947).*

Potsdam Declaration (July 26, 1945): *Stalin* did not join in this (the *Soviet Union* was not yet at *war* with Japan), but it was endorsed by *Harry Truman, Clement Atlee* and *Chiang Kai-shek*. It promised that the *Allies* would occupy and disarm Japan, called for *occupation* policies to purge it of *militarism* and proposed to limit its defense forces to the *home islands*. The declaration's central demand was for Japan's *unconditional surrender*, barring which it could expect "prompt and utter destruction." The threat was, of course, to use the *atomic bomb*--successfully tested just 10 days prior. However, the Japanese could not, and did not, know that.

poverty: Basically, even crudely, when personal or national income falls below the level needed to provide food and shelter. In political reality, the definition of poverty is a subjective and relative concept varying with each society and era. For it reflects wants and desires compared with the relatively privileged status of others in that society, and not just one's physical needs: to be poor in Germany or Japan is quite a different matter from being poor in Bangladesh or Mali.

POW: See *prisoner of war.*

power: (1) A relationship of economic, military or other superiority (inequality) that gives one *actor* the ability to sway the policy or behavior of others, and by that to produce the outcomes it wants. (2) Possessing great *capabilities* relative to other *states*, varying from issue to issue. (3) Anything that creates and helps one maintain control over the minds and actions of men and women [Hans Morgenthau]. By convention, the sources of national power are split into tangible and intangible components: {A} Tangible: *food* supply; economic strength (*competitiveness, productivity,* wealth); geography (*size, location, climate* and *topography*); *industrialization;* military capability; *natural resources; population;* and *technology;* {B} Intangible: generalship; *ideology; national morale; prestige;* and the quality of one's *diplomacy.* Cf. *coercion; influence; leverage; propaganda; soft power.*

power politics: The approach to international relations analysis, or to *statecraft* that sees *states* as ends in themselves, grades them according to their *capabilities,* and stresses the use of whatever means are necessary and at hand to the dedicated pursuit of the *national interest.* It is especially identified with the threat or use of force. Cf. *idealpolitik; Machiavelli; machtpolitik; raison d'etat; realism; realpolitik.*

power sharing: A constitutional division of powers that modifies strict democratic representation with a preserved bloc of seats for a given group. It was used in Rhodesia (Zimbabwe) to ease white acceptance of *majority rule,* and was proposed by some for South Africa, but not adopted.

power transition theory: The idea that *wars* are more likely as one *state* passes another in relative *power.* The trigger is this or that *crisis,* but the fundamental *cause* is the refusal of the weakening state to accept a loss of power and *prestige,* and fear that passivity while still in a superior position may cause it to be overcome by the rising rival at a later date.

Prague Spring: An unofficial term for the 1968 liberalization movement in Czechoslovakia under *Alexander Dubček.* It was crushed by an *invasion* by the *Warsaw Pact.* The reforms presaged the cultural, press and individual liberties that *Gorbachev* would introduce in the Soviet Union itself 20 years later--when they proved precisely as mortally threatening to the communist system as *Brezhnev* feared in 1968.

Pravda: "Truth." This (in)famous newspaper was the mouthpiece of the *Communist Party* of the Soviet Union for seven decades. Few today would claim it ever lived up to its masthead. *Boris Yeltsin* banned it in October 1993, after a failed communist rising led to street fighting in Moscow. Cf. *Izvestia.*

preamble: The prologue to a *treaty* or *final act,* usually dwelling on matters of general principle.

preemptive strike: A surprise attack on the enemy,

provoked by the belief that one is about to be attacked or to remove a basic threat, as in Israel's attack on an Iraqi nuclear reactor on June 7, 1981. It may also be aggressive, designed to achieve *strategic* superiority with a single blow, as in the Japanese attack on *Pearl Harbor*. Cf. *preventive war.*

preferential tariff/trade: Granting special *terms of trade* to certain states, by means of lower *tariffs* on their *imports* than apply to other states. Cf. *imperial tariff; most-favored-nation; STABEX.*

prelaunch survivability: The ability of a weapon to survive a direct attack and still launch. Cf. *postlaunch survivability.*

preliminary objection: The first notice by a *state* of objection to a legal proceeding, on grounds (procedure or *jurisdiction*) unrelated to the merits of the case.

preponderant power: A *state* that is markedly superior in economic or military power, and hence dominates all such arrangements in its region due to its sheer presence and expansive interests. It may also do this deliberately, in which case *imperialism* flows from its preponderance. But note that preponderance, even dominance, and imperialism may not be the same thing: the former may be unintentional or unavoidable; the latter is neither. Examples of preponderance, imperial or not: Japan in East Asia, 1895-1945; Germany in Central Europe 1870-1943, 1989- ; India in Southwest Asia 1965- ; Russia in the Caucasus c.1780- ; the U.S. in the Western hemisphere since c.1880, and globally c.1917-90. Cf. *primacy; primus inter pares.*

prescription: Uninterrupted *occupation* of a *territory* that formerly belonged to another *state*, leading to a *recognized* legal claim after the passage of time. It assumes the previous state is *extinct*, or acquiesces in the occupation. The necessary period for prescription to take hold remains highly moot.

Presidium: See *Politburo.*

prestige: Seeking acknowledgement and/or enhancement of one's ranking among the *states* is common to most diplomatic endeavors, even if seldom the prime goal of an initiative. Yet prestige is still best understood as an aspect, rather than a mere representation of *power*. It may be sought for domestic purposes--to provide an inflated sense of national importance among the general public that is *fungible* into support for certain foreign policies, or for a given regime, dictator or political party. Or, foreign acknowledgment of a state's power ranking may be sought out, as con-vertible into acceptance of one's foreign policy preferences. Prestige thus both reflects and influences the power evaluations made about one state made by all other states, and this has a real impact on foreign policy behavior. States are therefore about as jealous of their prestige (and as sensitive to slights against it) as, say, junior cabinet ministers, associate professors or LA gang leaders. See *force de frappe; May Day; middle power; Olympic Games; Partial Test Ban Treaty; power transition theory; preponderance; primacy; primus inter pares; protocol; save face; soft power; space race; SPUTNIK; weltpolitik.*

preventive diplomacy: Closely associated with *Dag Hammarskjöld*, it was originally the idea of *diplomatic intervention* in conflicts concerning areas not of direct concern to the major protagonists in the *Cold War*. It was designed to try to exclude the *superpowers* from carrying their competition into new areas and regions. Since the end of the Cold War, it has shaded somewhat into the idea of *peacemaking*. But it still means a primary emphasis on *advisory services, mediation, good offices* and so forth, rather than *multilateral* military action. See also *peacekeeping*. Cf. *CSCE; UN.*

preventive war: A near synonym for a *preemptive strike*, but implying a more extensive use of *force*; e.g., Israel's destruction of Arab air forces and subsequent land attacks during the *Third Arab/Israeli War*, in contrast with its sharp but limited attacks on *PLO* or *Hezbollah* bases in Lebanon.

price controls: Regulatory *intervention* in the marketplace to freeze prices, usually at artificially low levels. They are often used concerning *food* staples, especially bread, as a means of dampening political unrest by maintaining a minimum "social bargain" with the poorest members of society. Cf. *black market; free market; stabilization program.*

price elasticity: The rate at which, and the range within which, demand for a *good* or *service* changes in response to price. See *elasticity of demand.*

price supports: When a government *intervenes* in the marketplace to inflate the price of a *commodity* as an aid to domestic producers.

primacy: The condition of being first in *power* and *prestige*. Sometimes inaccurately used to mean *hegemony*. See *preponderant power; primus inter pares.*

primary producer: A *state* whose economy is heavily dependent on the *export* of *primary products* rather than manufactured *goods*. Such states must often re-import at much higher prices manufactured or processed goods made from their own lower-priced primary exports. This relation was a mainstay of colonial economics. For instance, *Gandhi* opened many eyes about the underlying economic nature of the *Raj* with a *boycott* of British cloth made from Indian cotton, then reexported to India. In *dependency theory*, primary producer nations invariably are portrayed as exploited by the structure of the *world capitalist system*.

primary products: Unprocessed or minimally processed *goods*; e.g., *oil* that is exported unrefined; or exporting logs, rather than paper; or exporting raw fruit, rather than tinned fruit.

Primo de Rivera, Miguel (1870-1930): Spanish general. Dictator 1923-30. His forces were defeated by the U.S. in the Philippines in 1898. After 1923 he tried to found a *fascist* regime on the Italian model. His efforts inspired formation of the *Falange* (founded by his son, José). He put down the *Rif Rebellion*.

primus inter pares: "First among equals." (1) The greatest among the *Great Powers*; the one enjoying the most *power* and status, such as the U.S. in *power* since 1917, and power and *prestige* since 1945; or Britain, France and Spain in earlier eras, or China in a different region and era. (2) The leading state in a region or on an issue, in any identifiable group of states. Cf. *preponderant power*.

Princely States: Some 700 quasi-independent statelets of varying size in India, connected to the *Raj* by *treaties* securing their *autonomy*. They were all dissolved into India and Pakistan in 1947, though the choice made by *Kashmir's* ruler has been disputed ever since.

principality: A state governed by a prince, duke, or some lesser nobility, but not a king; e.g., *Monaco*.

Principal Organs (of the UN): There are six: (1) the *Security Council*; (2) the *General Assembly*; (3) *ECO-SOC*; (4) the *Trusteeship Council*; (5) the *Secretariat*; (6) the *International Court of Justice*.

principal power: (1) A synonym for *Great Power*. (2) In an academic--and even then, idiosyncratic--usage, powers said to be "principal" in importance to some other country(ies), without themselves being Great Powers; e.g., the relationship of Australia and New Zealand to some of the South Pacific *microstates*.

principal state: One that accepts to exercise delegated authority over foreign policy and security, granted by an *associated state;* e.g., the U.S. in its capacity to-

ward the *Marshall Islands;* or New Zealand vis-à-vis the *Cook Islands.*

prisoner of conscience: An *Amnesty International* designation for political *dissidents*; it carries the proviso that they must not have advocated or used violence to advance their cause. This definition troubles those who might view this or that *war* for *self-determination* or an *uprising* against an unjust government as quite moral, and its practitioners as deserving of defense from persecution (or even prosecution). However, the restrictive definition has the merit of allowing AI to avoid having to make just such difficult, and inherently political, judgments about the causes dissidents espouse. It is widely believed that AI's resulting reputation for objectivity increases its persuasiveness, at least with some governments. Cf. *political prisoner.*

prisoner of war (POW): A legal status in which military personnel captured by the enemy have specific rights and duties as spelled out in the *Geneva Conventions*, distinct from those of *civilians*. These rights are conditional upon *belligerents* being party to the conventions, and even then are frequently ignored in the cruelty of combat and captivity. The *postwar* return of POWs has at times complicated *peace* negotiations, or a resumption of *normalized relations*. Tens of thousands of German and even some *Allied* POWs were kept in the Soviet Union after *WWII*, in the case of the Germans as a form of unilateral *reparations* (they were put to *forced labor* on *reconstruction* work, and many were never allowed home). Disputes and recriminations over forcible return of POWs drew out the *Korean Conflict* negotiations for many months. India and Pakistan have argued over POWs after their several wars, while some Arab countries refused to return or simply executed Israeli prisoners. U.S./Vietnamese relations remained strained for 20 years by unresolved cases of *MIAs* and reported POWs. Cf. *EPW.*

prisoner's dilemma: In *game theory*, a *mixed motive game* with two players and the following set up: If A defects and B does not, A scores zero while B scores -10; if both defect, each scores -5; if neither defects, each scores -1. What is interesting is the paradox that the choice to be made is not clearly "irrational" altruism vs. "rational" self-interest. It may be beneficial, even more rational, to play a seemingly irrational strategy: if both act on trust, each will receive a reduced penalty, but chance a heavy one. Choosing to defect will reduce the penalty only if the other player chooses to trust, and will if the defection is reciprocal, increase one's own penalty fivefold over a reciprocal decision to trust. It is applied by some, by analogy, to the study of international *crises* and cooperation.

privateer: (1) A merchant ship, armed and converted to wartime use. (2) Previously, a privately owned *warship*, hired by a state to harass, *capture* or destroy the enemy's shipping under *letters of marque*. It was made illegal by the *Declaration of Paris (1856)*.

private international law: The body of rules within *municipal law* that regulate private legal relations that have a foreign aspect. For instance, private debts held abroad, or child custody disputes between parents of different nationality and domicile.

private sector: All economic activity other than government purchases and expenditures.

privatize: To return to private control economic activities or facilities that had previously been run by the state. During the 1980s *Margaret Thatcher* undertook extensive privatization in Britain, reversing an economic trend within the *OECD* that dated back several decades. In the 1990s privatization is in vogue across the board, from Africa to China and India, in the former *Soviet bloc*, and within most OECD nations.

prize: Enemy *goods* or vessels seized or *captured* at sea in wartime. Cf. *booty*.

prize court: An *ad hoc*, international court established to decide conflicting claims over what is, or is not, *contraband*.

procrustean bed: From Procrustes, a mythical robber who cut off the limbs of victims to make them fit his bed; said of theories that try to do the same to the facts (produce conformity by arbitrary means).

product cycle theory: The idea that the motive force behind firms expanding into *multinational* activity is a threat to their existing *export* markets: they respond by building *subsidiaries* near these markets to lower prices and raise their access. Cf. *internalization theory*.

productivity: The amount of product created over a given period, as related to a single component of production, such as *capital* or *labor* ("labor productivity"). It measures economic *efficiency*. Relative national productivity is an important measure of economic *competitiveness*.

profit: A net positive return on an *investment*, due to an excess of return over expenditure. This is the form compensation takes for investors and entrepreneurs, as distinct from wages or income from rent.

pro forma: "As a matter of form (alone)." When a

thing is done, say a *diplomatic protest*, without serious intent to *influence* the other party, but merely to satisfy legal ritual or mislead *public opinion*.

prohibited weapons: Since the middle of the 19th century there have been attempts to prohibit the use of certain weapons in *warfare*, efforts that have met with mixed results. Since *WWI* numerous weapons have been restricted to various degrees, and a few banned outright. Perhaps most surprising to the average layperson, the one major class of weapons for which there is not even a minimalist convention in *international law* limiting use, and certainly no general outlawing, is *nuclear weapons*. However, there are efforts to contain *proliferation* through the *IAEA* and the *Nuclear Non-proliferation Treaty*. For the nature and state of other weapons types, see *biological weapons; Biological Warfare Treaty; chemical and biological warfare; chemical weapons; Chemical Weapons Convention; gas weapons; Geneva Protocol; mustard gas; nerve weapons*. See also *incendiary; land mine*.

proletarian revolution: In *marxism*, a *revolution* to overthrow the *mode of production* of *capitalism* and replace it with a *socialist* mode, by the ultimate winner of history, the *proletariat* or working class.

proletariat: (1) Members of the industrial working class, or persons who labor in exchange for wages. (2) In *marxism*, the class of wage laborers produced and exploited by *capitalism*, which is destined by the "iron laws of history" to overthrow that *mode of production*, institute a socialist mode, and transform global society into the communist nirvana. See *marxism; vanguard*.

proliferation: The spread of weapons systems, particularly *weapons of mass destruction*, to new countries. (1) Horizontal: acquisition of weapons systems by additional *states, terrorists* or others. (2) Vertical: quantitative increases in available weapons.

propaganda: The deliberate spread of ideas, images and information that is often (but need not be) untrue, to advance one's own cause and undermine the interests of opponents. The term derives from the 16th century Catholic committee "Congregatio de Propaganda Fidei," (Congregation for the Propagation of the Faith). It was established by Pope Gregory XV (1554-1623) to supervise foreign missions and proselytize among native populations. Propaganda is an ever-present element of international relations. All states (and not a few *international organizations, MNCs* and even *NGOs*) engage in it to some degree. Governments will always put the best possible light on their own actions and policies, and frequently will also use heavy-handed, even coarse distortion of the views and actions of enemies to advance their own interests. Propaganda is a potentially highly effective means of *influence*, given the right message and audience (and that can mean virtually anything and anyone). It is thus generally viewed by states as an integral component of *power*, though they almost always call such public persuasion campaigns something else. See *disinformation; doublethink; Goebbels; Greenpeace; national morale; NWICO; Pravda; psychological warfare; public opinion; Radio Free Europe; soft power; UNESCO.*

propinquity: Geographical proximity, or nearness. Some *states* have used this as justification for claiming special rights in a neighboring *territory*; e.g., Japan regarding China in the *Lansing/Ishii Agreement*, the U.S. in the *Monroe Doctrine* or post-1991 Russia in its stance toward the *near abroad*. Declared or not, it is an underlying assumption behind almost all claims to a *sphere of influence*. See also *regionalism.*

proportionality: In *international law* and in *just war theory*, a *rule* that a *state's* right to use *force* in *self-defense* or *retaliation* is limited by a requirement that the compulsion used correspond to the danger still posed, or the harm already done.

protecting power: In *international law*, a *neutral* acting to protect the nationals or property of a *belligerent*, or like Switzerland, protecting *POWs* on all sides though itself neutral.

protectionism: Any effort to alter or influence the flow of *trade*, especially by use of *protective tariffs, non-tariff barriers* and *subsidies* to defend domestic producers from more efficient foreign producers. See also *new protectionism.*

protective tariffs: Taxes on *imports* that aim to shelter domestic producers by excluding more efficient foreign competition within the home market. These are different from normal *tariffs*, which aim at extracting revenue for the government from foreign producers in exchange for the privilege of trade. Cf. *peak tariffs.*

protectorate: A *territory* declared or agreed by *treaty* to be dependent on, and defended by, a more powerful state. A kind of precolony, the larger ones were often converted to *colonies* after long possession led to acceptance of one's authority by the other *Great Powers*. It was one way imperial powers limited the chance of coming to blows over competing claims, through the *deterrent* effect of knowing certain areas would be defended by force although not formally annexed or colonized. See *associated state.*

protocol: (1) An international agreement supplementary to an existing *treaty*. (2) Ritual, ceremonial and formal courtesies used to signal the state of relations among *nations*. Elaborate measures are engaged not person-to-person, though that is how it may appear, but nation-to-nation. Giving deliberate offense to an *ambassador*, say by missing appointments or speaking brusquely, is therefore intended (and received) as a snub to the nation he or she represents. On occasion, diplomatic courtesy may be extended to non-diplomatic persons as an indication of a desire to elevate relations, or to signal a desire for a change in the political map of another country. For example, the West continued to receive "ambassadors" from the *Baltic States* during the *Cold War*, though those countries had been annexed by the Soviet Union; and France has since the late 1960s extended full diplomatic courtesy to the premiers of *Québec*, to signal support for *independence* without provoking an open confrontation with Canada. More subtle variations in the proper use of protocol can be used to signal disapproval of another government's policy or an impending shift in one's own. Cf. *prestige; provocation.*

Protocols of the Elders of Zion: An infamous forgery by the tsarist *secret police* (the *Okhrana*), purporting to document a Jewish conspiracy to set up a world dictatorship. It was seized upon by the *Nazis* for use in their hate campaigns against the Jews, and was used by some Arabs to the same purpose. Despite thorough and complete exposure as a forgery it is still cited by *neo-nazis*, and other latter day anti-Semites, as "evidence" that their fear and loathing of Jews is in fact well-grounded. See *anti-Semitism; Holocaust.*

provisional government: (1) One set up in the wake of *liberation, defeat* or *revolution*, pending establishment of a new constitutional order. (2) The government in Russia from March 12-November 6, 1917. It was nearly overthrown by a right-wing *coup*, launched a disastrous summer offensive while delaying domestic reforms, and was in the end displaced by the *Petrograd Soviet* and the *Bolsheviks.*

provocation: An act or gesture (say a breach of *protocol*) that is regarded as a violation of principles of the *comity of nations*. If severe (say a pattern of *incursions*), it may be responded to forcefully. In almost all cases a provocation will call forth a *diplomatic protest*. In some, it may lead to *war.*

proxy wars: The idea, true or not, that in an age of *nuclear deterrence* where direct force is denied to the *Great Powers* they will fight each other through proxies. Some point to Soviet support for N. Vietnam and use of Cubans in Angola and Mozambique, or to the *Reagan Doctrine* and U.S. support for the Afghan *mujahadeen* as examples of this.

prudence: (1) In *realism*: the cardinal political virtue, requiring restraint, taking only those limited actions necessary to pursuit of the *national interest*, and implying respect for the national interests of other *recognized* political communities. (2) In *just war theory*: The moral requirement that before resort is had to *force* to correct some evil, a calculation must be made as to whether *intervention* will cause even greater evil (e.g., would massive military intervention to stop the *ethnic cleansing* in Bosnia save lives, or lead to a widened conflict and greater destruction)?

Prussia: A north German state that was a rising military power during the 18th century, and formed the core of the *North German Confederation* and then of Imperial Germany in the 19th century. Much of the original Prussian state was divided among Lithuania, Poland and the Soviet Union after *WWII*, and the remainder broken into various states within Germany proper. See *Germany*, and see *Bismarck; Concert of Europe; Congress System; East Prussia; Franco/Prussian War; Frederick I; Frederick II; Frederick III; Frederick-William III; General Staff; Great Powers; Napoleonic Wars; partitions of Poland; realpolitik; Schleswig-Holstein; Seven Weeks' War; Tilsit.*

psychohistory: The attempt to apply psychological methods and theories to the interpretation of historical events, and/or the analysis of historical persons.

psychological warfare: Techniques of *disinformation*, *propaganda*, publicity, threats and other measures designed to influence or intimidate a foreign population, and by that undermine an enemy's *national morale*. It may be *covert* or *overt*.

public contracts: Contracts for *goods* or *services* made between *states* and private firms or individuals.

public debt: The total of government *debt* from all levels, federal, state and local. Cf. *national debt*.

public goods: Facilities such as communications, transportation electricity, and other publicly funded and regulated services necessary to conduct economic activity. A synonym is *infrastructure*.

public international unions: These were the first major *functional* organizations to develop. They did so in response to the extraordinary outburst of commercial and other *transnational* activity in the latter half of the 19th century. They were in no way the product of visionaries. Instead, they were the invention of bureaucrats reacting to pragmatic administrative needs by setting up contacts with their counterparts in other *states*, even those their political masters might not favor. The public international unions fed directly into the functional stream of modern international organization. For instance, see *International Telegraph Union; Universal Postal Union*.

public opinion: The collective opinion of a national community. Traditionally, *diplomacy* took place without regard for public opinion, which before the age of mass literacy was virtually non-existent when it came to *foreign affairs*. Given the rise of democracies to *Great Power* status, public opinion today plays a prominent role in relations among *states*. More often than not its function is negative: it is aroused in opposition to some proposed policy, say opening or maintaining *diplomatic relations*, engaging in a *war*, or a move toward *free trade* or regional *integration*. On occasion, it may spur a government to do something it otherwise is reluctant to undertake, say intercede on behalf of *human rights* or in relief of *famine*, or start a war. Cf. *national morale; propaganda; world public opinion*.

public sector: The total governmental portion of a national economy, federal, state and local, excluding all private expenditure and transactions.

Pueblo Affair: On January 23, 1968, the USS Pueblo (a spy ship) was seized by North Korea. The U.S. insisted the ship had been on the *high seas* and protested vehemently, with *public opinion* demanding forceful action by the *Johnson* administration. After 11 months of bitter negotiations, the U.S. signed an apology and the crew (but not the ship) was released. The apology was vitiated by an advance declaration that it had been coerced, and was immediately renounced by Washington upon release of the crew.

Puerto Rico: This Caribbean island was discovered by Columbus in 1493. It was claimed for Spain by Juan Ponce de Lion (1460-1521) in 1509. The Spanish imported African slaves to work the sugar fields (*slavery* was not abolished until 1873), over time giving the island its distinctive, mixed-race population. The Dutch and British both tried to seize Puerto Rico in the late 16th century, but Spain defended it until it fell to the U.S. in 1898 following the *Spanish/American War*. In 1916 its inhabitants were granted U.S. *citizenship* (Jones Act). In 1952 it was granted status as a self-governing commonwealth attached to the U.S. Puerto Ricans remain divided over whether they should seek U.S. statehood (they have no representation in Congress, and no electoral votes for president). In November 1993, in a *referendum*, they decided 50% in favor of the status quo as a commonwealth (in which they pay no federal income tax and headquartered corporations also receive tax breaks) to 46% for statehood. A mere 4% voted for *independence*. Extreme advocates of independence have in the past used bombings and assassinations on the U.S. mainland to advance their cause. Population: 3.4 million.

pump priming: When a government stimulates an economy by spending borrowed money. See *Keynes*.

punitive damages: *Damages* exceeding the harm actually done, exacted as punishment.

Punjab: A region of the *subcontinent* of India seared by violent division in 1947 between India and *West Pakistan*, with most *Muslims* going to Pakistan. The Punjabis of Pakistan have dominated that country's national politics and life more often than not. Those of India have been subdivided as of 1966 into *Hindu* and *Sikh* areas. Among the Sikhs there is considerable agitation for *secession* to form "Kalistan."

puppet regime/state: Often pejorative as well as descriptive, this term refers to a *state* that is not free of the direction of a more powerful state in its foreign policy, despite maintaining the fiction of *independence*. Positions it adopts, *wars* it fights, and so on are decided in a foreign capital. For instance, *Manchukuo*.

purchasing power: A method of comparing national income (or production) that seeks to go beyond simply translating per capita *GNP* figures into a standard *hard currency* and then measuring the differences. Instead, it assess purchases that might be made before comparing the relative buying power of each currency. Often, the results indicate a greater purchasing power in poorer countries than per capita income figures suggest.

purge: Mass elimination of political opponents from within one's own political party or movement. See *cultural revolution; gang of four; Great Proletarian Cultural Revolution; Night of the Long Knives; purge trials; Red Guards; Yezhovshchina*.

purge trials: Criminal/political proceedings, especially if rigged, used to remove, imprison or kill opponents of a given *regime*, whether the opposition was real or imaginary. Their most important function was to provide *propaganda* makers in *totalitarian* states with a set of scapegoats upon whom all failings of the promised *revolution* could be fastened, and through which the new *party line* was communicated by excoriation and example, even to a farflung and illiterate peasant audience. They were, when all was said and done, a form of political theater in which anticipation was built by baiting the defendant (victim), and the climax came with a confessional breakdown, arranged in advance by threats or *torture*. The denouement of sentencing hardly mattered--while death sentences were usually carried out, in some cases *reeducation* and *rehabilitation* was permitted to reinforce lessons of the purge/morality play. The most spectacular took place in the Soviet Union in the 1920s and 1930s, when star chambers condemned the usual suspects, on testimony from the usual witnesses who were then callously purged in their turn. In this way, the anger and frustration of urban workers--who were being squeezed by *Stalin's* exaggerated *five-year plans* on the one hand and whose *standard of living* was plummeting due to *collectivization* on the other--was focused on "wreckers," "saboteurs" and other supposed *counter-revolutionary* villains. See also *Beria; cultural revolution; Dzerzhinsky; gang of four; GULAG; KGB; Mao; NKVD; OGPU; Stalin; Vyshinsky; Yezhovshchina*.

putsch: A near synonym for a *coup*, but referring also to a sudden revolt or uprising. It is used especially about the several extreme right-wing attempts to take power in the *interwar* period in Germany. See *Beer Hall putsch; Kapp putsch*.

Pu Yi, a.k.a. Hsuan T'ung, a.k.a. K'ang Te (1906-67): "The Last Emperor." Proclaimed *Manchu* emperor of China at the age of two, he reigned but never ruled. The *Chinese Revolution* of 1911 led to his abdication in 1912. Taken north by a *warlord*, with the growing disruption in northern China in 1928, he sought *asylum* in Japanese controlled *territory*. In 1931 the Japanese made him the figurehead ruler of *Manchukuo*, proclaiming him the Emperor K'ang Te in 1934. With Japan's *defeat* he abdicated and was *interned* in the Soviet Union 1945-50. Handed back to China, he underwent political *reeducation* in communist labor camps. Eventually he was released into quiet, but always closely guarded, retirement.

pyrrhic victory: One obtained--in *politics* or in *war*--at a cost in lives and treasure so great that victory may not be distinguishable from *defeat*. For example, see *Iran/Iraq War; Verdun*.

Q

Qatar: Location: *Arabian peninsula*. Major associations: *Arab League, OAPEC, OPEC, UN*. Population: 500,000. Military: small, and dependent on Saudi Arabia and the *West* for protection. Long a minor province of the *Ottoman Empire*, in 1916 it became a British *protectorate* in exchange for permitting London to decide its foreign policy. As Britain prepared to withdraw from its *Persian Gulf* commitments in the late 1960s, Qatar sought *federation* with other former British protectorates. When this fell through, it declared itself an independent *sheikdom* in 1971. It is coterminous with a small peninsula, jutting eastward from Arabia proper, of the same name.

Quadaffi, Muammar (b.1942): Libyan dictator. An admirer of *Nasser,* he led a *coup* in 1969 that overthrew the Libyan monarchy. He has used Libya's oil wealth to elevate its international profile far beyond its real importance, not least by supporting *terrorism* against several countries, including Britain and possibly the U.S. In any case, he was blamed by *Ronald Reagan* for sponsoring terrorist attacks. On April 15, 1986, the U.S. bombed Libyan military installations and Quadaffi's living quarters in *retaliation* for what it said was support of terrorist actions against Americans in Europe. Quadaffi's young, adopted daughter was among the dead. His policies have led to clashes with nearly all neighboring states, including Chad, Egypt, Morocco, Sudan and Tunisia. Yet most of his stratagems have come to naught. Among his major setbacks: sending troops to aid *Idi Amin* against Tanzania in 1979, losing the *Chad/Libya War,* losing the *Auzou strip*, and repeated failure to construct a *pan-Arab* federation in North Africa. During the *Gulf War* he gave rhetorical support to Iraq. He has perennially sought to acquire *chemical, nuclear* and other *weapons of mass destruction*. Some analysts question his mental stability. See *line of death; Gulf of Sidra.*

Quadrilateral: A system of Austrian fortifications in N. Italy, based on the towns of Legnano, Mantua, Peschiera and Verona, designed to hold French *power* back from the peninsula. It was rendered strategically irrelevant by the unification of Italy in 1861.

Quadruple Alliance: The powers that defeated France 1814-15, formed the *Congress System* and, with the addition of France, ran the *Concert of Europe*: Austria, Britain, Prussia and Russia. Note: Not to be confused with the *Holy Alliance*. Cf. *Quintuple Alliance.*

Quai d'Orsay: A synonym for the French Foreign Ministry, from its site on the south bank of the Seine.

Quaker gun: A sham gun so emplaced as to fool the enemy into thinking the defensive strength of a *fortification* or ship is greater than it is in fact; coined in open mockery of the renowned *pacifism* of Quakers.

qualified majority voting: In the *EC* the *unanimity rule* applied, until this form of *weighted voting* was introduced by the *Single European Act*. Under this "qualified majority" system, it took two large countries and one small one to block new, single-market laws. In the *EU* votes are weighted so that on internal functions of the common market the four large states cannot block propositions or rule changes by themselves: they need three small states to join them to sustain an effective *veto* of 23 votes.

qualitative analysis: Analysis that seeks to penetrate to the core nature or essence of events or phenomena, or their constituent parts, using eclectic methodologies and expressing conclusions as general principles or judgments. For example: "Based on a close reading of archival material, interviews and public documents, it can be said that the main motives of the key participants in the crisis were. . . ." Its main strength is to incorporate the very real role of accident, *volition* and the subtext of human motivation and psychology into explanations of *economics, history* or *politics*. Yet such analyses have been accused of too often delivering up subjective judgments about what ought to be considered objective phenomena. Some qualitative analyses also use *quantitative* techniques, but usually only where clearly useful and appropriate, not out of a predilection to *scientism*. See also *traditionalism*. Cf. *behavioralism; post-behavioralism.*

quantitative analysis: Analysis that seeks to assess the proportional weight of different causes of events or phenomena, or their constituent parts, using statistical and other numerical devices and expressing conclusions in formulas and measurements. For instance, "X(t) = expenditures by nation X for conventional weapons in year t. $S_x(t)$ = stock of conventional weapons at time t. This can be reduced to: $S_x(t) = X(t) + S_x(t-1)$." For some, this approach promises "scientific" (that is, verifiable) conclusions, and perhaps a predictive *model* of economic or political life that will allow social engineering on a grand scale. At its best, quantitative analysis can deliver highly precise conclusions. However, it has been criticized for doing so about strictly limited, often less important or even trivial (but quantifiable), issues. Moreover, the inherent obscurity of much quantitative analysis and language renders it of little use to policy makers, and often makes it impenetrable as well by students or fellow researchers. Lastly, claims to a rapier like methodology may be blunted in the application. For example, one published study of *MNC* investment models in the *Third World* purported to find a value for $-R^2$, bravely defying the fact that a negative square number is, of course, a mathematical impossibility. See also *behavioralism; jargon; obscurantism; post-behavioralism*. Cf. *qualitative analysis; traditionalism*.

quarantine: A variant of *blockade*, invented by the U.S. during the *Cuban Missile Crisis*. It falls somewhere between a pacific blockade and a hostile, or bellicose, blockade. That is, it does not reflect a direct intention to perform *acts of war*, but nor does it exempt third party ships from *visit and search* (in the Cuban case, it was aimed mainly at Soviet ships).

quarantine flag: A (yellow) flag flown to signal that a ship is under medical quarantine because it is carrying diseases communicable to humans; or more often these days, because it has insects or plant diseases on board that might infect a port country's agricultural production, forests and so forth.

quarter: Refusal to fire upon or kill a defeated enemy. This is a basic expectation of *just war theory* and of the *laws of war*. However, there are permitted exceptions in both the theory and the law: (1) Where no quarter is offered by an enemy, none need be given either. (2) It is not required to give quarter twice; thus, if a foe fakes *surrender*, fire may be resumed and continued until the enemy position is utterly repressed (all defenders killed or *hors de combat*).

quasi delicts: Legal breaches that do not amount to *torts*, but are analogous to such acts. See *delict*.

quasi-international law: Legal relations in which an *object of international law* is treated on a factual footing with a *subject*, but where the ultimate *jurisdiction* is *municipal law*; e.g., private bank loans to a foreign government.

quasi states: The idea that some states, particularly in Africa, are sustained not by the old structures of "positive sovereignty" as laid out in the *Westphalian* system, but by *international law* and *international morality*. Although such states lack some or all of the empirical (*de facto*) aspects of *sovereignty*, they are buttressed by "negative sovereignty" deriving from juridicial (*de jure*) and moral acceptance and support for their continued existence.

Quasi War (1797-1800): In 1795, then again from 1797-1800, France seized hundreds of U.S. vessels trading in the West Indies. That policy was related to France's ongoing conflict with England. The U.S. retaliated in kind, though its naval resources were meager. Neither side *declared war*. More radical *Federalists* wanted *war*, and with the election of *John Adams* the *Directory* in France also raised the stakes close to war. The crisis worsened with the *XYZ Affair*, but eventually *Talleyrand*, who could see no advantage to France in a wider war, facilitated a settlement.

Québec: Formerly *Lower Canada*. The second largest (after Ontario) and second most populous province of Canada, with a predominant *francophone* population. In the 1960s agitation began for government promotion of the French language. As the movement spread beyond artistic and intellectual communities it developed a broad nationalist attraction, and some reforms were legislated in what is known as the "Quiet Revolution." Things turned violent by 1970, with a *terrorist* bombing campaign and then two political kidnappings (and one murder) by a small extremist group, the *Front de Liberation du Québec* (FLQ). The Federal response was to declare *martial law* ("War Measures Act"). But the mainstream of the nationalist movement rejected violence, turning instead to the *Parti Québecois (PQ)*. It won a majority in 1976 but lost a *referendum* on *secession* in 1980. From 1980-92 efforts focused on entrenching legal changes that gave preference to the French language (even in some private affairs of non-French speakers), and set up a monopoly for French in all public affairs. Federally, efforts were made to revise the constitution to make it acceptable to the government of Québec without alienating the other provinces (mainly by devolving powers to all of them). In 1992 these efforts came to naught: in a national *referendum* a majority of all citizens in a majority of the provinces, including Québec, rejected the compromise constitution devised by the politicians. In 1993 Québec *separtists* were elected to the Federal Parliament. Others anticipated a provincial election.

Queen Anne's War (1702-13): The North American extension of the larger conflict between England and France (then under *Louis XIV*), in which American colonists and English *regulars* fought French regulars, *Québec* colonists, and their Spanish and Indian allies. The French invaded New England, an action notable mainly for their massacre of the citizens of Deerfield, Massachusetts. As in *King William's War*, American colonists from the north responded with angry demands to invade Québec, while southerners wanted to attack south and west into French holdings in the Floridas and across the Mississippi. In the *Treaty of Utrecht* (1713) the British gained control of Acadia and Hudson's Bay, and secured *Newfoundland*. That settlement so emasculated *New France* geostrategically, it was only a matter of time before French power in North America was extinguished by Britain in the *Peace of Paris (1763)*.

Quemoy and Matsu crises (1954/1958): The main islands of an offshore group retained by the *Nationalists* after their evacuation to Taiwan. In 1953 and again in 1954 *mainland China* heavily shelled the islands, from which the Nationalists had launched several *commando* raids. That led to a U.S./Taiwan defense pact in December 1954. Undeterred, China retook some minor islands in the group in January 1955, but stopped short of attacking Quemoy or Matsu. A second crisis over possession erupted in 1958, but was resolved when *Eisenhower* threw a naval screen around the islands and made clear that Taiwan had full U.S. backing. A.k.a. "Crises of Formosa Strait."

***qui desiderat pacem, praeparet bellum*:** "Whosoever wants *peace* should prepare for *war*." Roman maxim, and the main principle of *deterrence*.

***quieta non movere*:** "Do not disturb settled affairs." A legal/political maxim advising one to let lie sleeping international *disputes*.

quiet diplomacy: Using direct, government-to-government channels of communication when making an appeal or *diplomatic protest*, rather than open or public channels. It assumes that governments will respond better to criticism when they can *save face;* or that *negotiation* is most effective when not conducted in the glare of media attention and subjected to the pressures of an aroused *public opinion*. It may therefore involve secret recourse to *mediation, good offices* or the like. It is the preferred path of most governments when dealing with highly contentious and emotional issues, say of *human rights*. Cf. *open covenants*.

Quintuple Alliance: The *Quadruple Alliance* plus France, after its readmission to the *Great Power* club at *Aix-la-Chapelle*.

Quisling, Vidkun (1887-1945): Norwegian traitor. *Military attaché* in Russia 1918-19, and in Finland 1919-21; Minister of War 1931-33. He conspired with *Hitler's* plans to invade Norway, and headed a Nazi *puppet regime* 1940-45. Tried and executed for *treason* after the war, his name has entered several languages as a synonym for treachery and betrayal. In English, it rivals in that regard the name of *Benedict Arnold*. Cf. *Pierre Laval; Wang Jingwei*.

quotas: A type of *non-tariff barrier*. There are two main types affecting trade: (1) *Import* quota: a blanket limit to the total amount of an import permitted in a specified period. (2) *Tariff* quota: a specified amount of imports are permitted in at one price, and subsequent volumes are subjected to higher tariff rates. Cf. *GATT; voluntary export agreements (VERs)*.

R

Rabin, Yitzhak (b.1922): Israeli statesman. Chief-of-Staff 1966-68; Ambassador to Washington 1968-73; PM, 1974-77, 1992- . A member of the *Haganah* who fought in the *First Arab/Israeli War.* As Minister of Defense in 1984, he oversaw Israel's withdrawal from Lebanon and definition of its "security zone." He long opposed efforts to trade the *West Bank* for a *peace* settlement. Yet in September 1993, he agreed to just that, after *back-channel* talks with the *PLO.*

racism: Economic, political or social discrimination against individuals or groups based on race or ethnicity. Among other entries, see *anti-Semitism; apartheid; boat people; Bosnia; Burundi; colonialism; Dumbarton Oaks; ethnic cleansing; fascism; genocide; Holocaust; human rights; Minorities Treaties; National Socialism; Oriental exclusion laws; overseas Chinese; Paris Peace Conference; power-sharing; Rwanda; social darwinism; tribalism; UDI; zionism.*

radiation effects: The immediate, as well as lingering lethality and physical harm caused by the flash (blindness) and a range of other radiation released in a nuclear explosion. Radiation sickness is typified by extreme nausea, vomiting, cramps, bloody diarrhea and so forth. Later genetic mutation is also not uncommon. Cf. *blast effects; fallout; neutron bomb; radiological weapons.*

radical/radicalism: Concerned with fundamental, even revolutionary change, that goes to the "root" of public affairs. Note: This can occur at either end of the political spectrum, but in recent discourse "radical" tends to be reserved to the far left. Cf. *reaction.*

radio: The first international efforts to regulate radio began in 1906. A major conference in 1927 set rules whereby radio broadcasters are required to obtain licenses from national authorities, and set regulations on the proper use of commercial and ham frequencies, and reserved special frequencies for emergency and communications purposes. In 1932 radio and other forms of telecommunications were brought under the regulatory authority of the *International Telecommunications Union.* It has since introduced rules against jamming legal broadcasts, *piracy* and related matters. A major supplementary convention on telecommunications came into effect in 1982.

Radio Free Europe: A U.S.-funded, though technically private, broadcast service set up during the *Cold War* to send news and other programming into the censored countries of the *Soviet bloc,* in their various languages. Accused by Moscow of carrying merely Western *propaganda,* its signal was jammed until the era of *Mikhail Gorbachev.*

radiological weapons: Non-explosive *nuclear weapons* that emit high levels of harmful radiation to poison people, and/or render useless other targets by making them radioactive. See *radiation effects.*

Rafsanjani, Ali Akbar Hashemi (b.1934): Iranian statesman; deputy speaker of the *Majlis* 1980-89; head of the armed forces 1988-89; President 1989- . He was the "moderate" leader the *Reagan* administration thought it could deal with in *Iran/Contra.* While he manifested more pragmatism than his predecessors, either from conviction or necessity he also bent to pressures from *fundamentalists* and *xenophobic* nationalists. While publicly condemning the introduction of Western troops into the region during the *Gulf War,* he must have welcomed the destruction of Iraqi military capability. To date, he has refused to lift the *Ayatollah Khomeini's* fatwah (edict) calling for the faithful to murder *Salman Rushdie.*

Rahman, Sheikh Mujibur (1920-75): PM of Bangladesh 1972-75; President 1975. He led the Awami League in its bid for *independence* for *East Pakistan.* When he won the 1970 election and demanded independence for *Bangladesh,* he was arrested. That occasioned the riots and West Pakistani *intervention* that ultimately brought on the *Third Indo/Pakistani War.* He set an unfortunate precedent for the country's political future by governing as a dictator. He was assassinated by elements in the army.

Rainbow Warrior incident: In July 1982, a *Greenpeace* vessel (Rainbow Warrior) was sunk in Auckland Harbour by French *intelligence* agents, killing one man. It had been about to sail in protest against French *nuclear weapons* testing in the South Pacific. The arrest of the agents led to a diplomatic row between France and New Zealand. In the end, New Zealand surrendered the pair to serve their sentences in French custody. After a token incarceration, they were released, decorated and resumed their careers.

raison d'état: "For reasons of state." A classical justification for policies that must (or merely do) depart from accepted norms of moral conduct or look past mere *dynastic* or class interest, actually or ostensibly in order to promote the *national interest.* It asserts that conventional moral categories should not apply to, and private interests should not be served by, the *state.*

Raj: The *British Empire* in India, some three quarters under *direct rule* as well as some 700 *Princely States*. See *India: The Raj*.

ramification: In *functionalism*, the idea that after *states* cooperate in technical areas, cooperation may cause a *spillover* into security issues.

rampart: A raised earthen or stone structure that shields defenders from enemy fire.

Rapallo, Treaties of: (1) 1920: Italy and Yugoslavia (United Kingdom) agreed to set aside their *disputes* over control of certain islands in the Adriatic, and pledged to oppose any effort to restore the *Hapsburgs* in Austria or Hungary. (2) 1922: This is the more important *treaty*, between *Weimar Germany* and the *Soviet Union*. It reestablished *diplomatic relations*, breaking the isolation of each nation; it mutually renounced all financial claims, which spoke to German resentment over *reparations* and Soviet refusal to pay Russia's *war debts* or *compensation* for *nationalized* property of foreigners; and it opened trade relations, vitally important to both. It also contributed to the development of secret military cooperation that enabled Germany to get past the *disarmament* provisions of the *Treaty of Versailles*.

Rapid Deployment Force (RDF): A highly mobile force for the *Persian Gulf*, set up by the U.S. after the *Iranian Revolution* and the start of the *Afghan/Soviet War*. It includes prepared bases and equipment stockpiles in the region, to permit quick air transport of troops. It was used to great effect in *Operation Desert Shield*. See also *Gulf Cooperation Council*.

Rapid Reaction Force (RRF): Since the end of the *Cold War*, this is part of a "new strategic concept" within *NATO*, replacing *forward defense*. It calls for a smaller, high-tech and mobile force to be ready for *intervention* in trouble spots, rather than to meet an enemy along a broad, prepared front.

rapprochement: Instituting improved, even cordial relations, following a period of *conflict* or *war*.

Rarotonga, Treaty of (1987): "South Pacific Nuclear Free Zone Treaty." An agreement making the *South Pacific* a *nuclear weapons free zone*, drafted by members of the *South Pacific Forum*. Most states in the region have signed it (excepting Tonga). The agreement does not ban port calls by, say, French or American nuclear *warships*. Cf. *ANZUS*; *Kiwi disease*.

Rasputin, Gregori (1871-1916): Priest and mystic. The Tsarina's belief in his ability to control the condition of the Tsarevich Alexi (who was a hemophiliac) gave him near controlling influence over her, and through her over *Nicholas II* and hence Russian foreign and domestic policies. It is thought he may even have interfered with military decisions during *WWI*. Infamous for drunkenness and debauches, he was murdered by aristocrats who wanted to end his hold over the Tsar. He took awhile to die: he was poisoned, then stabbed, shot and thrown into a river to drown.

Rathenau, Walther (1867-1922): German statesman. He directed the German economy during *WWI*, and *Weimar's* reconstruction from 1921. As Minister of Foreign Affairs, in 1922 he arranged reduced *reparations* and negotiated *Rapallo* with Russia. A Jew, he was assassinated by a fanatic *anti-Semite*.

ratification: (1) International: When the *executive* authority of a *state* formally confirms that the state it governs accepts a *treaty*, by delivering the *instruments of ratification* to another state if the agreement is *bilateral*, or an appropriate body such as the UN if it is *multilateral*. (2) Domestic: Acceptance by the requisite constitutional authority of a state's *adherence* to a treaty. This usually requires legislative approval and executive signature, but the process varies with each given constitution. The U.S. process is among the most complex, and can be highly troublesome (because it is uncertain) for other states. It is also frequently misstated, as in "the Senate ratified the treaty." Actually, the Senate gives "advice and consent" to treaties, but the president (chief of the executive) negotiates, signs and ratifies them. The Senate may attach amendments or *reservations* that subsequently influence the decision of the president to ratify. Depending on the extent of Senate revision, a president may choose to renegotiate a treaty, ratify it as amended (but only if he or she is able to obtain *consent* to the revisions from all other signatories) or refuse to ratify it. In the event the Senate withholds consent (rejects a treaty), the matter of ratification never arises.

ratio decidendi: "Reason for the decision." The legal principle upon which a court rests its *judgment*.

ratio legis: "Reason for the law." The reasoning that led to the *rule* used to decide a case.

rational actor: See *rational decision-making*.

rational decision-making: The assumption, basic to most analyses of foreign policy, that *decision-makers* are for the most part agreeable to reason; that is, that they assess, rank and then choose on a logical basis from a range of policy options those that are the most satisfactory (or the least unsatisfactory) and likely to advance their interests. This assumption has been challenged by suggestions that, in practice, other factors come between leaders and a purely rational choice. See *bureaucratic politics; cognitive dissonance; decision-making theory; groupthink; ideology; image; misperception; SOPs; organizational process model.*

rational player: In *game theory*, a player who chooses the most rewarding of all possible alternatives, and assumes that other players will act similarly. Cf. *prisoner's dilemma.*

rationing: Strict apportionment of *food*, fuel and other necessities of life among a population (*civilian* and/or military). This is a common practice during *war*, when great call is made upon the nation's resources to sustain a military endeavor at the *front line*, or because of a *siege*. It may also occur during peacetime as a result of *depression* in *market economies*, or crop failure or natural disaster in poorer countries. It was endemic in all countries with a *planned economy*, amounting to a basic feature of such inefficient systems.

raw intelligence: *Intelligence* data that has not yet been analyzed for its significance or accuracy, or vetted for *disinformation*. It is not, therefore, normally shown in this form to top *decision-makers.*

raw materials: Any material in its natural, or preprocessed state: iron ore, not iron; wheat, not flour; wool, not yarn; and so forth. An abundance of raw materials, or at least access to such materials, is widely considered a prerequisite of great national *power*. The drive to acquire raw materials has been a major component of *wars* and of *empire* building.

reaction/reactionary: Pejorative terms suggesting favoritism for the far (but not revolutionary, or *fascist*) right-wing of the political spectrum, or those whose prime political motive is a conservative, negative reaction to some great change that has taken place. It originally referred to those who responded with hostility to the *liberal* ideals of the *French Revolution*. But of course, what "far right" (or left) really means is dependent on time, context and speaker. Cf. *radical.*

Reagan, Ronald (b.1911): U.S. statesman. President 1981-89. Leaving a career in film, he was Governor of California 1967-74. He won a landslide victory over *Jimmy Carter* in 1980. He followed *monetarism* in his economic policy, while blanket anti-*communism* formed the core of his approach to security policy. He was not loathe to use limited, unilateral force to advance foreign policy goals, in *Grenada* (1983), *Lebanon* (1983-84) and *Libya* (1986); or indirect force through *aid* to governments (El Salvador, Guatemala, Honduras) or *covert aid* to *insurgents* (the *Contras*, Afghan *mujahadeen* and *guerrilla* groups in Angola and Mozambique). He relaxed *human rights* strictures on aid to *Third World* allies, while increasing them toward the *Soviet bloc*. His main concern was always the Soviet Union. During his first administration he continued the *arms buildup* begun in 1978 by Congress and carried over in the final Carter budget, until by 1985 both the U.S. armory and the federal *deficit* were bulging. From 1981-85 there was extreme, though mainly rhetorical, confrontation with Moscow over Afghanistan, Central America and Poland. A major *crisis* within *NATO* occurred in the early 1980s concerning Pershing and *cruise missile* deployments to counter a prior Soviet deployment. Reagan was also criticized for avoiding *summits*, although that was largely due to the rapidity with which Soviet leaders were dying and being replaced (*Brezhnev, Andropov* and *Chernenko* all died between 1982-85). When *Gorbachev* assumed power, he and Reagan struck a new chord in American/Soviet relations. The second Reagan term saw a winding down of the confrontation over Afghanistan and major breakthroughs in *arms control*. It was badly marred, however, by *Iran/Contra* and by still-rising deficits. His more uncritical admirers claim he "won the *Cold War*." While it is true that the Soviet collapse began on his watch, that exclusive claim ignores decades of sustained *containment* by eight Presidents, the Congress and many foreign allies. See also *authoritarianism; Reagan Doctrine; SALT; Strategic Defense Initiative; START.*

Reagan Doctrine: A promise made by *Ronald Reagan* in his 1985 State of the Union address to *aid* all anti-communist *insurgents*, to whom he referred as "freedom fighters" and compared to the *minutemen* of the *American War of Independence*. It served to justify *martial* and other assistance already underway to *guerrillas* in Afghanistan, Angola and Nicaragua. See also *authoritarianism; totalitarianism.*

realism, classical: A broad approach to international politics and history that focuses on the role of *power* and the *national interest*, with special concern for *national security*, admiration for the *balance of power*, and hardheaded respect for the utility of both *force* and *diplomacy*. In consequence, it is less concerned with issues of *low politics* or *distributive justice*, at times to the point of apparent indifference. Classical realism stems from a pessimistic assumption about the flawed nature of humanity (its penchant for evil). It consequently assumes/observes that all politics is a *struggle for power* under conditions of threat and fear, with power the coinage of measurement and defense of self-interest. Less well understood or appreciated, classical realism also argues that the balance of power ultimately rests on shared social and moral bases and practices among national communities. In particular, it requires of statesmen the virtues of *prudence* and self-restraint. It is merely a caricature (sometimes purveyed by cruder, self-proclaimed and proudly amoral realists themselves) that portrays realism as necessarily advocating *machiavellian* ethics. Nor is it unconcerned with *international law* or *international organization*, or inarticulate about human rights and community. At its best, realism supports law and organization as central mechanisms of diplomacy, as ends desirable in themselves, and as means advancing the order and civilization. Cf. *idealism; idealpolitik; Leviathan; liberal-internationalism; machtpolitik; neo-realism; Peloponnesian War; raison d'etat; realist; realpolitik.*

realist: (1) A person who analyzes and views the world the way it truly is, not giving in to sentimentalism or wishful thinking about how they might like it to be. (2) A person who thinks that they analyze and view the world the way it truly is, because they lack the imagination to conceive that it might be different, either already or in the future, from how they perceive it to be. (3) A person who approaches the analysis of *international relations* or the conduct of *statecraft* and *diplomacy* according to the principles and predilections of *realism.*

realpolitik: The practice of *diplomacy* based on an assessment of *power*, material and prudential matters, without undue concern for theoretical considerations, or restraint by ethical worries. The term was first used in 1859 by the liberal journalist and historian August Ludwig von Rochau to characterize the foreign policy of *Bismarck*, which he saw as abjuring from abstract principles (*idealpolitik*), and guided instead by "the reality of the natural law of power." Rochau said Bismarck's pursuit of *Prussia's* interests was conditioned as much by limitations as *capabilities*, and saw him as free from either soft sympathies or hard antipathies for other *states*. The term has since taken on (particularly in the U.S.) an implication of *machiavellianism* about both means and goals. That is a subtle shift in emphasis perhaps reflecting more than anything the distaste felt by *liberal* observers for the necessities, and not just excesses, of diplomacy. Yet detachment from sentimentality about relations among nations should not be mistaken for mere amorality, and remains a key component of realpolitik. See also *Machiavelli; machtpolitik; power politics; prudence; raison d'etat; realism; realist.* Cf. *Grotian; liberal-internationalism.*

rear echelon: Troops and other support personnel, like cooks or hospital staff, not in the *front line.*

rear guard: Part of a larger military force detached from and charged with defense of the rear of a position, especially when an army is moving in retreat.

rearmament: (1) Building up the armed forces after a period of *demobilization* or *arms control*, either in preparation for *war*, or to reinforce *deterrence*. (2) Upgrading the quality of one's armed forces, particularly their weaponry and equipment.

rebellion: Armed *insurrection* or resistance to an established government. The term is often used when the scale of violence is greater than a *mutiny*, but has not reached the point of *civil war* or *revolution*. See also *POW.*

rebus sic stantibus: See *clausula rebus sic stantibus.*

recall the ambassador: (1) For consultations: A tactic used to show displeasure with another government's policies or actions. It falls short of breaking *diplomatic relations*, and is more easily reversed. (2) Permanently: This occurs when fully severing diplomatic relations, or automatically upon the outbreak of *war*. See also *recognition; relations officieuses.*

recession: A short-term decline of economic activity, production, *investment* and *growth*, and a corresponding rise in unemployment. By convention, a recession is an economic downturn lasting a minimum of three consecutive fiscal quarters. Cf. *recovery.*

reciprocity: (1) In *international law*: {A} A basic principal that allows *reprisal* and bases procedures on a notion of equal rights and duties among *states*. {B} Specific to *extradition*, it involves advance agreement to surrender one's own citizens for trial in other countries, in exchange for the right to try citizens of those countries for offenses committed within one's own *jurisdiction*. (2) In *foreign policy*: Treating the actions of other states in a positive, or negative, tit for tat manner. (3) In *trade*: Mutual lowering or raising of *tariff* and other *trade barriers*. See *GATT; MFN.*

recognition: One of the fundamental principles of *international law*, it involves acceptance of the status of *international personality* of other political communities, and thereby of all their requisite claims of rights and duties under the law. It can be express or implied; it may be just *de facto*, or fully *de jure*. It is accomplished by an announcement, usually followed by a formal ceremony where *diplomatic credentials* are exchanged. "Nonrecognition" is a rather feeble, always symbolic policy sometimes adopted to express displeasure with or disapproval of a changed political situation in another *territory* (e.g., general refusal to recognize *Manchukuo*, or Western refusal to recognize Soviet annexation of the *Baltic States*, 1940-91). It should be noted that withholding recognition from a government is distinct from withholding recognition from a *state*. Thus, Western refusal to recognize the *Bolshevik* regime in Russia in the early 1920s or China after 1949 did not imply a lack of recognition that states called Russia and China existed. Similarly, general international withholding of recognition from the Vietnamese-supported regime in Cambodia from 1979-1992 did not mean that recognition of the state of Cambodia was at an end. On the other hand, refusing recognition to the *Kurds* in their aspiration for *Kurdistan* denies them full status and protections (as in Iraq), and the rights they would obtain were they in possession of a state. Similarly, *Biafra* never obtained sufficiently widespread recognition to permit Biafrans to also obtain adequate matériel help to sustain their political claims. A special, limited form of recognition is sometimes extended to successful *insurgencies,* elevating them to a status of *belligerent* (or "belligerent community"). This may occur (the decision is a political one) when the rebels have demonstrated clear control and substitute government functions in a portion of the territory of the affected state. Recognition in this form does not confer the status of international personality on the rebels, nor does it proffer to them other rights or incur obligations under peacetime international law. But it does afford them legal protections (and incur obligations) under the *laws of war*. Britain extended this type of recognition to the *Confederacy* during the *American Civil War*. More recently, some states recognized the belligerent status of anti-government rebels in the El Salvador civil war. See also *legitimate government; recall the ambassador; relations officieuses; sovereignty; two-Chinas policy.*

reconnoiter: To spy out an enemy's battle strength or position, or one's own possible line of movement.

reconstruction: (1) The period immediately following a destructive *war*, in which economic, political and social order is made over and rebuilt. (2) In U.S. history, c.1865-77: when recovery from the *American Civil War* and partial adjustment to the end of *slavery* took place, under conditions of such corruption and retribution that permanent bitterness marked the South.

recovery: A return to pre-*recession* levels of economic activity, production, investment and *growth*, and a corresponding rise in employment. By convention, a recovery is underway when an economic upturn lasts three consecutive fiscal quarters.

recruit: A newly enlisted soldier, whether a *conscript* or a volunteer.

Red Army: The Soviet army, organized by *Leon Trotsky* to defend the *Bolsheviks* during the *Russian Civil War*. It helped in forced *collectivization*, then became a target of the *Yezhovshchina* (great purge) before *WWII*. During that war it fought huge battles (e.g., *Stalingrad, Kursk*) against the *Wehrmacht*, taking staggering losses but prevailing in the end. During the *Cold War* it emerged as one of history's most formidable militaries. It was also a pillar of the communist order in the Soviet Union. It also enforced the allegiance of *Warsaw Pact* countries to the *Soviet bloc* in Hungary in 1956, Czechoslovakia in 1968 and elsewhere by the implicit threat of those examples. It was badly divided over the *Afghan/Soviet War*, losing some internal cohesion and much of its popular reputation. Some units supported the 1991 *coup* attempt against further decentralization of the Soviet federation, but others supported *Yeltsin*, thus dooming the coup. The army was then ordered back from its forward posts in the *Baltic States* and former Warsaw Pact countries, though some troops failed to return due to a lack of housing to receive them (and perhaps lingering imperial interests). The army too split apart with the breakup of the Soviet Union, with units joining the national armies of the post-Soviet republics. Some units, renegade or not, joined in fighting to support ethnic Russians in *Moldova*, and to support secessionists in *Abkhazia*. Others gave support to rebels in *Ossetia*. The long-term attitude toward reform of the now renamed Russian Army remains a matter of conjecture. In 1993 *Duma* elections the army vote went heavily to the neo-*fascist* party of *Zhirinovsky*.

Red Brigades: An *anarchist* and *terrorist* group active in Italy in the 1970s and 1980s, responsible for multiple bomb attacks and murders, including that of PM Aldo Moro (1916-78).

Red China: In disuse. See *China, People's Republic.*

Red Cross, International Committee of: A philanthropic agency founded in 1859 by Jean Henri Dunant (1828-1910; first *Nobel Prize* for Peace, 1901). It was charged in 1864 with overseeing implementation of the first *Geneva Convention* on humane treatment of the wounded and captive in *war*. It has been without peer in ensuring respect for the sanctity of hospitals and medical personnel, even in the midst of battle. It has helped advance into law, and with less success into actual practice, respect for *just war* notions of mercy for the wounded and the distinction between *combatant* and *civilian*. It has gained access to *POW* camps, and shipped mail and minor luxuries (soap, candy, etc.) to hard-pressed POWs. Yet it is not universally accepted, and states sometimes refuse its services and oversight of their conduct. It was awarded the Nobel Prize for Peace in 1917, 1944 and again in 1963. See also *Red Crescent*.

Red Crescent: An organization modelled on and resembling the *Red Cross* in its functions and organization, and often cooperating with that agency, but operating mainly in *Islamic* countries.

Red Guards: The youths sent out by *Mao Zedong* to *purge* the *Communist Party* during the *Great Proletarian Cultural Revolution*. Many Red Guards began as childish idealists, but ended as vicious thugs and killers. They publicly humiliated, beat and sometimes murdered those they accused of *counter-revolution*, *revisionism*, "capitalist-roadism" or other ideological crimes. Ultimately numbering several million, organized into military-style units, they persecuted tens of millions, caused untold cultural and economic destruction (a favored pastime was desolation of China's classical buildings and heritage), and not a few deaths. They rejected all tradition and authority, whether real or symbolic, including that of high party officials; they recognized only the personal authority of Mao. Scenes of hundreds of thousands of teenage Red Guards, frenetically chanting praise and loyalty to Mao while waving in unison the "little red book" of his political sayings, sent chills through Chinese society and the party. Once they menaced China with *anarchy* and perhaps even *civil war*, Mao turned to the *PLA* to restrain them. Many were sent to rural camps for their own taste of political *reeducation*, while Mao reclined into renewed personal mastery in Beijing.

redoubt: An isolated fortification defending an important position; or a small, self-contained fortification built within a larger structure as part of its layers of defense.

Red Scare (1919): In the wake of the *Bolshevik Revolution* in Russia a hysteria about possible *communist* plots and agitation swept the popular press and imagination in America. Some employers and government officials actually believed it; others used it as a pretext to smash unwanted unions, deport undesirable *aliens* or, in the South, target blacks who might organize others politically. A similar phenomenon occurred in Canada, where a *general strike* in the western city of Winnipeg led to bloodshed and death.

Red Sea: An extension of the Indian Ocean between Arabia and Africa, that connects with the Mediterranean through the *Suez Canal*.

Red Terror: The indiscriminate, *summary executions* carried out by the *CHEKA* in the wake of an assassination attempt against *Lenin* (it left him badly wounded). Many thousands were killed, especially in the cities. It was the first mass example of *secret police* ruthlessness and reliance on terror that would characterize Soviet politics for decades. Cf. *collectivization; Dzerzhinsky; KGB; NKVD; OGPU; war communism*.

reductionism/reductionist: The tendency to reduce explanation, say of foreign policy, to a single factor by gross *abstraction* or oversimplification.

reducto ad absurdum: "Reduction to the absurd." Taking an analogy or argument to the absurd extreme, simply by extension of its own logic.

reeducation: A euphemism for indoctrination, and even brain-washing, used by communist states about their treatment of political and social *dissidents*. The assumption was (is) that deviation from the *party line* was (is) caused by ignorance or "false consciousness," not rational or defensible disagreement. This was considered a merciful assessment, when compared to the punishments meted out for wilful *revisionism* or worst of all, *counter-revolution*. See *rehabilitation*.

referendum: When a population is asked to answer a specific question, say on *secession* or *union*. In the 20th century referenda have grown in use, until virtually no question about *self-determination* is now considered fully legitimate without popular ratification by plebiscite. For example, see *Cameroon; Palau; Saar; Schleswig-Holstein; Québec*.

reflation: Deliberate *inflation* caused by government spending that aims to stimulate economic *growth*.

reflexive development: When the process of *modernization* responds, like a reflex, to external conditions; that is, when an economy has high *vulnerability* to external economic factors that can alter its development in spite of local decisions.

Reformation, Protestant: The great shattering of the formal unity of Christian civilization, occasioned by new economic, social and political developments that created the opportunity to present an alternative to the dominance of Europe by the *Catholic Church*. It lasted some 300 years, c.1340-1648. Its fundamental tenet was that individuals needed no intermediary between themselves and God, no established and corruptible priesthood, no hierarchy of interpretive authority and no pope. Not all Protestants were that radical in the changes they sought, but that was the general form Protestantism took after decades of bloody struggle burned most of the bridges to Rome. It erupted in different forms in several countries from which it then spread, in Holland, Germany, Switzerland and, more for *dynastic* reasons, in England too. It led to numerous wars between Catholic and Protestant princes and states, of which the *Thirty Years' War* was the greatest and last. From the point of view of international history, it was vitally important because doctrinal quarrels and revolt soon became political rebellion, and then took on the aspect of far-reaching *revolution* and civil war within European civilization as a whole; and because Europe would emerge from the Reformation bursting with the political energy released by a new emphasis on *individualism*. That coalesced with the intellectual openness born of the earlier *Renaissance* to make Europeans the first to embrace a scientific world view, and proceed ultimately to *secularism*. Together, these changes empowered the rising *states* of Europe, enabling them to conquer most of the rest of the world, and to impose upon it the state system itself-- with its anti-ideological presumptions established at *Westphalia*, that great settlement that bought religious peace by elevating the state to a near absolutist position, in its relation both to superior authority and subject populations. Through this political innovation and the blood and conquest of the coming imperial age, for good and for ill, the globe was politically united for the first time in history. In sum, the Reformation so changed Europe it enabled Europeans to set the pace of global change for the next 500 years. Properly understood, therefore, the Reformation is a key act in the play of world history, not merely an upheaval internal to the European region.

reformism: An approach to *North/South issues* that argues the violent overthrow of the *world capitalist system* is not required, because it can be reformed.

reform liberalism: A revision of *classical liberalism* that has become dominant in the 20th century. It accepts the premise that the most *efficient* and desirable economic system is a *free market*. Yet it argues that a completely free market does not lead to inevitable harmonious results as classical liberal theory supposed, but to maldistribution of wealth and resources. Adherents thus accept government *intervention* in the economy as fitting and necessary to more fairly distribute wealth, but reject *central planning* as suffocating the sources of wealth creation. See also *capitalism; individualism; keynesian economics; market economy.*

refugee camp: Make-shift living quarters for *refugees* who await relocation to a country of final settlement, or merely wait to return home once a natural disaster or *war* subsides, or a political solution is found to restore them to their homes and former national status.

refugees: Persons who flee a situation of economic distress, persecution or *war*, and seek refuge in another part of their own country (internal refugees), or in a foreign country (external refugees). By convention, refugees are additionally classified as (1) economic: not officially counted, to whom little *aid* is offered, and who are subject to *deportation*; (2) political: for whom a welcome of varying warmth or coolness awaits in different host countries, but who are looked upon with relative favor; and (3) wartime: who may receive international assistance, but are seldom offered relocation as they are expected to resettle in their home countries once the fighting dies down. Internal refugees also are not officially counted, and do not come under international mandates except when faced with *famine* or *genocide*. In 1993 the *UN High Commissioner for Refugees* said there were 18 million refugees worldwide, up from 8 million in 1980 and just 2 1/2 million in 1970. To that figure must be added another 24 million internal refugees and an untold number of economic migrants. See also *boat people; displaced person; ECOSOC; Kurds; Palestinians; refugee camp.* Cf. *migration.*

regime: (1) Domestically: a synonym for government, but often pejorative, and implying lack of respect for democratic rights, as in "the *Nazi* regime." (2) Internationally: an umbrella term for any set of *rules, norms* and procedures that focus common concerns and are used to manage an issue (or "*issue area*") of common interest, as in "*nonproliferation* regime," or "*free trade* regime." It may incorporate *treaty* rules, but implies as well both a broader and more informal set of understandings than the precise index of *terms* in a treaty.

regional banks: See *African Development Bank; Asian Development Bank; Inter-American Development Bank.*

regionalism: (1) A policy favoring regional over universal associations as the optimum path to *international organization*. Some analysts view regionalism as merely an interim step to construction of global organizations; others see it as a possible serious obstacle to *universalism* should, say regional trade and/or political blocs develop. (2) A claim to exclusive *jurisdiction* over an issue or conflict, based on *propinquity*. For example, African states calling for an "African solution" to the *civil war* in *Liberia*; some Arab states calling for an *Arab League*, rather than *UN* solution to the Iraqi *invasion* of Kuwait; claims of the *CSCE* to responsibility for *peace* and *security* in Europe.

regional power: A state that can effectively project influence within a given region, but not globally. For instance, Nigeria in West Africa, China in *East Asia* or Egypt in the *Middle East*.

regional war: One that expands beyond just two states to include some or all neighboring states, but does not draw the *Great Powers* directly into the fighting. For instance, see *Arab/Israeli Wars* and *Balkan Wars*.

registration: Depositing a copy of a signed and ratified *treaty* with a public registrar, such as the UN, for purposes of publication and open dissemination. The idea was spurred by the *liberal peace program,* which insisted that there should be *open covenants, openly arrived at* as a means of avoiding a repeat of the calamity of *WWI* (thought by many--correctly or not--to have been caused by secret *alliances*).

regression: A statistical technique for identifying a functional relationship between two or among several *variables,* drawn from *empirical* examination of a set of data and where the relationship is expressed in the natural units of the variables. It is used by *quantitative* analysts to predict values for *dependent variables* based upon known values of *independent variables*.

regular army: The permanent, professional force that forms the core of the *standing army* and any expanded force, should *reserves* be called up or *conscription* introduced.

regulated coexistence (geregeltes Nebeneinander): A West German adjustment to the reality of *East Germany,* enunciated in 1967 and moving the country on a pragmatic basis roughly halfway from the rejectionist *Hallstein Doctrine* toward the accommodation of *Ostpolitik.* Cf. *peaceful coexistence.*

rehabilitation: When in a *communist* political system a former official or leader who has been *purged* is brought back into public life, following a (coerced) confession of wrongdoing, or the proclamation of a new *party line* with which the official is now in tune.

Reich: An *empire* of Germanic *peoples*. See *Austria; Germany; First Reich; Second Reich; Third Reich.*

Reichstag: The lower house of the German legislature 1871-1945. In 1933 it was set afire by a deranged Dutch communist (later beheaded by the *Gestapo*).

The Nazis used the fire to launch a *purge*, and suspend political rights. Within months they banned all other parties.

Reichswehr: "State defense." The German military, 1871-1933. See *Bundeswehr; Versailles; Wehrmacht.*

reify: To regard an abstract notion as if it were something material or concrete.

Reinsurance Treaty (June 18, 1887): A secret German/Russian agreement giving Russia freedom of maneuver toward Bulgaria, and guaranteeing German *neutrality* in all events save a Russian *war* with Austria or a German war with France.

relations officieuses: "Official relations," even in the absence of *recognition*. This condition arises where there is no *de jure* recognition and political obstacles arise to extending it, but a pressing, practical need yet exists to resolve common problems or *disputes*. For example, despite not recognizing its communist regime, the U.S. participated with China in negotiating the *Geneva Agreements*. Similarly, prior to recognition of the Soviet Union in 1934 the U.S. dealt with an unaccredited Soviet trade representative, including using him to pass non-commercial, diplomatic messages back to Moscow. See *special interest section.*

relativism: The view that ethical and social truths depend upon the individual (moral relativism) or group (cultural relativism) upholding them. Some go on to argue that any search for universal standards of *international law* or morality, such as concern for *human rights, distributive justice* or *just war* is inherently misplaced and even "imperialistic." Cf. *universalism.*

remedy: When a state agrees to make legal redress for some action it has taken that has been deemed unfair or illegal and has caused harm to an *alien*. Under *international customary law*, an individual seeking *damages* against a foreign *state* must first seek redress by all available local means, before his or her government is entitled to appeal under *diplomatic protection*. There has been a recent modification in multiple cases, by the practice of lump-sum or general settlements between governments.

remittances: *Profits* from foreign *subsidiaries* of *MNCs,* or wages from migrant workers to their families and accounts in their home country, *repatriated* from where they are earned abroad.

remonstrance: A synonym for *diplomatic protest*. See also *diplomatic note*; *pro forma.*

Renaissance: "Rebirth." The intellectual and cultural efflorescence that began in 14th century Florence, spread across northern Italy, influenced all of Europe by the 17th century, and greatly shaped the character of the modern age. It was distinguished by a revival of classical learning, in particular of natural science but also theological criticism and moral philosophy, through texts acquired in part from *Muslim* middlemen in great centers of Islamic scholarship such as Granada and Seville. Its central contribution to modern life was its celebration of humanism and rationalism, which would find full flower in the *Enlightenment*. It is also justly famous, though historically far less important, for its advances in the arts and literature. Often overlooked are the period's contributions (some might object to that word) to modern *diplomacy*, *international law* and to *war*, as developed in Italy during the era of the *city-states*. Explicit formulation of the idea of the *balance of power* dates from this time, as do notions of *machiavellian* ethical and political theory and constitutional *republics*. When the movement passed north of the Alps it reinforced a shift in *power* already underway from the Mediterranean to the Atlantic states: from Byzantium and the *Holy Roman Empire*, to England, France, the Netherlands, Portugal and Spain. In sum, the Renaissance marked the transition from the ancient and feudal eras to modern times, not just for Europe but through the subsequent expansion and global dominance of Europe in the age of *imperialism*, for the world. Its rational curiosity and impulse toward change in economics, politics, religion and technology echoes to this day.

rendition: Surrender of individuals between *states* that have an *inter se* relationship. Cf. *extradition*.

reparations: (1) Money or *goods* delivered abroad to make redress for a previous *illegal act*. (2) Money or goods extracted by a *victor* from a *defeated* power, often but not always based on the claim that the losing side provoked the *war*. For instance, Prussia exacted reparations from France in 1871; Germany extracted reparations from the *Bolsheviks* at *Brest-Litovsk*; the *Allies* demanded reparations of Germany after 1920; the Soviet Union and France took reparations from Germany in 1945; and the *UN* in 1991 forced Iraq to pay Kuwait reparations. Cf. *indemnity*.

repatriate: To return someone or something (e.g., *profits* or *remittances*) to his/her or its *state* of *citizenship* or origin. See *deportation; POW; refugee*.

representation: The right of *international personalities* (and very rarely, other entities) to send and receive agents abroad, to represent their positions and interests as a member of the *world community*. The most recent *codification* of these rights came in 1961, with the *Vienna Conventions*. The main functions of such representatives, or *diplomats*, are: information gathering (but not *espionage*) about the affairs of state, commerce, science, the military and so on in the host country, and communication of accurate reports to his or her *foreign ministry; negotiation; protocol;* seeing to due process and fair play for nationals in legal or other trouble with the host country; and representation of the *sovereign* power and the policies of his or her government both to the host government, and at times to the host population. In return for *diplomatic immunity*, a diplomat must refrain from *subversion,* espionage (many engage in this nonetheless), smuggling, counterfeiting and other merely criminal acts. A second category of representation involves *consuls*. These are commercial representatives (historically, they were often chosen by and from the corps of foreign merchants in a given *capital*). Consuls are official representatives of governments, but do not normally enjoy diplomatic immunity. Their main functions are: facilitating commercial and other transactions; administering travel documents, *passports* and *visas;* aiding fellow nationals in difficulties and before local courts, if necessary; and reporting on economic and other activity in the host country. See also *ambassador; attaché; chargé; envoy; envoy extraordinary; minister plenipotentiary; nonresident ambassador; persona grata; persona non grata; plenipotentiary; special interest section*.

reprisal: (1) In *international law*: an act normally illegal, but permitted if taken to punish the prior *illegal act* of another *state*; e.g., applying discriminatory *tariffs*, deportation of *diplomats* for cause as *persona non grata* and so forth. (2) In *war*: reciprocal punishment; e.g., Israel's bombing southern Lebanon in reprisal for *guerrilla* or rocket attacks launched from there. See also *letters of marque; Treaty of Paris (1856)*.

republic: (1) In classical usage: a constitutional *state* where the citizenry is said to be bound in a single community by a *social contract*, is regularly consulted on matters of governance and exercises power (or thinks it does) through chosen or appointed representatives. (2) In modern usage: any state headed by a president, elected or not, rather than a hereditary *monarch*; not necessarily a constitutional democracy.

Republican Guard: The *elite* corps of armored and other units within the Iraqi Army that backed the *Ba'ath* coup in 1968, supported *Saddam Hussein* in power and in his internal repressions; was bloodied but escaped destruction in the *Gulf War*, repressed the

Kurds and southern *shi'ites* after the war; and continued to sustain Saddam in power into the mid-1990s.

republicanism: Clear preference for constitutional government and an elected president and/or supreme legislature, rather than a personal *sovereign*. Cf. *absolutism; American Revolution; democracy; divine right of kings; Enlightenment; French Revolution; Kant; Machiavelli; monarchism; nonintervention; popular sovereignty; Rousseau; social contract.*

Republican Party (U.S): The second of the modern American political parties, it was founded as successor to the *Whigs* in 1854. Originally based in the west and still strongest there, it supported *free soil* farmers and rapid western settlement. It opposed any extension of *slavery* (an institution inimical to free farming in the west), the issue that tore apart the rival *Democratic Party* on north/south lines. The first Republican president was *Abraham Lincoln*. During *Reconstruction* and under *Grant*, the party adjusted so that its base included general business and industrial, as well as western and agrarian interests. It continued to dominate national politics for over three decades, losing the presidency only rarely before 1912. Under *McKinley* and *Teddy Roosevelt*, it took the U.S. into the *Spanish/American War*, its brief experiment with *imperialism*, and its emergence as a Pacific power. It split badly over *Taft's* reelection bid but remained powerful in Congress, where it helped block the *Treaty of Versailles*. After *WWI* its nativist and *isolationist* wing commanded, and it became home to most conservatives outside the "solid South," where the *Democratic Party* held sway. In the *White House* again from 1920-32 under *Harding, Coolidge* and *Hoover*, it governed passively. In opposition from 1933-53, and with many grassroots Republicans still convinced *laissez-faire* was next to godliness, it opposed both New Deal reforms and postwar *keynesian* initiatives. However, during *WWII* a majority of Republicans abandoned isolationism, embraced the UN and a more active American global role, especially toward China. Still, an isolationist minority hovered in the right-wing of the party, blocking *Eisenhower's* activist foreign policy. During the *Cold War* most Republicans were fiercely anti-Soviet. But unlike the Democrats who had an inclination toward *Atlanticism*, the Republican Party was drawn by its western roots into an emphasis on Asia over Europe. That led to a grand compromise, in which blanket anti-communism covered over regional party tensions. After 1968 the Republicans again came to dominate presidential elections, even despite the fiasco of *Nixon's* resignation and *Ford's* perceived ineptitude. The right wing was ascendant again in the 1980s under *Reagan*, though less so under *Bush*. But with the shat-tering of Cold War consensus old divisions over foreign policy reappeared. During and since the *Gulf War*, moderates and internationalists in the party have clashed with its isolationist and social conservative wing, with no victor yet in sight.

requisition: When an invading or other foreign army demands *billets*, food stuffs and other matériel necessities from the *civilian* population.

res communis: "Common things." Those things held to lie outside any *sovereign* authority (such as the air, as opposed to *airspace*, the *seabed*, the *Moon*, *satellite* parking orbits and *radio* band broadcast frequencies). This notion lies at the core of the *common heritage principle*.

reservation: A statement reserving *sovereign* rights by withholding *consent* from specific provisions of a *treaty*. It operates only if other parties to the treaty agree. If they do not, the reserving state must accept the whole treaty without reservation, or decline the treaty. See *derogation; ratification; understanding.*

reserve: (1) In *war*: that portion of an armed force held back from the *front line* for emergency defense or for *counterattack*. (2) In *peace*: that portion of the military not on active duty but maintaining respectable levels of training and preparedness.

reserve currency: Holdings of *hard currency*, used to finance trade arrangements and to pay the national *debt*. See *foreign exchange reserve.*

res extra commercium: A thing excluded from the sphere of private transaction.

res inter alios acta: A thing that is the exclusive concern of others. See *noninterference.*

resistance: A generic term for those actively opposed to foreign *occupation*. For France and several other European countries, "the Resistance" during *WWII* has assumed near-mythical proportions, sometimes obscuring the competing reality of extensive *collaboration*. In several Asian states, with the *defeat* and departure of the Japanese national resistance shifted against a re-imposition of European colonial rule. French *Resistance* fighters on Corsica were called "Maquis."

res judicata: A thing that is decided.

res nullius: A thing without ownership.

resolution: A consensus statement by a *multilateral*

body, whether the *UNGA* or a regional or *treaty* organization. Within the UN, General Assembly resolutions are non-binding, having at most quasi-legislative authority under *international law* and requiring formal *consent* in a follow-up *convention* to have binding force. Only the *Security Council* can make binding resolutions, and not even all of its fall into that category. Other *international organizations* have different *rules* concerning how their members are bound by resolutions. See below, and *declaration; qualified majority voting; weighted voting.* Cf. *declaration.*

Resolution 242, Security Council (November 22, 1967): It called for a "just and lasting peace" in the Middle East, based on "secure and recognized boundaries," with Israeli withdrawal from the *occupied territories* in exchange for *recognition.*

Resolution 338, Security Council (October 22, 1973): Often cited in tandem with *Resolution 242,* it called for an immediate *cease-fire* in the *Fourth Arab/Israeli War,* to be followed by implementation of 242 and *negotiations* leading to a final settlement.

Resolution 660, Security Council (August 2, 1990): It found Iraq's *invasion* of Kuwait a breach of the law and of *peace,* condemned it and demanded immediate and unconditional withdrawal. But 660 also called for follow-up *negotiations* with Kuwait over outstanding Iraqi grievances.

Resolution 678, Security Council (November 29, 1990): This resolution authorized members to use "all necessary means" to implement *Resolution 660* should Iraq fail to withdraw from Kuwait by January 15, 1991. It did, and so they did.

resolutive condition: In *international law,* a future event that, if it occurs, will have the effect of abrogating an existing right.

res petita: The object of a claim.

responsibility: A central principle of *international law* by which states must make *reparation* for any *illegal act* they make.

restitutio in integrum: See *restitution.*

restitution: In *international law,* returning some *object* of the law to the condition it enjoyed before a state committed an *illegal act* against it.

Restoration: (1) The return to France of the *Bourbons,* in the (enlarged) form of *Louis XVIII,* with the

aid of foreign armies in 1814, and so again after *Waterloo.* (2) Any return to power of the old order following a revolutionary interregnum. See also *Meiji.*

restrictive interpretation: Narrow, literal interpretation of the text of a *treaty.*

retaliation: (1) In *international law:* when one state suspends compliance with a *treaty* on the ground that another contracting party is not living up to its *terms.* (2) In *nuclear deterrence* theory: the threat of massive counter-destruction with *second strike* forces should an adversary contemplate or launch a *first strike.*

retorsion: Acts taken in *retaliation* by *states* that are quite legal, but might be considered unfriendly.

retrenchment: An interior fortification within a larger fortress, to which a defending force can retreat if the outer walls are breached.

retrofit: Upgrading weapons systems by fitting them with advanced modifications. Benefit: cheapness.

Réunion: An island forming an *overseas department* of France, west of Madagascar. It has been a French possession since 1665.

revaluation: Changing the official (as opposed to *black market*) rate of a *currency,* as measured against the *gold standard* or the value of *hard currencies.*

revanchism: From the French for "revenge," a policy of seeking to recover *territory* lost in an earlier *war.* See *Alsace-Lorraine.* Cf. *irredentism.*

revision: Reconsideration of a *judgment,* or the redrafting of a *treaty* to take account of changed circumstance.

revisionism: (1) Any foreign policy that seeks to amend a given status quo. (2) A generic term for histories that challenge established interpretations of events, from whatever point of view. (3) A term used about the *"Wisconsin school"* of economic reinterpretation of U.S. foreign policy, and other histories that portray the U.S. as primarily responsible for the *Cold War.* (4) A pejorative term used by the orthodox about those who reassessed or revised the basic tenets of *marxism.* It was a common charge in Russia during the *Yezhovshchina,* and again in China during the *Great Proletarian Cultural Revolution.* It was later used by China regarding the ossifying internal system of the Soviet Union and its foreign policy shift to *peaceful coexistence.* See *Sino/Soviet split.*

revisionist power: Any state that seeks to alter, especially by forceful means, the territorial or political status quo of a *peace* settlement or *balance of power*. The antonym is *status quo power*.

revolution: The forcible overthrow of a political system by a significant portion of a population, usually accompanied by mass violence and frequently resulting in *civil war*. The term derives from Nicolas Copernicus' "De Revolutionibus" (1543), which overturned the ancient, Aristotelian view of an earth-centered, static universe by demonstrating that the planets revolve around the sun. Most revolutions are of merely local importance, displacing this or that *regime* and perhaps, but far from always, increasing the quotient of social or political justice in a given society (e.g., Ethiopian, Mexican or Portuguese). Some have wider significance because they occur within a dominant *regional power* or otherwise affect surrounding countries (e.g., the *Chinese, Cuban* or *Iranian Revolution*). A rare few have had global significance owing to the twinning of universal claims made for the ideas they propound and the fact they took place within a *Great Power,* and thereby affected the entire *international system* (e.g., the *French* or *Russian Revolutions*). Proponents of such cataclysmic upheavals often assert that they are about the business of utter, *radical* transformation not of a given society but of human nature itself. Such movements usually begin by proclaiming dedication to a higher plateau of human liberation, but devolve into persecution of any who stand in the way of the purifying changes they propose (say, by individuals willfully and perversely continuing in the old habits of their lives!). This pattern was repeated during phases of the Chinese, French, Iranian and Russian revolutions, among others. See also *agricultural revolution; class struggle; cultural revolution; Enlightenment; green revolution; Industrial Revolution; marxism-leninism; modernization; paradigm; Reformation; Renaissance; revolution from above; rising expectations*. Cf. *coup d'etat; insurrection; rebellion*.

Revolutionary War: See *American War of Independence*.

revolution from above: Any major social or economic upheaval or fundamental reform instituted by the reigning political authorities in a country, often against lower-level resistance. For example, *Peter I* (the Great) and *Stalin* both forced major changes on resistant social groups in Russia, Peter on the *boyars* and Stalin on all those he identified as "class enemies," but especially the *kulaks*. Such "revolutions" can be just as permanent and violent as mass phenomena that overwhelm existing power structures. See also *Bismarck;*

collectivization; communism; cultural revolution; dictatorship of the proletariat; Mao; National Socialism; vanguard; war communism.

Revolutions of 1830: Several European countries experienced social and political unrest, but most incidents were minor--more liberal reform efforts than *revolutions*. The exceptions were in France, where the *Bourbons* were displaced by the *July Monarchy*; Belgium, which seceded from the Netherlands; and Poland, where a full-scale *insurrection* was bloodily put down by *tsarist* troops in 1831.

Revolutions of 1848: The clashes of this remarkable year arose from dislocation between the new, industrial sectors of national economies and an exodus of peasants from the countryside, in search of jobs and *goods* that did not yet exist in abundant *supply*. That set a match to the tinders of urban political dissent in Northern Europe and national discontent in Southern Europe. The situation was aggravated by the failure of Europe's potato crop. It was not just Ireland that experienced successive years of blight and food shortages in the "hungry '40s." Though Ireland suffered more than most, there were "potato riots" in several centers, including Berlin itself. Nearly every country in Europe experienced profound unrest, or outright *revolution*. An additional cause of the outbreak was the frustration of *liberals* with the stultifying effects of *Metternich's* system. The exceptions were (1) Belgium and Britain, where *industrialization* and (partial) representative government blunted the economic crisis and vented frustration into reform rather than revolutionary movements; and (2) Russia, which was so backward the dynamic of *rising expectations* did not occur. In short, the most liberal and the most repressive societies alone escaped the unrest. Elsewhere, the middle classes led the poor into the streets, then shuddered at what they had done and turned to the old order to save them from their folly. All the uprisings failed, some after bloody clashes (Berlin, Milan, Prague, Rome and Venice). The one success was in Paris, where the *Second Republic* was set up (if that benighted experiment can be called a success). Flaubert said of 1848: "It was an outburst of fear. . . . Intelligent men were made idiotic by it for the rest of their lives."

Rhee, Syngman (1875-1965): Korean statesman. President of South Korea 1948-60. A longtime supporter of Korean *independence* from Japan (which imprisoned him from 1897-1904). He went to the U.S. where he was influenced by *Woodrow Wilson*. He returned to Korea in 1910, but left again after a failed *insurrection* in 1919, heading a *government-in-exile*. He became the principal political figure in the U.S.

occupation zone after 1945. He was elected President in 1948. He was dissatisfied both with the levels of U.S. commitment to his government, and with *de facto partition* of the Korean peninsula. He led the South in the *Korean Conflict*, in which he enthusiastically endorsed the decision to cross the 38th parallel and unify the country by force. He proved an obstacle to *peace*, refusing for months to agree to forced *repatriation* of Northern *POWs*. He was ousted in 1960 following widespread rioting, and went into *exile* for the third and last time.

Rhineland: That part of Germany bordering France and the *Low Countries*, west of the Rhine. It was ceded to *Prussia* as part of the settlement of the *Congress of Vienna*. In the 19th century it became an area of paramount industrial importance, while also serving as a jump-off point for German *invasions* of France in 1870, 1914 and 1940. At the *Paris Peace Conference* France sought to detach the Rhineland and create a separate Rhenish state, as a *buffer* between itself and Germany. But that scheme was opposed by *Woodrow Wilson*. He proposed the compromise clause in the *Treaty of Versailles* permitting a 15-year French military *occupation*, and permanent *demilitarization* of the right bank of the Rhine. In 1923 a Rhenish *republic* was declared (with French connivance), but soon failed for lack of popular support. British troops withdrew in 1926. The French, who could not stand alone, pulled out in 1930. In March 1936, *Hitler* sent in just three battalions of troops to remilitarize the Rhineland. While a daring violation of Versailles and *Locarno*, they had secret orders to pull out if opposed. When the Western powers did nothing, Hitler was emboldened to revise other features of the Versailles settlement with greater speed. After *WWII* France again sought to detach the Rhineland from Germany, and was again opposed mainly by the U.S. The dispute seems resolved by *integration* of both countries' interests in the region within the *ECSC* and *EU*.

Rhodes, Cecil (1853-1902): British imperialist. He made his fortune in South African diamonds (De Beers Co.) at a tender age. He obtained a Royal Charter to develop *Rhodesia* (Zimbabwe). He was also Premier of *Cape Colony* from 1890-96, when he was forced out over his complicity in the *Jamieson Raid*. His fortune went to his alma mater, Oxford University, to fund the Rhodes Scholarship program.

Rhodesia: Formerly called Southern Rhodesia. It was a *charter colony* founded by *Cecil Rhodes* in 1897 and run by the British South Africa Company. It was taken over by Britain in 1923. Thereafter it was linked to Northern Rhodesia (Zambia) and Nyasaland (Malawi).

In 1961, with "winds of change" blowing across Africa, Rhodesia's whites entrenched their political and economic privileges in a reworked constitution. On November 11, 1965, PM Ian Smith made a "*Unilateral Declaration of Independence (UDI)*" to preempt a settlement from Britain that would have enfranchised the country's black majority. Britain obtained UN agreement to *sanctions*, first on oil and in 1968 on all trade. But London resisted calls for direct military action. Several *guerrilla* groups formed and waged a campaign against the illegal Smith regime (which was supported by South Africa and Portugal, until the latter's collapse into *revolution* in 1974). In 1978 a *power-sharing* agreement was signed. *Independence* as Zimbabwe came in April 1980. The most unreconstructable whites departed the country, emigrating mainly to such places as Australia, Britain, Canada and South Africa (they have since had to pack again), where their unrepentant attitudes helped worsen race relations. See also *Godfrey Huggins; Robert Mugabe*.

Rhodesia and Nyasaland, Federation of: A composite British colony in East Africa, 1953-63. It was broken into Malawi, Rhodesia (Zimbabwe) and Zambia. Also known as the Central African Federation.

Ribbentrop, Joachim von (1893-1946): *Nazi* diplomat. Ambassador in London 1936-38; Foreign Minister 1938-45. He negotiated the *Anglo/German Naval Agreement* in 1935. A true believer in Nazi *ideology*, he gave this gloss to foreign policy in agreements such as the *Anti/Comintern Pact*, *Axis* and *Tripartite Pact*. He negotiated, with *Molotov*, the *Nazi/Soviet Pact* of August 1939, which opened the floodgates of *WWII*. Convicted at *Nuremberg*, he was hanged.

Richelieu, Armand Jean (1585-1642): "*Éminence Rouge.*" Cardinal of the church, and French *statesman*. He schemed to destroy the enemies of France, as he perceived them, both at home and abroad. He bested the *Hapsburgs* of Spain with *dynastic* marriages and with *war*. He crushed French Protestantism when he destroyed the Huguenots, scattering them to *New France* and to southern Africa. In 1630 he invaded Italy, conquering Savoy. He was no Catholic ideologue, however: Paris, not Rome, hosted his cathedral. Thus he courted the great Protestant prince, *Gustavus Adolphus*, allying with Sweden and other Protestant powers during the *Thirty Years' War* against Catholic (but Hapsburg) Austria. His legacy was a more powerful French crown, a centralized and absolutist state, and the beginnings of regularization of modern *diplomacy, espionage* and the idea of the *national interest*.

rifled bore: A gun or cannon with a grooved, spiral

bore, that spins the projectile and gives greater accuracy and range to the marksman or gunner. For its revolutionary impact cf. *smooth bore.*

Rif (Riff) Rebellion/Republic (1922-26): The Rifs were fierce Moroccan tribesmen who rose against the Spanish in 1922, killing 12,000 Spanish troops and setting up a *republic.* They were overthrown by a combined French and Spanish force, under *Pétain,* in 1926.

right deviationists: A pejorative term used by *Stalin* against the opponents of his *collectivization* scheme, led by Bukharin, Rykov and Tomsky. Real or imaginary, hundreds of thousands of accused "right-deviationists" were *liquidated* in the *Yezhovshchina.*

righteous Gentiles: Non-Jews who, during the *Holocaust,* risked themselves to save Jews from *summary execution* or the *death camps.*

Rights of Man and Citizens, Declaration of: This influential statement of the original principles of the *French Revolution* was promulgated on July 27, 1789. Owing something to the American revolutionary example, but more to the *Enlightenment,* it inspired generations of *liberal* thinkers and reformers. Besides proclaiming basic civil and individual rights, its most important assertion was the idea of *popular sovereignty.* In the 20th century this declaration found resonance in the *Universal Declaration of Human Rights.*

Rimland: The theory of Nicholas Spykman (1893-1943), developed as a modification of the idea of the *World Island* promoted by *Halford Mackinder.* Spykman saw not *Eurasia* but its outlying promontories (Africa, the Middle East, India and SE Asia) as the key to world political dominance. Here is his revision of Mackinder's famous formulation about the influence of geography on history: "Who rules the Rimland rules Eurasia; who rules Eurasia controls the destinies of the world."

Rio Group: A forum in which Latin American *heads of state* or government meet to discuss common problems and regional issues.

Rio Pact (September 2, 1947): A regional defense *alliance* set up at U.S. behest. It includes all the major Latin American countries and is coordinated through the *OAS.* Cuba was barred from participation, also at U.S. insistence, in 1962. Echoing the *Monroe Doctrine,* it calls for mutual action not only against a direct, extrahemispheric attack, but against "indirect threats" as well. It arose from cooperation against German and Japanese forces in the Western Hemisphere during *WWII,* but spoke more to security concerns of the burgeoning *Cold War.* Cf. *isolationism.*

rising expectations, crisis of: This was (is) a phenomenon of the industrial age. During the first decades of *modernization* the vast mass of rural poor, displaced from the land or simply seeking fuller lives under bright city lights, found their expectations unfulfilled due to a shortage of jobs, housing and so forth. The cause was a delay in the ability of the modernizing sectors of the economy to meet the new demands of a rising consumer society, and extant needs no longer being fully met by the collapsing traditional economy. This created a vast reserve of frustrated, needful people, and much potential for social violence (as *Karl Marx* noticed outside the windows of the Reading Room in the British Museum). On the other hand, the history of the 19th and 20th centuries in Europe was to demonstrate that while short-term unrest increased with early industrialization, contrary to the predictions of orthodox *marxists,* social discontent decreased with full industrialization. That was because industrialization generally has been accompanied by social reform and welfare spending, supported by new wealth being created in the factories and through expanding trade. Astute observers have noted, and the Soviets learned firsthand in 1985-91, that there is a parallel to this phenomenon in politics; to wit: a bad government is never in so much danger as the moment it begins to reform itself. Cf. *Industrial Revolution.*

risorgimento: "Resurrection." The nationalist movement working for unification of Italy in the 19th century. See *Cavour; Garibaldi; Piedmont-Sardinia.*

Robespierre, Maximilien de (1758-94): "The Incorruptible." A *Jacobin* lawyer, revolutionary leader and puritanical megalomaniac, who believed he personally embodied the "general will" of France. His ascent to power came by way of voting for *Louis XVI's* death, but especially the terrible retribution of *The Terror* against all seen as enemies of the *French Revolution.* For Robespierre that came to include fellow Jacobins like *Danton.* His *radical* and increasingly irrational dictatorship, and an attempt to suspend all rights of defense from judgment by revolutionary courts, provoked a conservative reaction in 1794 ("*Thermidor*"). He was then guillotined in his turn.

robust regression: A *regression* that is fairly insensitive to errors in the data.

Rokossovsky, Konstantin Konstantinovich (1896-1968): Polish-born "Marshal of the Soviet Union." He fought at *Stalingrad* and *Kursk,* though not in supreme command. It was his army that paused to watch the *Nazis* crush the *Warsaw Rising*. He led one prong of the final assault on Berlin. He was Poland's Defense Minister 1945-56, using troops to crush worker uprisings in 1956. He returned to Moscow and served as deputy Minister of Defense before taking a final active command in *Transcaucasia*.

Romanov (a.k.a Romanoff): The ruling *dynasty* of the Russian Empire 1613-1917. *Catherine II* (the Great) introduced a German line, but this was not a widely or enthusiastically celebrated fact. The royal family, including several very small children, was massacred on *Lenin's* personal orders--an old rumor confirmed as fact from Soviet archives in 1993--and buried in secret. After revelations about Lenin's involvement the bodies were exhumed and reburied in marked graves.

Roman Question: "What should be the relationship of the Vatican to the Italian state?" For more than 14 centuries Rome was under the temporal control of the popes, and beyond Rome, so were the *Papal States*. From 1850-70, however, *Pius IX* was kept in Rome only by French troops. When these were pulled out for use in the *Franco/Prussian War*, Italian troops assaulted the city and incorporated it into Italy, making it the capital. The popes never accepted this, until the compromise with *Mussolini* drawn up in the *Lateran Treaty* (1929) that established the *Vatican*.

Rome, Treaty of (1957): Six West European *nations* (Belgium, France, Italy, Luxembourg, the Netherlands and West Germany) met in Rome in 1957 to sign a *treaty* setting up *EURATOM* and the *EEC*, and intending to "establish the foundations of an ever closer union among the European peoples." It provided for creation of a *common market* within 15 years, while permitting smaller *customs unions* to operate as well, such as the *BENELUX*. It committed signatories to free movement of *capital* and *labor*, progressive elimination of *tariffs* and other *trade barriers*, and common *investment* and social welfare policies. *Agriculture* was exempt, but was later brought under the *Common Agricultural Policy (CAP)*. The treaty established four major organs: (1) *European Commission*, as a semi-executive; (2) *Council of Ministers*, to coordinate the national governments (connected to the Commission by a consultative committee); (3) the *European Parliament*; and (4) the *European Court of Justice*.

Rommel, Erwin (1881-1944): "The Desert Fox." A hard-charger who always chose attack over defense, rather than a brilliant tactician, he led the Afrikakorps against the British in N. Africa. Although the military effect of his exploits was minimal, he was made a great war hero by Nazi propagandists. He later commanded *Hitler's* Atlantic defenses. Only once Rommel came to believe Germany was losing the war did he join the *July Plot* to kill Hitler and negotiate *peace*. To preserve Rommel's reputation as a *propaganda* support for the war effort, rather than execute him Hitler forced him to drink poison by threatening his family, and then announced he had died of battle wounds, giving his all for the *Third Reich*.

Roosevelt, Franklin Delano (1882-1945): U.S. statesman. Assistant Secretary of the Navy 1913-20; President 1933-45. His first administration was preoccupied with the national calamity brought on by the *Great Depression*. However, in foreign affairs he opened relations with the Soviet Union and announced the *Good Neighbor policy*. After 1936 he grew increasingly concerned with events in Europe and Asia, but offered only rhetorical support to proposals for *collective security* measures against Italy, Germany and Japan. He tried to convince Britain and France to work with *Stalin* against *Hitler*, but to no avail, as he insisted the U.S. would remain *neutral*. In 1940-41, however, he jumped ahead of *isolationist* public opinion with the *destroyers-for-bases* deal, *Lend-Lease* and the *Atlantic Charter*. The latter virtually declared American *war aims* although the U.S. was still a neutral power. After *Pearl Harbor* he agreed with *Churchill* and *Stalin* to concentrate on defeating Germany. He pushed successfully for creation of the *United Nations Organization* during 1944-45. He has been criticized for unilaterally declaring the *unconditional surrender* policy and for distrusting Britain almost as much, or more, than he did Soviet Russia. He negotiated at *Casablanca*, *Tehran* and *Yalta*, for which he received much unfair criticism for his supposed "sell-out" of Eastern Europe to Stalin (when what he did was accept to live with the reality of a *de facto* Soviet *sphere of influence*). With more justice, he has also been criticized for overestimating the importance of *Chiang Kai-shek* to China's future and America's *national interest*. He died while the *San Francisco Conference*, in which he stored great hope, was underway.

Roosevelt, Theodore (1858-1919): U.S. statesman. Assistant Secretary of the Navy 1897-98; Vice President 1898-1901; President 1901-08. At home he was an energetic reformer, but in foreign policy he was an enthusiastic imperialist (though he later came to have regrets about that). While with the navy, he sent the Pacific fleet to waters near the Philippines, in anticipation of acquiring those islands should *war* break out with Spain. He led the "Rough Riders" in a charge up San Juan Hill in Cuba during the *Spanish/American War*. His most famous admonition was to "speak softly and carry a big stick." He tried to do both when intriguing to create Panama so he could build a canal across it, and in his reluctance to *intervene* in Central America except when unavoidable (*Woodrow Wilson* would intervene more frequently than Roosevelt). He brought America onto the world stage with his successful *mediation* of the *Treaty of Portsmouth,* for which he won the 1906 *Nobel Prize* for Peace. In 1912 he split the Republicans by running against *Taft* on the "Bull Moose" ticket. In 1914 he argued for early entry into *WWI*, against what he saw as Wilson's excessive caution. He opposed the latter's call for a "peace without victors," arguing instead for a military *occupation* of Germany and the other *Central Powers.*

Roosevelt/Litvinov Agreements (1933): A set of paper understandings on consular arrangements, limited religious liberty, retrenchment of activities of the *COMINTERN*, trade and *war debts*, all negotiated by *Franklin Roosevelt* and *Maxim Litvinov.* They paved the way to U.S. *recognition* of the Soviet Union after 15 years of severed relations.

Root, Elihu (1845-1937): U.S. statesman. Secretary of War, 1899-1904; Secretary of State, 1905-09. His main concentration was on the *Root Arbitration Treaties,* for which he won the 1912 *Nobel Prize* for Peace. He also negotiated the *Root/Takahira Agreement* with Japan, and resisted unsuccessfully a precipitous decline in American/Russian relations and *abrogation* by Congress of a 72-year-old *commerical treaty* over the issue of Russian persecution of American Jews. See also *William McKinley.*

Root Arbitration Treaties: U.S. Secretary of State *Elihu Root* believed that even weak *arbitration* agreements were better than none, and negotiated 24 *bilateral* treaties (renewable at five-year intervals) with most leading states, except Germany. That added to the 10 that *John Hay*, his predecessor, had negotiated. Cf. *cooling-off treaties.*

Root/Takahira Agreement (1908): U.S. Secretary of State *Elihu Root* and Japanese Ambassador Baron Takahira agreed to confirm Japan's paramountcy in Korea, in return for a Japanese affirmation that it had no designs on the Philippines. Two years later, having thus eased the way, Japan *annexed* Korea.

Round Table Conference (1930-32): Abortive talks between the British and various Indian leaders, including *Gandhi,* on self-government for India.

Rousseau, Jean-Jacques (1712-78): Swiss philosopher. His influence spread widely, especially after many of his ideas were embodied and tested by the *French Revolution.* He was one of several *social contract* theorists whose views helped the doctrine of *popular sovereignty* surmount *absolutism.* His work influenced *Kant* and *Hegel,* though in greatly different directions. Rousseau wrote much, and like any prolific author, frequently appeared to contradict his earlier self. One can locate in his writings soaring and inspirational paeans to human freedom and the essential goodness of human nature, but also darker yearnings for political and social compulsion (that great temptation of all radical idealists). See also *Enlightenment; state of nature.*

Royal Navy: The Royal Navy was the basis of Britain's military power and the key to its imperial expansion. Its greatest moments were at *Trafalgar,* where it broke *Napoleon's* fleet, policing the ban on the *slave trade* off the east and west African coasts after 1833, enforcing the *blockade* of Germany during *WWI,* and in the *Battle of the Atlantic* during *WWII.* Britain sought to maintain a *two-power naval standard,* but abandoned that effort by 1912 in face of German strength and the *Dreadnought* revolution. It accepted parity with the U.S. Navy in 1922. Since WWII it has shrunk steadily, but still managed to project British power during the *Falklands War.* It otherwise operates within *NATO,* and is one of several nuclear navies.

Ruanda-Urundi: A *trust territory* in Central Africa under Belgian control 1946-62, when it was divided into the independent states of Rwanda and Burundi.

Ruhr: A major mining and industrial region of Germany, centered on the Ruhr Valley. It was occupied by French and Belgian troops from 1923-25 in an effort to compel *reparations* payments. That contributed to the German *hyperinflation,* and set the stage for *Hitler* to attempt the *Beer Hall putsch* (at the time, a minor incident). The *occupation* gained little for France that was concrete, and lost it valuable diplomatic support from Britain and the U.S.

rule of 1756: Now archaic, this maritime law said that trade between a *metropolitan power* and its *colonies* was designated "enemy trade" in wartime, even if carried by *neutral* shipping.

rule of double criminality: Of recent vintage, this *rule* now written into many *treaties* on criminal *extradition* holds that extradition of a fugitive may occur and a trial proceed only if the charges concern an act that is a crime in both countries concerned.

rule: In *international law*, the only binding measure.

The binding character of rules is derived mainly from *consent*, but also from the premise that there is broad agreement under *international customary law* as to the existence of commonly binding *norms* of *state* conduct. See *declaration; jus cogens; resolution; treaty.*

rules of engagement: The operational orders under which a military unit is authorized to use *force* in a *war zone.* Rules of engagement may be liberal (at the extreme, akin to "shoot whatever moves"), or highly restrictive (at the extreme, "fire only if directly fired upon and can identify the shooter and the gauge of weapon used, and then return fire only with the same gauge of weapon and using as many rounds as the perpetrator"). Worst of all is when rules of engagement forbid return fire due to the political delicacy of a situation (to troops on the ground, that amounts to the order "duck"). Restrictive rules have been the usual ones for UN *peacekeeping* forces, but became more liberal with the UN's move into *peace enforcement,* as in Somalia 1993- .

rules of the game: *Norms* of conduct tacitly agreed between or among *states* otherwise engaged in serious conflict, whose violation will escalate the conflict. *Nonintervention* in each others' *spheres of influence* is a grand rule; not assassinating leaders or *intelligence agents* may be a lower-level example.

Rumania: Location: E. Europe. Major associations: *CSCE, UN.* Population: 23.5 million. Military: old *Warsaw Pact* weapons, regionally capable. As the *Danubian Principalities,* it became *autonomous* within the *Ottoman Empire* in 1862. With Russian support, it became fully *sovereign* in 1878. It entered the *Second Balkan War* looking for *territory.* Ionel Brătianu (1864-1927) was PM intermittently, 1909-27. He tried to stay out of *WWI.* It remained *neutral* in 1914, but was bribed into the war on the side of the *Allies* in 1916 with promises of land at Austria-Hungary's expense. Instead, it was nearly overrun by Austrians and Germans, and was forced to make a *separate peace* in March 1918. However, by redeclaring war in November (just days before the German *surrender*), it could sit as a victor at the *Paris Peace Conference* and thereby gain huge new territories, including *Bessarabia* and *Transylvania.* It joined the *Little Entente* in the *interwar years,* but a large Rumanian fascist party (the *Iron Guard*) pulled it toward *Nazi Germany,* a process completed after the destruction of *Czechoslovakia.* Bessarabia was surrendered to the Soviets under pressure in 1940; Hungary and Bulgaria also took back some of their lost territory. Rumania joined the *Tripartite Pact* in 1940 and enrolled in the Nazi assault on Russia in 1941, in a bid to reclaim Bessar-

abia. Ion Antonescu (1882-1946), Rumania's fascist dictator, was overthrown in August 1944 (and shot in 1946). Rumania then tried to escape Soviet vengeance by switching sides and *declaring war* on Germany. But by early 1945, a *communist* regime had been imposed by Moscow, and Rumania entered the Soviet orbit for the duration of the *Cold War.* Under the dictatorial rule of Gheorghe Gheorghiu-Dej (1901-65), it negotiated the withdrawal of Soviet troops in 1958. *Nicolae Ceaușescu* became president and dictator in 1967. He ran a ruthless regime at home that yet won favor in the West for its occasional foreign policy independence from Moscow. In the 1980s he intensified discrimination against ethnic Hungarians, forcing many to flee to Hungary and embittering relations with that *Soviet bloc* neighbor. In 1989 his Securitate, a particularly brutal *secret police,* savagely repressed demonstrations in Timisoara. That set off a general uprising. Ceaușescu's family dictatorship was overthrown in four days, and he and his wife were shot. However, old communists in democrats' clothing rallied to win the 1990 elections and retard movement toward genuine reform. Rumanians have since been further distracted by fighting in Bessarabia, now an ethnically Rumanian part of Moldova, where *secessionists* drew support from units of the Russian Army.

Rumelia: A *Balkan* subdivision of the old *Ottoman Empire,* including Albania, Macedonia and Thrace. Eastern Rumelia later became southern Bulgaria.

ruse: A deliberately deceitful policy; a *stratagem.*

Rush-Bagot, Treaty of (1818): Acting U.S. Secretary of State Richard Rush and British Minister (Ambassador) Charles Bagot negotiated this first-ever naval *disarmament* agreement. It limited both *nations* to light naval craft, sufficient only for police and *customs* duties, concerning the Great Lakes and Lake Champlain. During the *American Civil War* the U.S. considered giving the required six-months notice of renunciation. It was reacting to the use of Canadian soil as a base for *Confederate* raids into Vermont, New York, and other far northern states. The *treaty* passed from Britain to Canada, and still remains in force. It underwrites part of the world's longest undefended frontier, some 3,800 miles of the Canada/U.S. border.

Rushdie, Salman (b.1947): British novelist. In February 1989, *Ayatollah Khomeini* condemned as blasphemous his allegory "The Satanic Verses," issued a fatwah (edict) calling for Muslims to strike him down, and offered a substantial gratuity for the act. Refusal by Iran to revoke this incitation to murder soured relations with Britain and the West, just as they had begun to improve. Rushdie remains in protective concealment, and is always under guard. In 1993 *William ("Bill") Clinton* met Rushdie, to demonstrate U.S. commitment to the principle of free speech.

Rusk, Dean (b.1909): U.S. statesman. Secretary of State 1961-69. He had a long career in the *State Department*, at the UN, and as an adviser to Presidents on Asian/Pacific affairs. He was a strong supporter of using U.S. military power to block local Asian communist movements, in *Korea* and again in *Indochina*. He saw these as threads in a larger tapestry of *subversion* and *expansion* woven by Moscow. He was intimately connected with policy toward the *Korean Conflict* and the *Vietnam War*. He reputedly did not warm easily to opinions different from his own.

Russia: Location: It sprawls over *Eurasia*. Major associations: *CIS, CSCE, permanent member of the Security Council*. Population: 150 million (85% Russian). Military: downsizing under *conventional* and *nuclear treaties*; still with over 2 million troops, a world-class navy, and thousands of nuclear *warheads*. This great *nation* has had an agonizingly complex history. It has been marked by *invasion, expansion* (sometimes defensive, but often opportunistic), and vacillation between internal reform and *modernization* vs. repression and *xenophobia*. The first identifiably Russian state was Kievan Rus (c.882-c.1240 A.D.), a loose feudal association with cultural, religious *(Orthodox Church)* and political ties to the Byzantine Empire. But it was weakened by *civil wars* and ultimately overrun by Mongol invaders. The Mongols ruled Russia for two centuries, establishing the Golden Horde and other states. They took much but gave little in return. (The poet Pushkin said of them, in comparison with the historical experience of the West, they were "Arabs without Aristotle or algebra.") This was the time of social chaos of "Appanage Russia," named for the splintered landholding (udel, or appanage) system that kept each local prince weak, but independent of the others. A strong state (Muscovy) slowly emerged in the north around the city of Moscow. When it broke the "Mongol yoke" in 1480 it looked to Byzantium, not Mongolia, as its model and inheritance, except in one regard: Russia was to be a harsher state and society for centuries of subjugation by the "Great Khans."

(1) Tsarist Russia (1480-1917): The *empire* established by Muscovy was ruled by *tsars*, from the renunciation of vassalage to the Mongols by *Ivan III (the Great)* in 1480, to the abdication of *Nicholas II* in 1917. Under *Ivan IV (the Terrible)* it expanded in all directions: south against the *Tartars*; west against Balts, Poles and Lithuanians; and east into the vast expanses of *Siberia*. From 1598-1613 was the "Time

of Troubles" (Smutnoe Vremia), defined by *dynastic* struggles, social unrest, *famine*, peasant *uprisings* and harsh repression. It ended with the establishment of the *Romanov* dynasty and the reforms of *Peter I (the Great)*. His reign was followed by another four decades of dynastic intrigue, but also continuing influence by *Westernizers* and Russia's further development as a European *Great Power*. Next came *Catherine II (the Great)* and more expansion, in wars against the *Ottoman Empire* and through the *partitions of Poland*. Catherine was followed by the brief enlightenment period of *Alexander I*, before his great struggle during the *Napoleonic Wars* contributed to a return to *despotism*. After the failure of the *Decembrist* revolt came the descent into full *reaction* under *Nicholas I*. The *Crimean War* shook Russia, leading to the great reforms of *Alexander II*, especially his *emancipation* of the serfs (1861). But Alexander's assassination in 1881 in turn propelled Russia partway back to reaction, and began several decades of the worst indulgence of its deeply rooted *anti-Semitism* and tolerance of *pogroms*. Yet, *industrialization* had come to Russia, and with it the growth of new social classes and demands for urban and political reform. With a new and powerful Germany at the center of Europe, Russia looked to the Far East--to *Manchuria* and Korea for additional gains. It built railways through Siberia, pushed development into Kamchatka and began to press into Manchuria. In 1904-05 its imperial expansion clashed with Japan's: it was humiliated at sea (though it held out on land) in the *Russo/Japanese War*. It then experienced the *Russian Revolution of 1905*, the first of several domestic *revolutions* that were to shake tsarism. But the system was really destroyed when things fell apart during *WWI*. Massive setback upon setback, and extraordinary casualties, broke the back of the system, which collapsed into the *Russian Revolutions of 1917*. The center could not hold: several years of savage civil strife and *anarchy* was loosed upon the empire.

(2) Soviet Russia 1918-91: Despite *defeat* in WWI, and in the *Polish/Soviet War* of 1920, Russia clung to the lion's share of its great empire between the wars, losing the *Baltic States*, Finland and Poland, but holding the Caucasus, Central Asia, Ukraine and Siberia. Under *Lenin, Trotsky* and the *Bolsheviks* the *Red Army* won the *Russian Civil War*, and reconstituted the empire as the Soviet Union (officially, "Union of Soviet Socialist Republics"). In theory, this was a great, voluntary federation of 15 "independent" republics, plus other quasi-autonomous zones. In reality the USSR was a *unitary*, overcentralized and highly repressive continuance of the Russian empire. Russia was the largest of the constituent republics, itself containing 16 "autonomous republics" and still more "autonomous regions." For decades this composite state

wore a cloak of *marxist* internationalism, an ideological fig-leaf to cover the naked verity that it was an imperial extension of the Russian nation. With the failure of the notion of *permanent revolution* it withdrew into a paranoid *isolationism* under *Stalin*. It pursued *socialism in one country* and successive *five-year plans*, and suffered the torments of forced *collectivization*, artificial *famine*, the *Yezhovshchina* and the *GULAG*. Soviet Russia sensed the danger from Nazi Germany and Imperial Japan somewhat earlier than the West, but was rebuffed in the mid-1930s in its efforts to form a collective front against *fascism* (partly because it refused to give up its own *subversive* efforts through the *COMINTERN*). Excluded from the *Munich Conference*, Stalin looked to a separate deal with *Hitler*, signing the *Nazi/Soviet Pact* in August 1939. After partitioning Poland with Germany he took advantage of German preoccupation with war in the west to launch the *Winter War* against Finland (1939-40), annex the Baltic States (1940) and force *cession* of *Bessarabia* and *Bukovina* from Rumania. The Soviet Union lost all that *territory*, and one-third of European Russia, including Ukraine and the *Crimea*, when Hitler launched *Barbarossa* in June 1941. With *Lend-Lease* aid and an extraordinary industrial and military effort of its own, by the end of *WWII* the Soviet Union retook all the territory lost in 1918-20, all that lost in 1941-42, all gained by the Nazi/Soviet Pact, plus a good deal more: it reannexed the Baltic States, and annexed parts of northern China, Czechoslovakia, eastern Germany, Finland, Hungary, Japan, Manchuria, Mongolia, Poland and Rumania. By that it alienated all those nations to some degree. This was not seen by the West as the realization of the agreements hammered out at *Tehran, Yalta* and *Potsdam*, but as their disavowal. The *Cold War* dominated the next four decades, highlighted from 1947-68 by the *Berlin air lift* and *Berlin Wall*, the *Korean Conflict, Hungarian Uprising*, the *adventurism* of *Khrushchev* before and during the *Cuban Missile Crisis*, indirect confrontation with the U.S. in the *Vietnam War*, direct confrontation with China in the *Sino/Soviet split* and invasion of Czechoslovakia to end the *Prague Spring*. In response to West Germany joining *NATO* in 1955, Moscow put together the *Warsaw Pact*; in response to the *Non-Aligned Movement* and U.S. *deterrence* policy, it promoted *wars of national liberation* and *peaceful coexistence*. The 1970s brought *détente* and the *SALT* treaties and setbacks in the Middle East, but also Soviet geopolitical thrusts into the Horn of Africa and the Arabian peninsula. The *Afghan/Soviet War* marked a new departure and the beginning of the final erosion of the communist system and Soviet power. The early 1980s witnessed a crisis of leadership with *Brezhnev, Andropov* and *Chernenko* all dying within three years.

They were followed by *Gorbachev*, who stumbled from bold beginnings in 1985 to economic and political collapse in 1990-91. A coup attempt by the old guard in the *Communist Party* and the army failed in August 1991. On December 25th, the Soviet Union suffered *extinction* by internal demand and international consent, and 15 *successor states* formed from its breakup. Despite this huge loss of territory, the Russian state remains by far the largest in the world.

(3) Contemporary Russia: Under President *Boris Yeltsin* Russia confirmed the change in its foreign policy from confrontation and obstruction to creative engagement and facilitation of international cooperation. It ceased to use its *veto* at the UN to block *collective security* or *peacekeeping* actions. Indeed, it supported the UN during the *Gulf War* and in its *intervention* in *Somalia* and *Bosnia*. It began cooperating with *NATO* and played a more positive role within the CSCE. It applied to join the *IMF* and the *G-7*, for reasons of both economic need and desire for *prestige* in a time of sinking *national morale*. It drew upon some Western aid, but struggled into 1994 without completing the transition to a *market economy*. Under Foreign Minister Andrei Kozyrev, Russia announced a liberal policy toward the 25 million Russians living in the *near abroad*: the best way to protect their rights, it said, is to encourage local governments to respect human rights and democracy, while securing both in Russia itself. Still, by mid-1993 it had sent troops back into Tajikistan to intervene in a civil war, and was accused by Georgia and Moldova of allowing Russian Army units to support *secession* movements. Its worst quarrel was with Ukraine, over the division of the *Black Sea Fleet* and the disposition of 1,800 *nuclear weapons* left in Kiev's hands with *partition* of the old union. An interim settlement, on Russia's terms, was reached as Ukraine's economy collapsed. In October 1993, the last important vestiges of communist power appeared to be crushed during a day of street fighting in Moscow. But elections for a new parliament, held in December, returned large numbers of extreme right-wing delegates, and a goodly number of unreconstructed communists. Yet the key fact seemed the passage of a new constitution, creating the strongest presidential power (rule by edict is a real possibility) of any country still maintaining a legitimate claim to representative government. Russia had not exhumed its tsars, but for good or ill, after seven decades of communist misrule it had returned to the path of its pre-Soviet history and traditions. See also *anarchism; apparat; Bakunin; Beria; Birobizhan; CO-COM; containment; CHEKA; CIS; Dzerzhinsky; Eastern Question; KGB; Kirov; Kuriles; Minatom; Molotov; narodniki; NKVD; nomenklatura; OGPU; Old Believers; Pamyat; Port Arthur; purge trials; revolu-*

tion from above; Russian America; Sakhalin; space race; SPUTNIK; START; Straits Question; Tilsit; Vyshinsky; X article; Zhirinovsky; Zhukov; Zinoviev.

Russian America: In the 19th century Russia laid claim to large swaths of the west coast of North America, primarily in Alaska but also in northern California, where a few small settlements were set up. California was not targeted for colonization after declaration of the *Monroe Doctrine*, while Alaska was sold to the U.S. in 1867.

Russian Civil War (1918-20): *White* military units, often led by former *tsarist* generals and officers, began to skirmish with the *Red Army*, then being assembled among supporters of the *Bolsheviks* by *Trotsky*. Whereas the latter fought under a unified, and often ruthless command, the Whites never formed a single force, and sometimes fought each other. Balts and Finns (the latter under *Mannerheim*) succeeded by 1920 in forcing the Bolsheviks to accept the loss of several tsarist provinces. In the Ukraine, Whites, Reds and Poles tangled in a bloody mêlée that saw Poland take some Ukrainian *territory*, and several groups of Whites eventually crushed. In the *Crimea*, armies of *Cossacks* seemed to fight everybody, penetrating the Ukraine proper before being defeated by the Reds. The special areas were North Russia (near Murmansk) and *Siberia*. In North Russia the Western *Allies* intervened in 1918, with a small U.S. backup force sent most reluctantly by *Woodrow Wilson*. The initial plan was to prop up the *eastern front* and prevent the Germans from capturing large military stockpiles. But with *Brest-Litovsk* that purpose evaporated and the Americans withdrew. That forced the Allies out too. In Siberia motives for *intervention* from 1918-22 were more varied: Britain (with *Churchill* in the lead) and France wanted to overthrow the Bolsheviks, and perhaps wreak some vengeance for Brest-Litovsk. Japan clearly sought to detach part or all of Siberia from Russia, intending its own imperial penetration of that area and *Manchuria*. The U.S. again refused a forward role, and seems to have gone along mainly to keep an eye on the Japanese, whom it suspected of wanting to close the *Open Door* throughout the Far East. A secondary aim was to aid the *Czech Legion*. The Siberian Whites, under *Kolchak*, were ultimately defeated by the Red Army.

Russian Empire: See *Russia.*

Russian Revolution (1905): Discontent with the *reactionary* and incompetent rule of *Nicholas II* built for years. Fuel was added by defeats in the *Russo/Japanese War*, but the tinder was lighted by a massacre of demonstrators on *Bloody Sunday* (1905). Strikes, a naval mutiny and creation of the *St. Petersburg Soviet* under *Trotsky* compelled the Tsar to agree to set up the *Duma*. The right-wing then turned on the Jews, and a wave of *pogroms* swept Russia more violent and vicious than any seen in 150 years. Russian *liberals* accepted reforms that seemed to promise a constitutional *monarchy*, but the soviet did not and was bloodily repressed (as were the peasants). When the crisis eased, the Tsar returned to a more *autocratic* style.

Russian Revolution (February/March 1917): Its deepest roots lay in the *rising expectations* brought about by the pace of *industrialization* Russia was experiencing at the turn of the century. But also important was the frustration of *liberals* who saw the gains of 1905 eroded to nothing by a tsarist regime increasingly distant from the reality of the nation, and lost in the mystic miasma cast over the royal family by *Rasputin*. However, the *sine qua non* of 1917 was the fact that Russia was losing the *war*, and in the process taking insupportable casualties (close to 6 million, killed and wounded). When the troops lost confidence in their officers and began to *vote with their feet* for *peace* and political change, the professional revolutionaries moved to seize the moment. The majority were liberals or democratic *socialists* who sought varying degrees of constitutional and social reform. Many also supported the war effort, though not the regime. More *radical* were the *Bolsheviks* and their allies of the moment, *Trotsky*, the Social Revolutionaries (SRs) and the *soviets* that began to spring up in cities and towns. But it was the liberals who made the March Revolution (February in the old, Julian calendar). The affair was relatively bloodless: *Nicholas II* was forced to abdicate on March 13th, after failing to abolish a *Duma* which finally stiffened its back after years of docility. Subsequently, the great political struggle was between the *Provisional Government* and the *Petrograd Soviet*, with the first deciding to continue the war, and the latter obstructing government policy in the hope of further radicalizing events. The *Bolsheviks* came to dominate the soviets, but when they contemplated a *coup* in July they were faced down and *Lenin* had to flee to Finland. However, *Kerensky's* decision to launch a summer offensive proved disastrous. It broke the will of the army, split the Provisional Government, permitted Lenin to return and opened the way to a successful Bolshevik coup in November.

Russian Revolution (October/November 1917): *Lenin* and the *Bolsheviks* launched their *coup* on November 6, 1917. It succeeded where their July effort failed, mainly due to the exhaustion of the Russian population caused by a pervasive sense that the *Provisional*

Government would not quit the *war*, but wanted to continue a fight for which the *nation* no longer had the stomach. The Bolsheviks capitalized on this mood in brilliantly effective slogans, such as "All power to the *soviets*!" and most famously, "Peace, Land, and Bread!" By promising and then delivering *peace*, albeit the *diktat* of *Brest-Litovsk*, Lenin got large components of the armed forces to support him (excluding most *officers*). Soldiers and workers came together in the All-Russian Congress of Soviets to sanction Bolshevik policy and vote support for the *Red Army* in the *Russian Civil War*, 1918-20. Real power passed into the hands of Lenin and his closest associates, among them *Trotsky* and *Stalin*. By quickly enacting land reform the Bolsheviks gained peasant support, despite their essentially urban agenda, and took the peasants out of the coming fight with the *ancien régime*. And by promising to correct the food shortages in the cities they gained support among industrial workers and their families. But real peace waited until 1920, after the ravages of the civil war; the land would be taken back in the 1930s through forced *collectivization*; and the bread (and meat and grain) was brutally confiscated from the peasants to feed the Bolsheviks' worker base in the cities, under the policy of *war communism*. Anyone disaffected with these arrangements, and desperate or foolish enough to say so, was *summarily executed* during the *Red Terror* or sent to swell the *forced labor* system in the *GULAG*.

russification: A policy practiced on and off by both tsarist and Soviet Russia, aiming at assimilation of ethnic and religious minorities by insisting on the use of the Russian language, and the imposition of Russian over minority or local culture.

Russo/Japanese War (1904-05): It sprang from a clash of Russian and Japanese imperialist interest in penetrating and controlling *Manchuria*, and to a lesser extent *Korea*. That led to a surprise Japanese attack on, and destruction of, the Russian fleet at anchor in *Port Arthur*, on February 8, 1904. Russia sent its troops into Manchuria and Korea. It then dispatched its Baltic fleet on a seven-month journey to the Pacific (it was refused passage through the *Suez Canal* by Japan's ally, Britain). On the way, the fleet aggravated relations with Britain in the *Dogger Bank incident*. When it arrived, it was annihilated at the *Battle of Tsushima Straits*. A *stalemate* developed on land, after initial Japanese victories. With Russia approaching the *Revolution of 1905*, and Japan nearly bankrupted by its war effort and unable to make headway on land

against the huge numbers of the tsarist army, Tokyo appealed to *Teddy Roosevelt* to *mediate* an end to the war. The parties met in New Hampshire, and terms were agreed in the *Treaty of Portsmouth*.

russophile/phobe: A person who loves/fears Russia, and things Russian.

Ruthenia: An alternate name for Carpatho-Ukraine. It was given to *Czechoslovakia* in the *Treaty of Trianon* in 1920; ceded to the Soviet Union in 1945; and is today a region of eastern Ukraine.

Rwanda: Location: Central Africa. Major associations: *OAU, UN*. Population: 7.5 million. Military: small, with connections to Belgium and France. For several centuries the warrior *tribe* of Tutsi (Watusi) dominated the Hutu majority (90% of the population) of Rwanda, just as they did in *Burundi*. In 1890 Germany claimed the *territory* and incorporated it into German East Africa. In 1916 it was captured by Belgian forces, and after *WWI* it was made a *mandate territory* (*Rwanda-Urundi*) under Belgian control. Converted into a *trusteeship territory* after *WWII*, it became an independent republic, separate from Burundi, in July 1962. Ethnic conflict continued throughout the 1960s and 1970s with the Hutu gaining the upper hand. In 1990 *exiled* Tutsi (RPF) based in Uganda attempted an *invasion*, but were repelled with Belgian and French assistance. In 1992 fighting created one million *refugees*, nearly 1/7th of the total population. In 1993 a *demobilization* agreement was signed under UN auspices, but ethnic relations remained taught. The situation was exacerbated by massacres of Hutu in Burundi. With Burundi's Tutsi military abusing *hot pursuit* to drag Hutu back across the border to kill them, war threatened with Rwanda. In April 1994, the Rwanda and Burundi presidents (both Hutu) were killed when their aircraft was shot down. That sparked a frenzy of--possibly preplanned--killing of Tutsi by the Hutu government. The RPF *guerrilla* army advanced on Kigali. An airlift was mounted to get most foreigners out, while all around perhaps 500,000 Tutsi were butchered and refugees from both tribes poured over the borders. The UN first pulled out its *peacekeeping* forces, then sought to reinsert them, after the main massacres were over.

Ryukyus: Japan retained only "residual *sovereignty*" over this chain of 55 islands after *WWII*, according to the *Japanese Peace Treaty*. U.S. *occupation* lasted until they were returned to Japan in 1972. The largest island in the chain is *Okinawa*.

S

SA (Sturmabteilung): "Storm Battalion." The *Nazi paramilitary* formation used for political thuggery and murder during the 1920s and 1930s. In 1933 it reached a strength of 400,000, or four times that permitted the *Reichswehr* under the *Versailles Treaty*. Its leadership had pretensions to one day displace the *Wehrmacht* (the renamed regular army), but after the *Night of the Long Knives* it was a tamed force. Within the Nazi Party, it thereafter fell under the shadow of the rising and even more sinister *SS.*

Saar: A coal-rich valley in western Germany. It was placed under administration of the *League of Nations*, as a *condominium* from 1919-35, when it was returned to Germany after a *plebiscite*. During that period France controlled its coal resources, in lieu of *reparations* for French mines the *Reichswehr* had flooded while retreating in 1918. After *WWII* France reoccupied the Saar, returning it to *West Germany* in 1957.

Sabah: The northernmost part of the island of Borneo (formerly British North Borneo), that with *Sarawak* joined Malaysia in 1963. The Philippines maintained a dormant claim to this *territory* for decades.

saber rattling: Explicitly threatening to use *force* to decide a *dispute*, or displaying one's capability for using force (say by full-scale *maneuver* or an *incursion*) as an implicit threat.

sabotage: The destruction of economic or military *infrastructure* necessary to prosecute a *war*. This is one of the main *tactics* of *guerrillas* or *partisans* in warfare. It may also be the object of *covert action*.

SAC: See *Strategic Air Command.*

Sadat, Muhammad Anwar el- (1918-81): Egyptian statesman. VP 1969-70; PM 1973-74; President 1970-81. As a young man and a nationalist, during *WWII* he supported *Nazi Germany* against the British. In 1952 he participated in the *coup* that overthrew *Faruk*. Succeeding *Nasser*, he expelled 20,000 Soviet advisers and began to plan for the *Third Arab/Israeli War,* which he believed was necessary to break the diplomatic logjam in the Middle East. It did: thus armored, he flew to Israel and called for *peace*. This moved Egypt into the American orbit, spurred talks at *Camp David* and led to peace with Israel by 1979. Disregarding his warmaking, the world honored him with a *Nobel Prize* (for Peace); remembering and hating his peacemaking, some men plotted to kill him. In 1981 he was assassinated by Muslim *fundamentalists.*

safe conduct: A letter granting permission to pass through a *territory* in time of *war*, given to persons such as eminent civilians, *Red Cross* personnel, *neutrals* or diplomats.

safe havens: Areas of *civilian* refuge in a *war zone*. For instance, America, Britain and France jointly declared and enforced these for *Kurds* in northern Iraq and marsh Arabs in southern Iraq, in the aftermath of the *Gulf War*. The *UN* and *NATO* declared six safe havens in Bosnia in 1993, but gave these no more than paper existence until they were pressed in 1994.

safe house: In *intelligence,* a (presumed) secret location where *cipher* and other *covert* activities can be carried out, or *agents* may hole up or be *debriefed,* confident that the locale is not being watched or bugged by opponents.

Sahel: The arid, semidesert region in Africa bordered by the Sahara Desert to the north and the true savannah to the south. Its peoples are mostly *Muslim*, and extremely poor. Since the 1970s the area has been afflicted by drought, *famines* and *wars*.

Sakhalin Island: In 1858 this large N. Pacific island was divided between Japan and Russia. In 1875 Japan gave up its half to Russia. It regained southern Sakhalin in the *Treaty of Portsmouth* in 1905. After *WWI* and the *Bolshevik Revolution,* Japan seized the northern half as well. Under U.S. pressure, Tokyo withdrew from northern Sakhalin in 1925, and it reverted to the Soviet Union. Southern Sakhalin was taken from Japan by decision of the *Cairo Conference,* and given to the Soviets by agreement at *Yalta*. All Sakhalin is now part of Russia.

Sakharov, Andrei Dimitrievitch (1921-89): Soviet nuclear physicist and *human rights* activist. After helping to design the Soviet *hydrogen bomb* he became a *dissident* under the powerful influence of his wife, Yelena Bonner. He was as crushed by the ending of the *Prague Spring* as were the Czechs, and publicly advocated radical change in the Soviet Union. He won the *Nobel Prize* for Peace in 1975. His stature preserved him from the punishment camps, but only until he organized a *Helsinki watch group*, wrote to *Jimmy Carter* and criticized the *invasion* of *Afghanistan* in 1979. He and Yelena Bonner were *exiled* to the gray, provincial city of Gorky. His case was prominent on the Western/Soviet agenda. In 1986 he was finally released by *Gorbachev*. That was taken as a sign that things were truly changing in Moscow. When he died in 1989 he was given a *state funeral* by the system he had once served, and then opposed.

salami tactics: A crude metaphor suggesting that an *aggressor* will seek to expand one slice of *territory* at a time, pausing to digest each meal and to gauge the response of possible opponents. See *opportunism.*

Salazar, Antonio (1889-1970): Portuguese dictator. PM 1932-68; Foreign Minister 1936-47, Minister of War 1936-44. His semi-*fascist* government kept Portugal out of *WWII*, but fought drawn-out colonial wars in Angola, Guinea-Bissau and Mozambique. As with *Franco* in Spain, Salazar's domestic misrule kept Portugal out of the mainstream of European *integration* and other developments until his death.

Salisbury, Robert Arthur (1830-1903): British statesman. Secretary for India 1866, 1874-76; Foreign Secretary 1878-80, 1886-92, 1895-1900; PM 1885-92, 1895-1902. To Salisbury is often attributed the policy of *splendid isolation*, but it might be fairer said that he pursued limited cooperation with other *Great Powers* when it suited his sense of Britain's *national interest*. His diplomacy was not therefore *isolationist*, so much as *ad hoc* and pragmatic. On the other hand, he was entirely devoted to empire and a firm supporter of maintaining Britain's naval superiority. See also *Anglo/German Naval Arms Race; Boer Wars.*

SALT I and II: See *Strategic Arms Limitation Talks.*

salt march (March-April, 1930): A protest organized by *Mohandas Gandhi* against the imperial monopoly on salt production, and thus the whole exploitative relationship of Britain in India. With elegant simplicity, he walked to the coast, gathering support along the way, and made salt from the sea. He then refused to pay the British salt tax. He was arrested, along with tens of thousands, but the point was made and never thereafter forgotten by Indians, or the British *Raj.*

salvo: A phalanx of *artillery* or rifles fired at once, for maximum destructive and psychological effect.

samizdat(*sam izdate/stvo*): "Self-publishing." Laboriously typed and copied, privately circulated, illegal literature. This method was used by *dissidents* to keep alive ideas, books and pamphlets that the various *Soviet bloc* states had banned. Some samizdat was smuggled out, published in the *West* and smuggled back into the Soviet bloc. It has since become a generic term for dissident literature within closed societies.

Samoa: This Pacific *territory* was an American/British/German *condominium* from 1889-1900, when it was split into *American Samoa* and *Western Samoa.*

samurai: The warrior caste of feudal Japan, surviving as a class into the *Meiji* period. At their height, tens of thousands served as retainers to the *daimyo.*

sanction: To declare approval of some act or policy, usually by a formal announcement or similar procedure, as in "the administration sanctioned [such-and-such] as policy." Note: This usage should not be confused with the idea of *sanctions.*

sanctions: Enforcement of a state's international obligations or policy, or of *international law,* by means of cultural, diplomatic, economic, and in the last resort, military pressure, punishment or coercive *intervention* by other states. This can be done bilaterally as a *reprisal* (e.g., the U.S. against Cuba or Vietnam, or Britain against Rhodesia); or multilaterally (e.g., *League of Nations* over Italy's attack on Ethiopia, or the *UN* toward Haiti, Iraq, Serbia or South Africa). Sanctions are a major component of the theory of *collective security.* See also *boycott; disinvestment; embargo.*

Sandinistas: Members of the Frenté Sandinista de Liberacíon Nacional (FSLN), a guerrilla/revolutionary movement named for Augusto Sandino (1896-1934), a Nicaraguan rebel in the 1920s and 1930s. The FSLN was a broad front that opposed the *Somozas* from 1961-79. But as it came to power in Nicaragua from 1979-90 it was increasingly dominated by *marxists* under the leadership of *Daniel Ortega.* Since 1990, it has participated in a coalition government, while still controlling the army and police.

Sandwich Islands: Former name of *Hawaii.*

San Francisco Conference (April 25-June 26, 1945): The follow-up to *Dumbarton Oaks,* where the main outlines of the *United Nations Organization* had been decided. San Francisco was the less important, just more public, of the meetings. Fifty-one nations (including Poland, whose government was in dispute between the *Allies*) attended, in contrast to the *Big Four* at Dumbarton Oaks. After adjusting working proposals to please smaller powers and achieving agreement on the scope of the *veto* among the *permanent members of the Security Council,* the conference accepted the *Charter of the United Nations.* See also *human rights.*

San Marino: A European *microstate* that officially styles itself the "Serene Republic of San Marino," it is located in the eastern part of the Italian peninsula, and claims to be the oldest independent country in Europe.

It is just 38 sq. miles in size. It has had close trade and other connections to Italy since 1862. From 1947-57 and from 1978-86 it was governed by a coalition that included communists, as was much of northern Italy. Population: 24,000.

San Martin, José de (1878-1956): South American revolutionary. He led armies against the Spanish in what is modern-day Argentina, Chile and Peru. He wanted to establish a unified Latin American *monarchy*, but when by 1822 it was clear that separate *republics* would be set up, he retired to Europe.

***sans-culotte*:** "Without breeches." Named for their distinctive dress, these were the urban poor in Paris who were extreme *republicans* and supporters of *radicalization* of the *French Revolution*. The term has passed on to refer to any grass roots, poorer sort of urban revolutionary.

San Stefano, Treaty of (March 3, 1878): This abortive agreement ended yet another Russo/Turkish *war*, this one from 1877-78. It proclaimed Montenegro and Rumania *independent*, enlarged Serbia, declared Bulgaria (including Macedonia) *autonomous* within the *Ottoman Empire* and expanded Russian *influence* in the *Caucasus*. This alarmed the Austrians and angered the British, who reversed south *Slav* gains later that year at the *Congress of Berlin*. San Stefano's lasting importance, therefore, was symbolic: Bulgarians and Serbs never forgot the vainglorious dreams of "Greater Bulgaria" or "*Greater Serbia*" it briefly fulfilled.

Santa Anna, Antonio López de (1797-1876): Mexican statesman. He was a man with nine political lives, and he used up all of them. He led a *coup* in 1822, making himself President in 1833. He was overthrown in 1836, after losing *Texas*. He led an *invasion* of Texas, but was defeated. In 1838 he lost his leg to a cannon ball. In 1846 he became President again, only to face the humiliation of the *Mexican/American War*, which cost Mexico a vast, resource rich *hinterland*, and Santa Anna his office once more. In 1853 he returned to the presidency, a supposedly lifetime appointment that was cut short two years later when his political enemies (who were legion) drove him from Mexico. Even his devious skills could not bring him back to power during the French years of *Maximilian*. In 1867 he tried to invade his own country but was captured and condemned to death. Pardoned, he retired to New York until 1872, when he was given amnesty.

São Tomé and Principe: Location: off the W. African coast. Major associations: *OAU, UN*. Population: 125,000. Military: minimal. A *colony* of Portugal from

1521-1974, it was originally settled by Portuguese convicts and by Jews fleeing the Catholic *Inquisition* and other persecution in *Iberia*. The *slave trade* then became an economic mainstay, and the races melded over time. In 1975 it became independent. In 1991 it held its first free elections in many years.

Sarajevo: Capital of *Bosnia-Herzegovina*. After Bosnian *independence* Serb *militia* laid *seige* and shelled it throughout 1992-93. It became a center of UN relief efforts and international media attention. In 1993 it was declared a UN *safe haven*, though hardly anyone living there noticed until *NATO* enforced this in 1994.

Sarawak: The northern part of Borneo. It was a British protectorate 1888-1946, and a Crown colony from 1946-63. With *Sabah* it joined Malaysia, over the objections of Indonesia. See *Konfrontasi*.

Sardinia, Kingdom of: This large Mediterranean island formed the core of an independent kingdom 1720-1860, along with Genoa (after 1815), Piedmont and *Savoy*. It merged with the mainland in the unification of *Italy* in 1861, ceding Savoy to France. It was really dominated by Piedmont after 1748, and hence is usually referred to as *Piedmont-Sardinia*. See also *Cavour; Garibaldi; risorgimento*.

satellites: While no formal legal *regime* yet governs these devices, tacit *rules* exist in practice. (1) Satellite passes over national *territory* are tolerated in a way that aircraft overflights are not. (2) Information of an economic nature (location of minerals, environmental degradation) gleaned by an advanced country's satellites about a non-space-faring nation should, in general, be made available to the country concerned. (3) *States* are liable for harm caused should their satellites crash on the territory of another country (e.g., in the 1980s the U.S. vehicle "Skylab" crashed in Australia; after several years delay, the Soviets paid millions of dollars to clean up nuclear contaminants from a satellite reactor strewn accross the Canadian *arctic*).

satellite state: An astronomical metaphor for when a *state* is nominally *sovereign*, but so controlled in its foreign and domestic affairs by another power it is said to "orbit" (be under the dominant *influence* of) the larger power. Cf. *client state*.

satisfaction: Under *international law*, when *reparation* is made for non-material *damage* done by some state action.

satisficing: In *game theory*, choosing a satisfactory, rather than an optimal solution. By analogy, some see this *decision-making* pattern as suggesting that statesmen and other *decision-makers* tend to settle for the first minimally acceptable solution, not the best.

Sato Eisaku (1901-75): Japanese statesman. PM 1964-72. He revised Japan's *security treaty* with the U.S. and secured the return of *Okinawa*. He also improved relations with South Korea. He utterly disavowed *nuclear weapons* for Japan. He was awarded the 1974 *Nobel Prize* for Peace.

saturation attack: Overwhelming enemy defenses in specific areas by mass use of weapons and/or troops.

Saudi Arabia: Location: major part of *Arabian peninsula.* Major associations: *Arab League, OAPEC, OPEC, UN.* Population: seven million. Military: small, but the best that *oil* money can buy; hi-tech and with U.S. training. Founded by *Ibn Saud* in 1926, its importance stems from two facts: it sits atop a major share of the world's known oil reserves, and it contains the *Hejaz,* the spiritual focal point for the *Islamic world,* constituting one billion members of humanity. The Hejaz has been there for 1,300 years, but the oil was only discovered in the 1930s (the first exports were in 1938). *Modernization* has come slowly, and with great resistance from the conservative *sunni* dynasty that rules the country: the House of Saud. For instance, *slavery* was only made illegal in 1962, and laws restricting the public life of women abound. In the 1960s Sheik *Yamani* led Saudi Arabia into *OPEC,* and took over its lead during the 1973 and 1979 *oil shocks.* Saudi Arabia sent contingents to fight Israel in 1948 and in 1973. During the *Cold War* it was nominally *non-aligned,* but in fact deeply anti-Soviet. After the *invasion* of Afghanistan it gave financial and other support to the Afghan *mujahadeen*). It supported Iraq during the *Iran/Iraq War,* a conflict that drove it closer to the West out of fear of radical *shi'ites* in Iran. It broke *diplomatic relations* with Iran in 1988, and agreed to preparations necessary to receive the *Rapid Deployment Force.* In August 1990, the Saudis welcomed U.S. and other foreign troops and themselves participated in *Operations Desert Shield* and *Desert Storm.* They cut back contributions to the *PLO* after the *Gulf War,* owing to its support for Iraq. Saudi Arabia is currently rearming against possible threats from either Iran or Iraq. It also faces domestic religious and political unrest. In 1980 the Great Mosque in *Mecca* was attacked by militant shi'ites from the deep desert. Portions were severely damaged when the Saudi military shelled it, leading to much criticism in other Islamic countries. In 1987 shi'ites from Iran and elsewhere rioted, leaving hundreds of dead. During the 1990 *Haj* nearly 1,500 pilgrims were killed in a riot/

panic. And since the Gulf War, there is Western and some internal pressure for limited political representation and civil and political rights for women.

Saud, Ibn Abd al-Aziz (1880-1953): King of Arabia 1926-53. He waged a rebellion against Turkish rule from 1901-15. However, out of rivalry with *Ibn Ali Hussein* he refused to join *T. E. Lawrence* and the *Arab Revolt.* After *WWI* he fought against and defeated Hussein and other Arab leaders. He invaded the *Hejaz* in 1924, and with the help of the *fundamentalist* sect *Wahabi,* installed the Saud dynasty in Arabia in 1926. He oversaw the first *oil* deals with the *West* in the 1930s and was loyal to the *Allies* in *WWII.*

save face: Said of a policy maneuver that helps the losing/concessionary side in a *conflict* or *dispute* preserve some *prestige,* while still conceding the main points at issue. It is generally considered something of a lubricant of agreement, and as such, an important part of bargaining and *crisis management.*

Savoy (Savoie): A region in SE France (conquered by *Richelieu*), once part of the Kingdom of *Sardinia,* but ceded back to France in 1860 as part of the settlement permitting the unification of Italy.

Scandinavia: Denmark, the Faroe Islands, Iceland, Norway and Sweden (and sometimes, Finland).

Scapa Flow: After *WWI,* surrendered German *warships* were sailed by their crews to this British naval base in the Orkneys. When it became clear that Britain would seek to retain the German fleet to add to its own, the crews scuttled their ships. Thus, ingloriously, ended the great *Dreadnought* race.

Scharnhorst, Gerhard Johann von (1775-1813): Head of the Prussian *General Staff.* He oversaw the great reorganization of the Prussian army which had been badly beaten by *Napoleon,* but that reemerged victorious in 1813-14 and was decisive at *Waterloo.*

Schleswig-Holstein: These Duchies on the lower Jutland peninsula were under Danish rule for centuries, despite having a predominantly German-speaking population. Denmark lost Holstein in 1815, as part punishment for having allied with *Napoleon I.* During the turmoil of 1848 Denmark tried to *annex* both duchies, but popular opposition and Prussian *intervention* prevented this. In 1864 *Bismarck* seized the duchies in a sharp, summer war, annexing Schleswig in 1864. A *condominium* was set up in 1864, with Prussia administering Schleswig and Austria controlling Holstein. However, Bismarck never intended this to be permanent, and annexed Holstein in 1866, after crushing Austria in the *Seven Weeks' War.* After *WWI,* the *Treaty of Versailles* committed to a *plebiscite* in the northern part of Schleswig, where there were many Danes; the area voted to join Denmark. After *WWII* the remainder of Schleswig-Holstein voted for incorporation in West Germany.

Schlieffen, Alfred von (1833-1913): Chief of the Imperial German *General Staff.* He oversaw the massive German *arms buildup* on land after 1895. Rejecting the caution of the elder *Moltke,* whose greatest fear was a *two-front war,* Schlieffen devised (1897) and modified (1905) the *Schlieffen Plan.*

Schlieffen Plan (1905): Named for *Alfred von Schlieffen,* it was premised on the likelihood of a *two-front war.* It proposed a swift blow in the west to knock out France, while remaining strictly on the defensive against Russia in the east. It was assumed (correctly, as matters turned out) that French élan and national pride would cause a headlong rush by the bulk of their army into *Alsace-Lorraine.* Germany would permit that, defending with about one-third of its western forces while hastening the other two-thirds around fortified French positions via a huge *flanking* maneuver through the *Low Countries.* That might bring Britain into the war under terms of the *Treaty of London (1839),* but not before Germany had bypassed Paris to slam an iron door behind the French Army, trapped now by its earlier advance. France would be beaten and Britain would then have to withdraw from the continent. With the *western front* won, the full might of the German armed forces could be turned on Russia, and *Mitteleuropa* constructed in due course. It is seldom noted, though nonetheless true, that besides reckless and arrogant dismissal of *international law,* the Schlieffen plan also ignored the interests of Germany's ally, Austria: Vienna was left to defend against Russian attack as best it could while Berlin sought victory in the west. With modifications (Holland was ignored), this plan was implemented in 1914, and almost worked. It failed largely due to *civilian* panic in Berlin as Russian armies advanced in the east, requiring that troops be taken from the western offensive to defend (or rather, calm) the home folks. It also failed because the Belgians, British and French put up more effective resistance than was anticipated, especially at the first *Battle of the Marne.*

Schmidt, Helmut (b.1918): West German statesman. Minister of Defense 1969-72; Minister of Finance 1972-74; Chancellor 1974-82. He continued the *Ostpolitik* of his predecessor, *Willy Brandt,* striving to maintain *détente* in the face of deteriorating Ameri-

can/Soviet relations in the latter half of the 1970s. He was the first postwar chancellor of Germany ever to criticize an American president (*Jimmy Carter*) in public. That revealed the rising importance of Germany and frustration with the erratic shifts Schmidt saw in U.S. diplomacy toward Europe during the *Ford,* Carter and *Reagan* presidencies. He was a strong supporter of responding to Soviet *missile* deployment in the late 1970s with new *NATO* missiles in the early 1980s, and encouraged a reluctant U.S. to do so. He succeeded in carrying out the policy, but it cost him the support of the left wing of his *Social Democratic* party, and he was ousted in 1982. He has been a prolific and respected writer on foreign affairs since then. See also *neutron bomb.*

Schuman, Robert (1886-1963): French statesman. Minister of Finance 1946-47; PM 1947-48; Foreign Minister 1948-52; President of the European Assembly 1958-60. A member of the *Resistance* during *WWII,* he is most famous for the *Schuman Plan,* and most praised for forging the Franco/German *alliance* that has been at the heart of European *integration* since 1950. He also played a role in founding *NATO.*

Schuman Plan: The plan for building the *European Coal and Steel Community,* proposed by *Robert Schuman* in 1950 and set up in 1952. His intention was to build political *union* not all at once, but by a sustained effort at *integration* of Europe's economies and societies across a broad front of activities.

Schwartzkopf, H. Norman (b.1934): U.S. general. He commanded the *Gulf Coalition* that fought Iraq in the *Gulf War,* coordinating operations of more than 1/2 million troops drawn from 28 countries. The plans used in *Operation Desert Shield* and *Operation Desert Storm* were adapted from contingency exercises he and his staff had designed, and practiced, long before the Iraqi *invasion* of Kuwait. Reportedly, his temper and rages almost led to his dismissal from command during the *campaign.* His main role was coordinating with Arab allies; his major *tactical* decision was to disapprove proposals for an amphibious landing.

scientism: Preference for pseudo-scientific language and aping of the scientific method in non-scientific disciplines, such as the humanities or social sciences.

scissors crisis: The twin dilemma of mounting foreign *debt* at a time of shrinking *export* earnings, leading to a severe crisis for weaker economies by cutting domestic savings and government revenues.

scorched earth: A tactic used by retreating armies in

which all land and resources to be abandoned are torched (and bridges are blown, mines flooded, dams broken etc.) to deny their use to the enemy. This lengthens the enemy's *supply lines* and forces it to waste troops and resources in *requisition* and resupply, thus slowing any advance. The Russians used the tactic to great effect against the French in 1812. The *Union* used it offensively against the *Confederacy*, 1864-65, and all sides used it both ways in *WWII*. In contrast, Iraq's firing of Kuwaiti oil fields in 1991 was more an act of wanton spite than a military stratagem.

Scotland: Conquered by English arms, it was united with England and Wales in the *Act of Union* of 1707. Since the 1930s there has been a slowly growing movement for "devolution," or *autonomy*. Since the 1970s and discovery of North Sea *oil*, there has been some movement toward demands for outright *independence*, within the larger *European Community/Union*. While Scotland's ties to *Ulster* are strong, and it too is divided between Catholic and Protestant, the more important social cleavages were between the lowlands and highlands historically, between the Edinburgh/Glasgow urban axis and the countryside in the early 20th century, and among social classes today.

scramble for Africa: The rapid, competitive colonization of Africa in the latter 19th century. It included *conquest* of the white, *Boer* republics by Britain, leaving just Liberia and Abyssinia independent. See *Adowa; Berlin Conference; Boer Wars; Fashoda; imperialism* and various African countries.

SDECE (*Service de Documentation Extérieure et de Contre-Espionage*): As the name suggests, it is the *counterespionage* service of France. Cf. *Sûreté*.

SDI: See *Strategic Defense Initiative*

Seabed Treaty (1971): It proclaimed the seabed under the *high seas* beyond the *twelve-mile limit* to be a *nuclear weapons free zone* (which it was, and was likely to remain, anyway). It has been *adhered* to by most states. Note: It says nothing about *boomers* that operate beneath the oceans, hence even the Soviet Union and United States *ratified* it, as innocuous).

sea mine: An explosive capable of damaging or sinking a ship. It can be floating to detonate on contact, placed on the seabed and triggered by sound or magnetism or tethered below the surface and triggered by any of the above. Sea mines may be laid by ship, plane or less efficiently, by *submarine*. The *Hague Convention* of 1907 prohibited floating sea mines as indiscriminate and required *belligerents* to notify all

other governments of the existence of minefields at sea. However, in practice these provisions have been largely disregarded. For instance, huge minefields were laid in the Baltic and North Seas during *WWI* and *WWII*, by Germany and Britain, even in portions of the *high seas* and in the case of Norway, in the *territorial waters* of a *neutral* (pre-1940). The U.S. used sea mines against North Vietnam in the *Vietnam War;* and against Nicaragua in peacetime under the *Reagan* adminstration. The Persian Gulf was heavily mined during the *Iran/Iraq War,* leading to an international minesweeping operation by several navies.

sea power: (1) A nation that is in the first rank in naval strength. (2) A synonym for naval strength, implying an ability to project force far beyond one's own shores. In the 20th century, the great weapons of sea power have been the *aircraft carrier* and the *submarine.* (3) A theory developed in its most sophisticated form by *Alfred Thayer Mahan,* that says the key to dominant or even world power is naval strength, and views the oceans as avenues of contact rather than barriers between continents. See *Anglo/German Naval Agreement; Battle of the Atlantic; Battle of Tsushima Straits; battleship; Black Sea Fleet; blockade; boomer; Bosphorus; capital ship; convoy; cruiser; Dardanelles; destroyer; Dreadnought; English Channel; Five-Power Naval Treaty; frigate; geopolitics; Gibraltar; Gulf War; Jutland; London Naval Disarmament Conference; Mackinder; man-of-war; Midway; Nine Power Treaty; Panama Canal; Pearl Harbor; Rimland; Royal Navy; Scapa flow; ship-of-the-line; sloop-of-war; Straits Question; Suez Canal; Trafalgar; Tsushima Straits; two-power standard; U-boat; unrestricted submarine warfare; wolf pack; world island.* Cf. *air power; land power.*

search-and-destroy missions: A term used by the U.S. military during the *Vietnam War* to refer to its main *military objective* of searching out the enemy's armed forces, and destroying them. In the media and in *public opinion* it was associated with scenes of GIs burning out Vietnamese villages and other depredations against *civilians*, and came to mean something close to atrocity. Cf. *My Lai massacre.*

Sebastopol: Capital of the *Crimea.* Founded by *Potemkin,* it was besieged for a year by the British, French and Piedmontese during the *Crimean War.* In the *Treaty of Paris (1856),* it was *demilitarized.* Russia refortified it after 1870-71, making it again the main base of the *Black Sea Fleet.* It was bombarded and captured by Germany in 1942, but later liberated. It is now in Ukraine, presented as a "gift" by Russia in 1954. In mid-1993 the Russian parliament claimed the city, but *Boris Yeltsin* disavowed the land grab as a "shameful act." When Ukraine subsequently agreed to Russian possession of the Black Sea Fleet, it agreed to lease the fleet's Sebastopol base to Russia.

secession: Formal withdrawal from a political *union* or *federation*. Most secessions face forceful resistance, and may be treated as criminal rather than political movements. A few are peaceful. While encouraged by the principle of *self-determination,* they also face hostility from a *states* system that is inherently conservative about the survival of its members. Generally, it takes *intervention* by some outside power in the form of military *aid* or troops for secession to be realized. Yet there are enough bloody, self-won successes (such as Eritrea) and sufficient ethnically or otherwise repressive regimes to encourage more attempts. Among other entries, see *Biafra; Congo; Kurds; Québec.*

Second Empire: France, from the declaration of empire by *Napoleon III* in 1852, to his capture at *Sedan* and abdication in 1870. See *France.*

second front: The *WWII* demand from the Soviet Union, and the promise made repeatedly by the Western *Allies,* to relive pressure on the *eastern front* by attacking Germany in the west. It was mainly delayed by a lack of landing craft and transports, and by the prior necessity of winning the *Battle of the Atlantic.* The British were more reluctant than the Americans to proceed, having experienced the horrors of *Passchendale* and the *Somme* in *WWI,* and the disaster at *Dieppe.* Also, *Churchill* remained convinced that the *Balkans* were the "soft underbelly of Europe" through which a saber thrust might end the war more quickly (as well as cut the Soviets short of entering Central Europe). As the term refers to operations in France and NW Europe, the landings in North Africa, Sicily and Italy did not satisfy American demands for a quick opening of a second front, or allay Soviet suspicions that the Western Allies were determined to fight Germany to the last Russian. Cf. *two-front war.*

Second International (1889-1914; 1920-): After the failure of the *First International* this less ideological association was founded. It was broader-based than the first, and more genuinely representative of the range of socialist opinion than the *Third International.* Dominated by trade unions and parliamentary *socialists,* it still officially embraced many ideas drawn from *Marx.* Its hopes for a working class front against *war* did not survive the more general sundering of European and international life in 1914. It reformed after *WWI,* without the more *radical* socialist and *communist parties* that split to join the *COMINTERN.* It persists on the margins of political influence, as the Socialist International.

Second Moroccan Crisis: See *Agadir.*

Second Reich: Germany, from the proclamation of *empire* upon defeating France in 1871, to the abdication of Kaiser *Wilhelm II* in 1918. See *Germany.*

Second Republic: France, from the *Revolution of 1848* to the proclamation of the *Second Empire* by *Napoleon III* in 1852. See *France.*

second strike: Launch of a retaliatory strike of *nuclear weapons* that survive an enemy's *first strike.*

second-strike capability: The capacity to retaliate with a devastating *nuclear* strike even after suffering colossal damage from a *first strike.* It has been often, but wrongly, argued that second-strike capability distinguished the *superpowers* in the *Cold War.* In fact, Britain and France also had second-strike capability: once their *deterrent* was *submarine*-based it was not subject to a first strike, even should both home countries be utterly destroyed. See also *sufficiency.*

Second World: A synonym for the *communist* states during the *Cold War.* However, one must differentiate *Yugoslavia* from this group after 1947, China after the *Sino/Soviet split* and *Albania* after c.1958.

Secretariat: The *executive* or administrative body of an *international organization.* In the UN, it is the division that houses the main corps of international civil servants, and is headed by the *Secretary General.* Appointments are frequently made based on country or *caucus group,* as well as merit. However, since the mid-1980s pressure from major donors has meant the budget of the UN Secretariat has been trimmed, and a good deal of fat and corruption eliminated.

Secretary General: Chief administrative officer of the *United Nations Organization,* and head of its *Secretariat.* During the *Cold War* most Secretaries General were compromise candidates between the *superpowers.* Now, elections within the *UNGA* are more complex and more fluid. Election is by a 2/3rds vote of the UNGA, following a recommendation by the Security Council. The term of service is five years, and re-election is possible. Beyond administrative functions and performance of specific tasks set by the Security Council or the UNGA, the Secretary General has the right to bring to the attention of the UN any matter he or she regards as a threat to international *peace* and *security.* The personality of the various Secretaries

General has been a key determinant of how active or passive, and how effective the office has been. To date, there have been six Secretaries General. By date of first election: *Trygve Lie*, of Norway (1946); *Dag Hammarskjöld*, of Sweden (1953); *U Thant* of Burma (1961); *Kurt Waldheim*, of Austria (1972); *Javier Pérez de Cuéllar*, of Peru (1982); and currently, *Boutros Boutros-Ghali* of Egypt (1992).

Secretary of Defense: In the U.S., the *cabinet* officer in charge of the Department of Defense (*Pentagon*), the *Joint Chiefs*, Air Force, Army, Marine Corps and Navy, and all military matters relating to national security; until *WWII* called the "Secretary of War."

Secretary of State: In the U.S., the *cabinet* officer in charge of the *State Department,* who is formally responsible for formulating and overseeing implementation of *diplomacy*; elsewhere, the *Foreign Minister*.

secret diplomacy: For some in the *intelligence* community, this euphemism is preferred to *covert action.*

secret police: A euphemism for political police, which are secret and powerful services used in dictatorial and *totalitarian* societies to repress dissent and/or instill terror in the populace, as a deterrent to opposition to the government's policies. For example, see *Gestapo; KGB; NKVD; STASI.*

secret service: (1) In general: an alternate for *intelligence services.* (2) In the United States: that arm of the *Department of the Treasury* responsible for stopping counterfeiting, and for protecting the president, vice president, visiting *heads of state* or *government, cabinet* officers and former presidents.

secularism: A social and political philosophy that rejects all religion as inappropriate when applied to public affairs. It is a prominent characteristic of the industrial and post-*Enlightenment* age, whether openly admitted or not by *modernizing* political movements that must contend with organized religious belief in every society. The most *radical* secularists ever to take power gave the world the *Terror* during the French Revolution, and the multiple horrors of 20th century *communism*. Yet, it would be a mistake to confuse secularism per se with repression of *liberty*-- rather the reverse relationship is closer to the historical truth: secularists have worked to free social and other public policy from the strictures of religious *ideologies*. In general, they have been compelled to compromise with the public forms, if not the essence of religious faith. While they may coexist fairly easily with tamed religious communities, they remain in perpetual tension with proponents of *fundamentalism*. In the post-*Cold War* world some analysts suggest that this tension between modernizing secularism and *reactionary* fundamentalism will take on much greater significance, amounting to a "clash of civilizations" that will provide the major fault lines of world affairs. But even if that proves to be the case, such a division is not likely to lead to global conflict: major religious faiths are deeply divided from each other, less internally cohesive than sometimes thought, subject to schism and--in their political and social aspects--under intense assault even in deeply traditional societies by the combined effects of mass literacy, mass communications and modern consumerism.

security: See *international security; national security.*

security analyst: A specialist in questions relating to *national security* issues. Traditionally this meant questions of *defense* and *strategy* (and it still does), but of late it has expanded to involve questions of the economic basis of national strength as well as novel issues such as *environmental security.*

Security Council: The main organ of the *UN*, above the other five *Principal Organs*. It is charged with maintenance of *peace* and *security*, and is a law-making body when it passes binding *resolutions*. It was originally made up of the five *permanent members*, plus six non-permanent members drawn on a rotating basis from the *UNGA*. The latter group has been increased to 10. There is some discussion of elevating Germany and Japan to the first group, although that poses serious constitutional and political problems (both for them and for the UN). All decisions, whether procedural or substantive, require an affirmative vote (abstentions do not count) of nine members, while substantive questions and binding resolutions must not have among the negative votes (no *veto* by) any of the five permanent members. The Security Council was blocked from effective action during most of the *Cold War* by American and Soviet vetoes on issues, *wars* and *crises* that concerned them, but also by disagreement over the status of China, and on *decolonization* issues by British and French vetoes. From 1988 to 1993 it enjoyed a remarkably active period in which not one veto was cast (though China frequently abstained), a record broken by a Russian veto on the relatively trivial and non-ideological question of funding for *peacekeeping* operations in Cyprus. The Security Council may thus be emerging from its doldrums to be a major forum for resolution, as well as discussion, of international security issues. See also *collective security; Gulf War; Korean Conflict; Palestine; Resolutions, 242, 338, 660* and *678; sanctions.*

security dilemma: The theory that under conditions of international *anarchy* when one *state* seeks to improve its defenses those improvements will be seen as threats by other states, which must assume the worst. An *arms race* may result, as other states match the first increase in military preparedness. This in turn will be seen as a threat by the first state, which thinks its defensive intentions are obvious, and therefore that its neighbors are arming without cause, or to attack. So it raises the ante and arms some more, and so on. Of course, in its pure form this theoretical *model* ignores the reality of assessments of intentionality. For example, the arming of the U.S. during the *Cold War* never led to counterarming by Canada, Mexico, Britain or France, because those states saw no intended threat to themselves behind the U.S. buildup. However, it did contribute to arms procurement in countries like Cuba, which perceived a definite threat. In contrast, the buildup by the Soviet Union led most of its neighbors to counterarm, because they feared (or at least doubted) Soviet intentions.

security treaty: An agreement between or among *states* undertaking mutual military support in the event any signatory is attacked by a non-signatory. Some compacts will specifically name the third country or countries, and may or may not also delineate precise conditions under which the *treaty* may be invoked.

Sedan, Battle of (September 1, 1870): The decisive battle of the *Franco/Prussian War*, in which French resistance was broken (20,000 dead), the main French army (80,000) surrendered and *Napoleon III* captured.

sedes materiae: The locale of settlement.

Seeckt, Hans von (1866-1936): He served as a *staff officer* in *WWI*, then headed Germany's secret *rearmament* program 1919-26. Although politically neutral, his secret training of the *Reichswehr* in the Soviet Union built the core of an army that proved rapidly expandable by *Hitler* after 1933.

seisin of a court: Proceedings prior to judgment.

seizure: Detention of *contraband* or other cargo, pending judgment in a *prize court*.

self-defense: A fundamental legal principle upholding the right of a *state* to take a range of measures to protect its other legal rights, or to redress infringements of those rights by other states. Article 51 of the *Charter of the UN* recognizes a right of "individual or collective self-defense if an armed attack occurs against a Member." This right is limited by a require-

ment of *proportionality*. Article 51 was cited in founding *alliances* apart from the UN, such as *NATO*, and to justify coming to the aid of South Korea in the *Korean Conflict*, and Kuwait in the *Gulf War*. See also *aggression; Entebbe raid; preventive strike*.

self-determination: (1) Legally accepted: The right of a *sovereign* people (read: *state*) to choose their (its) own political institutions and government. (2) Controversial: The right of all peoples to separate, sovereign states. (3) In practice: At the *Paris Peace Conference* this right was proclaimed and upheld against the defeated *Central Powers*, but rejected for the subject nations of Russia (an erstwhile ally of the Western powers) or the colonial populations of the Western *empires*. Moreover, it was used to sanction the creation of *Czechoslovakia* and *Yugoslavia* (curiously enough, themselves *multinational* states). Since *WWII* it has been generally endorsed as expressing the right of colonial peoples to *independence* from Western empires, but denied to those such as *Biafrans* or *Kurds* who wished to exercise it against *Third World* nations. The 1993 acceptance of self-determination by *Eritrea* is an exceptional case, as that state had a prior, separate existence from Ethiopia and had clearly and effectively established its *de facto* sovereignty by force of arms. It remains unclear what the latest round of state-building accompanying the collapse of the *Soviet Union* and Yugoslavia means in practical terms for this principle. Will it continue as one of the dominant international political ideas into the next century, or be rejected with revulsion for the violence and disorder that so often attends its realization? Another question is whether political self-determination is coming into increasing conflict with economic efficiency and regional *integration*, or is being facilitated by those forces. See also *Fourteen Points; mandates*.

self-help: (1) In *international law*: the claim that as enforcement of rights is ultimately up to the victim of a violation, *unilateral* or *multilateral* action may be taken to redress certain legal wrongs without resort to a court. In ascending order of effectiveness, or at least of warning, peaceful self-help devices (a.k.a. *measures short of war*) available to the *states* include: *diplomatic protest, recalling the ambassador,* breaking *diplomatic relations, withdrawal* (from *international organizations*), *retorsion, reprisal, embargo, sanctions, pacific blockade* and *occupation* (if undertaken with both an announced and real intention not to proceed to *annexation*). Of course, the ultimate self-help device is *war.* (2) In international relations theory: some analysts see an assumed, underlying condition of international *anarchy* as dictating that each state must always look to its own *security*, making self-help an ineluctable characteristic of the *international system*. When this view is taken, use of unilateral force may tend to become more a first than a last resort.

self-preservation: Under *international law*, this plea may be used to defend taking what would otherwise be *illegal acts*. Cf. *necessity; self-defense; self-help.*

self-reliance: A national economic policy that aims at *self-sufficiency* in low-technology manufactured *goods*, especially for *Third World* countries, to lessen dependence on outside powers or global market forces. It involves *import substitution* and state-directed industrial development (*dirigisme*). Cf. *autarky.*

self-sufficiency: The attempt by a single national society to develop economically without major connections to world markets. *Dependency theory* advocates this option as the only means of "breaking free" of the structural ties of the *world capitalist system*. In this extreme form, self-sufficiency amounts to *autarky*. However, the term also describes efforts to preserve or develop national control over key industries or markets, without necessarily implying a withdrawal from world trade and finance. Cf. *mercantilism.*

sellers' market: One where the prices of *goods* and *services* are high. The antonym is *buyers' market.*

semiperiphery: In *dependency theory*, those areas occupying an intermediate position between the *core* and the true *periphery*, and possessing certain economic and political characteristics of both.

Sendero Luminoso: "Shining Path." A *maoist, terrorist* organization founded in Peru by a flaky philosophy professor, Abimael Guzmán. It has solid control of portions of the countryside, in cooperation with *drug cartels*. It wages sometimes spectacular bombing and assassination campaigns in the cities. Portly, middle-aged Guzmán was quietly captured in 1992, curtailing but not ending the violence.

Senegal: Location: W. Africa. Major associations: *ECOWAS; la francophonie; OAU, UN*. Population: 8 million. Military: small, with ties to France. The coast of this nation was probed by the Portuguese in the 15th century, but it was France that *colonized* Senegal in the 17th century. It was a slow process, with independent *sheikdoms* resisting French rule until 1893. In 1895 it was joined to *French West Africa*. During *WWII* the French in Senegal supported *Vichy*, leading to British shelling of Dakar (the capital and main port). The *Free French* took control in 1942. In 1958 it became *autonomous* within the *French Community*,

and gained full independence in 1960 (after a year joined with Mali in the abortive "Mali Federation"), under the leadership of *Léopold Senghor*. In February 1982, Senegal joined with Gambia in *Senegambia*, but this confederal experiment was abandoned in 1989. Persecution of ethnic Senegalese by Mauritania resulted in a spillover of refugees in 1988-89, and an undeclared border war in 1990. France continues to guarantee Senegal's security. Relations with Mauritania remain tense.

Senegambia: A *confederation* formed by Senegal and Gambia in 1981. It shared federal institutions and aimed at common defense and monetary policies. It was dissolved in 1989.

Senghor, Léopold (b.1906): President of Senegal 1960-80. A noted poet (he is a member of the Academie Française) and cultural leader, he was a founder of the *négritude* movement to revive and celebrate traditional African culture. A proponent of *pan-Africanism*, his several attempts at regional *federation* came to naught. He maintained close economic, political and security ties to France, the old colonial power. He was one of the first African leaders to leave power gracefully--and to be replaced by an effort at multiparty democracy--despite having run a *one-party state* for much of his tenure as president.

Senkaku (Diaoyu) Islands: Located north of Taiwan, between China and Japan, their ownership is disputed by all three countries.

sensitivity: Used to describe a level of *interdependence* where *internal affairs* in one *state* react easily to events within other states, especially on economic matters such as sudden changes in *interest rates* or *stock* prices. Societies may also be sensitive to political or cultural trends in neighboring states, or in states with similar ideological/political systems (witness the toppling of east European *communist* governments during 1989-90). Cf. *domino theory.*

sentry: A soldier or military unit placed on guard at the extremes of a set position.

separate opinion: When a justice on an international court agrees with a *judgment*, but submits a discrete opinion providing different reasoning.

separate peace: When one member of an *alliance* negotiates an exit from a *war* without consulting its allies, looking solely to its own interests. For example, Russia's bending to the German *diktat* at *Brest-Litovsk*, both threatened and deeply embittered the *Allies* and prompted their joint *intervention* in North Russia during the early part of the *Russian Civil War.*

separatism (*sépartisme*): A synonym for *secession.* In Canada the politically correct often wince at this usage, if applied to those from *Québec* who wish to form their own country. Instead, the term of preference is the uniquely awkward "sovereigntists."

Sepoy: Native soldiers, particularly in India, trained and enlisted in the British Army in imperial times.

Sepoy Rebellion: See *Indian Mutiny.*

Serbia: Location: *Balkans.* Major associations: Suspended from the *CSCE*; member, *UN.* Population: 10 million. Military: most weapons of the old Yugoslav army; supplemented by Serb *militia* from Bosnia and Croatia. A feudal Serb *empire* was conquered by the Ottomans (at the Battle of Kosovo) in 1389. Serbia remained a province of the *Ottoman Empire* until the 19th century. A Serb revolt from 1804-13 broke down in *civil war.* However, Serbia received *autonomy* within the empire in 1817, benefitting again in 1830 from the general weakness occasioned by Greek and Egyptian revolts, and by pressure from Russia. It received full *independence* in the *Treaty of San Stefano,* confirmed in the *Congress of Berlin,* both in 1878. After 1903 Belgrade was assertive about building *Greater Serbia* out of ethnically Serb lands then held by Austria but also by Turkey. During the first two *Balkan Wars* it gained large amounts of *territory.* By 1914 its policies led to the confrontation with Austria that triggered *WWI,* in which most of Serbia was overrun and occupied by Austrian and German troops. In 1918 it joined Croatia and Slovenia in the *United Kingdom of the Serbs, Croats and Slovenes* (renamed *Yugoslavia* in 1929), an association it dominated. During *WWII* Serbia was occupied by the *Nazis,* who set up a *puppet state* under Serb *fascists.* It was liberated by *Tito's* communist *partisans* and royalist *Chetniks,* whom Tito then *liquidated* in a short civil war. While Tito lived, he completely dominated Serbian politics—within the context of Yugoslavia. In the succession struggle that followed his death, Serbian nationalists again set out to construct Greater Serbia. Under *Slobodan Milošević* they took over the subregional governments in *Voivodina* (October 1988), *Montenegro* (January 1989), and *Kosovo* (February 1989). After June 1991, they supported militia attacks on *Slovenia* and *Croatia.* In 1992-93 the war spread to *Bosnia. Security Council* resolutions were ignored, as were all U.S. and *EC* warnings. Serbia was placed under *sanctions* by the UN on May 30, 1992, but still refused to accept the *Vance/Owen peace plan.* By June 1993, the Vance/

Owen plan was dead. Serbia had, *de facto*, attached to itself large parts of Bosnia, but at great cost: in 1993 its inflation hit 1900% per month (an annualized rate of four quadrillion percent)--and its *central bank* issued a 500 billion dinar note.

serfdom: Feudal servitude of the peasantry that could amount to effective *slavery,* extant in much of Europe into the early 19th century, and in Russia to 1861.

services: Intangible, non-material economic activities, like banking, computing, insurance or *tourism.* In the more developed economies services form an ever larger component of the *Gross National Product.*

servitude: When the exercise of *sovereignty* over a *territory* is limited by a binding legal obligation to other *states* to permit specific, limited uses of that territory (e.g., on all *coastal states* concerning fishing and transit rights, or on those states through which run international *canal zones*), or not to use it oneself for express purposes (e.g., the ban on military uses of the *Aland Islands,* or the *no-fly zones* imposed in 1992/93 on Bosnia and Iraq). Servitudes are not normally affected by *state succession.*

seven sisters: The seven largest, private oil companies that before the formation of *OPEC* colluded to set *oil* prices and control supply. The proliferation of state oil companies and the role of OPEC means that they no longer control the same market share or have the same influence they once did.

Seven Weeks' War (June-July 1866): *Bismarck* used his usual manipulative skills to start this *war* between *Prussia* and the *Austrian Empire.* His main aim was to end the competition with Austria for control of Germany, as a prelude to toppling France from its perch as the main power in Europe. He wanted the war so he could annex the *North German Confederation* to Prussia, and expel Austria from southern Germany. The combat was mercifully brief, which was also Bismarck's doing. He held back those dogs of war that most strained at their leash, demanding Austria be utterly crushed: the *Kaiser* and his generals. Bismarck proved magnanimous at the peace table, too. In the Treaty of Prague, Austria lost no *territory* other than the *cession* of Venetia to Italy (a small reward for Italian support of Prussia). But all the southern German states once within Austria's *sphere of influence* were attached to Prussia by secret *treaties.* At a blow, Austria ceased to be a German power, and turned exclusively toward the *Balkans.* The shift was accelerated by the *Ausgleich* that followed *defeat,* giving Hungary a share in imperial policy. In sum, for Berlin this war set the stage for the even more decisive *Franco/ Prussian War*, and Bismarck's creation of the *Second Reich*. But for Vienna it marked the transition point from imperial power to political question.

Seven Years' War (1756-63): England and Prussia faced Austria, France, Russia, Saxony and Sweden, in this, the climax of Anglo/French imperial competition overseas. England pressed the French in India, reducing them to the tiny *enclaves* of *French India*. In North America, English victory at the *Plains of Abraham* (1759) set the stage for the *conquest* of *Québec*, and left the rest of *New France* strategically untenable. The *Royal Navy* and its *privateer* allies drove the French from several Caribbean islands, including Guadeloupe (1759). In 1760 the English captured Montreal, and sealed the French failure in the Americas in 1762 with the capture of Grenada, Martinique and other island possessions. In Europe, *Frederick II of Prussia* defeated the Austrians and Saxons early on, and looked for *peace*. But his enemies would not quit, and several years later he had to beat back a Franco/ Austrian assault. The Russians he could not stop, however, and they burned Berlin in 1760. The British either could or would not send a large army to aid their continental ally (eliciting from Frederick that famous damnation of England, "Perfidious Albion!"). What saved Prussia was pure chance: the death of one tsar, and the brief ascent to the throne of another, Peter III (1728-62). Peter was an admirer of things German, and called off the war on that whim. English gains were codified in the *Treaty of Paris (1763)*.

Sèvres, Treaty of (1920): The agreement with Turkey to formally end *WWI*, negotiated at the *Paris Peace Conference*, signed but never *ratified*. It would have created independent *states* in Armenia, Mesopotamia and Syria, and called for *cession* of swaths of Turkish land to Greece (including *Smyrna*). It also would have created an independent *Kurd* homeland (*Kurdistan*). It was rejected by the Turks, who were able to outwait *Allied* unity and gain the more favorable *terms* of the *Treaty of Lausanne*, in 1923.

Seward, William (1801-72): U.S. statesman. Secretary of State, 1861-69. Having failed to win the presidency in 1860, he joined *Lincoln's* cabinet. During the *American Civil War* he was among the most important figures on the *Union* side. He recovered Lincoln's error in declaring a *blockade* of the *Confederacy*, and otherwise deflected foreign powers from granting *recognition* to the South. That contribution to the war effort was worth several battlefield victories, at least. His most delicate diplomacy came during the *Trent Affair*. He stayed on after the war in *Johnson's* cabi-

net. These were not happy years: he was an isolated *expansionist* in a nation exhausted of glory, and which remembered that the Civil War had roots in the acquisition of *territory* from Mexico in the 1840s. When in 1867 Seward purchased *Alaska* from Russia, the public dismissed his move as "Seward's Folly." Whatever his failings, he served the nation masterfully in its hour of worst crisis. For that, he is widely regarded as among the greatest of U.S. secretaries of state.

Seychelles: Location: Indian Ocean, N. of Madagascar. Major associations: *Commonwealth, OAU, UN*. Population: 72,000. Military: minimal. Occupied by France in 1768, these islands were seized by Britain during the *Napoleonic Wars* (1794). They were jointly ruled with Mauritius from 1814-1903, when they became a Crown Colony. *Independence* was granted in 1976 (it was not accepted entirely willingly). In 1979 the country became a *one-party state*. In 1981 a group of white *mercenaries* tried to overthrow the government, but were foiled (with the help of Tanzanian troops) and fled to South Africa.

Shaba: An alternate name for *Katanga* province of Zaire. See *Congo crisis*.

Shah: The title taken by the Pahlavi *dynasty* in Iran. See *Muhammed Reza Pahlavi; Reza Shah Pahlavi*.

Shaka Zulu (b.?-d.1828): A military genius and mad butcher, he became King of the *Zulus*, organizing them into a *martial* society with himself as supreme commander and absolute ruler. His chosen method of execution--and he murdered tens of thousands of his own people as well as prisoners and hostages--was impalement. He led the *mfecane*, a wildly rapid and successful *conquest* of the Ngoni peoples of southern Africa. The *imperialism* of Shaka and the Zulus might have led to creation of a vast, *martial* empire. But it ran into the contrary and technologically superior imperialism of the British, and the northward expansion of the *Boers*.

Shamir, Yitzhak (b.1915): Israeli statesman. Foreign Minister 1980-83, 1984-86; PM 1983-4, 1986-92. He was a member of the *Irgun*, then the *Stern Gang*. From 1948-65 he worked for *Mossad*. He opposed the *Camp David Accords*, supporting instead a creeping *annexation* via new settlements on the *West Bank*. During the *Gulf War* he agreed to U.S. requests for restraint in the face of unprovoked Iraqi *missile* attacks. Later, however, he refused to abandon his settlements policy or to join *peace talks* sponsored by the *Bush* administration. Shamir thus presided over the most precipitous deterioration in U.S./Israeli relations since the wartime crisis in October 1973. In 1992 he was defeated at the polls, and his policies on settlements and negotiation were both reversed.

Shanghai massacres: (1) 1925: British police fired on a Chinese crowd, killing some demonstrators who were protesting a strike against a foreign-owned firm. Massive protest strikes spread up and down the Chinese coast, hitting *Hong Kong* as well. The strikes and riots strengthened the *Guomindang* in the coastal areas. (2) 1927: Tens of thousands of Chinese communists were cruelly massacred by the *Guomindang* in many Chinese cities, starting in Shanghai. Coming after *Chiang Kai-shek's* victory over the main northern *warlords,* the bloodbath marked the beginning of the *Chinese Civil War.* Cf. *Partai Kommunis Indonesia.*

Shantung: The German *leasehold* base and *sphere of influence* in China. It was seized by the Japanese in 1914. In 1915 Chinese protests led Japan to issue the *Twenty-One Demands.* Japan retained Shantung until 1922, when they withdrew under *terms* negotiated at the *Washington Conference.* Japan retook the area in 1938, and held it until *defeated* in 1945, when it reverted to China. See *Kiaochow incident.*

sharia: Traditional *Islamic* law, based on "al Qur'an" (the Koran) and the "Sunna" (interpretations of the life of the Prophet Muhammad). It calls for, by modern *Western* standards, draconian punishments for criminal and civil offenses, including for adultery (stoning), consumption of alcohol (flogging) and theft (amputation). Its introduction by *fundamentalist* regimes has often alienated non-Muslims, more moderate Muslims and *secular* citizens. At times, introduction of the sharia has led to large-scale resistance and bloodshed, as in Iran and Sudan. Cf. *fundamentalism; secularism.*

Sharpeville massacre (March 21, 1960): South African police fired upon a crown of peaceful black demonstrators, most of them schoolchildren, killing dozens and wounding hundreds. The massacre led to an international outcry and convinced many hitherto peaceful opponents of *apartheid* that the system would have to be resisted with force.

Shatt-al-Arab: A waterway flowing into the *Persian Gulf,* lying between Iran and Iraq and formed by the junction of the Tigris and Euphrates Rivers. It contains several small islands, *oil* drilling and processing facilities, and controls riverine passage into the heart of the *Persian Gulf.* In 1975 the two nations agreed it should form their common *border.* On September 17, 1979 *Saddam Hussein,* dictator of Iraq, unilaterally denounced the agreement and five days later his troops suddenly attacked Iran. The *Iran/Iraq War* that followed may have taken upwards of one million lives (it ended in 1988). Saddam then threw away any small gains he had made, by invading Kuwait: hemmed in by the *Gulf Coalition* and UN *sanctions,* in 1990 he surrendered to Iran all *territory* taken in the earlier *war.*

sheikdom: A *state* ruled by a sheik (Muslim prince).

shell shock: A *WWI* term for *battle fatigue,* or any of the psychological disorders associated with sustained artillery barrages or other exposure to fire. It is today called (post) *traumatic stress disorder.*

Sheverdnadze, Eduard (b.1928): Soviet Foreign Minister 1985-90; President of Georgia 1991- . He was a major figure in ending the *Cold War,* freeing Eastern Europe, and negotiating major *arms control* agreements. He resigned in dramatic fashion before the Supreme Soviet while warning *Gorbachev,* who sat stiffly behind him, that he was consorting with enemies of *glasnost* and *perestroika* and drifting to dictatorship. Shevardnadze became President of Georgia in early 1992, where he faced growing unrest, *secession* in *Ossetia* and *Abkhazia,* and a widening *civil war.* In 1992 he converted to *Christianity* (Orthodox) from agnosticism. He accused Russian troops of aiding the rebels. Almost killed on July 4, 1993, he accepted *CIA* security assistance training for his guards.

shi'ia Islam: "The Party (of Ali)." The major sect that early on broke with *sunni Islam.* The shi'ites claim Ali (the Prophet Muhammad's son-in-law) as the rightful successor, and consequently disavow the three *caliphs* who in fact succeeded Muhammad. While the great corpus of shi'ia doctrine is akin to sunni practice, the shi'ites come closest to having an interpretive priesthood, in the form of "mujtahids." A minority of *fundamentalist* shi'ites reject the right of *Muslims* to select their rulers (who are to be anointed by Allah), and therefore work to replace *secular* regimes with Islamic ones. See *ayatollah; fundamentalism; Hezbollah; Iran; Iraq; Islam; Khomeini; mahdi; Mecca.*

shi'ite: An adherent of *shi'ia Islam.* They are found mainly in Iran, southern Iraq, parts of Lebanon and Pakistan, Yemen and the Saudi interior.

Shimonoseki, Treaty of (April 17, 1895): The agreement that ended the *Sino/Japanese War* of 1894-95. It confirmed Korea's *independence* and ceded Formosa, the *Pescadores* and the Liaotung Peninsula to Japan. It also forced China to pay a large *indemnity.* Two weeks later, Russian (and other *Great Power*) *intervention* forced Japan to return the Liaotung Peninsula, which included the highly strategic *Port Arthur*. See *Triple Intervention*.

Shining Path: See *Sendero Luminoso*.

Shinto: The indigenous religion of Japan, emphasizing ancestor worship and harmony with nature. Shinto is closely identified with the position of the *emperor* in Japan, before 1945 considered and treated as a god. When Emperor *Hirohito* died there was international controversy over the use of a Shinto ceremony to invest his son, *Akihito,* in the first open display of the old rites at a government level since *WWII*.

ship-of-the-line: Any *warship* in the age of sail powerful enough (double rows of cannon) to join a line of battle alongside the most powerful warships, without creating a weak point in the line. Cf. *frigate; galleon; man-of-war; sloop-of-war.*

shock treatment: A semi-slang term used about the choice to rapidly, rather than gradually, displace a *central planned economy* with the mechanisms of a *market economy*. Essentially, it involves eliminating *subsidies* to state industries and allowing prices to find their market levels, while controlling *inflation* by not printing extra *currency* or raising public sector wages to keep them level with prices. This has been done most deliberately (and successfully) in Poland, but also has been tried in Hungary and elsewhere.

shock troops: Military units that are specially trained and equipped to strike sudden, massive blows against an enemy position. *Napoleon I* used *cavalry* this way, to great effect. More loosely, it can mean the first line of troops sent in during an assault, who absorb the maximum shock force of enemy defensive fire.

Shogun (Sei-i-tai-shogun): "Great barbarian-subduing general." Title of the chief of Japanese *warlords,* from the 8th to 19th centuries, who came to rule Japan in fact while a succession of *emperors* remained in place as figureheads. The shoguns were dismissed with the *Meiji Restoration* in 1868. See *Japan* (especially the *Tokugawa period*). Cf. *generalissimo.*

short-term capital account: It measures the flow of short-term *investments* and payments made by a national economy.

show trial: A rigged legal proceeding, staged for *propaganda* purposes and to get rid of political enemies. Cf. *purges.*

shrapnel: Explosive shells containing miniballs, nails or metal fragments, designed to explode above or among enemy troops to cause maximum damage and shock. Loosely, the fragments of any exploding shell.

shuttle diplomacy: A term coined about *Henry Kissinger's* repeated trips to and within the Middle East in search of a negotiated settlement, following the *Fourth Arab/Israeli War.* It is now in general use about a sudden flurry of face-to-face diplomatic activity, especially during a *crisis.*

Siam: The former name of *Thailand.*

Siberia: The Asian portion of Russia, from the Ural Mountains to the Pacific. Russian expansion into this huge land was comparable to the settlement of the west in North America, except it took over 300 years. This was viewed by Russians almost as defensive expansion (Russia had been repeatedly invaded by Asian nomads, through Siberia). As in the Americas and elsewhere, *indigenous peoples* were conquered and assimilated, pushed aside to marginal areas or exterminated. Siberia's vast reserves of *natural resources* were exploited by both the Russian and Soviet empires. Both systems also used Siberia for their prison camps, and for internal *exile.* Since the breakup of the Soviet Union, eastern Siberia in particular has become more economically independent, looking not to Russia but to China, Japan and world markets. Some early talk has been heard of political *independence* or at least *autonomy* (which Siberia tasted briefly during the *Russian Civil War*). See also *GULAG; Kolchak.*

Siberian intervention (1918-22): See *Czech Legion; Russian Civil War.*

sick man of Europe: (1) The *Ottoman Empire*, so-called by *Nicholas I* just before he tried to *annex* several portions of it, leading to the *Crimean War.* (2) After *WWII*, a term applied to several nations, notably Italy then Britain, in reference to the poor relative performance of their national economies.

side payments: In *game theory*, payments in a common medium that is transferable among players.

Sidra (Sirte), Gulf of: An inlet of the Mediterranean off the Libyan coast. *Muammar Quadaffi* has asserted *sovereignty* over these waters, proclaiming a *line of death* across its mouth. However, the U.S. and other nations affirm it as international waters. The U.S. Navy has challenged Libyan claims with fly-overs and ship transits. Several times in the 1970s and 1980s there were clashes with the Libyan Air Force or Navy, which did not fare well against the Americans.

siege: Surrounding, isolating and attacking a *fortified* position or city.

Siegfried Line: (1) In *WWI*: A set of German trenches and fortifications to which the army fell back in 1917, not in retreat but for *tactical* reasons. (2) In *WWII*: German defensive works facing the *Maginot Line*, constructed during the 1930s. Most of its guns were stripped down from 1940-44 to feed active fronts, so that it posed a lesser obstacle to *Allied* advance in 1944-45 than had been feared/hoped.

Sierra Leone: Location: W. Africa. Major associations: *Commonwealth, ECOWAS, OAU, UN*. Population: 4.3 million. Military: small defense force. The capital, Freetown, was established by Britain in 1787 as a haven for freed *slaves* (Britain had declared some 15 years earlier that any slave arriving on its shores would win freedom). Freetown was made a Crown Colony in 1806. The interior, which was already populated by Africans, did not become a *protectorate* until 1896. The two administrative regions were joined as Sierra Leone (named for the lion-shaped mountain that dominates Freetown) in 1951, and became independent in 1961. The 1960s and 1970s were marked by political instability and a decaying and corrupt economy. In the 1980s economic and social frustrations led to outbreaks of tribal violence. Sierra Leone has a sizeable Lebanese commercial class, which grew with the *Lebanese Civil War.*

sigint: "Signals intelligence." Any and all information secretly gathered by intercepting and listening to signals, or messages sent by foreign governments, *diplomats* or *spies*. See also *cabinet noirs*.

signature: Provisional acceptance of a *treaty* by one or more contracting *states*, or other *international personalities*. It is preceded by *negotiation,* and followed (though not always) by *ratification*, and only then the treaty entering into force. Note: Signature alone does not make a treaty binding on the state concerned; a treaty must also be ratified (fully consented to) in order to be legally binding.

Sihanouk, Norodom (b.1922): Cambodian statesman. King 1941-55; PM 1955-70; President, *government-in-exile* 1978-92; King 1993- . He was installed as a nominal king by the French, but collaborated with the Japanese *occupation* in the hopes of achieving *independence*. In 1955 he abdicated to become PM following the *Geneva Accords*, which he helped negotiate. As *war* came to dominate the peninsula, he was ousted in 1970 by a pro-U.S. military *coup* led by *Lon Nol* (Sihanouk was outside the country making one of his

many films). He returned to Cambodia when the *Khmers Rouges* took power, but was soon placed under detention. He was released in 1978 and went into *exile* in China. In 1993 he returned following UN-brokered elections. He was greeted as the only candidate all Cambodian factions could agree to install as an interim *head of state*. He was then made a constitutional *monarch* again. But even with his son as PM, he found it difficult to rule as well as reign.

Sikhism: A blend of *Hinduism* and *Islam* that developed in the 15th century in the *Punjab* regions of India. The main holy site for Sikhs is the Golden Temple in Amritsar. It was the site of an occupation by militants and an assault by the Indian Army in 1984 that deeply angered Sikhs and provoked the *assassination* of *Indira Gandhi*. In the 18th and early 19th century a independent Sikh state existed, but was conquered by Britain in the "Sikh Wars" that ended in 1849. When the *Punjab* was partitioned between India and Pakistan in 1947, Sikhs joined Hindus in fleeing to India. In the 1970s a movement for *secession* from India and the creation of a Sikh homeland called "Kalistan" built steam. Its most radical proponents engaged in *terrorism* and assassination, provoking violent Indian repression in Punjab.

Sikkim: A former British *protectorate* bordered by Bhutan, Nepal and Tibet, with just 350,000 people in a region of giants. It was transferred to Indian protection in 1950. In 1974 it was made an associated state of India.

Sikorski, Wladislaw (1881-1943): Polish statesman. PM 1920-26. He commanded in the *Polish/Soviet War* and was PM until his former comrade-in-arms, *Pilsudski*, forced him to retire. He headed the Polish *government-in-exile* in London during *WWII* (until his accidental death in 1943). He was supported by *Roosevelt* and *Churchill*, but after the *Katyn massacre* the Soviets refused all further dealings with the London Poles, and his influence waned.

Silesia: A mineral rich province in Central Europe, the bulk of which was transferred to Poland from Germany by a decision taken at *Potsdam*. The German population was forcibly expelled, replaced by Polish *refugees* from the eastern provinces *annexed* by the Soviet Union.

silo: An underground launch facility, crew and *missile*. Silos are usually *hardened* against attack.

Sinai: An Egyptian peninsula lying east of the *Suez Canal*. It was captured by Israel in 1956, but returned to Egypt as part of the 1957 *cease-fire* agreements. UNEF *peacekeeping* forces were in place from 1957-67, when *Nasser* ordered them out. Sinai was captured by Israel again in 1967. It was all returned to Egypt by April 1982, under *terms* of the *Camp David Accords* and subsequent *peace treaty*. Those agreements succeeded despite a 1979 Soviet *veto* of a UN buffer force (it was replaced by a non-UN "Multinational Force of Observers"). See also *Arab/Israeli Wars*.

Sinatra Doctrine: A startlingly humorous reference in early 1989 by (till then) dour Soviet spokesman Genadi Gerasimov. He was asked whether Moscow still believed in the *Brezhnev Doctrine* for Eastern European *states*. He said that it would henceforth follow the "Sinatra doctrine: they can do it their way" (in reference to the one-time hit "My Way," by American crooner Frank Sinatra). It was an important signal to the *regimes* and reform movements in Eastern Europe, and especially Germany, that the Soviets would not *intervene* to prevent the decommunization of their erstwhile *allies*.

sine qua non: "Without which not." Something indispensable to an event or explanation. See *causation*.

Singapore: Location: SE Asia. Major associations: *ASEAN, Commonwealth, UN*. Population: 2.7 million. Military: minimal. The island was taken over by the *East India Company* in 1819. It was run by the governors of India from 1826-67, when it became a separate *colony* under the name "Straits Settlement." It was a major British military and naval base until its capture in February 1942 by Japanese forces, who attacked overland, to the rear of its fixed gun emplacements. Some 75,000 British and Commonwealth troops were captured. It reverted to Britain upon Japan's *surrender* in 1945. In 1959 it became independent. In 1963 it joined the Malaysian Federation, but left to become independent again in August 1965. Since then, it has concentrated on economic *growth*, emerging as one of the *Asian Tigers* under *Lee Kuan Yew* and his *one-party* system (People's Action Party). Its diplomacy is coordinated with that of ASEAN. In August 1993, it held presidential elections under a new constitution; the usual suspects from the PAP won again, essentially unchallenged.

Single European Act (1986): It suggested further *integration* of the *EC*, saying that by 1992 there should be a fully integrated market and a community "without frontiers," where *capital, goods* and people moved freely. France, Greece and Ireland objected to the speed of the proposals, and Britain, France and Germany all worried about the integrated market's effect on their national economies. It was in the end a compromise agreement that had few penalties for not meeting the deadlines for *integration*. Italy, Denmark and Greece at first refused to sign. It was also delayed until late in 1987 owing to a *referendum* in Ireland, ordered by the Irish courts because it was thought the Act violated Irish *neutrality*. It revised the original EC *treaties* and reflected the rising power of the *European Council* over the *European Commission* and *European Parliament*. In 1992--the "Year of Europe"--uncertainty caused by the reunification of Germany meant the times were more confused than celebratory. See also *qualified majority voting*.

single integrated operational plan (SIOP): The U.S. contingency plan developed during the *Cold War* for waging *war* following a failure of *deterrence*. It included the use of *nuclear weapons*.

sinification: To influence by, or make like or characteristic of, Chinese culture and values.

Sinn Féin: "Ourselves alone." A nationalist, mainly Catholic movement founded in 1902 and dominant in the *Irish War of Independence*. It split over the *peace treaty* and during the *Irish Civil War*, ceasing to dominate national politics. It reemerged as a *marxist* party fronting for the *IRA* (Provos) in *Ulster* after 1969.

sinologist: An analyst who studies the economics, history, politics and so forth, of China.

sinophile/phobe: Someone who loves/fears China and things Chinese.

Sino/Japanese War, First (1894-95): Where China had increasingly fallen under the sway of foreign powers and remained unyieldingly traditional, Japan had forged ahead with *modernization*, chiefly of the army and navy. In 1894 it sprang these on China to end a long *dispute* over Korea. When internal unrest led both powers to send in troops, a minor naval exchange was used as a pretext to declare war. Japan routed the Chinese armies, winning victory after victory, leading to the severe terms of the *Treaty of Shimonoseki*. So complete was the Japanese *victory* and so harsh the *diktat*, the *Great Powers* intervened to reverse certain *territorial* gains (in which Russia also had an interest). This deeply angered Japan. See *Triple Intervention*.

Sino/Japanese War, Second (1937-45): The Japanese took six years to digest *Manchuria* following their *invasion* in 1931. But all along the real ambition was to carve an *empire* out of China proper. A border skirmish in 1937, the *Marco Polo Bridge incident,* was seized upon as a *casus belli* by Japan, which invaded. The Japanese overran most of northern China, capturing and sacking *Nanking* and then advancing down the coast, taking city after city. Chinese forces were divided between the *Guomindang* under *Chiang Kai-shek,* and the Communists under *Mao* and *Zhu De.* These antagonists united to fight the Japanese, but only under great duress. China's cause was viewed most sympathetically in the U.S. (Europeans were preoccupied with Germany). Private aid and volunteers arrived in China, and some government assistance was sent as well. The war merged into *WWII* with the Japanese attack on *Pearl Harbor.* With the aid of war matériel and *air power* from the U.S. and Britain, the Chinese kept the bulk of Japan's land forces tied down while the Americans and *ANZAC* "island-hopped" toward and bombed the Japanese *home islands.* The war ended simultaneously with *WWII,* and Japan's formal *surrender* on September 9, 1945. See *Neutrality Acts.*

Sino/Soviet split: From the ascension to power of the Chinese communists in 1949 to the death of *Stalin* in 1953, Sino/Soviet relations were embittered by the old dictator's predilection to condescend and lecture the Chinese on how to construct *socialism* in their country. From 1953-58 the Chinese were accorded somewhat more status and received technical *aid,* but were still treated as subordinates by Moscow. Other irritants included special Russian privileges in China (including *Port Arthur*), many exacted by Stalin as the price for attacking the Japanese in *Manchuria* in 1945. These were the last foreign concessions in China, and grated painfully against Chinese memories of 150 years of *capitulations* to foreigners. In 1957 Moscow agreed to supply *nuclear weapons* technology to China, as part of a strategy to withhold the weapon in exchange for Washington's agreement to deny nuclear weapons to *West Germany.* But when this switch occurred in 1959, Beijing reacted with vehement denunciation of the Soviet Union. The split was real from this point, but the *West* hardly noticed or tried to take advantage. Although the fundamental clash was competition between rival, imperial *nationalisms,* it was disguised (possibly even to the protagonists) as an ideological contest between "*revisionists*" and "left-wing adventurists" (the respective accusations of the Chinese and Russian leadership against one another). In 1962 the struggle for leadership of the communist world was symbolized by competition for the loyalty of Albania, which shifted toward China. By 1964, with a small *détente* underway between the U.S. and the Soviet Union, the Soviets considered China the greatest threat to their regime. *Marxist-leninist* rhetoric about ineluctable conflict with the *capitalist* West was one thing;

Chinese troops, *missiles* and extreme hostility was another. In 1966 and again in 1969, elements of the *Red Army* and the *People's Liberation Army* clashed along the disputed Ussuri River border. During the second crisis the Soviets indirectly asked *Richard Nixon* what the U.S. response would be to a *preemptive strike* against China's nuclear facilities and weapons. Nixon warned off the Soviets and indicated the U.S. would *intervene*; that shattered some ideological barriers in Sino/American relations, and laid the basis for the subsequent *rapprochement* between Beijing and Washington. Sino/Soviet relations never recovered. However, after 1991 Sino/Russian relations began to improve on the basis of mutual interest in *trade.*

SIS: Secret Intelligence Service. The main *intelligence service* of Britain, and one of the most active and important during the *Cold War.* Cf. *MI5/MI6.*

situational factors: *Jargon* for the facts of the *balance of power, capabilities, national interest* and intentions of allies and opponents which a *statesman* must consider when making a foreign policy decision.

sitzkrieg: For the full meaning of this *WWII* pun, compare *blitzkrieg* and *Phony War.*

Six Day War: See *Third Arab/Israeli War.*

size: The actual, geographical extent of a *state* or an *empire.* Sheer size does not guarantee a *nation* great *power* (witness Australia or Canada), unless it also has the requisite *population* and technological means to exploit abundant *natural resources* and convert them into economic and military power. Size can even reduce national power by bringing a country into contact with many adversaries (e.g., the size of the *Soviet Union* gave it multiple borders). Still, smallness is more likely to handicap a country that seeks power and *influence* (say, Libya) than is largeness. That is so simply because if a country is big, ambitious leaders are more likely to have available to them a large population, plentiful resources and a solid economic base.

slash and burn: A land-clearing technique used by very poor, itinerant farmers in virgin forest areas. It leaves soil badly depleted and open to erosion after just a few crops are taken. It is of international concern because it threatens common environmental interests in the rain forests, especially in the *Amazon basin.*

Slav: Any of the Balkan, East or Central European peoples related by culture, ethnicity or language: (1) Eastern Slavs: Byelorussians, Moldavians, Russians, Ruthenians and Ukrainians. (2) South Slavs: Bulgars,

Croats, Serbs and Slovenes. (3) Western Slavs: Czechs, Moravians, Poles and Slovaks. The generic term derives from "slave," reflecting the horrific condition of these varied peoples during the Middle Ages and under the Mongol khanates. See also *lebensraum; pan-Slavism; slavophile; Yugoslavia.*

Slave Coast: Part of the West African coast (between the mouths of the Benin and Volta Rivers), named for the "primary product" taken from there during the 16th-19th centuries. Nearby sections were known as the *Gold* and *Ivory Coasts.*

slave labor/slavery: The ownership of one person by another, for purposes of exploiting their unpaid toil. Slavery is an institution as old as recorded history, appearing in some form in virtually every known ancient society (and many modern ones), irrespective of race or locale, and as far afield as Africa, Asia, Europe and the pre-Columbian Americas. From the 15th-19th centuries the international *slave trade* was mainly in West and Central African captives, brought to the *New World* to exploit its resources for the benefit of Europe. The American South, Brazil and the Caribbean and South American plantation economies continued to import African slaves well into the 19th century. The racial differences involved in the Atlantic trade made it a particularly pernicious variant. East Africans were also taken, in smaller numbers but for over 1,000 years, by Arab slavers operating from *Zanzibar.* That trade was not closed down until 1873. Slavery was not abolished in the U.S. until 1865 (13th Amendment), and in Brazil not until 1888. In terms of *international law*, the Convention of St. Germain (1919) made dealing in slaves on land or at sea an international crime. This was supplemented by another convention in 1926, a *protocol* in 1953, and a supplementary convention in 1956. In practice, however, slavery continued throughout the 20th century. It was reintroduced to Europe by the *Nazis*, who enslaved millions and literally worked them to death; and by the Soviets, in their forced labor and prison camp system in the *GULAG.* As many as 100,000 black slaves labored for Moorish masters in Mauritania into the 1980s, and under another name ("indentured servants") still toil and suffer there today. In Latin America a "debt peonage" system kept generations of poor families in bondage, and still survives in remoter areas. In Asia the *Khmers Rouges* and other radical movements used slave labor; and uncounted millions have drudged in China's vast, secret prison and work camp system. Near-slave conditions (including for children) are still found in illegal "sweat shops," debt-bondage systems and houses of prostitution in major world cities on every populated continent. See also *serfdom.*

slave states: Those 15 states of the American union where *slavery* was legal until the *American Civil War* finally settled the issue, and the 13th Amendment abolished the evil: the 11 states of the *Confederacy* (Alabama, Arkansas, Florida, Georgia, Louisiana, Mississippi, North Carolina, South Carolina, Tennessee, Texas and Virginia) and four *border states* (Delaware, Maryland, Kentucky and Missouri).

slave trade: The transport of persons from one locale to another, in order to sell them into *slavery.* Toward the end of the 18th century a humanitarian movement developed opposed to continuation of slavery and the slave trade. It caught hold most powerfully in the northern U.S. and Britain, where it was guided by the Christian philosophy of William Wilberforce (1759-1833); but it was not unconnected to the rise of industries in both areas that saw slavery and the agrarian interests it sustained as retrograde. In 1802 Denmark banned the slave trade. More important, in 1807 Britain followed suit. It was condemned by those gathered at the *Congress of Vienna*; but as only Britain had the naval capacity to enforce a ban, and other nations were loathe to hand over rights of *visit and search* to London, it was not made illegal. Britain thereafter pursued bilateral bans, and began unilateral enforcement. Spain and Portugal banned the trade in 1820. Two countries were even founded by freed slaves: Liberia and Sierra Leone (Freetown). But banning the trade did not stop the evil business. Trade in slaves continued just as long as slavery as an institution and economic system still thrived in the *Americas*, and elsewhere. To begin, banning the trade actually made the passage more lucrative for the slavers and vastly more dangerous for the slaves, who were the prime evidence of illegality should a slave ship be boarded. The more brutal slavers resorted to tying their captives together and weighing them down, to ensure they sank when thrown overboard upon the approach of a British *warship.* This heinous practice continued until the laws were amended to make the apparatus of slavery (chains, berths, whips, etc.) itself sufficient evidence for conviction. The exact number of slaves carried from Africa is unknown, but consensus estimates suggest 12 million-15 million persons, with untold additional numbers dying in the *wars* and transoceanic passages attendant on the vile trade. Note: Abolition of the slave trade should not be confused with the end of slavery; e.g., Britain abolished slavery within its empire many years after it banned the slave trade, in 1833; and it did so with full *compensation* to owners for the loss of their "property." The U.S. made importing slaves illegal in 1808, but the *slave states* winked at the practice in reality and protected the institution of slavery in law until the *American Civil War.*

slavophile: A Russian intellectual and cultural tradition maintaining that values drawn from *Slav* culture and institutions are superior, and more appropriate for Russia, than values imported by figures such as *Peter I*, *Alexander II* or *Boris Yeltsin*. This tradition also prefers harsh autocrats such as *Ivan IV* (the Terrible), *Nicholas I* and *Stalin*. Cf. *Pamyat*; *westernizer*.

sleeper: A *penetration agent* left inactive for years.

sloop-of-war: A mid-size *warship* in the age of sail, with cannon on just one deck; comparable to a *cruiser*. Cf. *man-of-war*.

Slovakia: Location: E. Europe. Major associations: *CSCE, UN*. Population: 5 million. Military: small. Formerly a province of the *Austro-Hungarian Empire*, after *WWI* it became part of *Czechoslovakia*, sharing the twists and turns of that country's fate until the end of 1992. The only interlude came during *WWII*, when a Nazi *protectorate* was set up in Slovakia under Josef Tiso (1887-1947). In 1941 it *declared war* on the Soviet Union and then on the U.S., in tandem with the German declarations. The Slovak population did not so readily embrace these policies, however. When the *Red Army* liberated Slovakia in 1945, Tiso was found hiding in a cellar, and shot. Slovakia resumed its prewar status as part of Czechoslovakia until that *federation* broke up at the turn of January 1, 1993. It continues to be reliant on heavy industrial production and *armaments* manufacture, which was disproportionately located on its *territory*, and it rapidly fell behind the more consumer-oriented Czechs. In 1993 it arranged its first *IMF* loan, and saw a rise in open discrimination against its *Gypsy* minority led by the PM and President. The anti-Gypsy drive had *fascist* overtones. Slovakia also has a Hungarian minority of 500,000.

Slovenia: Location: *Balkans*. Major associations: *CSCE, UN*. Population: 2 million. Military: minimal. It was part of the *Austrian Empire* from the 14th century. Along with other non-German provinces, it witnessed a rise in national consciousness after the *Revolutions of 1848*. It became a constituent republic of *Yugoslavia* at the end of *WWI*, with the *extinction* of the old empire. During *WWII* it was partitioned between Nazi Germany and *fascist* regimes in Hungary and Italy. Restored to Yugoslavia in 1945, it proclaimed its independence in June 1991, and was recognized by the *EC* (at Germany's urging) on January 15, 1992. It escaped the worst of the *Third Balkan War* because it was shielded from Serbia and Bosnia by the interposition of Croatian territory.

slump: A temporary decline in economic activity,
often affecting a single *service* or *commodity*; less pronounced than a *recession*.

smart bomb: See *bomb*.

Smith, Adam (1723-90): Scottish economist. His enormously influential book "The Wealth Of Nations" (1776) pioneered *liberal* economic theories on *labor*, markets, money and wages. He was a fierce critic of *mercantilism*, proposing instead *free trade*, a virtually unregulated market and even social *laissez-faire*.

Smithsonian Agreement (December 18, 1971): The first effort at agreement on *currency* realignment by the *Group of Ten*, in response to the *Nixon shocks*.

smooth bore: A musket or *cannon* with a bore that is not *rifled* but smooth, giving it less accuracy and range. Smooth bore weapons were the norm during the *Napoleonic Wars*, when their limited range was a key to *infantry* tactics. They were displaced by *rifled bore* firearms during the *Crimean War* and *American Civil War*. Generals were slow to adapt, however, leading to repeated massacres of charging *infantry*, who now could be accurately fired upon at 10 times the previous range. The new rifled weapons, including machine guns and *artillery*, contributed much to the tragedy of *trench warfare* in both those wars and in *WWI*.

Smuts, Jan Christian (1870-1950): South African statesman. He helped negotiate an end to the *Second Boer War*, negotiated (unsuccessfully) with Austrians looking for a *separate peace* in 1916; attended the *Paris Peace Conference*; and was PM 1919-24, and 1939-48. He played an active role within the *Commonwealth* group at the *San Francisco Conference*, and was highly regarded by *Churchill*.

Soccer War (1969): So-called because the trigger was a riot occasioned by a national match between Honduras and El Salvador. The real cause was *migration* of land-hungry peasants/squatters into Honduras, fleeing *overpopulation*, exhausted soil and feudal landholding laws in El Salvador. Several thousand were killed in the fighting. The *OAS* helped end it, by *mediation*.

Social Charter: The labor and social policy code of the *EU*. Conservatives, in Britain in particular, have objected to it as too "socialistic," but it was accepted nonetheless.

social contract: In political philosophy, an imaginary bargain that takes place in the *state of nature* in which individuals contract with each other to form *states*; these provide security and social welfare and set laws that regulate social relations. By extension, it is said by theorists that no social contract is possible among states, and therefore there can be no escape from the *anarchy* said to characterize the *international system*.

social darwinism: The intellectually crude and false application to the political, social and economic realms of theories of biological evolution developed by Charles Darwin (1809-82). This tendency was widespread in the decades following publication of Darwin's "Origin Of Species" (1859). It fed the urge to *imperialism* with rationalizations of domination, even by *liberal* societies, as a consequence of "natural selection" among civilizations. It also played well among those enamored of *militarism*. At its worst, it lent support to the spurious race theories of the *Nazis*, by supporting claims to special privileges for the *Aryan* race and helping to justify the subjugation and *liquidation* of "inferior races," such as *Slavs* or Jews. Cf. *geopolitik; Herrenvolk; war.*

social democracy: The parliamentary, and usually non-doctrinaire, philosophy of many modern *socialist* parties. It stresses the utility and justice of economic regulation and the benefits of a *mixed economy*. Social Democrats have formed governments in several western countries, including Britain, Canada, France, Germany and across *Scandinavia*. Cf. *socialism.*

social fascism: A spurious charge coming out of Moscow in the 1930s, that *social democracy* was not a rival for working class support on the left but instead was "the left-wing of *fascism*." This sort of tunnel vision delayed or prevented *Popular Front* governments from forming, thus helping the real fascists take power in several countries, including Germany.

social imperialism: When *nationalism* plays a unifying rather than divisive role in a society, by deflecting class and social tensions outward, in the form of an assertive, even *aggressive*, foreign and military policy.

socialism: (1) In general: an economic and political theory/system that advocates heavy regulation of economic and political affairs with the fundamental aims of more equality in wealth distribution and ending class distinctions and privileges. To varying degrees, socialists posit communal ownership not of all property but of the *factor endowments* of a national economy (very few, if any, socialists entirely reject private property). As distinct from *communism,* most variants of socialism developed within a broadly democratic and parliamentary tradition. (2) In orthodox *marxism*: the intermediate stage between *capitalism* and communism, where the *proletariat* has taken control of the *means of production* and established a socialist *mode of production*, but where the pure, classless society of communism is still distant and the workers must rely on the coercive apparatus of the *dictatorship of the proletariat*. Cf. *marxism; Social Democracy.*

socialism in one country: Predictions of general revolution following the *Bolshevik Revolution* failed to come to pass, creating a predicament for *Bolshevik* theory. This slogan was devised by *Stalin* to justify his concentration on consolidating control over the *Russian Empire*, during the power struggle that followed *Lenin's* death. *Trotsky* and the "Left Position" championed *permanent revolution*, and another faction proposed to continue the *New Economic Policy* indefinitely. But Stalin argued that it was possible to construct socialism in a Russia insulated from outside threats and influences, not least because of the huge *size* and abundant resources of the old *empire* inherited from the tsars. He triumphed, and "socialism in one country" became the *party line* at the 15th All Union Congress of the CPSU in December 1927.

Socialist International: See *Second International.*

socialist realism: The oppressive Soviet aesthetic doctrine that all art, literature and culture must help build *socialism* (in the orthodox marxist sense). It was a euphemism for thought control by the party and state. Some otherwise fine artists, such as Maxim Gorky, accepted its stultifying confinements.

social overhead capital: The physical *infrastructure* of a national economy, plus those socially provided assets such as health, education and technological skills, that enable human beings to make maximum productive use of *capital goods.*

soft currency: Money not freely convertible to other mediums (*hard currency* or precious metals) and thus not held in *foreign exchange* reserve accounts, for use in trade or *money market* intervention.

soft goods: Those with a limited life expectancy, such as processed food or clothing. Cf. *durable goods.*

soft loan: (1) Money lent to a *developing nation* on terms lower than market rates and with an easier repayment schedule; (2) such a loan made repayable in the local, *soft currency.*

soft power: Something of a synonym for *influence*, implying complete abstinence from the use of *force* or other coercive means, in favor of example (economic or ideological success), persuasion and rewards.

Solidarity (*Solidarnosc*): This Polish trade union/nationalist movement began in the 1970s in *Gdansk*, and grew to include 1/4 of all Poles. Led by *Lech Walesa*, it pressed ever-greater demands, until the *Soviet Union* threatened *intervention* as in *Czechoslovakia* and *Hungary*. The Polish army then stepped in with *martial law*, and Solidarity was banned (1982). It was relegalized in 1989. With the collapse of *communism*, to which it made a major contribution, it reemerged as a political movement. In 1990 it won a massive victory in free elections, making Walesa president of Poland. It subsequently fractured under the duress of Poland's adjustment to *market economics*, and moved into opposition. Walesa then resigned his membership. In 1994 it called its first, post-communist *general strike*.

Solomon Islands: Location: Pacific. Major associations: *ACP, Commonwealth, SPC, SPF, Spearhead Group, UN*. Population: 315,000. Military: 100. Although sighted by the Spanish in 1568, the first Europeans settled only in 1870. Britain made them a *protectorate* in 1899, administered from Fiji. They were *occupied* by Japan from 1942-43. Returned to Britain, they received *autonomy* in stages from 1952-70. *Independence* came in 1978. They oppose *nuclear* testing, support independence for *Kanaky*, and in 1984 seized U.S. fishing boats within their claimed *EEZ*. The U.S. responded with a brief *embargo*, lifted in 1985. The *dispute* was settled in a 1987 *treaty*.

Solzhenitsyn, Alexandr (b.1919): Russian novelist and nationalist. As a young officer in *WWII* he was taken from the lines and sent to the *GULAG* for the most minor of indiscretions. He did not come out again until the pardon that followed *Stalin's* death in 1953. During a brief literary *thaw* under by *Khrushchev*, he published his autobiographical novel "One Day in the Life of Ivan Denisovich" (1962), the first honest depiction of camp life under *stalinism* ever seen in Russia. His subsequent novels ("Cancer Ward," "August 1914") and his magnum opus, "The GULAG Archipelago," were banned in the Soviet Union but published in the *West*, and earned him the *Nobel Prize* for Literature in 1970. He was not permitted to leave to collect the prize, but was expelled in 1974. After startling Western audiences with harsh criticism of democratic-*capitalism* he settled into a reclusive life in Vermont, only occasionally firing off missives giving vent to his *slavophile* and *Orthodox* views. In 1994 he returned to Russia with his family, after an *exile* of 20 years.

Somalia: Location: *Horn of Africa*. Major associations: *Arab League, OAU, UN*. Population: 8.5 million. Military: splintered into a dozen *militia*, with the

country effectively under UN *occupation*. *Somaliland* was divided among the British, French and Italians after 1884. The French portion eventually became *Djibouti*. Italian Somaliland was overrun by the British in 1941 and occupied until 1949. In 1950 it became a UN *trust territory* under Italian authority, the only Trust Territory to be returned to one of the *defeated Axis* powers. In 1960 this Trust was united with British Somaliland to form Somalia. In 1969-70 a *marxist* military faction led by General Muhammad Siyad Barre took control, and opened Somalia's port facilities to the Soviet Union. In 1974 a more radical group took power in Ethiopia, and the Soviets shifted their attention from Somalia to a new *client state* just to the west. Somalia lent aid to ethnic Somali *guerrillas* fighting for *secession* of the Ogaden region of Ethiopia. In 1977 the *Ethiopia/Somalia War* broke out. After Somalia was beaten, largely by Cuban troops, it expelled all Soviet advisers and turned to the U.S. for aid. The U.S. agreed to support Barre, whose marxism looked increasingly tattered and inconvenient, and in return took over the Soviet naval facilities at Berbera. Throughout the 1980s border skirmishes continued with Ethiopia, producing a mass of *refugees* and contributing to *famine* and disease. A *peace* agreement was reached in 1988, propelled more than anything by the sheer exhaustion of both countries. Civil war then broke out. In 1990, with *Cold War* imperatives no longer pressing, all U.S. aid was cut and the base at Berbera closed. Barre fled on January 27, 1991. Clan divisions intensified during the succession struggle that followed, leading to a catastrophic famine and UN *humanitarian intervention* in 1991. The fighting was so severe the UN had to pull out as well, only returning behind a spearhead of 25,000 U.S. troops in December 1992. By the end of 1993 most of the country outside the capital showed signs of reconstruction, but famine and a return to anarchy remained real threats to the population. Mogadishu remained uncontrollable by any one party, and a political solution yet eluded negotiators meeting under UN auspices.

Somalia, UN intervention (1991-): The UN *intervened* in Somalia in March 1991, to negotiate a *cease-fire*, directly help 200,000 *refugees* hemmed into Mogadishu, and bring *food* relief to some 4.5 million Somalis threatened with *famine*. Immediate relief was to be followed with a "reconciliation conference" hosted by Nigeria on behalf of the *OAU*. However, the famine grew worse with the closing of most ports by gunmen from rival factions. UN *Secretary General Boutros-Ghali* therefore asked the U.S. to intercede with large-scale *force* to provide a minimum of security to food convoys. After some months of hesitation, while a UN consensus was built that accepted the use of U.S. troops for purposes of *humanitarian intervention* in Africa, the marines disembarked in December 1992. This was the first time in 47 years that the UN dispatched troops with liberal *rules of engagement* (essentially, to shoot anyone interfering with the humanitarian mission), and it did so without asking permission of the Somalis. The long-term plan was still for the OAU to play a role in *mediating* a settlement. In April 1993, the clans agreed to establish a 74-seat Transitional National Council. The UN committed 28,000 troops to replace the U.S. force; and the U.S. for the first time agreed to leave a contingent (of about 4,000 marines) under UN command. In July, the UN became engaged in a bloody battle with the *militia* of General Muhammad Farrah Aideed following an ambush that killed 24 Pakistani peacekeepers. The fighting raised frictions between Italy and the UN, when the Italians (the former colonial power) and some *Arab* states objected to the use of extensive force against Aideed. In subsequent fighting hundreds of Somalis and dozens of UN peacekeepers were killed--the worst UN casualty rate since the *Congo crisis*. TV pictures of some Somalis gleefully mutilating American corpses rapidly eroded public support in the U.S. for continued involvement in the UN effort. Still, U.S. troops remained in UN *reserve*. See also *peace enforcement; peacemaking; war crimes trials*.

Somaliland: The East African coastal region divided into *British, French* and *Italian Somaliland*.

Somme, Battle of (July 1-November 18, 1916): The most terrible battle of *WWI* for the British Army. In over four months of fighting the line advanced no more than 10 miles deep along a 20-mile front, with astonishingly high casualties on the Allied side (20,000 killed on the first day, and over 600,000 total casualties). Tanks were used here for the first time in warfare, but the British squandered any tactical advantage gained by failing to mass their *armor*, as they would later do at *Cambrai*. General *Douglas Haig's* continued use of frontal assaults in 1917 (he learned nothing from the carnage on the Somme) contributed to the army *mutinies* of that year. The Somme seared the memory of the British *elite* and *nation* for generations. It even indirectly affected UK strategy in *WWII*, away from a frontal assault on *Hitler's* "Fortress Europe" toward *flanking* operations in Greece, North Africa, Sicily and especially the *Balkans*.

Somoza, Anastasio (1896-1956): Nicaraguan dictator. In 1933 he headed the National Guard, which was trained by the U.S. to replace the marines it had kept in Nicaragua for nearly 20 years. It was these troops who killed the rebel Augusto Sandino, and propelled Somoza to power in a 1936 *coup*. His was a corrupt, personal dictatorship that *kowtowed* to the U.S. in foreign affairs and repressed efforts at rural reform. He was assassinated in 1956. His sons, Luis Somoza and *Anastasio Somoza Debayle*, followed him into the family business--dictatorship. See *Sandinistas*.

Sonderbund: A *league* of seven Catholic cantons, formed in 1845 out of opposition to federal reforms. It fought a losing *civil war* in 1847 against more liberal Swiss cantons.

Sonnenfeldt Doctrine (1976): Helmut Sonnenfeldt, a counselor in the *State Department*, gave voice to an idea that Western *diplomats* did not broach in public (for domestic political reasons): the U.S. had a *national interest* in orderly Soviet "management" of Eastern Europe and what is now called the *near abroad*. He suggested, therefore, that the U.S. ought to work not for the destruction of the *Soviet bloc* but for development of an "organic" relationship within it. When these private remarks to European ambassadors were reported in the "New York Times," they caused something of a tempest in a samovar. Cf. *pax sovietica*.

South: (1) The *developing countries* of Africa, Asia and Latin America, as opposed to the affluent *North*. It is an increasingly popular and "politically correct," though no more accurate, alternative to *Third World*. (2) The *Confederacy* in the *American Civil War*.

South Africa: Location: southern Africa. Major associations: *Commonwealth; UN*; negotiating entry into *OAU*. Population: 40 million (73% black; 3% colored; 3% indian; 20% white). Military: the best-equipped in Africa, but so deeply divided it has the potential to fracture over reform of the country and to lead it into *civil war*. It had a rich tribal mix before the arrival of European settlers: Hottentot, Swazi, Sotho, *Xhosa* and *Zulu* among the major *ethnic groups*. These *tribes* had their own history of *warfare* and *conquest*, however, such as the *mfecane* of Shaka Zulu. European settlers came in two distinct waves. Dutch and French (Huguenots) settled the Cape area in the 17th century, melded into the *Boer* people and began a slow *migration* inland. They overran the Hottentot and other tribes as they moved during the 18th and early 19th centuries, and then fought a fierce set of wars with the Zulu. The British followed, reestablishing *Cape Colony* before *encroaching* on the Boer lands in the latter half of the 19th century. The Boer moved on, in the *Great Trek*, and founded three republics (*Natal, Orange Free State* and *Transvaal*). After 1860 huge mineral deposits were discovered, especially of gold and diamonds. That only increased the three-cornered

(British, Boer and native) competition over the land. The British eventually won the three *Zulu Wars* and the two *Boer Wars,* with the latter foreclosing Boer *independence*. In 1910 the Union of South Africa was created out of Cape Colony and the three Boer states. Under *Louis Botha, James Hertzog* and *Daniel Malan,* South Africa lived uncomfortably with its British connection and sternly repressed its disenfranchised black majority. Under General *Smuts* the tie to Britain was more positive and the hand of the state somewhat less heavy. South Africa fought alongside Britain in both world wars. But in 1949 it took a hard turn to the right: *victory* of the *National Party* meant the introduction of *apartheid*, and the start of several decades of progressive isolation for all South Africans. Following the *Sharpeville massacre* (1960), the *African National Congress* and the *Pan-African Congress* reconsidered their non-violent policies and began to prepare for *guerrilla warfare*. In 1961 PM Hendrik Verwoerd (1901-66) took South Africa out of the Commonwealth and made it a *republic*. In the 1960s the first of a series of ever-tighter *sanctions* began to bite into the economy, though the strains would not show until the 1980s. In 1971 the *ICJ* declared South African refusal to surrender control of *Namibia* to the UN an illegal usurpation. Meanwhile, South Africa lent aid to the white minority, *UDI* regime in *Rhodesia* and to the Portuguese fighting guerrillas in Angola and Mozambique. Its mid-1970s creation of the *Bantustan* system was both ridiculed and rejected by the *world community*. Once all regional *allies* bowed to the inevitable (the Portuguese in 1974/75 and Rhodesia in 1980) South Africa was truly isolated. After 1976 Soweto and other black townships became hotbeds of unrest and resistance. Domestic casualties mounted even as Balthazar Johannes Vorster (1915-83), PM 1966-78, took the country into a drawn-out *intervention* in the Angola and Mozambique *civil war*s, including extensive combat with Cuban troops. Domestic controls were tightened even more in 1986, while *nuclear weapons* were built in secret. Yet the country was fast becoming ungovernable due to violence and civil disobedience in the townships and the rise of openly *fascist* movements among extremist whites. After a decade in *laager*, things finally began to change when *F. W. de Klerk* took office in 1989: Namibia was let go, the troops came home from foreign wars, the nuclear weapons were dismantled as secretly as they had been built, *Nelson Mandela* was released from 28 years in prison, the *ANC* was unbanned and sanctions were ended in 1993 as whites agreed to a multiracial constitution (69% voted yes to full democracy in the last whites-only *referendum*). A Multiracial Council took charge in September 1993 and a new constitution was adopted. Free elections held in April 1994 led to

an ANC majority and to Mandela assuming the presidency. It rejoined the Commonwealth in 1994.

South America: That portion of the Americas below the Panamanian isthmus.

South Asia: The countries between *West Asia* and *Southeast Asia*: Bangladesh, Bhutan, India, Maldives, Nepal, Pakistan, Sikkim and Sri Lanka.

South Asian Association for Regional Cooperation (SARC): It was formed in 1985 by Bangladesh, Bhutan, India, Maldives, Nepal, Pakistan and Sri Lanka. As with all regional associations, it is hampered by the great diversity, different *development* strategies, and ongoing conflicts among its membership.

South China Sea: Located within the circle of China, Malaysia, the Philippines, Taiwan and Vietnam, this shallow sea contains several disputed island chains and archipelagos, including the *Spratlys* and *Paracels*.

Southeast Asia: The countries east of India and south of China, to wit: Brunei, Cambodia, Indonesia, Laos, Malaysia, Myanmar (Burma), the Philippines, Thailand and Vietnam. By convention, Papua New Guinea is usually situated in the *South Pacific*. See also *Northeast Asia; Oceania; South Asia*.

South East Asian Treaty Organization (SEATO): A regional *security* organization set up in 1955 to carry out a *security treaty* signed the previous year by Australia, Britain, France, New Zealand, Pakistan, the Philippines, Thailand and the U.S. It never became involved in any of the key Asian conflicts of the day. Pakistan pulled out in 1973 and France left in 1974. SEATO was dissolved in 1977.

Southern Africa: The *states* of the southern third of the African continent, to wit: Angola, Botswana, Lesotho, Madagascar, Malawi, Mozambique, Namibia, Seychelles, South Africa, Swaziland, Zambia and Zimbabwe.

Southern African Development Coordinating Committee (SADCC): An association of the *front line* states and other states from *Southern Africa*, established in 1980 to coordinate *development* efforts and lessen their dependence on South Africa. It has had limited success to date.

South Korea: See *Korea, Republic of*.

South Pacific: The island states and *dependencies* of the south and central Pacific Ocean, including some north of the equator, such as the *Micronesian* states. The term generally excludes those islands, such as Hawaii or the Easter Islands, that are under clear control of states from outside the region (though it includes several disputed French possessions). It contains sovereign ex-*colonies*, states in *free association* with former colonial powers, as well as *protectorates*, dependencies and *Trust Territories*.

South Pacific Commission (SPC): A regional association established in 1947 by Australia, Britain, France, the Netherlands (later withdrew), New Zealand and the U.S. Eight island states joined between 1965-80. In 1983 all remaining *South Pacific* states and self-governing *territories* were admitted, making it the only body that gathers all regional governments. Before 1989 political matters were excluded from the agenda. That encouraged creation of the *South Pacific Forum* and led to rivalry and tension between the two associations, with the Forum at one point seeking to take over the Commission. Tensions eased after 1991. The Forum emerged as the region's political organization while the Commission serves as a conduit for extra-regional *aid*, and as a cooperative cultural, economic and technical association.

South Pacific Forum (SPF): It was formed at the urging of Fiji to address political issues explicitly excluded from the *South Pacific Commission*. Its founding meeting was in New Zealand in 1971. Other island nations and self-governing *territories* were invited to join, but the *Melanesian* members have resisted the inclusion of non-self-governing territories (mainly French and American). In 1985 the Forum agreed to designate the *South Pacific* a *nuclear weapons free zone*. That helped precipitate a crisis within *ANZUS*. In 1989 Britain, Canada, China, France, Japan and the U.S. were invited, as "friendly states," to attend post-forum regional discussions on an annual basis. The SPF has no charter, proceeding only by consensus. Consensus positions have been reached condemning French nuclear tests in the region, on the *law of the sea* (with a special regional interest in *EEZs*), decolonization issues, the environment and on various fishery questions. Several regional, *functional agencies* dealing with aviation, fisheries, shipping, and pollution have been established under SPF auspices.

South Vietnam: See *Vietnam, Republic of.*

South West Africa: Former name of *Namibia*.

South Yemen: See *Yemen*.

sovereign: (1) Adjective: A condition of legal *inde-*pendence. (2) Noun: A *monarch* or *emperor* actually exercising or merely symbolically representing a nation's *sovereignty*.

sovereignty: (1) Political sovereignty: actual, factual freedom from foreign control. On rare occasions historically, but more commonly in the 20th century, *recognition* has been withheld from a government with *de facto* control of a *territory*; e.g., initial Western refusal to recognize the *Bolshevik* victory in the *Russian Civil War*, the communist victory in the *Chinese Civil War* or the Vietnamese *puppet regime* in Cambodia, 1978-92. (2) Legal sovereignty: *independence* under *international law*. States may retain *de jure* status even without de facto control of territory; e.g., other states may refuse to recognize an *annexation* such as the 1940 Soviet takeover of the *Baltic States* or Iraq's 1990 annexation of Kuwait, both reversed in 1991. (3) Full sovereignty: a condition in which real control of a territory exists, and is recognized in law by other states. Weak states (and increasingly, strong states, too) find that even full sovereignty does not mean they are free from outside influences in economic or political decision-making. Note: *Civil wars* or *secessions* always raise questions of recognition and sovereignty. It is an open secret that no matter how vehement the initial objections, other states will, in the fullness of time, recognize whoever wins a struggle for control of a territory. See also *par in parem; popular sovereignty; quasi states; state obligations*.

Soviet bloc: The *Soviet Union* and its *satellites* and *communist* allies, but not its *client states*, 1945-1991. The ties that bound dissolved between 1988-91. The bloc centered on *Eastern Europe* but included Afghanistan (1978-88), Albania (until 1968), Angola (after 1975), Bulgaria, Cambodia (after 1978), China (until the *Sino/Soviet split*), Cuba, Czechoslovakia, East Germany, Ethiopia (after 1974), Hungary, Laos (after 1975), Mozambique (after 1975), Mongolia, Nicaragua (after 1979), Poland, Rumania, Somalia (1969-77), Vietnam (the North only after 1955, all Vietnam after 1975), South Yemen (after 1979) and Yugoslavia (but only loosely, and only until 1947). Cf. *COMINTERN*.

sovietize: To make similar to the social, economic and political forms of the *Soviet Union*, especially its *one-party, communist* political system and centrally *planned economy*.

Soviet legal thought: The *Soviet Union* took several distinct positions on matters of *international law*. Among the most important, Soviet writers and Soviet practice tended to divide law among *nations* into three types: (1) Law among *communist* states, where the

Brezhnev Doctrine was applied in practice long before it was promulgated as a principle of Soviet diplomacy. (2) Law among "bourgeois states" (or traditional international law). The Soviet Union proclaimed disinterest in this category, but actually participated more or less as a traditional power, largely adhering on a pragmatic basis to the established corpus of law, and (mostly) negotiating and keeping its agreements in *good faith*. (3) Law between communist and bourgeois (and other non-communist) states. In this last class, the Soviets played a double game: they elevated the notion of *sovereignty* to an absolute when it came to the affairs of the socialist camp, insisting on *nonintervention* and *noninterference*. Yet, simultaneously, they not only advocated a legal right to aid *rebellion* and *revolution* against Western states or colonial empires, they actively promoted *disinformation, propaganda, wars of national liberation* and other forms of *subversion*. See also *peaceful coexistence*.

sovietologist: A scholar or *intelligence* analyst who studied the history, economics and politics of the Soviet Union. After 1991 most hurriedly restyled themselves Russian or area specialists.

Soviet, Petrograd (1917): Reviving the institution of 1905, the Petrograd Soviet (and its imitators in dozens of other centers) was an intense rival to the *Provisional Government* throughout 1917. Established in March in the old *Duma* building, it was dominated until autumn by doctrinaire, orthodox *marxists*. They did not try to either share power with or wrest it from the liberals and "bourgeoisie" of the Provisional Government, thinking that the historical moment for *socialism* had not yet arrived on the tide of history. The Soviet played an important role in the demoralization and collapse of the army, by issuing a decree that *officers* would have to answer for their commands to a committee of soldiers. An all-Russian Congress of Soviets met in June, but failed to act decisively. *Lenin* thought the moment was ripe and struck for power. He was wrong: the attempted *Bolshevik* coup failed, and Lenin fled to Finland. But as the situation continued to deteriorate he returned. Delay and factionalism within the Soviet proved fatal (in time, literally, to many the Bolsheviks would later have killed): an undertow of unrest pulled moderates from control of the Soviets, and power was seized by the more radical, opportunistic Bolsheviks. By November (October) the Bolsheviks controlled the Petrograd Soviet and used it to propel themselves into power via a second, successful *coup d'etat*. See *Russian Revolutions, 1917*.

soviets: (1) Originally, elected councils of workers and soldiers in Russia; and similar councils and systems briefly established after *WWI*, in Hungary and parts of Germany. (2) The various peoples of the Soviet Union. See also *Béla Kun; Jiangxi Soviet; Petrograd Soviet; St. Petersburg Soviet*.

Soviet, St. Petersburg (1905): Its precise origins remain murky, due to conflicting claims/blame for its creation. It seems to have arisen fairly spontaneously from "Workers' Unions," and then was aided/joined by the professional revolutionaries. It first met in October, chaired by the *Mensheviks*. But it came increasingly under the influence of the more radical intelligentsia, including the *Bolsheviks* and then *Trotsky*. It was emulated by smaller *soviets* in over 50 provincial cities and some rural areas. Its real importance lies not in 1905, but in the precedent it set for a revival of the *soviets* in 1917, with all that meant for Russians, the subject peoples of the *Russian Empire*, and then the world at large. See also *Russian Revolution, 1905*.

Soviet Union: The *Russian Empire* 1918-1991 (with the formal name change coming in 1922). Formed at the end of the *Russian Civil War*, it suffered *extinction* in December 1991. Fifteen *successor states* were formed at its breakup: *Armenia, Azerbaijan, Belarus (Byelorussia), Estonia, Georgia, Kazakhstan, Kirghizstan, Latvia, Lithuania, Moldova (Moldavia), Russia, Tajikistan, Turkmenistan, Ukraine* and *Uzbekistan*. Note: While much more than just Russia, for convenience the main outlines of, and mosdst cross-references to, Soviet history are provided under *Russia (Soviet, 1918-91); Russian Civil War; Russian Revolutions, 1905* and *1917*. Additional information is given in multiple headings listed under *Cold War*, all constituent republics, various national leaders and autonomous regions. See also *Andopov; Brezhnev; Chernenko; Gorbachev; Gromyko; Lenin; Khrushchev; Molotov; SALT; Siberia; space race; Stalin; START; Trotsky; WWII; Yeltsin; Zhukov; Zinoviev*.

space race: Initiated by the launch of *SPUTNIK* in 1957, it was made a full-fledged matter of international *prestige* by *John F. Kennedy's* declaration that the U.S. would be the first to place a man on the moon, before the close of the 1960s. In 1969, in an exercise with little or no other justification than enhanced prestige through a demonstration of scientific and technical prowess, the U.S. put two men on the moon: their lunar lander set down in the Sea of Tranquility at 22.18 GMT, July 20, 1969. In other areas, such as unmanned exploration and building a space station, the Soviets excelled. During *détente* there was a brief period of *superpower* collaboration, but the space race always had a central and secretive military component for both nations. With the end of the *Cold War* space exploration and exploitation is no longer at base a geopolitical race. Military experimentation and research continues, but there is new emphasis on economics, and on multinational cooperation to develop new technologies and materials, and do "pure science." China, the *EU*, India and Japan are also increasingly involved in space. See *Moon Treaty; Outer Space Treaty; satellites; Strategic Defense Initiative.*

Spain: Location: W. Europe. Major associations: *CSCE, EU, NATO, OECD, UN.* Population: 40 million. Military: NATO member. In 711 A.D. Moors swept into Iberia from North Africa, claiming most of it for *Islam.* For the next eight centuries the peninsula saw *war* between Christian and Muslim states. With the union of Aragon and Castille through the marriage of *Ferdinand* and Isabella in 1469, the final battle got underway. In 1492, the same year Columbus was sent west by those two monarchs to search for the *East,* the last Moorish state (Granada) fell to their armies. What followed was an orgy of persecution of Jews and Moors by the *Inquisition.* Catholic, *Hapsburg* power now centered on a united Spain, grown mighty with *mercenary* armies bought with the *plundered* gold of the Aztec, Inca and Mayan Empires. Spain built an *empire* and became a *Great Power,* unthreatened to the south, stretching north to the Netherlands, east to Italy and parts of Germany and west across the Atlantic to the Americas. It repeatedly sent its armies against France, and once with less success, its Armada against *England* (1588), then an upstart, pirate nation in Spanish eyes. Its decline started with the breakaway of the Netherlands (1579-81), was well advanced by defeat in the *Thirty Years' War* and became precipitous by the time of the *War of the Spanish Succession.* Its humiliation came with *conquest* by *Napoleon,* even if some Spaniards first thought up *guerrilla warfare* during the *Peninsular War* against the French. That *defeat* cost it most of the empire: with Madrid down and out, Latin American *republicans* struck for *independence,* largely achieving it by 1825. The *Carlists* forced a succession struggle that led to *civil war* in 1834-37, and again in 1870-76. This quarrel kept Spain out of the larger political currents in Europe that were heading to the plunge of the *Revolutions of 1848,* but also held it back from faster *modernization* and *liberal* reform after that date. The rest of the empire was stripped away by another newcomer--the United States, during the *Spanish/American War.* Reduced to its own shores but for a lingering *imperial overreach* to some North and West African *colonies,* Spain entered the 20th century a backward and uncertain power. Convulsed by a sustained clash of *anarchism* and *fascism,* it stayed out of *WWI.* It then repressed the *Rif Rebellion* and sank into dictatorship under *Primo de*

Rivera. It then suffered the horrors of the *Spanish Civil War.* Quasi-*neutral* in *WWII* (it sent the *Blue Division* to fight the Soviets and gave the *Nazis* naval *intelligence*), it was under the iron hand of *Franco* from 1939-75. But when Franco died Spain enthusiastically embraced modernity, helped by the fact that after 1980 it enjoyed high *growth* rates and greatly increased and more equitably distributed prosperity. King *Juan Carlos* steered the difficult transition to *democracy* and the acceptance of a *socialist* government in 1982. Spain joined NATO that year and the *European Community* in 1986. See also *Basques; Ceuta; ETA; Gibraltar; Melilla; Spanish America.*

Spanish America: The mainly Spanish-speaking areas south of the United States, to wit: *Central America* except for Belize, *South America* except for Brazil and the Guianas, and parts of the Caribbean.

Spanish/American War (1898): Americans had long maintained an interest in Cuba; thus *insurrectionists* against Spanish rule could generate and steer public sympathy for their cause in the U.S. The Protestant religious press and the *yellow press,* in particular the Hearst chain, also stirred anti-Spanish sentiment. Spain's image and cause was not helped by the genuine cruelties it committed, including the use of *concentration camps,* nor by incidents where U.S. and Spanish *warships* exchanged fire. The *Republican Party* contained the lion's share of *jingoists* and imperialists, but this did not include President *William McKinley.* His fatal flaw was an inability to withstand the building sentiment for *war,* especially after the *Maine* was sunk. A U.S. *ultimatum* brought appeals by Spain to other European powers, but although most thought the U.S. was in the wrong none was willing to help. Madrid thus decided to concede on all points except complete Cuban *independence.* But the offer came just too late: Congress had decided for war, and McKinley went along rather than divide his party. To great fanfare, the U.S. inflicted *defeat* upon defeat on the ill-equipped Spanish, who were struck at wherever American forces found them, not just in Cuba. The U.S. public therefore found within 10 weeks that its crusade to free Cuba from *colonialism* had delivered into its hands an unwanted (by most) American *empire;* to wit, Americans found they controlled *Guam,* the *Philippines* and *Puerto Rico.* At a blow, the Spanish empire in the Americas was finished and the U.S. was transformed into an imperial republic, with looming interests in the Pacific and a budding *guerrilla war* against its own colonial mastery of the Philippines. See also *Theodore Roosevelt; white man's burden.*

Spanish Civil War (1936-39): It began as a revolt of

elements of the colonial army, led by *Franco* and supported by the *Phalange*, conservative Catholics and the church hierarchy (but not all priests). On the other side was the *Popular Front* coalition of the Republic. While the Western powers declared *neutrality*, the *fascist* states quickly *intervened*, sending *arms* (including German air force units) and "volunteers" to fight for Franco. The *Soviet Union* then counterintervened, becoming the main backer of the Republican side, along with the volunteers of the *international brigades*. In all, some 750,000 died. When the Soviets suddenly cut off *aid* to the Republicans in 1939, as part of the *rapprochement* with Germany leading to the *Nazi/Soviet Pact*, the Republic's forces collapsed. Terrible retribution followed. Come September, the British and French had cause to rue the fact they had not helped a fellow democracy survive. Yet, while Franco established a severe dictatorship he cunningly kept Spain out of *WWII*, other than for fascist volunteers sent to fight in the *Blue Division* on the *eastern front*. Something of the flavor of this war has been captured, in English, in Ernest Hemingway's "For Whom The Bell Tolls," and even more so in George Orwell's "Homage to Catalonia." See also *Fifth Column; Guernica; League of Nations; Neutrality Acts*.

Spanish Inquisition: See *Inquisition*.

Spanish Main: The Caribbean coast of Mexico and the United States, from whence treasure ships plied their way to Spain filled with *plundered, Aztec* gold, and where they were often preyed upon by *pirates*, English and otherwise.

Spanish Sahara: A West African *colony* given up by Spain in 1976, and immediately divided by Mauritania and Morocco. See *Western Sahara*.

Spartakists: German *socialists* and *communists* led by *Rosa Luxemburg* and Karl Liebnecht (1871-1919) who tried to take control of *Berlin* at the end of *WWI*. The revolt was put down not by *Weimar* authorities but by the *Freikorps*, who murdered Luxemburg and Liebnecht after taking them prisoner. The name refered, with romantic self-consciousness, to the Roman slave revolt in 73 B.C. led by Spartacus (d.71 B.C.).

SPC: See *South Pacific Commission*.

Spearhead Group: Formed in 1986 by Papua New Guinea, the Solomon Islands and Vanuatu to support *decolonization* demands of French South Pacific *territories*, to distance themselves from Australia and to work for *rapprochement* with Indonesia. Fiji declined to join, but it is expected that a *Kanak* government on

New *Caledonia* would. The exclusive character of this group may yet threaten to divide the *South Pacific* along *Melanesian/Polynesian* lines.

special drawing rights (SDRs): International *liquidity* reserves used by members of the *IMF*. Set up in 1967, they became available in 1970. SDRs are allocated by reference to fund contributions, and are designed to supplement other sources of global liquidity.

special interest section: An *ad hoc* arrangement made between *states* that wish or need to maintain *relations officieuses*, in the absence of full *diplomatic relations*. These are usually set up within the *embassy*, or under the custodianship, of a friendly or *neutral* power. However, on occasion the old embassy is used, but renamed and downgraded in status to special interest section. Officials of these estabishments are not usually covered by *diplomatic immunity*.

specialized agencies (of the United Nations): Those *functional* organs designated in Article 57 of the *UN Charter*, and later additions, now totalling sixteen: *Food and Agriculture Organization (FAO), International Bank for Reconstruction and Development (IBRD), International Civil Aviation Organization (ICAO), International Development Association (IDA), International Fund for Agricultural Development (IFAD), International Finance Corporation (IFC), International Labor Organization (ILO), International Monetary Fund (IMF), International Maritime Organization (IMO), International Telecommunication Union (ITU), United Nations Educational, Scientific and Cultural Organization (UNESCO), United Nations Industrial Development Organization (UNIDO), Universal Postal Union (UPU), World Health Organization (WHO), World Intellectual Property Organization (WIPO)* and *World Meteorological Organization (WMO)*. Related organizations not usually included in this list are the *General Agreement on Tariffs and Trade (GATT)*, the *International Atomic Energy Agency (IAEA)* and the *United Nations High Commission for Refugees (UNHCR)*. See also *UNICEF*.

special membership: Some organizations (e.g., the *Commonwealth*) grant this status to *microstates*, to enable them to enjoy full benefits of membership without incurring the costs of attending meetings or making donations. For example, see *Nauru; Tuvalu*.

SPF: See *South Pacific Forum*.

sphere of influence: (1) An area of small or weak *states* or portion thereof, dominated by a larger power purposefully or by virtue of its proximity, resources and expanded appreciation of self-interest. (2) An area declared by a *Great Power* to be its exclusive area of interest, where it acts to defend its dominance and to exclude other Great Powers. In the late 20th century, because of the sensitivities of *liberal-internationalism* and of newly independent states, spheres of influence are no longer so-called in diplomatic rhetoric, though they are no less real on the ground than before. See *Brezhnev Doctrine; China; CIS; Congress of Berlin; Eastern Question; Greater East Asia Co-Prosperity Sphere; hinterland; Manchuria; mare nostrum; Monroe Doctrine; Nazi/Soviet Pact; near abroad; Open Door; Poland; Potsdam; propinquity; protectorate; Shantung; sphere of interest; Sykes-Picot agreement; Tilsit; Twenty-One Demands; Yalta.* Cf. *empire.*

sphere of interest: A tighter concept than *sphere of influence*, implying a narrow, even territorial aspect. In colonial times, these were the areas of *hinterland* deemed to directly affect coastal settlements, and claimed as an extension of them. See also *Fashoda.*

Spice Islands: Former name of the Moluccas group, once a Dutch *colony* and now part of Indonesia.

spies: Spies are members of the second oldest profession. Most states regard spying as an entirely legitimate, if secret, business (certainly when they are doing it, and even to a large degree when done by opponents as well). All *states* engage in spying to the degree their resources and human and technical talents permit, at least on an *ad hoc* basis. Originally, spying was a principal function of *diplomats*, so valued by both sides that it was openly tolerated, in a curious application of the idea of *reciprocity*. Today, states maintain secret *intelligence services* and installations, specifically dedicated to gathering information abroad. States will try to block other states from spying, but most often will not maim or kill a foreign *agent* in peacetime. One special practice concerns spying on enemies in wartime, and is worthy of note. Although wartime spying is not prohibited under *international law*, it is so threatening to the nations being spied upon that spies are denied the status of *POWs*. Instead, they are *summarily executed*, pour encourager les autres ("to encourage the others"), as the dry, French saying has it. See *active measures; agent of influence; agent provocateurs; agitprop; assassination; attaché; cabinet noir; counter-intelligence; covert action; cipher; cryptology; dead letter drop; debrief; disinformation; double agent; double cross; economic espionage; elint; espionage; Alger Hiss; honey trap; humint; illegal agent; intelligence; legal agent; listening post; mole; overt/covert action; penetration agent; persona non grata; psychological war-*fare; safe house; sabotage; satellite; secret diplomacy; sigint; station; surveillance; tradecraft; wet affair.*

spillover: In *integration* theory, the suggestion that successful cooperation among *states* in one *functional* area encourages cooperation in others, builds trust and mutual interest and one day, perhaps, will lead to political *union.*

splendid isolation: A term often used about British diplomacy under *Palmerston*, usually seen as ending with the *Anglo/Japanese Alliance* (1902). It is more accurate to say Britain followed a policy of limited arrangements and commitments, befitting a fluid situation. In its narrowest meaning, it suggested Britain's unique ability to stand on the strength of its navy and empire without formal allies, at least until c.1902-05. The term will mislead if taken to mean Britain stood aloof from international disputes or *Great Power* rivalry in Europe, on anything like the American model.

spot market: That where buying or selling takes place at the market price of the day, in cash or cash equivalent, and for immediate delivery. For instance, the spot market for *oil* is constantly active and an influential indicator during times of crisis. Cf. *forward market.*

Spratly Islands (a.k.a. *Nansha*, a.k.a. *Truong Sa*): An archipelago of 500 coral reefs and islands, only 30 of which are substantial in size. Their control or ownership is contested by six nations: Brunei (which claims only *territorial waters*, not the islands per se), China, Malaysia, the Philippines, Taiwan and Vietnam. Previously, France and Japan maintained claims. This sprawling archipelago straddles a busy sea lane connecting the South China Sea to the Pacific and Indian Oceans. Its waters contain rich fish stocks, and it is thought that a major *oil* field lies below the region. The main *tension* is between China and Vietnam, each of which claim all the islands, reefs and territorial waters. In 1974 they fought an air and naval battle over the Spratlys and *Paracels*. China pushed Vietnam out of the latter in another clash in 1982. In 1988 Chinese *warships* took six of the Spratlys from Vietnam, leaving an estimated 100 Vietnamese dead. Vietnam had a military presence on 21 islands in 1992. China occupied seven, but in 1992 attacked two more Vietnamese-held islands and now holds nine; it does not keep troops on these, but maintains what it calls "sovereignty posts" and keeps up naval patrols. Taiwan makes the same claims as *mainland China* and occupies the largest of the Spratlys, Ito Aba (Taiping). It has had 400-500 troops there since 1958, and has previously fired on Soviet and Vietnamese aircraft. In one of the more curious results of these overlapping claims, Taiwan has said that it would come to China's aid against Vietnam--but added, rather unnecessarily, that China did not appear to need the assistance. Malaysia claims only three islands, on which it keeps troops. In 1992 it acquired Russian *MIGs* that can provide air cover for its claim. The Philippines lays claim to eight islands that it calls the "Kalayaan Archipelago." It has an air base on Pagasa (Thitu on world maps). Concern over these tensions led in 1992 to Indonesia's call for a 10-nation conference on the future of the Spratlys. *ASEAN* too has called for creation of a "Zone of Peace, Freedom and Neutrality" (ZOPFAN), but no nation has yet renounced its claims. In 1993 China and Vietnam opened bilateral talks on resolving this dispute, and another over oil exploration in the Gulf of Tonkin.

SPUTNIK: "Fellow Wayfarer." The first earth-orbital, artificial *satellite* ever launched (October 4, 1957), by the Soviets. Its sending of an elementary signal as it circled the globe shocked the *West*, gave a huge boost to the *prestige* and (misplaced) confidence of the Soviets and further spurred the *space race*.

Sri Lanka: Location: SW Asia. Major associations: *Commonwealth, NAM, SARC, UN.* Population: 17.2 million (Sinhalese 72%, Tamils 18%). Military: mainly Sinhalese. Formerly called Ceylon. Its *indigenous people* were conquered by *Buddhists* from India c.545 B.C. These settlers make up the modern Sinhalese, about 4/5ths of the island's population. The other 1/5th is *Hindu* and Tamil. After 1505 the Portuguese made their presence known along the coastal areas, facing competition for trade from the Dutch who eventually displaced them, and from the English and French. The *East India Company* seized and claimed the Dutch coastal towns in 1796, briefly leaving the interior *autonomous*. The *conquest* was completed by British troops in 1814. From 1815-47 Ceylon was a British *colony*, sustaining the empire's appetite for tea (and rubber and other tropical goods) with the output of its plantations. Some local representation was permitted after 1920. Ceylon became an independent *Dominion* in 1947. Solomon West Bandaranaike (1899-1959) was PM, 1956-59. A Sinhalese nationalist who alienated the minority Tamils with his domestic policies, he also reduced the British presence, closing naval bases and moving more clearly into the *Non-Aligned Movement*. Upon her husband's death Sirmavo Ratwatte Bandaranaike (b.1916) became the first woman PM, 1960-65, and again 1970-77. Ceylon in 1970 became the Republic of Sri Lanka. In 1978 ethnic and religious tension led to *terrorist* attacks by the *Tamil Tigers*. In 1983 the conflict flared into bloody *civil war*. A *state of emergency* was declared, as the Tigers

made early gains and seized control of the Jaffna Peninsula. In 1987 some 50,000 Indian troops *intervened* as invited "peacekeepers," but soon found themselves fighting the Tigers. They were withdrawn in 1990 in exchange for the opening of *peace talks*. In 1993 these talks stalled and heavy fighting resumed. Some 20,000 are known dead in the civil war so far (another 16,000 have "disappeared").

SS (*Schutzstaffel*): "Protective detachment." This evil *elite* began as *Hitler's* bodyguard, but surpassed the *SA* in size and importance after it was called upon for the bloodbath of the *Night of the Long Knives*. It was later subdivided into the Allgemeine or General SS, and the Waffen or Armed SS. The latter ended up as ideological *shock troops* and a pampered rival to the *Wehrmacht* during *WWII*. Commanded by *Himmler*, it carried out the dirtiest tasks of the Nazi Party and regime, including the murder of millions of Jews, Gypsies, homosexuals and others (the SS was in charge of the *death camps*). SS officers and men were rewarded with all the perquisites--financial, social and sexual-- that imperial *conquest* affords such a praetorian guard.

St. Germain, Treaty of (September 10, 1919): Negotiated at the *Paris Peace Conference*, this was the *peace treaty* formally ending *WWI* with Austria. It was based on Points 10 and 11 of the *Fourteen Points*, which forced Austria to renounce all claims to non-German areas of its erstwhile *empire*. But it went against the principle of *self-determination* by simultaneously stripping Austria of about 1/3rd of its German population. Moreover, any *Anschluss* with Germany was prohibited. The non-German portions of the old empire either became independent (Hungary), part of the new state of *Yugoslavia* (Bosnia-Herzegovina, Dalmatia, Slovenia), or were incorporated into existing states (Bohemia and Moravia to Czechoslovakia, Bukovina to Rumania, Galicia to Poland, and South Tyrol to Italy). At a blow, Austria was made a minor power.

St. Helena: A British island in the S. Atlantic, where *Napoleon* spent his second *exile* from 1815 to his death in 1821. Examination of a hair sample (his corpse lies embalmed in the Invalides in Paris) performed in the 1980s suggested that the British might have slowly poisoned his food with arsenic.

St. Kitts (Christopher) and Nevis: Location: *Lesser Antilles*. Major associations: *CARICOM, Commonwealth, OAS, OECS, UN*. Population: 40,000. Military: none. Discovered by Columbus in 1493, they were colonized by Britain after 1623. France sought possession until its defeat in 1713. They were joined to the Leeward Islands Federation from 1871-1956, and then the *West Indies Federation* 1958-62. They became *associated states* in 1967, and independent in 1983. They supported the *invasion of Grenada* by the U.S. and OECS.

St. Laurent, Louis (1882-1973): Canadian statesman. Minister for External Affairs 1946-48; PM 1948-57. Strongly anti-Soviet, he was a supporter of the formation of *NATO* and Canada/U.S. defense cooperation in *NORAD*. He led Canada into the *Korean Conflict*, and agreed to build the *St. Lawrence Seaway*.

St. Lawrence Seaway: A vast system of locks and canals connecting the commercial centers of the Great Lakes with the Atlantic *trade routes*. It was a joint construction venture of Canada and the U.S. from 1954-59, and is today administered by both powers.

St. Lucia: Location: *Lesser Antilles*. Major associations: *CARICOM, Commonwealth, OAS, OECS, UN*. Population: 155,000. Military: none. An eastern Caribbean island ceded to Britain by France as part of the settlement of 1814-15. It was given *autonomy* in 1967 as an *associated state*, and *independence* in 1979. It supported the *invasion of Grenada*.

St. Petersburg: Founded as the Russian capital by *Peter I (the Great)* to serve as a window on the *West*, for 200 years it served as the political and cultural capital of the Russian Empire (1703-1917). A *soviet* was established there in 1905, and again in 1917. Its name was changed to Petrograd in 1914, to make it sound less German. It was changed to Leningrad in 1924 by the *Bolsheviks*, and ceased to be the Russian capital (which moved to Moscow, the old capital of Muscovy). It was defended valiantly during a Nazi seige of nearly 900 days in *WWII* that caused widespread famine, and even some cannibalism. At the behest of its population, it was renamed St. Petersburg in September 1991.

St. Pierre et Miquelon: The two largest of a group of small islands off *Newfoundland* that form an *overseas department* of France. Overlapping *EEZ* claims, especially regarding fish stocks, led in the 1980s to diplomatic controversy and even some comically pretentious *saber rattling* by Canada toward France.

St. Vincent and the Grenadines: Location: *Lesser Antilles*. Major associations: *CARICOM, Commonwealth, OAS, OECS, UN*. Population: 105,000. Military: none. Discovered by Columbus in 1498, possession was disputed by Britain and France until the *Seven Years' War*, when the islands were seized by Britain. They became an *associated state* in 1969, and

independent in 1979. They supported the *invasion of Grenada*.

STABEX: "*Stab*ilize *Ex*ports." Created under the *Lomé Conventions*, this agency seeks to stabilize export earnings from certain key commodities. It established a *compensatory financing* fund paid into by *EC/EU* members that makes *soft loans* or grants credits to *ACP Nations* when commodity prices fall below set trading levels. Cf. *COMPEX*.

stability: (2) In *economics*: When an economy is productive and growing within a steady range for a sustained period, without wide fluctuations in the *business cycle*. (1) International: when most *Great Powers* in a given period or region accept the existing *balance of power* and work to preserve it. (3) In *politics*: When a *regime* is safe from fundamental challenge, either because it enjoys *legitimacy* with most of the population or because it is effective at repression.

stabilization program (IMF): After borrowing passes the *First Tranche*, the *IMF* may decide to impose certain conditions on further borrowing that aim at stabilizing a national economy so that repayment is a real possibility. Such programs vary from *state* to state, but usually share three main components: (1) *devaluation* of the national currency to cheapen *exports*, earn *foreign exchange* and improve the *balance of payments;* (2) cuts in government spending to curb consumer demand, decrease *inflation* and boost domestic staple producers; (3) price liberalization through cuts in consumer *subsidies* and elimination of *price controls*, even on staples, in the hope this will stimulate domestic production while lowing government expenditures. This program was designed for application to *OECD*-type economies, where it has had great success. It has enjoyed less success or favor in the *Third World*, where it is often unevenly applied, exports suffer from *inelasticity* of demand, and cheapness does not so much increase volume of exports as lower revenues.

stab-in-the-back, theory of: This accusation from the far right in Germany held that in signing the *Armistice* the *liberal* and *socialist* politicians of the *Weimar Republic*, and not the army, lost *WWI*. The theory was patent nonsense. Yet, it had a certain plausibility for troops who in July 1918, just before the second *Battle of the Marne*, stood astride one-third of Russia, much of the *Caucasus* and the *Baltic States*; were across the Italian frontier and within shell-shot of Paris; and who with their allies controlled all the *Balkans* and much of the *Middle East*. But all that was really but a great chimera: Austria and Turkey were both exhausted and soon to collapse, and the gains in Russia depended on the outcome on the *western front*. Most important, the German army itself was beaten in the west by September 1918. And it was the army, in the form of *Hindenburg* and *Ludendorff*, who told the *Kaiser* to *ask for terms*. Yet the *Nazis* and others made much of this thesis, feeding off the wounded *nationalism* of soldiers who had not, themselves, surrendered. Partly to avoid a repeat of this after *WWII*, at the *Casablanca Conference* the *Allies* demanded *unconditional surrender* from Germany, and agree on its *occupation* after the war. Cf. *mutilated victory*.

staff officer: One who works in a headquarters, helping higher level, senior command officers with administration, battle plans and logistics. Cf. *line officer.*

stages of growth: (1) A general idea that *economies* progress from less to more-advanced levels of *development*, organization and sophistication. (2) An argument about *modernization* of the *Third World* based on *capitalism* and scientific *technology*, and modeled on the Anglo/American experience with the *Industrial Revolution*. It was made most forcefully and famously by W. W. Rostow, in his influential book "The Stages of Economic Growth," first published in 1960. Rostow said that economies progressed to the point that *take-off* (toward sustained *growth*) occurred. He identified five stages along the path to a "mature economy:" traditional (subsistence), transitional (preparation for take-off), take-off, progress toward maturity and full maturity as an industrial, consumer society. Cf. *dirigisme; marxism; sustainable growth.*

stagflation: The combination of slow or stagnant economic *growth* with high *inflation*. This occurred on a wide scale in the early 1970s, and encouraged *beggar-thy-neighbor* policies and *protectionism.*

stagnation: When economic *growth* falters, as production fails to expand. It is attended by rising unemployment, business failures, and also rising public debt due to increased social welfare spending occasioned by higher unemployment rates.

stalemate: A military outcome in which no side is the clear victor. When this occurs, the immediate *postwar* settlement may lead to a *peace* that is merely a period of disguised rearming and refitting for *war*. Or a stalemate may help both sides recognize the futility of further attempts to win a disputed point by force. For example, after the effective stalemate of the *Russo/Japanese War* Russia and Japan reached a series of secret accommodations dividing *Korea* and *Manchuria*, the *territories* over which they fought in 1904-05. Cf. *defeat, in war; victory, in war.*

Stalin, Joseph Vissarionovich, né Dzhugashvili (1879-1953): Soviet dictator. A Georgian by birth, an *Orthodox* seminarian by training and a Great Russian nationalist, as well as a *marxist-leninist*, by conviction. He was an active organizer in the pre-revolution *Bolshevik* party. His adopted name meant "Man of Steel." Twice sentenced to *exile* in *Siberia* for political crimes, he rose steadily within the party. He returned from exile when the *Russian Revolutions of 1917* broke out. He was Commissar for Nationalities 1921-22, and General Secretary 1922-53. Using his control of the Party administrative apparatus he forced *Trotsky* out of office in 1927 and out of the country in 1929 (he later had him killed). He eliminated lesser rivals by murder or *purge*, clearing the way for an unchallenged personal dictatorship. His policies were: *socialism in one country*, centralized *five-year plans*, and forced *collectivization*. In the process he called for "liquidation of the *kulaks* as a class," created a deliberate *famine* in Ukraine that consumed millions of lives, and launched the *Yezhovshchina* and other terrible purges. In his masterful study, "The Great Terror," Robert Conquest estimated the total number of Stalin's non-wartime victims at 20 million dead, a claim for which Conquest was roundly criticized in certain circles during the *Cold War*, for supposed gross exaggeration. In 1989 official Soviet figures placed the number of victims at closer to 40 million from 1929-53 (and poor Conquest was criticized again, for underestimation!). In either case, the numbers make Stalin the greatest mass murderer in human history, surpassing even *Hitler's* staggering body count (only *Mao's* figures may yet rival, depending on what China's closed *archives* one day reveal). In foreign relations, Stalin first followed a policy of *isolationism*, but then sought to form a front with the U.S. against Japan after 1931. He did not achieve that goal, but did *normalize relations* in 1934. That same year he took the Soviet Union into the *League of Nations*. He also tried to form a front against Hitler, but *Neville Chamberlain* would have none of it. So after *Munich* Stalin moved to negotiate a separate *spheres of influence* deal with Germany. The *Nazi/Soviet Pact* divided Eastern Europe between the two great tyrants, with Stalin attacking Poland on September 17th, by prior agreement with Hitler. He then attacked Finland, without Hitler's agreement, on November 30th. In 1940 he fulfilled the terms of the pact by annexing the *Baltic States* and parts of Rumania. He ignored warnings about *Barbarossa* from the West, and from his own *intelligence* and *front line* troops. He was stunned by the fact and the fury of the German onslaught. With *Lend-Lease*, and his own factories behind the Urals, he recovered and directed the Soviet *counterattack* and drive to *victory* in *WWII*. To do so, he compromised most revolutionary principles to the expedient needs of the moment, reintroducing *military ranks*, opening the doors of the churches and appealing to Russian *nationalism* as a more powerful motivator than communist *internationalism*. He negotiated at *Tehran, Yalta* and *Potsdam*--probably in bad faith--with enormous consequence for the course of the *Cold War*. Just as he had immediately before WWII, right after it he abandoned his earlier caution and pursued an opportunistically aggressive foreign policy. From 1944-49 he set up *puppet regimes* throughout Eastern Europe, and launched the Soviet *nuclear weapons* program. But he then grew cautious again, refusing to be drawn directly into the *Korean Conflict* even while backing and supplying North Korean *aggression*. He was for decades the center of a grotesque *personality cult*, and by all accounts, an utter paranoid constantly planning *purges* to forestall plots, real or imagined. For this he was belatedly denounced by *Khrushchev*. Yet despite all the terror and bloodshed, to this day he retains a following among old and true believers in the army and former communist party, and has not received from all historians the full moral disapprobation his life and acts certainly deserve. Attributed remarks: "You cannot make a *revolution* with silk gloves." "One death is a tragedy, a million deaths is a statistic." See also *Alexander I; Stalingrad; stalinism; stalinization; de-stalinization.*

Stalingrad, Battle of (September 5, 1942-January 31, 1943): Germans and Russians both chose to emphasize the symbolic importance of this city, named for the great tyrant who had fought there during the *Russian Civil War*, but in 1942 brooding in Moscow. (It had been called Tsaritsyn, and was subsequently renamed Volgograd.) Neither side gave *quarter* in this battle of bloody and unmerciful *attrition* that raged around, through and over the city, scattering its population like so many disturbed ants. Much of the fighting was hand-to-hand. As the tide slowly turned in favor of the Soviets, the German Sixth Army under General Freidrich von Paulus (1890-1957) asked *Hitler* for permission to retreat, but was ordered to take "not one step back." *Göring* boasted that the *Luftwaffe* could resupply von Paulus, but it failed miserably, and the Sixth Army was encircled and slaughtered. Only 90,000 frozen survivors heard von Paulus disobey direct orders and *surrender* (the night before, Hitler had made von Paulus a Field Marshal, knowing no officer of such high rank had surrendered in German military history--in short, hoping he would commit suicide). Von Paulus was released from a Soviet prison in 1953, and spent his last years as a lecturer to the East German military. Most other German prisoners were not so lucky: after years of imprisonment and *forced labor*, nine out of ten never returned to Germany. In 1992 it was revealed that Soviet casualties were far higher than earlier believed, at a staggering 1.3 million. Still, Stalingrad was one of several great turning points in *WWII*: for the first time, German soldiers had tasted *defeat* on the *eastern front*. After Stalingrad, a worm began to burrow in the mind of the German *nation* that it could, after all, lose the war.

stalinism: Of or like the political style and system of *Joseph Stalin*: rigid, absolute control from the top; centralization of all *decision-making* and *collectivization* of the economy; political paranoia, accompanied by *purging* and *liquidation* of perceived enemies; strenuous efforts at thought control; a doctrinaire ideology that yet shifts with tactical needs; crushing all internal party and bureaucratic resistance with a hammer of textual manipulation, on an anvil of orthodoxy; and all supported by a pervasive *cult of personality*.

stalinization: Forcible conversion of a social and political order to make it conform to the principles and practices of *stalinism*. Cf. *de-stalinization.*

standard: A *norm* that may be adopted as a binding *rule* into a *treaty*. For example, a treaty that agrees to use *jus soli* as the basis for *naturalization*.

standard deviation: The degree to which individual values vary from the mean, established by taking a measure of a spread of values around an arithmetic average. See *quantitative analysis.*

standard of living: An *indicator* of social and economic *development* that attempts a statistical representation of the grade of material wealth, and comfort and concomitant well-being, enjoyed by individuals, classes or whole societies. It is a complex, composite measure of the availability of *consumer goods* and *public goods*, individual *purchasing power* and access to social resources such as education and employment.

standard operating procedure (SOP): The pattern of routine implementation by which a bureaucracy carries out decisions made at a higher level. Its implication for foreign policy is that SOPs may skewer decisions in ways unforeseen by policy makers, especially when routine procedures are applied in crises.

standards of civilized behavior: Moral standards from which a *derogation* may be asserted only if a fair claim is substantiated that the requirements of war-making warrant such a waiver. This is a main pole of tension in *just war theory*; the other is *necessities of war.*

standing army: The professional army of a nation, not including *reserves* or potential *conscripts*.

stare decisis: "Standing for things already settled." The general rule that courts should apply prior legal *judgments* (precedent) in cases of a similar nature. In *international law*, this is very weakly applied.

START I/II: See *Strategic Arms Reduction Treaties*.

Star Wars: See *Strategic Defense Initiative*.

STASI: The *secret police* as well as main *intelligence agency* of *East Germany*. It also had a *counterespionage* function. Its massive *archive* of files destroyed lives and careers even after 1989, as they revealed who had *collaborated,* or informed on family, friends, workmates, even spouses. In its heyday it had 100,000 full-time employees, its files covered half the population and it used one citizen in seven as informers. Its headquarters was stormed by an angry crowd after the *Berlin Wall* fell. Public release of some files caused a moral and political dilemma after reunification, as so many former East Germans were implicated. Cf. *HvA*.

state: (1) An organized political entity that occupies a definite *territory*, has a permanent *population*, and enjoys stable government, *independence* and *sovereignty*. (2) A synonym for government or *regime*. States have dominated world affairs for 500 years. They have together divided the continents and regulated the seas, skies, space and all of teeming humanity (as well as ownership and/or stewardship of other species). They have made themselves the sole entities with a legal right to wage *war*--although if one wages illegal war successfully and secures a territory, one may become a state. Even then, to gain all the rights of statehood one must win *recognition* by other states. At present there are some 190 recognized states in the *international system*, ranging from the perhaps absurdly small (8,000 people), to the possibly unmanageably large (1.2 billion). See *associated state; city-state; colony; dependency; empire; extinction; microstate; nation; nation-state; occupation; protectorate; quasi state; self-determination; state creation; state obligations; state succession; world community*.

state capitalism: (1) A version of *capitalist* development with a high degree of government ownership of the nation's *factor endowments*, and centralized direction and regulation of *capital* and *labor* markets. (2) A fashionable, but inaccurate, dismissal of the *marxist* origins of the *Soviet* system, by those who still wish to avoid the intellectual discomfort that would be occasioned by an attempt to reconcile Russia's dingy

historical experience with *Marx's* sparkling theoretical elegance. Cf. *dirigisme*.

statecraft: The art of conducting the public affairs of a *state*. Specific to *international relations*, it is a near synonym for *diplomacy*, but more clearly implies the direction of domestic policy and *war* as components of foreign policy, as well as peaceful *negotiation*.

state creation: The process of founding new *states* from the dissolution of *empires*, via *secession*, or through the *extinction* of previous *international personalities*. Cf. *successor states*.

State Department: See *Department of State*.

state funeral: A funeral for a *head of state* or *government*, or more rarely, another person of national importance or prominence. See *funerals*.

state immunity: From antiquity, *sovereigns* were regarded as immune from harm in their persons, if not their office, and treated as such by each other. In the Middle Ages in Europe, personal immunity was extended to *ambassadors* and then to state property, for the same, pragmatic reasons of avoiding *reprisals* and facilitating communication. It is now established tradition that diplomatic communications are inviolable in law (with the exception in practice of *espionage* against them), and that diplomatic ships cannot be boarded or *embassies* entered or searched. Also, *diplomats* and embassies are free of taxation, may not be sued and are not subject to civil or criminal prosecution. Efforts have been made to restrict this right, yet it is still widely regarded as absolute. Still, administrative restrictions have grown more common during recent years. In general, a distinction has been drawn between activities related to diplomatic functions, and the private activities of diplomats. One example: In 1993 the U.S. began using administrative sanctions and penalties to limit the abuse of immunity from civil fines by which many diplomatic missions obstructed traffic and parking in New York and Washington. See also *persona non grata; Vienna Conventions*.

state interest: Anything declared by a given *state* to be of foreign policy concern to it. See *vital interests*.

stateless person: An individual without *citizenship* in any *state*. International *human rights* law now declares against statelessness. However, this condition of legal limbo still affects many *refugees*. Cf. *citizenship*.

state obligations: As *sovereign* members of the *world community*, *states* have legal obligations toward, as well as rights against, other members of the community. They must abstain from illegal *intervention* and *subversion*. They are required not to pose a threat to international *peace* and good order, to abjure the use of *force* as a means of settling *disputes*, and in general to conduct their affairs in *good faith* and in accordance with the accepted principles and *rules of international law*. When judged to have injured an *alien*, they must accept to pay *damages*. If members of the *UN* (as all but a few small states are), they have additional duties under the *Charter of the UN*: they must advance the aims declared in the Charter, including *nonintervention, noninterference,* and (paradoxically) respect by all for fundamental *human rights;* they must not aid any state targeted by the UN for *sanctions* or other penalty or enforcement mechanism; and they must refuse to *recognize* any *territorial* acquisition obtained through *aggression* (such as Iraq's annexation of Kuwait). Other, quite extensive duties may be voluntarily incurred through *consent* to *treaties.*

state of emergency: A suspension of normal legal rights and privileges in the interest (or just the name) of *national security* and restoration of order. Such decrees may accompany *insurrections*, as in Sri Lanka in the 1980s; serve to repress dissent, as in the Philippines under Marcos or South Africa under *apartheid;* or be occasioned by natural disasters, to deter looting.

state of nature: A hypothetical condition posited by political theorists, as a means of illustrating arguments about the origins and nature of social and political formations prior to the invention of governments or structured social relations. It presumes perfect freedom for the individual (in *Rousseau's* famous depiction, "Man is born free, yet everywhere we find him in chains"). Optimists about human nature, such as Rousseau, tend to view the subsequent construction of social and political order as necessary but also as suffocating natural freedoms, and they seek ways of lightening the heavy hand of the *state* on human affairs. For these thinkers the state is the main obstacle to recovering human freedom and happiness, and for the most *radical* it is an unnecessary evil. Pessimists, such as *Hobbes*, call the state of perfect human freedom by another name: *anarchy*. In the Hobbesian view, life in the state of nature is "solitary, poor, nasty, brutish and short." The construction of the state and social relations, however crippling of personal freedoms, is the only means to a modicum of personal and social security. Government is an evil entirely necessary if one is to escape the greater dangers of unadulterated liberty.

state of war: (1) An actual condition of *armed hostilities* between or among *nations*, with or without for-

mal *declarations of war.* (2) A legal condition of armed hostility, engaging the *laws of war* and begun and ended by formal, legal acts.

statesman/stateswoman: (1) In polite company: any person responsible for the conduct of *diplomacy,* or other public affairs, at the highest levels of *decision-making* and political responsibility. (2) In the judgment of *history*: a person who conducts diplomacy or other public affairs wisely.

states' rights: All rights not vested by the U.S. Constitution in the federal government, or forbidden by it to the separate states. This was the rallying cry of those favoring *secession* and formation of the *Confederacy*. Later, it was a rallying cry for *isolationists* and southerners, who used states' rights to defend segregation and raise objections to ratification of UN covenants on *human rights*.

state succession: In *international law*, the doctrine that a *state* following another on the same *territory* or part thereof, inherits all or some duties and *treaty* obligations of the state that has suffered *extinction*; this includes the set of *rules* and procedures used to bring succession to pass. Generally, state succession occurs via mutual agreement (*decolonization*), violent seizure of *independence* by a *dependent* territory from a controlling (colonial or imperial) power, *annexation* or *cession* of territory by agreement between controlling powers, formation of a *union* or *conquest* and *subjugation*. (1) Universal: when one state absorbs completely the *international personality* of another by conquest, merger or *federation*, the rights and obligations of the prior state totally end. (2) Partial: This is more complex. While public property passes without *compensation*, private property rights are unaffected. Foreign *debts* can cause trouble, with *successor states* often reluctant to assume old burdens. Bilateral treaties remain in effect only by agreement of the new power, but *servitudes* are not generally affected.

state terrorism: (1) When a state provides logistical or other support to terrorists to further certain foreign policy goals. Western nations have designated certain states as purveyors of *terrorism* (among them, Iran, Iraq, Libya, Syria and Yemen), and have on occasion applied bilateral *sanctions*. In 1993 the UN applied mandatory sanctions against Libya for its refusal to *extradite* two suspects in the bombing of a Pan Am plane over Lockerbie, Scotland, which killed hundreds. (2) The use of repressive police power within a state, or when, as in the practice of *ethnic cleansing*, it directly seeks to intimidate a *civilian* population for political purposes.

station: An *intelligence* unit, usually set up in a foreign trade mission, *embassy* or some other legal cover, that "runs" *legal* and/or *illegal agents*.

status mixtus: A condition of muted hostility and conflict existing somewhere in the twilight zone between real *peace* and open *warfare*. This notion is not yet an accepted part of *international law*. Cf. *inter bellum et pacem; quarantine; reprisal*.

status quo ante bellum: Conditions before a *war*.

status quo post bellum: Conditions after a *war*.

status quo power: Any *state* that seeks to preserve the political and *territorial integrity* of a *peace* settlement or established *balance of power*. The antonym is *revisionist power*.

stealth bomber: Popular name for the *B-2* Strategic Bomber.

stealth fighter: Popular name for the *F-117A*, and sister craft, first used in combat in Panama in 1988, and much more extensively during the *Gulf War*.

stealth technology: A crude version was first developed by Germany in *WWII* to conceal the conning towers of *U-boats*. Another early form was used in the American *U-2* spy planes. Modern stealth technology was first seen in public in the late 1980s. It makes aircraft virtually undetectable with new materials and unusual angular designs. In designer *jargon*, stealth aircraft have "low observables" in their contrails, infrared, noise, optical visibility, radar and smoke.

Stern Gang: Founded in 1939 by radical *zionists*, it employed terror tactics against the British in *Palestine*, and against the *civilian*, Arab population. Some members later merged into the Israeli Defense Force; those who showed themselves incapable of adjusting to *peace* were repressed. Cf. *Count Folke Bernadotte; Yitzhak Shamir*.

Stimson, Henry L. (1867-1950): U.S. statesman. Secretary of War 1911-13, 1940-45; Governor of the Philippines 1927-29; Secretary of State 1929-33. In 1927 he mediated an uneasy *peace* in Nicaragua (the Tiptitapa Agreement). He tried to alert *Hoover* and others to the rising danger of Japanese *aggression*, but due to the opposition and influence of *isolationists* was unable to elicit more than the rhetorical commitment of the *Hoover/Stimson Doctrine* to the "*territorial integrity*" of China." He attended the *London Naval Disarmament Conference*. In 1939-40 he strongly backed

Franklin Roosevelt's preparedness measures and supported *Lend-Lease*. Although he had previously served three *Republican* Presidents, he was appointed Secretary of War by FDR. During *WWII* he supported most administration policies, including the decisions to bomb *Hiroshima* and *Nagasaki*. He also served *Harry Truman* briefly in 1945.

Stimson Doctrine: See *Hoover/Stimson Doctrine*.

stock: Ownership of a corporation or other enterprise, normally divided into shares represented by certificates (stocks) that may be bought and sold on the *stock exchange*.

stock exchange/market: An organized and regulated marketplace where *capital* may be raised for a variety of purposes, by the exchange of *stocks* and securities. The major stock markets are located in Frankfurt, Hong Kong, London, New York, Paris and Tokyo. Others of rising importance are in Beijing and Seoul, and still others exist among the numerous financial centers in nearly every country that is already a *market economy*, or moving in that direction.

stock market crash: See *Black Tuesday*.

STOL (Short Take-Off and Landing): A genus of military aircraft designed to operate without full-length airfields. They were used effectively by Britain during the *Falklands War*.

Stolypin, Peter (1862-1911): Russian statesman. Minister of the Interior 1906; PM 1906-11. Paradoxically, a moderate reformer who savagely repressed peasant unrest in the wake of the *Russian Revolution (1905)*. His reforms opened the way for entrepeneurial peasants (the *kulak* class), but he was also a vicious *anti-Semite* who encouraged a new wave of *pogroms*. He would not agree to U.S. concerns about treatment of Jews. That led by 1912 to abrogation of a 72-year-old *commercial treaty* and the nadir of relations between the U.S. and *tsarist Russia*. He was assassinated.

stormtroopers: The *SA (Sturmabteilung)*, or any private *militia* or gang of political street thugs comparable in its character and makeup to the SA. See also *Freikorps; SS*. Cf. *death squads*.

straight baseline: Since *UNCLOS I* (1958), an increasing number of *states* have taken advantage of a variation on the *baseline* method of determining the *territorial sea* that was first designed to accommodate the peculiarities of Norway's deep coastal indentations (the fjords). Instead of hugging the shoreline, the straight baseline method permits states to determine the outer limit of their territorial waters from a straight line drawn across the outer points of land, following the overall contour of the shore. This has the effect of marginally increasing the area of the *high seas* claimed as home waters for highly irregular coastlines. However, it greatly increases the territorial sea when applied to more normal coastlines (for instance, in the claims made by Canada off its *Arctic* shore).

strait: A natural passage that links two seas or oceans; not a canal.

Strait of Hormuz: A narrow *strait* connecting the *Persian Gulf* and the Gulf of Oman. Three small islands there were seized by Iran in 1971. In 1980 Iraq attacked to regain these islands, beginning the *Iran/Iraq War.* Any effective *blockade* of the strait would shut down tanker traffic from the *Gulf States,* as well as from southern Iraq and Iran.

Straits Question: The dispute between the *Great Powers* over passage of *warships* through the *Dardanelles* and *Bosphorus.* Throughout the 19th century the *tsars* sought to compel the *Ottoman Empire* to close the straits to all warships save Russian. Meanwhile, the British wanted to keep the straits closed to the Russian *Black Sea Fleet,* bottling it into its home waters. In 1833 Russia signed a secret *treaty* with Turkey (Treaty of Unkiar Skelessi) granting it all it had ever sought. This was changed by the Straits Convention of 1841 (Austria, Britain, France, Prussia and Russia) and the *Treaty of Paris (1856),* which together closed the straits to all warships when Turkey was at *peace.* This arrangement too was amended, in 1871 and again at the *Congress of Berlin* in 1878, to take account of Russia's decision to remilitarize the Black Sea (it had been *demilitarized* after the *Crimean War*). The changes permitted transit to all navies if the sultan appeared unable to act alone to defend the status of the narrows. The straits were closed by Turkey (with the support of Russia) to Britain in 1885, and to Russia (with British help) during the *Russo/Japanese War.* After *WWI,* which shattered Ottoman power, the *Treaty of Lausanne* demilitarized the straits. But it allowed free passage of all warships when Turkey was at peace, provided any force sent north was not larger than the (then Soviet) Black Sea Fleet. The *Montreux Convention* of 1936 was even more advantageous to the Soviet Union, reflecting its status as an emerging *superpower.* During the *Cold War* Soviet traffic through the straits was monitored by *NATO.* See map.

stratagem: Any artifice, plan, scheme or ruse designed to surprise or deceive an enemy or opponent.

strategic: (1) Considerations: Anything related to a nation's overall *power,* whether economic, military or political. (2) Plans: Those concerning the ability to strike an enemy at the sources of its military or political power, and relating to the game of ruse and discovery of military *stratagem.* Cf. *tactical.*

Strategic Air Command (SAC): The command structure within the U.S. Air Force responsible for *strategic* (including nuclear-armed) *bombers* and *ICBMs.*

Strategic Arms Limitation Talks/Treaty (SALT): Two sets of nuclear *arms control* agreements during the *Cold War,* spanning a decade of negotiation: (1) SALT I: Talks between the U.S. and the Soviet Union were held from 1969-72, aiming at heading off a full-scale *arms race* in defensive weapons systems, expansion of the *Partial Test Ban Treaty* and placing limits on offensive *strategic nuclear weapons.* An *Anti-Ballistic Missile (ABM), Missile Treaty* was agreed, and agreement was reached limiting the number of *launchers* each side could deploy. However, setting the limit above extant levels and not including a ban on *MIRVs* undercut the entire agreement, by encouraging a build-up to the permitted limits and leaving each launcher far more threatening than in pre-MIRV days. (2) SALT II: Talks were held from 1973-79. They focused on solving the MIRV problem and placing a permanent cap on strategic weapons. A second *treaty* was signed, but ran into opposition within the U.S. Senate even before the Soviets invaded Afghanistan. With that event, *Jimmy Carter* withdrew from Senate consideration a treaty he knew had no chance of passing. Even without formal acceptance, both sides observed most of the provisions of the agreement through the 1980s, until the changing dynamic of U.S./Soviet relations made a *START* agreement possible.

Strategic Arms Reduction Treaties (START): Agreements to reduce, not just limit, the nuclear arsenals of the U.S. and Soviet Union (succeeded in December 1991 by Russia, Ukraine, Belarus and Kazakhstan). (1) START I: negotiations began in 1982 toward major cuts in *nuclear weapons* arsenals. The *treaty* did make reductions, but was overtaken by events even as implementation began in the early 1990s. Both sides announced unilateral cuts to their arsenals that meant START I needed an overhaul, fast. Ukraine was the only former Soviet republic not to have *ratified* START I by mid-1994. The treaty is to be reviewed in 1995. (2) START II: It was signed by *Bush* and *Yeltsin* in January 1993. In combination with START I, it committed the U.S. and Russia to a reduction of stocks of strategic nuclear *warheads* from roughly 22,000 each to 3,500 each by 2003. That gave Russia formal, nuclear equality with the U.S. despite the fact it would have had to reduce anyway, given its grave economic distress. Yeltsin indicated that if Ukraine failed to ratify START I, Russia would not be bound by either START treaty. Ukraine repeatedly promised to ratify, but held off to extract funding and other concessions from the U.S. That threatened U.S. *adherence* to START II as well, as the U.S. position was premised on Russia eventually becoming the sole nuclear successor to the defunct Soviet Union.

Strategic Defense Initiative (SDI): "Star Wars." An extremely ambitious *ballistic missile defense* (BMD) research program announced by *Ronald Reagan* in 1983. It originally sought a total defense against *strategic nuclear weapons* and *missile* systems. It called for a complex, integrated structure of non-nuclear, land, air and space-based defensive systems, most of which were yet untested, designed or developed. SDI proposed to intercept missiles and *warheads* at all four stages of their flight-path: boost, post-boost, mid-course and terminal. At each stage, enemy weapons that "leaked" through the previous stage would be further "attrited." In this version, SDI was widely criticized as unrealistic, even unscientific, and as destabilizing of *MAD.* (One of the more curious features of the policy debate was how some longtime critics of *deterrence* suddenly found MAD a virtuous doctrine, when faced with the prospect of SDI.) Some SDI proponents responded by reducing the promised scope to a defense of the U.S. nuclear deterrent force, arguing that would reinforce MAD. Others went beyond the original conception, to one made nuclear with the addition of space-based, *charged particle beam* weapons (with beams to be generated by channeling the explosion of a *hydrogen bomb*). Research continued at a decreasing levels of funding for 10 years. In May 1993, the *Clinton* administration scaled SDI back to a limited, strictly ground-based and non-nuclear BMD program. Among other countries, in the 1990s Japan began researching BMD. See also *Edward Teller.*

strategic doctrine: The complex of fundamental military and geopolitical assumptions and *targeting doctrine* that make up a country's war-fighting strategy.

strategic materials: Food stuffs, minerals for making high-tech alloys, *oil* and all other items necessary to run a modern *war* or *economy*. See also *strategic stockpiles.*

strategic nuclear parity: *Essential equivalence* in the *nuclear weapons* systems of the Soviet Union (now Russia) and the United States, as measured in *launchers, warheads* or *megatonnage.*

strategic nuclear response: The launch of *strategic nuclear weapons*, in response to an enemy *first strike*. A synonym for *retaliation.* See *second strike.*

strategic nuclear weapons: *ICBMs* capable of striking targets on a different continent, whose launch would signal Armageddon. The line between *strategic* and *tactical* is blurring, as once short-range weapons systems increase in strike ability.

strategic stockpiles: Reserves of *strategic materials*, considered vital for national economic or military performance in case of *war* or *boycott.*

strategic triad: The three launch modes of *nuclear weapons*: land-based, ship or *submarine*-based *ICBMs*, and *bombers.* Having all three reinforces *deterrence.*

strategic weapons: Long range weapons that permit one to strike an enemy at its main sources of military and/or political power; e.g., a *blue water navy, ICBMs, submarines* or long range *bombers* like the *B-2.*

strategy: (1) Any grand plan designed to obtain an ultimate military or political goal, as in "it was *Bismark's* strategy to keep Germany preeminent by diplomatically isolating France;" or "the U.S. and its allies adopted an island-hopping strategy in the Pacific war." (2) Strategy in its fullest sense refers to the art and science of best using the largest scale *capabilities* of a nation to secure its defense, advance its *foreign policy* goals, or win its *wars*. This involves a great deal of planning over a long period, and the full resources of *diplomacy.* Cf. *geostrategic; tactics.*

Stresa Front: At a conference held from April 11-14, 1935, Britain, France and Italy agreed to oppose *Hitler's* declared intent to rearm Germany. The front was gutted by the separate *Anglo-German Naval Agreement* and then by the *Abyssinian War* later that year. Never again would these former *WWI* allies stand together against Hitler.

Stresemann, Gustav (1878-1929): German statesman. Chancellor 1923; Foreign Minister 1923-29. He advocated meeting Germany's commitments under *Versailles*, achieving a reduction in *reparations*. He accepted the *Locarno Pact*, took Germany into the *League of Nations*, agreed to the *Dawes* and *Young Plans*, and was awarded the *Nobel Prize* for Peace in 1926 (with *Aristide Briand*). He was less accommodating concerning the German lands lost to Poland in 1919, but took no forceful action to recover them.

Stroessner, Alfredo (b.1912): General and dictator of

Paraguay 1954-89. He led a *coup* in 1954, took the presidency in a rigged election, and set up a strict, even brutal, regime. Backed by the army, he stayed in power by proclaiming anti-communism in domestic and foreign affairs. He governed on behalf of commercial and landowning interests, but carried out enough in the way of social programs to stave off outright revolt. However, by 1989 he lost his grip on Paraguay as a movement toward representative government swept across Latin America, and the U.S. placed greater overt emphasis on *human rights* in its *aid* policies.

structural adjustment loans: Money provided, usually by the *IBRD* or the *IMF,* to see a country through a period of basic economic reform (adjustment of the structure of its economy). Such loans are given in accordance with certain *macroeconomic* policies specified by the lender. See *stabilization program.*

structural determinism: When a theory concludes that the *structure* or *architecture* of a system is what solely decides the behavior of the *states* in the system, and thus dismisses *free will,* or *volition.*

structural realism: See *neo-realism.* Cf. realism.

structure: The shape of the *international system* as defined by the distribution of *power* among the *states.* Some theorists simply assume an underlying structure of *anarchy*; others use descriptions that focus on the number of major powers (*unipolar, bipolar, multipolar*); still others see the system as determined by class relations and an international division of labor.

struggle for power: A classical *realist* phrase, suggesting that no matter what the final ends states or other political *actors* aim at, the struggle to increase one's relative *power* is always the immediate aim. This thesis has sometimes been misconstrued as arguing that the struggle for power in politics among nations is an end in itself, and then roundly condemned as amoral or immoral. Yet the phrase does little more than state the truism that all political actors strive to increase their *influence,* so that they may better achieve ("maximize") their interests. What the medium of power is (money, *prestige,* votes or brute force) will depend on specific circumstances, just as what interests are advanced will depend on specific players, their values, constituencies, wit, wisdom or stupidity.

subcontinent: Bangladesh, Bhutan, India, Nepal, Pakistan, Sikkim and Sri Lanka.

subjects of international law: Any entity with *international personality* (but mainly the states).

subjugation: The complete military suppression of an enemy, entailing utter destruction of all *state* apparatus and *extinction* of the *international personality* of the *defeated* state, following suppression of all armed and civil resistance, at home and abroad. This goes further than *conquest,* which it must follow. Cf. *debellatio.*

Sublime Porte: The self-styled title of the government of the *Ottoman Empire,* taken from one of the gates leading into *Constantinople.*

submarine: A submersible ship capable of navigation and weapons firing underwater. The first primitive submarines were put into service by the *Confederacy* during the *American Civil War.* Widely viewed by naval strategists as a curiosity or a reconnaissance boat rather than a *strategic weapon,* their value was demonstrated (for those with eyes to see) during *WWI.* Neglected again between the wars, in *WWII* German submarines inflicted unprecedented damage on the *Allied* navies until they were beaten back by a combination of *convoys,* land-based *bombers* and the *aircraft carrier.* American submarines also took a heavy toll of Japanese shipping. During the *Cold War* nuclear powered and nuclear *missile*-bearing *submarines* emerged as the most powerful weapons ever constructed by the twisted genius of humanity. Each such ship represents a multi-billion dollar investment (they are the size of *battleships*), and each is capable of independent delivery of dozens of nuclear *warheads.* A single *boomer* thus contains more sheer destructive power than has been expended by all the armies, air forces and navies of all nations in the entire history of warfare. See also *Anglo/German Naval Agreement; Battle of the Atlantic; hunter-killer; Nine Power Treaty; London Naval Disarmament Conference; Trident; U-boats; unrestricted submarine warfare; wolf pack.*

submarine launched ballistic missile (SLBM): *ICBMs b*ased on and launched from *boomers.*

submission: A brief to an international court.

subnational forces: Cultural, economic and social groups or forces within existing national societies that threaten their political disintegration, or major reorganization on non-traditional lines. This is a topic of much contemporary research focus. Cf. *ethnic cleansing; ethnic group; nationalism; rising expectations; technology; tribe; self-determination; separatism.*

subrogation: The assumption of an *extinct* state's rights and duties by a *successor state.*

sub-Saharan Africa: Africa below the Sahara desert,

distinguished ethnically and culturally from the Arab and Berber nations to the north. This is the preferred form for what once was called "Black Africa."

subsidiary: A firm owned and controlled by another firm, often a foreign-based *multinational corporation.*

subsidies: (1) Payments made in support of domestic producers by a government that bring no *hard good* or *service* in return, but are made anyway for political (e.g., *protectionism*) or *strategic* (e.g., preserve defense industries) reasons. (2) Payments made by large states to smaller ones, to sustain a friendly regime in power or underwrite other foreign policy objectives. For example, massive Soviet subsidies to Cuba kept the *Castro* regime afloat; U.S. subsidies to Israel and Egypt facilitated the *Camp David Accords.*

substantiation: The formal *justification* offered for an international legal claim.

subversion: In law and in political perception, the effort by one *state* through *covert action, disinformation, propaganda,* or funding *guerrillas* or *terrorists,* to undermine, destabilize or promote *insurrection* or *treason* against another state or its government.

succession of states: See *state succession.*

successor states: *States* that emerge on *territory* where a prior *international personality* has suffered *extinction.* For example, the following arose in whole or part from the extinction of larger states: (1) *Austro-Hungarian Empire,* 1918-20: Austria, Czechoslovakia, Hungary, Poland, Rumania and Yugoslavia (and part of Italy). (2) *Soviet Union,* 1991: Armenia, Azerbaijan, Belarus (Byelorussia), Estonia, Georgia, Kazakhstan, Kirghizstan, Latvia, Lithuania, Moldova (Moldavia), Russia, Tajikistan, Turkmenistan, Ukraine, Uzbekistan and counting. (3) *Czechoslovakia,* 1992: Czech and Slovak Republics. (4) *Yugoslavia,* 1991-93: Bosnia-Herzegovina, Croatia, Macedonia, Serbia and Montenegro, Slovenia and counting. See also *capitulations; Ottoman Empire; state succession.*

sudan (Fr: *soudan*; Ar: *al-sudan*): That part of Africa lying south of the arid and drought-striken *Sahel,* but north of the tropical forests of Central Africa.

Sudan: Location: Central/East Africa (the largest country, by area, in Africa). Major associations: *Arab League, OAU, UN.* Population: 25 million. Military: *counterinsurgency* focus. Ancient Sudan was known as Nubia to the Egyptians, the land of the Queen of Sheba. For centuries it was heavily influenced by the *Coptic Church* and other Egyptian institutions. With most Egyptians converted to *Islam,* northern Sudanese followed. But the south remained defiantly Christian and/or animist, leading to a religious conflict at the center of Sudanese life. Sudan was conquered by Egypt 1820-22, and it was Egyptians who founded its modern capital, Khartoum. Sudan was then used to supply the Arab *slave trade.* It revolted under the *Mahdi* from 1883-98 inflicting a severe defeat on the British under *Gordon,* but the revolt was ultimately repressed by British forces. In 1898, Sudan was re-organized as an Anglo-Egyptian *condominium.* In 1951 Egypt abrogated the condominium agreement, and Sudan became independent in 1955. Almost immediately, it succumbed to *tribal* and religious conflict and fell into a state of chronic *civil war.* In 1958 a military dictatorship was set up by General Ibrahim Abboud (1900-83), who increased persecution of southerners. In 1969 another *coup* brought General Muhammad Jaafar el Nimeri (b.1930) to power. He imposed a harsh order by 1972, ending the civil war by granting southern *autonomy,* while introducing the *sharia* legal code in the north. In 1983 he extended Islamic law to the Christian south, provoking a renewal of the civil war. He was overthrown in 1985 in a bloodless *coup.* Elections were held in 1986, but in 1989 another coup brought a militantly *fundamentalist* regime to power in Khartoum. It adopted policies of forced conversion and even *genocide* (according to various human rights groups) that aggravated the horrors of civil war and *famine* that had begun in 1983. The regime declared *jihad* its foreign and domestic policy. In 1992-93 the military balance shifted in favor of the government. The SPLA alliance of southern Christians and animists split, opening up a three-way civil war. The government, under General Omar Bashir, insisted that sharia must be applied to all Sudanese, of whom only 70% are Muslim. This drew in the *Vatican,* which wanted Sudan's 3.5 million Christians exempted. Other than a few human rights NGOs, no one has spoken out for the five million animists. Sudan has been accused by both Egypt and the U.S. of fomenting *state terrorism,* notably that purveyed by the *Muslim Brotherhood.*

Sudetenland: The German (before 1945) area of western Bohemia, granted to *Czechoslovakia* in 1919. From 1933-38 local *Volksdeutche* lobbied for an *Anschluss.* Although it contained the main Czech defensive fortifications and lines, it was handed over to *Hitler* at *Munich* in 1938. After *WWII* it was returned to Czechoslovakia; 2.5m Germans were expelled, the innocent alongside the guilty. After 1989 the issue of compensation soured Czech/German relations.

Suez Canal: The great and vital canal across the Suez

isthmus that connects the Mediterranean and Red Seas. It is 107 miles long, and was built from 1859-69 by the controversial French engineer Ferdinand de Lesseps (1805-94). In 1875 Britain bought a controlling interest in the Suez Canal Co. In 1888 a *convention* was agreed by the *Great Powers* declaring the canal open to all even in wartime. In practice, Britain denied access to its enemies in wartime and on occasion to the enemies of its allies as well (such as the Russians, who were refused passage for their Baltic fleet on its way to the *Battle of Tsushima Straits* with Japan). Egypt denied access to Israel from 1948-67. In 1956 the canal was *nationalized* by *Nasser,* unilaterally ending a long *servitude* on Egypt but also thereby precipitating the *Suez Crisis.* The canal was blocked by sunken ships from the *Third Arab/Israeli War,* and opposite banks were held by the Egyptians and Israelis. It was dredged, mineswept and reopened after 1975 as part of the *Camp David Accords.* In 1980 it was widened and deepened to oblige modern ships.

Suez Crisis: President *Nasser* nationalized the Suez Canal Co. on July 26, 1956, to claim its revenues to build the *Aswan Dam,* for which he had been refused Western loans. It was learned in London and Paris that Israel, for reasons pertaining to the origins of the *Second Arab/Israeli War,* was planning to attack Egypt. On September 1st Israel was informed that France would welcome a joint attack. From October 22-24, at Sèvres, British, French and Israeli representatives met but could not agree on a joint plan. Instead, Israel attacked on its own, on October 29th. Two days later, Britain and France piggybacked their attack onto the Israeli thrust. There was a huge international outcry against the triple *invasion,* including fierce Soviet and U.S. opposition. *Eisenhower* was especially angry at the distraction of world attention from the *Hungarian Uprising.* The crisis became deadly serious when the Soviets threatened to use force to expel the invaders from its *client,* Egypt, and hinted at nuclear strikes on London and Paris: the Soviets were alternately hopeful that Suez would breakup *NATO* and fearful that Hungary would destroy the *Warsaw Pact.* Eisenhower decided that a Soviet move into Suez would have to be met by U.S. armed forces, and worried that the crisis was escalating toward a nuclear confrontation. He made it patently clear that the U.S. vehemently opposed the invasion, and insisted Britain and France accept a UN proposal for a *peacekeeping* force interposed in the Sinai. All three invading countries were thus forced/persuaded to cease operations within a week. The British and French withdrew in disgrace (both governments soon fell). Israel pulled back too, but kept the Sinai until 1957. It was the last time during the *Cold War* that either Britain or France tried to act as a *Great Power* in a globally *strategic* region without advance clearance from Washington.

sufficiency: An idea introduced into U.S. *strategic doctrine* by *Richard Nixon,* in which a *first-strike capability* was disavowed, and research, development and deployment aimed only at providing weapons sufficient to guarantee *deterrence.*

Suharto, Radan (b.1921): Indonesian statesman. President 1968- . He fought alongside the Japanese in *WWII,* and as a *guerrilla* leader against the return of Dutch rule from 1946-49. During the attempted *coup* by the *Partai Kommunis Indonesia* in 1965 he led the government forces that massacred as many as 600,000 suspected PKI members. He displaced *Sukarno* from power in early 1967, ending the *Konfrontasi* and formally assumed the title of President the next year. Under his leadership Indonesia moved to support the U.S. in the *Cold War,* while still maintaining an official stance of *nonalignment.* It also seized *East Timor,* where it has been accused by some of conducting a *genocide,* and has staked out its claim to the *Spratlys.* Domestically, Suharto has tolerated little opposition to his rough, *authoritarian* style of government.

Sukarno, Achmad (1901-70): Indonesian statesman. President 1949-68. He was imprisoned by the Dutch 1929-31 for his early political activity. He collaborated with the Japanese during *WWII,* but as the Japanese resistance to the *Allies* collapsed across Asia he unilaterally declared Indonesian *independence* (August 1945). In 1949, after four years of *guerrilla warfare,* the Dutch finally accepted him as first President of an independent Indonesia. He hosted the *Bandung Conference* in 1955, but never emerged as a key leader of the *Non-Aligned Movement.* As the economy declined from 1956-65, his *authoritarian* tendencies came to the fore. In 1963 he began the *Konfrontasi* that almost led to *war* with Malaysia. In 1965 he was pushed aside by General *Suharto,* who put down an uprising by the *Partai Kommunis Indonesia.* He lost real power in 1967 but retained the title of president for about a year after that.

sultan: (1) The *sovereign* of an *Islamic* nation such as Oman. (2) A traditional Islamic ruler, above an *emir,* such as the Sultan of Sokoto in Nigeria. (3) The ultimate title of rulers of Muslim *empires,* including the *Ottoman Empire* to 1918, and implying authority over all *Muslims.* It has not been claimed by any significant leader in that sense since the fall of the Ottomans.

sultanate: A *territory* ruled by a *sultan,* as a secular prince, religious authority, or both. Cf. *caliphate.*

Sumatra: A large island comprising an important province of modern Indonesia.

summary execution: Execution on the spot, after instant judgment, with no appeal permitted and often without formal legal proceedings of any kind, or at best following a drumhead court martial.

summary procedure: When by agreement of the *states* party to a case, resolution follows a simplified and abbreviated judicial process.

summit/summitry: Meetings and talks, sometimes including real *negotiations*, between or among those at the summit of political power in the nations concerned. This is largely a 20th-century development. In an age of high-tech communications and mass media it clearly has much to do with good public relations. The first U.S. president ever to leave the country while in office to personally conduct foreign affairs was *Woodrow Wilson*, and he was heavily criticized for going to the *Paris Peace Conference*. There were several critical wartime summits, namely *Casablanca, Tehran, Yalta* and *Potsdam*. During the 1950s and 1960s Soviet/U.S. summits were rare and rarely successful. But after *Richard Nixon* held several important summits with Chinese and Soviet leaders, summitry was taken by the media and public as a sign of positive relations and seen as a critical mechanism for ending the *Cold War*. Subsequently, presidents were sharply criticized if they did not arrange summits with Soviet counterparts. The U.S. press still tends to use the term mainly about top-level American/Russian or *G-7* meetings. Yet any formal meeting of any top national leaders qualifies as a summit. Cf. *funerals*.

Sunda (Soenda) Islands: An important group of large islands in the Malay archipelago, including Borneo, Java, Celebes, Sumatra and Timor.

sunni **Islam:** The main body of *Islam*. It accepts the historical succession of *caliphs* and honors the Sunna, or Tradition (life example) of the Prophet. There are four streams of interpretation within sunni Islam, each reasonably tolerant of the others: (1) Hanafi, officially sanctioned by the *Ottoman Empire* and dominant in Central Asia, India, Iraq, Syria and Turkey; (2) Maliki, predominant in North and West Africa and Sudan; (3) Shafii, spread through Arabia, East Africa, Egypt and SE Asia; (4) and Hanbali, the official doctrine of the Saudis. Cf. *Ismaili; shi'ia Islam.*

Sun Yat-sen, a.k.a. Sun Yixian (1866-1925): Chinese revolutionary. Through *propaganda* work and political organizing, he brought together most of the factions opposing the *Manchus* by proclaiming three principles for the *revolution: democracy, nationalism* and *socialism*. He founded the *Guomindang* as a broad-based nationalist movement. He returned to China from the U.S. when the 1911 *Chinese Revolution* broke out, and briefly became nominal President in 1913. In the 1920s he made approaches to the Chinese *communists* and set up ties to the *Soviet Union*, trying as always to build national unity and avoid *civil war*. His death left China without a unifying figure, and it soon fell into the internecine carnage he so feared.

Super 301 Procedures: Deriving from a 1988 Omnibus Trade and Competitiveness Act, this is a *protectionist* mechanism that permits U.S. trade officials to unilaterally identify as "priority countries" states deemed to be trading "unfairly." They may then force trade negotiations or impose high *tariffs* after three years. Most U.S. trading partners regard the 301 law as a violation of *GATT*.

superior orders: The claim "I was just following orders" issued by a superior *officer*, made to mitigate one's responsibility for *war crimes*. This defense was rejected at the *Nuremberg* and *Tokyo war crimes trials*, and does not find favor within most systems of moral reasoning. However, it is as old as soldiering: "We know enough if we know we are the King's men. Our obedience to the King wipes the crime of it out of us." [Shakespeare, "Henry V," Act 4, Scene I].

supernational: Movements or ideas that span national loyalties and divisions by appeal to some arguably higher, or at least wider community. For example, *communism; liberal-internationalism; pan-Africanism; pan-Arabism; pan-Slavism.* Cf. *supranational.*

superpowers: A term concocted during the *Cold War* to distinguish the *Soviet Union* and the *United States* from even the other *Great Powers*. The term was mostly intuitive, speaking to the global reach and declared interests of those two *states*, and no clear definition ever developed. The one sometimes offered --that the superpowers were those states with a *second-strike capability*--failed to account for the fact that once Britain and France acquired *submarine*-based nuclear systems they too had such an ability. Since the collapse of the Soviet Union there has developed a regrettable pattern of abuse of this term, as in "Nigeria is a West African superpower," or "Japan and Germany have joined the ranks of the superpowers." What is really meant is that Nigeria is a major *regional power* and that Japan and Germany have rejoined the ranks of the Great Powers. Cf. *hegemon; hegemonic stability; preponderant power; primus inter pares.*

supply: The availability of *goods* and *services* in a given economy. Demand is the appetite for consumption of these goods and services. See *elasticity*.

supply lines: The air routes, roads, rails and other means of transport to the rear of an army, along which it must bring ammunition, food, fuel and medical supplies, and send back its wounded and perhaps its dead. A principal *tactic*, if it can be accomplished, is to cut the enemy's lines of supply in order to hamper, slow or with luck, even stop military operations.

supply-side economics: A qualified return to *laissez-faire* notions, as compared with *keynesian economics*. Where *Keynes* suggested governments attempt to manage demand, "supply siders" argue for greater attention to *supply*. They say *deficit spending* to satisfy demand has caused gross distortions in national economies. Their preferred means of managing supply is to stimulate production by cutting taxes that keynesians, it is charged, have raised too high on the path to social redistribution of demand (consumption). Supply-side economics came into vogue in the 1970s, and reflected a rising concern with that decade's runaway *inflation*, rather than with unemployment. It was partly implemented by the *Reagan* administration in the early 1980s, along with policies of *monetarism*.

supranational: Organizations or processes that are in some sense "above" the individual state, by virtue of networks of *functional* connectons. For instance, some facets of the *EU*. See *integration*. Cf. *supernational*.

Supreme Allied Commander in Europe (SACEUR): The commander-in-chief of *NATO*. Throughout the *Cold War* this position was always held by an American (*Eisenhower* was the first). The command now rotates among the major *allies*.

Supreme Command of Allied Power (SCAP): A coordinating committee headed by *Douglas MacArthur* in post-*WWII* Japan. It *repatriated* and *demobilized* Japanese troops who had surrendered all over the Pacific *theater*, as well as Japanese civilians. It oversaw the dismantling of Japan's war industries, conducted the *Tokyo war crimes trials* and drafted and set up the country's new constitution.

Supreme Headquarters of Allied Forces in Europe (SHAPE): *NATO's* theater headquarters, in Belgium.

Supreme Soviet: The bicameral (Soviet of the Union/Soviet of Nationalities) legislature of the Soviet Union. It was a rubber-stamp body for decisions made in the *Politburo* by the Central Commitee of the Party.

Sûreté: The French security and foreign *espionage* service. In addition to political and security *intelligence* gathering, it was among the first services to turn to *economic espionage*. Long before the *Cold War* was over, it was already spying on corporations in the U.S. and other allied countries, and handing such technological and other trade information to French companies and state corporations.

surface-to-air: Weapons fired by ground units or surface ships, against aircraft or other *missiles*.

surface-to-surface: Weapons fired by ground units or surface ships against ground targets or surface ships.

surface-to-underwater: An anti-*submarine* weapon, whether a *missile* or torpedo, fired from a surface ship to dive and seek its submerged target.

surgical strike: (1) Conventional: The idea that targets can be removed (destroyed) without *collateral damage*. (2) Nuclear: Attempting to use precise and low-yield *nuclear weapons* for *counterforce* attacks.

Suriname: Location: S. America. Major associations: *OAS, UN*. Population: 420,000. Military: minimal; connections to Holland. Formerly Dutch Guiana. The Netherlands acquired this *colony* in 1667 from England in a trade for New Amsterdam (New York). It was run as a giant plantation, using African *slave labor*. Once the slaves were freed, indentured wage laborers were brought in from the *Dutch East Indies* (Java) and from India. Time and human nature gave Dutch Guiana a distinctive Creole population. In 1954 the colony was incorporated directly into the Netherlands in a constitutional *union*. The minority Indian population opposed *independence* out of fear for their civil rights, and many migrated to Holland before the area was given outright independence, as Suriname, in 1975. In 1980 a military *coup* ended *democracy*. After years of economic decline, political instability and low-level *insurgency*, elections were held in late 1987. Suriname has an ongoing *border* dispute with Guyana, which has harbored Surinamese *guerrillas*.

surplus value: In *marxism*, the difference between wages and the value of the *good* that a worker produces. This is supposed to reflect the sole source of *profit* to a *capitalist*, who "expropriates" the "surplus value" of the workers. This idea ignores other factors besides *labor* that go into production, such as *capital*, management, risk and interest.

surrender: (1) In the field: yielding to a superior military force, in the expectation that *quarter* will be given, and of becoming a *prisoner of war*. (2) Between states: submission to demonstrated, superior, military force, and thereby conceding one's case in the *dispute(s)* that were considered *casus belli* to decision by the dictates of an opponent. It may also mean agreeing to legal limitations on one's subsequent claims or action that go beyond the original points at issue (e.g., *cession* of *territory* or *reparations*). Cf. *defeat; stalemate; unconditional surrender; victory*.

surveillance: In *intelligence,* keeping secret watch on the activities, contacts, mail and so forth of a foreign *agent, terrorist,* potential *defector* or other target.

suspension: (1) Of a *treaty*: placing a treaty in temporary abeyance, but not renouncing or abrogating it. (2) From an *international organization*: a rare punishment for egregious behavior by *states* (whose fellows are normally a most tolerant sort, having much to tolerate in themselves). In the UN, suspension requires a majority vote of the *UNGA* following a recommendation by the *Security Council*. The procedure has not been used. Cf. *expulsion; withdrawal*.

suspensive condition: In *international law*, a future event that if it occurs will have the effect of creating a legal right.

sustainable development: The idea that *appropriate technologies*, moderation of national consumption patterns, and bringing the rate of *exploitation* of *natural resources* into balance with their renewal, are essential measures for future economic development. It posits that practices common to *modernization* and *industrialization*, as they have evolved to date, cannot be sustained for much longer without destroying the resource and environmental base that supports them. This approach searches for equilibrium between exploitation and replenishment of renewable resources, and conservation of non-renewable resources. Cf. *environmental security; growth*.

sustainable growth: (1) A long-term rise in national per capita incomes. (2) In theories of the *stages of growth*, the stage that follows *takeoff.*

Suvorov, Alexander (1729-1800): Russian general. He was the leading soldier in Russia's several *wars* with the *Ottomans, Prussia* and *Sweden*. He also led *Catherine II's* troops in the *partitions of Poland*, and repressed a Polish *rebellion* in 1795. He had considerably less success against *Napoleon I*.

suzerain: The ruler of a semi-independent *state*; not a full *sovereign*. For instance, see *Mehemet Ali*.

Swaziland: Location: Southern Africa. Major associations: *Commonwealth, OAS, SADCC, UN*. Population: 6.8 million. Military: minimal. This traditional African kingdom has been ruled by the same dynasty for over 400 years, although the *territory* occupied shifted in 1820 when the Swazi were forced to migrate to their present lands by *Shaka Zulu* during the *Mfecane*. Swaziland was guaranteed independence by Britain and the *Boers* until the end of the *Second Boer War*, when it was made a British *protectorate*. It became fully *sovereign* in 1968. During the struggle against *apartheid* in South Africa, the large, powerful neighbor that nearly engulfs it, Swaziland allied itself rhetorically with the *front line states*. But out of sheer necessity it moderated its actual policy and continued close economic links with the racist republic. In 1973 its democratic constitution was rescinded. It is today governed according to its traditional, African kingship system, where a council of elders advises but cannot restrain a near-absolute *monarch*.

Sweden: Location: *Scandinavia*. Major associations: *CSCE, EFTA, Nordic Council, OECD, UN*. Population: 8.5 million. Military: first-rate equipment, troops and training; sizeable *reserves*. Sweden was an ancient Viking kingdom until it fell under Danish control in 1397. It revolted in 1523 and rose to become an important power by the mid-16th century. In the *Thirty Years' War* it championed the Protestant cause. During the 17th-18th centuries it numbered among the *Great Powers*, with an *empire* to rival Russia's. It launched a disastrous *invasion* of Russia in 1708, under *Charles XII*. After 1716 its power was spent and it began to lose its outlying possessions to the rising Great Powers of Prussia and Russia. In 1809 it was forced to cede Finland to Russia. It joined in the *War of the Fourth Coalition* but was not a major contributor to the defeat of *Napoleon I* and therefore made no great gains at the *Congress of Vienna*. In fact, it lost Pomerania to Prussia, although in exchange it received Norway from defeated Denmark. Under *Charles XIV,* and within the *Concert of Europe*, its ambitions were tamed. It grew content to be a *regional power*, isolated from armed conflict (it has not been at *war* since Napoleonic times) and enjoying its Nordic prosperity and security. It also evolved its Viking parliament into a modern democratic institution, and gave Norway *independence* in 1905. Sweden has always taken its *armed neutrality* seriously. It is a heavily armed country that maintains effective *deterrence* and is actively jealous of its *territorial* rights--it has regularly attacked intruders, such as Soviet *submarines* traversing its coastal waters. Its flexible, neutralist diplomacy has appeared to some as *appeasement*, as during *WWII* when it continued to supply *Nazi Germany* with iron ore. But others regard it as a model of how *neutrality* can be made to work when given steel teeth, and enacted as more than a policy of platitudes. To maintain its military independence it has become a significant *arms exporting nation*. Despite this, in the 1960s and 1970s it acquired a global reputation for supporting *disarmament*. Its *Social Democratic* party held power for over four decades after WWII. Many on the democratic left throughout Europe and North America looked to Sweden as a model of social engineering and a working welfare state, and it gained much *prestige* from this. In the late 1980s, however, Sweden too began to make cuts in social programs owing to mounting budget *deficits* and a building, citizen tax revolt. It was accepted to become a full member of *EU* on January 1, 1995.

Switzerland: Location: W. Europe. Major associations: *CSCE; UN (specialized agencies* only). Population: 6.8 million. Military: first-rate equipment, training, strategy and reserves. The region was organized as a loose association of independent cantons from the 15th-18th centuries, a time when Swiss *mercenaries* served in many foreign armies, including that of the popes. From 1798-1802 a French *puppet state* was in place. At the *Congress of Vienna* the *Great Powers* agreed to respect Swiss *neutrality*. Since then it has never been involved in a foreign *war*. One reason is that it practices *armed neutrality* by requiring all fit males between 18 and 55 to serve two years in the military, followed by one month active duty per year. As a result, within 48 hours Switzerland can put about 800,000 well-equipped and trained troops into the field. Of course, it also enjoys tremendous natural defenses on its frontiers: the Alps. The final *federation* of the country did not occur without conflict, however, including a brief *civil war* (the *Sonderbund*) in 1847. Its present constitution of self-governing cantons within a loose federation dates from 1848. Women were excluded from the national franchise until 1971, and in the 1980s one canton's male voters still refused women the vote in a local *referendum*. Switzerland has a tradition of support for cooperative international organizations, despite not belonging to the UN. It is home to the *Red Cross*, Geneva was the city of the *League of Nations*, and today Switzerland plays host to many UN agencies and commissions. It is also active within the *CSCE*. But the Swiss remain deeply and contentedly neutralist: they voted in national referenda (the Swiss hardly do anything without holding a plebiscite!) against joining the *EC* or the UN. And the work of the Red Cross notwithstanding, Switzerland is not a country overly fond of *refugees* or immigrants. It is a global banking and financial center, has one of world's top *hard currencies* and an enviably high *standard of living*. Its *citizenship* is one of the most sought after, and difficult to obtain.

Sykes/Picot Agreement (1916): A secret understanding between Mark Sykes (for Britain) and George Picot (of France) to *partition* most of the *Ottoman Empire* at the end of *WWI*. It undercut promises made to the *Arabs*, then fighting the Turks, and conflicted with *Woodrow Wilson's* championing of *self-determination*. It was among the secret *treaties* published by the *Bolsheviks* in 1918. It promised most of *Arabia, Iraq, Palestine* and *Transjordan* to Britain, while giving France parts of Asia Minor, as well as *Lebanon* and *Syria. See Arab Revolt; Lawrence (of Arabia).*

synthesis: (1) General: combining disparate analytical elements into a single whole. (2) In Hegelian method: a higher truth resulting from a clash of *thesis* and *antithesis* that becomes a new thesis. See *dialectic*.

Syria: Location: *Middle East*. Major associations: *Arab League, UN*. Population: 12.5 million. Military: although the armed forces are relatively large, their aging Soviet equipment needs replacing or upgrading. Civilization in what is today the Syrian Arab Republic dates back even before the Seleucid Empire, which predated the Roman. The Romans were followed by the great Arab *caliphates*, and then centuries of struggle between rival centers of *Islamic* power: Baghdad in Mesopotamia, Cairo in Egypt, and Damascus in Syria. After the Arabs came the *Ottomans*, who ruled over Syria for 400 years (from 1516-1918). Ottoman power was broken on the wheel of *WWI*, with Damascus falling to the *Arab Revolt* in October 1918. But unbeknownst to the Arabs who fought their way past and through the Turkish guns, Syria had already been secretly awarded to a French *sphere of influence* under terms of the *Sykes-Picot Agreement*. When this became known, it was contested by *Faisal I* on behalf of the Arabs. Nonetheless, Syria was turned into a French *mandate* in 1920. This too was contested by Arab leaders, and from 1925-27 by the *Druse*, who rebelled and briefly took Damascus from the French. In 1936 *Léon Blum* promised Syrian *independence*, but his government fell before that decision could be carried out. During *WWII* Syria was a battleground for *Vichy* and *Free French* forces, until the latter won out. After the war the French sought to return to the *status quo ante bellum*, and fought Syrian nationalists until April 1946. But then France withdrew and Syria became fully independent. Syria joined the fight against Israel in the *First Arab/Israeli War*. It then aligned with the Soviet Union and fought Israel again in the *Second, Third* and *Fourth Arab/Israeli Wars*, losing most badly in 1967 and 1973. It became embroiled in the *Lebanese Civil War,* especially after 1976. In June 1982, it almost fought Israel again over control of southern Lebanon. In 1986 Britain broke *diplomatic relations,* accusing Syria of *state terrorism;* in 1993 the U.S. still listed Syria as a state that sponsors terrorism. Yet, Syria established its dominance over most of Lebanon (with U.S. acquiescence) in the dual wash of the collapse of its Soviet patron and the *Gulf War,* in which Syria sent 20,000 troops to fight Iraq. In 1992 it participated in multilateral *peace talks,* for the first time negotiating directly with Israel over the return of the *Golan Heights.* Domestically, it was politically unstable for much of the 1950s. From 1958-61 it joined with Egypt in a dubious *union* called the *United Arab Republic.* The *Ba'ath Party* seized power in March 1963, and *Hafaz al Assad* took power. He was still in control in 1994, but was in poor health; a succession crisis was building behind the scenes.

systematic interpretation: Reading clauses of a *treaty* with careful reference to their overall context.

systemic: Affecting the whole, or flowing from the root structure of the *international system.*

systemic war: A general or *world war* involving all or most of the *Great Powers.* In modern times, to some degree they also involve or affect all other *states* in the *international system.* By consensus, there have been four in the last 400 years: the *Thirty Years' War;* the wars of the *French Revolution, WWI* and *WWII.* Such all-out wars among the Great Powers may be no longer possible, or at least no longer winnable, because they are not survivable in an age of *weapons of mass destruction.* The *Cold War* demonstrated a considerable awareness of this reality among the *elite* leadership of both the U.S. and the Soviet Union. It too was a systemic conflict, but of a new sort.

System of National Accounts (SNA): First developed in 1968, this is a *macro*-level system of reporting on national income (whole economies). The original system was praised for its handling of basic features of buying and selling *goods* and *services.* But it was criticized for failing to take proper account of non-market economic activity, such as household consumption and government provision of services such as health and education; for inadequately measuring the value of *investment* in basic research and product development; and for excluding sources of natural wealth such as *land* and *natural resources.* The new system was introduced in February 1994, after ten years of consultation among Eurostat (the accounting arm of the *EU*), the *IBRD, IMF, OECD* and *UN.* It treats non-market activities as part of the overall economy (though it still cannot account for in-home services such as housework, which do not usually involve payment). It introduced reporting on national wealth in land and resources, but does not yet calculate long-term environmental damage or short-term disasters against national income.

systems analysis/theory: An approach to the study of *world politics* that looks primarily at the *structure* and processes of what it sees as an *international system,* rather than to internal events in particular *states* (or other *actors* within that system). A system is taken to be any whole, or set of relationships, where the parts are *interdependent* in the sense that changes in one *variable* (a given *cause*) bring about variations (*effects*) in combinations of other variables. Systems may be loose or tight, stable or unstable; and may contain subsystems (e.g., the Middle East *balance of power* as a subsystem of the global balance of power system; or the *EFTA* as a subsystem of the world economy). The brand names, or *"taxonomies,"* applied by systems theorists to their shifting speculations continue to proliferate (cascade, some might say). A sampling: action, analytical, concrete, *hegemonic,* homeostatic, mechanical, steady-state and so on, seemingly ad infinitum. The proffering of various systems theories as *grand theory* has been widely criticized for exhibiting some or all of the following: apolitical content, conservatism about the possibility of systemic change, excessive *abstraction,* celebrating form over substance, strained assumptions, tautological argument and--this author's personal favorite--*procrustean* amputation of the facts. See also *anarchic; bipolar; city-state system; endogenous; events data; exogenous; multipolar; sensitivity; unipolar; vulnerability; Westphalian; world capitalist.*

T

tacit alliance: When *states* informally coordinate their foreign policies on matters of mutual interest.

tacit consent: Silence on an international legal matter may be taken as implicit *consent*. Cf. *acquiescence.*

tactical: (1) The use of *force* on a limited scale, with a limited purpose in mind. (2) Relating to battlefield considerations alone. Cf. *strategic.*

tactical nuclear weapons: Short-range systems for use against enemy military (generally, 200 miles/300 km range), not those *intermediate* or *intercontinental* systems used to destroy *strategic* bases of power.

tactics: Short-range considerations relating to the details of deployment and use of troops or weapons systems in combat. The term is also used to refer to the ploys and *stratagems* of political and diplomatic maneuvering. Cf. *strategy.*

Tahiti: See *French Polynesia.*

Taiping Rebellion: The largest of a series of internal disturbances in China between c.1850-73, itself lasting from 1850-64. It was led by a half-mad visionary, Hung Hsiu-ch'üan (1812-64). Feeding off economic dislocation and fear of foreign influence, this *uprising* coursed over south and central China. For nearly 10 years that part of China centered on the Yangtze was under the rule of the Taiping. In the end, it was not the *Manchu* center but armies from the regions that crushed the *rebellion.* Perhaps 20 million lives were lost in this and related risings, and the Manchu hold on China was correspondingly weakened.

Taiwan (Formosa), a.k.a. Republic of China: Location: E. Asia. Major associations: *APEC.* Population: 21 million (85% Taiwanese, 15% Nationalist). Military: Excellent equipment and training; it presents a significant deterrent to *invasion.* A large island off the Chinese coast, it was ruled by the Netherlands from 1620-62, before reverting to China. It was ceded to Japan under terms of the *Treaty of Shimonoseki* (1895) and remained under Japanese *occupation* until 1945. In 1949 the *Guomindang* retreated there after *defeat* in the *Chinese Civil War,* still claiming to be the *legitimate* government of all China. From 1949-75 it was ruled by *Chiang Kai-shek,* continuing its tense stand-off with the communist People's Republic for all that time. The most dangerous crises came over *Quemoy and Matsu,* from 1953-58. Taiwan held the China seat on the *Security Council* and the *UNGA*--upheld by

U.S. *veto*--until it was *expelled* in October 1971, so that *mainland China* could be seated instead. Even so, some 25 countries still recognized Taiwan in 1994, and called for its readmission to the UN. Of these, the most loyal were in *Central America,* where Taiwanese *aid* and *investment* dollars purchased diplomatic support from all seven *republics.* Chiang Ching-kuo (1910-88), son of Chiang Kai-shek, took control from 1978-88. In his time Taiwan prospered, emerging as one of the *Asian Tigers* and a valued trade partner of many *nations,* despite its deepening diplomatic isolation. In 1987, 38 years of *martial law* was lifted. Since 1988 Taiwan has made tentative moves toward multiparty democracy, although this has opened old wounds between the native Taiwanese and the dominant, immigrant Nationalists and their descendants. It retains close ties to the U.S., which in 1992 approved advanced *fighter* sales to Taipei, displaying a continuing commitment even at the expense of warm relations with Beijing. Taiwan makes the same claim to the *Spratly Islands* as does the People's Republic. In early 1993 it made the first, tentative and "unofficial" diplomatic contacts with China, where its business people have become important investors. The two Chinas met officially for the first time later that year, at an *APEC* summit in Seattle. See *two-Chinas policy.*

Tajikistan: Location: *Central Asia.* Major associations: *CIS, UN.* Population: 5.2 million (55% Tajik; 25% Uzbek; 15% Russian--some 100,000 Russians left in 1992 alone). Military: revamped *Red Army* units; Russian units now in-country. Over the centuries this area has been overrun by successive waves of nomadic invaders from Asia. In the 17th and 18th centuries it was home to small, independent khanates that existed uneasily between the contracting *Persian Empire* and the expanding *Russian Empire.* In the 19th century it fell to the latter. Kept in the *empire* by the *Bolsheviks,* it was joined loosely with Uzbekistan within the *Soviet Union* in a 1924 reorganization of the "nationalities problem" by *Stalin.* In 1929 it split from Uzbekistan to form the Tajik (Tadzhik) ASSR, a purely administrative change then, but one that left it an independent nation following the *extinction* of the Soviet Union in December 1991. After *independence* the local communists kept power, opposed by democratic reformers and Islamic *fundamentalists* alike. By December 1992, ethnic and religious conflict drove 60,000 *refugees* into Afghanistan. The UN later oversaw *repatriation* of some of these refugees. In the first six months of 1993 over 100 border *incursions* took place, by Tajik rebels and anti-communist Afghans fighting the government in Dushanbe. In July 1993, Russian troops were drawn into the fighting, with some killed. Russia agreed to a Tajik government request to station troops as a unilateral "*peacekeeping* force" in Dushanbe. In December, Tajikistan agreed to monetary union with Russia (which already provides half the national budget), bringing into question its real independence.

takeoff: In various theories of the *stages of growth*, that which precedes mature, *sustainable growth* and the critical point denoting the transition from traditional economic modes to a modern economy.

Talleyrand, Charles Maurice de (1754-1838): French statesman. Foreign Minister 1797-99; 1799-1807. This wiley bishop had one of the most storied careers in all *diplomacy*. He joined in support for the early stages of the *French Revolution*, even backing confiscation of church property (he lost his own see in 1791), for which he was excommunicated by Rome. He left France for the U.S. during *The Terror*, but returned to serve the *Directory*. He was Foreign Minister 1797-99. He then joined and served *Napoleon I* as Foreign Minister 1799-1807. He secretly communicated with Napoleon's enemies, however, and in 1814 managed to switch sides again, joining the *Restoration*. He represented France brilliantly at the *Congress of Vienna*, gaining agreement that it be treated as a *Great Power*. He then encouraged the growing split in the *coalition* that defeated France. In 1830 he turned against the Bourbons and helped install the *July Monarchy*, which he served as Ambassador to London 1830-34. At the end of his life this irrepressible opportunist even managed to reconcile with the church. One may only wonder what deals he has since made with the deity, and how long secret talks have been underway with the emissaries of Hades. See also *XYZ Affair.*

Tamil Tigers: *Guerrillas* based mainly in the Jaffna peninsula, and enjoying considerable support from the Tamil population. Their fight is for *secession* from Sri Lanka, which is dominated by a Sinhalese majority. The Tigers, led by Vellupillai Prabhakaran (b.1956), are demanding 1/3rd of the island of Ceylon. In early 1993 some discussion was heard of a negotiated settlement based on a new federal system, with guarantees of Tamil *autonomy*. However, at the end of the year both sides returned to the gun. See *Sri Lanka.*

Tanganyika: For 1,000 years it was exploited as a source of slaves for the Arab *slave trade* run from *Zanzibar*. It formed part of the composite settlement *German East Africa*. After *WWI* it was renamed "Tanganyika Territory" and became a British *mandate*. In 1945 it was made a UN *trusteeship territory*. It was given *independence* in 1961, and in 1964 joined in a union with Zanzibar. In 1993 a serious rift opened with Zanzibar, threatening the union. See *Tanzania.*

Tangier: This Moroccan city facing *Gibraltar* was part of Spanish Morocco from 1912-23, when it was *neutralized* and declared an *international city*. It was a seven-nation *condominium* from 1923-56. It was occupied by Spain from 1940-45, but was reinternationalized until 1956, when it joined Morocco.

Tannenberg, Battle of (August 26-30, 1914): The Germans encircled and defeated a large Russian army here. However, the victory came after the Russians had penetrated deep into Germany, causing panic in Berlin and forcing the *High Command* to pull back badly needed troops from the offensive in the west. The Russians thus helped save France from a quick *defeat*, though at a tragically high cost in lives. A semi-fictionalized, but powerful, account is *Alexandr Solzhenitsyn's* "August 1914."

Tanzania: Location: E. Africa. Major associations: *Commonwealth, OAU, UN*. Population: 26 million, Military: small, and with an apolitical tradition rare in Africa. Formed in April 1964, by a *union* of *Tanganyika* and *Zanzibar*. From 1964-85 it was led by *Julius Nyerere* who set up a *one-party state* and attempted to set up a variant of "African socialism" based on historic, communal property patterns laid out in the *Arusha Declaration*. By the 1970s the economy was failing, in part due to the fact Tanzania was surrounded by regional conflicts. It was a leader of the *front line* states in their opposition to *apartheid* and to *UDI* in Rhodesia, but was forced by geographical and economic reality to deal with South Africa on a practical basis. In 1970 it was one of only four African states to recognize *Biafra*. From 1970-75, with Chinese help, it completed the Tan-Zam railway linking it to Zambia and reducing its export dependence on South Africa. In 1979 Nyerere approved an *invasion* of Uganda and the overthrow of *Idi Amin*, after Ugandan troops had crossed the border in *hot pursuit* of anti-Amin *guerrillas*. In 1981 Tanzanian troops helped Seychelles repel an invasion by *mercenaries*. Since 1985 Tanzania has changed course. It now seeks to build a *market economy* and a multiparty democracy. In 1993 a serious constitutional issue erupted with the discovery that Zanzibar had secretly joined the *Islamic Conference* in violation of the country's *secular* constitution. The crisis was so deep it threatened the union. Nyerere was brought back to *mediate.*

targeting doctrine: Any principles set in advance to govern the selection of targets, the order of attack and the weapons to be used in case of *war*. These principles may or may not incorporate reasoning from *just war theory*.

tariff: A tax on *imports*; very rarely, a tax on *exports*. They are used to raise revenue for governments, but even more as a mechanism of *protectionism*. See *peak tariff; preferential tariff; protective tariff.* Cf. *common market; customs union; free trade; free trade area; GATT; new protectionism; non-tariff barriers; quota.*

Tartar (a.k.a. Tatar): A generic term for the Mongol and Turkic peoples that overran much of the south Russian steppes and the *Caucasus* during the Middle Ages. They established khanates in Astrakhan, Kazan and the Crimea, and waged *war* along the southern border of Muscovy for several centuries, marauding in search of *booty* and *slaves*. They were helped by Turkish *Janissaries*, and counted the *Ottomans* as *allies*. Muscovy gained the upper hand beginning in the reign of *Ivan IV (The Terrible)*, and ultimately subdued the Tartars and annexed their lands. In 1945 *Stalin* expelled 200,000 Crimean Tartars (but not the Kazan Tartars) to Siberia, unjustly accusing them en masse of *collaboration* with the Nazis. After the collapse of the Soviet Union they began to migrate back to the *Crimea*, where the Ukrainian government initially welcomed them as diluting the local Russian majority and thereby reinforcing Ukrainian claims to the peninsula. However, relations with local authorities soon cooled as Tartars competed with Ukrainians and others for housing, jobs and land.

task force: A momentary gathering of divers military units under a single command, for purposes of fulfilling a single major task, such as an *invasion*.

tax haven: A country that deliberately maintains very low corporate or income tax levels, and other incentives to attract foreign corporate headquarters or *subsidiaries*, or private savings. This permits *multinational corporations* in particular to avoid heavy taxes in their home countries. Switzerland has played this role for centuries; some Caribbean nations, such as the Bahamas, have joined the game more recently.

taxonomy: A $100 bit of *jargon* for the dime-a-dozen term "classification," self-consciously adapted by the social sciences from its origin in the natural science of classifying organisms. See *scientism; systems theory.*

technical intervention: See *intervention.*

technocracy: A theory advocating that decisions regarding industrial policy, the form and character of government and economic arrangements should be made by technicians following the dictates and findings of science and *technology*. Cf. *dirigisme.*

technocrat: A person who advocates or practices *technocracy*.

technology: The knowledge of how to do, or make, something: applied science, ballistics, computing, chemical, genetic and mechanical engineering are leading examples. It has been extremely dynamic since the end of the 18th century, driving enormous changes in economic, social and political organization and underlying much of *modernization*. It is enormously important for developing or maintaining national *power* and wealth. Also, technological innovations have always greatly affected *warfare*, by giving one side a (usually temporary) advantage. That was as true of the invention of the stirrup as of high explosives and ballistic science, or the machinegun or *ICBM*. See also *Industrial Revolution; technology transfer.*

technology transfer: When productive (or military) activity in one *nation* gains access to, and takes advantage of, *technology* hitherto available only abroad. Technology may be transferred by: importing advanced *goods* or *services, foreign direct investment, foreign aid,* student and professional exchanges, openly published scientific literature, *economic espionage* or theft. Access is limited by secrecy inherent to both military and competitive economic activity, patents and explicit export restrictions. See also *COCOM; turn-key factory; WIPO.*

Tehran Conference (November 28-December 1, 1943): *Stalin* finally agreed to meet with the other major *Allied* leaders, something *Churchill* eagerly accepted and *Roosevelt* had long wanted. The major issues discussed were the date for opening the *second front,* Russian entry into the war against Japan and the basic shape of the *United Nations Organization*. While disagreements existed over the future of *Poland,* the *Baltic States* and the *Balkans,* none emerged so clearly into the open that the *United Nations alliance* was threatened. This was still a meeting of wartime allies preoccupied by the immediate needs and purpose of prosecuting the war, but for the first time confident of winning it and beginning to look to their future divisions in the *postwar* world. Cf. *Potsdam; Yalta.*

telecommunications: See *International Telecommunications Union (ITU); piracy; radio.*

Teller, Edward (b.1908): Nuclear physicist. He worked closely with *J. Robert Oppenheimer* on the *Manhattan Project,* 1941-46. He always refused to accept that there may be overriding moral implications to *nuclear weapons* work. When Oppenheimer refused to press ahead on the *hydrogen bomb,* Teller was chosen to head the project, bringing it to fruition in 1952. Hungarian-born, he was a fierce anti-*communist* who seemed forever in search of a "technical fix" to the *Cold War* political problem. As head and then chief guru of the Lawrence Livermore Laboratory (second only to *Los Alamos* in terms of U.S. nuclear weapons research) he was enormously influential over several decades. It was Teller who personally convinced *Ronald Reagan* to authorize research funds for *SDI,* circumventing entirely the *Defense Department* with his direct access to the president. But where Reagan hoped and called for a non-nuclear "shield" against incoming *ICBMs,* Teller planned to incorporate new generation nuclear weapons into SDI, as a power source for *charged particle beam* defenses.

tension: A widely used physical metaphor describing a state of affairs when relations between or among *states* are strained by serious unresolved *disputes,* especially if there lurks in the background the possibility of one or other using *force.* Tension can build into a *crisis* if not addressed or eased.

terminal defense: The *active defense* of one target.

terminal guidance: Making corrections to the flight path of *missiles* during the final approach to target.

terms, ask for: A request for enumeration and explanation of the conditions on which a *surrender* will be accepted. This is a first step in ending a *war.*

terms of a treaty: Point-by-point declarations of principle, enumeration of agreement, postponement of disagreement, specific conditions imposed, or mechanisms of dispute resolution contained in a *treaty.*

terms of trade: The ratio of the price of *imports* to the price of *exports.* When import prices outpace exports, a *nation* suffers declining terms of trade. Thus, *natural resource* exporters have found their prices falling steadily compared to the manufactured and high-technology *goods* they must import. Terms of trade suggest the general direction of the *purchasing power* of a national economy: purchasing power rises if the value of exports outpaces that of imports.

terrae dominium finitur, ubi finitur armorum vis: "Dominion over the land ends where the cannon's fire stops." See *cannon-shot rule.*

terra incognita: "Unknown land." A term from the

"Age of Exploration" for lands hitherto undiscovered, at least from the point of view of Europe in the case of Africa, the Americas and Asia. See *discovery.*

terrain contour matching: Computer systems that match the terrain actually overflown by a *missile* with high-quality maps, permitting mid-course corrections. These can be substantial changes for *cruise missiles,* but are only minor for *ballistic missiles.*

territorial defense: A defensive posture centering on protection of the homeland, and showing little forward or offensive capability; e.g., see *Maginot Line.*

territorial integrity: A phrase used to suggest that *sovereignty* is indivisible, and that existing *states* should only be broken apart or their *borders* significantly rearranged in extremis. See *Open Door.*

territoriality (of criminal law): An international legal doctrine that *municipal law* may concern itself only with criminal offenses committed inside the *territorial jurisdiction* of the state concerned. Cf. *universality of criminal law.*

territorial jurisdiction: The legal competence of a *state* over the *territory* recognized as belonging to it.

territorial sea/waters: Adjacent waters of a *coastal state,* between the *baseline* and the *high seas.* Formerly confined to the *three-mile limit,* it was extended by *UNCLOS III* to a maximum of a *twelve-mile limit.* A special case is the *Arctic,* where several nations have claimed "sectors" defined by points drawn from the Pole to the furthest east/west extremities of their northern *territory.* A unilateral claim was made by Indonesia (and some other archipelagic nations) for an "archipelagic regime," in which all waters within a designated perimeter surrounding an archipelago were claimed as *internal waters.* In UNCLOS III a compromise was struck, placing a limit of 100 nautical miles on archipelagic baselines. A unique case is North Korea's unilateral declaration of a 50-mile "military zone" projected from its baseline, in which it insists on exclusive economic and military rights. See also *contiguous zone; straight baseline.*

territorium nullius: "No one's land." *Territory* not under the *sovereignty* or *jurisdiction* of any *state.* For example, *Antarctica,* the *moon* and the deep *seabed.*

territory: A marked area under *jurisdiction* of a *state* or rarely, some other *international personality,* including its airspace, inland waters, minerals and subsoil. If a *coastal state,* it also has claims to an *EEZ* corresponding to its *continental shelf* and to *territorial waters*. Territory can be acquired, legally or not, by the following means: *accretion, annexation, cession, conquest, discovery, occupation, peace treaty, prescription, union* or *secession*. Normally, additions or subtractions to territory caused by annexation or cession do not affect the underlying international personality that governs the territory; that is not the case with conquest, occupation, union or secession. Cf. *global commons; territorium nullius.*

terrorism: The use of indiscriminate violence by private (*non-state*) groups to cause mass fear and panic with the ostensible purpose of advancing revolutionary political goals, but often expressing a more prosaic criminal element and motivation as well. Though seldom without purpose or internal rationality, it is nonetheless always outside the norms of civilized society. In the 19th century *anarchists* (especially Russians and Spaniards) were the dominant group engaged in terrorism. In the 1920s and 1930s most terrorists came from the extreme right-wing. Thus, the *League of Nations* drafted the first international *convention* on terrorism in 1937 (it never came into force), in response to the assassination of *Alexander I of Yugoslavia* by a Macedonian nationalist (who fled to, and had support from, *fascist* Italy). In the 1960s and 1970s most active terrorists were on the left, or had agendas derived from the several conflicts in the *Middle East*. The *UNGA* and several regional organizations responded with conventions making terrorism a crime (the main UN instrument came into force in 1977). Other conventions followed in the 1980s. In the 1990s the nature of political terrorism has been blurred by the adoption of terrorist methods by organized crime, from the *drug cartels* of Colombia to the Italian and Russian mafias. It is noteworthy that terrorist groups have seldom, if ever, achieved their stated political goals. Indeed, terrorist tactics have more often than not damaged causes and delayed implementation of political agendas that otherwise might be viewed as having some merit. See *anarchism; assassin; Baader-Meinhof; Black Hand; Black September; Entebbe raid; Euskadi Ta Askatasuna; Freikorps; Front de Liberation du Québec; Hamas; hijacking; hostage taking; IRA; Irgun; narco-terrorism; Olympic Games; Palestine Liberation Organization; Red Brigades; Sendero Luminoso; Stern Gang; state terrorism; Ulster.* Cf. *guerrilla war; insurgency.*

Terror, the: In April 1793, the *French Revolution* took a *radical* turn under the "Committee of Public Safety." In October, *Girondins* were overthrown and guillotined by the more radical *Jacobins.* During 1793-94 *Robespierre* and *Danton* struggled to control the Rev-

olutionary Convention. With the former's victory, Danton and his supporters were put to death, and The Terror entered a new phase. Nearly 13,000 were guillotined in the cities, while in the *Vendée* a virtual *genocide* took place. The Terror ended after July 1794, with the arrest and guillotining of Robespierre. In its day, it shocked and shook the conscience of Europe, but by modern standards of state murder the number of its victims seems quite modest (e.g., it does not equal even a single day of those murdered by the *Nazis* at the height of the *Holocaust*). Cf. *Cultural Revolution; Red Terror; Yezhovshchina.*

Teschen: Part of Silesia, ruled by the Hapsburgs from 1772-1918. In the confusion engendered by division of the Austro-Hungarian lands it was simultaneously claimed by Czechoslovakia and Poland, between whom there was some fighting into 1919. In 1920 it was *partitioned* by the *League of Nations,* leaving both sides discontented and posing an obstacle to collaboration within the *Little Entente.* After *Munich,* the Czech portion was claimed by Poland, but after *WWII* and the incorporation of both countries into the *Soviet bloc,* Moscow imposed the old 1920-38 border.

Test Ban Treaty: See *Partial Test Ban Treaty.*

Tet Offensive (January 29-February 25, 1968): An attack on the cities of South Vietnam by the *Viet Cong* (VC) that coincided with the Tet, or lunar, holiday. During the VC *occupation* of the cities many massacres took place. After heavy fighting, South Vietnamese (RVN) and U.S. forces repressed the rising, with massive losses incurred by the VC. This was followed by reprisal massacres of perhaps 30,000 VC prisoners and supporters by the RVN. The combat losses and the massacre finished the VC as an effective fighting force, and they were subsequently replaced in the field by North Vietnamese regulars. Tet was thus a military and political disaster for the Viet Cong. However, it proved to be one of the decisive turning points in the *Vietnam War,* and a strategic *victory* for the North. It took place just after the *Johnson* administration assured the U.S. public that the war against the VC was about won. The sudden onslaught by thousands of VC, some fighting right inside the American Embassy compound in Saigon and all reported nightly on network TV, shook public confidence in the administration's truthfulness. More important, Tet made victory look ever more distant, and with the South's reputation blackened by the massacre, large numbers of Americans turned against the war.

Texas: Originally part of *Spanish America,* it became part of Mexico in 1821. After 1830, fighting between

Mexicans and American settlers began, leading to a proclamation of *independence* in 1836. In 1845 it was *annexed* by the U.S., an act not accepted by Mexico until its *defeat* in the *Mexican/American War*. During the *American Civil War* Texas seceded and joined the *Confederacy*. In 1865 it was forced back into the federal union.

textiles: Woven fabric, or any fibre (jute, wool, etc.) capable of being woven. Until the *Uruguay Round* of *GATT* trade in these materials was managed under the exceptionally complex, Multi-Fibre Arrangement; that will be phased out from 1994-2004. Textiles are distinct from clothing, which is any manufactured garment rather than just fabric, and to which a different schedule of *tariffs* may apply. Textiles and clothing are both labor-intensive industries. This makes then important to Southern exporters, but for the same reason (jobs) they have been heavily protected by *OECD* countries. See also *NAFTA*.

Thailand: Located: SE Asia. Major associations: *ASEAN, UN*. Population: 55 million. Military: dwarfed by Vietnam's; moderately well equipped; self-defense orientation. Formerly Siam. It managed to survive the Imperial Age without being colonized by a European power, the only SE Asian nation to maintain *independence*. However, it did not escape entirely unscathed: while serving as a *buffer* between the British in India and the French in Indochina, Siam was stripped by France of its own *vassal states* in *Cambodia* and *Laos*. Around the turn of the 20th century it began to both *modernize* and *westernize*, while retaining its absolute *monarchy* until a bloodless revolt in 1932 converted it into a constitutional *monarchy*. In 1938 that reform was overturned by Pibul Songgram (1897-1964), who moved toward dictatorship during his first premiership 1938-44. Siam changed its name to Thailand in 1939. It was *occupied* by Japan in 1941, by agreement with Pibul Songgram who sought to recover Thailand's Indochinese *territories* under the *fascist* "New Order" in Asia. While his government supported Japan, many Thai *guerrillas* joined the *resistance* to the Japanese. Following a *coup*, Songgram returned as PM from 1948-57, *aligned* with the Western powers against local Asian communist movements, and took Thailand into *SEATO*. During the American phase of the *Vietnam War*, Thai bases were used by the U.S. to bomb North Vietnam, the *Ho Chi Minh Trail* and *Khmers Rouges* positions in Cambodia. In 1967 it joined ASEAN. During the 1980s Khmers Rouges settled along the border and sometimes just inside Thailand, from where they conducted guerrilla operations against the Vietnamese-backed government in Cambodia. That kept *tensions* high with Vietnam. With *peace* in Indo-

china, Thailand sought to more closely coordinate its diplomacy with other ASEAN members. In the 1980s it underwent an economic *boom*, though in the early 1990s there was some retrenchment from uncontrolled *growth*. In 1993 a *cease-fire* was signed with rebels in the Kachin region, who had been fighting the central government since 1961. Five other *ethnic groups* are still fighting, with the most significant *rebellion*, among the *Karen*, dating from the 1940s.

Thalweg: In *international law*, the *rule* that on a navigable waterway the *boundary* between two *states* shall run down the middle of the main channel, thus giving each state equal access to commercial uses, traffic and so forth. If *accretion* occurs, the boundary shifts to track the center of the channel; but if *avulsion* takes place, the original boundary remains.

Thatcher, Margaret, *née* Roberts (b.1925): British stateswoman. PM 1979-90. She moved Britain to the right, domestically and in foreign affairs. She was suspicious of connecting British *diplomacy* to the *EC*, preferring close, personal cooperation with *Ronald Reagan*, over whom she had considerable *influence* on *Cold War* policy. She focused on domestic policy, where she emphasized *monetarism, denationalization* and curtailment of the power of the trade unions. She led Britain during the *Falklands War* and supported the U.S. bombing of *Libya* in 1986. She was angered by the U.S. *invasion of Grenada*, over which she was not consulted despite its being a *Commonwealth* member. She faced sustained criticism from the Commonwealth over her refusal to impose mandatory *sanctions* against South Africa. Yet she led the West in recognizing that *Gorbachev* was different from other Soviet leaders, declaring "I can work with this man." Her opposition to the *EU*, combined with an unpopular poll tax proposal, led to an internal *Tory* "coup," and her forced resignation in 1990. In April 1993, from her new seat in the House of Lords, Lady Thatcher called for *intervention* by *NATO* in Bosnia. That momentarily shook Western leaders, but did not influence their policy in any meaningful way.

thaw: A journalistic, but not inaccurate, metaphor describing improvements in interstate relations that are less than a full *rapprochement*, but notably warmer (less tense) than a preceding period.

theater nuclear weapons: Systems limited in range to one region, or *theater of war*.

theater of war: (1) In combat: A strategically and geographically distinct area within a larger conflict, as in "the Pacific theater during *WWII*." (2) In *interna-*

tional law: the locale(s) where *acts of war* may lawfully be carried out.

theocracy: Rule by a priesthood, acting as deputies (soi-dissant) of the deity. See *fundamentalism; Inquisition; Iran; Sudan.* Cf. *secularism*.

theorem: A proposition capable of being deduced from the assumptions of a theoretical system.

theory: (1) Any statement generalizing about economic, political and/or historical facts and purporting to explain their causal relations. (2) A working hypothesis (*theorem*). (3) A systematic view, or body of theorems. (4) An unproven assumption (colloquial sense). See *behavioralism; bicycle theory; causation; collective security; decision theory; decision-making theory; dependency theory; deterrence; game theory; falsification; geopolitics; hegemonic stability; idealism; imperialism; just war theory; keynesian economics; labor theory of value; liberal-internationalism; long-cycle theory; macro; maoism; marxism; marxism-leninism; mercantilism; micro; monetarism; neo-realism; pacifism; paradigm; parsimonious; post-behavioralism; post-imperialism; qualitative; quantitative; rational decision-making; realism; scientism; structuralism; supply side; systems theory; traditionalism.*

Thermidor (July 27, 1794): (1) A conservative *reaction* and *coup* that marked the end of *The Terror* in France, and start of the *Directory*; named for the 11th month of the *French Revolution* calendar, "Thermidor" (July 19-August 17). (2) Any comparable conservative reaction to preceding, revolutionary events.

thermonuclear bomb: See *hydrogen bomb*.

thesis: (1) A proposition to be considered against logical or empirical objections raised against it. (2) In Hegelian method, a proposition capable of generating an opposing proposition (*antithesis*). See *dialectic*.

Thieu, Nguyen Van (b.1923): President of South Vietnam 1967-75. He came to power just before the *Tet Offensive*. He did little about the corruption of South Vietnamese government and society. That weakened its war effort and wore down the morale of its military and its U.S. ally. He reluctantly adapted to *Nixon's* policy of *Vietnamization* of the war, and he fought on after the U.S. pulled out in 1972. In 1975 he fled to Taiwan to escape the Northern armies that swept over the South, an outcome he continued to blame on the U.S., charging it with faithlessness and abandonment.

Third (Communist) International: Founded by the Bolsheviks in 1919, it institutionalized the split already evident in international *socialism* between those radicals who sought immediate *revolution*, soon renamed *communists*, and those who accepted a democratic and trade union agenda of reform. Much feared by conservatives, it proved a not-too-effective front for Soviet foreign policy. More often than not, it aimed at countering the electoral appeal of *social democracy* as a rival for working class support, rather than combatting the rising threat of *fascism* or subverting *capitalism*. It was dissolved as a placatory gesture in 1943 by *Stalin*, at *Franklin Roosevelt's* request, out of concern its existence might threaten *postwar* cooperation by overexciting Western *public opinion*. It was also called the Communist International, or COMINTERN.

Third Reich: Germany, from *Hitler's* ascent to power in January 1933, to the German *surrender* in May of 1945. See *Germany*.

Third Republic: France, from the defeat of 1870 to the defeat of 1940. Legally, it survived until the creation of the *Fourth Republic* in 1946, but politically it ended with *Vichy*. See *France*.

Third World (*tiers monde*): A *Cold War* term referring to the *developing nations* of the non-Western world (the majority of African, Asian and Latin American nations). It referred especially to the facts that their economies and living standards did not rank with the *OECD* nations, while non-*communism* or *nonalignment* placed them outside the *Soviet bloc*. Later, some Third World countries joined the Soviet bloc, while others sided with the *West*. The term then assumed its primary, economic sense as a nearly exclusive connotation. During the 1960s and 1970s it took on an additional imputation, one of Western responsibility to help meet the socioeconomic needs of Southern peoples, based upon moral claims growing out of complaints about *imperialism* and *neo-colonialism*. By the 1980s, however, it evoked images of harsh, corrupt and abusive regimes that denied *basic rights* to impoverished populations even while also failing to satisfy their *basic needs*. In the 1990s it was displaced by *South* as a term of preference by those who wished to escape some or all of these negative meanings. See *ACP nations; appropriate technology; ASEAN; Bandung; debtor cartel; debt crisis; dependency theory; development; G-77; Generalized System of Preferences; graduation clause; IBRD; IMF; Lomé Conventions; MNC; modernization; NIEO; NWICO; Non-Aligned Movement; North/South issues; OAS; OAU; regional banks; rising expectations; SPC; SPF; STABEX; stabilization program; UNCTAD; UNDP; UNGA.* Cf. *First; Second;* and *Fourth Worlds*.

Thirty Years' War (1618-48): The first half of the 17th century in Europe was riven with crisis: economic, political, social, intellectual and religious. This ferment was both reflected in, and worsened by, the Thirty Years' War, which was not really one war but several, and which did not really begin in 1618 or end in 1648. Yet those conventional dates cover well a series of related wars, mostly centered in or fought over Germany. The main protagonists at first were Catholics and Protestants and the states each controlled, but *mercenaries* too were important participants, while princes from different faiths soon schemed with each other against coreligionists. Moreover, the war ended not with the triumph of one religious party over the other, but with a great compromise based on entirely *secular* principles. In its course and destructiveness, it took the religious question out of European and *Great Power* politics (at least, as a major subject of *diplomacy*); jolted the convictions of princes even as it shook the land; and reorganized the *states* system around agreement that members should conduct their affairs based upon *raison d'etat*, rather than differences of opinion on the question of transubstantiation or the transmigration of souls. It was nothing less than a *revolution* in the affairs of states, which would have lasting, global significance.

(1) Bohemian phase, 1618-25: It began with a Protestant revolt against the Catholic (*Hapsburg*) rulers of Bohemia. That threatened the religious balance among the "Electors" who chose the Holy Roman Emperor (Bohemia held the seventh vote, where the first six were divided three/three between Catholic and Protestant electors). The revolt thus struck at the heart of Hapsburg and Catholic power in Germany, while encouraging one Protestant prince, Frederick of the Rhineland (the "Winter King"), to *intervene* in support of protestantism in Bohemia. Catholic Europe responded with a *coalition* that overthrew Frederick, using mainly Spanish troops. It then imposed a draconian punishment on all Bohemia, instituting the full weight of the *Counter Reformation* and the cruel *tortures* and doctrinal rigors of the *Inquisition*.

(2) Danish phase, 1625-29: The King of Denmark wanted lands for his son to rule. He saw the chance to play to Protestant and French fears of Catholic Spain, whose power extended now into Germany. But a Protestant coalition failed to form, and after four years of fighting that devastated north Germany, Denmark was beaten into submission. Catholic and Imperial power was ascendant. It was a time for grace and magnanimity if the spate of war was to end. Instead, the Emperor tried to turn back a century of compromise with Protestantism by an edict that would have forced princes and Free Cities alike to yield, and even to convert back to "the one true Faith" (from the other

one). Even Catholic princes saw this as a Hapsburg grab for *hegemony*, not a Catholic policy.

(3) Swedish phase, 1630-35: The Imperial edict brought Protestant Sweden and Catholic France together, in defense of local *autonomy* against Imperial authority and Spanish hegemony. Now *Gustavus Adolphus* intervened, seeing an expansion of Swedish power as nicely linked to the Protestant cause in Germany. Though he died in battle, his *intervention* altered the whole course of the war (and modern history): it saved the Protestant cause, but also converted the conflict into a raw struggle for political *power*, regardless of faith: Catholic France led by a prince of the church (Cardinal *Richelieu*), entered the war not on the side of the Catholic cause, but in *alliance* with Protestant princes in Germany and Sweden, and even the Ottoman *sultan*, to fight Catholic Austria and Spain.

(4) General phase, 1635-48: For 13 years Catholic, Protestant and private armies marauded over Germany, sacking its cities and terrorizing the populace. Catholic now fought Catholic, and Protestant killed Protestant, even while both murdered, raped, tortured and burned out the other, spreading *famine*, pestilence, *refugees*, cruelty and death through the heart of Europe. Entire cities, such as Magdeburg, were put to the sword, leaving parts of Germany denuded of half their population. That general mêlée meant the end of an era of war between religious communities and the beginning of the era of war among the states, for raison d'état. Relief finally arrived in 1648, in form of the *Peace of Westphalia*, that great agreement so vital to the development of the modern state system. The other major consequence of the war was to leave Germany divided and weak (over 300 distinct German entities were *recognized* at Westphalia), and so on the margins of world history and politics for another 150 years. The age of popes and the *Holy Roman Empire* was over; the age of states had begun. And *primus inter pares* among the myriad states and statelets of Europe and then the world for the next two centuries, was France.

thousand bomber raids: Massive air raids against German cities and industrial plant, mounted by the U.K. and U.S. during *WWII*. The British bombed by night and the Americans by day, until plane and crew losses grew so heavy the switch to night bombing was made. The raids pulverized Germany's cities, but it is less clear what damage they did to its *war* production as most factories were already underground. Losses became less heavy in late 1944 and 1945, as *Luftwaffe* pilot losses proved irreplaceable (not even the first jet *fighters* could compensate). Paradoxically, they raised German *national morale*, rather than shattering it as hoped. Since the war, they have been criticized on *just war* grounds as disproportionate and *indiscriminate*.

But the hard truth is that at the time, they provided grim satisfaction to *Allied* publics, who more or less felt that Germans deserved a taste of what the *Nazis* had rained down on others. Such is war.

three-mile limit: The minimum extension of *territorial waters* agreed upon before *UNCLOS III.* It originates from the *cannon-shot rule* championed by the Netherlands in the 17th century, in opposition to a Danish view that the territorial sea should have an agreed upon, gauged width. Three nautical miles out (from low tide) was a nice compromise between these positions. Cf. *twelve-mile limit.*

throw weight: Discounting fuel and rocket weight, this is the *payload* carried by a *missile.* It includes all *penetration aids,* single re-entry vehicles or *MIRVs,* *warheads,* and release and guidance devises.

Tiananmen Square massacre (June 4, 1989): In 1988 the pro-democracy movement in China led to mass student demonstrations in Beijing to honor the death of reformer *Hu Yaobang.* After considerable hesitation by the central authorities, and growing international attention, the students were literally crushed under *PLA* tanks. That act of callous barbarism was watched live on international television, until the signal was cut off. Several thousand may have died, their bodies buried in secret; others were arrested and executed, and thousands sent to *reeducation* camps. China was widely condemned, and briefly withdrew into wounded *isolationism.* However, the end of the *Cold War* and the thrust of reform in China meant the massacre only temporarily interrupted its economic opening to the world.

Tibet: Tibet moved in and out of Chinese control over the centuries, according to the strength of the emperors. By 1900 the *Manchus* were moribund as a political force, and Tibet correspondingly independent. This *de facto* situation was confirmed in 1913 when the *Dalai Lama* returned from *exile* in India and agreed to rule Tibet as a British *protectorate.* But British power had waned by the close of *WWII,* while China was ascendant under the communists in 1949. In 1950 China invaded Tibet and declared it a province once again. In 1959 the Tibetans rose, but were defeated after heavy fighting and much bloodshed. The current Dalai Lama fled into exile, where he continues to lobby a mostly indifferent world on the cause of Tibetan *independence.* In 1965 Tibet was made an "autonomous region" within China. During the *Great Proletarian Cultural Revolution* it was harshly treated, with Buddhist temples not merely closed but destroyed by rampaging *Red Guards,* and thousands of monks

and others killed. In 1988-89 widespread unrest was again savagely repressed. China has deliberately encouraged Han *immigration* into Tibet to reinforce its claim. This cynical policy is working: native Tibetans now are an ethnic minority in their own land.

tied aid: Attaching procurement "strings" to grant *aid,* so that the money either goes directly to purchases from local producers in the *donor country,* or later recycles back to the donor economy for follow-up *services.* It is criticized for undercutting the development impact of aid by converting it into a manufacturing export support or job program for the donor economy, and by forcing recipients to purchase inappropriate or expensive *goods.* Its proponents argue that it helps sustain a domestic constituency for aid that otherwise might dry up. Most donor nations have agreed to significantly reduce the percentage of the their aid that is tied; a few have even done so.

tied loan: A loan where the borrower must spend the monies solely in the lending country. It has the same benefits to lender, and the same problems for the borrower, as experienced with *tied aid.*

Tientsin (Tianjin), Treaty of (1858): China was forced to sign this humiliating agreement with Britain (quickly followed on the *most-favored-nation* principle by similar *treaties* with France, Russia and the United States). It opened more of its coastal cities to foreign trade, allowed foreigners to import opium for sale to its addicts, gave additional guarantees to missionaries and set disadvantageous *tariff* terms. It was related to British *victory* in the second *Opium War,* though fighting in that war continued to 1860.

Tigre: A province of *Ethiopia,* bordering *Eritrea,* where in the 1970s and 1980s a *secessionist* movement fought a *guerrilla war* in conjunction with Ethiopia's other *wars* in Eritrea and with *Somalia.*

Tilsit, Treaties of (July 8, 1807): Two agreements setting up French and Russian *spheres of influence* in Europe, negotiated by *Napoleon I* and *Alexander I.* (1) Public: Russia accepted French dominance of Europe, the reduction in *size* of its *defeated* ally *Prussia* and the creation of a *vassal state* (the Grand Duchy of Poland) on its own doorstep. (2) Secret: Russia agreed to join Napoleon's *Continental System* on the condition that Britain refused to make *peace* with France; and France agreed to *partition* the European possessions of the *Ottoman Empire* with Russia, should the *sultan* not make *peace* with the *tsar.* Russia also was granted rights to Finland, which it forced Sweden to cede two years later. The agreements were invalidated when the two nations went to war again in 1812. See *retreat from Moscow; War of the Fourth Coalition.*

tilt: To gradually change from a policy of *neutrality* to favoring one side in a *conflict*; or to change slowly from supporting one side to supporting the other.

Timor: Largest of the Lesser *Sunda Islands*, it was once divided between Indonesia and Portugal but since 1975 has been completely controlled by the former. See *East Timor.*

Tirpitz, Alfred von (1849-1930): German grand admiral. He persuaded *Kaiser Wilhelm II* to build a great battle fleet to challenge Britain at sea, not by promising a German *victory* but by denying a British one; and he oversaw its construction. During *WWI* he was a vigorous proponent of *unrestricted submarine warfare*, but resigned in a Prussian huff in 1916 when temporarily overruled on that issue.

Tito, *né* Josip Broz (1892-1980): Yugoslav dictator. A veteran of the *Russian Civil War*, he led Serb-communist *partisans* in *WWII*, establishing an independent *communist* regime without Soviet *aid* in 1944/45. He immediately *liquidated* the *Chetniks* and the remaining *Uštaše*; as many as 200,000 died upon his orders to wreak vengeance. In 1948 he broke with Moscow, and later became a leader within the *Non-Aligned Movement*. While he *normalized relations* with Moscow in 1955, he never accepted orders from the Soviets, criticized the crushing of the *Hungarian Uprising* and rejected both the *invasion* of *Czechoslovakia* in 1968 and the *Brezhnev Doctrine*. Domestically, he favored the Serbs, but not so much as to cause the breakup of the *federation*, which he ruled with an iron hand, crushing efforts at reform.

titoism: Archaic. The assertion of the *national interests* of a communist *state* against the international interests of the *communist* movement as defined by Moscow (from the practice of *Tito* of *Yugoslavia*).

Tlatelolco, Treaty of (1967): "Treaty for the Prohibition of Nuclear Weapons in Latin America." An agreement declaring the Latin American region a *nuclear weapons free zone*, signed by 14 states in February 1967, and in effect as of April 1968. By 1990 almost all Latin American states had adhered. All declared *nuclear states* have accepted to honor the zone. However, that does not account for *near-nuclear states*, including Argentina and Brazil, which both were secretly researching *nuclear weapons* until the 1980s. Like all such agreements to date, it offers no safeguards against cheating or altered geopolitical

circumstance. Nonetheless, it is widely regarded as a useful, regional supplement to the *Nuclear Non-Proliferation Treaty*.

Tocqueville, Alexis de (1805-59): French historian, and perhaps the single most astute observer of American *politics* and society. His 1835 classic "Democracy In America," actually written as an instruction to his countryfolk, remains a masterful distillation of insight into American government and character. Wittily presented, it is, as the cliché goes, "indispensable reading."

Togo: Located: W. Africa. Major associations: *ECOWAS, la francophonie, OAU, UN*. Population: 3.5 million. Military: 15,000 strong. This area was combed for *slaves* from the 15th-18th centuries. It became a German *colony* called *Togoland* in 1884, and remained so until 1919, when it was divided into British and French *mandates*. The French portion became modern Togo in 1960. It quickly fell into the familiar, post-colonial African pattern of military *coups* followed by creation of a *one-party state* as a cover for personal and *tribal* dictatorship. As the *Cold War* closed and Western *aid* budgets tightened after 1990, it appeared to move in the direction of political openness. But in 1993 President Gnassingbé Eyadéma claimed a 96.5% victory in a farcical and rigged election that was condemned by international observers.

Togoland: A German *protectorate* in West Africa until 1919, the western part was made a British *mandate* 1922-46, and *trusteeship territory* 1946-57, when it joined the Gold Coast (Ghana). The eastern part was a French *mandate* 1922-46, and trusteeship territory 1946-60, when it became *Togo*.

Tojo, Hideki (1885-1948): Japanese general and dictator. Vice-Minister for War and chief of the *secret police* 1937-39; Minister for War 1940-44. He was the driving personality within the "war party" faction of the Japanese *elite*, pushing for an aggressive policy in China and arguing for *war* with the United States in 1941. Once he was convinced by the navy to strike south rather than do as the army wanted and strike west against Russia, he moved with alacrity to order the attack on *Pearl Harbor*. When the war went very badly he lost *Hirohito's* confidence and resigned (July 9, 1944). After Japan's *surrender* he was arrested by the *Allies*. He attempted but failed to commit suicide. He was condemned as a war criminal at the *Tokyo war crimes trials*, and was hanged.

Tokelau: A South Pacific *dependency* (pop. 1,600) administered by New Zealand since 1925. Despite its paucity of numbers, it claims a 200-mile *EEZ*.

Tokugawa: The powerful military family that provided Japan 15 *shoguns* from 1606-1867. See *Japan*.

Tokyo Round (of GATT): The 7th *GATT* round, held from 1973-79. The unpropitious context was *stagflation*, uncertainty in the *currency* markets, and *recession*. Tokyo continued the basic thrust of *tariff* reduction, but also addressed *non-tariff barriers* (NTBs) and tried to speak to *LDC* concerns and agricultural products. It succeeded in further reducing *tariffs* and in somewaht adjusting to LDC interests. It was most significant for beginning to limit NTBs such as manipulation of technical standards, import *licensing* and *customs* regulations. It completely failed to bring *agriculture* under the GATT. Cf. *Uruguay Round*.

Tokyo war crimes trials: They began in May 1946, by order of *Douglas MacArthur*. The judges were drawn from Australia, Canada, Nationalist China, New Zealand, the Philippines, the U.S. and the Soviet Union (11 in all). Some 28 senior Japanese leaders were tried on charges ranging from *crimes against humanity* and *war crimes* such as inhumane treatment of *POWs* and the wounded, to the more controversial charge of *crimes against peace*, tenuously resting on citation of the *Kellogg-Briand Pact*. Unlike the *Nuremberg Trials*, simple majority rule was used to decide judgment and sentences. At MacArthur's insistence, *Hirohito* was never charged. The U.S. feared that trying the emperor would turn the Japanese forever against their conquerors. Yet there was much sentiment to proceed against him among *Allied* jurists (and populations). Seven of the defendants were sentenced to death. Several thousand lesser war criminals were convicted by various national courts. The U.S. paroled the last convicted Japanese war criminals in its charge (approximately 100) in 1960. See also *superior orders; Tojo; Yamashita; war crimes trials*.

Tonga: Location: Pacific. Major associations: *Commonwealth, SPC, SPF*. Note: it has not joined the *UNGA*, though it does participate in UN *specialized agencies*. Population: 110,000. Military: just 200 police/military personnel, but the only South Pacific state in formal *alliance* with the U.S. (via an 1888 *treaty*, reaffirmed on its centenary). Tongolese kings ruled much of *Polynesia* before arrival of the first European settlers in 1826. King George Tupou I converted to *Christianity*, unified Tonga, and over his long rule in the 19th century held the colonizing powers at bay via treaties with Britain, France, Germany, Spain and the U.S. It was a British *protectorate* from 1901, but with significant *autonomy*. Queen Salote ruled from 1918-65. In 1970 Tonga became independent, still under *authoritarian* monarchs. It refused to sign the *Treaty*

of Rarotonga, and has welcomed nuclear ships to its ports. It has troubled relations with Fiji: both claim the Minerva reefs.

Tonkin: A historic state in the north of the *Indochina* peninsula, for centuries it waged defensive wars against China to the north and *expansionist* wars against neighbors such as *Cochin China*. It was conquered by the French after heavy fighting from 1882-95, and merged into *French Indochina* in 1887, before complete *pacification*. It was the heart of *North Vietnam*, and is today a key region of northern Vietnam. Demarcation of the Gulf of Tonkin, an adjacent bay, is disputed by China and Vietnam.

Tonkin Gulf Resolution (August 7, 1964): A joint resolution of Congress that presented President *Lyndon Johnson* with a "blank check" to use *force* in support of *South Vietnam*. It followed an attack by North Vietnamese patrol boats on the *destroyers* USS Maddux and USS Turner Joy, in the Gulf of Tonkin, alleged to have occurred on the nights of August 2nd and 4th. Hanoi admitted the first attack, claiming it was in *retaliation* for U.S. assistance to South Vietnamese *commando* raids against its coast, but it denied the second incident ever took place. Whatever the truth, Johnson was delighted at the result. In private, he compared the Tonkin Gulf resolution to "granny's nightshirt--it covers everything."

topography: The relief features of a surface area. Topography has historically had a great effect on international relations, in both military and political realms. *Tactics* frequently depend heavily on the terrain of a battlefield, and even grand *strategy* must account for physical barriers: the *Schlieffen Plan* sought to avoid the forested Ardennes region and invade via the lowland plains of Belgium and Holland; Russian topography explains much of that country's historic fear of *invasion*, and therefore something of its policy of defensive expansion; all island nations enjoyed unique advantages before the invention of *air power* and the *ICBM* (see *English Channel*). Topography may permit ethnic groups to live side by side in compartmentalized *peace* or set them at each other's throats, should they so choose, fighting for every piece of high ground or defensible valley (e.g., the situation on Israel's northern border, or in Bosnia).

tort: An unjustified breach of international legal obligations. Cf. *delict*.

torture: Deliberately inflicting great physical pain or mental anguish as a means of coercion, punishment, extraction of information or just sadistic pleasure. It has been on the increase this century. *Amnesty International* regularly reports that the majority of *states* use a range of barbaric tortures on an almost daily basis. The *UNGA* passed a non-binding *Declaration on Torture* in 1975, and some regional organizations (*EU, OAS*) have banned the practice in law. A major UN *convention* came into force in 1987, making torture a crime under *international criminal law*. Torture may also be a *war crime*, if it occurs during a *war*.

Tory: (1) An English political party from the 17th century to c.1832, that tended to favor the *monarch* over the rights of Parliament, and preservation of a social order based upon aristocratic landholding. Its hold was eroded by the progressive self-assertion of Parliament and the arrival of the *Industrial Revolution*, which raised up new, middle and working class interests against it. It was succeeded by the *Conservative Party*. (2) A common nickname for broadly conservative parties in English-speaking, parliamentary democracies, or (lower case) for individuals who advocate conservative political principles. (3) A royalist ("Loyalist") in the *American War of Independence*. With delicious multiple irony, the original term derives from the Gaelic for "highwayman," which in Irish history meant a landless, persecuted peasant.

totalitarianism: Absolute control by the state of most aspects of the daily lives of its *citizens*, according to the dictates of a ruling party that professes some exhaustive ideology (say *fascism* or *communism*). It may also be said to exist where a priesthood interprets a *fundamentalist* religious vision as the basis of government policy, and political and social morality. Note: Some critics object to lumping divers political ideologies under this single rubric; others insist that there are traits in common. See *Bolshevism; Iran; maoism; marxism-leninism; nazism; North Korea; stalinism; Sudan; theocracy.* Cf. *anarchism; authoritarianism; laissez-faire; liberal-internationalism.* Among the most penetrating insights into the character of totalitarianism are those of George Orwell in "Animal Farm" and "1984," and Hannah Arendt in "Totalitarianism."

total war: (1) A *war* fought with unlimited means, on a vast scale and for unlimited *strategic* purposes. (2) The tendency in modern times for whole societies to feel committed to and engage in *warfare*. This contrasts with the age immediately preceding the modern, when combat was less destructive because of the skittishness of *mercenary* armies, and because *limited wars* engaged the passions and the fate only of dynasties, monarchs or local *warlords*, but rarely *peoples* or *nations*. This changed forever with the development of modern bureaucracy (and its capacity for organiza-

tion), and the explosion of *nationalism* during the French Revolution. The transformation was reflected in the *levée en masse* and greatly influenced the *Napoleonic Wars* and *Napoleonic warfare*. Added to that were exacerbating 19th century processes of *industrialization* and *technology*, growing class hatred in the new urban centers, the rise of 20th century *ideologies* and techniques of *propaganda*, and specious and pernicious social theories such as *social darwinism*. Yet it should be remembered that earlier ages and wars, too, had their passionate ideologies and hatreds that raised levels of destruction beyond even the normal horrors found acceptable (e.g., the *Thirty Years' War* or the Crusades). Also, some medieval and ancient peoples (the Greeks at Melos, the Romans at Carthage, or the Mongols wherever their horses took them) waged war with a ruthlessness and savage efficiency that approached totality. See *Carthagenian peace; Peloponnesian Wars.*

tourism: Touring, for pleasure's sake. Once the preserve of the high-born and wealthy, with the new affluence created by the *Industrial Revolution* international touring became a middle-class activity around the mid-to-late 19th century. It expanded even into the working classes in the 20th century. Today it is a large *service* industry and an important part of the world economy. It provides significant economic benefits to those countries receptive to tourists (and not all are). Tourism is additionally important as a major vehicle for the spread of ideas, cultural awareness--or sometimes misunderstanding--and disease.

Toussaint L'Ouverture (1743-1803): Born into *slavery* in Haiti, in 1791 he joined and then led slave insurgents against French rule. In 1797 he was made commander-in-chief on the island by the French, and subsequently drove out the British and Spanish, establishing a working government. In 1800 *Napoleon* decreed that slavery be re-established in Haiti, but L'Ouverture refused to comply. Defeated and then betrayed, he died after a year in a French dungeon. His followers gained *independence* for the Dominican Republic in 1804.

TOW: **T**ube launched, **O**ptically tracked, **W**ire-guided *missile*. With it, even illiterate *infantry* can undercut a sophisticated enemy's advantage in *air power*, as many *mujahadeen* did in the *Afghan/Soviet War.*

tracer: Ammunition, often for anti-aircraft guns, containing chemical compounds that when ignited (by firing the shell) emit light or smoke. That allows the shooter to observe where the *ordnance* flies or falls, and adjust aim.

trade: The buying, selling or barter of *goods* and *services* between or among nations.

trade agreement: A *treaty* specifying the conditions regulating *trade* in *goods* and *services*. See *FTA*.

trade balance: A measurement of the movement of *goods* and *services* between one *state* and all others.

trade barrier: See *new protectionism; non-tariff barriers; protectionism; tariff; quota.* Cf. *free trade; GATT.*

tradecraft: The various techniques used in the conduct of *intelligence*, or how intelligence gathering is actually carried out by professionals. Well-known examples of tradecraft include *cryptology, penetration agents* or setting a *honey trap;* more mundane is knowledge of how to conduct and/or evade *surveillance*, or use of *ciphers* and *listening posts.*

trade related investment measures (TRIMs): Local content and equity requirements, restrictions on *remittance* of *profits, export* requirements and *technology transfer* measures. An effort was made to bring these into the *Uruguay Round*, representing the first venture by *GATT* into *investment* issues that pertain to *trade.*

trade routes: The overland trails or sea-lanes used to carry international *trade* (and along which historically also flowed armies, culture, religion and *technology*). Arab power in the Middle Ages was largely based on the wealth derived from controlling the overland routes from Asia to Europe, which also aided the spread of *Islam.* The Age of Sail permitted Venetians, Portuguese and others to bypass the *Middle East*, thus sending Arab economies and civilization into a decline that some say has yet to be arrested. Much of the history of *colonialism* is the story of the consolidation and protection of the trade routes to India and China from Europe (from the discovery of the Americas to securing the Cape of Good Hope as a way station to India; or the *Sinai* to build a canal to end the need to circumnavigate the Cape), with guardpost colonies at *Aden, Malta* and *Gibraltar.* Modern transportation has made trade routes more varied and less individually important. Still, some routes (such as those through the *Panama* and *Suez Canals*, or the *Straits of Hormuz*) remain key choke points of global commerce.

traditionalism: An approach to the study of world affairs that stresses the study of diplomatic *history*, *international law* and political and moral philosophy, and rejects most *quantitative* analyses as arid, amoral, misplaced and/or *reductionist*. Cf. *behavioralism; post-behavioralism; qualitative analysis.*

Trafalgar, Battle of (October 21, 1805): A British naval victory over a combined French and Spanish fleet, and the decisive naval action of the *Napoleonic Wars*. The British, whose *tactics* and discipline were vastly superior to their foes, did not lose a single *ship-of-the-line*; the French and Spanish lost 20, almost two-thirds of their complement. However, the British commander *Nelson* was killed at the moment of his triumph. The setback prompted *Napoleon I* to curse: "Wherever wood can swim, there I am bound to find this damned flag of England!"

transatlantic: Crossing or spanning the Atlantic Ocean, whether in interests, threats or trade.

Transcaucasia: The portion of *Caucasia* lying south of the Caucasus Mountains. Once the eastern half of the Byzantine Empire, it was overrun by Turkic *tribes* in 1071. It is a patchwork quilt of *nations*, and ethnic and religious hatreds. In 1993/94 *wars* or *rebellions* were underway in *Abkhazia, Ajaria, Armenia, Azerbaijan, Georgia; Nagorno-Karabakh, Ossetia* and *Turkey.* Iran, Russia and Turkey are historic, *regional powers.*

Transcaucasian Soviet Federated Socialist Republic (SFSR): A composite "republic" within the *Soviet Union*, created in 1922 from *Armenia, Azerbaijan* and *Georgia.* When it was broken apart by *Stalin* in 1936, he made certain that ethnic *enclaves* were left isolated, so they would have to turn to Russia as mediator and referee of all regional conflicts. The world lives with that legacy still. Cf. *Nakichevan; Nagorno-Karabakh.*

Trans-Dniestra: A region in eastern *Moldova*, across the Dniester River, occupied mainly by ethnic Russians and Ukrainians. Upon Moldova's *independence* in December 1991, rebels in Trans-Dniestra drew support from the Russian 14th Army. In 1993 they also got some diplomatic support from Russia. The *CSCE* then became involved in *conciliation.*

transformation: In British legal thinking, the doctrine that changes in *international law*, because it lacks a strong sense of *stare decisis*, can be directly incorporated into domestic law even in the absence of legislation by Parliament expressly recording the change.

transgovernmental: Relations, ties or connections, often *functional*, spanning governments at levels below the political.

Transjordan: Originally part of *Arabia* when that area was a province of the *Ottoman Empire*. It was later used by Britain to link Egypt with Iraq. In 1949 the major part, also part of *Palestine*, became *Jordan.*

transnational: *Non-governmental organizations*, activities, connections, loyalties or transactions crossing national *boundaries*, including any private *actors* with interests in foreign countries. In international relations literature, the main concern has been with the transnational character and influence of *multinational corporations*, but some have written cogently on the role of ideas, culture, religion and professional connections.

transnational corporation: See *foreign direct investment; multinational corporation.*

transpacific: Spanning the Pacific Ocean, whether in interests, *influence*, threats or *trade*.

transparency: The notion that agreement on *Confidence and Security Building Measures (CSBMs)* in an otherwise hostile relationship reduces possibilities of miscalculation and *accidental war*, by making capabilities and intentions plain.

Transvaal: A state established "Across the Vaal River" in 1853, by the *Boers*. It was *annexed* by Britain in 1877, by agreement with the Boers who were seeking protection from *Zulu* raids. That contributed to the *First Boer War*, after which it was given *independence* again. It was reannexed after the *Second Boer War*, but given *autonomy* in 1906. It joined the Union of South Africa in 1912.

Transylvania: A region between Hungary and Rumania (within modern Rumania), and constantly a subject of dispute between them. It was ruled by the *Ottomans*, then the *Hapsburgs*. Following the *Ausgleich*, it became part of Hungary. In 1916 Rumania was bribed into *WWI* on the side of the *Allies* by a secret promise of gaining possession of Transylvania (which it later did, in the *Treaty of Trianon*). In 1940 *Hitler* imposed a settlement dividing the province between his two east European allies--a rare instance indeed, of Hitler as peacemaker! In 1947 the entire region was ceded to Rumania. During the *Cold War*, friction continued between what had become *Soviet bloc* allies. In the 1980s Rumania openly persecuted its ethnically Hungarian minority. Once a *pax sovietica* no longer applied after 1989, the issue of ownership re-emerged. In 1993 Hungary hinted that it might no longer accept the Trianon borders, thereby reopening the historic question of ownership of Transylvania. That same year, Rumania granted minority language rights to the 1.7 million Hungarians in Transylvania.

traumatic stress disorder: A psychoneurosis, or other pyschological reaction, resulting from exposure to combat; formerly called *shell shock* or *battle fatigue*.

traveaux préparatoires: Work done preparatory to a *treaty*, used to clarify later interpretations.

treason: Betrayal of a *state* by one of its *citizens*. What constitutes betrayal is, of course, a slippery idea. The U.S. defines it narrowly, limiting it to mean making *war* against one's own country, aiding and abetting the enemy in wartime or committing peacetime *espionage*. Other states do not count peacetime espionage as treasonable, merely criminal. But some define treason so broadly it becomes indistinguishable from dissent. The usual penalty is death. Cf. *war treason*.

treaty: A binding agreement between or among *states*, or with other *international personalities*, enumerating *rules*, and creating mutual rights and obligations under *international law*. Treaties may, but need not, establish *ad hoc* or even permanent mechanisms for resolving *disputes*. They always require *consent* (with the rare but notable exception of a *diktat*). They may and do cover virtually any subject, from the usual concerns with *security* and *commerce* to migratory bird protection and long-term disposition of the mineral resources of the *moon*. Treaties are created and undergo *adoption* by a four-step process: *negotiation, signature, ratification* and--only then--entry into force. Subsequently, they may or may not be offered for *registration*. If points of disagreement arise, they are addressed by one or more of these methods of interpretation: *grammatical, historical, logical, restrictive, systematic*. The nomenclature used for treaties is varied, but of minor consequence. There are two truly important distinctions among treaties: (1) Treaties are executed or executory. The first are very precise, usually have an agreed time frame or specific object in view, and once their designated task is completed they pass into history. The second are not time bound, govern ongoing transactions, and may even anticipate future conditions and developments. (2) Treaties are self-executing or non-self-executing. The first do not require implementing legislation to take effect in domestic law; the second do (but note, if signed and ratified, but not implemented, the failure to implement domestically does not absolve the state concerned from incurring an international *delict*). Lastly, treaties may be terminated in a variety of ways: by fundamentally altered circumstances that render them moot, by the *terms* of the treaty itself (either completion of the object in view, or reaching a specified date for termination), by mutual consent, by *violation*, by *war* or by *extinction* of one of the parties (though even here, some obligations and rights might accrue to a *successor state*). See also *accession; adherence; archive; bilateral; clausula rebus sic stantibus; convention; covenant; declaration; derogation; executive agree-*

ment; *Final Act; friendship treaty; illegal act; instruments of ratification; judicial legislation; jus cogens; law-making treaties; multilateral; nonaggression pact; notification; pact; peace treaty; protocol; obscuritas pacti nocet; reservation; resolution; security treaty; state succession; suspension; trade agreement; tribe; understanding; validity; verification regime.*

treaty ports: Fifty coastal cities of China, including Amoy and Canton, forced open to foreign *trade* by the *Treaty of Nanking, Treaty of Tientsin* and related *diktats.* Treaty ports also existed in Korea and Japan.

Treaty Power/State: (1) In *international relations:* a *state* that has *adhered* to a given multilateral *treaty*, as in "China has a direct interest in [such and such a matter] because it is a Treaty Power." (2) In the United States: Article II(2) of the Constitution, requiring the "advice and consent" of the Senate for subsequent *ratification* of a treaty by the president.

trench warfare: Combat characterized by both sides occupying opposing systems of trenches, from which they launch assaults, patrol perimeters and so forth. Extensive trench warfare occurred in the *Crimean War, American Civil War, Iran/Iraq War* and especially *WWI.* Conditions were so appalling from 1914-18, several diseases were named for their high incidence among the soldiery, to wit: trench fever, trench foot, trench mouth, etc. These horrors have been nowhere so well depicted as in Erich Maria Remarque's "All Quiet on the Western Front" (banned by the *Nazis* for its inherent *pacifism*), and Robert Grave's "Goodbye To All That." See *no-man's-land.*

Trent Affair: This incident during the *American Civil War* aroused widespread anti-*Union* feeling in Britain, and led to a major crisis that almost resulted in *war.* Union *blockade* ships seized two *Confederate* diplomats from a British vessel (the Trent), denying them *diplomatic immunity* because they were rebels. The British chose to view this as a national affront, and threatened war. The crisis was resolved when Russian *mediation* led to a Union apology (which *Seward* convinced a reluctant *Lincoln* to make), and release of the Confederates into British custody.

triad: The three "legs" of the U.S. *strategic weapons* forces: land-based *ICBMs, submarine launched ballistic missiles (SLBMs)* and strategic *bombers.*

Trianon, Treaty of (June 4, 1920): The agreement formally ending *WWI* between the *Allies* and Hungary. It left Hungary truncated from its prewar position, with 2/3rds of its *territory* and a sizeable portion of its

population gone to build up its neighbors: Czechoslovakia received most of Slovakia (Poland got the rest) and *Ruthenia,* Italy took *Fiume,* Rumania got *Transylvania* and *Yugoslavia* (then the *United Kingdom*) took *Croatia* and *Voivodina.* Like Germany, Hungary was restricted to a small army (35,000) and made to pay proportionate *reparations.*

tribalism: When *politics* is characterized by a shattered mosaic of loyalties to competing *tribes* or *ethnic groups.* This can lead to the worst kind of *civil war,* with overtones of *genocide.* See *Bosnia; Rwanda.*

tribe: Any group of people united by common ancestry, custom, language or religion. Politically, the difference from a *nation* or a *people* is really only one of scale. Yet the term is sometimes unconsciously used in the pejorative, as in referring in the same breath to African tribes but Asian or European peoples. It may also be used to deliberate pejorative effect, to belittle the national aspirations of a subject people (say the *Kurds*), or an established people perceived to be acting in barbaric fashion ("the Serbian tribe" rather than nation). Under *international law,* tribe has a tightly circumscribed meaning. It is a political community that lacks full membership in the *world community,* in the legal sense, and hence may not exercise *sovereign* rights such as contracting binding *treaties.* More than once, a colonial power or settler state such as Canada, New Zealand or the United States, has made use of this distinction to deny retroactively the binding character of treaties drawn up with tribes of *indigenous peoples.* Of course, this had led to bitter recrimination and much legal confusion about the international status of tribal land claims and other "treaty rights" that may have been agreed or conferred. If and when tribes acquire *states* they are immediately elevated in diplomatic discourse, in law, and usually also on the editorial pages, from the status of tribe to that of nation. See *Manifest Destiny; Maori Wars; Zulu Wars.*

tributary: A small state that pays tribute (treasure) to a larger power, as acknowledgement of its political subjugation.

Trident: U.S.-built, *boomers* that each carry 24 *MIRVed, SLBMs* (128 *warheads*). Britain also purchased several of these *nuclear weapons* platforms, but announced in 1993 it would limit its Trident to 96 warheads each (its Polaris boats carried 48). Trident *submarines* are quite simply the most awesome, destructive weapons systems created in history.

Trieste: It was made a *free city* by the Italian *treaty* among the *Treaties of Paris* (1947). However, Yugoslavia disputed control until 1954, causing the British and Americans to garrison the city. It was then agreed that Trieste, whose population is mostly Italian, should revert to Italy (confirmed in 1975).

Trinidad and Tobago: Location: Caribbean. Major associations: *CARICOM, Commonwealth, OAS, UN.* Population: 1.3 million. Military: minimal. Discovered by Columbus in 1498, the islands were turned into a raft of *slave labor* plantations for several centuries. Tobago became a British *protectorate* in 1763 (taken from France) and Trinidad followed in 1802 (taken from Spain). They were ruled as a single British *colony* from 1888-1958, when they were made part of the *West Indies Federation.* In 1962 they withdrew in favor of *independence* within the Commonwealth. In 1976 they changed to a *republican* form of government. They are rich in *oil* and other *natural resources,* and are among the most prosperous of Caribbean nations. In 1990 their island peace was disturbed by a quirky revolt by 100-120 Muslim *fundamentalists,* who for six days held the PM and others *hostage.*

Tripartite Pact (September 27, 1940): An agreement signed by Nazi Germany, Fascist Italy and Imperial Japan, undertaking an *alliance* in the event any of them was attacked by an (unnamed) third power with whom they were not then at *war.* It was clearly intended to deter U.S. entry into *WWII,* but had rather the reverse effect: it caused many Americans to see less and less difference between Japan and the European *fascist* states. It was subsequently *adhered* to by Bulgaria, Hungary and Rumania. A Yugoslav government signed in March 1941, but was then overthrown and the *pact* repudiated, leading to a German *invasion.* The Nazi *puppet states* of Croatia and Slovakia also signed, later in the war. Cf. *Axis.*

Triple Alliance: (1) 1668: A *league* of England, the Netherlands and Sweden, against France. (2) 1717: A league of Britain, France and the Netherlands against Spain. (3) 1882-1915: A secret *alliance* between Austria-Hungary, Germany and Italy, pledging mutual assistance in the event of an attack by France. As it was Germany that attacked France in 1914, Italy was entirely within its legal rights in refusing to accept that the *treaty* had come into effect. However, it was an entirely different matter when Italy abrogated the Triple Alliance by joining the *Allies,* and *declared war* on Germany and Austria in 1915.

Triple Entente: A loose term used for the three-way British, French and Russian cooperation between 1907 and 1914, and the military *alliance* signed on September 3, 1914 (and sometimes confused with the *Entente*

Cordiale). The 1914 military *pact* was disavowed by the *Bolsheviks* when they signed a *separate peace* with Germany at *Brest-Litovsk* in 1918.

Triple Intervention: Within six days of the end of the *Sino/Japanese War,* France, Germany and Russia counseled Japan to renounce the claim to the Liaotung Peninsula it had just wrested from China. Japan agreed to be pushed out of *Manchuria,* but regarded the *intervention* as little more than a veiled threat from imperial rivals. Within 10 years Japanese troops returned in force, and stayed for 40 years.

tripolarity: A theoretical structure for the *international system* in which three main centers of great *power,* or poles, are said to attract lesser powers into their orbit. Some theoreticians maintain that such a system would be inherently unstable, as each of the three *Great Powers* would seek to be in the party of two while fearing a betrayal might leave it the party of one; that effect would be magnified for smaller powers. Cf. *biploarity; multipolarity; unipolarity.*

Tripoli (a.k.a. Tripolitania): One of the *Barbary States,* and later an Italian *colony* that put up heavy *guerrilla* resistance to *conquest* 1922-30. See *Libya.*

Tripolitan War (1801-07): Following *independence* the U.S. *merchant marine* was no longer protected by the *Royal Navy,* and fell victim to predations by the *Barbary pirates.* In the mid-1790s, with a dozen ships captured and 100 (white) Americans taken as *slaves* or *hostages,* Congress agreed to pay annual ransom to the Dey of Algiers, and made similar *treaties* with *Tripoli* and *Tunisia (Tunis).* All these treaties were violated by the "pirates." President *Thomas Jefferson* sent a punitive expedition in 1801, but the underequipped, outgunned Americans suffered several defeats. Despite a minor victory in 1805, the U.S. continued to ransom its *citizens.* Jefferson withdrew the navy, which he had consistently underfunded, in 1807. After the buildup of the *War of 1812* a much stronger American force returned in 1815, joined by flotillas from several European nations, and ended the *piracy.*

Troppau, Congress of (1820): Austria, Prussia and Russia met, with Britain and France as observers, to deal with an outbreak of liberal *revolution* in the Italian and Iberian peninsulas. Britain agreed to Austrian *intervention* in Italy, but rejected the general premise of the three conservative powers, especially Russia, that intervention was justified to suppress any reform or revolt in Europe.

Trotsky, Leon Davidovich, *né* **Bronstein (1879-1940):**

Russian revolutionary. He allied with *Lenin* in 1902 but did not join the *Bolsheviks*. In the *Russian Revolution of 1905* he founded the *St. Petersburg Soviet*. In 1917 he headed the *Petrograd Soviet*, and this time joined Lenin and the Bolsheviks. As Commissar for Foreign Affairs he negotiated the *Treaty of Brest-Litovsk*. He led and organized the *Red Army* in the *Russian Civil War*, during which he showed a capacity for ruthlessness rivaled by few. After Lenin's death *Stalin* maneuvered Trotsky out of power, and in 1929 sent him into *exile*. The policy of *socialism in one country* thus won out over Trotsky's more romantic, and *adventurist*, notion of *permanent revolution*. He founded the *Fourth International* in 1938 to oppose Stalin, whom he regarded as having betrayed the *revolution*. In 1940 Stalin sent an assassin to murder Trotsky in his home in Mexico. The deed was done by means of several blows to the head with an icepick.

trotskyites: Followers of the theories of *Leon Trotsky*, forming into marginal groups within the wider *marxist* movement after 1928. Highly critical of *stalinism*, they yet indulged in rather a *cult of personality* of their own. Their main, historic importance was to feed *Stalin's* paranoia about a conspiracy to overthrow his *regime*. Trotskyites are famous for arcane, doctrinal quarrels (prompting the jest that wherever one finds two trotskyites one also finds three "tendencies").

trouble spot: A journalistic euphemism for an area of endemic international conflict and violence, such as the *Balkans* or the *Middle East*.

Troubles, the: A popular euphemism for the *Irish War of Independence*, 1918-21, sometimes including the *Irish Civil War*, 1922. This term has been revived and used since 1969 for the ongoing sectarian violence in *Ulster*.

truce: Suspension of fighting for a specified time. It may be used, loosely, as a synonym for *armistice*.

Trucial Oman (a.k.a. Trucial States): Seven *sheikdoms* on the south, or Trucial, coast of the *Persian Gulf*: Abu Dhabi, Ajman, Dubai, Fujairah, Ras al-Kaimah, Sharjah and Umm al-Qaiwain. They maintained a *treaty* relationship with Britain from the 19th century, when they were compelled to cease their *piracy* in the Gulf. They became in effect a British *protectorate* in 1914, after Turkey entered *WWI*. In 1971 they formed the *United Arab Emirates*. In an earlier era, they were called collectively by the British the "Pirate Coast." Cf. *Barbary Coast*.

Trudeau, Pierre Elliot (b.1919): Canadian statesman.

Minister of Justice 1967; PM 1968-79, 1980-84. His main concentration during his whole time in office was the problem of *Québec*. In 1970 he introduced *martial law* ("War Measures Act") in response to a few *terrorist* incidents in Québec; it was lifted within weeks, but has generally been judged a gross overreaction to events. He sought to confirm that province within the Canadian confederation after 1980 by *repatriation* of the constitution from Westminster. One of his first actions in foreign affairs was to cut Canada's troop commitment to *NATO* by 50%. That was coupled with a new emphasis on promoting precise national, including economic and symbolic, interests as opposed to the postwar *liberal-internationalism* pursued by his predecessors. He spoke of finding a "Third Option" for Canada, by which he essentially meant less reliance on the U.S., and of increasing *foreign aid*. But shifting trade toward the *EC* or the *Pacific Rim* was more easily said than done (the percentage of Canadian trade with the U.S. remained near 80%); and budget and domestic pressures meant Canada never met its promised aid targets. As the 1970s and *détente* both waned, Trudeau reluctantly agreed to increase defense spending, paralleling a shift all across NATO countries. But he reacted less strongly than most other Western leaders to the Soviet *invasion* of Afghanistan (during which he was briefly out of office), and spoke with sympathy for the dilemma faced by General *Jaruzelski* in his decision to introduce martial law to Poland. As tensions grew between the U.S. and Soviet Union in the early 1980s, he launched himself on a multinational "peace mission" to stimulate *arms control* talks. Although politely received abroad and domestically popular, the effort led to no measurable, practical success.

Truk: See *Caroline Islands*.

Truman, Harry S (1884-1972): U.S. statesman. VP 1945; President 1945-53. He took office upon the death of *Franklin Roosevelt*, in the midst of the *San Francisco Conference*. He was a committed supporter of the *UN*, in particular of its *human rights* programs. Within weeks of taking power he went to the *Potsdam Conference*. Then he was faced with momentous decisions, in particular whether and how to use the *atomic bomb* against Japan. With the end of *WWII* he canceled *Lend-Lease*, some have said too quickly. Aided by a brilliant supporting cast including *Dean Acheson*, *Lucius D. Clay* and *George Marshall*, Truman oversaw the recovery from WWII, including rehabilitation of the *Axis* states. He directed the *Berlin air lift*, announced the *Truman Doctrine* and began *containment* with the *European Recovery Program* and the founding of *NATO*. His administration then was bogged down domestically in the tragi-farce of *McCarthyism,* and in its diplomacy in the morass of the *Korean Conflict*. During that *war* he took the courageous decision to fire *Douglas MacArthur* for his insubordination and reckless talk about war with China. He left office deeply unpopular, but has been judged by many historians as one of the more farsighted and decisive U.S. presidents in the 20th century.

Truman Doctrine (March 12, 1947): A promise of U.S. *aid* to all "free peoples who are resisting attempted subjugation by armed minorities or by outside powers." Its initial impetus was the perceived need to aid Greece against a communist *insurgency*, and prepare the American public for future engagements against the Soviet Union (including military *intervention* in what was otherwise peacetime) in the interests of *containment*.

trustee (a.k.a. trusteeship) powers: Those seven *states* charged with responsibility for one or more of the UN *trust territories:* Australia, Belgium, Britain, France, Italy, New Zealand and the U.S.

Trusteeship Council: One of the *Principal Organs* of the *UN*, charged by the *UNGA* with overseeing the *trust territories* (with the exception of the *Trust Territory of the Pacific Islands*, the sole *strategic* trust. It is technically overseen by the *Security Council)*. It replaced the *mandate* authority of the defunct *League of Nations*. Membership includes all *trustee powers*, all other members of the Security Council, and other states elected by the UNGA. Most of the work of the Trusteeship Council has been accomplished, including the difficult and legally tangled job of securing *independence* for *Namibia*.

trust/trusteeship territories: The 12 *territories* so designated by Article 77 of the UN Charter. By 1950, 11 territories were in the trust of seven *trustee powers*. All but Somalia were former *mandates*: *Cameroons* (Britain), Cameroons (France), *Nauru* (Australia), *New Guinea* (Australia), *Ruanda-Urundi* (Belgium), *Somaliland* (Italy), *Tanganyika* (Britain), *Togoland* (Britain), *Togoland* (France), *Trust Territory of the Pacific Islands* (U.S.) and *Western Samoa* (New Zealand). Of these, eight achieved self-rule by 1962. By 1989 only *Palau* (from the Trust Territory of the Pacific Islands) remained in trust, and it voted for *free association* with the U.S. in 1993. The most difficult case was the 12th: South Africa's refusal to submit *Namibia* (South West Africa) to UN authority. But even that was eventually resolved, with Namibian *independence* coming in 1990. In 1986 the UN declared *New Caledonia* in trust, over vehement French objection.

Trust Territory of the Pacific Islands: Some 2,100 islands spread over 3 million square miles of the Pacific. A U.S. *trust territory* from 1947, comprising the Caroline, Mariana and Marshall Island groups recaptured from Japan. It was the only *strategic* trust. Until 1952 it was administered directly by the U.S. Navy, then handed to the Department of the Interior (save the Marianas, which remained with the navy until 1962). In 1975 a *referendum* led to formation of a Commonwealth of the Northern Marianas, in *free association* with the U.S. That left only *Palau* in trust, and it too voted for free association in 1993. See also *Micronesia (Fedrated States); Marianas; Marshall Islands*. Cf. *Guam*.

Tsar: "Caesar." The title of the *emperors* of Russia.

tsarist Russia: The Russian Empire when ruled by the tsars, from the renunciation of vassalage to the Mongols by *Ivan III (the Great)* in 1480, to its end with the abdication of *Nicholas II* in 1917. Tsarism upheld principles of *autocracy* and paternalism, even under the most able reformers. See *Russia*.

Tshombe, Moïse (1920-69): He led the revolt of *Katanga* province during the *Congo crisis*, earning opprobrium among other African leaders for his use of white *mercenaries* in support of Belgian mining interests. He had *Patrice Lumumba* murdered. Upon the reunification of Katanga with Congo, he went abroad. He returned to office briefly as PM of the Congo Republic 1964-65, but he soon fell out with *Mobutu* and again fled. He was condemned to death *in absentia*, but died instead under mysterious circumstances in an Algerian jail.

T'su Hsi (1834-1908): "The Dowager Empress." She acted as regent for half a century, possibly even killing her own son to retain full powers. Deeply conservative and *xenophobic*, even after the *defeat* of the *Sino/Japanese War* she opposed reform, moving to stop the "Hundred Days of Reform" in 1898. She sought to preserve everything traditional in China, and hated all foreigners. She secretly supported the *Boxer Rebellion*, with dire results for the *Manchus*. Her *reactionary* rule left China backward relative to the Western powers and Russia. Most important, she left it vulnerable to a rising Japan, which chose a far different response to the foreign threat.

Tsushima Straits, Battle of May 27-28, 1905): Refused permission to use the *Suez Canal*, during the *Russo/Japanese War* the Russian Baltic Fleet was sent on a seven-month-long voyage to the Far East, to replace the fleet sunk by surprise Japanese attack in

Port Arthur in 1904. It almost caused *war* with Britain along the way, at *Dogger Bank*. It arrived at the Tsushima Strait (running through two adjacent islands between Korea and Kyushu, Japan) just in time to be nearly entirely sunk, with heavy loss of life. After that two-day battle, Russia agreed to meet to discuss *terms* at *Portsmouth*.

Tunisia (Tunis): Location: N. Africa. Major associations: *Arab League, Maghreb Union, OAU, UN*. Population: 8.2 million. Military: modest in size and equipment. During the 19th century Tunis was virtually independent from the *Ottomans*. Under the Bey of Tunis it was one of the *Barbary states*. In 1881, out of fear of Italian ambitions for North African *conquest*, the Bey signed an agreement with France accepting to become a *protectorate*. During *WWII* it was under *Vichy* rule at first, but became an *Allied* and *Free French* base for the *invasions* of Sicily and Italy in 1943. It became an independent *monarchy* in 1956. In 1957 the Bey was overthrown and Tunisia became a *republic*. Habib Bourguiba (b.1903) became Premier in 1956 and was President 1957-87. From 1954-62 Tunisia was used as a base for French operations during the *Algerian War of Independence*. After the Algerian war Bourguiba kept a low profile in foreign affairs, concentrating on a fairly progressive domestic agenda (by Middle East or N. African standards), and cultivating trade and political links with the *EC*. His diplomatic moderation drew criticism from more radical Arab neighbors. He initiated *mediation* of the Jordanian/PLO war in 1970. In the early 1980s Tunisia had to fend off Libyan raids and efforts to provoke a *rebellion* of its southern population, which harbors historic grievances against the north. Political dissent rose alongside living standards, and after 1985 the demand for political freedoms could not be resisted. Bourguiba was overthrown in 1987, and a multiparty system was set up in 1988. Like other North African states, Tunisia faces a domestic challenge to its *modernization* from Islamic *fundamentalists*.

turbulence: A term used by some theorists to describe high levels of complexity and dynamism said to be a special characteristic of modern *international politics*. This, they add, qualitatively alters the efficiency and utility, and increases the "permeability" to outside influences, of all *states*. As a result, the *international system* is seen as in transition to global, *complex interdependence*. Note: There is much confusion in the literature about whether advocates mean this phenomenon is a *cause* of large-scale changes, or an *effect* of those changes. At least one foremost proponent of the idea unapologetically uses it both ways, thereby illuminating neither side of the causal question.

Turkestan: An older, geographical/cultural term referring to the vast region of *Central Asia* populated mainly by Turkic speaking peoples. It includes northern Afghanistan and stretches as far as parts of southwestern China. Its main components are: Kazahkstan, Kirghizstan, Tajikistan, Turkmenistan and Uzbekistan.

Turkey: Location: *Middle East*. Major associations: *ECO, NATO, OECD, UN*. Population: 58 million. Military: NATO member, and while not *first-line*, NATO quality, still a formidable *regional power*. Turkey formed the core of the *Ottoman Empire* during its many centuries of *martial* glory, then slow decay and decline. The Turks rejected the *Treaty of Sèvres (1920)* and fought successfully to obtain the better terms of the *Treaty of Lausanne*. The modern *republic* was proclaimed by *Atatürk* in October 1923, with deliberate intent to sever it from its Ottoman and *Islamic* past and create a modern, *secular* state (the *caliphate* was renounced in 1924). It was for this reason the capital was moved to Ankara in 1923 from *Constantinople* (Istanbul). Turkey was a *one-party state* until 1950, after which it varied between civilian and military rule until in the present day it is in a civilian phase. In foreign affairs, it sat out *WWII*. Feeling pressure from the *Soviet Union* even in the 1930s (e.g., in the *Montreux Convention*), it joined NATO in 1952. But its foreign policy has really been dominated by three regional issues: (1) Relations with Greece, particularly over *Cyprus*, have always been bad. The conflict undermined its position in NATO and led to Turkey's *invasion* of Cyprus in 1974. (2) Relations with Armenians, both within Turkey and in the Armenian *diaspora*, have been terrible since the *Armenian genocide*. They worsened in April 1993, when Armenian gains in the *Armenia/Azerbaijan War* led Turkey to warn that it would not wait as it had in Bosnia, but would *intervene* unilaterally if necessary to stop any dismemberment of Azerbaijan. (3) Relations with the *Kurds* remain bad, with Turkey repressing its own Kurds and working with Iran and Syria to prevent the emergence of a Kurdish *state* in northern Iraq. Turkey did not join the *Gulf Coalition*, but during the *Gulf War* it lent its airfields to the coalition and agreed to block Iraqi *oil* shipments through a northern pipeline. It has since cooperated with UN *sanctions* against Iraq. The rise of *neo-nazism* in Germany meant relations were damaged by several murderous attacks on Turkish nationals who were "guest workers" in Germany, including firebombing deaths of women and children. Turkey hoped to join the *EU*, but the events of 1989-90 propelled several other countries ahead of it on the waiting list, raising suspicions (among Turks) that the EU has racial and/or religious prejudices against accepting them as members.

Turkish Republic of Northern Cyprus: Turkish Cypriots declared the northern 40% of the island independent in 1983, but this *vassal state* of Istanbul does not enjoy international *recognition*. See *Cyprus.*

Turkmenistan: Location: Central Asia. Major associations: *CIS, CSCE, UN.* Population: 3.5 million (70% Turkmen; 15% Russian; 10% Uzbek). Military: revamped *Red Army* units. This area has been overrun by successive waves of Asian nomads over several millenia. It was conquered by, and incorporated into, the *Russian Empire* in 1881. It was kept in the empire by the *Bolsheviks*, and became a consitutent "republic" of the *Soviet Union* in a reorganization by *Stalin* in 1924. It declared *independence* following a failed *coup* in Moscow in August 1991, but was not *recognized* until the *extinction* of the Soviet Union in December. It has rich mineral, *oil* and gas deposits. With independence it developed its own *currency* and sought *foreign direct investment.* Politically, it has changed hardly at all from the Soviet period: it remains deeply *authoritarian*, with a poor *human rights* record.

turn-key factory: An industrial plant built and managed entirely by a foreign concern, whether an *aid* agency or a *multinational corporation (MNC)*, until local management and *labor* are trained to take over. This is one example of *technology transfer.*

Tuvalu: Location: Pacific. Major associations: *ACP, Commonwealth, SPC, SPF, UN.* Population: 8,000. Military: none. Formerly the Ellice Islands, this *microstate* of fewer than 8,000 souls is isolated from population centers, cut off from sea lanes and lacking in mineral resources (although it does claim a sizeable *EEZ*). It was a British *protectorate* from 1892 as part of the Gilbert and Ellice Islands, and a *colony* after 1916. *Occupied* by Japan early in *WWII*, it was *liberated* and occupied by the U.S. from 1943-45. A UN supervised *referendum* in 1974 led to a split with the Gilberts (Kiribati), and it became independent as Tuvalu in 1978. As a *special member* of the Commonwealth, Britain still represents most of its foreign interests. As a low-lying atoll, its existence may be threatened by rising sea levels due to *global warming.*

twelve-mile limit: Over the course of the 20th century agreement on the *three-mile limit* broke down, as *coastal states* extended claims to exclusive fishing and the *territorial sea.* Much discussion failed to resolve the problem, including lack of progress at *UNCLOS I* and *II.* During the 1960s and 1970s a number of *states*, including several major maritime powers, declared they would honor a twelve-mile limit. Adjusting to a *de facto* situation, *UNCLOS III* endorsed this

change to the territorial sea. States may now assert their *sovereignty* to a maximum of 12 miles (some have set limits less than that).

Twenty-One Demands (January 18, 1915): In January 1915, the Japanese presented the Chinese government with twenty-one, secret demands, amounting to an *ultimatum* to become a Japanese *protectorate.* They were in five groups, with Group Five the most far-reaching: (1) confirmation of Japan's seizure of *Shantung* from Germany; (2) extension of the *leaseholds*, soon to expire, for *Port Arthur*, Darien and the South Manchurian Railroad from 25 to 99 years; (3) granting of Japanese industrial *monopolies* in central China; (4) non-alienation of China's coastal territory; (5) placing Japanese overseers in key government positions, grants of interior lands to select Japanese, joint control of China's police, and Chinese arms purchases to be made solely from Japan and with Tokyo's approval. China submitted to most of the demands, granting Tokyo the rights to the previous German *sphere of influence* and extending the leaseholds. But the Chinese leaked the note, leading to British *mediation* that prevented total capitulation, such as the placing of Japanese "advisers" at all levels of China's government. This creeping *aggression* against China greatly deepened long-term U.S. suspicion of Japan. In realizing only part of its extreme ultimatum, Japan lost face. But it soon redirected its aggression toward *Manchuria.* Cf. *Lansing/Ishii Agreement; unequal treaties.*

two-Chinas policy: An attempt in the early 1970s by several *nations* to give *de jure* sanction to the *de facto* separation of *Formosa* from China after the Communist *revolution* in 1949. The United States, in particular, was anxious to finally extend *recognition* to *mainland China* without cutting off its close ties to *Taiwan.* However, neither Beijing nor Taiping would permit joint recognition as each claimed full *sovereignty* over the other. This ultimately forced most countries to formally downgrade their relations with Taiwan. Some wag has truly said of this situation that the only thing the two Chinas agreed upon was that there was only one China.

two-front war: Where one has to fight two (or more) enemies on separate fronts, demanding a division of forces for both defense and offense. This was the *strategic* nightmare of German war planners that underlay the *Schlieffen Plan. Hitler* regarded fighting a two-front war as the *Kaiser's* major mistake, and was determined not to repeat it during *WWII.* But he did: failing to finish off Britain before attacking Russia probably was the decisive error of the war. The Soviets, too, feared such a war, but Japan attacked softer targets to the south rather than turn west against *Zhukov's* Siberian divisions. It is noteworthy that the U.S. also fought a two-front war during *WWII*, although the Pacific played second fiddle to Europe in terms of troops, *air power* and *landing craft*. That contrasted with the experience of the Soviet Union, which only entered the war against Japan three months after the *surrender* of Nazi Germany; and differed from Britain, which while at war with Japan, used mainly *Indian Army* and token naval forces in the Pacific *theater* until later in the war. In the post-*Cold War* era, it is stated U.S. policy to maintain a military capable of fighting two *Gulf War*-sized conflicts at the same time. Cf. *second front; unconditional surrender.*

two-plus-four talks (1989-90): *Negotiations* held concerning German unification, among the two Germanies (East and West) and the four *occupation* powers from *WWII* (Britain, France, the Soviet Union and the United States). These talks were essential to rapid reunification. They concerned matters of both internal (between the Germanies) and external (between Germany and the *Allied* powers) *sovereignty*, especially the fate of some 300,000 *Red Army* troops still in *East Germany* (full withdrawal took place in 1994), and whether the new Germany could remain in *NATO*. This eight month flurry of extraordinary *negotiation* and innovation resulted in several *bilateral* and *multilateral* treaties on *border* issues and *arms control*. It was without peer in postwar *diplomacy* in terms of peaceful accomplishments. The agreements reached formally concluded both WWII and the *Cold War*. See also *Oder-Neisse Line; Paris, Charter of (1990).*

two-power naval standard: The key to British naval policy from 1899-1912, a time of enormous naval construction and competition. It was Britain's stated goal, at a minimum, to maintain the *Royal Navy* at the equivalent strength of the next two largest navies combined. The standard was applied mainly to *capital warships* (then including only *battleships, battlecruisers* and *cruisers*, not yet *aircraft carriers* or *submarines*). In fact, the British standard was actually kept at higher than just equivalence. But the development of *Dreadnoughts* and Germany's construction of a major, surface battle fleet under *Tirpitz*, meant that Britain was pressed to abandon the two-power standard in 1912, in favor of a 60% margin over the next largest (that is, the German) main fleet. The U.S. refused to accept less than equality with the Royal Navy after *WWI*, and with Britain's economy already in decline, in 1922 the two-power standard was formally abandoned and new ratios accepted by London and written into the *Five Power Naval Treaty*.

Two Sicilies, Kingdom of: An intermittently independent kingdom founded by the Normans and existing from 1130-1861, when it was incorporated into modern Italy. Toward the end, it was really the Kingdom of Naples, with Sicily kept in submission.

two-speed Europe: The idea that those *states* interested in rapid political and defense as well as economic *integration* of the *EU* should push the process forward with due speed, in the expectation that others will eventually have to follow, or not.

Typhoon: U.S. term for a class of Soviet nuclear *submarine* that carried 20-24 *MIRVed, ICBMs.*

tyranny: (1) Unjust, arbitrary exercise of power by an absolute ruler, or tyrant. (2) Laws and actions by any government that are strongly felt to be oppressive.

tyrannicide: The killing of a tyrant. Cf. *assassination; wet affair.*

U

U-2 incident (May 1, 1960): A U.S. spy plane, the high-altitude U-2, was shot down over the Soviet Union. Its pilot, Gary Powers, was captured. *Khrushchev* used the incident as an excuse to break off his *summit* in Paris with *Eisenhower* two weeks later, pretending it was a U.S. *provocation*. Yet such flights had been going on for years: Powers was not the first (or the last) U.S. pilot shot down by the Soviets; however, the other incidents were kept secret, by both sides, until after the end of the *Cold War*. Powers was swapped to the U.S. for a captured Soviet *agent* in 1962. See also *Open Skies*.

Ubangi-Shari: See *Central African Republic*.

U-boat *(Unterseeboot):* A German *submarine* in *WWI* or *WWII*. See *Anglo/German Naval Agreement; Battle of the Atlantic; convoy; sea power; unrestricted submarine warfare; wolf pack*.

UDI (Unilateral Declaration of Independence): Made by *Rhodesia* on November 11, 1965, it was rejected by Britain and the *UN* as illegal and led to *sanctions*.

Uganda: Location: E. Africa. Major associations: *Commonwealth, OAU, UN*. Population: 18 million. Military: enmeshed in government; no offensive capability. It came under British *influence* after 1890, when the British East Africa Co. began to penetrate the interior. Missionaries followed, then British troops and conversion into a *protectorate* in 1894. Government was by a mixed pattern of *direct* and *indirect rule*. It became independent in 1962 with the Kabaka (king) of the Buganda *tribe* as president, the Buganda region semi-*autonomous*, and Milton Obote (b.1924) as PM. In 1966 Obote carried out a *coup* that overthrew the Kabaka and the privileges of Buganda. He was in turn overthrown in 1971 by *Idi Amin*, whose brutal reign lasted until he provoked a brief *war* with Tanzania in 1980. Obote returned to power on the bayonets of the Tanzanian army in 1980. His second presidency was an economic disaster and saw a bloodbath to rival that of Amin. He was overthrown and fled a second time in 1985. From 1971-86 perhaps one million Ugandans perished in war, massacres or *famine*. Out of this tribal violence and *anarchy*, in 1986 Yoweri Museveni (b.1944) led his National Resistance Army to power, seizing the capital and imposing order in the provinces. Uganda is now undergoing slow economic, political and social *reconstruction* from two decades of terror and destruction.

ukase: In Russia, a *tsarist* edict or decree.

Ukraine: Location: E. Europe/Near Abroad. Major associations: *CIS, CSCE, UN*. Population: 52 million. Military: 3rd largest nuclear power; significant navy; large conventional army, *strategic* air force capability. This vast, bountiful land was the center of the first Russian state--Kievan Rus (c.882-c.1240), which fell to internal divisions and Asian *invasions*. Ukraine was occupied for 200 years by the Mongols but was more deeply influenced by Russia, to which it was connected for the following 300 years. During the *Russian Civil War* Ukrainian *Whites* joined with Poles to fight the *Bolsheviks*, but ultimately lost. During *Stalin's* forced *collectivization* of *agriculture* Ukraine experienced an artificial, political famine and slaughter of the *kulaks* that may have taken as many as 15 million lives. Then *Nazi* armies tore across it, *pillaging* and murdering from 1941-44. Ukrainians both fought the Nazis and joined them: some helped with the extermination of the Jews, others formed divisions to fight the returning *Red Army*, while still others joined that army or *partisan* groups and killed Germans. Some *guerrilla* fighting against the restoration of Soviet rule over Ukraine lasted until the early 1950s, with a least minor support from Western *intelligence* agencies. After *WWII* new *territory* was added from Czechoslovakia, Poland and Rumania; the *Crimea* was a "gift" from Russia in 1954. Ukraine became independent, one of the *successor states* to the Soviet Union, on December 25, 1991. It has not ratified *START I*, as promised, leaving it with 176 strategic *missiles*. Of these, 130 are SS-19s, old missiles that leak. Ukraine appeared to be holding them to extort economic and disarmament assistance from the West. The real problem was its 46 SS-24s, the latest and best missiles built by the Soviet Union (in a factory now in Ukraine). Each can be *MIRV*ed with 10 *warheads*. It also had two divisions of Blackjack nuclear *bombers*, giving it in 1993 the third largest nuclear arsenal in the world. Some argued it should keep the weapons to guarantee its *independence* by *deterrence* of a Russian attack, as unlikely as that may seem. Other analysts suggested the weapons would be more likely to provide future targets than act as a deterrent. The issue seemed resolved when Ukraine's economy collapsed in midsummer 1993, and high *inflation* set in. Deeply indebted to Russia, it announced a swap of control of the weapons for debt relief. But gains by the hard right in parliamentary elections in Russia kept the issue in doubt. In January 1994, Ukraine, Russia and America agreed to a deal whereby Ukraine has seven years to give up its *nuclear weapons*, in exchange for a share of $12 billion committed by the U.S. to purchase Russian and Ukrainian surplus *uranium*, and promises of respect for its *territorial integrity.* Ukraine was told that it would be excluded from *NATO's* new *partnerships for peace* if it kept the weapons. It also argued with Russia after 1991 over the *Black Sea Fleet.* In 1993 Ukraine leased Russia its old base at *Sebastapol.* But the status of Crimea came into question again in 1994, when ethnic Russians voted in a *secessionist* party. Eastern Ukraine, too, is a problem for Kiev, as it contains 10 million Russians and is potentially a secessionist area. By 1994 Ukraine's neighbors were cutting off sales, due to unpaid bills. See also *Tartars; Uniate Church.*

Ulbricht, Walter (1893-1973): East German statesman. He was a communist deputy in the *Reichstag* from 1928 until the *communist party* was banned by the *Nazis* in 1933, when he escaped to Moscow. Ulbricht returned in 1945, arriving with the other baggage while the *Red Army* was visiting Berlin. He rose to head the German authority within the Soviet *occupation zone,* and remained in charge when it became the *German Democratic Republic* in 1949. He was a stern *stalinist* in all respects, slavishly adhering to the *party line* set out by his masters in Moscow.

Ulster: An independent Celtic kingdom during the Middle Ages, in more recent history it made up the nine northern counties of *Ireland.* As a reward for service in Britain's *wars,* Protestants settled in Ulster on land *expropriated* from Irish Catholic peasants (the "Plantation of Ulster"). As the *Home Rule* movement grew in the rest of Ireland in the 19th century, Ulster Protestants organized against it. Before *WWI* they threatened armed resistance under the leadership of Edward Carson (1854-1935). His organization of a Protestant *militia* (the Ulster Volunteers) nearly brought about *civil war.* That near-tragedy was averted only by the greater tragedy of the outbreak of *WWI.* After the *Irish War of Independence* Ulster ceded three of its most Catholic counties to the South, while the predominantly Protestant six remained part of the *United Kingdom.* After that, the gerrymandered Protestant majority insisted on perpetual *union* with Britain, and discriminated against Catholics in jobs and housing (in scarce supply due to economic decline). In 1967 a new round of sectarian violence required an increased British military presence, at first to protect Catholics (who patterned their civil rights movement on the American), then to deal with the *IRA,* which attacked the troops and regular police. In this confusion of loyalties, on "Bloody Sunday" (January 30, 1972) 13 protesters were killed in Londonderry by British troops. After that, rising levels of violence --the conflict claimed some 3,200 lives by 1994--led to *direct rule* by Westminster. Secret *peace talks* with the IRA took place in 1993. An Anglo/Irish "Framework Agreement" was signed as well, in which Britain agreed not to oppose all-Ireland union and Ireland agreed to respect a majority wish to forgo union, and to alter its constitution to meet Protestant concerns about minority rights. The agreement aims at new negotiating structures to help end the violence, and at cooperative governance of the province. In the longer term, demographic projections suggest Protestants will lose their majority sometime around 2020, making possible a majority decision to join the South. This impending change may permit either a reasoned settlement in advance of *secession,* or yet make possible a bitter *civil war* in Ulster, and even all Ireland.

ultimate destination: Under a *blockade,* the doctrine that *goods* may be seized as *contraband* if their final destination is enemy *territory,* no matter what the ship manifest says or whether they first stop in *neutral* territory. In short, goods are required to make a "continuous voyage" to a neutral port, if they are to be judged neutral goods. It was originally a British doctrine, held especially against the French after 1756. The U.S. accepted this rule during the *American Civil War,* and its Supreme Court repeatedly upheld this doctrine in contraband cases. See also *infection.*

ultimatum: A statement by one party of final and often peremptory terms of settlement of a *dispute,* which if ignored will result in a break in *diplomatic relations, sanctions* or *armed hostilities.* It may also be used as a grand, albeit highly risky, bluff.

ultramontane: Belief in the supreme moral and even political authority of the *Catholic Church* and withholding loyalty from any *state* that challenges church doctrine, authority or interests. See *Kulturkampf.*

ultra vires: In *international law,* beyond the scope or *jurisdiction* of the law.

UN: See *United Nations Organization.*

unanimity rule: A fairly standard rule in *multilateral diplomacy,* whereby action may only proceed with unanimous *consent.* It gives each participant a working *veto.* Cf. *qualified majority voting.*

unconditional surrender: An unusual demand, made only if one is or expects to be in a utterly overwhelming position on the battlefield. In fact, most *surrenders* take place under negotiated conditions. The most famous instance of unconditional surrender was the demand made of the *Axis* by *Franklin Roosevelt* at the *Casablanca Conference* in 1943 (later endorsed by *Churchill* and *Stalin*). It reflected determination not to repeat the "*stab-in-the-back*" theory about *WWI* that the *Nazis* used to such *propaganda* advantage, and to reassure Stalin that the West would not seek a *separate peace* with *Hitler* (and vice versa). The policy has been criticized for stiffening Axis resistance and possibly prolonging the *war*. Alternately, it has been credited with bringing home to the *defeated* states the depth of their loss, and thereby setting the *postwar* stage for genuine reform. Applied rigorously to Germany, it was waived to permit the single condition for Japan of retention of Emperor *Hirohito*, but not until *atomic bombs* had incinerated two cities.

underdeveloped nation: An older term for *developing nation,* no more in use due to its putative insensitivity.

underdevelopment: A concept from *dependency theory.* It implied not merely a lack of *development* in the *Third World* but a history of negative development, or "underdevelopment," caused by *imperialism* and *colonialism.* Using essentially *marxist* categories of analysis, it was posited by some writers (not all of whom were marxists) that for centuries *capitalism* had extracted *surplus value* from the *South* and transferred it to the *West.* From this premise several conclusions flowed: (1) continued attachment to the *world capitalist system* perpetuated unequal economic relations and *dependent development;* (2) the Third World was owed *reparations* in some form (*aid, preferential trade* and so on); and (3) domestic and foreign policies were needed in the South that aimed to retain the domestic "surplus" at home, to be plowed back into autonomous *growth.* Classical economists in the West, and their governments, never accepted these theses. But in the 1960s and 1970s the *G-77* got them adopted as something of an official *ideology* for such *international organizations* as *UNCTAD* and the *UNDP.* After that, their influence waned sharply and debate shifted toward *reformism.* See also *debt crisis; NIEO.*

underground economy: Economic activity that goes unreported to governments, primarily as a way of avoiding taxation. See also *black market.*

understanding: (1) In *diplomacy*: a written explanation of one *state's* policy given to another, usually in the form of a memo or *diplomatic note,* for purposes of clarification. (2) In *international law*: an explanation attached to a *reservation,* which is in turn attached to the *instruments of ratification* for a *treaty.* It spells out the attaching state's interpretation of specific aspects of the treaty, but without binding the other party(ies) to that interpretation.

unequal treaties: A series of agreements between China and various foreign powers in which China accepted onerous and unbalanced *terms of trade,* and permitted extraterritorial *capitulations* to foreign *citizens* and powers. The first unequal treaty was the *Treaty of Nanking* (1842), following the first *Opium War.* The second was the *Treaty of Tientsin* (1858). A spate of unequal treaties were signed in 1860, in which China was forced to legalize the opium trade, open more ports and the Yangtze to foreign trade, permit Christian missionaries direct access to its interior, and accept resident *ambassadors* from the European powers. The *Twenty-One Demands* made by Japan in 1915 were well within this tradition, though far more extreme than anything other foreign powers had attempted. *Tariff* control returned to China by the late 1930s, but some other provisions lasted until 1943.

UNESCO: See *United Nations Educational, Scientific and Cultural Organization.*

uneven development: (1) In *economics*: *growth* of sectors of a national *economy* at varying rates, with differential benefits accruing to individuals and social classes. (2) In *dependency theory*: the idea that *capitalism* inevitably produces an unequal and unjust spread of development benefits and burdens, both internationally and within societies.

Unfederated Malay States: Five small Malay *states* controlled by Britain after *WWII*; they eventually joined the Malaysian Federation.

unfriendly act: An action by one *state* directed against another that is hostile in intention, but not overtly illegal and not constituting a *casus belli* or an *act of war.* For instance, causing a deliberate slight to an *ambassador* or receiving persons, such as *terrorists* or *dissidents,* found objectionable by another state.

UNGA: See *United Nations General Assembly.*

Uniate: Those churches that maintain their own liturgy and rite, but acknowledge the authority of the popes on matters of faith and doctrine and maintain a formal union with the *Catholic Church.* They are found mainly in Eastern Europe and Ukraine, but also Armenia, Egypt, Ethiopia, Greece, Lebanon and Syria.

UNICEF: See *United Nations International Children's Emergency Fund.*

unilateral act: In *international law,* a self-binding declaration by a *state* of its intention to do, or to desist from doing, something. For instance, announcing a *moratorium* on weapons testing.

unilateralism: A preference for pursuing foreign policy interests independently of either the opportunities or constraints of *multilateral diplomacy*. This tendency is most pronounced among the *Great Powers*, where great *capabilities* often suggest, and sometimes actually enable, such *states* to act without restraint and in the face of broad international opposition.

unincorporated territory: A *territory* under the *sovereignty* of a larger, usually non-contiguous power, but not directly under the constitution of that power. For instance, *American Samoa, Guam*.

Union: The Northern states in the *American Civil War*: California, Connecticut, Delaware, Illinois, Indiana, Iowa, Kansas, Maine, Maryland, Massachusetts, Michigan, Minnesota, New Jersey, New Hampshire, New York, Ohio, Oregon, Pennsylvania, Rhode Island, Vermont and Wisconsin. Of the *border states*, Missouri and Kentucky were held by force, as was Maryland; but their populations were divided on the great question of *slavery*, and many from these states fought for the *Confederacy*. The war carved West Virginia out of old Virginia, and it hastened to join the Union.

Unionists: Protestants dedicated to defense of the political *union* of Northern Ireland with Britain, who have formed political parities and *paramilitaries* to that end. See *Ulster*.

union of sovereign states: There are several types of composite, *international personality*: (1) Personal union: When states share a *head of state*; e.g., previously, Denmark and Iceland; Belgium and the Congo; the *Holy Roman Empire;* and less clearly, members of the *Commonwealth* sharing *Queen Elizabeth II* as head of state: Australia, Britain, Canada, etc. (2) Confederation: An interstate association in which governments volunteer to limit application of normal *sovereign* privileges in pursuit of some common aim, but keep the shared organs distant from contact with their population, and do not surrender *sovereignty*; e.g., the *North German Confederation*, the *United Arab Emirates*. (3) Full (real) union: When states merge by *treaty*, assuming a single government and after that acting as a single entity in relations with the outside world. States in a real union may remain legally sovereign, but share only one international personality; e.g., *Austria-Hungary* after the *Ausgleich; Yugoslavia; Tanzania*, created in 1964 by the union of *Tanganyika* and *Zanzibar*, and in 1990, merger of the Yemens into the Yemeni Republic. More often, such efforts have failed; e.g., the Egyptian attempt to join with Syria in the *UAR*; Libya's several attempts seemingly to join with anyone willing; and *Senegambia*. Such failures can have lasting negative repercussions, leading to deep recrimination and soured relations between once close *allies*. See also *federation*.

Union of Soviet Socialist Republics (USSR): The formal title of the *Soviet Union*. See also *Russia*.

unipolarity: A hypothetical *international system* in which there is only one *Great Power*, or pole of *influence*. Some theorists present ancient Rome as a "unipolar system." But that is ahistorical, even *procrustean*, as it ignores Rome's many contacts and wars with barbarian kingdoms, not to mention Carthage, Egypt, Nubia and the Persian Empire. Other analysts point to the putative "unipolar moment" of the U.S. in 1945 (overlooking the Soviet and other *empires*), or the immediate post-*Cold War* period (neglecting Germany, Japan and other Great Powers). Cf. *bipolarity; hegemony; preponderant power; tripolarity; multipolarity*.

unitary actor: The assumption, made to ease discussion and permit generalization, that one can usefully speak of states as individual *actors* rather than the complex collective entities they really are.

unitary state: One in which there is a single center of supreme or constitutional authority; not a *federation*. Cf. *Leviathan*.

United Arab Emirates: Location: *Arabian peninsula*. Major associations: *Arab League, OAPEC, OPEC, UN*. Population: 2.3 million. Military: since the *Gulf War*, closely *aligned* with the U.S. and Saudi Arabia. A loose *federation* formed in 1971-72 by the *Trucial States*. It is held together by geography, and by *oil* revenues that make this one of the richest countries in the world, per capita.

United Arab Republic: A *union* formed by Egypt and Syria in 1958 in the name of *pan-Arabism*, that effectively ended with Syria's withdrawal in 1961, although Egypt incongruously carried the name forward into the mid-1970s. When Yemen is added, the term "United Arab States" is sometimes used.

United Empire Loyalists: During the *American War of Independence* the population of Canada was swollen by an influx drawn from that third of the American public that wished to remain subjects of the British crown. Most settled in the maritime provinces or Ontario; very few settled in *Québec*. They left an indelible anti-American and anti-republican mark on Canadian national life and politics.

United Irishmen: The name taken by Irish nationalists

who followed Wolfe Tone (1763-98) in opposing British rule in Ireland, ultimately by force from 1796-98. The climax came during the "Year of the French" (1798), when rebels set up a base in Co. Wexford in the hope that a French army would land to aid them. They were bitterly defeated, at the appropriately named battle of "Vinegar Hill." Two months later a small French force did land, and was routed.

United Kingdom of Great Britain and Northern Ireland (UK): Location: W. Europe. Major associations: *CSCE, Commonwealth, EU, NATO, OECD, UN (permanent member of the Security Council), WEU.* Population: 57.5 million. Military: first-rate NATO power; over 500 *nuclear weapons* and building to a total of 650. Partially occupied by the Romans from 43-410 A.D., Britain was a land of petty Saxon and Celtic kingdoms for the next several centuries. From the 8th to 11th centuries it was subjected to Viking raids all along its coasts, and then to the establishment of Viking kingdoms in the north (the Danegeld) that owed allegiance to Denmark and Norway. The last foreigner to successfully cross the *English Channel* with an army was William the Conqueror (1027-87), who made the short trip in 1066. *England* slowly evolved representative institutions in isolation from the Continent (the Magna Carta was forced on English Kings in 1215, followed by slow extension of the rights of Parliament). England conquered Wales in 1300, but *Scotland* and *Ireland* continued in clannish isolation. For centuries England fought to keep its *empire* in France, but was thrown off the continent by the *Hundred Years' War* (1338-1453). That *defeat* sparked a long dynastic struggle and *civil war*, the so-called War of the Roses (1455-85). With the consolidation of Tudor rule, England enjoyed a sustained period of prosperity and rising naval and commercial power. It was torn apart by the Protestant *Reformation*, which was radicalized during the English Civil War (1642-46) and under Cromwell's Commonwealth (1649-60). The Glorious Revolution (1688-89) secured Britain for Protestantism by expulsion of the Catholic James II and enthronement of the Protestants William and Mary (it has modern significance for *Ulster*, where it is still celebrated annually by Protestants in the face of Catholic resentment). Relations with Catholic France and Spain were hostile during the 17th century. In 1707 Scotland was annexed. Ulster had been subdued in the time of Cromwell; the remainder of Ireland was added in the 1800 *Act of Union*. England opposed the schemes for aggrandizement of *Louis XIV* and his successors, resulting in several wars that formed a near-seamless whole: *War of the Grand Alliance*

(1688-97), *War of the Spanish Succession (1701-1714), War of the Austrian Succession (1740-48)* and the *Seven Years' War (1756-63);* with their North American extensions: *King William's War (1689-97), Queen Anne's War (1702-13), King George's War (1744-48)* and the *French and Indian War (1754-60).* In these wars England *contained* French power in Europe and destroyed it in the Americas and *India,* greatly expanding its own empire in the process. Yet the victory in the Americas actually removed the main bond with 13 of its 17 colonies there, and the expense of fighting and the sacrifice of colonial to imperial interests strained relations past the breaking point. Between 1775-1783 England fought to preserve its preferences in America, but lost (mainly due to French, Dutch and Spanish *intervention*). This interrupted an otherwise spectacularly successful imperial policy.

England, or Britain as this island power was called after 1800, was at war with France almost without pause from the start of the *French Revolution* to the defeat of *Napoleon I.* Shrugging off the loss of its important North American colonies, which it fought again in the *War of 1812,* it created an even greater, second empire in Asia and Africa. Following the *Napoleonic Wars* it emerged as the greatest power of the 19th century, based on its early industrial advantage, the riches of its vast empire, the superiority of the *Royal Navy* and a fine diplomatic tradition. It built the *Raj* in India, took control of much of Africa, extended its holdings in Asia and underwrote the *Concert of Europe.* As the Concert decayed Britain propped up the *Ottoman Empire* against the *Russian Empire,* postponing a final answer to the *Eastern Question* by fighting the *Crimean War.* As the *pax britannica* waned with the turn of the 20th century, Britain moved from *splendid isolation* into *rapprochements* with America, France and Russia, and framed the *Anglo/Japanese Alliance.* But it saw relations with Imperial Germany deteriorate into the cataclysm of *WWI.* Britain was so badly wounded by that war it let Ireland break away in 1921, and began discussions on *Home Rule* for India. It pursued a shoddy policy of *appeasement* of Nazi Germany until after the *Munich Conference.* Yet when it had to fight anyway, it did so doggedly. It staggered to a *Cadmean victory* in *WWII,* largely with U.S. help. By 1947 it started to let go its overseas commitments, feeling the strain of *imperial overreach.* It pulled back from the eastern Mediterranean, replaced by the U.S. when the Soviets threatened Greece and Turkey; and it let India, the "jewel in the crown" of the British Empire, go free. In the 1950s and 1960s nearly all the rest of the empire followed suit, a loss of stature not concealed by the poor cloth of the Commonwealth. The humiliation of the *Suez Crisis* aside, Britain ceased to act independently of the U.S. in its major foreign policies. Still, it was a nuclear power, and remained a major player at the UN. In 1973 it joined the *EC*, but has always been uncomfortable with the notion of European political *union*. The *Falklands War* distracted it in 1982, and *Margaret Thatcher's* domestic policies preoccupied it for most of the 1980s. In 1990-91 it joined the *coalition* that fought the *Gulf War*, and stayed to police the *no-fly zones*. It was reluctant to intervene with force in Bosnia, or to develop the *WEU* as an alternative to NATO. See *Baldwin; Balfour; Bevin; Canning; Castlereagh; Chamberlain; Churchill; Dreadnought; English Channel; Gladstone; Liverpool; Lloyd George; John Major; Palmerston; Pitt; Sykes-Picot Agreement; two-power standard; Wellington; Harold Wilson* and other related personalities, crises and wars.

United Kingdom of the Serbs, Croats and Slovenes: The formal name of *Yugoslavia* from 1918 to 1929. It was run mostly by and for the Serbs.

United Nations alliance: The league that won *WWII*, then gave its name to the modern security organization its members founded in 1944-45. See *Allies*.

United Nations Conference on the Environment and Development (UNCED): Held in Rio de Janeiro in June 1992 (popularly called the "Earth Summit"). It was the largest conference to date in the history of *diplomacy*. Five *conventions/declarations* were signed: (1) Agenda 21, a non-binding "action plan" for environmental and development programs. Only the U.S. refused to sign (a decision reversed the next year by the *Clinton* administration). (2) The Rio Declaration on the Environment and Development, calling for $125 billion in new *aid* transfers to *Third World* states. (3) Declaration on Principles of Management and Sustainable Development for All Types of Forests. (4) Convention on Climate Change. (5) Convention on Biological Diversity.

United Nations Conference on Human Settlements (HABITAT): May-June 1976, Vancouver. It was the largest world conference ever held (since surpassed by the *Earth Summit*), with 131 participating states, focusing on new *UNEP* machinery to deal with the problem of housing ("human settlements").

United Nations Conference on the Law of the Sea (UNCLOS) I: Held in 1958, it addressed conflict over various extensions by *coastal states* of their claims to *territorial waters*, fishing zones and so forth. Its main innovations concerned *straight baselines,* and a redefinition of *baselines* (limited to 24 nautical miles) drawn across bays entirely abutting a single country. It also led to a *convention* on rights to *oil* and gas under the *continental shelf*, but largely failed to resolve other looming problems of *jurisdiction*.

United Nations Conference on the Law of the Sea (UNCLOS) II: A follow-up to *UNCLOS I* held in 1960. It failed in most respects, including on whether to extend the *three-mile limit* to a *twelve-mile limit*.

United Nations Conference on the Law of the Sea (UNCLOS) III: Talks were held from 1973-82. Much of the code of maritime law was overhauled to take account of new *territorial* claims and marine technologies. It set a *twelve-mile limit* and agreed to give *coastal states* 200 nautical mile *EEZs* and grant them more rights to the *continental shelf*. It also dealt with new regulations concerning marine pollution, designated *international waterways,* and addressed a host of traditional concerns. Most controversial, it established an "International Seabed Authority" replete with Secretariat, Council and Assembly (located in Jamaica), and related Tribunal (located in Hamburg). It then set down that deep seabed mineral deposits are "the common heritage of mankind" (at least, within the "Area" outside *territorial waters*). It gave "the Authority" *international personality,* and empowered it to oversee a mining company ("the Enterprise") and *regime* that guaranteed *Third World* countries access to all available, non-military mining *technology*. That dramatic initiative caused some states to balk. Originally not signing, though for varied reasons, were: Brazil, Britain, Ecuador, Israel, Peru, Switzerland, the U.S., the Vatican, Venezuela and West Germany. As these states have not contributed to *capitalization* of the Enterprise, and as *ratifications* have been slow (60 are required for the *treaty* to enter into effect), the more radical innovations of UNCLOS III have yet to make any mark. On the other hand, most states in practice already respect most of the less controversial features of the new code, giving them status under *international customary law*. See also *baseline; common heritage principle; contiguous zone; internal waters*.

United Nations Conference on Trade and Development (UNCTAD): The initiative for this 1964 conference came from the *G-77*. Southern countries sought trade reform through this forum because in it they commanded a majority, and hoped to have more influence than in the *GATT* or the *IMF*. Although they failed to significantly advance their trade agenda, they did achieve acceptance of UNCTAD as a permanent forum and a few symbolic modifications to the trade *regime*. UNCTAD quickly adopted a *dependency theory* view of the structure of the international economic system. However, the *OECD* nations declined to treat UNCTAD as a legitimate negotiating forum on trade matters. It also fell prey to internal divisions within the G-77. It has no compulsory mechanisms, and may only suggest courses of action. Combined with the economic marginalism of most Southern countries, that rendered it a largely ineffective institution. See also *Integrated Program for Commodities; NIEO*.

United Nations Development Program (UNDP): To provide a new avenue for development *aid*, the UN set up a "Special Fund" (SUNFED) in 1959. In 1965 the *UNGA* decided to merge SUNFED with the Expanded Program of Technical Assistance (EPTA), to form the UNDP. The UNDP now provides a single administrative center for UN *aid* and *development* projects. Its budget is small by the standards of major *donor countries* (about $1 billion in 1989, which was down from the high-water mark of 1979). If less aid in the future is *tied aid*, and if more states choose to deliver assistance through *multilateral* channels, the UNDP's role should expand. But into the mid-1990s most aid remained bilateral, or was distributed through the *IMF* and the *IBRD,* where donors retained full control.

United Nations Educational, Scientific, and Cultural Organization (UNESCO): A *specialized agency* set up to promote cooperation in the fields its title lists. It was immersed in controversy in the 1980s, when it promoted the *New World Information and Communication Order (NWICO)*. Criticism of the thrust of NWICO, budget overruns and poor management were the stated reasons for U.S. (1985) and British (1986) *withdrawal* from UNESCO. Other Western and some *neutral* states also criticized NWICO and UNESCO on those grounds, but remained members.

United Nations Environmental Program (UNEP): This forum became more prominent after the mid-1980s, with its support for scientific research that led to uncovering *ozone depletion*, and its drafting of *conventions* on *CFCs* and other harmful substances. It works closely with the *WMO*, and sponsored the *Earth Summit* in 1992 and follow-up meetings.

United Nations General Assembly (UNGA): The main body within the *UN system* in which all member *states* are represented on an equal basis (with the exception

that during the *Cold War* the Soviet Union had three seats, one each for *Russia, Byelorussia* and *Ukraine*). It can pass *resolutions*, issue reports, and discuss and deliberate on matters of interest to the members. Other UN bodies and agencies may report to it. However, the *Security Council* remains the focus of real *power* within the system. This caused considerable tension from the 1960s on, as a *Third World* majority began to use the UNGA as a platform for demands on establishing the *NIEO* agenda. However, by the late 1980s there was a less contentious atmosphere overall.

United Nations High Commission for Refugees (UNHCR): A position established in 1951 to replace the International Refugee Organization, a short-lived (1947-51) *specialized agency* set up to deal with the postwar *refugee* emergency left over after the work done by the *United Nations Relief and Rehabilitation Administration (UNRRA)*. Financing of the UNHCR is on a voluntary basis. Its main functions are to provide: legal protection for *stateless* persons, *repatriation* or resettlement of refugees, *good offices* to other relief agencies, publicity for refugee problems, and *advisory services*. Refugees who are nationals of countries granting *asylum* do not fall under UNHCR jurisdiction. The office won the *Nobel Prize* for Peace in 1954, and again in 1981.

United Nations Human Rights Commission (UN-HRC): The main body within the UN system dealing with *human rights*. Only *states* are represented, though some *non-governmental organizations* have been granted observer status. It reports to *ECOSOC*, and thereby to the *UNGA*. Its proceedings are highly political and its powers proscribed. It has a monitoring, rather than implementation, role regarding international *covenants* and *conventions*. With the *Cold War* logjam on human rights broken, a modest "thematic" approach emerged by which states are not singled out for political targeting, so much as general problems (such as *torture*) are addressed. Yet sharp divisions remain. The main one runs along *Southern* and collectivist notions of rights (a right to *development* as the primary international right) vs. Western (*Northern*) and individualist conceptions (civil and political liberties as a prerequisite to more just and equitable societies). See also *anti-Semitism; World Human Rights Conference*.

United Nations Human Rights Committee (HRC): It was set up under an *Optional Protocol* to the Covenant on Civil and Political Rights, to which few states have adhered. The Protocol is notable for permitting individuals to *petition* against their own governments, directly to the Committee. Adherence to the Protocol and acceptance of the oversight role of the HRC is separate from *ratification* of the Covenant.

United Nations Industrial Development Organization (UNIDO): One of the 16 *specialized agencies* of the UN, it was approved by the *UNGA* in 1965, and actually started up operations in 1967. Its main aim is to assist in *industrialization* within the *LDCs*. It promotes research and *advisory services*. It manages a small budget and, some critics charge, is but marginally useful in a field where market forces hold such sway. It coordinates its activities with the *UNDP*. It did not formally become a specialized agency until 1985.

United Nations [International Emergency] Children's Fund (UNICEF): It was set up in 1946 to provide emergency relief to the child victims and *refugees* of *WWII*. "International Emergency" was dropped from the title in 1953, as UNICEF gained permanency and moved into longer term programs, beyond Europe and Asia. Its funding is on a voluntary basis by member *states* (it is not a *specialized agency*), with large amounts of supplemental funds coming from millions of private individuals. Its programs focus on education, emergency *aid*, health care (including vaccinations) and nutrition. It sustains thousands of family care clinics and schools, annually servicing millions of the world's poorest and most destitute children. It won the *Nobel Prize* for Peace in 1964.

United Nations Organization (UN/UNO): The global *peace* and *security* organization agreed upon by the *Great Powers* at *Dumbarton Oaks* in 1944, and formally founded at *San Francisco* by some 50 charter members. In 1993, Macedonia, Eritrea, Monaco and Andorra joined, the 181-184th members, respectively. Some *microstates*, both Koreas and Switzerland remain non-members. As a recognized *international personality* all UN premises wherever located are immune from search, *expropriation* or any other interference. It is immune from financial controls (but not withholding of contributions), and from all taxes, duties and prohibitions on the imported *goods* it needs to function. Its assets are immune from legal process. It may have access to media, and is theoretically exempt from censorship. Its *archives* are immune. It may also encrypt messages and use couriers who enjoy *diplomatic immunity*. See the related entries immediately above and below, and among others, *Bosnia; Cambodia; collective security; Congo crisis; El Salvador; embargo; good offices; Gulf War; Korean Conflict; Namibia; peace enforcement; peacekeeping; peace-*

making; principal organs; Secretariat; Secretary General (and individual Secretaries General)*; Security Council; Somalia; specialized agencies; Suez crisis; veto; Western Sahara.*

United Nations presence: A term applied mainly to UN *peacekeeping* operations, but also to UN mediators, in-country staff or military observers, *advisory services* personnel and other official missions.

United Nations Relief and Rehabilitation Administration (UNRRA): This agency preexisted the *UN*: it was established by the *Allies* in 1943, with the lion's share of funding coming from the U.S. As the Allied armies moved into *liberated* areas the UNRRA followed in their wake (even in parts of Eastern Europe, where the Soviets otherwise kept out all foreign observers). It brought emergency relief to the *civilian* populations of devastated areas, and to the victims of the *concentration camps*. No one can say how many lives were saved by this effort. Until 1949 it continued its relief work, and began to direct some of its efforts into *reconstruction*. By then the *specialized agencies* were coming on-line to take over relief work, and reconstruction was the task of the *Marshall Plan*. So the UNRRA folded its tents, its job well done. Its remaining assets passed to *UNICEF*.

United Nations Relief and Works Agency (UNRWA): An agency set up in 1949 in response to the *refugee* problem generated by the *First Arab/Israeli War*. The U.S. is the major *donor nation*. The UNRWA is handicapped by the situation in the Middle East, where it is unable to *repatriate* or resettle *Palestinian* refugees because neither Israel nor the Arab states will accept them permanently. Instead, the UNRWA has branched into provision of services such as health care and schools (currently running over 600).

United States Agency for International Development (USAID): The main U.S. *aid* agency, in operation since 1961 and responsible for most non-military aid.

United States of America (U.S.): Location: North America. Major associations: *APEC, CSCE, NAFTA, NATO, OAS, OECD, UN (permanent member of the Security Council).* Population: 250 million. Military: the only state that can project *power* to any point in the world on short notice; the largest *nuclear power* and third largest (but best quality, overall) military; by far the best navy and air force in the world.

  (1) The Colonies: The arrival of the various peoples of Europe and Africa began after 1500 (and of

Asia after c.1850). Within 100 years of the voyages of Columbus most of the continental U.S. was claimed by France or Spain, with the Dutch and English making sizeable claims too. *Slavery*, too, arrived with European settlement and lasted 350 years. Very slowly, 13 of the 17 British *colonies* in North America gained a weak sense of common destiny, mainly out of fear of France. But they remained on the periphery of world affairs, trivial in number, and in fact and general perception but a minor extension of Britain's empire. European wars spilled into North America as *King William's War (1689-97), Queen Anne's War (1702-13), King George's War (1744-48)* and the *French and Indian War (1754-60)*. Those clashes entangled the colonies in conflicts that appeared far distant from local interests, yet when they were done they had broken French power in the hemisphere. They also had these other effects: (A) They shook the confidence of the colonies that in fighting for England their own interests were tended to as well: more than once, a *peace treaty* handed back to France *territory* hard-won in North America, in return for a concession to Britain in the Caribbean or in India. (B) The end of the wars with France dissolved the bond of a common enemy between the colonists and England. (C) With *war* and then again with *peace*, came higher taxes and *tariffs* to make the colonists pay for their own defense. When Britain decided also to maintain *mercantilist* tariffs against American goods there arose a demand for self-government, ultimately fulfilled by the *American War of Independence* (1775-83).

(2) The 19th century: The young republic that took shape from 1783-89 was weak for many decades, as reflected in the humiliation of the *Tripolitan War*. The *French Revolution* and *Napoleonic Wars* bitterly divided the nation, a split personified by the dispute between *Thomas Jefferson* and *Alexander Hamilton* over whether to form a French or British alliance. *George Washington* resolved the argument by keeping his weak and fragile nation *neutral*, and warning it against *entangling alliances*. That admonition was appropriate to his day, yet would hamstring policy well into the 20th century, far past the time when *isolationism* matched the country's rising power and requisite responsibilities. Moreover, as Americans were to find three more times in the next 200 years, their interest in trade and fondness for abstract principle meant they could not stay at peace when the *balance of power* and the idea of *liberty* was under challenge in Europe. With *Napoleon* commanding the continent and Britain ruling the seas, the U.S. was thus drawn into the fiasco of the *War of 1812*. Then came peace with Britain, the *Rush-Bagot Agreement*, and extension

of the isolationist doctrine to the whole hemisphere in the *Monroe Doctrine*. Next came a burst of expansion: into the Floridas, north toward Oregon, but especially west and south because of the *Mexican/American War*. The huge area found in that war gave the U.S. an imperial *hinterland* of continental proportions, but also brought the unresolved dilemma of slavery to the fore as new states applied for entry into the Union. The awful question of slavery was only resolved on the battlefields of the *American Civil War*. The U.S. emerged from that bloodiest of all its wars as a *Great Power* in industrial, military and technological terms. Americans then sought a return to *status quo ante bellum* simplicity and isolation, and their leaders declared that nothing had changed. But it had. Other major powers recognized this fact (even if most Americans did not), and adjusted their policy: Russia vacated *Alaska*, France left Mexico and Britain negotiated the *Treaty of Washington*, settling all outstanding *disputes*.

(3) The World Wars: After several decades of quiet in foreign affairs, marred only by occasional outbursts of pugnacity toward some small Latin American neighbor, the U.S. broke upon the world stage with the *Spanish/American War*. That contest left it a somewhat reluctant colonial power. More important, the acquisition of the *Philippines* projected U.S. interests deep into Asia--of America's five 20th-century wars, three would begin in Asia. This new involvement was reflected in *Teddy Roosevelt's* mediation of the *Treaty of Portsmouth*. From 1900-1933 the U.S. *intervened* almost by reflex in Central America, yet it found it difficult to appreciate that other Great Powers, in particular Japan, also regarded *propinquity* as justification for a *sphere of influence*. While conflict with Japan over its policy toward China simmered, there arose another threat to the European balance of power and transatlantic commerce. Germany's ambitions and U.S. commercial interests led to entry into *WWI*. The U.S. was already the dominant power in the world in 1919, a fact reflected in *Woodrow Wilson's* towering influence at the *Paris Peace Conference*. Yet, again, Americans sought a return to simpler days after a burst of enthused engagement with the wider and, so they thought, wilier world. The Senate rejected the *Treaty of Versailles* and with it membership in the *League of Nations*. Three successive isolationist presidents then took office: *Warren Harding, Calvin Coolidge* and *Herbert Hoover*. Just as a semblance of responsible *internationalism* was returning to U.S. diplomacy, with *Henry L. Stimson*, the *Great Depression* knocked out the will to act even as it raised up dangerous regimes in Germany and Japan. *Franklin D. Roosevelt* tried to stiffen U.S. and Western resolve against the threat

from *Hitler*, but as late as 1940 all Congress or the public gave him to work with was words. It would take a direct attack by Japan to fully awaken America's interest in world affairs. *Pearl Harbor* ultimately meant that *WWII* would complete what WWI had started: exposure of the vast economic and latent military *power* of the U.S. to all concerned, and the education of its *elite* and population to the enormous responsibility that comes with *preponderant power*.

(4) The *Cold War*: As WWII ended the U.S. was already engaged in the task of *reconstruction*: it had hosted the *Dumbarton Oaks, San Francisco* and *Bretton Woods* conferences, and was largely responsible for the shape taken by the *GATT*, the *IBRD, IMF* and UN. *Harry Truman* took the U.S. into the United Nations and set out the parameters for *containment* with the *Marshall Plan* and the founding of NATO. With these changes the U.S. finally rejected its isolationist traditions and accepted that it was a Great Power, with commensurate obligations. Indeed, it sometimes took to its new role with more verve than *prudence*, as during expansion of the *Korean Conflict* into a war of *liberation* of North Korea, and by intervention in the *Vietnam War*. Conflict with the Soviet Union (and China) pervaded nearly all foreign policy during the *Eisenhower* administration and the *Kennedy* years. But this struggle took on a more limited quality after the *Cuban Missile Crisis*, then under *Lyndon Johnson* and during *détente*. Relations eased with China and the Soviets during the *Nixon* years. While the end of U.S. involvement in Indochina forced a reconsideration of means, the main outline of U.S. policy remained a sustained effort to block any Soviet advance, real or perceived, in Europe, Asia, Africa or the Middle East. Therefore the use of force by the Soviets in Afghanistan, which lay outside their traditional and accepted sphere of influence, provoked a strong U.S. reaction. Congress and *Jimmy Carter* after 1978, and the *Reagan* administration in the 1980s, displayed a renewed willingness to use U.S. economic and military power to advance foreign policy goals. There was division over Reagan's preoccupation with minor states such as *Grenada, Libya* and *Nicaragua*, but the broad thrust of a renewed hard line toward Moscow had wide public support. After 1985 tensions with the Soviets dissipated as their empire collapsed; and *arms control* agreements rather than weapons proliferated. After 45 years of Cold War the world was again greatly complex and diverse. Yet, world order and *international organization* had been significantly reshaped by American power, and broad pursuit of *liberal-internationalist* ideas about *world governance*.

(5) Post-Cold War: With the *extinction* of the Soviet Union at the end of 1991 relations with Russia became genuinely warmer, despite worries about regional conflicts within the old Soviet sphere. In 1990-91 *George Bush* assembled an unprecedented *coalition* to fight the *Gulf War*, parlaying that success into multilateral *peace talks* in the Middle East (but not electoral survival at home). Just before leaving office he also committed U.S. forces to support UN efforts in *famine* relief and social reconstruction in Somalia. In the first year of the *Clinton* administration the U.S. faltered briefly on NAFTA, and showed only intermittent interest in involvement in Bosnia. Neither the national will nor the international climate any longer appeared conducive to clear U.S. leadership or intervention: by mid-1994 the U.S. public and Congress had turned solidly against the Somali operation, opposed large-scale intervention in Bosnia, and wanted only limited involvement in restoring democracy in Haiti. And the Clinton administration had yet to enunciate any clear doctrine or vision for future U.S. engagement in regional crises.

Uniting for Peace Resolution: Passed during the crisis leading to UN intervention in the *Korean Conflict*, it authorizes the *UNGA* to assemble on 24 hours notice in an emergency. It has been invoked concerning: the *Suez Crisis* (1956), *Hungarian Uprising* (1956), Lebanon crisis (1958), *Congo crisis* (1960), Middle East (1967), Afghanistan (1980), Palestine (1980), Namibia (1981), *Occupied Territories* (1982), Kuwait (1990) and Bosnia (1992).

units: *Jargon*. Used in *political science* to refer "objectively" to whatever political communities are under study, which nonetheless are almost always the *states*.

Universal Declaration of Human Rights: It was adopted by the *UNGA*, then meeting in Paris, on December 10, 1948. It is a non-binding statement of largely *liberal* principles and aspirations, but including as well *social democratic* notions of economic, social and cultural rights. Some lawyers and activists claim it has achieved the status of *international customary law*; others dispute that claim. Cf. *International Covenants*.

universalism: The view that ethical truths do not depend upon the group or individual upholding them but apply across cultures, as they derive from universal sources, alternately said to be God, human needs or nature, or reason. When applied as an adjective (to an idea, institution, *norm*, principle or *rule*) it implies near-global acceptance, relevance, scope or timelessness. Cf. *human rights; natural law; relativism*.

universality (of criminal law): The doctrine that *municipal law* on criminal matters may take note of violations wherever they occur. It is heavily limited in practice. Cf. *territoriality of criminal law*.

Universal Postal Union (UPU): First established as a *public international union* in 1874, as of 1947 it has been a *specialized agency* of the UN. It operates under a *convention*. It standardized postal service and made handling the world's mails a remarkable story of international cooperation (appearances to the contrary in your local post office, notwithstanding).

unrestricted submarine warfare: When *WWI* began the U.S. declared its *neutrality*. But it wished to continue trade with all *belligerents*, and so asserted a traditonal doctrine of *neutral rights* and respect for the *Declaration of Paris*. The problem was that neutral trading rights clashed with the British and German *blockades*. Furthermore, the Paris code in practice favored Britain's superiority in surface *warships*, as it took no account of *submarines* (because it was drafted before their invention, or at least application to naval warfare). Unanticipated by any strategist, it was the German *U-boats*, not its *Dreadnoughts*, that became the main threat to the *Royal Navy*. In short order, Germany grew desperately dependent on its U-boats to strangle Britain, as both before and after *Jutland* the bulk of its surface navy was bottled into its Baltic home ports. That neutral merchant ships were often sunk in the course of U-boat combat was, from the German point of view, simply part of the fortunes of war. But Americans, not fully appreciating the degree to which the combat in Europe had become a no-holds-barred affair, were outraged. That reaction was aggravated by the failure of U-boats to observe the Paris (and later) rules on "cruiser warfare," which required a warning to merchant ships and provision of aid to the people on board. Germany had ceased these practices after some of its surfaced U-boats were fired upon by armed merchant ships, or were rammed; also, there was hardly room on a WWI submarine for its own crew, let alone *POWs* or *civilians*. That led to charges of *piracy*, and greatly inflamed *public opinion*. The British *blockade* of the *Central Powers* began to bite hard by early 1915. The German *High Command*, stymied on land by the failure of their great offensive strategy, the *Schlieffen Plan*, ordered all-out submarine warfare. This sharply altered the character of relations with the U.S., until then on a fairly good footing. *Wilson* and *William Jennings Bryan* took a hard-line on neutral rights. Then, on May 7, 1915, the passenger liner Lusitania was sunk off Ireland, leading to a crisis

that threatened war and lasted until early 1916 (see *Lusitania Notes*). Other liners were sunk after the German apology for Lusitania in early 1916. Wilson protested in the strongest terms. Not yet willing to add America to its formidable list of enemies, Germany backed down and restricted its U-boat campaign. However, in January 1917, Germany again rolled what *Bismarck* called "the iron dice of war." It decided to revert to a policy of unrestricted submarine warfare, knowing this would tumble the U.S. into the war. This was the great gamble of the High Command: it counted on defeating Russia in the east and starving Britain into submission in the west, thereby forcing France to terms before an aroused United States could bring its full power to bear and decide the conflict in favor of the *Allies*. On February 1, 1917, the U-boat campaign duly resumed. Shortly thereafter, the British handed Wilson their intercept of the *Zimmermann Telegram*. And on April 2nd, when he could delay no more, Wilson asked for and received from Congress a *declaration of war* on Imperial Germany.

Untermenschen: "Lesser (literally, under) men." In *nazism*, the non-*Aryan* peoples and races, such as Jews or *Slavs*, considered racially inferior to *Herrenvolk*.

untouchables (Harijans): In *Hinduism*, and specifically the Vedic tradition, those of the lowest caste or even outside the caste system. Discriminated against for centuries, they were brought into political life by *Mohandas Gandhi*. "Untouchability" became illegal in the new, *secular* India, though it was still widely practiced. In the early 1990s the Harijans gained a large share of state jobs through a federal affirmative action program, and what in the U.S. are called "set-asides" (reserved, public contracts). This caused much resentment among the educated and middle classes.

Upper Canada: A British *colony* comprising southern Ontario 1791-1840, named for its location on the St. Lawrence River. It received the bulk of the *United Empire Loyalists* after the *American War of Independence*. It was briefly invaded by the U.S. during the *War of 1812*, and was the locale of a failed *rebellion* against the British in 1837 that had support from Irish-Americans (*Fenians*) and some northerners. See *William Lyon Mackenzie*. Cf. *Lower Canada*.

Upper Volta: Former name of *Burkina Faso*.

uranium: See *plutonium*.

Uruguay: Location: S. America. Major associations:

LAIA, OAS, UN. Population: 3 million. Military: small. Settled by Europeans later than most South American areas, the Spanish and Portuguese did not displace the Indian population until after 1625. Like other Latin states, it rebelled against Spain during the *Napoleonic Wars*. There was periodic fighting from 1810 until effective *independence* in 1825, with full *sovereignty* in 1828. The liberal, Colorado Party ruled uninterruptedly for 86 years (1872-1958). After 1963 a left-wing *guerrilla* group, the Tupemaros, conducted a random, anarchic campaign of *terrorism* that was not entirely put down until the late 1970s and at considerable cost to civil liberties (the military took control from 1973-85). The economy has declined from its premier position in the early 1960s, and external *debt* has risen. Still, Uruguay remains one of the most stable of Latin American countries.

Uruguay Round: The 8th round of *GATT* negotiations. It began in 1986 and was to have ended in 1990, but was not agreed until December 1993. It brought the hitherto excluded sectors of *agriculture*, *services* (worth $4 trillion in 1993) and intellectual property under the GATT. It also reformed GATT's institutions and further reduced general *tariffs*. Additional features: an agreement on farm trade that replaced *quotas* with tariffs ("tariffication"); major cuts in tariffs on tropical produce; a 10-year phase out of tariffs on *textiles* and *clothing* (an end to the multi-fiber arrangement that previously managed trade in these areas); weak, but additional, rules on *anti-dumping laws* and *subsidies*; an effort to limit use of *voluntary export restraints (VERs)* and other *non-tariff barriers (NTBs)*, such as import *investment* and local procurement rules. Lastly, there was discussion of transforming GATT into (and renaming it) a "Multilateral Trade Organization." Entrenched disagreements and a papered-over, last-minute compromise between the U.S. and the *EU* (pushed by France) reduced the planned freeing of financial *services*; kept very high tariffs on agricultural imports; and excluded films and television ("audio-visuals") from the agreement on the basis of a French assertion of the need to protect national "culture" (language, film and printing).

Urundi: Former name of *Burundi*.

U.S.: See *United States of America*.

USSR: See *Soviet Union*.

Uštaše: A Croatian *independence/fascist* movement that collaborated with the Nazi *occupation* of *Yugo-slavia* and set up a Croatian *puppet state*, 1941-45. The Uštaše pursued *genocide* (or *ethnic cleansing*, as it is called in the 1990s) against Jews, Gypsies, Muslims and Serbs. They also massacred as many as they could of both *Chetniks* and members of *Tito's* communist *partisan* units (who answered tit for tat). They may have killed as many as 350,000 in all, in what amounted to a Yugoslav *civil war* within the confines of WWII. During and after *liberation* in 1944-45, Tito had 200,000 Uštaše hunted down and killed.

U Thant (1909-74): Burmese and world statesman. *Secretary General* of the *UN*, 1961-71. He succeeded *Dag Hammarskjöld* when the latter was killed during the *Congo crisis*, which U Thant finally helped *mediate* to an end in 1964. He also oversaw the sending of UN *peacekeeping* forces to *Cyprus* that year. However, the limits of his office were made clear during the *Cuban Missile Crisis*, the *Third Arab/Israeli War*, the *Nigerian Civil War*, the *Vietnam War* and other major conflicts where he exercised little influence.

utopian socialism: This derisory term was applied by *Karl Marx* to all non-*marxist* visions of new social relations, especially those that called for a voluntary shift from unregulated, early *capitalism* to more cooperative production, and various schemes of collective endeavor and ownership. He used it to elevate his own theories, which he claimed derived from "scientific" insight into the "laws of history" which predicted an ineluctable movement toward violent *class struggle*. Among the notables so dismissed were French thinkers Claude Henri Saint Simon (1760-1825) and François Marie Fourier (1772-1837), and the Welsh reformer Robert Owen (1771-1858).

Utrecht, Treaty of (1713): A singular name for a collection of *treaties* negotiated between 1713-14. They gave *Gibraltar* to England, and much weakened *New France* by also giving England *Newfoundland*, Nova Scotia (Acadia) and title to the Hudson's Bay region. The Dutch gained a measure of *security* and *independence* from Spain, permanent separation of the Spanish and French monarchies was confirmed, and Spain lost *territory* in the Netherlands and the Mediterranean to the *Hapsburgs* of the *Austrian Empire*. In the east, *Frederick II* was confirmed in the right to style himself King, and his Prussian lands a kingdom. *Louis XIV's* ambitions for *hegemony* were utterly frustrated, and English *power* was ascendant: over the rest of the century, much of what was left of the French empire overseas would pass to England. Moreover, France was exhausted, and would not try on Europe again until its power was inflated by the *French Revolution* and its better sense dazzled away by *Napoleon I.*

Uzbekistan: Location: *Central Asia/near abroad.* Major associations: *CIS, CSCE, UN.* Population: 20 million (70% Uzbek; 15% Russian). Military: revamped *Red Army* units. This region of Central Asia was overrun by the Mongols, under the "Great Khan," Ghengis Khan himself, in the 13th century. It subsequently became the center of an independent Mongol empire (under the Timurids) that held sway over the Turkmen, Tadjik and other Central Asian peoples. In the 16th-18th centuries it broke into separate, feudal khanates. Thus weakened, it was conquered by and incorporated into the *Russian Empire* in a series of expansionist wars in the 19th century. Held in the empire by the *Bolsheviks,* it was briefly joined with Tajikistan within the *Soviet Union,* before becoming a separate, "autonomous republic" in 1925. It declared *independence* after a failed *coup* attempt in Moscow in August 1991, but was not *recognized* until December. The most populous of the Central Asian republics, it sees itself as historic leader of the region. In 1993 it joined Russian in sending troops into Tajikistan. Its current *regime* also shares with Russia an antipathy to Muslim *fundamentalism:* Islamic parties are banned, and opposition generally repressed. In January 1994, it signed an agreement with Kazahkstan allowing freer movement of *labor, goods* and *services.* See also *cordon sanitaire.*

V

V-1 and V-2 rockets (*Vergeltungswaffe*): "Reprisal weapon." The V-1 was a subsonic, "flying bomb" (a crude precursor to the *cruise missile*). The V-2 was the first true *ballistic missile.* Developed by *Nazi Germany,* they were used as terror weapons against British cities in *WWII.* See *Peenemünde.*

Valera, Eamon de (1881-1975): American-born, Irish nationalist, PM of Ireland 1932-48, 1951-54; and President from 1959. He was an *IRA* commandant during the *Easter Rising.* Condemned to death, he escaped to fight in the *Irish War of Independence* and led IRA opposition to the Free State forces in the *Irish Civil War.* He kept Eire *neutral* during *WWII,* and maintained close ties with the Irish *diaspora* in the U.S.

validity: The degree to which a *treaty* is binding on states giving their *signature* and *ratification.* Theoretically, treaties are fully binding. Yet, circumstances may arise that erode this quality and deplete treaty obligations. Thus, the validity of treaties may be brought into question if the person(s) who negotiated them are later shown to have lacked proper authority, or to have exceeded their authority, to act on behalf of the *states* concerned. Treaties may also be invalidated by the following: if forced upon one party (made "in duress"); if bribery is discovered to have influenced the agent(s) of one state; if one of the parties lacks standing under *international law* to make a binding agreement (e.g., a *tribe*); if treaty rights of a third state, stemming from a prior agreement, are abridged without that state's *consent;* if there is a fundamental conflict with established, basic principles of *international law;* if the agreement aims at an illegal or immoral object; or due to *error.* Cf. *clasula rebus sic stantibus; pacta sunt servanda.*

Vance/Owen peace plan: A *UN* (Cyrus Vance) and *EC* (Lord Owen) plan drafted in 1992, aiming at a single Bosnian *state* divided into a *federation* of 12 ethnic subregions. It was killed by June 1993, as Croat and especially Serb *militia* pounded the Bosnian Muslims in an effort to compel *partition.*

Van Daemon Land: The former name of the island of Tasmania, which was used by the British as a penal colony. It is now a province of Australia.

Vandenberg, Arthur (1884-1951): U.S. *Republican* senator and statesman. Originally a leader among Senate *isolationists,* during *WWII* he was persuaded by events (and by *Franklin Roosevelt*) of the need for an American commitment to postwar *reconstruction* and *security* through the *United Nations.* He served on the U.S. delegation at *San Francisco,* authored the *Vandenberg Resolution* and steered financial and other support in the Senate to back the *Truman Doctrine* and the *European Recovery Program.* His death left Congressional Republicans bereft of conservative-internationalist leadership, even as the party captured the *White House* for the first time in 20 years.

Vandenberg Resolution (June 11, 1948): It paved the way for U.S. participation in *NATO.* It relied on Article 51 of the *Charter of the United Nations,* permitting the right of collective *self-defense.* Given *Arthur Van-*

denberg's support, it passed with just four votes against, taking *Cold War* issues out of the 1948 presidential campaign and laying the basis for two decades of bipartisan foreign policy. See *containment.*

vanguard: (1) In military usage: troops at the head of a moving army. (2) In *marxism-leninism*: a self-designated, revolutionary *elite* that guides the *proletariat* and takes power after the *revolution* succeeds.

Vanuatu: Location: Pacific. Major associations: *Commonwealth, NAM, SPC, Spearhead Group, SPF, UN.* Population: 150,000. Military: police force, undergoing some military training. The name means "Our Land" (formerly called New Hebrides). In 1887 France and Britain agreed to a Naval Commission, and in 1906 to set up a joint *condominium* to forestall *annexation* by Germany. The island group therefore is divided between *anglophone* and *francophone* communities. The 1970s saw belated national sentiment overcome linguistic barriers. It was the only *South Pacific* territory to witness violence during the *decolonization* process, and then only on Espiritu Santo and Tannu, where Papua New Guinea sent troops to repress an attempt at *secession* in 1980. *Independence* came under the name Vanuatu. It has been the most *radical* of the region's *microstates*. Stiffly anti-nuclear, until 1988 it was the only regional member of the *Non-Aligned Movement*. It also opened relations with Libya, Cuba, Nicaragua, North Korea, the PLO and Vietnam (then all Soviet *allies* or friendly to the *Soviet Union*), and twice expelled a French ambassador, in 1981 and 1987. Vanuatu claims two dependent islands of, and supports independence for, the French possession of *New Caledonia*. Despite this diplomatic tweaking, France remains an *aid* donor.

variable: In *quantitative* analysis, anything apt or able to vary, and therefore subject to measurement, that might bear a causal relation to something else one is attempting to explain. Cf. *causation; cause; dependent variable; effect; independent variable; intervening variable; operationalize.*

variable sum game: From *game theory*, one where gains and losses for the players are not equal. By analogy, a situation where *states* may make mutual gains, or both suffer losses.

variance: The square of the *standard deviation*; a measure of the spread of a set of values.

vassal state: A synonym for *puppet state.*

Vatican: Location: 108 acres within central Rome.

Population: the residents and employees of the Vatican. Military: ceremonial only (Swiss Guards). Major associations: *CSCE, Universal Postal Union; observer missions (UN)*. In 1871 the *Papal States* were absorbed by Italy, causing a 58-year breach in relations between the popes and the Italian state. An annual allowance set aside for the pope remained in *escrow*, unclaimed as a matter of disputed principle. On February 11, 1929, *concordats* (the *Lateran Treaties*) were signed *recognizing* "The State of the City of the Vatican" as a *city state* distinct from Rome and Italy, and establishing Catholicism as the state religion of Italy (this was revised in 1976). The *sovereign* of the Vatican is the pope, who is pledged to perpetual *neutrality* in temporal affairs, with the exception of performing *arbitration* when asked (this request is now made less commonly than previously). The depth of papal silence was tested, most controversially, during the *Holocaust* (see *Pius XII*), and again by the Vatican's anti-*communism* during the *Cold War*. However, temporal self-denial has not prevented comment by the Vatican when laws or secular affairs in other states touch upon "matters of faith, morals or doctrine." Nor has it prevented the establishment of *diplomatic relations* with over 100 states. Yet, there have been breaches. The U.S restored relations in 1984--they had been barred by an 1867 Act of Congress voicing little more than anti-Catholic bigotry. Long-strained relations with Israel improved at the end of the 1980s, with a papal apology for the historic *anti-Semitism* of the church and many Catholics, and deferral of the question of the status of *Jerusalem*. In December 1993, an agreement was signed to move to mutual recognition. Relations with Russia also improved, with religious freedoms granted after 1989. In 1993 the Vatican criticized Sudan--an unusual gambit--for persecution and *genocide* of Christians by Sudan's *fundamentalist*, Islamic government. It is also deeply interested in the fate of *East Timor*, where many of Indonesia's Catholic minority are concentrated. See also *Catholic Church; Roman Question; Vatican Councils.*

Vatican Councils: There have been two great church councils in the modern era, each with a significant impact on the lives and politics of hundreds of millions of people in dozens of countries. (1) First (1869-70): Its most controversial doctrine was proclamation of the infallibility of the popes "on matters of faith and doctrine." That led to sustained conflict with secular authorities in several nations, especially Prussia. It was followed by the incorporation of Rome into Italy, which began a 58-year dispute between the popes and the Italian state. (2) Second (1962-65): It represented an effort to reform and modernize the *Catholic Church*. It made many changes to liturgy and stressed *ecumenism* in relations with other Christian faiths. Whether it succeeded in its set task is a matter of conjecture and, to a degree, of historical and personal viewpoint. Cf. *John XXIII; Kulturkampf; Pius IX.*

VE (Victory in Europe) Day: May 8, 1945, when *Nazi Germany* surrendered to the *United Nations alliance*.

velvet revolution: The disintegration of *communist* rule in Czechoslovakia in 1989. The term derives from the fact that after initial repression of a mass demonstration on November 17, 1989, there was little violence. The *communist party* simply stood aside, and democracy was established under *Václav Havel.*

Vendée, rebellion in (1793-1800): The Catholic peasants of this region of western France, led by clergy, rebelled against the *secularism* of the *French Revolution.* The *Jacobins* put down the initial *rebellion* with characteristic brutality, but discontent and opposition remained until 1800, when *Napoleon* sent an army to hammer peasant resistance flat, while buying off the church hierarchy with concessions. Recent historical work suggests the reprisals taken in the Vendée were truly horrific, perhaps even *genocidal.*

Venezuela: Location: S. America. Major associations: *LAIA, OAS, OPEC, UN.* Population: 20 million. Military: moderate, local/regional forces. Charted by Columbus in 1498, it was part of the larger Spanish holdings in South America until 1821, when *Simón Bolívar* helped it secure *independence* from Spain as part of the larger state of *Colombia.* In 1830 it became a separate *republic.* From 1895-96 it was involved in a serious *dispute* with Britain over the *border* with *British Guiana,* in which Venezuela was robustly supported by the U.S., much to the surprise of Britain. From 1902-08 Venezuela was under *blockade* by several European powers for declining to pay *compensation* sought for their nationals for various injuries. That dispute too was *mediated* by the U.S. In the 1920s it began to exploit its *oil* reserves, becoming a major exporter in the 1940s-1960s. In 1959 it returned to civilian rule after several decades of government by *junta.* In 1960 it instigated the founding of OPEC. In the 1970s and 1980s it squandered much of its oil revenue on wasteful megaprojects and unregulated development. Riots ensued in 1989, after a strict austerity program was put in place. Two coup attempts failed in 1992. Venezuela maintains a standing claim to a share of the *territory* of Guyana.

Venice, Republic of: For nearly 800 years after c.1000 A.D. Venice was the commercial center of the Mediterranean, a conduit of ancient and Muslim learning to Europe and a military power in its own right. It was one of the main *city-states* of the Italian *Renaissance.* Its formal *independence* ended with *conquest* by *Napoleon I* in 1797, but it had ceased to be truly *sovereign* much earlier, with the French conquest of Italy at the close of the Renaissance. It was ceded to Austria after 1815. In 1848 it briefly declared itself a republic once again, but that move was crushed by Austrian arms. In 1866 it was ceded to Italy by *Bismarck,* as a reward for aid in the *Seven Weeks' War.*

venire contra factum proprium: In *international law,* a subsequent act in conflict with a prior act.

Venizelos, Eleutherios (1864-1936): Greek statesman. PM 1910-15, 1917-20, 1924, 1928-32, 1933. He declared the *union* of Crete with Greece in 1905, and led Greece in the *Balkan Wars,* gaining control of *Macedonia.* He tried to bring Greece into *WWI,* siding with the *Allies,* but was dismissed from office. He returned from *exile* in 1917, deposed the king, and *declared war* on Germany and Bulgaria. He represented Greece at the *Paris Peace Conference,* but his efforts to take *territory* (part of *Anatolia*) from Turkey led to more *war* and *defeat.* Out of office in 1935, he staged an abortive uprising that led to a brief *civil war,* after which he fled to exile in France.

venture capital: High-risk *investments* made in search of high *profits.* Venture capital has been an important part of international relations at least since the South Sea Bubble (1720). For instance, it backed the construction of the *Suez Canal,* opened *Siberia* and the American West and was in play behind many a colonial adventure. It can be a critical component of national *power,* since it supports economic *competitiveness.* The global demand for venture capital grew at a tremendous pace at the end of the 1980s, as new market opportunities opened in the former *Soviet bloc* countries, Chinese opportunities continued, and certain *Third World* economies entered periods of rapid *growth.* Also called "risk capital." Cf. *patient capital.*

Verdun, Battle of (February 21-December 16, 1916): From the soldier's point of view, this was perhaps the worst battle of *WWI,* fought bitterly and often hand-to-hand for over 300 days. Nearly three quarters of a million men were casualties in this war of *attrition* between distant generals, *Falkenhayn* for the Germans and *Pétain* for the French. The battle destroyed French morale, contributed to the *French Army mutinies* of 1917 and rendered the French Army incapable of an independent offensive. Yet it may have cost Germany the war: it used precious *reserves* and compelled the *High Command* to make the decision in January 1917 for *unrestricted submarine warfare* that finally brought the *power* of the U.S. down upon them in 1918. Falkenhayn was dismissed when his strategy failed to finish the French. Pétain became one of the greatest heroes of the war on the French side, but never again had the stomach for a fight. His *defeatism* pervaded the French military during the 1920s and 1930s, and he *surrendered* to Germany at the first available opportunity in 1940.

verification regime: Any set of agreed rules, procedures and mechanisms, cooperative or independently operated (e.g., *satellite* surveillance) used to verify that each party is actually complying with a *treaty*. It is used especially about *arms control* agreements.

Verona, Congress of (1822): Austria, France, Prussia and Russia met, with Britain as observer, in the final, full meeting of the *Congress system*. The main issue was a French proposal to invade *Iberia* to repress *liberal* rebellion. *Metternich* of Austria agreed, in part hoping to prevent a Russian army from marching across Europe, as *Alexander I* was threatening. The British were opposed, not so much from principle as because Portugal was an *ally*. They also wanted to see Spanish ports remain open to free commerce, and so also contested a royal *restoration*, there or in Latin America. The possibility of Russian *intervention* in the Americas led *Canning* to approach *John Quincy Adams*, and by that route to the *Monroe Doctrine*.

Versailles: The palace built by *Louis XIV*, outside Paris. It is often used as a shorthand for the *Paris Peace Conference* held there and in Paris from January 1919-January 1920. Note: It may be used interchangeably, to refer to the peace conference as a whole or just the *Treaty of Versailles* (one of several war-ending instruments negotiated at Paris).

Versailles, Treaty of (June 28, 1919): The *peace treaty* between the *Allies* and Germany, negotiated at the *Paris Peace Conference*. It formally ended *WWI* between all *states* and Germany (except the United States, which signed but did not ratify it, and negotiated a separate *treaty* in August 1921). (1) Territorial adjustments: *Alsace-Lorraine* to France; all German colonies relinquished (later converted to *mandates*); *Danzig* made a *free city* under *League of Nations* administration, and connected to Poland via the *Polish corridor;* much of *East Prussia* and *Silesia* to Poland; *Eupen and Malmedy* to Belgium; *Memel* to Lithuania; northern *Schleswig* to Denmark (pending a *plebiscite*). (2) Other terms: *Anschluss* with Austria forbidden; *demilitarization* of the *Rhineland;* the *Saar* under French *occupation* and League administration for 15 years; large-scale *reparations* (to be fixed by a commission); an upper limit of 100,000 in the armed forces of Germany, and no *General Staff* permitted; a ban on any air force, *conscription, gas weapons* or *armor;* no *capital warships* over 10,000 tons and no *U-boats,* with the extant German fleet at *Scapa Flow* to be handed over to Britain. Among the most controversial provisions, the treaty contained a so-called *war guilt clause* and called for *war crimes trials* of *Wilhelm II* and the *High Command* (these never took place, although some lesser officers were tried). A right-of-way *servitude* was placed on the Kiel Canal. Versailles also contained the *Covenant of the League of Nations,* an inclusion with manifold and deleterious effects on later events. Lastly, Germany was barred from the League until it passed a period of "probation." These *terms* weighed heavily on the *Weimar Republic* without entirely satisfying British or especially French *public opinion,* or *security* concerns. Long before the *Nazis* took power, the German military devised ways to evade the disarmament provisions (for instance, by secret training in Russia after *Rapallo*), and without British or American support, France alone was unable to enforce the harsher clauses. *Hitler* disemboweled the treaty after 1933. See also *Anglo/German Naval Agreement; Clemenceau; defeat; diplomacy; entangling alliance; Foch; Lloyd George; stab-in-the-back; Stresemann; Woodrow Wilson.*

vertical escalation: Increasing levels of military response, rather than expanding or widening a combat area. Cf. *horizontal escalation.*

vertical proliferation: Quantitative increases in available weapons systems. Cf. *horizontal proliferation.*

vertical take-off and landing (VTOL): A (self-descriptive) genus of aircraft designed for forward, battlefield conditions, where full-length airfields are in short supply. They also permit design of short-surface *aircraft carriers.*

veto: A by-product of situations where the *unanimity rule* is in effect, whereby any one *state* refusing *consent* blocks or invalidates an agreement. This *rule* may be qualified according to the organization concerned. Under terms of the *Charter of the UN* it is a right limited in the UN to the five *permanent members of the Security Council,* the only states empowered to stop substantive (but not procedural) decisions simply by casting a negative vote. Note: mere abstention by a permanent member does not constitute a veto. Nor does even their negative vote block measures or resolutions in the *UNGA,* where they sit and vote in legal *equality* with the discontented, the middling and the weak and powerless among nations. See also *liberum veto.* Cf. *qualified majority voting; weighted voting.*

viceroy: A ruler of a country, such as colonial India, who serves in lieu of an absent *sovereign.*

Vichy: Unoccupied France, plus its overseas possessions, July 1940-November 1942. It was named for its capital, which was the provincial town of Vichy (the Germans were touring Paris at the time). The Vichy *regime* willingly *collaborated* with the Nazi occupiers. Some Vichy commanders fired on the *Allies,* while its police aided the *Gestapo* and government officials helped transport non-Jews to *forced labor* camps and Jewish citizens to the *death camps.* It was anti-*republican,* and at least partly *fascist* itself. *Pétain's* declared reason for heading it, that it would preserve at least part of France from direct *occupation,* was invalidated in November 1942, when the Germans occupied the whole country. Top Vichyites continued to collaborate even then, until forced to flee to Germany in July 1944. The full extent of collaboration has never really been admitted within France, which tends to look on *WWII* through *Resistance*-colored glasses. See also *Darlan; de Gaulle; Free French; Laval.*

Victor Emmanuel III (1869-1947): King of Italy. On the throne for 46 years, from 1900-1946, he watched Italy enter *WWI* for *territorial* gain, only to be humiliated in the field and denied *Italia irredenta.* He collaborated with *Mussolini* and the Italian *fascists,* accepting to become "Emperor of Ethiopia" in 1935. He tried to distance himself from them when they brought Italy to *defeat* and foreign *occupation* during *WWII.* He agreed to dismiss Mussolini as part of the coup that brought *Pietro Bodoglio* to power. Widely viewed as having served too many masters too easily, he was deposed in 1946.

Victoria (1819-1901): Queen of the *United Kingdom* 1837-1901; Empress of India 1876-1901. Her efforts to interfere with foreign affairs were easily deflected, and her reign saw the complete and final subordination of the British *monarchy* to parliamentary authority. For students of *international relations* she is notable mainly as a symbol of British *power* at its greatest, and most detached, imperial heights.

victor's justice: When a *victor* in war tries and punishes the *defeated,* which may or may not mean justice is done. Usually pejorative. See *war crimes trials.*

victory, in war: When an enemy concedes one's superiority in combat by asking for *terms,* with the consequence that one's interests in the *dispute(s)* occasion-

ing the war are advanced at the expense of the loser. That qualified definition should not surprise: no victory is absolute (though some defeats are), because all wars are inherently political as well as military, and hence reflect competing interests and continuing opposition to the absolute triumph of any one group, nation or idea, regardless of momentary ascendancy in matters of combat. Cf. *defeat; pyrrhic victory; war.*

Vienna, Congress of (September 1814-June 1815): The meeting of the four main victors over *Napoleon* and France: Austria, Britain, Prussia and Russia. It was held over the winter of 1814-15. Its main purpose was to discuss a host of questions pertaining to territorial settlement, *restoration* of the *monarchs* of Europe deposed by the *French Revolution* and by Napoleon, and other questions left in the wake of French *defeat.* It was interrupted by Napoleon's return for the *Hundred Days.* When it resumed, France received less generous terms than before, including some minor loss of *territory.* Yet while France was not fully accepted back into the fold, under *Talleyrand's* masterful diplomacy it was still treated with the respect accruing to a *Great Power.* Vienna was the first, and most important, of the meetings of the *Congress System.* It laid out a comprehensive settlement following a quarter century of *war,* and in so doing set the basic mold of Great Power relations that would last until the *Crimean War.* (1) Territorial provisions: It created a united kingdom of Belgium, Luxembourg and the Netherlands; set up the *German Confederation*; gave Britain the Cape of Good Hope (*Cape Colony*), Ceylon, *Heligoland, Malta,* Mauritius, St. Lucia and Tobago; united Norway to Sweden; reinstated and made *neutral* the Swiss Confederation; confirmed control of *Venice* and parts of the *Balkans* by Austria, and *Poland* by Russia; and granted *Danzig* and other Baltic areas to Prussia. (2) Other clauses: It denounced the *slave trade;* recommended constitutional protections for Jews in Germany; *internationalized* the Rhine and the Meuse; barred France from involvement in the politics of the Italian peninsula (a traditional French *sphere of influence*); and revamped diplomatic procedures and *protocol,* regularizing the titles, rights and duties of *ambassadors, ministers, envoys* and *chargés.* Unlike the *Paris Peace Conference* a century later, Vienna did not enunciate general principles and then apply them (with varying degrees of integrity). Instead, it made deals and arrangements that flowed from *power* and political realities, from which later observers extrapolated principles said to govern the *Concert of Europe. Liberals* came to view the Congress of Vienna with general disdain, for its territorial adjustments that took little or no regard of *self-determination.* For instance, *Woodrow Wilson* said at Paris that he wished to avoid the "odor of Vienna." More conservative observers, by contrast, have admired and acclaimed the settlement for its *realism* about Great Power relations, and for helping keep the *peace* for several decades.

Vienna Convention on Consular Relations (1961): Negotiated alongside more important *Vienna Conventions* cited below, it regularized and codified the rights, duties and status of *consuls* and *consulates*.

Vienna Convention on Diplomatic Privileges, Intercourse and Immunities (1961): It was drafted in 1961 and came into effect in 1964. It codified existing, *international customary law* on the status and functions of *diplomats* and *embassies*, carrying forward the clarifying and regularizing work begun at the *Congress of Vienna* (1815). It affirmed the rights of all *sovereign* states to *representation*, and to *recall an ambassador* or break *diplomatic relations*. It also affirmed the ranking of diplomats, as follows: (1) *ambassadors* and *high commissioners;* (2) *envoys, envoy extraordinary, minister plenipotentiary;* (3) *ministers resident;* and (4) *chargés.* Below these ranks are quasi-diplomatic positions: (5) *attaché,* and (6) *consul.*

Vienna Convention on the Law of Treaties (1961): It codified well-established *international customary law* govering *treaties.* See also *validity; violation.*

Viet Cong *(Viet Nam Cong San)*: "Vietnamese Communists." A *guerrilla* army organized under the umbrella of the National Liberation Front (NLF), drawn from volunteers and dragooned *conscripts.* They fought the armed forces of South Vietnam and the U.S. from 1959 to the end of the *Vietnam War.* The VC were a determined foe with *logistical* and other backing from North Vietnam, which was in turn backed by China and the Soviet Union. Nonetheless, they were largely eliminated as a fighting force during the *Tet Offensive,* after which North Vietnamese Army (NVA) regulars took the field.

Viet Minh *(Viet Nam Doc Lap Dong Minh Hoi)*: "Vietnamese Independence League." A communist-led, Vietnamese nationalist organization that took the lead in the fight against the Japanese *occupation* of Vietnam 1941-45. From its base in northern Vietnam it then fought the French 1945-54, the South Vietnamese 1954-75, and the United States 1964-72.

Vietnam: Location: SE Asia. Major associations: *UN.* Population: 70 million. Military: 4th largest in the world (one million troops); outdated Soviet equipment and a shrinking budget are made up in part by the well-deserved reputation of Vietnamese soldiers as fierce and resolute enemies. (1) Pre-*WWII*: Historical knowledge of Vietnam dates back centuries before the present era. In 111 B.C. it was conquered by and became a *vassal state* of China, a condition that lasted over 1,000 years. In 939 A.D. it achieved some significant *autonomy*, but for centuries yet had to fight off Chinese and then Mongol efforts to reconquer it, not always succeeding. The French began to penetrate the Indochinese peninsula after 1850, and between 1858-84 progressively extended their dominion over *Annam*, *Cochin China* and *Tonkin*, uniting them with other colonies in the composite state called *French Indochina*. In 1940 Japan forced *Vichy* authorities to cede military bases in Indochina, which it used in 1941 to complete *conquest* of the peninsula. The *Viet Minh* fought the Japanese from 1941-45, then the French in the *French/Indochina War* (1946-54). The *Geneva Agreements* divided Vietnam at the 17th parallel, into the Democratic Republic and the Republic of Vietnam, or North and South Vietnam, respectively. The two states existed in uneasy, suspended hostility until 1959, when the climactic installment of the *Vietnam War* broke out.

(2) Democratic Republic of Vietnam (North Vietnam): *Ho Chi Minh* was the guiding light of North Vietnam, established in 1945, maintained against the French and confirmed in 1955 in the Geneva Agreements. Ho and the Viet Minh introduced a modified *stalinist* system in the 1950s, including forced *collectivization* of the villages and massacres of "landlords" (better-off peasants). When economic collapse threatened they backtracked, with Ho admitting "some errors have been made." The North aligned with China and the Soviet Union and kept ties with both despite the *Sino/Soviet split* over other issues. It drew upon the larger communist powers for assistance in *industrialization*, but mainly it called upon their military prowess and weaponry to build itself into a formidable *martial* state. During the *Vietnam War* it took a terrific pounding from the U.S. Air Force without flinching from its determination for reunification under communist rule, an objective accomplished in 1975.

(3) Republic of Vietnam (South Vietnam): The Emperor *Bao Dai* was *head of state* from 1949-55, when it became a *republic* under *Ngo Dinh Diem*. From 1959 on it faced a loss of control over the countryside as the *Viet Cong* murdered thousands of local officials. The *Kennedy* administration responded by raising the number of U.S. advisers from around 600 to over 16,500 just before JFK was assassinated in November 1963. Diem's response was too timid for some of his own military, and apparently also for the U.S. At first supported by the U.S., Diem was overthrown in a *coup* directly approved by Kennedy (though JFK did not approve of Diem's murder). Un-

der *Lyndon Johnson*, who took charge of U.S. policy shortly thereafter, the number of U.S. advisers soared, and after the *Tonkin Gulf Resolution* the U.S. became directly involved in large-scale combat. The American phase of the war raged until 1973 and the *Paris Peace Accords*. South Vietnam fought on alone, until it succumbed to a full-scale *invasion* in 1975 and became *extinct* by incorporation with the North.

(4) After the war: The united, Socialist Republic of Vietnam bent to the task of *reconstruction* after 1975, aided by the Soviet Union but hamstrung by a U.S. *embargo* that was not fully lifted until early in 1994. It joined *COMECON* in 1978, but that organization had little to offer beyond *barter* markets and limited choice and supply. The consequence of rigid *ideology* and economic mismanagement, embargo and continuing *war* with several neighbors was nearly two decades of decline. Meanwhile, all around in SE Asia former colonies were emerging as prosperous *Asian Tigers*. In 1978, after running border skirmishes with its former *ally* the *Khmers Rouges*, Vietnam invaded Cambodia. It would not vacate that country until after 14 years of war (including a major clash with China in 1979 and battles with Thai troops in 1985). With its economy in shambles and its Soviet ally gone, Hanoi pulled out all its forces in late 1992. But the occupation of Cambodia set Vietnam at odds with *ASEAN* and more importantly with China. After 1980 large numbers of *boat people* began to leave Vietnam. Along with other communist countries, Vietnam began to experiment with market reforms ("Doi Moi") after 1987. In 1990 inflation surpassed 1,100% per annum. In 1992 Vietnam signed a "Treaty of Amity and Cooperation" with *ASEAN*, as a first step toward membership. It maintains a strong claim to the *Paracels* and the *Spratlys*, where its forces clashed with Chinese naval and marine units. However, in November 1993, it signed an agreement with China mutually renouncing the use of force over border disputes. Relations with the U.S. remained constrained by a lack of full *diplomatic relations*, and American insistence on a satisfactory accounting (whatever that means, and if it is still physically possible) by Vietnam of all American *POWs* and *MIAs* from the war. In mid-1993 *William Clinton* lifted a ban on joint business ventures and the U.S. *veto* on *World Bank* loans, and at the end of the year approved business participation in internationally approved and funded trade ventures. In February 1994, he ended the *embargo*, over objections from MIA families and others, but with wide support from the business community.

Vietnamization: A policy announced by *Richard Nixon* as a key to phased American withdrawal from the *Vietnam War*. It called for arming and training of South Vietnamese soldiers in sufficient numbers and quality to replace the American GIs in the field. That was supposed to allow the U.S. to remain committed only with naval and *air power.* Nixon later complained that Congress gutted his policy, by refusing to continue large-scale military *aid* to the South and prohibiting the use of American air power against Northern *incursions*. He asserted, in short, that the war was winnable (South Vietnam could survive) even after U.S. withdrawal. But it seems highly unlikely that a downsized bombing operation would have saved the South, when an eight-year commitment of up to 550,000 U.S. troops and the most intensive bombing campaign in history had not. Nor is it likely the determined, even fanatical leadership of the North could have been stopped short of complete *victory* by anything other than ultimate U.S. force, which was (wisely) never used.

Vietnam War (1959-75): Some say the Vietnam War lasted from 1940-75, encompassing the fight led at first by *Ho Chi Minh* for *independence* and then unification against the Japanese, French, Americans and most of all, other Vietnamese. Others date it from the start of heavy U.S. involvement in 1964. In any case, the phase from 1959-75 was the most violent. It began when *cadres* of *Viet Cong* (VC) finally began armed attacks. They had been organized in the South by the North as early as 1957, but stayed restlessly quiet on orders from Ho until sufficient strength was built up to really threaten the *Diem* regime. From 1959-61 the VC assassinated about 10,000 South Vietnamese officials. American advisers were sent in by *Eisenhower*, but barely topped 500 when he left office. They poured in under *Kennedy*, multiplying 32-fold (to over 16,500) and taking on additional, often quasi-combat tasks. Actual U.S. combat troops (joined by small numbers from *ANZUS*, as well as Koreans and Filipinos) were not committed until after the *Tonkin Gulf Resolution*, engineered by *Lyndon Johnson*. After 1964 the war was largely Americanized in its direction, *strategy* and weapons. By 1965 some 200,000 American combat troops were in Vietnam. They numbered over 540,000 by 1968 (the turning point year), when General William Westmoreland (U.S. commander, 1965-68) asked for 200,000 more, and was refused by an administration grown confused, internally divided, and deeply unpopular because of the war.

The VC strategy was elegantly simple: make the country ungovernable by anyone but themselves and their sponsors in the *Viet Minh*, who already ran the North. So too were their tactics of terror and assassination, right at the village level, highly effective. They infiltrated supplies and reinforcements down the *Ho Chi Minh Trail*, drawing upon the North, but also

China and the Soviet Union for *logistical* support. The U.S. and South Vietnamese (RVN) forces tried to defeat the VC conventionally through *search-and-destroy* missions, politically through village *pacification*, and unconventionally with borrowed tactics of assassination and *guerrilla warfare* run by the *CIA*. Meanwhile, they penalized and sought to coerce North Vietnam with massive bombing strikes on its military along the Ho Chi Minh Trail (including secret bombing of the Trail's Cambodian and Laotian ancillaries), and against Northern *infrastructure* and cities--and that meant killing large numbers of civilians as "collateral damage." By 1968 the U.S. military claimed, believed and probably actually was winning the war against the VC. But the war's crucial political context changed dramatically with the *tactically* disastrous (for the VC and the North), but propagandistically and ultimately *strategically* decisive (also for the North), *Tet Offensive*. By the end of 1968 the decision was taken in Washington to phase out American involvement in the war. The *home front* had folded after Tet, which made *victory* look as or more distant than before, and raised suspicions about the truthfulness of U.S. government statements. After that, most arguments were over how fast, not whether, the U.S. should pull out. *Richard Nixon* introduced *Vietnamization* (reversing the pattern of Johnson's *escalation*). He then traveled to Moscow and Beijing to get agreement to a prolonged *truce* (or what *Henry Kissinger* once called in private "a decent interval" between a U.S. withdrawal and the South's *defeat*). But Nixon was not loathe to strike out at North Vietnam with large-scale force in the interim. He thus authorized a secret *incursion* into eastern Cambodia, in an extended search-and-destroy mission in 1971-72; and he several times renewed bombing of Northern installations and cities, and mining of Northern harbors. Those U.S. actions, continuing Northern infiltration and ongoing fighting in the fields and jungles took place while *peace talks* were underway in Paris, from 1969-72. The *Paris Peace Accords* in 1973 led to a pullout of all American ground forces. In 1975, with the "decent interval" over, the Viet Minh completed via an *invasion* of the South what it began 30 years earlier: unification of all Vietnam under its rule. Here is the roll call of the dead: 6,000 from the minor allies of South Vietnam; 58,000 Americans; 200,000 RVN; 1 million (or more) VC and NVA regulars; and some 2 million civilians. Cf. *containment; domino theory; national liberation, wars of; Nguyen Giap; Robert McNamara; mutiny; My Lai massacre; Nixon Doctrine; Wise Men*. And see map.

Villa, Francisco (1877-1923): "Pancho Villa." Mexican revolutionary. He deliberately provoked U.S. *intervention* in Mexico by attacking a Texas town in 1916, in the apparent belief he could then play the role of defender of all Mexico against the Yankee. *Woodrow Wilson* rose to the bait, and the U.S. army had to be recalled from chasing Villa when war was declared on Germany in April 1917. He died by assassination.

Vilna (Vilnius): The ancient *capital* of Lithuania. It was seized by Poland in 1920, but returned in 1939, as part of the settlement in the *Nazi/Soviet Pact*.

Vimy Ridge, Battle of (April 1917): A prolonged assault by Canadian troops on entrenched German positions during *WWI*. They took the ridge where other troops had failed, but their casualties were appallingly heavy. The battle helped arouse interest in an independent foreign policy after the war, the intent being to avoid repeating such carnage on behalf of others, for reasons so little understood.

violation: When one party to a *treaty* acts against one or more of the *terms* of the agreement. This gives ground for *termination* by the other party(ies).

Virgin Islands of the United States: These three Caribbean islands were discovered by Columbus in 1493. They were claimed by the Spanish, who went on to utterly destroy the native population by 1596, supplanting it with European settlers. In 1917 the islands were purchased by the U.S. for naval use, and then made an *unincorporated territory*. In 1927 residents were granted U.S. *citizenship*. Since 1973 they have had limited, non-voting representation in the U.S. House of Representatives. Population: 102,000. Military: U.S. base.

visa: A permit or pass stamped or written on the *passport* of one country by a *consul* or *customs* official of another, allowing the bearer to enter or exit the second country. Visas may allow passage but still place considerable restrictions on the bearer, such as excluding areas that may be visited, compelling currency *exchange* at set government rates, prohibiting censored literature or, in many Muslim countries, barring importation of alcohol or pornography. Visas may be temporary (*tourist*, transit or work visa) or permanent (*immigration* visa).

visé: To issue, or to check, a *visa*.

visible trade: Trade in tangible *goods*; not *services*.

Visigrad countries: Czech Republic, Hungary, Slovakia and Poland.

visit and search: (1) The right of a *belligerent* to stop on the *high seas* and search for *contraband* any or all *neutral* shipping. (2) The right of any *state* to stop and inspect a foreign merchant ship if it suspects that ship of *piracy*, engaging in the *slave trade*, or concealing its *nationality* under a flag of false registration.

vis major: See *force majeure.*

vital interests: Any *national interest* that is, or is deemed to be, indispensable to the prosperity, future *development* and most of all the *security* of a given *state.* A vital interest might be virtually anything perceived in such terms, including but not limited to access to markets or a *strategic* commodity like *oil*, preventing encirclement by enemy powers, or preempting another state's acquisition of a *weapon of mass destruction.* When a state declares that it regards such-and-such as among its vital interests, it is almost always indicating that it is prepared to use *force* to defend those interests. Cf. *self-help.*

VJ (Victory in Japan) Day: August 15, 1945 (GMT), when Japan indicated it would *surrender* to the *United Nations alliance.* The instruments of surrender were signed later, aboard a U.S. *warship* in Tokyo Bay.

Voice of America: A division of the U.S. Information Agency that makes worldwide shortwave broadcasts in multiple languages. During the *Cold War* its broadcasts were a supplement to the more clearly political work of *Radio Free Europe.*

Voivodina: Once part of the *Austrian Empire*, it was ceded to *Yugoslavia* in the *Treaty of Trianon.* As an "autonomous region" it was attached to *Serbia* while both were part of Yugoslavia, except briefly during *WWII* when Hungary occupied and annexed it. It was retained by Serbia after the breakup of the Yugoslav federation. It has a large Hungarian minority.

volition: Choices made or decisions taken by freely willing individuals. Whether decisions are heavily conditioned by circumstance or not, *decision-makers* always operate within a realm where some free choice is possible, and hence where moral and political accountability remain active. Cf. *determinism.*

Volksdeutsche: Germanness, ethnically defined. For *Hitler*, Volk and völkische conveyed all the meanings of the English words "folk" and "race," while adding the German sense of "Kultur" (a superior civilization imbued with a historic "soul"). The Volk was supposedly rooted in the "Volksgemeinschaft," or "organic community." These terms were used by the *Nazis* to define *nationality* in terms of ethnicity rather than

citizenship, and thus include Germans living beyond the borders of the *Reich* while excluding others living in-country (such as *Gypsies* or Jews). Alleged repression of the rights of the outer Volksdeutsche then became a favored ploy in agitating German-speaking populaces against governments in Austria, Poland and Czechoslovakia. In contemporary Germany, ethnically defined rights of citizenship mean that a Turk living always in Germany can have more difficulty securing citizenship than an ethnic German from Polish *Silesia* or Russia, who has never before set foot on German soil. Cf. *Fifth Column; Minorities Treaties.*

Voltaire, né François Marie Arouet (1694-1778): French "philosophe." A leading figure in the *Enlightenment*, he corresponded with and advised *Catherine II (the Great), Frederick II* and other monarchs. His writings had such an impact his history of *Louis XIV*, "Siècle de Louis Quatorze," gave the name of that brilliant, brooding king to the Age itself. His novel "Candide" likewise did much to expose the myth of benevolent *colonialism* through its savage honesty about conditions on the plantations of the Americas ("this," says a beaten and dying slave to Candide, "is the price of sugar in Europe"). Voltaire's satire was biting, his pen acid, his irreverence revolutionary, his wit politically infectious and his influence lasting. See, for example, *Holy Roman Empire.*

voluntary export restraints (VERs): Also called voluntary restraint agreements (VRAs). These are actually involuntary export restrictions that everyone agrees to pretend are voluntary so as to limit the political fallout from a serious trade *dispute.* The first major industry affected by VERS, which are a form of *non-tariff barrier*, was steel. But the most important to date has been Japanese automobiles, targeted for VERS by the U.S. and Western Europe starting in the 1980s. Japan agreed to curtail its exports and to negotiate VER limits under threat of unilateral, mandatory *quotas.* A near-synonym is "orderly market arrangements." See *protectionism.*

voting with their feet: (1) A coinage of *Lenin's,* in response to queries about the democratic legitimacy of the *Bolshevik* regime. He maintained, radical tongue planted firmly in cheek, that Russia's soldiers and peasants had voted for *revolution* "with their feet" when they threw down their rifles and walked home from the *eastern front.* By the same token, erecting the *Berlin Wall* and drawing down the *iron curtain* demonstrated how little Soviet leaders trusted their chances of reelection. (2) Any similar mass movement, especially a *migration*, that effects basic political change without formal consultation.

vulnerability: Under *interdependence,* when changes in conditions within one *state* have sharply adverse consequences for another. This is true of most small powers on most issues in their relations with larger powers. It also applies to *Great Powers* on issues such as access to foreign reserves of *strategic resources,* or sudden fluctuations in *exchange rates* due to a change in *interest rates* set by a major trading partner.

Vyshinsky, Andrei Yamuareivich (1883-1954): Soviet Foreign Minister 1949-53. He was a front man for *Stalin,* both as Foreign Commissar in the 1940s and earlier, when he carved out a noxious reputation for baiting and vilifying defendants during the *Yezhovshchina.* Nightmare states like Stalin's are constructed on pylons sunk into the small talents and perverse loyalties of such gray functionaries as Vyshinsky.

W

Wahhabi: A strict, conservative, even puritanical *Islamic* sect founded in 18th century Arabia. The Wahhabi supported *Ibn Saud* in his bid for power over the *Hejaz,* and still sustain the Saudi *dynasty* against radical *shi'ites* from the interior.

Waitangi, Treaty of (1840): A *treaty* between Britain and approximately 500 *Maori* chiefs, granting British *sovereignty* over New Zealand in exchange for protection of Maori land claims from white settlers. When the British failed to uphold their guarantee, the *First Maori War* began. See also *tribe; validity.*

Wake Island: Located on the Hawaii-to-Hong Kong *trade route,* it was claimed by the U.S. in 1898. It was captured by Japan early in *WWII,* but was later retaken. It has no *indigenous population* and since 1972 has been administered by the U.S. Air Force. *Guam* claims Wake, as does the *Marshall Islands.*

Waldheim, Kurt (b.1918): Austrian and world statesman. *Secretary General* of the *UN* 1971-82; Austrian Foreign Minister 1968-70; President 1986-92. He was ineffective at the UN because of his election as a compromise candidate, a chronic impasse in the *Security Council* and his passive personality. Files released in the mid-1980s revealed he had covered up his war record and suggested he might have participated in *Nazi* atrocities. In 1988 an international panel of historians concluded that Waldheim had known of *war crimes* committed in *Yugoslavia* during *WWII* and had not intervened to stop them. However, it said he had not participated actively. A highly unusual diplomatic boycott of Austria ensued, with many states (led by Israel) refusing to maintain full relations as long as Waldheim remained President. He stayed popular in Austria, however, where local opinion grew more defiant even as world opinion became more critical.

Walesa, Lech (b.1943): Polish statesman. Former worker and trade union leader in the *Gdansk* shipyards, he founded and led *Solidarity* from the 1970s, through its banned period under *martial law,* and then to electoral victory in 1989 and 1990, with himself chosen as President of Poland. He was awarded the *Nobel Prize* for Peace in 1983. Admiration for him in the West, and his close relationship with Pope *John Paul II,* gave Poland a profile it otherwise might not have had. In 1992 he apologized to all Jews and to Israel for remarks tainted with *anti-Semitism* he made as President. In 1993 Walesa resigned from Solidarity, citing its refusal to accept his reform proposals.

Wallis and Fortuna Islands: Once a *colony* of *Tonga,* these sparsely populated archipelagoes became French *protectorates* in 1887. In 1957 they voted to become French *overseas territories.* There is little apparent sentiment for *independence.*

Wall Street Crash: See *Black Tuesday.*

Walvis Bay: A British *colony* deep inside South West Africa (Namibia), annexed to *Cape Colony* in 1878. In 1910 it was incorporated as an exclave of the Union of South Africa. In 1993 it was ceded to Namibia.

Wang Jingwei, a.k.a. Ching-wei (1883-1944): Chinese traitor. He was one of *Sun Yat-Sen's* main lieutenants, and was prominent in the early years of the *Chinese Revolution.* In the 1920s he was on the left of the *Guomindang,* but joined *Chiang Kai-shek* and served as head of the administrative council and party president from 1932-35, after heading the regional government in Wuhan from 1927. He was nearly assassinated in 1935. He fled to *Hong Kong* in 1938. After the Japanese *invasion* he *collaborated,* becoming a vassal PM of occupied China, with his "capital" in the city where the Japanese butchered 200,000 civilians during the *sack of Nanking.* He died in Japan, probably of natural causes. Cf. *Pierre Laval; Vidkun Quisling.*

Wannsee conference (January 1942): See *final solution to the Jewish problem; Holocaust.*

war: (1) *Armed hostilities* within, between or among states or other political communities (*ethnic groups, tribes*) in which economic and political outcomes are decided mainly by superior *force*, not equity, *negotiation* or reason. By convention, such outbreaks of organized political violence are termed wars when 1,000 or more are killed. (2) A legal condition of open and declared hostility between or among states, wherein they may use any force deemed fit or effective, subject only to the *laws of war* and perhaps to notions of *just war*. In this sense, war is the ultimate *self-help* device. (3) The narrowest meaning of the term is the art and science of military operations. Discourse on war usually divides the phenomenon into an ascending scale of participation, thus: *rebellion, insurrection, insurgency, guerrilla, civil, local* or *regional wars*; and then three synonyms, global, *systemic* and *world war*. Or it divides by weapon type, as in *conventional/nuclear war*; or it types by scope and objective, as in *limited war* and *total war*. War has, of course, disparate purposes. At its crudest, it may be little more than organized theft. Or it may be undertaken in the belief (mistaken or not) that it will serve the *dynastic*, social, or *ideological* purposes of rulers and *elites*; or to gratify the collective egoism of national, ethnic or tribal groups. Often (mis)quoted on this aspect of war, as essentially political in nature, is *Clausewitz*: "War is not merely a political act, but also a political instrument, a continuation of political relations, a carrying out of the same by other means." Yet war has important legal purposes and ramifications as well. At a more sophisticated level than that of unadulterated *power politics*, it has two recognizable legal objectives when indulged in by *states*, and especially by a *Great Power*: (1) It is a device for enforcing political claims based on asserted legal rights. (2) It is a means of overturning an existing legal order, either to unilaterally alter it to one's own advantage (e.g., Iraq's 1990 attempt to deny Kuwait's *sovereignty* by *occupation* and *annexation*, or China's 1962 alteration by force of its *border* with India); or to compel other states to adjust to fundamentally changed conditions in the *international system* of which the law has not yet taken account (e.g., *Bismarck's* reordering of Germany's place in Europe, first in fact and then in law, through demonstration of its *preponderance*). Among lesser legal ramifications of war are: it automatically severs *diplomatic relations* (if accompanied by a *declaration of war*); it has a mixed effect on *treaties*, dissolving some, placing most in abeyance (*suspension*), but calling all those connected to the laws of war into operation and effect; and it severs all legal relations among *citizens* of the bel-

ligerent states. Thus, war should be understood not simply as the moral crudity of superior physical *power* carrying the day on a given question, but as a complex recipe of legal, as well as economic and political, motives, tactics and effects. See also *accidental war; ace; active defense; act of war; aggression; airborne; airburst; aircraft carrier; air drop; air power; angary; anti-ballistic missile, missile (ABM); anti-personnel weapon; anti-satellite weapons (ASAT); anti-submarine warfare (ASW); area defense; armed hostilities; Armed Neutrality; armistice; armor; arsenal; artillery; atomic bomb; atomic demolition mine (ADM); attrition; ballistic missile; ballistic missile defense (BMD); barrage balloon; battlecruiser; battle fatigue; battleship; beachhead; belligerency; belligerent rights; besiege; billets; binary weapons; biological agents; blast effects; blitzkrieg; blockade; blue water navy; bomb; bombardment; bomber; booty; bridgehead; bus; C³; C³I; camouflage; campaign; cannon; cannon fodder; capital warships; capture; casus belli; cavalry; ceasefire; chemical and biological warfare; chemical agents; civil defense; civilian; cobelligerency; coercion; collaboration; collateral damage; combat area; commando; conquest; conscription; convoy; counterattack; counterinsurgency; crimes against humanity; crimes against peace; cruise missile; cruiser; D-Day; death squad; defeat; defeatism; defense; defense area; defense-in-depth; defilade; demilitarized zone (DMZ); depth charge; destroyer; deterrence; disengagement; diversionary war; dog fight; Dreadnought; dynastic war; emplacement; enceinte; enemy prisoner of war (EPW); enfilade; entrench; envelopment; escalation control; escalation dominance; ethnic cleansing; feint; field artillery; fighter; fighter-bomber; firebreak; first line; first strike; first use; flagship; flak; flank; foot soldiers; force; fortification; forward defense; fraternize; friendly fire; frigate; front line; gas weapons; General Staff; Geneva Conventions; Geneva Protocol; genocide; grapeshot; guerrilla warfare; guided missile; gunnery; Hague Conferences; Hague Conventions; heavy (bomber etc.); high command; home front; hostilities; hot war; hunter-killer; hydrogen bomb; impressment; incendiary weapons; incursion; indiscriminate bombing; Intercontinental Ballistic Missile (ICBM); interdiction; internment; intervention; intrawar deterrence; intrusion; invasion; ironclads; jihad; jus ad bellum; jus in bello; kamikaze; landing craft; land mine; land power; launcher; launch on warning; letters of marque; levée en masse; liberation; limited nuclear war; limited war; line officer; living off the land; logistics; low-intensity conflict; Luftwaffe; manned penetrator; man-of-war; measures short of war; mercenary; military government; military law; military necessity; military objective; military ranks; military science; military units; militia;*

MIRV; mobilization; munitions; mustard gas; Napoleonic warfare; navy; necessities of war; necessity; nerve weapons; neutrality; neutralization; neutral rights and duties; neutron bomb; no-fly-zone; no-man's-land; noncombatants; nuclear agents; nuclear winter; occupation; officer; officer corps; ordnance; outflank; pacification; pacifism; Panzer; paramilitary; Paris, Declaration of; partisan; passive defense; penetration aids; pillage; piracy; PLA; plunder; plutonium; pocket battleship; poison; police action; pontoon bridge; postwar; preemptive strike; preventive war; prisoner of war (POW); privateer; prize; prohibited weapons; proportionality; proxy wars; prudence; psychological warfare; quarantine; radiation effects; radiological weapons; rampart; qui desiderat; rationing; rear echelon; rear guard; recognition; reconnoiter; Red Army; Red Cross; redoubt; refugees; regular army; reprisal; requisition; resistance; retaliation; rifled bore; Royal Navy; rules of engagement; ruse; sabotage; salvo; scorched earth; sea mine; sea power; search-and-destroy; second strike; self-defense; sentry; shell shock; ship-of-the-line; shock troops; siege; sloop-of-war; smooth bore; staff officer; standards of civilized behavior; standing army; state of war; Strategic Defense Initiative (SDI); strategic nuclear response; strategic nuclear weapons; strategy; submarine; summary execution; superior orders; supply lines; surface-to-air; surface-to-surface; surface-to-underwater; surgical strike; surrender; tactical nuclear weapons; tactics; targeting doctrine; task force; technology; terminal defense; terms, ask for; territorial defense; theater nuclear weapons; thousand bomber raids; topography; torture; TOW; tracer; traumatic stress disorder; trench warfare; truce; two-front war; two-power naval standard; U-boat; unconditional surrender; unrestricted submarine warfare; V-1 and V-2 rockets; vanguard; vertical escalation; victory; visit and search; war aims; war contagion; war crimes; war debts; warfare; war fighting strategy; war games; warhead; warlord; warmongering; warplane; war planning; warship; wars of independence; war termination; war treason; war weariness; war zone; weapons of mass destruction; Wehrmacht; withholding strategy; wolf pack; yield; zeppelin; zero hour; and see the discrete wars synopsized in this volume. Cf. *inter bellum et pacem; peace; status mixtus.*

war aims: The declared and secret economic, political and *strategic* goals and ambitions a *state* engages in *war* to fulfill or advance.

War Between the States: The *American Civil War,* as known below the *Mason-Dixon line.* For southerners who remain utterly unreconstructed the preferred reference may even be "The War of Northern Aggression."

war communism: The *Bolshevik* practice of *nationalization* of finance and industry, from 1918 until adoption of the *New Economic Policy* in 1921. It was also used as a euphemism for *forced labor,* and brutal and often bloody *requisition* of grain and other foodstuffs from the peasants during the *Russian Civil War.*

war contagion: A common metaphor likening *war* to a disease, and implicitly warning against allowing it to spread by contact or neglect. By extension, it implies that one ought to pursue an interventionist *diplomacy,* in which measures are taken to lance the conflict (or cut out the canker, depending on one's chosen image).

war correspondent: A journalist reporting on a war.

war crimes: The third in a category of criminal acts concerning war, along with *crimes against humanity* and *crimes against peace,* for which individuals may be held accountable. War crimes may be a violation of either *international criminal law,* as laid out in the *Geneva Conventions,* or of the municipal law of the place the act was committed. Traditionally, there were two defenses against a charge of war crimes: *act of state* and *superior orders.* However, this has changed since 1945. New principles were developed at the *war crimes trials* at *Nuremberg* and *Tokyo,* and in *treaties* such as the *Genocide Convention,* in which for certain acts defined as war crimes the defenses given above did not sway tribunals, and no longer appear to convince most legal thinkers. In addition to normally criminal acts (murder or *torture*), the following are generally considered war crimes: (1) killing or wounding enemy *combatants* who ask to *surrender;* (2) firing on a flag of *truce;* (3) abusing a flag of truce or request for mercy to gain a military advantage and continue hostilities; (4) hiding military targets under the emblem of the *Red Cross* or *Red Crescent,* or otherwise abusing the privileges attached to those emblems, such as firing from the sanctuary of a hospital; (5) hiding among a *civilian* population by discarding one's uniform and wearing civilian clothes, if done in order to better commit hostile acts (not if done to effect escape); (6) killing, wounding or maliciously neglecting *POWs,* or using them for medical or other experimentation; (7) killing or wounding civilians, unless as a form of *collateral damage;* (8) using *prohibited weapons* of war, such as *biological, chemical, gas* or *nerve agents* (possibly to one day include *land mines* as well); (9) targeting militarily insignificant areas; (10) *pillaging;* (11) using POWs as slave or *forced labor* on military installations; (12) accepting *surrender* terms, then disregarding them; (13) using torture to elicit information about the enemy from its civilian population; (14) abusing the dead in any way;

(15) sacking hospitals or similarly protected buildings; (16) deliberate terror attacks on a civilian population; (17) forcing a POW to serve in one's own armed forces, or auxiliary units, against his/her former comrades; (18) concealing oneself in the uniform of the enemy, for purposes of deceit and advantage in combat. With appropriate adjustments, these same rules apply to naval and air warfare (no false flag or markings, no firing from or on hospital ships or planes, no indiscriminate *bombardment* or bombing, no killing after surrender and so on). Additional prohibited acts were added to this list by a *UN* tribunal organized in 1993 to try suspected war criminals from the *Third Balkan War*. Its most notable additions to date have been prohibitions on *ethnic cleansing* and rape. See also *war crimes trials; war treason*.

war crimes trials: International (as opposed to municipal) criminal proceedings were set up after *WWI* by the *Treaty of Versailles*, in the hope of trying *Wilhelm II* and other German leaders. American opposition to this procedure--and then failure to *ratify* the *treaty*--combined with German obstruction to turn the proceedings into a farce. In the end, a mere handful of junior officers (mainly from *U-boats*) were convicted, and then conveniently allowed to escape by their German jailors. After *WWII*, two international and multiple national tribunals were established. The international tribunals sought convictions of those deemed to have committed *crimes against humanity* and *crimes against peace*, in addition to *war crimes*. The trial body for Germans and Austrians met at *Nuremberg*, and another for Japanese met in *Tokyo* (a separate, U.S. military tribunal for Japanese met in the Philippines). These proceedings were spectacular (the top leaders were tried), but also short-term and limited. It was actually the national military tribunals and civilian courts that brought most war criminals to justice: by 1960 the Western *Allies* had tried over 5,000 war criminals, executing nearly 500 of those convicted. Meanwhile, the Soviets tried over 10,000 Germans after WWII, executing a high proportion. West Germany tried many more of its citizens, and Israel hunted down some German war criminals, most notably *Eichmann*. Also, many occupied countries tried their own citizens for *collaboration* in German, Italian or Japanese war crimes (but note, not their own military for the commission of war crimes). While there is little legal controversy over trials and convictions on strict charges of war crimes, the introduction at Nuremberg and Tokyo of charges of crimes against peace and against humanity raised two main criticisms of the proceedings, then and since: (1) No specific laws about crimes against humanity or peace existed before the war, and therefore no crime, in a legal sense,

could have taken place, however reprehensible the moral transgressions of the defendants. (2) The tribunals represented *victor's justice*, as only persons from or allied with the *defeated* nations were tried (e.g., no Soviet was tried for the *Katyn massacre*, nor Westerner for the *indiscriminate bombing* of cities). On the other hand, few among the convicted were condemned solely on the basis of a charge of crimes against humanity; most were also convicted for war crimes.

Other instances: (1) In 1971 Bangladesh began war crimes proceedings against nearly 200 West Pakistanis, but dropped the charges with return of its detained *POW*s. (2) The U.S. tried a small number of its own men for war crimes in *Vietnam*, and specifically for the *My Lai massacre*. (3) In February 1993, the *UNGA* authorized the *Secretary General* to develop rules and procedures to open war crimes trials concerning the *Third Balkan War*. That recommendation, from a five-nation commission, listed suspected war criminals, including *Slobadan Milošević*, charged with approving *ethnic cleansing* and other atrocities taking place in Bosnia and Croatia. This was the first time the international community warned in advance that leaders may be held accountable for their actions and decisions (during WWII the Allies warned *Axis* leaders about *postwar* retribution, but that warning came from a hostile *alliance* and did not carry the sanction of the *world community*). The commission made several recommendations: (A) no trials *in absentia*; (B) for the first time, rape to be a war crime; and (C) ethnic cleansing to be a war crime. (4) In 1993 Canada began court-martials of several of its soldiers accused of *torture* and murder of *civilians* while their unit was on UN *peacekeeping* duty in Somalia. These proceedings were confused by a revival of the defense of *superior orders* when the commander, who had signed the charges, was himself implicated.

war debts: Debts accumulated by heavy borrowing to pay for a *war*. War debts add greatly to the general burden of *reconstruction*. After *WWI* the U.S. was owed huge amounts by Britain and France, lesser sums by Russia. Britain and France tried to use German *reparations* to repay the U.S. until the *Hoover moratorium* of 1931, after which both countries defaulted. The *Bolsheviks* repudiated Russia's war debts, mostly hurting its largest creditor, France.

warfare: Actual hostilities, not merely a legal state.

war-fighting strategy: A *strategic* posture where one's ability to fight and win (survive) a *nuclear war* denies the opportunity of *victory* to the adversary, thereby reinforcing *deterrence*. Some said this was the main posture of the Soviet military, c.1947-89.

war games: Military exercises simulating combat conditions, used to train *officers* and troops and test operational plans and strategies. Cf. *maneuvers*.

war guilt clause (of the *Treaty of Versailles*): Article 231, which identified Germany as responsible for *WWI*, to provide a legal basis for its obligation to pay *reparations*. The psychological harm done to *Weimar* democracy by the clause probably outweighed any good or justice obtained by including it in the *treaty*, although an argument for inclusion on those grounds can certainly be made.

warhead: The business end of a *missile*, rocket or torpedo. It can be *conventional* or *nuclear*, or contain *chemical, biological* or *nerve agents*; and it can be a single device or part of a *MIRV*ed system.

warlord: (1) A military commander who has seized political power over part of a country, as in China 1911-28; Russia, 1918-21; or Somalia 1988-93. (2) A national leader whose political power largely derives from, and whose survival may depend upon, a continuing ability and willingness to wage successful *war*. Cf. *generalissimo; shogun*.

warmongering: Advocating or attempting to precipitate an *aggressive* or otherwise needless war.

warm water port: One that does not freeze in the winter. Not having enough of these has been a major geopolitical problem for Russia, especially as its Crimean ports could be made useless by corking the Black Sea bottle at the *Bosphorus* and *Dardanelles*. See *Port Arthur; Straits Question*.

War of 1812: This *war* between the U.S. and Britain sprang from the strain the British *blockade* of Europe placed on the U.S. economy. Additional grievances included the *impressment* of U.S. citizens into the *Royal Navy*, and rumors that the British in Canada were stirring trouble among the frontier Indian *tribes*. Having allowed the *navy* built by *John Adams* to rot in port, *Madison* could not strike at the most valuable British possessions, those in the Caribbean; so he hit the British the only way and place he could, overland in Canada. American *militia* invaded from New York, in ragtag fashion, in 1812. During a second *invasion* in 1813, U.S. troops set fire to the provincial capital at York (Toronto). In retaliation, British troops set fire to Washington, including the *White House*, when they counterinvaded in 1814. Canadian militia and some Indian *allies* also skirmished with American militia, farther west. The war ended indecisively, with a settlement *mediated* by Russia. That saved the U.S. from

having to face the seasoned veterans of the *Napoleonic Wars*, perhaps under *Wellington* himself, just freed by *victory* over *Napoleon*. Terms were agreed at *Ghent*, Belgium, in December 1814, after which a bloody and entirely useless battle was fought at *New Orleans*. The peace avoided all points at issue in the war, as befitted a *stalemate*; that left serious questions between Britain and the U.S. unresolved for decades more. Americans and Canadians alike tend to exaggerate and even misinterpret this conflict: the former as a spirited and decisive victory over Britain, and even as a "second War of Independence," though it was neither; the latter as evidence of always simmering Yankee plans for *annexation*, when the furthest U.S. thinking went along those lines was perhaps to capture Canada as a bargaining chip. The British view the war more for what it actually was: an unfortunate and entirely avoidable side action to their much larger and more important conflict with France.

War of Attrition (March 1969-June 1970): Egypt and Israel engaged in this conflict along the *Bar-Lev Line*, in the manner its name suggests. It was announced with promises of *victory* by *Nasser*, who hoped to use Egypt's large army to wear down Israeli morale by inflicting a stream of casualties. Instead, Egyptian casualties reached unsustainable levels, and the campaign faded.

War of the Austrian Succession (1740-48): Austria, England, Hanover, Hesse and the Netherlands fought France, Prussia, and Spain for control of the Austrian (*Hapsburg*) lands. The conflict was touched off by the death of a Holy Roman Emperor, Charles VI, in 1740, raising rival claims to the succession from royal houses in Bavaria, Saxony and Spain. The weakness at the center of the Hapsburg empire tempted *Frederick II*, of Prussia, to invade *Silesia*, setting off the conflagration. The *war* ended formally with the Peace of Aix-la-Chapelle (1748), but that is misleading, as other than Prussia (which kept Silesia), no major power was satisfied with the settlement. It was among the first modern wars (that is, among *nations*) but masqueraded still as a *dynastic* conflict. Therefore, fighting continued even after settlement of the succession, which in the end went to *Maria Theresa*, daughter of Charles VI. Prussia consolidated its gains, and Austria and Spain licked their wounds. But England and France broadened the fight into the *Seven Years' War*, linking their struggles over control of North America and India with the contest in Europe. This fighting was not resolved until the *Peace of Paris* in 1763. See also *King George's War*.

War of the First Coalition (1792-97): Austria and

Prussia waged *war* on Revolutionary France, joined over the next two years by Britain, the Netherlands, Spain, Naples, the *Papal States* and *Piedmont-Sardinia*. The *levée en masse* and superior generalship of *Napoleon Bonaparte* enabled France to hurl back the invaders; conquer Naples, the Netherlands, *Piedmont*, and the *Papal States*; force Prussia and Spain out of the war in 1795; and force the Austrians to terms in 1797. That ended the *coalition*, leaving only Britain still at war.

War of the Fourth Coalition (1813-14): Following the *retreat from Moscow*, Prussia entered the *war* with its reformed army against France, encouraged by British funds but also a thirst for revenge for the defeats of 1807. This last and greatest of the anti-French *coalitions* was assembled by *Castlereagh* over the summer of 1813. He brought (some say bought) the Austrians, Prussians and Russians together as major *allies*, then added Bavaria, Sweden, Saxony and Würtemburg. Coalition armies ("the Grand Alliance") entered Paris on March 31, 1814, forced *Napoleon I* to abdicate two weeks later, and began the *Restoration*. That process would yet be interrupted by the *Hundred Days* and *Waterloo*, but the back of French power was already broken by the great *defeat* of 1814.

War of the Grand Alliance (1688-97): Also called the War of the League of Augsburg. *Bavaria*, Brandenburg-*Prussia*, *England*, the *Holy Roman Empire*, the *Netherlands*, the Palatinate, *Savoy*, *Spain* and *Sweden* all allied to oppose France. The North American phase was called *King William's War*. It ended in *stalemate*, as was reflected in the Treaty of Ryswick, which restored all *conquests* and thereby set the stage for more Anglo/French conflict in the years ahead.

War of the League of Augsburg: See *War of the Grand Alliance*.

War of the Pacific (1879-84): Fought between Bolivia, Chile and Peru 1879-81, but not formally ended until the U.S. *mediated* two *peace treaties*, in 1883 and 1884. The main issue was control of a desert region valued as a source of fertilizer, as it was rich in guano and nitrates. Chile was the main victor, keeping in the peace treaties all *territory* it seized on the battlefield.

War of the Second Coalition (1798-1801): Britain was joined in its dogged *war* against *Napoleon I*, and his reluctant *ally* Spain, by Austria, Naples, Portugal, Prussia, Russia and Turkey. Intercoalition arguments led to Russia's withdrawal in 1799. Napoleon then knocked Austria out of the war in 1801, after one of his more brilliant *campaigns*. Turkey had withdrawn

in 1800, and in 1801 Spanish and French forces compelled Portugal to resign the contest. Britain made peace at *Amiens* in March 1802, but was back at war with France by May 1803.

War of the Spanish Succession (1701-13): Austria, England, the Netherlands and Prussia allied against France and Spain. This was the last of the *wars of Louis XIV*. It broke his power, and left France intact but exhausted and frustrated in its imperial ambitions. England emerged the big winner, expanding its overseas holdings, particularly in the Canadas, at the expense of France. It ended with the *Treaty of Utrecht*.

War of the Third Coalition (1805-07): Britain again brought Austria and Russia into *alliance* against *Napoleon I*, but within months both continental powers were defeated at *Austerlitz*. The Austrians left the *war*, and the Russians retreated. Britain secured itself by the great victory at *Trafalgar*, and continued the fight. Prussia joined the *coalition* in 1806, but was quickly defeated (at Jena and Auerstadt). *Frederick-William III* was forced out of the war when Napoleon occupied Berlin. Napoleon met *Alexander I*, on a barge on the River Niemen, to arrange the *Tilsit* understanding on *spheres of influence* in Europe. That left Britain isolated until 1812, when Napoleon turned on Russia.

War of the Thousand Days (1899-1902): A *war* of *secession*, prompted and aided by the U.S., in which Panama broke away from Colombia. It was followed by a swift agreement with the U.S. to build the *Panama Canal*.

War of the Triple Alliance (1865-70): Argentina, Brazil and Uruguay joined to strip Paraguay of much of its *population* and *territory* (by some estimates it lost 65-70% of its population).

warplane: Any aircraft armed for combat or designed for other military functions, such as *espionage* or transport.

war plans/planning: Preparation by a *General Staff* of details of *mobilization*, logistics, *tactics* and *strategy*, in the event *war* should occur. See *Schlieffen Plan*.

War Powers Act (1973): An Act of the U.S. Congress aimed at limiting the independent ability of the President to commit armed forces to combat. It requires notification of military commitments to Congress within 60 days (extended to 90 upon request), after which the president must ask Congress for a *declaration of war* or withdraw the forces. It arose in response to *executive* abuse of the *Gulf of Tonkin Reso-*

lution, and the sense that an "imperial presidency" had overcommitted the U.S. militarily, and to fruitless conflicts. However, it has been mostly ignored by presidents from both parties. That defiance has not gone unchallenged politically, yet the act has never been tested by congressional appeal to the Supreme Court. The likely reason is that it may prove an unconstitutional burden on presidential authority (the Court has consistently found in favor of the executive in foreign affairs), and Congress would prefer to keep it as a political prop rather than lose it forever.

Warsaw Pact: See *Warsaw Treaty Organization.*

Warsaw Rising (1944): When the *Red Army* advanced on Warsaw in the early summer of 1944 it asked the Polish *resistance* to rise and harass the German rear to hasten the Soviet advance. The Poles seized most of Warsaw. Then the Red Army, commanded by *Rokossovsky,* stopped in its tank treads. The Germans moved in reinforcements to systematically destroy Warsaw and slaughter the *resistance* fighters. For 63 days, despite pleas from *Roosevelt* and *Churchill* and the Polish fighters, the Soviets sat and watched from across the Vistula as the Germans eliminated the only force that might resist the imposition of Moscow's authority over Poland. It was a cynical betrayal of the first order, and smolders still in Polish national memory. See also *Katyn massacre.*

Warsaw Treaty Organization (WTO): The military *alliance* formed by the *Soviet bloc* in 1955, in response to rearmament of *West Germany* and its inclusion in *NATO.* It gave legal sanction to an already existing state of affairs: the presence of Soviet troops in several east European countries. Where NATO was essentially a guarantee of U.S. *aid* to Western Europe, the WTO was a guarantee of *Eastern Europe's* allegiance to the Soviet Union. Thus, when Hungary announced the next year that it would withdraw, the Soviets invaded and crushed the *Hungarian Uprising.* Similarly, the WTO invaded Czechoslovakia in 1968, crushing the *Prague Spring.* Only Albania, because it was buffered by the interposed *territory* of *Yugoslav*ia, left the Pact without suffering an *invasion* in consequence--and only because it found the Soviets insufficiently *stalinist* after 1958! With the events of 1989, the WTO ceased to be an effective alliance. It was dissolved on March 31, 1991. Its membership: Albania (ceased participation in 1962, withdrew formally in 1968), Bulgaria, Czechoslovakia, East Germany, Hungary, Poland, Rumania and the Soviet Union.

warship: Any government commissioned ship armed for combat that displays national colors and markings, is captained by a *commissioned officer,* and operated by a navy crew. Such a ship enjoys total immunity from *visit and search* or any other oversight by any government whatsoever (except its own), while on the *high seas.* Other ships may arm for defense, such as merchant craft refitted with deck guns or *depth charges,* but any vessel using offensive force that does not meet the criteria above may be classed as engaged in *piracy.* Cf. *aircraft carrier; battlecruiser; battleship; capital warship; cruiser; destroyer; frigate; galleon; man-of-war; pocket battleship; privateer; sloop-of-war; ship-of-the-line; submarine.*

wars of independence: See particular *wars,* listed by country name; e.g., *American War of Independence.*

war termination: The process of making the transition from combat back to *negotiation* and *peace.* The first task is to begin a process of physical disengagement of *combatants,* usually through a *cease-fire* agreement that (a) stops the shooting at a designated time; (b) includes a waiting period to satisfy both sides that the other is not merely seeking a pause for resupply or some other advantage; (c) moves the *front line* troops back a specified distance, so they are no longer in direct contact and hence in danger of accidentally or through passion restarting the fighting. After that the assessment of who, if anyone, has "won the war," and the degree of *victory* and *defeat,* will drive negotiations over the terms to govern an *armistice.* This usually includes such questions as whether and how one army or both will *demobilize,* whether *territory* is to come under *occupation,* and even whether the existing governments may remain in place or must give way to acceptable (to the victors) substitutes. Much later, there may be a formal *peace treaty* to legally end the *state of war,* spell out permanent territorial adjustments (if any), whether there are to be *war crimes trials,* the amount and schedule of *reparations* (if any), and resolve other *casus belli* that led to war in the first instance. However, quite a few wars end without the *states* involved proceeding to reestablish peace, in the legal sense of that word, or at least taking many years to reach such an agreement. This can occur by simple cessation of the fighting without any formal agreement, not even a cease-fire; or by failing to press on from a *truce* or cease-fire to a peace treaty (the only instrument that can legally end a state of war between or among surviving *international personalities*). It is also possible for a war to end legally through *conquest* followed by *subjugation,* in which no need for a peace treaty arises as one party has become *extinct.* See also *surrender.*

war treason: Acts seen as criminal by most *states* in

times of *war*, and usually carrying a death sentence. These include giving information to the enemy, enticing soldiers to desertion, harboring enemy personnel, and all *sabotage*. Cf. *treason; war crimes*.

war weariness: (1) Fatigue with the privation and death attendant on *war*, that undercuts *national morale* during a prolonged armed conflict. (2) The idea that after a long and bloody war a nation will avoid bellicose policies and be more amenable to negotiated settlements; at least until the next generation of leaders and young men (and now, perhaps, young women too) begin to romanticize about national glory and yearn to test their mettle in combat. For instance, immediately after the *Napoleonic Wars* Europeans exhibited a generalized longing for *peace* and *international order* that may even have helped sustain the *Concert of Europe*. But after several generations of peace, and forgetfulness, the troops that volunteered in 1914 did so to the sound of marching bands and cheering crowds (these remarkable scenes were not repeated in 1939). Similarly, after the *American Civil War* most Americans opposed new annexations (the purchase of *Alaska* was widely dismissed as "Seward's Folly"), and resisted calls to fight Spain in aid of a rebellion in Cuba. Yet, 30 years later, a new generation demanded war with Spain over a similar Cuban *rebellion*, and launched the U.S. into a period of "imperial democracy."

war-widening strategy: See *horizontal escalation*.

war zone: (1) A synonym for combat area, or place where *armed hostilities* are underway. (2) A zone on the *high seas* where the normal rights of *neutral* shipping are prohibited by declaration of the *belligerents*. See *Lusitania Notes; theater of war.*

Washington, George (1732-99): American general, and first President 1789-97. He led the Continental Army against Britain in the *American War of Independence*. He leaned toward *Alexander Hamilton* and the Federalists in their plans for construction of a stronger central government, but he opposed their *anglophilia*. He adopted a policy of *neutrality* toward the great contest between France and Britain, but one tempered by preparation for *war*, such as construction of a navy. In his vaunted "Farewell Address" he warned against permanent *alliances*. That was subsequently mistaken by *isolationists*, who were fond of quoting Washington, as a prohibition against all alliances. It was not: it was a practical expedient by a small power faced with a clash of titans, and while successful in his time, it proved inappropriate as a guideline for U.S. diplomacy after the country emerged as an unquestioned *Great Power*.

Washington Conference (November 1921 to February 1922): It dealt with naval *disarmament* and Asian *security* issues. It was attended by all the major naval and/or Asian powers, among whom the most important were Britain, France, Italy, Japan and the U.S. It arrived at nine *treaties* and 12 *resolutions* on Asian affairs. The three key agreements were the *Five Power Naval Treaty*, the *Four Power Treaty*, and the *Nine Power Treaty*. These understandings helped maintain stability in Asia for 10 years. In the end, however, they were reliant on *good faith* to maintain the *balance of power* and the *peace*, and good faith--like *oil*, rice and rubber--was in short supply in Tokyo after 1931. Cf. *London Naval Disarmament Conference; Shantung; two-power standard.*

Washington, Rules of (1871): Laid out in the *Treaty of Washington*, they spelled out rights of *neutrals* in sea warfare, laying to rest a long and bitter dispute between Britain and the U.S. They reflected a fresh U.S. appreciation of Britain's historic defense of *belligerent rights*, born of the *Union's* experience with *blockade*, and the new U.S. status as a major *sea power*.

Washington, Treaty of (1871): This agreement represented a major advance for *arbitration* as a mechanism of resolving non-vital *disputes*. There were four sets of long-standing disagreements to be resolved: (1) The main issues involved British claims about its *neutral rights* to have traded with the *Confederacy* against U.S. assertions of *belligerent rights* in enforcing its *blockade*. Britain conceded most of the points at issue in advance, in order to set a precedent with Washington on interpretation of *belligerent* vs. neutral rights. That was very clever. London knew that as the world's greatest *sea power*, and given America's penchant for *isolationism*, the future was likely to reverse roles and place Britain in the position of making the belligerent claims against U.S. assertions of neutral rights; and of course that is just what happened in 1914-17, and again 1939-41. (2) A fisheries agreement was signed concerning the U.S./Canada border, where the Canadians had shut out American fishermen in *retaliation* for high U.S. *tariffs* on other Canadian goods. The border was set by an arbitration commission. (3) The issue of ownership of the San Juan Islands, in the Strait of Juan de Fuca off Vancouver Island, was finally settled, with arbitration by the *Kaiser*. (4) The *Alabama claims* were resolved by an *ad hoc* international tribunal, in exchange for Britain assuming the obligation to make financial redress of Canada's grievance over Fenian raids launched from U.S. soil in 1866-68. The *treaty* thus cleared away the dross of decades of lingering animosity and distrust between the U.S. and Britain, opening the path to the great *rapprochement* that was vital to the history of the 20th century. And it fortified Canada/U.S. relations as entirely peaceful, even harmonious.

water: Water, as a *vital interest* and source of conflict, is often overlooked. Yet water (or more precisely, water shortage) has the potential to send states to *war*. For instance, lack of potable water or competition over hydroelectric power generation underlies in significant ways several of the political fault lines in the *Middle East*. Also, large numbers of people live and grow crops where fresh water does not naturally flow in abundance (e.g., *North Africa,* the Middle East, *Sahel, California*), and desalination *technology* is at best a limited solution. Conversely, most of the world's fresh water (which is only 3% of all water on the planet) is located where there are no, or almost no people: about 70% of all fresh water is frozen into the *Antarctic* ice sheet, a resource currently forbidden to *exploitation* by the rigors of nature and the *terms* of the *Antarctic Treaty system*. Other sizeable amounts of fresh water flow unused, or are trapped as ice sheets, over the various *Arctic nations*. For instance, 10% of world supplies flow largely unexploited over Canadian soil. Yet, any suggestion that these waters might be rechanneled and sold for use elsewhere raises howls of environmental and/or nationalist protest. See *Aral Sea; Euphrates River; Third Arab/Israeli War; West Bank*.

Watergate scandal: Essentially a domestic crisis, but one that so eroded the ability of the *Nixon* administration to govern it had serious foreign policy implications as well. During the summer lead-in to the 1972 presidential election a group of five *White House* "plumbers" (so-called because they were supposed to fix information leaks) were caught inside the *Democratic Party* National Headquarters in the Watergate Hotel complex in Washington. A spate of denials of White House involvement was followed by revelations that "hush money" was being paid to keep the plumbers quietly in prison. A sorry tale then unraveled of "dirty tricks," illegal wiretaps of domestic opponents of the administration, and most damaging of all, a cover-up of these activities that seemed directed out of the Oval Office. In time, Nixon's chief aides and his attorney general were indicted (and later convicted) on various charges, mostly to do with obstructing justice. Impeachment proceedings began against Nixon, and became unstoppable once the Supreme Court ordered him to surrender tape recordings of his office conversations concerning Watergate. These revealed that while he had not known of the burglary, he was directly involved in obstructing investigations by the Justice Department and Senate. On August 9, 1974, he became the only U.S. president to resign. For 18

months, while the nation transfixed on itself, foreign policy was hamstrung. And the next five years saw a newly "imperial congress" attempt to displace the "imperial presidency" from its lead role in foreign policy, attaching hitherto unheard of constraints on presidential conduct of foreign affairs.

Waterloo, Battle of (June 18, 1815): A bitter, one-day contest fought within earshot of Brussels, in the culminating phase of the *Hundred Days*. The British under *Wellington* were nearing *defeat* when Prussian reinforcements arrived, led by *Gebhart von Blücher*. His late yet decisive advent routed the French, winning the battle and ending *Napoleon's* career. Bonaparte abdicated, for the second and final time, four days later.

weapons grade material: Elements that can sustain an uncontrolled *fission* or *fusion* reaction, and are thus suitable for making bombs. See *plutonium*.

weapons of mass destruction: *Nuclear weapons*, but also *chemical, biological* and *nerve weapons*, that can destroy whole populations. Ever since the *WWI* experience with *poison gas*, there have been efforts to limit the production and use of such weapons. The motive forces behind that effort have been a complex mix of pragmatic and moral concerns.

Wehrmacht: "Armed power." The German armed forces 1933-45. In 1937 they came under command of the OKW (Oberkommando der Wehrmacht), which *Hitler* personally headed. His conviction after 1941 that he knew better than his generals how to wage *war* helped the *Allies* win *WWII*. Cf. *Reichswehr*.

weighted voting: Where the principle of *equality* is waived so that *states* making, say, the greatest financial contribution to the *IMF*, have the most influence in deciding how funds are used. Depending on the forum, voting may also be weighted by *population, size* or some other criterion. See *qualified majority voting*.

Weimar Republic: Popularly named for the city where its constituent assembly met, its official name was the German Federal Republic. It lasted from 1918-33. See *Germany, Weimar Republic*.

Weizmann, Chaim (1874-1952): President of Israel 1948-52. His real importance came as a *zionist* leader before the founding of Israel, particularly his success in obtaining British *recognition* of the *Jewish Agency*.

Wellington, Arthur Wellesley (1769-1852): "The Iron Duke." British general and statesman. He made his military reputation in the *Peninsular War* and at *Wa-*

terloo. He commanded the *occupation* in France 1815-18, often moderating Allied policy. He attended several meetings of the *Congress system,* but *statecraft* was not his forte. He entered *politics* at the top, as PM from 1828-30, successfully completing *Catholic Emancipation* (he was Secretary for Ireland 1807-08). But his innate conservatism caused him to oppose further reform of Parliament, and on this issue he lost office. He was PM again for just two months in 1834, but was more comfortable as Foreign Secretary 1834-35, and Commander-in-Chief 1842-52. Some blame him for failing to adopt *Prussian*-style military reforms, and hence for the debacles of British *arms* during the *Crimean War,* and the Army's retrograde professionalism during the 19th century (e.g., until 1871 *officer* commissions could still be purchased by the wealthy, rather than earned by training or merit).

Weltpolitik: "World policy." (1) A term first applied to Kaiser *Wilhelm II's* foreign policy of making Germany a first-rank, *world power.* It abandoned *Bismarck's* caution and satisfied continentalism in favor of *adventurism,* shrill insistence upon *prestige* and "national honor," construction of a navy to rival Britain's and belated joining in the *scramble for Africa* and for *spheres of influence* in China. Its main effects were to provoke formation of the *Triple Entente* and earn Germany a reputation for bluster and bullying. (2) An overarching concern in foreign policy with geopolitical *strategy* and *prestige,* as opposed to regional stakes and interests.

West: (1) Historically: European civilization, and its colonial extensions, extending into the Middle East under the Byzantine empire, and into the vast lands of Russia, before Mongol *conquest* cut off that nation from intercourse with the Latin world. (2) In modern times: the industrial democracies of the *OECD,* including Japan and Turkey after *WWII.*

West Asia: Asia west of the Hindu Kush pass in the Himalayas: from Afghanistan through *Central Asia,* and including all the *states* of the *Middle East* lying west of the *Suez Canal.*

West Bank: The part of *Palestine* west of the Jordan River. It was annexed by *Transjordan* in 1948. Captured by Israel in 1967, it became the larger part of the *occupied territories.* Two of Israel's three main aquifers lie under the West Bank. Given a 1993 accord between Israel and the *PLO,* the likely future of the West bank is to form the core of an *autonomous* Palestinian area, and in the fullness of time either a separate Palestinian *state* or one *federated* with Jordan. See *Gaza; Jerusalem.*

West Berlin: The combined American, British and French *occupation zones* in Berlin. See *Berlin; Berlin air lift; Berlin Wall.*

westernize: To imbue with the values, practices and habits of mind of Western civilization. It refers in particular to the West's emphases on *individualism* and *secularism,* its preference for *market economics,* and its liberal-democratic values and institutions. See also *cosmopolitan values; human rights; liberalism; liberal-internationalism; modernization.*

westernizer: A designation of a Russian intellectual and cultural tradition believing that values drawn from the *West,* including modes of economic, political and social organization, are necessary and proper for Russian *modernization.* Among leaders identified with this tradition are *Peter I (the Great), Alexander II,* and lesser lights *Gorbachev* and *Yeltsin.* Cf. *slavophile.*

Western European and Other Group (WEOG): A *caucus group* of Western states in the UN and other forums of *multilateral diplomacy.* The "Other" refers to the United States and Canada. The U.S. has not always caucused with WEOG, depending on the forum.

Western European Union (WEU): It was formed as a follow-up to the *Brussels Treaty* in a compromise with France, to permit West Germany and Italy to rearm under close supervision after 1955. It lay dormant for three decades until in the mid-1980s European federalists sought to revive it as the core of an independent *EC* military. Portugal and Spain joined in 1988. In 1994, it contained all *EU* countries except Greece, Denmark and Ireland. Britain wants it to become the European pillar of *NATO;* France would like it disconnected from the U.S., to serve as the defense arm of the EU. Germany has yet to choose between those alternatives. In 1992 it agreed to help enforce *sanctions* against Serbia, alongside NATO.

western front: In both *WWI* and *WWII,* the front line between forces of the Western *Allies* and the German Army. During WWI it ran from the *Low Countries,* through France, and into Italy (after 1915). In WWII, it ran from Norway, down the coast of France (after 1940, but moving inland after *D-Day*). It did not include Italy, *North Africa* or the *Balkans.*

Western Hemisphere Free Trade Area (WHFTA): A proposal by *George Bush* to extend *NAFTA* to all the Americas. It remains a very long-term prospect.

Western Sahara: Location: W. Africa. Formerly Spanish Sahara. Spain withdrew in 1976 and this *territory* was immediately *partitioned* between Mauritania and Morocco, an action not recognized by the *OAU* or *UN*. By 1979 *POLISARIO* forced Mauritania to abandon its claim, but Morocco then seized that portion of Western Sahara as well. The fighting continued for 12 years. King *Hassan II* of Morocco persisted in opposing POLISARIO in defiance of most African and international opinion, even constructing hundreds of miles of wall in the desert to block access by the nomad population that supports POLISARIO, and present barriers to the *guerrillas*. In 1984 the OAU admitted POLISARIO as if it was the government of an established *state* in Western Sahara. That led to Morocco's *withdrawal*. In 1988 a UN special *envoy* was sent to mediate a *cease-fire* between the guerrillas and Morocco. An agreement was signed in August, which called for a *referendum* on the future of the territory. The OAU agreed to appointment of the *Secretary General* as "the sole authority over all issues related to the referendum," and the UN set up an *observer mission* (MINURSO). By 1991 there were 400 UN observers in place. But problems remained, including disputes over the census and Morocco's preventing nomads from voting by claiming they were not "permanent residents."

Western Samoa: Location: Pacific. Major associations: *Commonwealth, SPC, SPF, UN.* Population: 170,000. Military: no defense *pacts* or (known) enemies. The German portion of Samoa, divided from *American Samoa* in 1899 (Britain was *compensated* with several of the Solomon Islands). New Zealand captured it in 1914, and after 1919 ran it as a *mandate* and then *trusteeship territory.* U.S. troops were based there 1942-45. *Independence* came in 1962, after a *plebiscite* by which Samoans disenfranchised themselves in favor of a tribal council. Insistence on traditional, communal ownership of property overseen by this council has discouraged foreign investment, led to considerable corruption and to *IMF* controls in the 1980s. It joined the UN in 1976. It has ties to Australia and the U.S. but is most closely oriented to New Zealand. Reflecting old ties, trade with Germany is still extensive. In a 1990 plebiscite a slim majority reinstated universal adult suffrage.

West Germany: See *Germany.*

West Indies: The three island groups forming a large archipelago lying between the American continents, comprising the *Greater Antilles,* the *Lesser Antilles* and the *Bahamas.*

West Indies Associated States: The smaller colonies in the east of the *West Indies* that became *associated*

states with Britain in 1968: Antigua, Dominica, Grenada, St. Kitts-Nevis-Anguilla and St. Lucia.

West Indies Federation (1958-62): An *extinct* effort at forming a *federation* of the British *colonies* in the *West Indies,* out of concern that individually *independence* was not viable. It comprised Barbados, Jamaica, Trinidad, Tobago, the Windward and Leeward Islands and the *West Indies Associated States.* It collapsed when Jamaica withdrew, out of reluctance to subsidize the poorer island members. It was quickly followed out by Trinidad and Tobago.

West Irian: See *Irian Jaya.*

Westminster, Statute of (1931): An act of the British Parliament, granting powers over foreign affairs well beyond the domestic *autonomy* already enjoyed by the main *Dominions* (Australia, Canada, Eire, New Zealand, Newfoundland and South Africa). Despite this, the Dominions coordinated policy with Britain, to the point of again joining its *war* effort in 1939 after *pro forma* gestures of independent decision-making (except *Eire,* which remained *neutral*). Real *independence* in foreign policy came after *WWII,* that crucible to burn away old sentimentalities about the imperial tie (excepting South Africa, which had never felt much regard for things British and broke away more sharply with the introduction of *apartheid* in 1949).

West Pakistan: From 1947-71 it dominated *East Pakistan,* which is now Bangladesh. After the *secession* of East Pakistan most references to West Pakistan simply dropped the geographical indicator.

Westphalian: Of or like the principles of *diplomacy* and law laid out in the *Peace of Westphalia* (1648).

Westphalia, Peace of (1648): The great settlement that ended the *Thirty Years' War.* That conflagration left no single German *state* in a position to dominate the others, a situation France appreciated and worked to sustain. The *terms* elevated Sweden and France to formal guarantors of Germany *security,* which cleared the way for a century of French intrusion into German affairs (Sweden would shortly fall from the ranks of the *Great Powers,* a victim of its own ambitions and the rise of Russia). But most important, the Peace of Westphalia laid the groundrules for the modern state system. The principle of *sovereignty* permeated the settlement, raising with it as absolute standards of interstate conduct subordinate principles such as *nonintervention* on all *internal affairs,* and especially on religious matters. The *wars* occasioned by the great ideological schism of the previous three centuries were ended with ratification of the principle of the Peace of Augsburg, decided in 1555 but largely ignored since: "cuius regio, eius religio" (who rules, decides the religion). In fact, *secularism* was to be the new order in politics. The states (which meant the princes), and not religious authorities, were henceforth to be the supreme temporal rulers. The quasi-feudal relations, and in particular the pretensions to universal empire of the *Holy Roman Empire* were dismissed. The popes, too, were now to be largely ignored, including by Catholic powers just as jealous of sovereign prerogative as their Protestant counterparts. So angry did this make Innocent X, he condemned the accord as "null, void, invalid, iniquitous, unjust, damnable, reprobate, inane, empty of meaning and effect for all time." But rail as the enraged pontiff might, the *Reformation* and the *Counter Reformation* had both failed to triumph, and were well and truly over. In their place, an age of absolute sovereignty had begun. With it came a pattern of Great Powers lording it over the small, and of *raison d'etat*, the *balance of power* and *power politics*. Not until the *French Revolution* tempted the continent's greatest power to revive the old ambition to universal political dominion, would European civilization again so badly and bloodily divide against itself. Also see, *Gustavus Adolphus; Richelieu; world community.*

wet affair: *Intelligence* slang for *assassination*, presumably in reference to the spilling of blood.

whaling: Whaling was a major industry at the turn of the 19th century, so much so that concern grew as stocks became depleted. An International Whaling Commission (IWC) was set up in 1946, charged with deciding the length of hunting seasons for each species and setting national quotas. In the 1960s scientists warned that many whale species were on the verge of extinction. Several countries announced unilateral hunt *moratoria*, but historic whaling nations such as Iceland, Japan, Norway and the Soviet Union refused to submit to a general ban. Pressure then built for a 10-year moratorium. In 1979 the IWC banned whaling in the Indian Ocean. By 1980 the major whaling nations accepted restrictive quotas, but not the idea of a global moratorium. Bans were then introduced on a species-by-species basis. Beginning in 1986 a worldwide general ban was imposed by the IWC; though with a loophole permitting each of Iceland, Japan, Norway and South Korea to hunt a limited number of whales, ostensibly for scientific purposes. Several very small whaling states (such as Mauritius) pulled out of the IWC when the ban was imposed. In 1993 Norway announced it was resuming commercial whaling, in violation of the ban. In 1994 the IWC declared a kill-free zone around *Antarctica*, that may or may not be enforceable.

Whigs: (1) In Britain: A major party from 1679-1832. It generally favored reform, and evolved into the Liberal Party. (2) In the United States: {A} a supporter of the revolt against Britain; {B} a party formed in 1834 and lasting to 1855. It opposed the *Mexican/American War*, any expansion of *slavery* into new states, and pushed for a high national *tariff* to protect industry. It was succeeded by the *Republican Party.*

White Dominions: An informal but formerly oft-used term for those British *colonies* with large white settlements: Australia, Canada, Irish Free State, Newfoundland, New Zealand and South Africa. They were given *autonomy* within the evolving British Commonwealth by the *Statute of Westminster.*

Whitehall: A common, shorthand reference for the British government and its policies, derived from the location of the major government offices on Whitehall Street in London.

White House: (1) The working residence of the president of the United States, containing the Oval Office. It was burnt by the British during the *War of 1812*. The term is used as a shorthand reference for the *executive* power and policies of the U.S. (2) The former Soviet/Russian Parliament. It was used as a headquarters by *Boris Yeltsin* during the August 1991, *coup* attempt by the communist old guard and elements of the *Red Army*. In 1993 he abolished the old, Soviet-era parliament and sent troops against the White House when hardcore members and their supporters holed up within, and called for a national political and military revolt. See *Duma.*

White Lotus Rebellion: This peasant and *Buddhist uprising* against the *Manchus* broke out in 1796, and took many years and lives to crush. It sprang from: (1) pressures built up in previous decades by a *population* increase in China that marginalized peasants on already overworked land; (2) the ever-growing distance of the Manchu rulers from the mass of people.

white man's burden: This phrase was widely used in English-speaking *nations* from c.1900-1945, to refer to the ostensible historical and moral obligation of the white nations to guide and govern the non-white, colonized peoples of Africa and Asia. It was taken from a bit of doggerel of the same title written in 1899 by the bard of *imperialism*, Rudyard Kipling (1865-1936). Kipling hoped to exhort the U.S. to join the imperial nations by full *annexation* of the *territories* it had just captured from Spain: "Take up the White Man's burden, send forth the best ye breed; Go, bind your sons to exile, to serve your captive's need." One honest

British newspaper printed this rejoinder: "Pile on the brown man's burden, to satisfy your greed." Cf. *manifest destiny; mission civilatrice*.

White Russia: See *Byelorussia; Belarus*.

White Russians: (1) Natives of Belarus. (2) Anti-*Bolshevik* Russians. See *Whites*.

Whites: (1) The Royalist supporters of the *exiled* kings of France, who opposed the *French Revolution*; taken from the white flag of the House of *Bourbon*. (2) Tsarist *officers*, aristocrats, *cossacks*, democrats and others who opposed in arms the Bolshevik dictatorship (often preferring one of their own) during the *Russian Civil War*. Sometimes called *White Russians*.

Wilhelm II (1859-1941): *Kaiser* of *Germany*, King of *Prussia* 1888-1918. A crass, pompous martinet, in 1890 he forced the cautious *Bismarck's* resignation, preparatory to endorsing a reckless foreign policy that contributed much to the outbreak of *WWI*. On the other hand, he also fell increasingly under the military's influence and authority, and directed affairs of state but little. In 1918 he abdicated and went into *exile* in the Netherlands. The *Allies* wanted to bring him to trial, but the *neutral* Dutch refused *extradition*. In 1940 *Hitler* invited him to transfer his retirement home to Germany, but he refused. See *adventurism; Kruger telegram; First Moroccan Crisis; Weltpolitik*.

William III, Prince of Orange (1650-1702): Stadholder of the Netherlands and King of England 1689-1792. He led the Netherlands in a drawn-out conflict with *Louis XIV* of France, making *peace* in 1678. In 1688 he landed a Protestant army at Torbay. The Catholic James II (1633-1701) fled; his partisans held out in parts of Scotland and Ireland, to 1691. This *conquest* of Catholic power in the British Isles is still celebrated annually in *Ulster* by the *Orangemen*, to the chagrin of the native Irish.

Wilsonian: Of or like the policies of *Woodrow Wilson*. Often a pejorative. See *liberal-internationalism*.

Wilson, James Harold (b.1916): British statesman. PM 1964-70, 1974-76. In foreign affairs he was preoccupied with repairing the damage done by *de Gaulle's* veto of British entry into the *EC*, and by several messy endings to British imperial rule in Africa. Of these the most bloody was the *Nigerian Civil War*, in which Wilson never wavered from support for the Federal cause despite widespread popular belief (later proved false) that *genocide* was occurring in *Biafra*. But the most troublesome was *Rhodesia*,

where he faced calls for British military *intervention* from African leaders and domestic opinion split along ugly, racially informed lines. Wilson also supported restrictions on *immigration* from *Commonwealth* countries and announced that the UK would withdraw all military forces "east of Suez." In short, he presided over the painful but inescapable retreat of Britain from the status of great imperial power to that of modest, European *regional power*.

Wilson, Woodrow (1856-1924): U.S. statesman. President 1912-20. Elected as a progressive reformer, he remarked in private that it would be a great irony should his administration become concerned primarily with foreign affairs. It did. In 1913 he refused to recognize the revolutionary government in Mexico, the first time *recognition* was ever withheld by the U.S. based on the internal nature of a *regime*. He would also *intervene* in Mexico and Central America to a greater extent than any previous president. He tried to keep to a policy of strict *neutrality* after *WWI* started in Europe in 1914, but his own sympathies and that of the public leaned increasingly toward the *Allies*. His offers of impartial *mediation* were repeatedly rebuffed, by both sides. He almost made the decision for *war* in 1915, during the first *U-boat* crisis with Germany. But he returned to impartiality when Germany pulled back from *undeclared submarine warfare*. When that policy was resumed in 1917 he took America into the war, pronouncing it necessary to "make the world safe for democracy." He welcomed the *March Revolution* in Russia, and was disappointed but not overly concerned by the *November Revolution*. He tried to bring the various Russian factions into the *peace* process, but the effort went nowhere. He was a most reluctant interventionist in the *Russian Civil War*, ordering American forces kept to a token level, and pulling them out at the first opportunity, but also refusing to recognize *Bolshevik* victory in 1920. In January 1918, he announced the *Fourteen Points*, which became the basis for the *Paris Peace Conference*, where he was the major figure. He was the first President to leave the country while in office, traveling to Paris for three months to negotiate the *peace treaties* and oversee creation of the *League of Nations* and its *collective security* system. He refused to compromise with *Republican* senators during the debate over the *Treaty of Versailles*, and may by that have lost a winnable fight for American entry into the League, his great hope for a lasting peace. He was awarded the *Nobel Prize* for Peace in 1919. He suffered two strokes during his second term; the second left him nearly incapacitated, and much policy was made secretly by his personal secretary, Joseph P. Tumulty, and his wife, Edith. Many of his initiatives went down in ruins in the *interwar* period (but then, whose did not?). Yet as the century closes he appears a more lastingly important and historically influential figure than even his great contemporary, and rival visionary, *Lenin*. See also *Harding*.

Winter War: See *Finnish/Soviet War*.

Wisconsin school: An economic interpretation of American history, and especially foreign policy, promulgated by Fred H. Harrington and his more famous student, William Appelman Williams, and others from the University of Wisconsin. Although non-*marxist*, it borrowed heavily from marxist notions and the populist, American *radical* tradition. Its basic assumption was that *capitalist* countries were inherently *expansionist* and *aggressive*. All American foreign policy thus could be usefully understood as the more or less rapacious pursuit of the *Open Door*, and the U.S. viewed as an "imperial democracy" from its very founding, or before. But American *imperialism* was different than the British, French, German or Russian kind: it sought markets, not *colonies*. It was thus superficially anti-imperial, in that its own drive required the breakdown of the closed, *mercantilist* systems of the old *empires* and substitution of informal mechanisms of *hegemony;* hence pursuit of the Open Door and of *dollar diplomacy*. For this school, individual *decision-makers* were relatively unimportant: *Polk, Wilson, Roosevelt, Johnson*, yes even *Lincoln* had taken the country to *war* to gain or preserve access to the markets of Europe and Asia (in Lincoln's case, to crush the last domestic resistance to capitalism), and made *peace* always in ways that expanded the "American empire." American capitalism was fundamentally responsible for the *Cold War*, too, it was argued, because in its greed it tried to force open the door to *Eastern Europe*, which lay well within Russia's *sphere of influence*. The response of *Stalin* in consolidating that sphere--with the *Red Army* and proxy *communist parties*--was thus understandable, hardly more than a defensive reaction.

Wise Men: An informal designation for six American *statesmen*, all friends and/or old classmates, who laid the intellectual foundations for, and then constructed, U.S. *Cold War* policy: *Dean Acheson*, Charles Bohlen, *Clark Clifford, George Kennan, W. Averell Harriman*, Robert Lovett and *John McCloy*.

withdrawal: Owing to the underlying reality of *sovereignty*, a state may withdraw from an *international organization* any time, bound only by legal requirements (should they exist in a given *treaty*) to give formal *notification* and wait the required period. Withdrawal may carry little or very heavy political pen-

alties. Germany (1933), Japan (1933) and Italy (1937) all withdrew from the *League of Nations* without consequence to themselves (though with great consequence for the League), as did some minor powers, such as Brazil. Only one state withdrew from the *UN*: Indonesia in 1965 (and it rejoined in 1966). Lesser organizations such as the *Commonwealth* have seen more withdrawals. Cf. *expulsion; suspension*.

withholding strategy: A theory of *nuclear war* fighting, proposing that by not striking at all the enemy's targets in the first wave of *missiles* launched, one might preserve enough of value to the adversary nation to provide it with an incentive to join in mutual de-escalation of the conflict.

Witte, Serge (1849-1915): Russian statesman. He constructed the trans-Siberian railroad and the Chinese Eastern Railroad (in *Manchuria*), and guided a surge in industrial development. But he was displaced by *imperialists* in such a hurry to acquire Manchuria they provoked the *Russo/Japanese War*. In 1905 he was brought back to negotiate the *Treaty of Portsmouth* with Japan. He served briefly as PM but again fell victim to court intrigues. After this final dismissal he remained out of office, and in rather a bad temper, for 10 years. He also opposed Russia's entry into *WWI*.

wolf pack: *U-boats* hunting together, coordinating patrols and attacks. It was a tactic developed by *Doenitz*, and nearly turned the *Battle of the Atlantic* in Germany's favor. It was designed to counteract the *convoy* system by setting up a "picket line" of U-boats to improve the chances of contact with the enemy, and then coordinate hit-and-run attacks so that the escorts were confused and exhausted.

working class: See *proletariat*.

world affairs: A synonym for *international relations*.

World Bank: See *International Bank for Reconstruction and Development*.

world capitalist system: In *dependency theory* this is the underlying economic structure that determines the relations of the *core* to the *periphery*. The theory posits the dominance of a global *capitalist* class with powerfully shared interests, and is dismissive of the role played by individual *states* or by the states system. It focuses instead on efforts of the mass population of the periphery to break free of the putative *exploitation* of its resources and labor by the dominant *elite* controlling the core, and its servants in the *comprador classes* running the periphery.

world community: (1) All *states*, and in some ill-defined and immeasurable sense, their publics too. (2) On occasion, a euphemism to avoid saying "the West," when what is meant in a discussion of the "norms of the world community" is the prevailing values of Western states and their political and legal traditions. (3) In *international law:* the "community of nations," a.k.a. *civilized states.* It is generally taken to have originated with the *Peace of Westphalia (1648),* but for 200 years applied only to the "Christian states" of Europe and then the Americas (the U.S. and the Latin *republics*). The formal admission of the *Ottoman Empire,* in the *Treaty of Paris (1856),* was a turning point. It was followed by quick expansion to the *Balkans* and Asia (*China, Japan, Persia* and *Siam*). By the end of *WWI* the term was taken to include all fully *sovereign* states. After *WWII* another rapid expansion occurred, with admission of the new states born of *decolonization.* A similar augmentation took place from 1989-93, with admission of a wave of *successor states* from the breakup of *Czechoslovakia, Yugoslavia* and the *Soviet Union.* In sum, the world community or "community of nations" includes: all fully independent states, all *unions, neutralized states* and even divided states (such as China/Taiwan, Cyprus, the Koreas and formerly, the two Germanies) where *sovereignty* is in dispute. It also includes, with qualifications, the *Vatican* and various *microstates.* Entities not members of the community of nations, in the legal sense, include: *associated states, condominiums, trusteeship territories,* unrecognized *belligerents, international organizations* (not even those with a degree of *international personality*) and *tribes.* See also *state obligations.*

World Council of Churches: A *transnational* organization founded in the Netherlands in 1948 to pursue *ecumenism* among the Christian churches, and in particular to bridge the historic divide between the *Catholic Church,* various Protestant churches, and the *Orthodox* churches of Eastern Europe and the former Soviet Union. It has increasingly moved past doctrinal matters, to a public concern with *disarmament, human rights* and *North/South issues.*

World Court: The informal, journalistic and popular name for the *International Court of Justice,* and before that the *Permanent Court of International Justice.*

World Disarmament Conference (1932-34): See *Disarmament Conference, Geneva (1932-34).*

world federalism: The idea, fluctuating in popularity among theorists (and the public) from decade to decade, of a global *federation* in which the existing *states* merge at the political level first, with *integration* to

follow on *functional* lines. Cf. *world governance; world government.*

World Food Program: A UN food *aid* program set up in 1963. It coordinates *multilateral* relief during *famines* and is also involved in some agricultural *development* projects.

world governance: The art of governing world affairs in the absence of a *world government.* This demands and receives a high degree of cooperation among *states,* but through the decentralized mechanisms they have already developed for this grand task: the *balance of power, diplomacy, international law, international organization, moral norms, sovereignty* and *spheres of influence.* Cf. *anarchical society; anarchy.*

world government: The idea of a lawmaking and enforcing, supreme global authority to replace the present system of *states.* While usually spoken of hopefully as a democratic and federal model, it is conceivable that a world government might take the form of a global *tyranny.* In either case, it should be clearly understood that the *United Nations system* is not even the beginning of a world government (just as the *World Court* is not a supreme court for the world). For good, for ill or more likely for both, *sovereignty* remains the fundamental principle of international political life at the end of the 20th century. That said, the UN does represent an aspect of *world governance.*

World Health Organization (WHO): A *specialized agency* of the UN founded in 1948 and headquartered in Geneva. It is perhaps the one with the most sterling record of success. It provides *advisory services* as well as direct assistance, sponsors research and conducts educational programs that have helped eradicate several epidemic diseases, and controlled many others. By 1977 it had eradicated smallpox, and so targeted six other major child killers: diphtheria, measles, polio, tetanus, tuberculosis and whooping cough. By the 1990s nearly 80% of the world's children were vaccinated against these diseases under WHO's Expanded Program of Immunization. It plays a smaller role in the *Children's Vaccine Initiative.* Its record is not unblemished, however. For instance, under pressure from *Islamic* and certain *African* nations, it failed until the 1980s even to discuss *female circumcision,* which afflicts millions of women and children each year.

World Human Rights Conference (June 1993): This was the first global conference on *human rights* since a meeting in Teheran in 1968. It confirmed a continuing, fundamental split between those nations (mostly, though not exclusively, in the *West*) that see human rights as centering on the individual, and those (mainly in the developing world) that argue--either sincerely, or merely as a protective cover for privileged classes and repressive *regimes*--that individual civil and political rights must be subordinated to collective rights, such as a "right to *development*." A major shift from the *Cold War* came with Russian support for a "High Commissioner for Human Rights," leaving China alone among the *permanent members of the Security Council* still opposing that initiative. China also blocked an appearance before state delegates by the *Dalai Lama*, who was relegated to speaking to *NGOs*.

World Intellectual Property Organization (WIPO): A forum devoted to standardization of the highly diverse laws governing copyright on intellectual property, importantly related to trade to hi-tech *services*. It largely failed to perform this function, causing the issue to move into the *GATT* as part of the *Uruguay Round*.

World Island: In the theory of *Halford Mackinder*, the adjoining continents of *Africa, Asia* and *Europe*.

World Meteorological Organization (WMO): A *specialized agency* of the UN, set up in 1947 to coordinate information about climate, weather patterns and related phenomena. It is headquartered in Geneva. It did its work quietly and effectively for years, until it came to public attention in the late 1980s by coordinating and publicizing research revealing that *ozone depletion* had caused holes to appear in the ozone layer over both poles. It is now also concerned with setting up a global data bank, and other initiatives, concerning *global warming*.

world politics: A synonym for *international politics*.

world power: A state capable of moving events on a global scale, and seeing itself as having worldwide *national interests*. Not even all the *Great Powers* qualify as world powers, which emerged in the 17th-18th centuries with the expansion of European *imperialism* into Latin America, Asia and Africa, and in the 19th century with the *Industrial Revolution* and comparable revolutions in communications and transportation technology. World powers to date have been, in rough order: France, Britain, Germany, Russia and the United States. Of these, since 1991 only the U.S. meets both criteria. China and Japan may be emerging as world powers, and Germany may be reemerging, although all those states still give an extraordinary stress to regional affairs in their diplomacy. Cf. *hegemon*.

world public opinion: An amorphous concept, varying with (and usually saying most about) the user. (1) It may be employed as a rhetorical device to claim universal support for one's own position, based on some immeasurable and unsubstantiated sense of how "plain folks" the world over must regard an issue. It is usually wielded in conjunction with that other resort of the incompetent debater or the scalawag, the appeal to "common sense" (after all, relying on our common senses should lead us to the uncommon belief that the sun revolves around the earth). Any claim to know what opinions the world holds is, of course, an imaginative leap of the first order of arrogance. It also makes the rather large assumption that most people in the world actually have opinions on international affairs, when national polling data from various countries suggests only a minority in each has anything more than a superficial knowledge of, or low interest in, world politics. (2) The term is sometimes used, with only slightly more accuracy, to mean the collective opinion of the world's governments, say as voiced in *resolutions* in the *UNGA* and *Security Council*--in which case it would be more factual to say just that.

World Slump: The *Great Depression* of 1929-39.

world system theory: A view of the world as a single, *capitalist* system, with an international division of *labor* wherein *core* states monopolize capital-intensive industries and exploit resources and labor of the *periphery*. See *dependency theory*.

World Trade Organization: See *GATT*.

world war: A *systemic war* involving all or most of the *Great Powers*, which overturns the old *balance of power* and sets up a new one. Even Great Powers may be destroyed in such wars.

World War I (WWI): The "Great War," and the "war to end all wars." Through the streets, farms and cafes of Europe in the summer of 1914 there whispered the old lies about glory in combat. Few young men knew or cared about the carnage that had been seen in the trenches of the *Crimean War*, or the killing fields of the *American Civil War*. Most dreamed of the offensive, of storybook charges and rapid promotion, of honor and glory; few understood what it meant to truly "meet one's Waterloo." Even the *General Staffs* of the major protagonists thought little of defense. Their secret war plans, too, were visions of great sweeping assaults, *envelopments* and quick victories. *Mobilization* was accompanied by bands and parades, by wives or parents cheering the troops, in country after country. "Auf nach Paris!" "Au Berlin!" "Victory by Christmas!" Such were the illusions, the eagerness and excitement with which Europe plunged the world into the greatest *war* humanity had yet suffered through. In the first two weeks of 1914 some 20 million young men donned uniform and rifle and entrained for the front; that was 10% of the entire population of Europe. In nearly every sector what met them was not glory, but mass death amidst the muddy trenches, shell-holes, barbed wire, bayonets, grenades, *artillery* barrages, corpse-fattened rats, machine guns and *poison gas*. And it went on and on, summer into winter into spring, for four awful years. Except for a brief phase of movement in the summer and fall of 1914, and again in 1918, for over three years--despite one major *campaign* after another--the *western front* moved no more than 10 miles. In the east, things were more fluid, as on a larger canvas, but in the end it amounted to the same thing. WWI killed 15 million people, mostly soldiers, and wounded and maimed in body or mind at least as many more. Three million of the dead were German. Another two million French died; and a million each from Austria and Britain. About 600,000 Italians fell, along with hundreds of thousands from Belgium, Canada, Turkey, the U.S. and a dozen more nations. Russian losses were so great they remain forever uncounted, but reached at least five million. After it was over another 20 million or so civilians died, from pestilence carried worldwide by returning soldiery, and made more deadly by years of *home front* deprivation. The war broke open three *multinational* empires (the *Austrian, Ottoman* and *Russian*), spilling their diverse peoples into new and untidy arrangements in the Balkans, and Central and Eastern Europe; and it left a global legacy of bitterness that would take a second world war to quell. Through it all, the inscription on the belt buckles of German soldiers read "Gott mit uns" (God is with us), which only expressed an arrogance common to all armies: Russians fought for "God and the Tsar." The British said the battle was for "God, King and Country" and the "rights of small nations." And Americans felt called upon by Providence itself to "make the world safe for democracy." All who felt they marched in the footsteps of the deity might have learned from *Frederick II (the Great)*, who knew war. "God," he once said, "is always with the strongest battalions." And so it was to be the big battalions grinding each other down over four years of bloody murder that decided this, the greatest of wars to that time.

The proximate cause of WWI was a prolonged crisis in the Balkans driven by territorial disputes, as evident in the *First* and *Second Balkan Wars*. The immediate cause was Austrian resistance to Serbian provocation, which drew in the other *Great Powers* during the *mobilization crisis* of June-August 1914. The more fundamental causes are moot. After all, *Bethmann-Hollweg* said of the reasons why on the

night of Britain's *declaration of war*, "if we only knew." Still, there is general agreement that among the main antecedents were: the fading of Ottoman *power*, or the *Eastern Question*; a corresponding decline of Austrian power, which Vienna was desperate to arrest; the bitter legacy of the *Franco/Prussian War;* the dangerous *Weltpolitik* pursued by Germany after 1890, and the sense among its leaders that a window of opportunity existed to use German power for *aggrandizement,* but that it would close by c.1920; Britain's reluctance to adjust to a relative decline in its status vis-à-vis Germany; the existence of broad *alliances* or near-alliances that helped spread the war beyond the Balkans; abrasive colonial rivalries; and a series of key *crises* and war scares that raised general *tensions* from c.1900-1914. Even deeper causes were the volcanic tensions in Europe between the rising promise of *liberalism* throughout the 19th century and the widespread reality of *reaction*, beneath which moved a magma of frustrated national ambitions, ethnic resentments, and religious and social hatreds. WWI was, when all is said and done, not merely a war over the *balance of power*, or of classes, exclusive economic interests, colonial empires, muddled *imperialisms* or inept or evil rulers, though it was all that. More deeply, it was a long-awaited and even longed-for clash of entire *nations* and *peoples*, some of which had harbored enmities for decades, or even centuries. Once the drift to war began *statesmen* and generals thus found it could not be easily channeled, or arrested.

Its course: (1) In the west: After an initial German thrust toward Paris in 1914, both sides began *flanking* movements which eventually took them to the Atlantic (the so-called "race to the sea"). They then dug in, and slugged it out for the next three years from Belgium to the Alps. There were many battles. The Allies tried to break the *stalemate* by attacking in the south, at *Gallipoli*, but failed. In 1916 the Germans attacked at *Verdun*. To relieve the terrible pressures on the French the British counterattacked in the *Somme*. The slaughter of that summer was unparalleled in history. The Germans tried to break the stalemate in 1917 by returning to *unrestricted submarine warfare*. But despite *mutinies* in the Western armies, the lines held. Berlin's all-or-nothing gamble came to a head in 1918. The front was broken open that summer, after the Germans exhausted their *reserves* in a final, spring offensive, turned back by seasoned *Allied* and fresh American troops (the U.S. had *declared war* on Germany, but not on the other *Central Powers*, in April 1917). (2) In the south: Italy entered the war in 1915, but Allied hopes it would crack the Austrian Army faded, and by 1917, after *Caporetto*, the British and French had to come to Italy's aid. Serbia was overrun in 1915-16, by Germans, Austrians and Bulgarians (who entered the war in 1915). (3) In the east: The Russian advance into Germany in 1914 drew troops away from the western front, and helped save Paris and perhaps France. But by autumn, Russia was driven back at the battles of *Tannenberg* and the Masurian Lakes. Another Russian offensive against Austria in 1916 had early successes, but overall the east was characterized by German offense and a slowly weakening Russian defense. By March 1917, the tsarist regime collapsed. A failed offensive in the summer finished the Russian army, and hastened the *Bolshevik Revolution* in November. At *Brest-Litovsk*, the Bolsheviks made a *separate peace* with Germany. (4) In the Middle East: Turkey, which joined the Central Powers at the end of 1914, held off the British at Gallipoli but was pushed back from Palestine and Syria by the *Arab Revolt*, in support of British forces. Turkey also gave way to Russia in the Caucasus. (5) In Asia: Japan took advantage of Europe's war to seize German holdings in China in 1914, and issue the *Twenty-One Demands* in 1915. (6) In Africa: Extensive fighting occurred in southern Africa, where the Germans were finally defeated in their *colonies* only a few days before the *Armistice* in Europe. (7) At sea: There was only one major battle, at *Jutland*. The main action came with the use of unrestricted submarine warfare by Germany, which eventually brought the U.S. into the war. The war at sea also witnessed the development of the *convoy* system and of *aircraft carriers* as defensive measures against the *U-boat*. On October 4, 1918, Austria and Germany asked for terms, and on November 11, the *Armistice* was signed. The *peace treaties* with the defeated Central Powers, or their *successor states*, were drafted at the *Paris Peace Conference* 1919-20. See also *Agadir; armed neutrality; Bosnian crisis; Bryan; Cambrai; Churchill; Clemenceau; Constantinople Agreement; Falkenhayn; Francis Ferdinand; Foch; Fourteen Points; Lloyd George; Edward Grey; Entente Cordiale; Douglas Haig; Hindenburg; Jean Jaures; Kerensky; Kitchener; Lenin; Ludendorff; London, Treaties of (1839 and 1915); Lusitania Notes; Marne; Moroccan crises, First and Second; Military Conversations; Helmut von Moltke; mustard gas; no-man's-land; Nicholas I; Vittorio Orlando; Passchendale; Pétain; Rasputin; Schlieffen Plan; stab-in-the-back; Sykes-Picot Agreement; Triple Entente; Wilhelm II; Woodrow Wilson; Ypres; Zimmermann telegram;* the *Treaties of Neuilly, St. Germain, Trianon* and *Versailles;* and other participant states and leaders.

World War II (WWII): There is an increasingly prevalent tendency to see WWII as a continuation of the unfinished business of *WWI*. While that is no doubt true in many ways, this even greater conflict also had distinctive roots. The social origins of the war lay in the *Great Depression*. That was the *sine qua non* of the rise to power of German *fascism*, a contributing factor to the growth of *militarism* in Japan and national bombast in Italy, and the great handicap on a dynamic response by the democratic states. But the Depression did not of itself cause WWII. The central, political origin of the war was German unwillingness, intensified after 1933, to continue to live within the strictures laid down in the *Treaty of Versailles*. At first Germany was opposed, even if meekly, by all the other *Great Powers* in Europe, including Italy and the Soviet Union. However, by the mid-1930s a combination of political divisions (most notably, mutual distrust between the West and *Stalin*, but also the rise of Italy's own ambitions to empire) and adroit Nazi diplomacy prevented those states from forming a solid front against German *revisionism*. With the failure of the *Stresa front* and the shift of Italy into the German camp, the western democracies turned to a policy of *appeasement*. That pushed the Soviet Union back into its earlier, brooding *isolationism*. Meanwhile, from the U.S. all that arrived was exhortation and platitudes, but no willingness to commit to *collective security* against the fascist powers. A series of crises followed: the *Abyssinian War,* the *Rhineland,* the *Spanish Civil War* and, lastly, *Hitler's* threat to Czechoslovakia that culminated in the *Munich Conference*. Shortly after Munich, Western opinion began to shift and harden, and a full-scale *arms race* was soon underway. But Stalin's thinking was changing too, toward the prospect of the separate and secret deal with Hitler that came in the *Nazi/Soviet Pact* in August 1939.

Its course: (1) In Europe, 1939-41: On September 1, Germany asserted that Poles had attacked it, and attacked Poland without a *declaration of war*. On the 3rd, Britain and France issued *ultimata* demanding Germany pull out; when they expired at midnight all three countries were in a *state of war* (Japan, Italy, Russia and the U.S. stayed *neutral*). Poland was crushed within a month, first by German then by Soviet troops (who attacked on September 17th). What followed in the west has been caustically called the *sitzkrieg,* or *Phony War,* although at sea the vitally important *Battle of the Atlantic* was being fought in deadly earnest. In November, Russia attacked Finland, beginning the discrete but related *Finnish/Soviet War.* In April 1940, Germany attacked and *occupied* Denmark and Norway. On May 10th, it attacked Belgium, France and the Netherlands. While the German *blitzkrieg* rolled over those countries in days or weeks, in the east the Soviets forced Rumania to cede *Bessarabia* and annexed the *Baltic States. Mussolini* declared war on Britain and France in order to pick up easy spoils, which angered Hitler. German plans to invade Britain were abandoned after defeat in the *Battle of*

Britain. That turned Hitler's attention eastward, always his main interest. Mussolini invaded Greece, but found the going much rougher than expected, as he also did in North and East Africa, where the British enjoyed their few successes on land, against the Italians. Hitler came to his friend's aid, throwing the British out of Crete (the first paratroop invasion in history), sending the Afrikakorps to Tripoli, and invading Greece and Yugoslavia (with Bulgaria as an ally) in April 1941. Operation *Barbarossa,* the German attack on Russia that was to give WWII the additional character of a *genocidal* race war against *Slavs* and Jews, was finally launched on June 22, 1941. By Christmas, the Germans and their Finnish, Hungarian, Italian and Rumanian allies had captured three million Soviet soldiers, shattered and destroyed entire armies, overrun Kiev (where they were initially welcomed as liberators), Minsk and dozens of lesser cities, besieged Leningrad and shelled Moscow. It seemed the flags of fascism were destined to fly over the *Kremlin* itself. Hitler's empire stretched from the Atlantic to the heart of European Russia, and from the Baltic to North Africa. But also by Christmas, Japan had attacked the United States and Germany and America were at last at war. The Japanese thus did at *Pearl Harbor* what *Roosevelt, Churchill* and even Hitler had not in the two years previously: they joined otherwise separate Atlantic and Pacific conflicts, and thereby caused the U.S. *intervention* that was to be decisive for both.

(2) In the Pacific, 1939-45: The main prewar *tension* was between the U.S. and Japan, over the ongoing Japanese war against China, but also over suspicions of larger Japanese ambitions (later called the *Greater East Asian Co-Prosperity Sphere*). The war in Europe presented Tokyo's *warlords* with a dilemma: the army wanted to strike west, further into China and ultimately, *Siberia.* But the navy was drawn south, toward the ripe pickings of now lightly defended European colonial empires in Southeast Asia, especially after the Nazi *conquest* of France and Holland and the drawing back of British forces from Burma, Hong Kong and Singapore. In other words, the Japanese had to choose whether they wanted to fight Russia, then desperately defending itself against the Nazi onslaught, but with 40 Siberian divisions in place under *Zhukov,* who in 1939 had bloodied the Japanese in an undeclared war; or attack America, the only power with the naval resources, but perhaps not the will, to stand against a thrust toward Southeast Asia, and eventually India. With the fall of France, Tokyo forced the Vichyites in *French Indochina* to accept Japanese terms, and such easy conquest helped the navy view prevail. From 1940-41 the U.S. offered a diplomatic and strategic accommodation, but on terms that included Japan's withdrawal from China, something deemed unac-

ceptable by Japanese imperialists. The U.S. therefore imposed an ever-tighter *embargo* on Japan's purchase of war matériel, and on *oil.* Tokyo saw this as unfairly constricting its national ambitions and economic needs, and on December 7, 1941, Japan struck at the U.S. at *Pearl Harbor.* Within days, for reasons that remain murky, Germany and Italy declared war on the U.S., linking the two distant *theaters* (and making Churchill the happiest man in Britain). The Japanese at first enjoyed victory after victory, on Guam and Wake; in the consolidation of their hold on Indochina; in Hong Kong, Burma, Singapore and the Philippines. But they were stopped by *ANZAC* and American forces in New Guinea, and then suffered a series of naval setbacks. Within just six months the Japanese were thrown onto the defensive, after *Midway.* The Americans then adopted an "island-hopping" strategy, by which they bypassed and isolated Japanese island garrisons while progressing toward the recapture of islands from which *strategic bombers* could hit the Japanese *home islands.* Meanwhile, in bitter jungle fighting, British and Indian troops threw the Japanese back from India, and began to push them out of Burma. The fall of Saipan in July 1944, was another turning point, allowing easy, round-trip bombing of the Japanese home islands from the *Marianas.* The Philippines was retaken, after vicious fighting, 1944-45. The main land warfare was in China, however, where Allied supplies and *air power* aided Chinese Nationalist and Communist armies, who had paused their civil war to fight the foreign invader. The steady sinking of Japan's *merchant marine* by U.S. *submarines* strangled supplies. But it was the constant strategic air attack and threat of imminent invasion that pushed the Japanese to *surrender.* Tokyo was considering capitulation even before the dropping of *atomic bombs* on *Hiroshima* and *Nagasaki,* on August 6 and 9, 1945. Yet even after those instant incinerations of Japanese cities, there was fanatic, last-ditch resistance by thousands of younger officers. The Soviet Union entered the Pacific War in the same week of the atomic attacks, pushing the Japanese back in *Manchuria* and northern China. Japan surrendered on August 15, 1945. The terms were signed aboard the USS Missouri, in Tokyo Bay, on September 2nd. Some 3.1 million Japanese were killed between 1937-45, along with millions more Burmese, Chinese, Filipinos, Vietnamese and thousands of ANZUS, Americans and others.

(3) In Europe, 1942-45: At first 1942 looked like it would bring more German victories. *Rommel* was still bedeviling the British, soon to be joined by the Americans, in North Africa. Meanwhile, new thrusts were made into the *Crimea,* and deeper into Russia. But Leningrad refused to fall, Hitler's legions were pushed slowly back from Moscow, and in October the

British inflicted a major defeat at *El Alamein*. Then, in January 1943, the German Sixth Army was annihilated at *Stalingrad*. The tide turned. Anglo/American forces pushed the Germans out of North Africa by May 1943, then quickly invaded Sicily and Italy, toppling Mussolini and taking Italy out of the war in September. The Soviets, too, moved to the offensive after Stalingrad, decisively winning at *Kursk*, one of the largest and most important battles of the entire war. Less effectively, *partisans* resisted the Nazis, from Norway and France to Yugoslavia, Greece and the Ukraine (where cheers had turned to tears over the reality of Nazi *occupation*). The Western Allies landed in Normandy on June 6, 1944. After a brief period of consolidation of the beachhead, the Americans under *Patton* broke into southern France and raced for the *Ziegfried Line*, while British and *Commonwealth* troops under *Montgomery* moved more slowly up the coast into Belgium and Holland, toward the Rhine. By this time, Germany had for two years been suffering from Anglo/American *thousand bomber raids*. Now it was in a *two-front war*, and by midwinter its armies were fighting on their own soil for the first time. A last-ditch effort was made at the *Battle of the Bulge*, but it spent German *reserves* and broke morale. The *Wehrmacht* began to *surrender* en masse in the west, while fighting a disciplined retreat in the east. But the *Allies*, so soon to fall out, would not do so--openly-- while Hitler and his henchmen lived. The *Red Army* advanced into Berlin itself, expending 100,000 Soviet lives to take the city. On April 30, 1945, with fighting going on barely 100 meters from his subterranean bunker, Hitler and several others of the Nazi leadership killed themselves; others were captured, or not, in later days and weeks. On May 2nd Berlin fell, and on May 8th Germany surrendered unconditionally. The "Thousand Year Reich" had lasted but 12 years, but to bring it and its allies down took the combined forces of over 40 nations, and cost 55 million lives. The roll of the dead: 20 to 25 million Soviets, 8 million Germans, 6 million Jews (including 3 million Polish Jews), 5 million Chinese, 3 million Japanese, 3 million non-Jewish Poles and several millions more drawn from scores of countries. See also *Anti-COMINTERN Pact; Atlantic Charter; Axis; Badoglio; Bataan death march; Cairo; Canaris; Casablanca; Neville Chamberlain; Ciano; de Gaulle; Doolittle Raid; English Channel; final solution; Four Freedoms; Japanese Peace Treaty; Goebbels; Göring; Hirohito; Holocaust; kamikaze; Lansing/Ishii Agreement; Manhattan Project; Morgenthau plan; National Front governments; nazism; Neutrality Acts; Nuremberg trials; Pact of Steel; Treaties of Paris (1947); Potsdam; Resistance; Ribbentrop; Rokossovsky; Saar; second front; Second Sino/Japanese War; Sikorski; Teheran; Tojo; Tripartite Pact; unconditional surrender; United Nations alliance; V-1/V-2 rockets; Vichy; war crimes trials; Warsaw Rising; Yalta; Yamamoto; Yamashita;* and other individuals, leaders and states.

WTO: See (1) *Warsaw Treaty Organization;* (2) *World Trade Organization (GATT).*

X

X article: In July 1947, "Foreign Affairs" magazine published an article entitled "The Sources of Soviet Conduct," identifying the author only as "X." In fact, it was by *George Kennan*, writing under a pseudonym owing to his position as a government official. Kennan pointed to the Soviets as the central threat to global *security*, and proposed a strategy of flexible *containment* to forestall a shift in the *balance of power*--so recently restored--out of America's favor. He argued that U.S. foreign policy must aim at keeping the two remaining centers of great industrial capacity, Western Europe and Japan, out of Soviet hands. As these regions were struggling to recover from *WWII*, it was imperative to oppose the threat of *communist* takeovers with diplomatic, political and most important, economic support. Containment was not depicted as an offensive strategy, nor as primarily a military one: Kennan did not believe the Soviets had any clear intention of invading Western Europe; he simply wanted to ensure they were never presented with that temptation by a failure of resolve in the West. Counterforce might have to be used on occasion, but *deterrence* was the preferable course. Most important was denial of political opportunity to the Soviets through support for the continuation of liberal-democracy in those countries that already enjoyed it, and cultivation of democratic virtues and habits of mind in the defeated *Axis* states. This could be accomplished through application of the anaesthetic of prosperity to Western Europe and Japan, in the form of a U.S. led and underwritten *aid, trade* and credit *regime*. That was, of course, something entirely in U.S. economic interests as well: a fulfillment of its long-standing interest in the *Open Door*. Kennan was confident. He regarded the West as by far the stronger party, and saw the Soviet Union as so full of systemic and structural contradictions it must surely collapse if expansion was

denied it. "No mystical, messianic movement can face frustration indefinitely," he wrote, "without eventually adjusting itself in one way or another to the logic of that state of affairs." The Soviet state and system might not fall soon, but given time and containment, it would surely fail, and then fall. Cf. *Cold War; domino theory; double containment; Long Telegram; Paul Nitze; NSC-68; peaceful co-existence.*

xenophobia: An unreasonable fear of foreigners, or of foreign values. Cf. *chauvinism; ethnocentrism; isolationism; jingoism; nationalism; racism; slavophile.*

Xhosa: The second-largest *ethnic group* in South Africa, after the *Zulu*, against whom they fought desperate *wars* in the time of *Shaka Zulu*. The Xhosa also fought the British and the *Boers*, both of whom were *migrating* northward from the Cape after 1800. These so-called "Kaffir Wars" were waged intermittently before 1880, ending in Xhosa defeat and subordination. With *apartheid*, many Xhosa were herded into *Bantustans* and became supporters of the *African National Congress*, whereas some Zulu supported *Inkatha*.

XYZ Affair: U.S. President *John Adams* wanted to defuse the growing crisis with France that faced his new administration in 1797, and send a delegation to Paris. The delegates were asked for a bribe by the wily *Talleyrand* before he would even receive them, but they did not have the money and the mission failed. Adams was shocked at the slight and considered *war*, but announced only limited hostilities. He told Congress of the bribe demand, substituting the initials "X," "Y" and "Z" for names of the French *agents*. National indignation resulted that fueled conflict with France for years, and led to the first significant appropriations to build a *navy*. See *Quasi War.*

Y

Yahya Khan, Agha Muhammad (1917-80): President of Pakistan 1969-71. His troops repressed an *uprising* of the Awami League (a Bengali political party) in *East Pakistan* with such *genocidal* cruelty that a full-scale *civil war* broke out. The *refugees* pouring into India numbered in millions, and rumblings of a wider *war* were heard. Yet, he refused to quell the violence or take steps to placate India, partly out of a mistaken belief in the superiority of Pakistani armed forces over their Indian counterparts. When *Indira Gandhi* delivered an *ultimatum* he reportedly fumed that such an insult should come from a woman, and sent some 85 aircraft to attack India. All that did was provoke a punishing Indian attack on *West Pakistan,* and significantly widen the war. When his repressive policies led to *defeat* and national dismemberment (*independence* for *Bangladesh*), he resigned.

Yalta Conference: A wartime meeting held in the *Crimea* from February 4-11, 1945, between *Winston Churchill, Franklin Roosevelt, Joseph Stalin* and their top advisers. It was critical to the shape of the *postwar* world and the origins of the *Cold War*. They discussed some military matters concerning the final phases of *WWII*, but focused on four main postwar topics: (1) What to do with Germany? It was decided to demand *unconditional surrender*, hold *war crimes trials* and impose militarily *occupation*. It was not proposed to divide Germany, however, other than into administrative zones. The longer term division of Germany resulted from the Cold War, not directly from WWII. (2) What to do about Asia? As the *atom bomb* was yet untested and the *invasion* of Japan promised to be very bloody in terms of American and British lives, Roosevelt and Churchill urged Stalin to bring Russia's vast reserves of manpower into the Asian war. They offered the *Kurile Islands, Sakhalin Island, Outer Mongolia* and restoration of Russia's pre-1904 rights in *Manchuria* as an incentive. Stalin agreed to attack Japan three months after Germany *surrendered*, a promise he kept. In return, he recognized the *Nationalists* in China. It was also decided to jointly occupy Korea. (3) What to do about *Eastern Europe*? This proved the most difficult and controversial of issues. It was agreed to join the Polish *government-in-exile* in London with the Soviet-backed "Lublin Poles," pending free elections in Poland and other *liberated* countries, as promised in the *Declaration on Liberated Europe*. (4) What about the UN? The scope of the *veto* and other unsettled issues were discussed, pending final resolution at the *San Francisco Conference*. Within three weeks of Yalta, serious disagreements and mutual charges of violation were exchanged (the main points of controversy concerned Soviet actions in Rumania and Poland, and Moscow's refusal to permit Western observers into those areas. By *Potsdam* the *alliance* was crumbling fast, and over the next two years it completely fell apart. Cf. *Casablanca; Tehran.*

Yamagata, Aritomo (1838-1922): Japanese statesman. Minister of War 1873; PM 1889-93, 1898-1900; *éminence grise* 1900-1921. Something of a convert to *modernization*, he helped build up the Japanese army and oversee its operations in *Guandong*, Korea and the *Russo/Japanese War.*

Yamamoto, Isoroku (1884-1943): Japanese admiral. He saw action as a young *officer* during the *Russo/Japanese War.* He commanded the fleet that attacked *Pearl Harbor*, and directed subsequent Japanese naval operations in the Pacific *theater*. He had lived, studied and worked (as naval *attaché*) in the U.S. and opposed *war* with America. He also opposed Japan joining the *Axis* alliance. But when the order for war came, he saluted stiffly and set about putting his considerable *tactical* and *strategic* talents to work on behalf of Japanese imperial expansion. Yet he suffered from forebodings of *defeat*. Immediately after Pearl, when he learned Japan's *declaration of war* had come only after the attack began, he said of America: "I fear all we have done is awaken a sleeping giant, and fill him with a terrible resolve." His forces were pushed back at the *Coral Sea*, and his battle plan for *Midway* went badly awry, largely because U.S. and British *intelligence* had broken some Japanese codes, but partly owing to the varying luck and/or courage of pilots and commanders on both sides. When U.S. intelligence intercepted a message saying precisely where and when Yamamoto would be on April 17, 1943, his plane and escorts were duly intercepted by an entire U.S. *fighter* squadron, and shot down.

Yamani, Ahmad Zaki (b.1930): Saudi statesman. *Oil* Minister 1962-86. Harvard educated, he was the leading individual behind the creation and management of *OPEC*, including its use of oil *embargoes* in 1973 and 1979. He was ousted in 1986 after a six-year drop in world oil prices (that continued into the mid-1990s).

Yamashita, Tomoyuki (1885-1946): Japanese general. In 1940 he was at the head of a mission to *Nazi Germany* sent to study German *war* methods and *tactics*. He commanded the Japanese army in Malaya, and accepted the British *surrender* at Singapore in February 1942. He then took command of the Japanese *campaign* in the Philippines, capturing Bataan and

Corregidor. The *Bataan death march* took place under his command. He was tried and hanged in Manila, for the many *war crimes* and atrocities his troops committed, and he had tolerated or ordered, especially after Japan was clearly losing the war during 1944-45.

Yap Island: One of the Caroline chain, it caused friction between the U.S. and Japan in the 1920s, when it was run by the latter as a *mandated territory*. At the *Washington Conference* it was agreed to give the U.S. cable and other rights equal to Japan's, in return for *recognition* of Japanese *mandates* north of the equator (discrete recognition was necessary as the U.S. was not a *League of Nations* member, and hence had not formally approved the mandate system).

Yaoundé Convention (1969): Some 18 African states signed this *preferential trade* and *aid* agreement with the *EC*. It was superseded by the *Lomé Conventions*.

Yellow Peril: The pre-*WWII* fear, deriving in part from racist attitudes and partly from *security* concerns, that Japan might overrun territories, such as Australia or the west coast of North America, already settled by whites (who had themselves overrun the native population). It gained currency after Japan's surprisingly successful performance in the *Russo/Japanese War*.

yellow press: Media that indulge in or encourage shrill *nationalism* or *jingoism*, especially in times of *crisis* and *war*. The term was originally applied to U.S. newspaper baron William Randolph Hearst (1863-1951), whose several chains whipped up war-fever before the *Spanish/American War.*

Yeltsin, Boris Nikolayevich (b.1931): Russian statesman. *Gorbachev* promoted him to head the Moscow party in 1985, viewing him as an ally. After 1987 he grew openly critical of Gorbachev, pushing him toward more radical and faster reform. Yeltsin won an overwhelming popular victory in May 1990, when he was elected President of the Russian Federation (or *Russia*, as opposed to the *Soviet Union*, which Gorbachev headed). When Yeltsin joined other republic leaders in calls for decentralization under a new "Union Treaty," Gorbachev floundered, and briefly turned to the old communist right. During the August 1991, *coup* attempt, Yeltsin acted bravely and decisively, emerging as the undisputed spokesman for Russia. He next publicly humiliated Gorbachev, and pushed for creation of the *CIS*, which led to the *extinction* of the Soviet Union on Christmas Day, 1991. He has since cooperated extensively with the West on *arms control*, on the *Gulf War*, and even on *Bosnia*, where Russian conservatives preferred support for the Serbs. In return

he received promises of extensive *aid*, renewed at a Vancouver summit with Clinton in 1993. He improved relations with China, but quarreled seriously with Ukraine over many issues, and could not resolve the impasse with Japan over the *Kuriles*. He showed up for the *G-7* summit in Tokyo in July 1993 (where he was politely received but did not attend meetings). He was rewarded with $3 billion in aid and confidently predicted that he would soon return at the head of a Russia that was a full member of a new "Group of Eight." But his biggest battles were at home. From 1991 on, he was locked in a mortal struggle with the entrenched interests of the old Soviet system, in particular over the division of powers between the presidency and the parliament in any new constitution, and the pace and depth of economic reform. In October 1993, he moved to settle the question by forcibly crushing an armed *rebellion* by the parliament, which refused his order to disband. But as he pushed through a new constitution granting the presidency unprecedented powers, he saw his parliamentary supporters lose ground to *fascists* and old guard *communists*.

Yemen: Location: *Arabian peninsula*. Major associations: *Arab League, UN*. Population: 13 million. Military: two separate armies maintained after the 1990 *union*. For four centuries the part of this land formerly known as the Arab Republic of Yemen was a province of the *Ottoman Empire* (1517-1918). To its immediate east lay the port and later British *protectorate* of *Aden*. Yemen became an independent *monarchy* in 1918, then spent several decades in tribal quarrels. After the assassination of its first king in 1948, his malevolent son took Yemen into the camp of *radical* Arab states, first associating closely with *Nasser* then approaching the *Soviet bloc* directly and supporting anti-British rebels in Aden. Saudi *intervention* in a Yemeni succession struggle in 1962 (when a *republic* was declared) prolonged a civil/tribal war that lasted until 1970. Meanwhile, after a radical *rebellion* in *Aden* in 1967, the British withdrew and the People's Republic of Yemen (a.k.a. South Yemen) was set up, with assistance from the Soviets and Chinese. In 1979 it fought a brief war with its neighbor and ethnic kin, fed by several hundred thousand *refugees* who fled north. It also signed a *friendship treaty* with Moscow, leading to stationing of Soviet troops in South Yemen. That got in the way of an Arab League effort to bring about unification of the two states. In 1986 there was a bloody uprising in South Yemen against continuation of the Soviet tie. An enlarged republic was formed in 1990, when the erstwhile enemies formed a union. During the *Gulf War* Yemen lent diplomatic support to Iraq. That strained already uneasy relations with Saudi Arabia, which expelled 1 million Yemeni workers. In 1993 Yemen was accused by Egypt and the U.S. of fomenting *terrorism* by *fundamentalist* Muslims. The union was unstable: the urban south (3 million, but with oil) was at odds with the rural north (10 million, but poor). This cleavage led to renewed civil war and dissolution of the union in 1994.

Yenan: The provisional capital of the large area in China's interior controlled by the Chinese *Communist Party* after the *Long March*. See *Chinese Civil War.*

Yezhovshchina: There were several terrible *purges* in Russia during the 1930s, all accompanied by huge *propaganda* campaigns, elaborate legal paraphernalia and spectacular *show trials*. The bloodiest lasted from 1934-38, and was named for Nikolai I. Yezhov (1894-1939), head of the *NKVD*, 1936-38. Under *Stalin's* direction, Yezhov beheaded the *Red Army* by decimating the senior *officer corps*, eliminated nearly all the *Old Bolsheviks,* wiped out whole classes of "state enemies" real or imagined, and utterly terrorized the populace. Estimates vary, but the purges as a whole took at least 10 million lives (*Khrushchev's* number). Overall, Stalin killed at least 20-25 million (Western estimates), and may have slaughtered as many as 40 million (a shocking Soviet figure--probably compiled by the *KGB*--released in 1989). After serving as Stalin's willing and eager executioners, Yezhov and other top NKVD officers were themselves purged. See *Beria; GULAG archipelago; Kirov; Molotov; Vyshinsky.*

yield: A measure of the energy released, and therefore the destructive power of a *nuclear weapon*, or any other explosive. See *kiloton; megaton.*

Yom Kippur War: See *Arab/Israeli War, Fourth.*

Yorktown, Battle of (October 19, 1781): Site of the *surrender* of the British under Cornwallis (1738-1805) to the Americans under *George Washington*. It convinced France to *declare war* on Britain, an outcome and decision far more decisive to the *American War of Independence* than the battle per se.

Yoruba: A numerous West African people, living mostly in western Nigeria (where they are one of the three main *ethnic groups*, with the *Ibo* and *Hausa*), but also in neighboring Benin and Togo. Many of those carried away by the *slave trade* were Yoruba, prisoners from the many Yoruba wars, sold into European *slavery* by their African captors. During the *Nigerian Civil War* the Yoruba backed the Federal side. In 1993 there was much unrest among Nigerian Yoruba, over a cancellation of the victory of one of their own as president.

Yoshida, Shigeru (1878-1967): Japanese statesman. PM of Japan 1946-47, 1949-54. He was a principal architect of the pro-Western foreign and domestic policies that led to astonishing electoral success for the *Liberal Party* in Japan, and the country's remarkable postwar recovery. He accepted the *Japanese Peace Treaty* in 1951.

Young Ireland (Young Italy, etc.): 19th century nationalist and *liberal* movements in several European countries, that sought independent *republics*.

Young Plan (1929): Named for Owen Young (1874-1962), the American who headed an international committee on German *reparations*, charged with revising the *Dawes Plan*. It proposed reduction of the amount owed and spacing payments out until 1988. The *Great Depression* rendered it moot. It was overtaken by a severe capital shortage, and then *Nazi* refusal in 1933 to make any more reparations payments. The Nazis used opposition to the Young Plan to great effect in two elections prior to 1933.

Young Turks: (1) The movement of Turkish army officers founded c.1889, that sought rapid *modernization* of the *Ottoman Empire* from 1908-14, when they deposed the *sultan*. Many participated in (though they no longer led) the *secularization* of Turkish politics and society after *WWI*. (2) Anyone, but especially if relatively young, who is aggressive in advocating rapid social or political change.

Ypres, Battles of: From 1914-18, this small Belgian town witnessed several great and bloody battles. It is particularly remembered by the British and Canadians, both of whom who took extremely heavy losses.

Yugoslavia: The name meant "South Slav State." It was created after *WWI*, when the *Slav* areas of the *Austrian Empire* (*Bosnia, Croatia* and *Slovenia*) were free to attach themselves to *Serbia and Montenegro*, which formed the core of Yugoslavia. The country was put together in the *Pact of Corfu*, creating the "United Kingdom of the Serbs, Croats and Slovenes," which was dominated by the Serbs. The name was officially changed to Yugoslavia in 1929. During the 1930s Yugoslavia drifted toward association with German policy, although it remained *neutral* in 1939. Following a pro-British *coup* in late March 1941, Germany invaded in early April. The country effectively broke apart during *WWII*, with Serb nationalist partisans (*Chetniks*) fighting both the Germans and Serb communist partisans, led by *Tito*. The British, who coordinated *Allied* policy in Yugoslavia, first supported the Chetniks but later switched to Tito's communists. Meanwhile, *fascists* set up a Nazi *puppet state* in Croatia, setting off a vicious multisided *civil war* fought within the parameters of the larger conflict with Germany and Italy. With British *aid* and Allied *recognition*, at war's end Tito was well placed to set himself up as Yugoslav leader, brutally repressing all remaining Chetnik and Croatian resistance and uniting in a federal, communist dictatorship, six republics: *Bosnia, Croatia, Macedonia, Montenegro, Serbia* and *Slovenia.* Yugoslavia's *postwar* communist regime thus came to power under its own steam, without Soviet *occupation* or assistance. It moved into the Soviet camp in the early *Cold War*, but always had its own agenda (e.g., for entirely noncommunist reasons, it disputed control of *Trieste* until 1954, when it finally agreed to let the city join Italy). Its refusal to toe the *party line* after 1948 undermined the support it had

given to Greek communists, then fighting their own civil war. Its break with Moscow was much praised in the *West*, but little exploited with aid or diplomacy. In 1953, with *Stalin's* death, Yugoslav/Soviet relations underwent something of a *thaw.* After 1955 Tito took a leading role in the *Non-Aligned Movement.* Violence erupted among the various *ethnic groups* in 1968, and again in 1981 in *Kosovo* province. During 1990-91 the country broke apart: Slovenia, Croatia and then Bosnia and Macedonia moved to non-communist government, and then severed their ties with Serbia and Montenegro, where communists redressed as nationalists under *Slobodan Milošević* clung to power. For the moment, Serbia retains legal title to the name "Yugoslavia," but in everyday discourse this state is already taken to be *extinct.* See also *ethnic cleansing; Third Balkan War; successor states.*

Z

zaibatsu: Great industrial cartels, that first appeared in Japan during the *Meiji* period, and grew to dominate its economic life. After *WWII*, U.S. *occupation* authorities at first tried to break up the zaibatsu. But by 1947 this effort was put aside, as American policy shifted from basic reform of Japanese national life to rapid *reconstruction* of its economy, so as to have a rebuilt Japan act as a bulwark against Soviet penetration of Asia.

Zaire: Location: Central Africa. Major associations: *OAU, UN.* Population: 36 million. Military: used solely to sustain the *regime* through repression. From 1879-84 the Belgians penetrated the Congo, following the mapping expedition of the British explorer Henry Stanley (1841-1904; "Dr. Livingstone, I presume?"). King Leopold II of Belgium (1835-1909) financed Stanley. Leopold then set up a company to exploit the region abutting the Congo river. At the *Conference of Berlin* he was made personally *sovereign* over the "Congo Free State." His malign neglect and coarse exploitation led to widespread disturbances from 1903-05, and to an international campaign to relieve him of the Congo. In 1908 it was annexed directly to Belgium. The worst abuses ceased, but the Belgian government did little better than Leopold over the next 50 years in allowing political expression or providing education and social amenities to the Congolese. Then in 1960, in a move widely criticized as precipitate and irresponsible, Belgium suddenly withdrew and gave Congo its *independence.* That provoked the *Congo*

crisis. Fighting continued until 1965, when *Mobutu Sese Seko* took power in a *coup.* In 1967 Mobutu barely survived a *mercenary* revolt and attempted invasion by Congolese exiles, attacking from bases in Rwanda. Until 1971 the country was called the Republic of the Congo; it was renamed Zaire. In 1977 and 1978, *Katanga (Shaba)* province was invaded by *mercenaries*, leading to French and Belgian *intervention.* Otherwise, Mobutu presided undisturbed over perhaps the most corrupt and inept government in *sub-Saharan Africa.* In spite of enormous natural mineral and other wealth, Zaire was misgoverned into pervasive poverty, persistent social unrest, and continuing political instability. Mobutu's hold on power has grown tenuous since 1990, especially with the example of other African nations converting from one-party dictatorships to incipient multiparty democracies. The Zairean economy is also nearing total collapse, and *anarchy* has taken hold in parts of the countryside: in 1993 annual *inflation* reached 7,000%. In January, French and Belgian paratroops intervened to rescue European nationals endangered by Zairean troops rioting over the *inflation* rate and Mobutu's failure to pay them. In the confusion the French ambassador was killed, reportedly while peering out his window at the rioters. Zaire additionally faces, as it has its entire national existence, the constant threat of *secession* in Katanga. In June the U.S. *embargoed* arms, and with France and Belgium denied *visas* to Mobutu's officials.

Zambia: Location: Central Africa. Major associations:

Commonwealth, OAU, UN. Population: 8.2 million. Military: no offensive capability. Known in colonial days as Northern Rhodesia, it was acquired for Britain by the machinations of *Cecil Rhodes,* and run by the British South Africa Company from 1889-1924. It then became a *protectorate,* and later still, part of the *Federation of Rhodesia and Nyasaland.* The drive for *independence* was led by Kenneth Kuanda (b.1924), who wished to break particularly with the whites who controlled Southern Rhodesia (later called Rhodesia, then Zimbabwe). The *sovereign* republic of Zambia emerged in 1964. For its first several decades of independence Zambia was handicapped by being one of the *front line states,* first concerning *UDI* in Rhodesia, then *apartheid* in South Africa. In 1991 Kuanda was voted out, and left office with good grace, in a model of transition to a multiparty system. Since then *IMF*-backed economic reforms have been in place.

Zanzibar: This east African island was home to the Arab *slave trade* for over 1,000 years, under local *sultans* with ties to *Oman*. Portugal ran the Zanzibar trade for 200 years, but the sultans reestablished themselves c.1700. The British and Germans competed for trade concessions (cloves and clove oil replaced slaves) until 1890, when a British *protectorate* was established in exchange for *Heligoland.* In December 1963, it joined the *Commonwealth* as an independent state, but within weeks the sultanate was overthrown and a few months later Zanzibar joined with *Tanganyika* in a *union.* That gave Zanzibar distinct advantages: it gained access to the resources of the mainland without having to surrender its local *autonomy* (Tanganyikans by law may not hold office or own land on Zanzibar, but the reverse is not true). In 1993 it was uncovered that Zanzibar had secretly joined the *Islamic Conference,* violating the union constitution. *Julius Nyrere* mediated, and persuaded Zanzibar to withdraw, but the issue has raised doubts about the viability of the union. Population: 700,000. See *Tanzania.*

Zapata, Emiliano (1877?-1919): Mexican revolutionary, agrarian reformer and *guerrilla* leader from 1911-16. He fought independently from the other revolutionary groups, though he cooperated importantly with *Pancho Villa.* He retired from active fighting after 1916 to concentrate on his land reforms in the south. He was ambushed and killed by troops loyal to *Carranza,* whom Zapata opposed.

Zeitgeist: The spirit of the time or place, as in "the zeitgeist of *interwar* France was one of *defeatism* and wilful denial."

zemstvo: A system of local government set up in

Russia by *Alexander II* after the abolition of noble councils in 1864. It promised, but never delivered representative government. It was swept aside by the *Russian Revolutions of 1917.*

zeppelin: A class of large, hydrogen-filled dirigible, named for its German inventor (Ferdinand von Zeppelin, 1838-1917). They were used in *WWI* for bombing missions against the English coast, until 1916. They were militarily ineffective (the raids killed mainly *civilians*), and anti-zeppelin defenses soon made them too costly in crew lives to continue. The experience of city bombing, however, further lowered *jus in bello* expectations and hardened attitudes toward the eventual *peace.* Their use as civilian passenger liners ended with the newsreel-recorded, "Hindenburg" tragedy in Lakehurst, N.J., on May 6, 1937, which killed 36.

zero hour: The time set to begin an attack.

zero-population growth (ZPG): When the birth rate reaches replacement levels with the death rate.

zero-sum game: From *game theory*, a situation where if one party wins a confrontation the other necessarily loses, with the sum of gains and losses always equaling zero. It is widely applied, by analogy, to situations of intense conflict. Some analysts suggest that escaping the *perception* of international relations as a zero-sum game is the key to successful *negotiation* and *conflict management.*

Zhirinovsky, Vladimir Wolfovich (b.1944): Russian politician and *fascist* buffoon. In elections in December 1993, his "Liberal Democratic Party" (the name an utter malapropism) gained the most seats in Russia's first freely elected parliament (the State *Duma*), marshaling about 1/4 of the national vote, and more in the army. This sent shock waves through Russia's reformers and Western capitals, as Zhirinovsky's views were both fascist and *imperialistic.* The latter appeared not to matter too much, as Russia's ability to project *power* or control events beyond the *near abroad* was more limited than before, and historically discredited. But his views still boded ill for the survival of democracy in Russia--which some analysts began to compare to *Weimar Germany.* Also, his reckless speeches raised tensions in the *CIS,* and made it less likely that Ukraine would give up its *nuclear weapons* and agree to *START.* One sample of his threatening bombast was a public assertion that if Japan demanded the *Kuriles* "I would bomb the Japanese. . . . If they so much as chirped I would nuke them." Within weeks he was expelled from Bulgaria for interfering in its politics, and barred from Germany for associating with *neo-*